Published in 1981 by
BELL & HYMAN LIMITED
Denmark House
37–39 Queen Elizabeth Street
London SE1 2QB

First published in 1980 by
Mills & Boon Ltd

Reprinted 1982
Second Edition 1984
Reprinted, with corrections, 1984

British Library Cataloguing in Publication Data

Simpkins, J.
Advanced biology—2nd ed.
1. Organisms
I. Title II. Williams, J. I. III. Simpkins, J.
Biology of the cell, mammal and flowering plant
574 QH307.2

ISBN 0 7135 1387 X

Printed and bound in Great Britain by
William Clowes Limited, Beccles and London

List of contents

ACKNOWLEDGEMENTS ix

PREFACE xi

1 THE STRUCTURE OF CELLS

1.1 Cell structure as interpreted by the light microscope 2
1.2 Cell ultrastructure as revealed by the electron microscope 5
1.2.1 Cell membranes 8
1.2.2 Endoplasmic reticulum 9
1.2.3 The Golgi body 11
1.2.4 Vacuoles 12
1.2.5 Lyosomes 12
1.2.6 Ribosomes 13
1.2.7 Centrosomes 13
1.2.8 Mitochondria 14
1.2.9 Chloroplasts 16
1.2.10 The nucleus 18
1.2.11 The plant cell wall 20
1.3 A comparison of light and electron microscopes 21
1.4 Cell fractionation 24

2 WATER AND AQUEOUS SOLUTIONS

2.1 The water molecule 26
2.2 Properties of water 27
2.2.1 Thermal properties 27
2.2.2 Density and viscosity 29
2.2.3 Surface tension, capillarity and tensile strength 29
2.2.4 Penetration by light 29
2.2.5 Dissociation of water 30
2.2.6 Water as a solvent 31
2.3 Some properties of aqueous solutions
2.3.1 Acids, bases and buffers 33
2.3.2 Colligative properties 34
2.4 Uptake and loss of water by living cells 35
2.4.1 Osmotic behaviour of plant cells 35
2.4.2 Osmotic behaviour of animal cells 38
2.4.3 Non-osmotic movement of water 40

3 THE CHEMICAL CONSTITUENTS OF CELLS

3.1 Carbohydrates 41
3.1.1 Monosaccharides 41
3.1.2 Disaccharides 44
3.1.3 Polysaccharides 46
3.2 Lipoids 49
3.2.1 Fats and oils 49
3.2.2 Phospholids 51
3.2.3 Waxes 52
3.2.4 Steroids and sterols 52
3.3 Proteins 52
3.3.1 Amino acids 53
3.3.2 Polypeptides and proteins 55
3.4 Biochemical techniques 60
3.4.1 Chromatography 60
3.4.2 Electrophoresis 66

4 ENZYMES

4.1 The structure of enzymes 67
4.2 Enzyme action 68
4.2.1 Enzyme catalysis 69
4.2.2 The lock and key mechanism 69
4.2.3 Enzyme specificity 70
4.2.4 Control of enzyme action 70
4.3 Factors affecting enzyme action 70
4.3.1 Co-factors 71
4.3.2 Inhibitors 71
4.3.3 Temperature 72
4.3.4 pH 73
4.3.5 Enzyme concentration 74
4.3.6 Substrate concentration 74
4.4 The classification of enzymes 75
4.4.1 Hydrolases 75
4.4.2 Oxido-reductases 76
4.4.3 Transferases 76
4.4.4 Isomerases 77
4.4.5 Ligases 77
4.4.6 Lyases 77

5 ENERGY CHANGES IN LIVING CELLS

5.1 Respiration 78
5.1.1 Adenosine 5′-triphosphate 78

5.1.2 Oxidation of respiratory substrates 79
5.1.3 Energy yields from respiratory substrates 83
5.1.4 Measuring the rate of respiration 85
5.1.5 Respiratory quotient 87
5.2 Photosynthesis 88
5.2.1 Light-dependent reactions 88
5.2.2 Light-independent reactions 93

6 NUCLEIC ACIDS AND PROTEIN SYNTHESIS

6.1 The nucleic acids 98
6.1.1 Deoxyribonucleic acid 98
6.1.2 Ribonucleic acid 101
6.1.3 DNA as the hereditary substance 102
6.1.4 Replication of DNA 105
6.2 Protein synthesis 107
6.2.1 Role of the nucleic acids 107
6.2.2 The genetic code 110
6.2.3 Regulating the synthesis of proteins 112
6.3 Genetic engineering 114

7 CELL DIVISION

7.1 Mitosis 117
7.1.1 Mitotic nuclear division 118
7.1.2 Cytoplasmic cleavage 120
7.1.3 The significance of mitosis 122
7.2 Meiosis 123
7.2.1 The first meiotic division 124
7.2.2 The second meiotic division 125
7.2.3 The significance of meiosis 127
7.3 Genetic variation 130

8 GAS EXCHANGE IN MAMMALS

8.1 Gas exchange and evaporation 132
8.2 Breathing 133
8.2.1 The breathing mechanism 133
8.2.2 Control of breathing 137
8.2.3 Oxygen debt 139
8.3 Oxygen uptake and carriage 139
8.3.1 Oxygenation of the blood 139
8.3.2 Gas exchange in the tissues 142
8.3.3 Adaptations to high altitude 144
8.3.4 Pregnancy and foetal haemoglobin 146
8.3.5 Myoglobin 147
8.4 Respiratory physiology of diving mammals 148
8.4.1 Aquatic mammals 149
8.4.2 Diving and man 149

9 BLOOD, LYMPH AND CIRCULATION

9.1 Circulation of blood and lymph 151
9.1.1 The heart 153
9.1.2 Exchange of materials between 163 blood and tissues 163
9.1.3 Lymph formation and circulation 165
9.1.4 Circulation in the mammalian foetus 167
9.2 Blood cells 169
9.2.1 Erythrocytes 169
9.2.2 Leucocytes 170
9.2.3 Thrombocytes and coagulation 171
9.2.4 Lymphocytes and antibodies 173
9.3 Vaccines 178
9.4 Allergy 178
9.5 Blood groups 179
9.6 Organ transplantation 181

10 THE MAMMALIAN URINARY SYSTEM

10.1 The urinary system 182
10.2 The functions of nephrons 186
10.2.1 Ultrafiltration 186
10.2.2 Reabsorption 187
10.2.3 Regulation of nephron function 191
10.3 Extreme cases of water economy 192
10.4 The role of the kidneys in acid-base balance 193
10.5 Kidney machines 195

11 UPTAKE AND TRANSPORT OF WATER IN FLOWERING PLANTS

11.1 Transpiration 197
11.2 Factors affecting the transpiration rate 199
11.2.1 Climate 199
11.2.2 Leaf structure 202
11.2.3 Xerophytic plants 204
11.3 The effects of transpiration 206
11.3.1 Water movement through the shoot system 206
11.3.2 Water absorption by roots 209
11.4 Root pressure 212
11.5 Tracheids, vessels and capillarity 214

12 PHOTOSYNTHESIS AND TRANSLOCATION OF PHOTOSYNTHETIC PRODUCTS

12.1 The leaf as a photosynthetic organ 217
12.1.1 Penetration of light 217
12.1.2 Supply of water 219
12.1.3 Uptake of carbon dioxide 219
12.1.4 Opening and closing of stomata 221
12.2 Factors affecting the rate of photosynthesis 223
12.2.1 Temperature 226
12.2.2 Light intensity 226
12.2.3 Concentration of carbon dioxide 227
12.3 Productivity of plants and plant communities 228
12.3.1 Leaf area index 228
12.3.2 Unit leaf rate 229
12.3.3 Net primary productivity 229
12.4 Translocation of photosynthetic products 229
12.4.1 The pathway of translocation 230
12.4.2 The mechanism of translocation 235

13 MINERAL NUTRITION OF FLOWERING PLANTS

13.1 Mineral requirements of flowering plants 240
13.1.1 Water culture experiments 240
13.2 Function of minerals in flowering plants 242
13.2.1 Macronutrients 242
13.2.2 Micronutrients 244
13.3 Toxic minerals 245
13.4 Soil as a source of minerals 245
13.5 Mineral absorption by plants 246
13.5.1 Roots as organs of mineral absorption 246
13.5.2 Mechanisms of mineral absorption 247
13.6 Transport of mineral in plants 249
13.6.1 Passage across the root tissues 250
13.6.2 Movement into the shoot system 250
13.6.3 Circulation of minerals in plants 250
13.7 The nutrient-film technique 253

14 THE MAMMALIAN ALIMENTARY SYSTEM

14.1 Mammalian nutritional requirements 254
14.1.1 Organic nutrients 254
14.1.2 Vitamins 255
14.1.3 Inorganic nutrients 256
14.2 Mammalian dentition 256
14.2.1 Structure and development of teeth 256
14.2.2 Variety of mammalian teeth 258
14.3 Digestion 264
14.3.1 The mouth 264
14.3.2 The stomach 267
14.3.3 Rumination 270
14.3.4 The small intestine 271
14.3.5 The caecum 275
14.4 Absorption 275
14.5 The liver 278
14.5.1 Structure of the liver 278
14.5.2 Functions of the liver 280

15 NERVOUS CONTROL AND CO-ORDINATION IN MAMMALS

15.1 Electrochemical basis of nervous activity 283
15.1.1 The resting potential 284
15.1.2 The action potential 286
15.1.3 The nerve impulse 287
15.1.4 Membrane recovery 289
15.1.5 Rate of impulse conduction 289
15.1.6 Synaptic transmission 293
15.1.7 Neuroeffector junctions 296
15.1.8 Muscle and contraction 296
15.1.9 Cartilage, bone and joints 299
15.2 The mammalian nervous system 302
15.2.1 The peripheral nervous system and reflexes 303
15.2.2 The autonomic nervous system 307
15.2.3 The central nervous system 310

16 THE MAMMALIAN EYE AND EAR

16.1 The mammalian eye 317
16.1.1 Structure of the eye 317
16.1.2 Focusing 319
16.1.3 Defects of the eye 321
16.1.4 Photoreception 322
16.2 The mammalian ear 327
16.2.1 Structure of the ear 327
16.2.2 Hearing 327
16.2.3 Balance 330
16.2.4 Defects of the ear 332

17 THERMOREGULATION IN MAMMALS

17.1 Heat production 334
17.1.1 Measuring metabolic rate 335
17.1.2 Distribution of body heat 336
17.2 Heat loss 337
17.2.1 Radiation 337
17.2.2 Evaporation 337
17.2.3 Conduction 338
17.2.4 Surface area and body volume 338
17.3 Thermoregulation 340
17.3.1 The thermoregulation centres 340
17.3.2 Regulating heat production 341
17.3.3 Regulating heat loss 341
17.3.4 Hibernation 347

18 ENDOCRINE CONTROL IN MAMMALS

18.1 The thyroid and parathyroid glands 349
18.1.1 The thyroid gland 349
18.1.2 Control of thyroid activity 351
18.1.3 Measurement of thyroid activity 351
18.1.4 Malfunction of the thyroid gland 352
18.1.5 The parathyroid glands 353
18.1.6 Role of the thyroid gland in calcium control 355
18.1.7 Malfunction of the parathyroid glands 356
18.2 Control of blood glucose 357
18.2.1 Insulin and glucagon 357
18.2.2 Cortisol 360
18.3 Control of blood sodium and potassium 361
18.3.1 Aldosterone 362
18.4 The adrenal medulla 363
18.4.1 The medullary hormones 363
18.5 The pituitary body 364
18.5.1 The anterior pituitary 364
18.5.2 The posterior pituitary 367

19 REPRODUCTION IN FLOWERING PLANTS

19.1 Sexual reproduction 368
19.1.1 Flower structure 368
19.1.2 Development of pollen and ovules 370
19.1.3 Fertilisation and its consequences 375
19.2 The life cycle of a flowering plant 379
19.3 Pollination 380
19.3.1 Mechanisms for ensuring outbreeding 380
19.3.2 Pollination mechanisms 382
19.4 Asexual reproduction 384
19.4.1 Diploid parthenogenesis 384
19.4.2 Haploid parthenogenesis 384
19.4.3 Vegetative propagation 384
19.4.4 The consequences of asexual reproduction 386
19.5 The physiology of angiosperm reproduction 386
19.5.1 The physiology of flowering 386
19.5.2 Physiology of pollen growth 389
19.5.3 Physiology of seed and fruit formation 390
19.5.4 Physiology of fruit ripening 391

20 SEED STRUCTURE AND GERMINATION

20.1 Seed structure 392
20.2 Morphological aspects of seed germination 392
20.2.1 Germination of broad bean 392
20.2.2 Germination of sunflower 394
20.2.3 Germination of maize 395
20.3 Physiology of germination 396
20.3.1 Mobilisation of stored food 396
20.3.2 Factors affecting seed germination 399
20.3.3 Seed dormancy 403

21 GROWTH AND DEVELOPMENT OF FLOWERING PLANTS

21.1 Morphological and anatomical aspects of growth and development 406
21.1.1 Primary growth and development 406
21.1.2 Secondary growth and development 418
21.2 Physiological aspects of growth and development 422
21.2.1 External factors 422
21.2.2 Internal factors 425
21.2.3 Practical uses of plant hormones 432

22 MAMMALIAN REPRODUCTION

22.1 Testes 434
22.1.1 Structure of the testes 435
22.1.2 Spermatogenesis 436
22.1.3 Male hormones 437

22.2 Ovaries 438
22.2.1 Structure of the ovaries and oogenesis 438
22.2.2 Hormonal control of ovulation 440
22.2.3 The oestrus cycle 440
22.2.4 Other effects of female hormones 443
22.2 Reproduction 443
22.3.1 Copulation 443
22.3.2 Fertilisation and implantation of the embryo 444
22.3.3 The placenta 445
22.3.4 Birth and lactation 448

23 GENETICS

23.1 Autosomal inheritance 450
23.1.1 Monohybrid inheritance 450
23.1.2 Dihybrid inheritance 453
23.1.3 Polyhybrid inheritance 453
23.1.4 Co-dominance and incomplete dominance 455
23.1.5 Multiple alleles 455
23.1.6 Gene interaction 455
23.1.7 Linkage 456
23.1.8 Chromosome maps 458
23.2 Non-autosomal inheritance 460
23.2.1 Inheritance of sex 460
23.2.2 Sex linkage 461
23.3 Inheritance of quantitative characteristics 463
23.4 Population genetics 463
23.4.1 Inbreeding and outbreeding 463
23.4.2 Clones 464
23.4.3 The Hardy-Weinberg law 465
23.4.4 Genetic polymorphism 466

24 THE ORIGIN AND EVOLUTION OF LIFE

24.1 The origin of life 467
24.1.1 Monomer synthesis 467
24.1.2 Polymer synthesis 468
24.1.3 Polymer isolation and replication 468
24.1.4 The first cells 469
24.2 Evidence of evolution 470
24.2.1 Fossils 470
24.2.2 Affinities 476
24.2.3 Geographical distribution 478
24.3 How evolution came about 479
24.3.1 Lamarckism 479
24.3.2 Darwinism 480
24.3.3 Variation 481
24.3.4 Selection 483
24.3.5 Isolating mechanisms 486
24.3.6 The formation of species 488

25 VARIETY OF LIFE: MICRO-ORGANISMS AND PLANTS

25.1 Nomenclature and classification 489
25.2 Viruses 490
25.2.1 Structure 490
25.2.2 Replication 490
25.2.3 Importance to man 492
25.3 Bacteria (*Schizomycophyta*) 492
25.3.1 Structure 492
25.3.2 Nutrition 494
25.3.3 Respiration 494
25.3.4 Reproduction 494
25.3.5 Endospores 494
25.3.6 Importance to man 494
25.4 Fungi (*Eumycophyta*) 498
25.4.1 Structure 498
25.4.2 Nutrition 500
25.4.3 Reproduction 500
25.4.4 Importance to man 502
25.5 Algae 505
25.5.1 *Cyanophyta* (*Myxophyta*) 505
25.5.2 *Chlorophyta* 506
25.5.3 *Phaeophyta* 508
25.5.4 *Rhodophyta*, *Bacillariophyta* and *Euglenophyta* 509
25.6 *Bryophyta* 510
25.6.1 *Hepaticae* 510
25.6.2 *Musci* 512
25.7 *Pteridophyta* 513
25.7.1 *Selaginellales* 513
25.7.2 *Equisetales* 515
25.7.3 *Filicales* 515
25.8 *Spermatophyta* 517
25.8.1 *Gymnospermae* 518
25.8.2 *Angiospermae* 521

26 VARIETY OF LIFE: NON-CHORDATE ANIMALS

26.1 *Protozoa* 523
26.1.1 *Sarcodina* (*Rhizopoda*) 523
26.1.2 *Mastigophora* (*Flagellata*) 524
26.1.3 *Ciliata* (*Ciliophora*) 526
26.1.4 *Sporozoa* 527
26.2 *Porifera* 529
26.3 *Cnidaria* 530
26.3.1 Cell differentiation in cnidarians 530
26.3.2 Variety of cnidarians 532
26.4 *Platyhelminthes* 536
26.4.1 *Turbellaria* 536
26.4.2 *Trematoda* 538

26.5 *Nematoda* 541
26.6 *Annelida* 542
26.6.1 *Polychaeta* 542
26.6.2 *Oligochaeta* 544
26.6.3 *Hirudinea* 546
26.7 *Arthropoda* 547
26.7.1 *Onychophora* 548
26.7.2 *Crustacea* 549
26.7.3 *Myriapoda* 551
26.7.4 *Insecta* 551
26.7.5 *Arachnida* 555
26.8 *Mollusca* 556
26.8.1 *Gastropoda* 557
26.8.2 *Lamellibranchia* (*Bivalvia*) 558
26.8.3 *Cephalopoda* 558
26.9 *Echinodermata* 559
26.9.1 *Asteroidea* 560
26.9.2 *Echinoidea* 560

27 VARIETY OF LIFE: CHORDATE ANIMALS

27.1 Protochordates 561
27.1.1 *Ascidiacea* 561
27.1.2 *Cephalochorda* 562
27.2 *Vertebrata* (*Craniata*) 563
27.2.1 *Agnatha* 563
27.2.2 *Chondrichthyes* (*Elasmobranchii*) 564
27.2.3 *Osteichthyes* 567
27.2.4 *Amphibia* 569
27.2.5 *Reptilia* 572
27.2.6 *Aves* 574
27.2.7 *Mammalia* 578

28 ECOLOGY 1: DISTRIBUTION OF ORGANISMS; ASSOCIATIONS

28.1 Factors affecting the distribution of organisms 583
28.1.1 Biotic factors 584
28.1.2 Abiotic factors 588
28.1.3 The factor complex 596
28.2 Associations between organisms 597
28.2.1 Parasitism 597
28.2.2 Symbiosis 600
28.2.3 Commensalism 605

29 ECOLOGY 2: POPULATIONS, COMMUNITIES AND ECOSYSTEMS

29.1 Populations 606
29.1.1 Population growth 606
29.1.2 Growth of human populations 607
29.1.3 Population dynamics 609
29.2 Communities 613
29.2.1 Succession 613
29.3 Ecosystems 616
29.3.1 Trophic relationships 616
29.3.2 Energy flow 617
29.3.3 Ecological pyramids 622
29.3.4 Cycling of matter 624
29.3.5 Soil as an ecosystem 627

30 POLLUTION AND CONSERVATION

30.1 Pollution of the atmosphere 638
30.1.1 Carbon dioxide 638
30.1.2 Sulphur dioxide 639
30.1.3 Particulate matter 641
30.1.4 Carbon monoxide 641
30.1.5 Oxides of nitrogen 642
30.1.6 Metals 642
30.2 Pollution by heavy metals 642
30.2.1 Lead 642
30.2.2 Mercury 644
30.2.3 Other heavy metals 645
30.3 Pesticides 646
30.3.1 Herbicides 646
30.3.2 Fungicides 647
30.3.3 Insecticides 647
30.4 Radiation 651
30.4.1 Forms of radiation 651
30.4.2 Sources of radiation 652
30.4.3 Biological effects of radiation 653
30.5 Pollution of aquatic habitats 655
30.5.1 Freshwater pollution 655
30.5.2 Marine pollution 659
30.6 Conservation 661
30.6.1 The case for conservation 661
30.6.2 Conservation in action 661

QUESTIONS 664

INDEX 682

Acknowledgements

We gratefully acknowledge the assistance of:

Our editor, Margaret Sands, for constant encouragement and helpful guidance.

Joan Bryant of Mills and Boon Ltd., and Antonia Murphy of Bell and Hyman Ltd., for their endless patience and thoughtful advice in ensuring the completion of the project.

Dr. R. Jones, Dr. P. M. Davies and Dr. D. M. Holdich of the Department of Zoology, University of Nottingham; Dr. I. Mackenzie and Dr. A. F. Braithwaite of the Department of Botany, University of Nottingham; Dr. A. Booth of the Department of Botany, University of Sheffield and Dr. G. Triggs of Liverpool Polytechnic who devoted much time to reading the typescript. Their comments were immensely helpful.

Dr. D. Brindley of the Queen's Medical Centre, University of Nottingham for his useful advice on biochemical nomenclature.

The Joint Matriculation Board, the Schools Examination Department of the University of London and the Joint Committee for Ordinary National Certificates and Diplomas for their permission to use recent examination questions.

Mr. J. Kugler of the Queen's Medical Centre, University of Nottingham and Mr. D. Wark of King's Mill Hospital, Sutton-in-Ashfield, without whose expertise and hard work the task of obtaining most of the photographs would have been immensely more demanding. Nearly all of the photographs not acknowledged below or in the text were provided by Mr. Kugler and Mr. Wark.

Mrs. M. Hollingsworth of the Department of Anatomy, University of Sheffield, Mrs. A. Tomlinson of the Queen's Medical Centre, University of Nottingham, and Mr. B. Case of the Department of Botany, University of Nottingham, who kindly gave their time and skills in preparing some of the photographs.

Mr. P. Bailey and Mr. A. Bezear of the Queen's Medical Centre, University of Nottingham who supplied the photographs and drawings for Figures 7.15(b), 9.7(a), 9.8, 10.17(a), 15.36, 18.8, 18.29, 18.30 and 22.16.

Philip Harris Biological Ltd., for contributing photographs for Figures 1.21(b), 2.12, 7.1(b), 7.11, 7.13(a), 7.14(a), 7.14(b), 7.15(a), 8.7, 12.15(f) and 19.2(c). Also for supplying microscopic preparations from which many other figures were produced.

Professor R. M. H. McMinn of the Department of Anatomy, the Royal College of Surgeons of England, for kindly providing Figures 9.3(c) and 15.38 as well as the photograph used on the front cover.

Dr. M. Davey of the Department of Botany, University of Nottingham for his generosity in providing Figures 1.5(a), 1.16(a), 1.19, 1.20, 1.21(a), 3.11(a), 3.14, 5.5(a), 12.16, 21.28 and 28.29(a).

Dr. J. Freer of the University of Glasgow for providing Figures 25.1(b) and (c) and 25.4(b) and (c).

Dr. M. A. Tribe of the School of Biological Sciences, University of Sussex for his help in acquiring Figure 5.18.

Mr. D. Gould, of the Department of Dental Surgery, General Hospital, Nottingham for providing Figure 14.3.

Mrs. S. York, of the EEG department, Leicester Royal Infirmary, for providing Figure 15.50(a).

Mr. S. Hyman of the University of Leicester for providing Figure 25.1(a).

Table 24.2 was redrawn from Hollingsworth and Bowler, "Principles and Processes of Biology", published by Chapman and Hall. Table 24.3 was redrawn from Marshall, "Biology—Advanced Level" published by Macdonald and Evans as was Table 24.4 and Figure 24.15. Figure 23.13 was re-drawn from Carter, "Human Heredity" page 105 and was reprinted by permission of Penguin Books Ltd. Figure 30.14 was re-drawn from "Evolution by Natural Selection", Open University Science Foundation Course (S100) Unit 19.

The many other individual and institutions who provided or who gave permission to use illustrative material. They have been credited in the text alongside the appropriate figures.

Any errors in the book are entirely the responsibility of the authors and the publishers.

Preface

In recent years there has been a change in emphasis in the content of GCE Advanced Level syllabuses in biological sciences. As well as traditional topics, students are now expected to cope with the complexities of biochemistry and the molecular basis of genetics. Most Examination Boards have also altered their style of assessment. Less weight is now placed on memorising facts and more on understanding principles and interpreting data. The applications of biology are currently stressed more than ever. It is with these changes in mind that this book has been written.

The major topics of all GCE Advanced Level syllabuses in Biology are included. The contents are also relevant to courses leading to the Technical Education Council Diploma in Sciences. Technician students enrolled for TEC Certificate programmes will find the objectives of the Standard Units Biology II, Cell Biology II, Mammalian Physiology II and III, and Biochemistry III well covered. Our many years' experience in teaching and examining at this level have been instrumental in determining the appropriate depth of treatment of the subject matter.

We have consciously attempted to write in a style and language which the average sixth former can readily understand. The chapters can be read in any order. However, in our opinion the subject matter is more intelligible if the topics are studied in the order in which they are set out. The first seven chapters provide a foundation in biological, biochemical and physical knowledge and principles which should make it easier to understand the topics in the remainder of the book. Key words have been presented in bold type to emphasise important facts and concepts and for ease of revision.

Biology is a practical subject but in the space available we could not include details of practical work. However, second-hand evidence from experimental work is quoted extensively in the text and in a number of the questions. It is hoped that this will encourage students to realise that factual evidence is essential if valid conclusions are to be arrived at in biological science. Where we have written about debatable issues an attempt has been made to strike a reasonable balance in the conflicting evidence available. The practical uses to which biological knowledge can be put have been mentioned where appropriate.

J.S.
J.I.W.
Nottingham, 1983.

the structure and activity of which were thought to mirror that of the whole organism. Recently there has been more interest in the ways in which different types of cells interact in the functioning and development of multicellular organisms.

1.1 Cell structure as interpreted by the light microscope

The compound microscope is still used by most biologists to examine cells and tissues (Fig. 1.2(a)). With this instrument it is possible to observe living material. Good images showing much detail can be obtained, especially if the microscope is of the **phase-contrast** type (Fig. 1.2(b)). A phase-contrast microscope exaggerates small differences in refractive index of cell components to create an image in which the components are more clearly distinguished by the human eye. Nevertheless, most of what was known about the structure of cells up to the 1940s was obtained from observations on dead tissue which had been treated with preservatives. The technique, which had been developed for over a hundred years, first involves immersing the tissue in a fixative such as methanal or ethanol in order to prevent deterioration and to keep the structure as life-like as possible. Following **fixation** the tissue is **dehydrated** with ethanol and then **cleared** with an organic solvent such as dimethylbenzene which is miscible with paraffin wax. The next stage is to **embed** the tissue in molten wax which on hardening supports the tissue while thin sections, 2–10 μm thick, are cut using a microtome. After attaching the sections to microscope slides the wax is removed before the tissue is **stained**. Staining changes the refractive index of

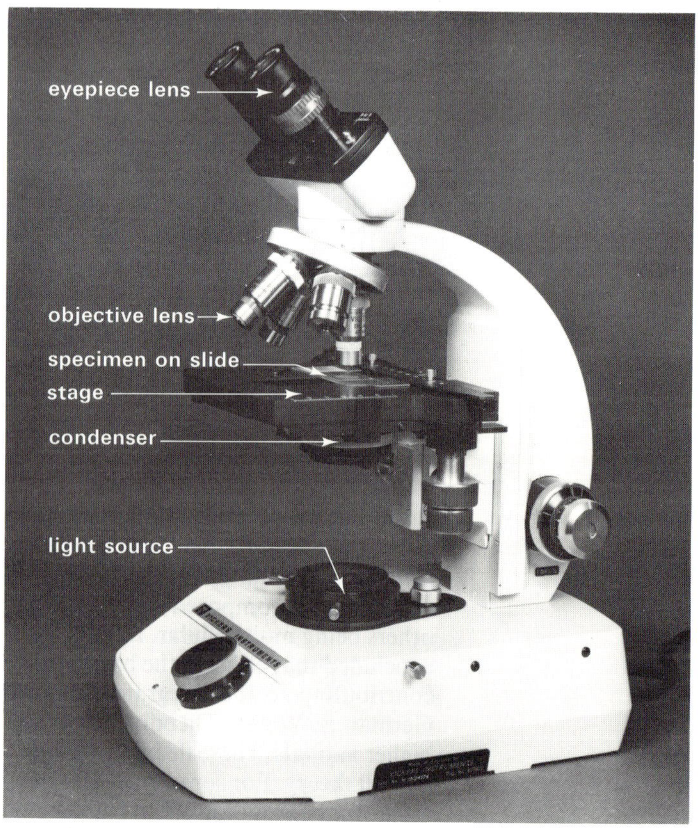

FIG. 1.2 (a) *A modern compound microscope* (courtesy Vickers Instruments)

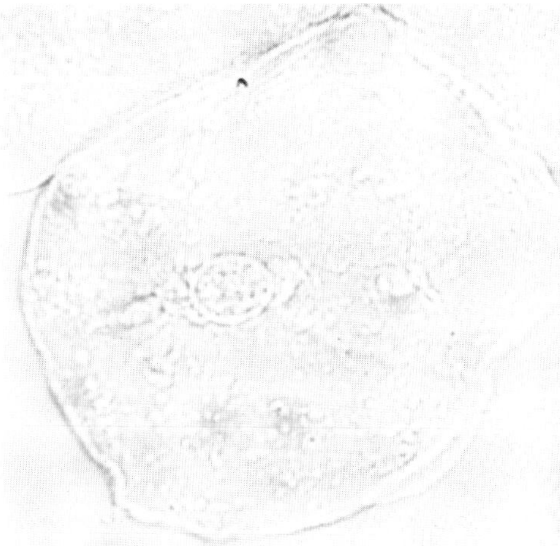

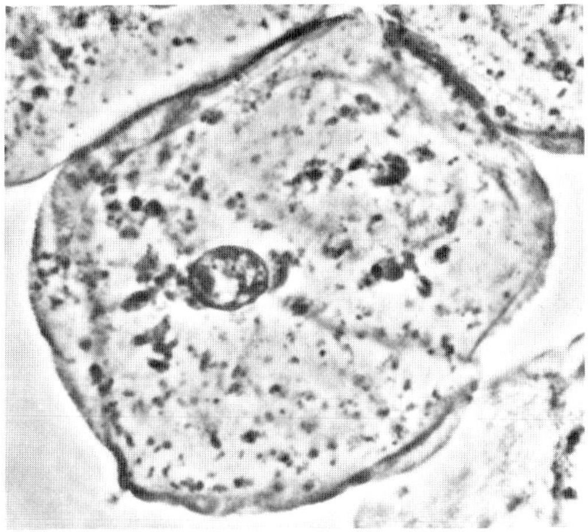

FIG. 1.2 (b) *An epithelial cell from the mouth lining*

(i) *as seen with a conventional light microscope, × 900*
(ii) *as seen with a phase-contrast microscope, × 900*

cell components so that they are more easily seen when the material is examined microscopically. Any of the above steps can lead to distortion of the specimen, so it is necessary to guard against artificial structures, called **artefacts**, which appear in the specimen during treatment but are not present in living cells.

Using such methods, coupled with observations on living cells, it is possible to build up a fairly detailed picture of cell structure (Fig. 1.3(a) and (b)).

The living material of cells is called **protoplasm** and is enclosed in a **plasma membrane**, an elastic outer layer. In plant cells the protoplast, the unit of protoplasm found in a single cell, is surrounded by an inert **cell wall**. The main ingredient of plant cell walls is a glucose polymer called cellulose. Adjacent plant cells are held together by a thin layer composed mainly of calcium pectate and known as the **middle lamella**. Another distinctive feature of many plant cells is the presence of pigment-containing bodies called plastids, the most common of which are the green **chloroplasts**. Large sap-filled **vacuoles** are also frequent.

FIG. 1.3 *Structure of cells as revealed by a compound microscope*

(a) (i) *section of a leaf mesophyll cell as seen with a light microscope × 1200*

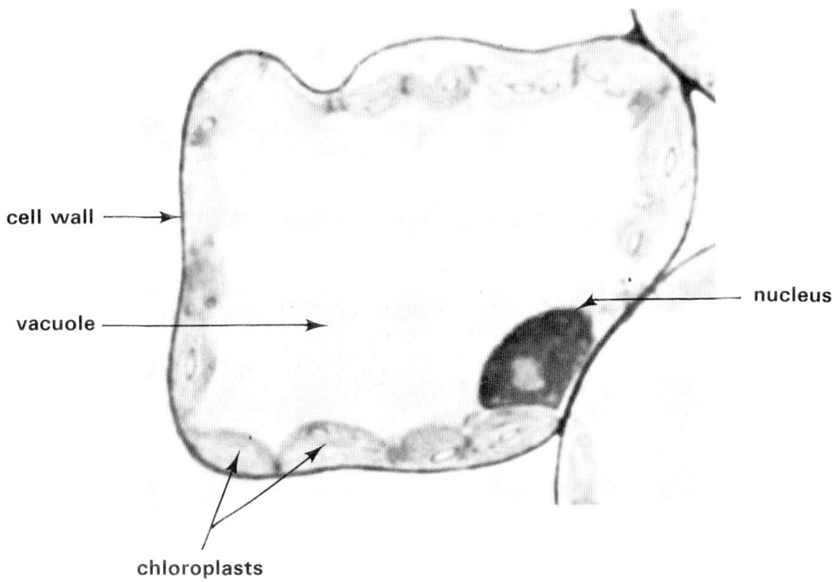

cells immediately die. Secondly, sections of cells and tissues must be extremely thin (0·01–0·5 μm thick) otherwise electrons will not pass through them. For **fixation** osmium(VIII) oxide which stains lipids and proteins is often used. Otherwise gluteraldehyde which fixes the material without rendering it electron-dense is used. The sample is next **dehydrated** with ethanol as described for light microscopy, then **cleared** ready for embedding. Paraffin wax fragments if cut into very thin sections so is unsuitable as an embedding substance for electron microscopy. Instead, clear plastic epoxy resins such as *Araldite* are used. The material is cleared in liquid resin which is hardened by gentle heat. The sample is now embedded in a tough, clear supporting substance which can be cut into very thin slices.

Sectioning is carried out with an **ultra-microtome**, the blade of which is usually made by breaking a thick piece of glass to give a hard cutting edge. The sections are then transferred to tiny circular copper grids on which they can be **stained**. Solutions of lead salts are taken up by lipid components in the specimen whilst uranyl salts react with protein and nucleic acid. The effect is to make the lipids, proteins and nucleic acids electron-dense so that they contrast with other cell components in the final image. A special holder is used to place the sections, still supported on their grids, in the electron microscope which is evacuated of air before the electron beam is switched on (Fig. 1.4(b)).

FIG. 1.4 (b) *Stages in the preparation of thin sections for electronmicroscopy*

(i) *cutting the sections with an ultramicrotome*

(ii) *mounting the sections on to copper grid*

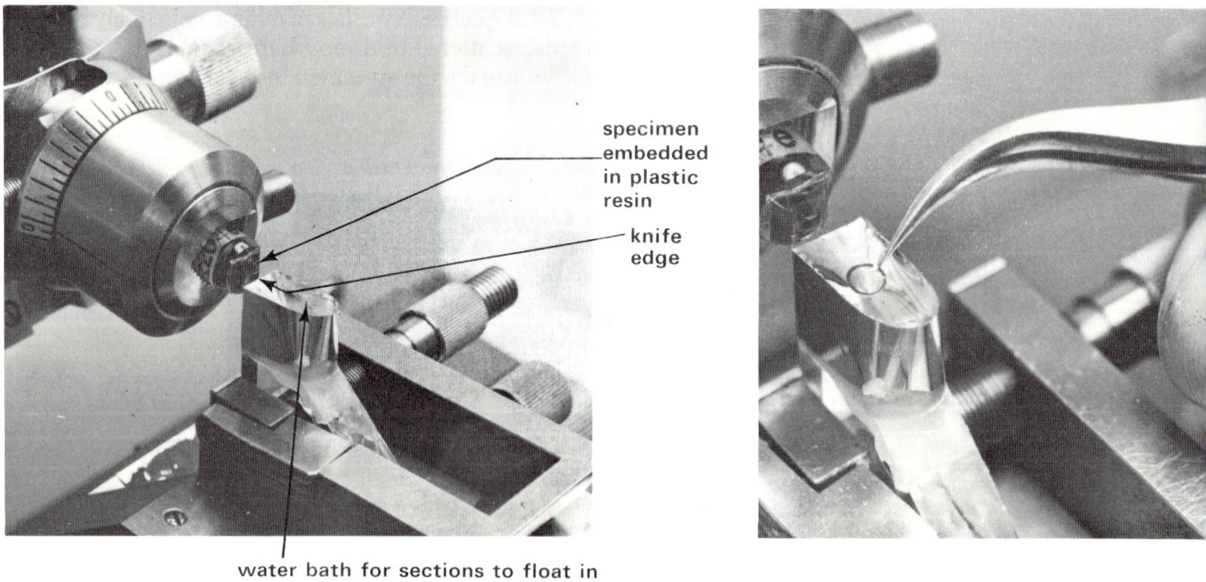

When electron microscope techniques were used for the first time both plant and animal cells were shown to have a detailed structure previously undreamed of. Not only were some components discovered for the very first time, others already well-known were found to be incredibly complex in structure (Fig. 1.5). Furthermore the subcellular components called **organelles** common to plant and animal cells were seen to be remarkably similar in appearance.

1.2.3 Th
body

FIG. 1.5 (a) *Electronmicrograph of a section through two adjacent cells from a tobacco leaf, × 15 000*

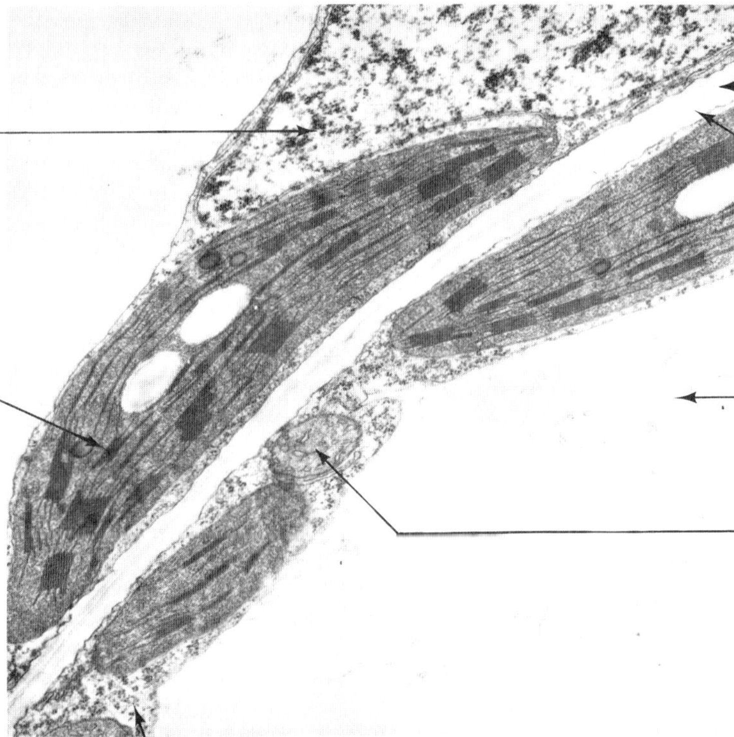

FIG. 1.10 *Ele*
a thin sectio
body, × 24 0

FIG. 1.5 (b) *Electronmicrograph of a cell from the pancreas of a mammal, × 10 000*

FIG. 1.11 *Th*
drawing of p
body

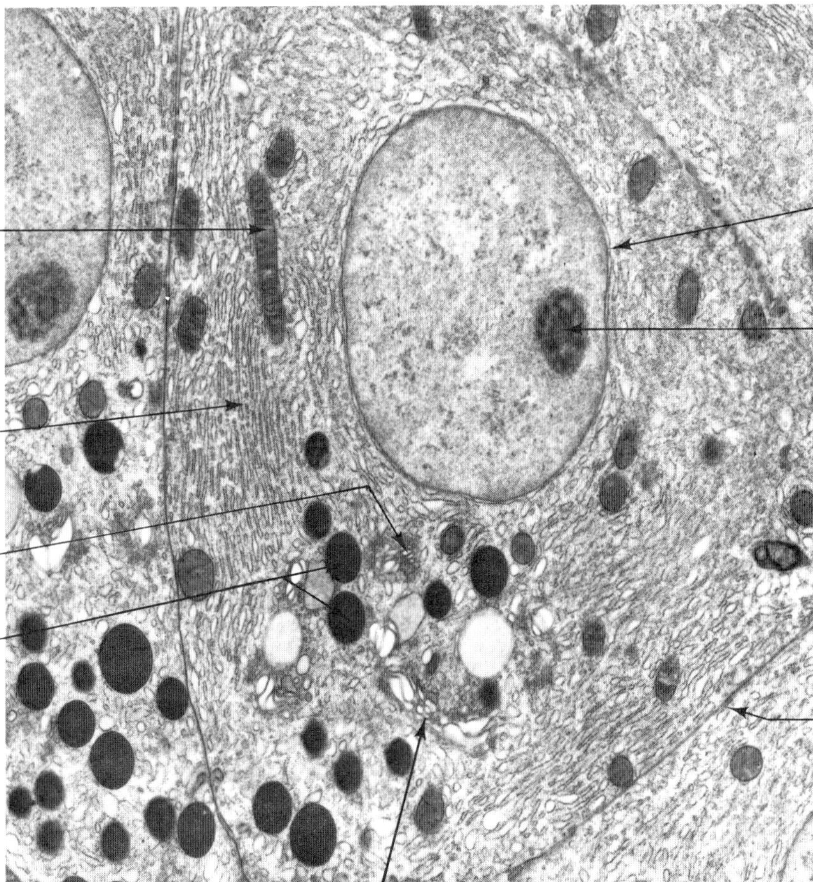

FIG. 1.13 (a) *Electronmicrograph of a section through a centrosome, ×65 000. The two centrioles are at right angles to each other. The upper centriole has been cut longitudinally, the other one transversely*

moves to opposite poles of the cell. They produce a system of microtubules called **spindle fibres** radiating towards the equator of the cell. Chromosomes become attached to the spindle equator before migrating to the poles of the cell, seemingly connected to the microtubules (Chapter 7).

In motile cells centrioles divide to produce basal bodies from which flagella and cilia develop.

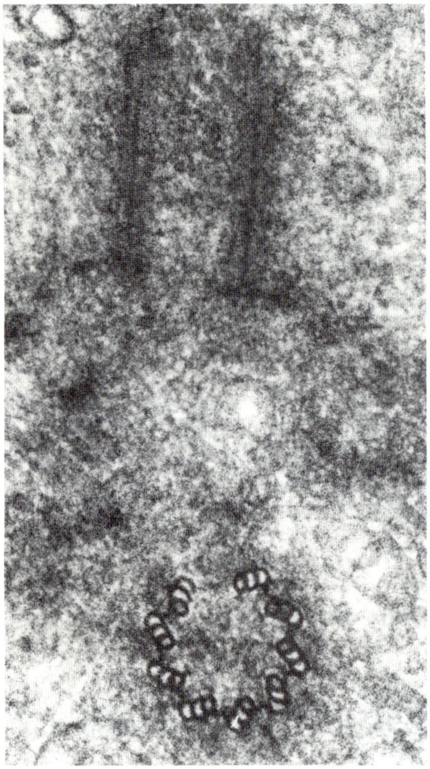

FIG. 1.13 (b) *Diagrammatic representation of the structure of a centriole*

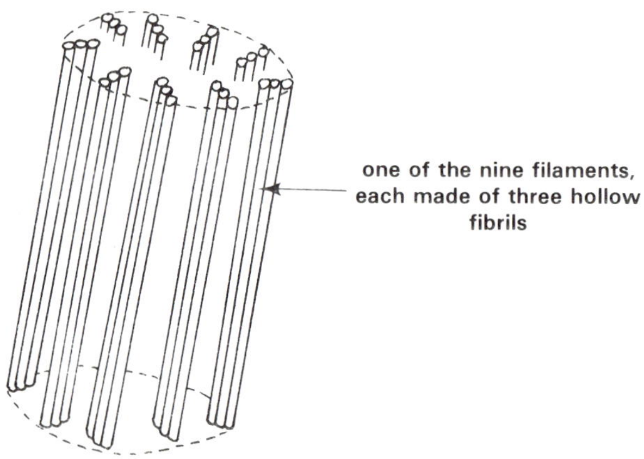

1.2.8 Mitochondria

The presence of small elongate bodies in the cytoplasm of plant and animal cells was first reported in the 1850s. The name **mitochondria**, meaning thread-granules, was later given to these structures which are just visible as very small grains with a light microscope. It was not until a hundred years later that thin sections of mitochondria examined under the electron microscope showed that they had a structural complexity previously unsuspected. Mitochondria from different organisms are similar in structure. They have a smooth outer unit membrane and a much folded inner unit membrane. The folds, which are called **cristae**, increase the surface area of the inner membrane thus providing a large number of sites for biochemical activity. Between the two membranes is a fluid-filled **intracristal space** while the inner membrane encloses a space containing a mixture of protein, lipid and nucleic acids called the **matrix**. In some electronmicrographs small stalked spherical bodies about 9 nm in diameter have been seen attached to the matrix side of the cristae (Fig. 1.14).

The shape of mitochondria is variable, from rod-shaped to spherical, spiral and even cup-shaped. They also vary in size depending on their source. The mitochondria from mammalian liver cells measure 1–2 μm long and 0·3–0·7 μm wide, while those from pancreatic cells, although of the same width, are up to 10 μm long. Cells which are metabolically very active contain large numbers of mitochondria. Insect flight muscles for example have numerous mitochondria packed between the muscle fibres (Fig. 1.15). The companion cells of phloem (Chapter 12) and the tubule cells of kidney nephrons (Chapter 10) are also packed with mitochondria.

FIG. 1.14 (a) *Electronmicrograph of a section through a mitochondrion, ×81 000*

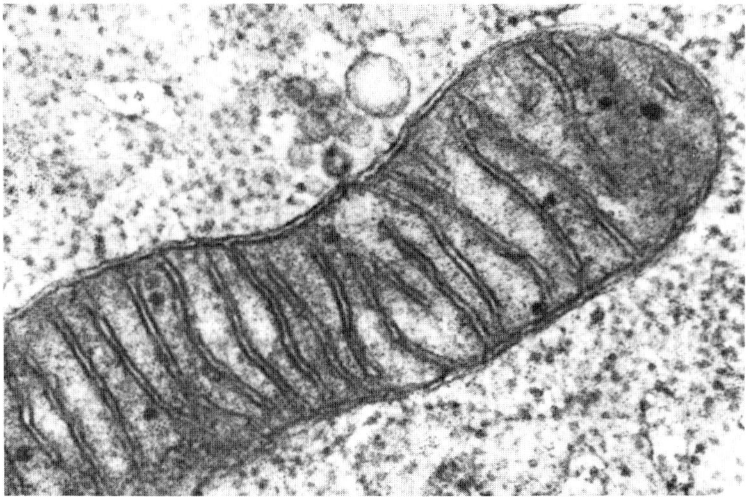

FIG. 1.14 (b) *The internal structure of a mitochondrion*

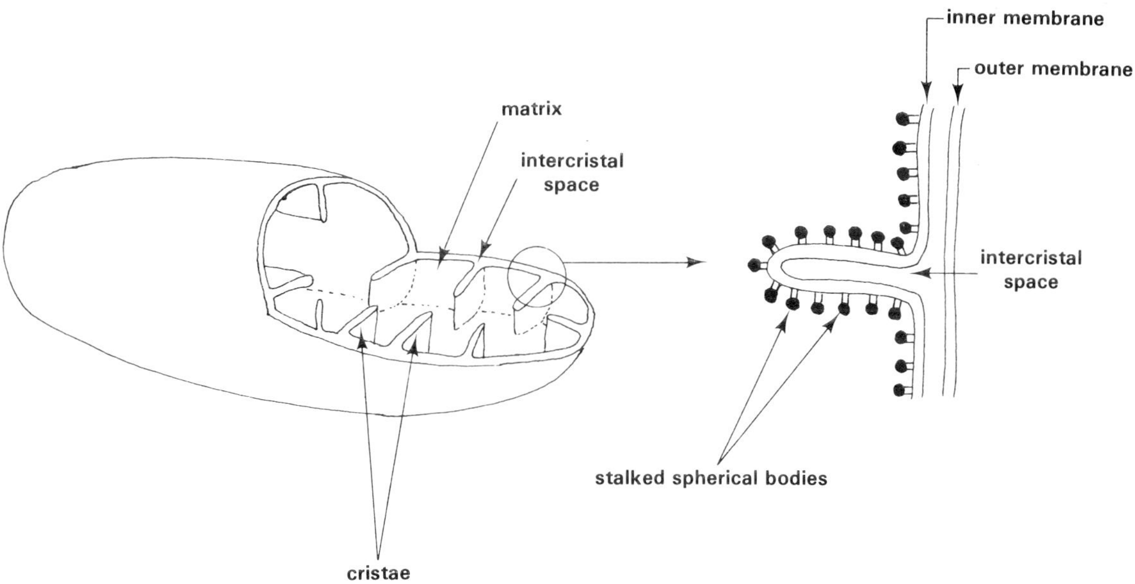

Structurally, mitochondria provide sites isolated from the rest of the cytoplasm on which enzyme-catalysed reactions occur. Their main function is the production of **adenosine 5′-triphosphate (ATP)** from adenosine 5′-diphosphate (ADP) and inorganic phosphate ions. The conversion of ADP to ATP is an energy-consuming reaction. Energy for the reaction is obtained from the oxidation of energy-rich substrates such as pyruvic acid which is derived from sugars metabolised in the cytoplasm. The oxidation process is called **respiration**, the biochemistry of which is described in detail in Chapter 5.

In some cells it is possible to observe mitochondria dividing. In others they appear to arise from immature mitochondria called **promitochondria**. The evolution of mitochondria is the subject of great controversy. Some cell biologists believe they were originally formed from infolding of the plasma membrane while others consider mitochondria to be degenerate symbiotic bacteria!

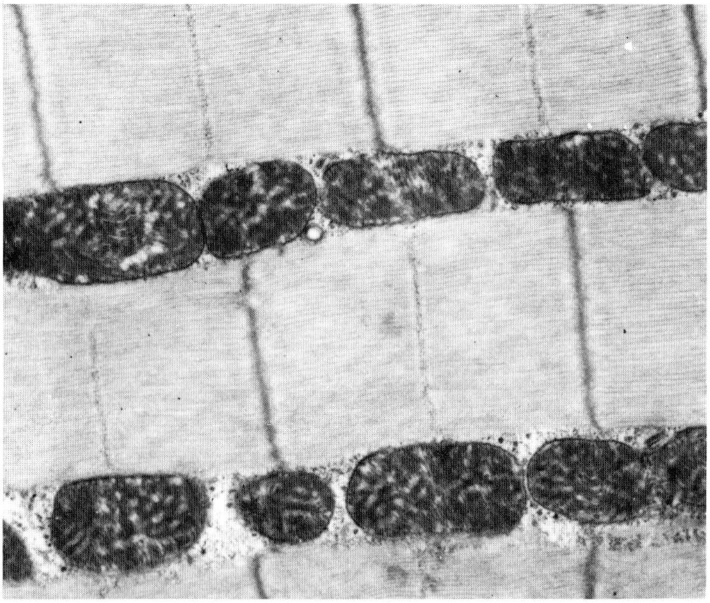

FIG. 1.15 *Electronmicrograph of a section through the flight muscles of a housefly, ×58 000*

1.2.9 Chloroplasts

In all photosynthetic plants apart from the blue-green algae and photoautotrophic bacteria the light-absorbing pigments are housed in complex organelles called **chloroplasts**. In the cells of higher plants chloroplasts are shaped like biconvex lenses 4–10 μm in diameter and 2–3 μm thick. They are found chiefly in the mesophyll cells of leaves. Being so large chloroplasts can be seen with a light microscope and they have been studied from the mid-seventeenth century onwards.

Thin sections of chloroplasts viewed under an electron microscope show them to be bounded by a double unit membrane. The outer membrane is smooth while the inner is extended inwards as a system of layers called **lamellae** in which the photosynthetic pigments are located. In places the lamellae appear as flat discs known as **grana** piled on top of each other. These are connected by **intergrana lamellae**. The entire system of internal membranes is suspended in an aqueous matrix called the **stroma** which contains protein and nucleic acids. Following a period of illumination, photosynthetic end-products such as **starch grains** and **lipid globules** appear in the stroma (Fig. 1.16).

The arrangement of chlorophyll and other photosynthetic pigments in the chloroplast membranes is highly organised and concentrated in the grana which are just visible with a light microscope as darker green spots inside chloroplasts. Figure 1.17 shows the way in which the pigments are probably distributed in a granum. It has been suggested that the pigment layers consist of particles called **quantasomes** which are thought to be the basic photosynthetic units.

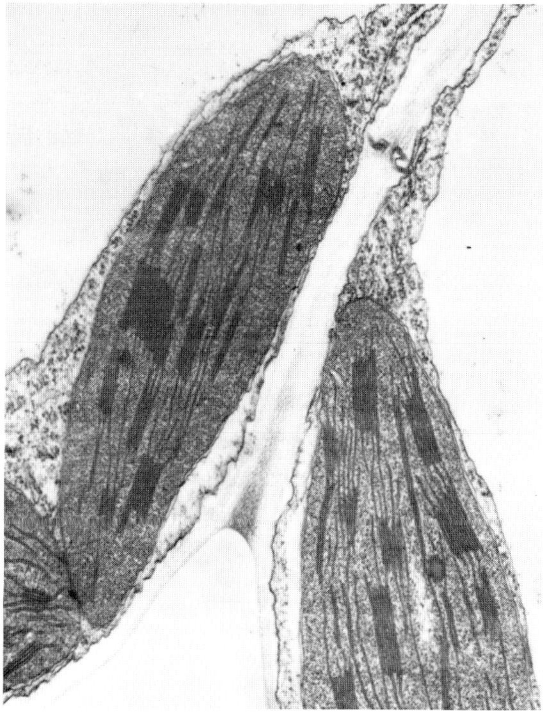

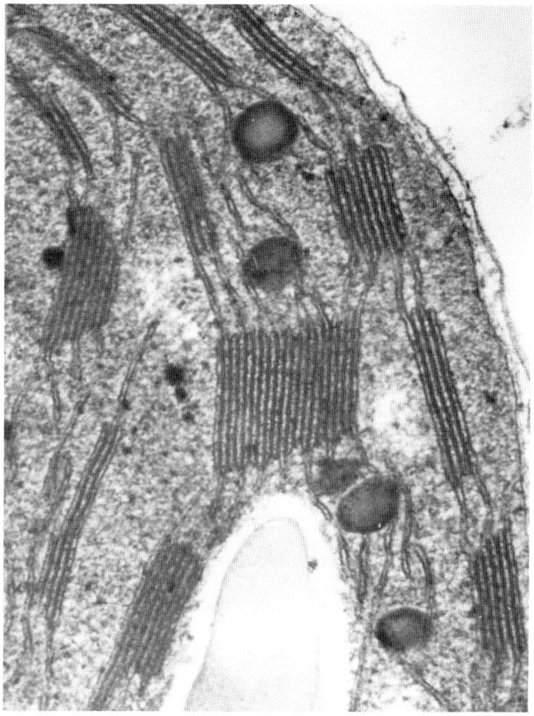

FIG. 1.16 (a) *Electronmicrographs of sections through chloroplasts*

(i) *whole chloroplast from a tobacco leaf cell, × 30 000*

(ii) *part of a chloroplast from a* Petunia *leaf cell, × 75 000*

FIG. 1.16 (b) *Drawing of a thin section of a chloroplast*

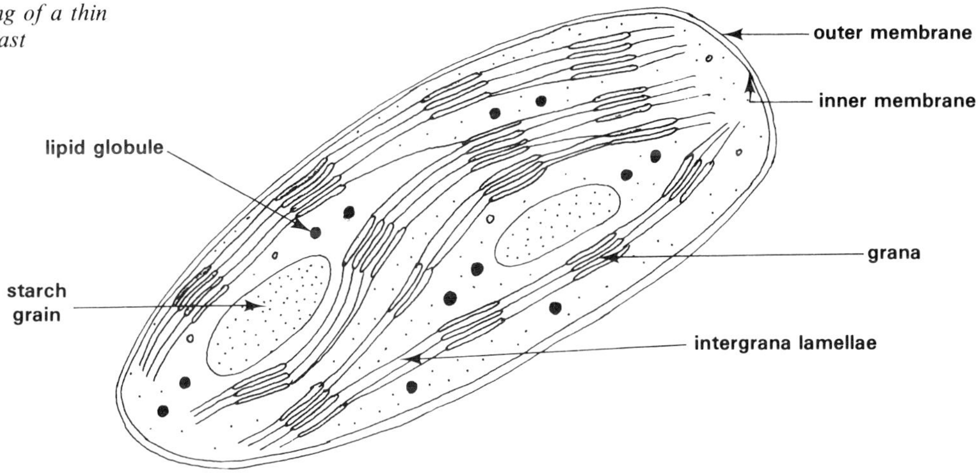

FIG. 1.17 *Probable distribution of pigments in a granum*

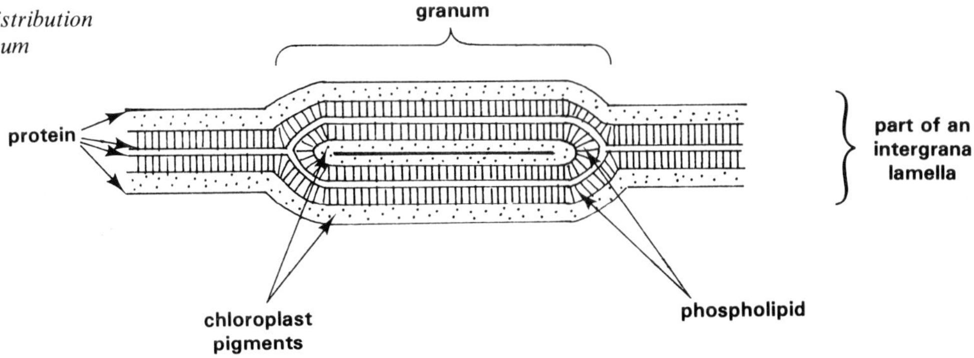

Chloroplasts provide sites on which the biochemical and photochemical reactions of photosynthesis can proceed without interference from those going on in the rest of the cytoplasm. Details of the reactions are given in Chapter 5. In the pigment-containing membranes, and especially in the grana, solar energy is used to produce reduced **nicotinamide-adenine dinucleotide phosphate** (**NADPH**) and ATP in the light-dependent reactions of photosynthesis. The stroma contains the enzymes necessary for the light-independent reactions in which NADPH, carbon dioxide and energy from ATP are used to synthesise energy-rich organic compounds such as sugars and starch. Chloroplasts are thus the organelles in which energy from sunlight is converted to chemical bond energy.

The chloroplasts of higher plant cells originate from simple organelles called **proplastids** which are abundant in actively dividing cells. The proplastids divide and during mitosis (Chapter 7) pass into newly formed cells. Later they differentiate into chloroplasts. There is just as much speculation about the evolution of chloroplasts as there is with mitochondria. A recent hypothesis favours the idea that chloroplasts are the vestiges of primitive algae which once lived symbiotically in the cells of non-green organisms.

1.2.10 The nucleus

The **nucleus** is usually the largest of the cell's organelles and can thus be seen easily with a light microscope. Van Leeuwenhoek is credited with the discovery of the nucleus in the red cells of salmon blood towards the end of the seventeenth century. A distinct nucleus is present at some stage in the cells of all forms of life apart from bacteria, blue-green algae and viruses. Although usually more or less spherical the nucleus can be more complex in shape. For example, the nucleus of a phagocytic white blood cell is lobed (Chapter 9).

In electronmicrographs the nucleus is seen to be bounded by a double-layered **nuclear membrane** (Fig. 1.18). Each layer is a unit membrane, the outer one often covered with ribosomes and continuous with the endoplasmic reticulum. Between the two layers is a **perinuclear space** about 20 nm wide. A prominent feature of the nuclear membrane not seen in the covering membranes of mitochondria and chloroplasts is the presence of numerous **pores**. These may occupy up to 15 per cent of the membrane's surface area, each pore being approximately 50 nm in diameter (Fig. 1.19). The pores provide routes for the passage of materials from the nucleus to the cytoplasm and vice versa.

Inside the nuclear membrane are found two main ingredients, **nucleic acids** and **protein**. Both **ribonucleic acid** (**RNA**) and **deoxyribonucleic acid** (**DNA**) are present, the nucleus being the main store of the cell's DNA.

Nuclear DNA is bound to a number of proteins collectively called **histone**. When the nucleus is not dividing the nucleic acid-protein complex appears as tiny granules of **chromatin**. Among the chromatin granules are one or more densely granular bodies called **nucleoli** composed mainly of DNA.

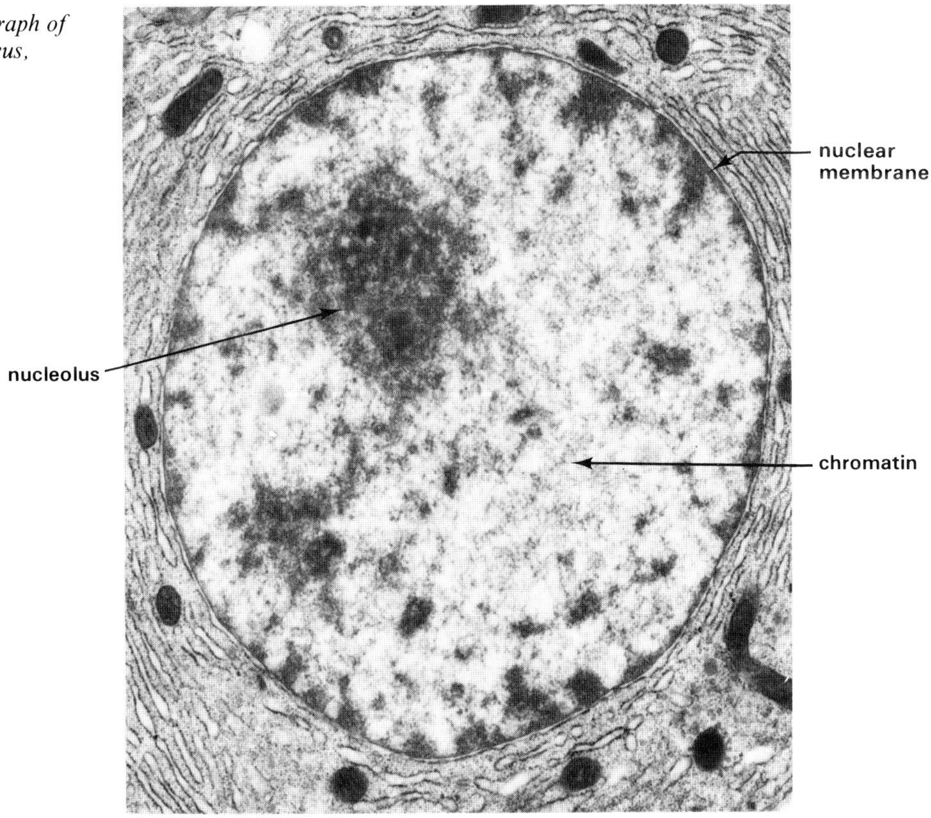

FIG. 1.18 *Electronmicrograph of a section through a nucleus, × 14 000*

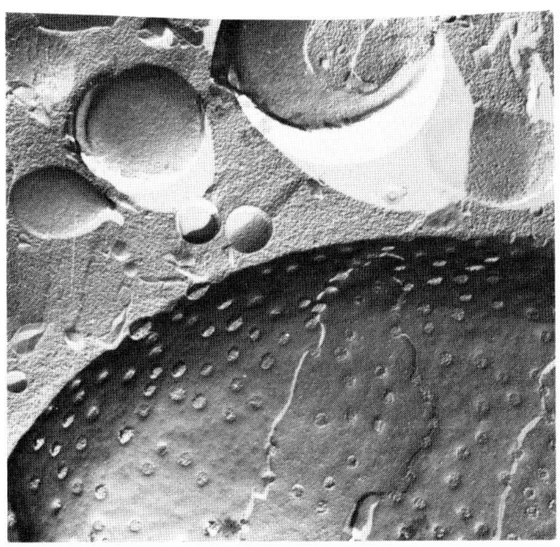

FIG. 1.19 *Electronmicrograph of freeze-etched nuclear membrane of a carrot cell, ×37 000*

During nuclear division the nuclear membrane and nucleoli disappear and the chromatin becomes visible as thread-like bodies called **chromosomes**. At telophase (Chapter 7) the nucleoli reappear near the **nucleolar organiser**, a secondary constriction of one of the pairs of homologous chromosomes. It is thought that nucleoli code the manufacture of tiny globular bodies consisting of protein and RNA. After passing through the nuclear pores the bodies are changed into ribosomes.

The way in which the nucleus transmits hereditary materials is described more fully in Chapter 7. In Chapter 6 you can read about the way in which the nucleic acids provide the genetic code for protein synthesis at the ribosomes.

1.2.11 The plant cell wall

A characteristic of plant cells is that they have a **cell wall**. Structurally the cell wall is like fibre-glass, consisting of fibres embedded in an amorphous matrix. The fibres are of **cellulose**, an unbranched polymer of up to 10 000 β-D-glucose units (Chapter 3). Each fibre is made of several hundred microfibrils in which about 2000 cellulose molecules are held together by hydrogen bonds. The matrix consists of **pectic acid** and its salts calcium and magnesium pectate, and **hemicelluloses** which are polymers of various pentose and hexose sugars. Pectic substances also make up most of the **middle lamella** which binds adjacent plant cells to one another.

The cell wall is secreted by the protoplast it encloses. In young undifferentiated cells, such as those cut off by root and shoot apical meristems, the wall is thin and is called the **primary wall**. The cellulose fibres are orientated at random (Fig. 1.20) so that the primary wall is highly porous. This arrangement allows for considerable stretching when cells grow. Adjacent protoplasts are joined by **plasmodesmata**, threads of cytoplasm which extend through the pores. As a cell grows more cellulose fibres are laid down on the inside of the primary wall forming a thicker **secondary wall**. The cellulose fibres of the secondary wall are closely packed and laid down in an orderly way giving considerable rigidity to the cell wall. Plasmodesmata still exist but the pores through which they pass are now deeper and are called **pits** (Fig. 1.21).

FIG. 1.20 (a) *Electronmicrograph of freeze-etched primary wall of a carrot cell, ×37 000. Note the random arrangement of the cellulose fibres*

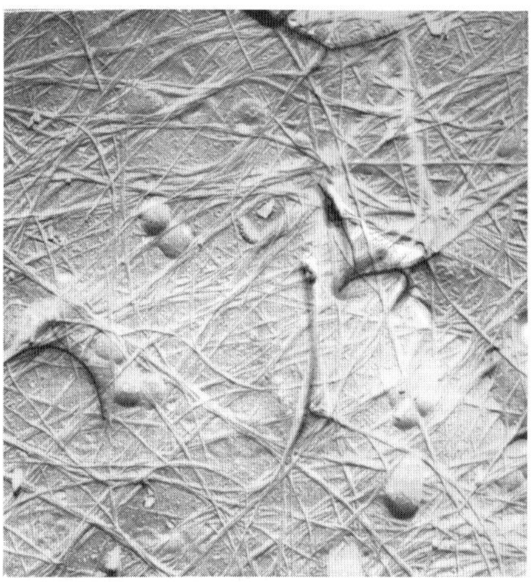

FIG. 1.20 (b) *Electronmicrograph of primary walls of adjacent cells of deadly nightshade, ×35 000*

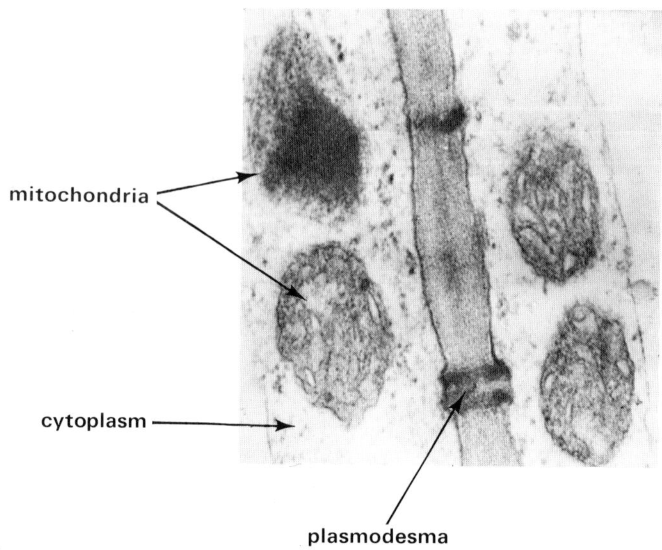

FIG. 1.21 (a) *Electronmicrograph of freeze-etched secondary wall of a carrot cell, × 37 500. Note the orderly arrangement of the cellulose fibres*

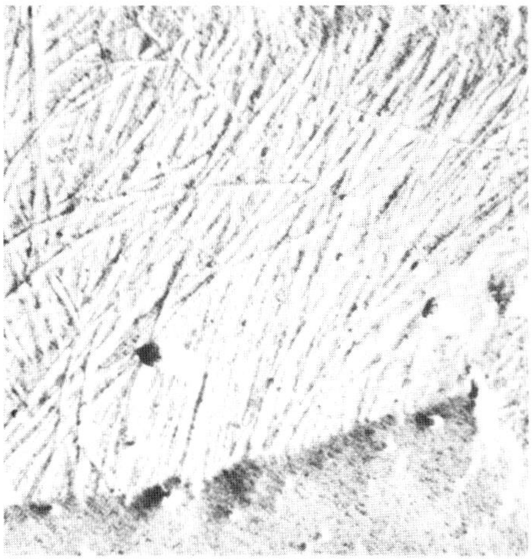

FIG. 1.21 (b) *Electronmicrograph of a freeze-etched bordered pit* (courtesy Philip Harris Biological Ltd.). *The torus is the thickened remains of the plasma membrane. It can be pushed against the border to close the pit* (see Fig. 11.20)

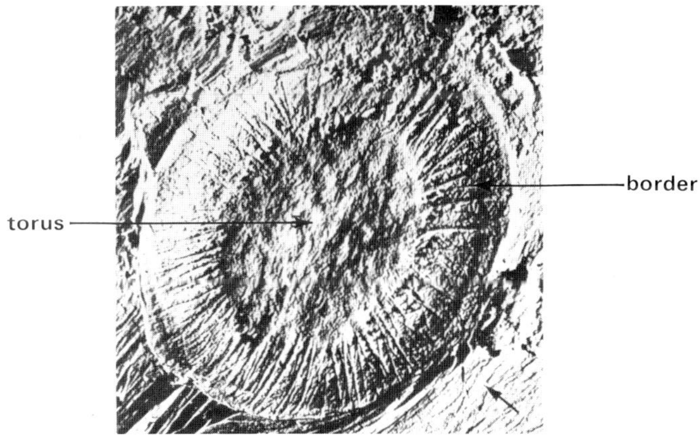

During the differentiation of specialised cells such as xylem vessels, tracheids and sclerenchyma fibres the secondary wall often becomes extremely thick. Together with the primary wall it becomes impregnated with an alcohol polymer called **lignin** which gives the wall great strength. In cork tissue **suberin** impregnates the cell wall, while in the outer walls of epidermal cells of leaves and young stems **cutin** appears instead. Both suberin and cutin are waxy materials which provide an effective waterproof covering to the aerial surfaces of plants (Chapter 11).

1.3 A comparison of light and electron microscopes

Why is it that so much more detail can be made out when specimens are examined with an electron microscope as opposed to a light microscope? Before we can answer this question it is necessary to compare the principles on which light and electron microscopes work.

Figure 1.22 shows the paths of radiation in the two instruments. In both microscopes a tungsten filament lamp is used as a **source of radiation** but whereas the light microscope uses **visible light** to create the final image, the electron microscope uses a **beam of electrons**. The radiation is focused on to the specimen by a **condenser**, which in the light microscope consists of thick glass lenses mounted beneath the stage. Glass is opaque to electrons so in electron microscopes the condenser is a vertical magnetic field produced by a large cylindrical electromagnet which straightens and intensifies the electron beam. The light rays or electrons, as the case may be, now pass through the **specimen** after which the radiation is focused by an **objective lens**. An **eyepiece lens** in the light microscope further enlarges the image. The human eye cannot see electrons so in the electron microscope the final image is projected on to a viewing screen coated with a fluorescent compound such as zinc sulphide. When irradiated with electrons the fluorescent substance emits light visible to the human eye. A comparable process is used to create a picture on a television screen. With both microscopes it is possible to photograph the final image to produce **photomicrographs** and **electronmicrographs**.

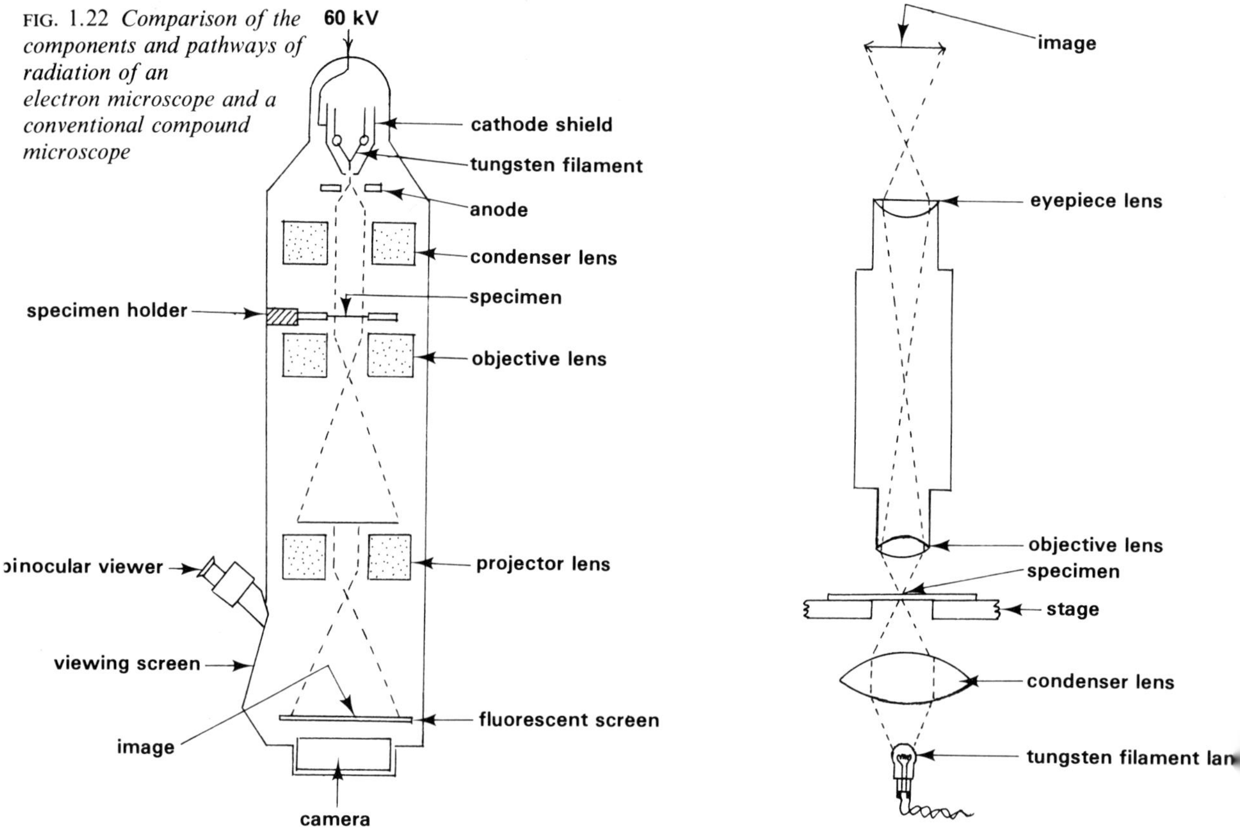

FIG. 1.22 *Comparison of the components and pathways of radiation of an electron microscope and a conventional compound microscope*

Perhaps the most obvious difference in the final images is the extent to which the specimens are magnified. With a high quality compound microscope fitted with an oil-immersion objective a magnification of about 1500 times is possible. An electron microscope can magnify up to 500 000 times. However, it is the **resolving power** of the electron microscope rather than its magnifying power which enables it to produce images containing so much more detail. Resolving power or **resolution** is the ability to make out as separate entities bodies which lie close to one another.

The power of resolution (R) of a microscope depends mainly on the wavelength of the radiation used and on the numerical aperture of the objective lens.

$$R = \frac{0{\cdot}5\,\lambda}{n\,.\,\sin\theta}$$

Where λ = wavelength of radiation

n = refractive index (RI) of medium between specimen and objective lens

$\theta = \frac{1}{2}$ angle of aperture (Fig. 1.23(a))

The expression $n\,.\,\sin\theta$ is called the **numerical aperture** (**NA**) of the objective. The smaller the value of R, the better is the resolving power of the microscope. Using a compound microscope fitted with an oil-immersion objective, R = 210 nm (Fig. 1.23(b)). In other words this instrument is theoretically capable of resolving particles lying as close as 210 nm to one another. In practice it is difficult to achieve a value of R as small as this when viewing unstained preparations with a conventional compound microscope. The phase-contrast microscope provides better powers of contrast but does not improve resolution.

FIG. 1.23 *Angle of aperture and resolution. Calculate the resolution* R *of each of the objectives*

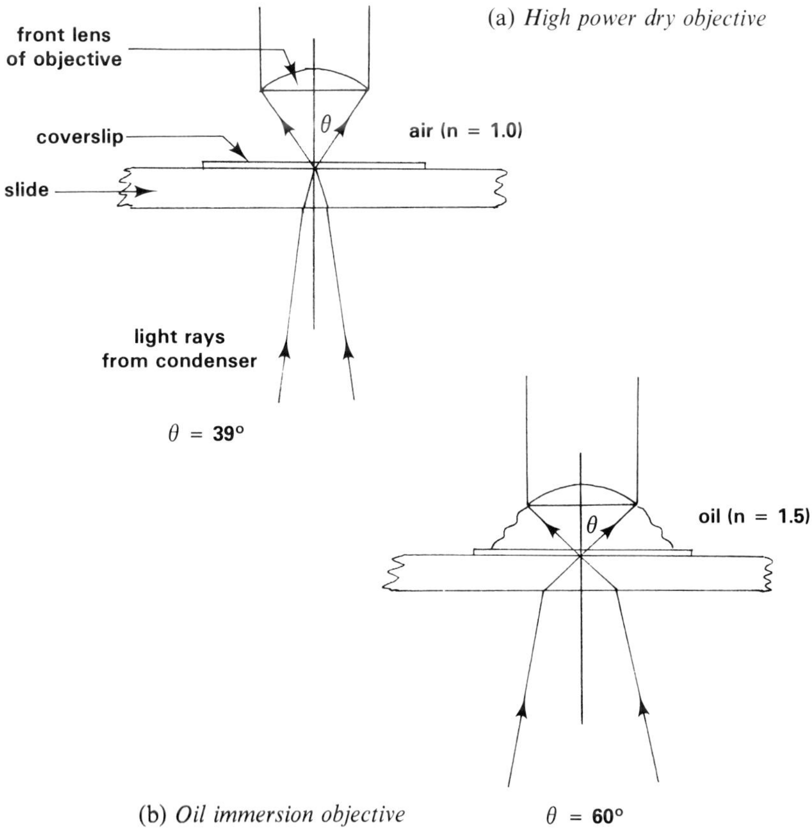

With an electron microscope λ is 0·05 nm which is 10 000 times shorter than the average wavelength of white light. Other things being equal this should produce a corresponding increase in resolution but there are technical difficulties preventing this from being realised in practice. Present-day electron microscopes have resolving powers of about 0·5 nm, about 400 times greater than the light microscope. Compare these figures with the resolving power of the human eye which is about $1{\cdot}0 \times 10^8$ nm.

The major disadvantage of the electron microscope is that it cannot be used to examine live specimens. Because it is necessary to process cells and tissues before they are used for electronmicroscopy, artificial bodies called **artefacts** may appear in electronmicrographs. With this instrument we see mainly the static aspects of cell biology.

How then is so much known about the functions of the various components of cells? One technique which has been of enormous help involves separating or **fractionating** the organelles. The activities of the organelles can then be studied without interference from all of the other reactions which take place in whole cells.

1.4 Cell fractionation

Live tissue is first chopped up in a cold **isotonic buffer** solution. The isotonic solution prevents distortion of the organelles. The chopped tissue is then ground up in an **homogeniser**. A domestic blender can be used for this purpose but it usually breaks most of the organelles. For sophisticated work a motor driven ground glass pestle which fits into a tube is used. This type of homogeniser develops shearing forces just sufficient to rupture the cells. Cells can also be ruptured using ultrasonic waves. The homogenate is then transferred to a **centrifuge** in which the mixture is spun at known speeds whereby the organelles are sedimented separately. The main factors governing sedimentation are the magnitude of the centrifugal force, which depends on the spinning speed, and on the size and density of the suspended particles relative to the medium in which the organelles are suspended. Exact times and speeds of centrifugation vary from one tissue to another and are determined by trial and error.

Centrifugal forces of up to 1000 times the force of gravity ($1000 \times g$) can be attained with simple bench centrifuges used in school laboratories. Large organelles such as nuclei and chloroplasts can be sedimented by spinning at $500–600 \times g$ for 5–10 minutes. If the supernatant liquid is spun at $10\,000–20\,000 \times g$ for 15–20 minutes, mitochondria and lysosomes are sedimented. Fragmented endoplasmic reticulum with attached ribosomes, collectively called **microsomes**, can be sedimented from the supernatant liquid by spinning it for 60 minutes in an **ultracentrifuge** (Fig. 1.24) in which

FIG. 1.24 *An ultracentrifuge* (courtesy Beckman–RIIC Ltd.). *B shows one of the buckets in which the homogenised cell suspension is placed for centrifugation*

forces of 100 000 × g and above are developed. Figure 1.25 summarises the various steps in fractionating cell organelles by differential centrifugation.

Of course, the separation of organelles in this way can lead to their physical and chemical damage. They may not then behave as they normally do in the intact cell where their activities are closely co-ordinated. Nevertheless by suspending the separated components in a medium which closely resembles the intracellular environment some of the functions of organelles can be investigated.

FIG. 1.25 *Flow diagram showing the major stages in the fractionation of organelles by differential centrifugation*

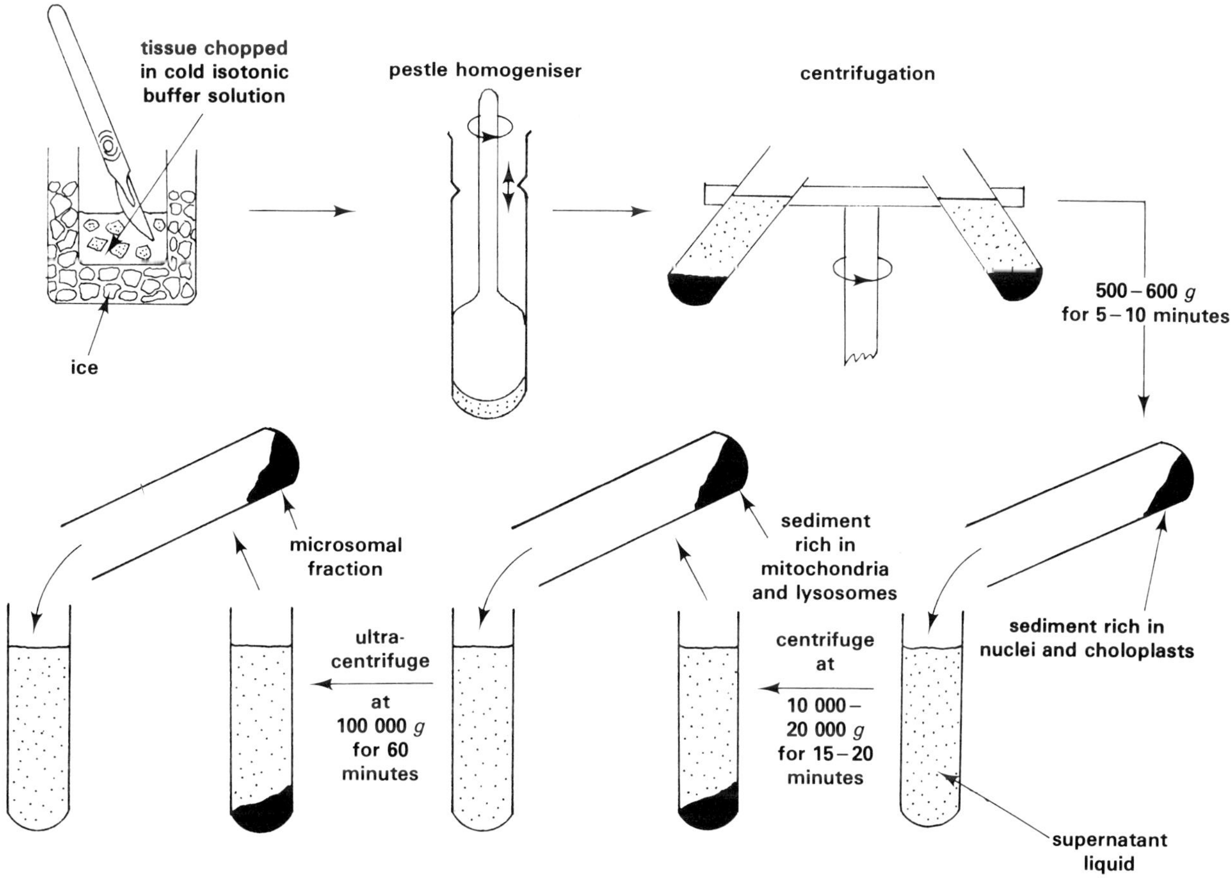

The wealth of information we have about cell structure has clearly depended on technological improvements in microscopy. The electron microscope is the most sophisticated of instruments available to date for probing the fine structure of cells. Useful as it is to know the detailed structure of cells, electronmicrographs tell us little about the functions of the various cellular components. Cell biologists therefore make use of a variety of techniques in investigating the relationship between structure and function. Some of the techniques such as cell fractionation have already been described in this chapter. Details of other techniques are given at appropriate places in the following chapters.

Chapter 2 Water and aqueous solutions

Water is the most common substance on earth. Vast quantities of frozen water make up the ice caps of the north and south poles. Even larger volumes of liquid water fill rivers, lakes and oceans. The atmosphere contains an enormous volume of water vapour. Wherever there is water there is life. Yet the importance of water to living organisms is often overlooked.

Life is thought to have originated in water (Chapter 3) and many present-day species of plants and animals live either in fresh water or in the sea. Irrespective of whether a creature lives in water or on land its life processes cannot occur without water. The living cells of all organisms contain a high proportion of water (Table 2.1) and it is in aqueous solution that metabolic reactions take place. However as we shall see in this chapter there are many other ways in which water is indispensable to all living creatures.

Table 2.1 Water content of living organisms

SPECIMEN	WATER CONTENT PER CENT FRESH MASS
lettuce leaf	93–95
carrot taproot	89–91
strawberry fruit	88–90
jellyfish	95–98
earthworm	82–84
mammal	63–68

In order to appreciate why water is so important to living organisms it is first necessary to know some of the characteristics of water molecules.

2.1 The water molecule

A water molecule consists of two atoms of hydrogen and one atom of oxygen. The atoms are joined in such a way that the single electron of each of the hydrogen atoms is shared with electrons in the outer shell of the

FIG. 2.1 *Formation of a molecule of water*

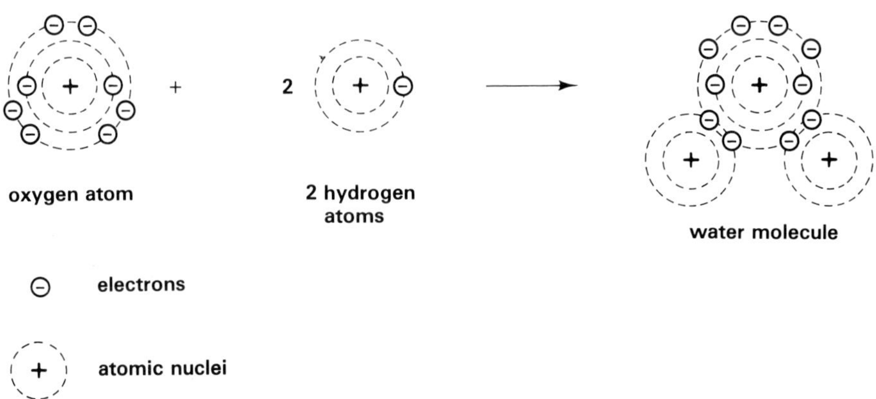

oxygen atom (Fig. 2.1). The unshared pairs of electrons repel the shared pairs so that the hydrogen nuclei are pushed towards one another. As a consequence the molecule is bent (Fig. 2.2). The end of the molecule where the hydrogen nuclei are located is positively charged while the other end where the oxygen atom is found is negatively charged.

Such a molecule is said to be **polar** because the positively charged end differs from the negatively charged end in the way it reacts with ions and charged molecules. The polarity of water molecules accounts for many of the properties of water which are of importance to living organisms.

FIG. 2.2 *The non-linear water molecule*

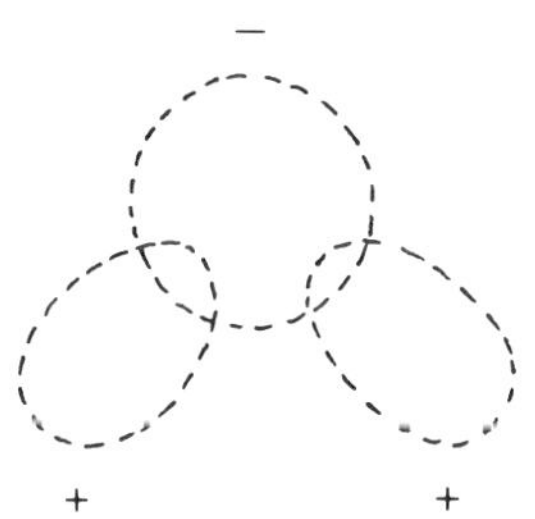

2.2 Properties of water

2.2.1 Thermal properties

Compared with other compounds of about the same relative molar mass, water has higher melting and boiling points and is liquid over a wider temperature range (Table 2.2). The reason for this can be understood by looking at the way in which water molecules react with each other. Because particles of opposite charge attract each other, the negative pole of a water molecule is drawn towards the positive pole of another. Weak **hydrogen bonds** are formed between linked water molecules. In this way a water molecule can bind with up to four others, two attracted to the oxygen atom and one to each of the hydrogen atoms (Fig. 2.3). Water therefore exists as **molecular clusters** rather than as individual molecules.

Table 2.2 Some thermal properties of water and compounds of comparable relative molar mass

SUBSTANCE	FORMULA	RELATIVE MOLAR MASS	MELTING POINT/°C	BOILING POINT/°C
water	H_2O	18	0	100
ammonia	NH_3	17	–78	–33
methane	CH_4	16	–184	161

Temperature has an effect on the amount of bonding between water molecules. At 0°C, the freezing point of water, the molecules are arranged in a regular, hexagonal, crystalline network in which each water molecule is hydrogen-bonded to four others (Fig. 2.4(a)). At temperatures just above 0°C some of the bonds are broken producing clusters of molecules which fit together more compactly than the evenly spaced water molecules in ice (Fig. 2.4(b)). This is why liquid water is denser than ice. Water is most dense at 4°C.

Changes in the density of water are important for the survival of many aquatic organisms. The temperature of a body of open water such as a pond or a lake is affected by the temperature of the air above the water.

FIG. 2.3 *Hydrogen bonding between water molecules*

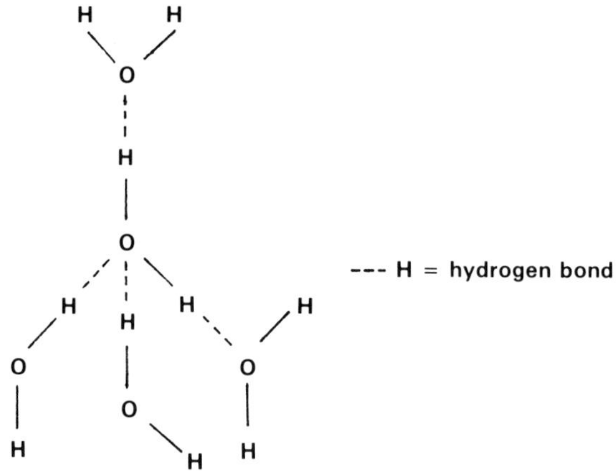

Very cold air causes a body of water to cool from the surface downwards. When the temperature of the upper layers falls to 4°C the dense water sinks bringing warmer water to the surface. Convection currents of this sort delay the freezing of a body of water. Ultimately a point may be reached when the water near the surface freezes. The ice so formed, being less dense than the water beneath, floats on the surface where it insulates the water from further heat loss. Consequently liquid water, in which aquatic life can survive, remains beneath the ice.

FIG. 2.4 (a) *Crystalline structure of ice*

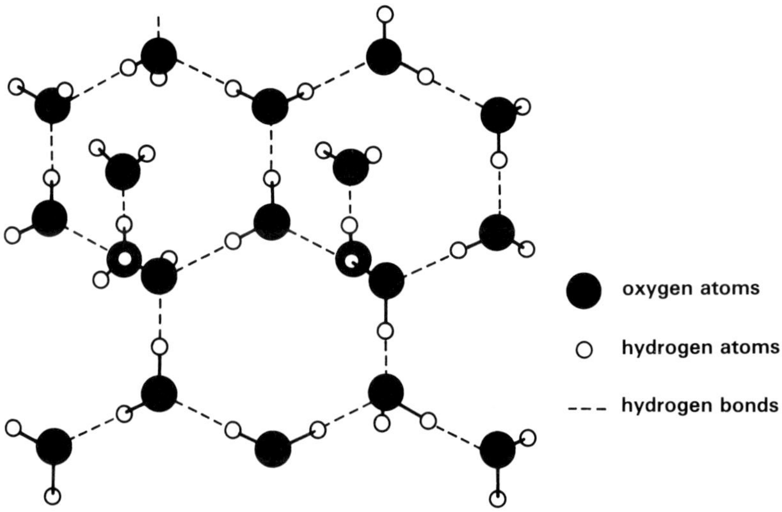

FIG. 2.4 (b) *Packed molecules in liquid water*

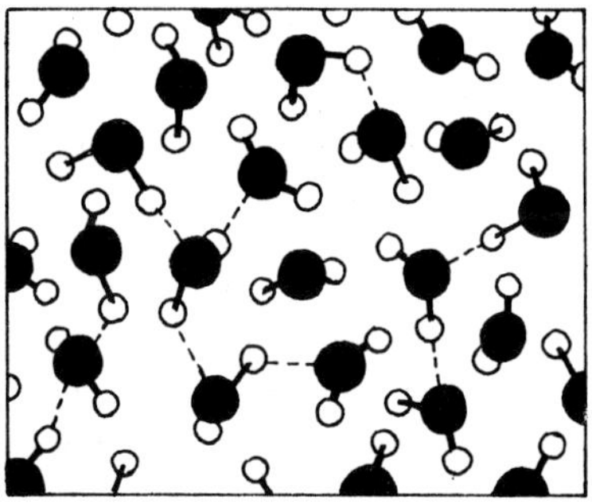

It should by now be evident that heat energy can break the bonds between water molecules. Because of the extensive hydrogen-bonding in ice, a relatively large amount of heat, called the **latent heat of melting**, is required to convert ice to liquid water. This is why water has a relatively high melting point. The formation of water vapour involves the breaking of hydrogen bonds between molecules of liquid water. Evaporation uses a lot of heat energy called the **latent heat of vaporisation**. This is why water has a relatively high boiling point. It also explains why a considerable cooling effect occurs when water evaporates from the bodies of living organisms.

Where do you suppose most of the heat energy for this evaporation comes from? The evaporation of water from terrestrial organisms plays an important role in preventing them from becoming overheated (Chapters 11 and 17).

The amount of heat required to raise the temperature of a given mass of a compound is called the **specific heat capacity**. Water has a much higher specific heat capacity than other compounds of similar relative molar mass. Why do you think this is so? The significance of water's high specific heat capacity to living organisms is that water does not quickly heat up or cool down as air does. It is for this reason that large bodies of water such as oceans and lakes which are inhabited by living organisms have a steady temperature. The ability of water to act as a **thermal buffer** also helps to prevent rapid changes in body temperature of terrestrial organisms. Remember that land-dwelling creatures, like all forms of life, contain a large volume of water.

2.2.2 Density and viscosity

Compared with many other substances water has a high **relative density** (specific gravity). It is for this reason that many living organisms readily float in water. Water is thus a means of external support for aquatic organisms. The buoyancy of water also helps the swimming of motile gametes and in the dispersal of fruits, seeds and spores.

Viscosity is a measure of the difficulty with which molecules slide over one another. You may be excused for thinking that the hydrogen bonds between water molecules should cause water to be highly viscous. However, this is not so. The hydrogen bonds are continually broken and re-formed so that water molecules slide over each other with relative ease. The viscosity of water is thus relatively low and enables water to flow rapidly through the bodies of terrestrial plants (Chapter 11).

Aqueous solutions on the other hand can be very viscous. The high viscosity of blood plasma and lymph is of importance in the smooth flow of body fluids in mammals (Chapter 9).

2.2.3 Surface tension, capillarity and tensile strength

FIG. 2.5 *Pond skaters suspended on the surface film of water*

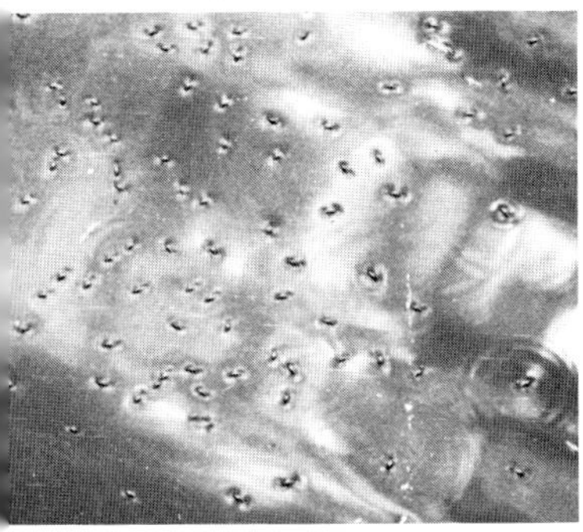

Yet another property of water attributable to the polarity of its molecules is its high **surface tension**. At the surface of an aqueous solution water molecules are pulled downwards and inwards by the hydrogen bonds which join them to water molecules just below the surface. The result is that the surface area of the water shrinks and forms an elastic skin. Some aquatic organisms such as pond skaters and duckweed are sufficiently light to be supported by the elastic skin (Fig. 2.5). Others, such as mosquito larvae, can remain suspended from the underside of the skin.

Surface tension is also mainly responsible for the capillary movement of liquids through fine tubes. **Capillarity** is one of the forces which helps bring about the transport of water through terrestrial plants (Chapter 11).

The individual hydrogen bonds between two linked water molecules are not very strong. However, the combined hydrogen bonding between a large number of water molecules can be strong enough to prevent a column of water from breaking when the column is stretched. Water thus has a high **tensile strength**. This property can be important in the upward movement of water through the vascular tissue of terrestrial plants (Chapter 11).

2.2.4 Penetration by light

Light rays can penetrate water with relative ease because water is transparent. The depth to which light can penetrate is of course reduced if the water is turbid due to suspended particles. In clear water red and yellow light can reach to a depth of 50 m while blue and violet rays can go down to 100 m.

The ability of light to penetrate water enables photosynthetic organisms to inhabit the vast surface volumes of lakes and seas. It also means that light can easily penetrate the transparent water-filled epidermis of leaves and reach the underlying cells which contain the light-absorbing pigments (Chapter 12).

2.2.5 Dissociation of water

The way in which electrons of two hydrogen atoms are shared with electrons of the outer shell of an oxygen atom when a water molecule is formed is described in section 2.1. The nucleus of a hydrogen atom consists of a single positively charged particle called a **hydrogen ion** (H^+), also called a proton. In an aqueous solution small numbers of water molecules lose their hydrogen ions. The remainder of the water molecule is called a **hydroxyl ion** (OH^-). Such molecules are said to be **dissociated**. The process is usually written as:

$$\underset{\text{water}}{H_2O} \rightleftharpoons \underset{\text{hydrogen ion}}{H^+} + \underset{\text{hydroxyl ion}}{OH^-}$$

In reality the hydrogen ions become attached to the oxygen ends of other water molecules to form **oxonium ions** (H_3O^+):

$$2H_2O \rightleftharpoons \underset{\text{oxonium ion}}{H_3O^+} + OH^-$$

What do you think causes the hydrogen ions to bind with the oxygen end rather than the hydrogen end of other water molecules?

In pure water the concentration of hydrogen ions $[H^+]$, or more correctly the oxonium ions, is 10^{-7} mol dm^{-3} at 298 K. The product of the concentrations of hydrogen and hydroxyl ions, which is called the **ionic-product of water K_w**, is always 10^{-14} mol dm^{-3} in any aqueous solution at 298 K:

$$\underset{\substack{\text{ionic-product}\\ \text{of water}}}{K_w} = \underset{\substack{\text{concentration}\\ \text{of } H^+}}{[H^+]} \times \underset{\substack{\text{concentration}\\ \text{of } OH^-}}{[OH^-]}$$

Thus for pure water at 298 K:

$$K_w = 10^{-7} \times 10^{-7} = 10^{-14} \text{ mol dm}^{-3}$$

Remember to add the indices when multiplying numbers expressed in this way.

K_w is the basis of the **pH scale**, a means of indicating the concentration of hydrogen ions in an aqueous solution. The pH of a solution is defined as:

the logarithm to the base 10 of the reciprocal of the hydrogen ion concentration of the solution.

$$\text{pH} = \log_{10}\frac{1}{[H^+]}$$

$$\text{or} \quad \text{pH} = -\log_{10}[H^+]$$

A solution of pH 7·0 is a **neutral** solution. If the pH is less than 7·0 the solution is **acidic** but if the pH is greater than 7·0 the solution is **alkaline**. The pH of pure water at 298 K is:

$-\log_{10} 10^{-7} = 7{\cdot}0$, so pure water is neutral.

Table 2.3 Concentrations (mol dm^{-3}) of H^+ and OH^- in solutions of pH ranging from 0–14

pH	0·0	1·0	2·0	3·0	4·0	5·0	6·0	7·0	8·0	9·0	10	11	12	13	14
$[H^+]$	1·0	10^{-1}	10^{-2}	10^{-3}	10^{-4}	10^{-5}	10^{-6}	10^{-7}	10^{-8}	10^{-9}	10^{-10}	10^{-11}	10^{-12}	10^{-13}	10^{-14}
$[OH^-]$	10^{-14}	10^{-13}	10^{-12}	10^{-11}	10^{-10}	10^{-9}	10^{-8}	10^{-7}	10^{-6}	10^{-5}	10^{-4}	10^{-3}	10^{-2}	10^{-1}	1·0

In all solutions $K_w = [H^+] \times [OH^-] = 10^{-14}$ mol dm^{-3}

Table 2.3 gives the concentrations of hydrogen and hydroxyl ions in solutions ranging from pH 0–14, the full range of the pH scale. How many times more concentrated are the hydrogen ions in solutions of pH 4·0 and 5·0 respectively compared to a solution of pH 7·0?

The pH of cellular fluid is normally between 6·5–8·0. The body fluids of higher animals also have a pH within this range. Even more significant, the hydrogen ion concentration in living organisms is kept fairly constant. Examples of the way in which this is achieved are described later in the chapter. One of the advantages of maintaining a relatively fixed pH inside living organisms is that it enables enzymes to catalyse metabolic reactions efficiently. Should the pH of body fluids go outside the pH range of 6·5–8·0 most enzymes will not work (Chapter 4).

2.2.6 Water as a solvent

A wide range of inorganic and organic substances readily dissolve in water. The reason why water acts as a **solvent** for so many inorganic compounds can be understood by considering the way in which a simple salt such as sodium chloride reacts with water. In a crystal of sodium chloride the sodium and chloride ions are held together by electrovalent bonds. When placed in water the positively charged sodium ions (Na^+) are attracted to the negatively charged oxygen ends of water molecules. Conversely the negatively charged chloride ions (Cl^-) are pulled towards the positively charged hydrogen ends of water molecules. As a consequence the sodium and chloride ions become separated by clusters of water molecules and an **aqueous solution** of sodium chloride is formed (Fig. 2.6). The polarity of water molecules is clearly a key factor in the ability of water to dissolve inorganic substances.

FIG. 2.6 *Reaction between sodium chloride and water*

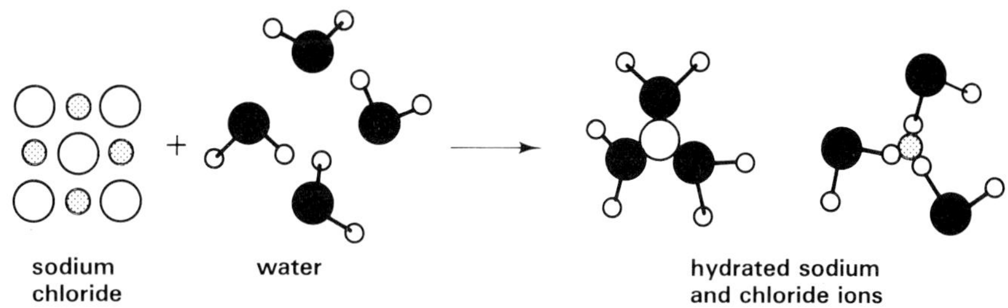

Many biologically important organic substances do not ionise yet they also dissolve in water. This is because they form hydrogen bonds with water. The hydroxyl (—OH) groups of sugar molecules, imino ($>$NH) groups of amino acids and proteins, and carbonyl ($>$C = O) groups of organic acids react with water in this way. Molecules of such organic compounds thus become surrounded by water molecules and go into solution.

1. TRUE SOLUTIONS

For the reasons outlined above many inorganic and organic particles smaller than 10^{-5} cm in diameter dissolve quickly in water to form what is called a **true solution**. The dissolving power of water is particularly important in the uptake by, and transportation of substances inside the bodies of plants and animals (Chapters 9, 11, 13 and 14). Metabolic reactions catalysed by enzymes also take place in aqueous solution (Chapter 4).

2. THE COLLOIDAL STATE

Particles between 10^{-3} and 10^{-5} cm in diameter such as polysaccharides and proteins of high relative molar mass do not form true solutions with water. Such particles attract water owing to hydrogen-bonding between water molecules and hydroxyl, imino and carbonyl groups. A colloidal state then exists with water acting as a **dispersion medium** in which the particles, known as the **disperse phase**, are permanently suspended. Substances which react with water in this way are called **hydrophilic colloids**. Cytoplasm is a good example of a colloid, suspended protein molecules providing cells with a vast number of fixed sites on which metabolic reactions can occur (Chapter 1). The plasma of mammalian blood is another example. Here the blood proteins which form the disperse phase play important roles in blood clotting, combating infection and in the formation of tissue fluid (Chapter 9). Hydrophilic colloids cling to water and so help to prevent the evaporation of water from organisms which live on land.

3. SUSPENSIONS

Particles larger than 10^{-3} cm in diameter do not dissolve in water but can be temporarily dispersed in water to form a **suspension**. On standing, the disperse phase of a suspension gradually separates from the dispersion medium. A suspension is formed when fats and oils are emulsified in the mammalian gut (Chapter 14). The disperse phase has a large surface area on which fat-splitting enzymes can work.

The dissolving power of water is very important for many of the activities of living organisms. Nevertheless, we should not overlook the fact that the inability of some substances to dissolve readily in water sometimes poses serious problems to plants and animals. For example, if we compare the volumes of some common gases in air and in water in direct contact with air we immediately see some startling differences (Table 2.4). Whereas carbon dioxide dissolves in water with ease, oxygen and nitrogen do not. Oxygen for respiration is thus much less available to aquatic as opposed to terrestrial organisms. It also means that the transport of oxygen in aqueous solutions inside the bodies of living organisms is inefficient unless an oxygen-carrying pigment is present (Chapter 9). Even though the relative volumes of carbon dioxide in air and in aerated water are similar, the rate at which gases diffuse through water is much slower than through air. For this reason the rate at which carbon dioxide diffuses through the protoplasm of photosynthesising cells before reaching the chloroplasts is a factor which limits the productivity of plants (Chapter 12).

Table 2.4 Amounts of some common gases in air and in water in direct contact with air

	PERCENTAGE COMPOSITION		
	OXYGEN	NITROGEN	CARBON DIOXIDE
air	20·95	78·0	0·03
water (at 10°C)	0·64	1·2	0·03

2.3 Some properties of aqueous solutions

Some of the properties of aqueous solutions have already been touched on in this chapter. It is worthwhile exploring a number of these properties more fully. Two properties in particular are important to living organisms. Firstly there are those properties governed by the nature of the solute. Of special importance in this context are **acids**, **bases** and **buffers**. Then there are the **colligative properties** which are governed by the number of solute particles per unit volume of water, that is the concentration of an aqueous solution.

2.3.1 Acids, bases and buffers

An **acid** is a substance which dissociates in solution to release **hydrogen ions** (H^+). Most organic acids are called **weak acids** because few of their molecules dissociate. Conversely, many inorganic acids are **strong acids** because most of their molecules dissociate. Both weak and strong acids are found in living cells. Carboxylic acids are weak acids produced by all living organisms. Hydrochloric acid produced by cells in the stomach lining is a strong acid.

Substances which accept H^+ are called **bases**. A reaction between an acid and a base involves a **conjugate acid-base pair** which consists of a H^+ donor and a H^+ acceptor. Acid-base pairs are found in solutions containing weak acids and their salts. Let us consider a mixture of ethanoic acid and sodium ethanoate. The acid, being a weak acid, dissociates to yield a small number of ions:

$$\underset{\text{ethanoic acid}}{CH_3COOH} \rightleftharpoons \underset{\text{hydrogen ion}}{H^+} + \underset{\text{ethanoate ion}}{CH_3COO^-}$$

However, the salt dissociates to produce a large number of ethanoate ions:

$$\underset{\text{sodium ethanoate}}{CH_3COONa} \rightleftharpoons \underset{\text{ethanoate ion}}{CH_3COO^-} + \underset{\text{sodium ion}}{Na^+}$$

Because the ethanoate ions have a high affinity for H^+, they remove a large proportion of H^+ added to the mixture so the pH of the solution remains almost constant. This effect is called the **buffering capacity** of the acid-base pair.

The main buffer which prevents large fluctuations of pH in cells is the dihydrogenphosphate and hydrogenphosphate acid-base pair. The blood and tissue fluids of higher animals are buffered by the carbonic acid–hydrogencarbonate acid-base pair (Chapters 8 and 9). The importance of buffers in living organisms cannot be overstressed. They help to stabilize the pH of cellular and body fluids, so helping to maintain suitable conditions for enzymes to efficiently catalyse metabolic reactions (Chapter 4).

2.3.2 Colligative properties

Biologically, the colligative properties of most interest are **depression of the freezing point** and **elevation of the boiling point** of aqueous solutions and the fact that aqueous solutions have **osmotic properties**.

1. DEPRESSION OF THE FREEZING POINT

When a mole of a non-electrolyte such as a sugar is dissolved in 1 dm^3 of water the solution so formed of concentration 1·0 mol dm^{-3}, has a freezing point of $-1·86$°C. More concentrated solutions freeze at lower temperatures.

Because the water in living cells contains dissolved substances it follows that cellular fluid freezes only when exposed to temperatures below the freezing point of pure water. The body fluids of fish living in seas near the north and south poles are rich in solutes. Some of the solutes are similar to anti-freeze compounds used to stop the cooling system of a motor car engine freezing during winter. Even when the sea in which these fish live becomes frozen solid their body fluids remain liquid. A similar effect occurs to a lesser extent in all living organisms. The chances of damage to body tissues due to the formation of razor-sharp ice crystals inside living cells is thus minimised.

2. ELEVATION OF THE BOILING POINT

A solution of a non-electrolyte of concentration 1·0 mol dm^{-3} has a boiling point of 100·54°C compared with 100°C for pure water. The more concentrated the solution the higher is the temperature at which it boils.

The higher boiling point of a solution compared with pure water is of some importance to land-dwelling organisms. It means that slightly more heat is required if water is to evaporate from their bodies. As a result the chance of desiccation is lessened.

3. OSMOTIC PROPERTIES

When pure water is separated from an aqueous solution by a selectively permeable membrane there is a net flow of water into the solution (Fig. 2.7). The process by which the net flow of water occurs is called **osmosis**. Entry of water into the solution can be stopped if pressure is applied at C. The pressure required to prevent water passing from A to B is called the osmotic pressure of the solution. The Dutch chemist Van't Hoff discovered that the size of the osmotic pressure depends on the concentration of the solution. He found that solutions of non-electrolytes such as sugars of concentration 1·0 mol dm^{-3} have an osmotic pressure of -2270 *k*Pa ($-22·4$ atm) at STP compared with pure water which has an osmotic pressure of 0 under similar conditions. Today the term **osmotic potential** is used instead of osmotic pressure.

In the arrangement shown in Figure 2.7 the water molecules on either side of the membrane have kinetic energy and move about at random. The total amount of kinetic energy of water on either side of the membrane is called the **water potential**. Pure water at STP has a water potential of 0. Water molecules moving near the membrane may hit the solid parts of the membrane and bounce off or they may slip through the pores. In this way water moves either way through the membrane from A to B and from B to A. The movement of water from A to B is impeded only by other water molecules whereas movement from B to A is impeded by dissolved solute molecules to which water molecules are attracted. The water molecules in A therefore have more kinetic energy than those in B. In other words the water potential in A is higher than in B. Because diffusible substances move from areas of high potential to areas of low potential, water passes from A to B. One way of defining osmosis is therefore:

the net diffusion of water through a selectively permeable membrane from a place of high water potential to a place of low water potential.

It should be apparent that a net osmotic flow of water from A to B will occur if a solution is placed in A instead of pure water providing the solution in A is less concentrated than in B. Attempt to explain why this happens in terms of a difference in water potential.

FIG. 2.7 *A simple osmometer*

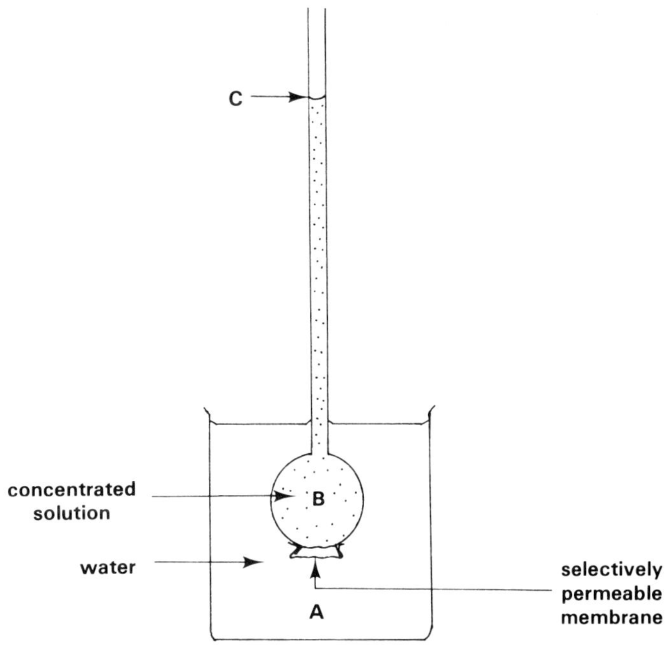

2.4 Uptake and loss of water by living cells

One of the ways in which water enters and leaves living cells is by osmosis. It is convenient to look at the osmotic behaviour of plant and animal cells separately.

2.4.1 Osmotic behaviour of plant cells

The main part of the body of most terrestrial plants consists of a tissue called parenchyma (Chapter 21). Parenchyma cells have a **wall** made of a jelly-like mixture of hemicelluloses and pectic compounds in which fibres of cellulose are enmeshed. The wall is porous and permeable to aqueous solutions. In contrast the outer boundary of the protoplast called the plasma membrane is **selectively permeable**. Whereas water can move freely through the plasma membrane, dissolved solutes cannot. The protoplast contains **sap**, an aqueous solution of inorganic and organic substances.

Much of the sap is localised in one or more conspicuous vacuoles each bounded by a selectively permeable membrane called the tonoplast (Fig. 2.8).

FIG. 2.8 *A parenchyma cell*

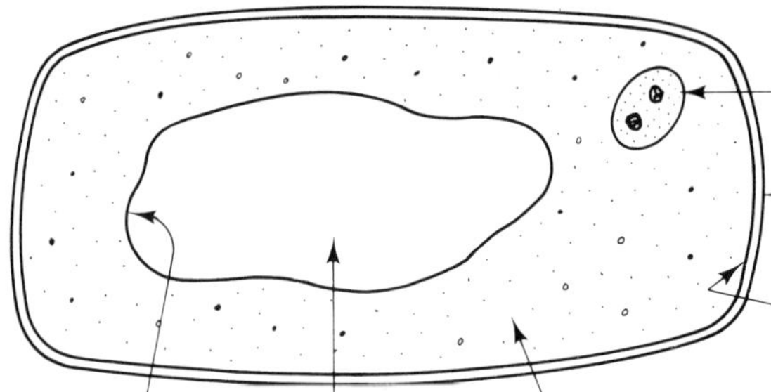

If the protoplast is sufficiently swollen to press firmly against the wall the cell is **turgid**. Should the protoplast be too small to create such a pressure the cell is **flaccid**. When a flaccid cell is immersed in water there is a net inward osmotic flow of water because the selectively permeable plasma membrane separates a place of low water potential, the cell sap, from a place of higher water potential, the water outside the cell. As water enters the cell the protoplast enlarges until it presses against the cell wall with a force called **turgor pressure**. The cell wall opposes the turgor pressure with a force of equal magnitude known as **wall pressure**. If water continues to enter the cell the wall pressure ultimately becomes so great that any further net osmotic uptake of water stops. At this stage the cell is fully turgid. The term **pressure potential** is used to indicate the tendency for water to be forced out of an expanding cell due to turgor pressure and wall pressure. Pressure potential is usually a positive force.

The ability of a cell to absorb water by osmosis is called its **water potential**. Remember that pure water has a potential of 0 at STP. Also keep in mind that cell sap has a lower, that is a negative water potential compared with water. The two factors which determine the size of the water potential of a plant cell are the osmotic potential of its sap (OPi) and the pressure potential (PP) of the protoplast. The following equation shows how the factors are related:

$$\underset{\text{water potential of cell}}{\mathrm{WP}} = \underset{\text{osmotic potential of cell sap}}{\mathrm{OPi}} + \underset{\text{pressure potential}}{\mathrm{PP}}$$

For example, if

$\mathrm{OPi} = -1013\,k\mathrm{Pa}\,(-10\ \mathrm{atm})$ and $\mathrm{PP} = +506{\cdot}5\,k\mathrm{Pa}\,(+5\ \mathrm{atm})$:

$\mathrm{WP} = -1013 + 506{\cdot}5 = -506{\cdot}5\ k\mathrm{Pa}\,(-5\ \mathrm{atm})$

The osmotic behaviour of a cell immersed in an aqueous solution depends on the difference between the water potential of the cell and the water potential and thus the osmotic potential of the solution (OPe). A non-turgid cell absorbs water so long as its water potential is more negative than that of the solution. A solution which has this effect is said to be **hypotonic**.

For example, if

$OPi = -1013\ kPa\ (-10\ atm)$, $PP = +506{\cdot}5\ kPa\ (+5\ atm)$

and $OPe = -303{\cdot}9\ kPa\ (-3\ atm)$:

$WP = -1013 + 506{\cdot}5 - (-303{\cdot}9) = -202{\cdot}6\ kPa\ (-2\ atm)$,

so the cell absorbs water.

If, however, the water potential of the solution is lower than that of the cell, water is withdrawn from the cell. As water is lost the protoplast shrinks and soon ceases to press against the cell wall. This condition is called **incipient plasmolysis**. Further withdrawal of water causes the protoplast to display **total plasmolysis**. When this happens the protoplast becomes a spherical mass at the centre of the cell. A solution which has this effect on the cell is said to be **hypertonic**.

FIG. 2.9 *Epidermal cells of beetroot petiole, ×250*

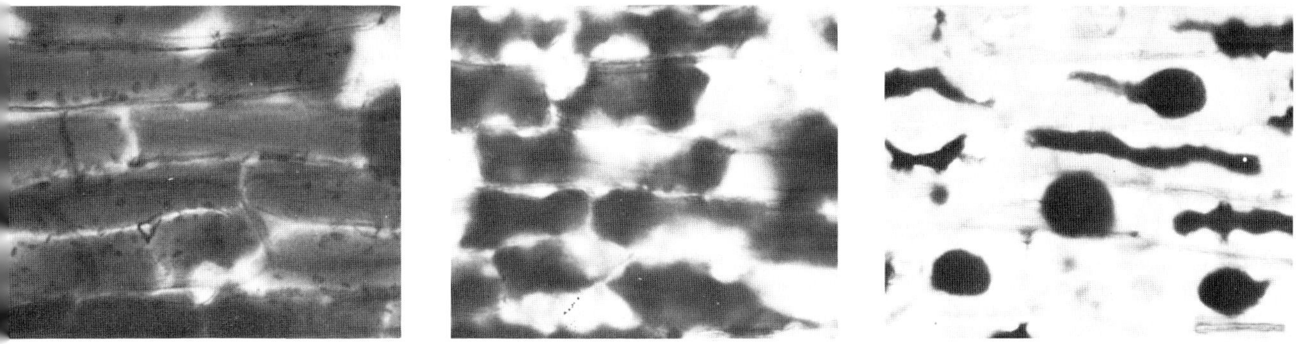

partial turgidity (ii) *incipient plasmolysis* (iii) *total plasmolysis*

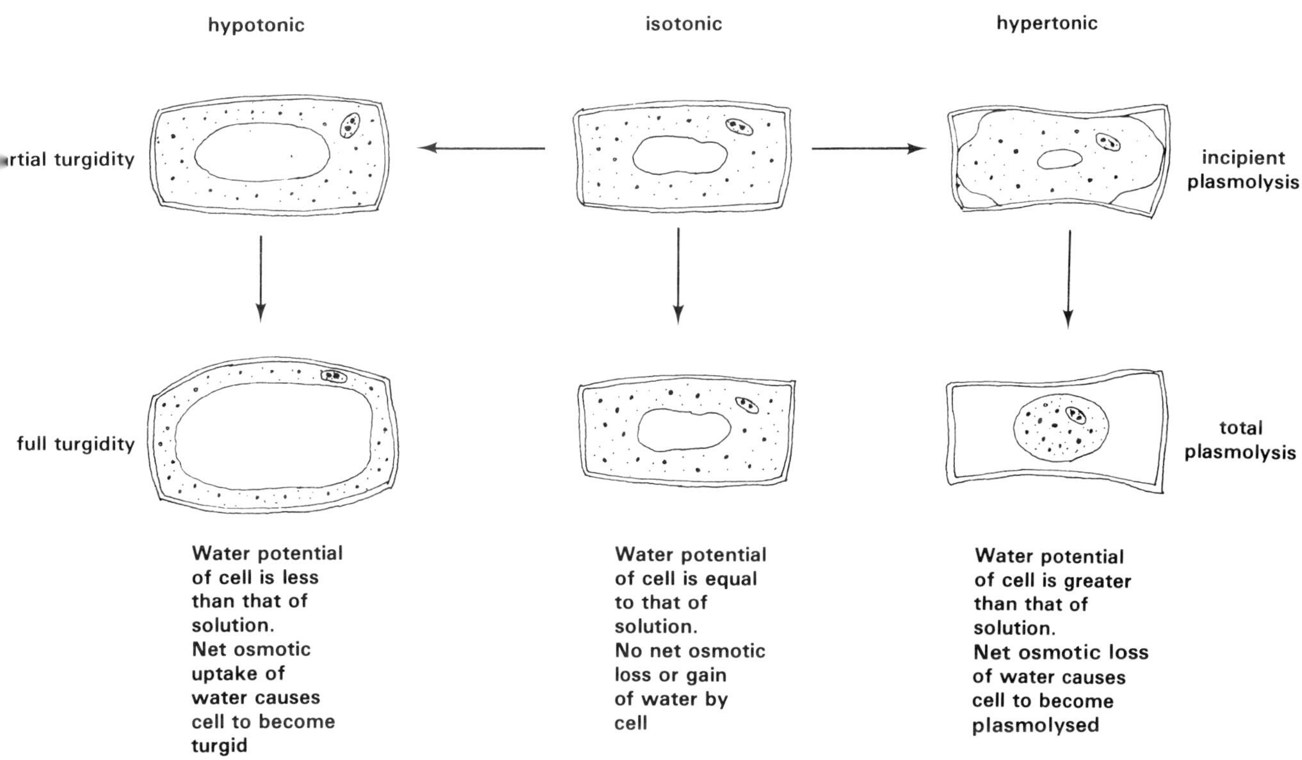

For example, if

$OPi = -1013\ kPa\ (-10\ atm),\ PP = +506{\cdot}5\ kPa\ (+5\ atm)$
and $OPe = -1215{\cdot}6\ kPa\ (-12\ atm)$:

$WP = -1013 + 506{\cdot}5 - (-1215{\cdot}6) = +709{\cdot}1\ kPa\ (+7\ atm)$,
so the cell loses water.

The third possibility is that the osmotic potential of the solution is such that there is no net loss or gain of water by the cell. In other words the water potential of the cell and the external solution are equal. Such a solution is said to be **isotonic**.

For example, if

$OPi = -1013\ kPa\ (-10\ atm),\ PP = +506{\cdot}5\ kPa\ (+5\ atm)$
and $OPe = -506{\cdot}5\ kPa\ (-5\ atm)$:

$WP = -1013 + 506{\cdot}5 - (-506{\cdot}5) = 0\ kPa\ (0\ atm)$,
so there is no net loss or gain of water by the cell.

The events outlined above are illustrated in Figure 2.9. Figure 2.10 shows the relationship between the various factors which affect the osmotic behaviour of plant cells. The way in which osmosis participates in the movement of water through terrestrial plants is described in Chapter 11.

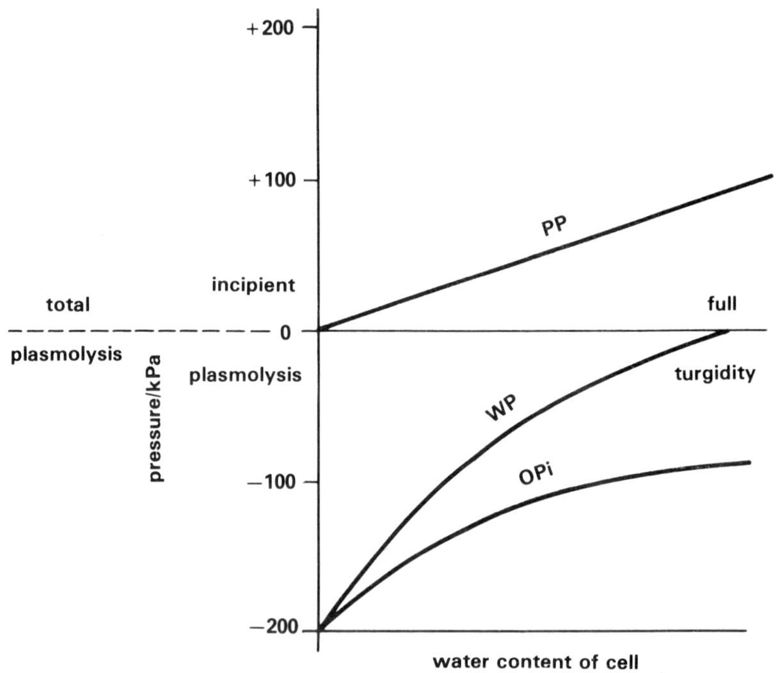

FIG. 2.10 *Graphical relationship between the factors affecting the osmotic behaviour of plant cells*

2.4.2 Osmotic behaviour of animal cells

Animal cells do not have a cell wall so wall pressure is not among the factors affecting their water potential. The osmotic potential of the cell sap (OPi) is the main factor which determines the water potential of animal cells.

When immersed in an aqueous solution animal cells behave in three different ways depending on the osmotic potential (OPe) of the external solution. If placed in a hypotonic solution there is a net osmotic uptake of water by the cell which therefore becomes turgid. If a large volume of water is absorbed the plasma membrane bursts and the contents of the cell are spilled into the solution. The bursting of red blood cells in this way is called **haemolysis**. If immersed in a hypertonic solution there is a net osmotic loss of water by the cell which therefore shrinks. Red blood cells take on a **crenated** appearance when this happens. Finally when placed in an isotonic solution there is no net loss or gain of water by the cells. In this solution the cell's water content remains steady. Figure 2.11 illustrates the osmotic behaviour of red blood cells when placed in solutions of different osmotic potential.

FIG. 2.11 *Osmotic behaviour of a red blood cell following immersion in different solutions*

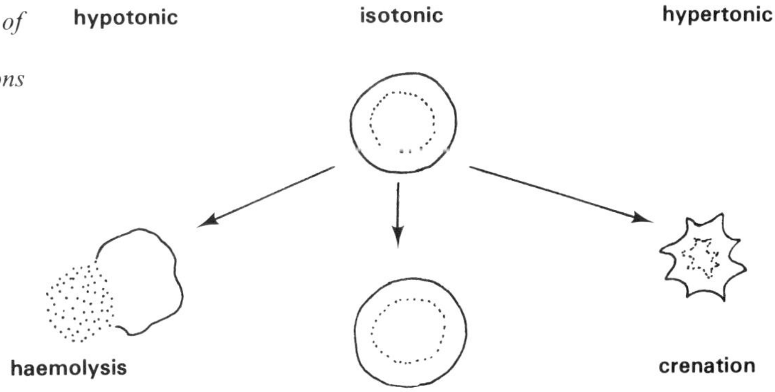

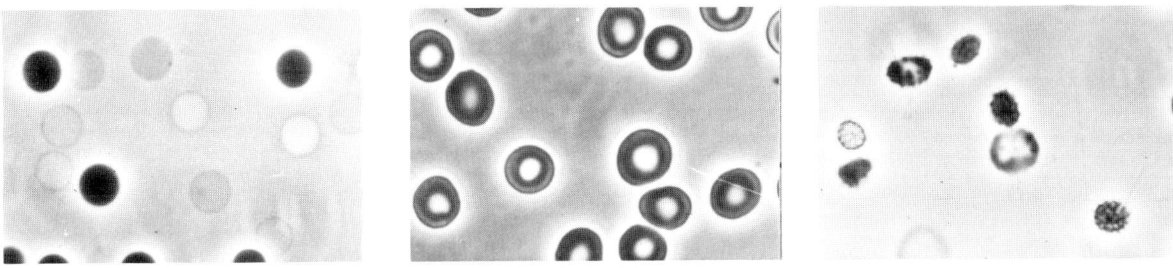

(i) *haemolysis* (ii) *red blood cells,* $\times 800$ (iii) *crenation*

A variety of mechanisms has evolved among animals which protect their cells from excessive intake or loss of water by osmosis. One of the simplest devices is seen in fresh-water protozoans such as *Amoeba* and *Paramecium* where the **contractile vacuole** eliminates excess water absorbed from the environment (Fig. 2.12). In mammals the means of keeping the tissue fluid isotonic with cellular fluid is an elaborate process in which the kidneys play a key role (Chapter 10).

2.4.3 Non-osmotic movement of water

Osmosis is not the only process responsible for water movement in and out of the cells. Water is taken in by cells when pockets are formed in the plasma membrane during **pinocytosis** and **phagocytosis** (Chapter 1). Cells also contain hydrophilic substances such as polysaccharides and proteins which chemically attract water, a phenomenon called **imbibition** (section 2.2.6). The absorption of water by dry seeds during the early stages of

FIG. 2.12 *The protozoan* Paramecium *as seen with a phase-contrast microscope* (courtesy Philip Harris Biological Ltd.) × *700*

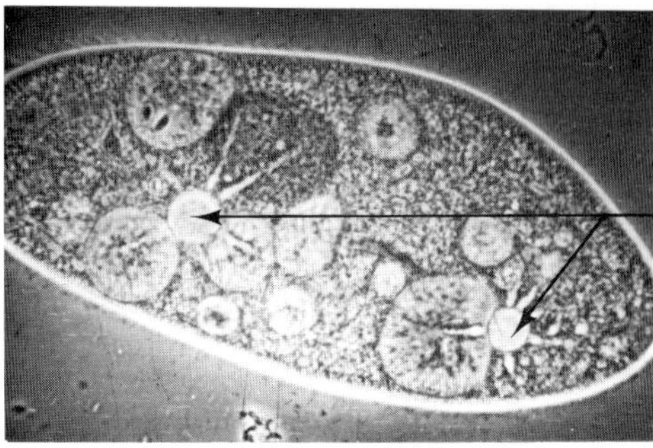

germination is largely due to imbibition (Chapter 20). The imbibing power of the polysaccharides in cell walls also probably plays a substantial role in the transport of water through terrestrial plants (Chapter 11).

Diffusion is the name given to the process whereby particles move from a place where they are highly concentrated to places where they are less concentrated. Osmosis is a special case of diffusion because of the involvement of a selectively permeable membrane. However, there are instances when water diffuses without passing through membranes. The **evaporation** of water and its subsequent diffusion into the atmosphere is the main cause of water loss from terrestrial organisms. Such processes are also of significance in the transport of water through land-dwelling plants. These and other aspects of water movement in whole organisms are described more fully in Chapters 9 and 11.

Chapter 3

The chemical constituents of cells

Many of the compounds commonly found in living organisms are **carbon compounds**. Carbon has properties which make it specially suited as an essential component of most biochemicals. The outer shell of a carbon atom requires four electrons for it to be completed. It means that there are four positions at which other atoms can become covalently bonded to carbon by sharing electrons in their outer shells. For this reason, carbon is said to be **tetravalent**. The atoms of most other elements have fewer bonding sites.

Stable covalent bonds are formed when carbon joins to a variety of other atoms such as hydrogen, oxygen, nitrogen, phosphorus and sulphur. Carbon, nitrogen and oxygen atoms can also share one or two pairs of electrons to form single or double bonds. Consequently a variety of **functional groups**, such as amino, carboxyl, hydroxyl and phosphate, are components of the diverse range of carbon compounds found in living organisms.

Carbon atoms can also join covalently to other carbon atoms. In this way rings of carbon atoms form the **skeleton** of sugar molecules, while the **backbone** of the hydrocarbon chains of fatty acids is a chain of carbon atoms. Many other carbon compounds are built in this way. To add to this, the atoms which bond with carbon are arranged spatially in **three dimensions** (Fig. 3.1). For this reason, carbon compounds are of widely differing shapes and sizes.

3.1 Carbohydrates

Sugars, starch, glycogen and cellulose are well-known examples of a vast group of compounds called **carbohydrates**. They all consist of just three elements: carbon, hydrogen and oxygen.

3.1.1 Monosaccharides

Monosaccharides are carbohydrates of low relative molar mass. They have an empirical molecular formula $(CH_2O)_n$. All monosaccharides are white, crystalline solids which are sweet to taste and dissolve readily in water. They can be classified according to the number of carbon atoms present in each molecule (Table 3.1).

Table 3.1 Some examples of monosaccharide sugars

	MOLECULAR FORMULA	EXAMPLES
trioses	$C_3H_6O_3$	glyceraldehyde
pentoses	$C_5H_{10}O_5$	ribose, ribulose
hexoses	$C_6H_{12}O_6$	glucose, fructose

The molecules of all monosaccharides have an unbranched backbone of carbon atoms, all but one of these atoms having an attached hydroxyl ($-OH$) group. The exceptional carbon atom is part of a carbonyl ($>C=O$) group. In **aldose sugars**, for example **glucose**, the carbonyl group is situated at one end of the molecule where it forms part of an aldehyde ($-\overset{\diagup H}{C}=O$) group. Where the carbonyl group occurs at any other position, as in **fructose** molecules, it is part of a ketone group and the substance is called a **ketose sugar**. The carbonyl group has a strong tendency to donate electrons and it is this property which is responsible for the **reducing powers** of monosaccharide sugars. In Fehling's test the carbonyl group reduces copper(II) ions to copper(I) ions.

Reaction on mixing Fehling's solutions 1 and 2:

$$\underset{\text{copper(II) sulphate}}{CuSO_4} + \underset{\text{sodium hydroxide}}{2NaOH} \longrightarrow \underset{\text{copper(II) hydroxide}}{Cu(OH)_2} + \underset{\text{sodium sulphate}}{Na_2SO_4}$$

Reaction with reducing sugar:

$$2Cu(OH)_2 + R-\overset{\overset{H}{|}}{C}=O \longrightarrow \underset{\substack{\text{copper(I) oxide}\\\text{(brick red}\\\text{precipitate)}}}{Cu_2O} + \underset{\text{sugar acid}}{R.COOH} + 2H_2O$$

Molecules of nearly all the monosaccharide sugars have one or more **asymmetric carbon atoms**, that is carbon atoms bonded to four different functional groups. Glyceraldehyde has one such carbon atom and because of this can exist in two forms (Fig. 3.1). The D- and L-forms differ only in the spatial disposition of the functional groups attached to the asymmetric carbon atom. The two forms are called **stereoisomers** and the D-form is a non-superimposable mirror image of the L-form. Only D-isomers are commonly found in living organisms.

FIG. 3.1 *Stereoisomers of glyceraldehyde*

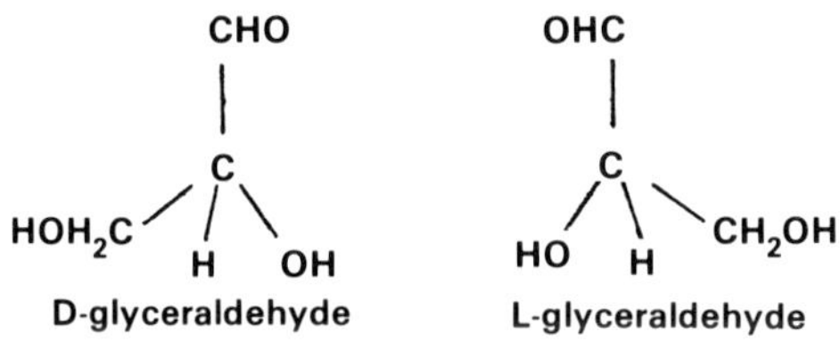

The number of isomers of any compound is determined by the number of asymmetric carbon atoms in one of its molecules. Some hexose sugars have 4 such atoms so 16 isomers are possible (derived from the formula 2^n, where n = no. of asymmetric carbon atoms). The molecular structures of some biologically important D-sugars are shown in Figure 3.2.

FIG. 3.2 *Molecular structure of some D-sugars*

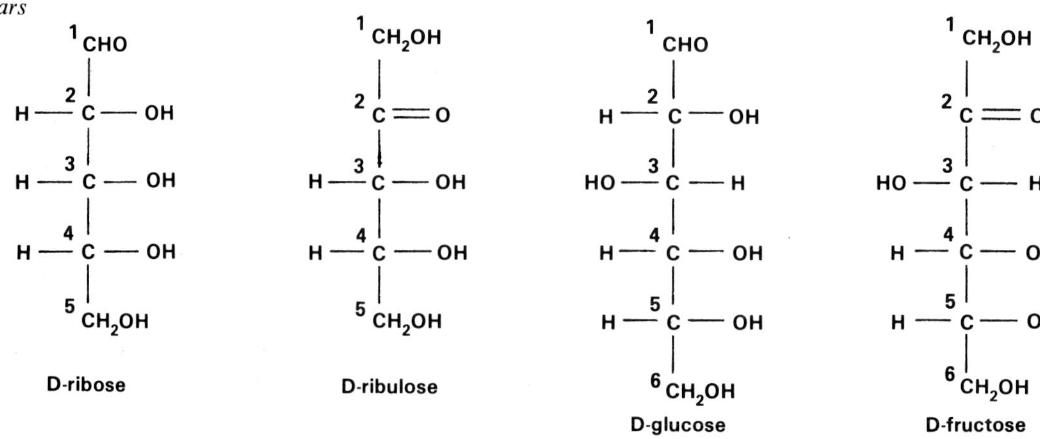

When dissolved in water many monosaccharides have an additional asymmetric carbon atom. For instance, D-glucose in aqueous solution occurs in two forms called α- and β-D-glucose. These are six-sided ring molecules in which the carbonyl group at carbon atom *1* reduces the hydroxyl group attached to carbon atom 5. As a consequence carbon atom *1* is now asymmetric because it has four different functional groups attached to it. The only difference between α- and β-D-glucose is the spatial orientation of the hydrogen and hydroxyl groups at carbon atom *1* (Fig. 3.3).

FIG. 3.3 *Ring forms of D-glucose*

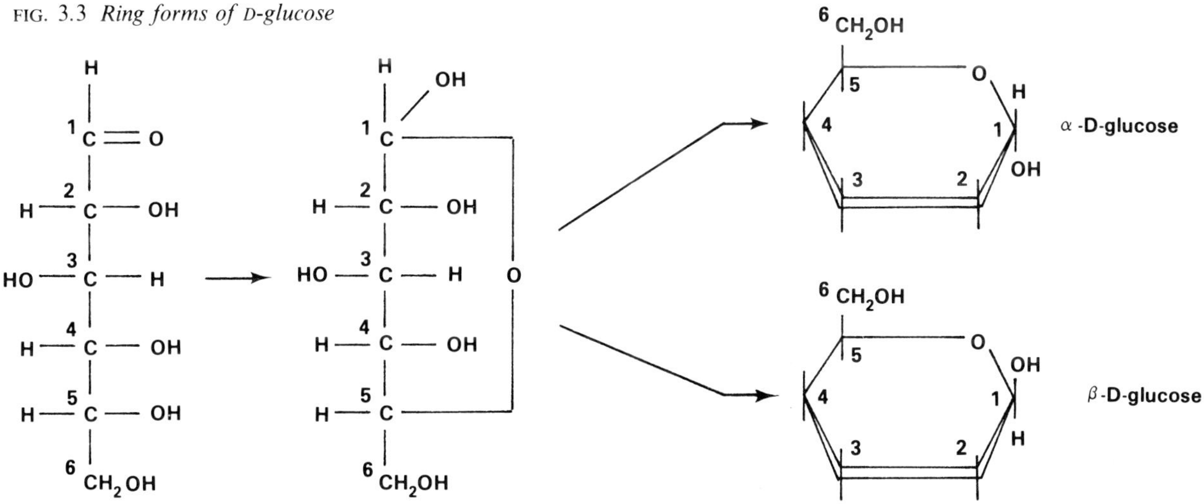

Fructose can also exist in a six-sided ring form but it more frequently exists as a more stable five-sided molecule in which the carbonyl group at carbon atom *2* reduces the hydroxyl group at carbon atom *5* (Fig. 3.4).

FIG. 3.4 *Ring forms of D-fructose*

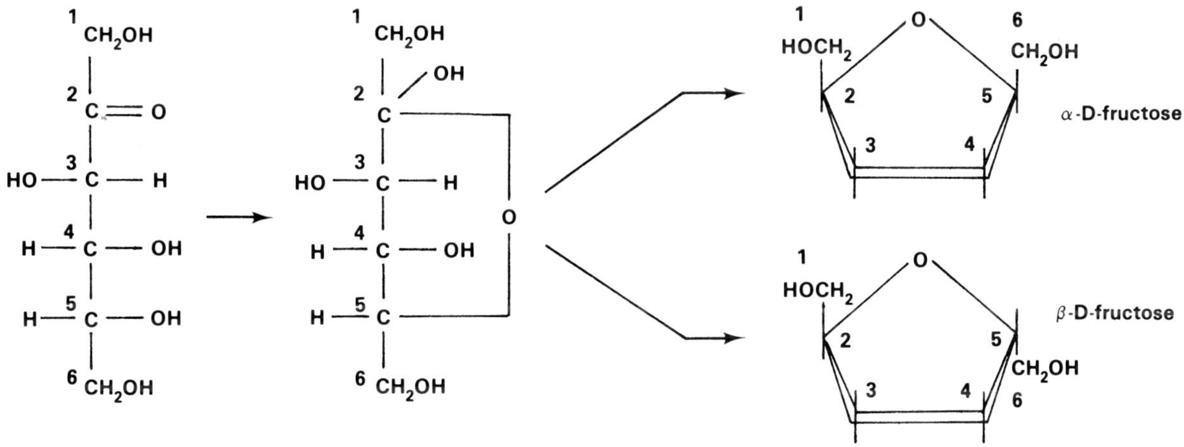

The ways in which the ring-forms of glucose and fructose have been drawn may lead you to think that the molecules are flat. This is not so. Normally the molecules have an elaborate three-dimensional structure, which in the case of glucose is often described as chair-shaped (Fig. 3.5). This has important implications in the chemistry of the more complex carbohydrates described later.

FIG. 3.5 *Chair-shaped glucose molecule*

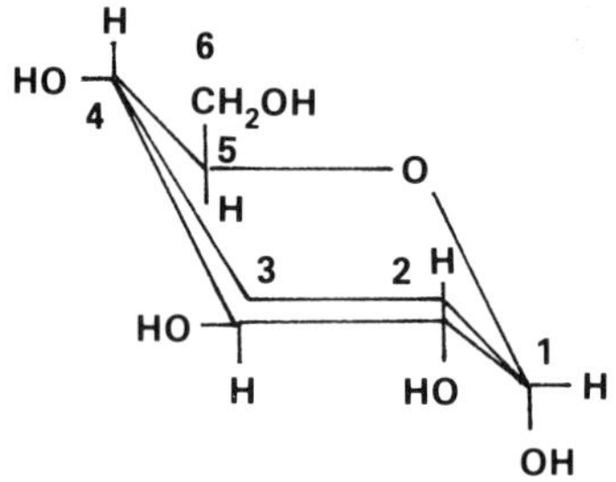

3.1.2 Disaccharides

Sucrose and maltose are the two **disaccharide sugars** most often found in living organisms. Disaccharides are formed when two hexose sugar molecules unite in a type of chemical reaction called condensation. In condensation reactions water is often one of the products:

$$\underset{\text{hexose}}{2C_6H_{12}O_6} \longrightarrow \underset{\text{disaccharide}}{C_{12}H_{22}O_{11}} + \underset{\text{water}}{H_2O}$$

Sucrose is found in most plants. It is stored in large amounts in sugar cane and sugar beet which are cultivated on a large scale to provide our supply of sucrose (Fig. 3.6).

FIG. 3.6 *A sugar-beet plant*

Sucrose is formed when a molecule of α-D-glucose and one of β-D-fructose join by condensation. The reaction involves the creation of a bond between carbon atom *1* of the glucose ring and carbon atom *2* of the fructose ring (Fig. 3.7). It is at these two carbon atoms that a carbonyl group occurs in the glucose and fructose molecules. This means that there are no free carbonyl groups in a molecule of sucrose which is therefore a **non-reducing sugar**. However, sucrose can be readily hydrolysed into its constituent monosaccharide reducing sugars. Hydrolysis can be achieved by boiling sucrose with dilute acid or mixing it with the enzyme sucrase (invertase).

Maltose is an intermediate product released from starch which has been hydrolysed by the complex of enzymes called amylase. Starch hydrolysis occurs in the mammalian gut (Chapter 14) and in germinating seeds (Chapter 20). A maltose molecule consists of two α-D-glucose rings joined together by an α(1→4)glycosidic linkage (Fig. 3.8). The linkage involves the aldehyde group of only one of the glucose rings. Maltose therefore has one free carbonyl group and is a **reducing sugar**.

FIG. 3.7 *Formation of a molecule of sucrose*

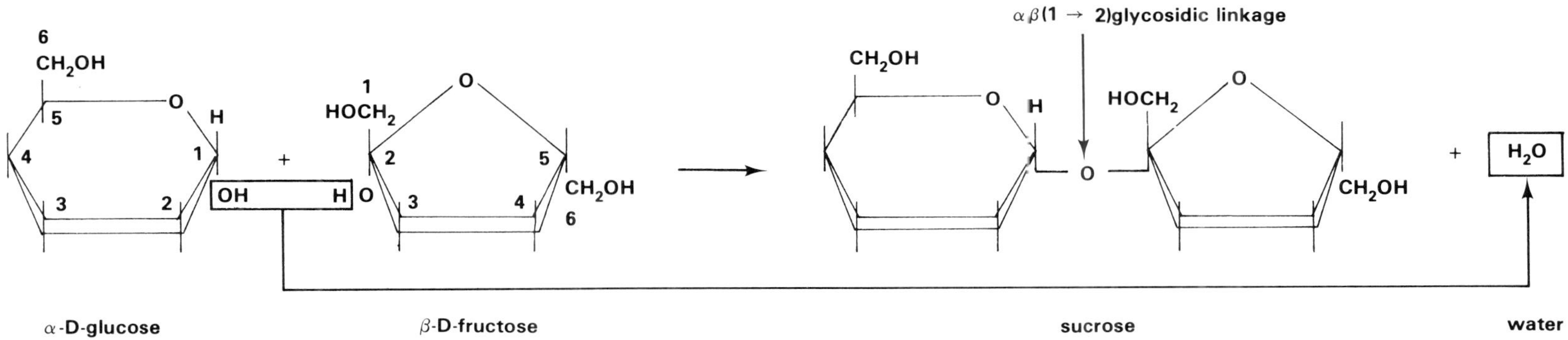

FIG. 3.8 *Formation of a molecule of maltose*

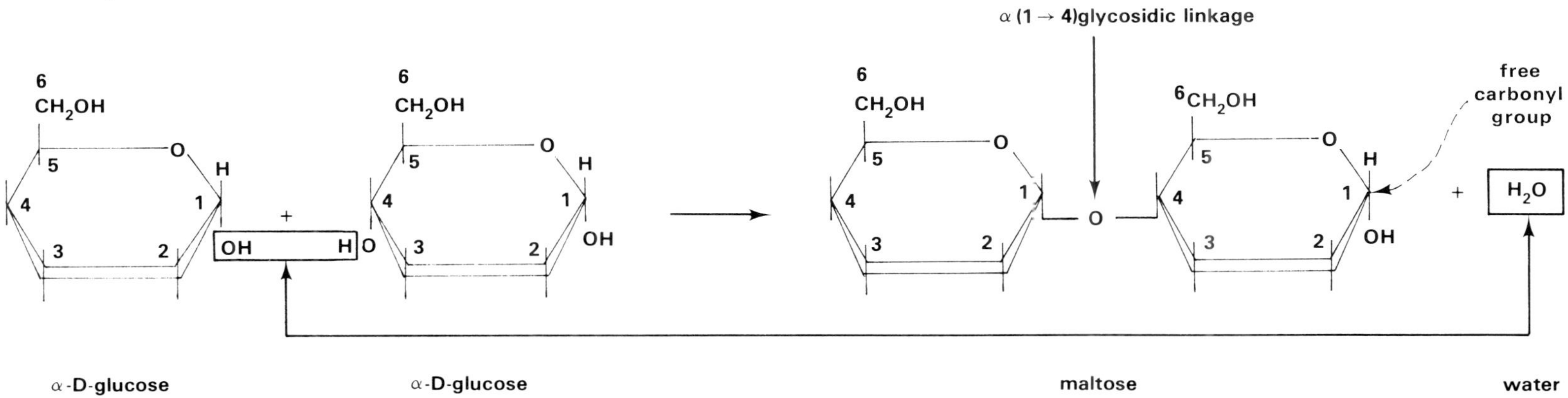

Simple chemical tests such as Fehling's test can be used to distinguish between pure solutions of reducing and non-reducing sugars. How is it possible to identify a number of different sugars in a mixture? Chromatography has revolutionised the art of separating and identifying many naturally occurring compounds. Descriptions of chromatographic and other techniques are given in section 3.4 of this chapter.

3.1.3 Polysaccharides

FIG. 3.9 *Helix of amylose*

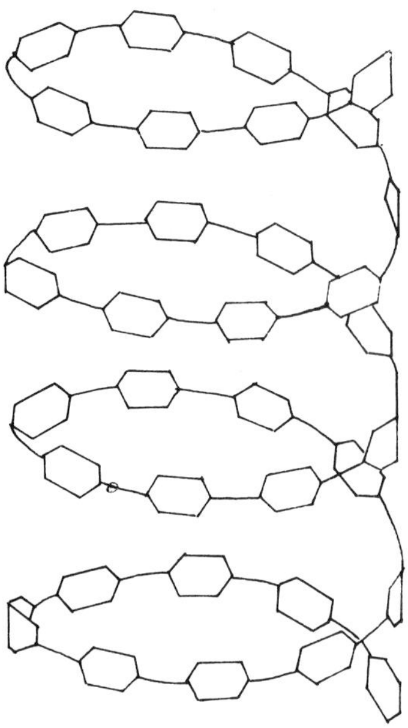

A **polymer** is a substance of large relative molar mass and is formed as a result of the joining together of a large number of basically similar smaller molecules. Polysaccharides are polymers formed by the condensation of many monosaccharide molecules. D-glucose is the main sugar involved and the products serve as storage and structural materials in plants and animals.

Starch is the main storage material of green plants. Its molecules have two components, **amylose** and **amylopectin**. The proportion of each varies from one type of starch to another. Soluble starches consist mainly of amylose. Amylose does not truly dissolve in water but forms a colloidal suspension. Amylose is a polymer of several hundred to a few thousand α-D-glucose rings joined by α(1→4)glycosidic linkages. The resulting molecule is unbranched and wound into a helix (Fig. 3.9). The bore of the helix is just big enough to trap iodine molecules. It is this reaction which produces the blue coloured complex when starch is mixed with iodine in potassium iodide solution. The iodine test is frequently used to investigate the presence of starch in materials of plant origin.

In contrast amylopectin is a branched molecule though again it is a polymer of α-D-glucose. The backbone of the molecule is held together by α(1→4)glycosidic linkages as in amylose. Branches arise about every tenth glucose ring where α(1→6)glycosidic bonds occur (Fig. 3.10). The branches which consist of 15–20 glucose rings joined by α(1→4)linkages may themselves be branched. Altogether several thousand glucose rings are present. Like amylose, amylopectin forms a colloidal suspension when mixed with water. The suspension reacts with iodine in potassium iodide solution giving a red-violet colour.

FIG. 3.10 *Part of a molecule of amylopectin*

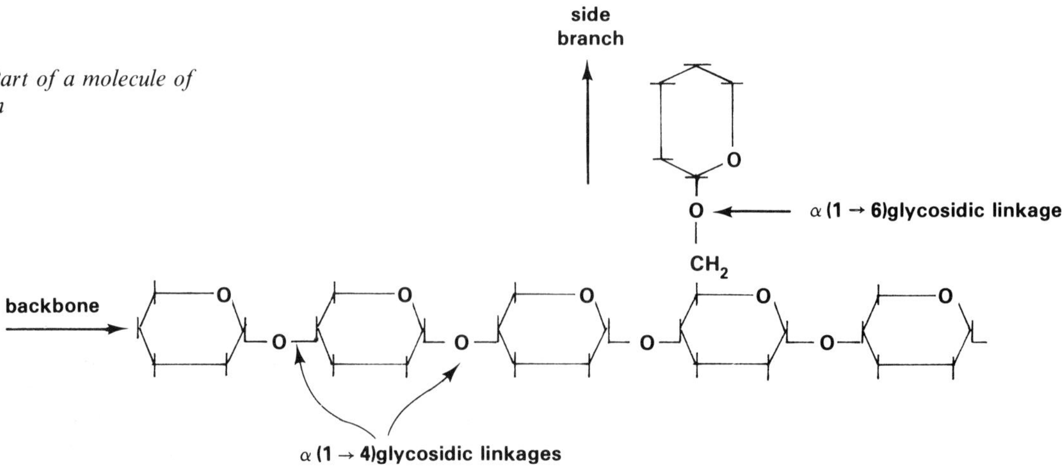

The two components of starch fit together to form a complex three-dimensional structure in which amylose helices are entangled in the branches of amylopectin molecules. Because starch is insoluble in water, it can be stored in large amounts without having any great effect on the osmotic potential of cells. It is usually stored as grains which appear in chloroplasts and in the tissues of storage organs such as potato tubers (Fig. 3.11).

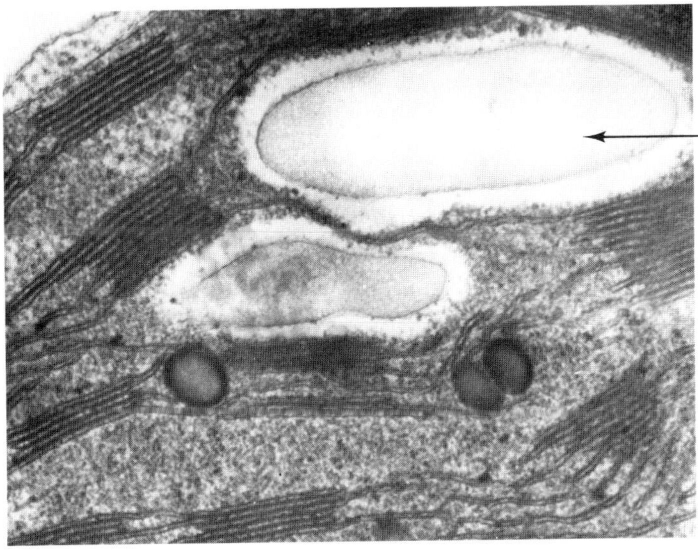

FIG. 3.11 (a) *Electronmicrograph of a section through a chloroplast from a leaf cell of* Petunia, *showing a starch grain* × *75 000*

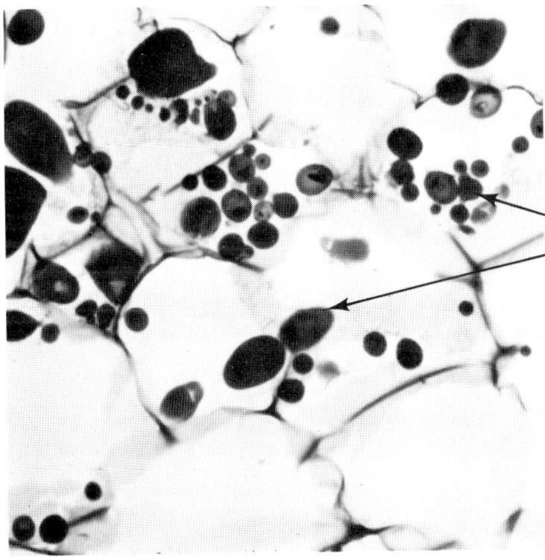

FIG. 3.11 (b) *Starch grains in a section of potato tuber,* × *200*

Glycogen is a storage polysaccharide found mainly in muscle and liver tissues of animals. In molecular structure it is very similar to amylopectin except that side branches occur more frequently and are somewhat longer. Glycogen is insoluble in water and therefore is ideal as a storage material because it has little effect on the osmotic potential of cellular fluid. It is usually stored as granules in animal cells (Fig. 3.12) and its reaction with iodine is similar to that of amylopectin.

FIG. 3.12 *Electronmicrograph of a liver cell containing glycogen granules,* × *28 000*

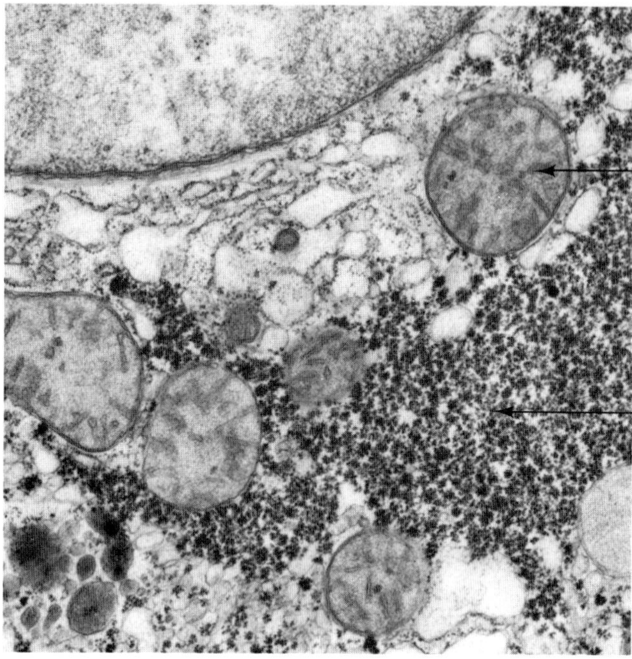

Cellulose is the most abundant structural polysaccharide in living organisms, although it is found only in plants. Unlike starch and glycogen it is a polymer of β-D-glucose. Several hundred to a few thousand glucose rings are joined by $\beta(1 \rightarrow 4)$glycosidic linkages in the long, unbranched molecules of cellulose (Fig. 3.13(a)). Attraction between hydroxyl (−OH) and hydrogen (−H) groups of the glucose rings of adjacent cellulose molecules results in the formation of hydrogen bonds which bind the molecules in a regular crystal-like lattice (Fig. 3.13(b)). The crystalline property of cellulose has been known for a long time but the way in which cellulose is laid down in the walls of plant cells was not known until the electron microscope came into use. Electronmicrographs show that plant cell walls consist of many fine **fibres** of cellulose which in some instances are laid down in parallel bundles but in others are distributed at random (Fig. 3.14). Each fibre contains a large number of cellulose molecules.

FIG. 3.13 *Structure of cellulose*
(a) *part of a cellulose molecule*

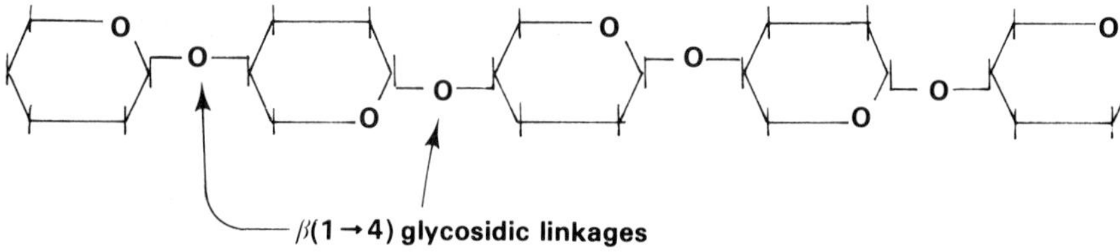

(b) *crystalline lattice of cellulose molecules*

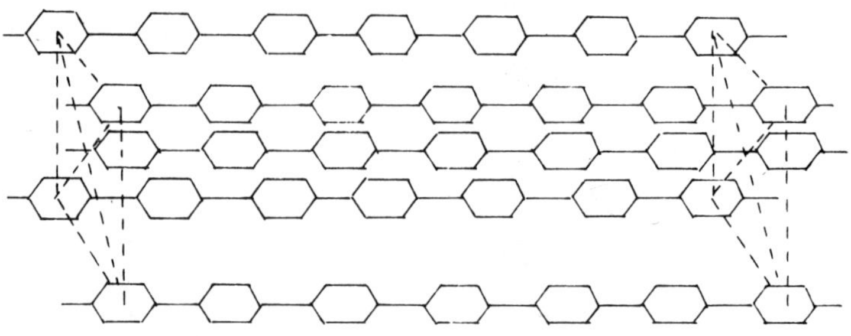

Hemicelluloses and pectic compounds hold the fibres together. Such a complex of materials is elastic enough to allow for cell growth yet has sufficient tensile strength to withstand turgor pressure which pushes the protoplast against the cell wall (Chapter 2). In sclerenchyma fibres and in xylem elements the walls are thickened with extra cellulose and stiffened with deposits of an alcohol polymer called lignin. This gives the tissues considerable rigidity enabling them to help support the shoot system in the air.

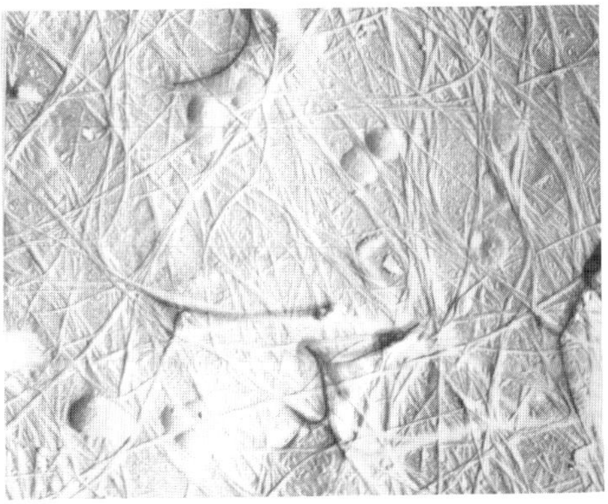

FIG. 3.14 *Electronmicrograph of freeze-etched primary wall of a carrot cell, showing cellulose fibres, × 37 500*

Cellulose reacts with iodine to form a yellow-brown complex. With chlor-zinc iodide cellulose is stained a violet colour. Lignified cell walls stain a yellow-orange colour when treated with phenylamine dyes.

3.2 Lipoids

The word **lipoid** is a collective term used to describe a range of organic compounds which can be extracted from living tissue using non-polar organic solvents such as benzene and trichloromethane. Lipoids are insoluble in polar solvents such as water and they include such diverse substances as fats, oils, phospholipids, waxes, steroids and sterols.

3.2.1 Fats and oils

Fats and **oils** are made from two ingredients, glycerol and monocarboxylic acids which are generally called **fatty acids**. Glycerol is an alcohol derivative of the triose sugar glyceraldehyde. Each molecule of glycerol has three hydroxyl (–OH) groups (Fig. 3.15(a)). Over seventy different fatty acids have been isolated from natural sources. Unlike glycerol, fatty acids are insoluble in water. All fatty acid molecules have a long hydrocarbon chain and a terminal carboxyl ($-C{\scriptstyle\begin{matrix}\nearrow OH\\ \searrow\!\!\searrow O\end{matrix}}$) group. The length of the hydrocarbon chain differs from one fatty acid to another. In some fatty acids the outer electron shell of each carbon atom in the chain is completed by sharing electrons with an adjacent carbon atom and with attached hydrogen atoms. In this way the valency of each of the carbon atoms is satisfied by the formation of four single covalent bonds. These are the **saturated fatty acids**. In contrast the hydrocarbon chain of **unsaturated fatty acids** has one or more double covalent bonds formed by the sharing of electron pairs between adjacent carbon atoms. Fatty acids therefore differ in the length of the hydrocarbon chain and in the number and positions of the double bonds, if any, in the chain. The fatty acids most frequently found in living organisms have hydrocarbon chains containing 15 to 17 carbon atoms (Fig. 3.15(b)).

FIG. 3.15 (a) *Molecular structure of glycerol*

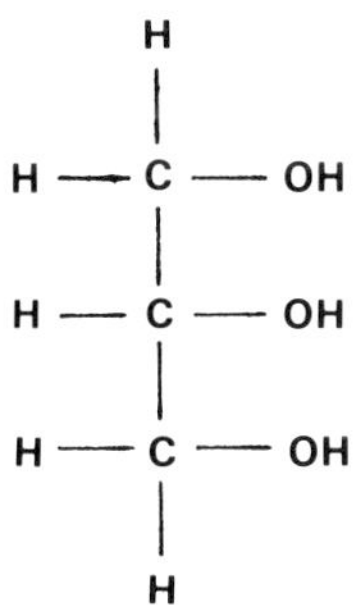

FIG. 3.15 (b) *Molecular structures of two fatty acids*

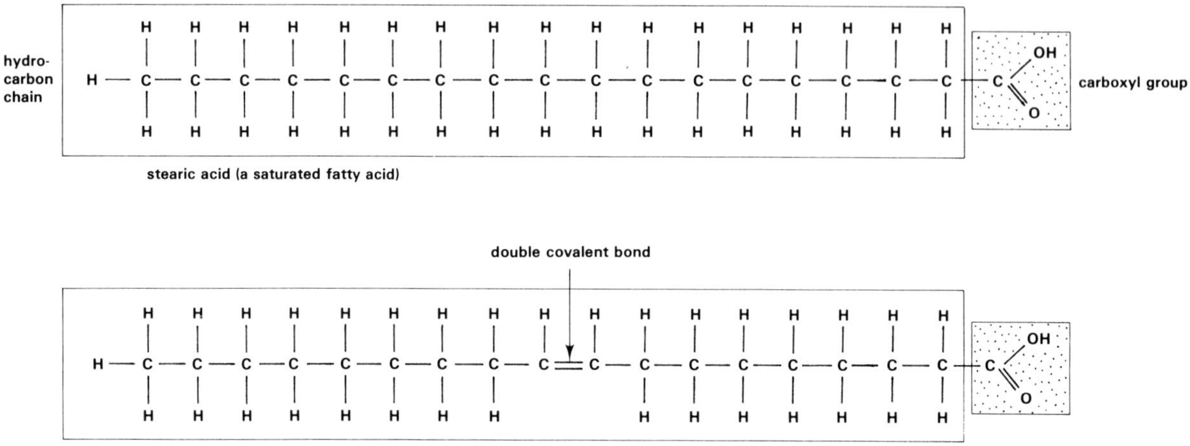

Condensation reactions between the carboxyl groups of fatty acid molecules and the hydroxyl groups of glycerol produce **acylglycerols** and water (Fig. 3.16). The oxygen bridges joining the two components are called ester linkages and this type of reaction is known as **esterification**. Fats and oils are triacylglycerols in which all three of the hydroxyl groups of glycerol are used up in this way. Acylglycerols formed from unsaturated fatty acids have relatively low melting points and are liquid at 15–20°C. They are generally called oils. Most vegetable oils such as olive oil, peanut oil and corn oil are derived from unsaturated fatty acids. Many acylglycerols of animal origin are derived from saturated fatty acids and have higher melting points. They are called fats. Butter and lard are animal products which consist almost entirely of fats.

Fats and oils are non-polar compounds and are therefore insoluble in water. For this reason they can be stored without affecting the osmotic potential of plant and animal cells. In mammals, fats are stored in adipose

FIG. 3.16 *Formation of a triacylglycerol*

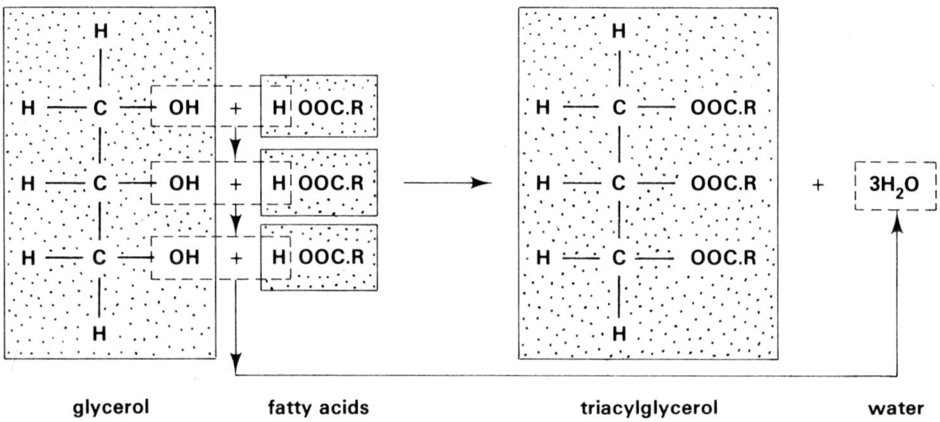

tissue beneath the dermis of the skin and around the internal organs (Fig. 3.17). The seeds of flowering plants are often the sites of oil storage.

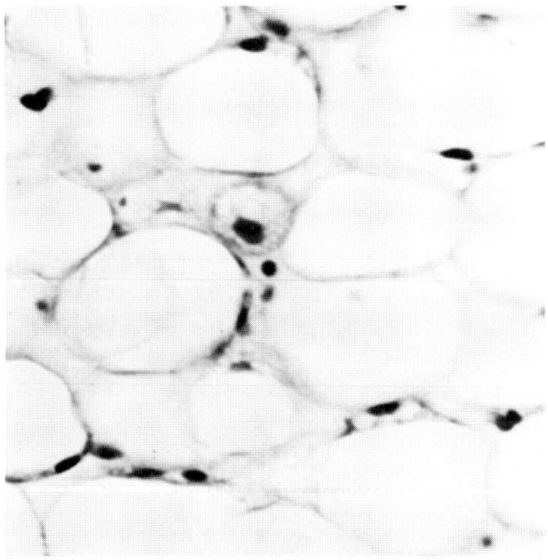

FIG. 3.17 *A section through adipose tissue, × 400. Each cell is virtually filled with fat so that the cytoplasm and nucleus are pushed close to the cell membrane*

Crude demonstrations of the presence of acylglycerols in tissue extracts or slices involve the use of fat-soluble dyes such as Sudan III. More sophisticated procedures such as chromatography are required for analysing the acylglycerol content of natural products (section 3.4).

3.2.2 Phospholipids

Phospholipids are triacylglycerols in which one of the hydroxyl groups of glycerol is esterified by **phosphoric acid** (H_3PO_4) rather than by a fatty acid. Also one of the hydroxyl groups of the phosphoric acid forms an ester linkage with an **amino alcohol**. Choline is one of the most common amino alcohols used for this purpose. The phospholipid so formed is called glycerophosphocholine (Fig. 3.18). An important property of a phospholipid molecule is its polarity. The phospho-choline 'head' is charged and

FIG. 3.18 *Formation of a phospholipid*

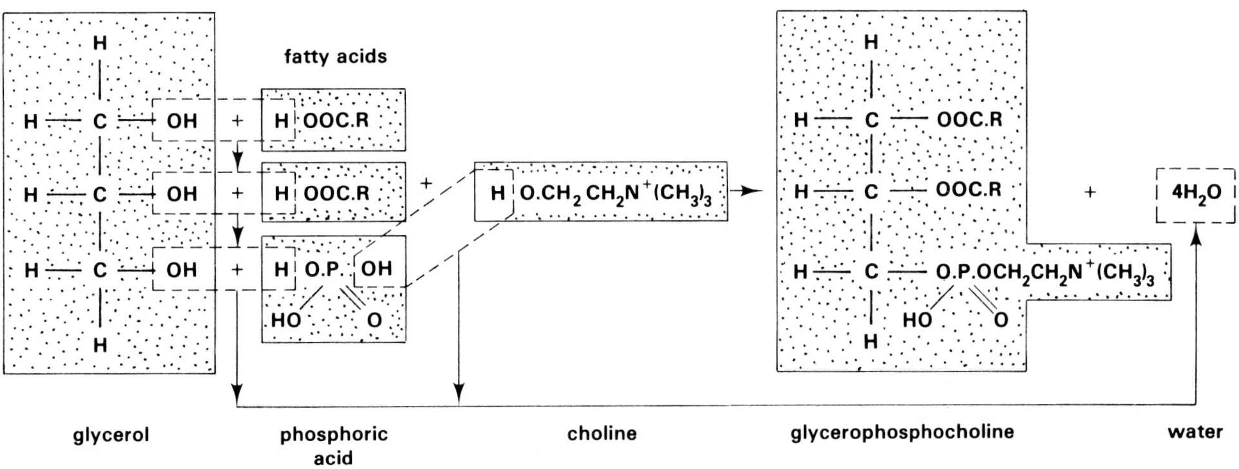

is therefore soluble in polar solvents such as water while the 'tail' of two hydrocarbon chains is non-polar. Such molecules do not truly dissolve in water but in certain conditions become arranged as a double layer called a **bimolecular leaflet** (Fig. 3.19). This arrangement is seen in the ultrastructure of unit membranes (Chapter 1).

FIG. 3.19 *A bimolecular leaflet*

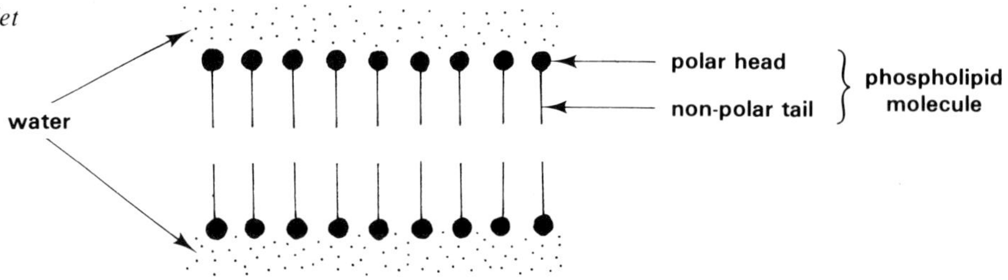

There is no simple procedure whereby the presence of phospholipids can be demonstrated in cell membranes. Osmic(VIII) acid, a solution of osmium(VIII) oxide, is used as a phospholipid fixative in preparing material for electron miscroscopy (Chapter 1). The oxide is reduced by the carbonyl groups in the hydrocarbon chains to lower oxides of osmium making the phospholipid component of membranes electron-dense.

3.2.3 Waxes

Waxes are esters of fatty acids with long hydrocarbon chains and alcohols of high relative molar mass. The alcohols have only one hydroxyl group compared with the three hydroxyl groups of glycerol. For example:

$$\underset{\text{carnaubic acid}}{C_{23}H_{47}COO\boxed{H}} + \underset{\text{carnaubyl alcohol}}{C_{24}H_{49}\boxed{OH}} \rightarrow \underset{\text{wax (carnaubyl carnaubate)}}{C_{23}H_{47}COOC_{24}H_{49}} + \underset{\text{water}}{\boxed{H_2O}}$$

Waxes are thus compounds of very high relative molar mass. They form waterproof coverings on the exterior surfaces of higher plants and animals. In terrestrial plants the **cuticle** is a waxy coating secreted by the epidermis of leaves and stems which prevents excessive evaporation from the shoot system. The sebaceous glands of mammals produce a waxy product called **sebum** which is released on to the surface of the skin (Chapter 17). Sebum helps to reduce evaporative losses from the bodies of terrestrial mammals. It also acts as a barrier which prevents waterlogging of the fur of aquatic mammals such as the otter.

3.2.4 Steroids and sterols

This group of compounds has little in common with the lipoids so far described except that like fats, oils and waxes they are soluble in non-polar solvents. **Steroids** have a complex molecular structure. They include the bile acids, hormones of the adrenal cortex and the male and female sex hormones (Chapters 14, 18 and 22). **Sterols** are alcohol derivatives of steroids. They include cholesterol, a component of the plasma membranes of cells and a precursor in the formation of steroid hormones.

3.3 Proteins

Proteins are compounds of extremely high relative molar mass. As much as 50 per cent of the dry mass of living organisms consists of protein. All proteins are polymers of **amino acid** molecules.

3.3.1 Amino acids

Nearly all amino acids consist of just four elements: carbon, hydrogen, oxygen and nitrogen. A few amino acids contain sulphur too. Every amino acid molecule has at least one amino ($-\mathrm{N}{<}^{\mathrm{H}}_{\mathrm{H}}$) group and one carboxyl ($-\mathrm{C}{<}^{\mathrm{O}}_{\mathrm{OH}}$) group. The empirical formula for an amino acid may be written thus:

$$\mathrm{R.NH_2.CH.COOH}$$

FIG. 3.20 *Structural formula of an α-amino acid*

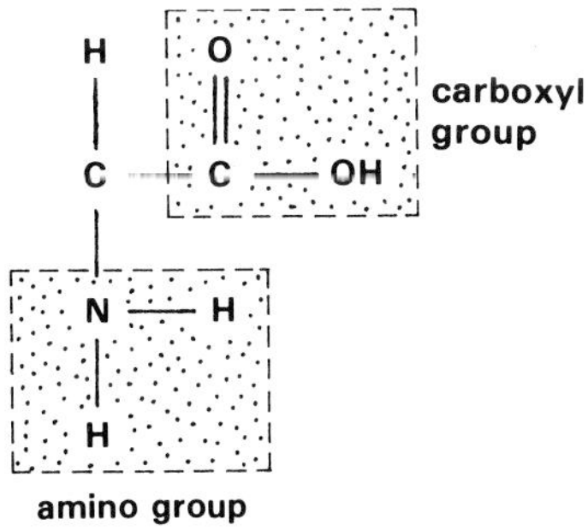

The structural formula is given in Figure 3.20. Because the amino group is bonded to the carbon atom next to the carboxyl group such compounds are called **α-amino acids**. Twenty different α-amino acids have been isolated from the proteins of higher plants and animals (Table 3.2). In glycine, the simplest amino acid, R is a hydrogen atom. In alanine it is a methyl ($-CH_3$) group, while in tyrosine it is a derivative of benzene. Cysteine is an example of an amino acid having a thiol ($-$SH) group (Fig. 3.21).

Table 3.2 α-amino acids commonly found in plant and animal protein

alanine	leucine
arginine	lysine
asparagine	methionine
aspartic acid	phenylalanine
cysteine	proline
glutamine	serine
glutamic acid	threonine
glycine	tryptophan
histidine	tyrosine
isoleucine	valine

FIG. 3.21 *Molecular structures of some amino acids*

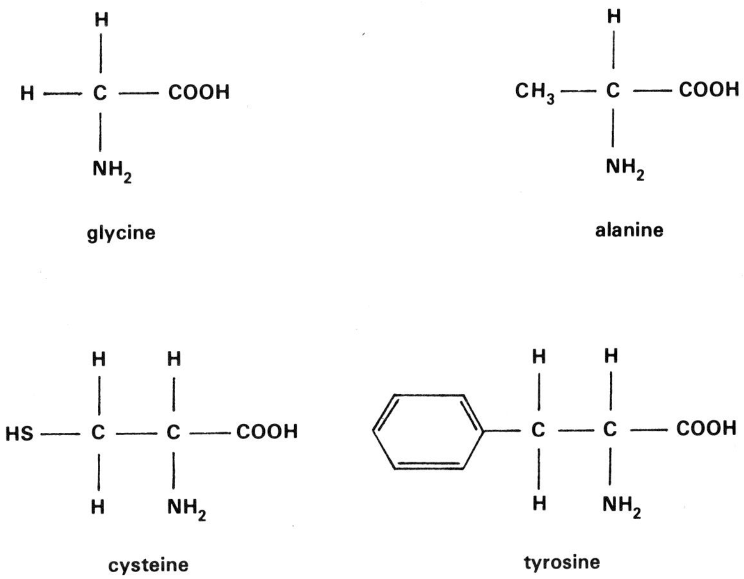

With the exception of glycine all amino acids have an asymmetric carbon atom and thus display stereoisomerism. Alanine, for example, can exist in two forms, D- and L-alanine (Fig. 3.22). As with glyceraldehyde (section 3.1.1), the two forms are non-superimposable mirror images. Interestingly, all of the amino acids which exist in proteins are L-isomers.

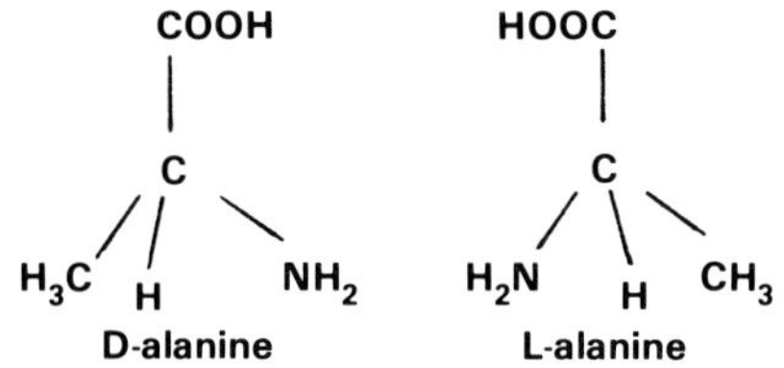

FIG. 3.22 *Comparison of the molecular structures of the stereoisomers of alanine and glyceraldehyde*

Note that the carboxyl group of alanine is in the same position as the carboxyl group of glyceraldehyde. Which groups in glyceraldehyde are in the same positions as the amino and the methyl group of alanine?

Table 3.3 Classification of α-amino acids by polarity of R group

POLARITY OF R	EXAMPLE	POLARITY DUE TO
non-polar	alanine	non-polarity due to CH_3 group
polar, but neutral	tyrosine cysteine	polarity due to OH group polarity due to SH group
negative	aspartic acid glutamic acid	polarity due to COOH group polarity due to COOH group
positive	lysine arginine	polarity due to NH_2 group polarity due to NH_2 group

A useful way of classifying amino acids is based on the polarity of R. According to such a scheme there are four main groups of amino acids (Table 3.3). A knowledge of polarity is important in understanding some of the methods which can be used to separate a mixture of amino acids (section 3.4) and in appreciating some of the properties of proteins. In neutral aqueous solutions amino acids with non-polar R groups exist as dipolar ions called **amphions** in which the carboxyl group donates a hydrogen ion (H^+) to the amino group:

$$\mathrm{R{-}\underset{\underset{NH_2}{|}}{\overset{\overset{H}{|}}{C}}{-}COOH} \rightleftharpoons \mathrm{R{-}\underset{\underset{\overset{\oplus}{NH_3}}{|}}{\overset{\overset{H}{|}}{C}}{-}COO^-}$$

Amino acids can therefore act as donors and as acceptors of hydrogen ions and are said to be **amphoteric**. In acid solutions, where the hydrogen ion concentration is high, amino acid molecules are able to bind some of the hydrogen ions, while in alkaline solutions amino acids can donate hydrogen ions to the excess hydroxyl ions (OH^-):

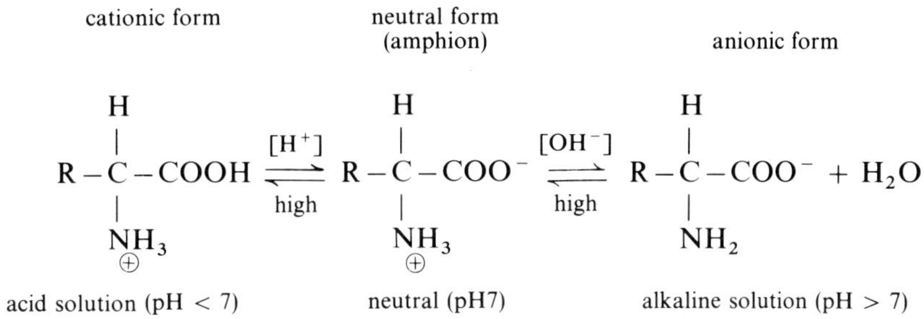

The ability of substances such as amino acids to control fluctuations in pH is called **buffering capacity** (Chapter 2).

The equilibrium point for the reactions described above depends on the hydrogen ion concentration, $[H^+]$. Where R is polar the situation is rather more complicated. However for every amino acid a particular $[H^+]$ causes amphions to predominate. The pH of the solution at which this occurs is called the **isoelectric point**, which for most amino acids is between pH 6 and 7. At this point the amino acids, being neutral, will not move towards the anode or to the cathode when an electric current is passed through the solution.

3.3.2 Polypeptides and proteins

In suitable conditions amino acids polymerise. They react in such a way that the α-amino group of one molecule becomes joined to the carboxyl group of another. The condensation reaction results in the formation of **peptide linkages** (Fig. 3.23). The free amino and carboxyl groups at each end of the dipeptide can form peptide linkages with other amino acid molecules so building up a chain of amino acid residues. Some short-chain peptides are of biological importance. Vasopressin (antidiuretic hormone) and ocytocin, two mammalian hormones, are each made from just nine amino acid molecules (Chapter 18). Long chains of amino acid residues are called **polypeptides**. One or more polypeptide chains are used in the formation of a protein molecule. The number of amino acid molecules ranges from about forty in the smallest proteins to several thousand in the largest. The relative molar mass of proteins ranges from 6000 to over 1 000 000.

FIG. 3.23 *Formation of a peptide linkage*

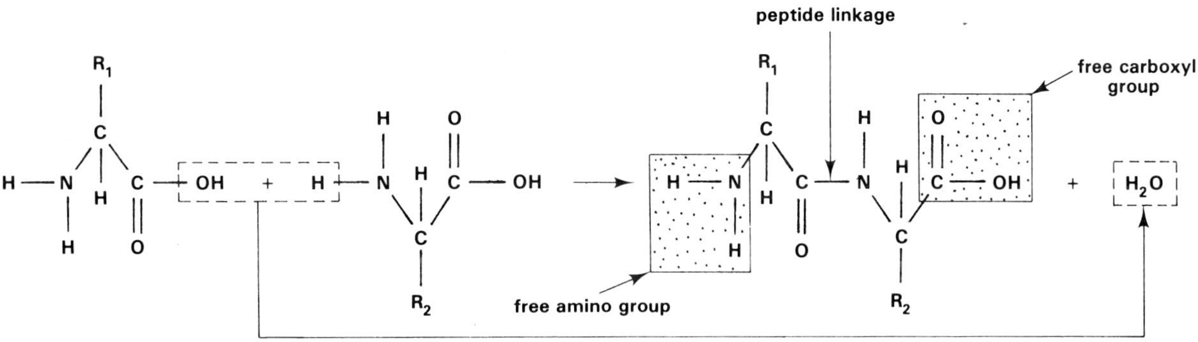

The amino acid composition of a few proteins was known in the 1940s. In the 1950s chromatographic techniques made it possible to identify the variety of amino acids in many other proteins. However, the sequence of amino acids in any protein molecule was a mystery until 1953 when Frederick Sanger published the findings of his research on the structure of the mammalian hormone insulin. Sanger showed that insulin consists of two polypeptide chains bonded to each other by **disulphide bridges** (Fig. 3.24). One chain contains 21 amino acid molecules the other 30. In the late 1950s and during the 1960s, the amino acid sequences of other small protein molecules were determined. Corticotropin (ACTH) was found to contain 39 amino acid molecules, ribonuclease has 124 while the α- and β-globins of haemoglobin have 141 and 146 respectively. More recently proteins of much higher relative molar mass have been analysed and a great deal of information has been compiled on the composition and amino acid sequences of a range of proteins from many different sources.

Such studies have shown that few proteins contain all twenty α-amino acids. Insulin, for example, has seventeen different amino acids. Some proteins consist of a small range of amino acids, in others a much wider range is found. The results of the sequence analyses revealed two general principles. Firstly, the sequence of amino acids differs from one type of protein to another. Secondly, the sequence in any one type of protein is precisely fixed. The findings have had a dramatic impact in molecular genetics (Chapter 6).

FIG. 3.24 *Structure of insulin*

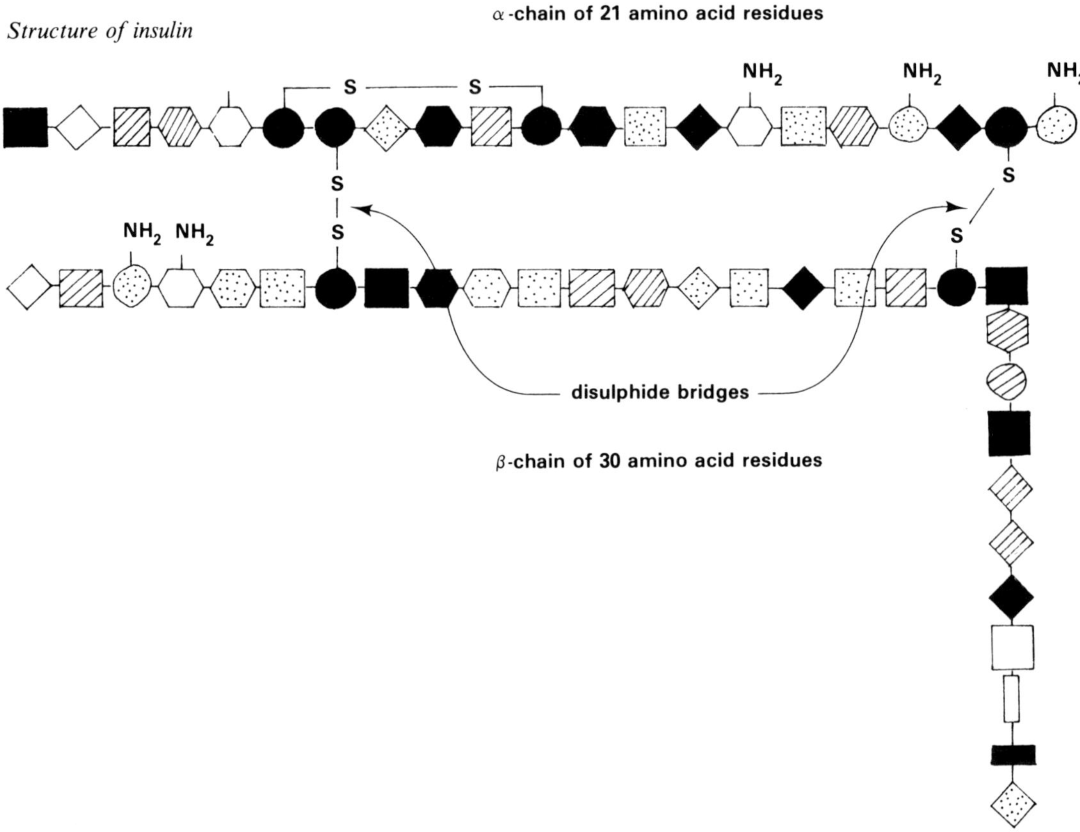

Without question, amino acid composition and sequence studies have yielded much valuable information about proteins. Yet proteins display many properties which cannot be accounted for from the results of such studies. In order to understand some of these properties it is necessary to know something about protein structure.

1. PROTEIN STRUCTURE

The name **primary structure** is given to the sequence and three-dimensional arrangement of amino acids in a polypeptide chain. Protein molecules have a very complex three-dimensional shape which cannot be explained in terms of the primary structure of their polypeptide chains. **X-ray diffraction analysis** has been a very important tool in unravelling the spatial arrangement of the atoms in protein molecules. In this technique molecules are bombarded with a beam of X-rays. Some of the rays are deflected by atoms in the molecules and are then passed through a photographic film to give a **diffraction pattern**. From the pattern, which is characteristic for a particular compound, the shape of the molecules can be deduced. It all sounds very simple but the interpretation of the pattern necessitates the use of a computer.

In 1939 Astbury obtained an X-ray diffraction pattern for keratin, a fibrous protein found in hair. The pattern indicated that the polypeptide chains in keratin were twisted or folded in a regular manner. Pauling and Corey in 1951 showed that the chains were twisted into a right handed helix. In this α-helix the peptide linkages form the backbone from which the R groups of the amino acids jut out in all directions. Stability of the helix is maintained by hydrogen bonds which occur between the keto ($>C=O$) and imino ($>N-H$) groups of every fourth peptide link (Fig. 3.25). It is now generally agreed that many fibrous proteins have a **secondary structure** of this kind.

FIG. 3.25 *The α-helix (simplified)*

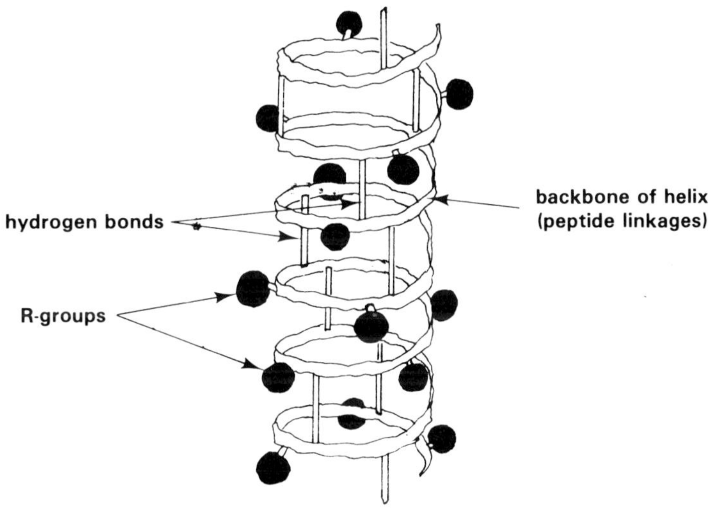

In keratin three to seven α-helices are coiled around each other like the strands of a rope. The strands are held together by disulphide ($-S-S-$) cross linkages between the thiol ($-SH$) groups of cysteine molecules. Earlier we saw that this type of bond holds together the two polypeptide chains of insulin (Fig. 3.24). The rope-like arrangement has considerable strength and elasticity. The helices are spring-like and are capable of extending and contracting. Proteins of this kind perform useful supporting and contractile functions in the mammalian body. They include myosin of striped muscle (Chapter 15) and elastin of yellow elastic tissue. In collagen of white fibrous tissue the polypeptide chains are permanently extended. Three such chains are wound around each other and are bound to one another by hydrogen bonds. This arrangement gives less elasticity but has considerable tensile strength (Fig. 3.26).

FIG. 3.26 *Tertiary structure of collagen*

The grouping together of several α-helices gives a protein its **tertiary structure**. Globular proteins such as myoglobin, haemoglobin and enzyme proteins have a less regular tertiary structure. Again using X-ray diffraction analysis, J. C. Kendrew in the late 1950s showed that myoglobin, the oxygen-carrying pigment in muscles, consists of a single polypeptide chain folded asymmetrically. The chain has eight relatively straight segments in which the polypeptide is coiled in an α-helix. The segments are united by bent peptide bonds and the chain bonded to an iron-containing haem group (Fig. 3.27). Disulphide, hydrogen and electrovalent bonds help to stabilise the three-dimensional shape of such molecules (Fig. 3.28).

FIG. 3.27 *Tertiary structure of myoglobin*

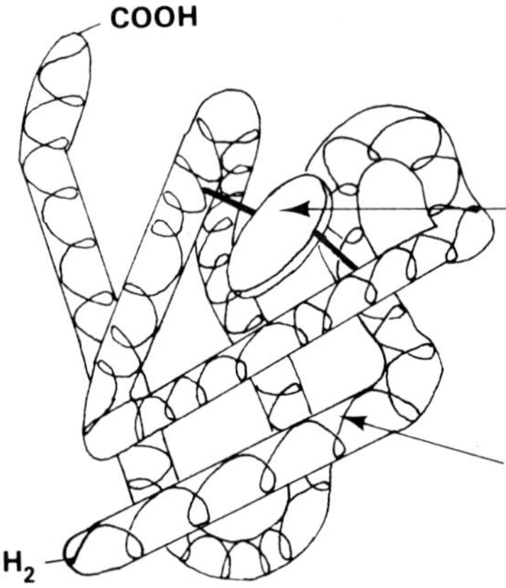

Most globular proteins with a relative molar mass of more than 50 000 consist of two or more polypeptide chains. The way in which they fit together is called the **quaternary structure** of the protein. Haemoglobin for example consists of four chains, two of α-globin and two of β-globin, each bonded to a haem group. The α- and β-chains are very similar in structure to myoglobin (Chapter 8).

FIG. 3.28 *Some of the bonds which maintain the three-dimensional structure of a globular protein*

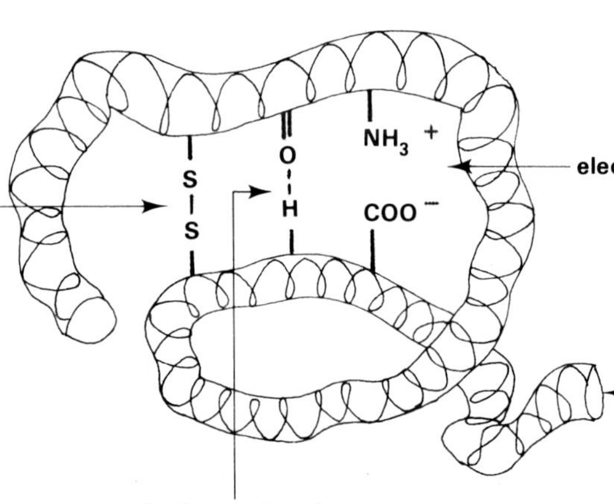

2. SOME PROPERTIES OF PROTEINS IN AQUEOUS SOLUTIONS

(i) SOLUBILITY. Globular proteins are generally **soluble in water** because the polar R groups jutting outwards from the α-helix attract water molecules. Enzymes are globular proteins which function in aqueous solutions. Some globular proteins of high relative molar mass form **colloidal suspensions** in water. They include the proteins which are present in cell membranes, ribosomes and in chromosomes (Chapter 7). The **insolubility** of fibrous proteins in water is accounted for by the large number of non-polar hydrophobic R groups on the outside of the α-helix.

(ii) BUFFERING CAPACITY. The ability of a protein to accept or donate hydrogen ions (H^+) depends on the number and charge of ionisable R groups on the surface of its molecules. The most important R groups in this respect are the amino ($-NH_2$) and carboxyl ($-COOH$) groups. Amino groups bind H^+ in acid solutions ($pH < 7$) while carboxyl groups donate H^+ in alkaline solutions ($pH > 7$). In this way proteins act as **buffers** in stabilising the pH of their surroundings.

(iii) ISOELECTRIC POINT. At a precise pH in aqueous solution each protein exists as an **amphion** which carries no net electric charge. This is called the **isoelectric point** of the protein. If the protein has a large number of free amino groups the isoelectric point is at a pH above 7 while proteins with a large number of free carboxyl groups form amphions at a pH below 7. Why is this so? The electrical properties of proteins are exploited in separating mixtures of proteins by electrophoresis and ion-exchange chromatography (section 3.4).

3. PROTEIN DENATURATION

Most proteins function effectively only within a limited range of temperature and pH. At extremes of temperature and pH proteins undergo physical changes called **denaturation** which generally result in their precipitation from solution. Further details of protein denaturation are given in Chapter 4.

It is an interesting fact that denatured protein molecules often spontaneously return to their original form when placed in ideal conditions of temperature and pH, providing denaturation was not too extreme.

4. FUNCTIONS OF PROTEINS

Proteins are used for an extraordinary range of activities in living organisms. Some of their more important functions are summarised as follows:

(i)	Enzymes	e.g. pepsin, amylase, lipase
(ii)	Contraction	e.g. actin and myosin in muscle
(iii)	Protection	e.g. antibodies, fibrinogen and prothrombin in mammalian blood
(iv)	Hormones	e.g. insulin, somatotropin, corticotropin
(v)	Transport	e.g. haemoglobin and myoglobin which carry oxygen in mammalian blood and muscle
(vi)	Support	e.g. collagen, elastin
(vii)	Storage	e.g. albumin in egg white, gliadin in wheat seeds.

5. BIOCHEMICAL TESTS FOR PROTEINS AND AMINO ACIDS

One of the most common biochemical tests used to demonstrate the presence of amino acids in extracts from living organisms is the **ninhydrin**

reaction. When heated with ninhydrin the α-amino group forms a blue coloured complex. Proline gives a yellow colour in this reaction.

The **biuret test** is frequently used to investigate materials of living origin for the presence of compounds with peptide links. Proteins and polypeptides form a violet complex when their peptide linkages react with alkaline copper(II) sulphate solution.

Millon's reagent is a solution of mercury(II) nitrate in nitric acid. Mercury reacts with thiol groups of amino acids such as cysteine which is found in many proteins. At the same time electrostatic forces in the protein molecules break due to the high concentration of hydrogen ions from the acid. The protein becomes denatured and a white precipitate is formed. When heated the precipitate takes on a red coloration.

3.4 Biochemical techniques

Breakthroughs in scientific knowledge often flow from the development of new procedures and techniques. Advances in biochemical knowledge have been no exception. Some technological developments used in biochemistry such as X-ray crystallography have already been mentioned earlier in this chapter. Let us now look at other techniques which have been used even more widely during the past twenty-five years or so to provide a wealth of information about the organic compounds found in living organisms. Some of the techniques are simple and you can use them for yourself. Scientific progress does not rely exclusively on sophisticated equipment and complicated technology. The techniques described here are mainly concerned with the separation and identification of biological compounds in mixtures and the analysis of complex molecules.

3.4.1 Chromatography

Chromatography is a technique used to separate the components of mixtures. It is based on the partitioning of compounds between a **stationary phase** and a **moving phase**. In **partition chromatography** the stationary phase is a liquid while in **adsorption chromatography** the stationary phase is a solid.

Partition chromatography depends mainly on the relative solubility of substances in two or more solvents. When a solute is added to a mixture of equal volumes of two immiscible solvents it may dissolve entirely in one or other of the solvents. If the solute dissolves in both solvents it may not dissolve to the same extent in each solvent.

The ratio: $\dfrac{\text{concentration of solute in solvent 1}}{\text{concentration of solute in solvent 2}}$ at equilibrium is called the **partition coefficient**. Use is made of differences in the partition coefficient to separate components of mixtures and to identify the components of mixtures extracted from living organisms.

Adsorption chromatography relies mainly on electrostatic interaction between solutes and the stationary phase. In partition chromatography the liquid stationary phase is held in position by a solid **support medium**. During separation of the components of a mixture some of the components may be adsorbed to the support medium. Thus in practice there is often no clear distinction between partition and adsorption chromatography.

Paper, column, thin-layer, gas-liquid and ion-exchange are examples of the various forms of chromatography commonly used by biochemists.

1. PAPER CHROMATOGRAPHY

Paper chromatography is used extensively in biological research yet it is a simple technique and is often practised in school laboratories. A **starting line** is drawn in pencil about half an inch from one edge of a sheet of absorbent paper which is the support medium. On the line a number of **origins** about half an inch apart are marked. A drop of solution of the mixture to be analysed is placed on one of the origins. On each of the remaining origins is placed a drop of a pure solution of a substance suspected to be in the mixture. The technique is extremely sensitive and can be used to detect minute quantities of unknown substances. For this reason a micropipette is used to spot the origins.

The paper is placed vertically in a tank so that the starting line touches a solvent which runs up (in **ascending chromatography**) or down (in **descending chromatography**) the support medium by capillarity. The known compounds and the components of the unknown mixture are carried different distances according to their partition coefficients between the solvent and water present in the paper. Adsorption to the support medium also affects movement of the solutes.

FIG. 3.29 *Flow diagram showing the main stages in ascending paper chromatography*

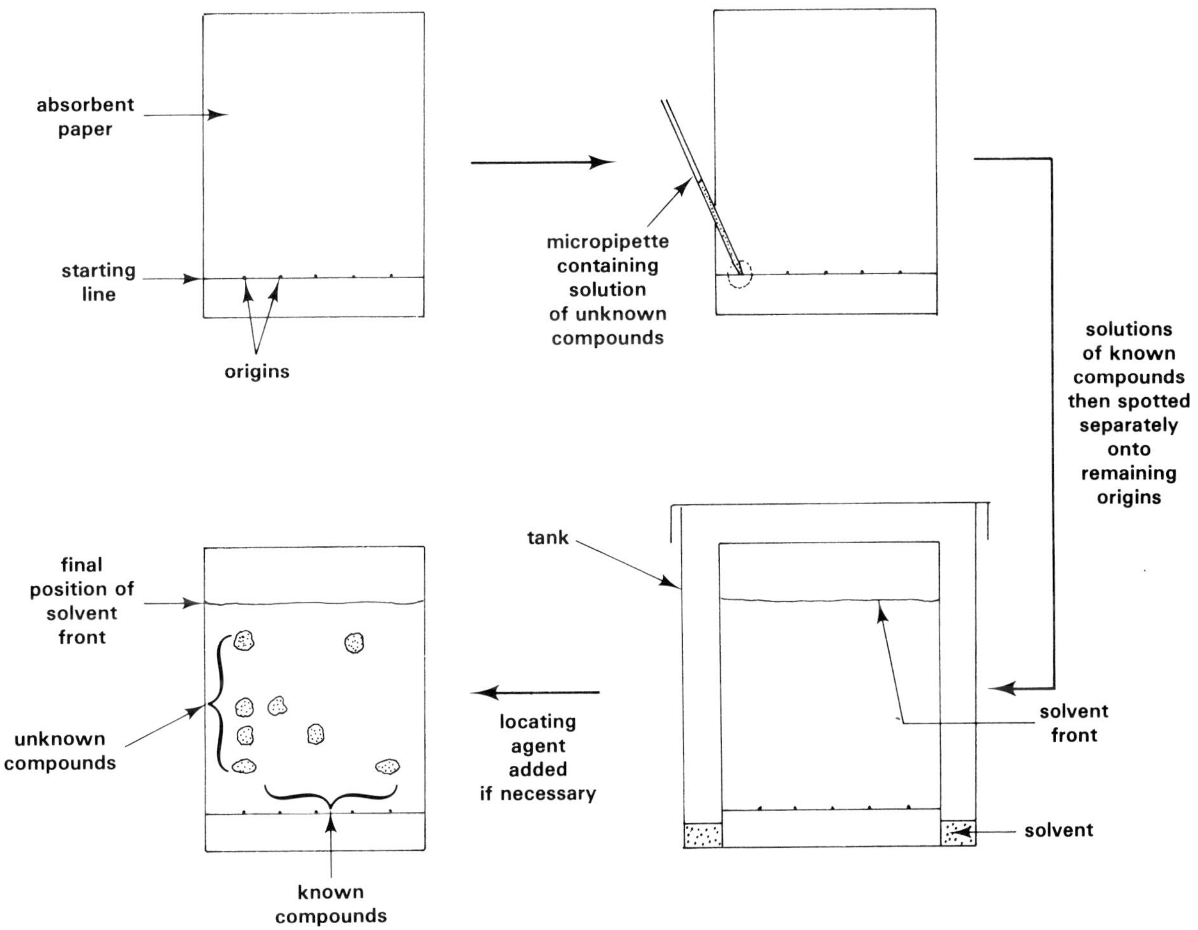

When the solvent has travelled most of the length of the paper, the distance it has moved, the **solvent front**, is marked and the paper is dried. If the solutes are coloured, as in the case of leaf pigments, the positions of the components can be seen without further steps. The positions of colourless substances have to be detected using a **locating agent** which reacts with the compounds under investigation to form coloured end products. Ninhydrin, for example, is used to locate amino acids (section 3.3.2).

The ratio: $\dfrac{\text{distance travelled by a compound}}{\text{distance travelled by solvent front}}$ is called the **retardation factor (R_f value)**. For a given solvent at a given temperature every compound has a characteristic R_f value. Thus by comparing the R_f values of the components of a mixture with those of the known compounds it usually is possible to identify some if not all of the substances in the mixture (Fig. 3.29). Should the first solvent not produce a satisfactory separation of all the compounds in the mixture the absorbent paper may then be turned through 90° and a second solvent run along it. This is **two-dimensional chromatography.**

The amounts of substances which have been separated can also be determined. The first step is to cut out the coloured spots and place them separately in a standard volume of a solvent. This procedure is called **elution**. After a standard period of time the paper discs are removed and the intensity of colour in the solvent is measured using a colorimeter.

FIG. 3.30 (a) *Stages in the separation of the components of a mixture by column chromatography*

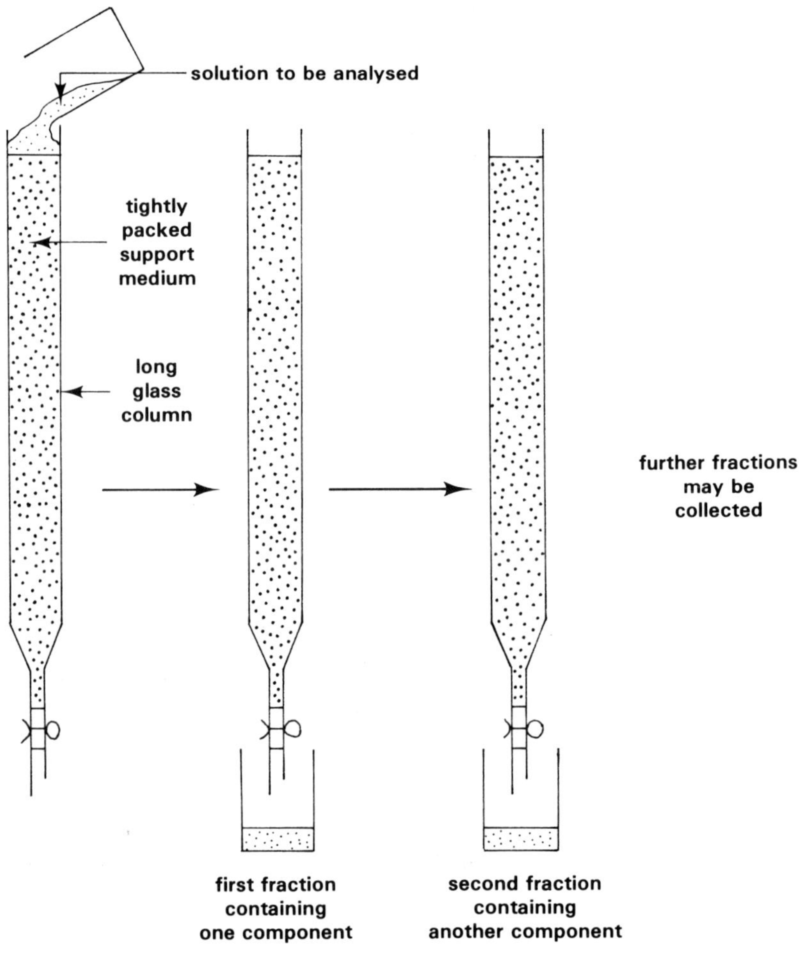

FIG. 3.30 (b) *A column chromatogram showing separated photosynthetic pigments*

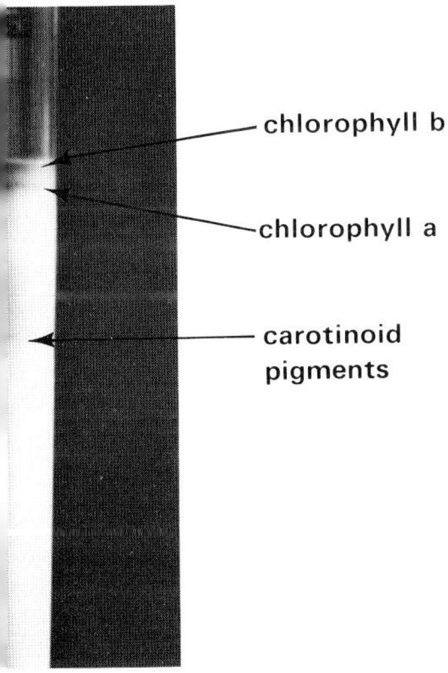

2. COLUMN CHROMATOGRAPHY

A long glass tube is packed with a support medium such as hydrated starch, silica gel or diatom shells called kieselguhr. A solution of the mixture to be analysed is poured into the top of the column. The components of the mixture move down the column at different rates. Differences in partition coefficients between the solvent and water in the support medium and adsorption to the support medium account for the rates at which the solutes travel. Again, the separation of coloured compounds such as leaf pigments can be seen without further steps. When the solvent begins to run out at the bottom of the column, fractions collected at staggered intervals of time will contain different components of the mixture. The separated components can be identified and their amounts can be measured using a colorimeter (Fig. 3.30).

3. THIN-LAYER CHROMATOGRAPHY

A glass plate is covered with an aqueous slurry of a support medium, for example, silica gel or cellulose powder. The plate is dried in a hot air oven and the mixture to be analysed, together with known compounds, spotted on to separate origins on the starting line. The plate is placed vertically in a tank so that the solvent almost touches the starting line. As in paper chromatography the solvent rises by capillarity and the components of the mixture become separated according to their partition coefficients and adsorption to the support medium. When the solvent front has moved a sufficient distance to separate the components of the mixture the plate is removed from the tank, dried, and if necessary a locating agent sprayed on to the support medium. The procedure can be made two-dimensional if the first solvent gives an incomplete separation. Once more the amounts of substances in the mixture can be determined. After scraping off the coloured spots and eluting the coloured complex, the intensity of colour can be determined with a colorimeter.

Sugars, amino acids and pigments in biological extracts can be separated and identified using any of the methods of chromatography described above. Thin-layer chromatography is often used to analyse the acylglycerols in natural fats and oils.

4. GAS–LIQUID CHROMATOGRAPHY

Analysis of the fatty acids in a mixture is normally carried out using **gas–liquid chromatography**. In this technique the vaporised methyl esters of the fatty acids are transported along a heated capillary tube using an inert carrier gas such as nitrogen. The tube is packed with a finely powdered support medium coated with paraffin grease or other similar high melting point substance. Because they have different partition coefficients between vaporised and liquid grease, the esters are separated and are carried out of the tube to a detector at different times. The time between the introduction of a sample into the tube and the appearance of a component in the detector is called the **retention time**. Each component has a characteristic retention time. Changes in potential difference between two electrodes when the component is burned in a hydrogen flame is one of several methods used to detect the amount of the component in the sample (Fig. 3.31).

FIG. 3.31 (a) *Gas–liquid chromatography*

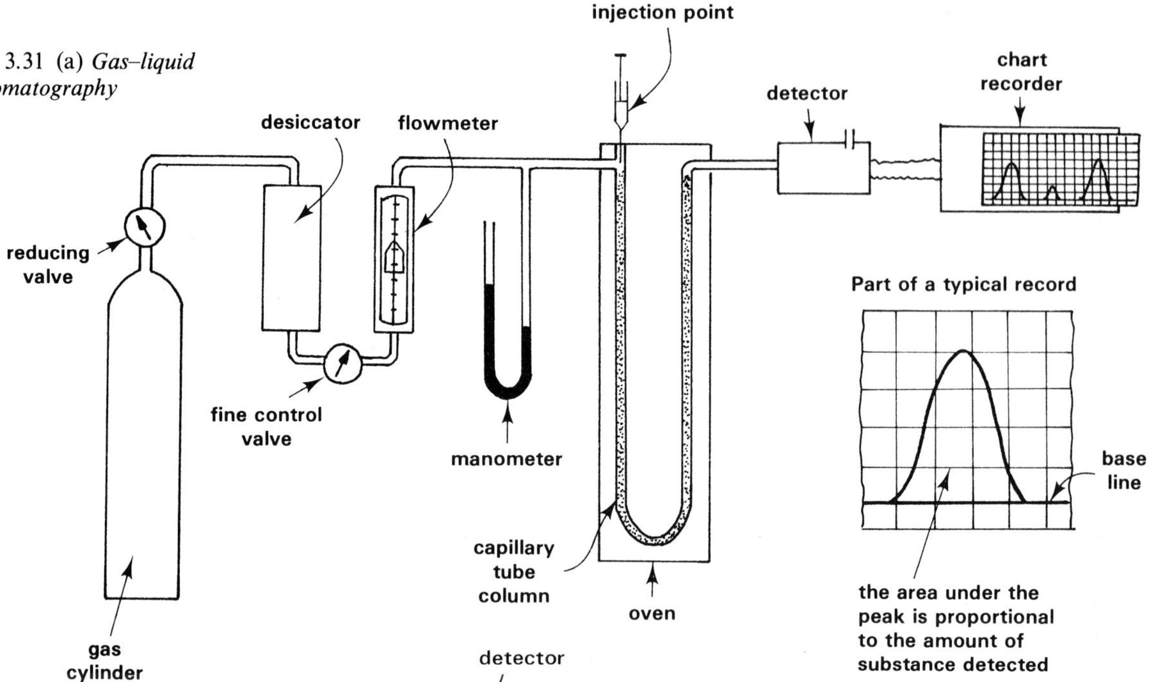

FIG. 3.31 (b) *Equipment for gas–liquid chromatography*

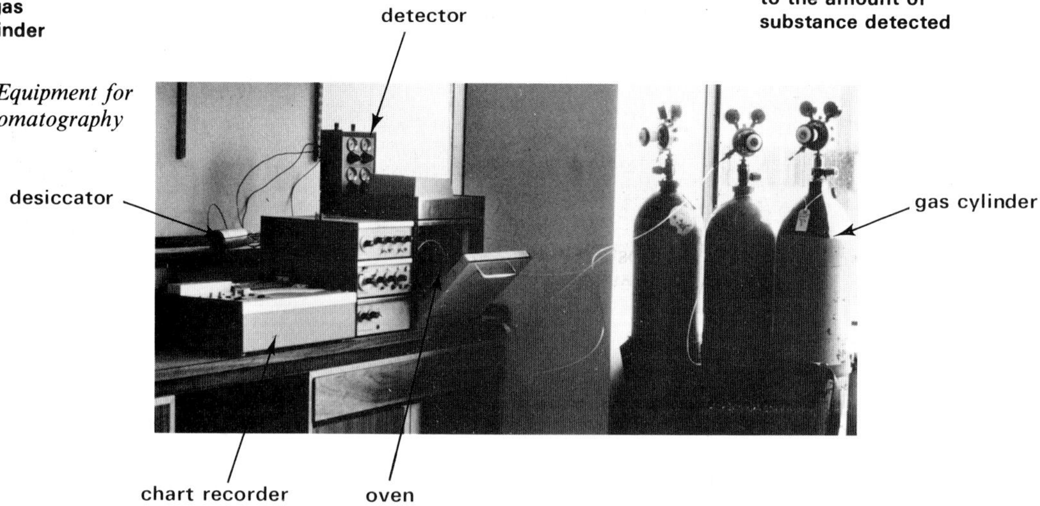

5. ION-EXCHANGE CHROMATOGRAPHY

Ion-exchange chromatography depends on the polarity of molecules and is therefore used to separate charged molecules. A long glass column is packed with a synthetic resin possessing charged functional groups. If the groups are positively charged the packing material is called a **cation exchange resin**, if negatively charged it is called an **anion exchange resin**.

Mixtures of amino acids are often separated using cation-exchange resins. Columns filled with sulphonated polystyrene beads are suitable. The polystyrene resin is first saturated with sodium hydroxide solution so that the beads are fully charged with sodium ions (Na^+). The amino acid mixture is adjusted to pH3 so that the acids are cationic (positively charged). Why does this happen? On pouring the mixture into the column the amino acids displace Na^+ ions from the resin. The amount of displacement depends on the polarity of the acids. Basic amino acids with an additional amino group such as lysine and arginine displace two Na^+ ions and are bound more firmly to the resin than acidic amino acids such as glutamic

FIG. 3.32 (a) *An amino acid analyser* (courtesy LKB Instruments Ltd.)

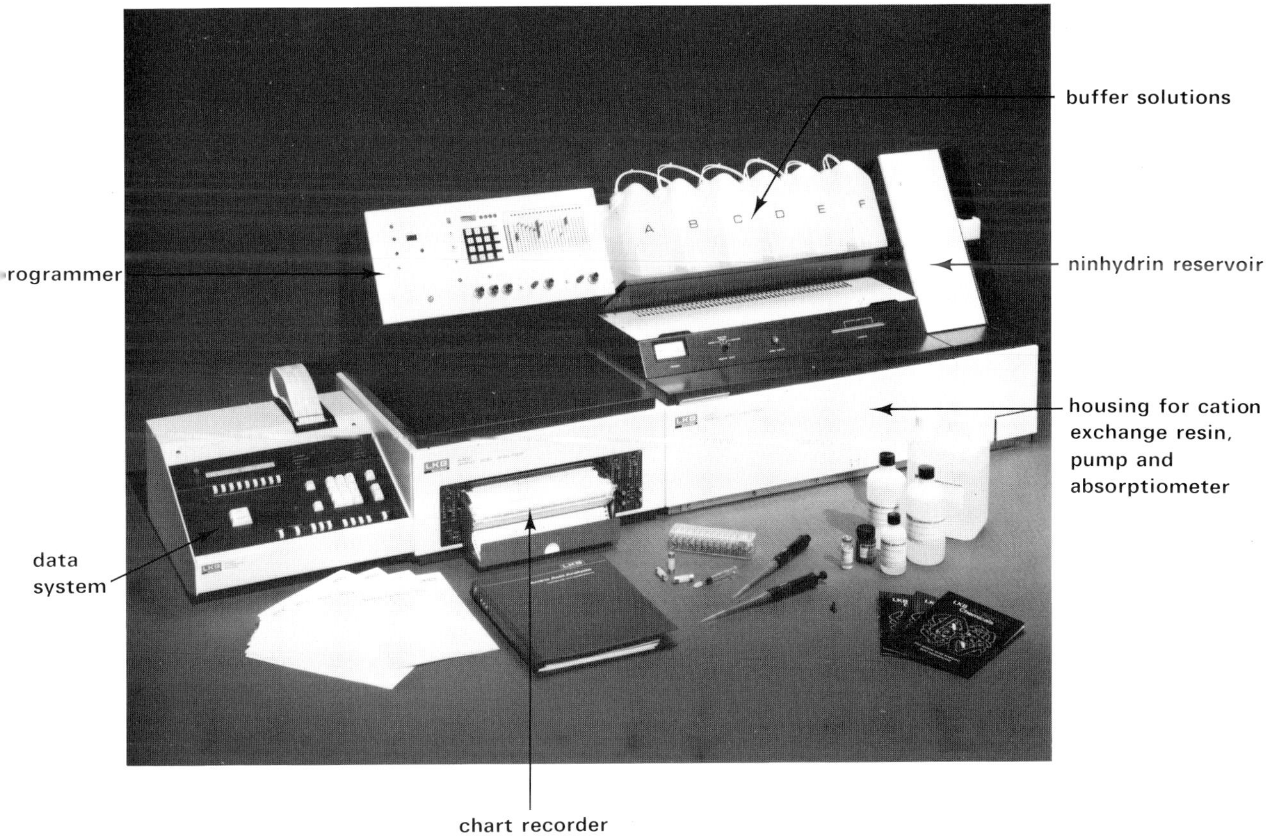

FIG. 3.32 (b) *Trace obtained from an amino acid analyser. The area under each peak is a measure of the amount of each amino acid in the mixture*

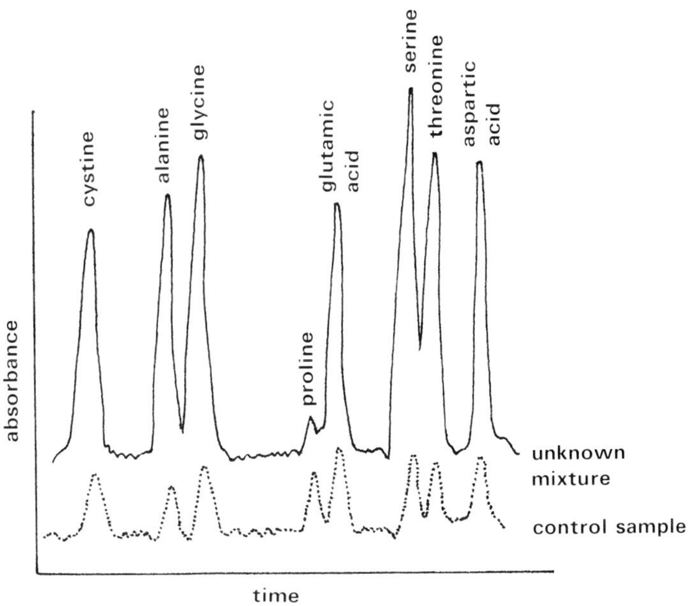

and aspartic acids which displace one Na^+ ion. For these reasons some amino acids move more quickly down the column than others. Samples collected from the bottom of the column at staggered time intervals contain different amino acids the amounts of which can then be measured by colorimetry. The collection of samples and their colorimetric determination can be performed automatically in **amino acid analysers** (Fig. 3.32).

3.4.2 Electrophoresis

The polarity of amino acids and proteins is exploited in separating mixtures of the compounds by **electrophoresis**. At its isoelectric point (section 3.3.2) a protein or an amino acid molecule is neutral and will not move to the positive pole (anode) or to the negative pole (cathode) if an electric current is passed through a solution in which the molecules are dissolved or suspended. At a pH above the isoelectric point amino acids and protein molecules have a net negative charge and move towards the anode. At a pH below the point they have a net positive charge and move towards the cathode.

In **paper electrophoresis** an aqueous solution or suspension of amino acids or proteins is applied to a starting line marked across the centre of a strip of filter paper or cellulose acetate paper soaked in a buffer solution.

FIG. 3.33 *Equipment for paper electrophoresis*

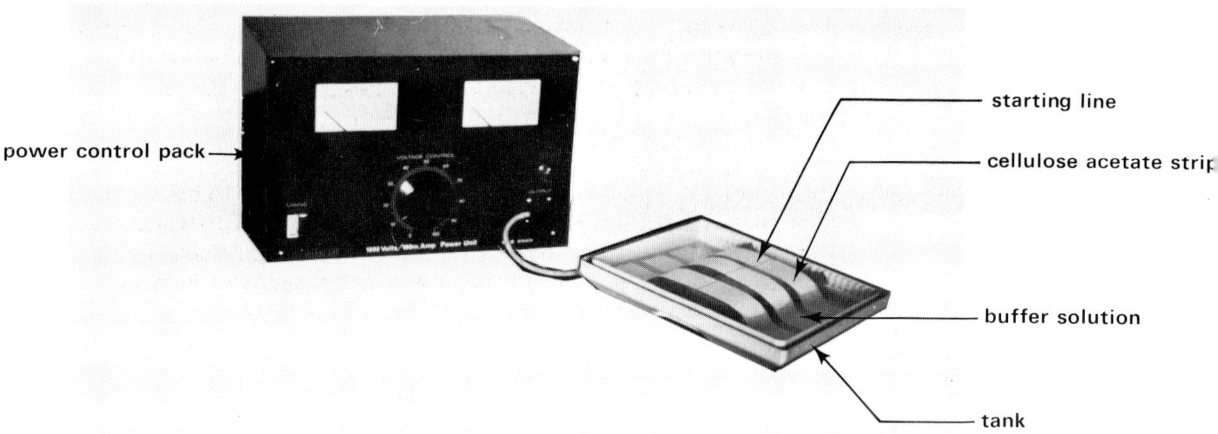

An electric current is passed through the buffer and the molecules move to either the anode or to the cathode at a rate depending mainly on the pH of the buffer, the net electrical charge of the molecules, and the voltage applied (Fig. 3.33). After a period of time the current is switched off and the positions of the separated components of the mixture identified using a locating agent. The pattern of separation is compared with that of known mixtures to identify the amino acids or proteins in the unknown mixture. Electrophoresis is used extensively in medicine to analyse blood proteins such as the immunoglobulins (Chapter 9).

It is impossible in a text of this nature to give more than a brief survey of some of the more useful biochemical techniques available today. Reference is made to other procedures at appropriate places in the book. Even now technical difficulties deny to man much biochemical knowledge and the search for new and improved techniques continues.

Chapter 4 Enzymes

In living cells hundreds of different biochemical reactions take place rapidly and simultaneously. The reactions go on at relatively low temperatures (4°C to 60°C) and are normally controlled in such a way that useful products are made and wastes removed at rates which satisfy the metabolic needs of cells. How is it possible for there to be such orderliness in what must be a potentially chaotic situation? How can reactions take place so rapidly at such modest temperatures? The answers to these questions come from a study of **enzymes**.

Enzymes were isolated almost accidentally in 1897 by Hans and Eduard Buchner. They were interested in making extracts of yeast cells for medical purposes. One of the problems the Buchner brothers were faced with was how to preserve the yeast juice. They tried various methods one of which involved adding large amounts of sucrose to the juice. To their surprise they found that the sugar was fermented even though there were no live yeast cells in the mixture. Up to this time it was thought that fermentation could only take place in the presence of living organisms.

The word enzyme, meaning 'in yeast', was used to describe the substance or substances in yeast juice which brought about the fermentation of sucrose.

4.1 The structure of enzymes

To appreciate the structure of enzymes it is necessary to have a knowledge of protein structure (Chapter 3). Over 90 per cent of enzymes are simple, **globular proteins**. The remainder are conjugated proteins which have a non-protein fraction called the **prosthetic group**. Most enzymes have relative molar masses of between 50 000 and 200 000.

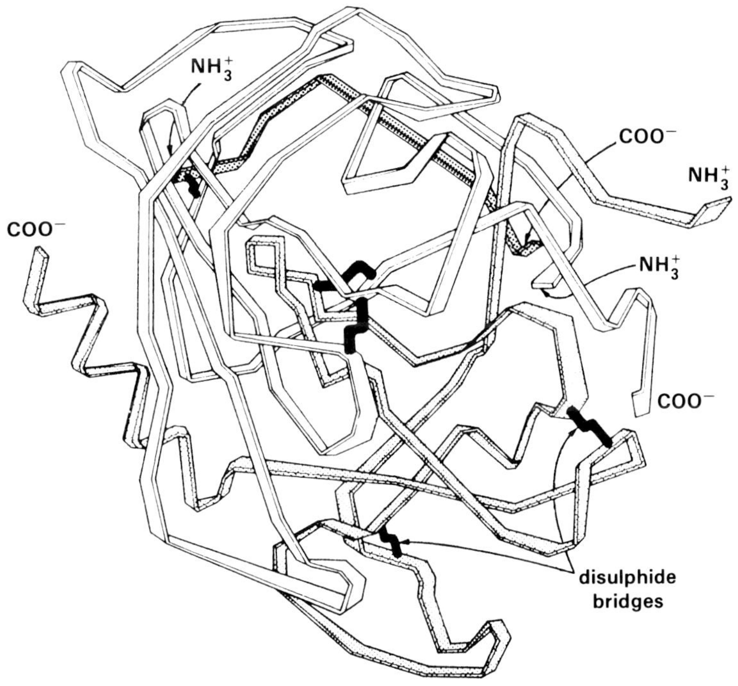

FIG. 4.1 *Three-dimensional structure of chymotrypsinogen* (after P. B. Sigler *et al.*, J. Mol. Biol., 35: 143 (1968))

Amino acid analysis, X-ray diffraction studies and other techniques have in recent years provided a lot of information about the structure of enzymes (Chapter 3). The three-dimensional structure of a number of enzymes is now known in detail. Chymotrypsinogen, an inactive precursor of the pancreatic enzyme chymotrypsin, consists of 245 amino acid residues which are bonded to form three polypeptide chains (Fig. 4.1 and Chapter 14).

4.2 Enzyme action

Enzymes are soluble in water and work in aqueous solution in living cells. They are sometimes described as **organic catalysts**. A catalyst is a substance which affects the rate of a chemical reaction. The biochemical reactions catalysed by enzymes are mainly **reversible reactions**. An example of a reversible reaction is as follows:

$$\underset{\text{reactants}}{A + B} \rightleftharpoons \underset{\text{product}}{C}$$

At equilibrium the rate at which A and B are converted to C is equal to the rate at which C is converted to A and B. The position of the equilibrium depends on the energy difference between the reactants and the product. Enzymes do not alter the direction of a reaction, they speed up the rate at which equilibrium is reached. In so doing they can catalyse reversible reactions in either direction providing it is energetically feasible. Let us look at the way in which enzymes can speed up biochemical reactions.

FIG. 4.2 *Energetics of a biochemical reaction*

(a) *Uncatalysed*

(b) *Catalysed by an enzyme*

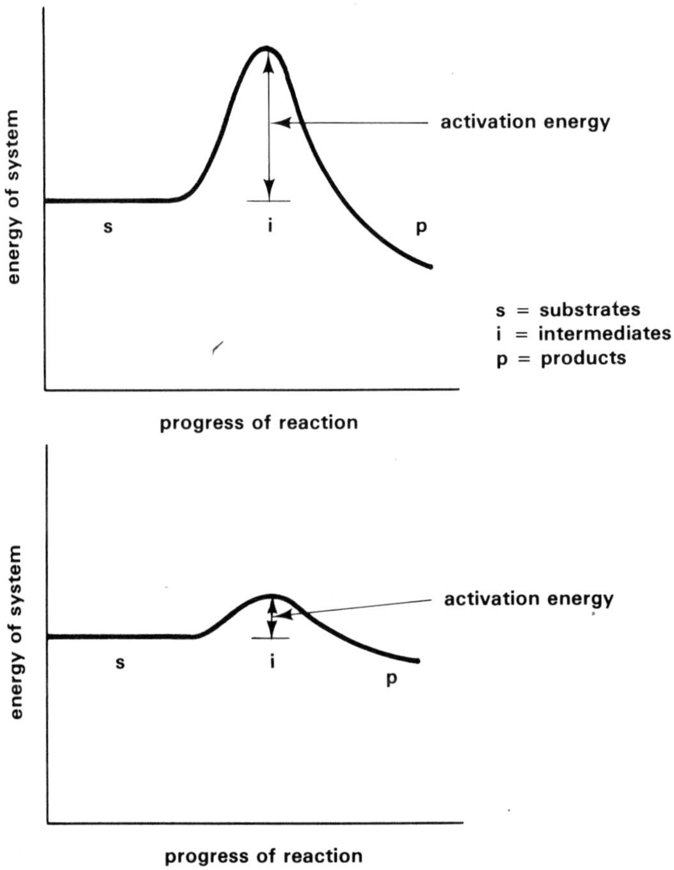

4.2.1 Enzyme catalysis

Biochemical reactions involve the formation or the destruction of chemical bonds. When two or more reactants are joined, chemical bonds are formed. When a complex molecule is split into simpler components chemical bonds are destroyed. In either case energy is required to bring about the changes. The energy required for a chemical reaction to proceed is called **activation energy** (Fig. 4.2(a)). Heat can be used as a source of activation energy. Indeed some reactions do not proceed quickly unless the reactants are raised to relatively high temperatures. In living cells however, reactions take place rapidly at relatively low temperatures. Enzymes lower the amount of activation energy needed, making it possible for reactions to occur at temperatures which are otherwise energetically unfavourable (Fig. 4.2(b)).

4.2.2 The lock and key mechanism

For chemical reactions to take place the reactants must be brought into contact. The quicker the reacting molecules collide the quicker is the reaction rate. One of the characteristics of enzymes is that they increase the chances of molecular collisions by drawing reactants together. They do this by what is called a **lock and key mechanism**.

Emil Fischer in 1894 proposed the lock and key hypothesis to explain how enzymes and reactants called **substrates** behave when mixed. Fischer suggested that enzyme and substrate molecules combine to form an **enzyme-substrate complex** before the products of the reaction are released (Fig. 4.3).

FIG. 4.3 *The lock and key mechanism of enzyme action*

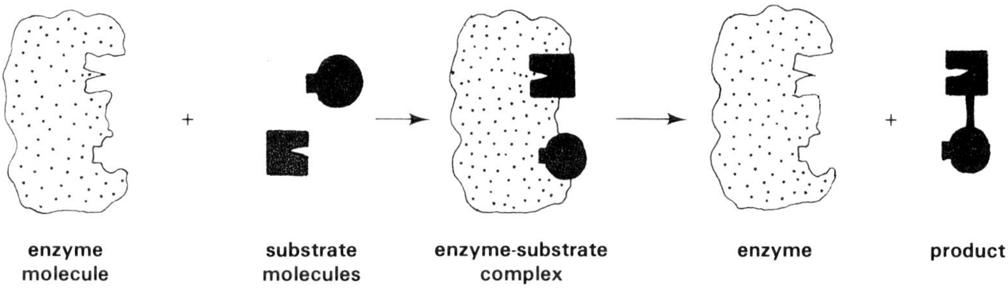

The sites on enzyme molecules where substrates fit are called **active centres**. Spectroscopic evidence supports the lock and key hypothesis (Fig. 4.4) as do the results of studies on enzyme inhibition (section 4.3.2) and the effect of substrate concentration on enzyme activity (section 4.3.6). Additional support comes from studies on enzyme specificity.

FIG. 4.4 *Change in absorption spectrum of NADH on addition of alchohol dehydrogenase*

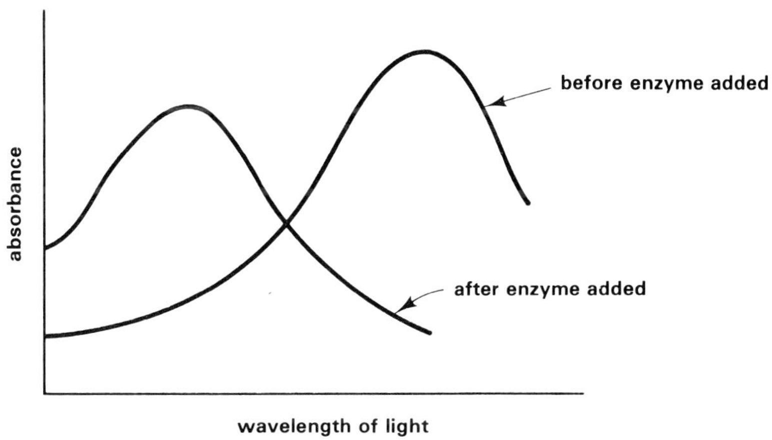

4.2.3 Enzyme specificity

Because enzyme and substrate molecules are three-dimensional structures the formation of an enzyme-substrate complex requires that the shapes of the reactants and the active centres of enzymes are **complementary**. Otherwise the enzyme and substrate cannot unite (Fig. 4.5). The phenomenon whereby most enzymes work with only one or with a limited range of substrates is called **enzyme specificity**.

One of the systems used to name enzymes is based on the substrates with which the enzyme combines. For example lipases react with lipids. What types of substrates do you think carbohydrases and peptidases react with?

FIG. 4.5 *Enzyme specificity*

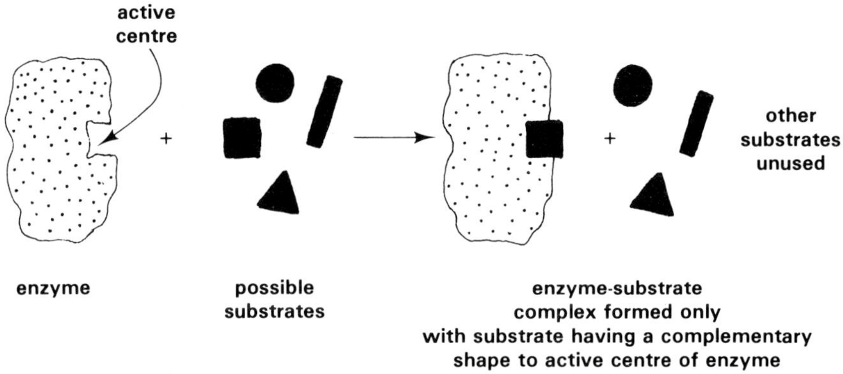

4.2.4 Control of enzyme action

Biochemical pathways usually involve a number of linked reactions. Each reaction is catalysed by a specific enzyme:

$$A \underset{}{\overset{\text{enzyme X}}{\rightleftharpoons}} B \overset{\text{enzyme Y}}{\rightleftharpoons} C \overset{\text{enzyme Z}}{\rightleftharpoons} D$$

In some instances accumulation of one of the products formed near the end of the chain inhibits the action of an enzyme used in one of the earlier reactions. In the hypothetical example shown above the presence of a high concentration of product D for example may slow down the rate at which enzyme X converts A to B. This is an example of **negative feedback inhibition**, an important device in the co-ordination of the metabolism of cells.

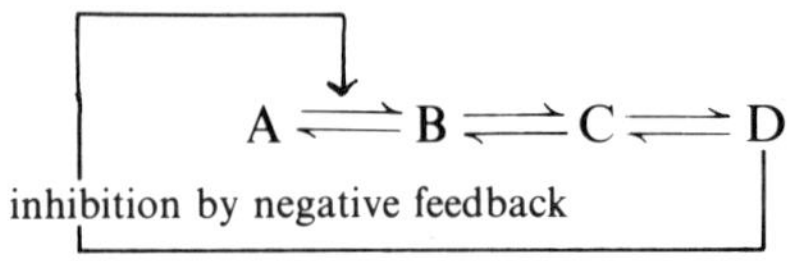

Negative feedback ensures that reactants are used efficiently and prevents the excess manufacture of end products. Like other homeostatic devices described elsewhere in this book the control of enzyme action helps to maintain a stable internal environment in living organisms.

4.3 Factors affecting enzyme action

To function at all some enzymes need the presence of **co-factors**. To function efficiently enzymes need a suitable **temperature** and **pH** and there must be enough **substrate** available. Enzyme action can be stopped partially or completely if **inhibitors** are present in the reaction mixture.

4.3.1 Co-factors

A **prosthetic group** is an essential co-factor attached to the protein part of a conjugated enzyme. If the prosthetic group is removed the enzyme fails to function. The prosthetic group sometimes contains a heavy metal such as iron (Fe), molybdenum (Mo), copper (Cu) or manganese (Mn).

Mineral ions must be mixed with the reactants before some enzymes will work. Many trace elements behave as **enzyme activators** in this way. It is partly for these reasons that minerals are essential to living organisms (Chapters 13 and 14).

In other instances enzymes do not function unless **co-enzymes** are present. Co-enzymes are organic, non-protein substances which are not bonded to enzyme molecules like prosthetic groups. Several important co-enzymes are vitamin-derivatives. **Nicotinamide-adenine dinucleotide (NAD)** and its phosphate ester **nicotinamide-adenine dinucleotide phosphate (NADP)** for example, contain a derivative of nicotinamide, a B-group vitamin (Chapter 14). Riboflavin (vitamin B_2) forms part of **flavin-adenine dinucleotide (FAD)**. NAD, NADP and FAD function as hydrogen acceptors in reactions catalysed by dehydrogenase enzymes (section 4.4).

4.3.2 Inhibitors

Many substances inhibit the activity of enzymes. **Inhibitors** fall into two categories, **reversible** and **non-reversible**.

1. REVERSIBLE INHIBITORS

Reversible inhibitors are substances which prevent enzymes from combining with substrates. Activity of the enzyme is restored when the inhibitor is removed.

Competitive inhibitors affect enzyme action by becoming attached to active centres, so stopping the substrate from binding to the enzyme. A well-known example of this behaviour is inhibition of the enzyme succinic dehydrogenase by malonic acid. Succinic dehydrogenase catalyses the oxidation of succinic acid to fumaric acid in the Krebs' tricarboxylic acid cycle (Chapter 5). In the presence of malonic acid the reaction rate is slowed down. Malonic acid has a molecular structure which is very similar to that of succinic acid. Inhibition happens because some of the dehydrogenase enzyme's active centres become occupied by malonic acid rather than by the normal substrate succinic acid. In effect malonic acid and succinic acid are competing for the same active centres of the enzyme (Fig. 4.6). The degree of inhibition by a competitive inhibitor is less if the ratio of substrate to inhibitor molecules is high. Why is this so?

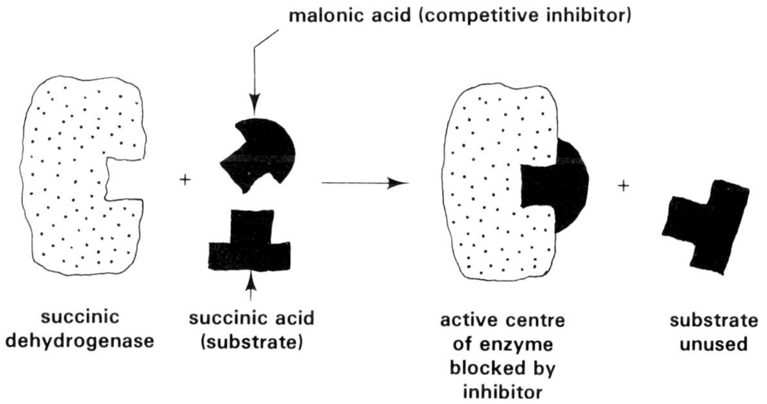

FIG. 4.6 *Competitive inhibition of an enzyme*

The degree of inhibition by **non-competitive inhibitors** cannot be reduced by increasing the number of substrate molecules. Here the inhibitor becomes attached to the enzyme at a position other than the active centre. Nevertheless the enzyme, the substrate, or possibly both become changed so that enzyme activity stops. Disulphide bridges are important in maintaining the tertiary structure of enzyme molecules (Chapter 3). If the disulphide bridges are broken the three-dimensional shape of the enzyme changes. The ions of heavy metals such as mercury (Hg), silver (Ag) and copper (Cu) affect enzymes in this way. Hg^{2+}, Ag^{+} and Cu^{2+} ions combine with thiol ($-SH$) groups in enzymes, so denaturing enzyme molecules and inhibiting enzyme activity. Cyanide is another non-competitive inhibitor. It blocks the action of some enzymes by combining with iron which may be present in a prosthetic group or which may be required as an enzyme activator. It is not surprising therefore that the salts of heavy metals and cyanide are potent poisons to living organisms.

2. NON-REVERSIBLE INHIBITORS

Organophosphorus compounds which are used as insecticides are good examples of non-reversible inhibitors. They bind with enzymes in such a way that activity of the enzyme is permanently stopped. Insecticides of this type inactivate the enzyme cholinesterase which is essential for the functioning of the nervous system (Chapter 15).

4.3.3 Temperature

Heat provides activation energy and therefore chemical reactions are more likely to occur at high temperatures. Secondly, heat supplies kinetic energy to reacting molecules, causing them to move more rapidly. The chances of molecular collisions taking place are increased at high temperatures so it is more likely that enzyme-substrate complexes will be formed. However, heat energy also increases the vibration of the atoms which make up enzyme molecules. If the vibrations become too violent chemical bonds in the enzyme break and the precise three-dimensional structure, so essential for enzyme activity, is lost. At high temperatures therefore enzymes become **denatured**.

When the effect of temperature on enzyme activity is investigated ex-

FIG. 4.7 *The effect of temperature on the rate of an enzyme-catalysed reaction*

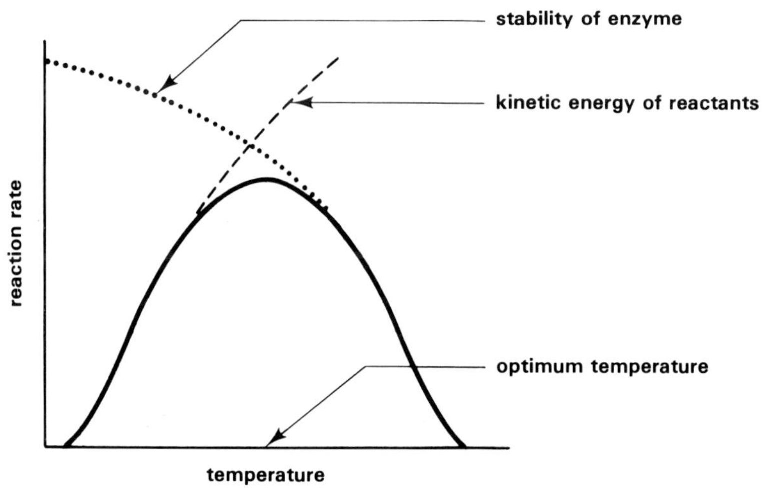

perimentally a temperature usually called the **optimum temperature** is observed at which the reaction proceeds most rapidly. This temperature is not necessarily that at which the enzyme is most stable. It is the resultant of the contrary effects of temperature on the movement of reactants and enzyme denaturation (Fig. 4.7).

The term **temperature coefficient** (Q_{10}) is used to express the effect of a 10°C rise in temperature on the rate of a chemical reaction.

$$Q_{10} = \frac{\text{rate of reaction at t + 10°C}}{\text{rate of reaction at t°C}}$$

Between 4°C and the optimum temperature the Q_{10} for enzyme-catalysed reactions is 2.

4.3.4 pH

The symbol **pH** refers to the concentration of hydrogen ions in solution (Chapter 2). The concentration of hydrogen ions $[H^+]$ affects the stability of the electrovalent bonds which help to maintain the tertiary structure of protein molecules (Chapter 3). Extremes of pH cause the bonds to break resulting in enzyme denaturation. For every enzyme there is an **optimum pH** at which the reaction it catalyses proceeds most rapidly (Fig. 4.8). Many enzymes work within a pH range of 5–9 and catalyse reactions most efficiently at pH 7. There are exceptions. For example, pepsin and rennin secreted in the mammalian stomach work best at pH 1·5–2·5 (Chapter 14).

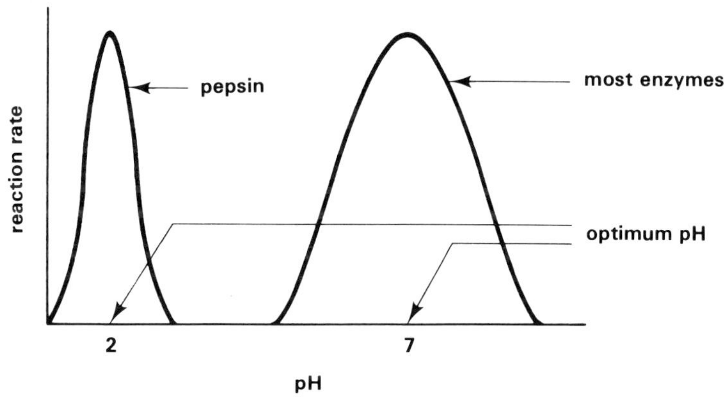

FIG. 4.8 *The effect of pH on the rates of enzyme-catalysed reactions*

It must be remembered that even small changes in pH mean relatively large changes in $[H^+]$. A change of 1 on the pH scale involves a ten-fold change in $[H^+]$ while a change in pH of 2 represents a hundred-fold increase in $[H^+]$ (Chapter 2). Thus even small changes in pH can have a great effect on enzyme activity.

Apart from the effect in denaturing enzymes, changes in $[H^+]$ can change the ionisation of the amino acid residues at the active centres of enzymes. Ionisation of the reactants can also be affected. The formation of enzyme-substrate complexes sometimes depends on the active centres and substrate molecules having opposite electrostatic charges. If the charges are altered by changes in pH some enzymes fail to function (Fig. 4.9).

FIG. 4.9 *One way in which pH may affect an enzyme*

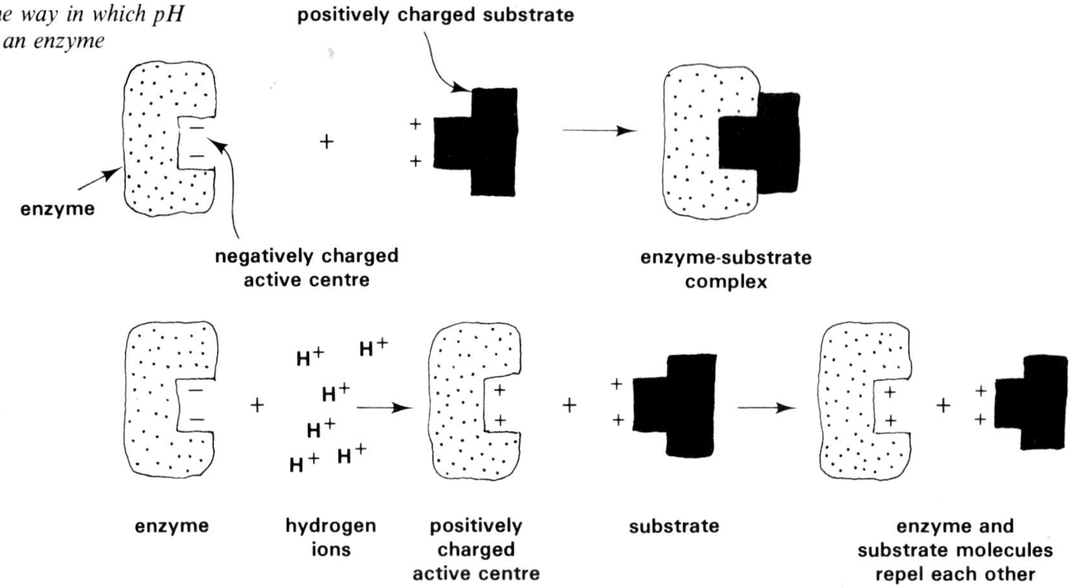

4.3.5 Enzyme concentration

Enzymes catalyse reactions rapidly at very low **enzyme concentrations**. This is because enzyme molecules form complexes with substrates only very briefly. The products of the reaction are quickly released and the enzyme is then available for further activity.

The rate at which enzymes use substrates is described as the **turn-over number**. For some enzymes the turn-over number is very high. Catalase for example breaks down 40 000 molecules of hydrogen peroxide into water and oxygen every second! Even the slowest of enzymes have turn-over numbers of 100 sec^{-1}. The larger the number of enzyme molecules present the greater is the amount of substrate used in a given period of time provided that there is an excess of substrate available (Fig. 4.10).

FIG. 4.10 *The effect of enzyme concentration on the rate of an enzyme-catalysed reaction*

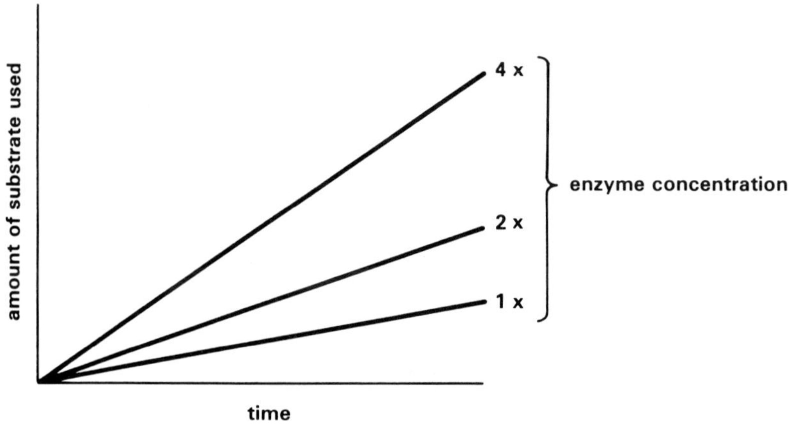

4.3.6 Substrate concentration

Figure 4.11 shows the effect of **substrate concentration** on the rate of a biochemical reaction when the amount of enzyme is limited. At low concentrations of substrate there is a linear relationship between the reaction rate and substrate concentration. In these conditions the ratio of enzyme to substrate molecules is high. Consequently some active centres are always free for reactants to bind with the enzyme. However, a point is reached when a further increase in substrate concentration does not cause the reaction to go any faster. The enzyme to substrate ratio is then lower and there are more substrate molecules present than there are free active centres with which to bind. Adding more substrate will not make the reaction go more quickly.

The concentration of substrate at which the reaction rate is half of its maximum is characteristic for each combination of enzyme and substrate. It is called **Michaelis' constant**.

FIG. 4.11 *The effect of substrate concentration on the rate of an enzyme-catalysed reaction*

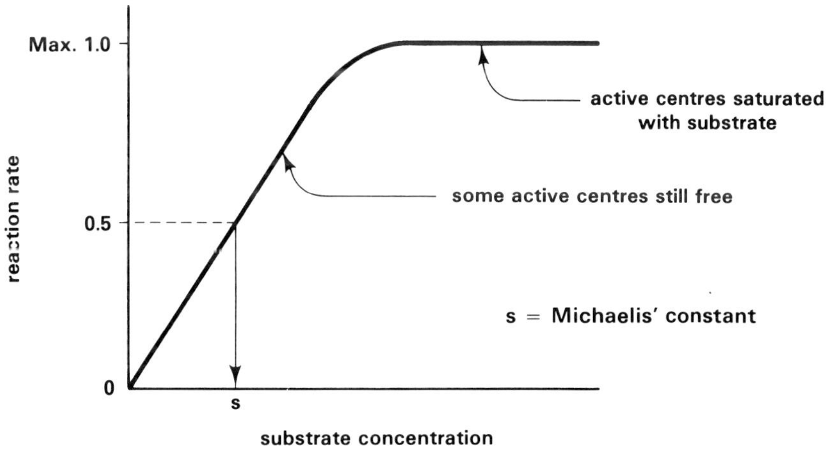

4.4 The classification of enzymes

In the past twenty years many new enzymes have been discovered. Older methods of classifying enzymes have become unpractical and for this reason, in the early 1960s the International Union of Biochemistry (IUB) recommended a new system for the classification and naming of enzymes. According to the IUB system there are six groups of enzymes.

4.4.1 Hydrolases

These enzymes catalyse reactions in which substrates are hydrolysed into simpler products. During **hydrolysis** hydrogen atoms from water enter one of the products while the hydroxyl groups end up in the other product. The reaction is shown in a simplified form as follows:

$$\underset{\text{substrate}}{AB} + \underset{\text{water}}{H.OH} \rightleftharpoons \underbrace{AH + B.OH}_{\text{products}}$$

Figure 4.12 shows how some important substrates found in living organisms are hydrolysed. Hydrolases bring about the breakdown of materials in lysosomes (Chapter 1), the digestion of food in the guts of mammals (Chapter 14) and the mobilisation of food reserves in plants (Chapter 20).

FIG. 4.12 *Hydrolysis of some important biological compounds*

(a) *Glycosidic linkage in a disaccharide*

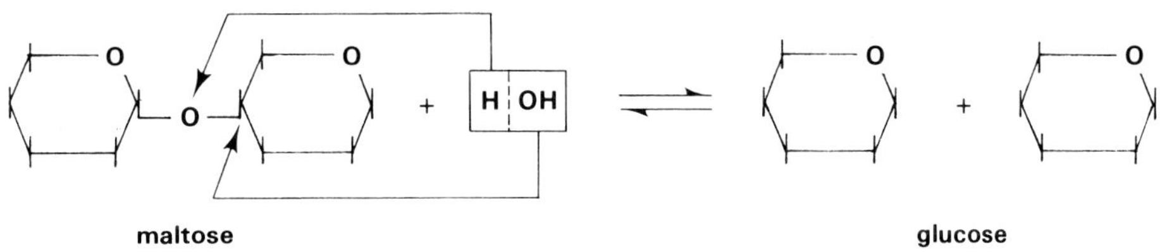

(b) *Peptide linkage in a protein*

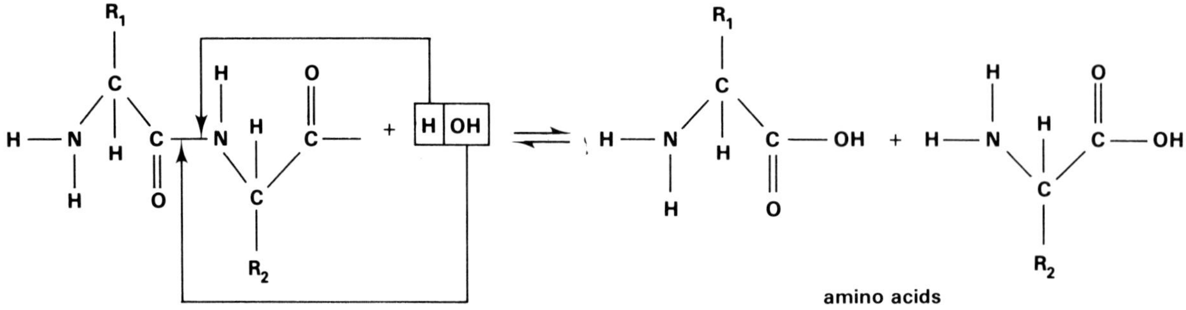

(c) *Ester linkages in a fat or oil*

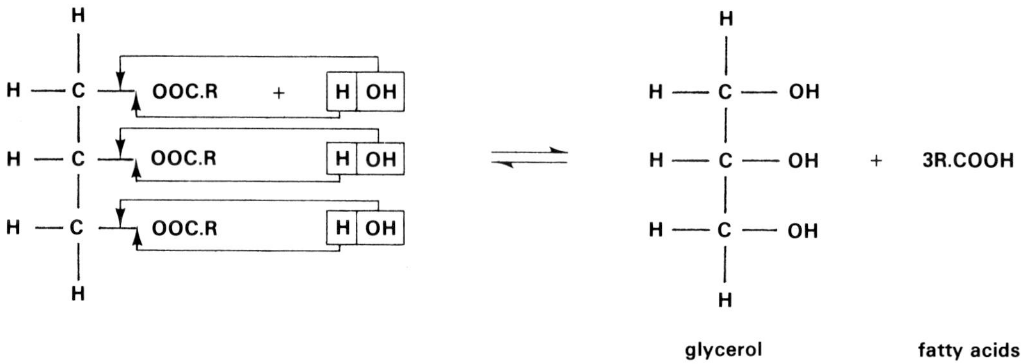

4.4.2 Oxido-reductases

The **oxidation** of substrates is catalysed by this group of enzymes. There are two kinds of oxido-reductase enzymes:

1. OXIDASES catalyse the transfer of hydrogen atoms to molecules of oxygen. A simplified way of expressing the reaction is as follows:

$$\underset{\text{substrate}}{AH_2} + \underset{\text{oxygen}}{\tfrac{1}{2}O_2} \rightleftharpoons \underset{\substack{\text{oxidised}\\\text{substrate}}}{A} + \underset{\substack{\text{water}\\\text{(reduced oxygen)}}}{H_2O}$$

Hydrogen peroxide is sometimes formed instead of water.

2. DEHYDROGENASES catalyse the oxidation of substrates by transferring hydrogen atoms to co-enzymes such as NAD and NADP:

$$\underset{\text{substrate}}{AH_2} + \underset{\text{co-enzyme}}{2NAD^+} \rightleftharpoons \underset{\substack{\text{oxidised}\\\text{substrate}}}{A} + \underset{\substack{\text{reduced}\\\text{co-enzyme}}}{2NADH}$$

Alternatively, electrons are transferred. In reactions catalysed by oxido-reductases, substrates are oxidised while oxygen or co-enzymes are reduced. Oxidation-reduction reactions usually release energy. The importance of these reactions is described more fully in Chapter 5.

4.4.3 Transferases

Transferases catalyse the transfer of functional groups from one substrate to another:

$$AB + C \rightleftharpoons A + BC$$

Two important kinds of transferases are **transaminases** which are concerned with the transfer of amino groups (Fig. 4.13 and Chapter 14) and **kinases** which control the transfer of energy-rich phosphate groups (Chapter 5).

FIG. 4.13 *Transamination*

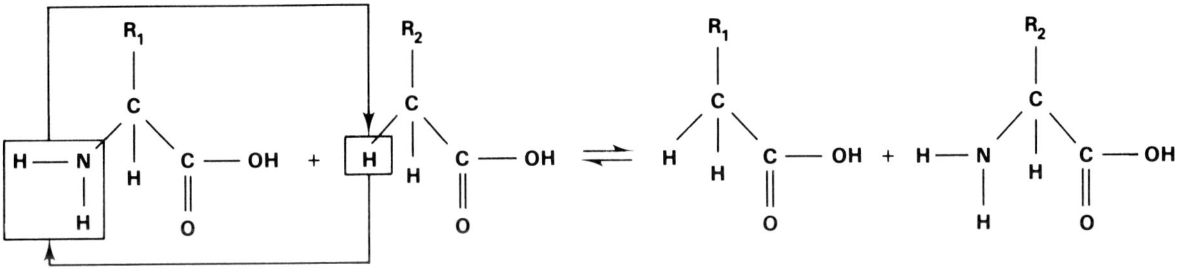

4.4.4 Isomerases

Isomerases convert one isomer of a compound to another isomer of the same compound:

$$ABC \rightleftharpoons ACB$$

Isomerases are involved in the interconversion of sugar isomers in glycolysis (Chapter 5).

4.4.5 Ligases

This group of enzymes catalyses reactions in which new chemical bonds are formed. **Ligases** control the synthesis of macromolecules such as proteins and nucleic acids (Chapter 6). ATP provides the energy to make the new chemical bonds.

4.4.6 Lyases

Lyases catalyse the breakdown of complex substrates into simpler products but water is not used as in hydrolytic reactions:

$$AB \rightleftharpoons A + B$$

Carboxylases which regulate the release from or the addition of carbon dioxide to substrates are examples of lyase enzymes. The roles of carboxylases in respiration and photosynthesis are described in Chapter 5.

Much of what is known about enzymes has come from investigations carried out *in vitro* on purified enzyme extracts. In vitro means in glass, indicating that it is easier to obtain information from test-tube studies than it is *in vivo*, in living cells. The way in which enzymes control vast numbers of different reactions taking place simultaneously in microscopic packets of protoplasm is therefore all the more remarkable. Compartmentalisation of cells (Chapter 1) undoubtedly helps. Each of the organelles of a living cell has a specific range of enzymes so that different kinds of metabolic reactions are separated. Even so, the way in which enzymes regulate the many, rapid and complex metabolic reactions in living cells surely gives cause for wonder.

Chapter 5 Energy changes in living cells

The composition of living organisms is very different from their surroundings. Whereas the environment consists of relatively simple substances such as gases, water and minerals, living organisms are made up of very complex molecules (Chapter 3). Most of the atoms in the environment are distributed in energy-poor compounds. In contrast, the atoms which make up living organisms are mainly found in energy-rich compounds.

Living organisms constantly use energy to synthesise the compounds of which they are made. They also use energy to perform osmotic, mechanical and electrical work (Chapters 2, 10, 11, 13 and 15 respectively). Where does the energy come from and how is it used?

The sun is the ultimate source of energy available to the living world. Energy in sunlight is changed to **chemical energy** in green plants in a process called **photosynthesis**. The products of photosynthesis are complex energy-rich molecules from which energy can be released to do work in living organisms. Green plants are called the **producer organisms** of ecosystems. Organisms which cannot photosynthesise are called **consumers**. Primary consumers acquire energy-rich compounds by feeding on green plants. Secondary consumers feed on primary consumers. Whatever the trophic level an organism belongs to, energy is made available when energy-rich substances are oxidised in living cells during **respiration**. Thus photosynthesis and respiration bring about the conversion of sunlight into energy which can be used to do work in living organisms.

5.1 Respiration

Respiration is the oxidation of energy-rich substrates. Carbohydrates, sugars especially, are the **respiratory substrates** most used by living organisms although lipids and proteins can also be oxidised. Polysaccharides are first hydrolysed to the hexose sugar glucose, lipids to glycerol and fatty acids, proteins to amino acids.

Most forms of life are **aerobes**. They respire using oxygen. Many aerobic organisms can respire for short periods of time in the absence of oxygen. They are called **facultative anaerobes**. A few species of bacteria are **strict anaerobes** and respire only in the absence of oxygen. Whatever the kind of respiration it is important to understand what energy is provided and how this energy is used in processes which could not occur without respiratory energy. In this context it is useful to know about a substance called adenosine 5′-triphosphate.

5.1.1. Adenosine 5′-triphosphate

Adenosine 5′-triphosphate (ATP) has the structure shown in Figure 5.1. ATP was first isolated by Lohmann from muscle extracts in 1929. Ten years later Lipmann suggested that ATP transfers energy from energy-rich substrates to energy-requiring processes in living cells.

According to the First Law of Thermodynamics every chemical reaction involves energy changes among the reactants. In some reactions a lot of heat energy is made. Heat energy is of little use to living organisms except that it can help speed up enzyme activity (Chapter 4). Heat cannot be used to synthesise proteins and other essential macromolecules, nor can it bring about the contraction of muscle or a host of other energy-requiring reactions. Energy which is used to do work in living organisms is called **free energy**.

It has been calculated that when the bond holding the terminal phosphate group of ATP is broken by hydrolysis, 30·66 kJ mol^{-1} of free energy is released. The same amount of free energy is released when the terminal phosphate bond of **adenosine 5′-diphosphate (ADP)** is hydrolysed. However, when the phosphate bond of **adenosine 5′-phosphate (AMP)** is hydrolysed only 14·28 kJ mol^{-1} of free energy is released. The amounts of free energy released in living cells may be even higher than the figures quoted here.

FIG. 5.1 *The structure of ATP*

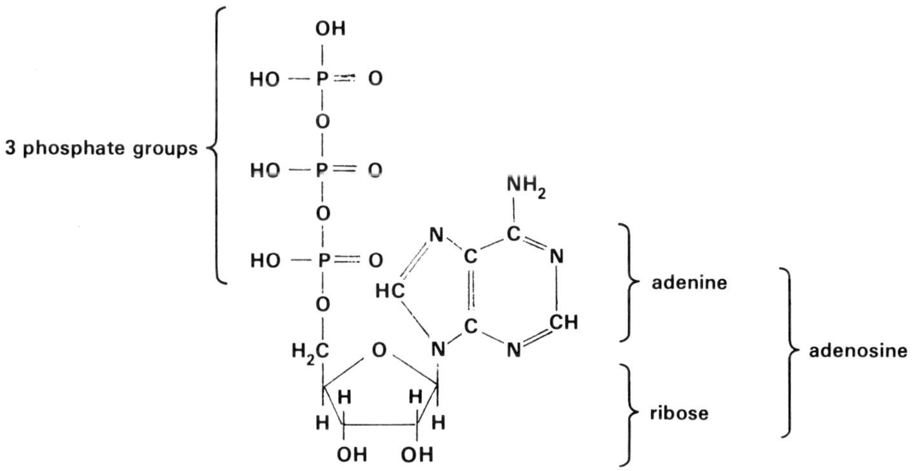

Similar amounts of energy are required to make the phosphate bonds. For example, when ADP and inorganic phosphate are converted to ATP, 30·66 kJ mol^{-1} of free energy is needed. The bonds between the first, second and third phosphate groups of ATP are called **high energy bonds** and adenosine 5′-triphosphate is sometimes written as:

$$A - P \sim P \sim P$$

where A = adenosine
P = phosphate group
$\sim$ = high energy bond
$-$ = low energy bond

The bonds in other substances found in living cells yield even more free energy than the high energy bonds of ATP. **Phosphocreatine** in striped muscle is an example of such a compound (Chapter 15). However, ATP is the only substance present in sufficient quantities in most living cells to be of general use as a provider of free energy. ATP is therefore indispensable in the transfer of free energy from energy-rich substrates to reactions in which free energy is used.

But how is ATP made in living cells and where does the energy for its synthesis come from?

5.1.2 Oxidation of respiratory substrates

In anaerobic conditions energy-rich substrates such as glucose are oxidised to lactic acid or to ethanol and carbon dioxide. Lactic acid is a product of anaerobic respiration in some bacteria and in animal cells. Ethanol and carbon dioxide are made by yeasts and higher plant cells when oxygen is absent. The overall processes can be summarised as follows:

lactic fermentation: $C_6H_{12}O_6 \longrightarrow 2CH_3CHOHCOOH$
glucose → lactic acid

alcoholic fermentation: $C_6H_{12}O_6 \longrightarrow 2CH_3CH_2OH + 2CO_2$
glucose → ethanol + carbon dioxide

The equations give us no idea of the amount of free energy released nor do they tell us anything about the way in which the substrate is oxidised. What is more they disguise the fact that the two processes are very similar, each sharing a number of common steps. **Glycolysis** (glyco = sugar; lysis = to split) is the name given to the common steps. Glycolysis also takes place when sugars are respired aerobically.

1. GLYCOLYSIS

Figure 5.2(a) shows the more important common steps in the oxidation of glucose, whether in anaerobic or aerobic conditions. Far from producing free energy, some of the earlier reactions need an input of free energy. The energy comes from the hydrolysis of high energy bonds of ATP. Without a supply of free energy from ATP the reactions could not proceed. The

FIG. 5.2 (a) *Glycolysis*

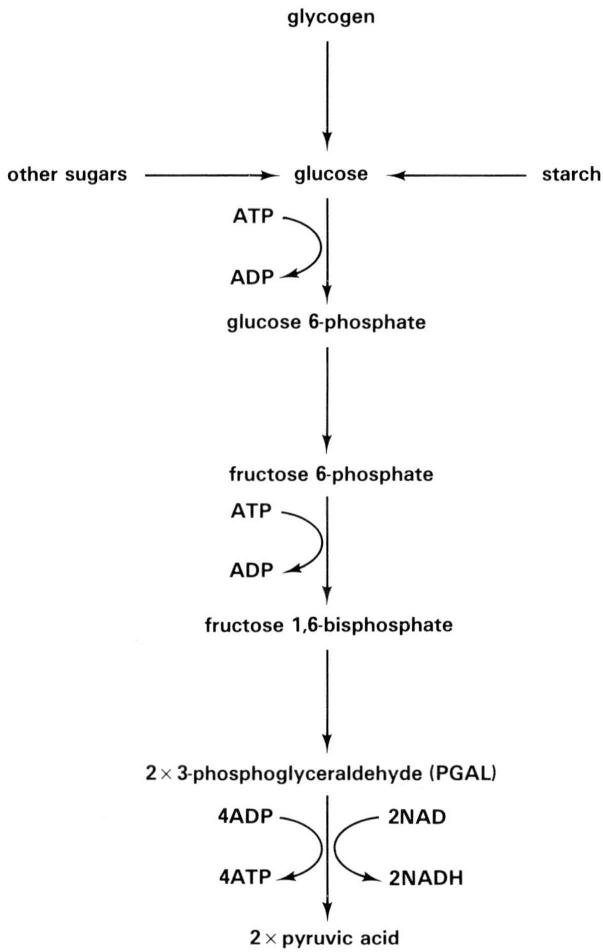

splitting of each **fructose 1, 6-bisphosphate** molecule yields two molecules of the triosephosphate called **3-phosphoglyceraldehyde (PGAL)** which is then oxidised to **pyruvic acid**. Oxidation of PGAL involves the removal of hydrogen and is catalysed by dehydrogenase enzymes (Chapter 4). At the same time the co-enzyme nicotinamide-adenine dinucleotide (NAD) becomes reduced to NADH. Oxidation of each PGAL molecule produces enough free energy for two ATP molecules to be synthesised from ADP and inorganic phosphate.

The fate of the pyruvic acid depends on the organism in which it was produced and on whether oxygen is available or not. If lactic acid is a product of anaerobic respiration the NADH formed in glycolysis transfers its hydrogen to pyruvic acid and **lactic acid** is formed. This is what happens in mammalian muscle cells when they have an oxygen debt (Chapter 8). Bacteria which sour milk also make lactic acid when oxygen is not available. If yeasts and higher plant cells are kept without oxygen, pyruvic acid is split into **carbon dioxide** and **ethanal**. The ethanal is then reduced to **ethanol** by hydrogen from NADH (Fig. 5.2(b)). Either way NAD is remade and once again acts as a hydrogen acceptor when more PGAL is oxidised.

FIG. 5.2 (b) *The fate of pyruvic acid in the absence of oxygen*

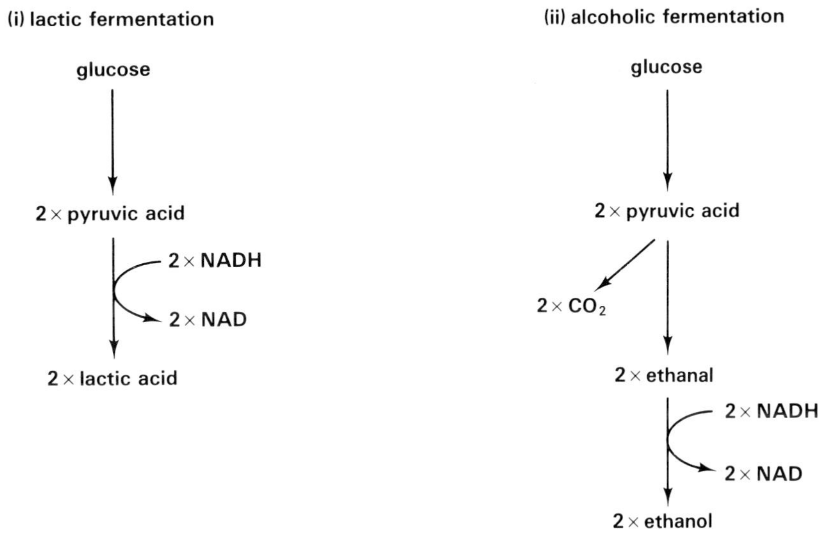

How has it been possible to unravel the steps of a complicated series of events such as glycolysis? The Buchner brothers in 1897 showed that extracts from yeast cells could ferment the disaccharide sugar sucrose (Chapter 4). In 1905 Harden and Young discovered that fructose 1,6-bisphosphate was formed in alcoholic fermentation which was stimulated by phosphate ions. During the 1930s Meyerhof observed that extracts of striped muscle broke down glucose to lactic acid. About the same time Embden accounted for the splitting of the hexose sugar into PGAL while Warburg found out how ADP and NAD are used in respiration. By discoveries such as these the intermediate compounds and end products were identified and a step by step scheme for glycolysis was pieced together. The enzymes which control glycolysis are found in the cytoplasm.

What happens to pyruvic acid if oxygen is available? In aerobic conditions the pyruvic acid is taken into the **tricarboxylic acid cycle**.

2. THE TRICARBOXYLIC ACID CYCLE

At the beginning of this century Thunberg discovered that animal tissues contain **dehydrogenase enzymes** which catalyse the transfer of hydrogen from carboxylic acids (Fig. 5.3). In 1935 Szent-Gyorgyi noticed that dehydrogenation of succinic acid in muscle is blocked by the competitive inhibitor malonic acid. Furthermore the inhibition stopped respiration of the muscle. Two years later Hans Krebs showed that respiration of pigeon breast muscle was stimulated by a specific variety of carboxylic acids. Krebs went on to carry out a series of brilliant experiments from which he

FIG. 5.3 *A Thunberg tube. The top of the tube is rotated so that the hole coincides with the outlet, and the air in the tube is then sucked out using a vacuum pump. The top is then turned to seal off the contents from the outside air. Finally the tube is inverted so that the blue dye mixes with the respiring cells and the dye is gradually reduced to a colourless compound. If air is left in the tube oxygen is reduced instead of the dye*

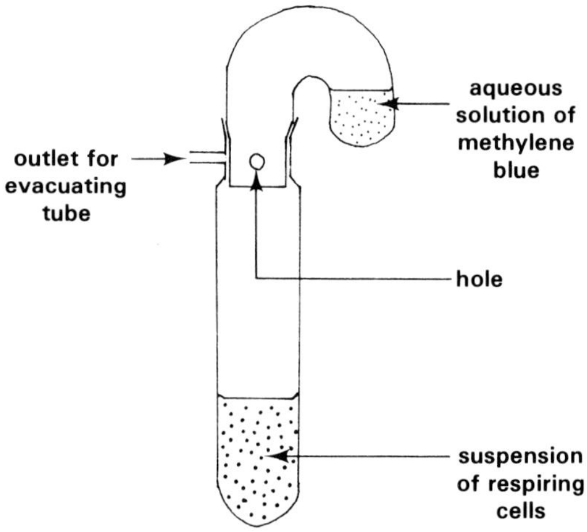

deduced that, in aerobic conditions, **pyruvic acid** combines with **oxaloacetic acid** to form **citric acid**. The citric acid is then dehydrogenated via a number of intermediate compounds back to oxaloacetic acid. One of the intermediates is **succinic acid**. Carbon dioxide is released in these reactions. It was some time later before it was found that pyruvic acid is converted to **acetyl coenzyme A** before it enters the cycle (Fig. 5.4). Today the citric acid cycle is called **Krebs' tricarboxylic acid (TCA) cycle**.

In the late 1940s mitochondria, separated from other cell components by differential centrifugation (Chapter 1), were found to break down pyruvic acid to carbon dioxide and water. The dehydrogenase enzymes which catalyse the oxidations in the TCA cycle are thus in the mitochondria. Biochemists are now fairly sure that the enzymes are in the matrix enclosed by the inner membrane of mitochondria.

So far so good, but what happens to the hydrogen removed from the carboxylic acids in the TCA cycle? Where does oxygen fit into the sequence of events?

In the TCA cycle oxidation of carboxylic acid molecules is catalysed by dehydrogenase enzymes. Dehydrogenation of the acids is accompanied by reduction of NAD to NADH. The fate of NADH in aerobic conditions is, however, different from NADH formed in anaerobic conditions. When oxygen is available the hydrogen from NADH is passed via a succession of hydrogen acceptors until it finally reduces oxygen to water. The succession is called an **electron transport chain** (Fig. 5.5). After NADH the hydrogen is passed to **flavin-adenine dinucleotide (FAD)**. The hydrogen atoms now split into electrons and protons. FADH transfers the electrons to the next acceptors called **cytochromes**. Reduced cytochromes then pass the elec-

FIG. 5.4 *Krebs' TCA cycle and some important biological pathways to which it is linked*

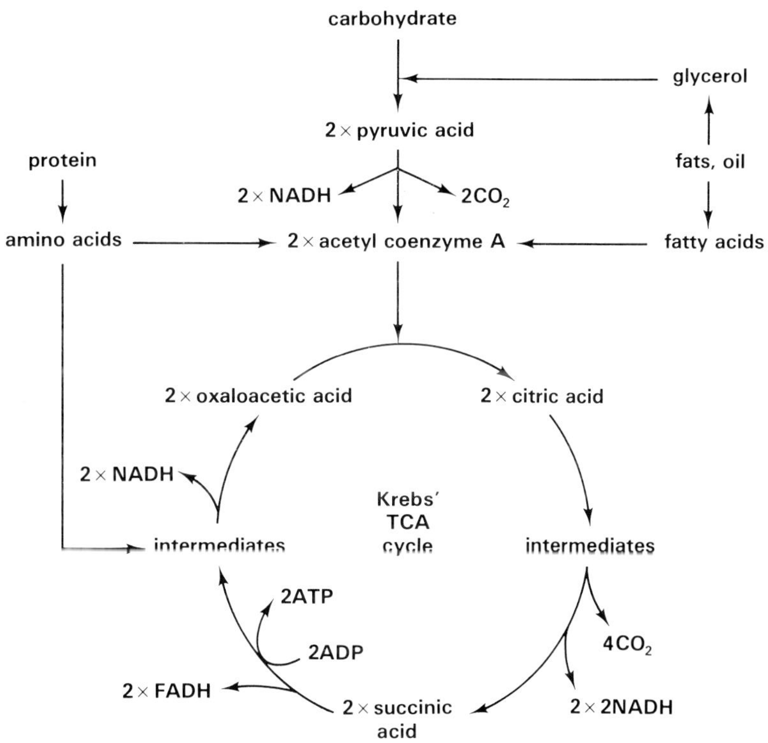

trons to **cytochrome oxidase**. Finally reduced cytochrome oxidase transfers the electrons back to the protons. The hydrogen so formed reduces oxygen to water. Each of the reactions in the chain is an oxidation-reduction reaction. As the hydrogen atoms and later the electrons move along the chain the reduced acceptors are oxidised and more hydrogen can be taken into the chain.

FIG. 5.5 *An electron transport chain*

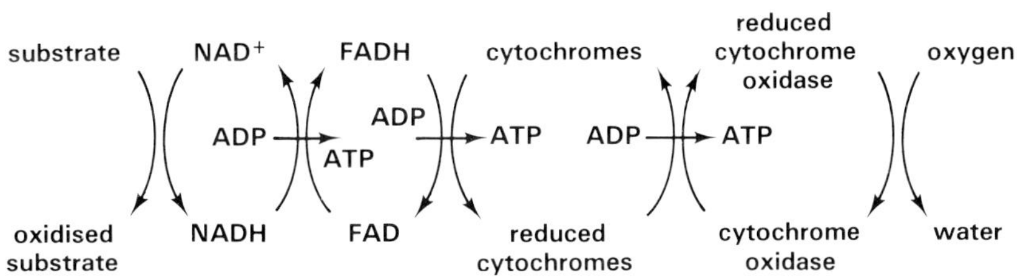

What is particularly important is that three of the oxidation-reduction reactions in an electron transport chain yield enough free energy to make ATP from inorganic phosphate ions and ADP. This type of reaction is called **oxidative phosphorylation**. It takes place in the stalked bodies projecting from the cristae of mitochondria. How many ATP moles are formed from each mole of glucose oxidised aerobically? How does this figure compare with the number obtained when glucose is oxidised anaerobically?

5.1.3 Energy yields from respiratory substrates

The breakdown of a mole of glucose in glycolysis uses the free energy from the terminal high energy bonds of two moles of ATP. On the other hand enough free energy is released in glycolysis to produce four moles of ATP from ADP and inorganic phosphate (Pi):

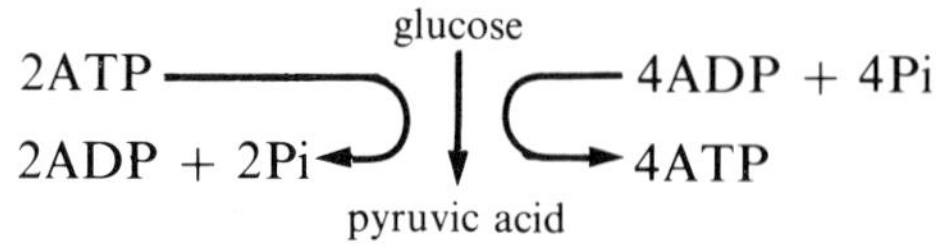

The net gain in free energy from a mole of glucose broken down to pyruvic acid therefore is the free energy released when the terminal high energy bonds of two moles of ATP are later hydrolysed. Thus living cells respiring anaerobically make 2 × 30·66 kJ of free energy for every mole of glucose oxidised.

In aerobic conditions ATP is made mainly in the electron transport chains into which NADH and FADH from the TCA cycle is fed. Altogether 38 ATP moles are made from each mole of glucose oxidised aerobically, 8 from glycolysis and 30 from the TCA cycle (Table 5.1). Living cells respiring aerobically thus release 38 × 30·66 kJ of free energy per mole of glucose. Aerobic respiration is clearly much more efficient than anaerobic respiration in releasing free energy.

Table 5.1 Origin of ATP formed in aerobic respiration of glucose

SOURCE	NO. OF ATP MOLECULES
glycolysis	2 (net gain)
NADH formed in glycolysis	6 (2 × 3)
NADH } formed in Krebs' TCA cycle	28(2 × 14)
FADH } direct synthesis in TCA cycle	2(2 × 1)
Total	38

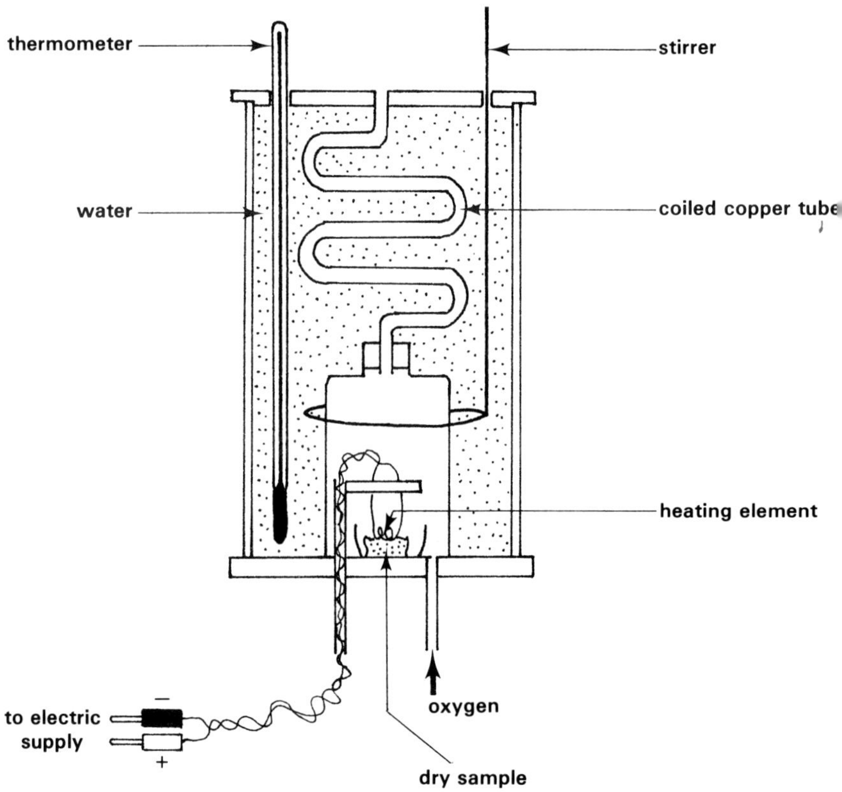

FIG. 5.6 *A simple calorimeter. When the supply of electricity is switched on the heating element becomes red hot and the sample ignites in the stream of oxygen. The heat given off by the sample causes the temperature of the water to rise. The amount of temperature rise, the volume of water and the mass of the sample are used to work out the calorific value of the sample*

What proportion of the energy in the respiratory substrate is used to do work in living cells? The amount of heat energy produced when glucose is burned to carbon dioxide and water can be measured using a **calorimeter** (Fig. 5.6). One mole of glucose releases 2880 kJ of heat energy. This is the amount of energy potentially available to do work. We can now calculate the efficiency of energy change in living cells when glucose is respired aerobically:

$$\text{Efficiency of energy change} = \frac{38 \times 30{\cdot}66}{2880} \times 100 = 44 \text{ per cent}$$

This means that less than half of the potential energy in glucose is used to do work.

You may wonder what has happened to the rest of the energy in the respiratory substrate. The Second Law of Thermodynamics states that whenever one form of energy is changed into another, some of the energy is converted into heat. In aerobic respiration over half of the energy in the substrate is released as heat. Heat energy helps to maintain the constant body temperature of warm-blooded animals (Chapter 17). However, remember that heat energy cannot be used to do work in living organisms.

5.1.4 Measuring the rate of respiration

In the 1930s Otto Warburg introduced a constant volume manometer to measure the rate of oxygen uptake by slices of living tissue. The apparatus is often called a **Warburg manometer** (Fig. 5.7). **Simple manometers** are often used in school laboratories for measuring rates of oxygen uptake by living organisms (Fig. 5.8).

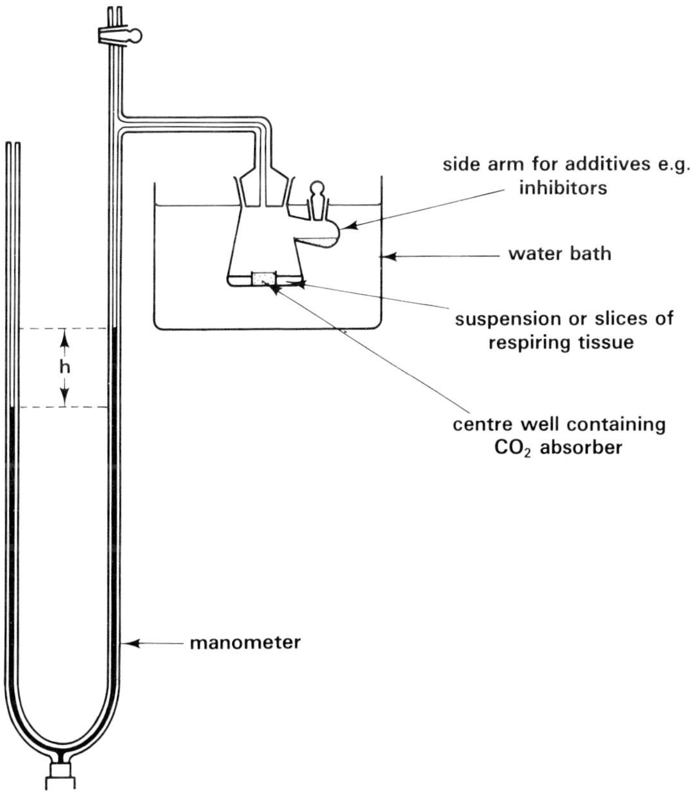

FIG. 5.7 *A Warburg respirometer. As the tissue respires the CO_2 it evolves is taken up by the CO_2 absorber. Consumption of oxygen by the tissue is then registered by a change in height* (h) *of the manometer fluid*

FIG. 5.8 *A simple respirometer*

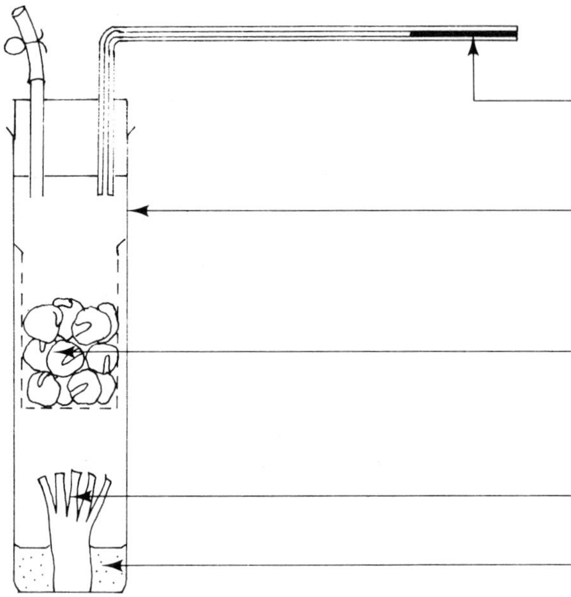

A known mass of live material is placed in the respiratory chamber. The apparatus is kept at a fixed temperature and the valve is closed. The potassium hydroxide absorbs the carbon dioxide given off in respiration. The volume of air in the respiratory chamber decreases as oxygen is used up. Consequently the coloured fluid moves towards the respiratory chamber. Knowing the distance moved by the meniscus of the coloured fluid and the bore of the tube the rate of oxygen uptake can be calculated. The results are normally expressed as mm^3 oxygen consumed g^{-1} tissue h^{-1} at t°C, where t is the temperature at which the measurements were made.

FIG. 5.9 *Haldane's method for measuring the rate of oxygen uptake*

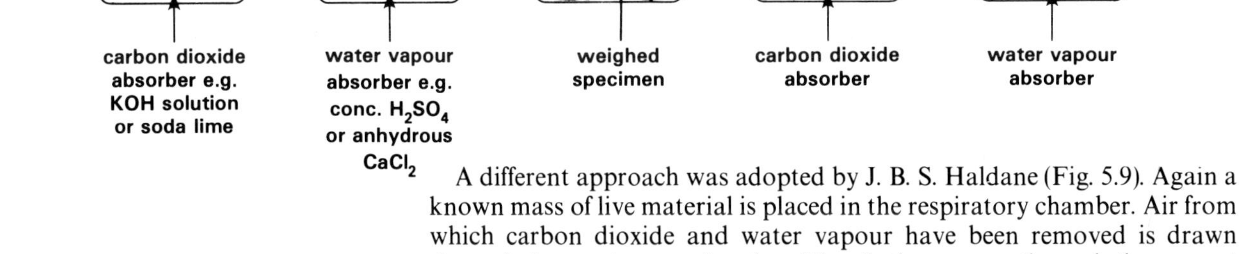

A different approach was adopted by J. B. S. Haldane (Fig. 5.9). Again a known mass of live material is placed in the respiratory chamber. Air from which carbon dioxide and water vapour have been removed is drawn through the respiratory chamber. The air then passes through the reagent bottles in which expired carbon dioxide and water vapour are separately trapped. The live material and the reagent bottles are reweighed after a fixed period of time. The rate at which oxygen was consumed is calculated on the assumption that any loss in mass of the material is due to expiration of the carbon dioxide and water vapour formed when the respiratory substrate is oxidised:

$$\underset{(1)}{\text{Respiratory substrate}} + O_2 \longrightarrow \underset{(2)}{CO_2} + \underset{(3)}{H_2O}$$

Knowing factors (1), (2) and (3) it is possible to calculate the rate of oxygen uptake.

Which of the two methods do you think provides the more accurate measurement of oxygen uptake?

Another method used to calculate the rate of respiration is to measure the rate at which living tissue gives off carbon dioxide. The method involves passing air devoid of CO_2 through the respiratory chamber in which a known mass of live material is placed. The expired air is bubbled through a solution of calcium hydroxide of known concentration (Fig. 5.10). The volume of carbon dioxide given off is determined after titrating the hydroxide with standard hydrochloric acid.

FIG. 5.10 *A method for measuring the rate of production of carbon dioxide by a living organism*

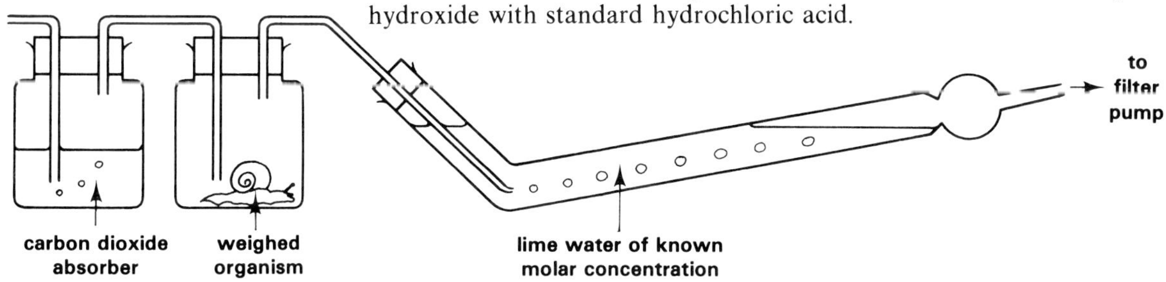

In each of the methods outlined above the respiratory chamber must be light-proof if the experimental subject can photosynthesise. Why do you think it is necessary to do this?

5.1.5 Respiratory quotient

The volume of carbon dioxide given off divided by the volume of oxygen taken up in a fixed period is called the **respiratory quotient (RQ)**:

$$RQ = \frac{\text{volume } CO_2 \text{ given off}}{\text{volume } O_2 \text{ taken up}}$$

RQ values indicate the type of respiration, aerobic, anaerobic or both. They also tell us which substrates are oxidised.

In aerobic conditions an RQ of 1·0 indicates that the respiratory substrate is a carbohydrate:

$$\underset{\text{carbohydrate}}{C_6H_{12}O_6} + 6O_2 \longrightarrow 6CO_2 + 6H_2O$$

For each volume of oxygen taken up a similar volume of CO_2 is given off:

$$RQ = \frac{6}{6} = 1{\cdot}0$$

When a lipid is oxidised aerobically the RQ is 0·7:

$$\underset{\text{tristearoylglycerol}}{C_{57}H_{110}O_6} + 81{\cdot}5\ O_2 \longrightarrow 57CO_2 + 55H_2O$$

$$RQ = \frac{57}{81{\cdot}5} = 0{\cdot}7$$

For the aerobic oxidation of protein an RQ of 0·99 is obtained. The aerobic breakdown of a mixture of carbohydrates, lipids and proteins gives an RQ of 0·8–0·9. Animals fed a balanced diet use carbohydrates and lipids as respiratory substrates and have an RQ of about 0·85. The RQ of starving animals is between 0·9 and 1·0. Can you explain why this is so?

A mixture of aerobic and anaerobic respiration takes place when there is a shortage of oxygen. Here the RQ is greater than 1·0. The exact value depends on the respiratory substrates used and on the relative rates of the two types of respiration. For example, when anaerobic and aerobic respiration of glucose occur at similar rates, an RQ of 1·33 is obtained.

anaerobic respiration $C_6H_{12}O_6 \longrightarrow 2CO_2 + 2CH_3CH_2OH$

aerobic respiration $C_6H_{12}O_6 + 6O_2 \longrightarrow 6CO_2 + 6H_2O$

Total $6O_2 \longrightarrow 8CO_2$

$$RQ = \frac{8}{6} = 1{\cdot}33$$

What might the RQ be if aerobic respiration takes place more rapidly, or more slowly than anaerobic respiration of glucose?

If oxygen is totally lacking the RQ is infinity. Why?

5.2 Photosynthesis

Photosynthesis consists of two main phases, the **light-dependent** and **light-independent** (dark) reactions.

5.2.1 Light-dependent reactions

White light is a mixture of light of different wavelengths (Fig. 5.11). Einstein and Planck suggested that light energy is transmitted as units called photons. Because the energy of light is inversely proportional to its wavelength it follows that light of short wavelength has more energy than light of long wavelength. Green plants convert the energy of light into chemical bond energy.

FIG. 5.11 *The visible spectrum*

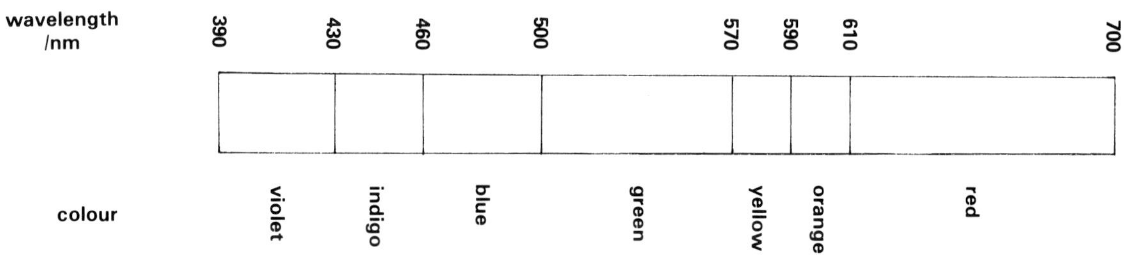

1. ABSORPTION AND ACTION SPECTRA

Green plants do not use energy from all of the components of white light for photosynthesis. This was neatly demonstrated by the German plant physiologist H. T. Engelmann in 1882. He placed filaments of the green alga *Cladophora* in a drop of water on a microscope slide. The filaments were illuminated with light of different wavelengths. He then watched the distribution of aerobic bacteria in the water. Engelmann noted that the bacteria clustered near to the filaments when blue light (450 nm) or red light (650 nm) was used (Fig. 5.12). Knowing that oxygen is given off during photosynthesis, Engelmann deduced that light of mean wavelength 450 nm and 650 nm is the most effective for photosynthesis. It has since been shown that photosynthesis in nearly all green plants occurs most rapidly when they are illuminated by blue and red light.

FIG. 5.12 *Engelmann's experiment*

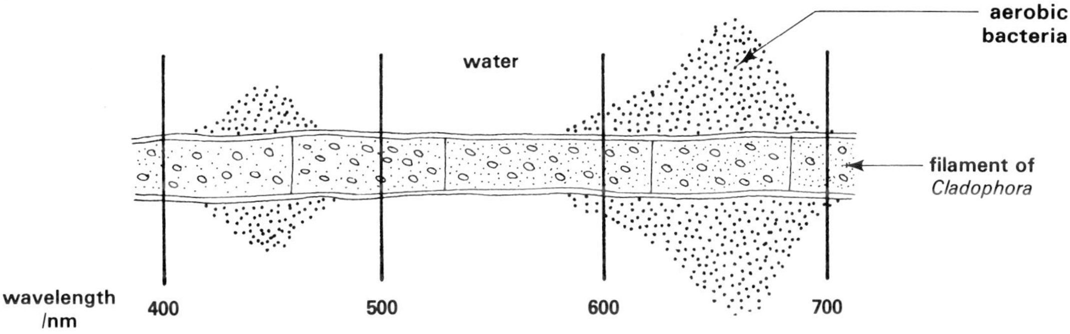

When the rate of photosynthesis is plotted against wavelength of light an **action spectrum** is produced (Fig. 5.13). The reason why light from the blue and red parts of the spectrum is effective is that it is absorbed efficiently by the pigments of green plants. The photosynthetic pigments most commonly present are chlorophylls and carotinoids (Table 5.2). Chlorophylls belong to a group of chemicals called porphyrins which includes the cytochromes and haemoglobin (Chapter 8). They all have four nitrogen-containing pyrrole rings (Fig. 5.14). In the chlorophylls a magnesium atom is held between the rings. In the cytochromes and haemoglobin there is an iron atom instead. Chlorophylls are green because they reflect green light.

FIG. 5.13 *An action spectrum for photosynthesis*

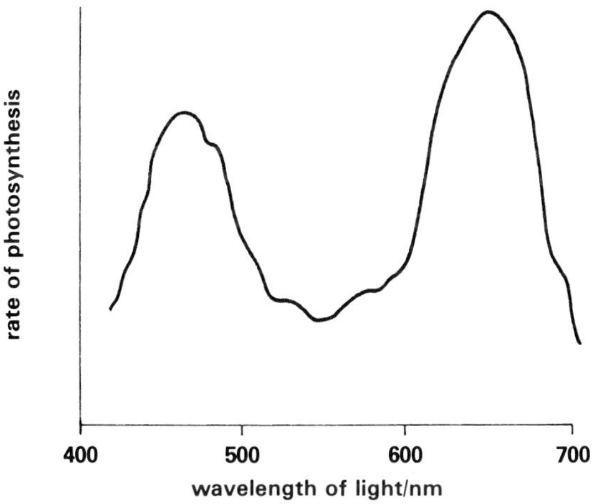

Table 5.2 Photosynthetic pigments commonly found in leaves of higher plants

GROUP	PIGMENT	FORMULA	COLOUR
chlorophylls	chlorophyll a	$C_{55}H_{72}O_5N_4Mg$	green
chlorophylls	chlorophyll b	$C_{55}H_{70}O_6N_4Mg$	green
carotinoids	xanthophyll	$C_{40}H_{56}$	yellow
carotinoids	carotene	$C_{40}H_{56}O_2$	orange

FIG. 5.14 (a) *Structure of chlorophyll*

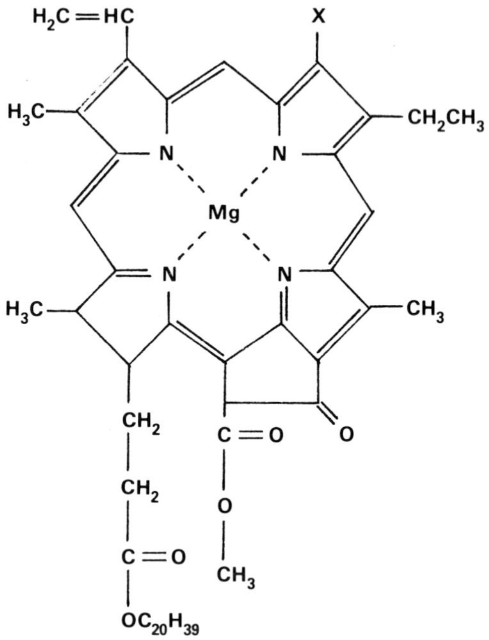

In chlorophyll a X = CH_3; in chlorophyll b X = CHO

FIG. 5.14 (b) *Structure of β-carotene*

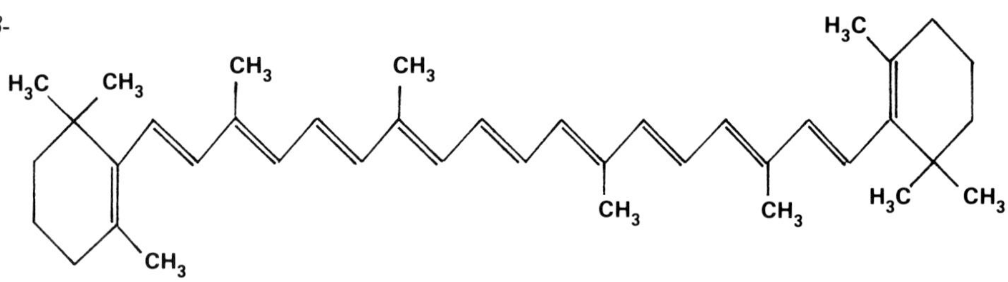

FIG. 5.15 *Absorption spectra of chloroplast pigments*

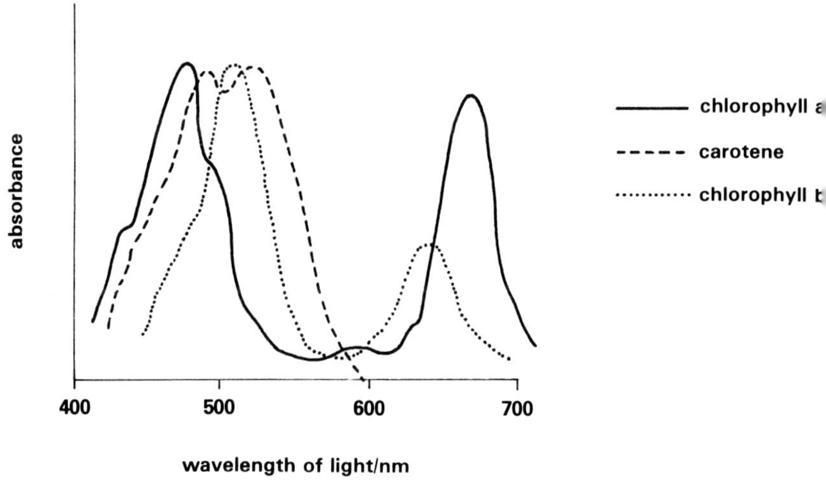

The wavelengths they absorb most strongly are in the blue and red parts of the visible spectrum. Carotene and xanthophyll are long chain hydrocarbons. Their colours indicate that they reflect orange and yellow light respectively. However, they absorb blue light effectively. If the percentage light absorption is plotted against wavelength of light an **absorption spectrum** is obtained for each pigment (Fig. 5.15). Notice the close correlation between the absorption and action spectra.

2. ELECTRON TRANSFER IN CHLOROPLASTS

What happens when chloroplast pigments absorb photons of light? One clue comes from the behaviour of the pigments extracted from leaves in warm ethanol or in propanone. When the solution is placed in white light the pigments give off red light. This is called fluorescence. It occurs because light energy temporarily raises the energy level of electrons in the outer shells of magnesium atoms in the chlorophyll molecules causing the electrons to become displaced. In their high energy state the electrons are said to be **excited**. Red light appears during fluorescence because shortly after being displaced the electrons fall back into position. The extra energy they held is emitted as red light.

What has just been described is of course an experiment. In living tissues the solvent is water. Green plants do not emit red light when they photosynthesise. Green plants also give off oxygen during photosynthesis. These facts strongly suggest that in living plants the energy of excited electrons is linked to reactions involving the release of oxygen. Where does the oxygen come from and what happens to the excited electrons?

Some idea of what happens to the excited electrons was established in 1937 by the English biochemist Robin Hill. He observed that an illuminated suspension of chloroplasts in water, while evolving oxygen, reduced iron(III) ions to iron(II) ions. This behaviour, called the **Hill reaction**, suggests that chloroplasts contain electron acceptors. In the 1950s it was discovered that the normal acceptor of excited electrons from chlorophyll molecules was **nicotinamide-adenine dinucleotide phosphate (NADP)**. Transfer of the electrons was later found to be catalysed by an iron-containing protein called **ferredoxin**. As we shall see later, other electron acceptors are also involved.

3. PHOTOLYSIS

Having given electrons to NADP, chlorophyll molecules are in an electron-deficient (oxidised) state. How is the pigment reduced to its former stable condition? One way it could be reduced is to receive electrons from another source. Water is the most likely source of the electrons. Water is a weak electrolyte and a small proportion of its molecules dissociate into hydrogen ions (H^+) and hydroxyl ions (OH^-):

$$H_2O \rightleftharpoons H^+ + OH^-$$

If electrons are removed from hydroxyl ions by oxidised chlorophyll, oxygen is given off:

$$2OH^- + \text{oxidised chlorophyll} \longrightarrow \tfrac{1}{2}O_2 + H_2O + \text{reduced chlorophyll}$$

Equilibrium is re-established as more water molecules dissociate. Thus one result of light absorption by chlorophyll is a rapid splitting of water molecules into hydrogen ions and oxygen. This is called **photolysis** (photo = light; lysis = to split). Using isotopes it is possible to prove that all of the oxygen given off in photosynthesis comes from water. When heavy water, that is water containing the heavy isotope of oxygen ^{18}O, is supplied to photosynthesising plants instead of normal water containing the isotope ^{16}O, heavy oxygen is given off.

$$CO_2 + 2H_2{}^{18}O \longrightarrow {}^{18}O_2 + (CH_2O) + H_2O$$

If a control experiment is also run in which the ^{18}O is supplied in carbon dioxide, while normal water is provided, the evolved oxygen is of the ^{16}O type.

What happens to the hydrogen ions from photolysed water is explained in the next section.

4. PHOTOPHOSPHORYLATION

Excited electrons displaced from chlorophyll *b* pass through an electron transport chain in which **cytochromes** act as electron carriers (Fig. 5.16(a)). As excited electrons pass through the chain some of their energy is used to make ATP. When they leave the chain the electrons have a normal, **ground-state** amount of energy. The ground-state electrons reduce chlorophyll *a* which has also lost excited electrons. The excited electrons from chlorophyll *a* pass through a second electron transport chain in which **ferredoxin** is the main electron carrier. Once again ATP is made. The production of ATP in the two electron transport chains is called **non-cyclic photophosphorylation**.

FIG. 5.16 (a) *Non-cyclic photophosphorylation*

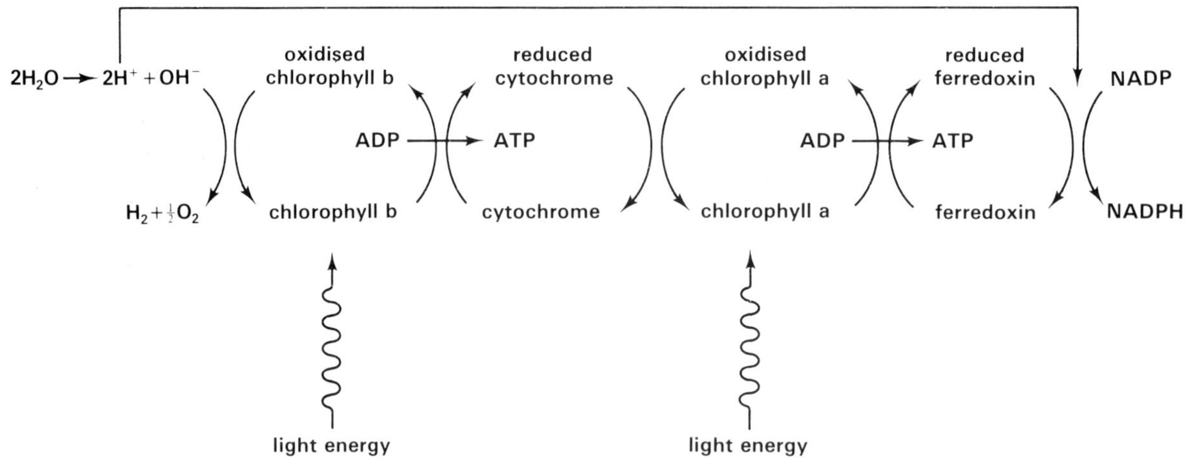

NADPH is another important product of the second electron transport chain. Hydrogen ions from photolysed water combine with ground-state electrons coming out of the chain. The hydrogen atoms so formed reduce NADP to NADPH. Oxygen is given off when hydroxyl ions from photolysed water donate electrons to oxidised chlorophyll *b*.

ATP is also made in a third electron transport chain called **cyclic photophosphorylation**. Excited electrons from chlorophyll *a* pass first to ferredoxin, then to cytochromes. The reduced cytochromes then pass the electrons back to oxidised chlorophyll *a* (Fig. 5.16(b)).

The important products of the light-dependent reactions of photosynthesis are ATP, NADPH and oxygen. ATP is a source of free energy required for the dark reactions. NADPH is also used in the dark reactions to reduce 3-phosphoglyceric acid (section 5.2.2). Oxygen given off in photosynthesis is used by living organisms for respiration.

No mention has yet been made of the role of the carotinoid pigments.

FIG. 5.16 (b) *Cyclic photophosphorylation*

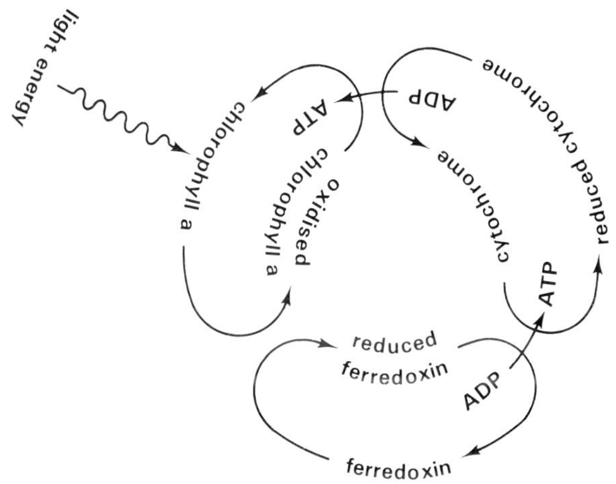

They are thought to shield the chlorophylls from excessive oxidation in intense light. The carotinoids are not involved in electron transfer. This is why photosynthesis occurs only in the green parts of variegated leaves.

5.2.2 Light-independent reactions

1. FIXATION OF CARBON DIOXIDE

For a long time plant scientists had little idea of what happens to carbon dioxide in photosynthesis. In the late 1940s Professor Melvin Calvin of the University of California decided that one way to find out was to allow plants to photosynthesise using carbon dioxide labelled with the radio-isotope ^{14}C. Calvin experimented with unicellular green algae such as *Chlorella* and *Scenedesmus* which he grew in a mineral solution held in flat glass containers he called lollipops (Fig. 5.17). The isotope was added as sodium hydrogencarbonate solution which breaks down to form $^{14}CO_2$. After a fixed period of illumination the algae were rapidly killed by running the mineral solution into a flask of hot ethanol. The cell contents were then analysed by **autoradiography** to find out which substances were labelled.

FIG. 5.17 *Calvin's experiment*

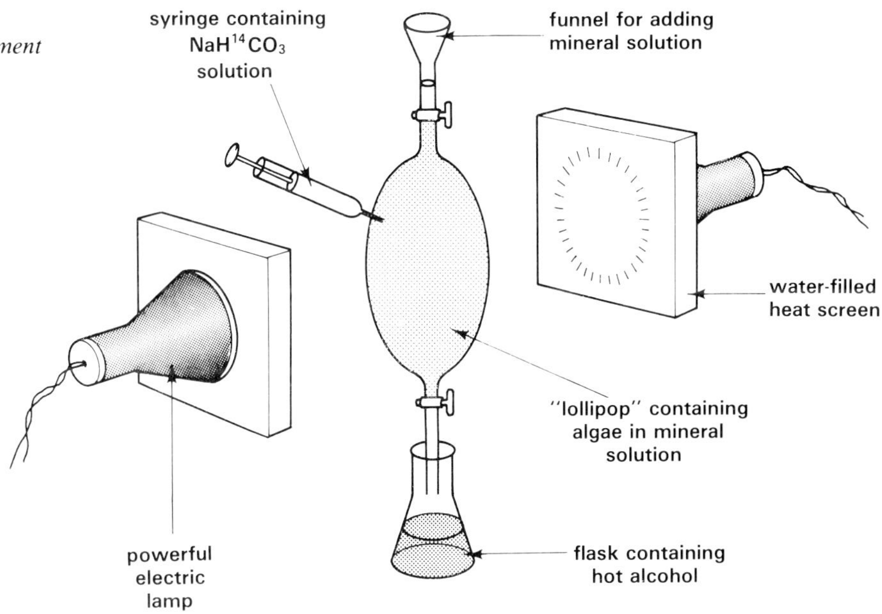

Hexoses are condensed into **disaccharides** and **polysaccharides**. Further reduction of PGAL yields glycerol which can be esterified to form **lipids**. Some PGA is fed into the Krebs' tricarboxylic acid cycle. Amination of some of the acids formed in the cycle results in the production of **amino acids** which are condensed into **protein** molecules. The polymerisation of higher carbohydrates and proteins and esterification of glycerol use the free energy provided when high energy bonds of ATP are hydrolysed. Thus a wide variety of complex organic substances, rich in chemical bond energy, results from photosynthesis (Fig. 5.20).

The synthesis of one mole of a hexose sugar uses 2880 kJ of energy

$$6CO_2 + 12H_2O + 2880 \text{ kJ} = C_6H_{12}O_6 + 6O_2 + 6H_2O$$

How much free energy is made available for work when a mole of glucose is oxidised in respiration?

3. OTHER PATHWAYS FOR CARBON DIOXIDE FIXATION

In the past few years it has been found that the fixation of carbon dioxide in some green plants occurs differently from that described above. The plants include some important tropical crops such as sugar-cane, maize and sorghum. When given $^{14}CO_2$ the carbon radioisotope first appears in **oxaloacetic acid**. Oxaloacetic acid contains four carbon atoms compared with PGA which contains three. This pathway, sometimes called the **Hatch-Slack** or **C4 pathway**, is outlined in Figure 5.21.

FIG. 5.21 *The Hatch-Slack (C_4) pathway*

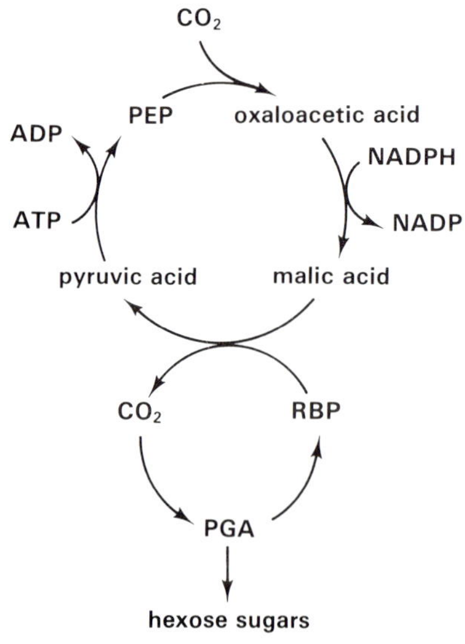

The source of energy for photosynthesis in C4 plants is sunlight, and ATP and NADPH are again the products of the light-dependent reactions. Some ATP is used to phosphorylate pyruvic acid with the formation of **phosphoenolpyruvic acid (PEP)**. On losing its phosphate group PEP releases free energy which is used to fix CO_2. Oxaloacetic acid is the first product of carbon dioxide fixation in C4 plants. NADPH reduces the oxaloacetic acid to **malic acid** which reacts with RBP to form **pyruvic acid** and **PGA**. The fate of PGA is the same as that described for C3 plants.

A similar process occurs in succulent plants including desert cacti. Here the events are called **Crassulacean acid metabolism** (**CAM**). The main difference is that CAM plants take in and fix carbon dioxide at night rather than during the daytime. This is of great importance to the water economy of such plants (Chapter 11). Malic acid is again the main product of CO_2 fixation. During the daytime it reacts with RBP and PGA is formed as described above.

Among the products of CO_2 fixation in all green plants is **hydroxyethanoic acid**. The acid is immediately oxidised in C3 plants in a process called **photorespiration** and carbon dioxide is given off. Up to 30 per cent of carbon dioxide fixed in photosynthesis can be recycled in this way. Consequently a considerable amount of the solar energy used to fix carbon dioxide is wasted. C4 plants do not photorespire so their photosynthesis is more efficient in making raw materials for growth. Furthermore, with a rise in temperature the rate of photorespiration increases more rapidly than carbon dioxide fixation. C4 plants are therefore much more productive than C3 plants, especially in tropical climates.

In this chapter we have concentrated on the energetics and biochemistry of respiration and photosynthesis. There are many questions about the two processes which we have not yet answered. How, for example, do cells respiring aerobically obtain a supply of oxygen? What happens to the carbon dioxide made in respiration? What is the source of carbon dioxide for photosynthesising cells and how does it reach the chloroplasts? How does light energy reach green cells? These and other aspects of respiration and photosynthesis are described in Chapters 8 and 12.

Chapter 6

Nucleic acids and protein synthesis

Progress in scientific knowledge normally comes a little at a time. There are occasions, however, when advances occur in leaps and bounds. This is aptly illustrated by a study of the structure and functions of the nucleic acids.

In 1869 a German physician called Meischer reported on a chemical analysis he had made of the nuclei of human pus cells collected from bandages. He found the nuclei to be rich in nitrogen, sulphur and phosphorus. Meischer set a pattern for investigating the composition of the nuclei of cells using the methods of the analytical chemist.

During the next eighty years analytical chemists provided small but significant facts about the composition of nuclei. Crude extracts of nuclei were found to be acidic in reaction, hence the term **nucleic acids** to describe the most important of substances present in nuclei. Gradually the building blocks which make up the nucleic acids were discovered. But the way in which the building blocks were put together and the roles of the nucleic acids in living organisms were still poorly understood at the middle of this century. It was then that giant strides in our knowledge and understanding of the nucleic acids were made.

The turning point came in the early 1950s when James Watson and Francis Crick proposed a structure for **deoxyribonucleic acid (DNA)**. The discovery of how exact copies of DNA are made in living cells soon followed and its biological significance was quickly realised. The momentum was maintained by the unravelling of the **genetic code**, the 'secret of life' as it has been called. We shall see in this chapter that great strides in unlocking the secrets of nucleic acids are still being made, one of which has recently confronted biologists with a moral dilemma.

6.1 The nucleic acids

Deoxyribonucleic acid (DNA) and **ribonucleic acid (RNA)** are the two main kinds of nucleic acids. DNA is found mainly in the nuclei of cells, small amounts occurring in mitochondria and chloroplasts. RNA is located mainly in the cytoplasm, particularly at the ribosomes.

Both DNA and RNA are polymers. The building blocks of which they are constructed are called nucleotides. For this reason the nucleic acids are described as **polynucleotides**.

6.1.1 Deoxyribonucleic acid

A nucleotide is made up of three parts, a **pentose sugar**, a **nitrogenous base** and **phosphate**. In DNA the sugar is **deoxyribose** (Fig. 6.1). Four different nitrogenous bases occur in DNA (Fig. 6.2). **Adenine (Ade)** and **guanine (Gua)** belong to a group of compounds called **purines**. **Cytosine (Cyt)** and **thymine (Thy)** are **pyrimidines**. The sugar, nitrogenous base and phosphate are bonded as shown in Figure 6.3 to form a **nucleotide**. In a DNA molecule the phosphate groups act as bridges joining together a chain of nucleotides by their sugar molecules (Fig. 6.4). During the early 1950s biochemists established that the number of adenine molecules in DNA from different organisms is the same as the number of thymine molecules. The ratio of cytosine and guanine molecules is also 1 : 1. However, the ratio of (Ade + Thy) : (Cyt + Gua) varies according to the source of the DNA. At this

FIG. 6.1 *Molecular structure of deoxyribose*

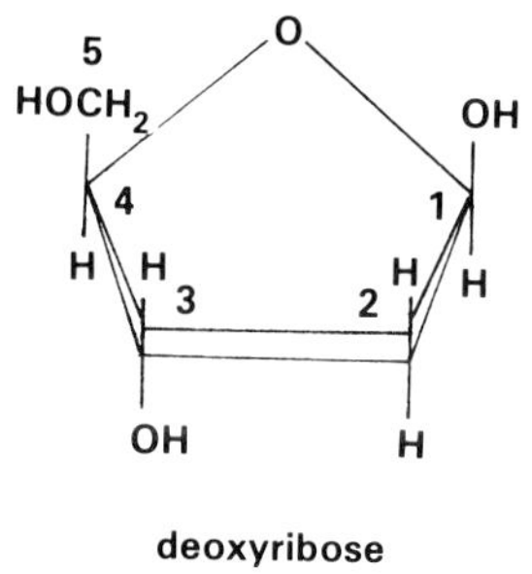

FIG. 6.2 *The nitrogenous bases of DNA*

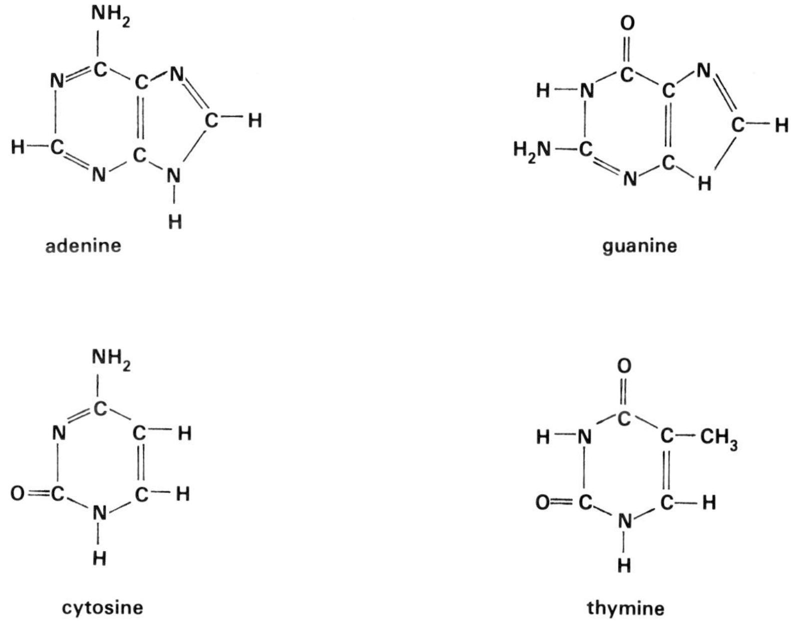

FIG. 6.3 *A nucleotide*

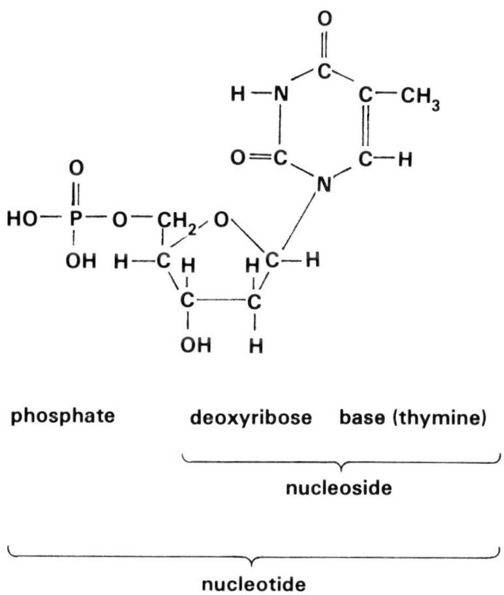

FIG. 6.4 *Part of a polynucleotide*

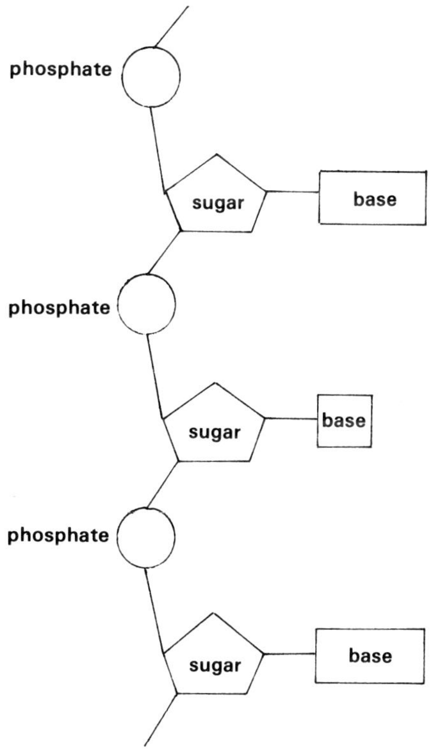

time Rosalind Franklin was working on the structure of DNA using X-ray crystallographic techniques (Chapter 3). Her results were part of the evidence which, in 1953, led James Watson and Francis Crick to propose that a DNA molecule consists of **two polynucleotide strands** each coiled in a **right-handed helix**. The two strands of the double helix are held together by hydrogen bonding between the nitrogenous bases of adjacent nucleotides. For each complete twist of the double helix there are 10 pairs of nucleotides, each twist measuring 3·4 nm in length (Fig. 6.5).

It is important to appreciate that the two polynucleotide strands of a DNA molecule are not identical. They are **complementary**. Where Ade occurs in one strand Thy is found in the other. Where Cyt appears in a strand Gua is present in the complementary strand. Watson and Crick were aware that such a structure could explain how exact copies of a DNA molecule can be made (section 6.1.4).

Altogether there can be several thousand pairs of nucleotides in a single molecule of DNA. The exact number depends on the origin of the DNA. The sequence in which the pairs of bases occurs also differs in DNA from different species. In theory the number of permutations of the bases is infinite.

During nuclear division the DNA of the nucleus is organised into visible threads called chromosomes (Chapter 7). The DNA double helix then has a coil of histone proteins wound around it. Under the electron microscope the DNA-histone complex making up the chromosomes has a woolly appearance (Fig. 6.6).

FIG. 6.5 (a) *Atomic model of DNA*

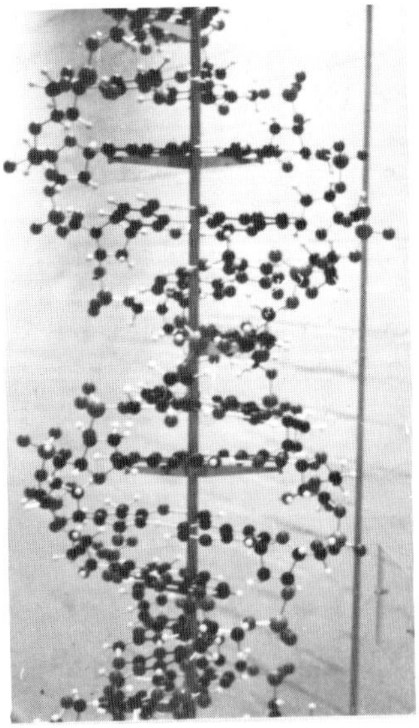

FIG. 6.5 (b) *The Watson–Crick model of DNA*

The double helix

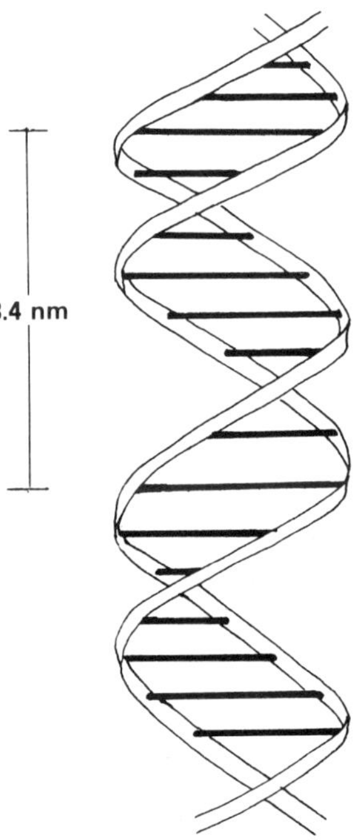

The pairing of the bases in the polynucleotides

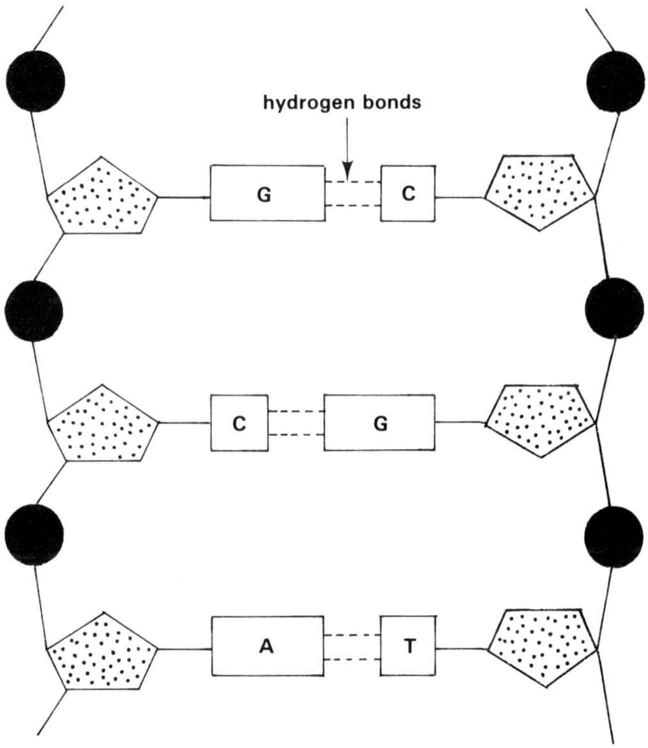

A = adenine T = thymine
G = guanine C = cytosine

6.1.2 Ribonucleic acid

FIG. 6.6 *Ultrastructure of a human chromosome (based on an electronmicrograph)*

The two chromatids consist of long, entangled chromatin fibres. The fibres contain about 75 per cent protein, 15 per cent DNA and 10 per cent RNA

There are three different kinds of ribonucleic acid, **messenger RNA (mRNA), transfer RNA (tRNA)** and **ribosomal RNA (rRNA)**. The nucleotides of which they are made contain the sugar **ribose** not deoxyribose as in DNA. Another difference is that thymine is not found in RNA. The nitrogenous base **uracil (Ura)** is present instead (Fig. 6.7(a)).

1. MESSENGER RNA

Between 3 and 5 per cent of the RNA in a cell is mRNA. The molecules of mRNA are single, helical strands made up of several thousand nucleotides. Messenger RNA is made in the nucleus by transcription (section 6.2.1). Its sequence of bases is complementary to that of one of the helices of DNA. The mRNA passes to the ribosomes where triplets of bases in the mRNA act as **codons** in the synthesis of proteins. The way in which the codons function is explained in section 6.2.1.

2. TRANSFER RNA

Transfer RNA makes up between 10 and 15 per cent of a cell's RNA content. The single strand of 75–90 nucleotides which make up a tRNA molecule is wound into a double helix which usually has three prominent bulges. In outline the molecule resembles a clover-leaf (Fig. 6.7(b)). One of the free ends of every tRNA molecule ends with nucleotides containing the following order of bases A ← C ← C ← with A at the very end. There are at least twenty different kinds of tRNA. They differ in the sequence of base triplets making up the **anticodon** by which tRNA binds to the codons of mRNA during the synthesis of proteins (Fig. 6.7(c)).

FIG. 6.7 (a) *Some components of RNA which are not found in DNA*

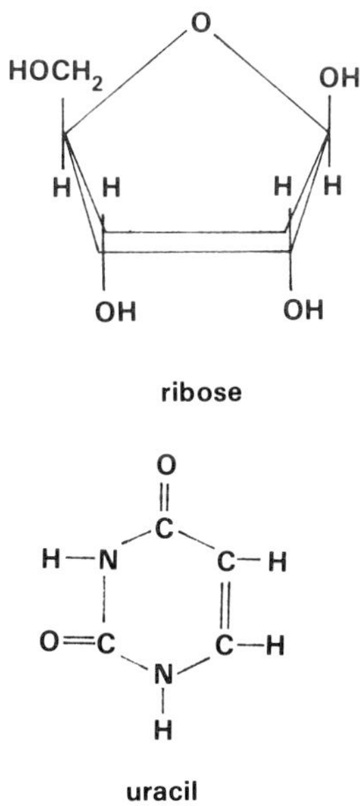

FIG. 6.7 (b) *Transfer RNA*

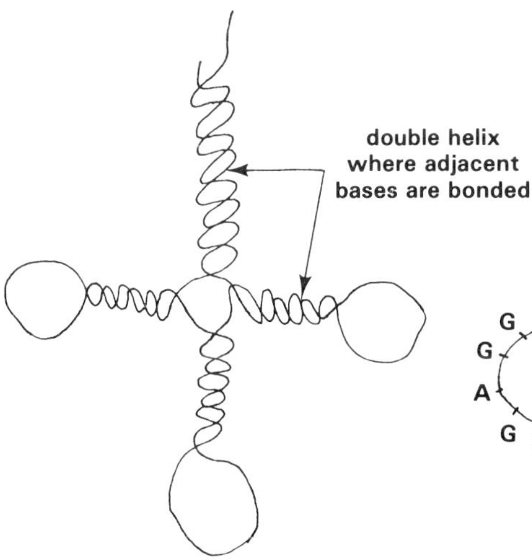

FIG. 6.7 (c) *An anticodon. The important difference between the 20 or so forms of tRNA is the sequence of bases in the anticodon triplet*

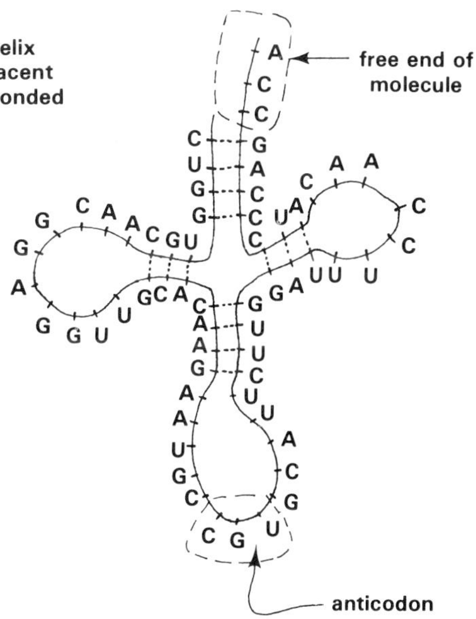

3. RIBOSOMAL RNA

The many thousands of nucleotides which make up a molecule of rRNA are wound into a complex structure consisting partly of single and partly of double helices (Fig. 6.8). Ribosomal RNA is made in the nucleus under the control of the nucleoli. It enters the cytoplasm and binds with protein molecules to become ribosomes. Over half the mass of a ribosome consists of rRNA and more than 80 per cent of the total RNA in a cell is rRNA. Even so, the precise function of rRNA is still not known.

FIG. 6.8 *Part of a molecule of rRNA*

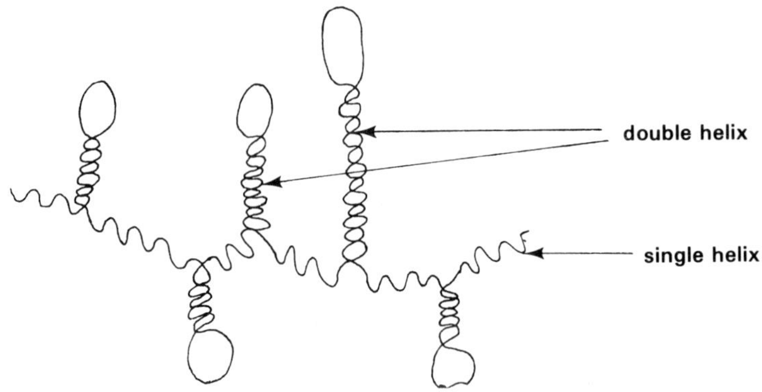

6.1.3 DNA as the hereditary substance

In 1928 Fred Griffith, an English bacteriologist, noted two distinct strains of the bacterium *Pneumococcus*. One called the **S-strain** has capsules, and when inoculated on to an agar-based medium it grows into smooth, glistening colonies. The other, called the **R-strain**, lacks capsules and its colonies have a rough, dull appearance. Griffith also observed that mice injected with the S-strain soon developed pneumonia and died. The R-strain is non-pathogenic and mice injected with it show no symptoms of illness. However, if heat-killed S-pneumococcus is mixed with the R-strain

FIG. 6.9 *Griffith's experiment*

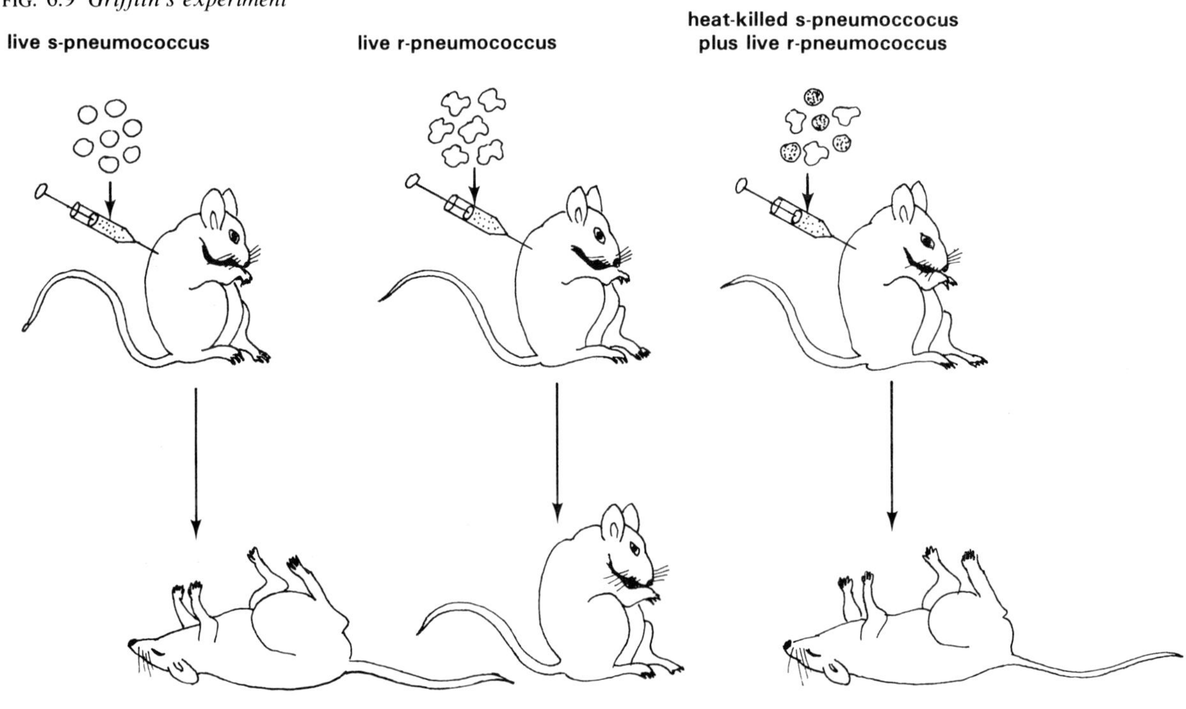

and then injected into the mice, the animals die of pneumonia. Moreover Griffith was able to isolate live S-pneumococcus from the mice subjected to this treatment (Fig. 6.9). He was, however, unable to explain his findings.

The reason for the peculiar behaviour of Griffith's *Pneumococcus* was given by Avery in 1943. Avery reported that the non-pathogenic R-strain could be converted to the S-strain by simply adding DNA from the S-strain to the medium in which the R-strain was growing. Furthermore, the newly-acquired characteristic was permanent and was passed to subsequent generations when the bacterium reproduced. Avery gave the name **transformation** to the process whereby the R-strain was converted to the S-strain. Here was a convincing piece of experimental evidence to suggest that DNA is the substance responsible for the characteristics of living organisms.

Another very important early piece of evidence confirming the role of DNA in inheritance came from experiments using bacteriophages. Bacteriophages are viruses which parasitise bacteria. Like all viruses they consist mainly of just two substances, protein and nucleic acid. A 'phage first becomes attached to the outer surface of a bacterium then injects its nucleic acid into its host leaving its protein coat outside. After some time complete new 'phages appear inside the bacterium which then bursts open. The entire sequence of events is called the **lytic cycle** (Fig. 6.10). In 1952 Hershey and Chase wrote about an experiment they had carried out using the T_2 'phage which attacks the bacterium *Escherichia coli*. The bacterium was first grown in a medium containing radioactive sulphur as $^{35}SO_4^{2-}$, or phosphorus as $^{32}PO_4^{3-}$. The T_2 'phage was then added and allowed to multiply as described in the lytic cycle. ^{35}S was used by *E. coli* to make sulphur-containing amino acids which were built into the protein coats of one of the sets of 'phages. The DNA of the other set of 'phages became labelled with ^{32}P. The labelled 'phages were then added separately to fresh cultures of *E. coli* growing in a non-radioactive medium. Shortly after the 'phages had become attached to the bacteria a homogeniser was used to chop off the protein coats of the 'phages adhering to the host cells. The cultures were then spun in a centrifuge. The bacteria formed a pellet at the bottom of the centrifuge tube, the 'phage coats remained in the supernatant liquid.

FIG. 6.10 *Lytic cycle of a bacteriophage*

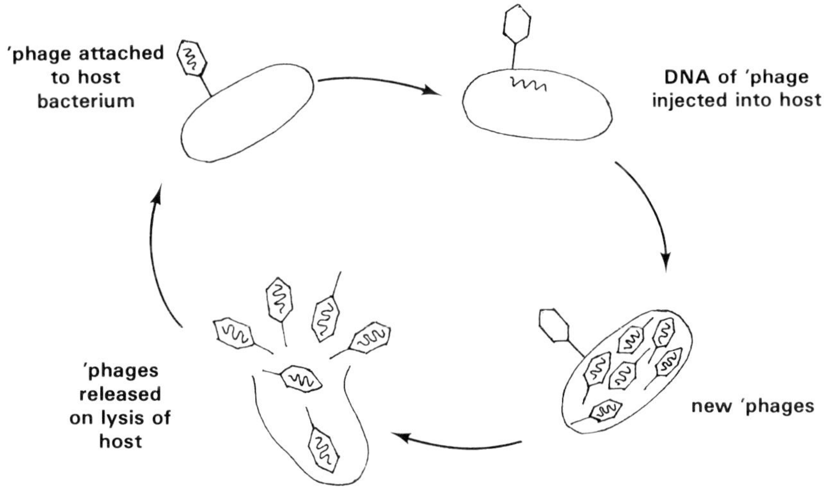

FIG. 6.22 *Two-dimensional analysis of haemoglobin. The haemoglobins were first broken down into peptide fragments using the enzyme trypsin. The peptides were then separated on paper by electrophoresis, after which the paper was turned at right angles and the peptides further separated by chromatography*

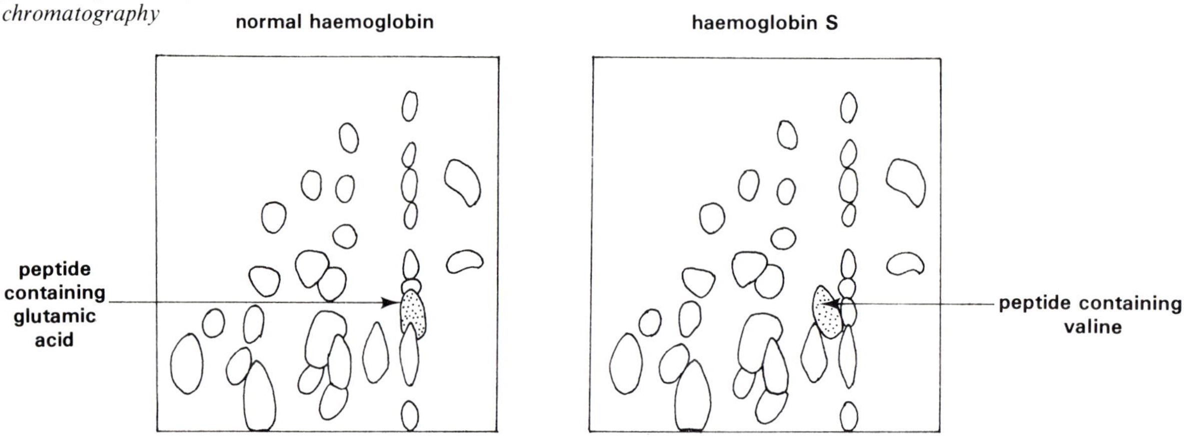

6.2.3 Regulating the synthesis of proteins

The ability of cells to regulate the amounts and types of proteins they make is important because it allows enzymes and metabolites to be produced as and when required. In this way the efficiency of metabolism is improved and a steady state can be maintained. One device which helps in **cellular homeostasis**, the maintenance of a steady state in living cells, is the temporary inhibition of an enzyme when the concentration of a substrate becomes too high (Chapter 4). Another is to regulate the synthesis of proteins.

In the late 1950s two French scientists, François Jacob and Jacques Monod, reported that the bacterium *Escherichia coli* was able to produce several enzymes 'on demand'. *E. coli* can synthesise all the metabolites and enzymes it requires from a medium consisting of glucose, mineral salts and water. Jacob and Monod observed that if lactose was substituted for glucose then *E. coli* makes an additional enzyme called β-D-galactosidase which hydrolyses lactose to glucose and galactose. When returned to the glucose medium the bacterium stops making β-D-galactosidase. The presence of lactose in the medium induces *E. coli* to make an enzyme capable of hydrolysing lactose. This is an example of **enzyme induction**.

E. coli can make all the amino acids it requires from a medium containing NH_4^+ as the only source of nitrogen. However, if the amino acid arginine is added to the medium the bacterium stops making the enzymes needed for the synthesis of arginine. In this case the presence of arginine in the medium inhibits the production of an enzyme, an example of **enzyme repression**.

Jacob and Monod produced a hypothesis to explain enzyme induction and repression. They proposed that the sequence of amino acids in an enzyme is determined by a **structural gene** which can be switched on or off by a **regulator gene**. The regulator gene transcribes the production of mRNA which has the codons to make a **repressor protein**. The repressor moves from the ribosomes where it is made to the nucleus. Here it binds with the structural gene stopping it from transcribing the manufacture of mRNA used in the synthesis of an enzyme. As a consequence, production of the enzyme is repressed. However, if an inducer substance is present it combines with the repressor. The inducer-repressor complex is unable to prevent transcription of the structural gene. Synthesis of the enzyme can then proceed. The formation of the inducer-repressor complex must be reversible because enzyme repression occurs when the inducer is removed. Induction and repression are thus linked. Induction is freedom from repression. The Jacob–Monod hypothesis is summarised in Figure 6.23.

FIG. 6.23 *The Jacob–Monod hypothesis*

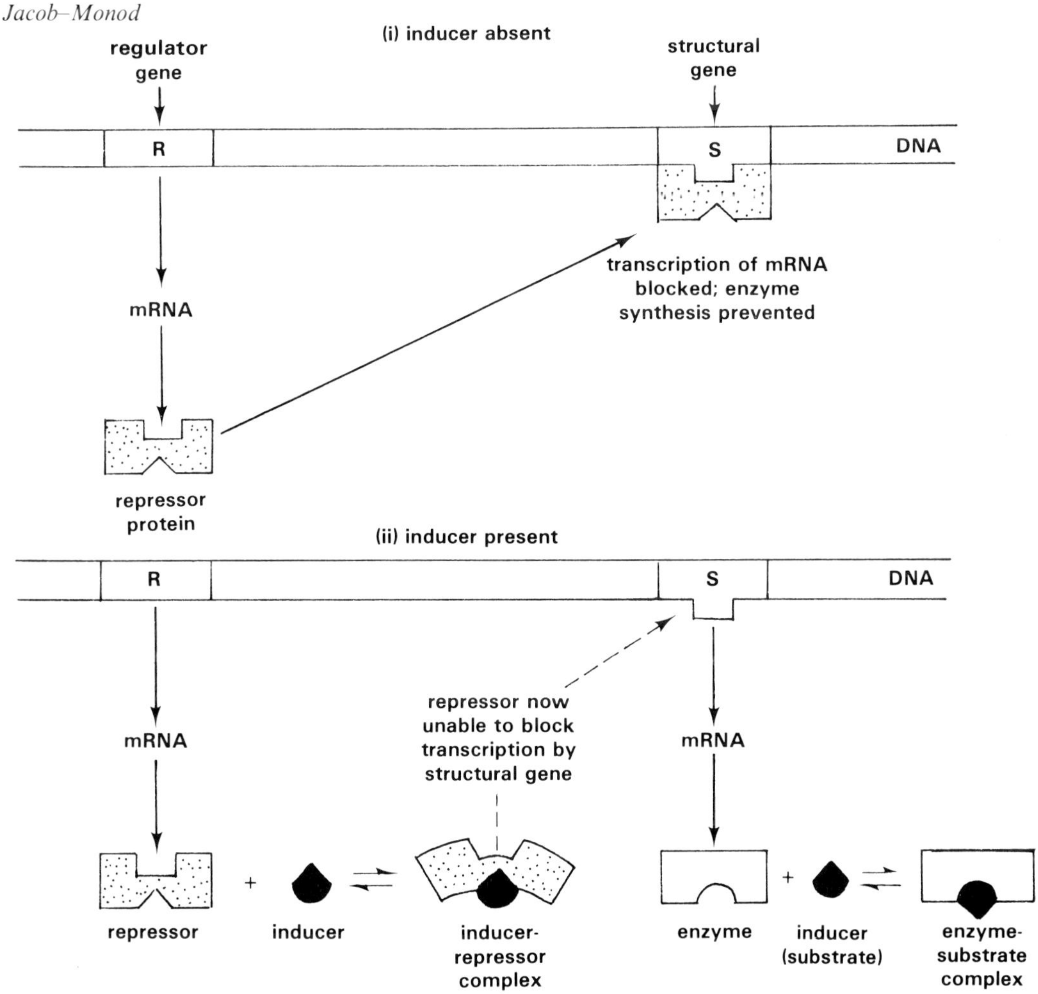

Recently it has been shown that induction and repression of enzymes also occurs in the cells of higher organisms. Liver cells of mammals are particularly efficient at regulating the types and amounts of enzymes they produce. In this way the liver can adjust to the fluctuating levels of substances it receives from the gut (Chapter 14).

Enzyme induction and repression are also important in the differentiation of living organisms. How it is possible for a one-celled fertilised egg to grow into a multicellular body made up of a number of different types of tissues is a process about which a lot has yet to be learned. However, induction and repression of enzymes probably enables the various types of tissues to differentiate by allowing different combinations of genes to be expressed at different stages during growth and development.

6.3 Genetic engineering

Avery in 1943 showed that it was possible to alter the genetic make-up (**genome**) of the R-strain of *Pneumococcus* by adding to its culture medium DNA from the S-strain (section 6.1.3). Since then biologists have devised sophisticated procedures whereby the genomes of experimental organisms such as bacteria can be altered with great precision. The experimental manipulation of the genomes of organisms is called **genetic engineering**. One of the methods used involves the transfer of genes from the cells of one organism to those of another. The DNA of the recipient is called **recombinant DNA**.

The technique involves isolating strands of DNA from one species and breaking them at specific points using **nuclease** enzymes. The same enzymes are then used to fragment strands of DNA from another species. Because of the specificity of the enzymes, the base sequence at the ends of some of the pieces of DNA from both sources are the same. They are said to have **sticky ends**. Recombinant DNA is formed when the two samples of DNA are incubated in the presence of DNA **ligase**, an enzyme which catalyses binding of the pieces of DNA at their sticky ends (Fig. 6.24). If the

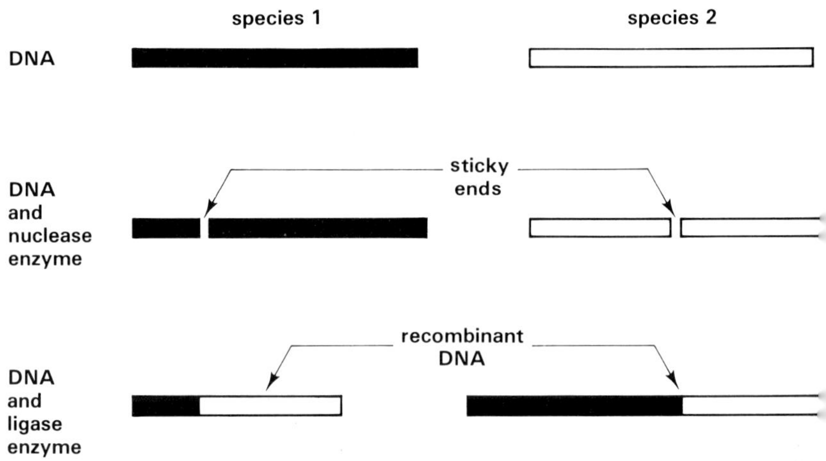

FIG. 6.24 *Genetic engineering*

recombinant DNA is then introduced into appropriate cells it replicates and the cells have characteristics of both species. So far most of the experiments in genetic engineering have been mainly with microbes. However there is no reason in principle why it should not be extended to other groups of living organisms.

Advantages of immense importance to the human race could arise from genetic engineering. For example, the roots of leguminous plants form a symbiotic relationship with the bacterium *Rhizobium leguminosarum* (Fig. 28.29). *Rhizobium* can fix nitrogen gas and some of the organic nitrogenous substances it makes are used by the leguminous host plants. The hosts as a result grow more profusely. Because many extensively grown crop plants such as peas, beans and clover are legumes the symbiotic relationship is of great importance to food production. But what of the many other types of crop plants which do not have this facility? The soil in which they are grown has to be treated with expensive artificial fertilisers or with manure (Chapter 13). Clearly it would be advantageous if non-legumes too could fix gaseous nitrogen which is plentiful in the atmosphere. For this reason attempts have been made to transplant the genes for nitrogen fixation into the cells of cereals and other non-leguminous plants.

Genetic engineering is also of interest to the medical world. When attacked by viruses mammalian tissues produce interferon, an antiviral agent (section 9.2.4). Until recently it has not been possible to manufacture adequate quantities of interferon for treating humans suffering from viral diseases. The very small amounts available came mainly from leucocytes taken from blood given by donors. However, within the past few years molecular geneticists have succeeded in incorporating the gene for making interferon from human leucocytes into the DNA of the bacterium *Escherichia coli*. When *E. coli* containing the gene is grown in laboratory conditions it secretes interferon into the medium. Mass culture of *E. coli* with recombinant DNA has thus substantially increased the manufacture of an important life-saving drug. Comparable procedures have been used to make a variety of antibodies as well as human growth hormone.

There is, however, another side to genetic engineering. Concern has been expressed about the danger of producing organisms whose new genomes pose a threat to the well-being of man. One of the organisms widely used in such experiments is the gut bacterium *Escherichia coli* which lives commensally in the bowels of humans and other vertebrates. What would be the consequence if a strain of genetically-engineered *E. coli* which was highly pathogenic became resident in a human population? As Dr. Erwin Chargaff, an eminent molecular geneticist has put it:

'You cannot recall a new form of life. Once you have constructed a viable *E. coli* cell into which a piece of eukaryotic DNA has been spliced, it will survive you and your children and your children's children. An irreversible attack on the biosphere is something so unheard of, so unthinkable to previous generations, that I could only wish that mine had not been guilty of it.'

The potential hazards of such experiments have led to a call for a halt to certain types of genetic engineering.

Chapter 7 Cell division

There are two types of cell division, **mitosis** and **meiosis**. Mitosis takes place when new cells are added to multicellular organisms as they grow (Chapter 21) and when tissues are repaired or replaced. Asexual reproduction can also occur as a result of mitotic division. Meiosis occurs in the production of gametes by organisms which reproduce sexually (Chapters 19 and 22).

During both types of division the DNA and histone proteins of the cell nucleus can be seen as threads called **chromosomes**. Chromosomes can be stained and are visible using a conventional compound microscope (chromo = coloured; soma = body). The number of chromosomes in the nucleus is fixed for each species of living organism. What is more, the chromosomes can be arranged in **homologous pairs**. In humans for example, the body cells contain 46 chromosomes, 23 homologous pairs (Fig. 7.1). The characteristics of living organisms are determined by many pairs of genes called alleles. One of a pair of allelic genes is found on a chromosome. The other is found on its homologous partner. Each chromosome carries a number of genes.

Mitosis normally ensures that the cells produced contain exactly the same number of chromosomes as the cells from which they were formed. The cells of the bone marrow of humans for example, constantly give rise to blood cells which have 46 chromosomes. On the other hand, cells produced by meiosis have half the chromosome number. For example, human sperm and eggs each have 23 chromosomes. However, there is much more to it than this. Let us take a close look at the two types of cell division to see in what other ways they differ.

FIG. 7.1 (a) *Chromosomes of a normal human, × 1000*

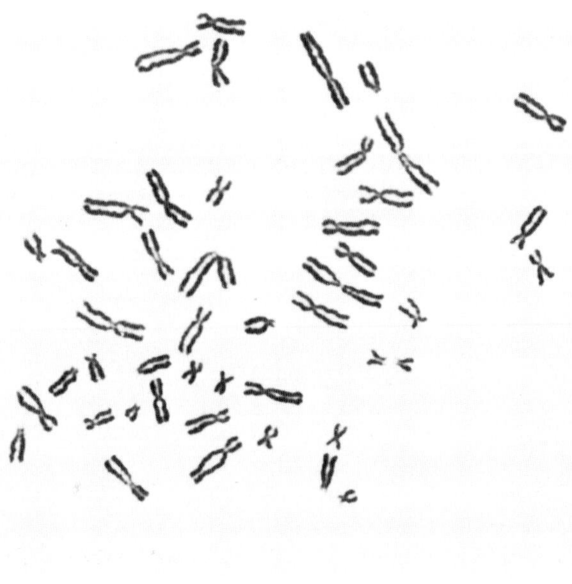

FIG. 7.1 (b) *Homologous pairs of chromosomes from a normal human male* (courtesy Philip Harris Biological Ltd.)

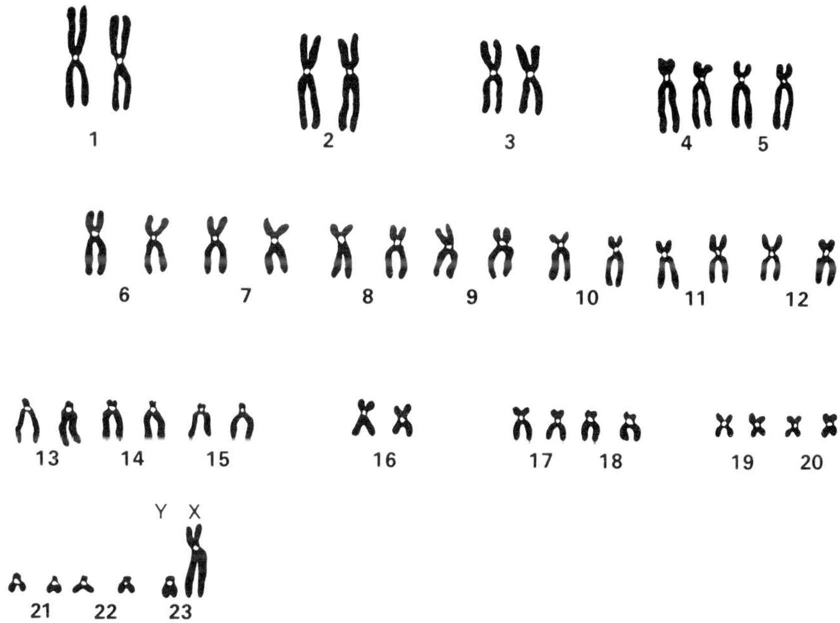

7.1 Mitosis

Before starting to divide a cell is at the **interphase** stage. The nucleus appears as a granular body. Inside the nuclear membrane are one or more dense nucleoli (Fig. 7.2). The absence of any visible signs of activity disguises the fact that intense metabolism is taking place. It is at this stage that replication of DNA (Chapter 6) and synthesis of nuclear proteins occurs. New ribosomes are also made at interphase. Mitochondria and centrosomes divide at this stage, so do proplastids from which chloroplasts originate. The proteins which later make up the microtubules of the spindle are also made at interphase although the spindle is not yet visible. The energy for the various forms of activity comes from respiration. It is therefore not surprising that the respiratory rate of cells at interphase is very rapid.

During both mitosis and meiosis the nucleus divides first, followed by cleavage of the cytoplasm.

FIG. 7.2 *Interphase*

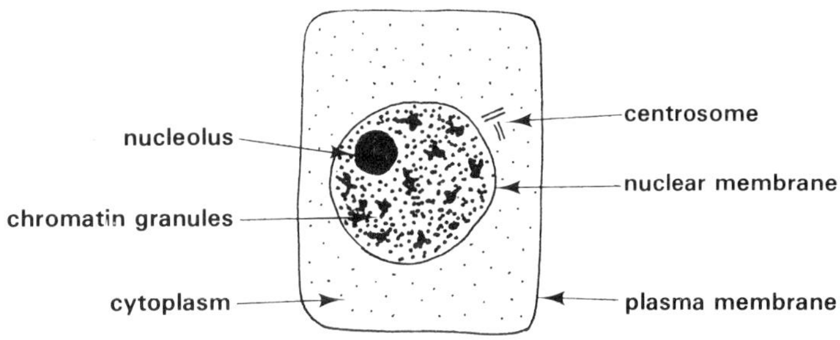

7.1.1 Mitotic nuclear division

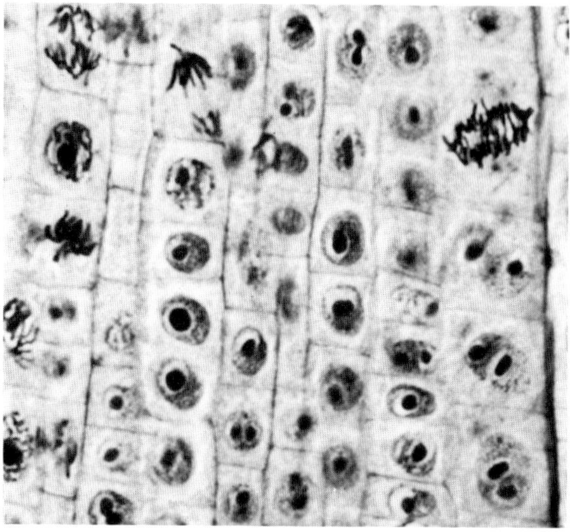

FIG. 7.3 (a) *Cells dividing near the tip of an onion root × 400*

FIG. 7.3 (b) *Mitotic nuclear division (only four chromosomes shown for clarity)*

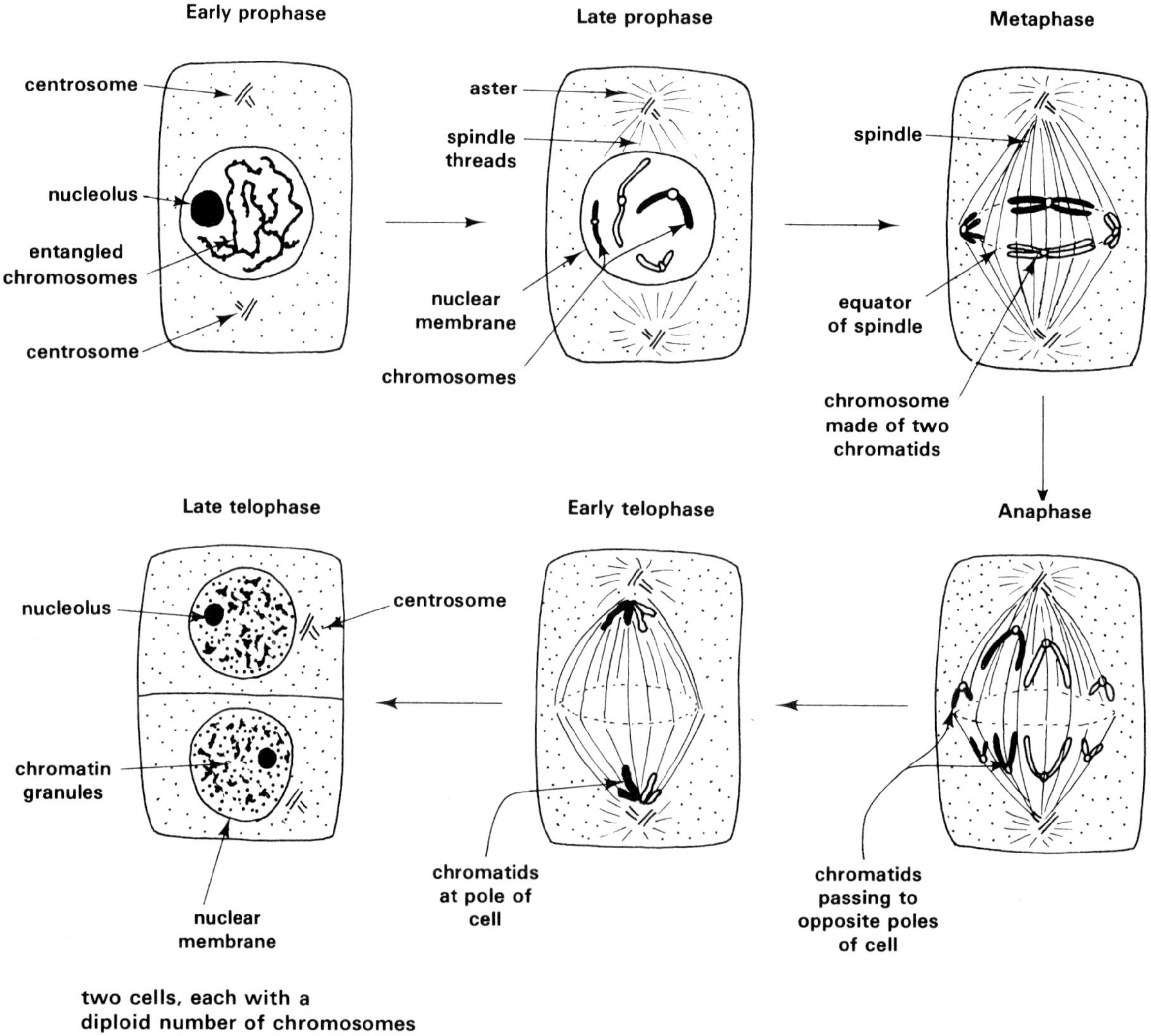

For convenience of description it is usual to separate mitotic division of the nucleus into four main stages. It is possible to see the various stages by examining stained sections and squashes of root tips or other suitable material under the microscope (Fig. 7.3). In this way what appears to be a series of static events can be observed. However, mitosis is an active process, the different stages merging into each other. Time-lapse photomicrography provides a means of seeing the dynamic nature of mitosis. Dividing cells are placed in a nutrient solution on a microscope slide and photographed through the microscope every 30 seconds or so over a period of several hours or even days. The exposed film is developed and run through a cine projector. It then becomes apparent that during division cells are particularly active.

1. PROPHASE

At the start of **prophase** chromosomes become visible inside the nuclear membrane. At first they are long, thin entangled threads. As time goes on the threads become shorter and thicker. The chromosomes disentangle and can be seen as separate structures. As the chromosomes become visible the nucleoli gradually disappear.

The centrosomes which duplicated at interphase begin to migrate to opposite ends (poles) of the cell. As they move apart the centrosomes lay down a large number of microtubules which extend from one pole of the cell to the other. The microtubules are the **spindle**, a fibrous structure which is widest at the centre (equator) of the cell. A mass of microtubules called an **aster** also radiates from the centrosomes at each of the poles of animal cells (Fig. 7.3(b)).

2. METAPHASE

The nuclear membrane breaks down. How and why this occurs is still a matter for debate. Mitochondria often congregate near the nuclear membrane at this stage. They may provide energy for some of the spindle microtubules to pull the nuclear membrane apart.

It is now possible to see that each chromosome consists of two threads called **chromatids** joined at a **centromere**. Unlike the rest of the chromosome the centromere is not easily stained. Independently of each other the chromosomes become attached by their centromeres to the equator of the spindle (Fig. 7.3(b)).

3. ANAPHASE

The centromere of each chromosome splits and the chromatids move to opposite poles of the cell. Separation of the chromatids appears to be caused by a shortening of the spindle microtubules to which the centromeres are attached. Consequently the chromatids are dragged, centromere first, away from the equator of the spindle. During their passage the chromatids slide over the other spindle microtubules which extend from pole to pole (Fig. 7.3(b)).

4. TELOPHASE

On reaching the poles of the cell the two groups of chromatids come together. Each group becomes surrounded by a newly formed nuclear membrane. It is not clear whether the new membranes are put together from fragments of the nuclear membrane destroyed in prophase or are made anew. Whatever their origin they are assembled from pieces of membrane. Inside the nuclear membranes the chromatids become uncoiled, nucleoli reform and the nucleus takes on the granular appearance it had at interphase (Fig. 7.3(b)).

Study the drawings of the various stages of mitotic nuclear division. Try to recognise the stages shown in the photographs in Figure 7.4.

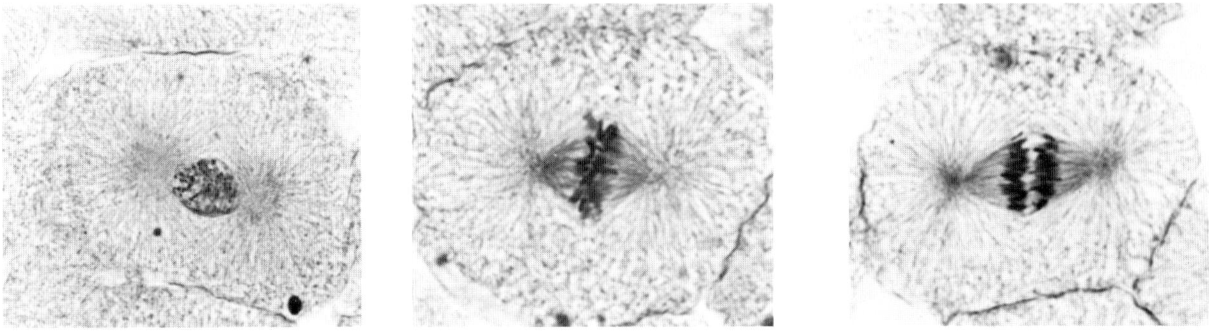

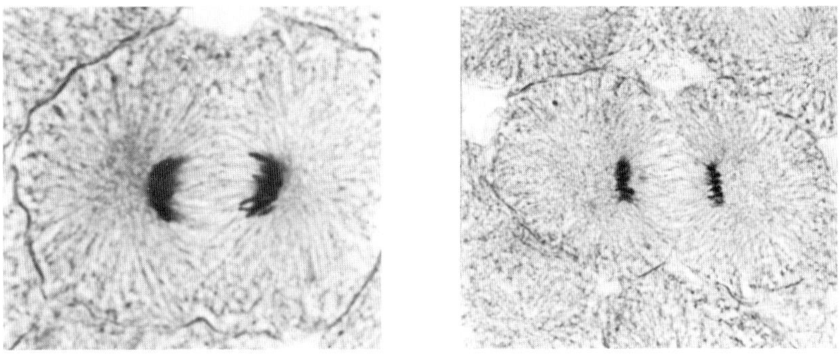

FIG. 7.4 *Mitotic division in a blastula cell from a fish, × 1000. Which stage of division is shown in each photograph?*

7.1.2 Cytoplasmic cleavage

Soon after nuclear division the cytoplasm is separated into two more or less equal parts, each part enclosing one of the newly formed nuclei. The way in which **cytoplasmic cleavage** occurs differs in plant and animal cells.

In the cells of higher plants a series of flat vacuoles surrounded by unit membrane, probably made by the Golgi body, appear at the middle of the cell. The vacuoles extend across an area of dense cytoplasm called the **phragmoplast** which contains numerous microtubules, the remains of the spindle. The membranes around the vacuoles fuse to form the **cell plate**, a double unit membrane which grows outwards and joins with the plasma membrane of the dividing cell. Cell wall materials are laid down between the two membranes of the cell plate and cleavage of the cytoplasm is thus achieved. By this time the phragmoplast has disappeared (Fig. 7.5(a)).

A ring of microfilaments appears around the middle of animal cells just inside the plasma membrane. A shallow **furrow** develops in the membrane, due it is thought to contraction of the filaments. Further shortening of the filaments ultimately pinches the cytoplasm into two more or less equal parts, each part surrounding a nucleus (Fig. 7.5(b)).

What has been described so far is sometimes called a **cell cycle**. The time taken by each of the stages varies considerably from species to species and depends on the conditions in which the cells are maintained. Mammalian skin cells kept at 36°C in an artificial culture medium divide every 24 hours or so. Average figures for the various stages are: prophase 35 minutes, metaphase 20 minutes, anaphase 10 minutes, telophase 40 minutes and cytoplasmic cleavage 25 minutes. This means that by far the longest period of the cell cycle is occupied by the interphase stage (Fig. 7.6).

FIG. 7.5. (a) *Cytoplasmic cleavage in a* Petunia *cell × 500*

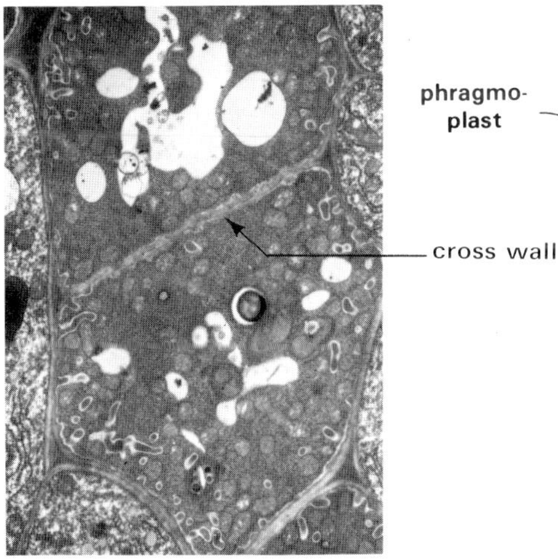

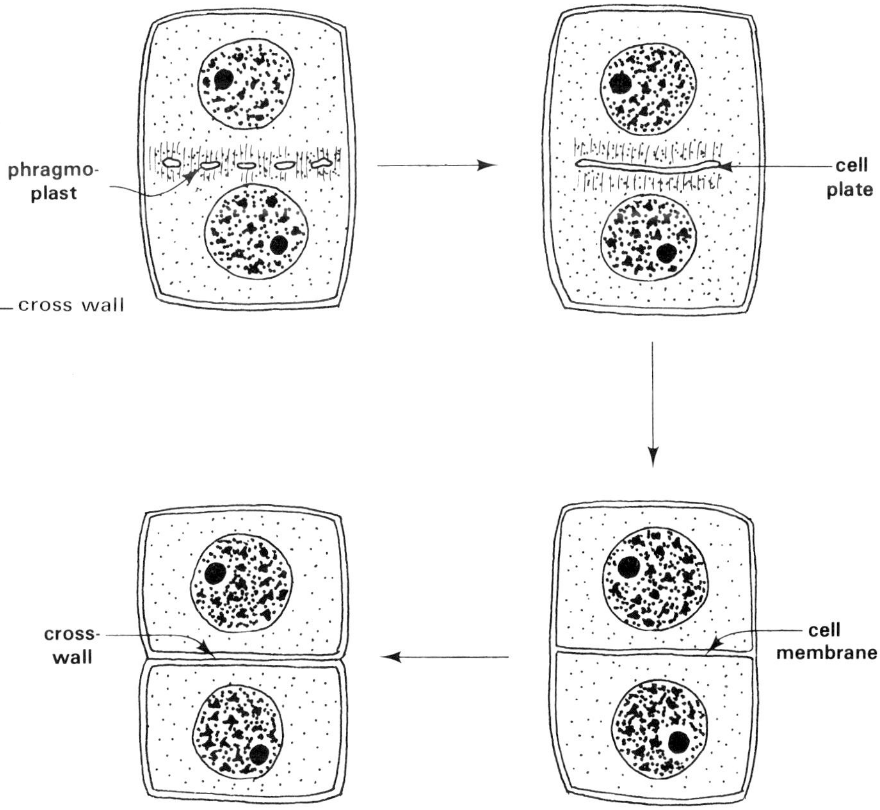

FIG. 7.5 (b) *Cytoplasmic cleavage in a cell from the bone marrow of a mammal, ×1800*

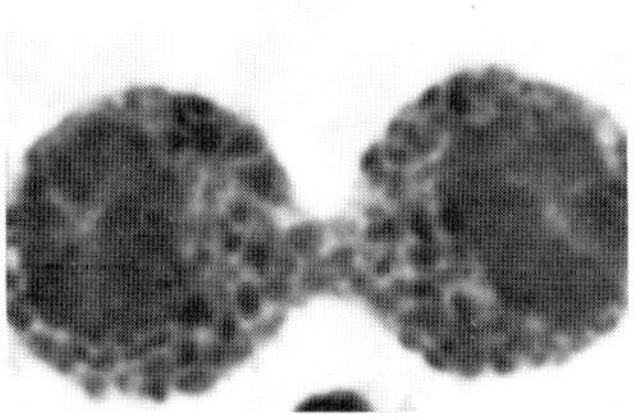

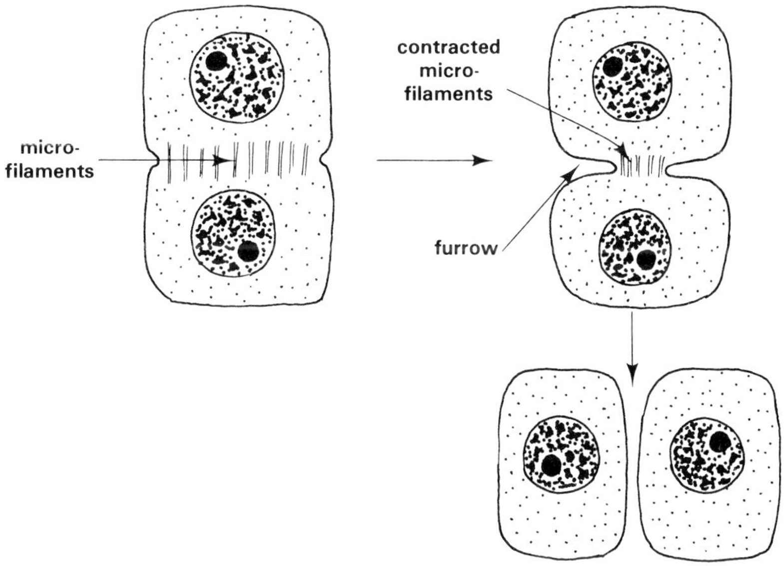

FIG. 7.6 *The cell cycle*

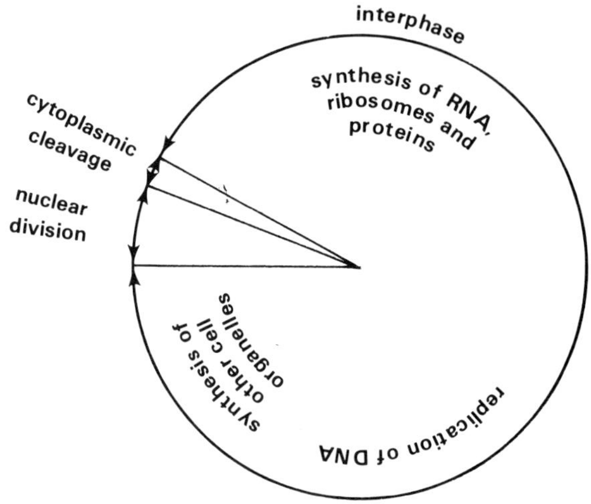

7.1.3 The significance of mitosis

The essential feature of mitosis is that it provides a means of distributing the hereditary material DNA equally between two cells. This does not mean that the DNA content is halved at each mitotic division. The hereditary material is normally reproduced in each cell exactly as it was in the parent cell.

FIG. 7.7 *Changes in the amount of DNA in a nucleus during mitotic division*

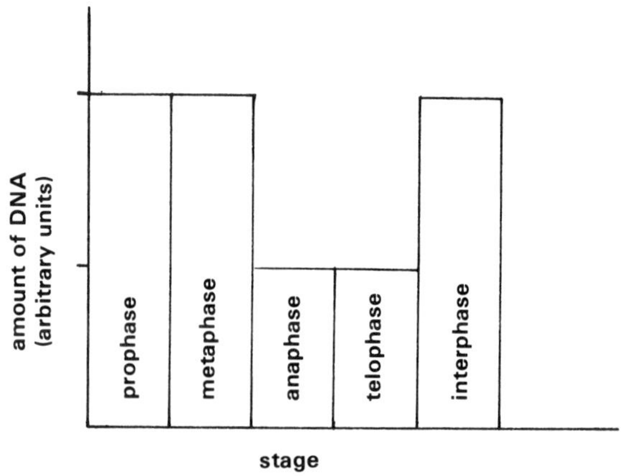

The way in which DNA is replicated is described in Chapter 6. What evidence is there that DNA replication occurs in the cell cycle? One way of finding out is to measure the amount of DNA in a cell at different times during mitosis. Figure 7.7 shows the results of such an investigation. The amount of DNA exactly doubles during interphase and is halved at anaphase. In this way each of the new cells receives the same amount of DNA as in the parent cell. It does not, however, prove that an exact copy of DNA is distributed to the new cells. Another approach is to use radioisotopes to label the DNA. Cells are grown in a nutrient solution containing thymine labelled with tritium (^3H) a radioisotope of hydrogen. As the cells divide the labelled thymine is incorporated into their DNA and after a while nearly all the DNA in the cells is radioactive. The cells are then placed in a non-radioactive medium. At each subsequent division some of the cells are removed and placed in photographic emulsion. Radiations given off by the labelled DNA cause the emulsion to develop giving labelled chromosomes a dark colour when viewed under a microscope. The results of such an experiment are shown in Figure 7.8. They prove conclusively that replication of DNA does occur during the cell cycle. Compare these results with the findings of Meselson and Stahl using the bacterium *Escherichia coli* (Chapter 6). There is thus no doubt that the same amount and type of DNA is normally distributed to each of the cells produced by mitosis.

FIG. 7.8 *Chromosomes of a Chinese hamster after labelling with ^{3}H thymidine (based on autoradiographs)*

(a) *metaphase immediately after labelling*

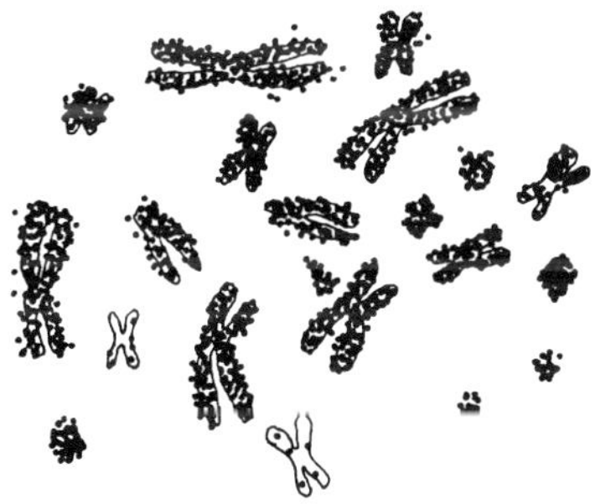

Both chromatids of most of the chromosomes are very radioactive. A few of the smaller chromosomes are only lightly labelled.

(b) *metaphase of next division*

Only one chromatid of most of the chromosomes is very radioactive.

The significance of what has just been described is that mitosis normally gives rise to cells with the same combination of genes (genome). Successful genomes can be perpetuated generation after generation in organisms which multiply asexually. In this way breeders can maintain pure strains of many useful plants which can be propagated vegetatively (Chapter 19). Some of these are important crop plants such as the potato.

Even so, variations do arise in organisms which do not reproduce sexually. The variation is due in some instances to gene mutations (Chapter 6). In others it is caused by chromosome mutations (section 7.3).

7.2 Meiosis

Meiosis occurs in the formation of gametes in organisms which reproduce sexually. Cell squashes made from the testes of insects and the young anthers of flowering plants are suitable specimens for observing the stages of meiotic division. In meiosis, nuclear division is followed by cytoplasmic cleavage but in contrast with mitosis there are two nuclear divisions not one. Thus four cells are formed from a cell which undergoes meiosis, not two as in mitosis. However, there are other differences which are just as important.

The interphase stage of meiosis is the same as in mitosis.

7.2.1 The first meiotic division

FIG. 7.9 *The first meiotic division (only four chromosomes shown for clarity)*

Once more, for convenience of description, division of the nucleus is separated into a number of stages. The Roman numeral I is placed after each of the stages in the first meiotic division of the nucleus to distinguish them from the stages of the second meiotic division.

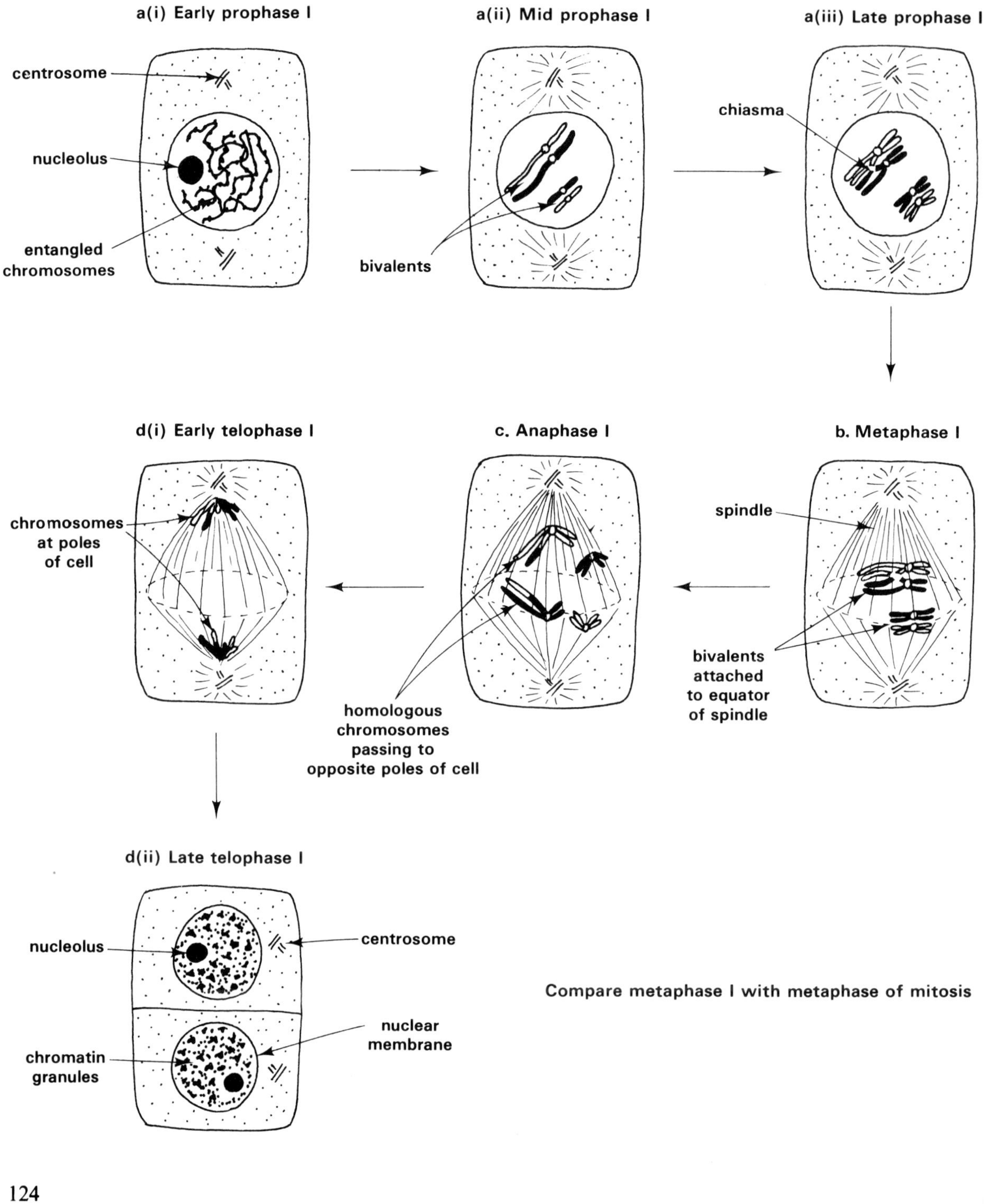

Compare metaphase I with metaphase of mitosis

1. PROPHASE I

The events of prophase I are much more complex than those which occur in prophase of mitosis. At the start of prophase I the chromosomes appear as long, thin entangled threads inside the nuclear membrane. They then come together in pairs called **bivalents**. Each bivalent is a homologous pair of chromosomes. The homologous chromosomes are positioned so that their centromeres and allelic genes are adjacent. Gradually the chromosomes shorten and thicken. At this stage the two chromatids making up each chromosome can be clearly seen. Cross-links called **chiasmata** frequently develop between the chromosomes and their homologous partners. Bivalents of long chromosomes often display several chiasmata (Fig. 7.9(a)).

Pairing of homologous chromosomes and the formation of chiasmata do not occur during prophase of mitosis. However, two other events which take place in mitotic prophase also occur in prophase I. The nucleoli disappear and a spindle is laid down in the cytoplasm by the centrosome which divided at interphase.

2. METAPHASE I

The nuclear membrane breaks down and the bivalents become attached by their centromeres to the microtubules at the equator of the spindle. One chromosome of each bivalent is directed towards one of the poles of the cell, its homologous partner towards the other pole. It is important to realise that each bivalent is orientated at random with respect to each of the other bivalents (Fig. 7.9(b)).

3. ANAPHASE I

Shortening of the spindle microtubules drags the homologous chromosomes of each bivalent apart, pulling them to opposite poles of the cell. As the chromosomes begin to separate the chiasmata become very evident (Fig. 7.9(c)).

4. TELOPHASE I

The two groups of chromosomes come together at opposite poles. Each group becomes surrounded by a new nuclear membrane. The chromosomes uncoil, the nucleoli reappear and the nuclei take on a granular appearance. Cleavage of the cytoplasm occurs as in mitosis (Fig. 7.9(d)).

The two cells possess half the number of chromosomes as the cell from which they were derived. For this reason meiosis is sometimes called **reduction division**. A short interphase may follow but there is no replication of DNA as happens during interphase of mitosis. Often there is no interphase and the two cells proceed directly to the second division of meiosis.

7.2.2 The second meiotic division

The Roman numeral II is used after each of the stages to distinguish them from the stages of the first meiotic division.

1. PROPHASE II

Chromosomes appear in both of the nuclei formed in the first division of meiosis. The centrosome of each cell divides and moves to opposite poles of the cells laying down the microtubules of the spindle. There is no pairing of chromosomes and chiasmata do not develop as in prophase I (Fig. 7.10(a)).

2. METAPHASE II

The nuclear membranes disappear and the chromosomes become attached by their centromeres to the microtubules at the equators of the spindles. The two chromatids of each chromosome are now easily seen. What is not so obvious is that the chromosomes are orientated at random with respect to one another (Fig. 7.10(b)).

FIG. 7.10 *The second meiotic division*

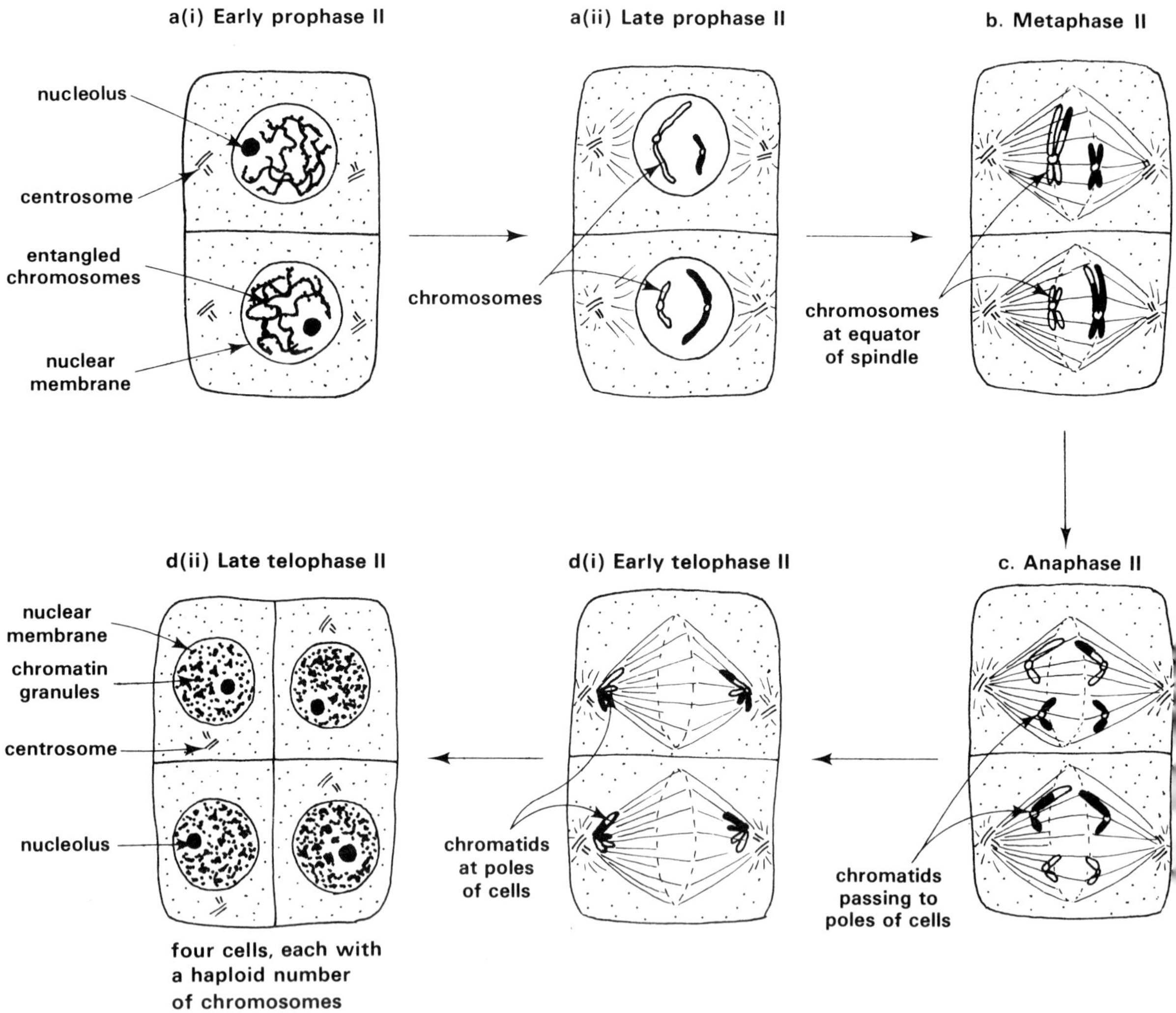

3. ANAPHASE II

The centromeres of the chromosomes break in two and the chromatids are pulled, centromere first, towards opposite poles of the cell (Fig. 7.10(c)).

4. TELOPHASE II

The chromatids come together at opposite poles of the cells where they become surrounded by nuclear membranes. The chromatids uncoil and nucleoli appear. The spindle disappears and cleavage of the cytoplasm follows (Fig. 7.10(d)). Altogether four cells, each with half the number of chromosomes, are produced from each cell which divides by meiosis.

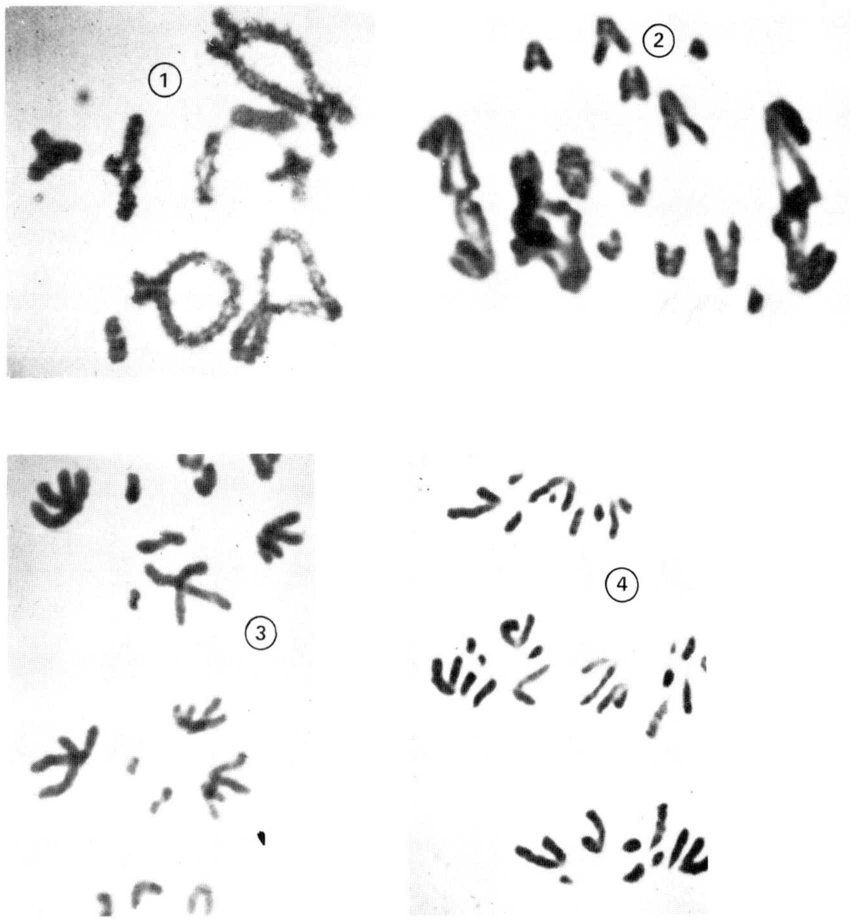

FIG. 7.11 *Meiotic division in the testis of a grasshopper* (courtesy Philip Harris Biological Ltd.). *Which stage of meiosis is shown in each photograph?* Compare with Fig. 7.4

Examine the photographs in Figure 7.11. Which stage of meiosis is shown in each picture?

7.2.3 The significance of meiosis

Whereas mitosis normally produces cells with an exact replica of the genetic material found in the parent cell, meiosis gives rise to cells with half the amount of genetic material. The body cells of higher organisms have a **diploid** number of chromosomes. Gametes made by meiosis have a **haploid** number of chromosomes. At fertilisation the diploid number is restored. In the life cycles of organisms which reproduce sexually, meiosis ensures that the chromosome number is normally kept constant in each generation (Fig. 7.12 and Chapters 19 and 22).

Another significant feature of meiosis is that it produces gametes with varied combinations of genes. There are two important events in meiosis which create new genomes.

1. CROSSING OVER

Crossing over takes place when bivalents appear in prophase I. Chiasmata are formed and homologous chromosomes exchange genes (Fig. 7.13(a)). The homologous chromosomes later separate and end up in different gametes. As a result of crossing over linked genes are parted and gametes with new genomes are produced.

FIG. 7.12 *Life cycles of a mammal and flowering plant (simplified)*

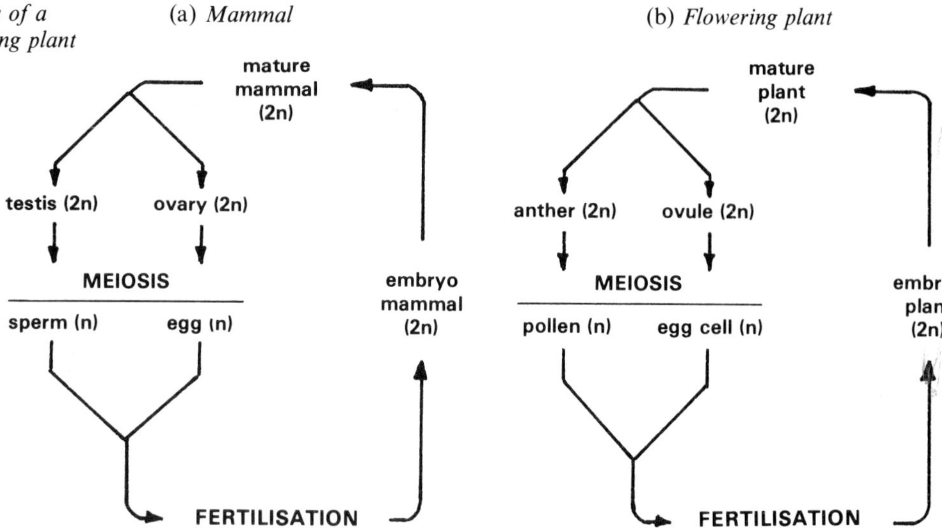

FIG. 7.13 (a) (i) *Crossing over. The photograph* (courtesy Philip Harris Biological Ltd.) *shows the chromosomes of a grasshopper*

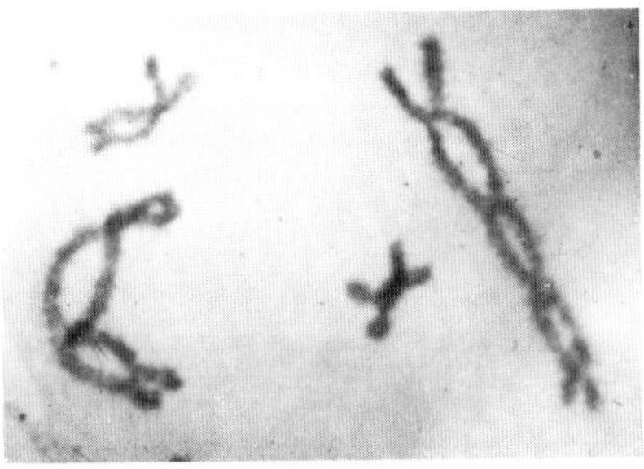

FIG. 7.13 (a) (ii) *Crossing over. For simplicity two pairs of alleles are shown. As a consequence of crossing over, the genes carried on the homologous chromosomes (linked genes) become separated. What combination of genes would result if there was no crossing over?*

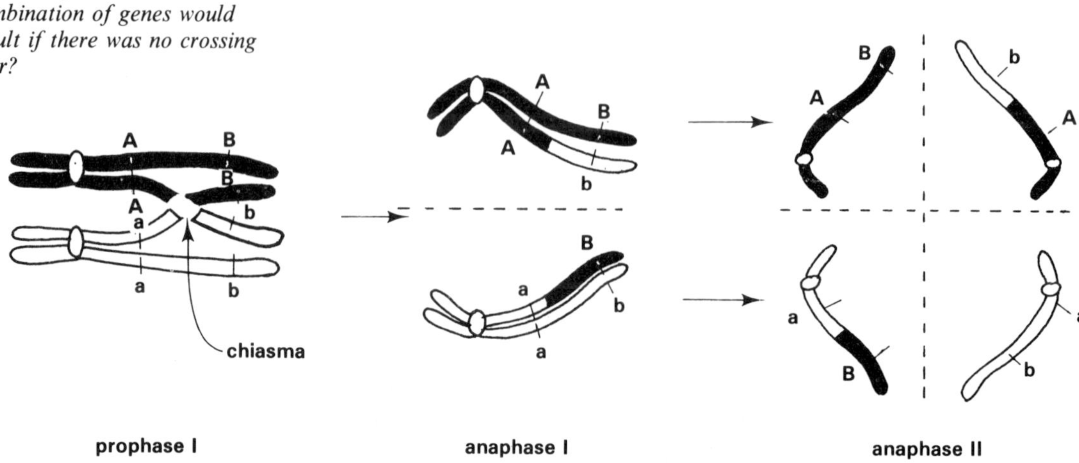

FIG. 7.13 (b) *The consequences of random orientation of chromosomes. The genes on one pair of homologous chromosomes separate independently of those on the other pair. For clarity, crossing over has not been shown*

2. RANDOM ORIENTATION OF CHROMOSOMES

The separation of a pair of homologous chromosomes at anaphase I is independent of the separation of other pairs. As the chromosomes are orientated at random the alleles on one pair of homologous chromosomes separate independently of the alleles on others (Fig. 7.13(b)). Because of random assortment a vast permutation of genes is possible in the gametes.

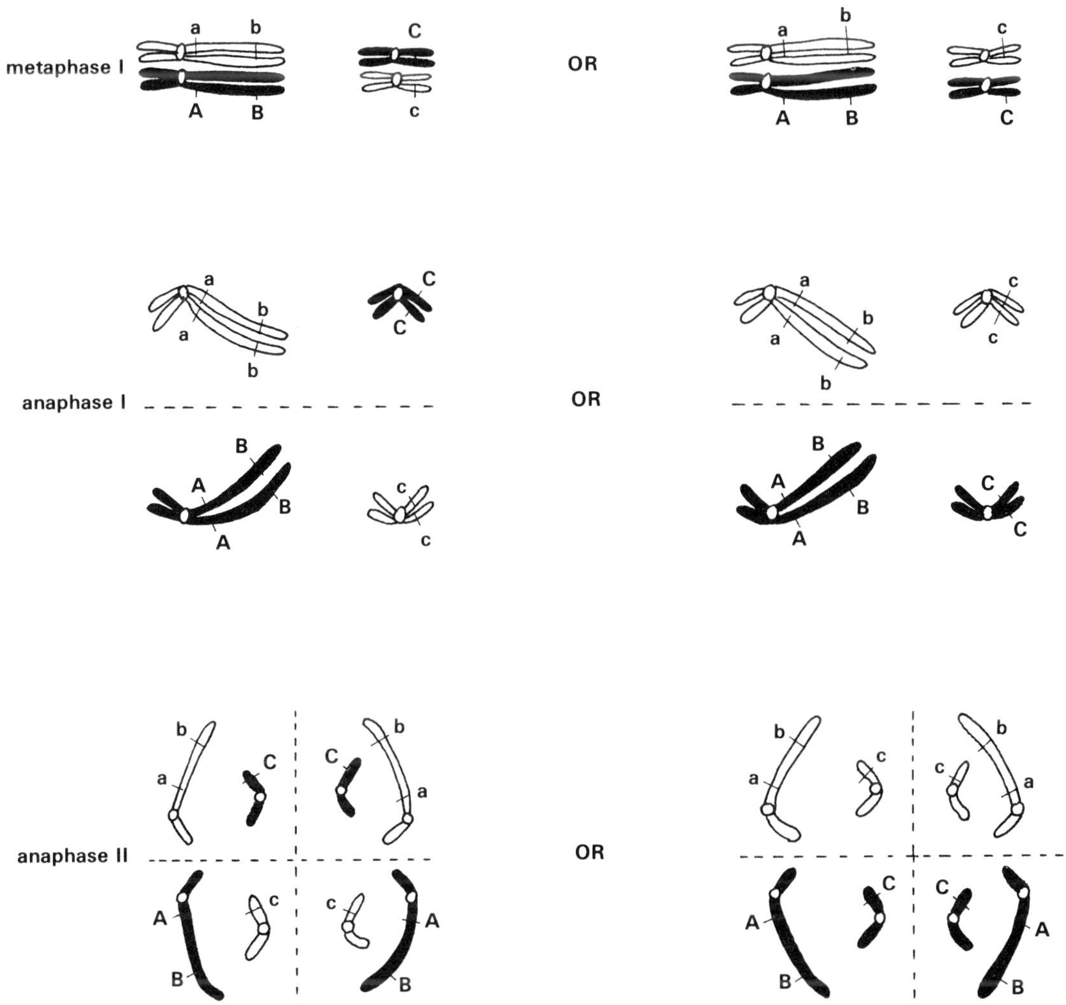

Crossing over and random assortment ensure that progeny resulting from sexual reproduction are genetically different from their parents. This is why no two humans for example, unless they are identical twins, have the same genome. Clearly meiosis is important in producing genetic variation in a species. There are however other ways in which genetic variation can arise (section 7.3).

7.3 Genetic variation

Do not forget that crossing over and random orientation of chromosomes in meiosis are important sources of genetic variation. Mutations are another important source of genetic variation. **Gene mutations** are described in Chapter 6. A second type of mutation which frequently occurs is called a **chromosome mutation**. There are several ways in which chromosome mutations can arise during either mitosis or meiosis.

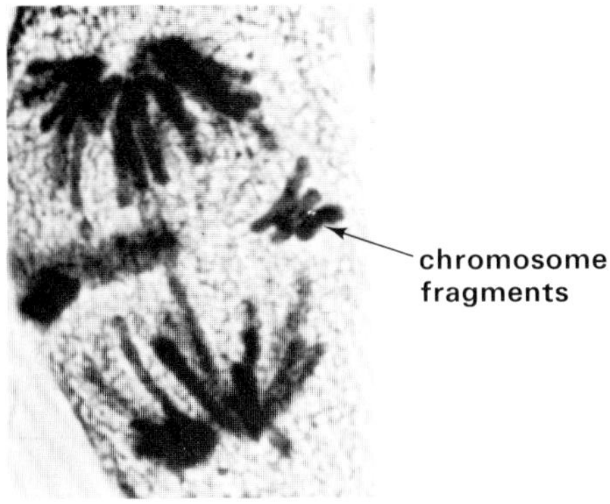

FIG. 7.14 (a) *Effect of radiation on chromosomes* (courtesy Dr. C. R. Davies and Philip Harris Biological Ltd.). *The chromosome fragments do not pass to the poles of the cell as do normal chromosomes*

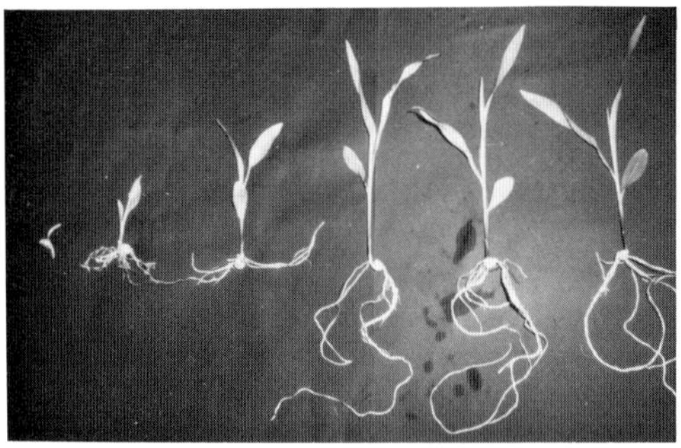

FIG. 7.14 (b) *Effect of γ radiation on the growth of maize seedlings* (courtesy Philip Harris Biological Ltd.). *The three seedlings on the right were grown from untreated seeds. Those on the left were grown from seed exposed to increasing doses of γ radiation*

Fragmentation of chromosomes often occurs when dividing cells are exposed to various forms of radiation such as X-rays (Fig. 7.14). The chromosome fragments pass at random into newly formed cells so producing cells with new genomes.

Failure of chromosomes to separate at anaphase gives rise to other types of chromosome mutation. If only one chromosome behaves in this way half of the new cells end up with an extra chromosome, the other half with one chromosome less than normal. Either condition is called **polysomy**. Down's syndrome (mongolism) in humans is a well-known example of polysomy (Fig. 7.15). Occasionally whole sets of chromosomes fail to separate. Half of the cells then receive twice the normal number of chromosomes, a condition called **polyploidy**. Polyploidy is more common in plants than in animals. Many modern varieties of cultivated plants are polyploids. For example, bread wheat has a diploid number of 42 chromosomes. Its ancestors have diploid numbers of 14 and 28.

Genetic variation is necessary for evolutionary change. If a new combination of genes enables its possessor to cope successfully with the pressures of its environment then the organism will survive. Should the organism reproduce asexually the new genome may be perpetuated unchanged for many generations. Equally well, the possessors of less effective genomes may not be able to compete successfully and will become extinct. This is the concept of **survival of the fittest**.

Charles Darwin was the first to draw attention to variation and survival of the fittest as the basis of evolution in his book *The Origin of Species by Natural Selection*. What has been outlined above is the genetic basis of evolution.

FIG. 7.15 (a) *Chromosomes of a male with Down's syndrome* (courtesy Philip Harris Biological Ltd.)

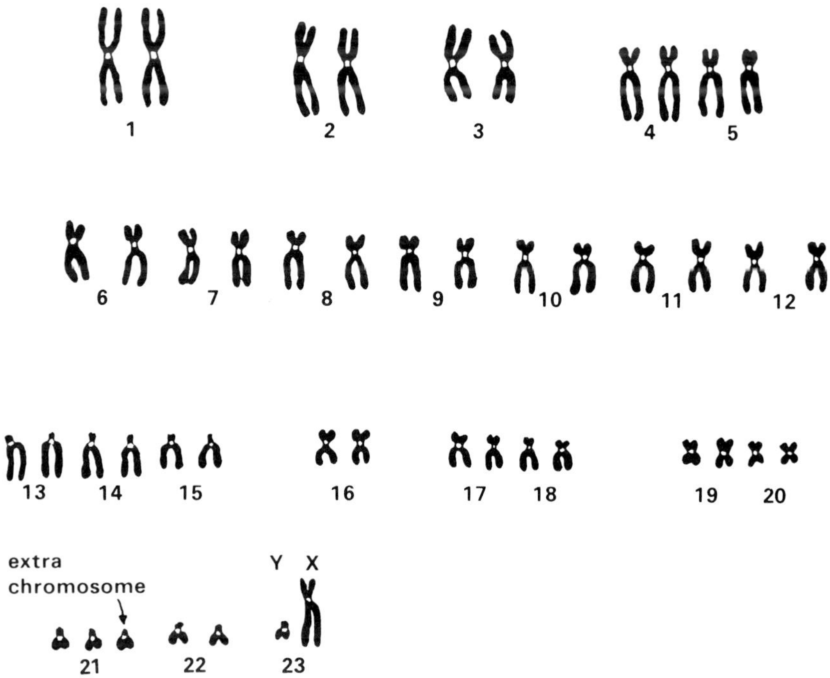

FIG. 7.15 (b) *A child with Down's syndrome* (courtesy A. Bezear and Heinemann Medical Ltd.)

Chapter 8

Gas exchange in mammals

Mammals respire aerobically so they need a constant supply of oxygen. The role of oxygen in cellular respiration is described in Chapter 5. Oxygen is consumed by mammals at a fairly rapid rate. This happens because respiration provides heat which helps to maintain a stable and relatively high body temperature (Chapter 17).

8.1 Gas exchange and evaporation

Mammals obtain their oxygen from the atmosphere. Oxygen makes up about 21 per cent of the atmosphere's volume, the rest being nearly all nitrogen. Before oxygen gas can diffuse through the outer surface of an organism and into its tissues, oxygen must first dissolve in water. Consequently the surface through which oxygen is absorbed must be moist. The moisture on any surface exposed to the air will usually evaporate. Some 500 cm^3 water are lost daily from the lungs of a man out of a total water loss of about 2500 cm^3. The rest is lost through the skin and in the urine and faeces. Water loss by **evaporation** may thus be a major physiological problem during gas exchange (Table 8.1).

Table 8.1 Loss of water vapour from several mammals

SPECIES	EVAPORATIVE WATER LOSS AS A PERCENTAGE OF TOTAL WATER LOSS
kangaroo rat	68
rat	65
camel	51
man	42
donkey	36

No biological system is perfect and physiological adaptations are usually compromises between advantage and disadvantage. To obtain enough oxygen to meet their metabolic needs, air-breathing animals such as mammals bring the air into direct contact with a relatively large area of moist lung surface. In doing so, water evaporates from the lungs resulting in substantial water loss. The rate of evaporation from a moist surface is affected by environmental factors such as temperature, atmospheric humidity and air movement. The ways in which such factors affect the loss of water vapour from terrestrial plants are described in Chapter 11. Climate similarly affects the rate of water loss from terrestrial animals.

Because mammals can regulate their breathing rate there is some control over water loss from their lungs. There is no such control in many terrestrial invertebrates such as earthworms and lower vertebrates such as amphibians which rely on a moist skin for gas exchange. Evaporative water loss is one of the main factors responsible for restricting such animals to moist habitats. Many mammals however live in deserts where evaporation is very rapid. Desert-living mammals possess adaptations which enable them to succeed where others would dry up and die within hours.

FIG. 8.1 *Kangaroo rat*

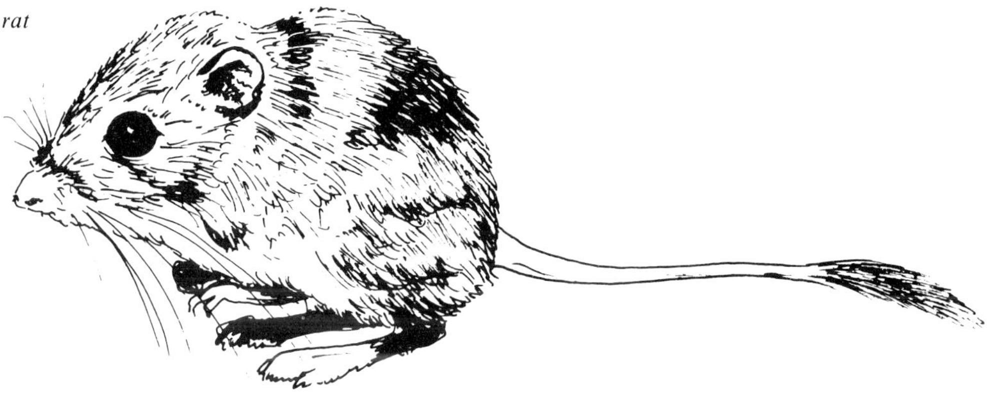

One of these mammals is the kangaroo rat, *Dipodomys*, an inhabitant of the deserts of the south-west United States of America (Fig. 8.1). The kangaroo rat has such fine regulation of its water content that although it lives in the desert it does not drink water. Since it has to match its water loss with a limited water intake the control of evaporation from its lungs is critical. Kangaroo rats have an efficient heat-exchange mechanism in their nasal passages which reduces the rate of water vapour loss during breathing. When breathing in, moisture on the inner surfaces of its nasal cavities evaporates, lowering the temperature of its nasal membranes. When breathing out, the moisture in the exhaled air condenses on the cooled nasal linings. Thus oxygen is taken in from the atmosphere with less of the accompanying water loss than occurs in most mammals (Fig. 8.2).

FIG. 8.2 *Moisture retention in the kangaroo rat during breathing*

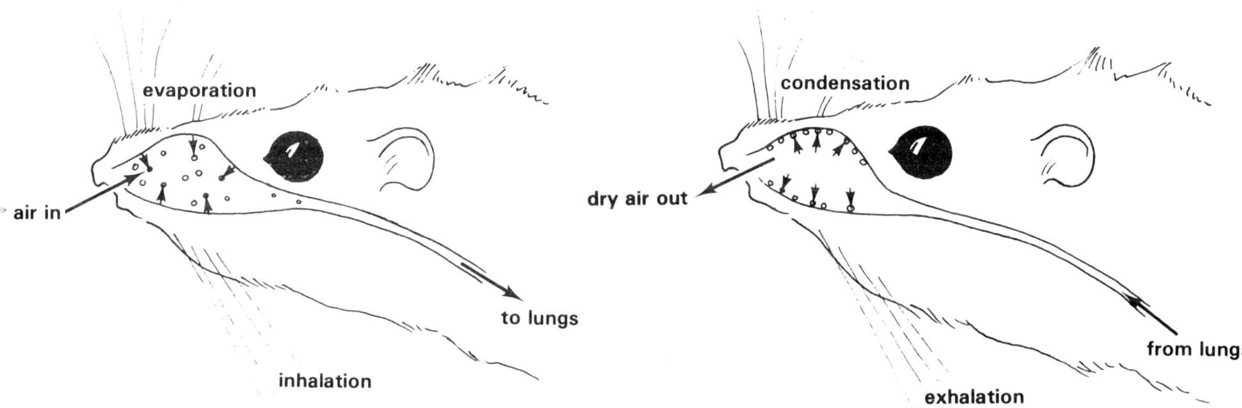

8.2 Breathing

8.2.1 The breathing mechanism

Mammalian **lungs** are compact organs. They are situated in the **thorax** which is separated from the abdominal cavity by a muscular **diaphragm** (Fig. 8.3). The lungs consist of millions of microscopic air sacs called **alveoli**. Each alveolus is surrounded by a network of fine capillary blood vessels (Fig. 8.4). It is across the delicate membranes separating blood from the alveolar air that diffusion of gases occurs. Oxygen is taken in from the alveolar air, carbon dioxide is released into it. Mammalian lungs have a considerable surface area for diffusion. For each gram of body mass there are about 7 cm^2 of lung surface in humans, 13 cm^2 in seals and 100 cm^2 in bats. This is a distinct improvement on the lungs of lower vertebrates which are little more than simple sacs (Fig. 8.5). In these animals the area of lung surface per unit mass of body is much less than in mammals.

FIG. 8.3 *The position of the lungs and air passages in the human thorax*

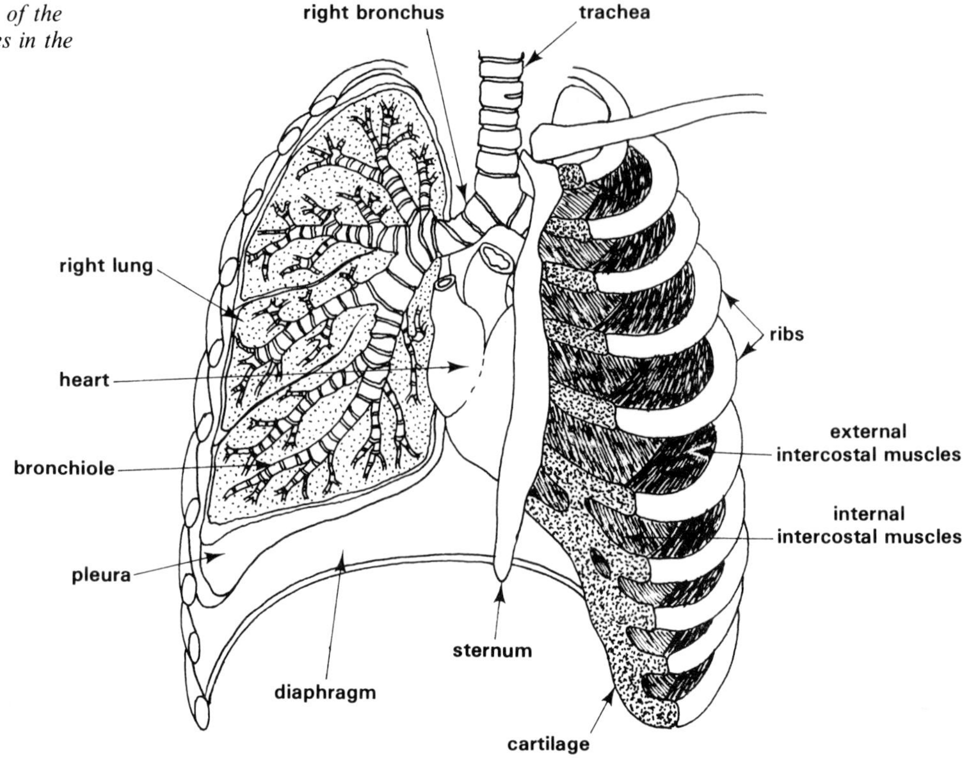

FIG. 8.4 *Photomicrograph of a thin section of cat lung, × 200*

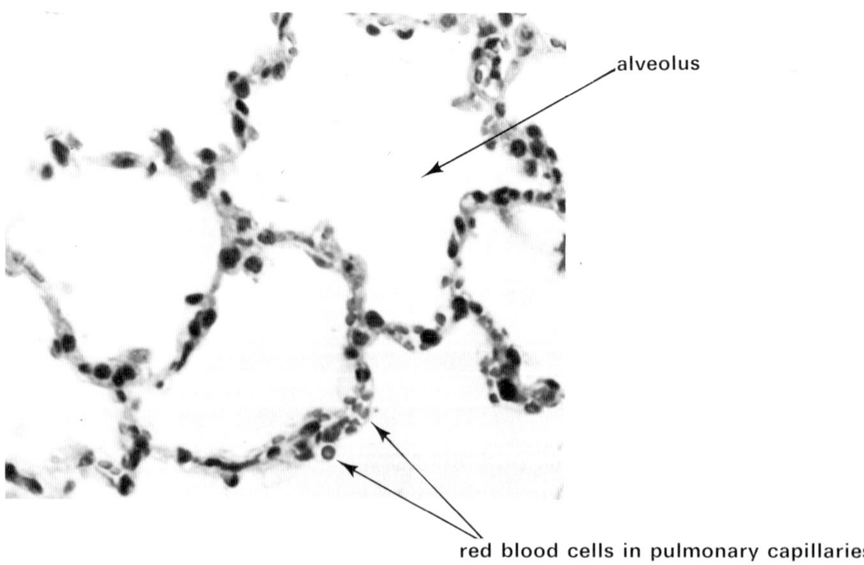

Fig 8.4

Breathing is a complex muscle-controlled activity in which the volume of the thorax is rhythmically increased and decreased. Air is sucked into and pushed out of the lungs when a mammal breathes. Breathing is brought about by movements of the ribs and diaphragm. Two sets of muscles, the **external and internal intercostal muscles** which work antagonistically, move the ribs. When the external intercostals contract, the internal intercostals relax and the ribs are forced obliquely out and up. Because they adhere to the inner wall of the thorax the lungs are stretched. At the same time the diaphragm contracts and pulls the lungs downwards towards the abdomen. These movements increase the volume of the lungs, thereby lowering the pressure of the air in them. As a result air is drawn into the lungs through the **trachea**, **bronchi** and **bronchioles**. Relaxation of the diaphragm and external intercostals together with contraction of the internal intercostals returns the thorax to its previous state. The pressure now applied to the lungs forces air from the lungs to the outside through the air passages (Fig. 8.6).

FIG. 8.5 *Longitudinal sections through the lungs of an amphibian and a reptile*

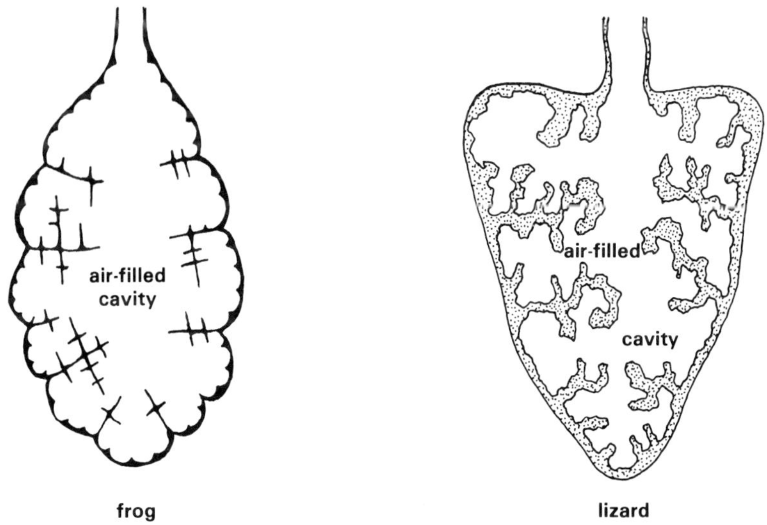

FIG. 8.6 *The process of breathing*

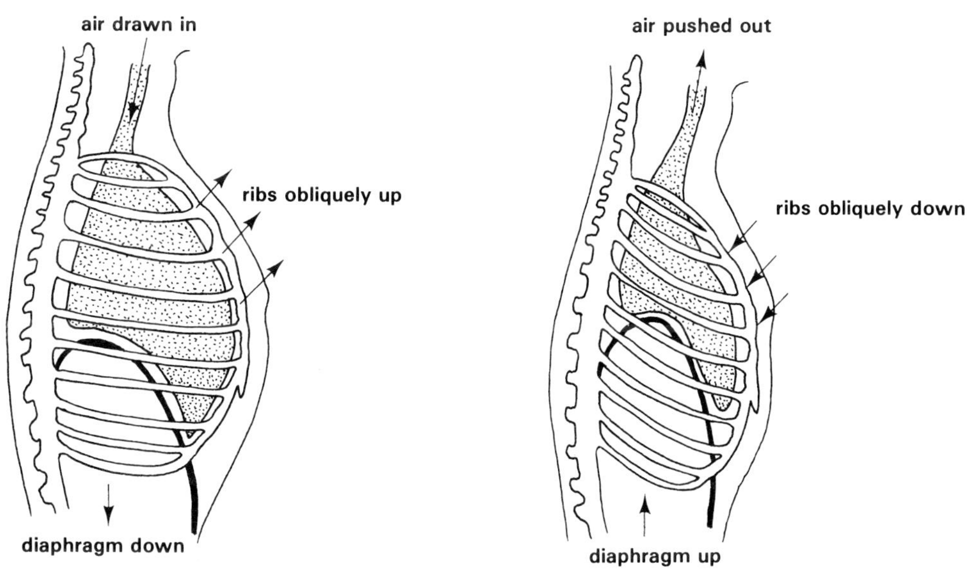

During each ventilation only about 10 per cent of the lungs' total air capacity is changed in most resting mammals. The volume of air exchanged with the atmosphere at each breathing cycle is called the **tidal volume**. A greater volume of air can be exchanged by forced breathing. The volume of air breathed out after breathing in to the fullest extent is called the **vital capacity**. About 70 per cent of the air breathed in enters the alveoli. The rest occupies **dead space** mainly in the bronchi and bronchioles. The total capacity of the lungs of an adult human is about 6 dm^3. Consequently during each ventilation of the lungs, only a small proportion of the alveolar air is replaced.

FIG. 8.7 *A spirometer being used to measure lung volumes* (courtesy Philip Harris Biological Ltd.)

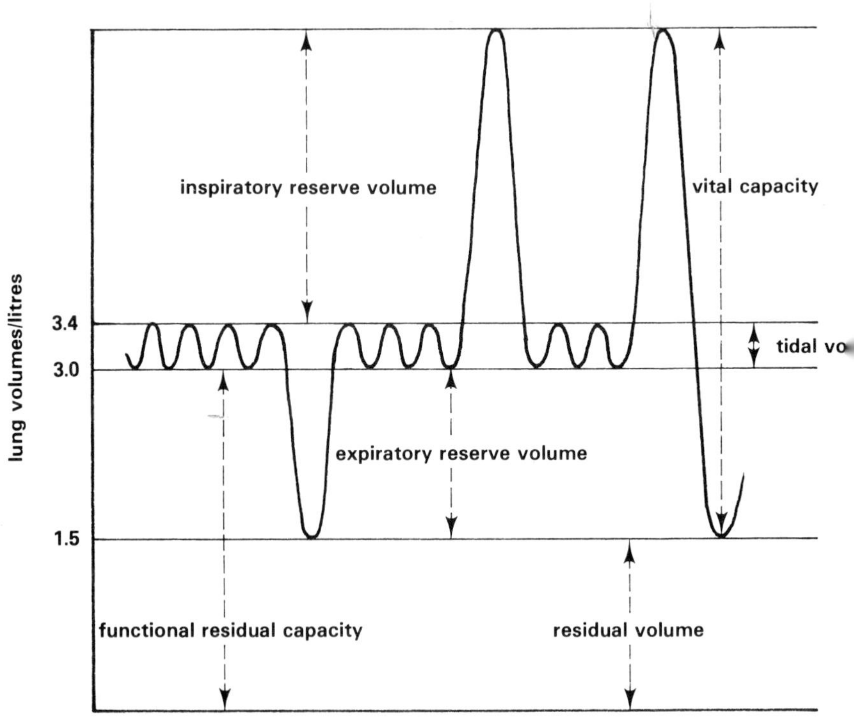

FIG. 8.8 *A spirometer tracing typical of a normal human adult. The inspiratory reserve volume is the maximum volume of air which can be inhaled during forced breathing. Similarly the expiratory reserve volume is the maximum volume of air exhaled. The residual volume is the minimum volume of air always present in the lungs*

Tidal volume, vital capacity and other lung capacities can be measured using a **spirometer** (Fig. 8.7). A spirometer is an air-filled chamber which rises and falls when a subject breathes into an attached mouthpiece. Movement of the chamber is recorded as a trace on a moving paper (Fig. 8.8). Spirometers are used in hospitals to measure lung capacities of patients suffering from respiratory ailments.

The tidal ventilation of lungs is very different from the continuous flow ventilation of the gills of many aquatic animals. In fish for example, oxygenated water is continuously moved over the surface of the gills and carbon dioxide is taken away in the same movement (Fig. 8.9).

FIG. 8.9 *A comparison of continuous flow and tidal ventilation*

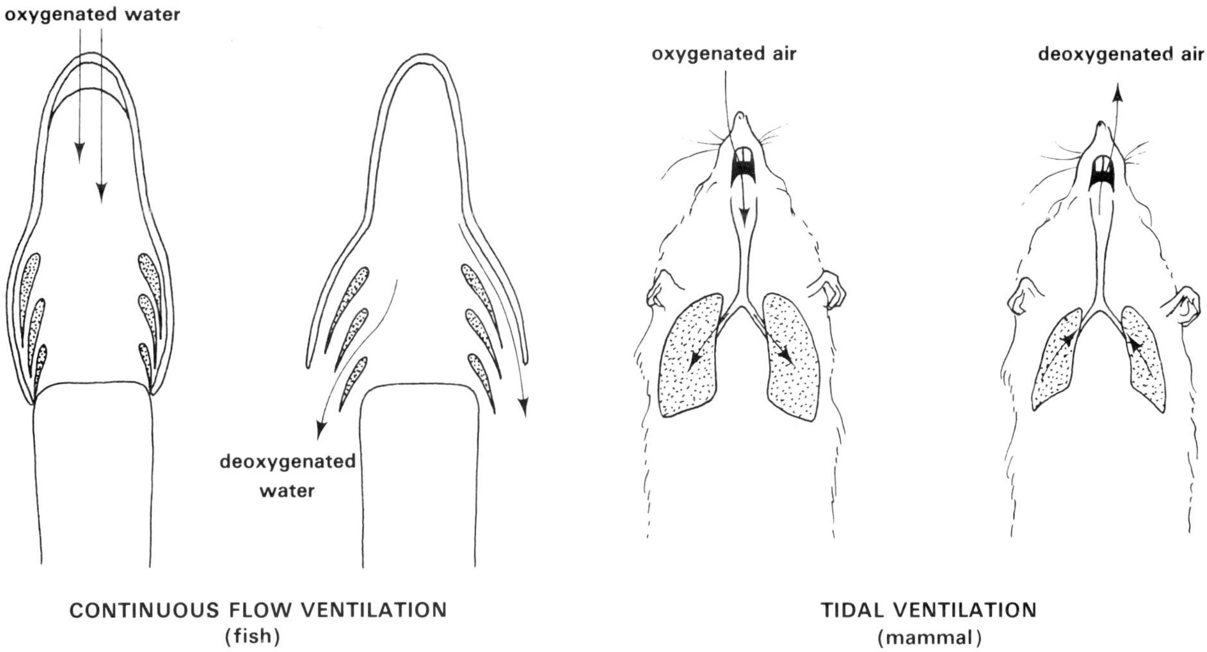

8.2.2 Control of breathing

The oxygen demand of an organism depends on the metabolic rate of its tissues. During periods of increased activity a mammal ventilates its lungs rapidly, so meeting the increased oxygen demand. Faster breathing also eliminates the extra carbon dioxide produced by increased respiration. Conversely the breathing rate slows down when the demand for oxygen drops during periods of rest. For example, a young woman resting on a bicycle may take in about 300 cm^3 oxygen per minute. When pedalling rapidly, oxygen consumption may rise to about 1500 cm^3 per minute. The fivefold increase in oxygen uptake is brought about by nearly trebling the breathing rate and nearly doubling the tidal volume. In other words she breathes faster and deeper. Changes in the rate and depth of breathing in response to exercise and rest are also accompanied by changes in the heart rate (Chapter 9).

The breathing rate is controlled by the **respiratory centre**, part of the medulla oblongata of the hindbrain (Chapter 15). Impulses from the respiratory centre travel along motor nerves to the intercostal and diaphragm muscles. The muscles respond by bringing about the thoracic movements necessary for lung ventilation. Whereas breathing is largely automatic, the responses of the intercostal and diaphragm muscles can be overridden by impulses from the higher centres of the brain. The pattern of breathing can thus be modified voluntarily. Activity of the respiratory centre is modified by several factors which indicate the need for a change in the breathing rate (Fig. 8.10).

FIG. 8.10 *Factors affecting the respiratory centre in the brain*

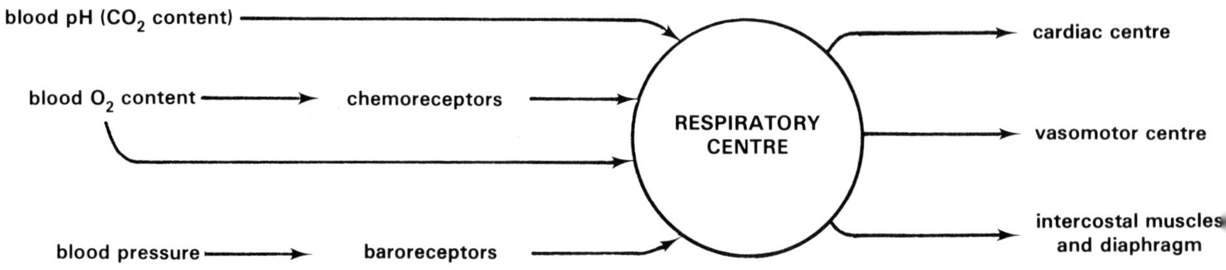

The respiratory centre is sensitive to the acidity of the blood flowing through it. Since the pH of blood is largely governed by the amount of carbon dioxide in it, increased breathing rate is an appropriate response as it leads to elimination of carbon dioxide from the blood. The carbon dioxide concentration of the blood is thought to be the main controlling factor in the automatic regulation of breathing.

The respiratory centre also responds to the oxygen tension of the blood. **Chemoreceptors**, cells sensitive to oxygen tension, are situated in small sinuses found in the aorta and carotid arteries. When the blood oxygen tension falls, the chemoreceptors stimulate the respiratory centre with impulses sent along sensory nerves. The respiratory centre then triggers off responses which bring about increased ventilation of the lungs.

FIG. 8.11 *Position of the baroreceptors (stippled) in the cat*

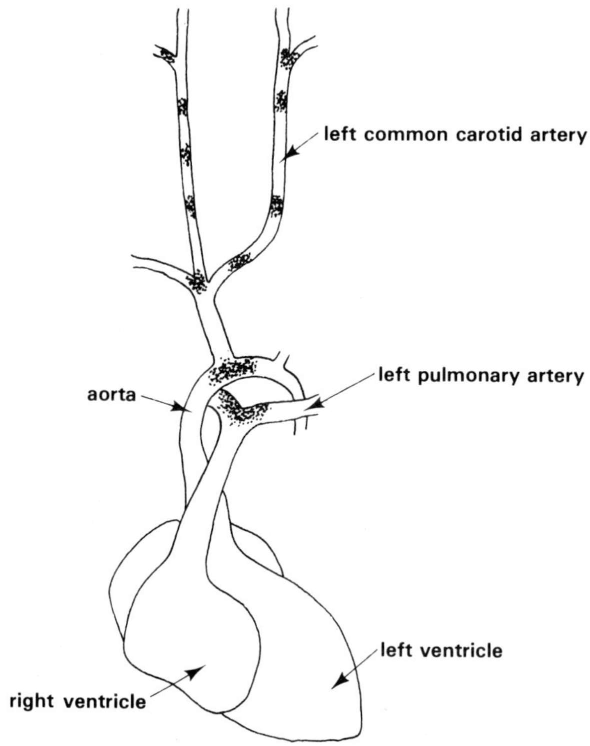

Cells sensitive to blood pressure, **baroreceptors**, are also found in the walls of the aorta, carotid arteries and pulmonary arteries (Fig. 8.11). Stimulation of the baroreceptors by a rise of blood pressure is monitored by the respiratory centre which reacts by triggering off responses which result in a decreased rate of lung ventilation.

Ventilation of the lungs in mammals is thus controlled by the net effect of the concentrations of carbon dioxide and oxygen in the blood, as well as blood pressure on the respiratory centre. In this way breathing and gas exchange are adjusted to meet the body's immediate needs. As with other homeostatic mechanisms the regulation of breathing involves **feedback** controls. The rate at which oxygen is taken in is regulated by factors which reflect the need for oxygen (Fig. 8.12).

FIG. 8.12 (a) *The main components of an automatic control system*

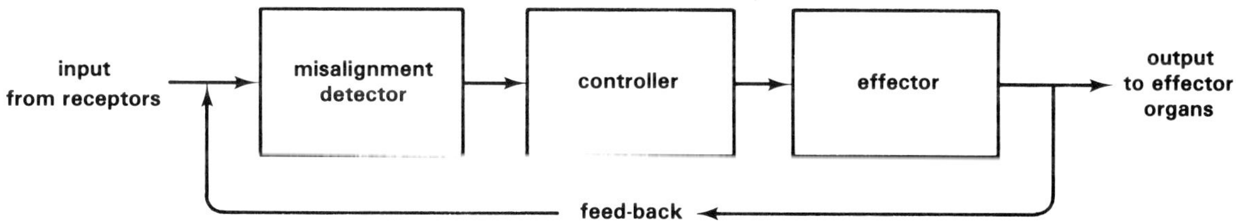

FIG. 8.12 (b) *The respiratory control system*

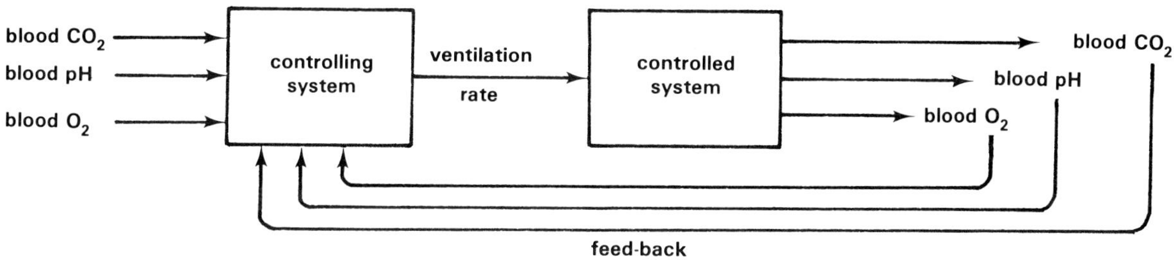

8.2.3 Oxygen debt

For short periods at a time the mammalian body can engage in severe exercise which requires more oxygen than can be provided by ventilating the lungs, whatever the rate of breathing. During intense exercise the reserves of free energy such as ATP and phosphocreatine are depleted. Anaerobic respiration occurs in the cells and lactic acid is produced (Chapter 5). During short periods of intense exercise an **oxygen debt** is built up. The debt is repaid by continued rapid and deep breathing when the period of exercise ends. The extra oxygen then absorbed by the blood corresponds to the oxygen debt and is used to oxidise the lactic acid produced in anaerobic respiration.

8.3 Oxygen uptake and carriage

One of the main functions of the lungs is to allow atmospheric oxygen to come into close proximity with the blood which can then absorb oxygen and transport it to the body organs and tissues.

8.3.1 Oxygenation of the blood

The red blood cells (**erythrocytes**) make up about 45 per cent of the total blood volume in man. Erythrocytes contain a respiratory pigment called **haemoglobin**. The main component of blood is plasma, a mixture of organic and inorganic materials dissolved in water. Oxygen is not very soluble in water. At 35°C, 100 cm^3 of water contains about 0·5 cm^3 oxygen. The blood of some mammals, such as the seal, can carry as much as 29 cm^3 oxygen per 100 cm^3 of blood. The ability of the blood to carry so much oxygen is due to haemoglobin (Table 8.2).

Table 8.2 Oxygen-carrying capacity of the blood of several mammals

SPECIES	cm^3 oxygen per 100 cm^3 blood
cat	15·0
rabbit	15·6
sheep	15·9
horse	16·7
kangaroo rat	17·5
rat	18·6
sea lion	19·8
man	20·0
porpoise	20·7
fox	21·7
llama	23·4
seal	29·3

Haemoglobin is a complex molecule made of four almost identical sub-units. Each sub-unit consists of a molecule of the protein **globin** attached to a central porphyrin group called **haem** which contains an iron(II) atom (Fig. 8.13).

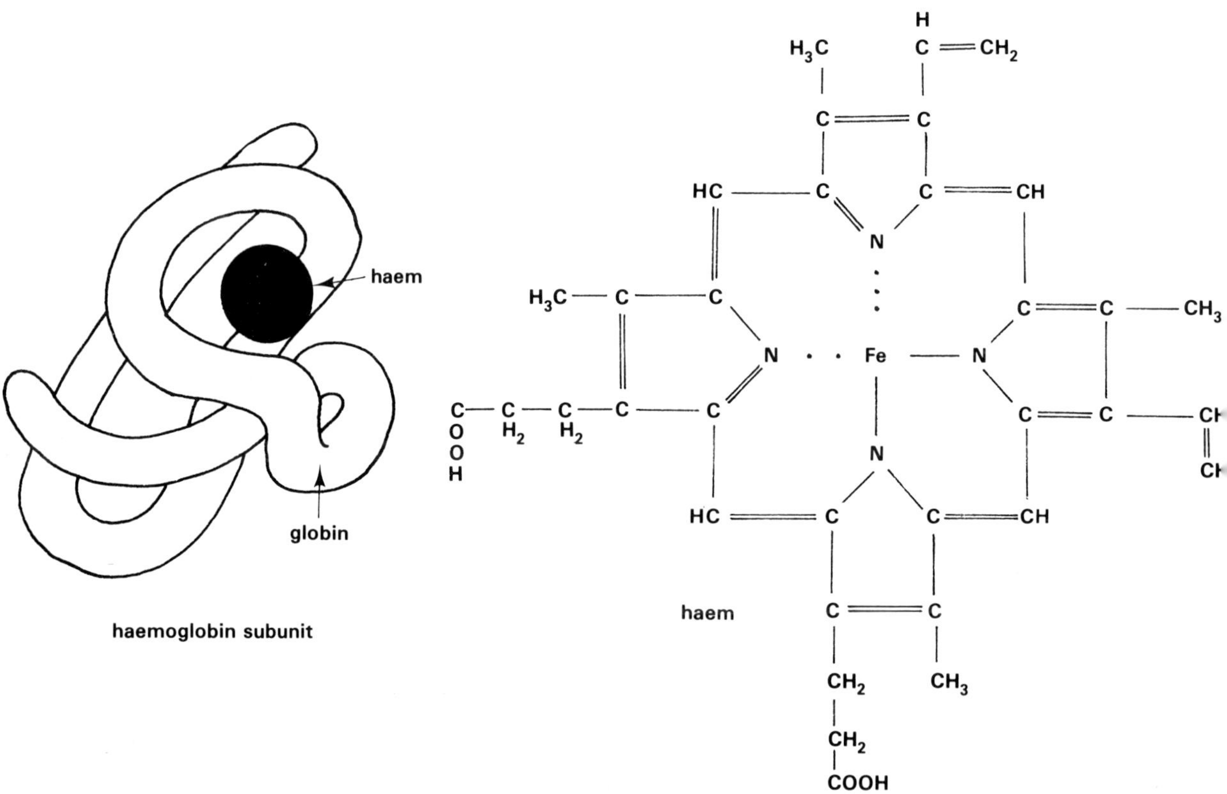

FIG. 8.13 *Haemoglobin structure. Each molecule consists of four sub-units. Each sub-unit contains an iron-centred haem group attached to the protein globin. The total relative molar mass is about 68 000*

FIG. 8.14 *Oxygenation of haemoglobin*

$$\text{haemoglobin} + O_2 \underset{\text{deoxygenation}}{\overset{\text{oxygenation}}{\rightleftharpoons}} \text{oxyhaemoglobin}$$

$$Hb_4 + O_2 \rightleftharpoons Hb_4O_2$$

$$Hb_4O_2 + O_2 \rightleftharpoons Hb_4O_4$$

$$Hb_4O_4 + O_2 \rightleftharpoons Hb_4O_6$$

$$Hb_4O_6 + O_2 \rightleftharpoons Hb_4O_8$$

In the capillaries of the lungs oxygen combines loosely with haemoglobin to form **oxyhaemoglobin**. The iron of the haem groups is not oxidised and remains as iron(II) (Fig. 8.14). Certain chemicals can oxidise the iron(II) to iron(III) producing derivatives of haemoglobin which cannot carry oxygen. Carbon monoxide poisoning, for example, is caused by the formation of carbon monoxide haemoglobin containing iron(III). Traces of carbon monoxide haemoglobin occur in the blood of non-smokers whereas up to 10 per cent is present in the blood of smokers. Oxygenation of haemoglobin takes place in the blood capillaries surrounding the alveoli. Here the haemoglobin becomes saturated with oxygen. The relationship between oxygen tension and haemoglobin saturation is usually shown as an **oxygen dissociation curve** (Fig. 8.15).

FIG. 8.15 *Oxygen dissociation curve of human haemoglobin*

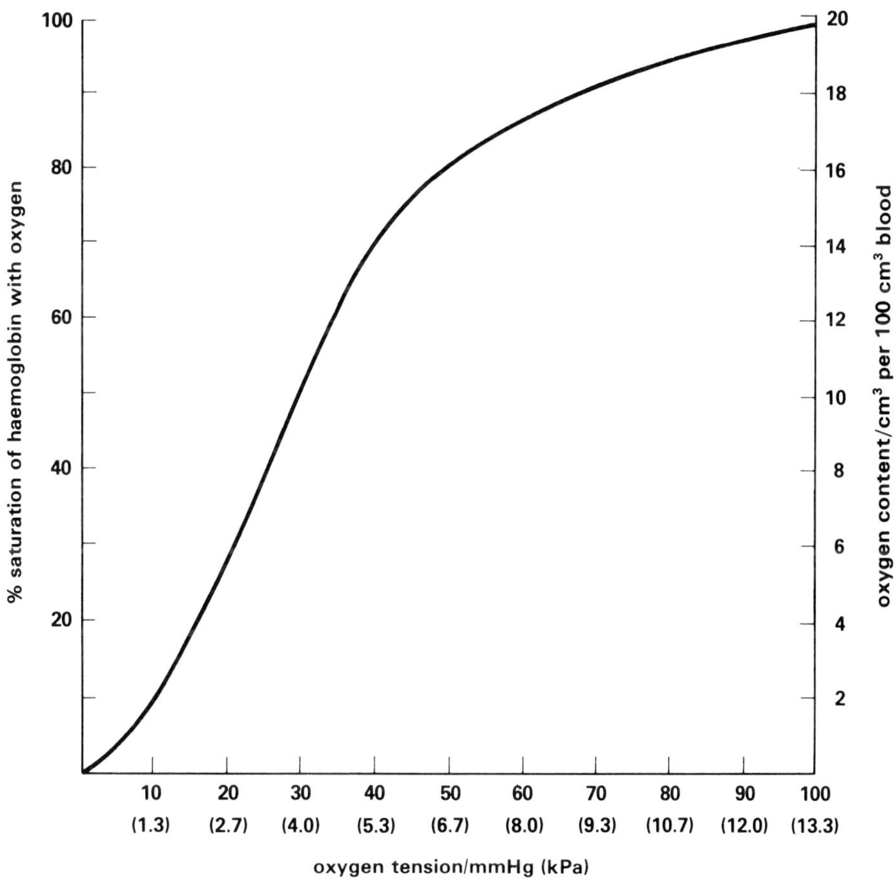

In air with a pressure of about 100 kPa (1 atm) the partial pressure exerted by the 21 per cent oxygen present is about 21 kPa. In the lungs, air breathed in is diluted with air in the dead space. Consequently the oxygen tension in the alveoli is lowered to about 13·3 kPa. Even so, blood circulating in the lung capillaries normally becomes fully saturated with oxygen from the alveoli.

8.3.2 Gas exchange in the tissues

Carbon dioxide is produced in body organs as a result of tissue respiration. The carbon dioxide diffuses through the walls of blood capillaries into the blood. In the red cells an enzyme called **carbonic anhydrase** greatly accelerates the combination of carbon dioxide with water to form carbonic acid:

$$\underset{\text{carbon dioxide}}{CO_2} + \underset{\text{water}}{H_2O} \xrightleftharpoons{\text{carbonic anhydrase}} \underset{\text{carbonic acid}}{H_2CO_3}$$

The carbonic acid partially dissociates into hydrogen (H^+) and hydrogencarbonate (HCO_3^-) ions:

$$\underset{\text{carbonic acid}}{H_2CO_3} \rightleftharpoons \underset{\text{hydrogen ion}}{H^+} + \underset{\text{hydrogencarbonate ion}}{HCO_3^-}$$

The HCO_3^- ions readily diffuse out of the red cells into the plasma. It is as HCO_3^- ions that most of the carbon dioxide is carried to the lungs (Table 8.3). In the lungs the reactions described above are reversed and the carbon dioxide gas so formed diffuses into the alveoli to be breathed out.

Table 8.3 Transport of carbon dioxide in the blood

	PERCENTAGE OF TOTAL CARBON DIOXIDE IN BLOOD
CO_2 in solution	7
carbon dioxide haemoglobin	7
hydrogencarbonate	86

FIG. 8.16 *Summary of red cell chemistry related to the carriage of respiratory gases*

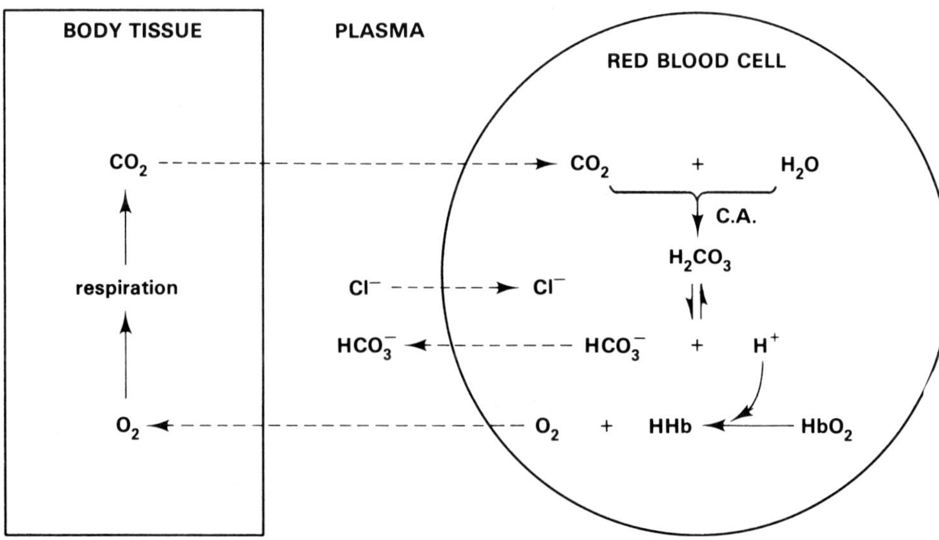

In response to the rapid loss of HCO_3^- ions from the red cells, an equal number of chloride ions (Cl^-) diffuse in the opposite direction. The **chloride shift** prevents electrochemical imbalances, particularly pH changes, which could adversely affect the red cells.

The H^+ ions which stay in the red cells cause the release of oxygen from oxyhaemoglobin:

$$\underset{}{H^+} + \underset{\text{oxyhaemoglobin}}{HbO_2} \rightleftharpoons \underset{\text{haemoglobinic acid}}{HHb} + \underset{\text{oxygen}}{O_2}$$

Gas exchange in the tissues takes place very rapidly. The reactions involved are summarised in Figure 8.16.

The main factor controlling the release of oxygen to the tissues is the volume of carbon dioxide produced by tissue respiration. As the carbon dioxide tension of the tissues and capillary blood rises the affinity of oxyhaemoglobin for oxygen is lowered. The phenomenon is called the **Bohr effect**. The oxygen dissociation curve moves to the right (Fig. 8.17).

Thus increased carbon dioxide production by respiring tissues causes the blood to release more oxygen. For example, assume that in a tissue somewhere in the body the oxygen tension is 4·0 *k*Pa. If the carbon dioxide tension increases from 5·3 *k*Pa to 9·3 *k*Pa then, from the oxygen dissociation curves, it can be seen that the saturation of haemoglobin is lowered from 55 to 35 per cent. As a direct result of such an increase in

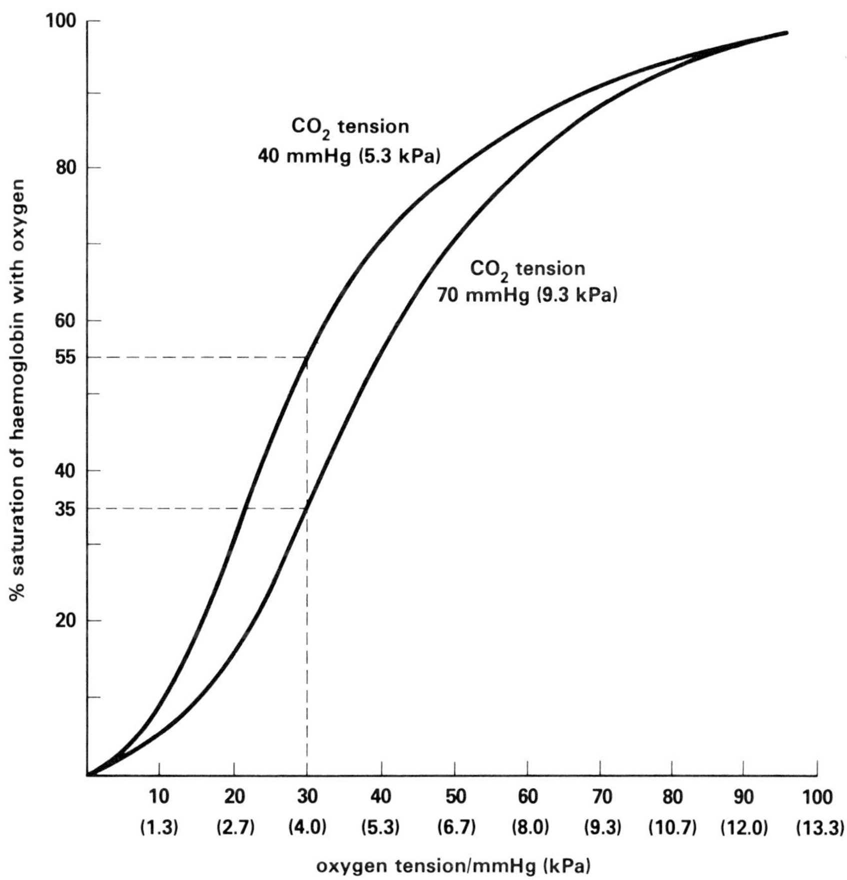

FIG. 8.17 *The effect of carbon dioxide tension on the oxygen dissociation curve of haemoglobin. The carbon dioxide tension in human arteries is about 40 mmHg (5·3 kPa). Tissue respiration increases this to about 46 mmHg (6·1 kPa). The oxygen tension of arterial blood is about 100 mmHg (13·3 kPa). Tissue respiration lowers this to about 40 mmHg (5·3 kPa).*

carbon dioxide production some 20 per cent of the haemoglobin releases its oxygen. The more carbon dioxide a tissue produces the greater is this effect. Consequently the tissues and organs such as muscles and the liver which have a relatively high respiration rate cause a rapid release of oxygen from the blood supplying them. Conversely those tissues with a low oxygen demand cause oxygen to be released less rapidly from the blood.

The carriage and exchange of respiratory gases also contributes to the regulation of the pH of blood and the body tissues (Chapter 2).

8.3.3 Adaptations to high altitude

As altitude is gained atmospheric pressure drops. The drop in atmospheric pressure is significant for organisms living at high altitudes because the partial pressure of oxygen in the atmosphere at high altitudes is less (Table 8.4).

Table 8.4 Approximate partial pressures of oxygen and nitrogen in the atmosphere at sea level and at 4848 metres

	PERCENTAGE	PARTIAL PRESSURE AT SEA LEVEL/*k*Pa	PARTIAL PRESSURE AT 4848 METRES/*k*Pa
oxygen	21	21	11
nitrogen	79	79	42
barometric pressure (approx)		100	53

The amount of haemoglobin and the number of red cells in the blood of mammals increase when they live at high altitudes (Table 8.5). This is a direct response to the smaller partial pressure of oxygen in the air. Red cell production occurs in the red bone marrow and is controlled by a hormone

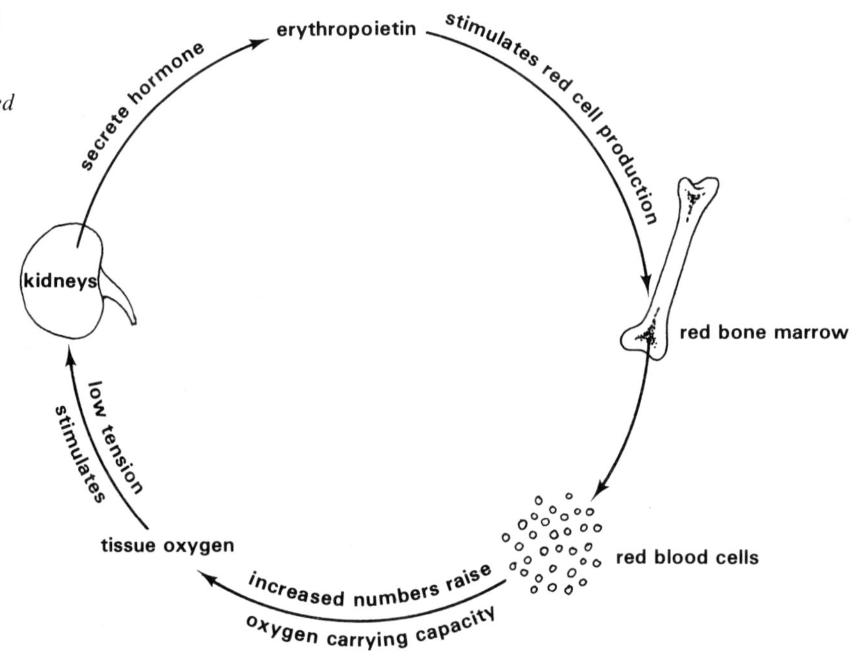

FIG. 8.18 *Hormone control of red cell production (erythropoiesis). Erythropoiesis is a continuous process and red cells have a limited life in the circulation, about 4 months in man*

called **erythropoietin** which is made in the kidneys. Secretion of erythropoietin is stimulated by low tensions of oxygen (Fig. 8.18). However, when a mammal moves from low to high altitude time is needed for an increase of haemoglobin and red cells. The problem was highlighted at the 1968 Olympic Games in Mexico City, 2460 metres above sea level. Athletes

Table 8.5 Numbers of red cells in the blood of several mammals at sea level and at high altitude

SPECIES	ALTITUDE	AVERAGE RED CELL NUMBERS $\times 10^{12}$ per dm^3
man	sea level	5·00
	5333 m	7·37 (residents)
		5·95 (transients)
sheep	sea level	10·50
	4673 m	12·05
rabbit	sea level	4·55
	5303 m	7·00
llama	sea level	11·40
	2800 m	12·30

FIG. 8.19 (a) *Oxygen dissociation curves of llama and horse haemoglobins*

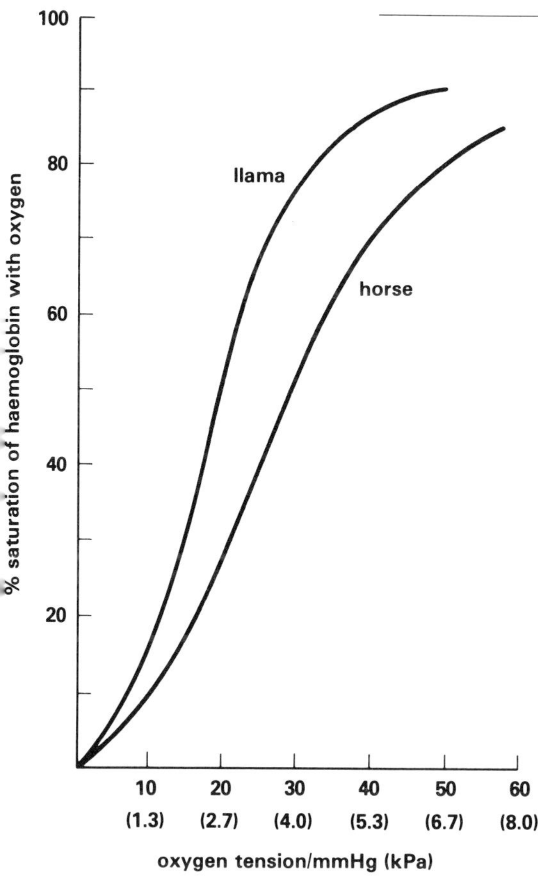

FIG. 8.19 (b) *Llama*

who were natives of high altitude countries or who had spent several months acclimatising to high altitude prior to the Games performed quite a lot better than those who had not.

Another adaptation which helps to overcome low oxygen tensions is seen in wild mammals living at high altitude. These animals possess haemoglobin which loads more readily with oxygen in the lungs. Haemoglobin of this sort has a dissociation curve to the left of normal haemoglobin (Fig. 8.19).

8.3.4 Pregnancy and foetal haemoglobin

During pregnancy several physiological changes take place inside the mother's body concerned with the provision of oxygen for the developing embryo. The changes occur partly as a result of the increased output of certain hormones during the gestation period (Chapter 22). For instance, the developing foetus in the uterus progressively displaces the mother's abdominal organs. The displaced organs push against the mother's diaphragm, as well as elsewhere, thus lowering the ventilating capacity of her lungs. Nevertheless, her rate of oxygen consumption increases by about 20 per cent as a result of widening of the thorax and an average 40 per cent increase in breathing rate.

Transport of the extra oxygen, partly to the foetus, is helped by an increase of about 1 dm^3 in the mother's total blood volume. The extra blood is circulated more rapidly than normal by increased cardiac output (Chapter 9) which rises from an average of 4·9 dm^3 per minute to about 6 dm^3 per minute. As it develops in the uterus, the embryo is attached to its

FIG. 8.20 *Oxygen dissociation curves of the adult and foetal haemoglobins of sheep*

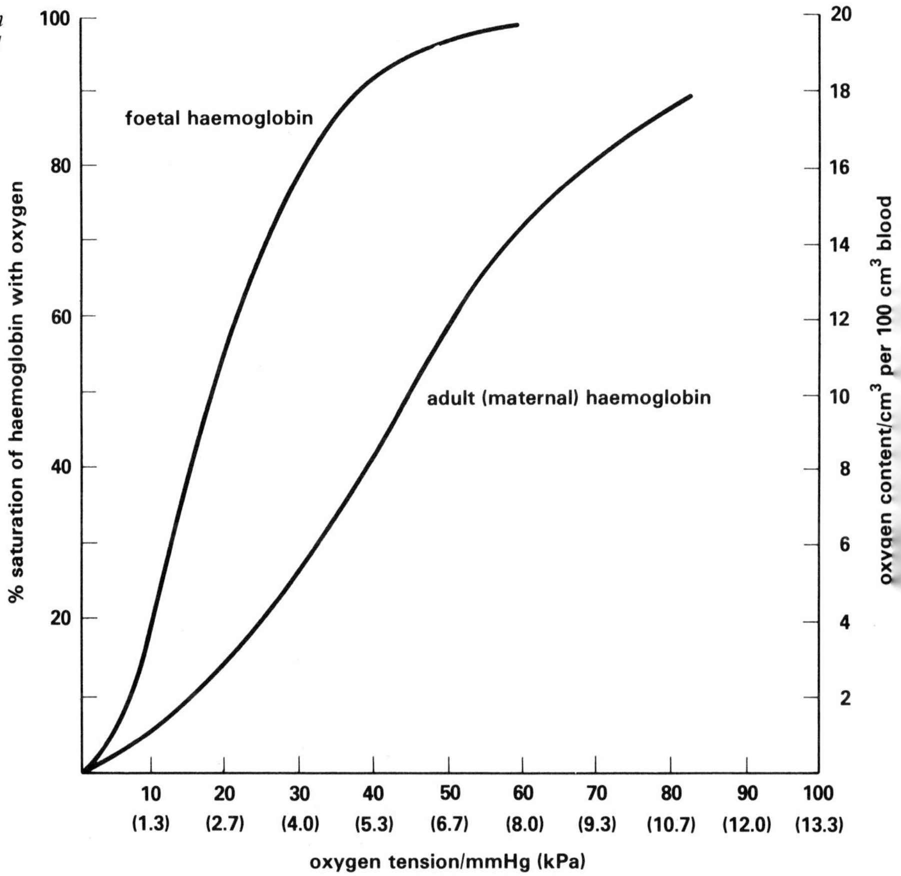

mother by a placenta (Chapter 22). Inside the placenta the maternal blood vessels lie very close to the foetal blood vessels. A two-way exchange of nutrients, wastes and respiratory gases occurs across the membranes separating the two circulations. Because of its rapid growth and development a mammalian foetus has a very high oxygen demand. Unloading of oxygen from the mother's blood to the foetal circulation is brought about because the foetal red cells contain a variant of haemoglobin which has a greater affinity for oxygen than the mother's haemoglobin (Fig. 8.20). This important functional difference between foetal and adult haemoglobin results from very small differences in the amino acid sequences of their globin proteins. **Foetal haemoglobin** is replaced by adult haemoglobin at birth. Can you think what advantage results from the replacement?

Not all changes in the haemoglobin molecule are advantageous. A serious disease of man called **sickle cell anaemia** results from the production of a haemoglobin variant differing from normal haemoglobin by only a single amino acid out of several hundred in the whole molecule (Chapter 6). When deoxygenated, the variant, called **haemoglobin S**, is a 100 times less soluble than the normal adult haemoglobin. At low oxygen tensions, haemoglobin S crystallises in the red cells distorting them into a sickle shape (Fig. 8.21). Many sickle cells are destroyed in the circulation causing an anaemia, which considerably lowers the oxygen-carrying capacity of the blood. Some sickle cells block the capillaries in vital organs and the disease may thus be fatal.

The incidence of haemoglobin S in certain parts of Africa and Asia is very high compared with other areas. People who inherit the gene for haemoglobin S from only one parent display the heterozygous condition called **sickle cell trait**. Sufferers of sickle cell trait are resistant to some forms of malaria and are therefore more likely to survive to adulthood. The resistance explains the high frequency of haemoglobin S among natives of regions where malaria is prevalent.

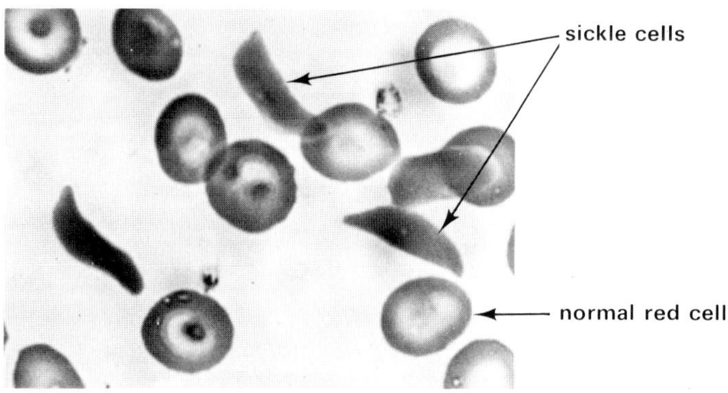

FIG. 8.21 *Photomicrograph of a smear of human blood showing sickle cells, (× 750)*

8.3.5 Myoglobin

The muscles of mammals contain a red pigment called **myoglobin** which is structurally similar to one of the four sub-units of haemoglobin (Fig. 3.27). Myoglobin has a higher affinity for oxygen than haemoglobin has and unloads its oxygen only when the blood is almost fully deoxygenated. This property is reflected in the oxygen dissociation curve for myoglobin which is further to the left than the curve for haemoglobin (Fig. 8.22).

Oxymyoglobin acts as an oxygen reserve in skeletal muscles which have a high oxygen demand during exercise. In this way the muscles can be provided with oxygen even though the blood flowing through them has all

FIG. 8.22 *Oxygen dissociation curve of myoglobin. That of haemoglobin is shown for comparison*

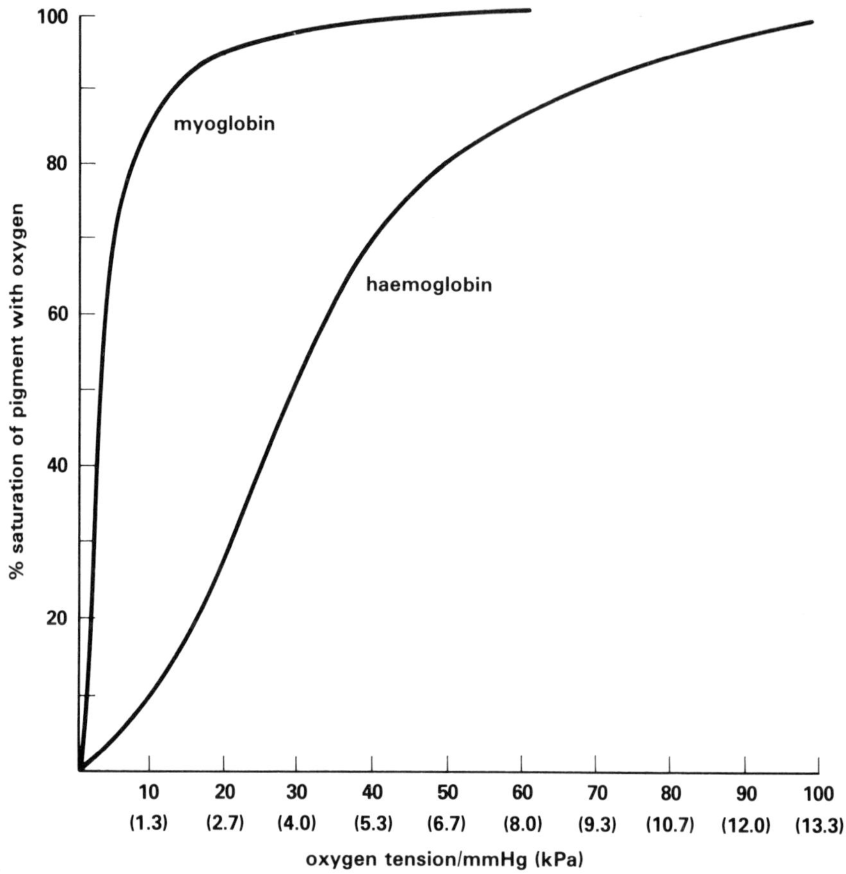

oxygen removed from it. Mammalian muscles display several other adaptations which enable them to sustain intense activity for short periods of time (Chapter 15).

8.4 Respiratory physiology of diving mammals

Many marine mammals can remain submerged in water for long periods, often at great depths (Table 8.6). Diving involves several adaptations of the respiratory system and tissue physiology. For example, the tidal volume, the volume of air exchanged with the atmosphere during each breathing cycle, is some 80 per cent of the total lung capacity in the porpoise compared with only 10 per cent in man. This means that any oxygen debt built up in a porpoise during prolonged submergence in water can be repaid quickly on surfacing. There are, however, other adaptations which are just as important.

Table 8.6 Diving times of several mammals

SPECIES	AVERAGE DURATION OF DIVE/min
man	2·5
seal	15
finback whale	30
sperm whale	60–90
bottlenose whale	120+

8.4.1 Aquatic mammals

P. F. Scholander was one of the first to investigate the physiology of diving mammals, mainly seals. The blood of the seal has a very high oxygen-carrying capacity, 29·3 cm^3 oxygen per 100 cm^3 blood (Table 8.2). Even though there is a lot of oxygen in the seal's blood when it submerges, much of its tissue respiration during long dives is anaerobic. This is because breathing may stop for up to fifteen minutes when the seal is under water. Lactic acid and carbon dioxide are produced as a result of anaerobic respiration (Chapter 5). The lactic acid can increase to seven times its normal concentration in the blood of seals without ill-effect. The respiratory centre of seals must be far less sensitive than that of non-diving mammals to high concentrations of carbon dioxide in the blood.

Another feature of seals when diving is a remarkable drop in heart rate from about 150 beats per minute to about 10 beats per minute. Blood is also redirected in the vascular system so that the supply to the brain is maintained while the amount of blood pumped to other parts of the body is lowered. In this way the oxygen goes to organs which cannot do without it. Seals also expel air from their lungs as they dive, lowering the volume of gases which are compressed on submerging. The danger of bubbles of nitrogen forming in the blood and tissues when the seal surfaces is thus minimised.

The mechanisms described above ensure the efficient use of oxygen during submergence and allow anaerobic respiration without damage to the tissues. Less is known of such mechanisms in whales. However, the muscles of whales contain high concentrations of myoglobin.

8.4.2 Diving and man

There has been much interest recently in the physiological problems of human diving. One reason for concern is the high rates of accidents and fatalities among divers engaged in oil exploration in the North Sea off the coast of Britain.

The main problems relate to the effects of pressure from the surrounding water as divers descend (Fig. 8.23). The pressure increases the volumes of gases entering the blood from the alveoli. At depths below about 60 m the increased oxygen content of the blood is such that the tissues receive more oxygen than they normally need. The increased supply of oxygen leads to abnormal metabolism and damage to brain cells can occur. Consequently the diver can quickly lose control of his actions. Oxygen poisoning may be overcome by adjusting the oxygen content of a diver's breathing mixture as he descends.

High levels of dissolved nitrogen in the body have an anaesthetic effect on the central nervous system. At depths below 60 m **nitrogen narcosis** can make a diver unconscious. Prior to this, a state similar to drunkenness can give a diver a false sense of security in which he cannot make rational decisions. In this state, he may endanger his life. Substitution of helium for nitrogen in the breathing mixture eliminates the danger of nitrogen narcosis. One amusing, if inconvenient, side effect of the use of helium for such purposes is that it affects the voice which becomes very high pitched and squeaky.

Rapid **decompression**, on sudden surfacing, can cause a further problem, that of gas bubble formation in the tissues and body fluids. At a depth of 60 m the nitrogen in a diver's body is at a pressure of about 517 *k*Pa, more than five times atmospheric pressure at sea level. At the surface however, nitrogen is at a pressure of 81 kPa. Sudden decompression causes rapid conversion of dissolved nitrogen in the blood into bubbles of nitrogen. The bubbles cause severe pain which in turn gives rise to terrible contortions of the body. For this reason, the condition is called the **bends**. The effects on the central nervous system can be severe and permanent. The bends or **decompression sickness** is prevented by controlling decompression at a rate slow enough for the extra nitrogen in the body to be gradually eliminated in the normal way by the lungs.

FIG. 8.23 *Relationship between pressure and depth beneath the sea*

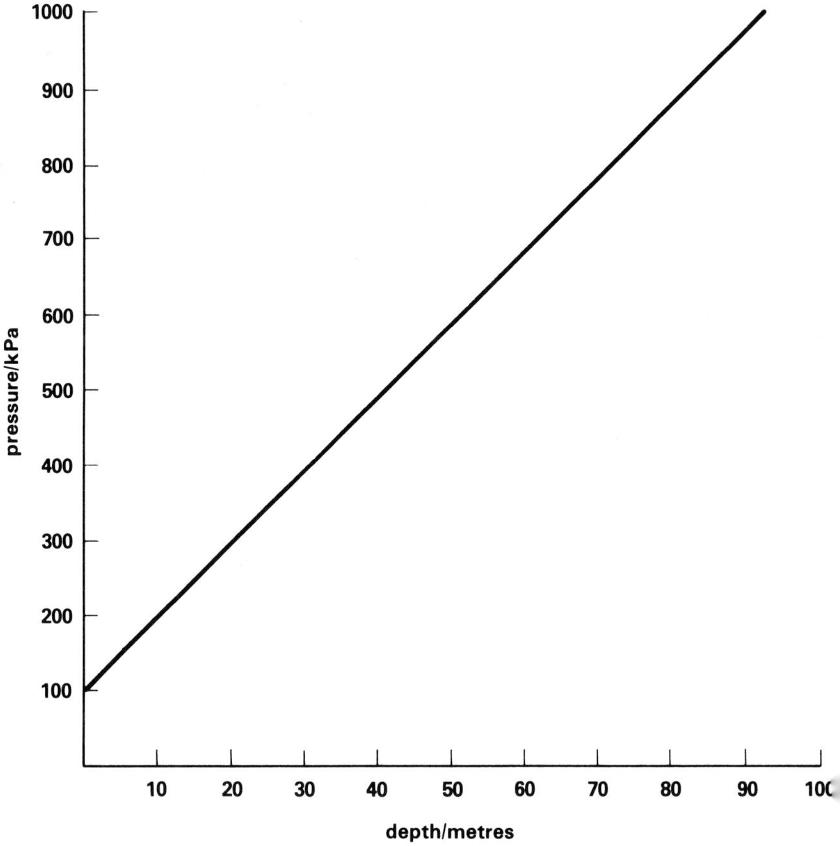

Chapter 9

Blood, lymph and circulation

Oxygen in the lungs and many nutrients in the gut enter the blood mainly by diffusion through the alveolar and intestinal surfaces respectively. Movement of dissolved metabolites around the body by diffusion alone, however, would be a very slow process. An inactive earthworm for example could only obtain about 10 per cent of its oxygen requirement if it had to rely on diffusion to distribute the gas throughout its body. Consequently all but the smallest of animals need a rapid means of internal transport. In mammals and other vertebrates transport is carried out mainly by the **blood**.

Blood distributes nutrients and respiratory gases to the tissues, transports hormones to target organs and carries metabolic wastes from the tissues to excretory organs. Blood also plays an important part in the defence against disease and in the repair of injured body tissues.

9.1 Circulation of blood and lymph

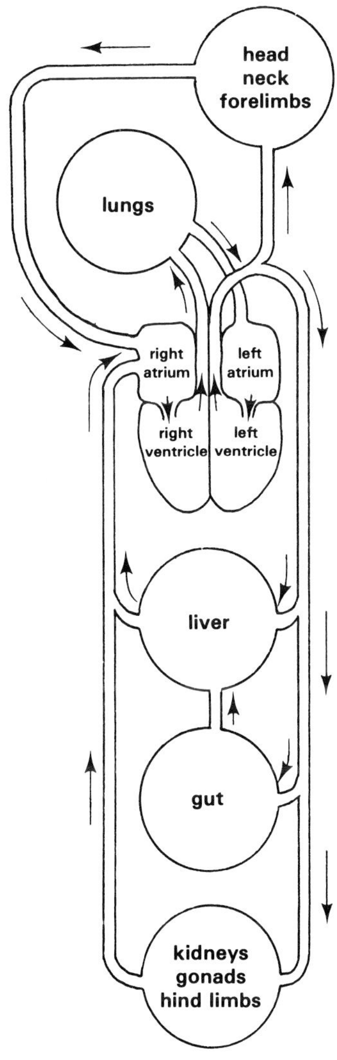

FIG. 9.1 *Diagram of the blood circulation of mammals*

FIG. 9.2 *The main arteries and veins in man. The pulmonary and gastrointestinal vessels are omitted for clarity*

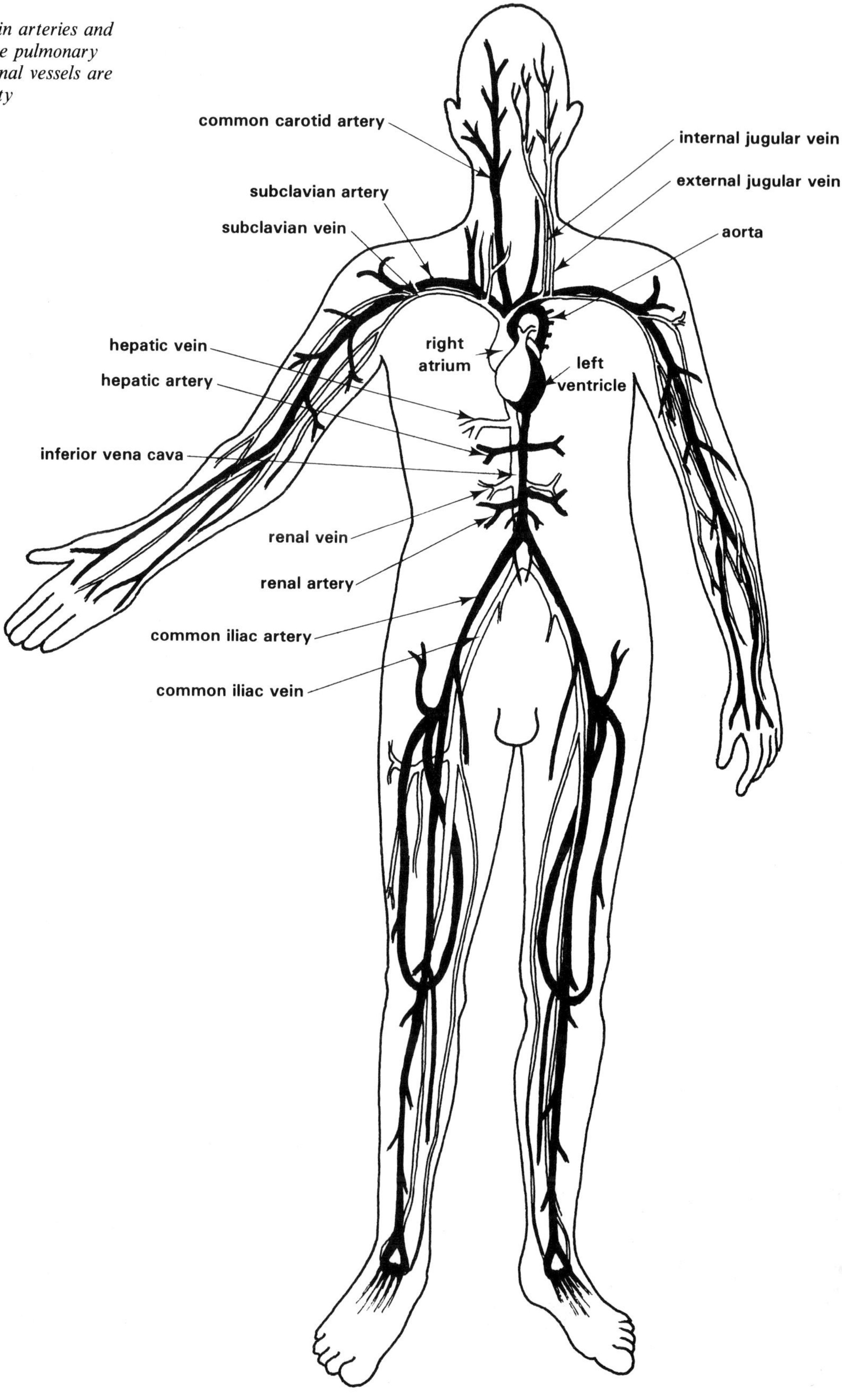

The volume of blood in mammals is substantial (Table 9.1). To act as a transport system large volumes of fluid require a powerful pump, the **heart**. From the heart blood is pumped through an extensive system of **arteries** and **arterioles** to all the organs of the body. It then passes through microscopic blood **capillaries** where metabolites and wastes are exchanged with the tissue fluid and cells of the organs. Blood drains from the organs in **venules** and **veins** which carry it back to the heart. Figures 9.1 and 9.2 illustrate the extent and complexity of the mammalian blood vascular system.

Table 9.1 Blood volume as a percentage of body mass in several mammals

SPECIES	BLOOD VOLUME AS PER CENT BODY MASS
goat	6·1
rabbit	6·5
man	7·0
cow	7·5
guinea pig	7·5
pig	8·0
dog	9·4

9.1.1 The heart

FIG. 9.3 (a) *The human heart, ventral view*

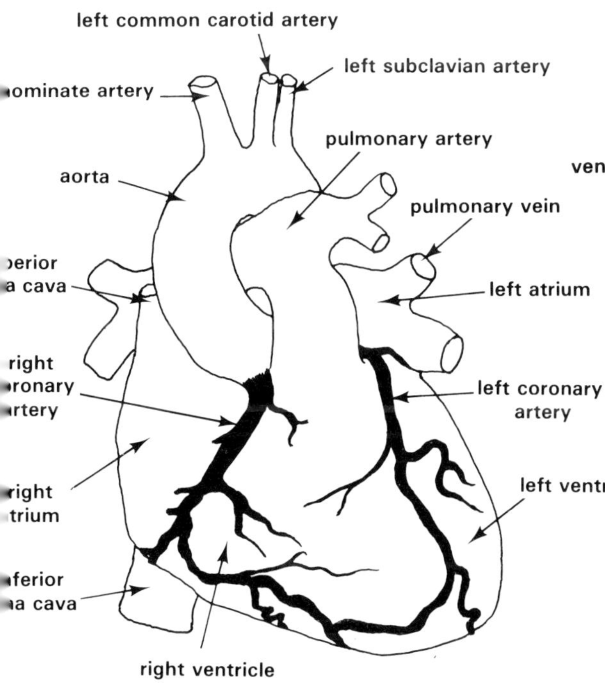

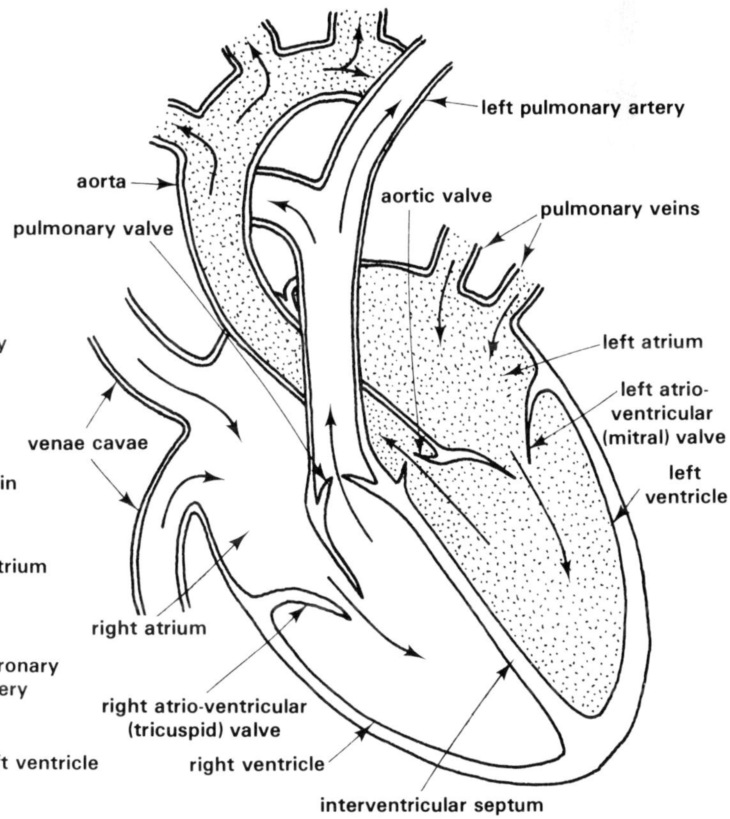

FIG. 9.3 (b) *Diagram of the mammalian heart indicating the direction of blood flow*

The mammalian heart is a remarkable organ. Functionally it is divided into right and left halves. The right half collects blood from the general body circulation and pumps it to the lungs where it is oxygenated (Chapter 8). The left half of the heart receives oxygenated blood from the lungs and pumps it into the general (systemic) circulation (Fig. 9.3).

1. THE CARDIAC CYCLE

The **cardiac output** is the volume of blood pumped from each ventricle in a minute. When the body is at rest the cardiac output of an adult human is about 4·9 dm^3 per minute. During severe exercise the output can rise to 30 dm^3 per minute. The pumping of blood requires considerable and sustained expenditure of energy. The mechanical work in pumping blood is performed by the **cardiac muscle** in the walls of the heart's four chambers. Cardiac muscle has inherent rhythmicity. Even if isolated from all its nervous supply it continues to contract and relax rhythmically (Fig. 9.4).

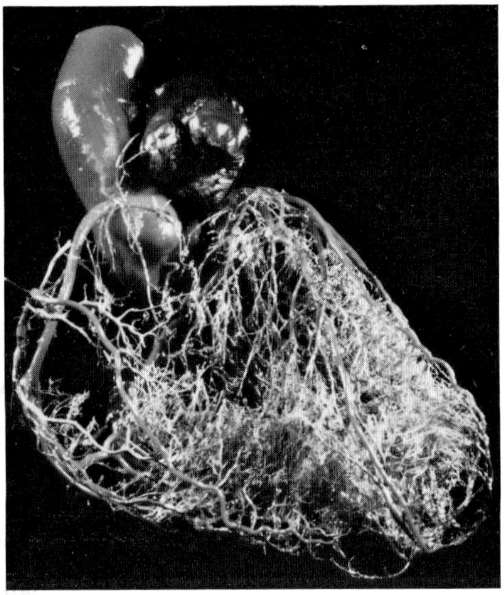

FIG. 9.3 (c) *Resin cast of the blood vessels of the human heart* (courtesy Professor McMinn, Department of Anatomy, The Royal College of Surgeons of England)

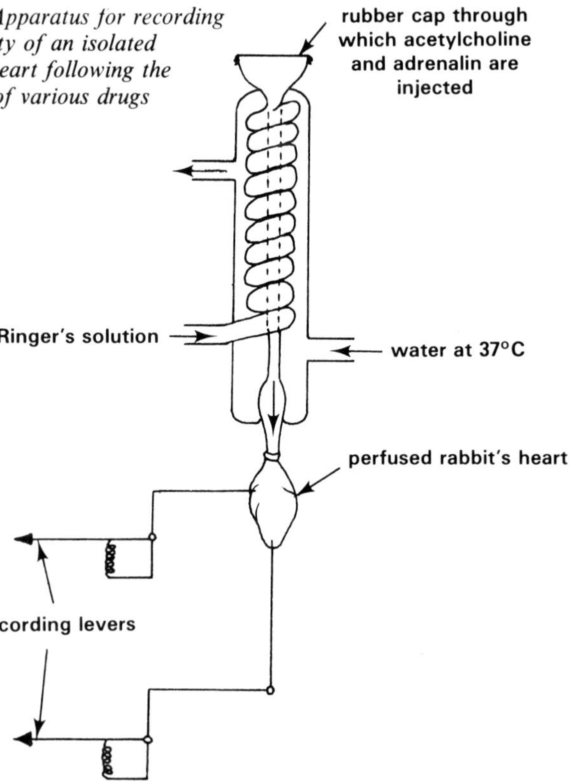

FIG. 9.4 *Apparatus for recording the activity of an isolated rabbit's heart following the addition of various drugs*

The **cardiac cycle** begins with atrial contraction. The electrochemical basis of muscle contraction is described in Chapter 15. The stimulus for the heart's rhythmic beat comes from a small part of the right atrium called the **sinu-atrial node** (**pacemaker**). From the pacemaker waves of electrical activity similar to nerve impulses spread out very rapidly over both atria. Each wave contracts the atrial muscle, forcing blood in the **atria** through a pair of **atrio-ventricular valves** into the **ventricles. Semi-lunar valves** prevent a backflow of blood into the veins supplying blood to the heart when the atria contract (Fig. 9.5(a)). The non-conductive septum between the atria and ventricles prevents the cardiac impulse in the atrial muscles from spreading directly into the ventricles. However, a second node, the **atrio-ventricular (AV) node**, also in the wall of the right atrium, picks up the atrial impulse. The AV node transmits the cardiac impulse along the conductive **bundle of His** and its branches in the interventricular septum. When the impulse reaches the apex of the heart it spreads rapidly up the ventricular walls in a network of conductive **Purkinje fibres**. The arrival of the cardiac impulse in the ventricles stimulates contraction there. Blood is forced upwards from the ventricles into the pulmonary arteries leading to the lungs and the aorta leading to the rest of the body (Fig. 9.5(b)). The atrio-ventricular valves prevent blood flowing back into the atria when the ventricles contract. When the ventricles relax, pulmonary and aortic semi-lunar valves prevent blood flowing back into the ventricles. The valves of the heart are non-muscular structures. They respond passively to blood pressure changes brought about by contraction and relaxation of the heart's chambers (Fig. 9.6).

FIG. 9.5 (a) *The cardiac cycle begins with the cardiac impulse passing through the atria. Atrial constriction forces blood into the ventricles. The aorta and pulmonary arteries are omitted for clarity*

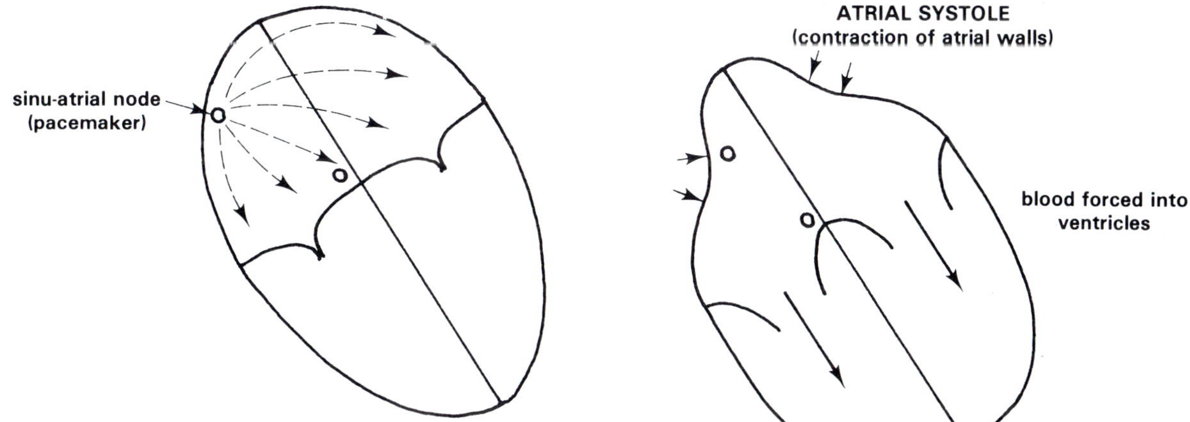

FIG. 9.5 (b) *The cardiac impulse reaches the ventricles along the conductive bundle of His. Ventricular contraction forces blood into the aorta and pulmonary arteries*

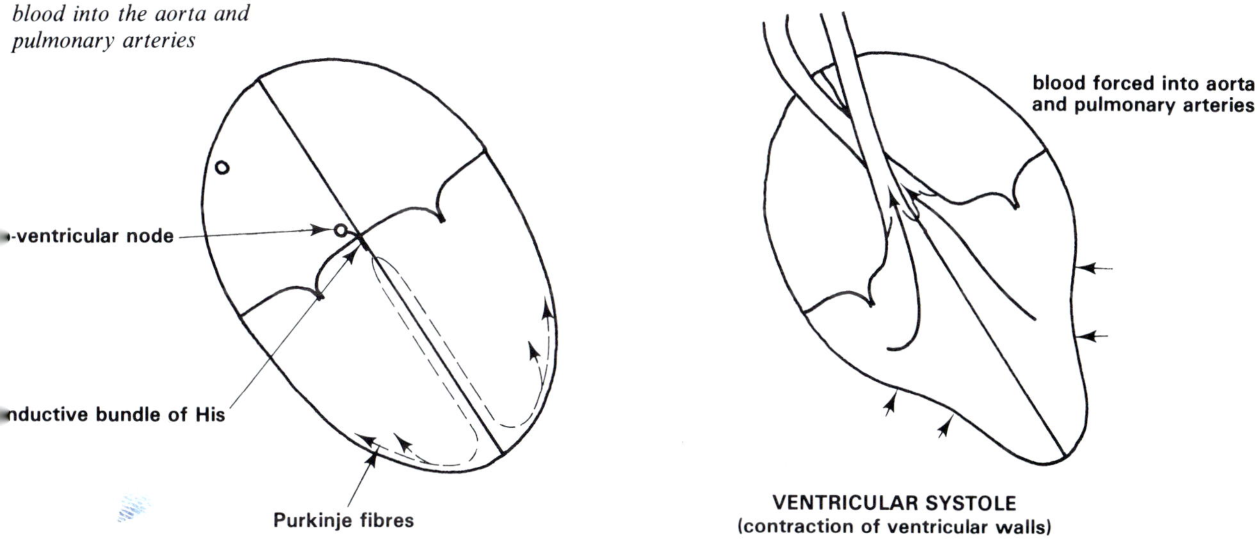

FIG. 9.6 *The passive action of* (a) *the mitral and* (b) *the aortic semi-lunar valves*

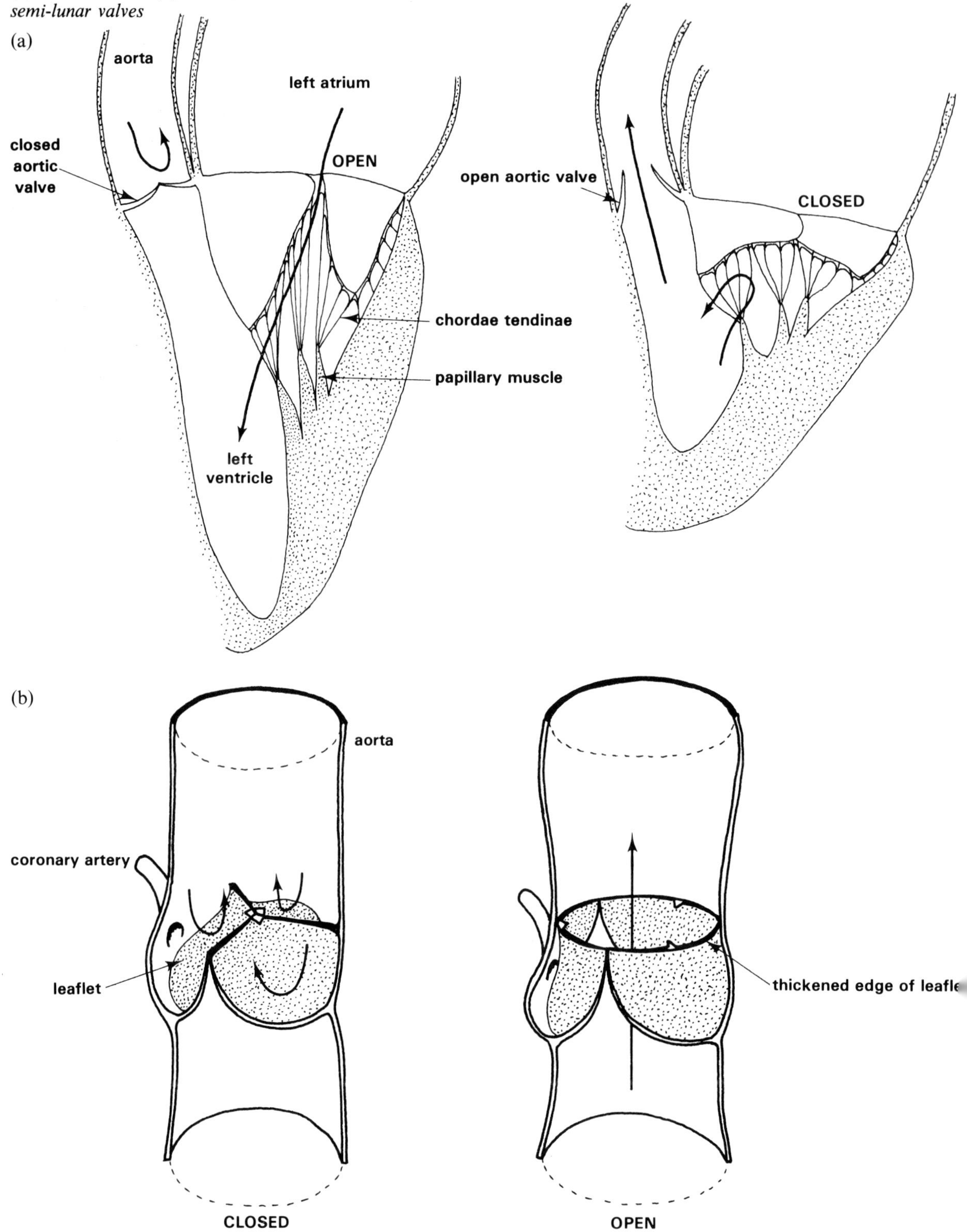

The electrical events which occur during each cardiac cycle can be displayed as an **electrocardiogram (ECG)**. Taking an ECG involves placing metal electrodes at specific sites on the skin. The simplest system uses four electrodes, one on the right wrist, one on the left wrist and one on the left ankle. The fourth electrode is connected from the right ankle to earth so that any electromagnetic disturbances in the room which are picked up by the body do not interfere with the recording (Fig. 9.7(a)).

The cardiac impulse spreads through the heart starting at the pacemaker. Small voltages also spread through the body fluids which, because they contain electrolytes, are electrically conductive. Voltage changes therefore occur at the body surface and correspond to the intensity and direction of the cardiac impulse in the heart. The electrical changes are measured as voltage differences between pairs of electrodes called **leads**. The differences are recorded on moving paper or displayed on an oscilloscope screen (Fig. 9.7(b)). A typical ECG consists of **waves** and **complexes** which correspond to particular cardiac events. The *P*-wave is generated by the cardiac impulse passing over the atria. The *QRS* complex is generated by the passage of the impulse down the bundle of His into the Purkinje network and through the walls of the ventricles. The *T*-wave corresponds to the electrical recovery of the ventricles. Deviations from the normal ECG are readily seen. Certain heart complaints result in typical abnormal wave forms (Fig. 9.7(c)).

FIG. 9.7 (a) *Patient with electrodes in position for the recording of his ECG*

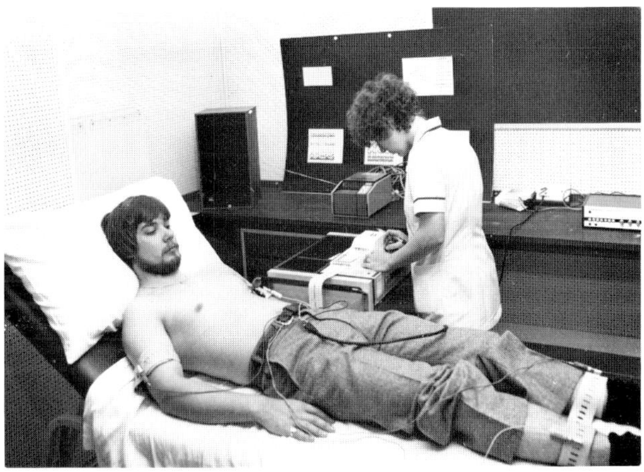

FIG. 9.7 (b) *A typical normal ECG pattern*

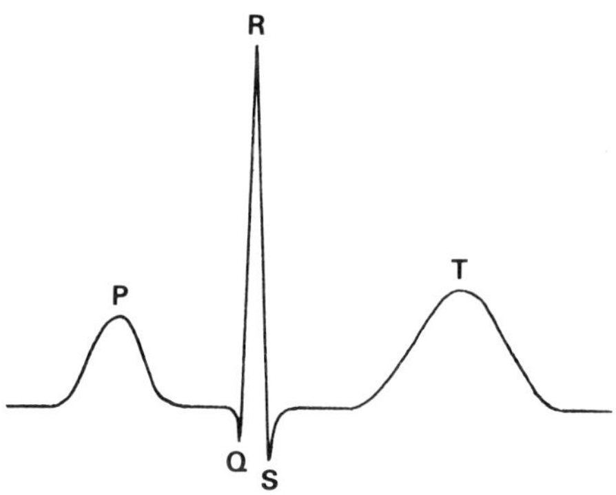

FIG. 9.7 (c) *Some abnormal ECG patterns*

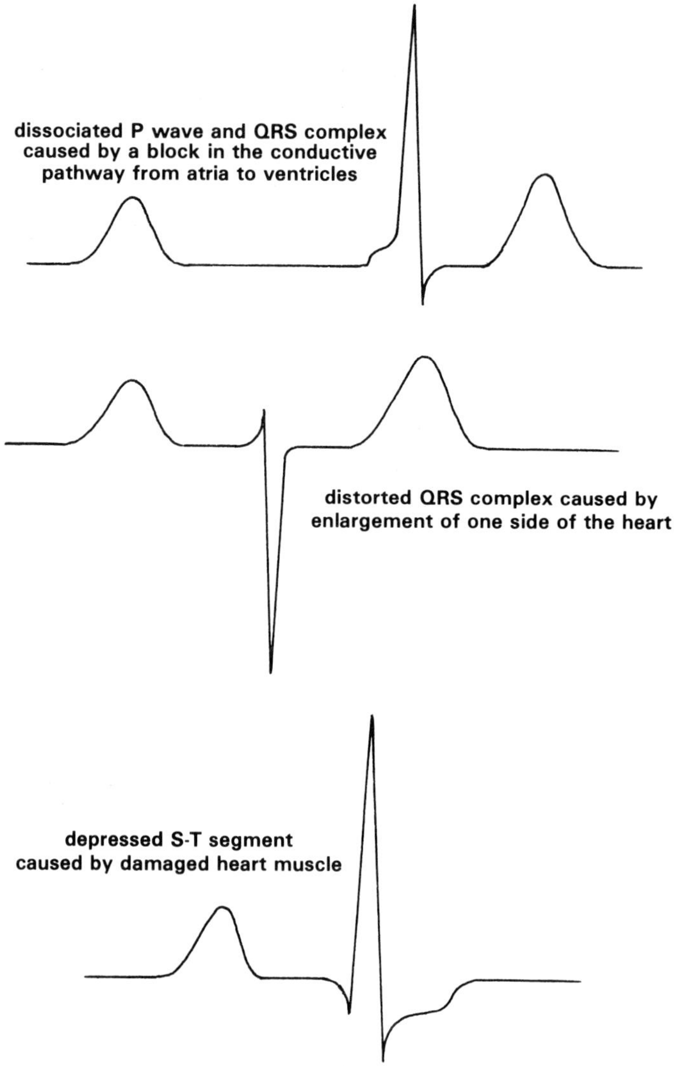

2. PRESSURE CHANGES IN THE HEART

Contraction of the atria, **atrial systole**, increases the pressure of blood in the atria. The rise in pressure forces the atrio-ventricular valves open and blood flows into the ventricles. Movement of blood from atria to ventricles is not entirely due to atrial systole. In a human heart about 70 per cent of the atrial blood is sucked into the ventricles as they relax, **ventricular diastole**, just before the atria contract. When the ventricles contract, **ventricular systole**, the pressure of the blood in the ventricles increases much more than atrial blood pressure. This is because the ventricles, especially the left one, have thicker and more muscular walls. During ventricular contraction blood pressure in man rises from zero to about 16 *k*Pa (120 mm Hg) in the left ventricle and about 3·3 *k*Pa (25 mm Hg) in the right ventricle. Blood enters the ventricles and stops for a moment before it is pumped into the arteries. The pumping action of the ventricles is so strong that it can be felt as the **pulse** in arteries far away from the heart. Although blood enters the arteries in spurts, its flow is continuous. How is this possible?

As the ventricles contract and the semi-lunar valves of the aorta and pulmonary arteries open, blood in the ventricles and arteries is continuous.

The blood pressure in the arteries is now the same as in the ventricles. Blood under pressure thus flows through the arteries causing the arterial walls to bulge. When the ventricles relax the main source of blood pressure is removed and the elastic arterial walls recoil keeping the blood in the arteries under pressure. In this way a continuous flow of blood is maintained. When the ventricular pressure falls to zero between contractions, aortic pressure drops to about 10·7 *k*Pa (80 mm Hg) and pulmonary artery pressure to about 1·1 *k*Pa (8 mm Hg). The term **blood pressure** as it is commonly used, refers to the pressure of blood in the aorta and the main arteries. Blood pressure in the arteries of the arm is often measured using a **sphygmomanometer** (Fig. 9.8).

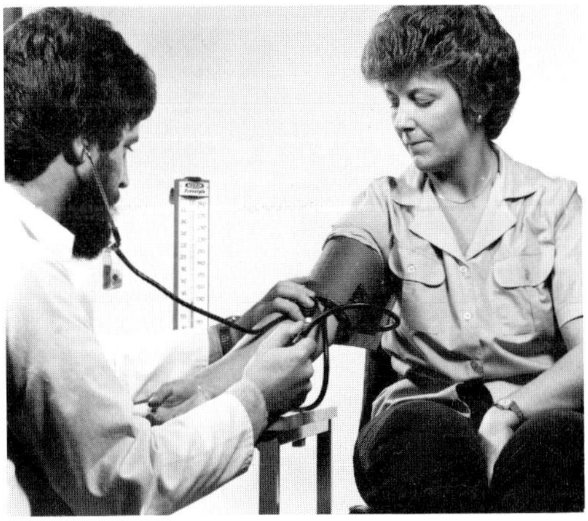

FIG. 9.8 *A sphygmomanometer being used to take the blood pressure of a patient*

3. HEART SOUNDS

As the blood flows through the heart, **heart sounds** are produced as the valves open and close. The sounds can be heard with the aid of a **stethoscope** and are often described by the words **lub** and **dup**. Simultaneous closure of the atrio-ventricular valves when the ventricles contract makes the first sound, lub. The second sound, dup, 0·3 seconds later is caused by the simultaneous closure of the aortic and pulmonary valves. Extra sounds called **murmurs** can be heard if the blood rushes into the ventricles faster than normal, possibly because one of the valves is defective.

When the body is at rest the human heart beats about 70 times a minute and each cardiac cycle lasts for about 0·8 seconds. During the cycle the atria contract for about 0·3 seconds, the ventricles for 0·5 seconds. When we consider that the heart may beat more than 200 times per minute during severe exercise and that it beats without stopping throughout life it is evident that the heart is a remarkably durable and efficient pump.

4. REGULATION OF THE HEART

Cardiac activity is **myogenic**, the contractions initiated by the heart muscle itself. The heart is supplied with nerves of the autonomic system (Chapter 15) which regulate cardiac contraction. Regulation is important since it allows the heart rate and cardiac output to be varied according to the body's metabolic demands especially for oxygen. When the body is active the heart pumps oxygenated blood more rapidly into the circulatory system. Conversely, when the body rests the heart rate and cardiac output fall.

Two **autonomic nerves** are involved in cardiac regulation, the **accelerator nerve** of the sympathetic system and the **vagus nerve** of the parasympathetic system. Each nerve affects the cardiac pacemaker in different ways. Impulses in the sympathetic nerve result in the secretion of small quantities of noradrenalin from the nerve endings onto the cardiac muscle. Noradrenalin is powerful in speeding up cardiac contractions and increases the volume of blood pumped by the heart at each beat. The **stroke volume** is usually about 70 cm^3 per ventricle but may rise to about 150 cm^3 during exercise. Impulses arriving at the parasympathetic nerve endings result in the release of small quantities of acetylcholine on to the cardiac muscle. Acetylcholine has the opposite effect to noradrenalin, reducing heart rate, stroke volume and hence the cardiac output (Fig. 9.9). It is the balance between sympathetic and parasympathetic nervous activity which adjusts the heart rate to meet prevailing physiological demands.

The questions now arise, what controls the autonomic nerves and how does the nervous system monitor the need to increase or decrease cardiac activity?

FIG. 9.9 (a) *The autonomic nerve supply to the cardiac pacemaker* (not drawn to scale) (after Green)

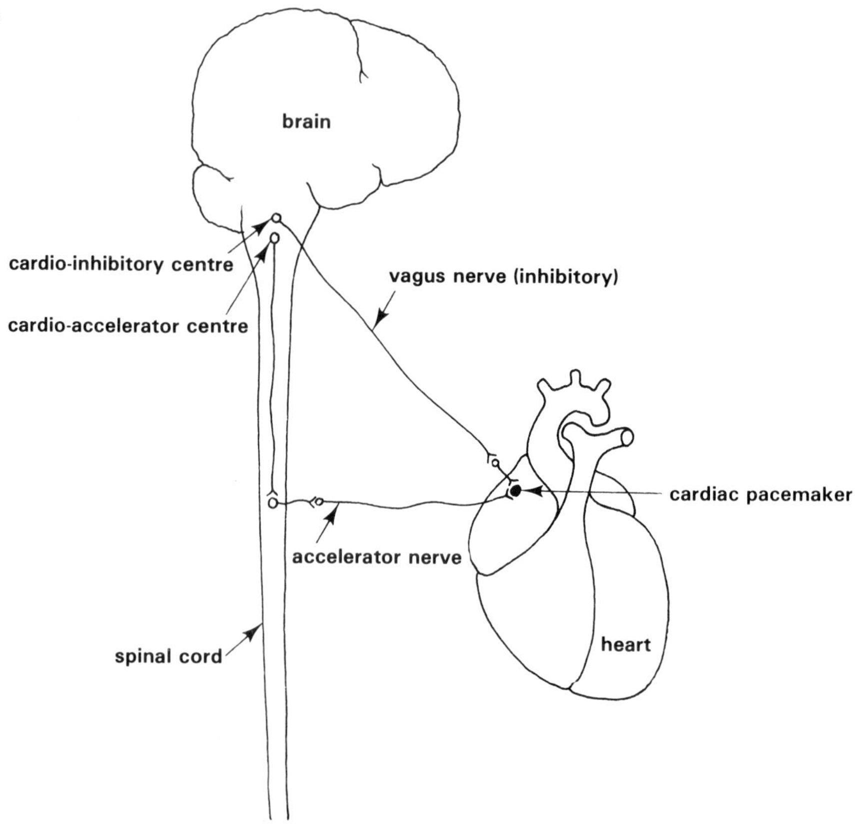

FIG. 9.9 (b) *Results of an experiment similar to that illustrated in Fig. 9.4, showing the effects on heart rate of the addition of adrenalin and acetylcholine*

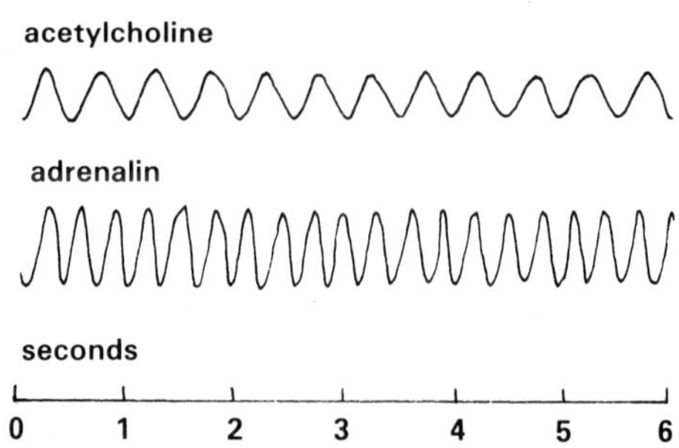

In the medulla oblongata of the brain there is a discrete region called the **cardiac centre** from which the nerves to the heart arise. The cardiac centre is sensitive to the tension of carbon dioxide in the blood which is high when the body is active and low when the body is at rest. In response to blood carbon dioxide tensions, impulses are directed from the cardiac centre along the autonomic nerves to the heart. The nerves regulate heart rate and cardiac output to meet the body's needs. A number of other sensory mechanisms monitor the extent of body activity. They include **chemoreceptors** in the walls of the carotid arteries which are sensitive to the oxygen tension of the blood. The oxygen tension is less when the body is active than when at rest. Near the chemoreceptors are patches of tissue called **baroreceptors** which are sensitive to increased blood pressure, a possible indication of an overactive heart. These sensory devices also help to regulate heart action via the cardiac centre in the brain (Fig. 9.10).

Reference is made in Chapter 8 to comparable mechanisms which control the breathing rate. Changes of breathing rate accompany changes in heart rate and enable efficient oxygenation of the blood as well as its distribution to body organs.

FIG. 9.10 *The main factors controlling the mammalian heart*

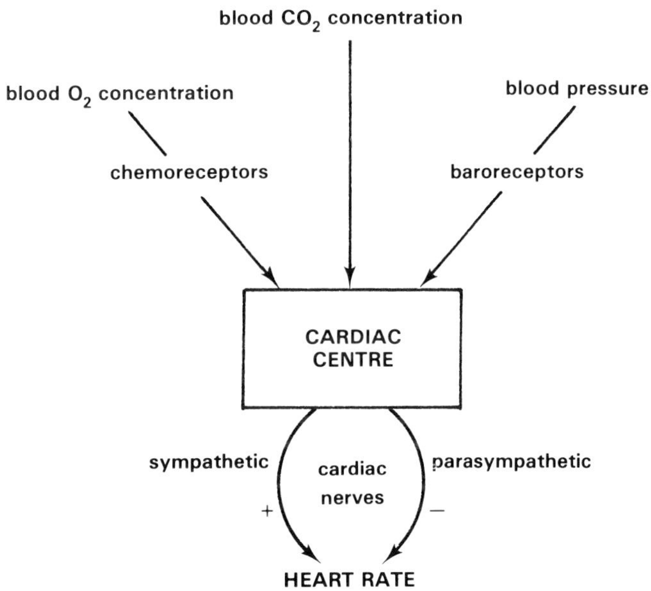

5. VASOMOTOR CONTROL

A further effect of stimulation of the baroreceptors is the transmission of nerve impulses to the **vasomotor centre**. Like the cardiac centre the vasomotor centre is found in the medulla oblongata of the brain. Sympathetic nerves originating in the centre lead to arterioles. By secreting noradrenalin from their endings the nerves bring about contraction of the smooth muscle in the walls of arterioles. As the muscle is arranged in a circular fashion its contraction results in narrowing of the arterioles called **vasoconstriction**. Conversely, decreased sympathetic activity from the vasomotor centre results in **vasodilation** (Fig. 9.11).

High blood pressure stimulates the baroreceptors which depress sympathetic output from the vasomotor centre. The resulting vasodilation lowers the blood pressure, an appropriate response to high blood pressure. Low blood pressure has the opposite effect (Fig. 9.12).

FIG. 9.11 *Photomicrographs of (a) dilated and (b) constricted arterioles seen in transverse section, × 400 and 270 respectively*

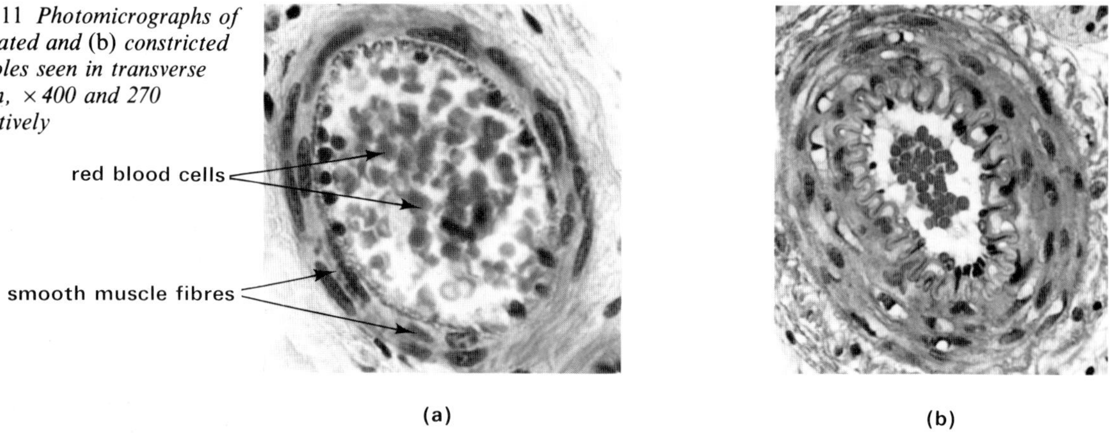

FIG. 9.12 *The main factors controlling mammalian blood pressure*

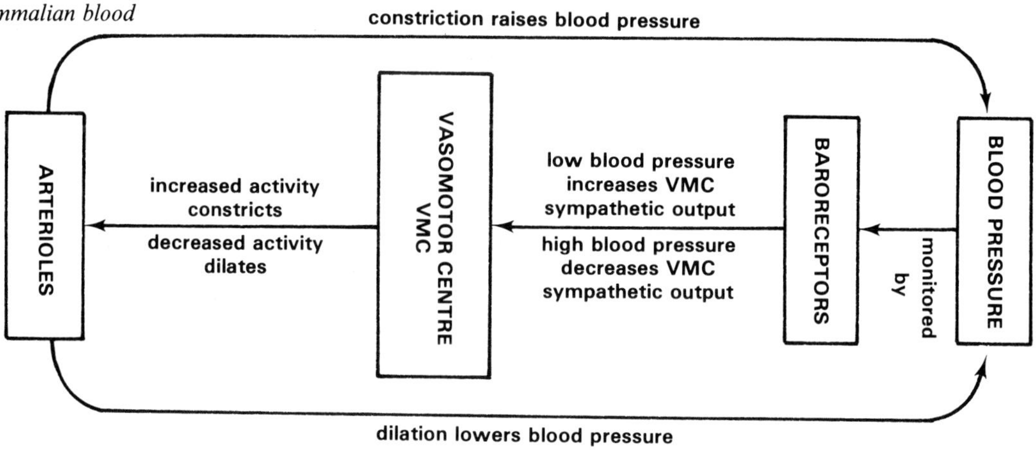

FIG. 9.13 *The control of breathing, heart rate and blood pressure in mammals*

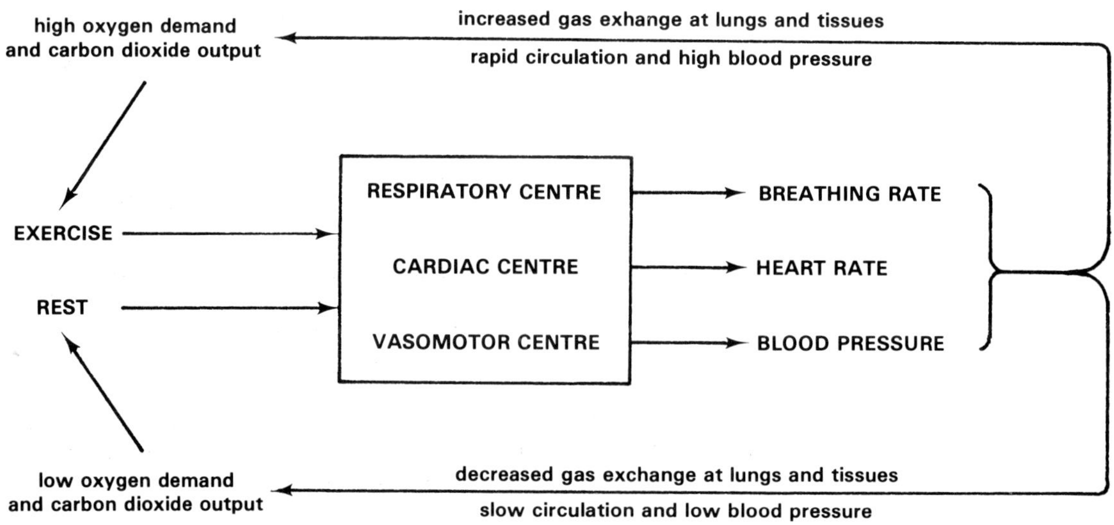

As with the cardiac and respiratory centres, the vasomotor centre is stimulated by changes in the tensions of oxygen and carbon dioxide in the blood. Generally all three centres respond to the same physiological stimuli (Fig. 9.13). Similar responses can be produced by secretions from the adrenal glands (Chapter 18).

9.1.2 Exchange of materials between blood and tissues

A major function of the circulatory system in mammals is to transport metabolites and wastes to and from the organs. Interchange of materials between blood and tissues occurs through the walls of numerous microscopic capillaries (Fig. 9.14). Each organ receives sufficient metabolites from the blood but not so much as to deprive other organs of vital materials. The means of controlling the release of oxygen from haemoglobin in the red blood cells is described in Chapter 8. Interchange of other substances is brought about by the interaction of two forces. The pumping action of the heart squeezes blood against the walls of the blood vessels, creating an outward-acting force called **hydrostatic pressure**. Counter to this is the attraction of certain blood constituents for water, the **colloid osmotic potential** of the blood. This is caused mainly by the plasma proteins which have a large relative molar mass.

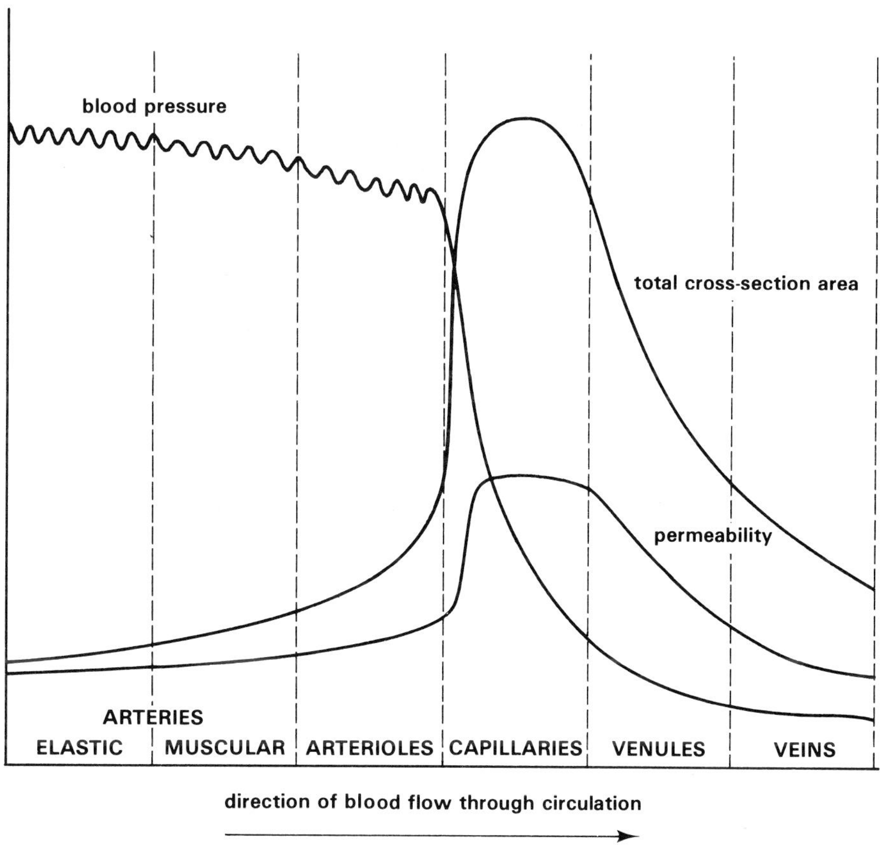

FIG. 9.14 (a) *Some characteristics of different blood vessels. Note that the capillaries have the greatest cross-section area and the most permeable walls. Nearly all the interchange between the blood and the tissues occurs in the capillaries*

The hydrostatic pressure of the blood entering capillaries is normally about 4·4 *k*Pa (32 mm Hg). Since the colloid osmotic potential is normally about −3·6 *k*Pa (−27 mm Hg), a **filtration pressure** of −3·6 + 4·4 *k*Pa = 0·8 *k*Pa (5 mm Hg) exists. Consequently, any constituents of the blood to which the capillary walls are permeable leave the vessels. They include all substances of small relative molar mass such as water, oxygen, glucose, amino acids, fatty acids, hormones and inorganic ions. The fluid so formed is called **tissue fluid**. Proteins of high relative molar mass and blood cells remain in the capillaries. Because of the reduction in blood volume the hydrostatic pressure in the capillaries drops (Fig. 9.14). A point is eventually reached at which the filtration pressure controlling the movement of fluid between the blood and the tissues is negative. Consequently, water containing dissolved metabolic wastes such as carbon dioxide and metabolites in excess of the tissues' needs is absorbed back into the blood. The process is illustrated by Figure 9.15.

FIG. 9.14 (b) *Photomicrograph of an artery and vein seen in transverse section, ×25*

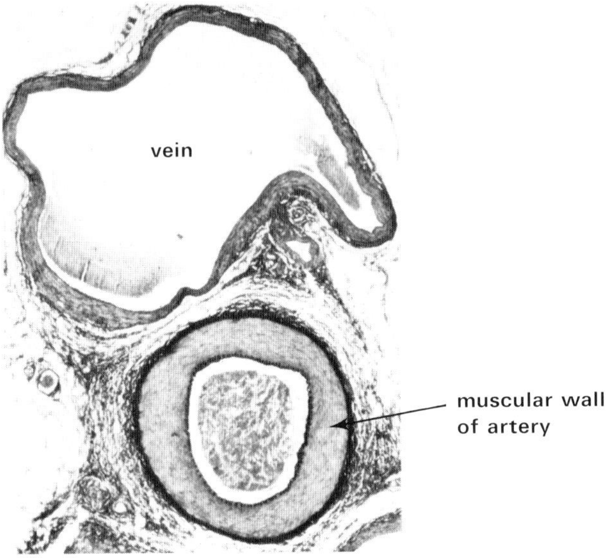

FIG. 9.14 (c) *Electronmicrograph showing a blood capillary in transverse section, ×6000*

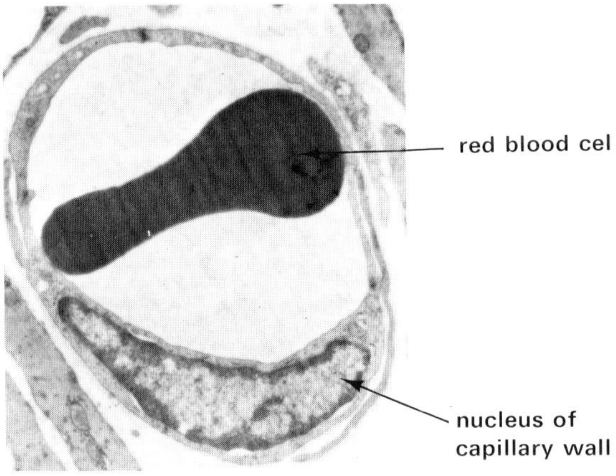

FIG. 9.15 *Diagrammatic interchange of metabolites between the capillary blood and tissue fluid*

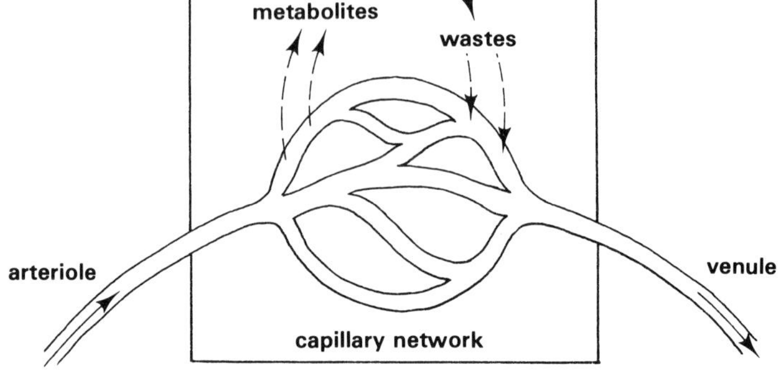

9.1.3 Lymph formation and circulation

FIG. 9.16 *The main vessels of the human lymphatic system. Those of the left limbs are omitted for clarity*

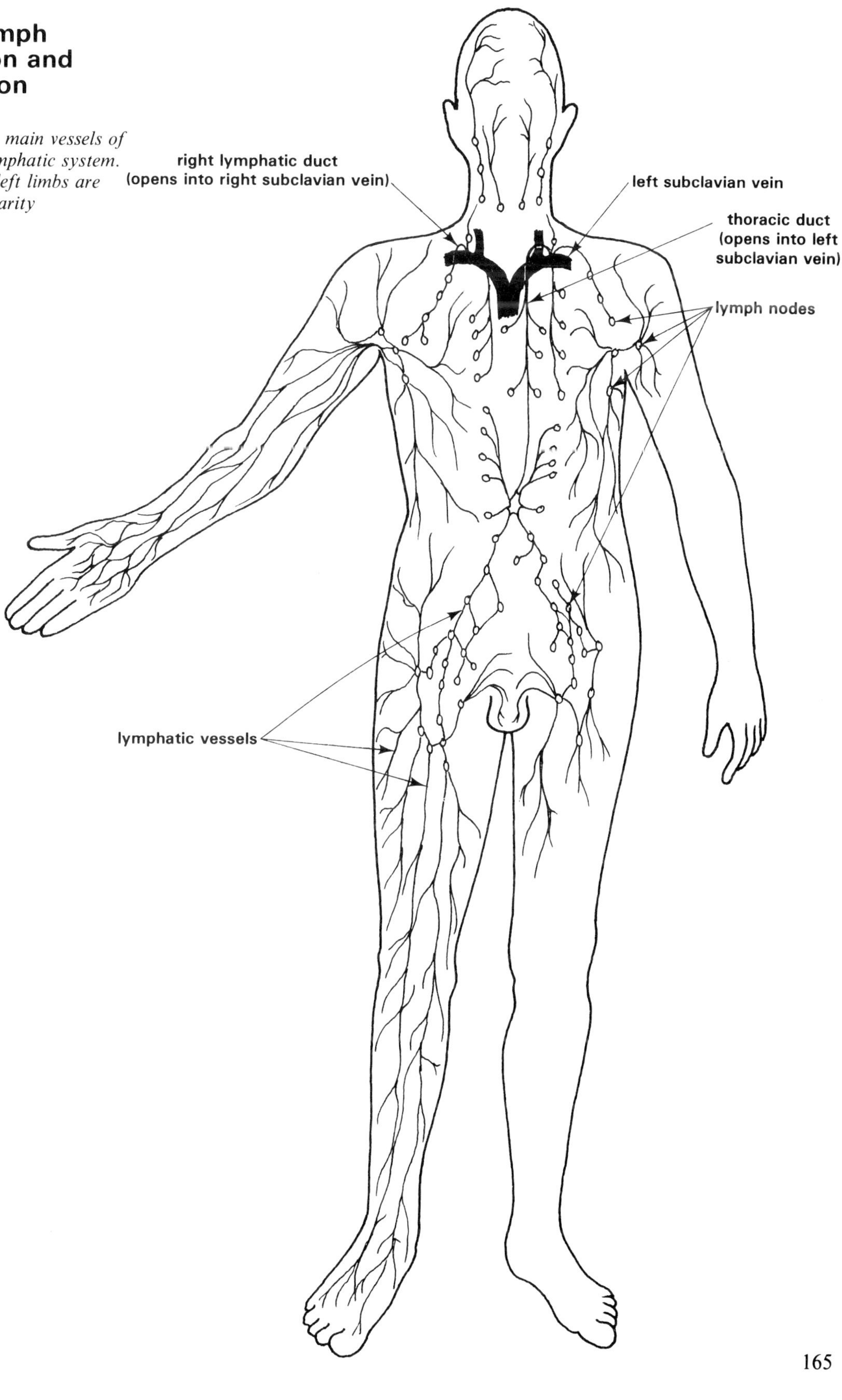

During the formation of tissue fluid a small proportion of plasma proteins leaves the blood and enters the tissue fluid. These are plasma proteins of small relative molar mass. Any fluid not reabsorbed by the blood capillaries enters another set of vessels called the **lymphatic capillaries** which are similar to blood capillaries and have selectively permeable walls. They drain all the tissues of the body into an extensive system of larger **lymphatic vessels** (Fig. 9.16). One of the main functions of the lymphatic system is to remove materials that might otherwise accumulate in the tissues and impair normal function. For example, accumulation of water in the tissue fluid creates a swollen condition called **oedema**. The delivery of metabolites from the blood to oedematous tissues is impaired as the materials have to diffuse greater distances to reach the cells.

The fluid collected by the lymphatic system is called **lymph**. In the average healthy human body 100 cm^3 of lymph are formed in an hour. The lymphatic vessels return lymph to the blood through ducts joining the left and right subclavian veins (Figs. 9.16 and 9.17). The lymphatic system does more than this, however. On its passage through the lymphatic vessels, lymph enters numerous **lymph nodes**. The nodes contain stationary phagocytes which engulf small particles, micro-organisms and toxins in the lymph. The possible harmful effects of such materials are thus neutralised (Fig. 9.17). The roles of the lymph nodes in antibody production are described in section 9.2.4.

FIG. 9.17 *Diagrammatic relationship between the blood vascular and lymphatic systems*

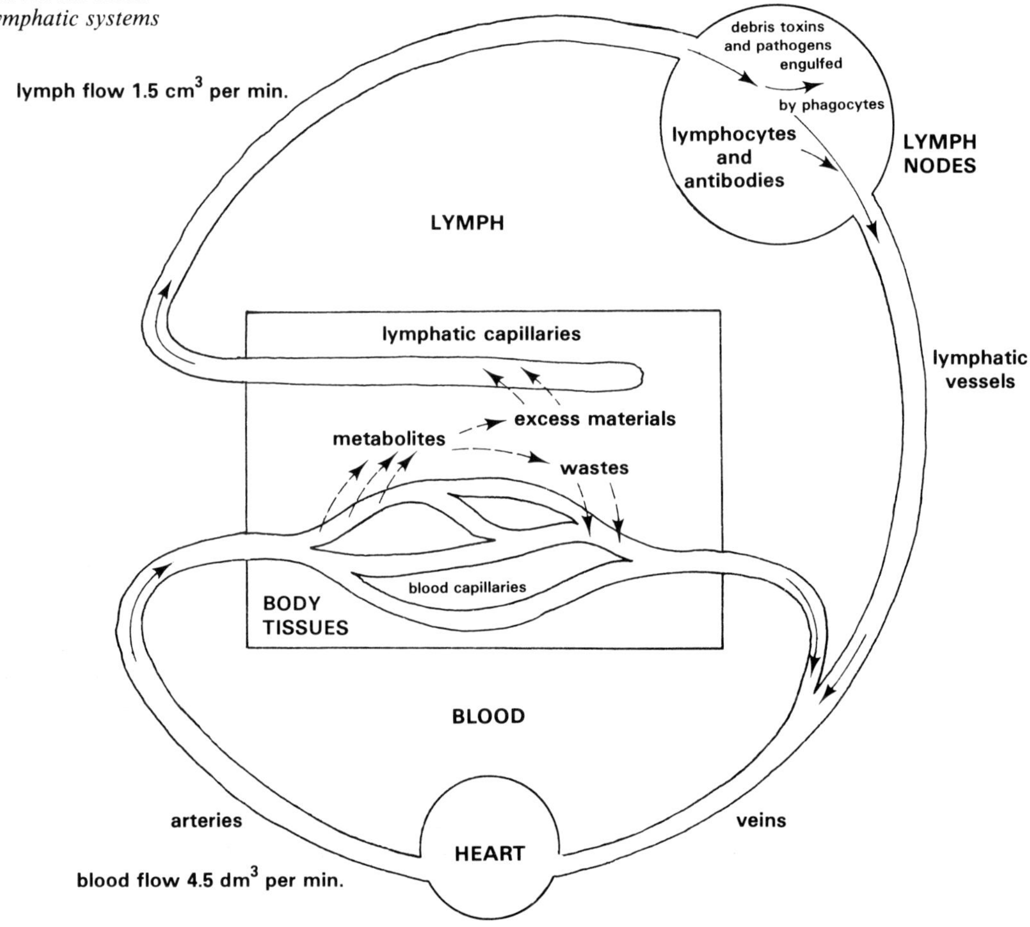

9.1.4 Circulation in the mammalian foetus

The mammalian foetus obtains its oxygen and nutrients from the **placenta** in the mother's uterus (Chapter 22). The placenta also removes wastes from the foetal blood. Maternal and foetal blood vessels come into close proximity to one another in the placenta (Fig. 9.18). The two-way exchange occurs mainly by diffusion. Thus the functions of the foetal lungs, kidneys and gut are performed by the placenta.

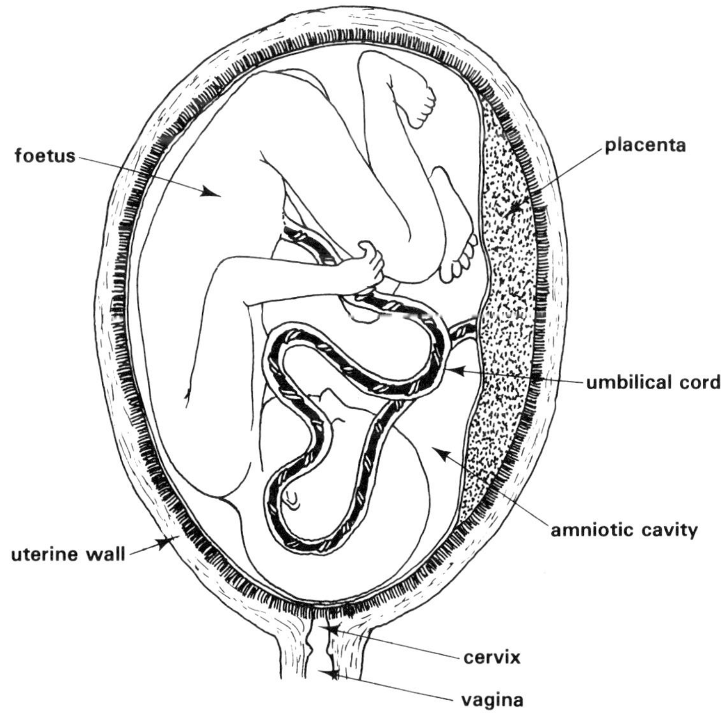

FIG. 9.18 *Human foetus and placenta inside the uterus*

The pattern of circulation in the foetal body is different from that of an adult. Figure 9.19 illustrates the circulatory system of a human foetus. Compare it with Figure 9.1. An obvious difference between the foetal and adult circulation is the presence of **umbilical blood vessels** in the foetus which carry foetal blood to and from the placenta. The umbilical vessels are found in the umbilical cord. The other main differences are concerned with the transfer of the functions of the foetal lungs to the placenta. The pulmonary circulation in the foetus is almost completely by-passed due to a **ductus arteriosus** between the pulmonary arteries and the aorta, and a hole called the **foramen ovale** between the right and left atria. Such an arrangement involves mixing of oxygenated blood from the placenta and deoxygenated blood from the foetal tissues in the posterior vena cava and in the heart. The relative loss of efficiency in the transport of oxygen is compensated for by the presence of **foetal haemoglobin** which combines more readily with oxygen than does adult haemoglobin (Chapter 8). Further, the heart of the foetus does not pump blood to its unaerated lungs so energy is saved. The **ductus venosus** directs blood from the placenta and the foetal gut to the posterior vena cava, thus by-passing the foetal liver. Since most of the functions of the foetal liver are performed by the mother's liver, a supply of blood to the liver of the foetus is less important. The foetal liver is, however, the only source of foetal blood cells.

Shortly after birth the ductus venosus, ductus arteriosus and foramen ovale normally close. Failure to do so is the cause of severe circulatory problems some of which can be corrected by surgery.

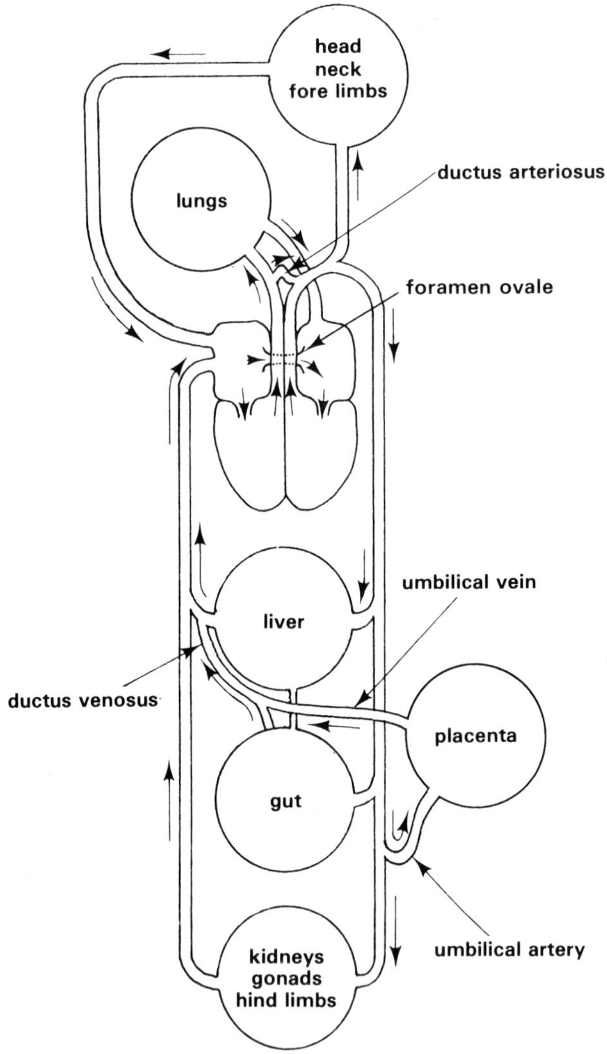

FIG. 9.19 *Diagram of the blood circulation of the mammalian foetus*

Table 9.2 Summary of the numbers and functions of human blood cells

CELL TYPE	AVERAGE NUMBERS × 10^9 PER dm^3 ADULT HUMAN BLOOD	FUNCTIONS
erythrocytes	3900–6500	oxygen carriage
neutrophils	2·50–7·50	phagocytosis
eosinophils	0·04–0·44	reduce inflammation; dissolve clots
basophils	0–0·10	unknown
monocytes	0·20–0·80	phagocytosis
lymphocytes	1·50–3·50	antibody production
thrombocytes	150–400	coagulation

9.2 Blood cells

Under the microscope **blood cells** are seen to be of several types. They make up about half the volume of mammalian blood (Table 9.2 and Fig. 9.20).

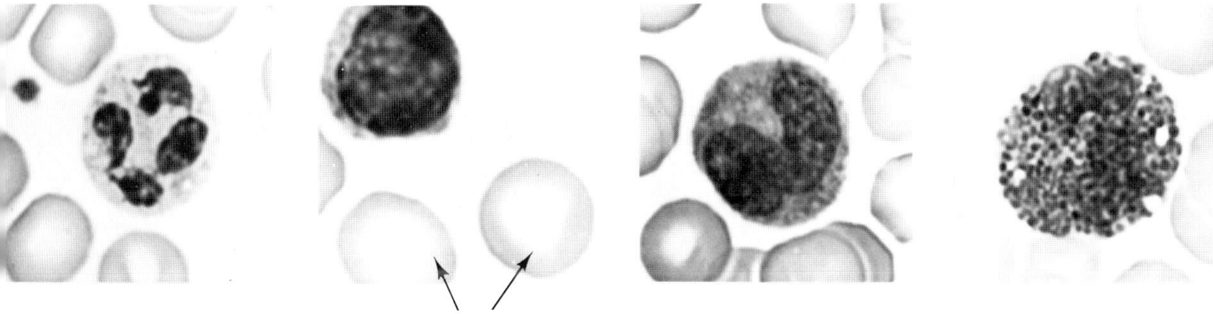

FIG. 9.20 *Photomicrograph of a smear of human blood showing* (a) *a neutrophil,* (b) *a lymphocyte,* (c) *a monocyte, and* (d) *an eosinophil, all* × *1500*

9.2.1 Erythrocytes

By far the most numerous of the blood cells are the red cells, **erythrocytes**. Their colour comes from the respiratory pigment **haemoglobin** which they contain. Human erythrocytes each contain about 30 pg of haemoglobin. Erythrocytes occupy between 40 and 60 per cent of the total blood volume in different mammals and their main function is to carry oxygen. Mammalian erythrocytes are biconcave discs and have a great surface area in relation to their volume. They are thus ideally shaped for the uptake of oxygen when in the pulmonary capillaries (Fig. 9.21). The function of haemoglobin in this respect is described in Chapter 8.

FIG. 9.21 *Scanning electronmicrograph of some human red blood cells,* × *1700*

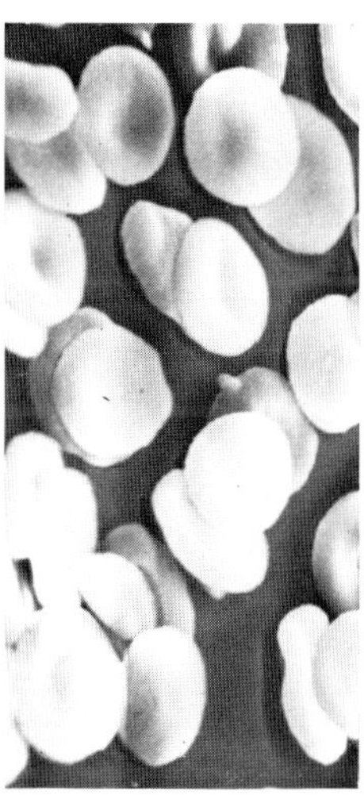

The absence of a nucleus in erythrocytes provides extra space for haemoglobin. The anucleate condition does have its disadvantages, however. In particular, erythrocytes have only a relatively short lifetime. Erythrocytes in man survive for about four months and have to be replaced continuously to keep a constant number in circulation. It is estimated that human erythrocytes are made at a rate of about 9000 million per hour. Erythrocyte production, **erythropoiesis**, occurs in the liver in the foetus but in adult life is restricted to the red marrow of certain bones. They include the cranium, vertebrae, ribs, sternum, parts of the pelvic girdle and some limb bones. Old erythrocytes are engulfed by phagocytic cells in the liver, spleen and red bone marrow. The haemoglobin is broken down and the iron it contains is retained for further haemoglobin synthesis. The rest of the pigment is excreted from the liver in bile (Chapter 14).

Impairment of the oxygen-carrying capacity of the blood is called **anaemia**. Anaemia can be caused by physical blood loss, **haemorrhage**, or functional blood loss, **haemolysis**. In haemolysis, erythrocytes are destroyed in the blood vessels and the haemoglobin is broken down in the blood plasma. Decreased blood production is another cause of anaemia. Anaemias in this category result from inadequate production of erythrocytes and haemoglobin in the bone marrow. **Impaired erythropoiesis** is often caused by deficiency of a vital nutrient in the diet. Iron deficiency is the commonest cause of human anaemia in the world today. Vitamin B_{12} is necessary for erythropoiesis. Absorption of vitamin B_{12} from the gut depends on the presence of a substance called intrinsic factor (IF) which is secreted in gastric juice (Chapter 14). Absence of IF leads to poor absorption of vitamin B_{12} and is the cause of **pernicious anaemia**. Production of abnormal haemoglobin is the cause of **sickle cell anaemia** (Chapters 6 and 8).

9.2.2 Leucocytes

FIG. 9.22 (a) *A neutrophil engulfing a chain of bacteria by phagocytosis*

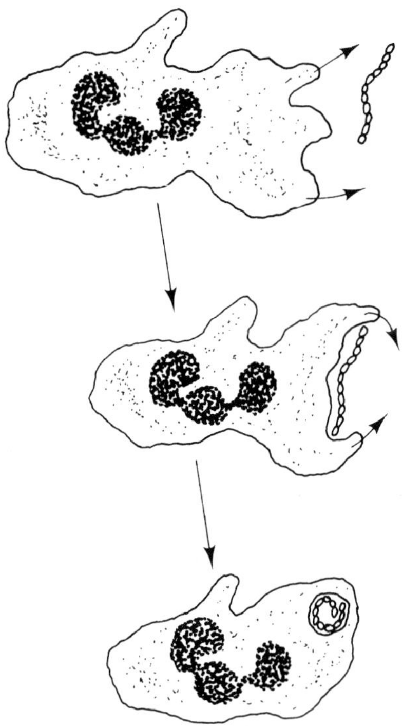

Far less numerous, but no less important than the erythrocytes are the white blood cells collectively called **leucocytes**. They include **neutrophils**, **lymphocytes**, **monocytes**, **eosinophils** and **basophils**. They are involved in defending the body against disease. The lymphocytes (section 9.2.4) are produced in lymphoid tissues, mainly the lymph nodes. Other leucocytes are made in the bone marrow. Leucocytes have a limited life time in the circulation and old leucocytes are disposed of by phagocytes in the liver and spleen.

Neutrophils and monocytes exhibit amoeboid movement. By extending pseudopodia they can encircle and engulf bacteria and other particles, a process called **phagocytosis** (Fig. 9.22). The phagocytic behaviour of living neutrophils can be observed microscopically and recorded by time-lapse photomicrography. Studies of this sort show that neutrophils can locate bacteria at a distance and actively seek them out for phagocytosis. This response is called **chemotaxis** and seems to be triggered off by chemicals released by the bacteria. Engulfed bacteria are taken into large food vacuoles where secretions of the leucocytes' lysosomes kill the bacteria after several minutes. When the bacteria are dead they are discharged from the trailing ends of leucocytes by reverse phagocytosis. Phagocytosis of some strains of virulent bacteria requires the presence of antibodies (section 9.2.4).

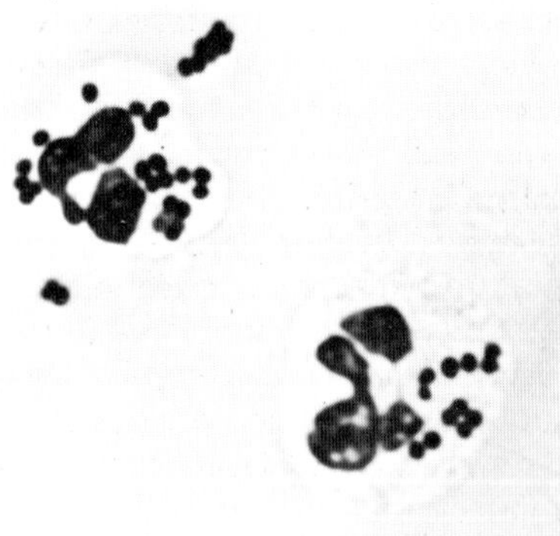

FIG. 9.22 (b) *Photomicrograph showing human neutrophils containing phagocytised bacteria, × 1400*

The numbers of phagocytes in the blood often increase in response to bacterial infection. Phagocytes can move in and out of blood capillaries by squeezing between the cells of capillary walls. They appear rapidly at sites of localised infection. As well as mobile phagocytes there are many fixed phagocytic cells in the mammalian body. Patches of fixed phagocytes are found in the lymph nodes, gut wall, alveoli, liver, spleen and red bone marrow. Fixed phagocytes form the **reticulo-endothelial system** which removes particulate debris including old blood cells from the blood and lymph.

Phagocytosis is thus a widespread and important means of neutralising infective agents and removing particulate debris generally from the body fluids.

9.2.3 Thrombocytes and coagulation

As well as erythrocytes and leucocytes, mammalian blood contains numerous anucleate cellular fragments called **thrombocytes** (platelets). Human blood contains between 150 and 400 thousand thrombocytes per mm^3. They originate in the red bone marrow from large cells called **megakaryocytes** from which the thrombocytes are budded off as fragments of cytoplasm (Fig. 9.23).

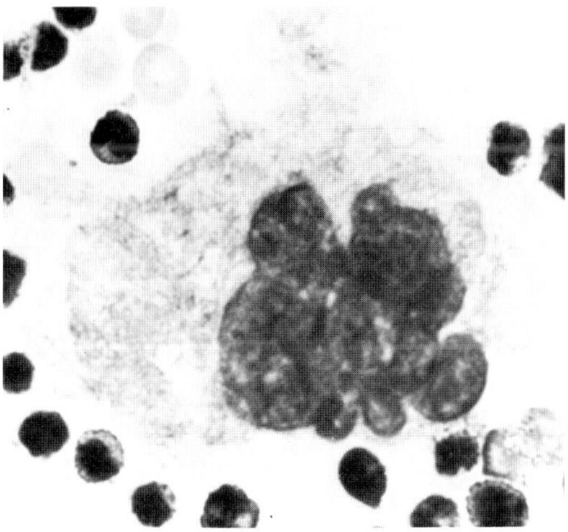

(a)

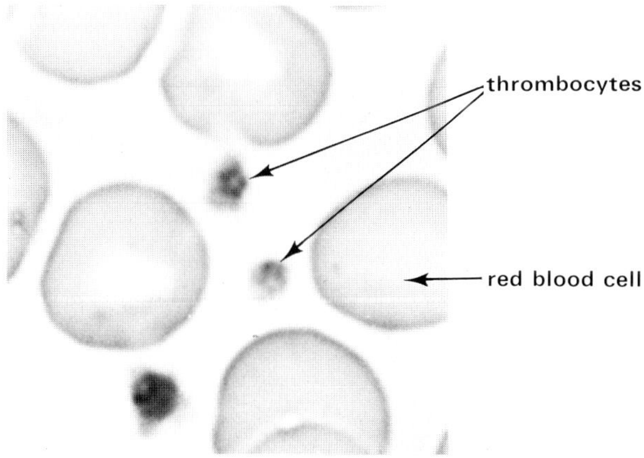

(b)

FIG. 9.23 *Photomicrographs showing* (a) *a megakaryocyte in a bone marrow smear from a guinea-pig, × 750,* (b) *a smear of human blood with thrombocytes (platelets), × 1500*

Thrombocytes are involved in the **coagulation** of blood, a response to injury which prevents excessive blood loss. Coagulation is a complex sequence of chemical reactions which results in the deposition of insoluble fibrous proteins to form a **clot**. It is the clot which blocks damaged blood vessels and may stop bleeding. Thrombocytes stick to the surfaces of damaged vessels. Healthy blood vessels secrete into the blood a substance called **prostacyclin**. Prostacyclin prevents thrombocytes from sticking together and to the walls of blood vessels. In the absence of prostacyclin, however, agglutination of thrombocytes occurs. They then burst releasing thrombocyte factors into the plasma. The **thrombocyte factors** react with other **blood factors** in plasma to produce **thromboplastin**. Thromboplastin can also be produced when certain **tissue factors** react with the blood factors, a reaction which occurs for example when blood vessels are injured.

The next stage of coagulation is the conversion of **prothrombin**, a plasma protein, into an active enzyme called **thrombin**. Thromboplastin activates the conversion which requires the presence of calcium(II) ions, a normal constituent of plasma. The final stage is the conversion by thrombin of the soluble plasma protein **fibrinogen**, into insoluble **fibrin**. The entire clotting mechanism is summarised in Figure 9.24. Fibrin is a fibrous protein which precipitates as strands around the thrombocytes and damaged edges of the vessel. The meshwork of fibrin traps blood cells which increase the size of the clot, eventually sealing off the damaged vessel (Fig. 9.25). Burst thrombocytes also release a substance called **serotonin**. Serotonin causes vasoconstriction which may be enough to stop blood loss from damaged capillaries.

Important though coagulation is it is equally important that coagulation is restricted to sites of injury. A complex set of factors exists in mammalian blood to ensure that this normally happens. Fibrin inhibits excessive conversion of fibrinogen by negative feedback:

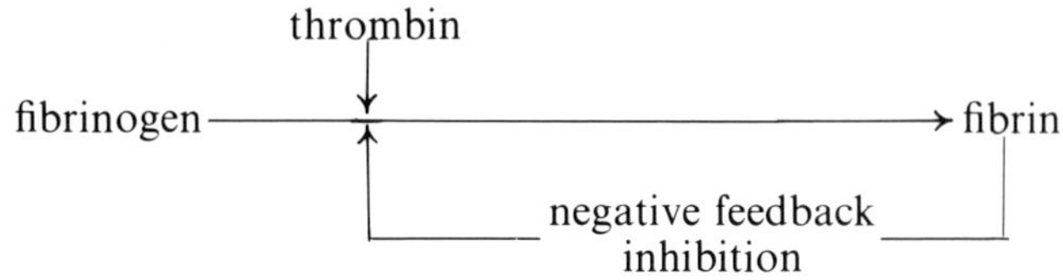

FIG. 9.24 *Summary of the coagulation mechanism*

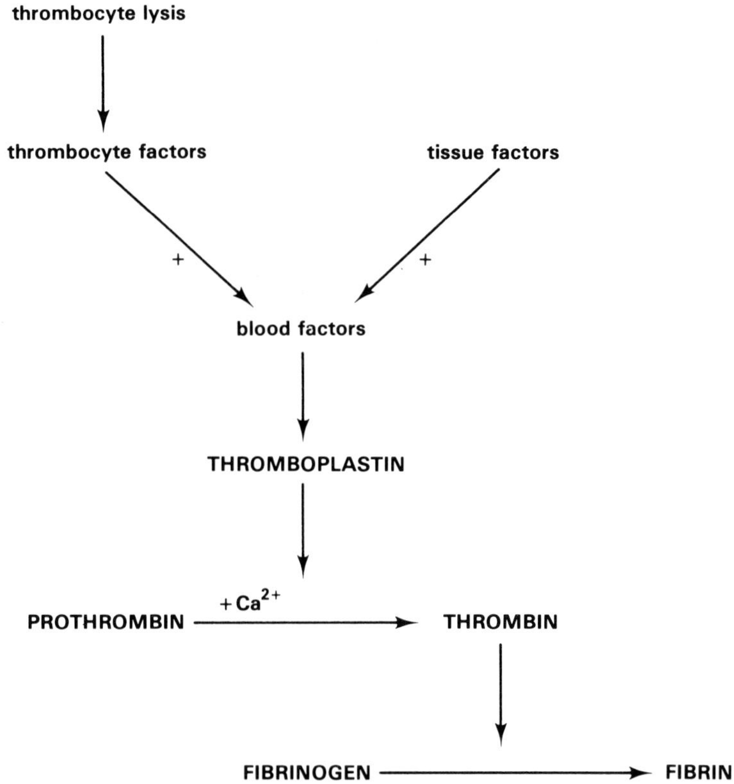

Enzymes capable of dissolving fibrin are carried in blood. The granules of eosinophils contain an inactive precursor called **profibrinolysin**. At sites of fibrin deposition profibrinolysin released by eosinophils is converted to **fibrinolysin** which helps to dissolve a clot after it has done its job.

The inner surfaces of blood vessels can become damaged, sometimes because of deposition of fatty substances particularly cholesterol. Deposits of this kind prevent secretion of prostacyclin and can trigger off coagulation, resulting in the formation of a clot inside the vessel. The clot is called an **intravascular thrombus**. Such a condition, commonly called **thrombosis**, can be very dangerous. For example, a thrombus in an artery feeding a vital organ such as the heart, can cause a sudden and fatal stoppage of blood to the organ. Coronary thrombosis accounts for a large number of deaths in industrialised countries. High-fat diets, sedentary jobs and tobacco smoking have been suggested as possible causes. An intravascular thrombus can occur in other vessels in the body such as a leg vein. If dislodged by the blood flow the thrombus is carried in the blood stream as an **embolus** which may eventually come to rest in the arteries of a vital organ. An embolus could for example be taken to the pulmonary arteries causing a **pulmonary embolism** which can cause death. The treatment of thrombosis and embolism involves administration of various anticoagulants such as warfarin which prevents coagulation by blocking the production of prothrombin in the liver. Other anticoagulants are used to dissolve the clot.

Evidently, normal coagulation depends on the delicate balance of many factors.

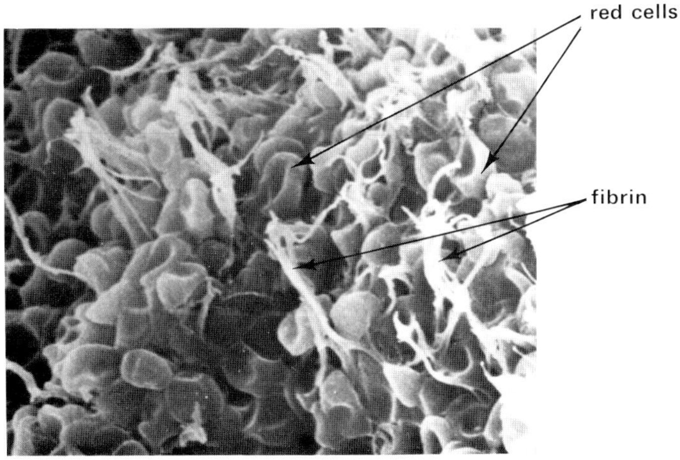

FIG. 9.25 *Scanning electronmicrograph showing some of the components of a blood clot, × 1000*

9.2.4 Lymphocytes and antibodies

The term **immunity** generally means the ability to resist disease.

1. INNATE IMMUNITY

All mammals have **innate immunity** because of:

(i) The **skin's resistance** to penetration by micro-organisms.

(ii) **Enzymatic destruction** in the stomach of most micro-organisms ingested with food. **Muramidase**, a powerful enzyme found in tears, can bring about lysis of bacteria.

(iii) The **acid environment** of the stomach and vagina inhibit the growth of most micro-organisms.

(iv) The **phagocytic activities** of neutrophils, monocytes and the reticulo-endothelial system.

(v) The action of certain chemicals produced in the body in response to microbial infection. For example, **interferon** is secreted by most mammalian tissues when they are attacked by viruses. Interferon is effective against many different viruses and it once looked like providing a major breakthrough in the medical treatment of viral diseases. Unfortunately interferon is species-specific. Mouse interferon works well in mice, but only human interferon is effective in man. Consequently it is difficult to obtain sufficient quantities of interferon for treating human diseases caused by viruses. Early experiments testing its use against diseases such as the common cold gave inconclusive results.

(vi) The **stickiness of mucus** which traps micro-organisms. Mucus is constantly produced by the linings of the respiratory and alimentary systems.

2. ADAPTIVE IMMUNITY

The means of protection outlined above are all general barriers to infection. Acquired or **adaptive immunity** is much more specific. It involves the production of specific **antibodies** directed against particular microbes or their toxins. Antibodies are produced by lymphoid tissue, as a direct response to the presence in the body of substances which are recognised as foreign or **non-self**. Such substances are called **antigens**. Antigens are mostly proteins, a few are carbohydrates, and are present on micro-organisms, transfused blood cells and transplanted organs. Antibodies are proteins of a specific kind (Fig. 9.26) which can locate and neutralise or destroy the antigens which triggered their production. Normally the immune system can recognise the constituents of its own body. It does not normally produce antibodies against **self** (section 9.6). However, in **autoimmune diseases** self-recognition fails. The body then makes antibodies against its own tissues. Rheumatic fever and some forms of diabetes mellitus are diseases of this kind.

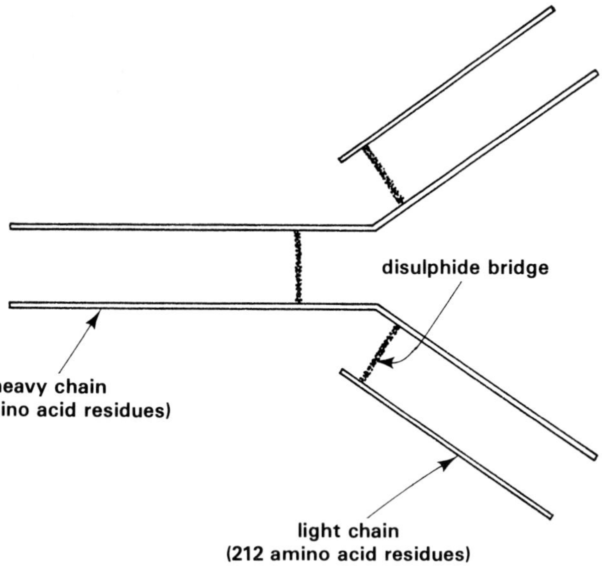

FIG. 9.26 *Diagrammatic structure of an immunoglobulin called IgG. It consists of two long (heavy) and two short (light) polypeptide chains joined by disulphide bridges. The sites for reaction with appropriate antigen are on the right where the molecule appears to gape open. The projection on the left may fix with complement*

Since the Second World War immunology has been an expanding science and is the focus of much research at the present time. Many theories of antibody action have been put forward and much is still not understood. Experiments indicate that as a result of stimulation by antigens, antibodies are made by lymphocytes in the lymph nodes. Antibodies enter the blood and are carried to sites of infection either in the plasma (**humoral immunity**) or on special lymphocytes (**cellular immunity**).

(i) **Humoral immunity**. On coming into contact with specific antigens, **B-lymphocytes** in the lymph nodes divide many times to produce a group of large **plasma cells**. The B-lymphocytes which react in this way are said to be **committed**. Plasma cells make the antibodies which are released into the lymph and eventually enter the blood. In the blood the antibodies form the γ-globulin (immunoglobulin) fraction of the plasma proteins (Fig. 9.27). Small numbers of committed B-lymphocytes remain in the lymph nodes for years, even after the antibodies have done their work and eliminated the original infection. This provides a very rapid response to any subsequent invasion by similar antigens.

(ii) **Cellular immunity**. In the lymph nodes other lymphocytes, called **T-lymphocytes**, may also be **sensitised** by antigens and become committed to produce specific antibodies. The antibodies remain attached to the T-lymphocytes which then enter the blood. About 80 per cent of the total lymphocyte population of human blood is of the T-variety. As in humoral immunity, a few committed T-lymphocytes remain in the lymph nodes and can respond to future invasion by similar antigens. Cellular immunity can be effective for the entire life-time of an organism.

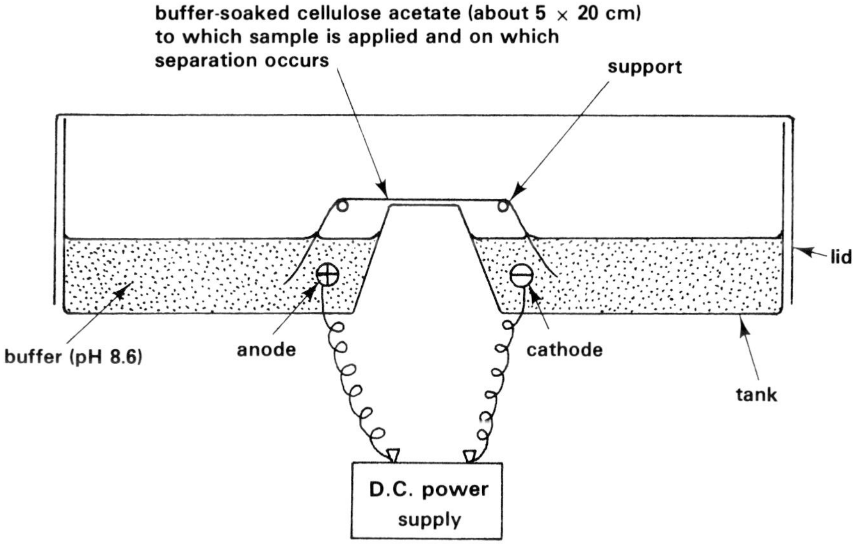

FIG. 9.27 (a) *The main fractions of plasma (or serum) proteins may be separated by* electrophoresis. *A sample of plasma (or serum) is subjected to an electric field in a special tank. At the pH used the different proteins in the sample carry different electric charges. Consequently the proteins migrate in different directions or at different speeds (some are heavier than others) when the current is switched on. Positive ions move towards the cathode, negative ions towards the anode*

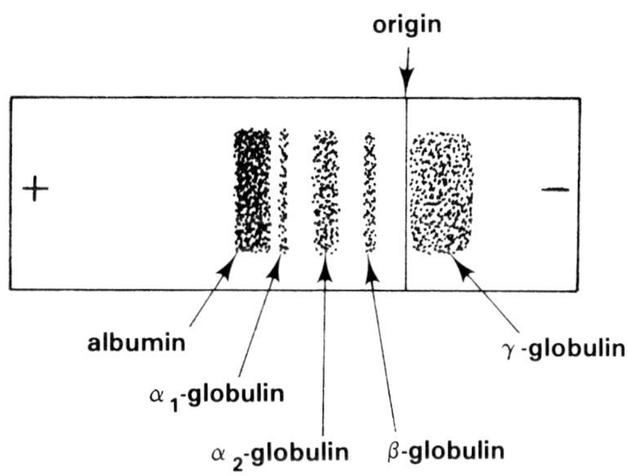

FIG. 9.27 (b) *When separation is complete the proteins are fixed and stained. The γ-globulin fraction contains the immunoglobulins*

Lymphocytes originate from **stem cells** in the bone marrow. The stem cells migrate to the lymph nodes before birth. On their way some of them enter the **thymus gland** lying near the heart. In the thymus gland the lymphocytes are exposed to self-components of the body. Those lymphocytes which react against self-components are destroyed. The remainder become T-cells ('T' for 'thymus-derived'). Removal of the thymus gland early on in life prevents T-cell processing and inhibits the development of the cellular immune system. Other stem cells are probably processed in the bone marrow. They produce B-cells ('B' for 'bone-derived'), the basis of the humoral immune system.

Some of the aspects of antibody production referred to above and the origins of lymphocytes are illustrated in Figure 9.28.

FIG. 9.28 *Diagrammatic origin of lymphocytes and their action in the immune response*

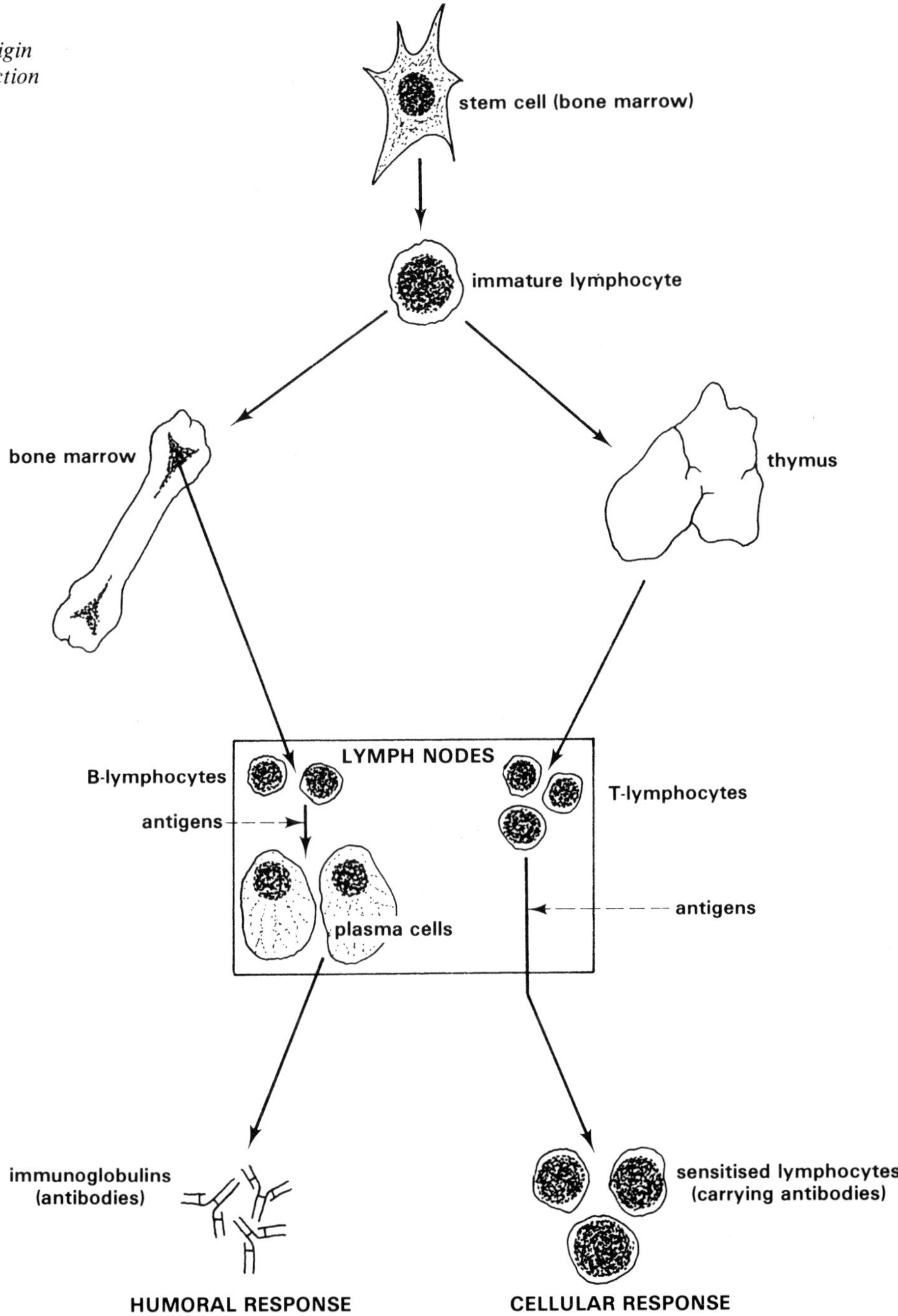

3. ANTIBODY REACTIONS

The basic function of antibodies is to react with and in some way neutralise antigens. In so doing, they eliminate or destroy the effect of the antigens. Since antigens usually are components of non-self cells, possibly pathogenic microbes, immunity results in resistance to disease. There are at least four types of antigen–antibody reactions, **neutralisation**, **precipitation**, **agglutination** and **lysis**. Some of the reactions make antigen-carrying cells susceptible to phagocytosis.

(i). **Neutralisation** is the reaction between antibodies and soluble antigens. Soluble antigens include toxins secreted by pathogenic microbes. The toxin produced by the bacterium *Clostridium tetani* which is the cause of tetanus is an example.

(ii). **Precipitation** involves the linkage of many antigen–antibody complexes to form a large insoluble lattice. Lattices are readily engulfed by phagocytes (Fig. 9.29).

FIG. 9.29 *The ability of most antibodies each to react with two antigen molecules may result in the formation of a large* lattice *structure. Insoluble, the lattice precipitates and is readily engulfed by phagocytes*

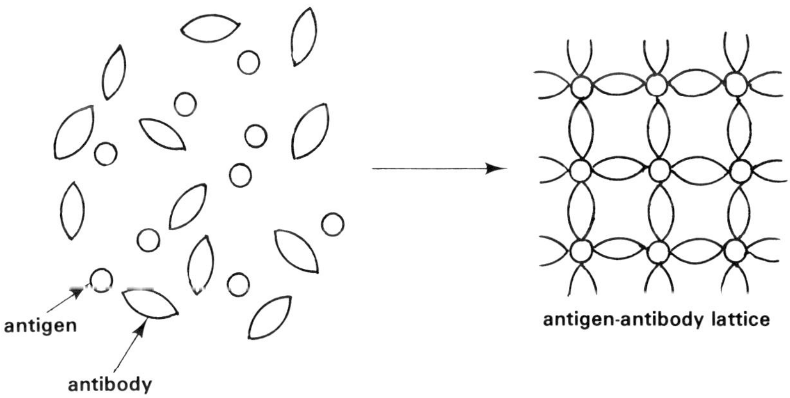

(iii). **Agglutination** is the clumping together of antigen-carrying cells. Mammalian plasma contains a set of proteins called **complement** which helps antibodies to surround invading organisms such as bacteria (Fig. 9.30). Such action often brings about agglutination and promotes phagocytosis.

FIG. 9.30 *The attraction of complement protein by antibodies fixed to a bacterial cell. The bacterium is now susceptible to phagocytosis. Without complement many bacteria are resistant to phagocytosis*

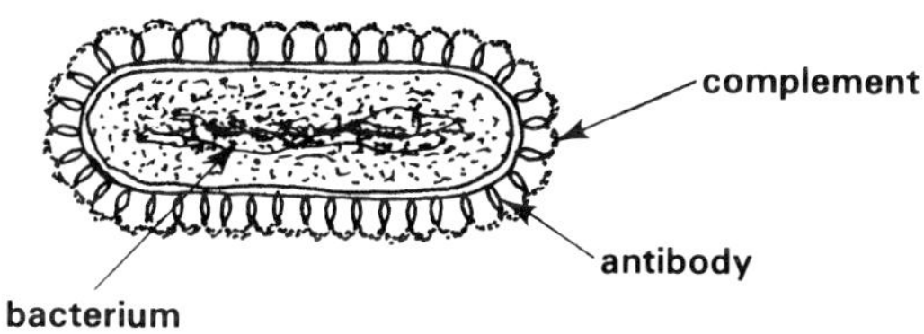

(iv). **Lysis** is the bursting of antigen-bearing cells. Complement, attracted to such cells by antibodies, contains digestive enzymes which dissolve the cells' outer covering (Fig. 9.31).

FIG. 9.31 *Photomicrograph of human blood showing red cells undergoing haemolysis. Haemolysis may sometimes result from the action of antibodies on the antigens of the red cell membranes* × *800*

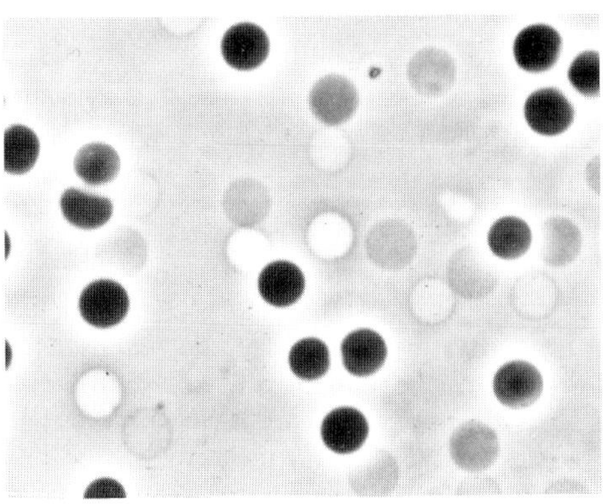

9.3 Vaccines

Among the main weapons in man's armoury against disease are **vaccines**. Vaccines are made from pathogenic microbes having the antigens which stimulate the body's immune system. The organisms are treated so that they do not give rise to disease when administered to a patient. The antibodies produced as a result of vaccination give immunity against disease following subsequent exposure to disease-causing microbes. Unfortunately it is not yet possible to make vaccines against all diseases of microbial origin.

In 1797 Edward Jenner, a Gloucestershire country doctor, was the first to use a vaccine successfully in preventing a human disease. He noticed that dairymaids who had milked cows suffering from cowpox were far less susceptible to the much more virulent and often fatal smallpox, although they often showed mild symptoms of the disease, such as hand sores. Jenner removed some of the liquid from a sore on the hand of a dairymaid and scratched it into the skin of a young boy, James Phipps. Later Jenner inoculated Phipps with material from the sores of someone suffering from smallpox. The boy was found to be immune to smallpox. Jenner had used an antigen to produce immunity against a dangerous pathogen. It is only relatively recently that mass vaccination programmes have virtually eliminated smallpox all over the world.

The reaction of the body to cowpox vaccine is an example of **active immunisation**. The body actively makes its own antibodies against the antigen. Protection against measles, whooping cough, poliomyelitis and tuberculosis is provided in this way. It is far too dangerous, however, to introduce some disease-causing organisms into the human body. Instead the pathogen is injected into another animal such as a horse. Antibodies soon appear in the horse's blood which is used to prepare an **antiserum**. The antiserum can then be injected into a human to provide **passive immunity**. It is in this way that humans are immunised against tetanus and diphtheria. Passive immunity is important in a foetus which absorbs antibodies from its mother across the placenta. The mother's milk also contains antibodies which provide passive immunity in the gut of new born mammals.

9.4 Allergy

About 10 per cent of the population in Britain has an **allergy**. Allergies include hay fever, asthma, childhood eczema and food allergies. An allergy is an immune response to an antigen called an **allergen**, to which most people show no reaction. Allergens are found on pollen grains, fungal spores, house dust, feathers, fur and in a variety of foods. Allergens on pollen for example, become attached to the mucus membranes in the breathing passages. The presence of allergens in people who suffer from an allergy stimulates the production of antibodies called **reagins**. It is thought that reagins are made in the lymph nodes. They circulate in the blood and become attached to cells throughout the body, particularly in the skin and mucus surfaces of the mouth, nose and breathing passages. The reagins can remain for years in these tissues which are said to be **hypersensitive**. Later, whenever there is exposure to allergens, an allergen–reagin reaction takes place. The reaction triggers a vigorous response involving the rupture of certain tissue cells and the release of **histamine**. Histamine causes inflammation of the affected tissues and constriction of the bronchi leading to breathing difficulties. Eosinophils increase in number during allergic responses. They are thought to have an anti-inflammatory effect by absorbing histamine from the tissues.

9.5 Blood groups

Since the pioneering work of Landsteiner in the 1900s it has been known that people can be categorized into one or more **blood groups**. A knowledge of blood groups is important because transfusion of blood from one person to another may cause an immune response in the recipient if the donor's blood is of a different group, that is if the donor's blood is **incompatible**. The response results in mass haemolysis of the donated red blood cells and oxygen carriage becomes affected. Before haemolysis some of the donor's red cells agglutinate and blockages occur in the capillaries of vital organs, usually with fatal results.

About twenty blood group systems have been described in man. They are based on the antigens which form part of the red cell membranes (Table 9.3). The best known blood group system is the **ABO system**. Human red cells possess one, both or neither of two antigens called **A** and **B**. Cells with A belong to blood **group A**, those with B belong to **group B**, those with both A and B belong to **group AB**. Cells with neither antigen belong to **group O**.

Table 9.3 The red cell antigens of the main blood group systems in man

SYSTEM	ANTIGENS
ABO	A_1 A_2 A_3 A_x B and others
Rhesus	D C c C^w C^x E D^u and others
MNSs	M N S s
P	P_1 P^k
Lutheran	Lu^a Lu^b
Kell	K k Kp^a Kp^b Js^a Js^b
Lewis	Le^a Le^b
Duffy	Fy^a Fy^b
Diego	Di^a Di^b
Yt	Yt^a Yt^b
I	I i
Xg	Xg^a
Kidd	Kj

In the plasma are two **isoantibodies** called **anti-A** and **anti-B**. Isoantibodies are not produced as a result of an immune response. Anti-A is found in the blood of group B individuals, anti-B in group A individuals. Both anti-A and anti-B are in the blood of group O individuals and neither antibody appears in the blood of group AB individuals. Table 9.4 shows the distribution of the antigens and antibodies of the ABO system. It can be seen that anti-A normally never encounters the A antigen, nor anti-B the B antigen. If they do, following incompatible transfusion for example, agglutination and haemolysis of the red cells occurs.

A person's blood group can be determined by mixing a small sample of blood cells with a variety of antisera. These are serum samples containing known blood group antibodies. Careful observation of which antisera agglutinate the red cells enables the selection of compatible blood for transfusion (Fig. 9.32).

The other well-known blood group system in man is the **rhesus system**. It was discovered from work on rhesus monkeys. The rhesus system involves several red cell antigens, mainly the **D-antigen**. About 75 per cent of the British population possess the D-antigen and are **rhesus-positive**. The rest without the D-antigen are **rhesus-negative**. There is no isoantibody to the D-antigen. However, if D-carrying red cells are transfused into a rhesus negative individual the recipient produces anti-D antibody by immune response. Anti-D antibody reacts with the D-antigen resulting in agglutination and haemolysis of the rhesus-positive cells. Consequently it is important to determine the rhesus group as well as the ABO group of blood before transfusion.

Table 9.4 The antigens and antibodies of the human ABO blood group system. There are sub-groups of A and AB called A_2 and A_2B but these have been omitted

Blood group	O	A	B	AB
red cell antigen	—	A	B	A + B
plasma antibody	anti-A + anti-B	anti-B	anti-A	—
British population/per cent	46·7	41·7	8·6	3

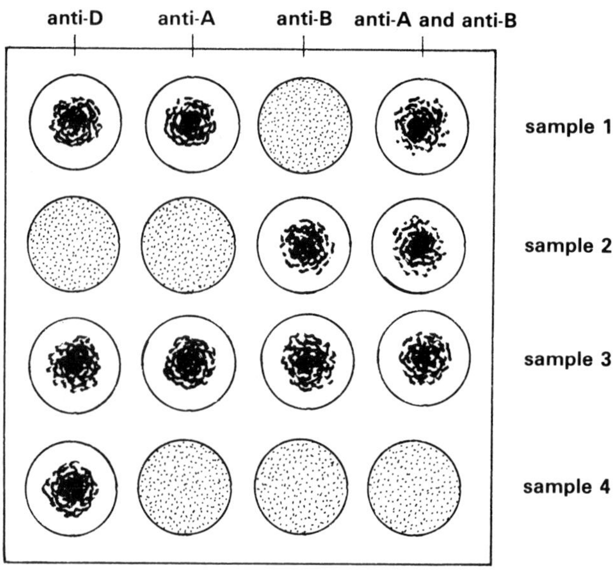

FIG. 9.32 *The results of blood group tests on four different samples. In each well blood cells to be tested are mixed with known blood group antibodies. What are the ABO and Rhesus groups of the four samples? What pattern of agglutination do you think cells of group O Rhesus negative would give in this test?*

A complication concerning the rhesus system can arise during pregnancy if a rhesus-negative woman is carrying a rhesus-positive foetus Normally the placenta keeps the D-carrying foetal red cells out of the mother's circulation. Nevertheless, the stresses caused by the muscular contractions of the uterus during birth can cause some foetal blood cells to enter the mother's blood. The mother's immune system recognises the D-antigen on the foetal cells as non-self and produces anti-D antibody. Since the anti-D antibody can pass across placental membranes, a rhesus-positive foetus of any future pregnancy is at risk. In about 10 per cent of such cases severe haemolysis of foetal red cells occurs during pregnancy

The reaction is the cause of a dangerous condition called **haemolytic disease of the newborn**. Transfusion of fresh blood into the foetus while still in the uterus may be necessary several times during the pregnancy. If the reaction can be predicted from a knowledge of the mother's rhesus group, such drastic measures can be avoided. Anti-D antiserum is injected into her blood immediately after the first birth. Any D-carrying foetal cells which may have entered her system are destroyed before they stimulate her own anti-D production. A rhesus-positive foetus of a subsequent pregnancy should be safe from haemolytic disease.

9.6 Organ transplantation

Another area of medicine in which the immune system plays an important part is **organ transplantation**. The surgical difficulties of transplanting organs such as a kidney or a heart from one person to another are not great. However, the transplanted organs carry about forty antigens which stimulate the production of antibodies in the recipient. The antibodies eventually **reject** the transplanted tissues. To a certain extent it is possible to match donor and recipient in a way comparable to the selection of compatible blood before transfusion. The antigens of tissues which make up organs are similar to those of the white cells in the blood and they can be categorised into one of several groups. The system most often used is the **histocompatibility** or **HL-A system**. Even so, perfect matchings are virtually impossible, even in closely related individuals whose antigens are most likely to be similar.

One means of minimizing the rejection of transplanted organs is to administer **immunosuppressant drugs**. The drugs counteract the immune system and block antibody production in response to the antigens of the transplanted organ. The main problem arising from the use of immunosuppressant drugs is that they prevent an adequate immune response to other antigens such as those of pathogenic microbes. Mild infections of common diseases may thus become fatal in immunosuppressed patients. Much research is necessary in this field before the problem of rejection is conquered. Recent work has shown that the HL-A antigens are the means by which the body's immune system recognises self and non-self. When body cells are attacked by viruses the HL-A antigens on the affected cells are modified by the virus. T-lymphocytes recognise the change as non-self, attack the infected cell and the viruses inside. Autoimmune diseases may therefore be due to a change in the HL-A antigens of body cells. T-lymphocytes then misrecognise self cells as non-self cells and destroy them.

Chapter 10

The mammalian urinary system

The complex and numerous activities of the mammalian body require a stable environment in which to take place. Even slight chemical or physical changes can upset the smooth functioning of the body. Many of the physiological activities of mammals regulate the constitution of the body's internal environment, and do so to within relatively narrow limits. Maintaining a stable internal environment is called **homeostasis**.

The very functions and activities which need a stable environment change it continuously. Metabolism involves the production of wastes. If wastes accumulate in the body they can become toxic. Consequently mammals like other animals eliminate or **excrete** their wastes. Excretion is the elimination of any substances which are present in the body in concentrations exceeding normal levels, whether metabolic wastes or not. Among the organs concerned with excretion and homeostasis are the kidneys which form part of the **urinary system**.

10.1 The urinary system

The **kidneys** are paired organs found in the abdominal cavity. They are held firmly in position by the peritoneum, a thin layer of tissue lining the abdominal cavity. The kidneys are usually embedded in fat (Fig. 10.1).

Each kidney receives blood from the general circulation through a **renal artery** and is drained of blood by a **renal vein**. In kidneys the blood circulates in a capillary network which surrounds numerous microscopic urinary tubules called **nephrons**. The nephrons remove excess and unwanted materials from the blood. The excretory products collect as **urine** which passes from the kidneys through the **ureters**. Urine is stored temporarily in the **urinary bladder** before it is eliminated from the body. Emptying of the bladder is called **micturition** and is controlled by the autonomic nervous system (Chapter 15). The exit from the bladder into the **urethra** is closed by contraction of a ring of muscle called the **bladder sphincter**. As the bladder fills, cells in the bladder wall which are sensitive to stretching trigger off a reflex action which results in relaxation of the bladder sphincter. Simultaneous contraction of the smooth muscle in the bladder wall forces the urine out through the urethra. Micturition can be controlled by voluntary nervous activity which is learned by humans in early life (Fig. 10.2).

A human kidney is a compact organ about 7–10 cm long and 2·5–4 cm wide. Inside, the tissues are in distinct regions. There is an outer **cortex** and an inner **medulla** (Fig. 10.3). The internal appearance of a kidney is due to the arrangement of the blood vessels and nephrons which make up most of the organ. The nephrons are the functional units of the kidney and there are about a million nephrons in each human kidney.

Nephrons are very small thin-walled tubules between 2 and 4 cm long in man (Fig. 10.4). At one end is a cup-shaped **Bowman's capsule** which encloses a small group of capillaries called a **glomerulus**. A Bowman's capsule and the glomerulus together are called a **Malpighian body**. The capsule leads into a coiled structure called the **proximal convolution** which opens into the **loop of Henle**. The loop of Henle consists of a descending limb and an ascending limb and leads into a second coiled tube, the **distal convolution**. The distal convolutions of many nephrons join a common **collecting duct** and many collecting ducts lead through the medulla to the **renal pelvis**.

FIG. 10.1 *The urinary system of the rat*. Compare with Figs 22.1 and 22.2

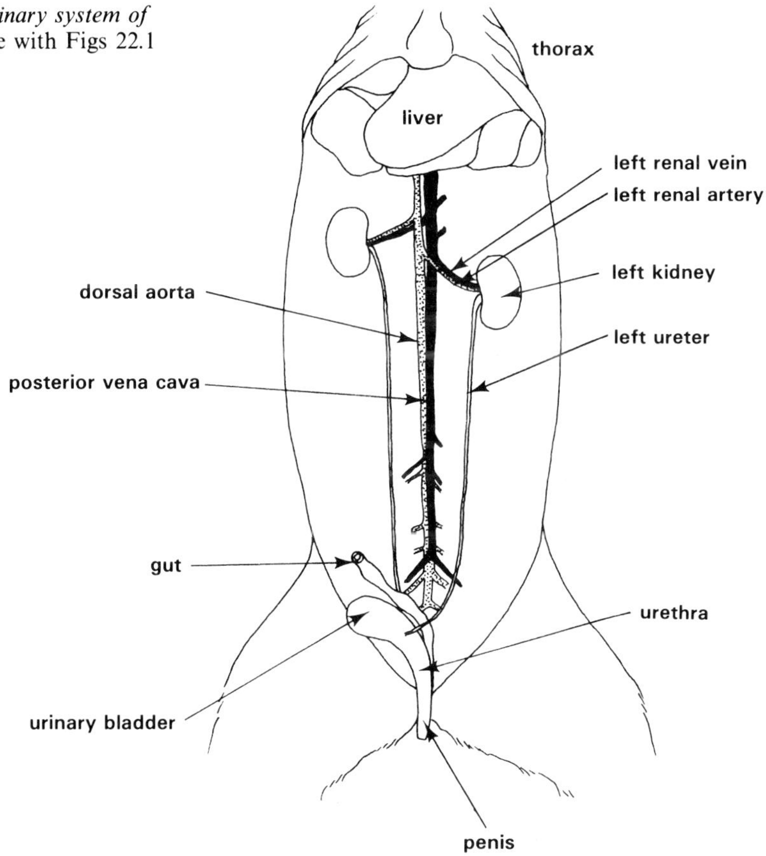

FIG. 10.2 *Autonomic supply to the urinary bladder and urethra*

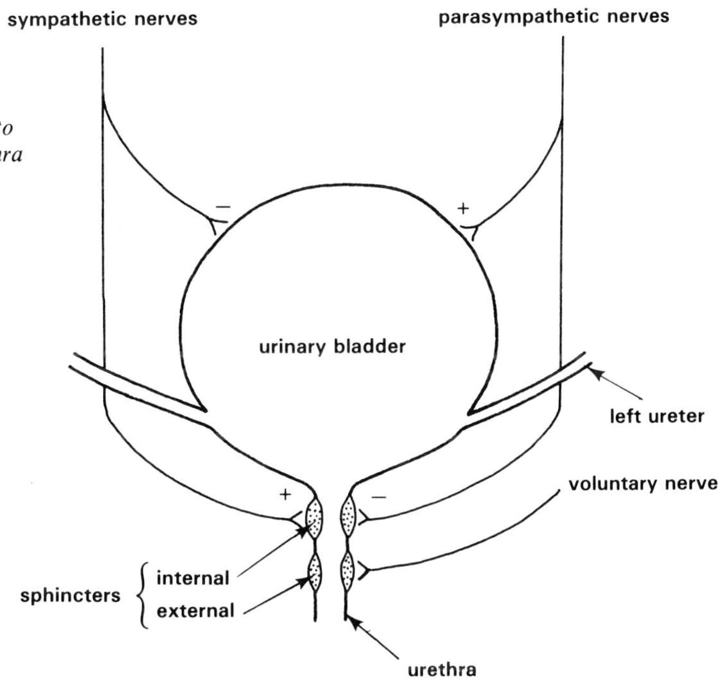

FIG. 10.3 (a) *Photomicrograph of a vertical section of a rat kidney, ×5*

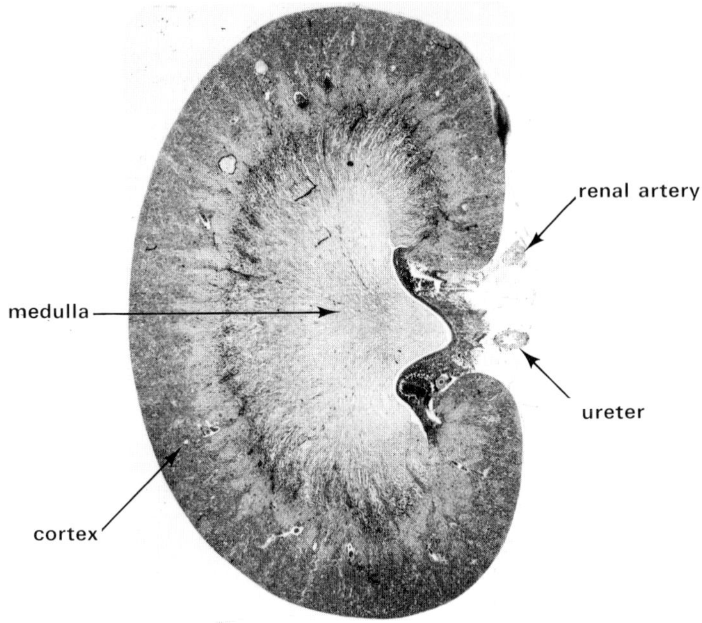

FIG. 10.3 (b) *Diagrammatic vertical section of human kidney. Note the arrangement of the medulla into a series of pyramids*

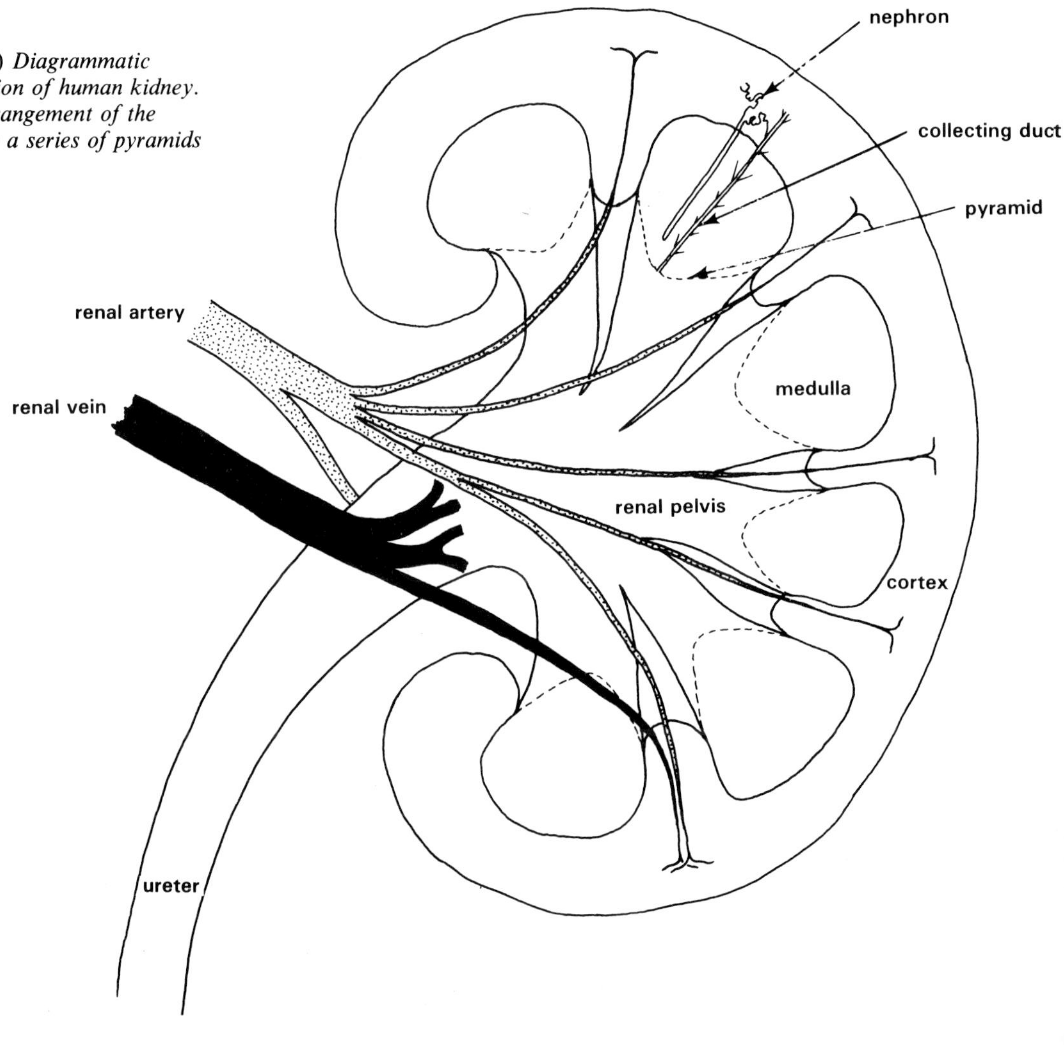

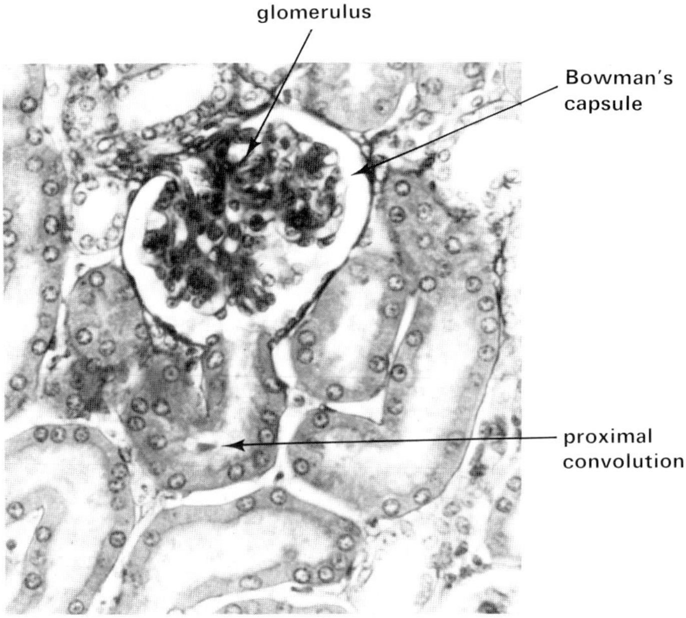

FIG. 10.4 (a) *Photomicrograph of a thin section of monkey kidney in the cortical region, ×300*

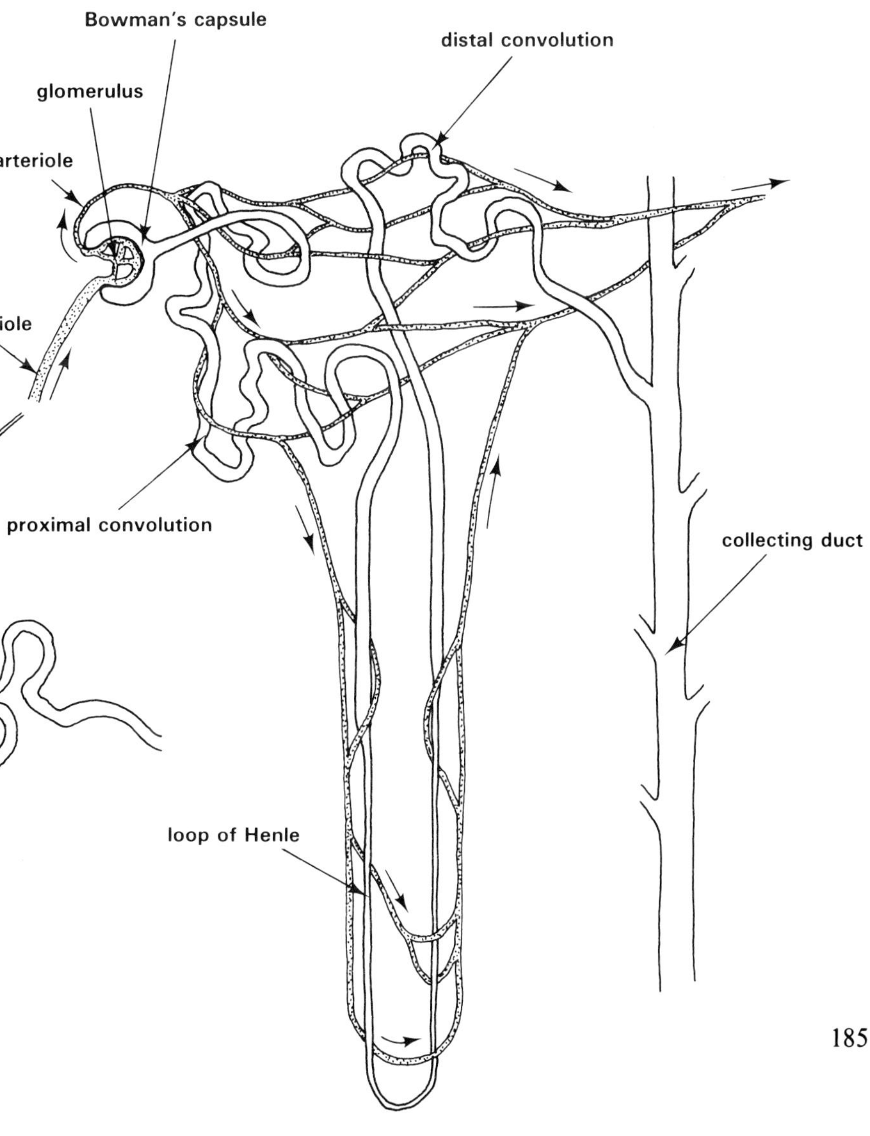

FIG. 10.4 (b) *A nephron and its blood supply*

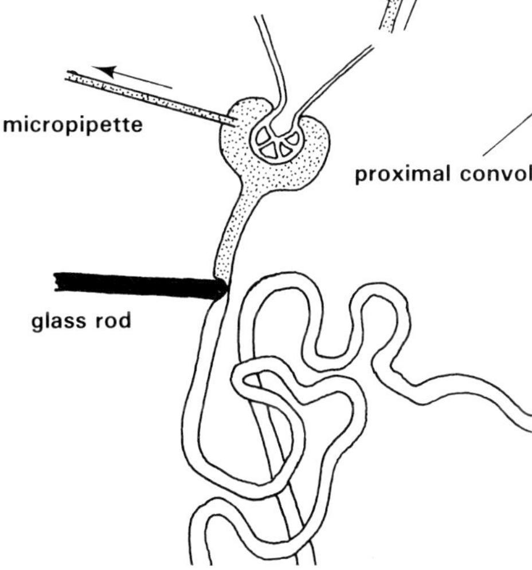

FIG. 10.5 *Removal of a sample of glomerular filtrate for analysis*

10.2 The functions of nephrons

Much of what is known of the functions of kidneys comes from quantitative analyses of the fluid inside nephrons. This involves the insertion of delicate micropipettes into nephrons of experimental animals. The fluid is drawn off carefully and analysed to determine what changes have occurred during its passage through a nephron (Fig. 10.5).

10.2.1 Ultrafiltration

The first activity of a nephron is the **ultrafiltration** of blood brought to the Bowman's capsule by arterioles. The aterioles branch into the capillaries of the glomeruli, tightly nestled in the capsules. Electron microscope studies of the capsules show that the only effective barrier between the blood in the glomeruli and the cavity of the capsules is a thin porous **basement membrane** (Fig. 10.6).

FIG. 10.6 (a) *Electronmicrograph showing a section through a podocyte and a glomerular capillary,* × *12 000*

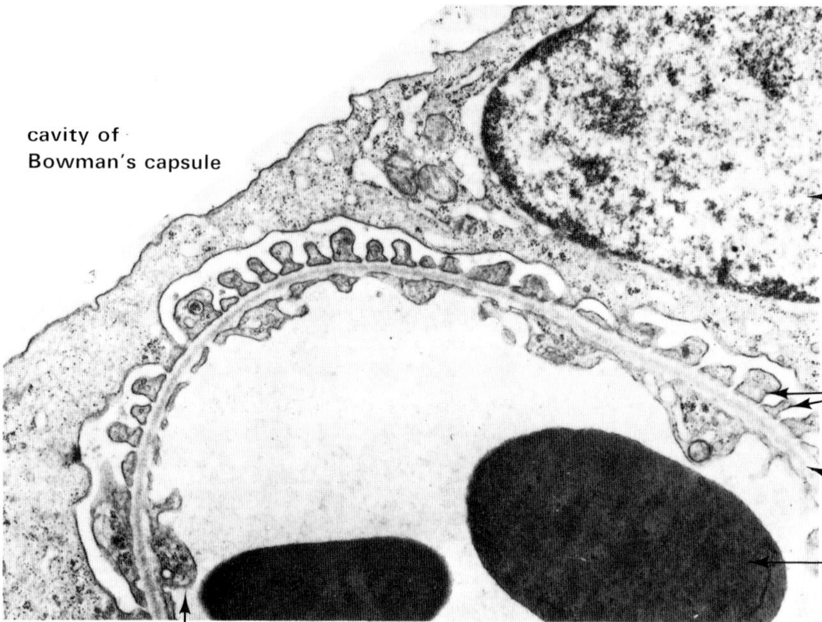

The hydrostatic pressure of blood in the glomerular capillaries is relatively high because the diameter of the afferent arterioles is greater than that of the efferent arterioles. Blood pressure is normally maintained by the pumping action of the heart. If the blood pressure falls too low, for example when much blood is lost in an accident, temporary use of a kidney machine may be required until the patient's blood volume and pressure are restored (section 10.5).

The basement membrane of the capsule is permeable to some blood constituents but not to others. Because the blood in the glomerulus has a **high hydrostatic pressure** it is filtered through the basement membrane. Apart from the blood cells and substances of high relative molar mass such as the plasma proteins, the chemical composition of the glomerular filtrate is virtually the same as the plasma. There is almost total transfer of materials from the blood in the glomeruli to the Bowman's capsules. The composition of urine, however, is very different. The filtrate is therefore modified considerably while passing along the nephrons. The volume of urine excreted is also much less than the volume of filtrate produced in a given time (Table 10.1).

FIG. 10.6 (b) *Diagram of the barrier between the glomerular blood and the filtrate in Bowman's capsule.* Compare with the electronmicrograph, Fig. 10.6 (a)

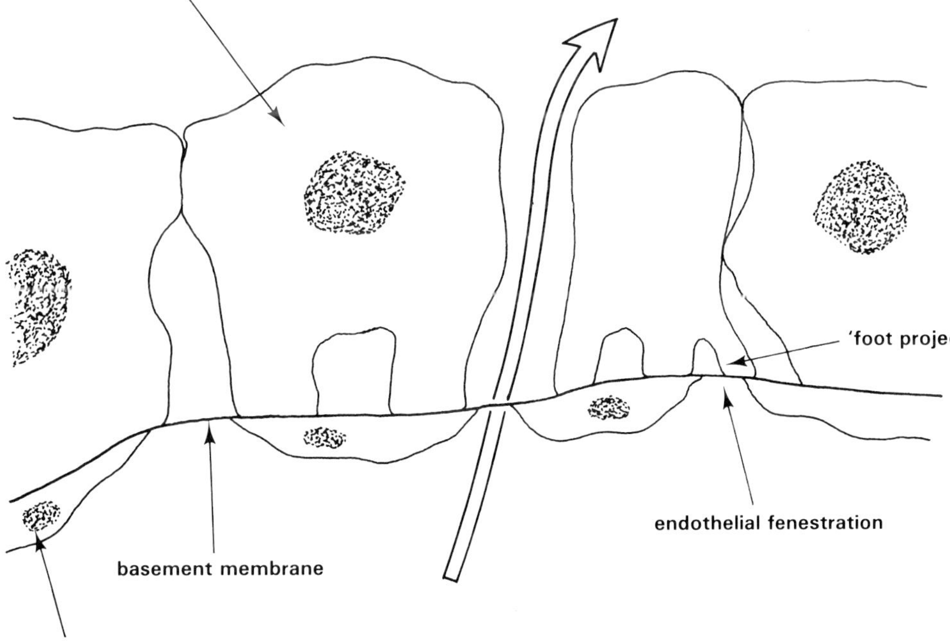

Table 10.1 Some human blood constituents and the quantities filtered and reabsorbed by the kidneys in a day

CONSTITUENTS	AMOUNT IN FILTRATE/g	AMOUNT IN URINE/g	PERCENTAGE REABSORPTION
sodium ions	600	6	99
potassium ions	35	2	94
calcium ions	5	0·2	96
glucose	200	0	100
urea	60	35	42
water	180 dm^3	1·5 dm^3	99

10.2.2 Reabsorption

Changes in the composition of the filtrate begin in the proximal convolutions. Here the epithelial cells of the nephron wall reabsorb a large proportion of the filtrate, passing it back into the blood flowing in the surrounding vessels. **Reabsorption** of individual substances is at a rate just sufficient to maintain normal concentrations in the blood. Any excesses stay in the nephron and are later excreted.

Since the transfer of materials from the filtrate into the blood is against a concentration gradient, reabsorption is active (Fig. 10.7). The energy for **active uptake** is provided by respiration in the nephron's cells which contain many mitochondria. The efficiency of reabsorption is helped by the presence of numerous **microvilli** which greatly enlarge the surface area through which the materials pass (Fig. 10.8).

FIG. 10.7 *Active solute reabsorption from the proximal convolutions against a concentration gradient as the levels of reabsorbed materials exceed those remaining in the filtrate*

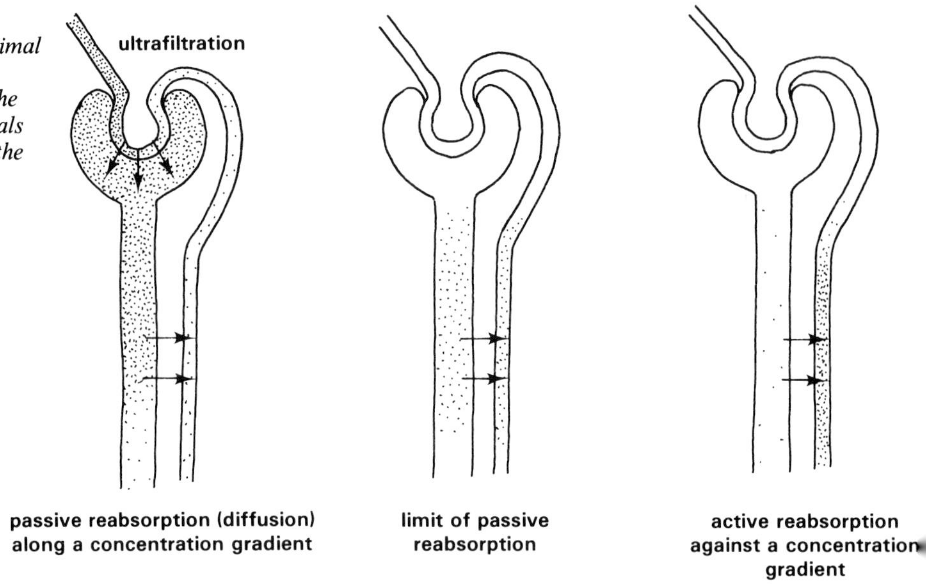

FIG. 10.8 *Electronmicrograph of a cell lining the proximal convolution of a nephron, ×5800*

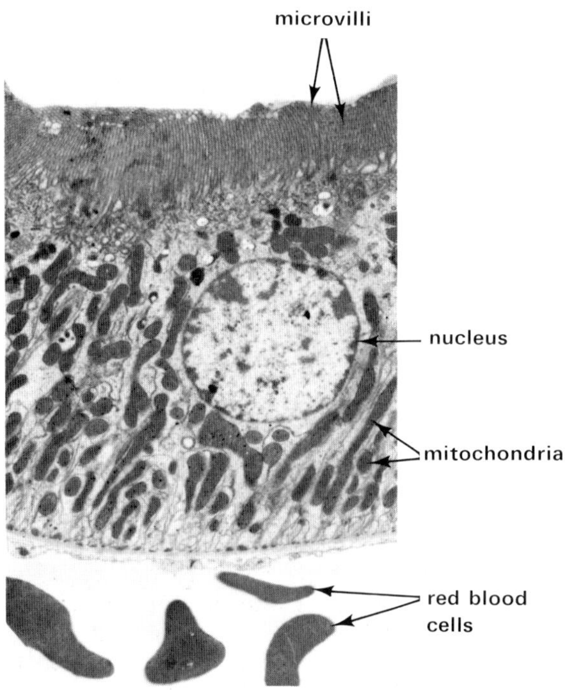

In humans about 120 cm^3 of water pass into the nephrons every minute. Of this, about 100 cm^3 per minute are reabsorbed passively from the proximal convolutions. The concentration gradient of solutes between the remainder of the filtrate in the proximal convolution and the blood in surrounding capillaries promotes **osmosis**. The osmotic reabsorption of water is further assisted by the colloid osmotic potential of the blood due to the plasma proteins (Chapter 9). Table 10.1 gives an indication of the extent of filtrate reabsorption from the proximal convolutions.

About 19 cm^3 of every 20 cm^3 of water left in the nephrons are re-absorbed every minute from the distal convolutions and collecting ducts. The extent to which water is reabsorbed from these parts of the nephrons depends on the body's state of hydration. If the body's water content is below normal the walls of the distal convolutions and collecting ducts become very permeable to water. If the body contains sufficient water, however, the walls of the distal convolutions become less permeable to water. Water is then reabsorbed slowly into the blood. Excess water then remains in the urine to be excreted (Fig. 10.9).

FIG. 10.9 *The fate of water in the distal parts of the nephron, depending on the body's state of hydration*

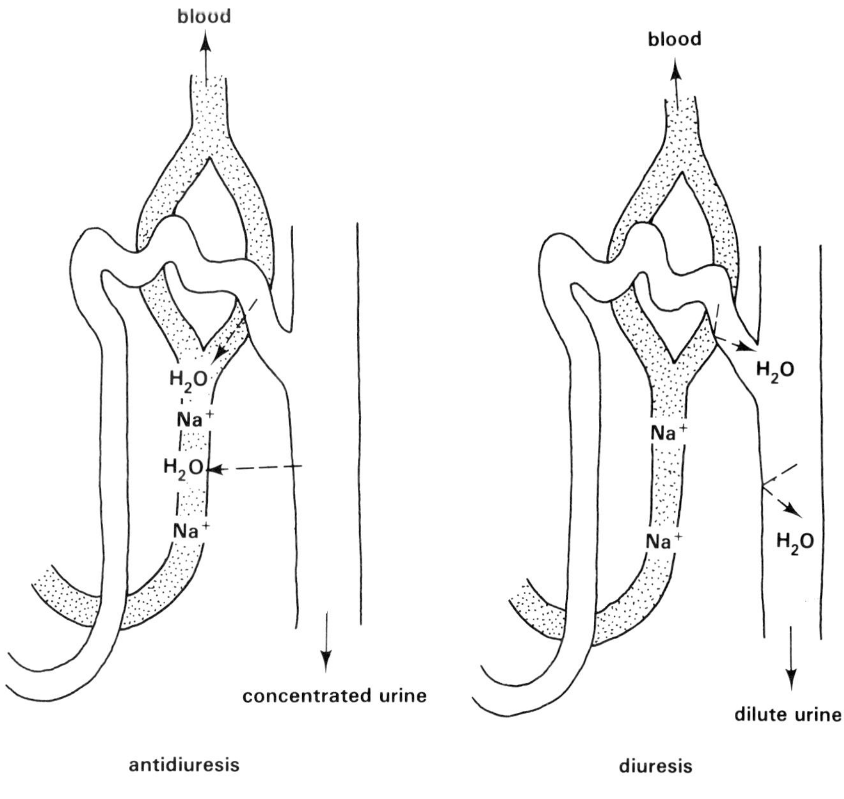

The arrangement of the loops of Henle and nearby blood vessels in the medulla of the kidney is important in efficiently maintaining the necessary water potential gradient for water reabsorption. The filtrate passing down the descending limb of the loop of Henle contains fewer sodium ions than the surrounding blood and tissue fluid which receive sodium ions pumped out of the ascending limb of the loop of Henle (Fig. 10.10). Consequently as the filtrate passes down the descending limb it loses water by osmosis. By the time the filtrate enters the ascending limb its sodium ion concentration is relatively high. The cells of the ascending limb expend only a little energy in pumping sodium ions out of the filtrate and into the blood and tissue fluid. This mechanism is called a **counter-current multiplication** system (Fig. 10.11).

FIG. 10.10 *Establishment of a high osmotic potential in the blood in the kidney's medulla*

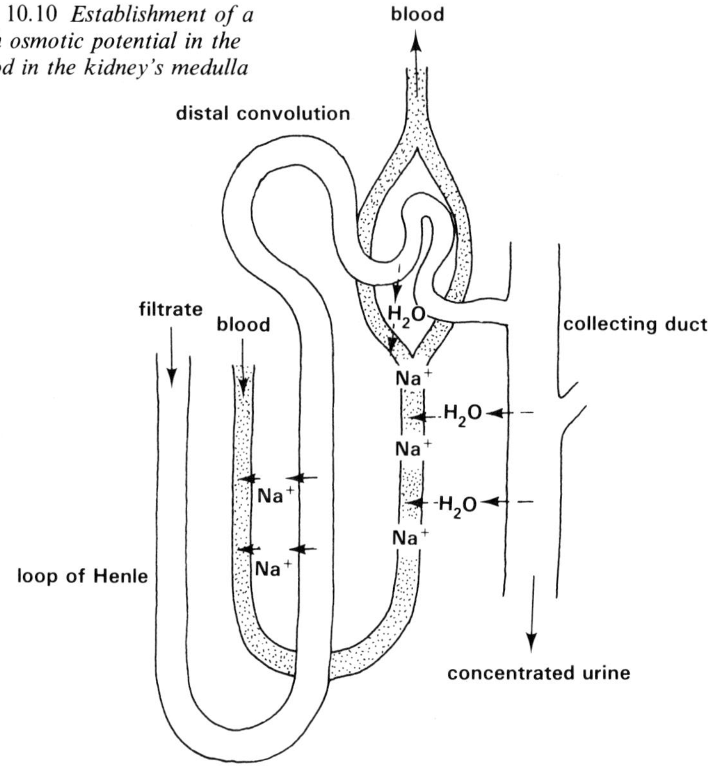

FIG. 10.11 *Counter-current multiplication system in the loop of Henle*

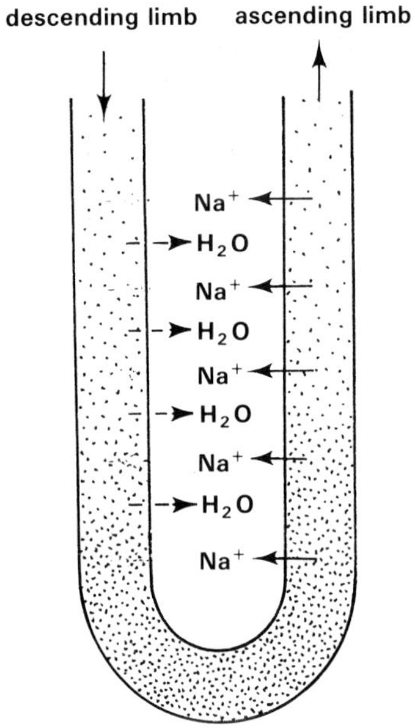

FIG. 10.12 *Relative proportions of the loops of Henle in the kidneys of three mammals living in different conditions*

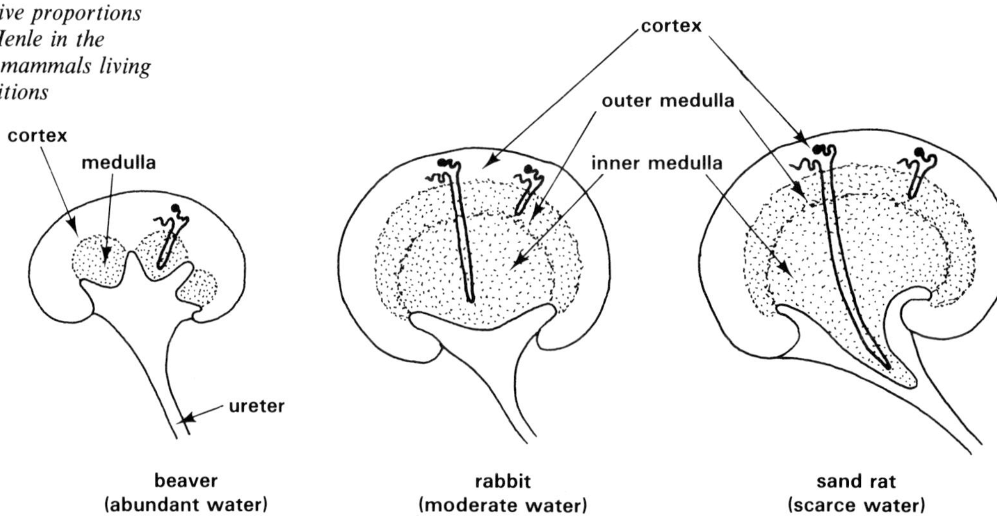

If the loops of Henle are long, more time is available for the filtrate passing down the descending limb to lose water to the medulla. The counter-current effect is then increased and the ascending limb can pump more sodium ions into the blood and tissue fluid. The water potential gradient between blood and filtrate in the distal convolutions and collecting ducts is then much greater. The ability to concentrate urine is important to mammals living in arid conditions. It is therefore of interest that the nephrons of many desert mammals have unusually long loops of Henle (Fig. 10.12).

10.2.3 Regulation of nephron function

The active reabsorption of solutes from the proximal convolutions is regulated by hormones. Reabsorption of water from the proximal convolutions is passive by osmosis. Osmosis normally accounts for the reabsorption of over 80 per cent of the water in the filtrate from the glomeruli. As we saw in the previous section, water reabsorption from the distal parts of the nephrons is also by osmosis. The extent of water reabsorption depends on the body's state of hydration and the permeability of the walls of the distal convolutions and collecting ducts. How does the body detect and monitor its water content? How is this information translated into permeability changes of the walls of the distal convolutions and collecting ducts?

FIG. 10.13 *Mechanism controlling water reabsorption from the distal parts of the nephrons*. See Fig. 10.9

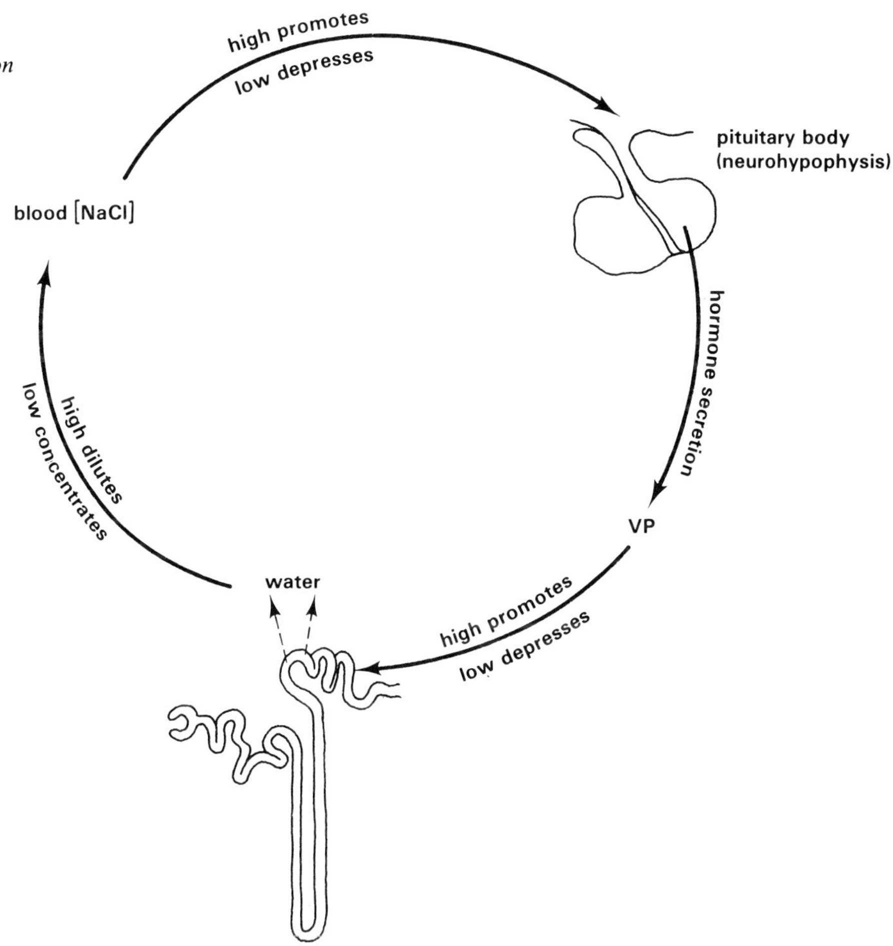

Beneath the **hypothalamus** in the brain and projecting downward from it is an endocrine gland called the **pituitary body** (Chapter 18). The hypothalamus is sensitive to the concentration of sodium chloride in the blood flowing through it. Since the concentration of sodium chloride is an indirect indication of the volume of water in the body, the hypothalamus is sensitive to the water content of the blood. If the water content is low the sodium chloride concentration is high. The pituitary body, stimulated by the hypothalamus, releases **vasopressin** (VP) sometimes called **antidiuretic hormone**. Vasopressin increases the permeability of the walls of the distal convolutions and collecting ducts to water, encouraging reabsorption of water into the blood. Consequently the small volume of urine eventually eliminated is relatively concentrated, a condition called **antidiuresis**. Conversely, if the body's water content is high VP output diminishes. The rate of water reabsorption from the distal ends of the nephrons then slows down. Urine flow increases and the urine becomes diluted, a condition called **diuresis** (Fig. 10.13).

Pituitary malfunction can lead to reduced VP output resulting in a daily urine production more than ten times the average 1·5 dm^3. This condition is called **diabetes insipidus** and is quite distinct from diabetes mellitus (Chapter 18).

10.3 Extreme cases of water economy

The camel is an animal which seems ideally fitted to life in the desert. Indeed, the camel can survive for many days without water. The exact length of time depends mainly on temperature and the availability of food. Camels have been reported to travel more than 900 km between watering points without drinking, taking three weeks to complete the trip.

For a long time it was assumed that the camel's hump, or even its stomach acted as a kind of water store. Investigations of the stomach ruled out such a function and the hump is filled with fatty tissue. Certainly the fat can be respired with the production of water (Chapter 5). However, in breathing, to obtain the oxygen needed for respiration, even more water is lost from the lungs by evaporation (Chapter 8). Schmidt-Nielsen and others have investigated the water relations of desert animals including camels. Their findings indicate that a camel's nephrons are particularly efficient in reabsorbing water from the glomerular filtrate. After allowing for differences in body size, the daily urinary water loss of a camel is only about 25 per cent that of a human.

More significant, however, is the camel's very great **tolerance of dehydration**. A camel can survive water loss of up to one third of its total body mass with no apparent ill-effects. This remarkable tolerance of dehydration cannot be matched by any other mammal. It is estimated that water loss of 15 to 20 per cent of total body mass would be fatal to a human. Recent work has revealed the presence of a special protein in the membranes of the red blood cells of camels. The protein strengthens the red cells and protects them against collapse when the surrounding plasma becomes concentrated because of water loss. Most mammals sweat and pant both of which help maintain a constant body temperature. By sweating and panting very little camels preserve water, but in doing so camels have to tolerate wide internal temperature fluctuations. A camel's temperature can vary from about 34·5°C to 40·5°C, a 6°C variation which would be very harmful to other mammals (Chapter 17).

Another mammal well fitted for survival in desert conditions is the kangaroo rat, *Dipodomys* (Chapter 8). This rodent has such a well-balanced water economy that it does not normally drink at all. Its total water requirement is provided by the small amount of moisture in the rather dry vegetation it eats and more important, the moisture produced by respiration of its food.

$$C_6H_{12}O_6 + 6O_2 \longrightarrow 6CO_2 + 6H_2O$$

Survival on **oxidation water** depends on reducing water loss to an absolute minimum. *Dipodomys* has highly efficient kidneys which produce very concentrated urine. The kangaroo rat also keeps to a minimum the amount of water vapour it breathes out (Chapter 8).

In most terrestrial animals, drinking sea water raises the osmotic potential of the blood plasma, resulting in dehydration of the body tissues by osmosis. Schmidt-Nielsen predicted that kangaroo rats concentrate their urine so much that they should be able to drink sea water without ill-effect. To test the prediction he fed experimental kangaroo rats with soya beans, the high protein content of which resulted in a high concentration of blood urea (Chapter 14). This led to excessive water loss during urination since urea is toxic and is eliminated by the kidneys. Kangaroo rats which were given sea water to drink after this treatment recovered just as well as a control group provided with fresh water. The experiment demonstrates the ability of kangaroo rats to eliminate excess salts, such as sodium chloride, in forming highly concentrated urine.

10.4 The role of the kidneys in acid-base balance

Buffers such as the carbonic acid-hydrogencarbonate acid–base pair (Chapter 2) are limited in the extent to which they can cope with excess hydrogen ions in the body. The final regulation of the pH of body fluids is carried out by the lungs and kidneys. Gas exchange in the lungs disposes of carbon dioxide (Chapter 8). This prevents the build up of carbonic acid in the tissues with accompanying high concentration of hydrogen ions.

Relatively small but significant quantities of acids enter the body daily in food. These and other acids are disposed of by the kidneys in such a way as to keep basic ions like Na^+ (sodium ions) in the body. Acid excretion in the kidneys takes place in the distal convolutions of nephrons. Here, inside the tubule cells, hydrogen (H^+) and hydrogencarbonate (HCO_3^-) ions are formed from carbonic acid. The carbonic acid comes from the carbon dioxide produced by respiration in the tubule cells (Fig. 10.14). The hydrogen ions are secreted into the tubule where they meet and react with disodium hydrogenphosphate in the glomerular filtrate. The hydrogen ions replace some of the sodium ions producing sodium dihydrogenphosphate. Sodium ions are then actively reabsorbed into the blood where they combine with the hydrogencarbonate ions from the tubule cells (Fig. 10.15).

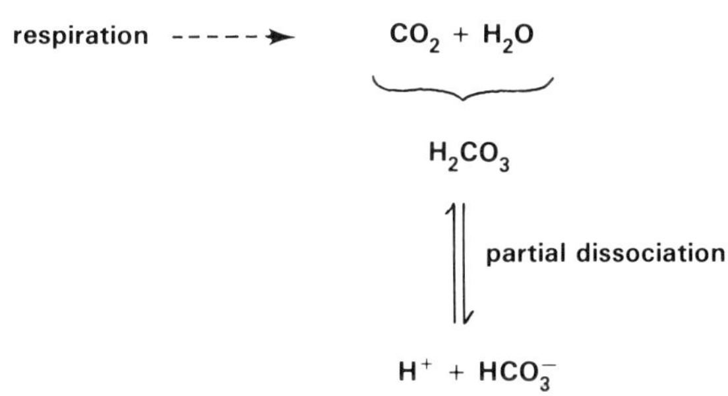

FIG. 10.14 *Production of hydrogencarbonate and hydrogen ions from respiration*

FIG. 10.15

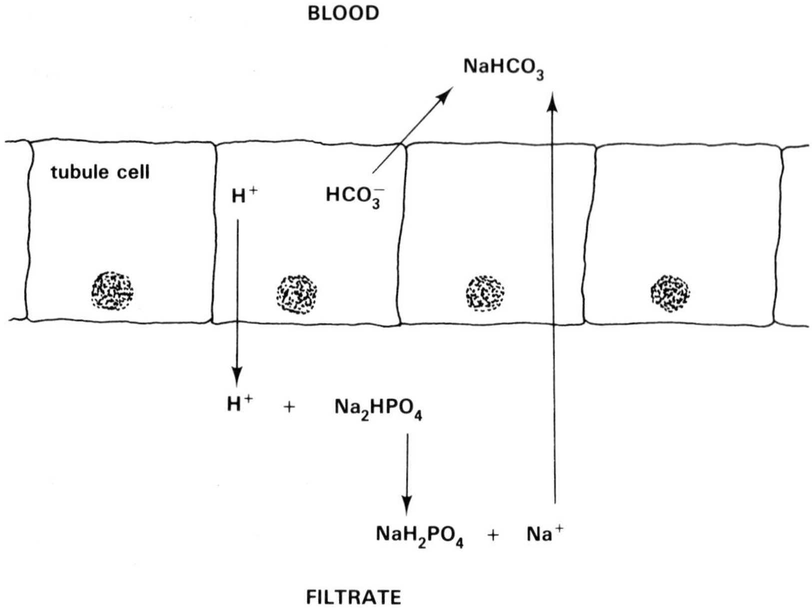

If the acid content of the blood is high, the resulting acidity of the glomerular filtrate stimulates the production of ammonia in the tubule cells. The ammonia completely replaces sodium ions from disodium hydrogenphosphate resulting in increased acid excretion and retention of Na^+ ions (Fig. 10.16).

FIG. 10.16

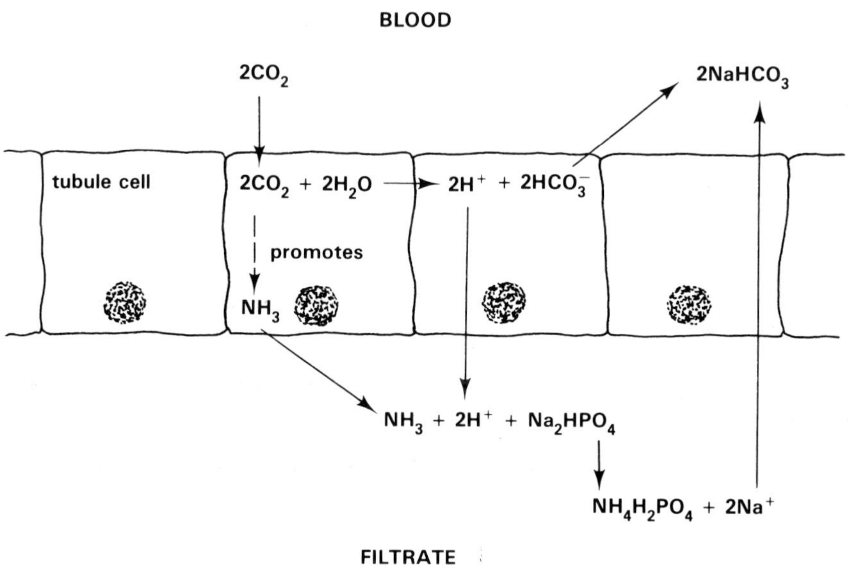

The pH of human blood lies normally between pH 7·35 and 7·45. A drop in pH below 7·30, a condition called **acidosis**, or a rise above 7·50 called **alkalosis**, results in metabolic malfunction. So sensitive are the body's physiological processes that failure to regulate the pH of the blood between 7·0 and 8·0 is usually fatal.

10.5 Kidney machines

Human kidney failure can be treated in two main ways. **Transplantation** of a healthy kidney from another person called a donor involves immunological reactions which have not as yet been completely overcome (Chapter 9). Alternatively, **kidney machines** can be used. A kidney machine is a mechanical device through which a patient's blood passes. The blood leaves the body usually from an artery in the forearm and returns to a nearby vein (Fig. 10.17). Inside the machine the blood flows over or between membranes which separate it from an aqueous **dialysing fluid** containing dissolved sugars and salts in concentrations normally found in blood. Soluble constituents in the blood in excess of normal concentrations diffuse across the membrane into the dialysing fluid. In this way wastes like urea which accumulate in the body are extracted. Blood cells and proteins remain in the blood. The process is called **renal dialysis** (Fig. 10.18).

FIG. 10.17 (a) *Patient connected to a kidney machine*

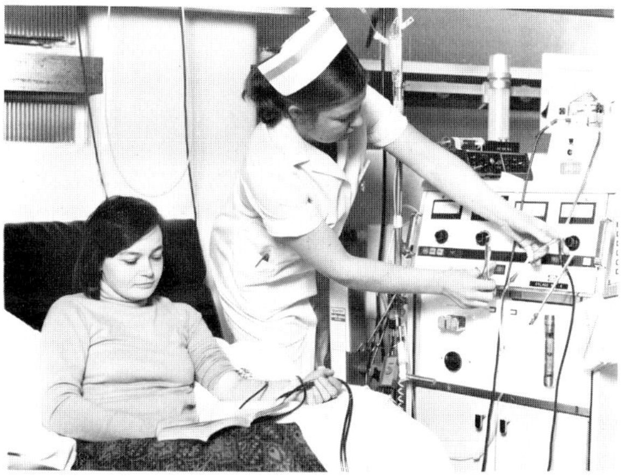

FIG. 10.17 (b) *Diagrammatic arrangement of the apparatus causing dialysis of a patient's blood in a kidney machine*

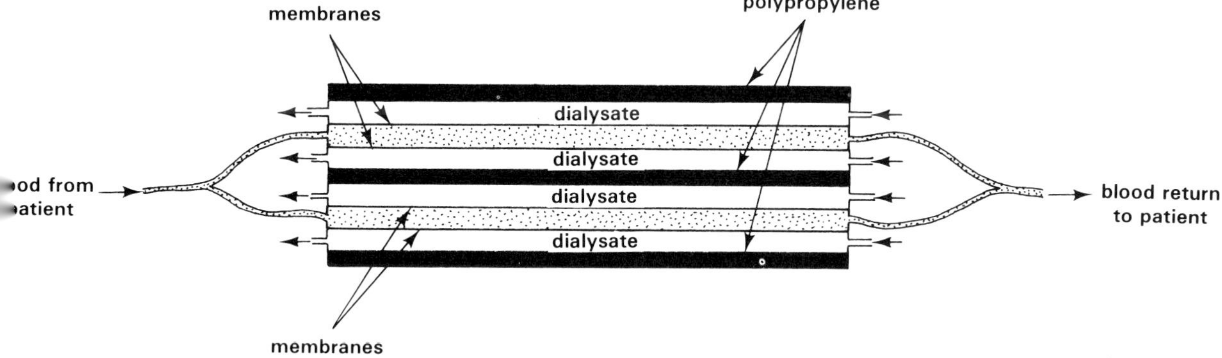

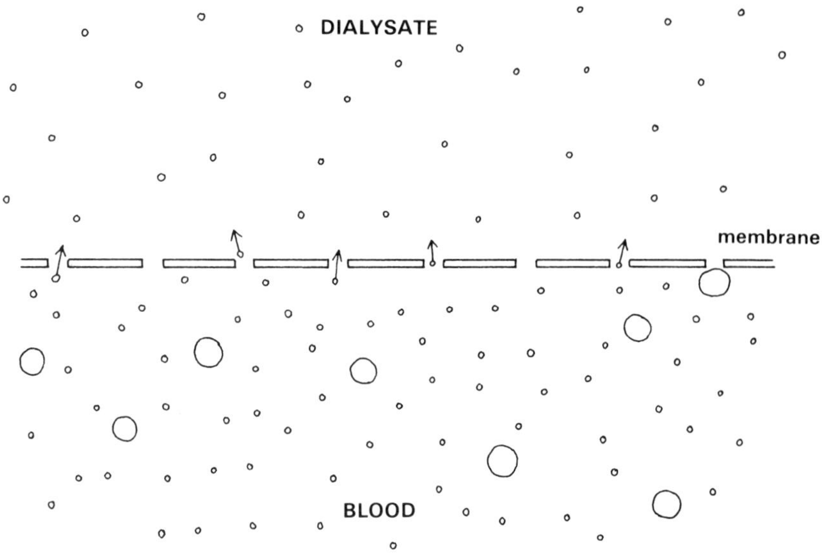

FIG. 10.18 *The mechanism of dialysis. Normal (for the blood) concentrations of dialysable substances (small circular symbols) in the dialysing fluid promote the diffusion of excesses and water from the blood across the membrane. The large circular symbols represent non-dialysable blood constituents such as proteins and cells. Dialysis continues until the concentration of dialysable substances on either side of the membrane are equal*

By using a clip to partially obstruct the tube carrying blood back to the patient's vein the blood pressure in the machine is increased. This makes it possible to remove water from the blood by **ultrafiltration**. Water is removed from the blood in a comparable way in a real kidney.

The pH of the blood falls from 7·4 to about 7·3 between two dialysis treatments. This is because the body's store of hydrogencarbonate ions is used to buffer the blood and in so doing is lowered to about 75 per cent of its normal value. The kidney machine replaces lost hydrogencarbonate. Earlier machines had sodium hydrogencarbonate in the dialysing fluid but sodium ethanoate is used now. The ethanoate diffuses into the blood and is metabolised in the body into hydrogencarbonate.

Usually a patient spends several hours about twice a week connected to a kidney machine during which time the dialysing fluid drains the blood of excess and toxic constituents. This is the basic function of healthy kidneys. However, man-made machines are not perfect. As we saw earlier in the chapter the activities of kidneys are regulated in response to changes in the body's internal environment. As yet kidney machines are not sufficiently sophisticated to be self-regulating. Furthermore, the machines are not designed to perform functions other than excretion. Kidneys functioning abnormally usually stop secreting the hormone **erythropoietin**. The hormone is necessary for normal red blood cell production (Chapter 9). Because of this, patients requiring dialysis are often anaemic. Nevertheless despite their shortcomings kidney machines very definitely have prolonged the lives of a large number of people.

In summary, the main functions of mammalian kidneys are to eliminate wastes and excesses from the blood. The kidneys thus help to maintain a stable internal body environment. Without the kidneys, changes in the composition of the body fluids soon occur. The body is then unable to maintain the optimum conditions for life.

Chapter 11 Uptake and transport of water in flowering plants

Water is essential to all forms of life. In plants, as in animals, water performs important functions as a solvent, as a thermal buffer and as a raw ingredient in hydrolytic reactions catalysed by enzymes (Chapter 2). There are some uses to which water is put in green plants alone. Water provides hydrogen to reduce the products of carbon dioxide fixation in photosynthesis (Chapter 5). In land plants the turgidity of water-containing cells helps to hold the shoot system erect in the atmosphere.

Most of the water required by a land plant is absorbed by its roots from the soil. The rate of water uptake is largely determined by the rate at which water is lost to the atmosphere from the shoot system. The loss of water vapour, called **transpiration**, also affects the rate at which water moves through the plant.

11.1 Transpiration

A major problem confronting all land-dwelling organisms is how to avoid desiccation. The chief advantages of a terrestrial as opposed to an aquatic existence for plants are direct access to sunlight, increased availability of carbon dioxide for photosynthesis and oxygen for respiration. However, in making the most of these advantages land plants continually lose water vapour to the atmosphere. Indeed, as much as 99 per cent of the water absorbed by a terrestrial plant can be lost by evaporation from the shoot system. Transpiration occurs most rapidly when the stomata are open and atmospheric gases come into direct contact with the internal tissues of stems and leaves (Chapter 12). Well over 90 per cent of the total water loss is due to **stomatal transpiration**. Water vapour may also pass directly through the epidermis of the shoot system, but this route is normally sealed by the waxy cuticle. **Cuticular transpiration** usually amounts to less than 5 per cent of the total water vapour loss. Woody stems lose small amounts of water vapour through lenticels by **lenticular transpiration**.

FIG. 11.1 *Venation of a leaf of elder, × 1*

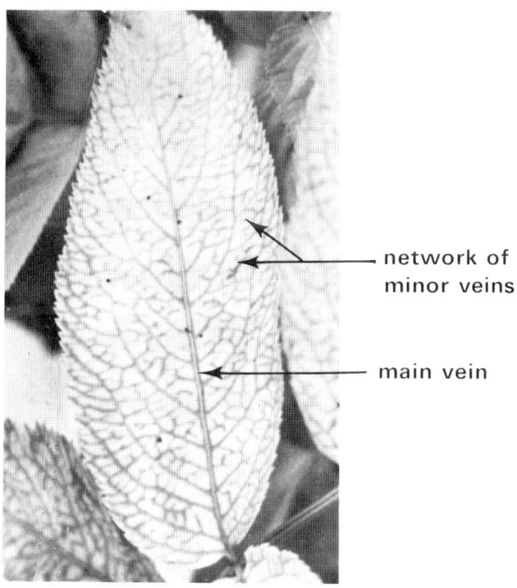

FIG. 11.2 (a) *Transverse section through part of the blade of a leaf of a dicotyledonous plant, × 100*

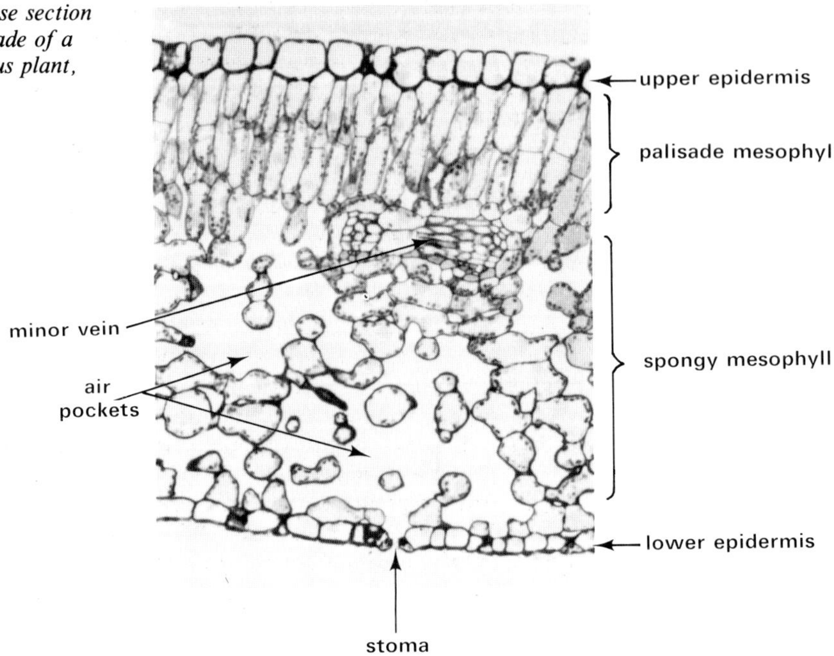

FIG. 11.2 (b) *Air pockets in the spongy mesophyll*

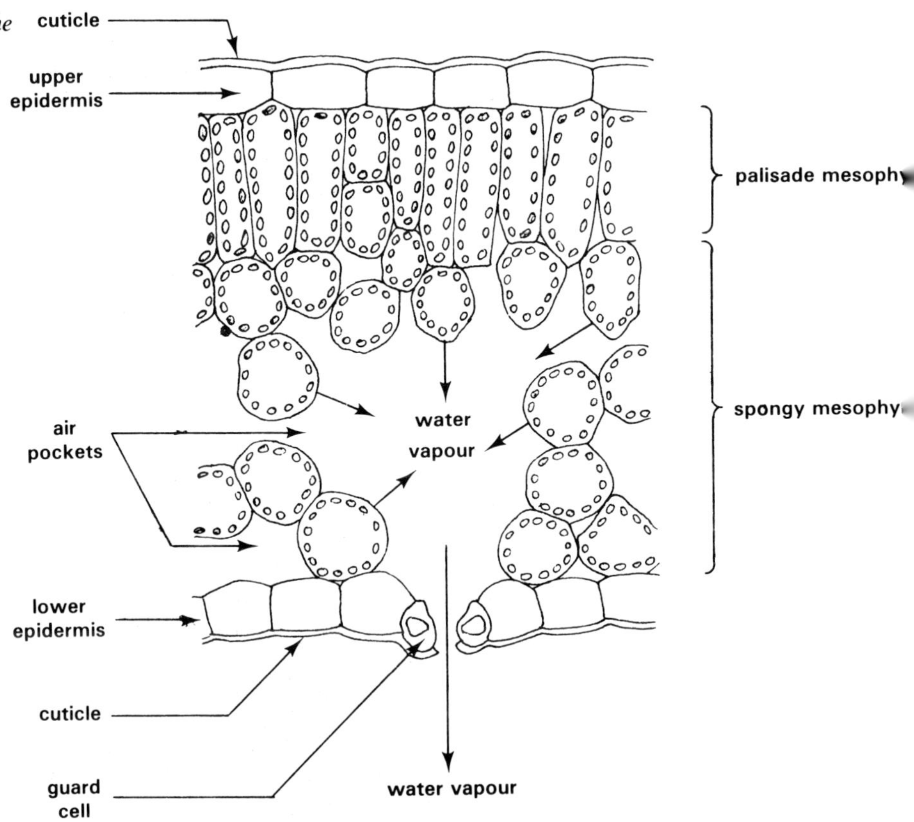

Because there are more stomata on the leaves than elsewhere on the shoot system it is evident that most of the water vapour is lost from the leaves. In many dicotyledonous species the leaves are broad, flattened organs with a vast network of minor veins (Fig. 11.1). Even the smallest vein contains transporting cells which supply the mesophyll tissue with water and dissolved minerals and remove soluble photosynthetic products. A conspicuous feature of the spongy mesophyll is the presence of numerous intercommunicating air pockets (Fig. 11.2). Water constantly evaporates into the air pockets from the walls of the mesophyll cells.

Since the mesophyll air pockets are enclosed spaces, the air in them is usually saturated or nearly so with water vapour. The air inside leaves therefore has a relatively high water potential (Chapter 2). The water potential of the atmosphere surrounding the shoot system fluctuates according to prevailing climatic conditions. In hot, damp greenhouses and in tropical jungles the atmosphere is extremely humid with a fairly high water potential. However, in most terrestrial habitats the atmosphere is generally much less humid and therefore has a relatively low water potential. Consequently when the stomata are open an area of high water potential is brought into contact with an area of low water potential and water vapour rapidly **diffuses** into the surrounding air down a **water potential gradient**. Clearly any factor which alters the size of the gradient will influence the rate of transpiration.

11.2 Factors affecting the transpiration rate

Climate is the product of a large number of interacting factors, notably the intensity and duration of sunlight, wind movement and precipitation, especially rainfall. The water potential of the atmosphere is determined by such interactions. As we have just seen, this affects the size of the water potential gradient between leaves and the surrounding atmosphere. However, the situation is complex because climatic factors may not affect leaves and the atmosphere in the same way or to the same extent. Although climate profoundly influences transpiration rates, other factors such as leaf structure, shape and physiology also determine the rate at which leaves lose water vapour to the atmosphere.

11.2.1 Climate

1. SOLAR RADIATION

Energy as heat and as light comes from the sun. About 10 per cent of **infrared radiation**, the main source of heat from the sun, falling on leaves is absorbed and is therefore potentially available to raise the temperature of leaves. However, most of this energy provides latent heat for the evaporation of water from the leaf cells. A drastic increase in leaf temperature is thus averted. Nevertheless, leaf temperatures of between 5–8°C above atmospheric temperature are common even in Britain. The effect of such temperature differences is described more fully in the next section.

Light intensity affects transpiration by controlling the degree and to some extent the pattern of stomatal opening (Chapter 12). The stomata of most plants open fully in daylight hours, bringing the saturated air enclosed in a leaf into direct contact with the surrounding atmosphere. This is why there is usually a close correlation between the rate of transpiration and light intensity (Fig. 11.3).

FIG. 11.3 *Correlation between rate of transpiration of oats and light intensity (after Sutcliffe 1968)*

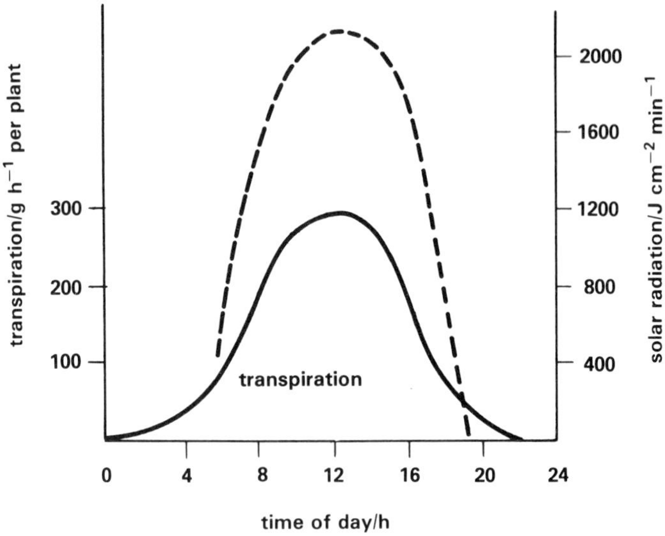

2. TEMPERATURE

A rise in temperature provides additional **kinetic energy** for the movement of water molecules. The effect is to accelerate the rate of evaporation of water from the walls of mesophyll cells and, if the stomata are open, to speed up the rate of diffusion of water vapour into the surrounding atmosphere.

The water potential of the atmosphere generally becomes lower as its temperature is raised and it can then hold more moisture. Table 11.1 compares the water potential at two temperatures of a fully saturated atmosphere, as exists inside a leaf, with one which is 60 per cent saturated, as may occur outside a leaf. It is evident that even a 5°C rise in temperature considerably increases the water potential gradient between a leaf and the air surrounding it.

Table 11.1 Comparison of the water potential, expressed as water vapour pressure, of air at 100 and 60 %RH at two temperatures

TEMP °C	WATER VAPOUR PRESSURE/*k*Pa		WATER VAPOUR PRESSURE GRADIENT/*k*Pa
	100 %RH	60	
15	1·70	1·02	0·68
20	2·33	1·40	0·93

The air inside a leaf normally remains saturated with water vapour when its temperature is raised because of increased evaporation of water from the walls of the mesophyll cells. Thus, as the leaf temperature rises so does the water potential of the air in the leaf. It is not likely that a similar situation exists in the surrounding atmosphere. The water potential here will increase only if there is a nearby source of liquid water from which evaporation can take place. Transpiration from plants and evaporation from the soil and from lakes and oceans are the main sources of water vapour in the atmosphere. If the upper layers of the soil are dry following a long period without rainfall, a rise in temperature has little or no effect on the water potential of the atmosphere in a terrestrial environment. In hot, dry weather, therefore, the water potential gradient between leaf and atmosphere is great and transpiration is very rapid.

The effect of infra-red radiation in raising leaf temperatures by several degrees above ambient (section 11.2.1(1)) accelerates the rate of transpiration. However, when a leaf is hotter than the air around it, convection currents develop bringing cooler air in contact with the leaf. To some extent the cooling effect counteracts the expected increase in the transpiration rate by lowering the leaf temperature.

3. AIR MOVEMENT

Transpiration in still air results in the accumulation of a **boundary layer**, several millimetres thick, of saturated air at the surfaces of leaves. The boundary offers considerable resistance to the diffusion of water vapour through stomata and cuticle, thereby reducing the transpiration rate. Movement of the surrounding air reduces the thickness of the boundary layer and results in increased transpiration (Fig. 11.4). Air movements can occur as a result of convection (section 11.2.1(2)) or wind currents. As still air rarely exists in nature for any length of time, air movement is important in increasing the loss of water vapour from terrestrial plants. However, air movement generally brings cool air into contact with leaves. As we have already seen, this may lower the temperature of leaves and help to reduce transpiration. Continuous exposure to wind of high velocity generally causes wilting of leaves. This is because the rapid loss of water vapour by transpiration is not balanced by absorption of water from the soil.

FIG. 11.4 *Effects of air movement on thickness of boundary layer*

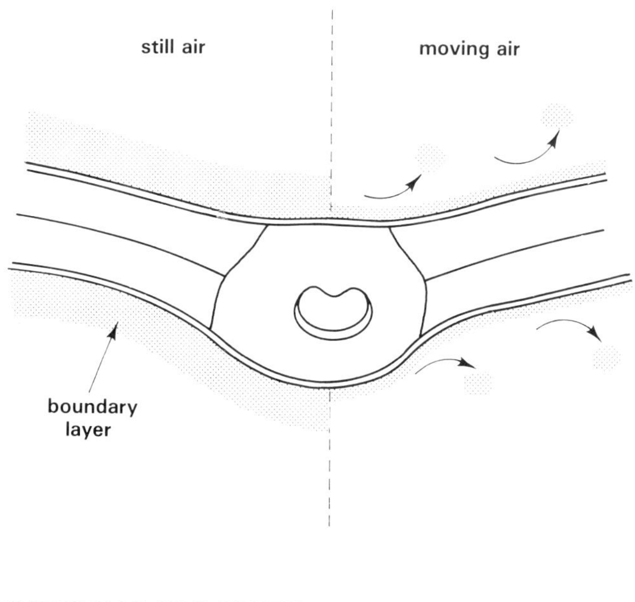

4. ATMOSPHERIC HUMIDITY

The water potential of air is usually expressed as **percentage relative humidity (%RH)**:

$$\%RH = \frac{\text{water vapour pressure of air at t°C}}{\text{water vapour pressure of saturated air at t°C}} \times 100$$

We have noted that the air inside a leaf is saturated with water vapour, that is at 100 %RH. Conversely the humidity of the atmosphere surrounding a leaf is changeable. Values exceeding 70 %RH are rare outdoors in Britain while figures as low as 30 %RH can occur following a long spell of hot, dry weather. In either case the water potential gradient between leaf and atmosphere is substantial and when the stomata are open water vapour rapidly diffuses from the leaf. As the %RH of the atmosphere falls the water potential gradient increases. There is thus a direct relationship between atmospheric humidity and the rate of transpiration (Table 11.2 and Fig. 11.5).

Table 11.2 Water potential, expressed as water vapour pressure, of air at four different humidities (readings taken at 20°C)

%RH	WATER VAPOUR PRESSURE/*k*Pa	WATER VAPOUR PRESSURE GRADIENT/*k*Pa
100	2·33	2·33 − 2·33 = 0·00
70	1·63	2·33 − 1·63 = 0·70
60	1·40	2·33 − 1·40 = 0·93
50	1·16	2·33 − 1·16 = 1·17

FIG. 11.5 *Effect of atmospheric humidity on the rate of transpiration*

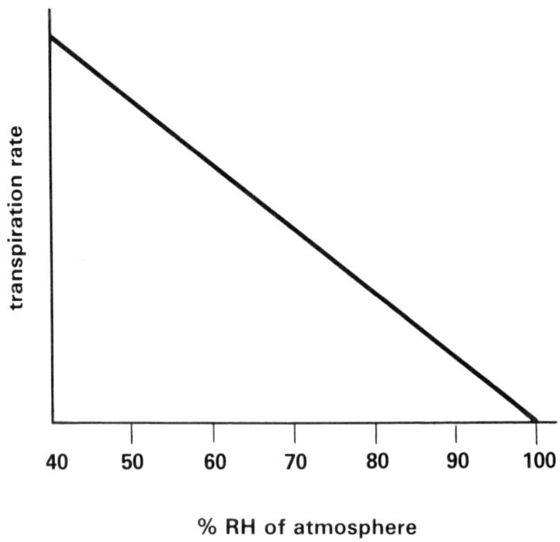

11.2.2 Leaf structure

Brown and Escombe in 1900 investigated the rates of diffusion of gases through membranes perforated by pores varying in size and number per unit area. Their findings of the movement of carbon dioxide and its implications in the absorption of the gas by leaves for photosynthesis are described in Chapter 12. Part of their work involved a study of the diffusion of water vapour. They observed that, providing the pores were not too close to one another, the rate of diffusion of water vapour through a perforated membrane is as much as 50 per cent of the total water loss from a body of water of surface area similar to the membrane. This occurred despite the fact that the pores occupied less than 3 per cent of the area of the membrane. Stomata usually account for about 5 per cent of the total area of a leaf. It may therefore be deduced that the epidermis is only a limited barrier to water loss when the stomata are open. The rate of diffusion of water vapour through stomata results, however, from the interaction of a number of factors.

1. PORE SIZE

As molecules of a gas such as water vapour escape through a pore into still air they spread out into concentric, hemispherical zones called **diffusion shells** (Fig. 11.6). The water potential of each shell diminishes the further it is from the pore. Water vapour molecules continually diffusing from the outer shell into the atmosphere are replaced by molecules diffusing from an inner shell. A continuous water potential gradient thus exists across the diffusion shells.

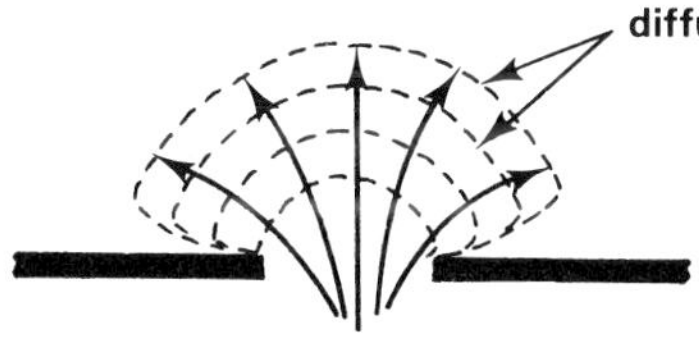

FIG. 11.6 *Diffusion of water vapour through a pore*

The rate of diffusion **per unit area of pore** is greater through small pores than through large pores (Chapter 12). Furthermore the diffusion rate is proportional to the **diameter** of the pore (Table 12.1). The effectiveness with which stomata control transpiration depends on the humidity of the surrounding air and on the extent to which the stomatal apertures are open. In still air when outgoing water vapour accumulates above stomata a reduction in pore size is less effective in lowering the transpiration rate than in moving air (Fig. 11.7). Why do you think this is so?

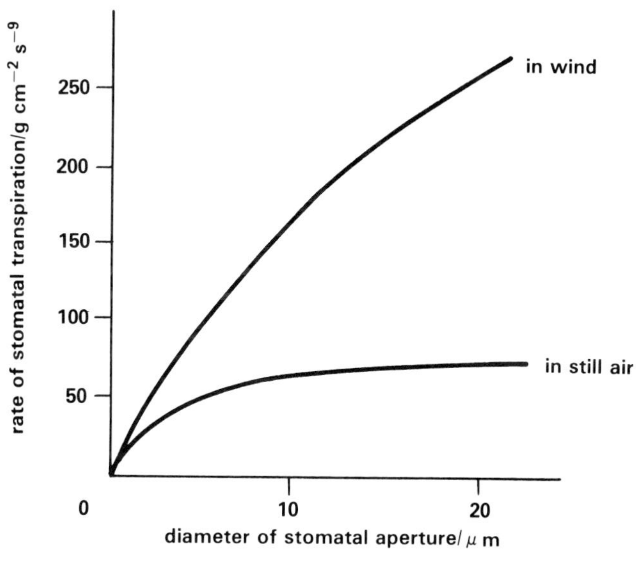

FIG. 11.7 *Effect of pore size in controlling transpiration rate in* Zebrina (after Bange, 1953)

2. PORE DENSITY

Where stomata are spaced wide enough apart there is no interference between the diffusion shells of water vapour above each pore. However, where stomata are close to one another, as occurs in most land plants, there may be considerable **overlap** between the diffusion shells above adjacent stomata (Fig. 11.8). The effect is to form one large area from which water vapour diffuses into the atmosphere. Because the rate of diffusion per unit area from a large area is less than that from a number of smaller areas of equivalent area the transpiration rate is reduced. Other ways in which leaf structure affect transpiration are mentioned in the next section.

FIG. 11.8 *Diffusion of water vapour through adjacent pores*

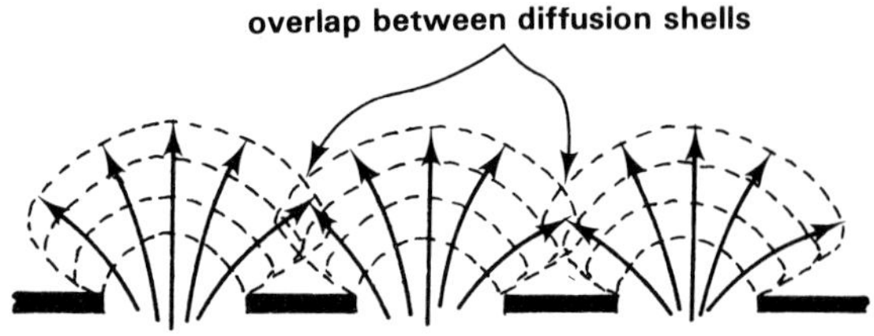

11.2.3 Xerophytic plants

There is a considerable variety of structure, stomatal distribution and physiology among higher plants. The differences often play a key part in determining the rate of transpiration. Species which inhabit areas where water is scarce are of particular interest in this respect. They are generally called **xerophytes** as opposed to most land plants known as **mesophytes** which inhabit areas where ample water is available and **hydrophytes** which live totally or partially submerged in water.

FIG. 11.9 (a) *Transverse section through a stoma of* Hakea, *×375*

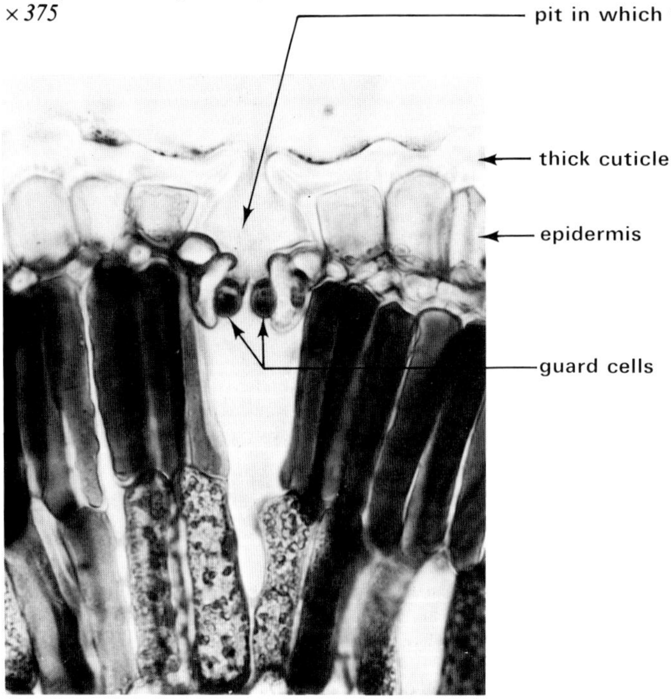

FIG. 11.9 (b) *Transverse section through part of a leaf of* Nerium, *×100*

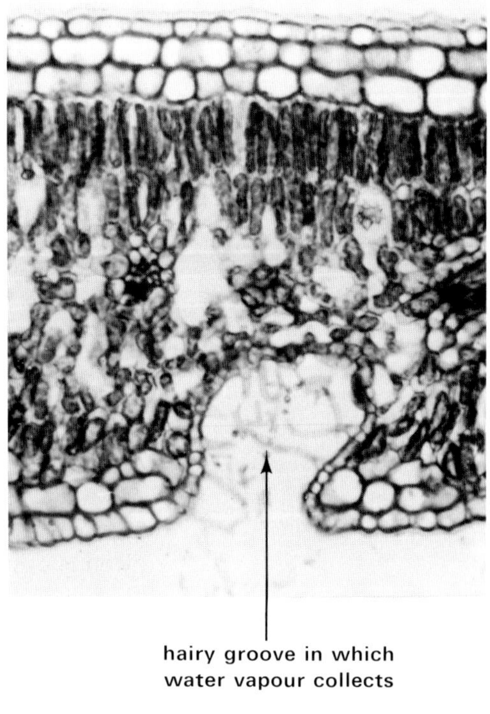

FIG. 11.9 (c) *Transverse section of a rolled leaf of marram grass, ×40. When the hinge cells lose water vapour excessively they become flaccid and the leaf rolls up as shown*

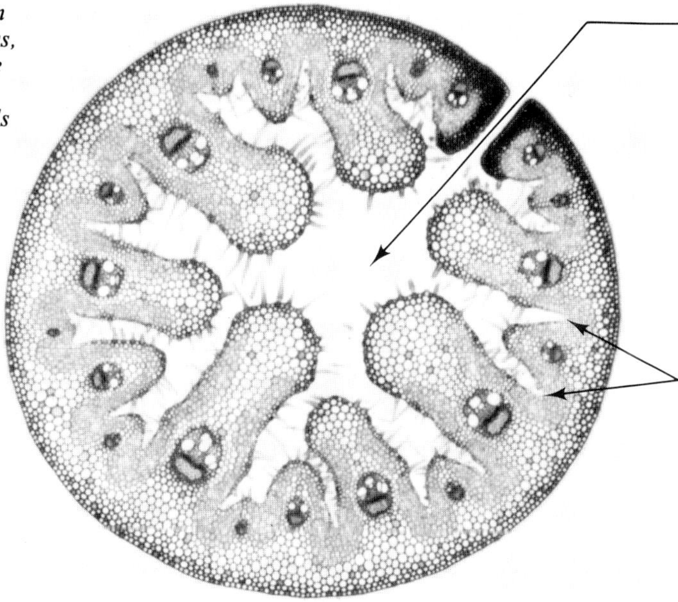

Frequently the guard cells of xerophytes are sunk in pits or in grooves well below the surface of the leaf or stem (Fig. 11.9(a)). Water vapour escaping through stomata accumulates immediately above the guard cells to form a **thick boundary layer** which reduces the transpiration rate even in moving air. Other modifications, such as **hairiness** of the shoot system and a relatively **thick cuticle**, also assist in minimising the rate at which water vapour is lost (Fig. 11.9(b)). In very dry weather the leaves of some xerophytes such as marram grass can even be **rolled** into a cylinder with the stomata on the inside. Water vapour is trapped inside the cylinder, so building up the humidity of the air into which transpiration takes place. Ultimately the water potential inside the cylinder becomes sufficiently high to stop transpiration (Fig. 11.9(c)).

Cacti are often thought of as plants ideally suited to conditions of drought. They are **succulent** plants and store water in a special tissue inside their bodies. The cylindrical shape of many cacti means that for each unit volume of tissue there is a small unit of surface area through which water vapour can be lost. Not all xerophytes are succulent. Some such as the creosote bush are highly lignified and can **tolerate** extremes of desiccation without wilting.

Perhaps even more significant is the rate at which some xerophytes fix carbon dioxide compared with mesophytes. Cacti and many other xerophytes are **C4 plants** (Chapter 5) and can make photosynthetic end-products more efficiently than C3 plants from the same volume of carbon dioxide. This means that the stomata of xerophytes need remain open for only short periods of time each day to acquire sufficient carbon dioxide. Cacti take in carbon dioxide at night when the air is cooler and conditions are less likely to encourage transpiration. Such adaptations considerably lessen the volume of water vapour transpired.

11.3 The effects of transpiration

One of the effects of transpiration has already been mentioned: the cooling effect which prevents drastic rises in leaf temperature. There is also little doubt that transpiration is the main factor affecting the rate of water movement through plants.

11.3.1 Water movement through the shoot system

A **potometer** (Fig. 11.10(a)) can be used to investigate the rate of absorption of water by a plant shoot. As the shoot transpires, the water vapour it has lost is replaced by liquid water drawn in from the potometer. What is more the rate of absorption is affected by the same factors which influence the transpiration rate. If the leafy shoot is replaced with a water-filled porous pot (Fig. 11.10(b)) comparable results are obtained. As water evaporates from the tiny holes of the porous pot it is replaced by liquid water entering the pores by **capillarity**. The capillary movement of water is due partly to forces of **adhesion** between water molecules and the walls of the pores and of **cohesion**, the forces of attraction holding the water molecules to each other. It is therefore logical to deduce that the forces responsible for water movement in the pot are also at work in the shoot system of a plant. Water evaporating from the porous walls of leaf mesophyll cells is replaced by capillarity. But where does the water come from and what effect does the refilling of the pores in the mesophyll cell walls have on the rest of the plant?

FIG. 11.10 (a) *A potometer*

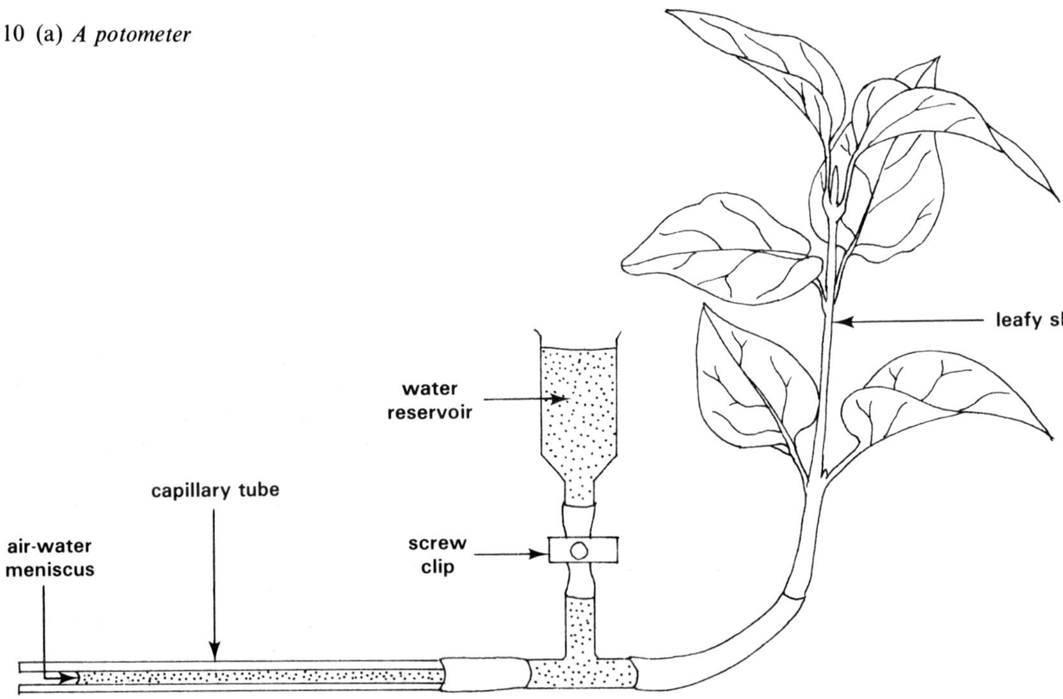

With the screw clip closed, the rate at which the meniscus moves along the capillary tube indicates the rate at which the leafy shoot is absorbing water. When all the water has been absorbed from the capillary tube it can be refilled by opening the screw clip.

FIG. 11.10 (b) *An atmometer.*

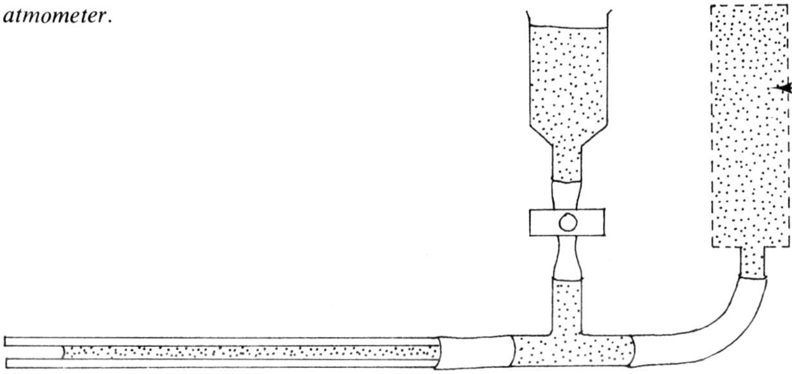

Readings are taken as with the potometer

Typical results

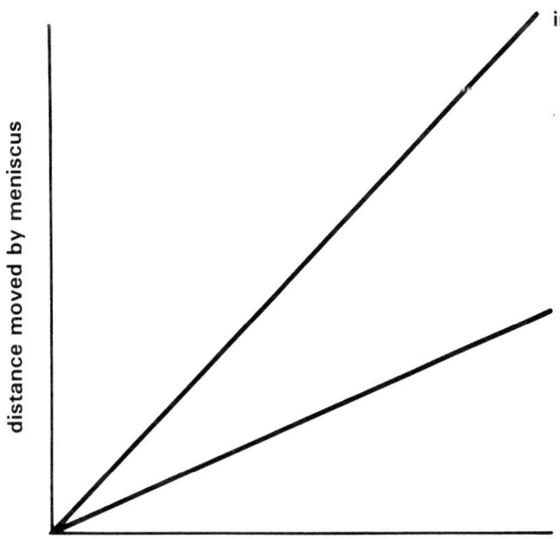

The nearest reservoir of water for capillarity is the protoplasts of the mesophyll cells. The effect of losing water in this way is to lower the water potential of mesophyll cells. If a source of water of higher potential is available nearby the protoplasts of the mesophyll cells could absorb water through their plasma membranes by **osmosis**. Alternatively water could be drawn by **capillarity** from the source directly into the mesophyll cell walls where evaporation is taking place. Whichever route is taken, the water comes from a minor vein containing water-conducting xylem elements. One effect of transpiration therefore is to create **leaf suction** which removes water from the veins of leaves. In turn the leaf veins become replenished by absorbing water from the xylem elements of the stem. Again the movement of water from stem to leaf is along a water potential gradient.

The cut shoot in the potometer has direct access to water in the apparatus and can draw freely on it. Does a similar situation exist in a whole plant? Some idea can be obtained by comparing the rates of transpiration and water absorption of an intact plant over a period of time (Fig. 11.11). Absorption lags behind transpiration, indicating that the roots are a barrier to a continuous flow of water triggered by transpiration. The effect of leaf suction and root resistance working in opposite directions places the water columns in the vessels and tracheids under strain or **tension**. Th columns are sufficiently elastic to take the strain so they do not normall break and the flow of water, **the transpiration stream**, continues. Wha prevents breakage of the water columns? The answer to this question is th **cohesive forces** which exist between water molecules (Chapter 2).

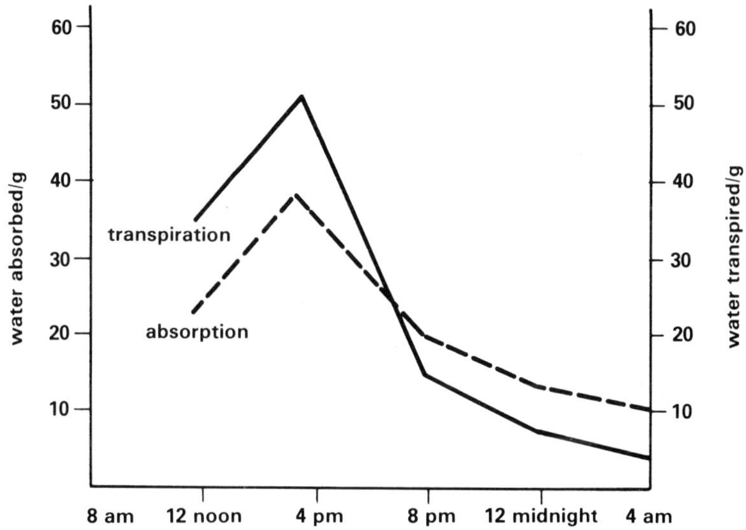

FIG. 11.11 *Comparison of the rates of transpiration and water absorption by sunflower plants* (after Kramer, 1937)

FIG. 11.12 *A giant California redwood* (*Sequoia tree*). (Photo Paul Conklin, permission Colorific)

The account of water transport given above is a summary of the **transpiration-cohesion-tension theory** described in 1894 by Dixon and Joly. What is of particular interest is that the proposed mechanism can account for the movement of water to the tops of extremely tall trees such as the redwood, *Sequoia*, which frequently grows to a height of well over 100 m (Fig. 11.12). Atmospheric pressure at sea level is 101·3 *k*Pa (1 atm) which can raise a column of water to a height of only 10 m, and is quite inadequate to move water to the top of a tall tree. Water potentials of up to −3000 *k*Pa (−30 atm) have been demonstrated in the mesophyll tissue of the leaves of tall trees. This means that leaves can generate a suction capable of pulling water to a height of 300 m. The tension required to stretch to breaking point columns of sap from the xylem of trees has been shown to be about 30 000 *k*Pa. This is well in excess of the tension normally generated in plants.

What we have seen so far is that transpiration can lead to an upward movement of water through the shoot system. But what about water transport in roots?

11.3.2 Water absorption by roots

Water is absorbed by the outermost layer of the root which is in direct contact with the soil. Between 4 and 10 mm behind the root tip the **epidermal cells** have **root hairs** which increase the surface area of the root several fold (Fig. 11.13). Because of the unceasing apical growth of the root tip, a root hair zone has a functional life of only a few weeks. It is continually replaced by a new zone in the freshly extended part of a root. In older parts of the root the epidermis is replaced by a suberised **exodermis**. If secondary thickening occurs a **periderm** becomes the outermost layer (Chapter 21). It is commonly thought that water uptake by a root is confined to the root hair zone. Yet it has been shown that water absorption can occur rapidly through the surface of older parts of the root even where an exodermis or a periderm is present (Fig. 11.14).

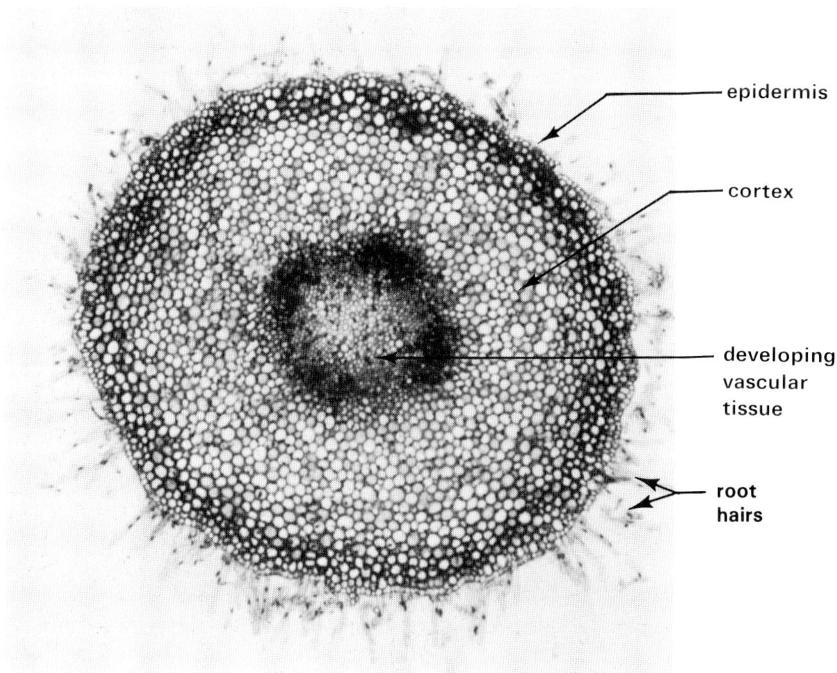

FIG. 11.13 (a) *Transverse section through the root hair zone of a broad bean root, ×40*

FIG. 11.13 (b) *Close-up view of some root hairs, × 100*

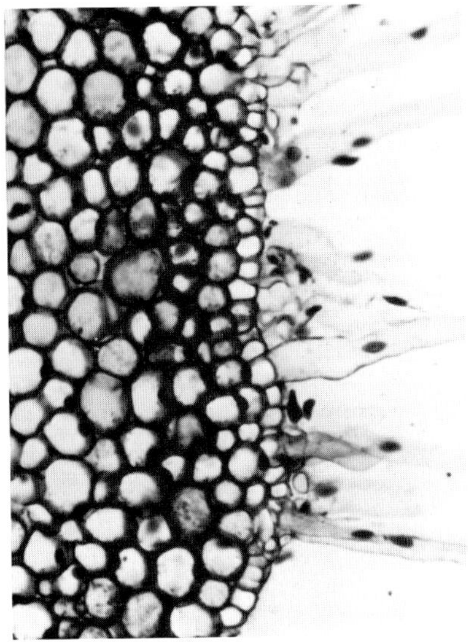

Inside the outermost root layer is the **cortex** of large, thin-walled, vacuolated parenchyma cells with conspicuous intercellular spaces. The innermost cortical layer is the **endodermis**, the cells of which, early in their development, have a suberised Casparian band on their radial walls. Later the suberisation becomes more extensive and covers the radial and inner tangential walls (Fig. 11.15). Immediately inside the endodermis is the **pericycle**, a region one to several cells wide of small, thin-walled parenchyma cells. The pericycle is the site of origin of lateral roots which may add greatly to the absorptive surface area of the root system. At the core of the root is the **vascular tissue**. In the root hair zone of the root of a dicotyledonous plant there are between two and five groups of **protoxylem** elements. At a later stage the central **metaxylem** elements differentiate and the primary xylem looks star-shaped in cross section (Fig. 11.16).

The transpiration stream drags columns of water upwards through the network of xylem elements which extend throughout the plant. The stream eventually lowers the water potential in the root xylem sufficiently to establish a gradient of water potential down which water is ultimately absorbed from the soil. There are forces which lower the water potential of the soil solution, thereby opposing absorption. The opposing forces include the osmotic potential of the soil solution, which is usually significant only in certain habitats such as salt marshes. Capillary and imbibitional forces also hold the soil solution in and between mineral particles and the humus fraction of soil. Nevertheless the transpiration stream can generate the necessary water potential gradient for water to pass from the soil solution across the root cortex and into the root xylem elements.

FIG. 11.14 *Water uptake by different parts of broad bean roots* (after Brouwer, 1965)

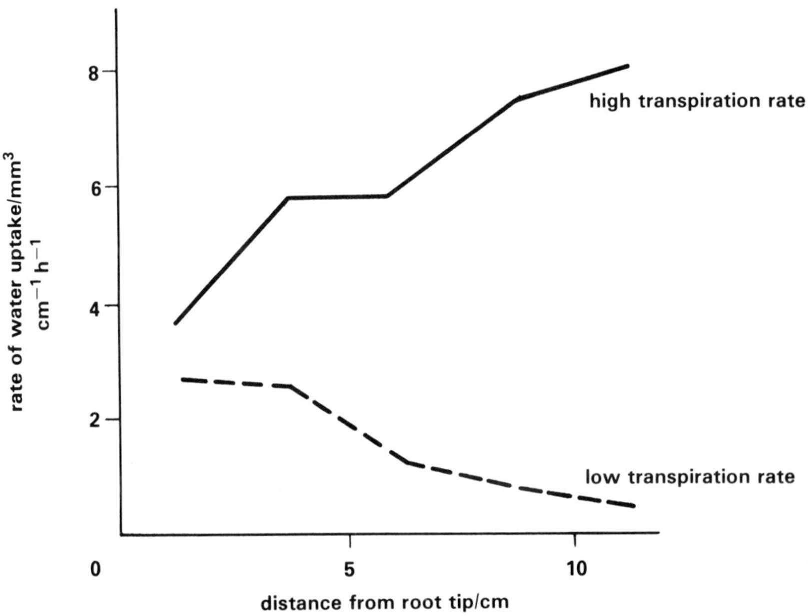

The classical view is that water moves through the living tissues of the root cortex from vacuole to vacuole by **osmosis**. However, as in the leaves it is possible that cell to cell transport by **capillarity** along the cell walls is also important. The wall route cannot be taken at the endodermis where the waxy Casparian band is impervious to water. At the endodermis water probably flows through the plasma membrane. The significance of this

FIG. 11.15 (a) *The endodermis* **(i) t.s. young endodermis**

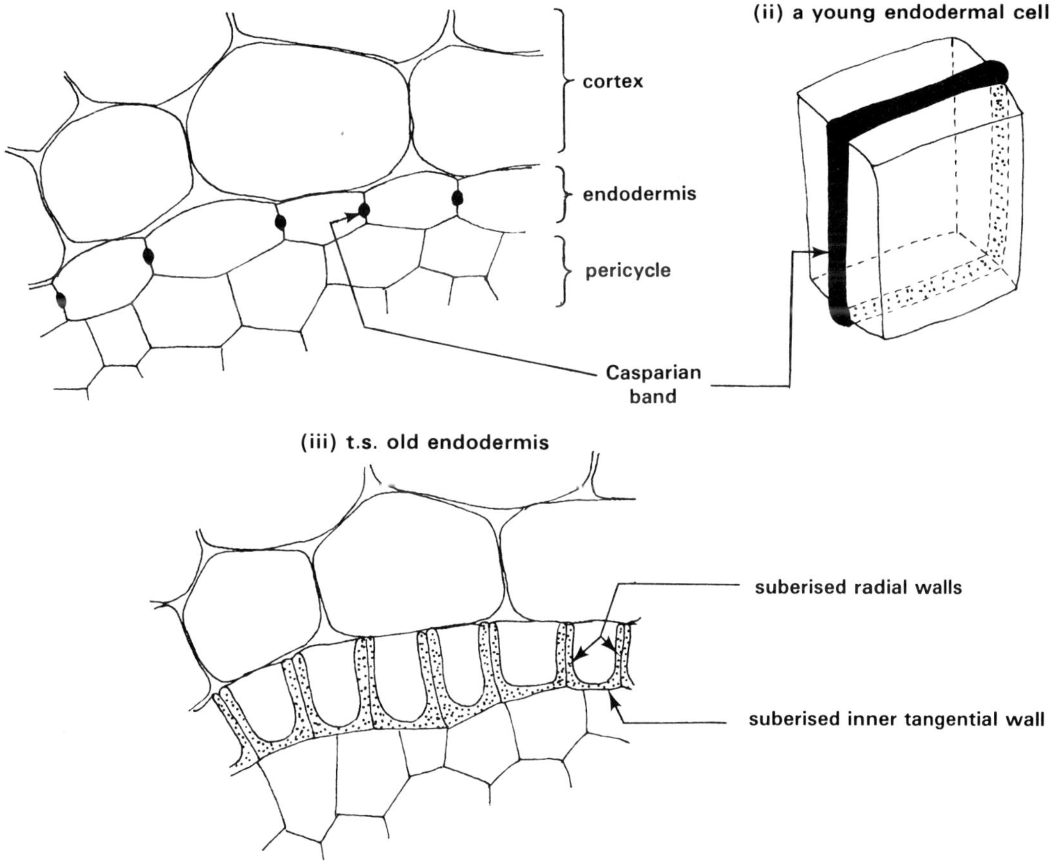

IG. 11.15 (b) *T.s. young ndodermis*, $\times 400$

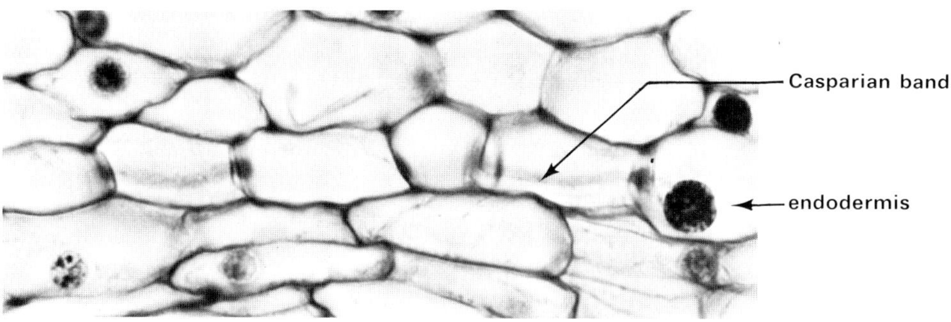

IG. 11.15 (c) *T.s. old ndodermis*, $\times 250$

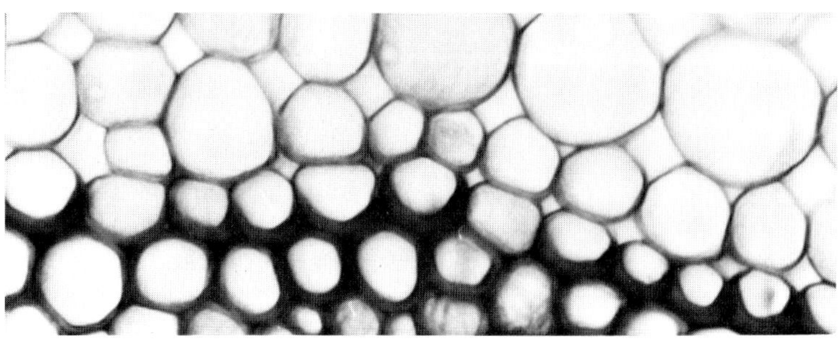

FIG. 11.16 *Transverse section through a root of a dicotyledonous plant,* ×200

pathway in controlling the entry of dissolved mineral ions is discussed in Chapter 13. Eventually the absorbed water reaches the xylem elements of the root from where it moves upwards into the veins of the shoot system.

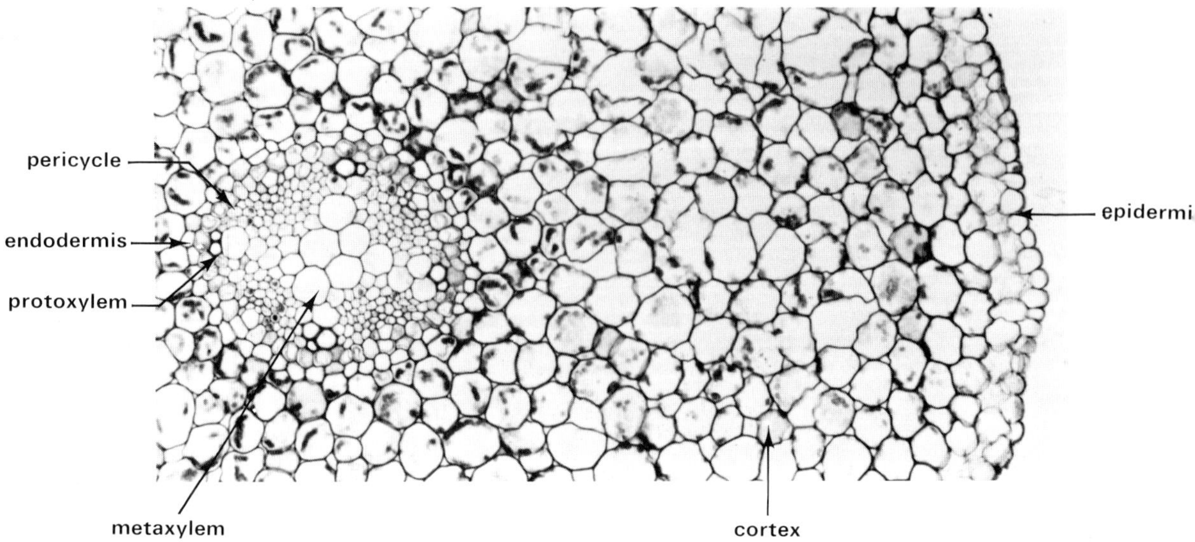

11.4 Root pressure

Few plant physiologists would challenge the role of transpiration in the movement of water through terrestrial plants. Yet there are other forces at work in plants which can take part in the flow of water. If, for example, a glass tube is attached to the stump of a freshly decapitated plant such as a vine, sap is pushed up the tube to a height of several metres (Fig. 11.17). Clearly the flow of sap from the stump cannot be linked with transpiration. The force responsible is called **root pressure**. In some species, notably low-growing plants such as grasses, root pressure is sufficiently strong at times to cause exudation of liquid water from special pores called **hydathodes** located at the edges of the leaves (Fig. 11.18). This phenomenon is called **guttation**. It is therefore possible that the flow of water through plants may sometimes be the combined result of the pulling effect of transpiration and the pushing effect of root pressure. However, the available evidence suggests that the forces generated by transpiration are usually more important.

Root pressure is most evident in conditions favouring rapid water absorption but limiting transpiration. For example, it is responsible for the rising of sap in the trunks of deciduous trees during spring before the leaf buds have opened. But even in these circumstances the pressure generated is rarely more than 200 *k*Pa (2 atm), a figure of minor importance compared with the transpiration pull. Furthermore the volume of sap exuded by the stumps of decapitated plants is generally little more than five per cent of the volume lost by transpiration from intact plants.

The development of root pressure seems to depend on the active secretion of mineral ions into the root xylem elements from surrounding parenchymatous transfer cells (Fig. 11.19). The effect of mineral secretion is to lower the water potential of the xylem sap leading to the absorption of water from the soil down a water potential gradient. Respiration by the transfer cells provides the energy required for movement of the ions against a concentration gradient. It is not surprising therefore that root pressure disappears when plant roots are treated with respiratory inhibitors such as potassium cyanide.

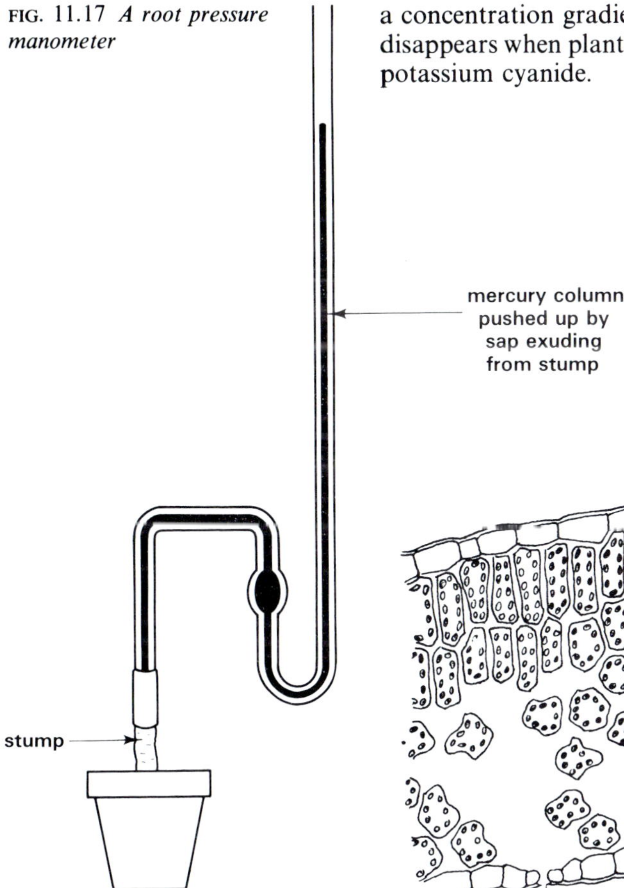

FIG. 11.17 *A root pressure manometer*

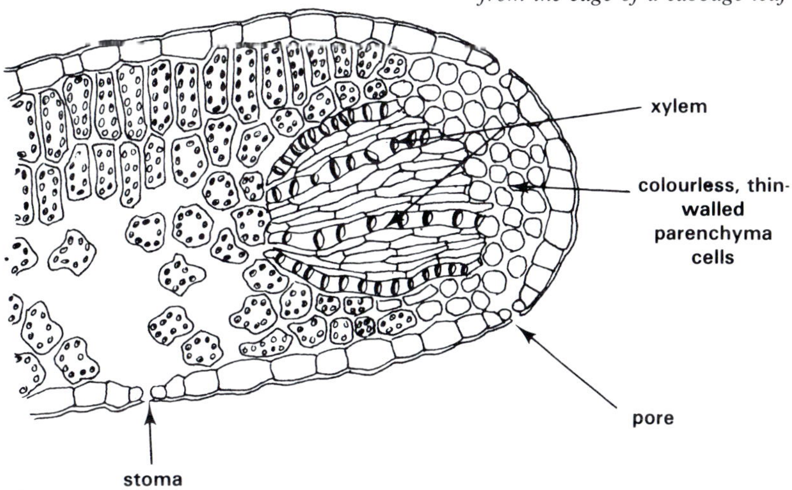

FIG. 11.18 *A hydathode in t.s. from the edge of a cabbage leaf*

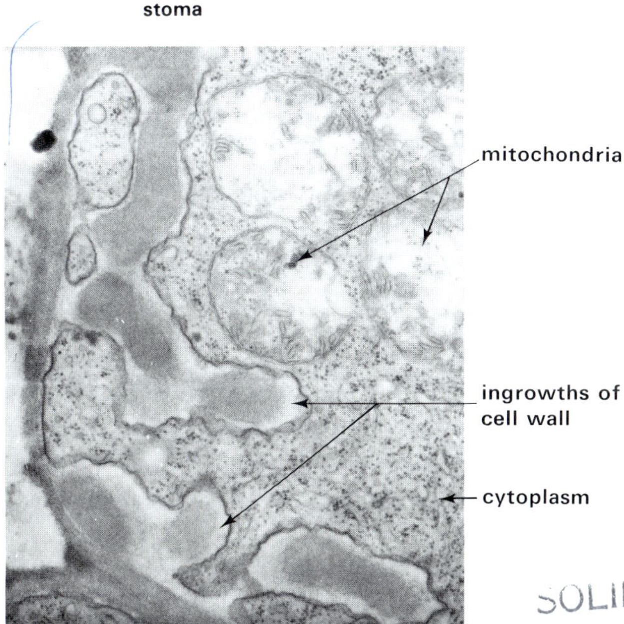

FIG. 11.19 *Electronmicrograph of a section through a transfer cell from the pericycle of a root of clover* (courtesy Dr. G. Briarty). *The cell wall ingrowths increase the surface area of the plasma membrane for the transfer of solutes. The mitochondria provide the free energy for active secretion of solutes*

11.5 Tracheids, vessels and capillarity

There is little doubt that xylem is the main water-carrying tissue of higher terrestrial plants. Proof of this comes from experiments in which the xylem elements of leafy shoots are blocked with wax and then given access to water. The leaves soon wilt compared with untreated shoots or where tissues other than xylem are blocked. As wax does not penetrate the

FIG. 11.20 (a) *Tracheids and vessels*

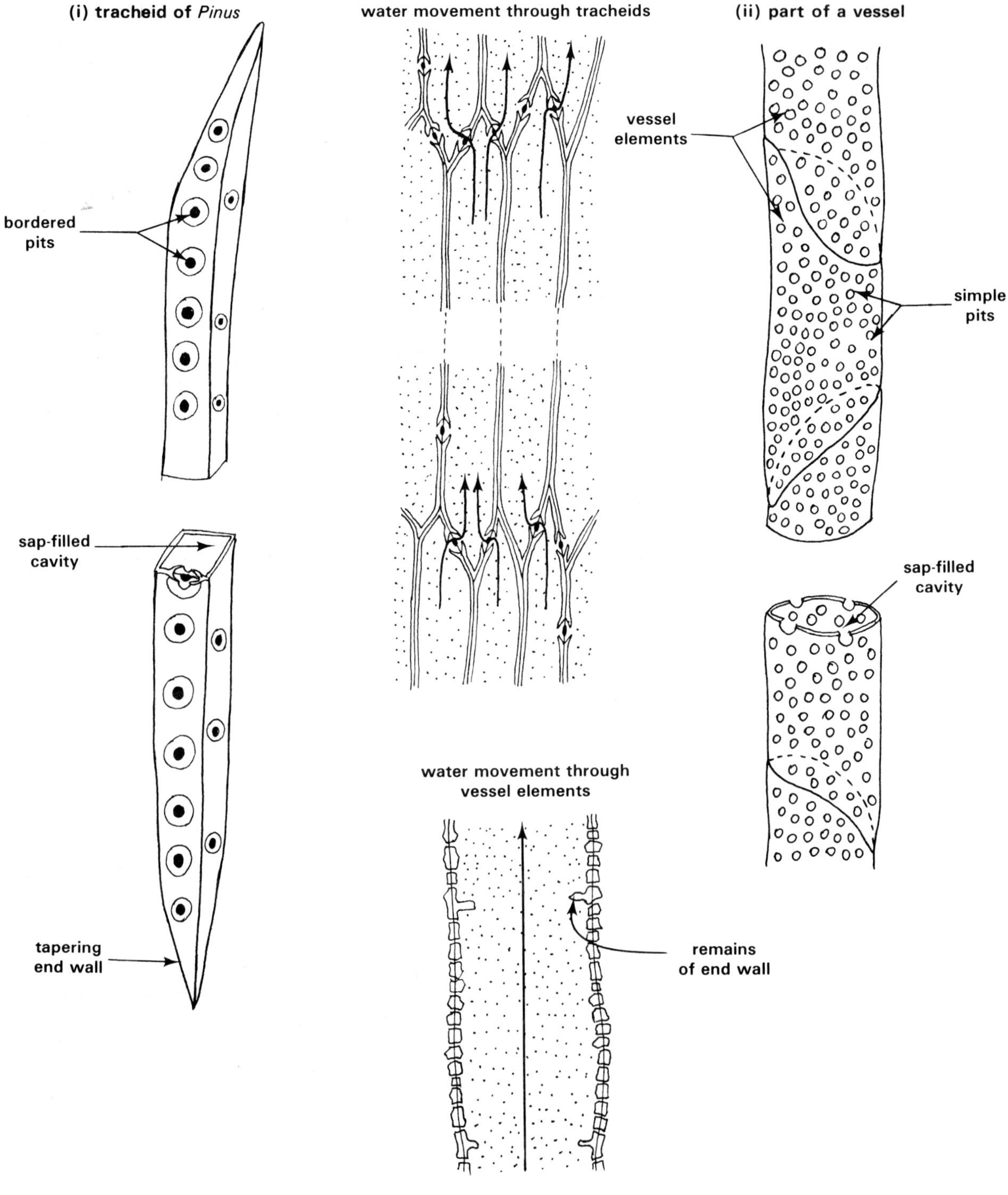

FIG. 11.20 (b) *Vessel elements, × 250*

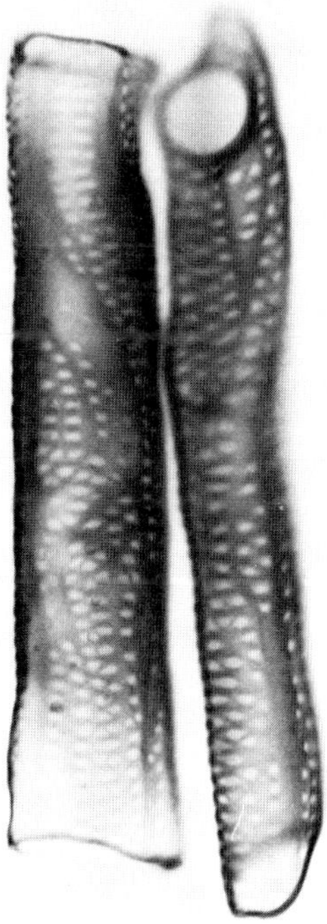

lignified walls of xylem elements it is clear that most of the water passes through the cavities of the xylem cells and not up the walls in a wick-like manner. These facts have recently been confirmed using isotopes of water.

The chief water-transporting cells found in flowering plants are **tracheids** and **vessels**. Tracheids were the water-carrying cells of the earliest land plants where they fulfilled the dual role of support and water conduction. They are still the main water-carrying cells in pteridophytes and gymnosperms. In conifers such as the pine, *Pinus*, mature tracheids are very long, narrow, angular cells measuring up to 5 mm long and 30 μm in diameter (Fig. 11.20(a)). Stiffening of the walls with lignin and interlocking of the tapered end walls are significant features in the role of tracheids as supporting cells. Water movement in the cavities of tracheids is helped by the lack of protoplasts. The presence of large, bordered pits allows the passage of aqueous solutions between adjacent tracheids.

Vessels are found in flowering plants. Unlike tracheids which differentiate from single cells derived from meristems, vessels originate from a vertical row of cells (Chapter 21). During differentiation the row of cells increases considerably in diameter, protoplasts are absorbed and the end walls between adjacent cells are partially or completely lost. Consequently, a long, open tube is formed, often several metres in length and averaging 250 μm in diameter (Fig. 11.20(b)). Because less resistance is offered, aqueous solutions can move three to six times more quickly through vessels compared with tracheids. As in tracheids, the walls of vessels are thickened with cellulose and hardened with lignin. The extent of wall thickening and lignification varies according to the stage of development of a plant organ when differentiation takes place. Protoxylem vessels which differentiate close to the apices of roots and stems have bands or spirals of strengthening material. The unthickened parts of the cell walls can be enlarged as the organs grow in length. Metaxylem vessels differentiate further back from root and shoot apices where growth in length has ceased. The walls of metaxylem vessels are more extensively thickened and cannot be enlarged.

Water rises in the bore of a fine tube by **capillarity** and plant physiologists have wondered whether capillarity is significant in the ascent of sap through the narrow cavities of xylem elements. Experiments have shown that water can rise to a height of 5–7 m in glass tubes with a bore comparable to the lumen of a tracheid. However, in wider tubes with bores similar to the lumen of a vessel the capillary rise is only a few centimetres. Even allowing for the fact that the many crevices in the walls of the transporting elements add to the capillary force it is generally considered that capillarity does not play an important role in the upward movement of sap through the xylem elements of land plants.

We have seen that the absorption of water and its transport through the body of a flowering plant is the consequence of several phenomena which are summarised in Figure 11.21. It is important to remember that water moves from one part of a plant to another and out into the atmosphere down **water potential gradients**. Heat from the sun is responsible for the largest water potential gradient between the shoot system and the atmosphere. Whereas emphasis in this chapter has been placed on the movement of water it should be mentioned that substances dissolved in the water are also moved simultaneously. The transport of mineral ions the main category of dissolved substances carried in xylem elements is described in Chapter 13.

FIG. 11.21 *Summary of water uptake and transport in a flowering plant*

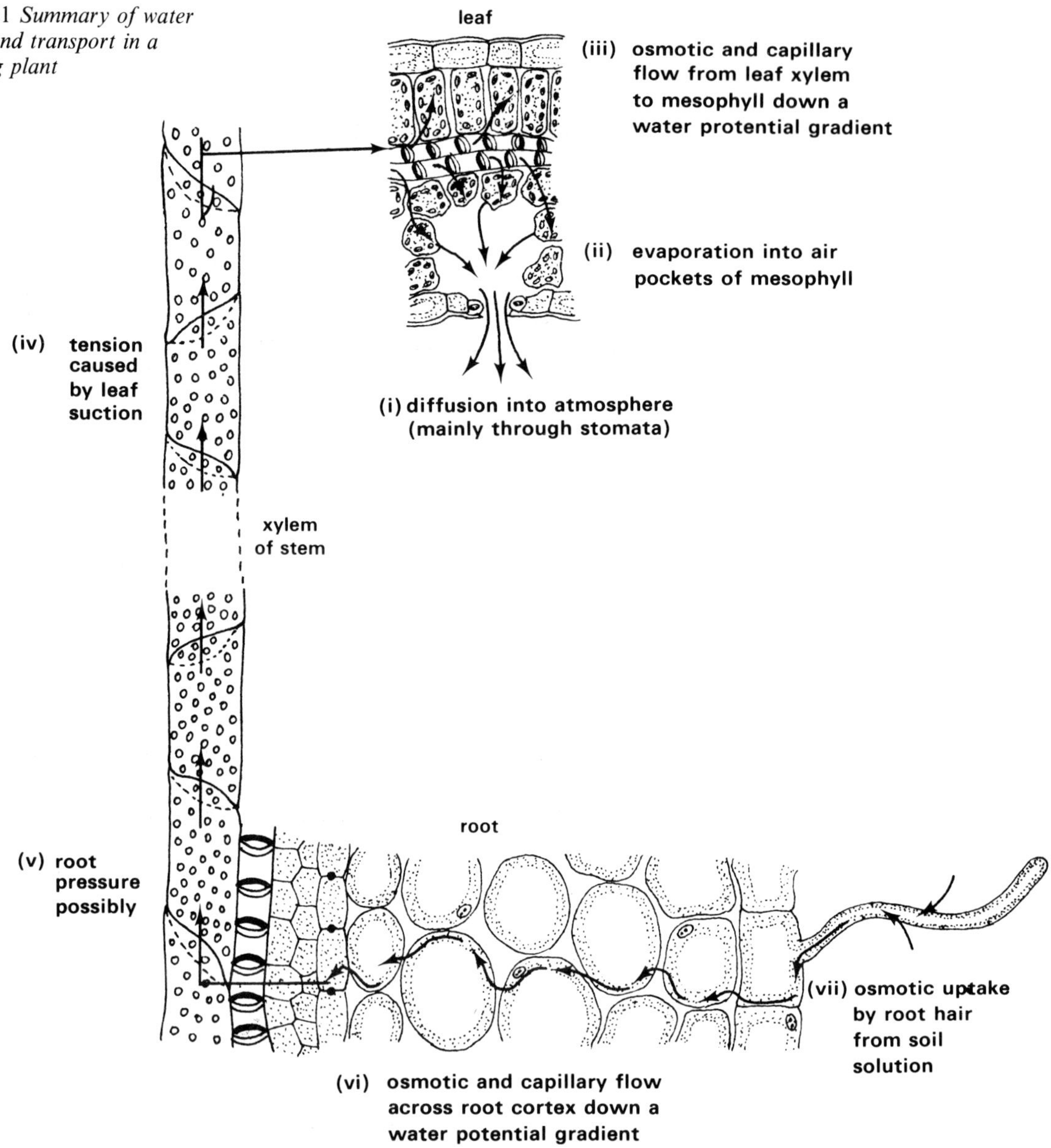

Chapter 12

Photosynthesis and translocation of photosynthetic products

Animals and green plants need a supply of raw materials and a source of energy to synthesise the many complex organic substances from which protoplasm is made. Animals get their energy from organic substances in their diets. Green plants obtain their energy from sunlight. The process whereby green plants use sunlight to produce organic molecules is called **photosynthesis**. Carbon dioxide and water are the raw ingredients for the process, which can be summarised simply in the following equation:

$$\underset{\text{from sunlight}}{\text{energy}} + \underset{\text{carbon dioxide}}{CO_2} + \underset{\text{water}}{H_2O} \longrightarrow \underset{\text{complex organic molecules}}{(CH_2O)} + \underset{\text{oxygen}}{O_2}$$

Photosynthesis is of the greatest importance to all living organisms. The organic substances made in photosynthesis can later be used by animals and other non-photosynthetic organisms. Thus in all ecosystems green plants are the **producers** on which the consumer organisms depend for energy and raw ingredients. On a global scale carbon dioxide is used in photosynthesis at a rate which more or less balances its output from respiration and the burning of fossil fuels such as coal and oil. What is more, the release into the environment of oxygen made in photosynthesis compensates for the uptake of oxygen by living organisms for respiration. Photosynthesis therefore helps to maintain an equilibrium or **steady state** in the environment.

Details of the way in which sunlight is converted into chemical bond energy in green plants are given in Chapter 5. In this chapter we shall examine how the structure of terrestrial plants enables them to obtain the raw materials and sunlight for photosynthesis. We shall also look at the ways in which various factors affect the rate of photosynthesis and what happens to photosynthetic products.

12.1 The leaf as a photosynthetic organ

The main organs of photosynthesis in terrestrial plants are the **leaves**. It is in the leaves that **chloroplasts** are present in abundance. If they are to function efficiently chloroplasts must have an adequate supply of **water** and **carbon dioxide**. They must also receive **light** of suitable wavelength and intensity. The structure of the leaves of mesophytes (Chapter 11) enables the photosynthetic requirements to reach the chloroplasts efficiently.

12.1.1 Penetration of light

The leaves of mesophytic plants are broad, thin, flattened structures. They thus have a relatively large surface area through which light can pass. The thinness of leaves means that light reaching the leaf surface has to pass only a short distance before reaching the mesophyll tissue where the chloroplasts are mainly located. Penetration of light to the mesophyll tissue is helped by the **transparency** of the leaf epidermis (Fig. 12.1(a)).

The leaves of many plants grow so that the leaf blade is usually at 90° to the sun's rays. Shading by leaves on the same shoot is often avoided because the leaves are normally arranged in a **mosaic** (Fig. 12.1(b)). These adaptations help to ensure that the maximum amount of available sunlight is received by each unit area of leaf surface. Leaves which are shaded, **shade leaves**, have a larger surface area than those exposed to full sunlight, **sun leaves**. Shade leaves are also thinner and have more chloroplasts. Because of this shade leaves make efficient use of the dim light they receive.

Inside chloroplasts the photosynthetic pigments are spread out in thin layers (Chapter 1). This arrangement presents a relatively extensive surface area for the absorption of sunlight. Chloroplasts can also change their positions to make the best use of available light (Fig. 12.1(c)).

FIG. 12.1 (a) *Passage of light through the outer surface of a leaf*

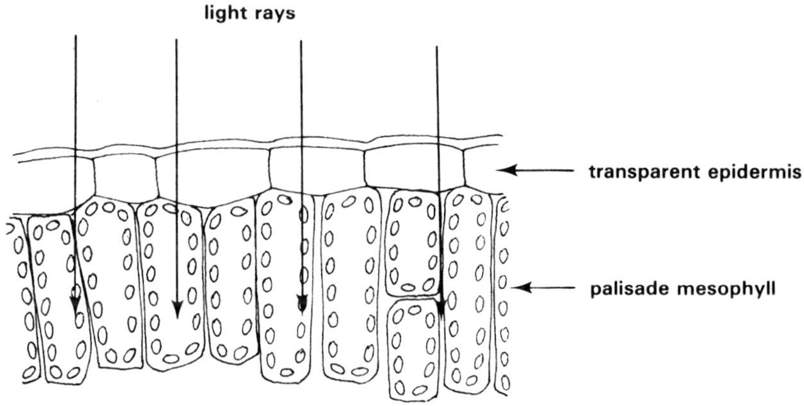

FIG. 12.1 (b) *Leaf mosaic of sycamore*

FIG. 12.1 (c) *Movement of chloroplasts in response to light intensity*

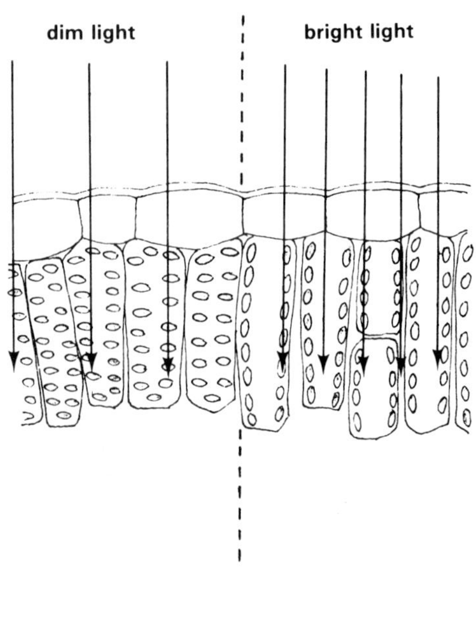

12.1.2 Supply of water

Water is carried into a leaf through a main vein in the midrib. An extensive network of minor veins arising from the main vein penetrates the mesophyll tissue. In an oak leaf for example, each mm^2 of leaf area contains a total length of about 10 mm of vein. Under normal circumstances the **xylem elements** of the veins maintain a continuous flow of water to the leaf tissues (Chapter 11). Another important function of the leaf veins is to carry away the organic products of photosynthesis to other parts of the plant. Phloem elements in the veins are responsible for this task (section 12.4).

12.1.3 Uptake of carbon dioxide

The waxy cuticle covering the epidermis of leaves is permeable to carbon dioxide in some plants. In other species carbon dioxide reaches the mesophyll tissue mainly through the **stomata**. There are three main patterns of stomatal distribution in leaves. In many mesophytic plants stomata are confined to the lower epidermis. The leaves of some mesophytes have a few stomata on the upper epidermis. Equal numbers of stomata occur on both surfaces in many monocotyledonous species. Each stoma consists of a pair of **guard cells** between which a **pore** is formed when the stoma is open. The walls of the guard cells are unevenly thickened. The inner walls where the two cells face each other is much thicker than the outer walls (Fig. 12.2). The guard cells are nucleate and several small chloroplasts are often present in the dense cytoplasm.

FIG. 12.2 (a) (i) *Surface view of stoma of privet*

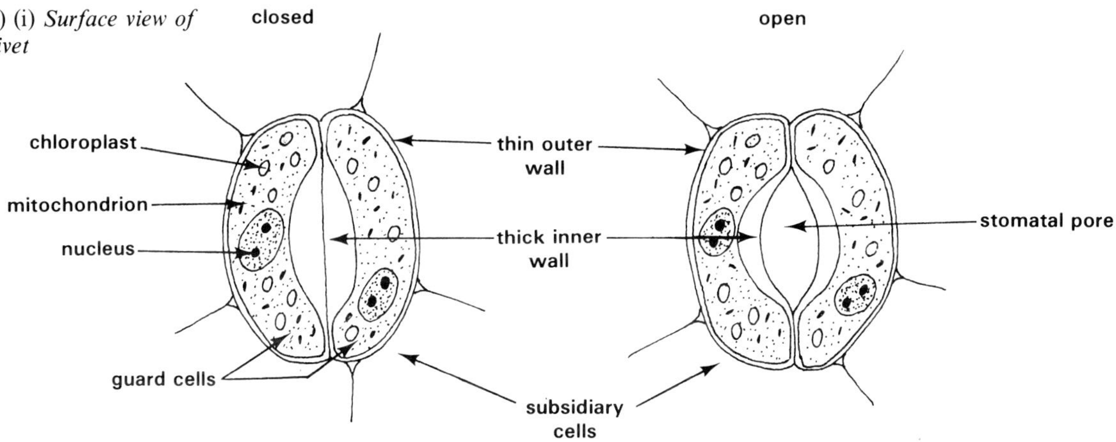

FIG. 12.2 (a) (ii) *T.s. stoma of privet*

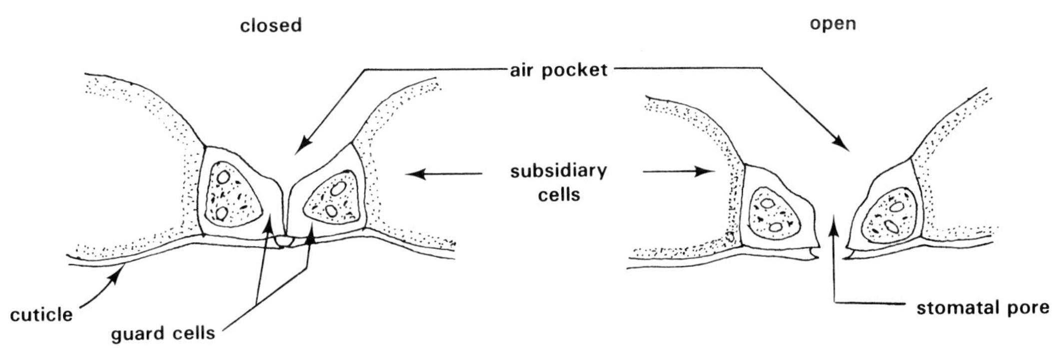

FIG. 12.2 (b) *Surface view of open stomata on the leaf epidermis of a dicotyledonous plant, × 300*

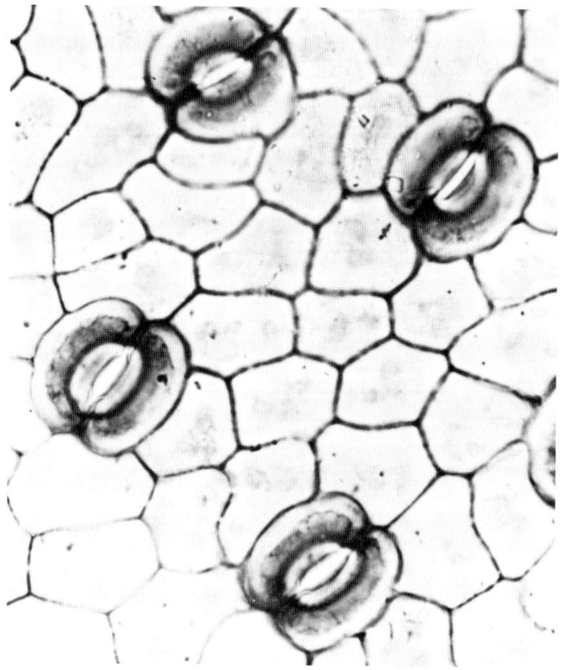

It might be expected that the tiny stomatal pores should offer considerable resistance to the passage of carbon dioxide from the surrounding air into the mesophyll tissue. However, experiments carried out by Brown and Escombe at the end of the last century demonstrate that gases can pass quickly through small pores (Table 12.1). The data shows that for a given area of pore, carbon dioxide flows more rapidly through small pores than through large pores. Stomatal pores are on average 10–30 μm long and 5–10 μm wide when fully open. The rate of gas flow per unit area through stomatal pores is much more rapid than that shown for the smallest pores used in the experiments.

Table 12.1 Diffusion of carbon dioxide through pores of different diameter (after Brown and Escombe, 1900)

DIAMETER OF PORE (mm)	cm^3 OF CO_2 DIFFUSING h^{-1}	cm^3 DIFFUSING h^{-1} cm^{-2} OF PORE
22·70	0·24	$5·9 \times 10^{-4}$
12·06	0·10	$8·8 \times 10^{-4}$
6·03	0·06	$21·0 \times 10^{-4}$
3·23	0·04	$49·0 \times 10^{-4}$
2·00	0·02	$64·0 \times 10^{-4}$

Plot the data given in Table 12.1 as a graph. Use the graph to calculate the rate at which carbon dioxide passes through pores 0·2 mm in diameter. Pores of this size are at least ten times larger than stomatal pores. Further experimental investigations by Brown and Escombe showed that the rate of diffusion of gases through porous membranes is also affected by the closeness of the pores (Table 12.2). It may therefore be anticipated that the uptake of carbon dioxide by a leaf to some extent depends on the number of stomata per unit area of leaf. Stomatal densities of between 50 and 200 per mm^2 of leaf area are commonly found on the leaves of mesophytes. The combined area of open pores is usually between 0·5 and 1·5 per cent of the total leaf area. Experiments and observations such as these suggest that atmospheric carbon dioxide enters the air spaces of leaves when the stomata are open almost as though there is no epidermis present at all.

Table 12.2 Diffusion of carbon dioxide through membranes with different densities of pores (after Brown and Escombe, 1900)

NO. OF PORES cm^{-2} OF MEMBRANE	% AREA PERFORATED	DIFFUSION AS % OF VALUE WITHOUT MEMBRANE
100·00	11·3	87·6
25·00	2·8	63·7
11·11	1·25	44·0

The mesophyll tissue is permeated by air-filled spaces which amount to 30–40 per cent of the total leaf volume in many species. The internal **air spaces** are very important because they allow carbon dioxide taken in from the atmosphere to diffuse rapidly to photosynthesising cells. If the carbon dioxide had to diffuse through water instead it would move 10 000 times less quickly. However, once inside the mesophyll cells carbon dioxide has to move through the aqueous cell solution to reach the chloroplasts. As the chloroplasts are situated just inside the plasma membrane the distance that carbon dioxide passes through water is minimal. Uptake of carbon dioxide by the mesophyll cells is enhanced by the enzyme **carbonic anhydrase** which catalyses the formation of carbonic acid:

$$\underset{\text{carbon dioxide}}{CO_2} + \underset{\text{water}}{H_2O} \underset{}{\overset{\text{carbonic anhydrase}}{\rightleftharpoons}} \underset{\text{carbonic acid}}{H_2CO_3}$$

In the air spaces of a photosynthesising leaf the concentration of carbon dioxide is lowered to 0·01 per cent compared with 0·03 per cent in the external air. The result is that atmospheric carbon dioxide diffuses down a concentration gradient through stomatal pores into the air spaces of the mesophyll tissue.

2.1.4 Opening and closing of stomata

The stomata of most terrestrial plants open in light and close in darkness. Water loss due to transpiration is thus confined to periods when the plant is obtaining carbon dioxide from the surrounding air. Conservation of water is essential in a terrestrial environment because of the dehydrating effect of the atmosphere. Some xerophytic plants open their stomata only at night when the drying power of the air is less intense (Chapter 11).

Changes in turgidity (Chapter 2) of the guard cells are responsible for the opening and closing of stomatal pores. When the guard cells are turgid the pores are open. The guard cells of closed stomata are flaccid. Stomata close in wilted plants because the guard cells lose turgidity following excessive water loss by evaporation (Chapter 11). The reasons for changes in the turgidity of guard cells of non-wilted plants, however, are still a matter for debate. The factors which are thought to be mainly responsible include photosynthesis by the guard cells, carbon dioxide concentration of the air inside leaves and the concentration of mineral ions in the guard cells.

1. PHOTOSYNTHESIS BY THE GUARD CELLS

The earliest theories state that the formation of sugars by photosynthesis in the guard cells is the key factor causing stomata to open. The water-soluble sugars lower the water potential of the guard cells causing water to enter by osmosis from surrounding epidermal cells. When exposed to light therefore the guard cells gradually increase in turgidity and the stomata open. However, not all guard cells contain chloroplasts. Think of those on the non-green parts of variegated leaves. Even guard cells with chloroplasts are unlikely to make sugars quickly enough to bring about the rapid increase in pressure potential necessary for opening stomata.

2. CARBON DIOXIDE CONCENTRATION INSIDE LEAVES

Guard cells are sensitive to changes in the concentration of carbon dioxide in the air around them. High concentrations of carbon dioxide cause stomata to close, low concentrations cause them to open. What is more there are fluctuations in the concentration of carbon dioxide in and around leaves each day. In darkness, when photosynthesis stops, respiratory carbon dioxide accumulates. During the daytime, however, carbon dioxide is used for photosynthesis. The concentration of carbon dioxide inside the leaf is then much lower than at night. But how can changes in carbon dioxide concentration bring about changes in turgidity of the guard cells? After a period of darkness most guard cells contain starch grains which are changed to sugar on exposure to light. Could it be that the conversion of starch to sugar is affected by carbon dioxide concentration, and if so how?

Leaf mesophyll cells contain the enzyme carbonic anhydrase which catalyses the reaction between carbon dioxide and water to form carbonic acid. The acid dissociates weakly into hydrogencarbonate (HCO_3^-) and hydrogen (H^+) ions:

$$\underset{\text{carbonic acid}}{H_2CO_3} \rightleftharpoons \underset{\text{hydrogencarbonate ion}}{HCO_3^-} + \underset{\text{hydrogen ion}}{H^+}$$

High concentrations of hydrogen ions therefore accumulate in leaf cells, guard cells included, in darkness. When light is available the carbonic acid is used for photosynthesis thereby lowering the hydrogen ion concentration $[H^+]$ in leaf cells during the daytime. But how are $[H^+]$ changes in leaf cells linked with changes in turgidity of the guard cells?

The starch-sugar conversion in guard cells is catalysed by a group of enzymes. Like most enzyme-catalysed reactions, the conversion is affected by pH. In acid conditions, high $[H^+]$, the enzymes convert glucose phosphate to starch. However at a lower $[H^+]$ the direction of the reaction is reversed and sugar accumulates in the guard cells:

$$\text{starch} \underset{\text{high } [H^+]}{\overset{\text{low } [H^+]}{\rightleftharpoons}} \text{glucose phosphate}$$

The daytime accumulation of sugar lowers the water potential of the guard cells. The guard cells take in water from nearby epidermal cells and become turgid. In darkness the sugar is converted to starch which, being insoluble in water, causes the water potential of the guard cells to be raised. Water now passes from the guard cells into surrounding epidermal cells down a water potential gradient. The resulting flaccidity of the guard cells closes the stomatal pores.

Plausible as this explanation is, it does not account for recent observations showing that there are fluctuations in the concentrations of certain mineral ions in guard cells during the opening and closing of stomata.

3. MINERAL ION CONCENTRATION OF GUARD CELLS

Increases in mineral ion content of the guard cells, especially of potassium ions (K^+), accompany stomatal opening (Fig. 12.3). ATP is produced rapidly in guard cells exposed to light. It is thought that energy from ATP may be used to work an **ion pump** which draws in K^+ ions from surrounding epidermal cells. The accumulation of K^+ ions could lead to the increase in turgidity of the guard cells which brings about stomatal opening.

However, there are simultaneous increases in concentration of other substances in the guard cells of open stomata. One of the substances is malic acid, a product of the breakdown of starch. Some plant physiologists think that an increase of hydrogen ions (H^+) in the guard cells due to accumulation of malic acid is prevented by exchanging the H^+ ions for K^+ ions from surrounding epidermal cells. The water-soluble malate ions help to lower the water potential of the guard cells leading to stomatal opening.

Although stomata have been studied for a very long time it is evident that there is still much to be learned about the mechanisms which control stomatal opening and closing. It may even be that different mechanisms operate in different species or that a combination of mechanisms is involved.

FIG. 12.3 *Relative amounts of potassium (continuous line) and phosphorus (dotted line) in guard cells of open and closed stomata* (after Humble and Raschke, 1971)

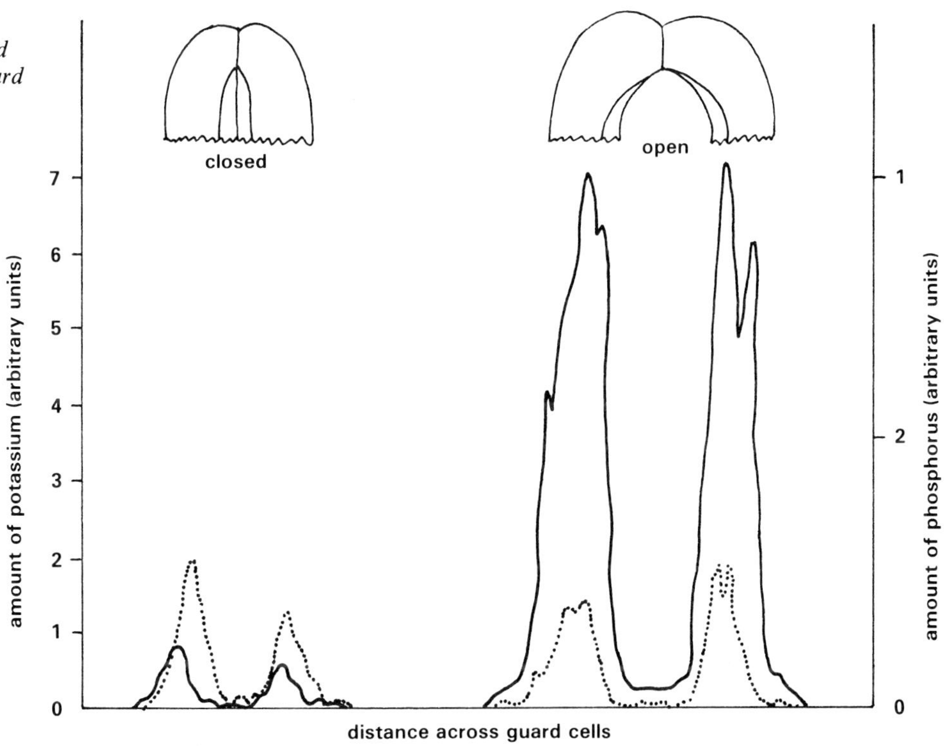

12.2 Factors affecting the rate of photosynthesis

The rate at which oxygen is given off by green plants can be used to measure the rate of photosynthesis. Aquatic plants such as *Elodea* are particularly suitable for this purpose. Bubbles of oxygen are given off from the cut end of the stem of *Elodea* when it is immersed in illuminated pond water or a dilute solution of sodium hydrogencarbonate (Fig. 12.4). Using this method in the 1930s the British plant physiologist F. F. Blackmann investigated the effect of light intensity on the rate of photosynthesis. The intensity of light was varied by increasing or decreasing the distance (D) between the lamp and the plant. Light intensity (I) is inversely proportional to the square of the distance ($I \propto \frac{1}{D^2}$). The results of the experiment are shown in Figure 12.5.

FIG. 12.4 *Measuring the rate of photosynthesis of the pondweed* Elodea

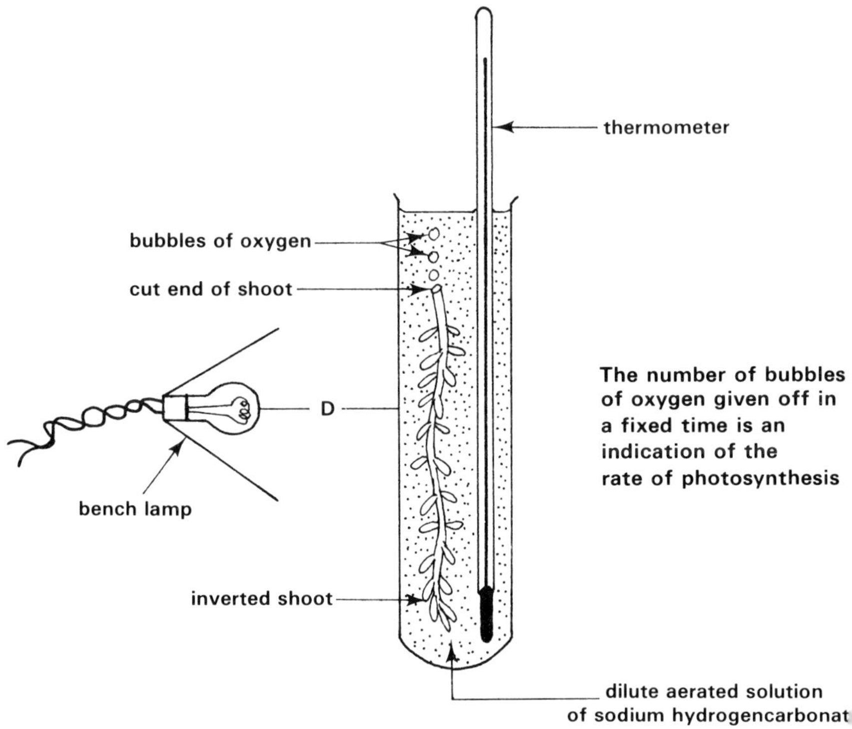

FIG. 12.5 *Effect of light intensity on the rate of photosynthesis*

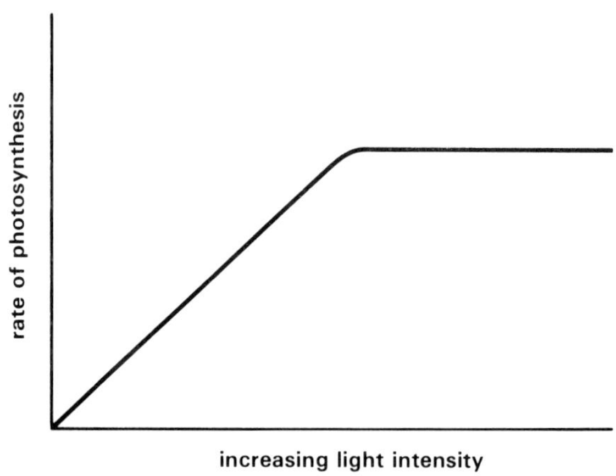

At low intensities of light Blackmann observed a straight line relationship between the rate of photosynthesis and light intensity. However, once a critical light intensity is reached the rate of photosynthesis remains constant. The results surprised Blackmann who reasoned that if photosynthesis is driven by light energy then it should go faster if more intense light is provided. He concluded that factors other than the availability of light energy limit the rate of photosynthesis at high light intensities.

Knowing that carbon dioxide is an essential raw ingredient for photosynthesis and that the process was probably catalysed at least in part by enzymes, Blackmann went on to investigate the effects of carbon dioxide concentration and temperature on the rate of photosynthesis. The results of these investigations are shown in Figures 12.6 and 12.7. Clearly photosynthesis is controlled by a combination of factors and it is apparent that the photosynthetic rate is limited by whichever factor is nearest its minimum value. This is a good example of the **law of limiting factors**.

FIG. 12.6 *Effect of carbon dioxide concentration on the rate of photosynthesis*

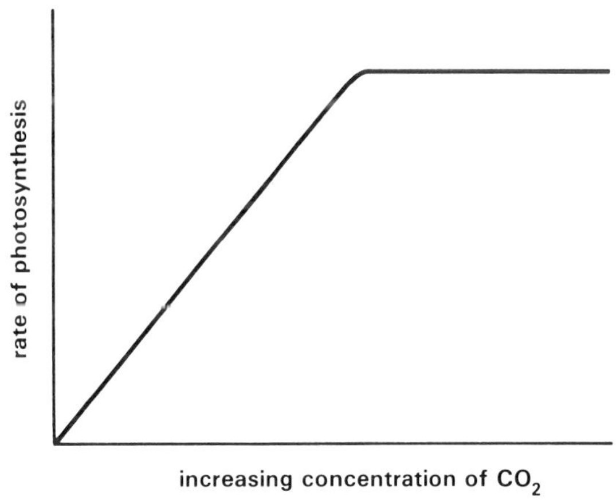

FIG. 12.7 *Effect of temperature on the rate of photosynthesis*

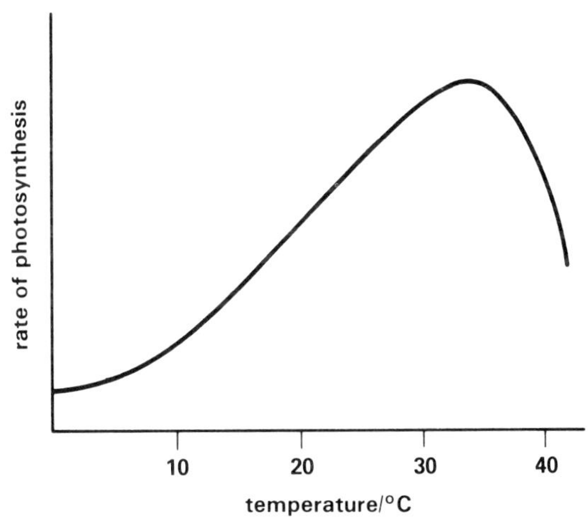

Blackmann did not attempt to find out whether the availability of water affects the rate of photosynthesis. In non-wilted plants there is always sufficient water for photosynthesis. The closure of stomata of wilted leaves may however limit the rate of photosynthesis by preventing the diffusion of carbon dioxide to the mesophyll tissue. In normal circumstances temperature, light intensity and carbon dioxide concentration are the factors most likely to limit the rate of photosynthesis.

12.2.1 Temperature

Photosynthesis consists of light-dependent and light-independent stages (Chapter 5). It is the enzyme catalysed reactions of the **light-independent stage** which are affected by temperature. The temperature coefficient, Q_{10} (Chapter 4), for the light-independent stage is between 2 and 3. Figure 12.8 shows the effect of temperature on photosynthesis at high and low light intensities. Notice that increasing the temperature has no effect on the rate of photosynthesis at low light intensity. Why is this so? For C4 plants the optimum temperature for photosynthesis is between 35–40°C and for C3 plants it is 20–25°C.

FIG. 12.8 *Effect of temperature on the rate of photosynthesis at two intensities of light*

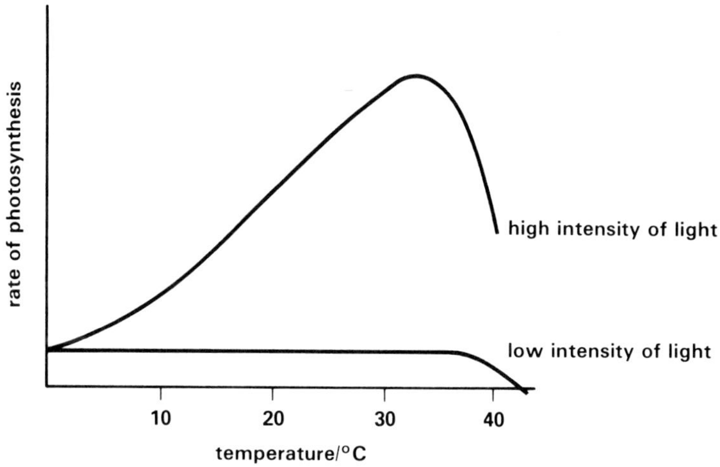

12.2.2 Light intensity

Light reaching the shaded leaves of a plant is less intense than light received by leaves exposed to full sunlight. Shade leaves compensate for this by structural adaptations which enable them to make the most of dim light (section 12.1.1). In some habitats such as dense beech forests and coniferous woodland the shade of the trees prevents the growth of herbaceous plants which normally appear as a field layer in open woodland where light can penetrate to the ground (Fig. 12.9).

FIG. 12.9 *Effect of shading on the field layer of a beech wood. The deep shade cast by beech trees prevents the development of a field layer, so the ground is bare*

In darkness photosynthesis cannot take place, although other metabolic processes such as respiration go on just as they do in daylight. In the absence of light, green plants give off carbon dioxide made in respiration. When light is available respiratory carbon dioxide provides a proportion of a plant's photosynthetic needs. The rest of the carbon dioxide is absorbed from the surrounding air. For a plant to grow it has to synthesise organic materials more rapidly than it oxidises them in respiration. When photosynthesis and respiration occur at rates such that there is no gain or loss of organic matter a plant is at its **compensation point**. The time taken for a plant which has been in darkness to reach the compensation point is called the **compensation period**. The most important factor governing the length of the compensation period in natural conditions is light intensity. Shade leaves have shorter compensation periods than sun leaves (Fig. 12.10). This is a physiological adaptation which enables shade leaves to make efficient use of light of low intensity.

FIG. 12.10 *Effect of light intensity on CO_2 exchange by sun and shade leaves*

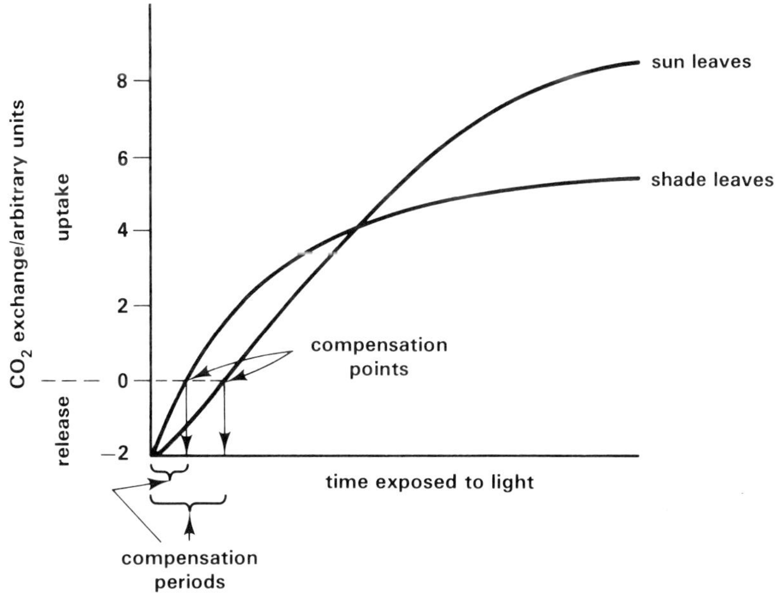

The stomata of most mesophytic plants open in light and close in darkness (section 12.1.4). In intense light stomatal pores are at their widest, enabling carbon dioxide to diffuse rapidly into the mesophyll tissue. Not all wavelengths of light are equally effective in stimulating photosynthesis. Blue and red light are more effective than others in this respect (Chapter 5).

12.2.3 Concentration of carbon dioxide

On a warm sunny day the concentration of carbon dioxide in the air is probably the factor which limits photosynthesis more than any other. Enriching air with carbon dioxide has a significant effect on crop plants grown in greenhouses (Table 12.3). It is now common practice for commercial growers of salad plants to raise the concentration of carbon dioxide of the air in greenhouses during daylight. The gas is either pumped in

Table 12.3 Yield of lettuces and tomatoes grown in normal air and in air enriched with carbon dioxide

CROP	WITHOUT ADDED CO_2	WITH ADDED CO_2	YIELD
lettuces	0·9	1·1	Fresh mass/ kg per 10 heads
tomatoes	4·4	6·4	Fresh mass/kg per plant

directly or is released by the burning of fuels such as paraffin, propane and natural gas which are used to heat greenhouses. Concentrations of up to 0·2 per cent carbon dioxide produce increases in crop yield which are economically worthwhile.

Of course, increasing the concentration of atmospheric carbon dioxide for crops grown in the open air is impracticable. On average the amount of carbon dioxide in the atmosphere outdoors is 0·03 per cent. It is controlled mainly by the rate at which living organisms give off carbon dioxide from respiration compared with the rate at which it is used by green plants for photosynthesis. An old-fashioned way of improving crop production in greenhouses was to add large quantities of manure to the soil. Carbon dioxide, released by soil micro-organisms which decomposed the manure, accumulated in the air and stimulated photosynthesis resulting in bigger crops.

12.3 Productivity of plants and plant communities

So far we have concentrated on the leaves of terrestrial plants as photosynthetic organs. It is just as important to consider photosynthesis in whole plants. After all, the entire plant is potential food for consumer organisms. Plants normally grow with others of the same species or of different species in **plant communities**. A field of wheat is an example of a man-made plant community. Natural forest and woodland are plant communities not made by man. The efficiency with which whole plants and plant communities produce dry matter determines how much food is available for the higher trophic levels in an ecosystem.

It is only recently that biologists have begun to appreciate which factors cause some plants and plant communities to produce dry matter more efficiently than others. Studies on crop plants show that two factors of fundamental importance to crop yield are **leaf area index** and **unit leaf rate**.

12.3.1 Leaf area index

Plants with a large surface area of leaves and other parts which can photosynthesise may be expected to produce more dry matter than plants having shoot systems with a small surface area. The area of leaves available for photosynthesis can be expressed as the **leaf area index (LAI)**:

$$\text{LAI} = \frac{\text{total leaf area of plant}}{\text{area of ground covered by plant}}$$

It indicates the amount of light intercepted by the shoot system of a plant. During the early stages of growth, crop plants have small LAI values because each plant has only a few small leaves and is surrounded by a patch of bare ground. As growth proceeds and the shoot system enlarges, the LAI increases. Maize grown in the U.S.A. achieves a maximum LAI of 4. Some crop plants have larger values than this. Sugar cane for example has a maximum LAI of about 7.

The shape of the shoot system is particularly important in determining the leaf area index of a plant. Plants which can be grown close to each other and which have leaves held vertically have higher LAI values than those with horizontally-held or drooping leaves. With this in mind plant breeders have produced new varieties of wheat and rice with erect leaves. The new varieties grow so that there is little mutual shading of their leaves and they yield extremely good crops of grain.

12.3.2 Unit leaf rate

Whatever the LAI value, increases in organic matter occur efficiently only if most of the photosynthetic products are converted to plant tissue or storage materials. If most of the products of photosynthesis are respired, dry matter accumulates slowly.

The term **unit leaf rate (ULR)** expresses the efficiency of dry matter accumulation by green plants. ULR is the mean rate of increase in dry mass of a whole plant per unit area of leaf. The ULR of a plant can be calculated from measurements of the leaf area and dry mass of a representative sample of plants at different stages of growth. Most species of crop plants grown in temperate areas have mean ULR values of between 4 and 6 g m^{-2} day^{-1}. In ideal growing conditions, when there are no factors limiting the rate of photosynthesis, the ULR can reach 15 g m^{-2} day^{-1}. Even so, some species have higher ULR values than others. Because they do not photorespire and have very short compensation periods C4 plants such as sugar cane and maize have a much greater unit leaf rate than most C3 plants (Chapter 5).

12.3.3 Net primary productivity

Synthesis of dry matter by green plants is called **primary production**. The total amount of dry matter produced per unit area of ground per year is called **gross primary productivity**. Some of the dry matter is used by green plants in respiration. What is left is called **net primary productivity (NPP)** and it is this which is available for consumer organisms including man.

$$\text{NPP} = \text{LAI} \times \text{ULR}$$

Clearly plants which quickly achieve high LAI values and which sustain an efficient ULR over a long growing period are highly productive. In attempting to raise the amount of food for human consumption plant breeders now have such factors foremost in mind.

12.4 Translocation of photosynthetic products

Leaves can be thought of as a **source** of photosynthetic products. Although leaves can store organic compounds such as starch, the products of photosynthesis are generally exported fairly quickly to tissues which actively use them or where they can be stored. Such places are called **sinks**. The meristems of root and shoot apices and the vascular and cork cambium (Chapter 21) are among the more important sinks for photosynthetic products. It is there that the organic materials made by leaves are used to produce new cells and provide the energy for growth. Most green plants have some means of storing food which can be used at a later stage. The cotyledons and endosperm of seeds are the only sites of food storage in many species (Chapter 20). In others, an enlarged part of the vegetative plant body acts as a storage organ (Fig. 12.11).

FIG. 12.11 *Storage organs of flowering plants*

The long distance movement of metabolites from sources to sinks is called **translocation**. The term translocation is often used to describe the movement of all water-soluble substances in the vascular tissue of plants. Here we shall confine our account mainly to the movement of organic substances made in photosynthesis.

12.4.1 The pathway of translocation

There is a lot of experimental evidence which suggests that the **phloem** is the tissue mainly concerned with the translocation of organic substances. An elegant technique applied to translocation studies makes use of the fact that phloem elements are penetrated by the mouthparts of **aphids** such as greenfly and blackfly when they are feeding on plant juices (Fig. 12.12). If a feeding aphid is anaesthetised and the mouthparts carefully cut across, the stylets left in the plant act as a tiny sampling tube at the end of which droplets of phloem sap soon appear. Analyses show that the phloem sap, unlike xylem sap, is rich in sugars, mainly sucrose, amino acids and potassium and phosphate ions (Table 12.4). Furthermore, the composition of the sap varies according to the photosynthetic activity of the plant. Sucrose for example is at its highest concentration a few hours after sunrise.

Table 12.4 Composition of phloem sap of the castor oil plant *Ricinus communis* (after Hall and Baker 1972)

COMPONENT	CONCENTRATION/mg cm^{-3}
sucrose	80–106
reducing sugars	0
protein	1·45–2·20
amino acids	5·2 (as glutamic acid)
carboxylic acids	2·0–3·2 (as malic acid)
phosphate(V) ions	0·35–0·55
sulphate(VI) ions	0·024–0·048
chloride ions	0·355–0·675
nitrate(V) ions	0
hydrogencarbonate ions	0·010
potassium ions	2·3–4·4
sodium ions	0·046–0·276
calcium ions	0·020–0·092
magnesium ions	0·109–0·122
ammonia	0·029
ATP	0·24–0·36
auxin	$10{\cdot}5 \times 10^{-6}$
gibberellin	$2{\cdot}3 \times 10^{-6}$
cytokinin	$10{\cdot}8 \times 10^{-6}$

FIG. 12.12 (a) (i) *Aphids feeding on a rose shoot*

FIG. 12.12 (a) (ii) *Ventral view of aphid × 50*

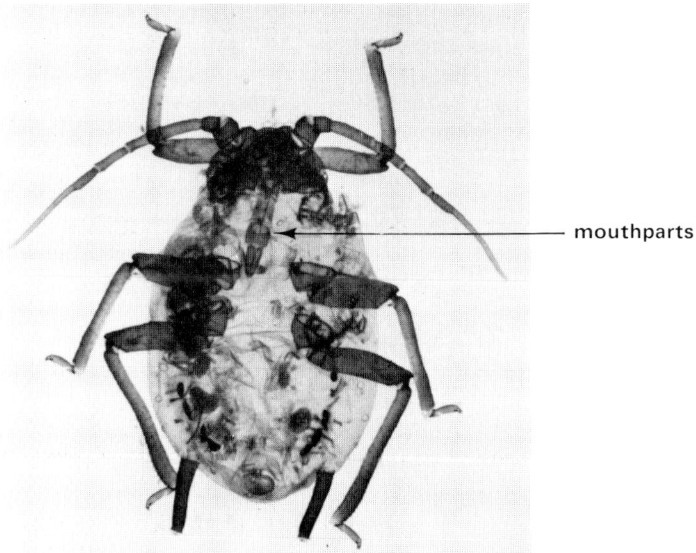

FIG. 12.12 (b) (i) *Aphid feeding on phloem sap* (modified after Dixon, 1973)

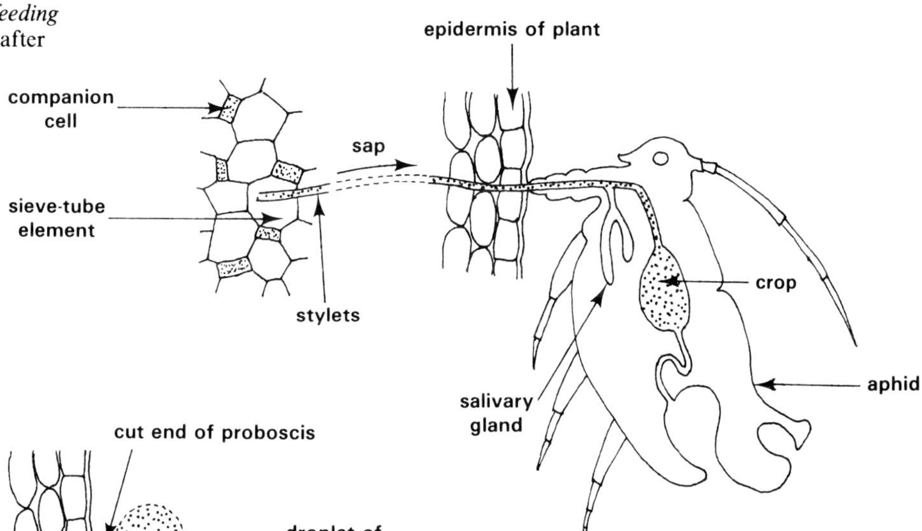

FIG. 12.12 (b) (ii)

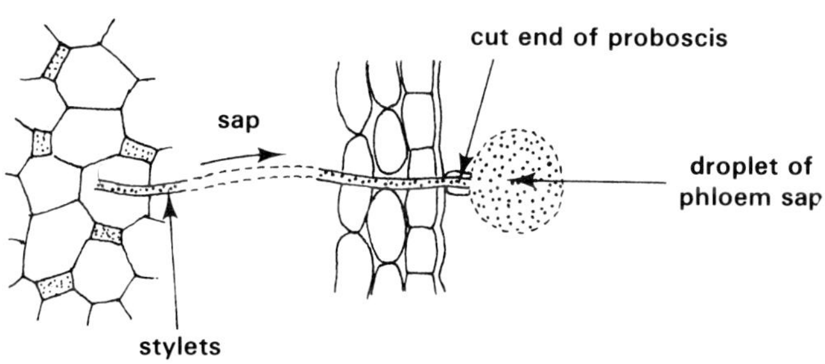

Another technique which has been used to great advantage in recent years involves supplying carbon dioxide containing the **radioisotope** ^{14}C to illuminated plant leaves. The isotope is fixed in the organic products of photosynthesis which are then translocated to other parts of the plant. The spread of radioactivity can be followed and is found almost entirely in the phloem (Fig. 12.13).

FIG. 12.13 *Investigating the spread of a carbon radioisotope in a plant*

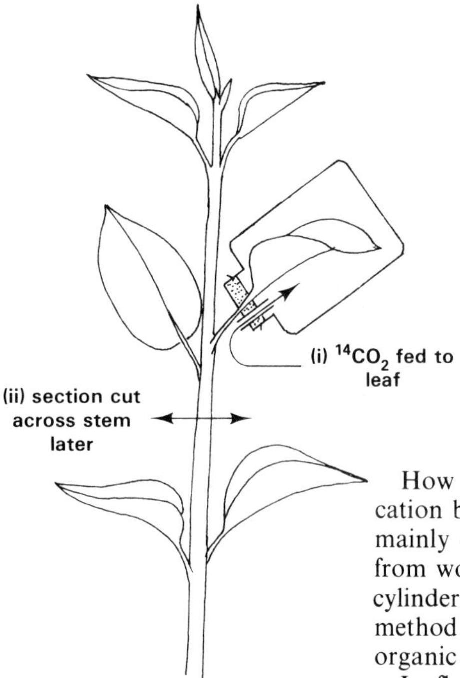

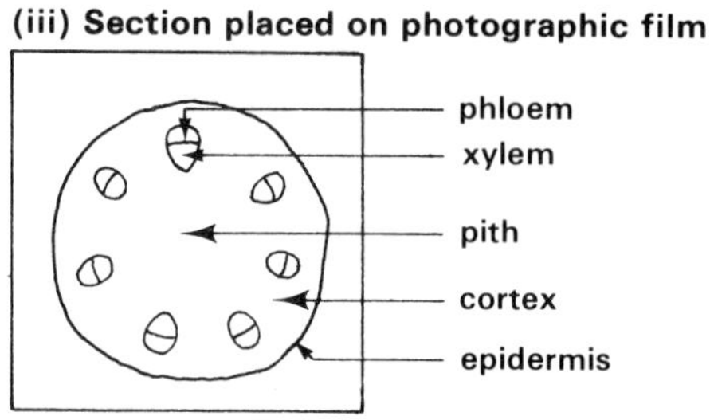

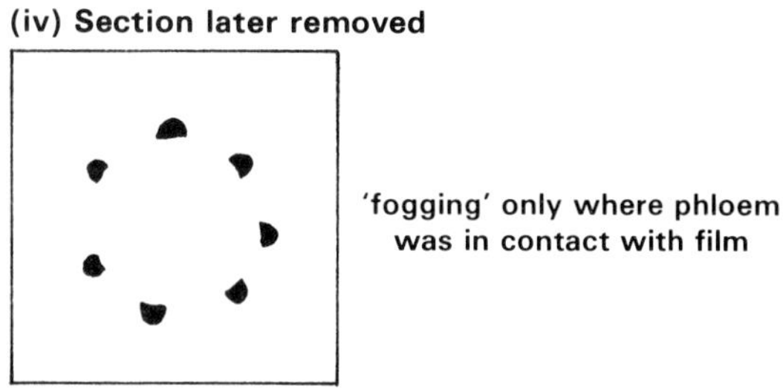

How did plant physiologists manage to learn anything about translocation before such sophisticated techniques were developed? They relied mainly on **ringing experiments** in which cylinders of bark were removed from woody stems and the contents of the phloem above and below the cylinder were later analysed (Fig. 12.14). Although crude, the ringing method provided some evidence that phloem is the main tissue in which organic compounds are translocated.

In flowering plants there are two conspicuous types of phloem cell concerned with translocation, **sieve-tubes** and companion cells. They lie alongside one another, derived from the same meristematic cell by longitudinal division (Chapter 21).

FIG. 12.14 *A ringing experiment*

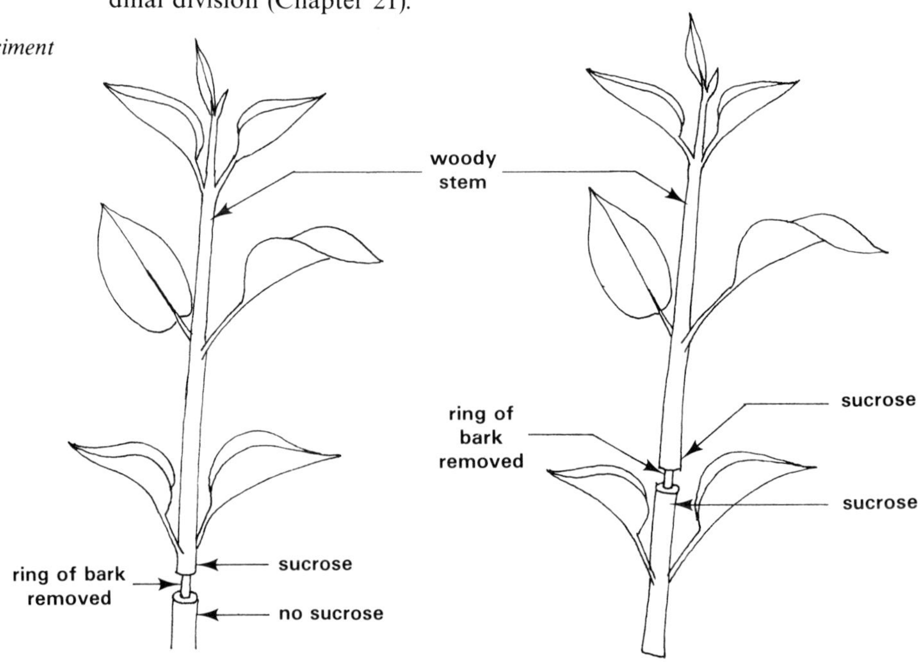

The bark includes the secondary phloem. What does the experiment tell us about the movement of organic materials like sucrose in the stem?

1. SIEVE-TUBES

Sieve-tubes are composed of a series of **sieve-tube elements** joined end to end. Each element is 10–50 μm in diameter and 150–1000 μm long. When first produced from a meristematic cell by mitosis, sieve-tube elements have a large nucleus and the usual cytoplasmic organelles. However, at maturity, when translocating organic materials rapidly in solution, the nucleus, ribosomes, Golgi body and tonoplast degenerate and the side walls are thickened mainly with cellulose. Small mitochondria remain, as does part of the endoplasmic reticulum which exists as parallel layers near the side walls. Plastids containing small starch grains are also present and the lumen is filled with slimy sap containing fibrils of a material called **phloem protein** (Fig. 12.15).

FIG. 12.15 (a) *L.s. of phloem as seen with light microscope*

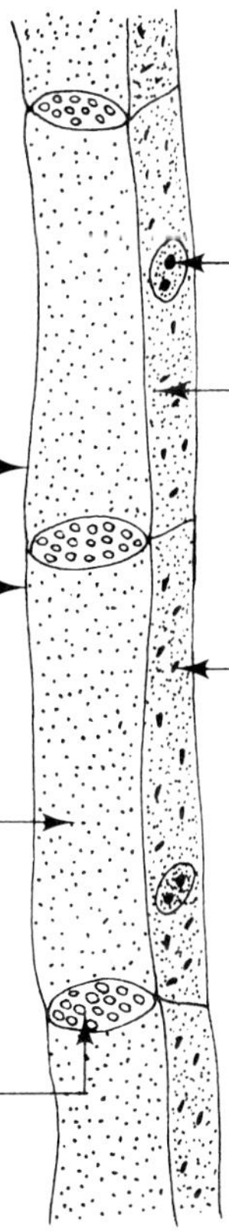

FIG. 12.15 (b) *Longitudinal section of phloem of marrow, ×350*

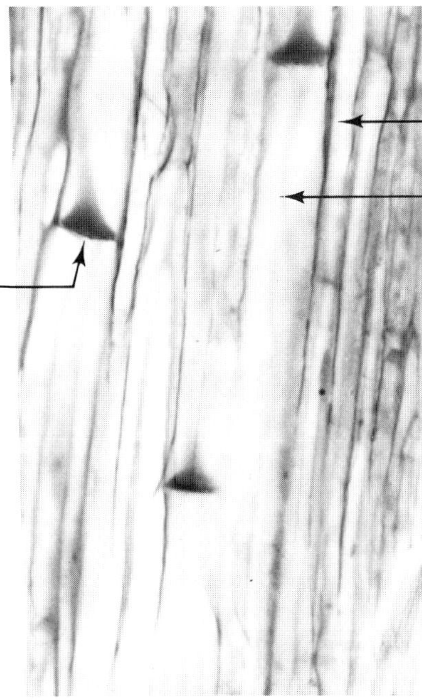

FIG. 12.15 (c) *Transverse section of phloem of marrow, ×800*

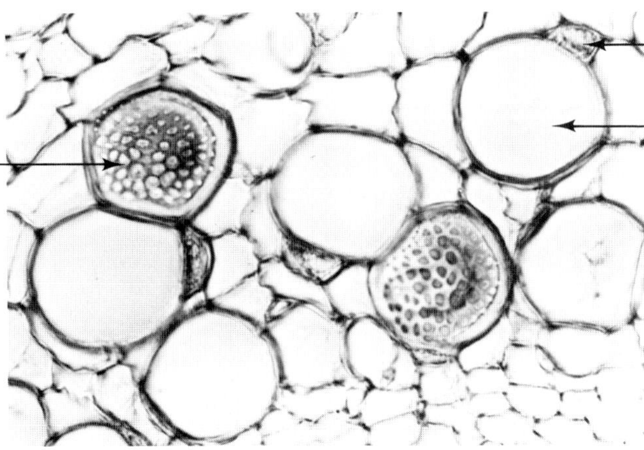

During differentiation the end walls between adjacent sieve-tube elements are modified to form **sieve plates** perforated by pores. The pores are lined with deposits, which vary in thickness, of a glucose polymer called **callose**. The mean diameter of the pores is 2–6 μm but where thick deposits of callose occur the pores appear to be blocked.

FIG. 12.15 (d) *Ultrastructure of phloem (based on electronmicrographs)*

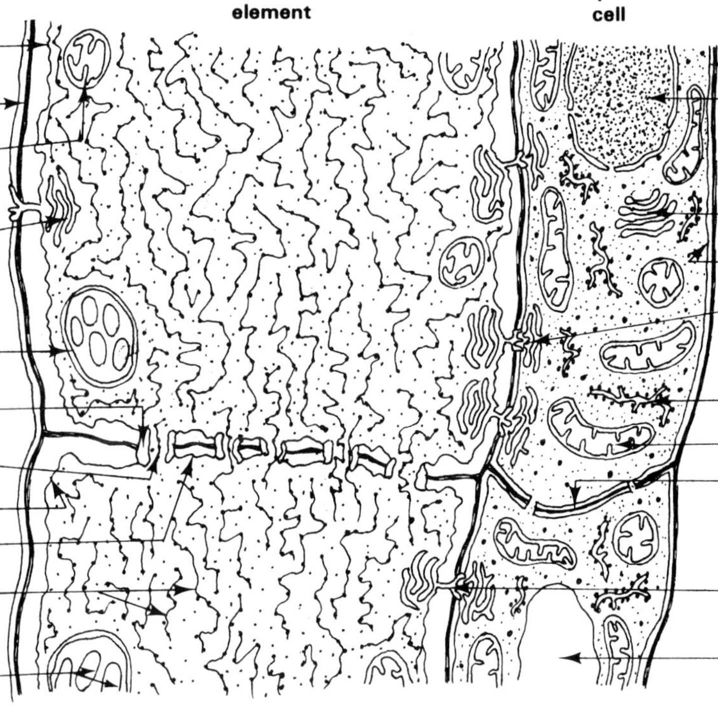

FIG. 12.15 (e) *Longitudinal section of part of sieve-tube showing transcellular strands (based on photomicrographs)*

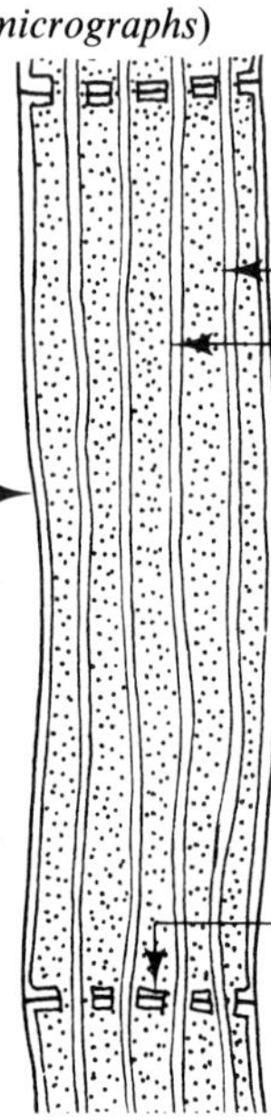

FIG. 12.15 (f) *Electronmicrograph of a longitudinal section through part of a sieve plate*

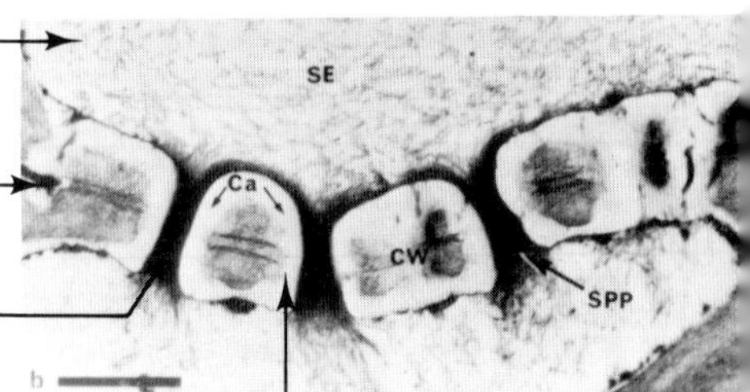

Although many biologists accept the interpretation of the ultrastructure of sieve-tubes given above, there are others who state that each sieve-tube element contains a number of parallel **transcellular strands** 1–7 μm wide.

The strands are thought to be hollow, membranous tubes which pass through the pores of sieve plates and extend through a series of sieve-tube elements (Fig. 12.15). Such a divergence of opinion may be due to differences in the species used for investigation. It may also result from differences in the techniques used to examine sieve-tubes.

2. COMPANION CELLS

A **companion cell** has a thin cellulose wall enclosing a protoplast which contains a prominent nucleus, numerous mitochondria, a well-developed endoplasmic reticulum with attached ribosomes, a Golgi body, small vacuoles and colourless plastids. The protoplasts of companion cells and adjacent sieve-tube elements are connected by many plasmodesmata (Fig. 12.15) suggesting that transfer of substances between the two types of cell can occur. At the ends of minor leaf veins the companion cells are much bigger compared with the sieve-tube elements than elsewhere in the plant. These companion cells also have ingrowths of their cell walls which greatly increase the surface area of the plasma membrane for the uptake of substances from surrounding mesophyll cells. The name **transfer cell** is given to specialised companion cells of this sort (Fig. 12.16).

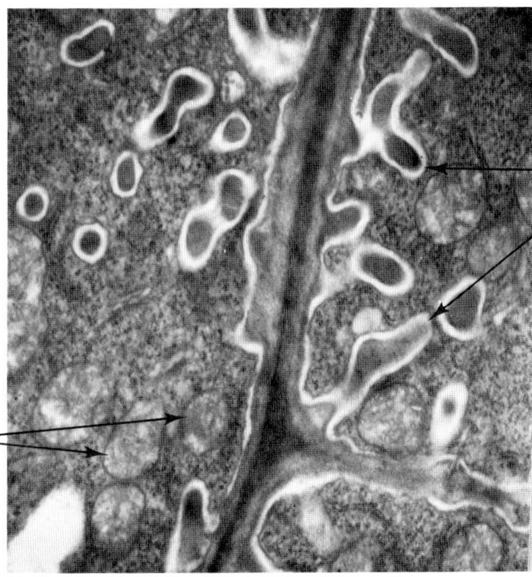

FIG. 12.16
Electronmicrograph of a section of part of a transfer cell from lentil, × 20 000. Note the ingrowths of the cell wall which increase the surface area of the plasma membrane for the transfer of solutes. What functions may the mitochondria have?

12.4.2 The mechanism of translocation

A common method used to determine the rate of translocation in phloem is to measure the rate at which growing organs increase in dry mass. If the area of cross-section of phloem supplying the organ is also measured it is possible to calculate the rate at which organic matter is transferred per unit area of phloem in a known period of time (Table 12.5). Another technique is to follow the spread of radioactivity in a plant after a labelled compound such as $^{14}CO_2$ has been supplied to a photosynthesising leaf. This procedure has been particularly rewarding when used in conjunction with aphids (Fig. 12.17). The results of such experiments clearly demonstrate that translocation is a rapid process, much too rapid to be explained by diffusion. Sugars such as sucrose are translocated at a rate of 25–200 cm h^{-1} in sieve-tubes compared with a meagre 0·2 mm day^{-1} possible by diffusion. How much faster does sucrose move when translocated compared with its movement by diffusion?

Table 12.5 Rates of translocation measured by transfer of dry mass

SPECIES	ORGAN	MASS TRANSFER/ g DRY MASS cm^{-2} PHLOEM h^{-1}
potato	tuber	2·1–4·5
marrow	fruit	3·3–4·8
grasses	leaves	4·4–14·9

Having dismissed diffusion as a possible mechanism of translocation it is not easy to provide a really convincing alternative. There are many theories but relatively few facts to support them. One of the more favoured explanations of translocation is the mass-flow hypothesis.

FIG. 12.17 *Use of aphids and radioactive carbon to measure the rate of translocation. Phloem sap at A and B is analysed for radioactivity at frequent intervals. The time taken for the radioactivity to spread from A to B is a measure of the rate of translocation*

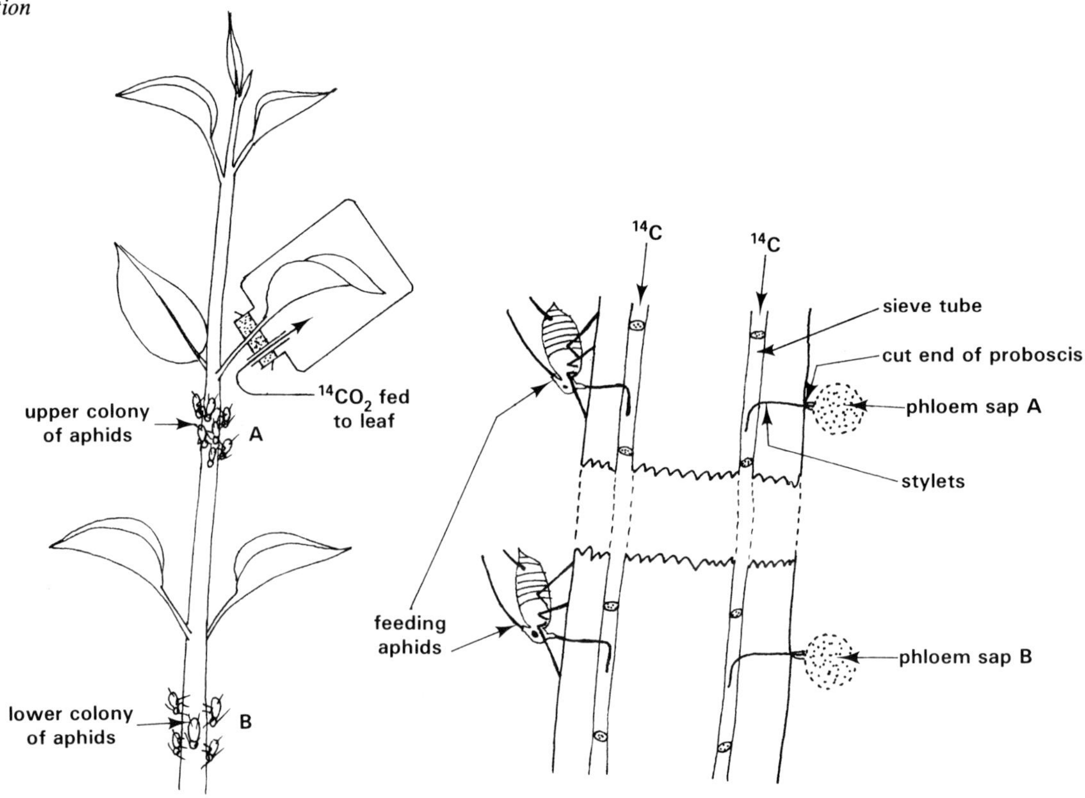

1. MASS-FLOW HYPOTHESIS

Figure 12.18 shows the principle of the **mass-flow hypothesis**. The sap in the sieve-tube elements next to leaf mesophyll cells, the **source**, is rich in organic solutes and thus has a low water potential. Water is absorbed into the sieve-tube elements by osmosis from surrounding tissues. A high pressure potential is thus created near the source and the solution inside the sieve-tube elements is pushed towards a sink along a pressure potential gradient. In this way organic solutes can be carried downwards to the roots of the plant or upwards to developing flowers, fruits and young leaves all of which are **sinks** (Fig. 12.19).

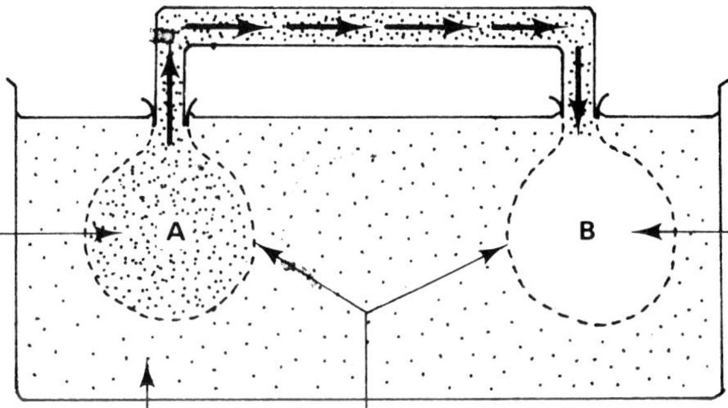

IG. 12.18 *Model to demonstrate he principle of the mass-flow ıypothesis. The sucrose solution, ıaving a relatively low water ɔotential, draws water into A by ɔsmosis. The resultant rise in ɔressure in A causes the sucrose olution to enter the connecting ube and pass into B. Starch, eing osmotically inactive, does ıot draw water into B from the ontainer. The model could be nade into a continuous-flow ystem if sugar could be ontinually added to A and emoved from B*

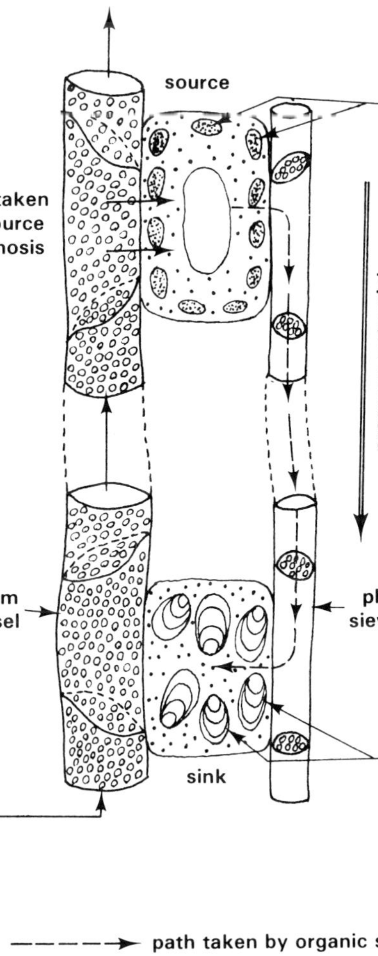

IG. 12.19 *Mass-flow of organic olutes in a plant*

The rapid and continued exudation of phloem sap from the severed mouthparts of feeding aphids shows that the contents of the sieve-tube elements have a high pressure potential. Furthermore, suitable concentration gradients of translocated substances exist between sources and sinks. Even so, the hypothesis does not account for all that is known of the physiology of phloem. There are doubts too that the structure of sieve-tubes in all plants is suitable for mass-flow. The main points of criticism of mass-flow are as follows:

(i) Phloem tissue has a relatively high rate of oxygen consumption (Table 12.6) and translocation is slowed down or stopped altogether if respiratory poisons such as potassium cyanide enter the phloem. Observations of this sort suggest that metabolic energy is used in translocation. The companion cells produce energy because they contain numerous mitochondria. Yet the mass-flow hypothesis is based on a passive, physical phenomenon and does not suggest a role for companion cells.

Table 12.6 Rates of oxygen uptake by various plant tissues (after Coult 1971)

TISSUE	mm^3 O_2 CONSUMED g^{-1} h^{-1}
vascular tissue	800
whole leaves	400
petioles	200
carrot taproot	30–40

(ii) It has recently been shown that plant hormones such as indole-3-acetic acid (IAA) assist the loading of sugars into sieve-tubes and their unloading into sinks. The mass-flow hypothesis makes no mention of hormones in translocation.

(iii) The sieve plates may offer a resistance which is greater than could be overcome by the pressure potential of the phloem sap. Higher pressure potentials than have been recorded would be necessary to squeeze sap through partially blocked pores in sieve plates. However, in view of the controversy centred around sieve plate structure this criticism may not be valid for all plants.

2. ALTERNATIVE HYPOTHESES

There has been no shortage of ideas about alternative mechanisms of phloem transport. One suggestion is that respiratory energy produced by companion cells maintains an electrical potential difference across sieve plates. The potential difference is achieved by the active removal of potassium ions (K^+) from one side of the plate by the companion cells and their secretion on the other side. The movement of K^+ ions through the pores of the sieve plate rapidly draws polar molecules of water and dissolved solutes through the pores. This phenomenon is called **electro-osmosis**. Experimental evidence to support the theory is sparse. Even so it is known that potassium ions stimulate the loading of phloem with sugars. Furthermore, potassium uptake is promoted by IAA.

Circulation of protoplasm has been observed in sieve-tubes and some physiologists have thought that this may be involved in translocation. It is unlikely though that **protoplasmic streaming** on its own would account for the speed at which substances are normally translocated.

Finally, supporters of the existence of transcellular strands have proposed that solutions may be pumped through the strands by **peristaltic waves** of contraction passing along the strands!

The various ideas embodied in the alternative hypotheses are summarised in Figure 12.20. There is obviously much debate surrounding the structure and physiology of phloem. At present, plant physiologists do not have a complete understanding of what appears to be a sophisticated and subtle mechanism of translocation.

FIG. 12.20 *Alternative mechanisms of translocation*

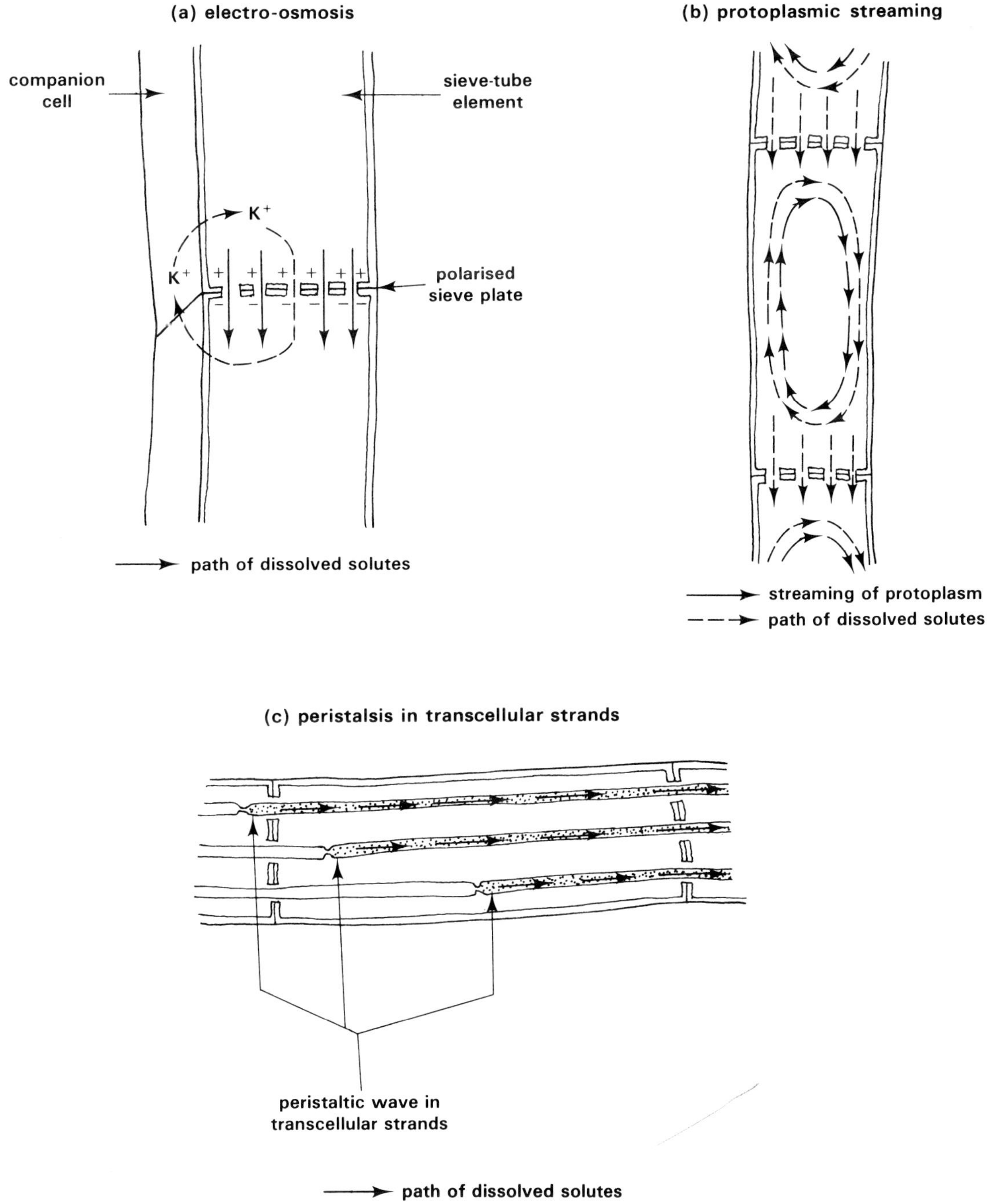

Chapter 13

Mineral nutrition of flowering plants

The great improvement in crop yields which has come from a combinatio of mechanisation on the farm, the application of fertilisers and pesticides t the land and the breeding of high-yielding varieties of crop plants has bee called the **green revolution**. Fertilisers improve the fertility of soils, that the ability of soils to sustain vigorous, healthy plant growth. **Mineral** inorganic chemical compounds, are used extensively as fertilisers in ag riculture and horticulture. Mixtures of minerals called compound fert lisers are applied to the soil before and at various times during the growt of a crop (Fig. 13.1). Few arable farmers in developed countries now gro crops without treating their land with fertilisers, especially those contair ing nitrogen, phosphorus and potassium.

FIG. 13.1 *Artificial fertiliser being applied to the land*

It is therefore evident that minerals perform a crucial role in the growt of flowering plants. But what minerals are required and what part do the play in the functioning of plants?

13.1 Mineral requirements of flowering plants

Seventeenth-century records indicate that scientists were then aware th plant growth depends on a supply of minerals. Yet it was two centuri later before any real progress was made in identifying precisely whic minerals are required by higher plants.

13.1.1 Water culture experiments

In 1860 the German plant physiologist Julius von Sachs described a syste for growing flowering plants without soil (Fig. 13.2). A few years later Knc published the formula of a liquid medium which was suitable for growing wide variety of plants (Table 13.1). The main advantage of using wat culture techniques to investigate a plant's mineral requirements is that t chemical composition of the liquid medium can be exactly fixed. Suc techniques make it possible to find out how plants respond to any con bination of minerals.

Table 13.1 Knop's culture solution (1865)

MINERAL	g dm^{-3} WATER
KNO_3	0·2
$Ca(NO_3)_2$	0·8
KH_2PO_4	0·2
$MgSO_4.7H_2O$	0·2
$FePO_4$	0·1

FIG. 13.2 *Equipment for water culture investigation using grass plants. The solution is aerated to encourage root growth. The light-proof cover discourages the growth of algae in the culture solution*

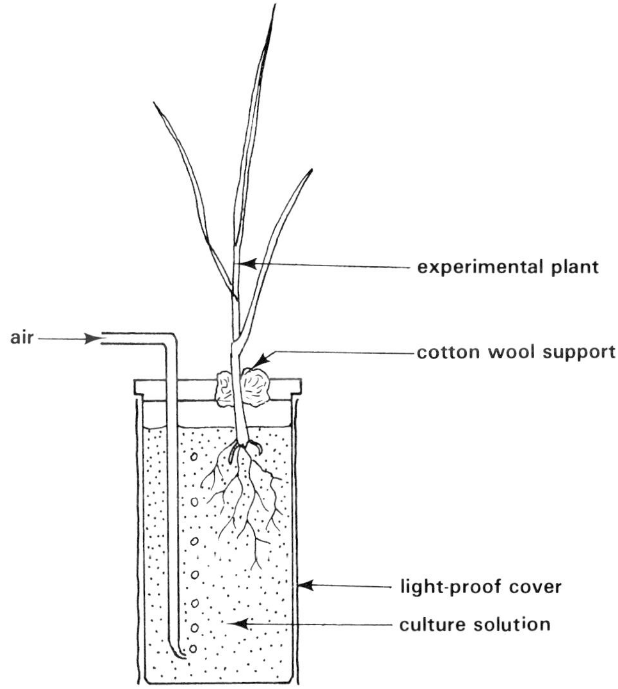

Sachs, Knop and others discovered that given a supply of carbon dioxide, water and light, flowering plants require seven chemical elements in relatively large amounts if they are to show healthy and vigorous growth. The seven **macronutrients** as they have since been called are **nitrogen (N)**, **phosphorus (P)**, **potassium (K)**, **calcium (Ca)**, **magnesium (Mg)**, **sulphur (S)** and **iron (Fe)**. It was later found that relatively small amounts of a number of other elements are also needed for normal plant growth. These are called **micronutrients** or trace elements. **Manganese (Mn)**, **zinc (Zn)**, **copper (Cu)**, **boron (B)**, **molybdenum (Mo)** and **chlorine (Cl)** are the most important micronutrients.

The reason why Sachs and his contemporaries failed to discover the importance of micronutrients was because the chemicals they used, although the purest available at the time, probably contained small amounts of trace elements as impurities. Liquid media used in present-day water culture experiments are prepared from pure chemicals dissolved in de-ionised water (Table 13.2). Glassware is cleaned with hot 50 per cent hydrochloric acid and then thoroughly washed with de-ionised water. Otherwise the vessels may be a source of minerals which the experimental plants can absorb.

Table 13.2 A modern culture solution (modified from Hewitt 1974)

MINERAL	g dm^{-3} WATER	g dm^{-3} WATER		
KNO_3	0·404	K	0·156	Macronutrients
		N	0·057	
$Ca(NO_3)_2$	0·656	Ca	0·160	
		N	0·113	
$MgSO_4.7H_2O$	0·368	Mg	0·036	
		S	0·048	
$NaH_2PO_4.2H_2O$	0·208	P	0·041	
Fe citrate.$5H_2O$	0·03350	Fe	0·005	

$MnSO_4.4H_2O$	0·00223	Mn	0·00055	Micronutrients
$ZnSO_4.7H_2O$	0·00029	Zn	0·00006	
$CuSO_4.5H_2O$	0·00025	Cu	0·00006	
H_3BO_3	0·00310	B	0·00054	
$Na_2MoO_4.2H_2O$	0·00012	Mo	0·00005	
NaCl	0·00580	Cl	0·00350	

The effects of mineral deficiencies on plants grown in water culture can be assessed in a variety of ways. One of the simplest is to compare the fresh and dry mass of whole plants or the organs of plants kept in a medium deficient in one or more elements with similar plants grown in a complete medium (Table 13.3). Differences in growth pattern and leaf colour can also be noted.

Table 13.3 Effect of mineral deficiency on growth of lettuce (after Strafford 1963)

ELEMENTS IN SOLUTION	AVERAGE FRESH MASS/g	
	SHOOTS	ROOTS
macronutrients only	71·4	14·5
macronutrients plus Zn, Cu, Mn, B, Cl	105·7	22·0

Good subjects for water culture work are seeds with small food reserves because they contain only small amounts of stored minerals. Many grasses produce seeds of this kind. Large seeds and cuttings are less suitable as they often have a substantial reserve of one or more minerals.

13.2 Functions of minerals in flowering plants

Valuable as the results of water culture experiments are, they rarely give a complete picture of the roles of minerals in the functioning of a plant. The results often need to be supplemented with data from metabolic studies in which the rates of processes such as respiration, photosynthesis and protein synthesis are measured. Analysis of the chemical composition of experimental and control plants may also be required.

13.2.1 Macronutrients

With the exception of iron, **macronutrients** are normally required at concentrations of 0·04–0·2 g dm^{-3} in mineral culture solutions to sustain vigorous, healthy plant growth (Table 13.2). About 0·005 g dm^{-3} of iron gives satisfactory results. For this reason iron is sometimes described as a micronutrient.

1. NITROGEN

Nitrogen is absorbed by plant roots as nitrate(V) ions (NO_3^-) or as ammonium (NH_4^+) ions. Insufficient NO_3^- or NH_4^+ in the soil is usually one of the factors which most limits the growth of crops on cultivated land. Some important crop plants such as clover, beans and peas have symbiotic nitrogen-fixing bacteria living in nodules in their roots. The bacteria can use nitrogen gas to form organic nitrogenous compounds, some of which are used by the higher plant partner.

FIG. 13.3 *A cabbage showing effect of nitrogen deficiency* (Crown copyright). *The young leaves at the top of the plant are green but the older, larger leaves are yellow*

In flowering plants nitrogen is found in amino acids, proteins, nucleic acids and chlorophyll. The functions of these important compounds are described in Chapters 3, 4, 5 and 6. Nitrate ions absorbed by roots are first reduced to ammonia which combines with carboxylic acids to form amino acids. Ammonium ions are used directly for amino acid synthesis.

Typical symptoms of nitrogen deficiency are reduced growth of all organs and chlorosis, a yellowing of the leaves due to inadequate production of chlorophyll (Fig. 13.3). Chlorosis appears first in older leaves.

2. PHOSPHORUS

Phosphorus is absorbed from the soil as dihydrogenphosphate(V) ions ($H_2PO_4^-$). The quantity of $H_2PO_4^-$ probably limits plant growth more than the amounts of NO_3^- or NH_4^+ in uncultivated soils (Table 13.4). Nucleic acids, phospholipids and ATP are among the phosphorus-containing compounds found in plants. The roles of these substances are described in Chapters 3, 5 and 6.

Table 13.4 Effect of N and P on dry mass of shoots of *Lolium perenne* **(after Goodman 1969)**

PHOSPHORUS/g kg^{-1}	NITROGEN/g kg^{-1} 0·000	0·040	0·100	0·200	MEAN DRY MASS/g
0·000	343	323	344	332	335
0·120	455	466	459	416	470

FIG. 13.4 *Spring barley showing effect of phosphorus deficiency* (Crown copyright)

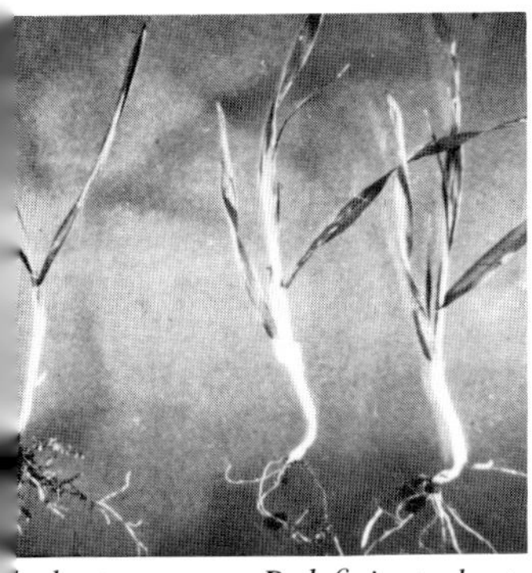

plants *P-deficient plants*

Severe lack of phosphorus obviously affects processes which use free energy provided by ATP. Poor growth, especially of roots (Fig. 13.4), and a reduction in uptake of all minerals are the usual symptoms of phosphorus deficiency.

3. POTASSIUM

Potassium is absorbed from the soil as potassium ions (K^+). Whereas nitrogen and phosphorus appear in complex organic compounds in flowering plants potassium does not. Nevertheless potassium is found in green plants in large amounts. An important function of potassium is to activate enzymes (Chapter 4). Over forty enzymes depend on potassium for optimum activity. Potassium is also probably essential for translocation in phloem sieve-tubes (Chapter 12).

A feature of plants grown in a potassium-deficient environment is the mottled appearance of the older leaves. The leaves may also display chlorosis (Fig. 13.5).

FIG. 13.5 *Apple leaves showing effect of potassium deficiency* (Crown copyright)

4. CALCIUM

Calcium is taken up by plant roots as calcium ions (Ca^{2+}). The main function of calcium in flowering plants is to form salt linkages between pectic acid molecules in the middle lamella which binds adjacent cells to each other (Fig. 13.6). Some enzymes are also activated by calcium.

Typical deficiency symptoms for calcium are chlorosis of young leaves, die-back of shoots due to death of apical buds and poor root growth.

FIG. 13.6 *The role of calcium in the middle lamella*

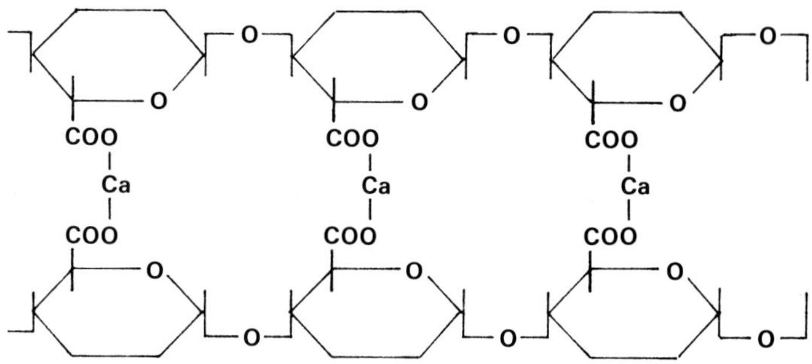

5. MAGNESIUM

Magnesium is absorbed from the soil as magnesium ions (Mg^{2+}). In green plants magnesium forms part of the chlorophyll molecule where it donates electrons in the light-dependent reactions of photosynthesis (Chapter 5). Magnesium also activates certain enzymes. Pronounced chlorosis beginning between the veins of older leaves is the main symptom of magnesium deficiency.

6. SULPHUR

Sulphur is taken up by plant roots as sulphate(VI) ions (SO_4^{2-}). It is needed for the formation of amino acids such as methionine and cysteine which contain thiol (−SH) groups. Sulphur-containing amino acids are present in most proteins. For this reason the symptoms of sulphur deficiency are very similar to those of nitrogen deficiency.

7. IRON

Iron is absorbed mainly as iron(II) ions (Fe^{2+}). Iron is present in cytochromes which act as electron carriers in photosynthesis and respiration and in the reduction of nitrate(V) ions. Iron is also required for the synthesis of chlorophyll and to activate certain enzymes.

Characteristic signs of iron deficiency are chlorosis, especially in young leaves, and inhibition of photosynthesis and respiration.

13.2.2 Micronutrients

A large number of chemical elements given to plants in very small quantities stimulate plant growth. However, not all of these elements are essential for plant metabolism. The **micronutrients** essential for plant growth are manganese, zinc, copper, boron, molybdenum and chlorine. Water culture experiments show that they are required at much lower concentration than the macronutrients (Table 13.2).

The main functions of the micronutrients are summarised in Table 13.5. Chlorosis can be a symptom of insufficient Zn, Cu, Mo or Cl. Even so, the deficiency symptoms for most of the micronutrients are so characteristic that certain plants may be used as indicator species in diagnosing soils which are deficient in trace elements (Fig. 13.7).

FIG. 13.7 *Cotyledons of pea seeds showing effect of manganese deficiency* (Crown copyright). *The symptoms shown are sometimes called marsh spot. They are typical of peas grown in reclaimed marshland soil which contains little manganese*

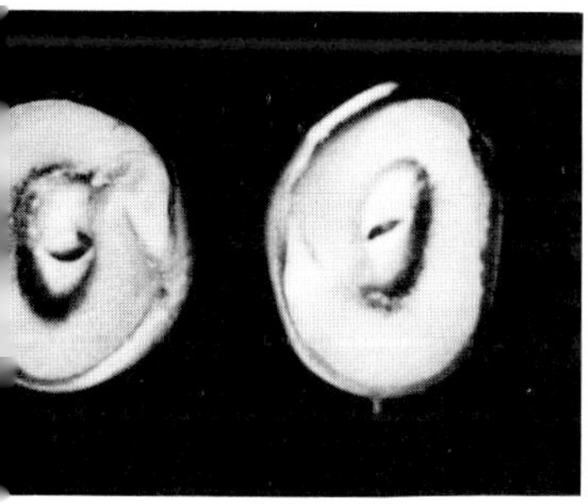

Table 13.5 Roles of micronutrients in plant metabolism

ELEMENT	ROLES
Mn	Activates carboxylase enzymes. May act as an electron donor for excited chlorophyll b.
Zn	Present in the enzyme carbonic anhydrase and also in various dehydrogenase enzymes.
Cu	Present in a number of oxidase enzymes. Also found in plastocyanin which acts as an electron carrier for chlorophyll a.
B	Not fully known. Essential for meristem activity and for growth of pollen tubes.
Mo	Required for nitrogen fixation. Activates the enzyme nitrate reductase.
Cl	Essential for oxygen evolution in photosynthesis.

13.3 Toxic minerals

In recent years large-scale reclamation of derelict industrial sites has taken place in Britain and in other parts of the world. One of the difficulties in work of this sort is to get vegetation to grow in such places where the soil, mainly derived from spoil heaps, is sometimes contaminated with heavy metals such as copper, lead, zinc and nickel. In spoil heaps the concentrations of these elements are toxic to most green plants.

Old spoil heaps from heavy metal workings are colonised by a select group of plants called **metallophytes** because of their tolerance to high concentrations of heavy metals. It is said that prospectors often located surface deposits of ores rich in heavy metals by the type of vegetation growing on the sites. One approach to the problem of getting vegetation to grow on spoil heaps has been to plant metallophytes. Varieties of grasses such as *Festuca ovina* and *Agrostis canina* tolerant of high concentrations of heavy metals have been used successfully in projects of this kind.

13.4 Soil as a source of minerals

Soil is much more complex than solutions used in water culture experiments. A fertile soil consists of a **mineral skeleton** derived from weathered rock, **organic matter** mainly as dead and decaying plant material, **water**, **air** and **living organisms** notably bacteria, fungi and soil-dwelling animals. The interaction of the various components mainly determines the availability of minerals to the roots of higher plants.

In natural soils nearly all the nitrogen comes from the breakdown of organic matter by **decomposer organisms** such as bacteria and fungi. Most of the sulphur, phosphorus, calcium, magnesium and potassium are also of organic origin. The rest, together with iron and the trace elements, are obtained from weathering of the mineral skeleton.

Cations such as Ca^{2+}, Mg^{2+} and K^+ are attracted to and held by the negative charges of clay and humus particles. However, the attraction is not permanent and the elements can be released by **ion exchange**. Anions such as NO_3^-, SO_4^{2-} and Cl^- are not usually held in this way and are found dissolved in soil water. Phosphorus is normally found in soil as insoluble phosphates of calcium, iron and aluminium.

In an undisturbed terrestrial ecosystem the soil is in a state of equilibrium. Minerals absorbed by plants are returned to the soil when the plants die and are decomposed. On the contrary, substantial quantities of mineral elements are removed annually from cultivated soils. Most of the loss is due to the high mineral content of the crop at harvesting (Table 13.6). Thus to maintain the fertility of land used for growing crops it is necessary to replenish the soil with minerals. This is done by applying **manures**, **composts** or **mineral fertilisers**.

Table 13.6 Mineral content of leaves of sugar beet (after Wallace 1961)

ELEMENT	Ca	Mg	K	P	Fe	Mn	B
% dry mass	2·64	0·55	4·21	0·35	0·0125	0·0046	0·0029

13.5 Mineral absorption by plants

Roots are the main organs concerned with mineral uptake by terrestrial plants although minerals can be absorbed through intact leaves. Foliar sprays containing fertilisers are now quite widely used to feed crops grown on a large scale.

13.5.1 Roots as organs of mineral absorption

The absorption of water by roots is described in Chapter 11. Minerals are taken into roots in aqueous solution yet there is no direct link between the absorption of minerals and water. Water uptake is controlled mainly by the rate at which a plant transpires. Mineral uptake can be rapid even when transpiration has stopped. Indeed, submerged aquatic plants absorb minerals even though they do not transpire. Most of a terrestrial plant's mineral requirements are absorbed by its roots from the top six inches of soil. It is here that roots grow profusely and minerals are most abundant.

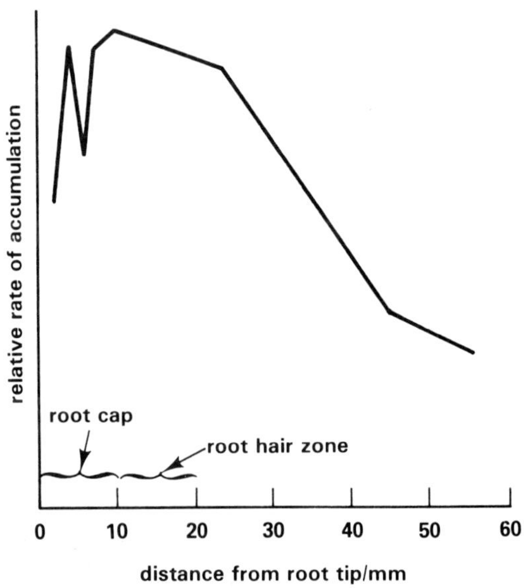

FIG. 13.8 *Mineral accumulation by different parts of barley roots* (after Kramer, 1969)

Roots which penetrate deeper into the soil absorb mainly water. By growing constantly in length, roots continually occupy new areas of soil from which minerals can be absorbed. All parts of the root system do not absorb minerals with equal efficiency. Mineral uptake takes place most rapidly in the zone of elongation just behind the apices of roots where root hairs are present (Fig. 13.8). The root hairs increase the area of contact between the soil and the root surface.

The roots of many terrestrial plants form a symbiotic association with the hyphae of certain species of soil-dwelling fungi. The association is called a **mycorrhiza**. Mycorrhizal roots absorb minerals more efficiently than ordinary roots (Table 13.7). What do you think are the reasons for this? In addition there are thriving populations of free-living saprophytic bacteria and fungi in the immediate vicinity of living roots. The micro-organisms feed on sugars and amino acids released into the soil by the root cells and on dead cells sloughed off as roots grow through the soil. The term **rhizosphere** is used to describe the soil around roots affected in this way. What effect do you think the rhizosphere micro-organisms have on mineral uptake by plant roots?

Table 13.7 Uptake of N, P and K by ***Pinus strobus*** **(after Hatch 1937)**

TYPE OF ROOT	NUTRIENTS ABSORBED/% DRY MASS		
	N	P	K
mycorrhizal	1·24	0·196	0·744
non-mycorrhizal	0·85	0·074	0·425

13.5.2 Mechanisms of mineral absorption

Minerals are usually absorbed against concentration gradients. Not all minerals are absorbed at the same rate and uptake is most rapid by tissues respiring aerobically. Let us examine two of the mechanisms which could account for mineral absorption.

1. DIFFUSION

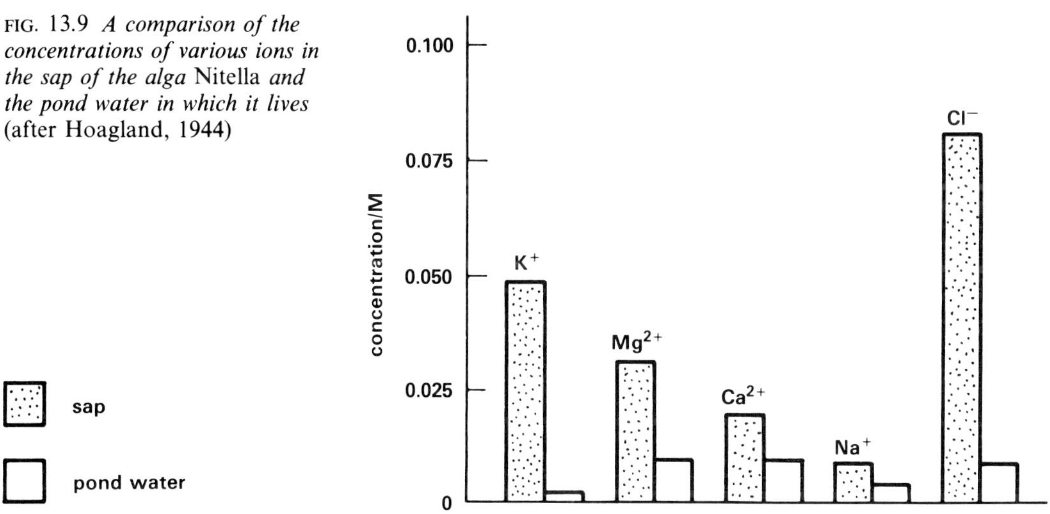

FIG. 13.9 *A comparison of the concentrations of various ions in the sap of the alga* Nitella *and the pond water in which it lives* (after Hoagland, 1944)

Diffusion is the random movement of ions or molecules down a concentration gradient. Most of the available evidence indicates that mineral absorption does not occur by diffusion. Minerals entering plants usually move against concentration gradients (Fig. 13.9). It is also difficult to explain why respiring cells absorb minerals more rapidly than non-respiring cells if diffusion is the mechanism of mineral absorption.

2. ACTIVE UPTAKE

When roots are transferred from distilled water to a dilute solution of a mineral salt the respiratory rate of the roots increases. Furthermore the increase in respiration is proportional to the rate of ion absorption (Fig. 13.10). It is thought that respiratory energy is used to absorb ions against a concentration gradient.

FIG. 13.10 *Relationship between the rate of respiration and bromide uptake by carrot root discs* (after Steward, Berry and Broyer, 1936)

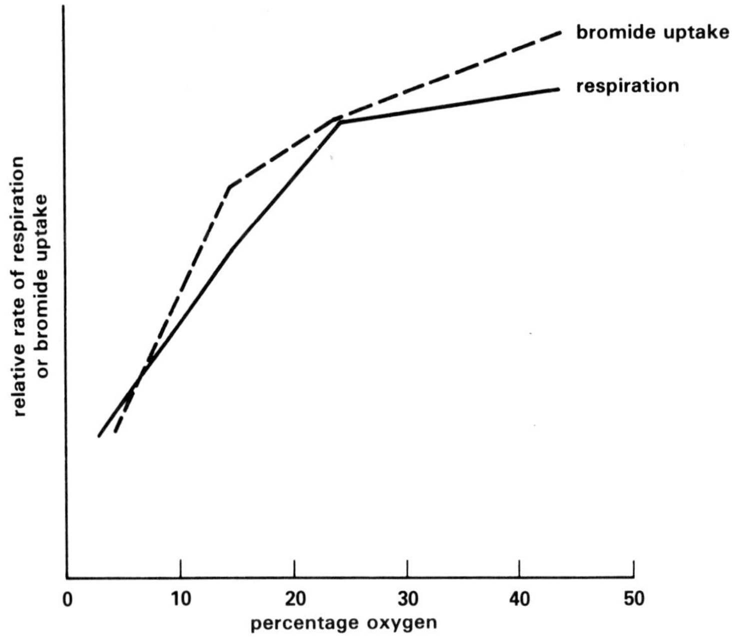

FIG. 13.11 *Two ways in which carrier molecules may be used to carry ions into cells*

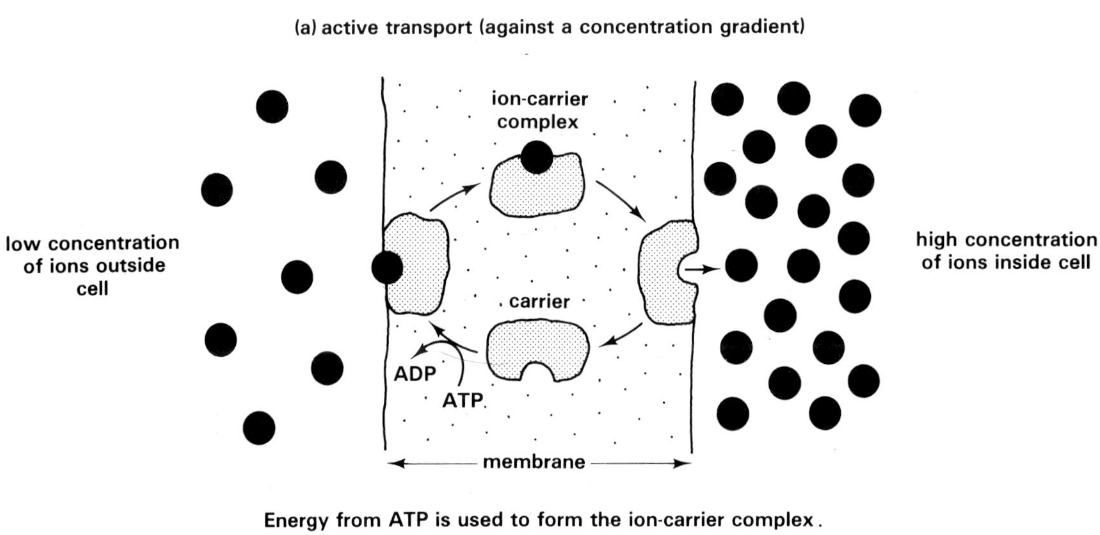

(b) facilitated transport (down a concentration gradient)

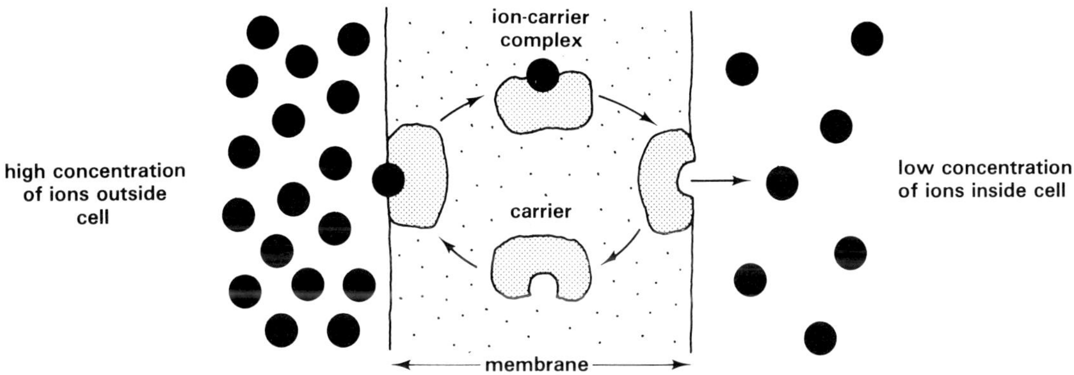

The carrier conveys the ions across the membrane without using energy.

Carrier molecules are probably used to transport mineral ions into cells (Fig. 13.11). Evidence that carriers are involved has come from experiments in which the rates of ion uptake are measured in the presence of increasing concentrations of mineral ions (Fig. 13.12). The results are similar to the relationship between the rate of an enzyme-catalysed reaction and substrate concentration (Chapter 4). The similarity in the relationships suggests that ions combine with carriers in much the same way as enzyme-substrate complexes are formed. In Chapter 4 it is explained how inhibitors compete for active sites on enzyme molecules. A comparable phenomenon occurs in mineral uptake when the presence of one mineral sometimes inhibits the uptake of another. Why do you think this occurs?

FIG. 13.12 *Effect of concentration of ions on ion uptake*

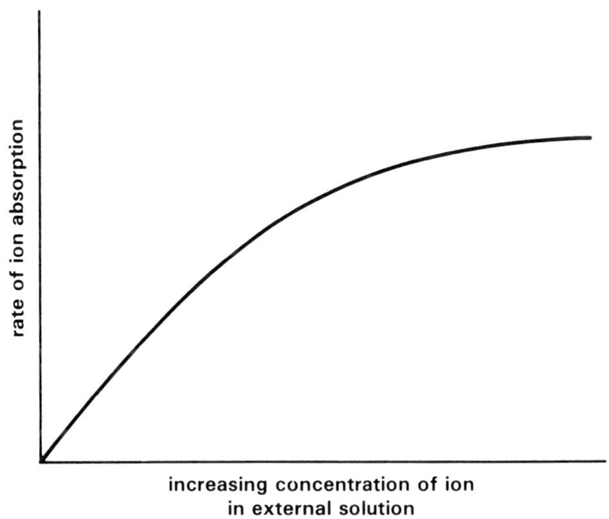

13.6 Transport of minerals in plants

Because they absorb minerals, roots can be thought of as a **source** of minerals for the rest of the plant. Actively growing tissues which have a demand for minerals can be thought of as **sinks**. Let us see how minerals move from a source to sinks.

13.6.1 Passage across the root tissues

After absorption by the epidermal cells of roots, minerals eventually enter the root xylem elements. Plant physiologists are still uncertain as to how the minerals cross the intervening tissues. The path of least resistance across the root cortex is probably through the cytoplasm, movement from cell to cell taking place along plasmodesmata. Alternatively mineral transport may take place along the walls of the cortical cells. At the endodermis the wall route is blocked by the suberised **Casparian band**. It is likely that minerals pass through the selectively permeable plasma membrane of the endodermal cells. Entry of minerals into the pericycle cells is controlled in this way. Movement of minerals from the pericycle to the xylem elements is thought to occur by **active transport**. The pumping of ions into the vascular tissue uses respiratory energy and is probably responsible for root pressure (Chapter 11).

Not all of the minerals absorbed by roots end up in the plant's vascular tissue. Some minerals are retained by the root cells for metabolic purposes. Metallophytes often store large deposits of heavy metals in the vacuoles and cell walls of the root cortex.

13.6.2 Movement into the shoot system

The ascent of solutes in the xylem elements of the stem can be demonstrated by placing the stalk of a leafy transpiring shoot in a solution of a dye such as eosin. Microscopic examination of thin sections of the stem cut a few hours later reveals the presence of dye in the vessels and tracheids. Some of the dye is found in the cell walls but the results of recent experiments with radioisotopes indicate that the cavities of tracheids and vessels are the most important route for mineral transport. The ascent of minerals is a **passive** process dependent on transpiration. A correlation between the rate of transpiration and the upward movement of solutes has been demonstrated with indicators such as dyes and radioactive isotopes. Although many minerals ascend the xylem as inorganic ions, some are carried as organic compounds. While most of the sulphur is transported as sulphate(VI) ions, a small proportion is moved as sulphur-containing amino acids such as cysteine and methionine. Nitrate(V) ions are generally converted in the roots to amino acids.

On reaching a sink in the **transpiration stream**, minerals are moved into the metabolising tissue. **Transfer cells** which have a large surface area to volume ratio are found in the minor veins of many species of flowering plants and are thought to transport minerals from the xylem into metabolising tissue (Fig. 13.13). Because transfer cells have large numbers of mitochondria it is probable that **active transport** is involved. Some lateral transport also takes place between xylem elements and adjacent tissues such as the vascular cambium and phloem.

13.6.3 Circulation of minerals in plants

What happens to individual mineral nutrients after they have been taken into a sink varies considerably. Calcium and iron accumulate in young leaves and display little movement into new organs formed later. The current needs of a plant for Ca and Fe are met by absorption from the soil. Thus deficiency symptoms of these elements often appear in the young leaves at shoot apices.

Most minerals are relatively mobile and after entering initial sinks they then pass into developing sinks such as young leaves, flowers and fruits.

For this reason deficiency symptoms of N, K, Mg, P and S are often seen in mature leaves. It has been shown that phosphate(V) ions are re-exported in phloem sieve-tubes and it is likely that other mobile elements follow the same pathway. The internal recycling of minerals enables plants to withdraw nutrients from old leaves before they fall off. The yellowing of older leaves for example is accompanied by the breakdown of nitrogenous compounds including chlorophyll and withdrawal of the end products into other parts of the plant. A small proportion of mineral nutrients, potassium especially, is leached from leaves by rainfall but the natural recirculation of the elements largely depends on the activities of micro-organisms in decomposing dead plant organs returned to the soil.

The main processes and pathways thought to be involved in mineral uptake and transport are summarised in Figure 13.13.

FIG. 13.13 *Summary of mineral uptake and transport in a flowering plant*

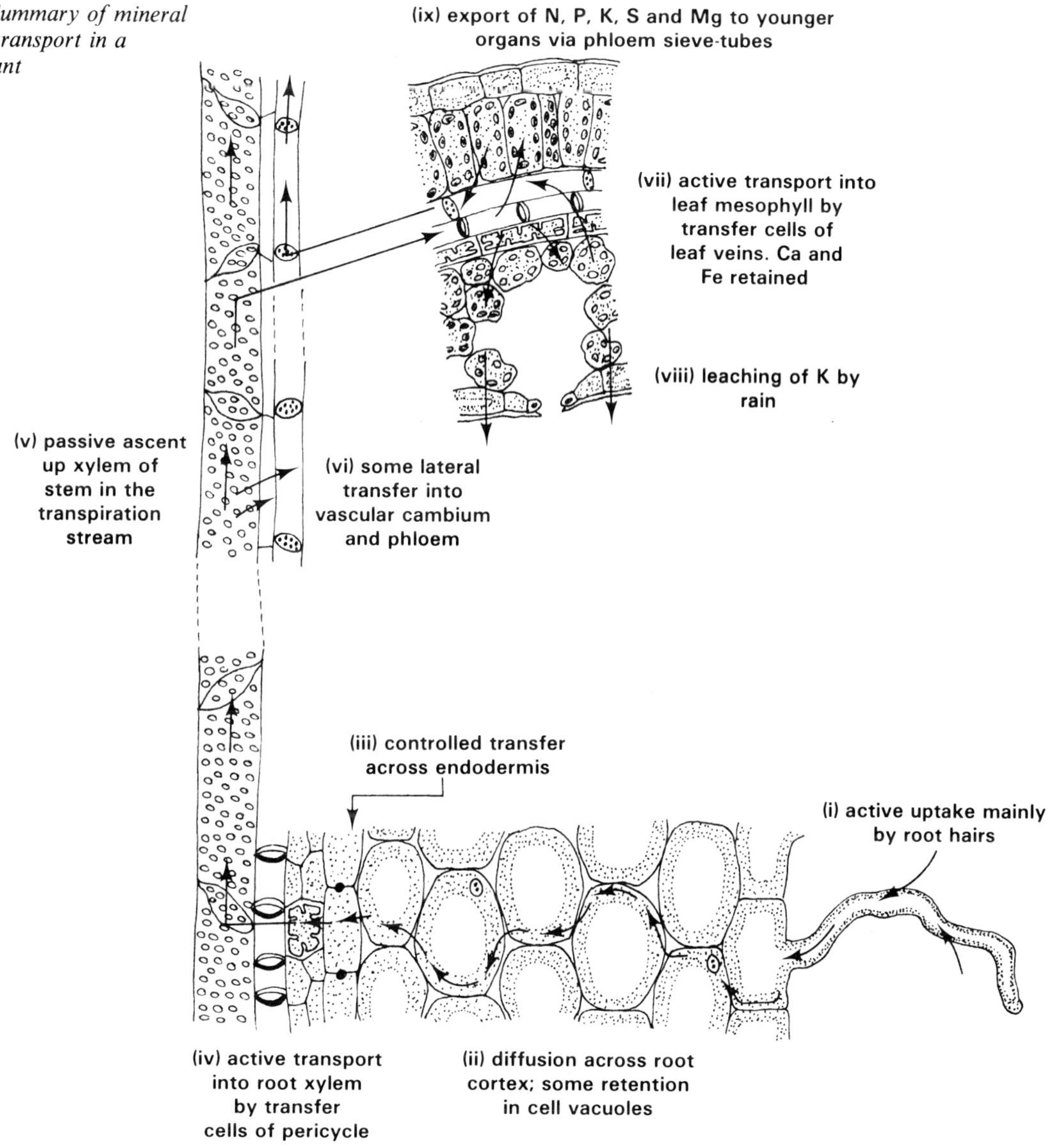

FIG. 13.14 (a) and (b) *The nutrient film technique* (courtesy Glasshouse Crops Research Institute)

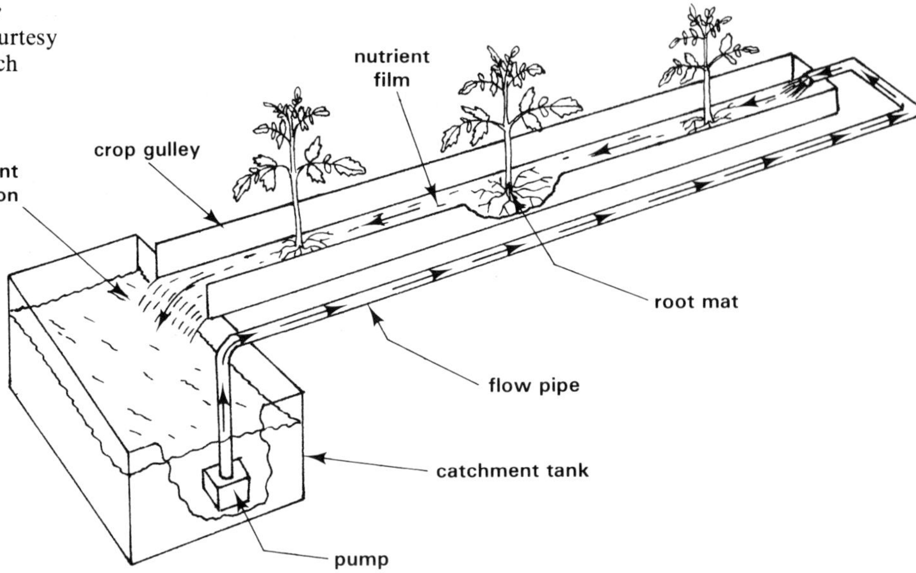

13.7 The nutrient-film technique

This chapter ends as it began with water culture techniques. In recent years a system has been developed at the Glasshouse Crops Research Institute in Britain for the large-scale cultivation of crops without soil. The system is called the **nutrient-film technique**. The plants are grown in plastic troughs through which circulates a film of water containing balanced amounts of macro- and micronutrients (Fig. 13.14). So successful is the system that commercial production of tomatoes, cucumbers and strawberries has now begun using the nutrient-film technique. One of the important advantages of this form of farming is that it dramatically increases crop production. One grower in Australia has obtained ten lettuce crops in a year using the technique. Another very useful benefit is that it can be used in arid areas because little water is lost from the troughs by evaporation.

Chapter 14

The mammalian alimentary system

A constant supply of organic and inorganic nutrients is required to sustain the many and complex activities which take place in the mammalian body

Organic nutrients such as proteins and lipids are the raw materials for the synthesis of cellular components in growth and repair. The energy needed to drive synthetic processes comes mainly from the oxidation of sugars in cellular respiration (Chapter 5). Mammals also require energy for movement and to help maintain a constant body temperature (Chapter 17). Vitamins are organic nutrients which participate in a wide range of body functions.

Inorganic nutrients (minerals) are needed to create and maintain electrical potentials across the membranes of nerve and muscle cells (Chapter 15). The coagulation of blood (Chapter 9), activation of enzymes (Chapter 4), growth of teeth and bones and maintenance of the osmotic potential of the body fluids are among the many other essential activities which depend on a supply of minerals.

Mammals obtain nutrients from their diet which consists of food and water. Food is a mixture of organic and inorganic nutrients. Water contains dissolved minerals. It is the alimentary system which first deals with food and water taken into the body.

14.1 Mammalian nutritional requirements

The nutritional requirements of mammals can be divided into three categories, **organic nutrients**, **vitamins** and **inorganic nutrients**.

14.1.1 Organic nutrients

The chemical nature of the main organic constituents of the diet is described in Chapter 3.

1. CARBOHYDRATES

About 50 per cent of the energy from the average human diet in Britai comes from **carbohydrates**. Glucose is the main respiratory substrate Reserves of carbohydrate are stored as glycogen in the liver and muscle (section 14.5.2).

2. PROTEINS

Proteins are necessary in the diet as a source of **amino acids**. Amino acid are respired in emergencies but only about five per cent of the huma body's energy requirement normally comes from amino acids. The mai function of amino acids is to provide the raw materials for the synthesis c proteins. A constant supply of amino acids is needed for the production c enzymes and cell membranes. Metabolism, growth and repair thus depen on the presence of proteins in the diet. Proteins are also made in secretor cells for export to other parts of the body. Plasma proteins in the blood fo example are made in the liver. Antibodies are proteins made in the lymp nodes. Digestive enzymes and certain hormones are proteins to **Transamination** in the liver enables some amino acids called **non-essenti amino acids** to be made from others (section 14.5.2). A few amino acid cannot be made in this way and these **essential amino acids** are a vit constituent of the diet.

3. LIPIDS

Lipids can be used as respiratory substrates. Fats and oils account for about 45 per cent of the energy obtained from the average human diet in Britain. The synthesis of cell membranes requires lipids as well as proteins. The fatty membranes of the myelin sheath around certain nerve cells is important in impulse transmission. Surplus fats are stored in mammals beneath the skin and around internal body organs such as the kidneys. As well as being a foodstore fat acts as a heat insulator which helps to keep a constant body temperature.

14.1.2 Vitamins

Vitamins are a range of substances necessary for good health. They affect a variety of body functions. Vitamins are varied chemically and are often required only in trace quantities. Some vitamins are soluble in fats and are absorbed from the gut dissolved in lipids. Others are water-soluble and are absorbed into the blood dissolved in water.

1. FAT-SOLUBLE VITAMINS

(i) VITAMIN A (retinol) is made from the plant pigment β-carotene and is needed for synthesis of the visual pigments rhodopsin and iodopsin. Deficiency of vitamin A can lead to **night blindness** (Chapter 16). Vitamin A is also essential for maintaining epithelial tissues in good condition. Infection of the epithelium of the respiratory tract often results from serious lack of vitamin A in the body.

(ii) VITAMIN D is a group of several sterols including ergocalciferol (vitamin D_2). Ergocalciferol is produced by the action of ultraviolet radiation from the sun on ergesterol in the skin. Vitamin D_2 stimulates the absorption of calcium from the gut. Deficiency of vitamin D_2 can lead to the release of calcium from the bones under the influence of parathyrin (Chapter 18). Malformation of the skeleton due to vitamin D_2 deficiency is called **rickets**.

(iii) VITAMIN E. The function of vitamin E in the human body is not fully understood. In rats it is essential for normal **spermatogenesis** (Chapter 22).

(iv) VITAMIN K is necessary for the production of **prothrombin** in the liver. Deficiency of vitamin K leads to impaired coagulation of the blood (Chapter 9).

2. WATER-SOLUBLE VITAMINS

(i) VITAMIN B is a complex of several vitamins most of which are components of **co-enzymes** (Chapter 4). **Vitamin B_1** (thiamin) is required to make the co-enzyme of carboxylases (Chapter 4). Deficiency of vitamin B_1 leads to **beri-beri** with malfunction of the nervous and cardiovascular systems.

Vitamin B_2 (riboflavin) is part of the co-enzyme FAD used as a hydrogen acceptor in Krebs' tricarboxylic acid cycle (Chapters 4 and 5). **Vitamin B_6** is required for **protein metabolism** including transamination (section 14.5.2 and Chapter 6). **Vitamin B_{12}** (cyanocob(III)alamin) is necessary for the production of red blood cells. Deficiency of vitamin B_{12} causes **pernicious anaemia** (section 14.4 and Chapter 9). Nicotinamide and nicotinic acid are other B-group vitamins. They are required to make the hydrogen acceptor co-enzymes NAD and NADP (Chapters 4 and 5).

(ii) VITAMIN C (ascorbic acid) is thought to act as an electron carrier in respiration. Recent evidence suggests that a high daily intake of vitamin C in the diet may have many beneficial effects including reduction of blood cholesterol (Chapter 9). Deficiency of vitamin C causes **scurvy**, symptoms of which include breakdown of connective tissues and blood vessels. Scurvy was once common among sailors who were deprived of fresh fruit containing vitamin C while on long voyages. When it was found that drinking the juice of citrus fruits prevented scurvy the Royal Navy provided lime juice on its ships for consumption by the crew.

14.1.3 Inorganic nutrients

Minerals are inorganic nutrients which participate in a wide variety of body functions. Some minerals called **macronutrients** are needed in relatively large quantities. Others called **trace elements** are needed in small amounts.

1. MACRONUTRIENTS

Sodium ions are more abundant than any other cation in the body fluids. Sodium ions play an important role in the electrochemical activities of nerves and muscles. Sodium chloride helps to maintain the osmotic potential of tissue fluid and blood plasma. **Potassium** ions are the most abundant of cations in cells. Potassium ions are involved, like sodium, in nerve and muscle impulse transmission. **Calcium** and **phosphate(V)** ions are the main mineral constituents of bone and teeth. Calcium ions are also required for coagulation of blood and for muscle contraction.

2. TRACE ELEMENTS

Trace elements must be provided in the diet to maintain health. Large quantities of trace elements can be poisonous.

Cobalt is a constituent of vitamin B_{12} (cyanocob(III)alamin) and is vital for the production of haemoglobin and red blood cells. Providing cobalt(II) ions are present, vitamin B_{12} can be synthesised by bacteria in the guts of ruminant mammals (section 14.3.3). Non-ruminants must have vitamin B_{12} in their diets. **Iodine** is a constituent of the hormone thyroxin and is absorbed from the blood by the thyroid gland. Lack of iodine in the diet leads to decreased thyroxin production and enlargement of the thyroid gland called a goitre (Chapter 18). **Copper** is vital for the activation of a variety of enzymes and for the production of haemoglobin. **Iron** is a constituent of haemoglobin and myoglobin (Chapter 8) and cytochromes (Chapter 5). Reserves of iron are stored in the liver (section 14.5.2). **Zinc** is an activator of several enzymes, including carbonic anhydrase (Chapter 8) and is required for synthesis of the hormone insulin (Chapter 18).

14.2 Mammalian dentition

Ingested food first enters the **mouth** where it is **chewed**. Chewing makes it easier to swallow food and helps the action of digestive enzymes secreted by the various glands which open into the gut. The cutting and grinding of food which takes place when food is chewed is the function of the **teeth**.

14.2.1 Structure and development of teeth

Tooth buds in the developing jaw give rise to the teeth. The buds each contain an enamel organ in which **ameloblast cells** produce **enamel** made of calcium salts. Enamel is the hardest material in the mammalian body and coats the protruding surfaces called the **crowns** of the teeth. Inside the cup-shaped enamel organ, **odontoblast cells** of the dental papilla produce **dentine** (Fig. 14.1). During tooth development, sockets of bone grow around the **roots** of the teeth (Fig. 14.2).

Many mammals including man, have two sets of teeth during their lives. The first set called **milk teeth** grow in early life and replaced by the **permanent teeth**. In children, tooth replacement begins usually at about five years of age and takes several years to complete. The final molars are called the wisdom teeth and usually emerge in early adult life. Permanent teeth develop from separate rows of tooth buds which arise under the buds from which the milk teeth grow (Figs. 14.1 and 14.3).

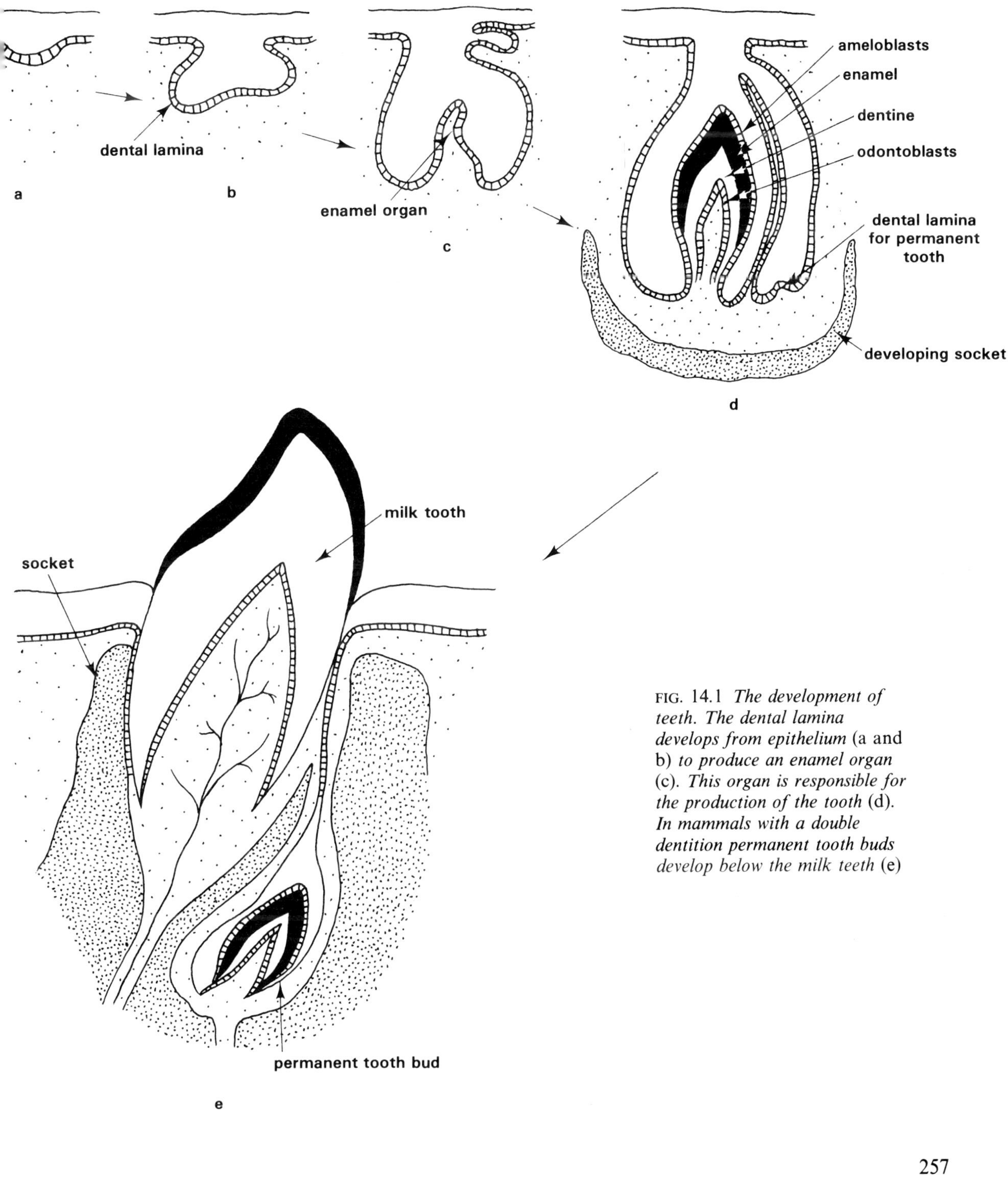

FIG. 14.1 *The development of teeth. The dental lamina develops from epithelium* (a and b) *to produce an enamel organ* (c). *This organ is responsible for the production of the tooth* (d). *In mammals with a double dentition permanent tooth buds develop below the milk teeth* (e)

FIG. 14.2 *Diagrammatic vertical section through a human molar. The root is held in the bony socket by cementum joined to a fibrous connective layer called the periodontal membrane. The elasticity of the fibres in this membrane allows limited movement of the root in the socket, thus acting as a 'shock absorber' during chewing*

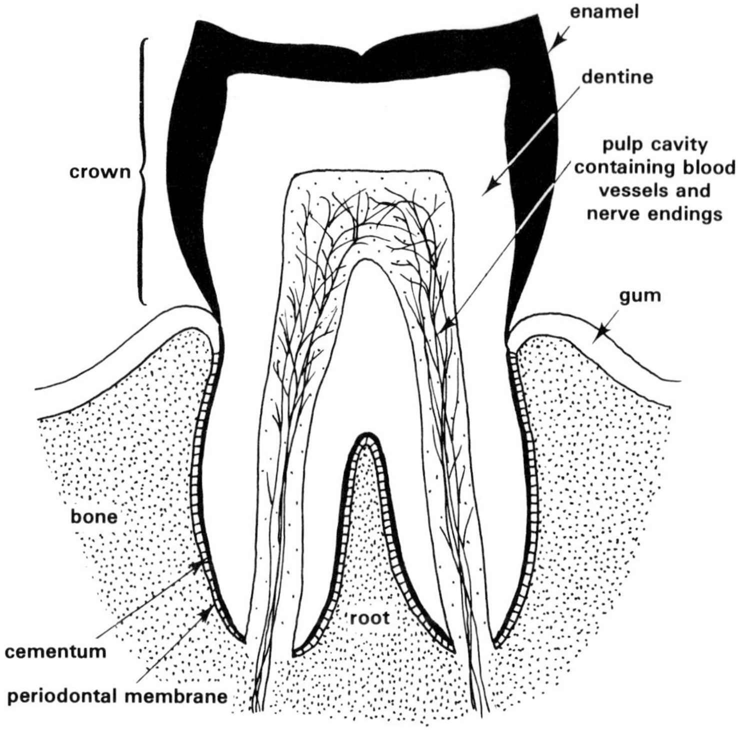

FIG. 14.3 *X-ray photograph showing the dentition of an 8-year-old child. Note the presence of both milk (deciduous) and permanent teeth* (courtesy Mr. Gould, Dental Department, General Hospital, Nottingham)

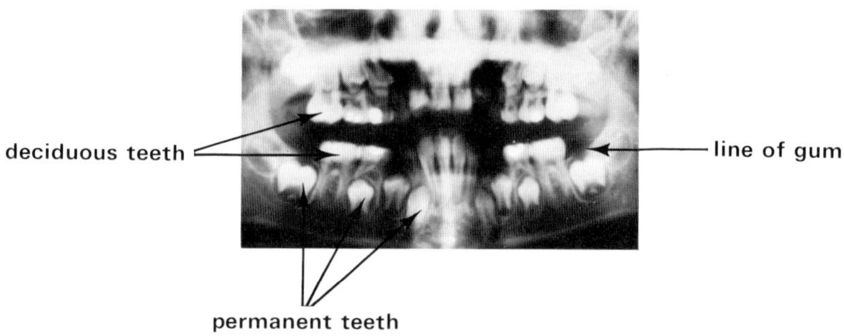

14.2.2 Variety of mammalian teeth

Mammals are **heterodont**. Their dentition includes several kinds of teeth. Moving from the front of the jaw to the rear there are **incisors**, **canines**, **premolars** and **molars**. The various kinds of teeth perform different functions during feeding.

Carnivores eat meat which is often captured alive. The teeth pierce and grip the prey to prevent it escaping and rip and cut it when chewing. In the dog these functions are performed mainly by the canine and **carnassial** teeth respectively. The latter are the fourth upper premolar and the first lower molar teeth (Fig. 14.4). Attachment of the lower jaw to deep grooves on the sides of the skull of the dog restricts the jaw to up and down movement, ideal for cutting flesh (Fig. 14.5). The molar and premolar teeth act like scissors, the upper teeth biting outside the lower ones.

Herbivores eat vegetation. The canine teeth are absent and a toothless space, the **diastema**, separates the incisors from the premolars (Fig. 14.6). In sheep the upper incisors are also missing. When grazing, the lower set of incisors bite against a horny pad in the upper jaw. The main chewing action in herbivores involves the premolars and molars. Because herbivores chew almost constantly the premolars and molars become very worn. The wearing is uneven, as the enamel on the outer surfaces of the teeth is harder than the dentine inside. Consequently the grinding surfaces of the premolars and molars develop a ridged pattern (Fig. 14.7).

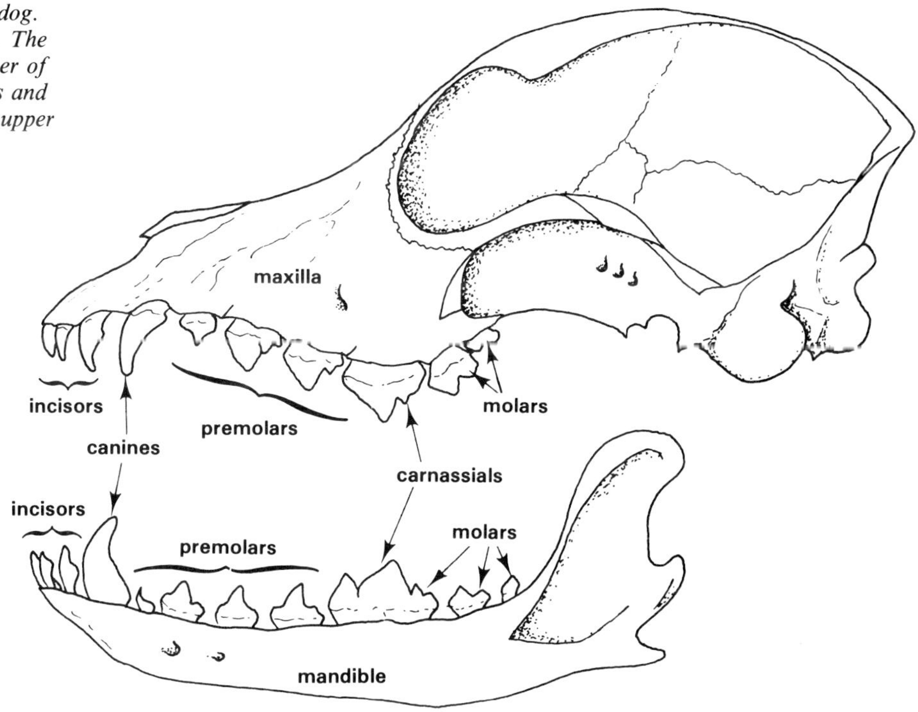

FIG. 14.4 *Dentition of the dog. The dental formula is* $\frac{3142}{3143}$. *The formula refers to the number of incisors, canines, premolars and molars on each side of the upper and lower jaws*

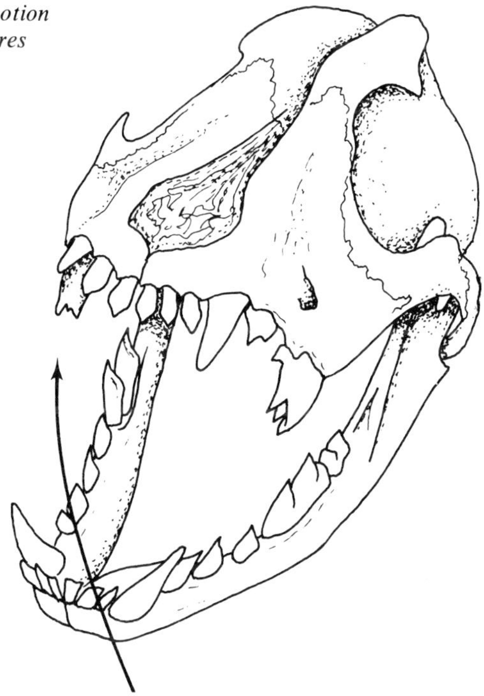

FIG. 14.5 *Vertical biting motion of the lower jaw in carnivores*

FIG. 14.6 *Dentition of the sheep. The dental formula is* $\frac{0033}{3133}$. Compare with Fig. 14.4

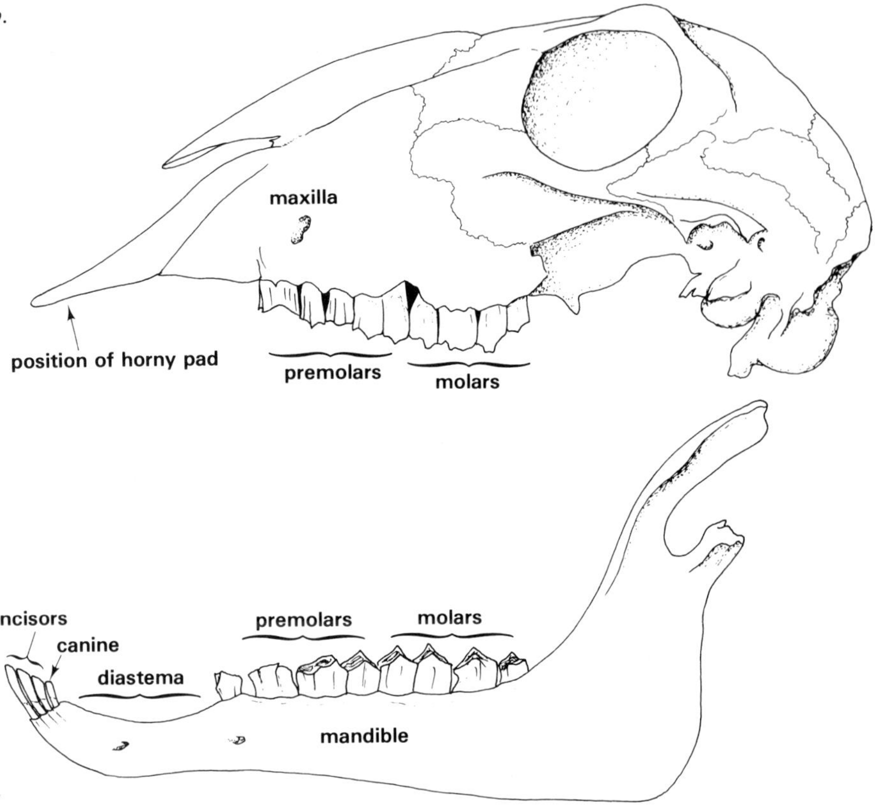

FIG. 14.7 *The grinding surfaces of a sheep's molars*

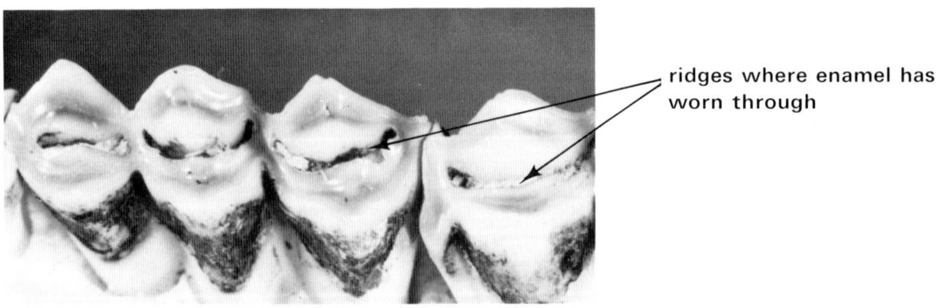

Attachment of the lower jaw to the skull allows a circular jaw motion in the horizontal plane. The ridges of the upper and lower premolars and molars slide over one another with the food in between (Fig. 14.8). In this way vegetation is ground to very fine particles before swallowing. Humans are called **omnivores** because we usually eat meat, fruits and vegetables. We have a relatively unspecialised dentition (Fig. 14.9).

The fossil record shows that primitive mammals had a **dental formula** of:

$$\frac{3 \quad 1 \quad 4 \quad 3}{3 \quad 1 \quad 4 \quad 3}$$

That is, three incisors, one canine, four premolars and three molars on each side of both upper and lower jaws, a total of 44 teeth. Present-day mammals have either this full dentition or, more usually, a reduced number of teeth. Some species of whales and a few other mammals have more teeth.

Modern mammals are thought to have evolved from early insect-eating species. Mammals belonging to the order *Insectivora* which includes shrews, hedgehogs and moles usually have a full dentition (Fig. 14.10).

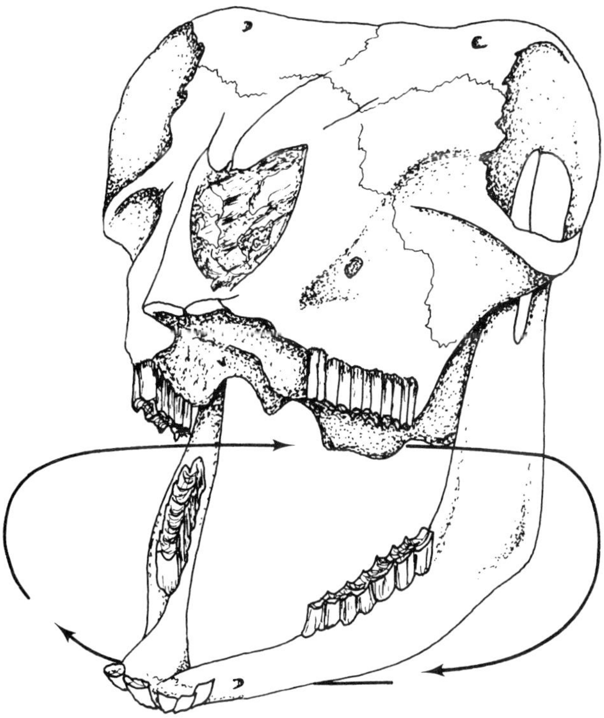

FIG. 14.8 *Circular grinding motion of the lower jaw in herbivores*

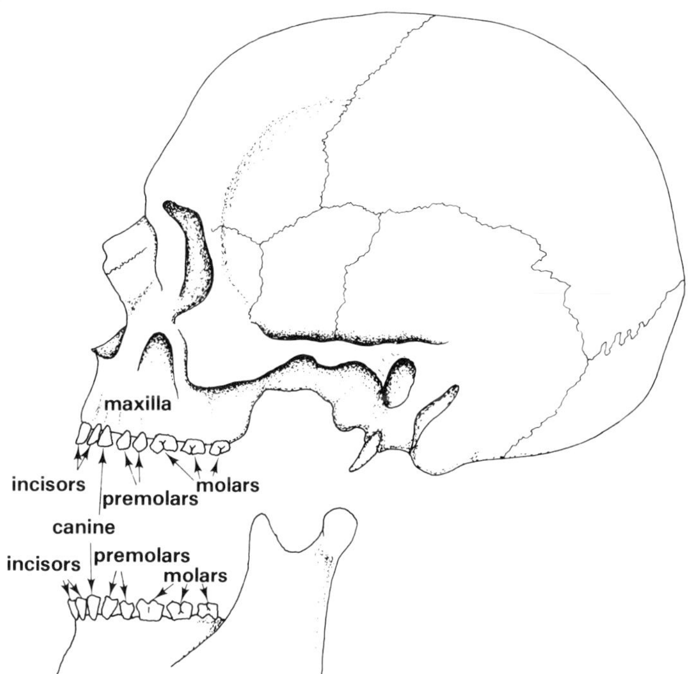

FIG. 14.9 *Dentition of man. The dental formula is* $\frac{2123}{2123}$. *Note the relatively unspecialised teeth compared with the dog and sheep* (Figs 14.4 and 14.6)

FIG. 14.10 *Dentition of the hedgehog*

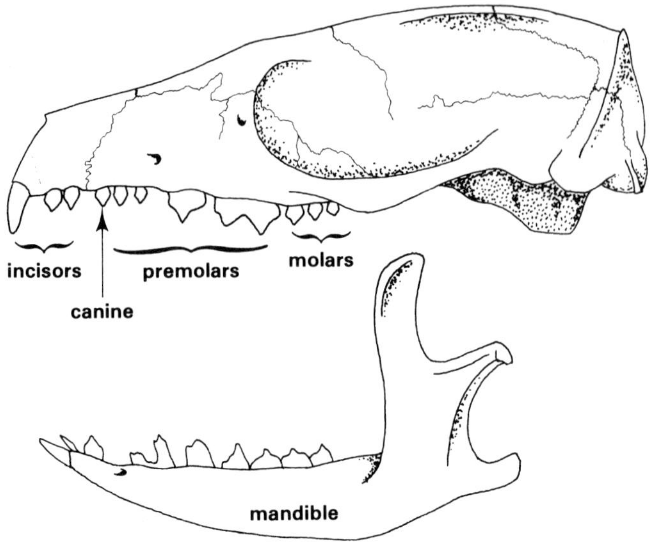

Rodents, such as rats, mice, squirrels, voles and beavers have incisors with **open roots** which allow the incisors to grow continually. Constant growth of the incisors is necessary to replace the tooth substance worn away by the gnawing action of the jaws. Enamel is present only on the outer surface of the incisors and a sharp sloping cutting edge is created as the teeth are worn. Rabbits and hares, which belong to the order *Lagomorpha*, have the same pattern of incisor growth. However, lagomorphs have a small second pair of incisors just behind the first pair (Fig. 14.11).

FIG. 14.11 (a) *Dentition of the rat. The dental formula is* $\frac{1003}{1003}$

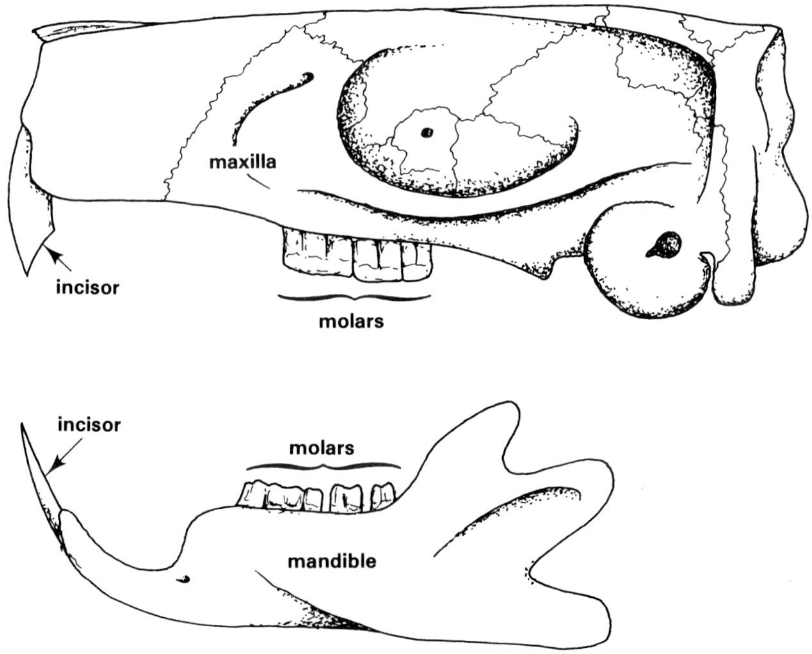

FIG. 14.11 (b) *Dentition of the rabbit. The dental formula is* $\frac{2033}{1023}$

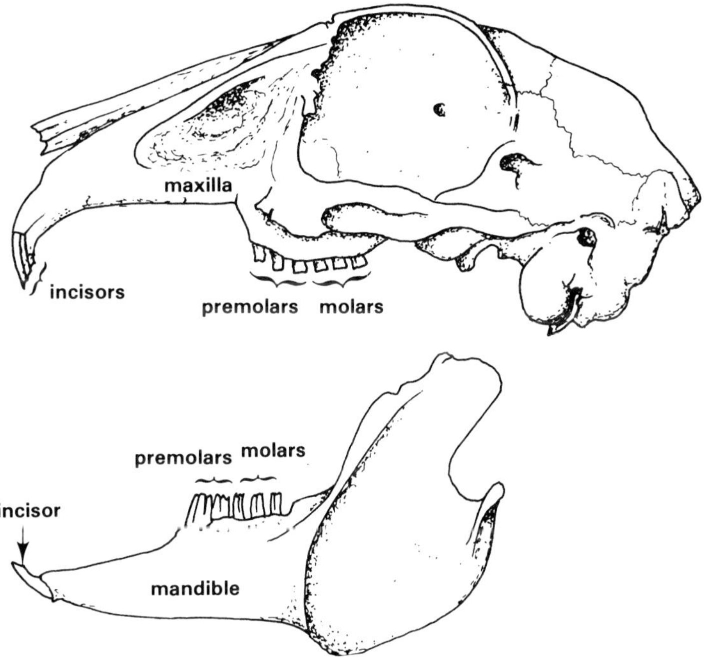

Toothed whales and **dolphins** are mostly flesh-eaters. They have very long jaws with rows of many peg-like teeth which are used to grip prey. **Whalebone whales** on the other hand feed on plankton. Only the foetus whalebone whale has teeth. In the adult, rows of large keratinous plates hanging transversely from the roof of the mouth trap plankton from sea water drawn into the mouth. The muscular tongue then forces sea water out of the mouth and the food is swallowed (Fig. 14.12).

Elephants have huge molar teeth with very large grinding surfaces. The large grinding area enables elephants to cope with the quantities of food necessary to support their massive bodies. The tusks of elephants are a single pair of continually growing upper incisors. They are composed of solid dentine except for a cap of enamel at their tips (Fig. 14.13).

FIG. 14.12 (a) *Dentition of a toothed whale*

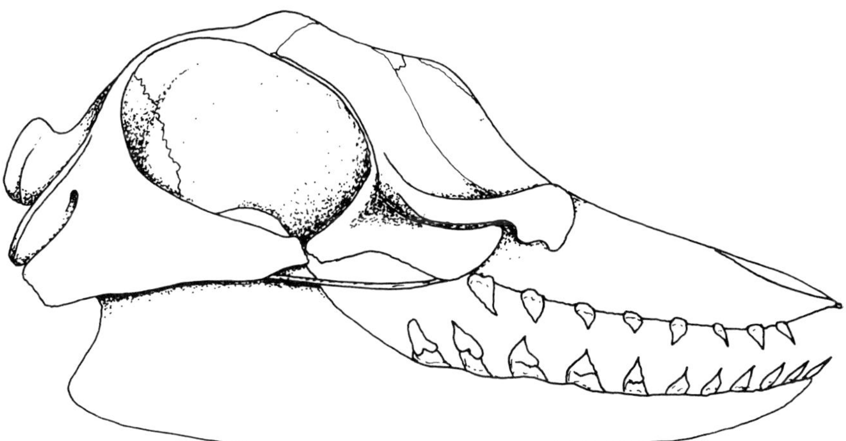

FIG. 14.12 (b) *Skull of a right whale, showing the baleen plates used for sieving food from the sea*

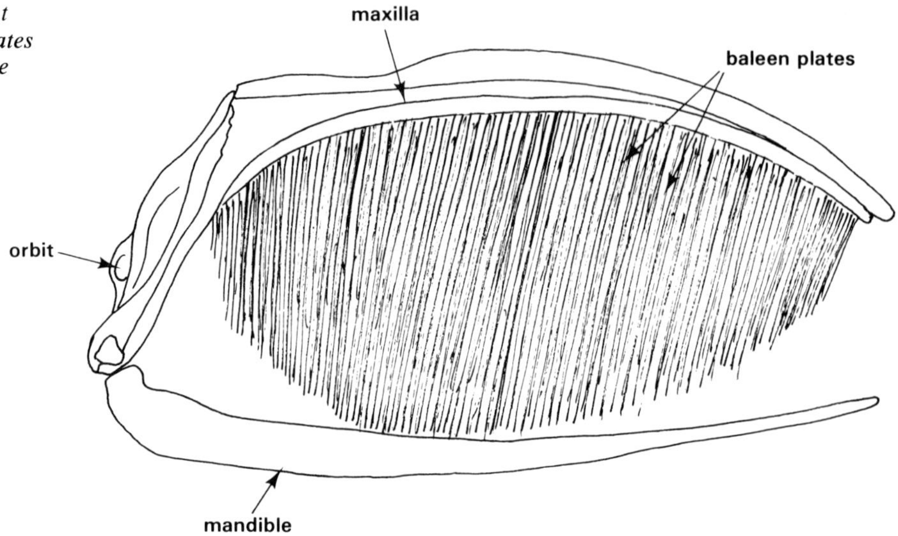

FIG. 14.13 *Dentition of the elephant*

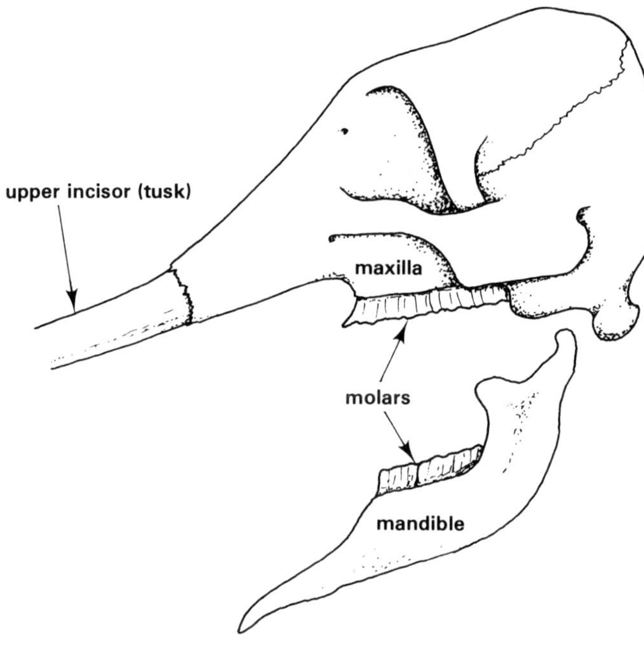

14.3 Digestion

Many of the organic nutrients in food such as proteins and polysaccharides are substances of high relative molar mass. They are insoluble in water and cannot pass through the membranes of body cells. It is necessary for such substances to be broken down into units small enough to be absorbed into the body fluids in which they can be transported to all parts of the body. The breaking down of food is called **digestion**. It takes place in the gut where food is acted on by hydrolytic enzymes (Chapter 4).

Except where otherwise stated the following account of digestion relates to man. The human digestive system is illustrated in Figure 14.14.

FIG. 14.14 *Diagram of the human digestive system*

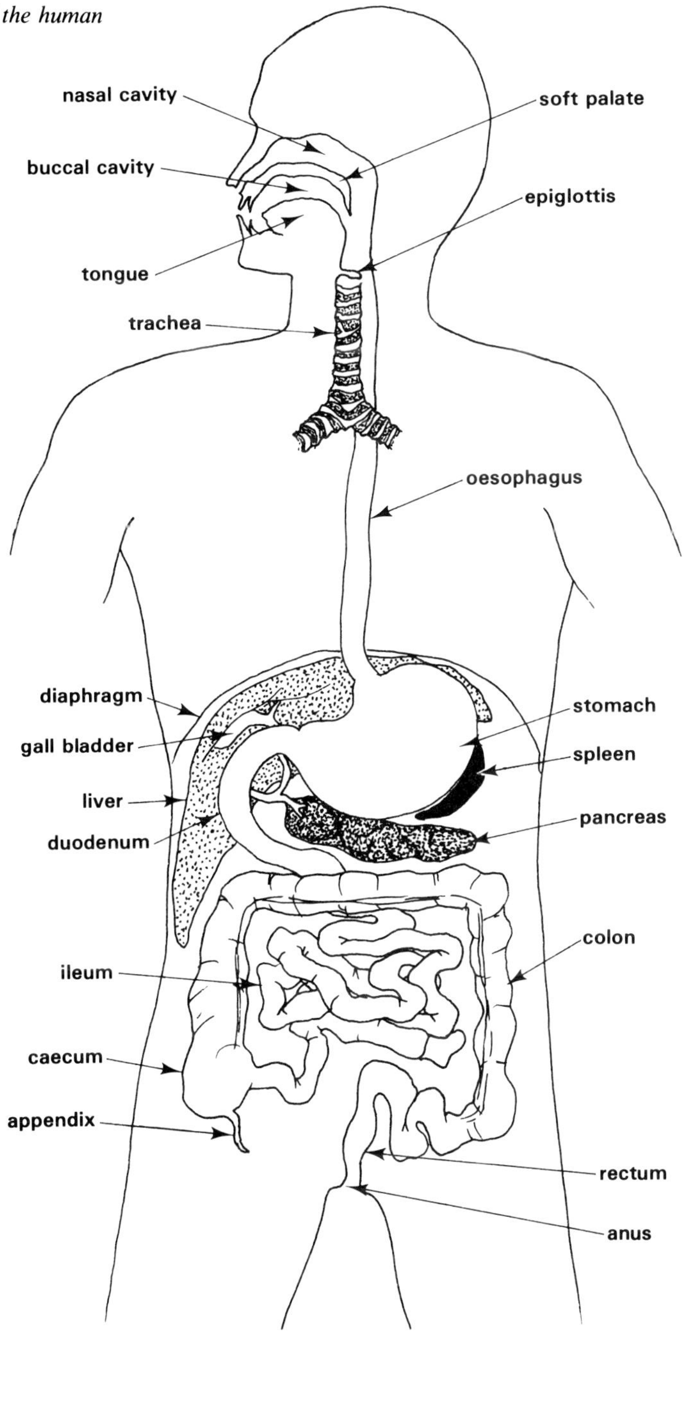

14.3.1 The mouth

The smell and sight of food as well as the mechanical stimulation of food in the mouth triggers a reflex action which results in the secretion of **saliva**. The reflex ensures a flow of saliva when food is in the mouth. Secretion of saliva slows down when a mammal is not eating. Saliva enters the mouth from three pairs of salivary glands (Fig. 14.15).

FIG. 14.15 *Position of the salivary glands in man*

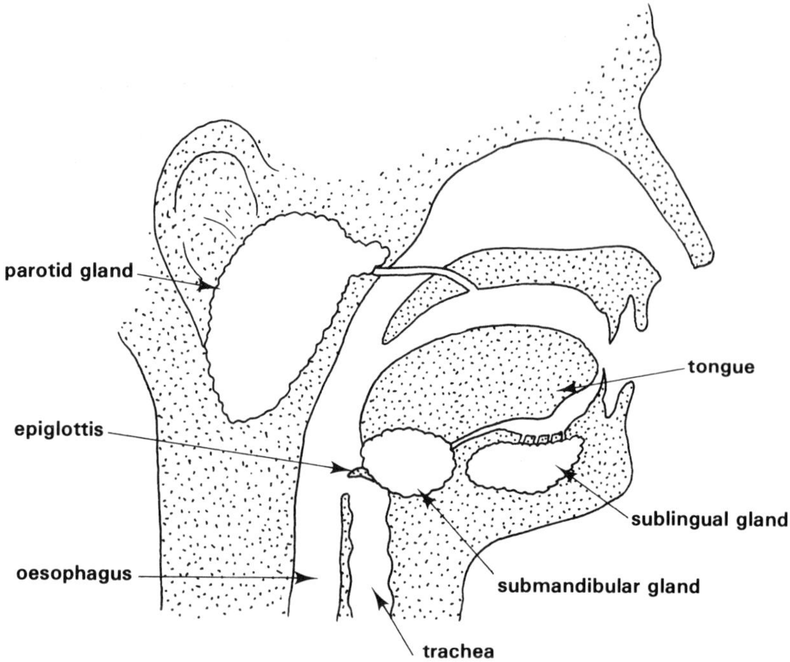

An enzyme called **salivary amylase** is usually found in saliva. Salivary amylase hydrolyses glycosidic linkages in **starch** breaking it down to the disaccharide sugar **maltose** (Chapter 3). Apart from in herbivores, salivary amylase probably contributes little to digestion. This is because most mammals hold food in the mouth for only a short time. Salivary amylase works best in neutral conditions and the pH of saliva is about 7. After swallowing, food passes down the oesophagus into the stomach where the pH is much lower. In acid conditions salivary amylase becomes inactive.

Saliva **lubricates** the pharynx and oesophagus making it easier for food to be swallowed. The food is moulded into a ball (bolus) by the tongue then pushed into the pharynx. Contraction of the pharyngeal wall pushes the bolus into the oesophagus. Rhythmical contractions of the oesophagus called **peristalsis** move the bolus towards the stomach. Peristalsis is a property of all parts of the gut and helps to move food along the alimentary canal. During swallowing the larynx is raised and the glottis is covered by the epiglottis so preventing food from entering the trachea (Fig. 14.16).

FIG. 14.16 *Peristalsis*

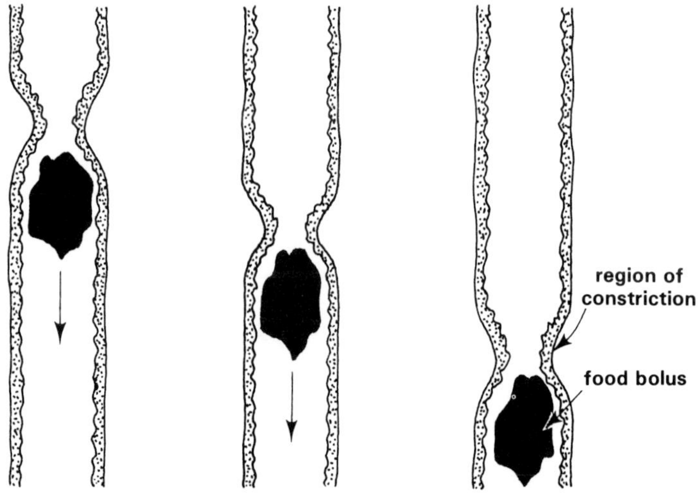

14.3.2 The stomach

The stomach is the first region of the gut where any significant digestion of food takes place. In man the stomach is a muscular bag with a volume of about two litres. It has a delicate inner folded membrane called the **gastric mucosa**. **Gastric juice** is secreted by numerous microscopic **gastric pits** embedded in the mucosa (Figs. 14.17 and 14.18). The juice is very acid with a pH of 2. The acidity is caused by **hydrochloric acid** secreted by **oxyntic cells**. **Peptic cells** secrete **pepsinogen** which on contact with the acid is converted to the peptidase enzyme **pepsin**. The gastric juice of many mammals contains a second peptidase enzyme called **rennin**. Rennin coagulates the milk protein casein and is particularly important in young mammals whose diet consists solely of milk. Pepsin hydrolyses peptide linkages in proteins producing polypeptides (Fig. 14.19).

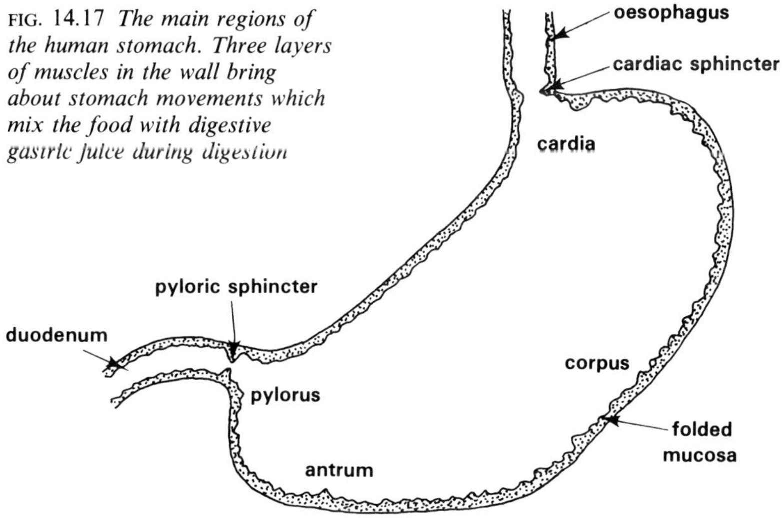

FIG. 14.17 *The main regions of the human stomach. Three layers of muscles in the wall bring about stomach movements which mix the food with digestive gastric juice during digestion*

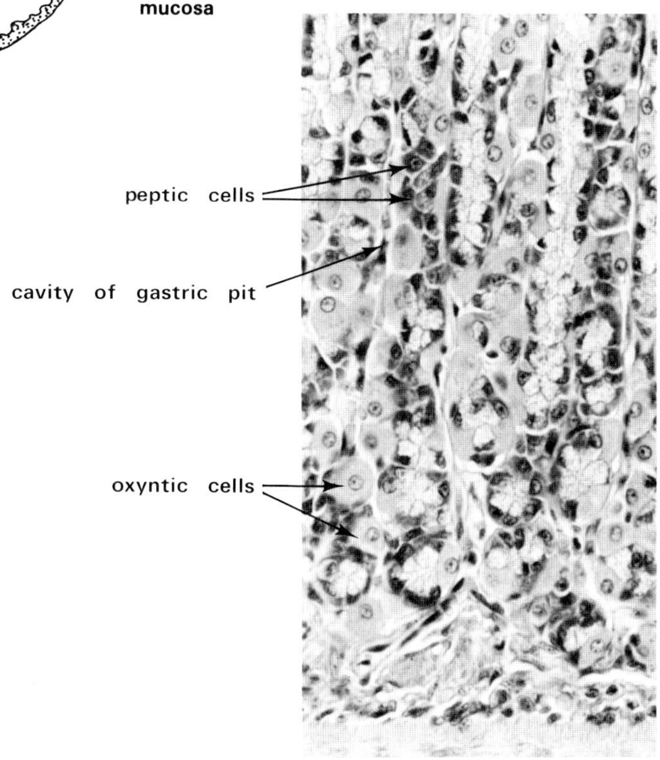

FIG. 14.18 (a) *Photomicrograph showing the gastric glands in a thin section of cat stomach, ×400*

FIG. 14.18 (b) *Diagram of a gastric gland*

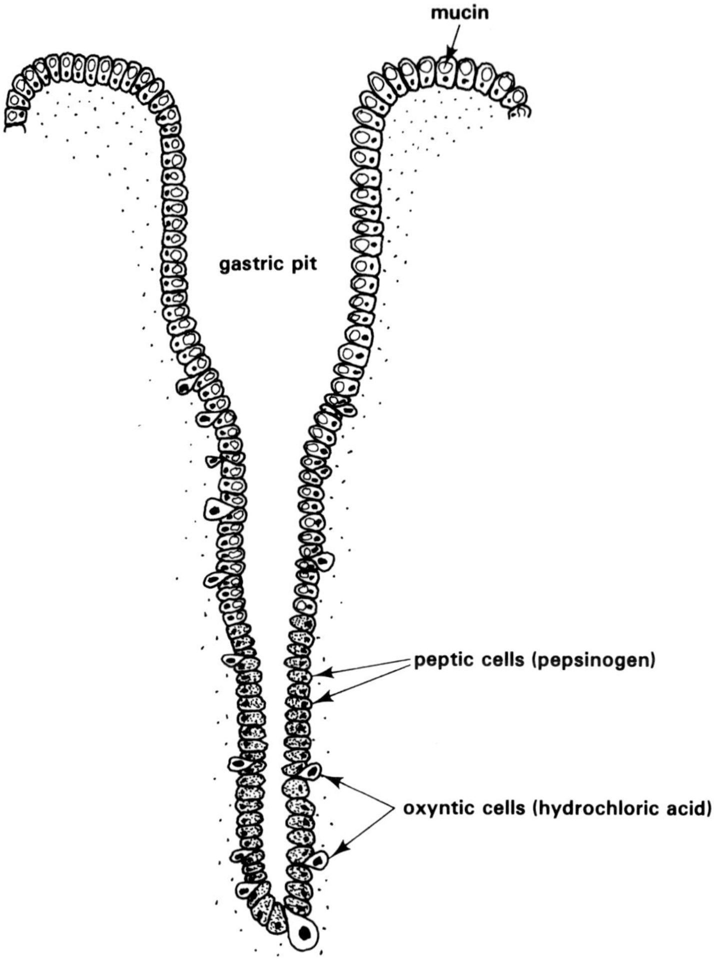

FIG. 14.19 *Action of rennin and pepsin. Gastric hydrochloric acid provides optimum pH for the action of these enzymes. Rennin is important in the stomach of many young mammals*

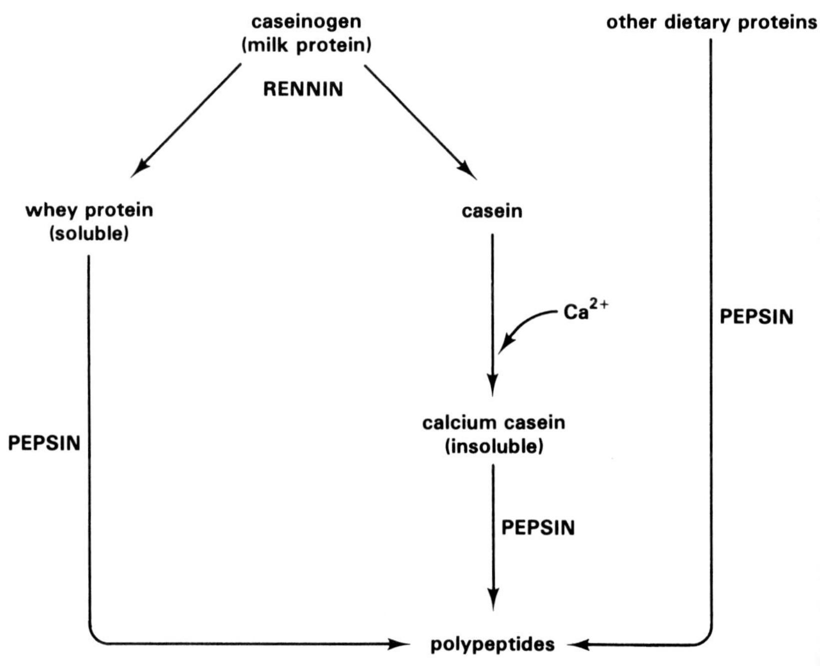

The corrosive and digestive properties of hydrochloric acid and pepsin place the delicate gastric mucosa at risk. Protection is given by a slimy glycoprotein called **mucin**. Mucin is secreted by goblet cells in the mucosa and forms a layer of mucus over the stomach lining. Mucus protects against mechanical as well as chemical injury. If the protection is not effective the mucosa and stomach wall are attacked by the gastric juice, causing an ulcer to form.

Like the release of saliva, gastric secretion is controlled by autonomic reflexes. Secretion of gastric juice begins when food is in the mouth. The presence of food in the stomach triggers the stomach lining to produce a hormone called **gastrin** which is taken into the blood. Gastrin stimulates continued secretion of gastric juice after the faster nervous mechanism has started it off (Fig. 14.20).

FIG. 14.20 *The relative importance of nervous (vagus) and hormonal (gastrin) influence on gastric juice secretion*

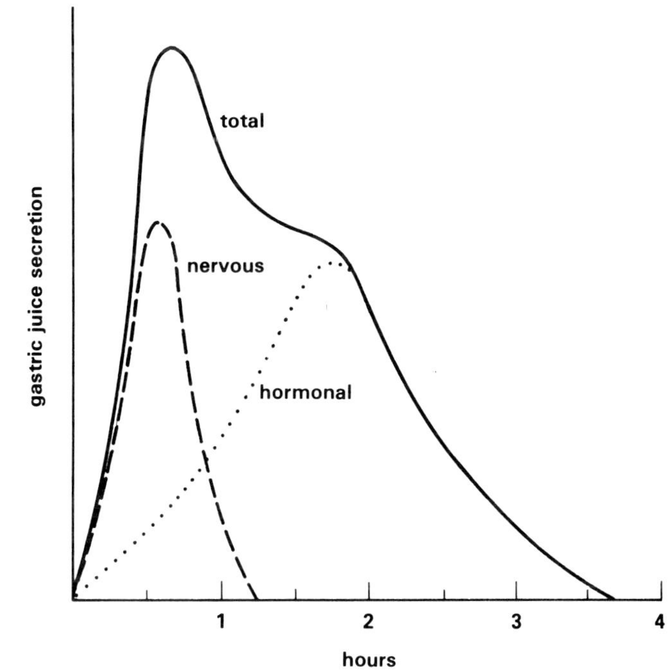

FIG. 14.21 *Churning action of the human stomach during digestion* (from X-ray photographs)

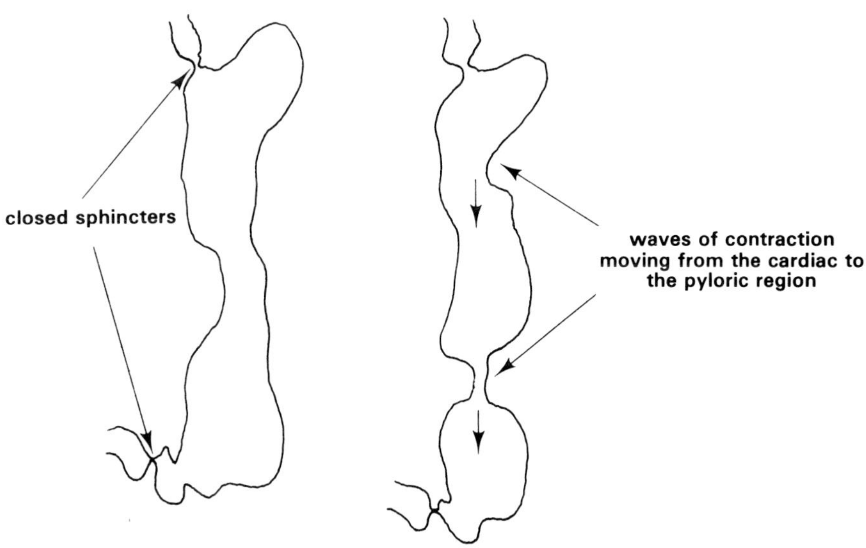

During the three or four hours food is held in the human stomach, rhythmic muscular contractions of the stomach wall churn the food, mixing it with gastric juice, so promoting digestion. The food is gradually converted into a creamy, acid suspension called **chyme** (Fig. 14.21).

14.3.3 Rumination

In **ruminant mammals** such as cattle and sheep, the stomach is large and modified for the digestion of vegetation. Cellulose in plant cell walls is the main carbohydrate constituent of the food eaten by ruminants. The ruminant stomach consists of four chambers, the **rumen**, **reticulum**, **omasum** and the **abomasum** (Fig. 14.22).

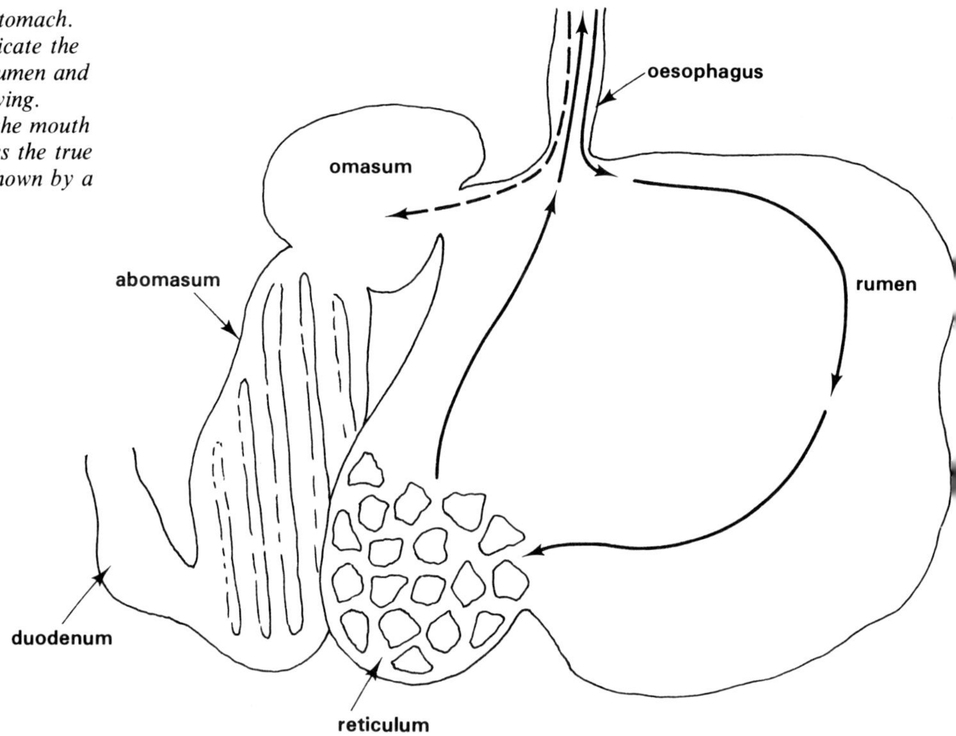

FIG. 14.22 *Ruminant stomach. Continuous arrows indicate the course of food in the rumen and reticulum after swallowing. Following a return to the mouth for cudding, food enters the true stomach by a course shown by a broken arrow*

Food is passed first into the largest chamber, the rumen, where huge populations of **anaerobic cellulolytic bacteria** begin the fermentation of cellulose. Fermentation continues in the reticulum into which the contents of the rumen are later directed. The partially digested food is then forced back into the mouth for further grinding called **chewing the cud**. Thorough grinding of plant material is essential if the cellulolytic bacteria are to be effective. On reswallowing, the semi-liquid cud is directed by closure of a groove on the side of the reticulum into a small chamber, the omasum. Inside the omasum, water is pressed out of the cud and is absorbed. The solid material passes into the abomasum. This is the true stomach and secretes an acid peptic juice.

The bacterial fermentation which occurs in the rumen produces sugars, methane gas and carboxylic acids such as ethanoic acid. Bacteria entering the abomasum with the cud are digested and add to the material available for absorption.

14.3.4 The small intestine

During gastric digestion, food is kept in the stomach by the constriction of two **sphincters**. These are circular muscles which seal off the stomach where it is joined to the oesophagus and small intestine (Fig. 14.17). Relaxation of the pyloric sphincter allows the propulsion of chyme into the small intestine by peristalsis of the involuntary muscles in the gastric wall.

From the stomach, chyme passes first into the **duodenum** which in man is about 30 cm long. Beyond the duodenum is the **jejunum** and then the **ileum** making up the rest of the small intestine (Fig. 14.14). The total length of the small intestine is about 6 m in man and 45 m in cattle.

In most mammals, digestion occurs mainly in the small intestine where enzymes complete the chemical breakdown of food into a soluble state suitable for absorption. The enzymes come from two sources, the pancreas and the glands in the wall of the small intestine. Food is also exposed to a non-enzymic fluid called bile made in the liver (Fig. 14.23).

FIG. 14.23 *Relationship between the liver, gall bladder, pancreas, stomach and small intestine in man*

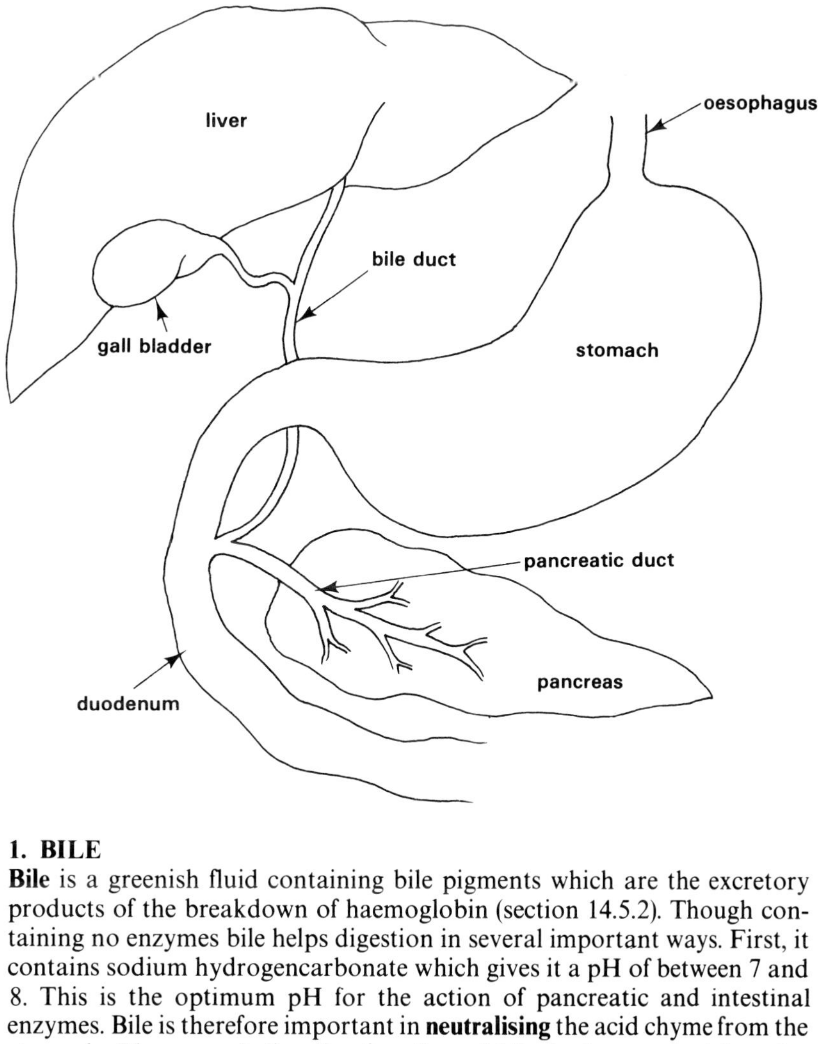

1. BILE

Bile is a greenish fluid containing bile pigments which are the excretory products of the breakdown of haemoglobin (section 14.5.2). Though containing no enzymes bile helps digestion in several important ways. First, it contains sodium hydrogencarbonate which gives it a pH of between 7 and 8. This is the optimum pH for the action of pancreatic and intestinal enzymes. Bile is therefore important in **neutralising** the acid chyme from the stomach. The second digestive function of bile is due to the bile salts, sodium and potassium glycocholate and taurocholate. They **emulsify lipids**, causing them to break down into numerous small droplets.

Emulsification provides a relatively large surface area of lipid for the action of lipase enzymes and hence speeds up digestion of fats and oils (Fig. 14.24).

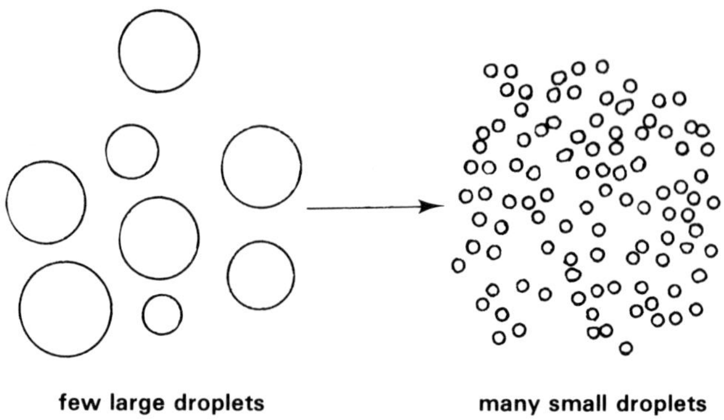

FIG. 14.24 *Emulsification of fat droplets*

2. PANCREATIC JUICE

The **pancreas** is situated just beneath the stomach and is connected to the small intestine by a pancreatic duct through which **pancreatic juice** is discharged. The bile duct joins the pancreatic duct in man. In some mammals the bile and pancreatic ducts are joined separately to the small intestine. The endocrine component of the pancreas, the islets of Langerhans (Chapter 18), plays no part in digestion.

Pancreatic juice contains four enzymes. **Pancreatic amylase** hydrolyses glycosidic linkages in starch, converting it to maltose in the same way as salivary amylase. Because food remains in the duodenum for some time there is more opportunity for hydrolysis of starch in the small intestine than in the mouth. **Pancreatic lipase**, probably a group of several lipase enzymes, hydrolyses lipids to fatty acids and glycerol (Fig. 14.25).

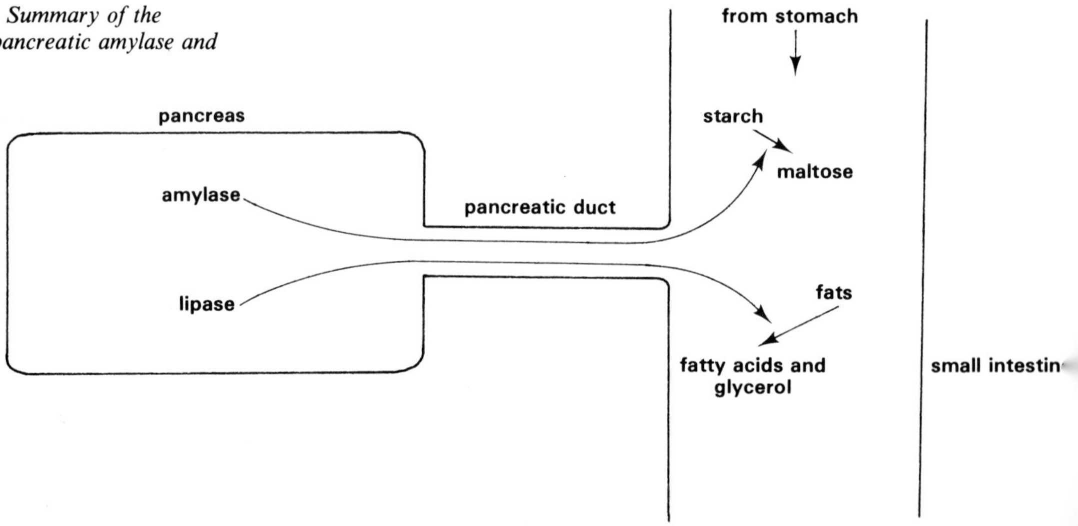

FIG. 14.25 *Summary of the action of pancreatic amylase and lipase*

Two inactive enzyme precursors are also found in pancreatic juice. They are **trypsinogen** and **chymotrypsinogen**. Trypsinogen is converted to the active enzyme **trypsin** by an activator called **enterokinase** made in the intestinal glands. Trypsin activates the conversion of chymotrypsinogen to

chymotrypsin. Trypsin and chymotrypsin are peptidase enzymes having an effect on proteins similar to that of gastric pepsin. They bring about a partial breakdown of proteins to polypeptides (Fig. 14.26).

FIG. 14.26 *Summary of the action of trypsin and chymotrypsin*

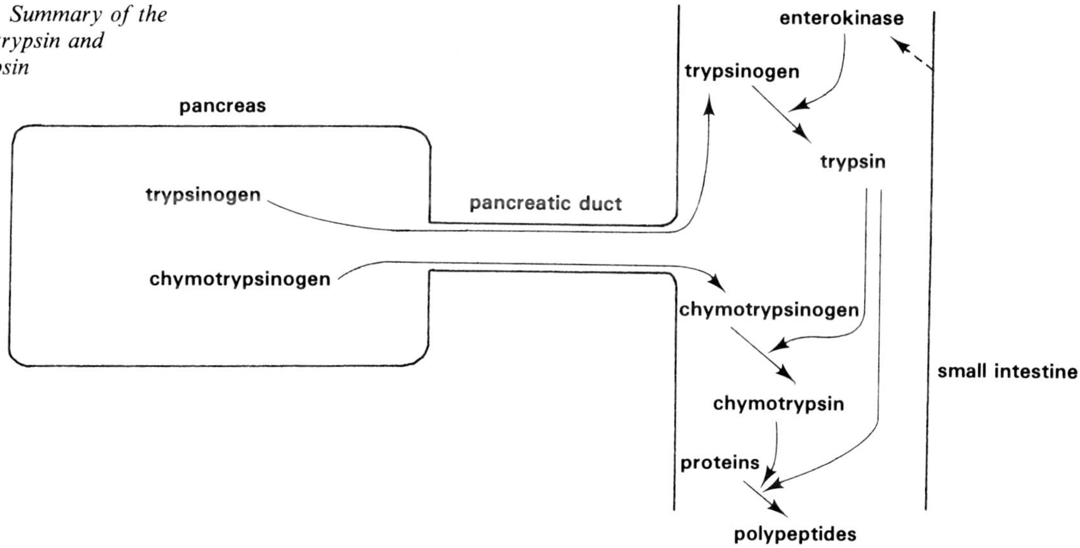

3. INTESTINAL FLUID

Embedded in the intestinal wall is a great number of microscopic pits called the **crypts of Lieberkühn**. In the duodenum, coiled **Brunner's glands** in the sub-mucosa secrete alkaline mucus into the crypts. Enzymes from the crypts complete the process of digestion started by the mouth, stomach and pancreas. Intestinal juice, called **succus entericus**, contains a large number of enzymes which convert complex carbohydrates to monosaccharide sugars, proteins and polypeptides to amino acids, and lipids to fatty acids and glycerol. The enzymes and their activities are summarised in Table 14.1. Some of the final stages in the digestion of carbohydrates and polypeptides occur in the cells lining the intestinal mucosa.

Table 14.1 Summary of the action of enzymes secreted by the small intestine

ENZYMES	SUBSTRATES	PRODUCTS
amylase	starch	maltose
maltase	maltose	glucose
sucrase	sucrose	glucose and fructose
lactase	lactose	glucose and galactose
peptidases	polypeptides	amino acids
lipases	fats	fatty acids and glycerol

The mechanisms controlling the release of bile, pancreatic juice and succus entericus are complex. They are triggered by the presence of chyme in the small intestine. Chyme stimulates the release of at least three hormones from the intestinal mucosa into the blood. **Pancreozymin** triggers

FIG. 14.27 *Summary of the gastrointestinal hormones involved in the release of bile and the digestive juices for the stomach, pancreas and small intestine*

the release of bile from its temporary store, the gall bladder, and the release of pancreatic enzymes. **Secretin** stimulates the flow of an alkaline fluid from the pancreas. **Gastric secretin** has an effect similar to secretin. Finally **enterocrinin** stimulates the intestinal glands to secrete their digestive juice (Fig. 14.27).

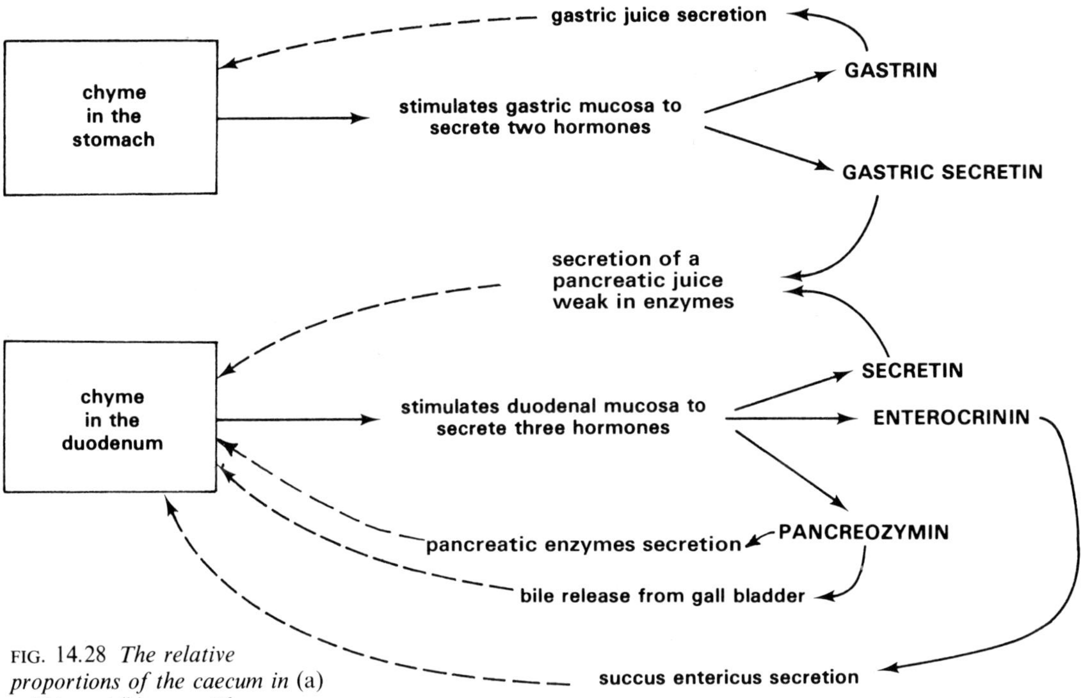

FIG. 14.28 *The relative proportions of the caecum in* (a) *rabbit and* (b) *man. The drawings are not to the same scale* (after Clegg and Clegg)

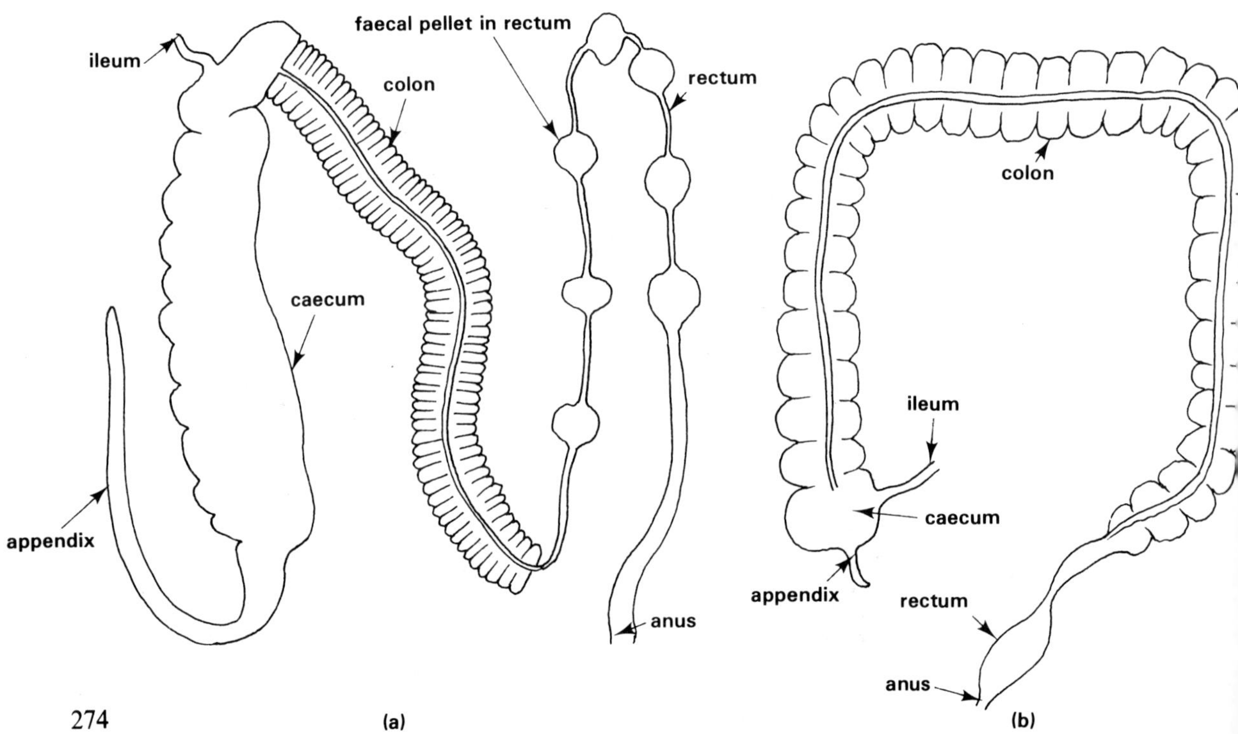

14.3.5 The caecum

In non-ruminant herbivores such as rabbits and horses fermentation of cellulose occurs in the caecum. The caecum is a bag-like structure and is the first part of the large intestine (Fig. 14.28). Inside the caecum **cellulolytic bacteria** perform the same function as those in the rumen of cattle and sheep (section 14.3.3). In many herbivores digestion and fermentation render the food soluble enough to be absorbed on its first passage through the gut. In others such as rabbits, the food must pass twice through the gut before it is sufficiently broken down for absorption to take place. For this reason rabbits eat the faeces formed from food which has passed once through the gut.

14.4 Absorption

Peristalsis of the small intestine helps to mix the digestive juices with chyme, so promoting hydrolysis of food by the enzymes. As a result, chyme is turned into a watery emulsion called **chyle**.

The **absorption** of nearly all the digestive products takes place through the extensive mucosa mainly in the duodenum and the first part of the jejunum. The internal surface area of the small intestine is greatly enlarged by its folded nature and even more so by numerous **villi**. Each villus is a microscopic tubular projection containing blood and lymph capillaries and covered with epithelium (Fig. 14.29).

Monosaccharide sugars and amino acids are absorbed into the **blood capillaries** of the villi. The capillaries drain into the **hepatic portal vein** which carries blood from the gut to the liver. While some fatty acids, glycerol and even lipid globules, are absorbed directly into the blood, they are mainly taken up by the lymphatic capillaries called **lacteals**. Fatty acids and glycerol are converted back to lipids in the epithelial cells of the villi. From here they are transferred into the lacteals. As a result, lymph in the lacteals appears white. Lymph eventually enters the blood through the thoracic ducts (Figs. 14.30 and 9.16).

FIG. 14.29 (a) *Photomicrograph of a transverse section of cat ileum. The blood vessels have been impregnated with a dye.* *×20*

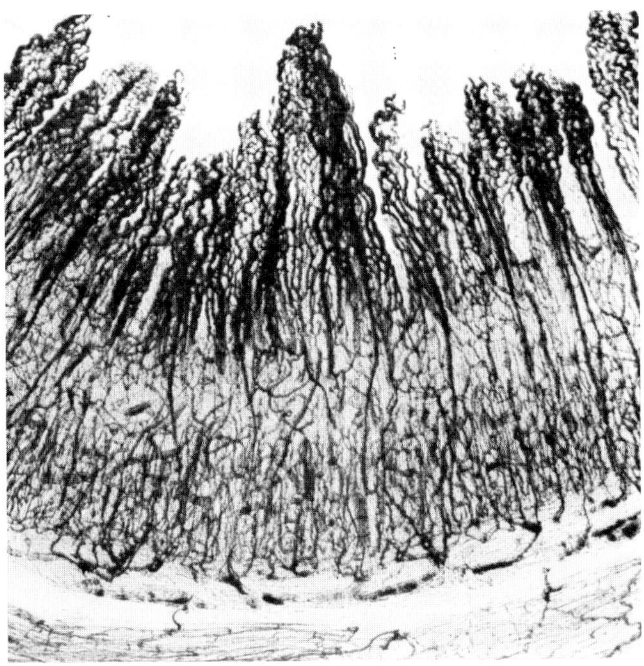

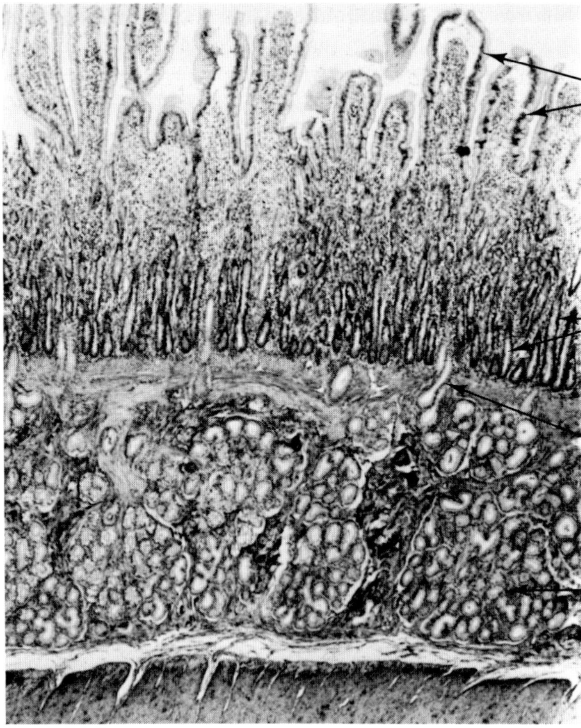

FIG. 14.29 (b) *Photomicrograph of a transverse section of cat duodenum,* $\times 45$

Table 14.2 Factors affecting the absorption of nutrients

Glucose	Active absorption may be linked with the transport of sodium ions across the membranes of mucosal cells.
Amino acids, some peptides	Active absorption may be affected by absorption of sugars and may also be linked with sodium ion transport through the mucosa.
Vitamin B_{12}	Absorption dependent upon presence of intrinsic factor (IF) in gastric juice.
Vitamin K	Absorption promoted by bile.
Calcium ions	Active absorption promoted by vitamin D_2 and probably also by parathyrin.
Iron ions	Absorbed in the iron(II) state. Rate of absorption depends on degree of saturation of transferrin with iron in the blood.
Water	Passive absorption by osmosis depends upon solute absorption.

The absorption of the products of digestion as well as inorganic minerals and vitamins which have not been changed by the gut enzymes involves **active and passive mechanisms**. Many substances require the presence of certain factors before they are absorbed in any amount. For example, the absorption of vitamin B_{12} requires intrinsic factor (IF), a mucoprotein component of gastric juice. Vitamin B_{12} is vital to red blood cell production and inability to absorb vitamin B_{12}, say through lack of IF, causes pernicious anaemia (Chapter 9). Reference is made in Chapter 18 to the role of parathyrin in the absorption of calcium ions. Table 14.2 summarises some of the factors concerned with the active absorption of nutrients from the gut.

It is in the large intestine, expecially the **colon**, that the absorption of water takes place. The digestive secretions of the gut contain a lot of water. If most of the water were not reabsorbed the loss would seriously reduce the body's water content. Faecal water accounts for about four to eight per cent of the total water loss in man.

Unabsorbed matter including the excretory products of bile is passed to the exterior through the **anus** as **faeces**.

FIG. 14.30 *Diagram of a villus*

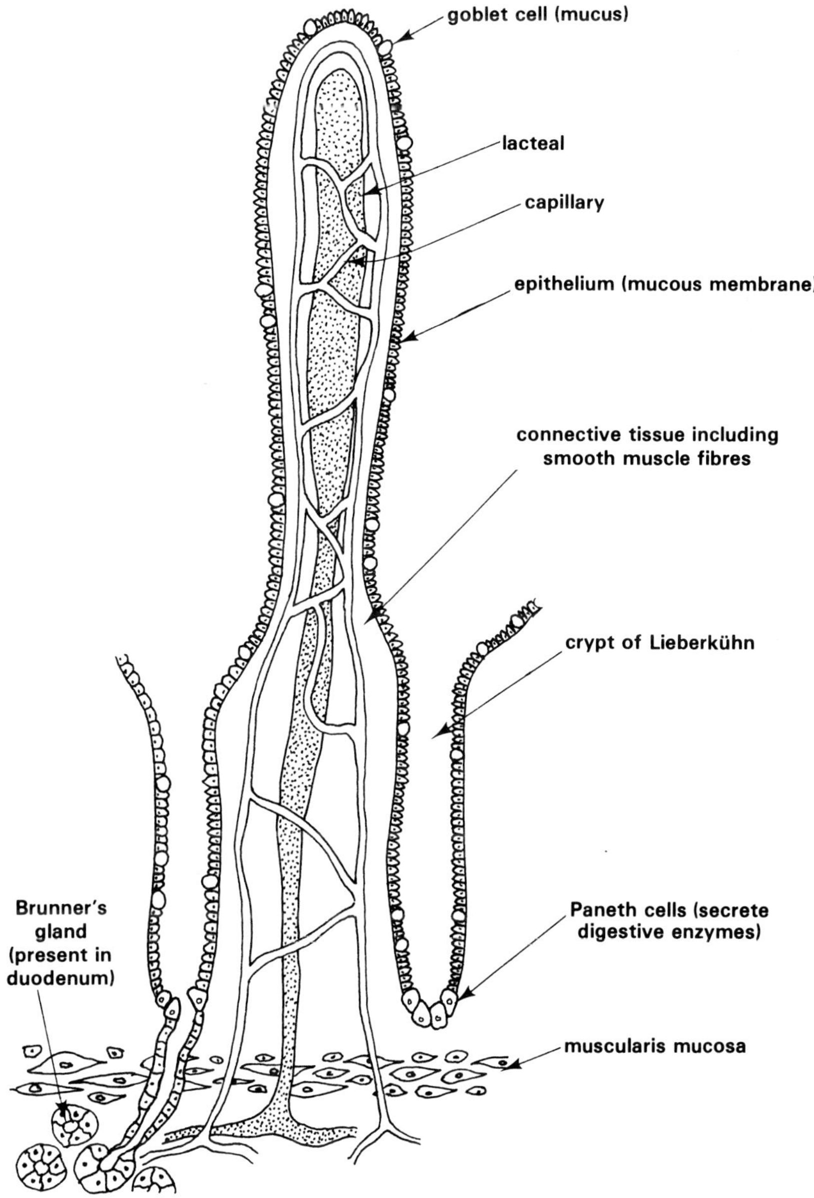

14.5 The liver

Several chapters in this book refer to **homeostasis**, the maintenance of a steady internal environment. Regulating the composition of blood and tissue fluid is an important aspect of homeostasis. The composition of blood leaving the gut in the hepatic portal vein is largely determined by the diet and thus the substances absorbed from the small intestine. However, the blood which enters the general circulation is often very different in composition. The hepatic portal vein carries blood to the liver. One of the functions of the liver therefore is to regulate the composition of blood. The liver is the largest organ in a mammal. It performs many functions, not all of which are concerned with homeostasis.

14.5.1 Structure of the liver

The mammalian liver consists of a large number of **lobules** (Fig. 14.31). Each lobule contains many vertical **plates of liver cells**, arranged radially around a central blood vessel which is a branch of the **hepatic vein**. The hepatic vein drains blood from the lobules and releases it into the general circulation. The blood supply to each lobule is from two sources, the **hepatic artery** and the **hepatic portal vein**. Branches of these vessels are found between the liver lobules. The artery delivers oxygenated blood from the general circulation and the vein delivers food-laden blood from the gut. Blood from the hepatic artery and hepatic portal vein flows between the plates of liver cells inwards and into the central vein in channels called **sinusoids**.

FIG. 14.31 (a) *Diagram of a liver lobule*

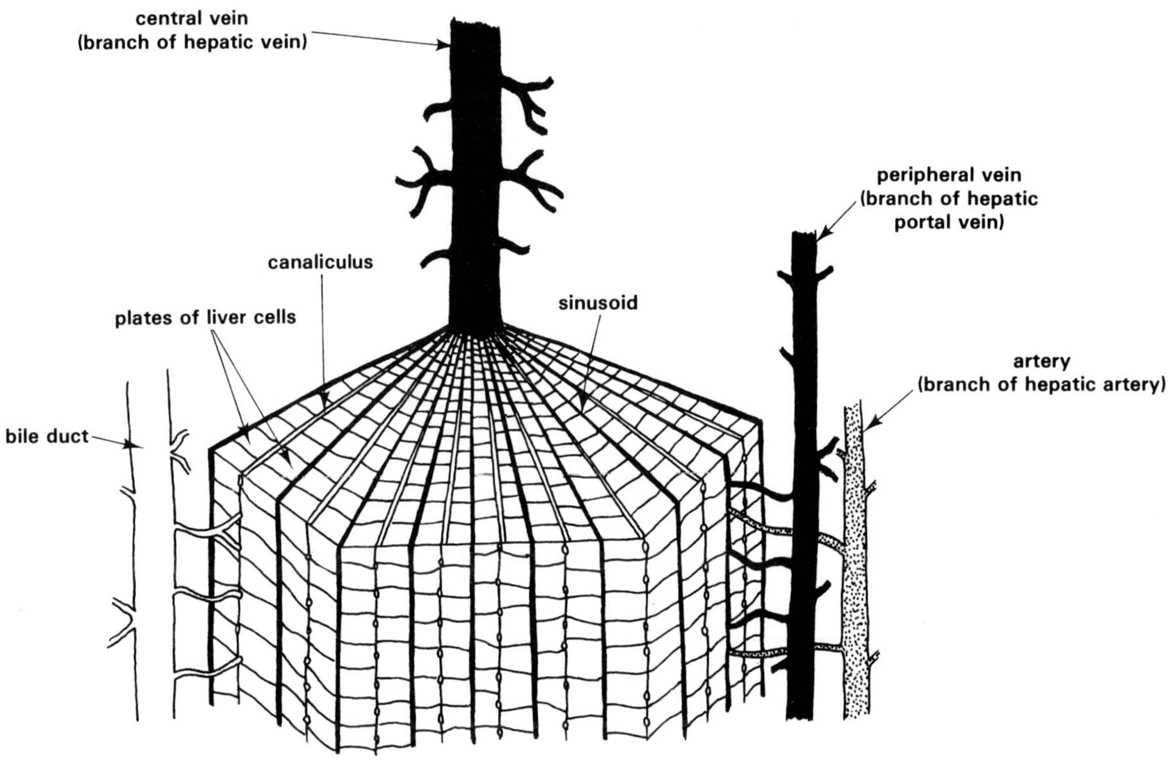

Between the plates of liver cells are channels called **canaliculi** which receive bile. The bile moves outwards to the periphery of the lobules where it collects into bile ducts. In most mammals bile is stored temporarily in a sac-like **gall bladder** before its periodic release into the small intestine.

FIG. 14.31 (b) *Photomicrograph of a transverse section of a lobule of pig's liver, ×45*

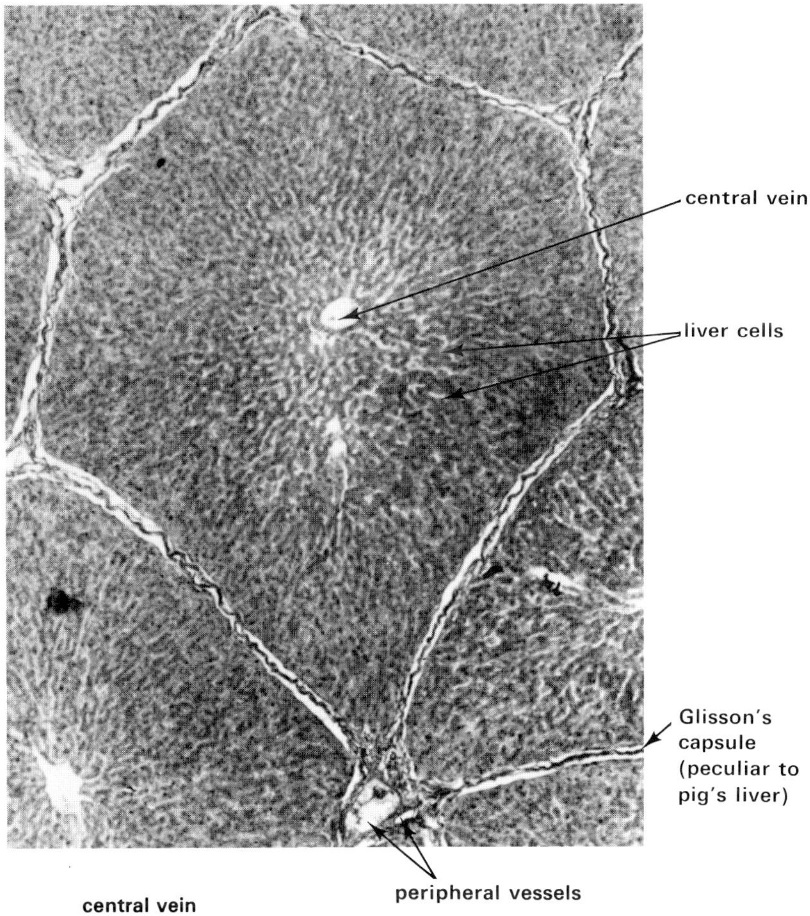

FIG. 14.31 (c) *Diagram showing the flow of blood and bile in a sinusoid and* canaliculus *of a liver lobule*

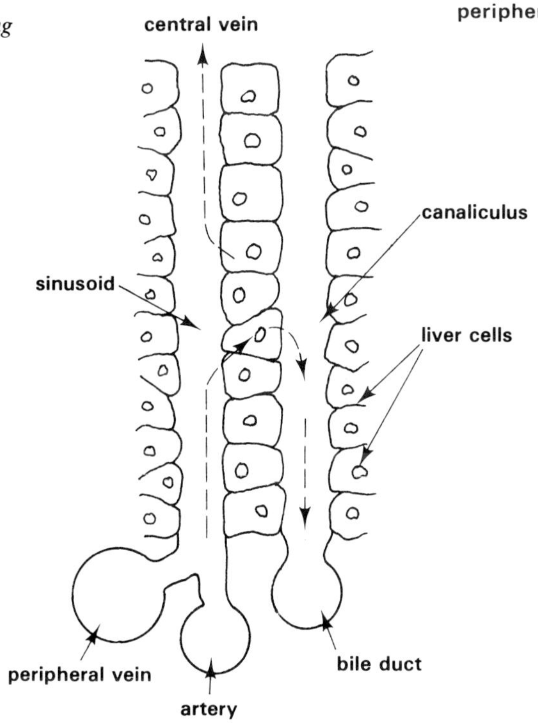

14.5.2 Functions of the liver

The functions of the liver are numerous and vital to life. For convenience they are described under three main headings.

1. METABOLISM OF ABSORBED FOOD

(i) CARBOHYDRATE METABOLISM. Soluble sugars, mainly **glucose**, are carried from the gut to the liver in the hepatic portal vein. Following a carbohydrate-rich meal the concentration of glucose in blood going to the liver is relatively high. When absorption is completed the glucose level drops. However, the concentration of glucose in the general blood circulation remains fairly stable. This is because excess glucose absorbed after a meal is converted in the liver cells to a storage polysaccharide called **glycogen**. The conversion is controlled by the hormone **insulin** from the islets of Langerhans in the pancreas (Chapter 18).

Glucose carried in the general blood circulation is used for tissue respiration throughout the body. It is replaced mainly from the liver's store of glycogen. The liver thus regulates the concentration of glucose in the general circulation irrespective of the rate of glucose absorption from the gut.

(ii) PROTEIN METABOLISM. Unlike carbohydrate, protein is not stored in the body. Amino acids from the gut pass through the liver and enter the **amino acid pool** in the general circulation. Amino acids are absorbed by the body cells and used for protein synthesis. The liver cells are important sites of **protein synthesis**, producing the plasma proteins (Chapter 9). A stable protein pool is established in the blood. Synthesis is balanced by an equal breakdown of plasma proteins which have a limited lifetime in the circulation.

Plasma proteins at the end of their lifetime together with excess amino acids absorbed from the gut are deaminated by liver cells. **Deamination** is the removal of amino groups and their conversion to ammonia. The remains of the acid molecules enter the Krebs' tricarboxylic acid cycle and are used to produce respiratory energy. Ammonia is very toxic and enters a sequence of reactions called the **ornithine cycle** which converts ammonia to the less toxic **urea** (Fig. 14.32). Urea is released into the general circulation and is excreted by the kidneys (Chapter 10).

Some of the twenty amino acids used for protein synthesis are **non-essential**. They can be produced from other amino acids in the liver by **transamination**. Liver cells contain a number of transaminase enzymes (Chapter 4) which transfer amino groups from amino acids to carboxylic acids, thus producing new amino acids. For example, glutamic-oxaloacetic transaminase (GOT) catalyses the following reaction;

FIG. 14.32 *The ornithine cycle*

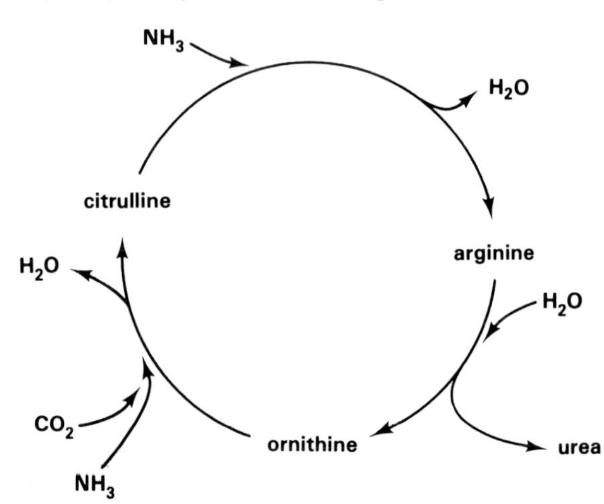

glutamic acid (amino group) + oxaloacetic acid (no amino group) $\xrightarrow{GOT}$ aspartic acid (amino group) + oxaloglutaric acid (no amino group)

Such enzymes enable the liver cells to make a wide range of amino acids even though the variety of amino acids in the diet is limited.
(iii) LIPID METABOLISM. Fats and oils absorbed from the gut can be converted to glycogen which is stored in the liver. Fat-soluble vitamins such as vitamins A and D are also stored in liver cells. **Cholesterol**, a sterol (Chapter 3) carried in the blood, is used in a variety of syntheses, particularly cell membrane production. The liver makes cholesterol when the dietary intake is inadequate. Excess cholesterol absorbed from the gut is eliminated in bile. Gross excesses of cholesterol however may be precipitated as gall stones in the bile ducts and gall bladder.

2. IRON METABOLISM

Some of the liver cells lining the sinusoids are part of the body's **reticulo-endothelial system**. The system removes particles of debris from the blood. The **Küpffer cells** are phagocytic liver cells which remove old red cells from the blood (Chapter 9). After old red cells have been engulfed the haemoglobin is split into two, an iron-globin complex and an iron-less haem group. The haem is then converted to **bilirubin**. Bilirubin combines with glucuronic acid to form the bile pigment **bilirubin diglucuronide** which is excreted in bile. In man about 7–8 g haemoglobin are removed from the circulation in this way each day.

FIG. 14.33 *Summary of haemoglobin breakdown in the liver and the fate of the products*

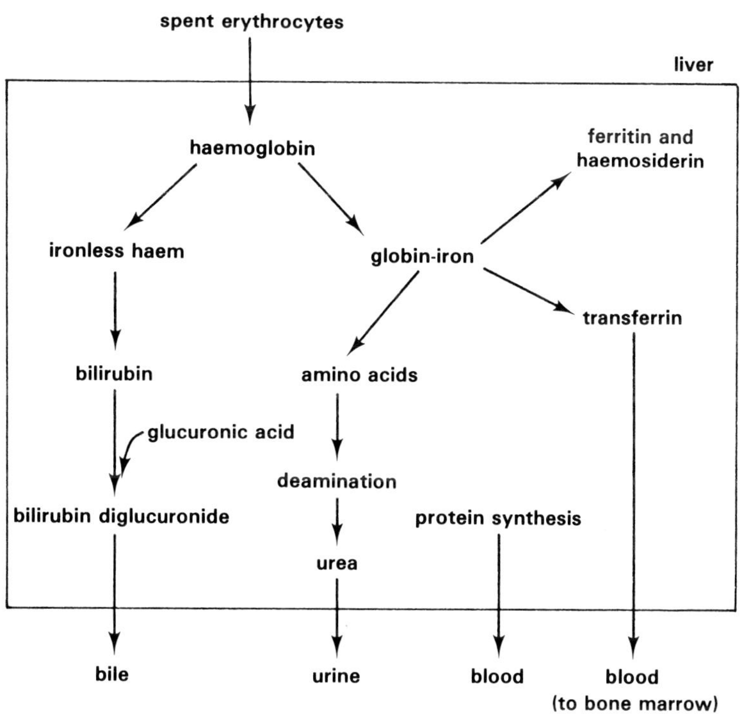

Any physical obstruction, such as **gall stones** in the bile ducts, or an increased breakdown of red cells results in an increase in the amount of bilirubin in blood. The skin takes on a yellow colour and the condition is called **jaundice**.

The iron-globin complex is metabolised further in the liver. The globin is broken down into amino acids which are used for protein synthesis. The iron is retained for the production of fresh haemoglobin. Haemoglobin synthesis and red cell production, erythropoiesis, occur in the liver of the foetal mammal. In the adult these processes are restricted to the red bone marrow (Chapter 9). Iron released from broken-down haemoglobin becomes attached to a plasma protein called transferrin and is transported in the blood to the bone marrow. Excess iron is stored in the liver cells as **ferritin** and **haemosiderin**.

The total iron content of the adult human body is normally between 3 and 5 g. Of this, about 1·5–5 g is in haemoglobin and about 1–1·5 g is stored in the liver. Pregnancy and lactation can lower a woman's total iron by as much as 20 per cent. This is why iron-containing tablets are given to pregnant women. Figure 14.33 summarises some of the factors involved in iron metabolism.

The liver helps erythropoiesis by producing a substance called the **haematinic principle**. Vitamin B_{12} is necessary for the production of the haematinic principle and deficiency of vitamin B_{12} causes pernicious anaemia (Chapter 9).

3. DETOXIFICATION

Many chemical substances which pass through the liver in the blood are modified by the liver cells. The substances include a variety of hormones. Much of the insulin from the pancreas is broken down by enzymes in the liver. Many sex hormones are also **inactivated** in the liver and **excreted** in the bile or released into the blood and excreted by the kidneys. Some chemicals are **destroyed** by liver cells, others are combined with various substances to render them less toxic. For example, benzenecarboxylic acid, a commonly used food preservative, is joined to the amino acid glycine to form N-benzoylglycine which is excreted in the urine. Certain chemicals such as tetrachloromethane, trichloromethane and ethanol damage the liver cells.

Within limits then, the liver acts as a filter, removing toxic substances from the blood, making them less harmful and preparing them for excretion. The liver performs a variety of other functions which are described elsewhere in the book. Notable among them is the contribution the liver makes to heat production in the body (Chapter 17).

Chapter 15

Nervous control and co-ordination in mammals

Changes constantly take place inside and outside the body. Mammals respond to the changes and their internal environment remains fairly constant. The ability to respond in this way is called **homeostasis**. An important aspect of homeostasis is the **co-ordination** of responses. A co-ordinating system contains several components. There are means of **detecting stimuli**, means of **transmitting information** about the stimuli and means of **responding to the stimuli**. The system also has a means of directing information along the most appropriate of many possible channels. Co-ordination also involves **feedback** which ensures that the degree of response is related to the intensity and direction of stimuli (Fig. 15.1). Note the similarity between Figure 15.1 and Figure 8.12 which summarises the mechanism controlling ventilation of the lungs. Other comparable examples are described elsewhere in the book such as control of the heart (Chapter 9) and body temperature (Chapter 17).

Mammals have two main co-ordinating systems, the **nervous system** and the **endocrine system**. Each system has different means of detecting and transmitting information. However, the two systems often work together (Fig. 15.2). The endocrine system is the subject of Chapter 18.

15.1 Electrochemical basis of nervous activity

The mammalian **nervous system** is an organised collection of numerous nerve cells called **neurons** (Fig. 15.3). Neurons consist of a bulbous cell body called the **soma** which contains a nucleus. Branched hair-like structures called **dendrites** which receive information from other neurons project from

FIG. 15.1 *Basic components of a feed-back control mechanism*

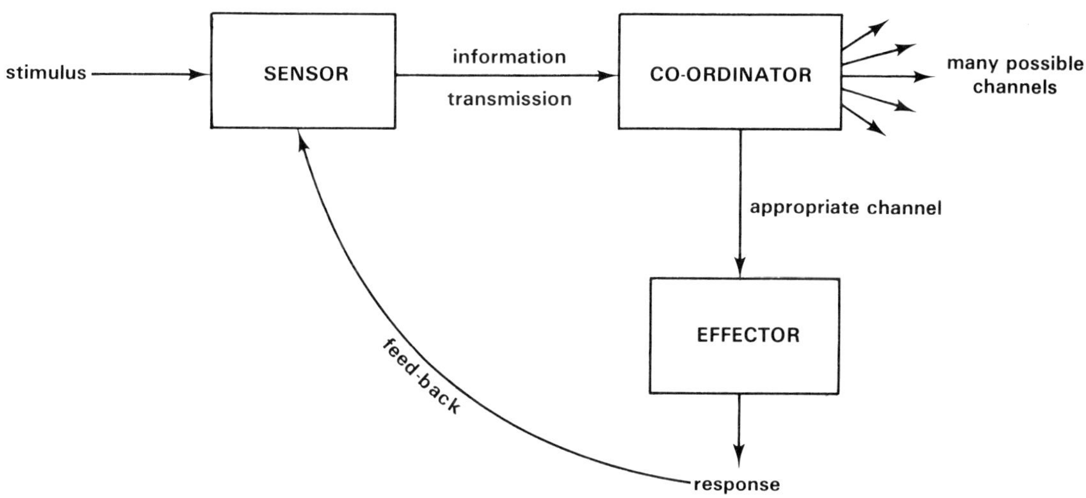

FIG. 15.2 *Interrelationships between the nervous and endocrine systems in mammals*

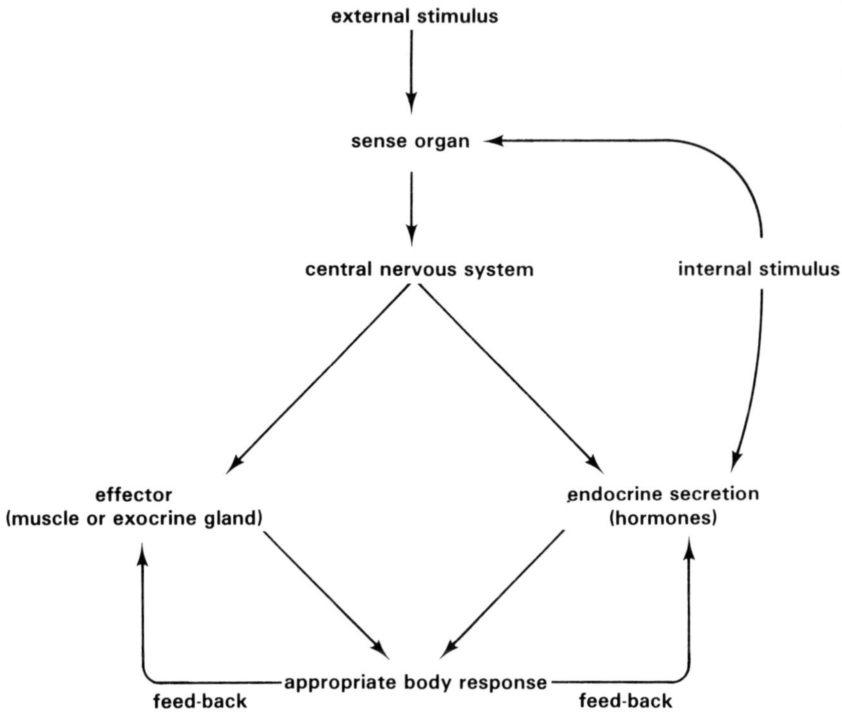

the soma. Some neurons have a long membrane-enclosed cytoplasmic thread called an **axon**. At their ends the axons divide into many branches which nearly touch the dendrites of adjacent neurons. Intricate pathways thus exist along which information can be transmitted very rapidly from one part of the body to another. The main function of neurons is to transmit nerve impulses over relatively long distances.

15.1.1 The resting potential

Analysis of the cytoplasm of the axon shows striking differences between its chemical composition compared with the surrounding tissue fluid (Table 15.1). The concentration of sodium ions [Na^+] in the tissue fluid greatly exceeds that in the **axoplasm**. Conversely the concentration of potassium ions [K^+] in the tissue fluid is far less than that in the axon. This state of affairs cannot be due to diffusion. Diffusion would result in equal concentrations of the ions on either side of the membrane. **Active transport** involving a sodium-potassium exchange pump is responsible for the non-random distribution of sodium and potassium ions. **Carrier molecules** in the axon membrane transport sodium ions out of, and potassium ions into, the axon against concentration gradients (Fig. 15.4). The pumping mechanism uses respiratory energy and is inhibited by metabolic poisons.

Table 15.1 Concentrations of various ions in cells and tissue fluids

ION	CELLULAR FLUID /m mol dm^{-3}	TISSUE FLUID /m mol dm^{-3}
sodium	16	140
potassium	100	4·4
chloride	4	103
hydrogencarbonate	8	27

FIG. 15.3 *A variety of mammalian neurons. The arrows indicate the direction of impulse transmission*

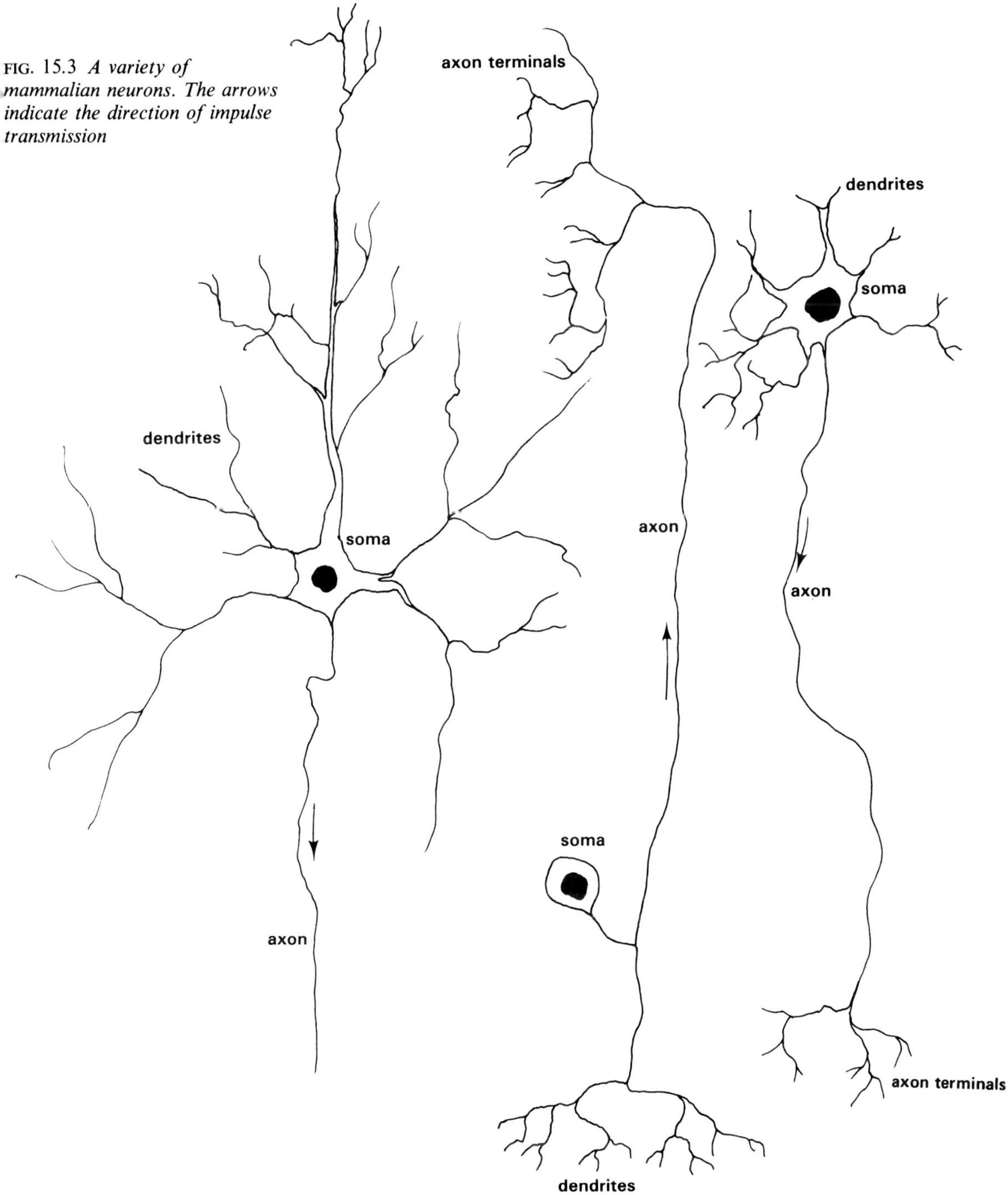

IG. 15.4 *The sodium–potassium xchange pump*

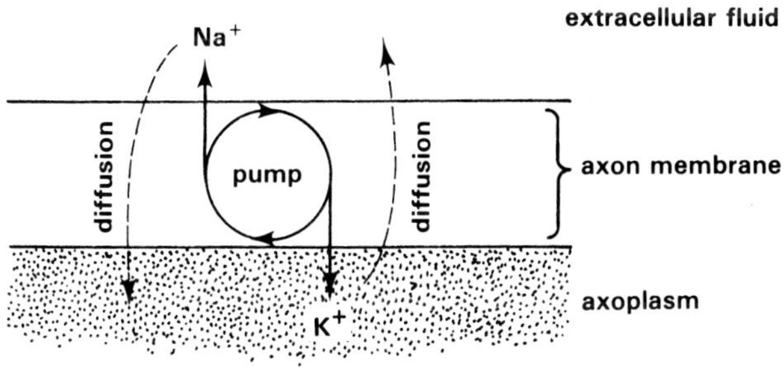

The axon membrane is about twenty-five times more permeable to potassium ions than to sodium ions. Consequently potassium ions can leave the axoplasm more rapidly than sodium ions can enter by diffusion. The net effect is a greater total concentration of both ions outside the axon:

$$\underset{\text{out}}{[\mathrm{Na}^+]} + \underset{\text{out}}{[\mathrm{K}^+]} > \underset{\text{in}}{[\mathrm{Na}^+]} + \underset{\text{in}}{[\mathrm{K}^+]}$$

Since both ions are cations the outer surface of the membrane has a net positive electric charge relative to the inner surface. In other words an electrical potential difference, the **transmembrane potential**, exists across the membrane. The membrane is **polarised**. Microelectrodes can be inserted into an axon and connected up with extracellular electrodes to a sensitive recording device such as a cathode ray oscilloscope (Fig. 15.5). A transmembrane potential of about −60 mV is recorded when neurons are not transmitting nerve impulses. This is called the **resting potential** and is the basis of the ability of neurons to transmit impulses. Even minor changes in the resting potential trigger off changes which may produce an electrochemical force. The force is propagated along the axon as a **nerve impulse**.

FIG. 15.5 *Measuring the transmembrane potential of an axon*

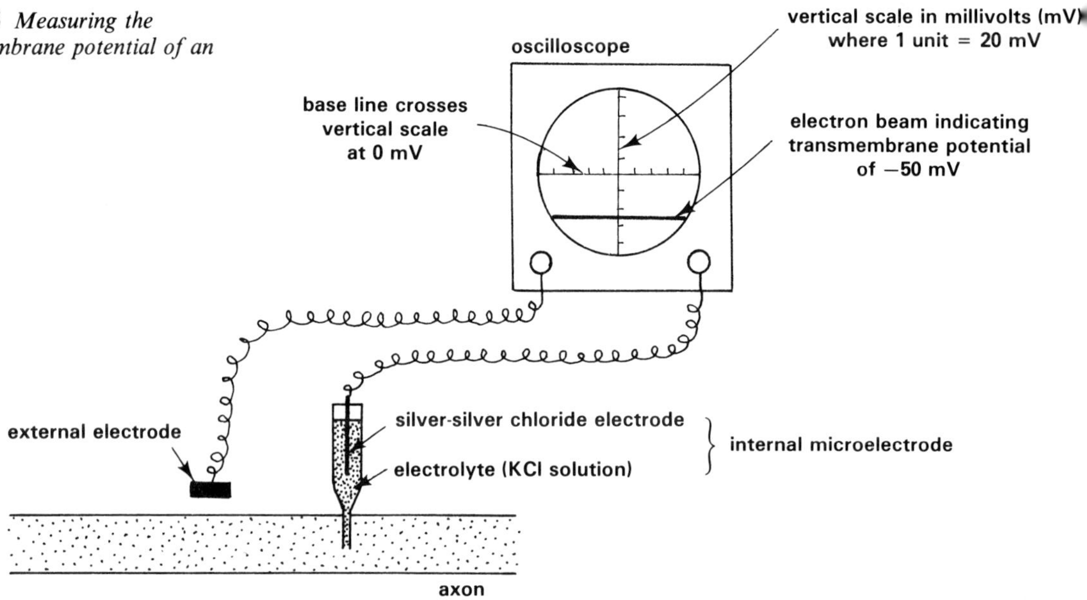

15.1.2 The action potential

Resting neurons are affected by a variety of stimuli including heat, stretching the membrane, electric currents and chemicals. Such stimuli change the permeability of the membrane at the point of application resulting in an influx of sodium ions. The membrane becomes **depolarised** (Fig. 15.6) and the transmembrane potential becomes progressively less. A point may be reached when the cation content of the axoplasm equals that in the tissue fluid. The electrical potential difference across the membrane is then zero. If the stimulus is sufficiently intense the polarity of the membrane is reversed. When the change of charge reaches a threshold value a nerve impulse results and the new transmembrane potential is called an **action potential**. If on stimulation the electrical change is not great enough the threshold is not reached and an impulse is not produced. This is the **all-or-none effect** (Fig. 15.7).

FIG. 15.6 *Depolarisation of an axon membrane following stimulation*

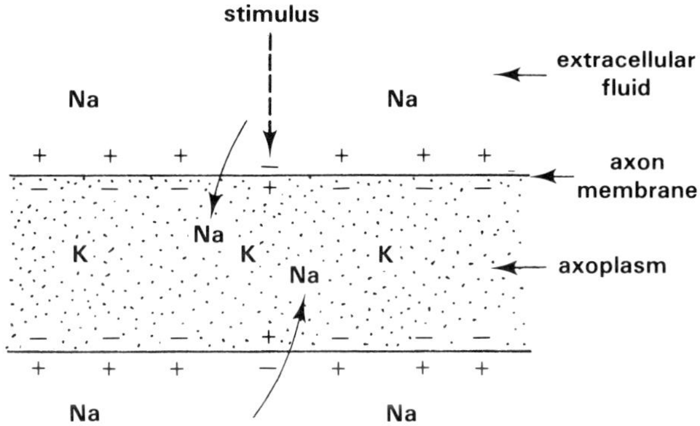

FIG. 15.7 *The all-or-none effect. Raising the stimulus strength from zero does not produce an impulse in the axon until a stimulus threshold is reached. Further increase in stimulus strength results in the same action potential across the axon membrane*

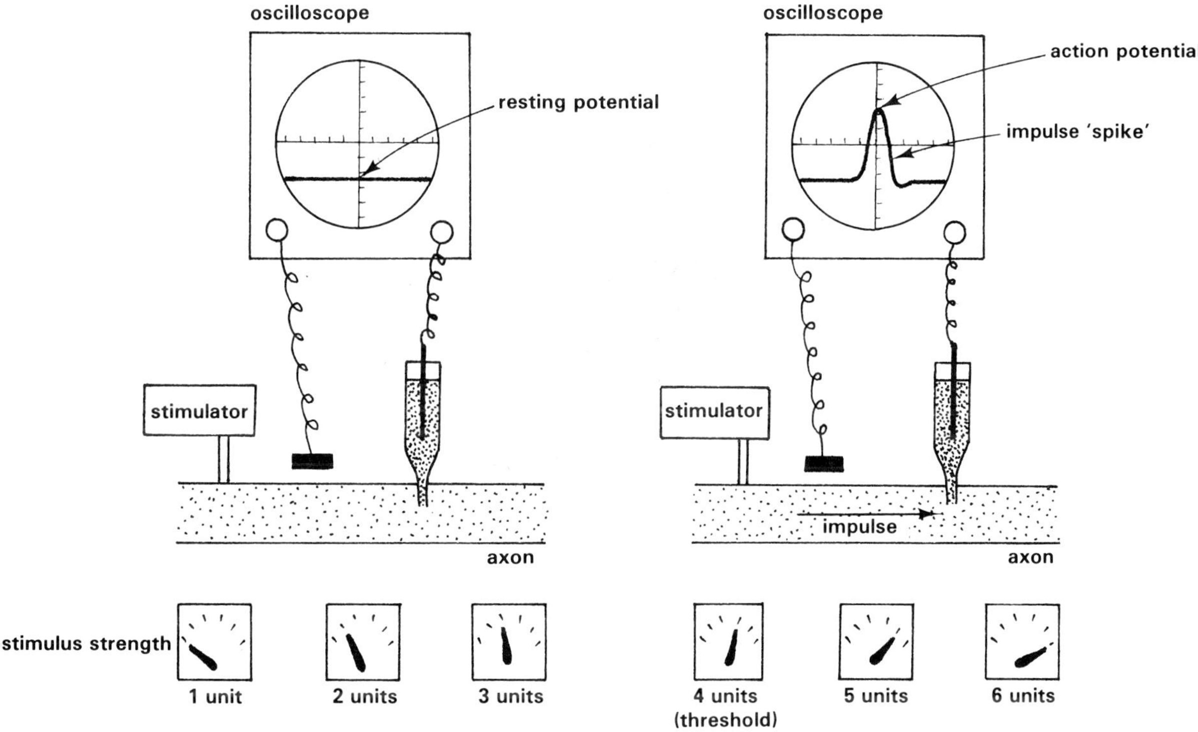

15.1.3 The nerve impulse

The production of an action potential causes the flow of a small electric current in the axoplasm and tissue fluid. The current crosses the axon membrane on either side of the point at which the stimulus is applied causing membrane depolarisation. In turn depolarisation spreads along the axon membrane and in this way a nerve impulse is **propagated** along the axon (Fig. 15.8). Recordings made using giant neurons of squids show that the membrane potential during passage of an impulse is reversed from a resting value of -60 mV to a peak of about $+45$ mV (Fig. 15.9).

FIG. 15.8 *The main stages in the transmission of an impulse along an axon*

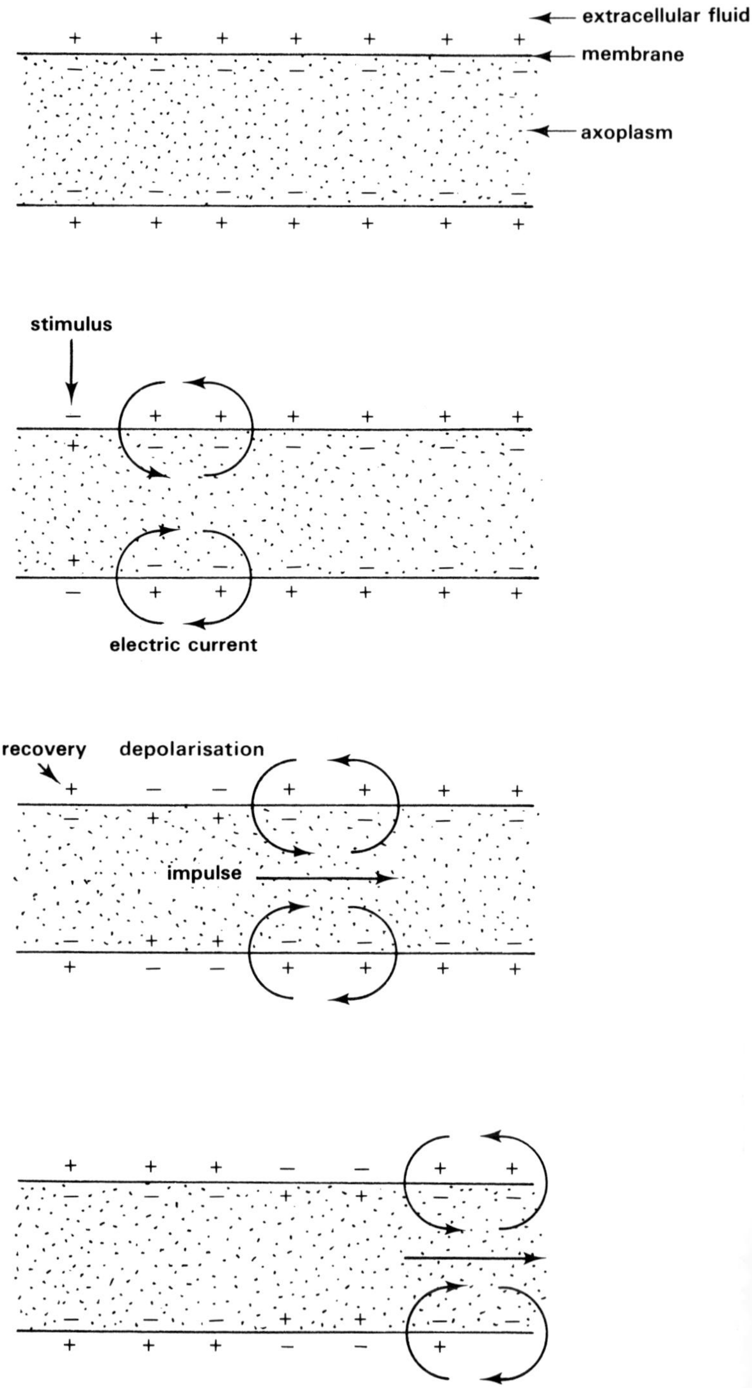

(a) The resting state

(b) Depolarisation of the membrane causing the flow of electric current

(c) Electric current stimulates the membrane nearby causing further depolarisation

(d) The process repeats itself along the axon

FIG. 15.9 *Oscilloscope display of the action potential produced during the propagation of an impulse along a giant axon from a squid. The vertical scale is graduated in millivolts (mV) where 1 unit = 10 mV. The horizontal scale is graduated in milliseconds (ms) where 1 unit = 0·25 ms*

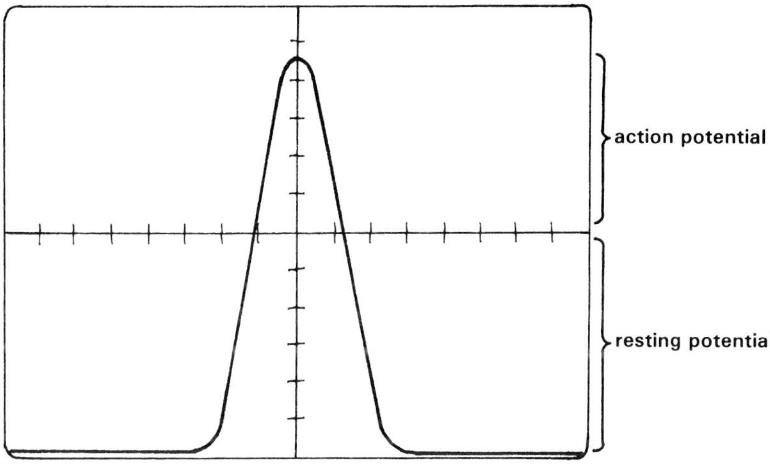

15.1.4 Membrane recovery

During the brief period of membrane depolarisation, which is only one millisecond, an axon cannot conduct a second impulse since impulse transmission depends on disturbance of the resting potential. Consequently a period of non-conductability called the **refractory period** follows each impulse (Fig. 15.10). During this time the membrane recovers its resting potential. Depolarisation is accompanied by diffusion of sodium ions from the tissue fluid into the axoplasm. In the refractory period potassium ions diffuse from the axoplasm into the tissue fluid. The sodium–potassium exchange pump now operates to restore the original ionic state of the neuron and the resting potential is recovered (Fig. 15.11).

FIG. 15.10 *Oscilloscope traces showing refractory period*

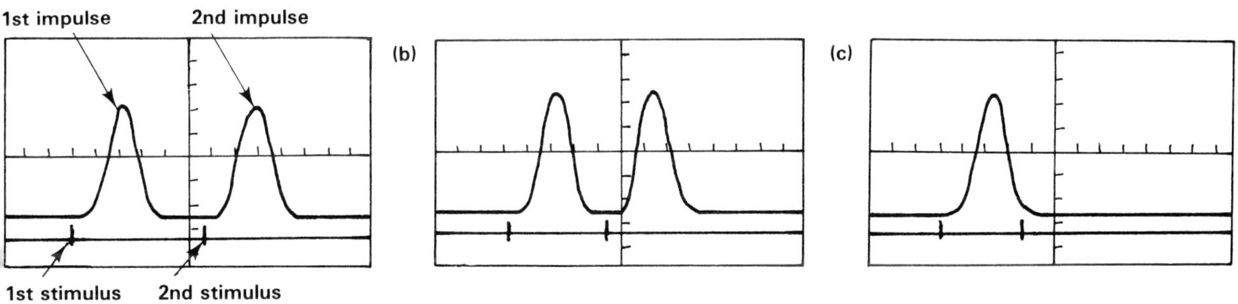

15.1.5 Rate of impulse conduction

Peripheral neurons are surrounded by **Schwann cells** which may respond to the proximity of neurons by growing around their axons. The axon is then wrapped in several membranous layers called the **myelin sheath**. The myelin sheath limits contact between the axon membrane and tissue fluid to only a few sites called **nodes of Ranvier** (Fig. 15.12). Because less of the axon membrane is used in impulse transmission the rate of impulse conduction in myelinated axons is greater than in unmyelinated axons (Fig. 15.13).

FIG. 15.11 *Membrane recovery*

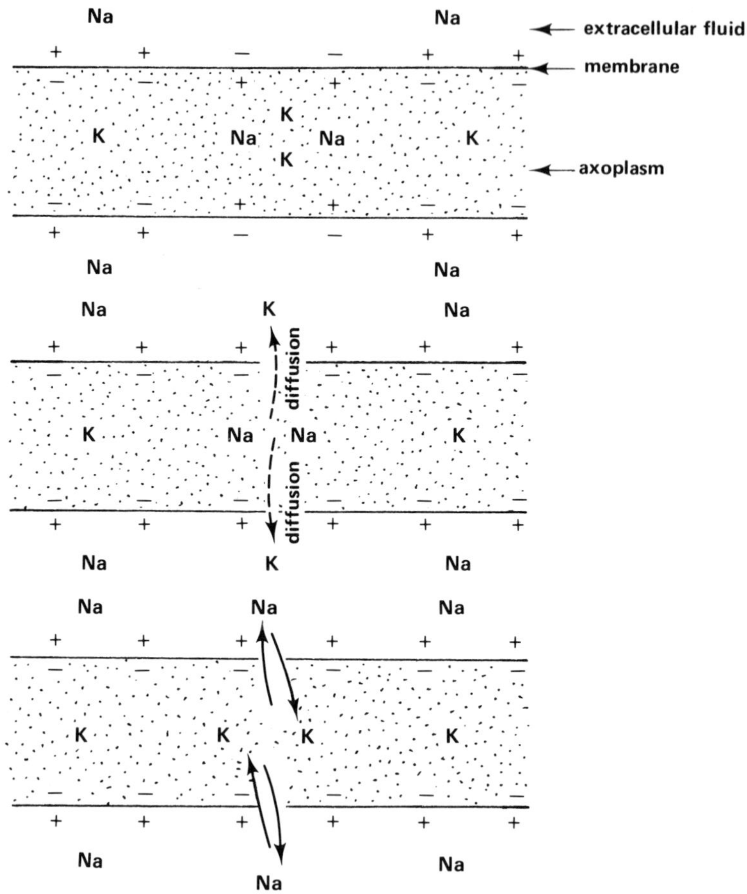

FIG. 15.12 (a) *Development of myelin sheath from Schwann cell seen in transverse section*

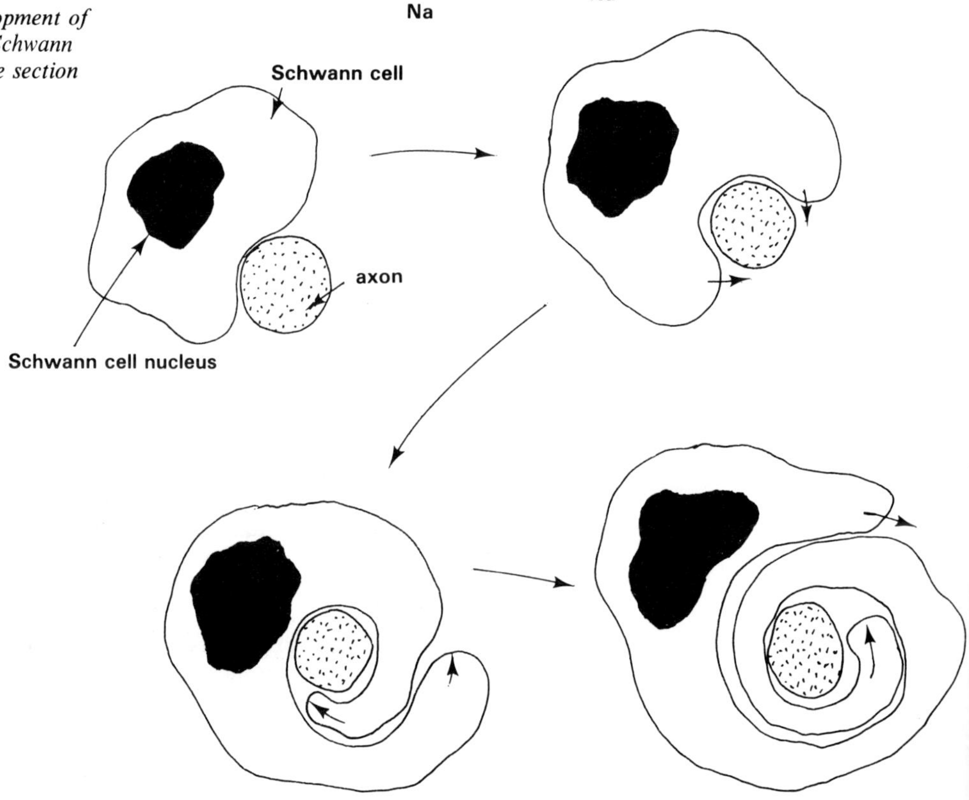

FIG. 15.12 (b) *Electronmicrograph of a transverse section of a myelinated axon, × 25 000*

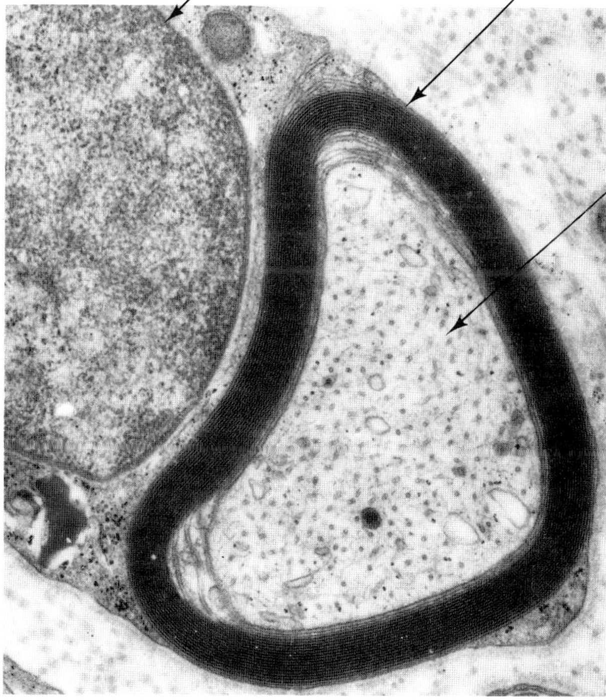

FIG. 15.12 (c) *Photomicrograph of some human myelinated neurons showing the nodes of Ranvier, × 400*

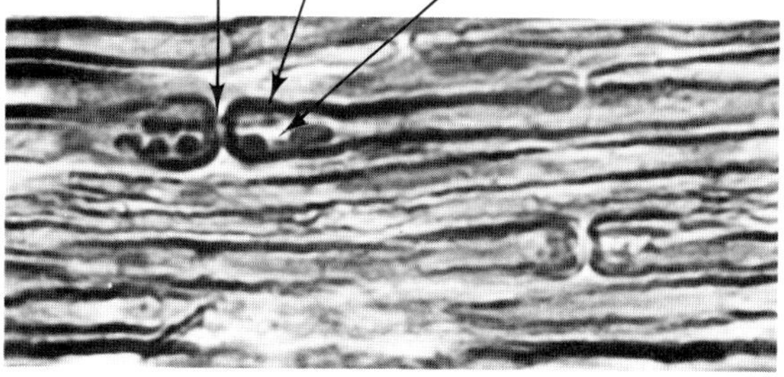

FIG. 15.13 *Electrochemical events at the nodes of Ranvier during the passage of an impulse along a myelinated axon.* Compare with Fig. 15.8

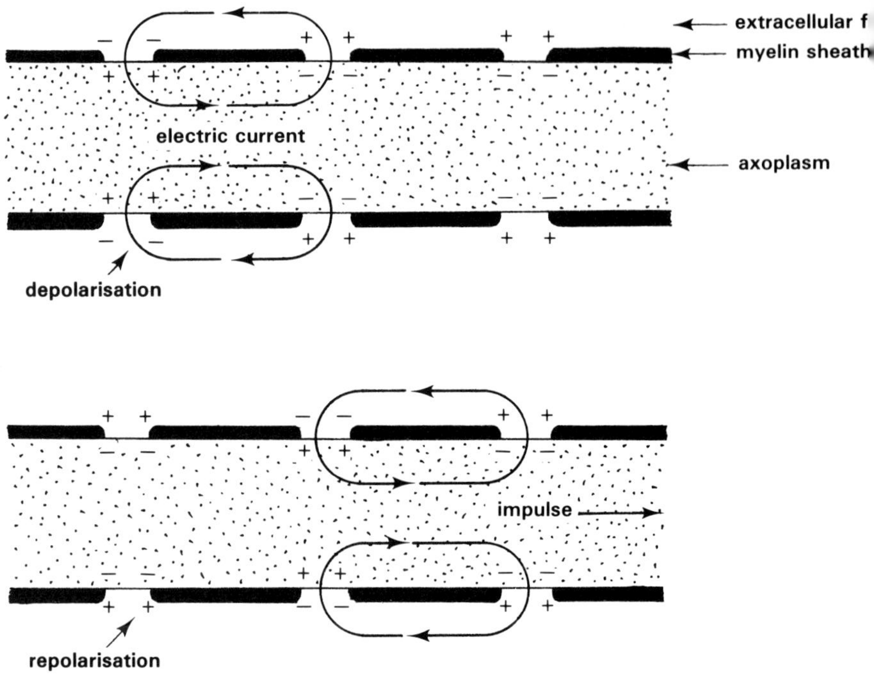

Another factor affecting the rate of impulse transmission is the diameter of the axon. The relationship for large myelinated mammalian nerve fibres is approximately:

$$v \infty 7 \times d$$

where v is the velocity of impulse conduction in m per sec and d is the fibre diameter in μm.

Thus, other factors excepted, a doubling of fibre diameter increases impulse velocity by about 14 times. Table 15.2 shows the conduction velocities of neurons from different animals. It was Helmholz in 1850 who first measured the velocity of a nerve impulse. He obtained a value of about 25 m per sec in a frog's nerve. Prior to his experiments impulses were thought to travel at about the speed of light!

Table 15.2 Speeds of impulse conduction in the nerves of various animals (from Bendal 1969)

TISSUE	TEMPERATURE /°C	FIBRE DIAMETER /μm	IMPULSE VELOCITY /m s^{-1}
crab nerve	20	30	5
squid giant axon	20	500	25
cat nerve (unmyelinated)	38	0·3–1·5	0·7–2·3
cat nerve (myelinated)	38	2–20	10–100
prawn nerve (myelinated)	20	35	20
frog nerve (myelinated)	24	3–16	6–32

15.1.6 Synaptic transmission

The junctions between neurons are called **synapses**. They are found where the branches of axons lie close to the dendrites of other neurons (Fig. 15.14). Electron microscopy has revealed a narrow gap about 20 nm across at the synapse. The gap has to be crossed when impulses are transmitted from neuron to neuron (Fig. 15.15). The transmission of impulses between neurons depends on **chemical transmitters** synthesised in the axon terminals and stored there in numerous small membranous vesicles. The arrival of a

FIG. 15.14 *Many axons terminate as synapses on the dendrites and soma of a neuron (light microscope view)*

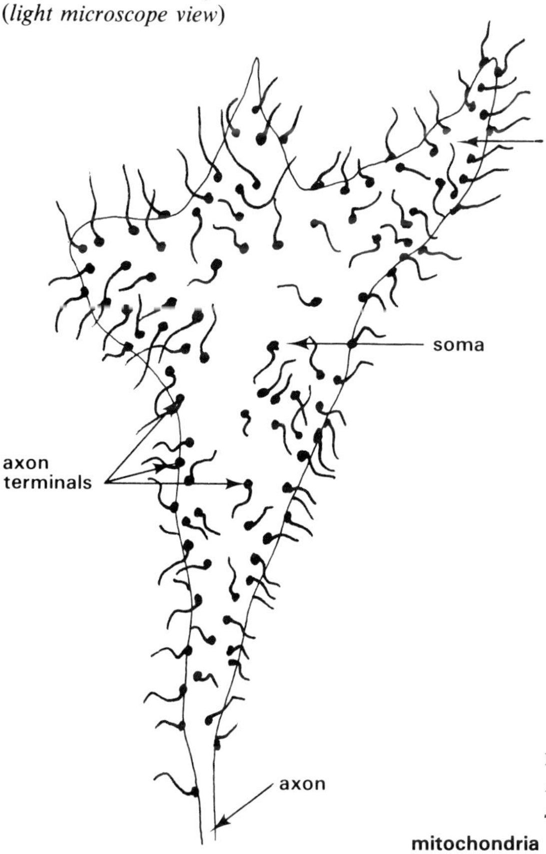

FIG. 15.15 (a) *A synapse* (from various electronmicrographs)

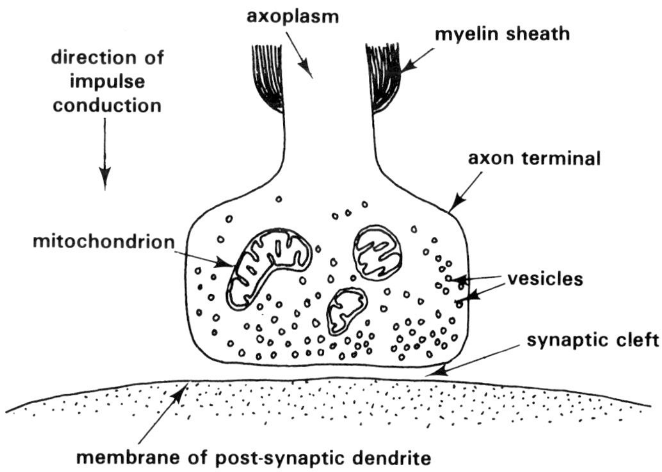

FIG. 15.15 (b) *Electronmicrograph of a synapse, × 24 000*

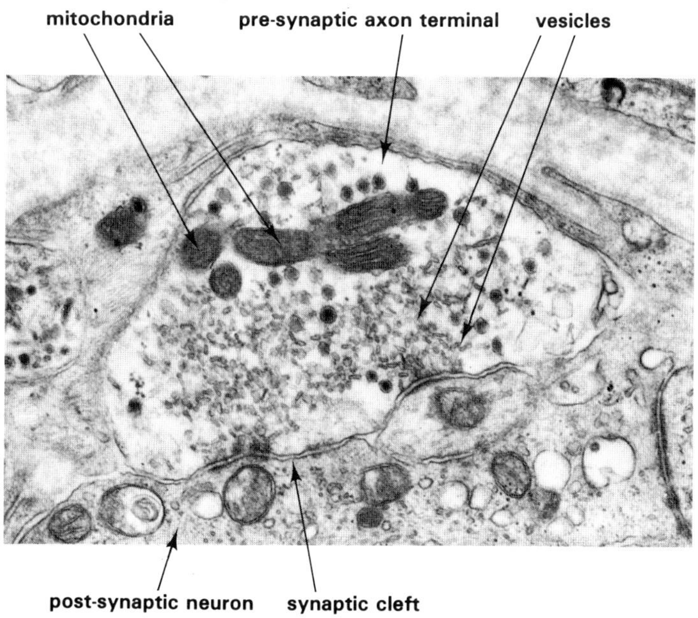

nerve impulse at an axon terminal triggers the release of small quantities of transmitter into the **synaptic cleft.** The transmitter becomes attached to receptive sites on the **post-synaptic membrane** of the dendrite of the next neuron. As a result the post-synaptic membrane is depolarised and an impulse may be transmitted along the second neuron (Fig. 15.16).

FIG. 15.16 *Synaptic transmission*

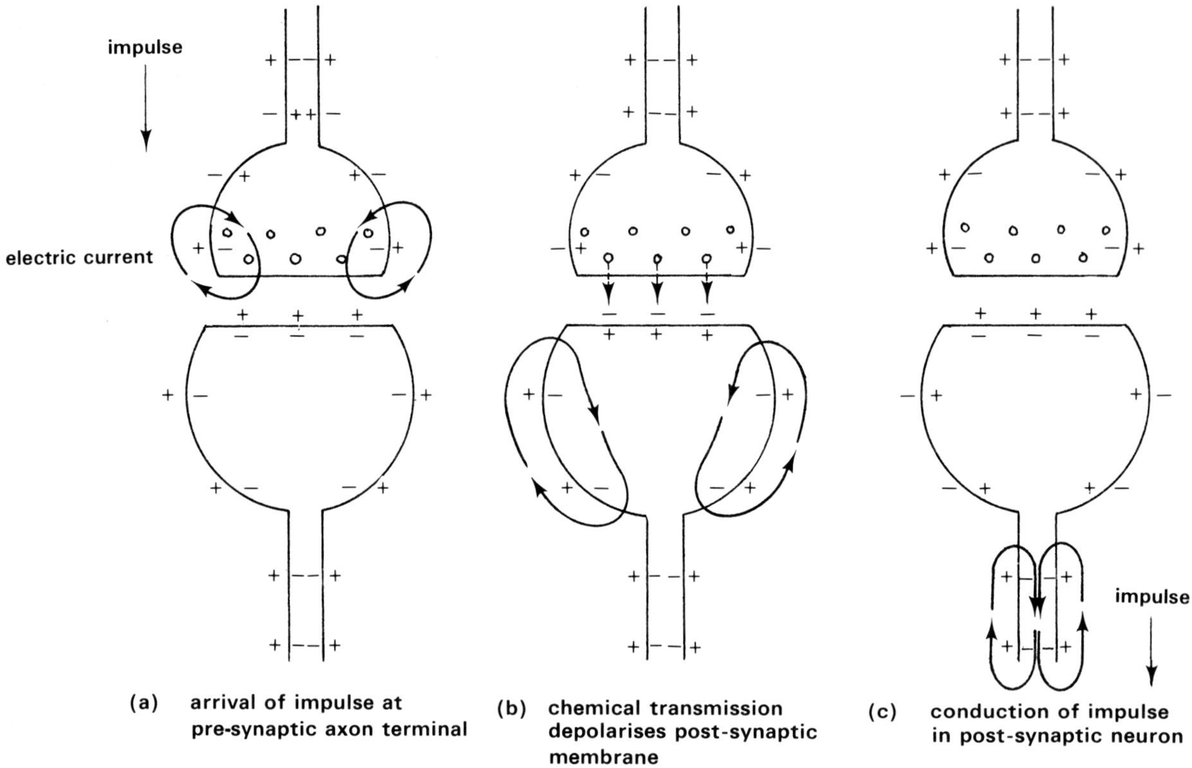

FIG. 15.17 *An inhibitory synapse*

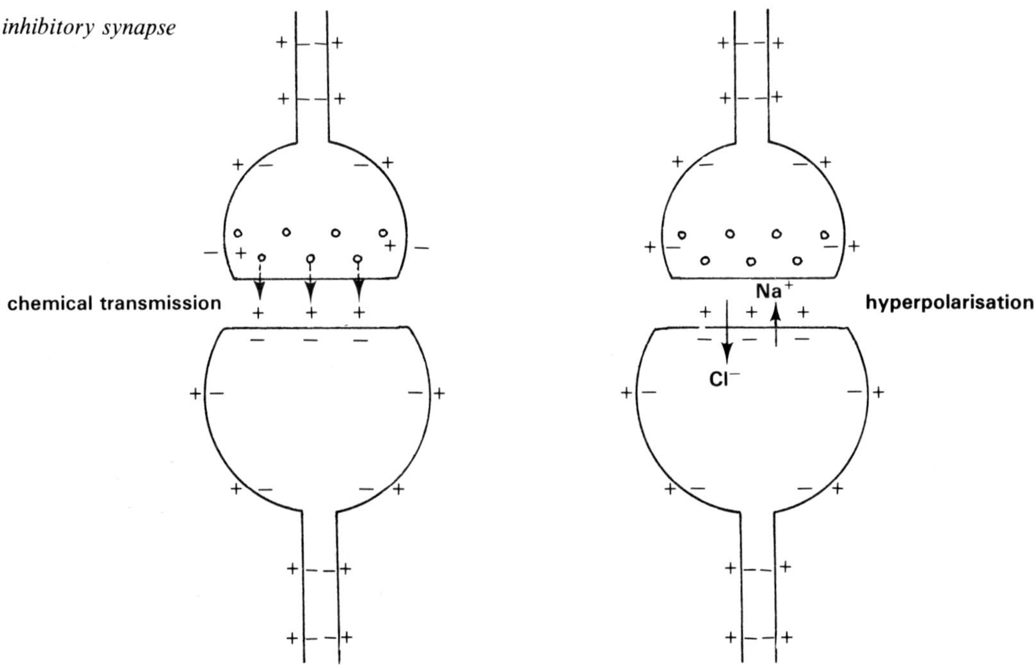

Excitation of the post-synaptic dendrite does not always occur. Impulses can be inhibited by some transmitters (Fig. 15.17). **Inhibitory synapses** are important in the overall control of the nervous system (section 15.2.1).

The transmitters released from the pre-synaptic terminals are quickly destroyed by enzymes in the tissue fluid. Consequently their effect is only temporary. One transmitter widely found in the mammalian nervous system is **acetylcholine**. After its secretion acetylcholine is broken down by the enzyme **cholinesterase** into the inactive end products choline and ethanoic acid. The end products are reabsorbed by the axon terminals and remade into acetylcholine using respiratory energy provided by mitochondria (Fig. 15.18). A general effect of transmitter destruction is to prevent the merging of successive impulses passing from neuron to neuron. The frequency of impulses in a sequence of neurons is determined primarily by the intensity of stimulus at the beginning of the sequence. If the frequency was amplified by uncontrolled synaptic transmission the response might be inappropriately excessive.

FIG. 15.18 *Cycle of release, breakdown, reabsorption and resynthesis of synaptic transmitter*

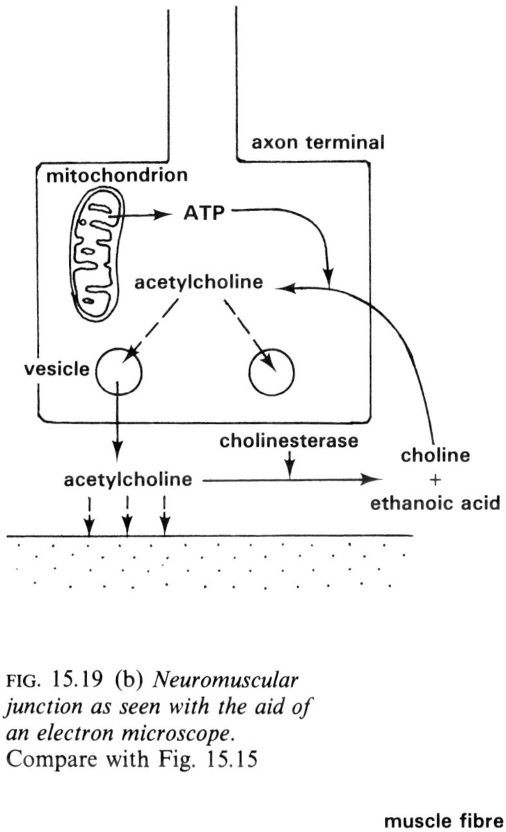

FIG. 15.19 (a) *Photomicrograph showing the junctions between motor nerve cell endings and striped muscle fibres, ×450*

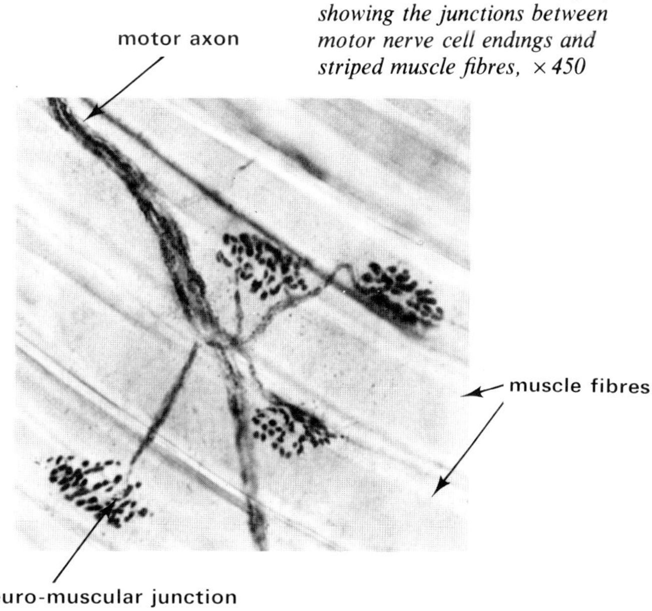

FIG. 15.19 (b) *Neuromuscular junction as seen with the aid of an electron microscope.* Compare with Fig. 15.15

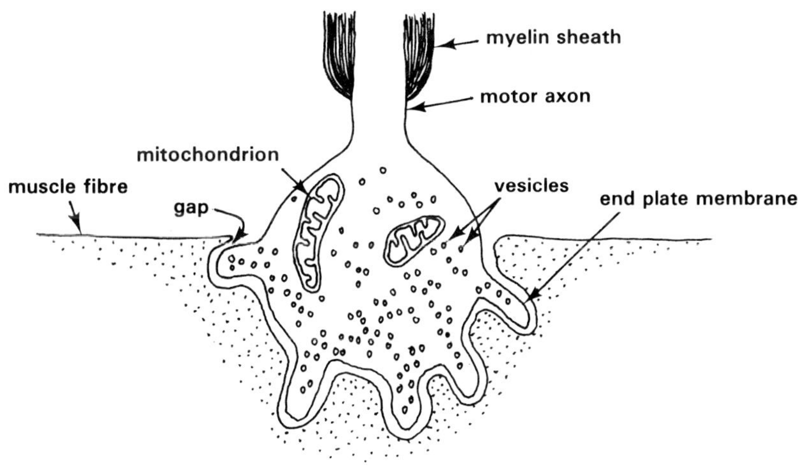

15.1.7 Neuroeffector junctions

The junctions between neurons and effectors such as muscles and glands are very similar to synapses (Fig. 15.19). The mechanism of impulse transmission from neurons to effectors also involves the secretion of transmitters. How does chemical transmission from a neuron bring about a response in an effector?

15.1.8 Muscle and contraction

Mammals have three kinds of muscle. The muscle used to move the skeleton is called **skeletal (striped) muscle**. The walls of the gut, urinogenital system and arteries contain **visceral (smooth) muscle**. Most of the heart is made of **cardiac muscle**.

Striped muscle consists of **fibres** which are made of many **myofibrils**. Each myofibril is divided by cross-partitions called **Z-lines** into numerous compartments called **sarcomeres** (Fig. 15.20). Chemical analysis and electron microscope studies show that the myofibrils have parallel strands. The arrangement of the strands, composed of the proteins **actin** and **myosin**, explains the striped appearance of the muscle when viewed with a light microscope. Compare Figures 15.20(a) and (b). Strands of actin project into the sarcomeres from the Z-lines. Between the actin strands, thicker filaments of myosin are held in position by molecular bonds.

FIG. 15.20 (a) *The structure of striped muscle*

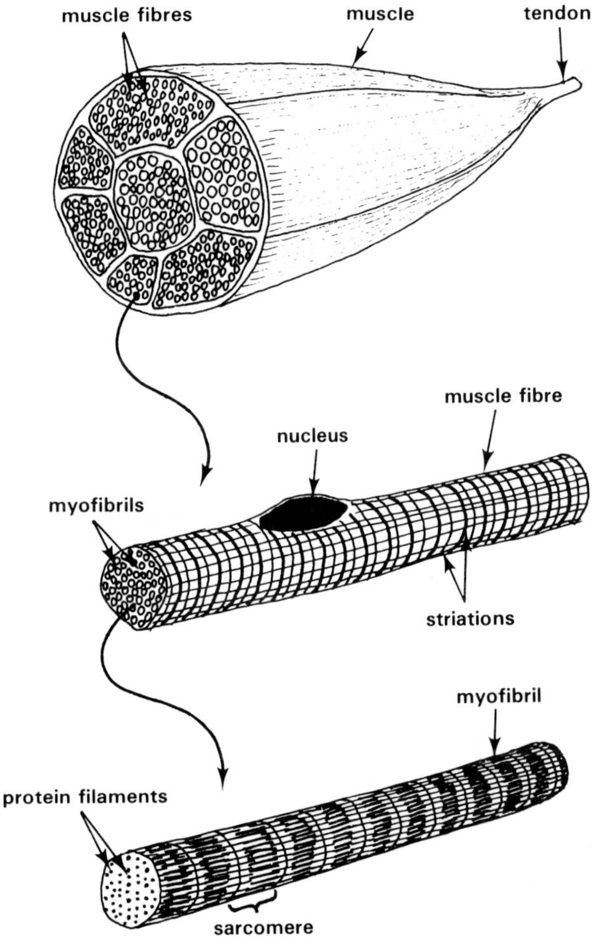

FIG. 15.20 (b) *Photomicrograph of some striped muscle fibres teased apart, ×600*

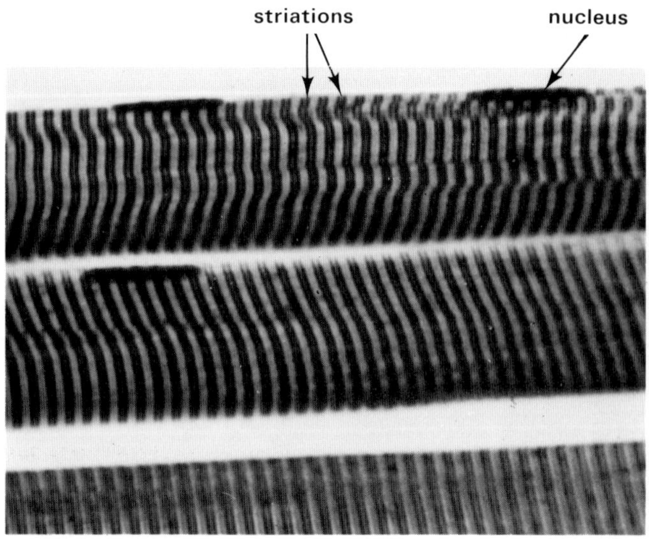

FIG. 15.20 (c)
Electronmicrograph of a myofibril showing a single sarcomere, ×65 000

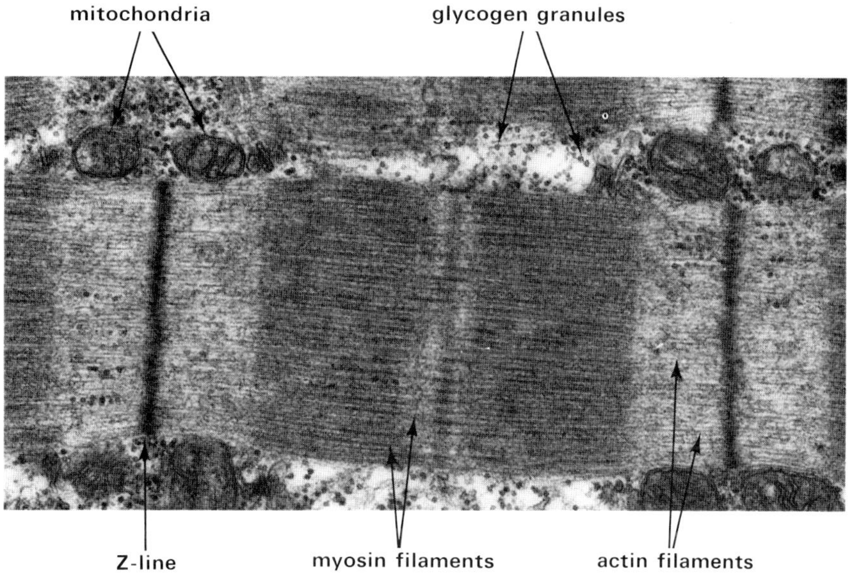

Isolated actin–myosin filaments contract when ATP is applied to them. As ATP is always present in living cells then muscles must contain an inhibitor, preventing continuous contraction. The inhibitor is neutralised by calcium ions. In relaxed muscle calcium ions and sodium ions are pumped out of the muscle fibres into the tissue fluid. The membrane of the fibres is thus polarised. Depolarisation of the membrane occurs when the muscle is stimulated and calcium ions enter the fibre. Here the calcium ions neutralise the inhibitor. This enables ATP to provide the energy for actin and myosin to interact resulting in muscle contraction.

Impulses spread rapidly all over the muscle in much the same way as nerve impulses are transmitted. Consequently stimulation of a muscle fibre by a nerve brings about impulse **propagation** in the muscle which causes contraction of the whole muscle. Using energy from ATP the bonds between actin and myosin break temporarily. The bonds reform further along the actin threads nearer each Z-line. The Z-lines of adjacent sarcomeres are thus pulled closer together, since actin and myosin do not stretch. In this way the sarcomeres shorten (Fig. 15.21). Because the stimulus to contraction spreads rapidly over the entire muscle all the myofibrils contract at once.

Muscle contraction requires a lot of free energy. It is therefore not surprising to find that muscles are well equipped to produce energy. Between the muscle fibres are numerous **mitochondria**. **Glycogen** is stored in muscle as a source of glucose, the main substrate used to provide free energy in respiration (Chapter 5). Muscle also contains a red respiratory pigment, **myoglobin**, which reacts with oxygen in much the same way as does haemoglobin, the pigment in blood. Oxygenated myoglobin acts as a reserve of oxygen in muscle (Chapter 8). Also peculiar to muscle is a substance called **creatine** which can become phosphorylated by transfer of high-energy phosphate groups from ATP. The ADP so formed is converted back to ATP in respiration:

respiratory substrate → oxidised respiratory substrate; ADP → ATP; ATP → ADP; creatine → phosphocreatine

FIG. 15.21 *Mechanism of sarcomere action*

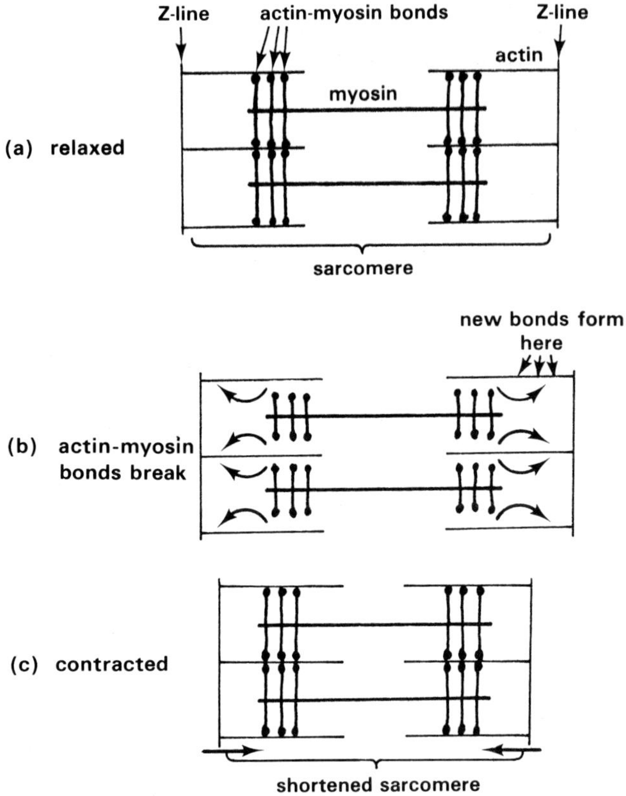

FIG. 15.22 *Photomicrograph of some smooth muscle cells from the urinary bladder of a cat, × 1000*

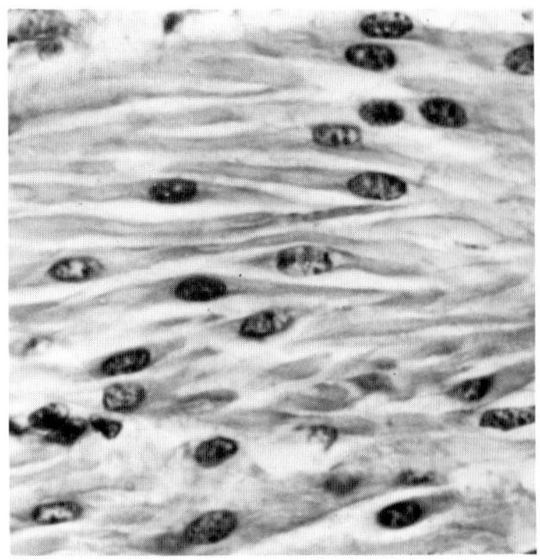

When ATP is used to provide free energy for muscular contraction, phosphocreatine replenishes the ATP supply in muscle fibres:

phosphocreatine ↘	↗ ADP ↖	↗ contracted actin-myosin
creatine ↙	↘ ATP ↗	↖ relaxed actin-myosin

Phosphocreatine therefore acts as an energy store in addition to ATP (Chapter 5).

Smooth muscle is made of fibres capable of slow but sustained contraction (Fig. 15.22). The electrochemical properties of smooth muscle are different from those of striped muscle. Smooth muscle has a lower and less stable resting potential. Changes of the resting potential result in the rhythmic production of action potentials. Hence smooth muscle exhibits **rhythmic contractions** even without nervous stimulation. This is called **myogenic** contraction as opposed to **neurogenic** contraction which requires nervous stimulation. Nerve fibres are usually present in smooth muscle but they regulate activity rather than initiate it (Fig. 15.23).

Cardiac muscle is structurally very similar to striped muscle (Fig. 15.24). However, like smooth muscle, cardiac muscle exhibits **rhythmic myogenic contractions**. The cross-connections between adjacent fibres of cardiac muscle enable contraction to spread through the heart wall. Cardiac muscle is also very conductive. These properties account for the ability of cardiac muscle to contract and relax smoothly and continuously when the heart beats (Chapter 9).

FIG. 15.23 (a) *Experimental arrangement to measure the contraction of smooth muscle in mammalian gut. Change in length of the gut piece is recorded as a fluctuation on a pen recorder*

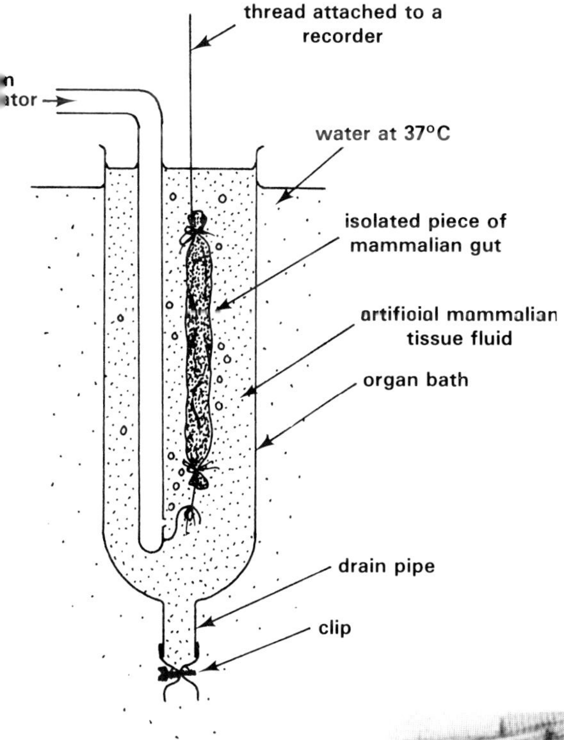

FIG. 15.23 (b) *Addition of adrenalin and acetylcholine to the isolated gut piece* (Fig. 15.23 (a)) *simulates the effects of the autonomic nerves on smooth muscle. Note the rhythmic myogenic contractions before the substances were added*

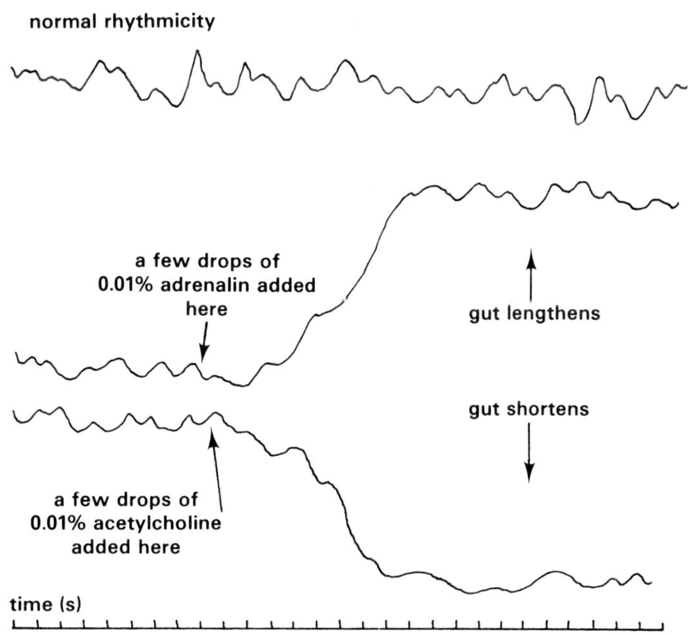

FIG. 15.24 *Photomicrograph of some human cardiac muscle fibres × 450*

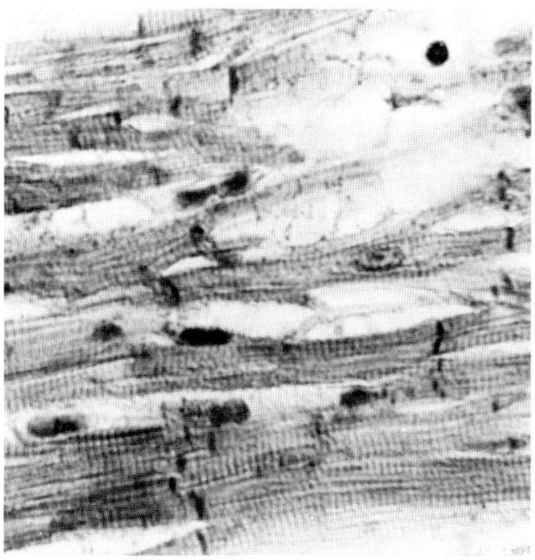

15.1.9 Cartilage, bone and joints

The mammalian skeleton is largely composed of **bone**. In the embryo, however, the first skeletal material to develop is **cartilage**. In chondrichthyean fish, the skeleton remains cartilaginous throughout life (section 27.2.2). In other vertebrates, embryonic cartilage ossifies during development to become bone. Some bones, called **membrane bones**, arise from embryonic connective tissue and do not begin as cartilage.

1. CARTILAGE

Hyaline cartilage consists of a matrix of **chondrin** containing collagen (section 3.3.2). Chondrin is secreted by cells called **chondroblasts** which lie in the matrix in small clusters (Fig. 15.25). Cartilage is bounded by a fibrous

FIG. 15.25 *Photomicrograph of hyaline cartilage, × 100*

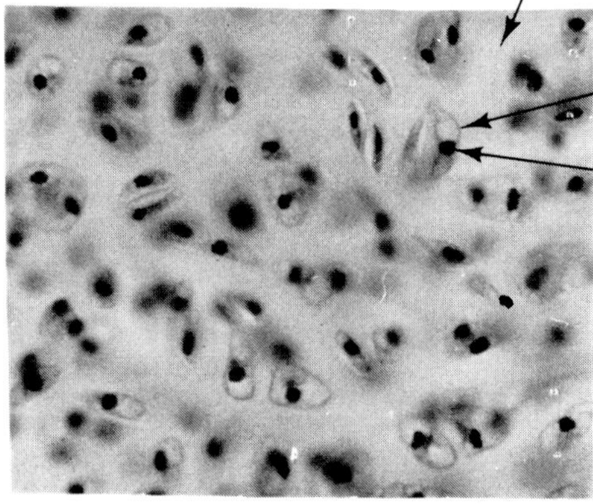

layer called the **perichondrium** in which there are blood vessels. It is here that new cartilage is laid down. In adult mammals, some hyaline cartilage remains in the skeleton. One of its main functions is to protect bones from abrasion where they articulate at joints (Fig. 15.29). Hyaline cartilage also joins the ribs to the sternum (Fig. 8.3) and allows limited flexing of the ribs during breathing. Rings of hyaline cartilage in the trachea and bronchi support the air passages and keep them open. **Elastic cartilage** contains yellow elastic fibres arranged in all directions in the matrix. The fibres allow greater flexibility compared with hyaline cartilage. Elastic cartilage is found in the epiglottis and in the pinna of the ear. **Fibro-cartilage** has many white fibres of collagen in the matrix. They resist stretching and give this type of cartilage considerable strength. Fibro-cartilage is found in the intervertebral discs of the spine. They cushion adjacent vertebrae in upright, bipedal vertebrates such as man. In fish the discs resist compression during swimming, yet allow limited bending of the spine (Fig. 27.9).

2. BONE

FIG. 15.26 *Diagram of the main parts of a bone*

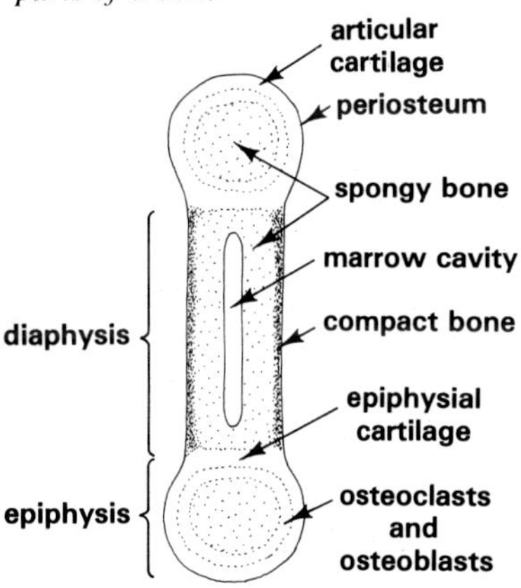

Most bones have a shaft called the **diaphysis**. It is usually hollow and contains the bone **marrow** which produces most of the various kinds of blood cells (section 9.2). Bone is covered by a tough, fibrous membrane called the **periosteum**. At the ends, bones are usually expanded to form the **epiphyses**. These are sites for the attachment of tendons and articulation with other bones (Fig. 15.26). In birds, hollow air spaces are found inside the **pneumatic bones**. They reduce the mass of the skeleton, making it easier for birds to fly (Fig. 27.31).

The substance of bones may be **spongy** or **compact** and is arranged to provide maximum strength with minimum mass. The matrix of the bone is a mesh of collagen fibres impregnated with concentric **lamellae** of calcium salts, especially phosphate (section 18.1.5). In the matrix is a system of **Haversian canals** arranged parallel to the longitudinal axis of the bone (Fig. 15.27). They contain nerves, blood and lymphatic vessels and connect with the periosteum and the marrow. Bone cells called **osteocytes** are found in concentric rings in the lamellae. The cells lie in cavities called **lacunae**

FIG. 15.27 *Photomicrograph of compact bone, × 100*

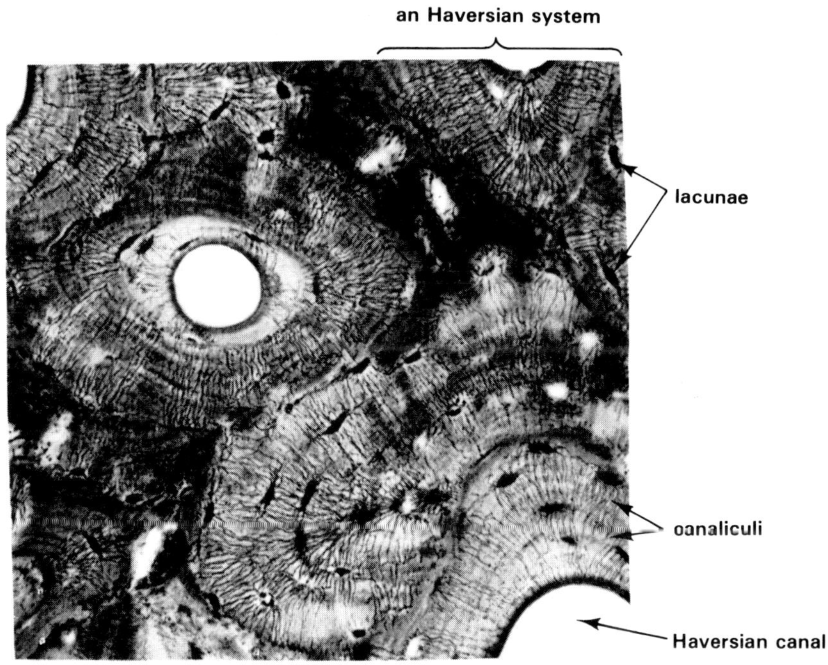

which are linked by a series of fine **canaliculi**. The osteocytes produce the bone matrix.

The production of bone from embryonic cartilage is called **endochondral ossification**. The limb bones are formed in this way. Chondroblasts multiply and become arranged in longitudinal columns. Then, starting from the centre, the chondroblasts deposit calcium salts in the matrix. The cartilage thus becomes ossified. Many of the chondroblasts degenerate and are replaced by large, amoeboid cells called **osteoclasts**. They cause erosion of much of the calcified cartilage, which then becomes invaded by blood vessels. Cells called **osteoblasts** now secrete a series of bony columns called **trabeculae** in the centre of the bone shaft. Ossification gradually spreads outwards towards the periosteum. At the same time, osteoblasts just beneath the periosteum produce dense bone. Some of the osteoblasts are enclosed in lacunae and become osteocytes (Fig. 15.28).

FIG. 15.28 *Diagram of the stages of ossification*

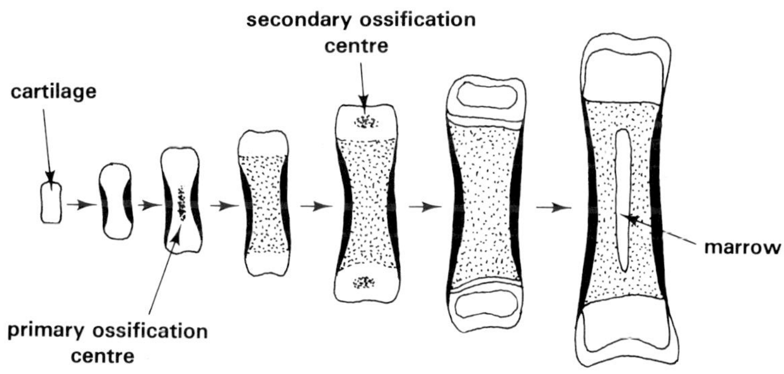

The production of bone from embryonic connective tissue is called **intramembranous ossification**. The bones of the skull are formed in this way. Fine

FIG. 15.29 *Diagram of a joint*

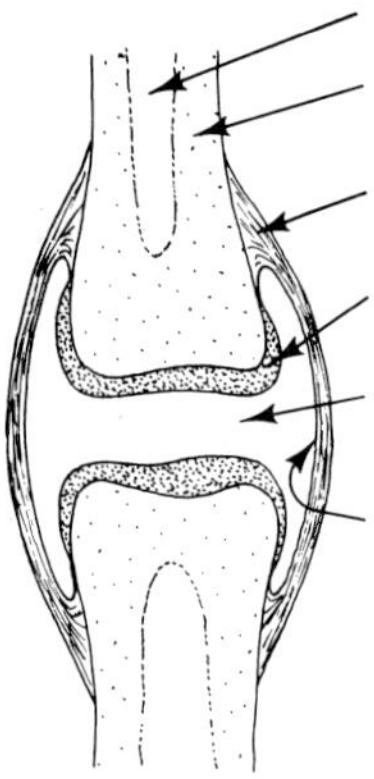

bundles of white fibres appear in the connective tissue matrix and calcium salts are deposited around them. Osteoclasts then erode much of the calcified matrix. Osteoblasts now form bony trabeculae, the periosteum appears and new bone is laid down beneath it.

3. JOINTS

The bones of the skeleton are moved by the action of muscles. For movement to occur smoothly, the bones articulate at **joints** (Fig. 15.29). The articulating surfaces of the bone are covered with pads of articular cartilage. The joint is enclosed in a fibrous **synovial capsule** which, with the aid of ligaments, keeps the bones together. The capsule is lined with a **synovial membrane**. It secretes **synovial fluid** into the capsule's cavity. The synovial fluid is a lubricant and allows free movement of the bones at the joint. Where free movement does not occur, as in the joints between vertebrae, the bones are separated by pads of fibro-cartilage.

15.2 The mammalian nervous system

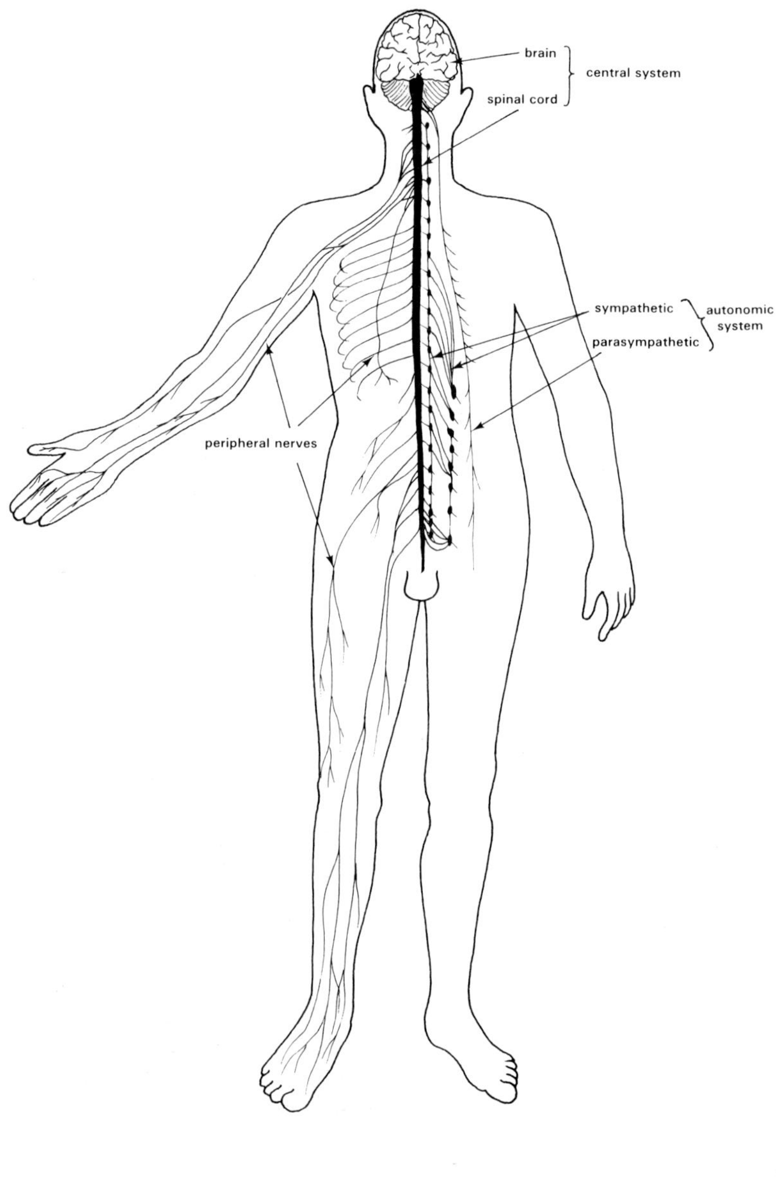

FIG. 15.30 *Diagram of the main divisions of the human nervous system*

While integrated into a functional unit the mammalian nervous system can be divided into several structural sections. The sections include the **peripheral, autonomic** and the **central nervous systems** (Fig. 15.30).

15.2.1 The peripheral nervous system and reflexes

The **peripheral system** includes **afferent (sensory) neurons** which receive impulses from **receptors (sense organs)** and transmit them to the central nervous system. Impulses may then be transmitted from the central system along **efferent (motor) neurons** of the peripheral system to **effectors**. Effectors are muscles and glands which respond to the stimulus (Fig. 15.31).

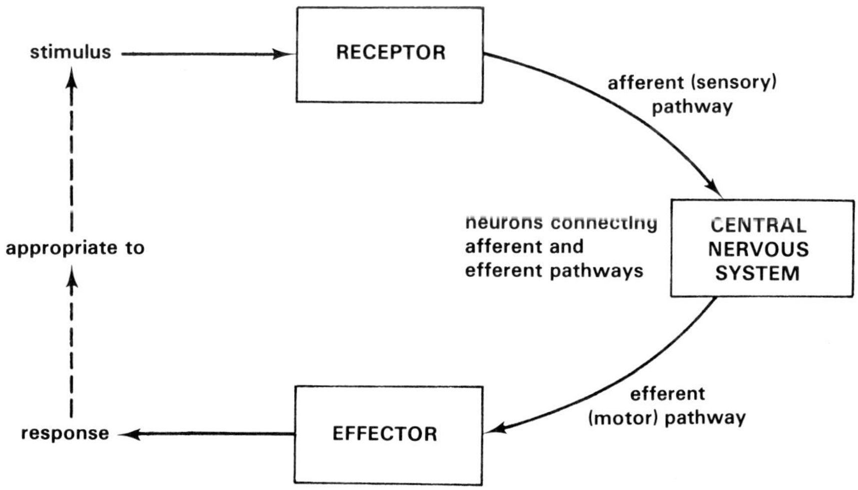

FIG. 15.31 *The main components of a nervous control mechanism.* Compare with Fig. 15.1

The type of activity in which the central system acts as a **relay** for incoming and outgoing impulses is the simplest form of nervous behaviour in mammals. Such **reflex activity** controls many aspects of mammalian behaviour. Reflex actions allow rapid responses to be made to a variety of stimuli without the conscious involvement of the brain. Most of the responses involve the control of posture and body movements under the subconscious control of the autonomic nervous system.

The involvement of the spinal cord in reflex actions is important since it connects afferent neurons to appropriate efferent neurons in different parts of the body. The mammalian **spinal cord** is a posterior extension of the brain and has a characteristic structure (Fig. 15.32). It contains **intermediate neurons** making up a central area of **grey matter** which relays information between afferent and efferent neurons. The grey matter is surrounded by **white matter**. White matter is composed mainly of the axons of longitudinal neurons connecting many parts of the body with the brain. Peripheral nerves contain afferent and efferent neurons lying side by side (Fig. 15.33). Near the spinal cord the afferent neurons enter the cord by pairs of **dorsal roots** and the efferent neurons leave in pairs of **ventral roots**.

An example of reflex activity is the body's response to changes of skin temperature. This is a convenient example to study in some detail as it illustrates how many co-ordinated responses can result from a single stimulus. Mammalian skin contains receptors sensitive to cold. When stimulated by low temperature, impulses are transmitted from the receptors along afferent neurons to the spinal cord. Here relays direct impulses along efferent neurons to a number of effectors. The effectors include skeletal muscles whose rapid contraction and relaxation result in shivering. Subcutaneous arterioles also constrict and the erector pili muscles at the base of the hair follicles contract causing erection of the hairs. Shivering produces heat. The other two responses minimise heat loss (Fig. 15.34). Control of body temperature in mammals is more complex than this and involves other reflexes described in Chapter 17.

FIG. 15.32 *Structure of the spinal cord. The central grey matter contains transverse fibres connecting afferent and efferent neurons in one spinal nerve. The outer white matter contains longitudinal fibres. Thick arrows indicate direction of impluses*

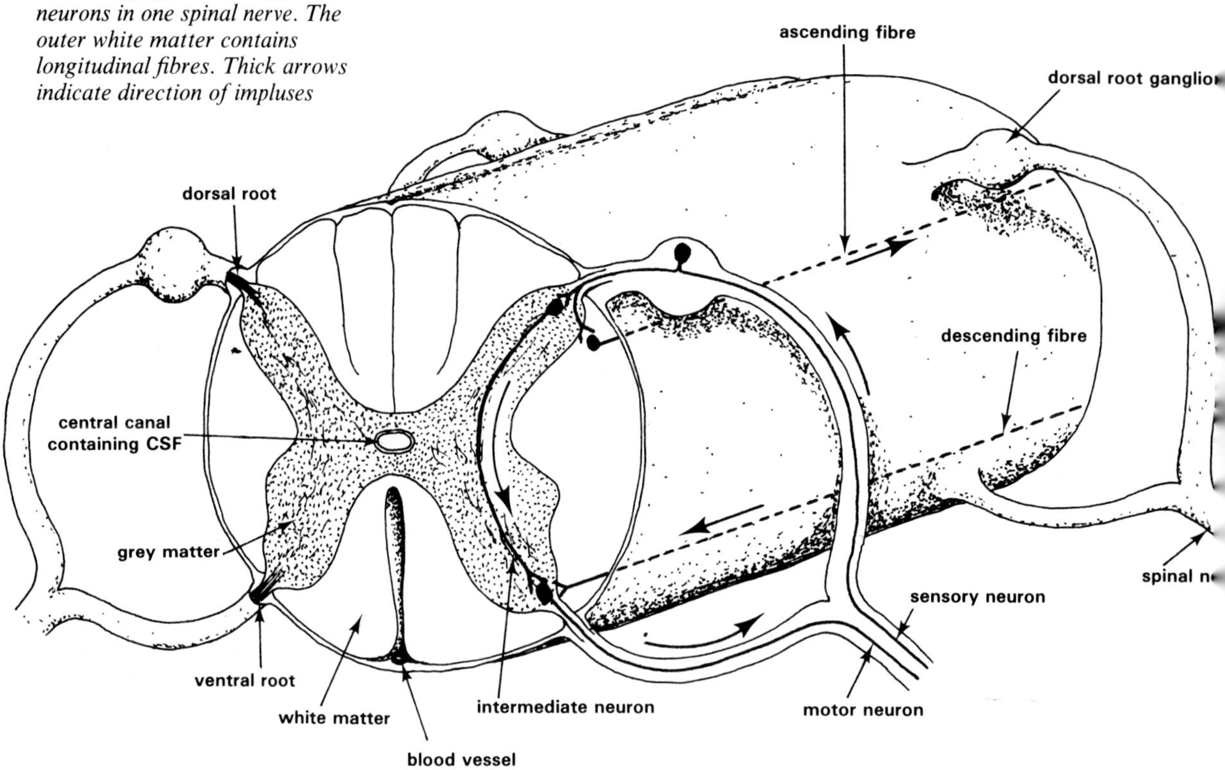

FIG. 15.33 *Photomicrograph of a transverse section of human median nerve. Note the variety of axon diameters.* ×*850*

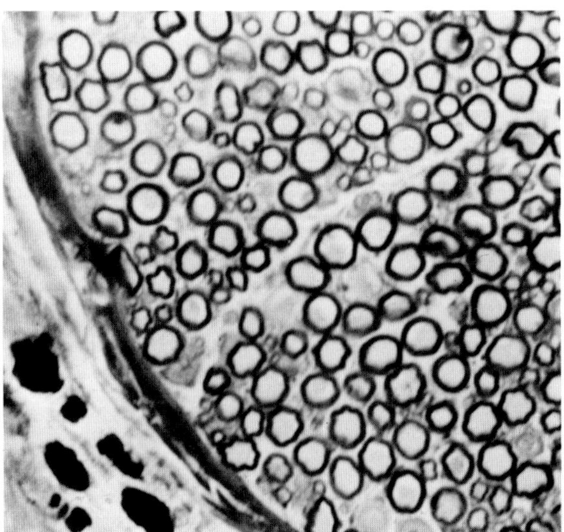

FIG. 15.34 *Nervous pathways involved in the responses to cold.* Compare with Fig. 15.31

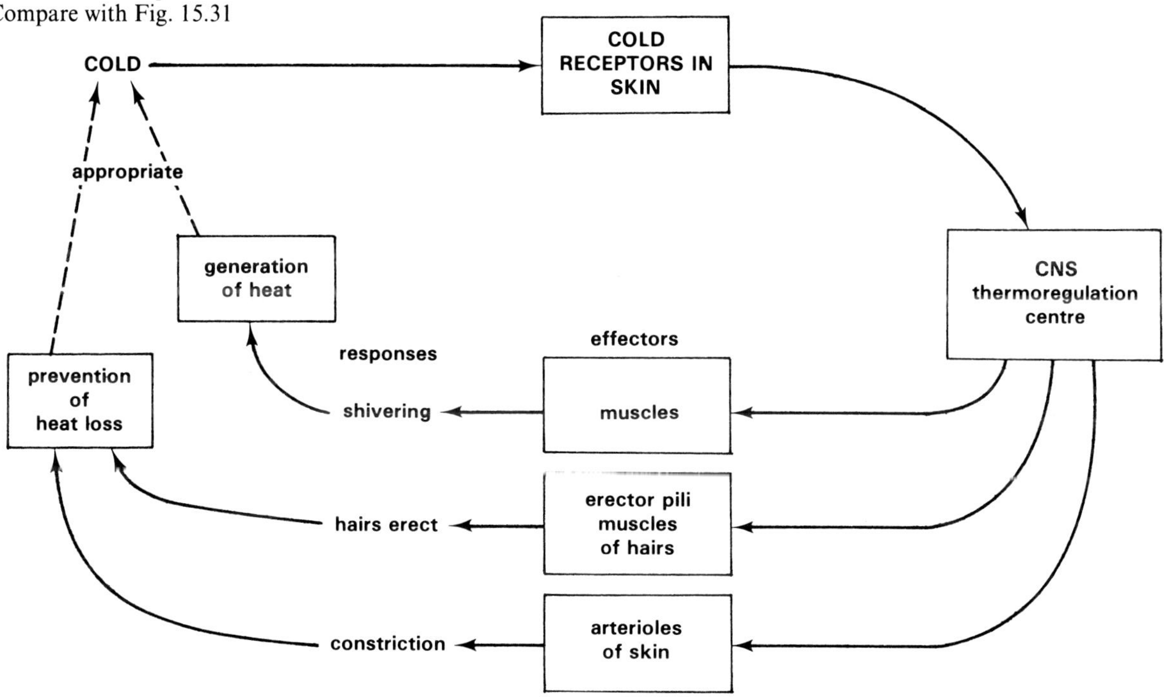

New-born mammals display a variety of **innate reflexes**. A baby for example will suck almost any object placed in its mouth. This is a vital reflex which activates the expulsion of milk from the mother's mammary glands during suckling (Chapter 22). Very young infants acquire additional reflexes and later override them at certain stages of their growth and development. Testing **acquired reflexes** is used to assess the developmental progress of premature babies (Fig. 15.35).

FIG 15.35 *Some infantile reflexes* (after Williams and Wendell-Smith)

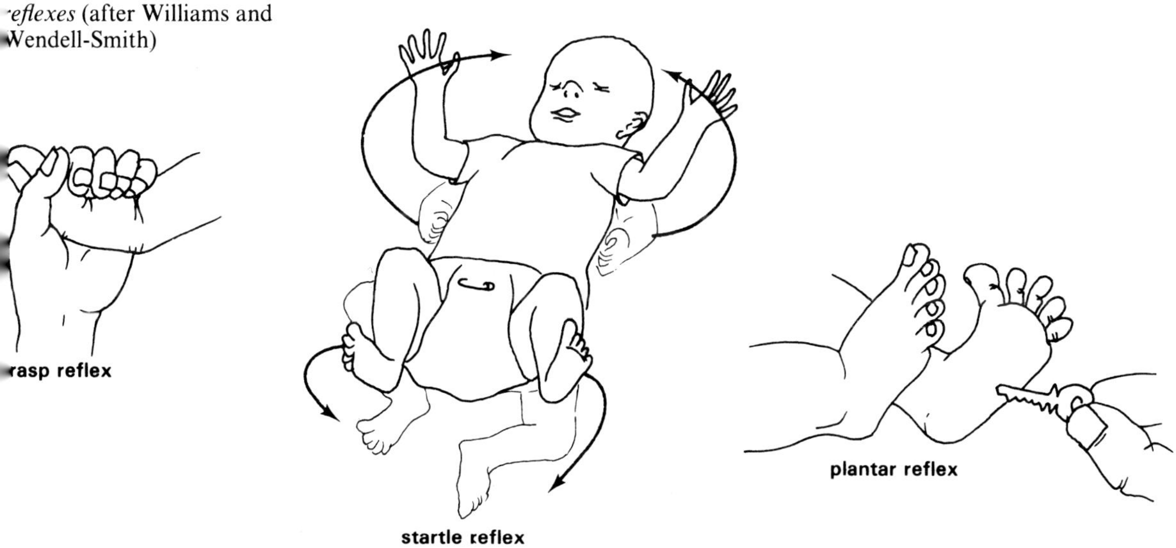

Pavlov in 1910 demonstrated another kind of reflex in mammals, the **conditioned reflex**. He noticed that hungry dogs salivate when presented with food, this being an innate reflex. He then observed that dogs salivate when exposed to a **secondary stimulus**, a ringing bell, at the same time as the **primary stimulus**, food. Pavlov discovered that in time the dogs learned to associate the secondary stimulus with food and salivated when a bell was rung even though food was not present (Fig. 15.36). This kind of conditioned reflex is common in mammalian behaviour. Knowledge of conditioning is very effectively used by the advertising industry. It is an interesting exercise to try to detect Pavlov's technique in television advertisements. How many describe the true nature of the product to be sold and how many associate it with something attractive but possibly quite unrelated to the product?

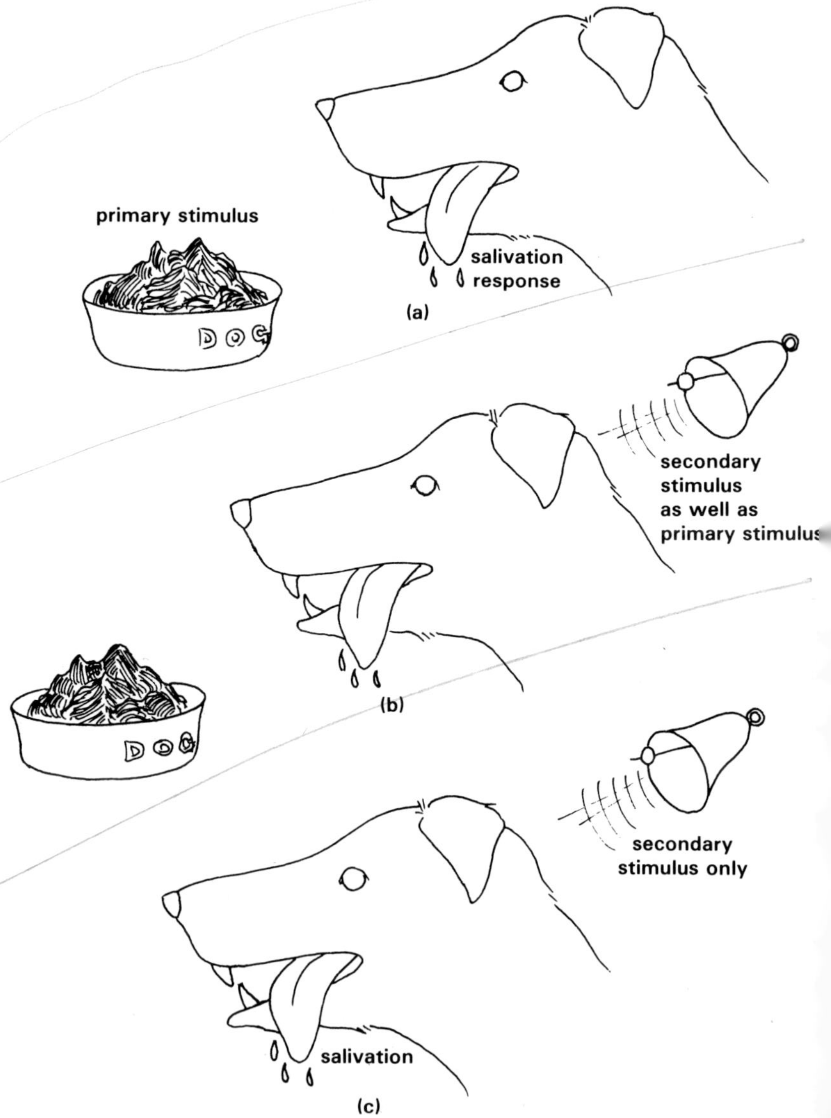

FIG. 15.36 *Pavlov's observations:* (a) *the hungry dog responds by salivating to the primary stimulus of food;* (b) *the dog is subjected to a period in which a second stimulus, a ringing bell, is presented with the primary stimulus to the salivation reflex;* (c) *eventually the dog salivates where only the secondary stimulus is given. The dog is said to be conditioned*

Body movements, often brought about by reflexes, involve the action of more than one muscle. Raising the forearm for example requires contraction of the **biceps (flexor) muscle** and relaxation of the **triceps (extensor) muscle** (Fig. 15.37). The nerve pathways in **antagonistic activity** of this sort excite one muscle and inhibit the other. The control mechanism is thought to involve excitatory and inhibitory synapses.

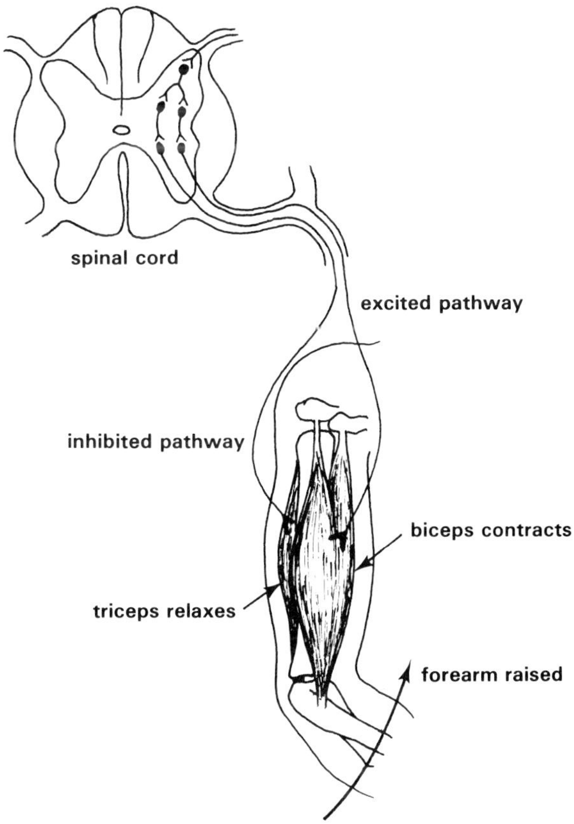

FIG. 15.37 *Reciprocal inhibition. During body movements involving the action of antagonistic muscles, one muscle is excited while the other is inhibited. Here, the flexing of the forearm is produced by contraction of the biceps and relaxation of the triceps. Nerve pathways involving inhibitory and excitatory synapses are thought to control this type of activity*

15.2.2 The autonomic nervous system

The **autonomic nervous system** consists of two sets of nerves, **sympathetic** and **parasympathetic** (Fig. 15.38). The autonomic nerves carry impulses to many organs in the body and the two systems normally act **antagonistically** (Table 15.3). The balance between the activity of sympathetic and parasympathetic nerves results in co-ordinated regulation of organs and glands, usually by reflex action. As with peripheral reflexes, the central nervous system is involved in autonomic activity. Many of the receptors which regulate autonomic activity are situated in the brain. They include the cardiac centre, the vasomotor centre and the respiratory centre (Chapters 8 and 9). The receptors detect body changes which require adjustment of the cardiovascular and gas exchange systems and convey appropriate impulses to the systems along autonomic nerves. However, unlike the peripheral system, the autonomic system is less easily controlled by conscious activity of the brain. Although it is possible to train an individual to reduce the heart rate for instance, autonomic function relies almost entirely on reflexes. The ability to control breathing consciously is due to the fact that the muscles involved are innervated by peripheral as well as autonomic nerves.

FIG. 15.38 *The autonomic nervous system*

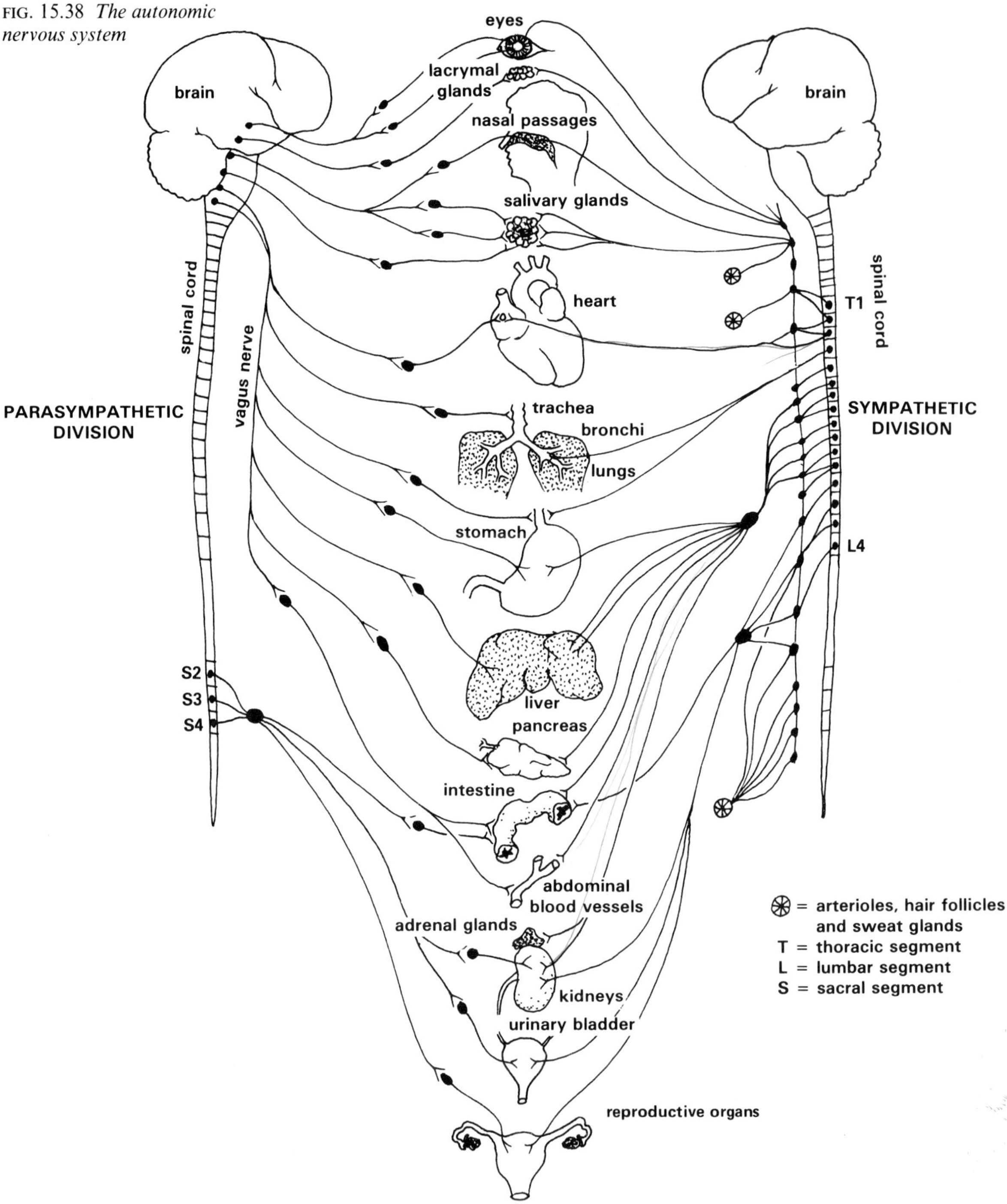

The antagonistic effects of sympathetic and parasympathetic nerves result from the different chemical transmitters secreted at their neuroeffector junctions. **Acetylcholine** is the transmitter secreted by parasympathetic neurons. For this reason parasympathetic neurons are **cholinergic**. Sympathetic neurons secrete **noradrenalin** and are **adrenergic** (Fig. 15.39).

Table 15.3 Summary of the effects of the autonomic nervous system

TARGET	SYMPATHETIC EFFECT	PARASYMPATHETIC EFFECT
iris of eye	extension	retraction
bronchi	dilation	constriction
heart	increase in rate	decrease in rate
sphincters of gut	constriction	dilation
urinary bladder	dilation	constriction
blood vessels	vasoconstriction	—
sweat glands	secretion of sweat	—
salivary glands	—	secretion of saliva
stomach	—	secretion of gastric juice
pancreas	—	secretion of pancreatic juice
genitalia	—	vasodilation of erectile tissue

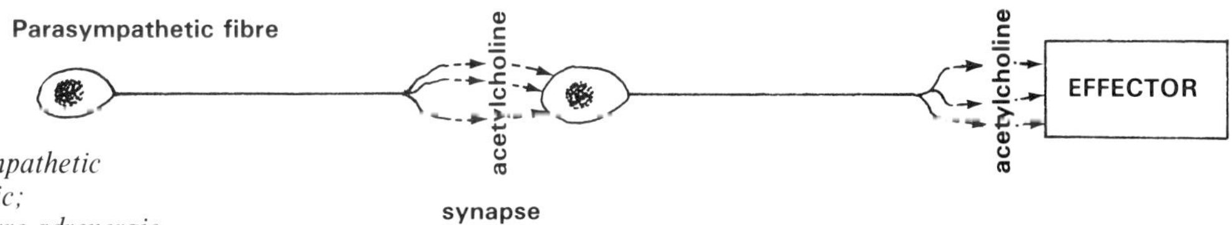

FIG. 15.39 *Parasympathetic fibres are cholinergic; sympathetic fibres are adrenergic*

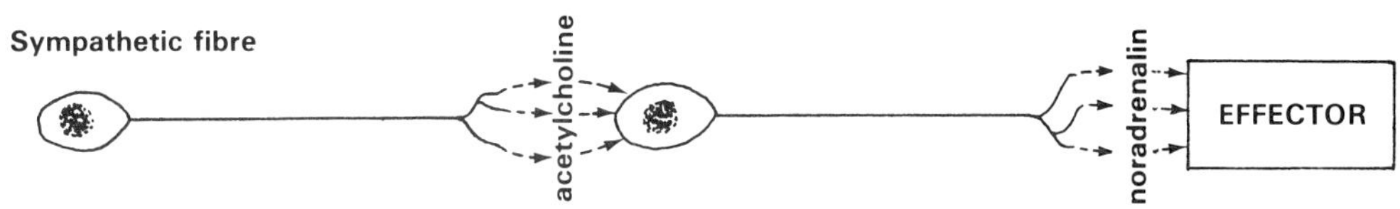

FIG 15.40 *Relative development of the main portions of the brain in amphibians, reptiles, birds and mammals. Note the relative size of the cerebrum in the mammalian brain*

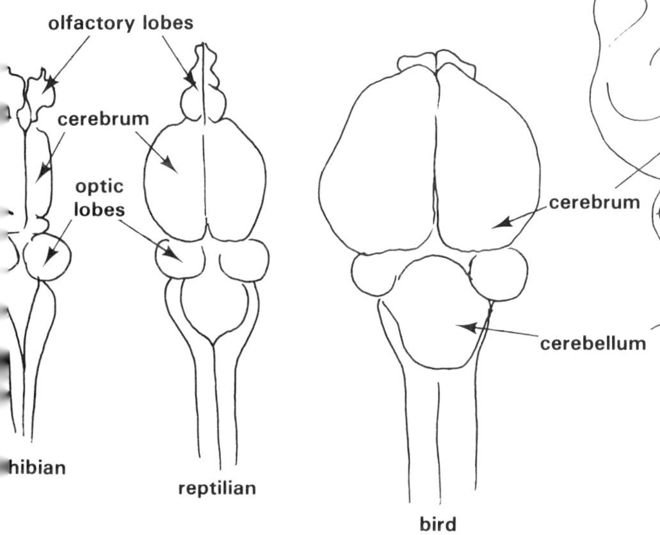
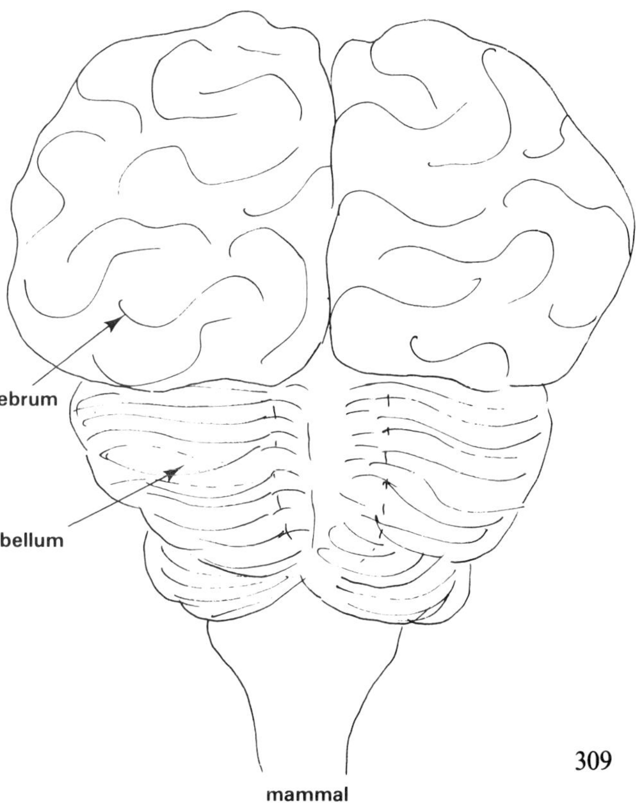

Adrenalin as well as noradrenalin is secreted into the blood from the medulla of the adrenal glands which are modified portions of the sympathetic system. In conditions of stress, secretion of adrenalin is increased. The significance of the response is discussed in Chapter 18.

15.2.3 The central nervous system

At the beginning of the chapter the basic components of a co-ordination system are listed. Stimuli are first detected by sensors called receptors. Information, conveyed in the nervous system as impulses, is then transmitted to a co-ordinator. The co-ordinator relays the impulses along appropriate channels to an effector which brings about the response (Fig. 15.1). The **central nervous system** comprising the **brain** and **spinal cord**, performs the role of the **co-ordinator** in the nervous system. We have already seen how the spinal cord relays impulses from afferent neurons to appropriate efferent neurons (section 15.2.1). However, the brain can act in much more complex ways.

1. STRUCTURE OF THE MAMMALIAN BRAIN

The mammalian brain is divisible into three main regions, **hindbrain**, **midbrain** and **forebrain** (Fig. 15.40). The hindbrain is continuous with the spinal cord which runs through the spinal canal of the vertebrae. The hindbrain consists of the **medulla oblongata** and a large dorsal structure called the **cerebellum**. The midbrain is relatively short in mammals, linking the hindbrain with the very large forebrain. The mammalian forebrain has two large dorsal structures called the **cerebral hemispheres** which make up the **cerebrum**. The hemispheres are so highly folded that only about a third of their surface area is visible on the outside of a human brain (Fig. 15.41). Projecting from beneath the forebrain is the hypophysis or **pituitary body** (Chapter 18).

FIG 15.41 *The human brain viewed from above*

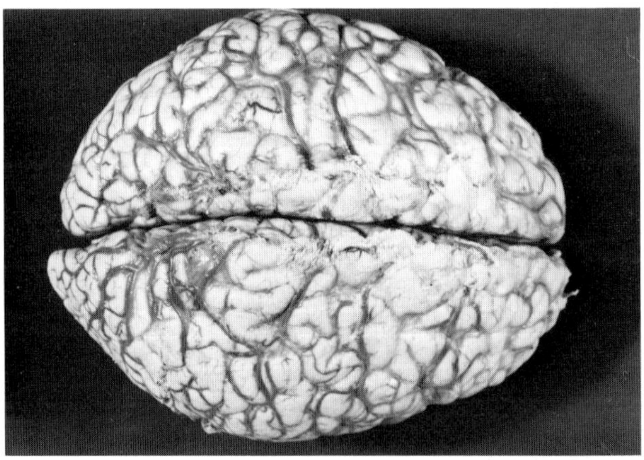

The entire central nervous system is surrounded by three protective membranes called the **meninges**. Between the inner two meninges is a fluid called the **cerebrospinal fluid (CSF)**. CSF is also found inside the brain, in four cavities called **ventricles** (Fig. 15.42). Ciliated epithelium lining the ventricles keeps the CSF in motion. Respiratory gases, nutrients and metabolic wastes pass between the CSF and the blood carried in capillaries which are plentiful in two of the ventricles. Disturbance of the blood supply can rapidly lead to permanent brain damage and may be fatal (Fig. 15.43). CSF also circulates in the central canal of the spinal cord. Impulses are transmitted to and from the brain along the spinal cord and twelve pairs of cranial nerves (Fig. 15.44).

The central nervous system is supported and protected by the **skeleton**. The **cranium** of the skull surrounds the brain and the **vertebral column** surrounds the spinal cord.

FIG. 15.42 *Main parts of the human brain as seen in a vertical section*

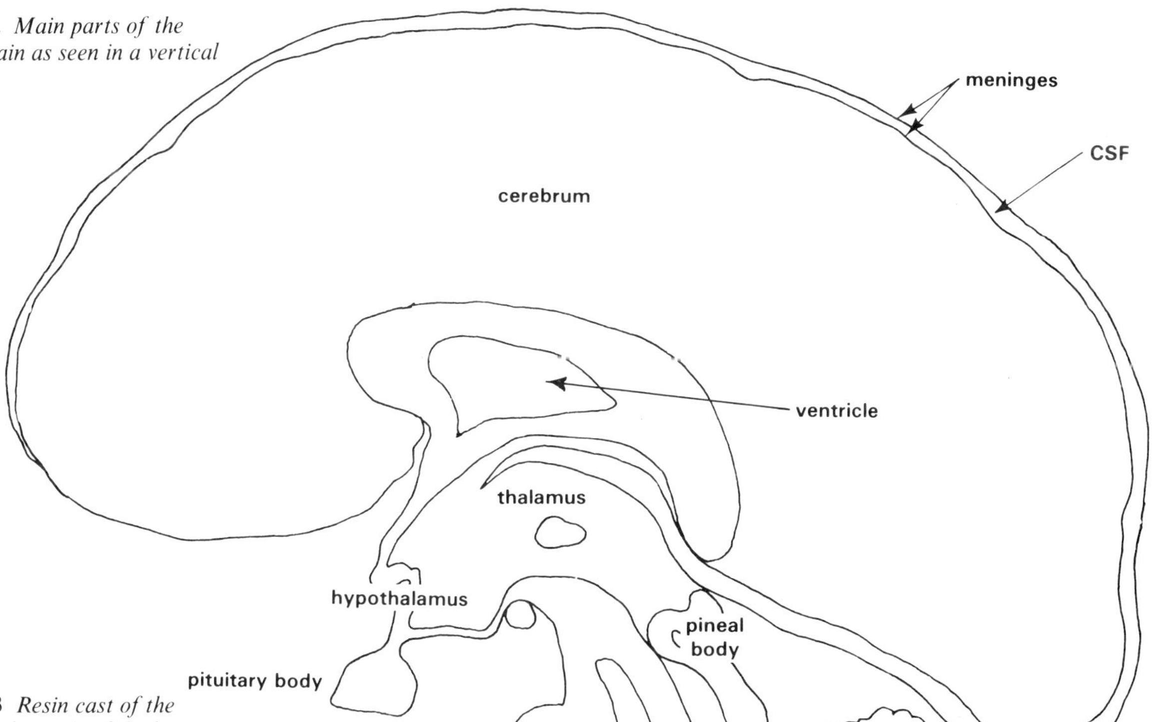
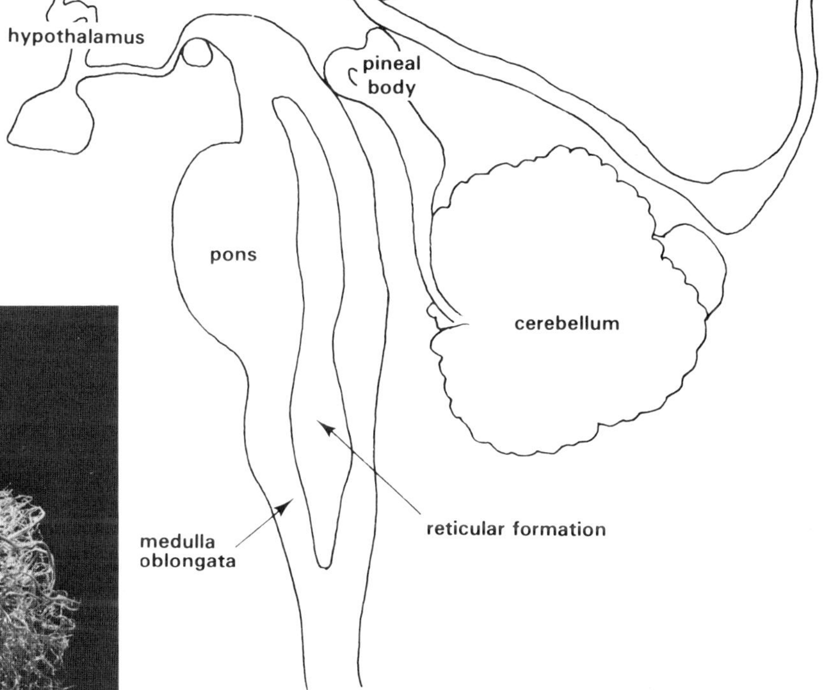

FIG. 15.43 *Resin cast of the main blood vessels of the human brain* (courtesy Professor McMinn, Department of Anatomy, The Royal College of Surgeons of England)

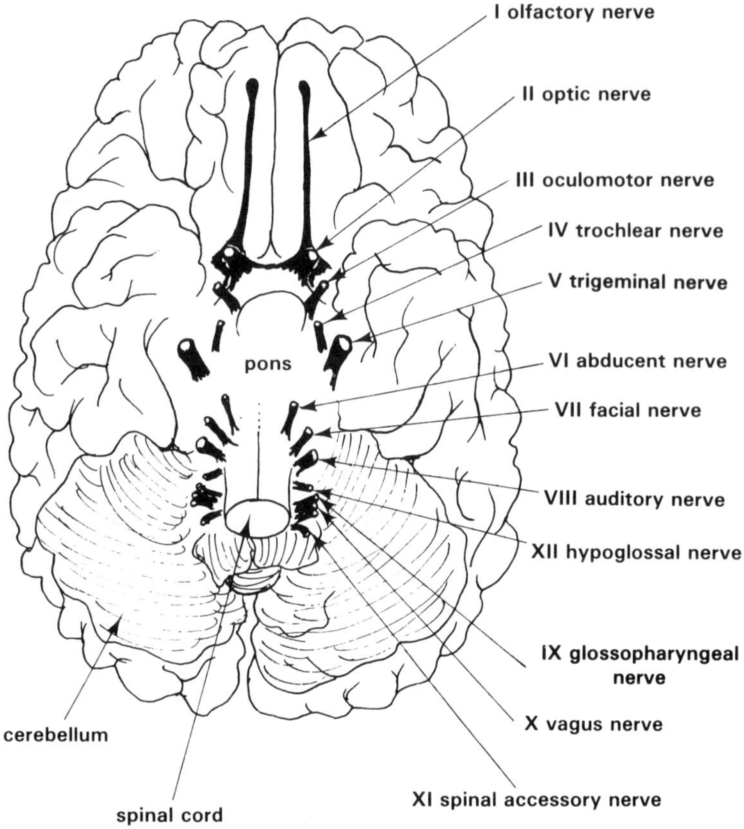

FIG 15.44 *The cranial nerves of the human brain (viewed from the base)*

2. FUNCTIONS OF THE MAMMALIAN BRAIN

The human brain contains more than a thousand million neurons. It has been estimated that in the cerebral cortex there are something like $10^{2\ 783\ 000}$ synapses! Considering the numbers of neurons and synapses in an organ weighing only about 1·3 kg it is evident how complex the human brain is.

(i) HINDBRAIN. The **medulla oblongata** contains the **cardiac**, **respiratory** and **vasomotor centres**. The centres contain neurons which are directly sensitive to blood carbon dioxide or more precisely hydrogencarbonate (HCO_3^-) concentration. An increase in blood carbon dioxide triggers off reflex activity starting in the centres and results in modifications of heart rate, breathing rhythm and blood pressure (Chapters 8 and 9). Refer again to Figure 15.1 and describe the roles played by the central nervous system in regulating cardiac and respiratory function.

The **cerebellum** is concerned with **co-ordination** of body movements and the **maintenance of posture**. Signals arising in the motor region of the forebrain travel through the cerebellum on their way to the spinal cord and the rest of the body. The cerebellum also receives sensory information from a variety of receptors. In some way, the cerebellum modifies the motor signals in the light of the sensory information received. The cerebellum thus ensures that appropriate body movements are made as intended and are not weakened or exaggerated in any way (Fig. 15.45).

FIG. 15.45 *Some nerve pathways illustrating the role of the cerebellum in modifying motor signals from the motor cortex of the cerebrum in the light of the degree of response produced. The stretch receptors in the muscle respond to muscle movements. If these movements are too great or too little the pathways illustrated enable 'damping down' or further stimulation* (after Guyton)

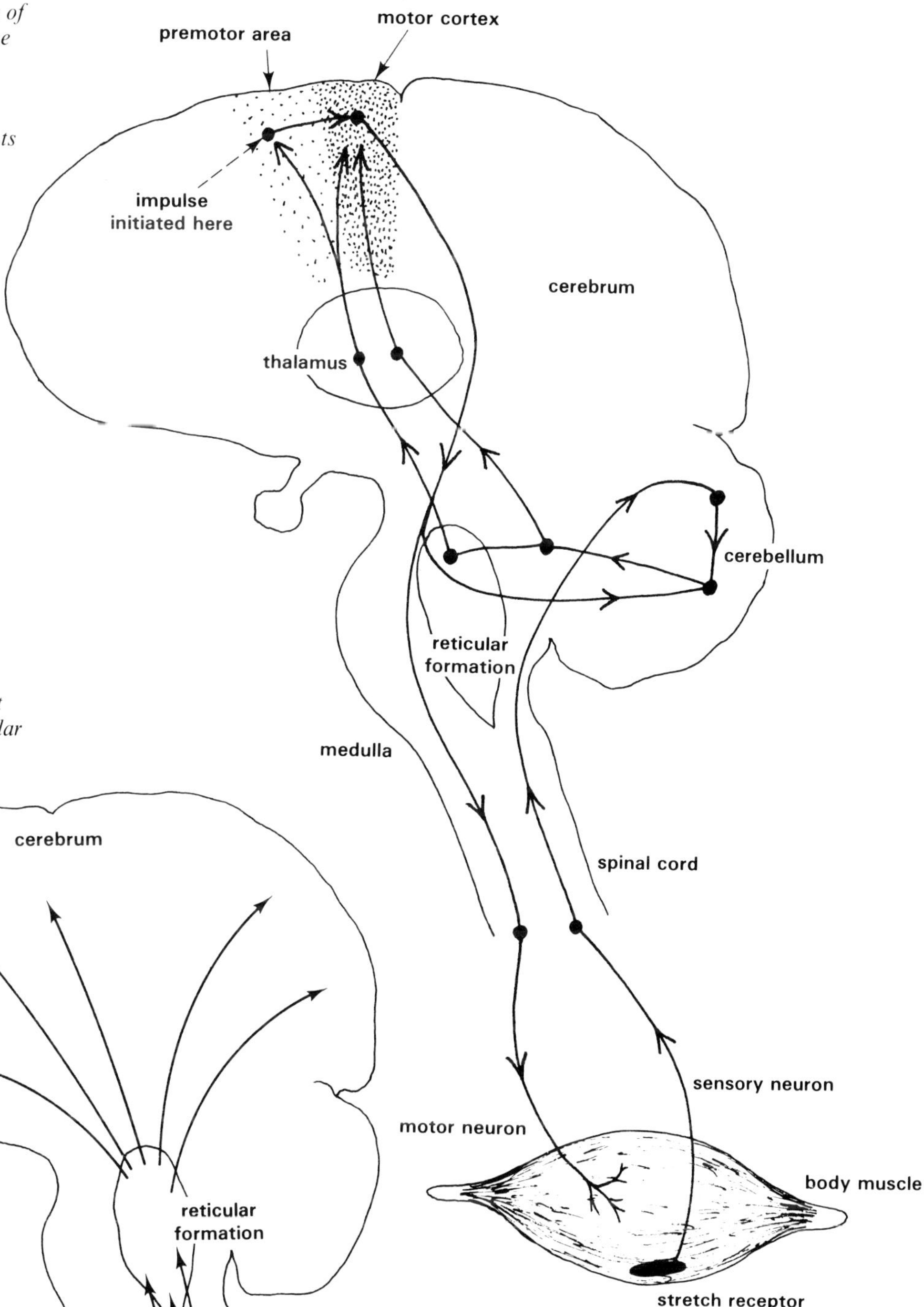

FIG. 15.46 *Sensory signals arriving in the cerebrum must first travel through the reticular formation for them to be 'registered' consciously*

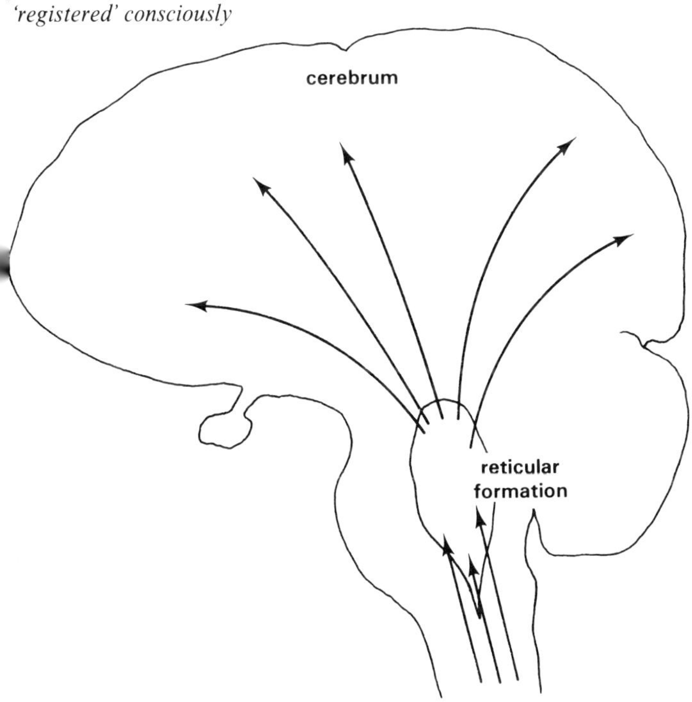

(ii) MIDBRAIN. As you sit reading this book you are bombarded by a variety of environmental stimuli. The more successfully you concentrate on your reading the less aware you are of outside distractions. When studying, unwanted stimuli may include the noise of traffic, people talking, a radio or television. You also constantly receive signals from your skin in response to the touch of your clothes or of a chair you may be sitting on. In other words, of the great number of environmental stimuli you receive at any one time, you are consciously aware of only a few whether you are studying or not. The **filtering effect** prevents overloading of your conscious awareness. Most people experience difficulty in concentrating on more than one thing at a time. The result of overloading the brain with many stimuli is lowered mental efficiency and often confusion.

One of the functions of the midbrain is to **activate the forebrain** with appropriate sensory signals. Lying in the midbrain is a group of nerve fibres called the **reticular formation**. Sensory pathways lead from the spinal cord to the reticular formation as well as directly to the forebrain. The forebrain does not respond to sensory signals unless it is activated by the reticular formation (Fig. 15.46).

Activation of the cerebral cortex by the reticular formation is necessary for **wakefulness**. The cortex is very active when you are awake and your nervous system constantly transmits impulses. Presumably as a result of neuronal or synaptic fatigue the system eventually needs rest. The reticular formation stops activating the cerebral cortex and a state of **sleep** follows. The full significance and physiology of sleep are not known at present. Sleep is nevertheless vital for the normal balance of nervous activity. Lack of sleep and excessive nervous fatigue can lead to serious mental disturbances. Sleep deprivation has been used to lower the mental resistance of prisoners prior to interrogation.

(iii) FOREBRAIN. The forebrain contains the dominant regions of the central system, notably the **cerebrum**. The cerebrum in mammals is very large relative to that of other vertebrates. It is in the cerebrum that higher mental processes occur, including conscious **thought**, **memory** and the detailed **interpretation** of sensory information. The main pathways of motor neurons originate in the cerebrum. Less than one per cent of the enormous number of neurons in the cerebrum synapse with fibres which transmit impulses out of the forebrain. Little is known of the significance of the rest of the cerebral neurons. The outer cortex of the cerebrum is grey in colour and contains dense masses of nerve cell bodies (Fig. 15.47).

FIG. 15.47 *Neurons in the cerebral cortex of a rat, × 75*

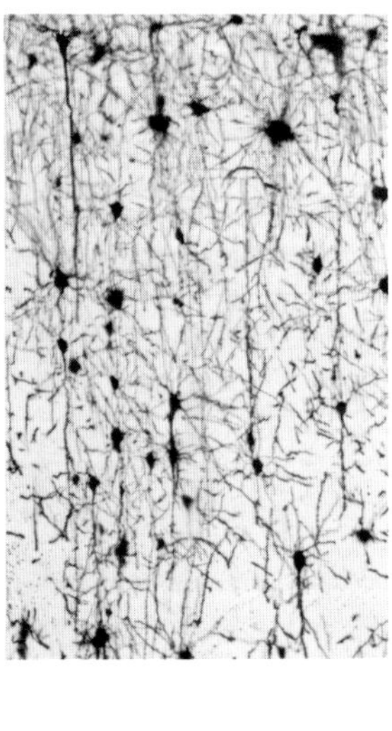

It is possible to map out distinct **sensory and motor regions** on the surface of the cerebrum. Localisation of function has been revealed by experiments with animals. Specific parts of the cerebral cortex can be stimulated with small electric currents and the response recorded. Deficiencies of sensation and motor activity have also been observed in people following injury to specific parts of the cerebrum. The sensory and motor regions are found on either side of a groove called the **central sulcus** which runs down the **parietal lobe** of each cerebral hemisphere (Fig. 15.48). Other regions of the cerebrum deal with **vision**, **hearing**, **speech** and **personality**.

The role of the **frontal lobes** in the maintenance of personality was first noted in the middle of the nineteenth century following the case of Phineas Gage. Gage was working in a quarry when an accident with explosives drove a metal bar through his head (Fig. 15.49). Even though the frontal lobes of his brain were severely damaged he survived with most of his bodily functions unaffected. However, Gage suffered a marked personality change, becoming irresponsible and vulgar. Before his accident he was a

FIG. 15.48 (a) *Location of the main motor and sensory regions in the human cerebral cortex*

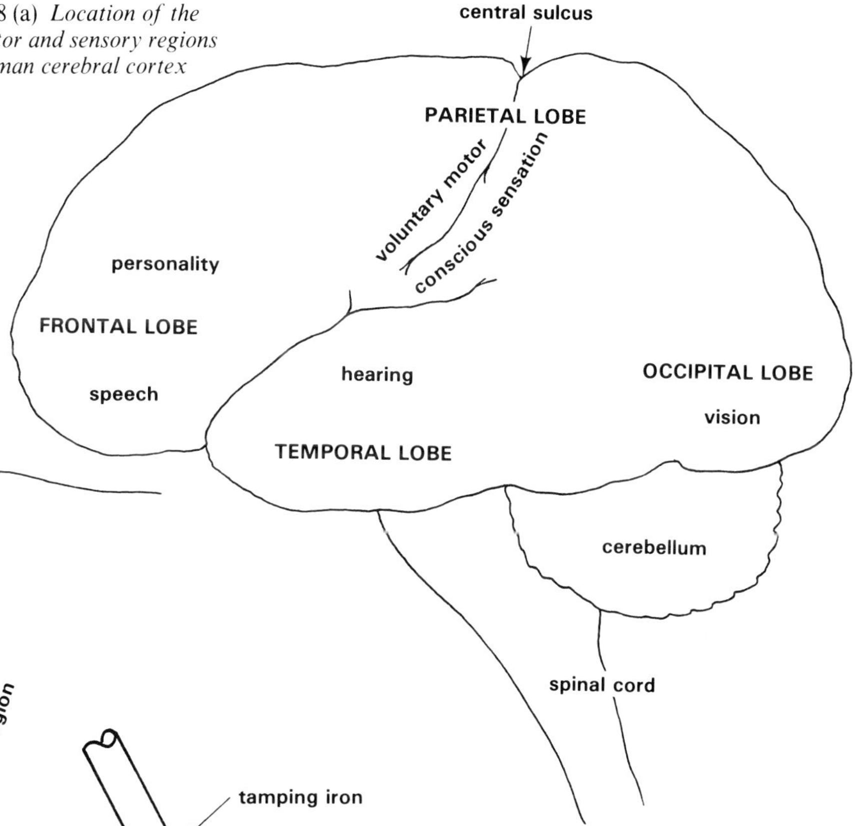

FIG. 15.48 (b) *Localised areas within the motor and sensory regions on either side of the central sulcus*

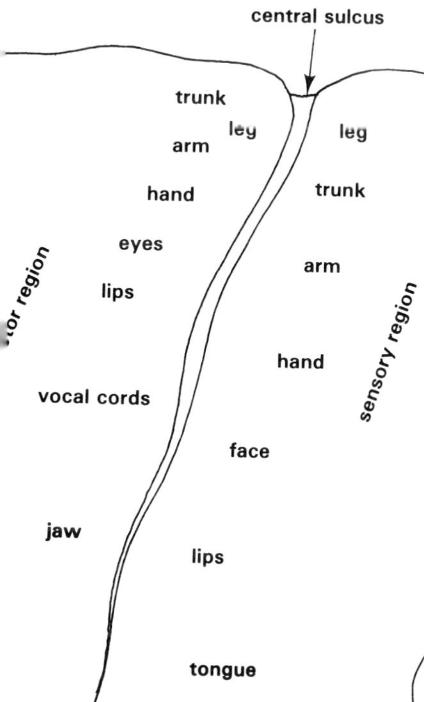

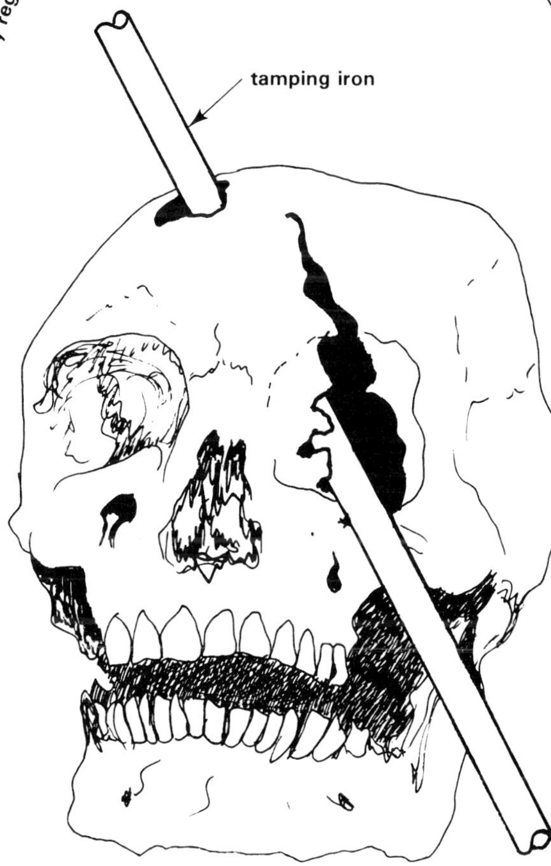

FIG. 15.49 *Skull of Phineas Gage showing the damage caused by the metal rod which pierced it during a mining accident*

FIG. 15.50 (a) *Electrodes being placed on the scalp of a patient prior to taking an electroencephalogram* (courtesy Sally York, Leicester Royal Infirmary)

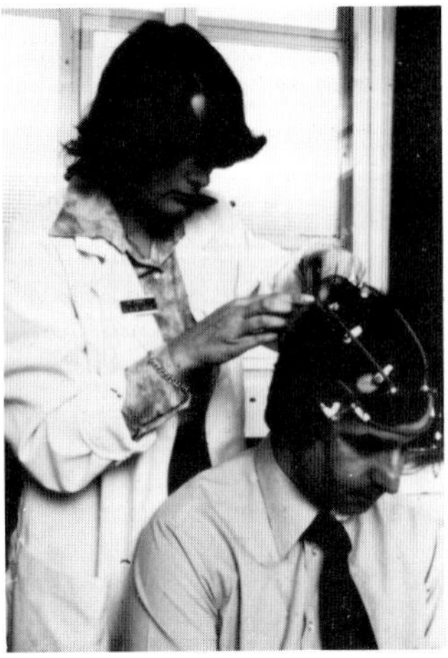

quiet, sober man. More recently, the frontal lobes have been surgically isolated in some mental patients in an attempt to cure severe personality problems. This practice of **prefrontal lobotomy** has now been replaced by the use of drugs.

The enormous numbers of neurons in the cerebral cortex are constantly active. The electrical activity accompanying transmission of impulses in the brain can be measured by placing electrodes on the scalp. Rhythmic waves are produced and these are displayed as an **electroencephalogram (EEG)**. Mental disturbances may produce EEG patterns which are abnormal and are of value in the diagnosis of some mental diseases (Fig. 15.50).

Sensory information reaching the cerebral hemispheres first passes through a region in the centre of the forebrain called the **thalamus**. The thalamus contains nerve pathways which activate appropriate regions of the cerebral cortex when sensory signals come in from the body's receptors. The function of the cortex is to interpret the details of the sensory signals and to link these with the memory of previous similar stimulations. The thalamus controls this function by channelling signals to the appropriate cortical region.

Beneath the thalamus is a part of the forebrain called the **hypothalamus**. The hypothalamus contains the **osmoregulation** and **thermoregulation centres**, important in regulating the body's water content and temperature (Chapters 10 and 17). Several **hormones** are made in the hypothalamus including ocytocin and vasopressin. Also made in the hypothalamus are hormones which control the release of tropins from the anterior pituitary (Chapter 18).

FIG. 15.50 (b) *EEG traces. The upper trace was recorded from the frontal region of a normal 18-year-old male. The lower trace was recorded from an individual with 'petit mal' epilepsy*

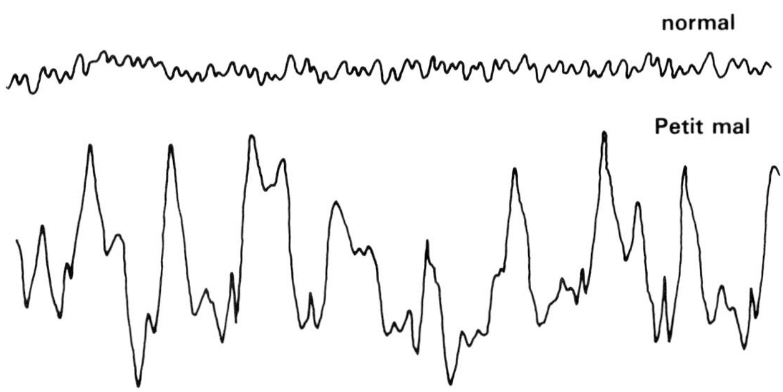

The brief survey of the brain given here serves to introduce some of the main functions of this highly complex organ. Many aspects of brain function are little known and still present one of the greatest challenges to science today.

Chapter 16

The mammalian eye and ear

The detection of stimuli depends on the conversion of the stimuli by **receptors** into impulses in the nervous system. The mammalian body contains a variety of receptors capable of feeding impulses into the nervous system about an equal variety of stimuli. Different receptors are sensitive to heat, light, sound, touch, stretching, spatial orientation and to chemicals.

The simplest receptors are single nerve cells which respond directly to a stimulus. Receptors in the skin are of this type (Fig. 17.11). Some receptors consist of groups of sensitive neurons such as the cardiac and respiratory centres in the brain (Chapter 15). Other receptors are grouped in complex **sense organs**. The structure of sense organs causes the stimulus to be channelled into a receptive region.

The way in which impulses are generated by receptor cells is important in discriminating between strong and weak stimuli. Measurement of action potentials (Chapter 15) in sensory neurons shows no significant difference between one impulse and another. However, a strong stimulus usually causes impulses to be generated rapidly in sensory neurons. The frequency of impulses generated by weak stimuli is lower. The appropriate sensory region of the cerebral cortex of the brain interprets the intensity of a stimulus according to the frequency with which it receives impulses.

The most obvious sense organs in mammals are the **eyes** and **ears**.

16.1 The mammalian eye

Most mammals depend greatly on vision to sense their environment. While reading this page your conscious awareness is almost totally stimulated by visual information.

16.1.1 Structure of the eye

Mammalian **eyes** are spherical structures (Fig. 16.1). The wall of the eye consists of three layers, the outer **sclera**, the middle **choroid** layer and the inner **retina**. The sclera is a tough, fibrous coating which protects the delicate inner layers. The sclera is white in appearance except at the front

FIG. 16.1 (a) *Photomicrograph of a longitudinal section of the eye from a monkey,* ×4

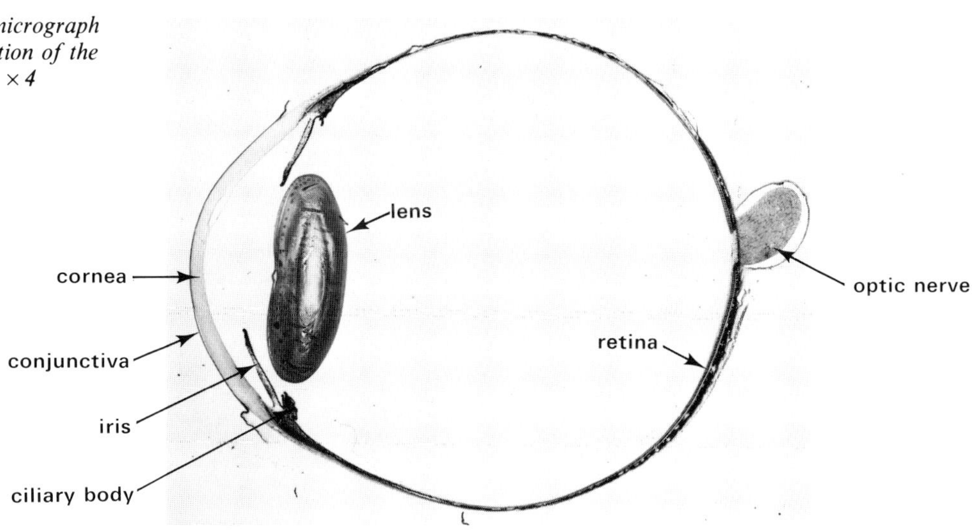

FIG. 16.1 (b) *Diagram of a vertical section through the eye of a mammal*

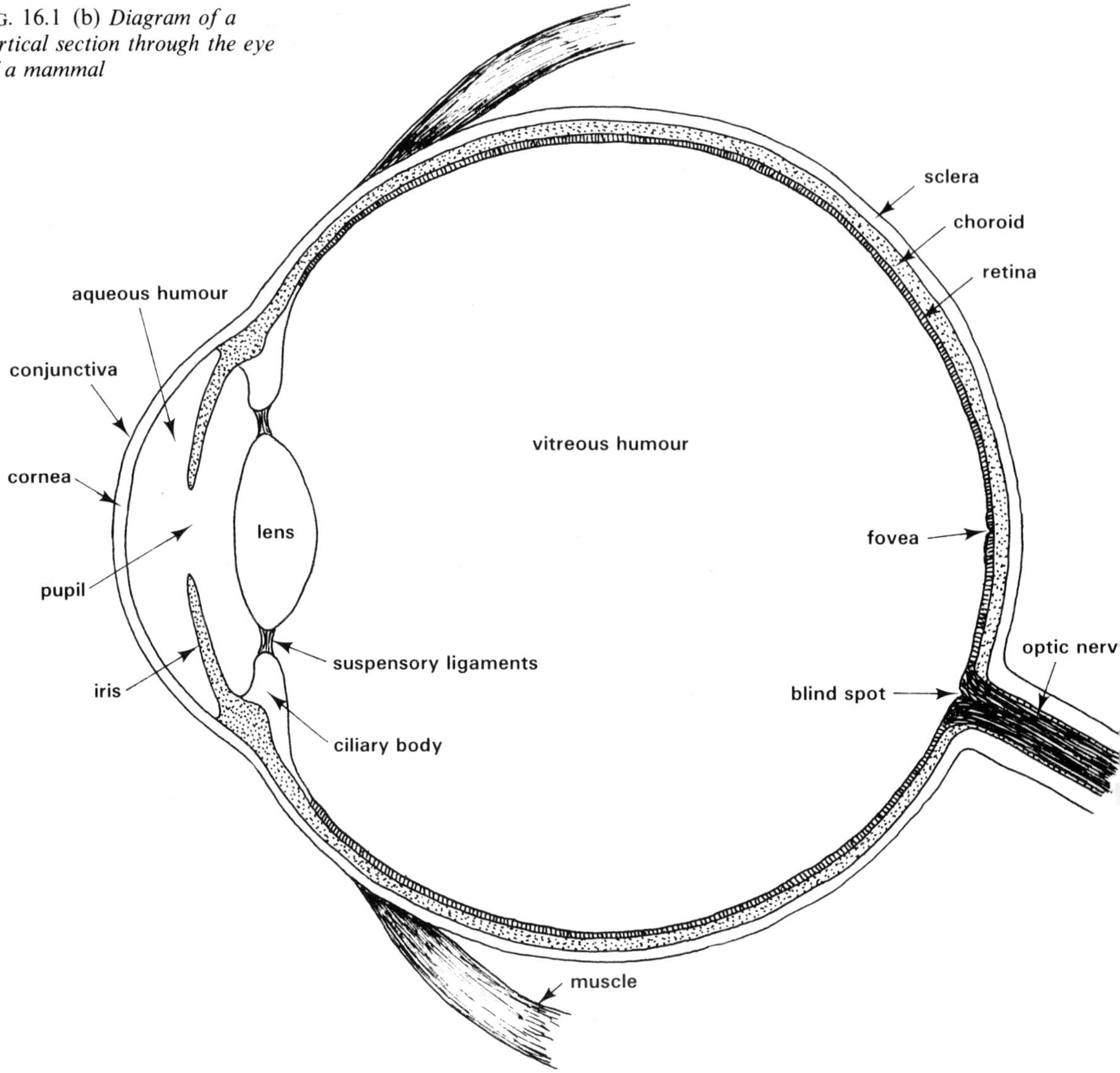

FIG. 16.2 *Angiogram showing the choroid blood vessels (injected with fluorescein) of the human eye*

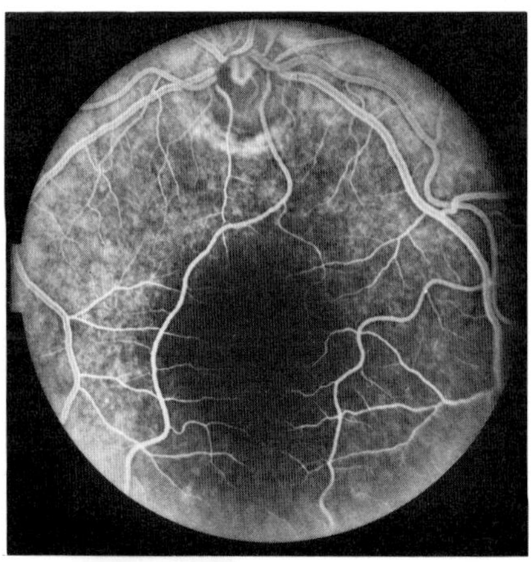

where there is a transparent area called the **cornea**. The cornea allows light into the eye. Tears secreted by the **lachrymal glands** lubricate the exposed surface of the eye, including the **conjuctiva** covering the cornea. The watery secretion helps to prevent abrasion of the eye's surface by dust particles and helps combat infection of the eye. Periodic closure of the eyelids, blinking, clears away debris.

Inside the sclera is thc choroid layer which contains numerous blood vessels (Fig. 16.2). At the front of the eye the choroid layer is modified as the **iris** containing pigments which give the eye its colour. The iris also contains radial bands of smooth muscle. Contraction of the radial muscles causes dilation of an aperture called the **pupil**, in the centre of the iris. Constriction of the pupil occurs when the radial muscles of the iris relax. Variation in pupil size is controlled by autonomic reflexes and is usually a response to change in the intensity of light entering the eye. In bright light the pupil constricts and prevents excessive illumination of the interior of the eye. In dim light the pupil dilates allowing the maximum amount of light to reach the photoreceptor cells.

The photoreceptors are located in the retina situated immediately inside the choroid layer. Fibres of sensory neurons lead from the retina at the back of the eye as the **optic nerve**. The optic nerve transmits impulses generated in the retina to the brain. The retina develops in the embryo as an outgrowth of the brain, and can be regarded as a modified part of the central nervous system.

Suspended in the fluid inside the eye and just behind the pupil is a biconvex, crystalline **lens**. The lens is held in position by **suspensory ligaments** attached to a ring of smooth muscle called the **ciliary body**.

16.1.2 Focusing

Light rays entering the eye are bent or **refracted**. Refraction occurs at three surfaces of the eye before the light reaches the retina. The first of the refracting surfaces is the cornea, then the front surface of the lens and finally the rear surface of the lens (Fig. 16.3).

Between the cornea and the lens is a colourless, watery fluid called **aqueous humour**. At the back of the eye between the lens and the retina is another fluid called **vitreous humour**. Vitreous humour is also clear and is made of a gelatinous mucoprotein. The humours are transparent so that transmission of light through the cavities of the eye to the retina is not normally impeded.

FIG. 16.3 *The three refracting surfaces in the mammalian eye*

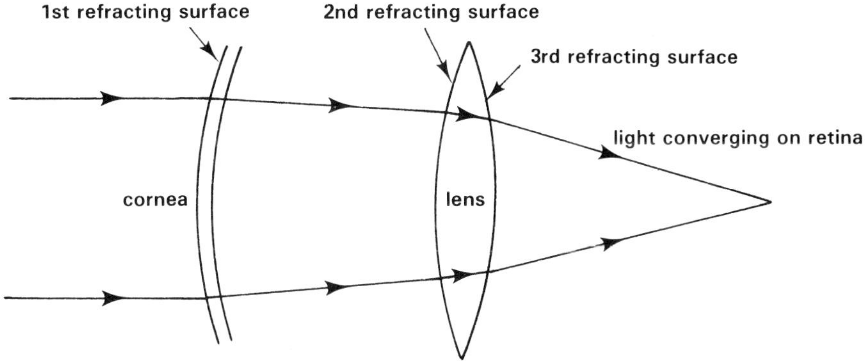

In the normal eye light rays are refracted sufficiently to be brought to a point on the retina. In this way the object viewed is brought into focus and a clear image is formed (Fig. 16.4). The **image** is **inverted** by the lens.

FIG. 16.4 (a) *Focusing of a light from a point source by the eye's lens. The cornea has been omitted for clarity*

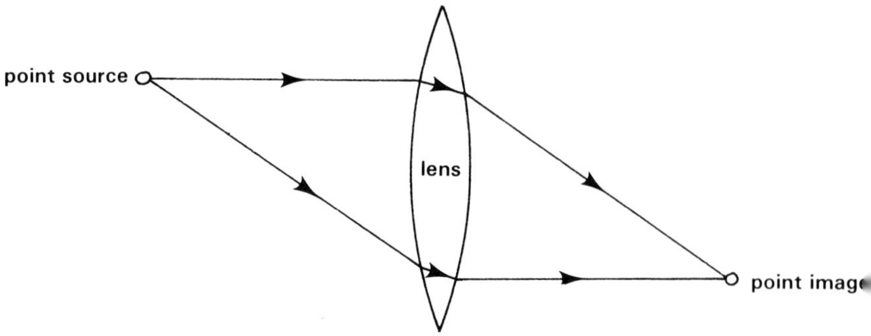

FIG. 16.4 (b) *Light from all points on an object are focused in such a way that the image on the retina is inverted. For clarity, only two light rays are shown here*

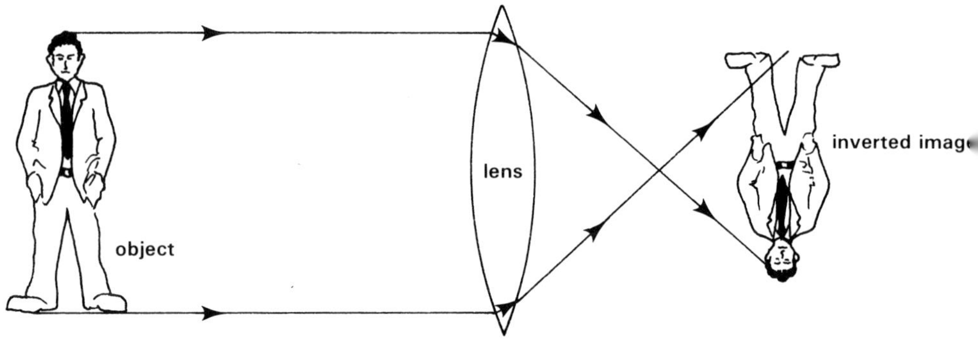

However, objects are seen the right way up because of the way in which the brain interprets images. Experiments have been performed in which human volunteers wore special spectacles, the lenses of which produced upright images on the retina. For a while the subjects in the experiment were confronted with an upside down world. However, after a few days they became used to the situation and their perception became adjusted so that once more they perceived things the right way up. When the spectacles were removed they again experienced a period of seeing things upside down before normal perception returned. Thus the mechanism of image interpretation, situated in the brain's cerebral cortex, is somewhat flexible.

FIG. 16.5 *Focusing (accommodation)*

(a) *Light from a distant object is focused on the retina by a flattened lens*

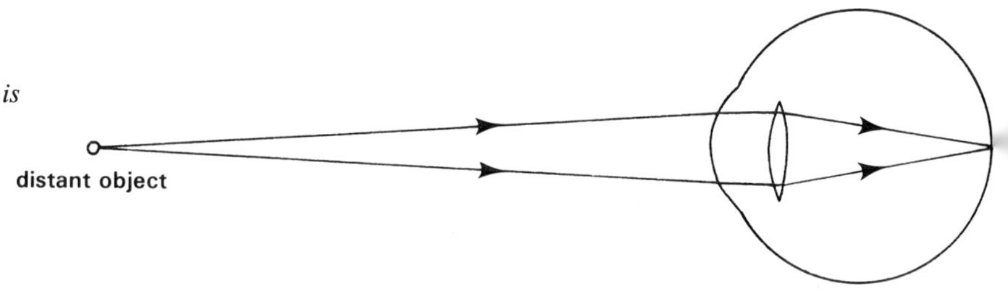

(b) *Light from a near object is focused on the retina by a near-spherical lens*

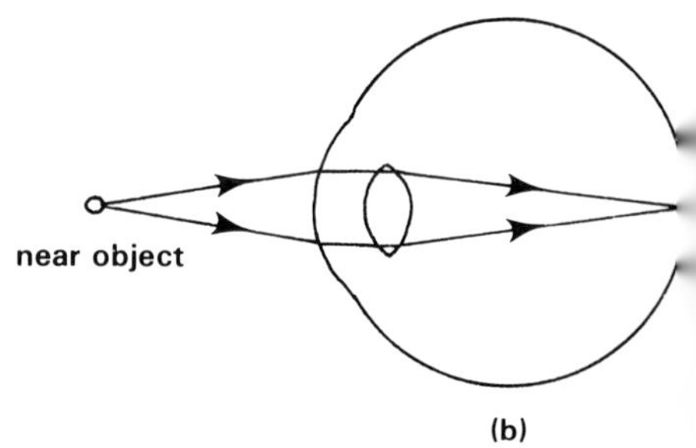

Light rays from an object near the eye strike the cornea and lens at an acute angle depending on the object's size. If the same object is moved further away from the eye the angle is less acute. Consequently the degree of refraction necessary to **focus** light rays on the retina is greater for close objects than for distant objects. Changes in the degree of refraction of light are achieved by altering the curvature of the lens' surfaces (Fig. 16.5). The ciliary body contains muscles the contraction or relaxation of which alters the tension of the suspensory ligaments which hold the lens in place. It is the tension of the ligaments applied to the lens which determines the shape of the lens. When the tension is increased the lens is pulled into a flattened shape suitable for focusing distant objects. When the tension is decreased, the lens becomes a more spherical shape suitable for focusing near objects.

16.1.3 Defects of the eye

A number of abnormalities of the eye's focusing mechanism exists in man and other mammals. The commonest are **myopia (short-sightedness)**, **hypermetropia (long-sightedness)**, and **astigmatism**, which is a mixture of the other two defects.

1. MYOPIA

Myopia results when the lens' curvature is too great (Fig. 16.6(a)). Light rays entering the eye are refracted more than is necessary. Consequently light is focused in front of the retina. By the time the light stimulates the retina it has diverged from the focal point of the lens. The image perceived is thus blurred. The condition is called short-sightedness because objects near the eye are less out of focus than those further away. This is because the light rays from near objects require greater refraction to be focused on the retina than rays from distant objects. Since the lens in a myopic eye refracts light excessively, distant objects appear more blurred than near ones. Myopia can be corrected by placing a **concave lens** in front of the eye. The surface of the concave lens refracts light rays in such a way that the rays diverge slightly from their original path. The lens of the myopic eye now refracts the diverged light rays into focus on the retina (Fig. 16.6(b)).

FIG. 16.6 *Myopia*

(a) *Light is focused on a point in front of the retina*

(b) *Light is focused on the retina by placing a concave lens in front of the eye*

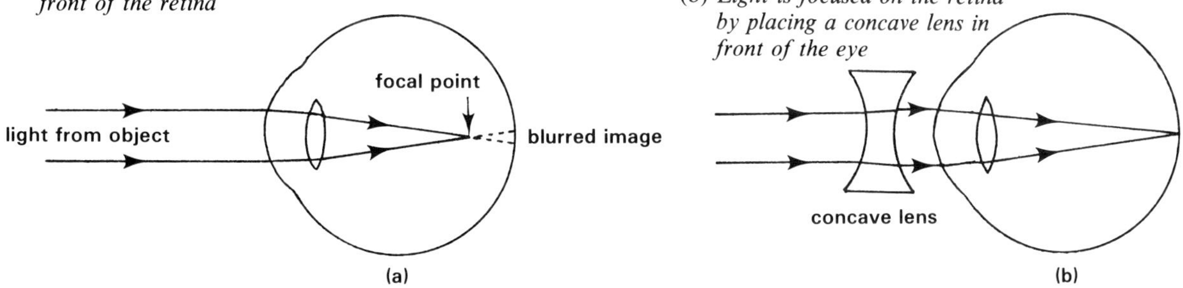

2. HYPERMETROPIA

Hypermetropia results when the curvature of the eye's lens is not great enough. Light rays are not refracted enough and are thus focused behind the retina (Fig. 16.7(a)). The condition is called long-sightedness because distant objects are less out of focus than near ones. This happens because light rays from distant objects require less refraction than rays from near objects. Correction of hypermetropia requires placing a lens in front of the eye. This time the lens is **convex**. The lens converges light rays before they enter the eye so that the eye's lens focuses the light correctly on the retina (Fig. 16.7(b)).

FIG. 16.7 *Hypermetropia*

(a) *Light is focused at a point behind the retina*

(b) *Light is focused on the retina by placing a convex lens in front of the eye*

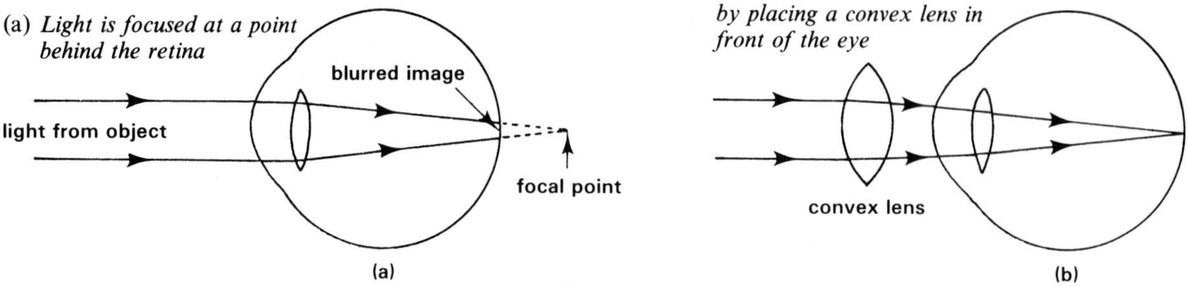

3. ASTIGMATISM

Astigmatism occurs if either the cornea or lens is distorted. One part of the focusing mechanism then refracts light rays too much, another not enough. Usually most of the image perceived is out of focus. Light rays from parts of the object are focused in front of the retina, as in myopia. Rays from other parts are focused behind the retina, as in hypermetropia. Astigmatism can be corrected by placing a lens in front of the eye. The curvature of this lens varies from one part to another to compensate for the eye's deficiencies.

The eye has often been compared with a camera. Look at Figures 16.1 and 16.8 and assess how valid the comparison is.

FIG. 16.8 *The main components of a simple camera*

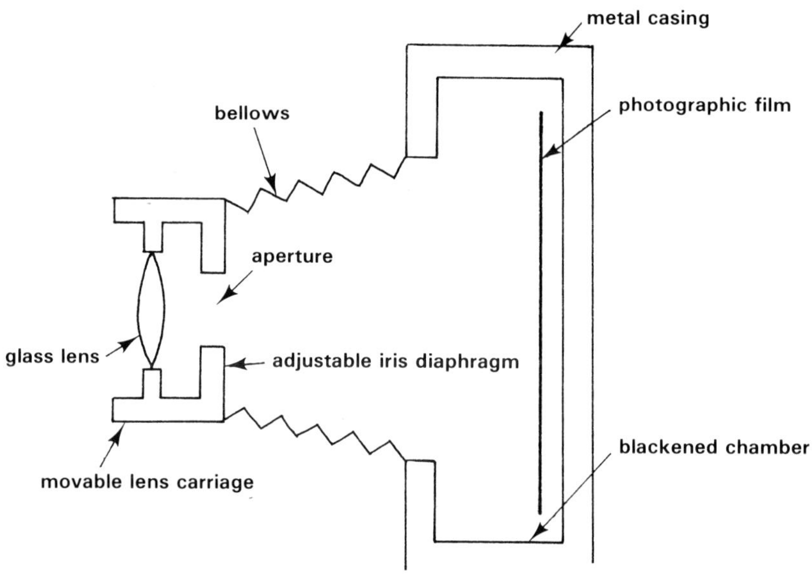

16.1.4 Photoreception

The transmission of nerve impulses to the brain in response to light is the function of the optic nerves and the **photoreceptors** in the retina. In human eyes and those of some other mammals there are two types of photoreceptors called **rods** and **cones**.

1. RODS AND CONES

Rods are sensitive to different intensities of light. Most mammals have only rods. **Cones** are sensitive to different wavelengths of light and enable some mammals to see things in colour. The assumption that an angry bull will charge a red object is somewhat misplaced, since the retina of a bull's eye has no cones. The bull is just as likely to charge an object of some other colour if it is annoyed.

2. DISTRIBUTION OF RODS AND CONES

The arrangement of photoreceptors in the mammalian retina is such that light has to travel through several layers of neurons which are not sensitive to light before reaching the rods and cones. The retina is **inverted** (Fig. 16.9).

FIG. 16.9 *The main cellular components of the retina*

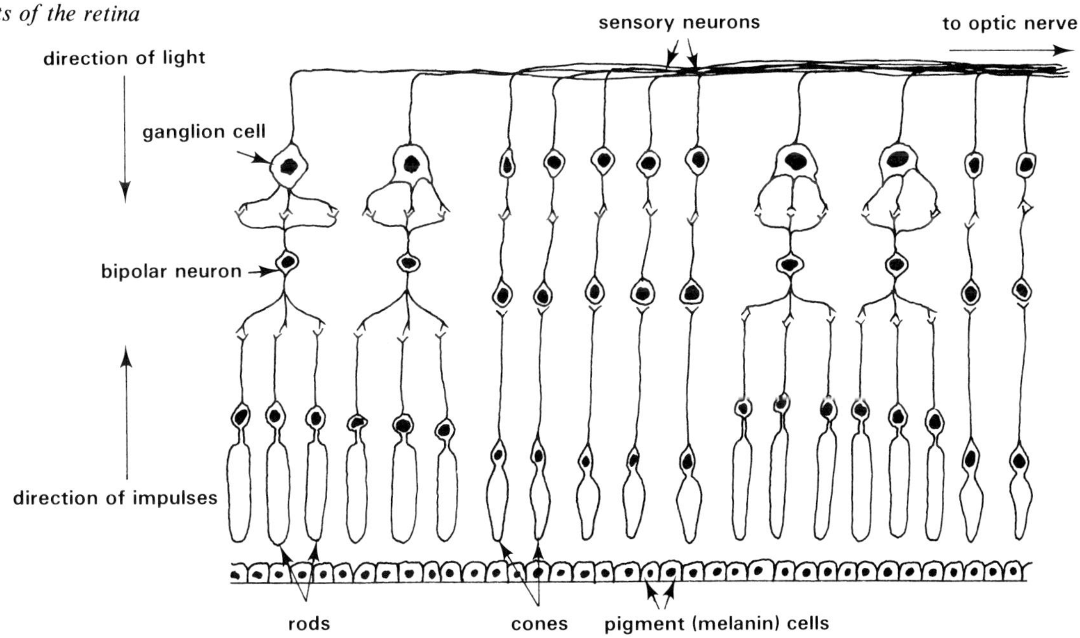

Beneath the photoreceptors is a layer of cells containing the black pigment melanin. Melanin is not sensitive to light but absorbs light rays which would otherwise pass through the retina. In this way the formation of hazy images caused by reflection of light to other parts of the retina is prevented. Some mammals have a reflective layer called the **tapetum** in the retina. The reflective 'cat's eyes' along the centre of roads create a similar effect to the reflective tapetum of real cat's eyes. A tapetum is common in nocturnal mammals and enables the maximum use of what little light is available at night.

Many synapses link the photoreceptors with sensory neurons. Impulses generated by the photoreceptors are first transmitted to a small region where the neurons project through the retina into the optic nerve. This region is called the **blind spot**, since no photoreceptors are located there (Fig. 16.1). It is possible to demonstrate that there are blind spots in your eyes by referring to the circle and cross illustrated below. Close your right eye and hold the page about 60 cm away from your open left eye. Keeping your left eye focused on the circle, the cross should be visible but slightly less clear. Now move the page slowly towards you and notice that at a distance of about 30 cm from your left eye the cross disappears. At this point light from the cross falls on the blind spot of your left eye. If you now move the page even nearer to your left eye the cross should reappear.

In this simple demonstration the circle appears clearer than anything around it in the field of vision. The reason for this is that when you direct your eye at the circle the light from it is focused on to a region of the retina called the **fovea**. Only cones are found in the foveas of the eyes of animals which have colour vision. Each cone forms a synapse with very few, sometimes only one, sensory neurons. Consequently the signals sent to the brain from each cone come from a small area of the retina on which a small part of the image is focused. The cones can thus discriminate between two points of the image which are close to one another. For this reason cones are said to have high **visual acuity**. On the other hand, many rods synapse with each sensory neuron. The signals transmitted to the brain from the rods therefore come from a relatively large area of the image (Fig. 16.10). The rods are distributed throughout the retina but are absent from the fovea. The part of the image focused on the fovea therefore appears much clearer than the rest of the image.

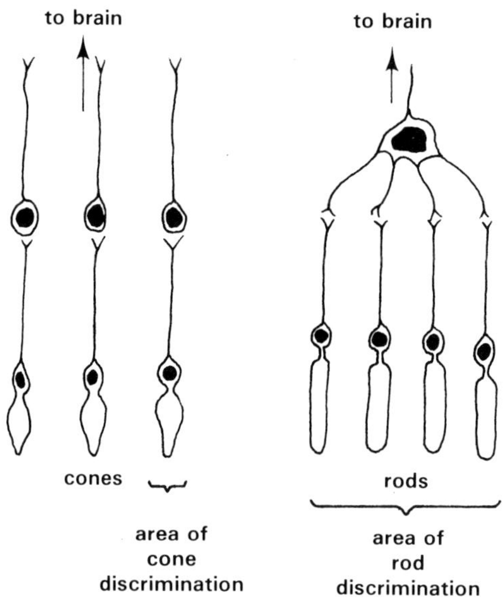

FIG. 16.10 *Cones synapse with single sensory neurons, whereas many rods synapse with a single sensory neuron. Cones are therefore important in the discrimination of close points in the image*

3. PHOTOSENSITIVE PIGMENTS

The functioning of rods and cones depends on **photosensitive pigments**. Electron microscopy has revealed the intricate subcellular structure of rods (Fig. 16.11). The outer segments of rods contain a great number of membranous, disc-like lamellae. The lamellae contain a photosensitive pigment called **rhodopsin**. Cones contain a pigment called **iodopsin**.

(i) RHODOPSIN consists of a protein called **opsin** attached to **retinal**, a derivative of vitamin A (Chapter 14). When exposed to light rhodopsin is split into opsin and retinal. The breakdown of rhodopsin produces a **generator potential** which is transmitted from the rod as an action potential to a sensory neuron. Rhodopsin, split in this way, has to be resynthesised to maintain the rod's ability to respond to light.

Resynthesis of rhodopsin requires energy and the rods have many mitochondria which make ATP for this purpose. However, rhodopsin resynthesis takes time. It is a common experience to suffer a brief period of poor vision after going from a well-lit room into darkness. When exposed to bright light rhodopsin is broken down rapidly and the reserve of rhodopsin in the rods is low. The eyes are **light-adapted**. If the retina is then exposed to dim light the rods show little response so vision is poor. The several minutes getting used to the dark is the time taken for enough rhodopsin to be resynthesised. When the retina is sufficiently sensitive for us to see in dim light the eyes are **dark-adapted**.

A brief period of poor vision is also experienced when you go from a very dark to a brightly lit room. When dark-adapted, the retina can work in dim light. Exposure of a dark-adapted retina to bright light overloads the photoreception mechanism. Light rays, even from the darker areas of an object in view, stimulate the rods which are now rich in rhodopsin. The eyes are light-adapted when excess rhodopsin is broken down and the retina once more adjusts to working in bright light. Prolonged exposure to very intense light, however, can reduce sensitivity of the retina too much. The rate of rhodopsin resynthesis may then be unable to keep pace with its breakdown. **Snow blindness** is caused by such an effect.

FIG. 16.11 (a) *Electronmicrograph of parts of several rod cells from the retina of a cat, ×5800*

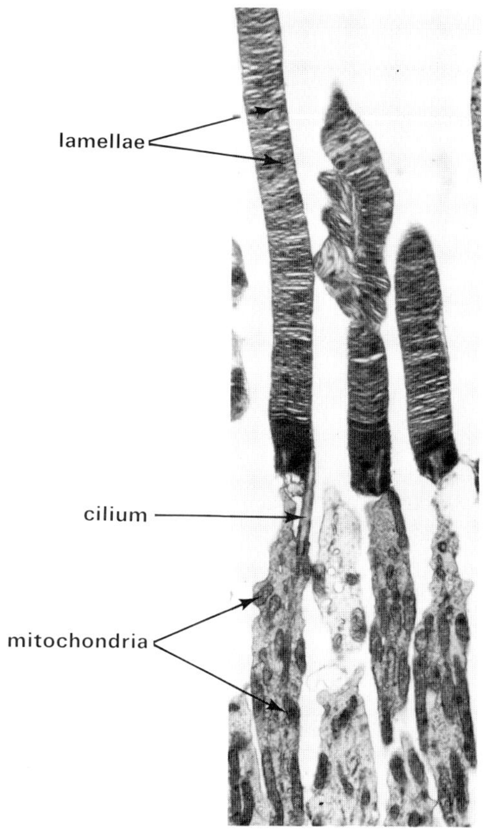

FIG. 16.11 (b) *Structure of a rod cell, based on electronmicrographs*

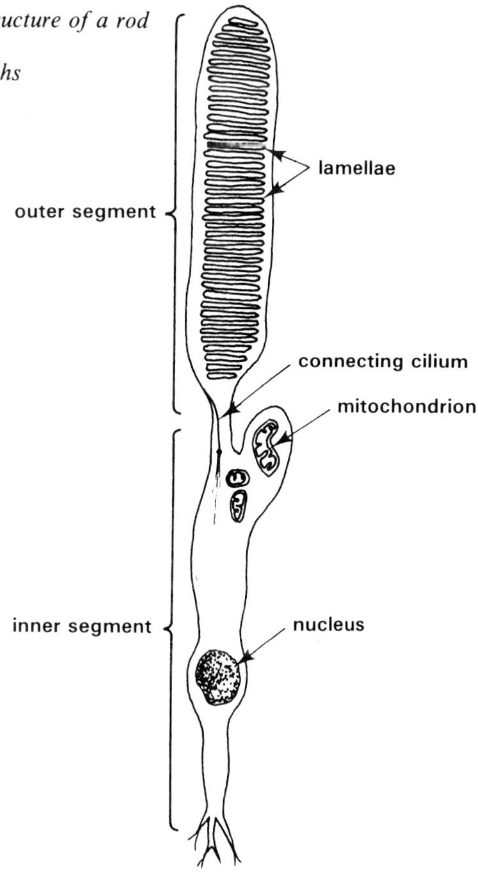

(ii) IODOPSIN is less sensitive to changes in light intensity than rhodopsin, so the cones are of little value in helping us to see in dim light. A popular theory of colour vision suggests that there are three variants of iodopsin each of which is sensitive to light of the primary colours, red, blue and green (Fig. 16.12(a)). For this reason the theory is called the **trichromatic theory** of colour vision. Each type of iodopsin is probably located in different cones. Light with a wavelength between those of the primary colours stimulates combinations of cones. Yellow light for instance, simultaneously stimulates cones which are sensitive to red and green light. The action potentials generated in the sensory neurons in response to generator potentials in the cones are interpreted by the brain as the appropriate intermediate colour, yellow in this case (Fig. 16.12(b)).

Deficiency of one or more of the three primary colour cones results in **colour blindness**. A glance at Figure 16.12(a) shows that there is some overlap in colour sensitivity between the three types of cones. For example, a green cone is sensitive to red light but its sensitivity to red is far less than that of a red cone. Absence of red cones therefore, means that it is still possible to perceive green, yellow, orange and red. However, the brain cannot distinguish satisfactorily between these colours because there are no impulses from red cones with which to contrast impulses from green cones. A similar effect occurs when green cones are absent. The condition is called **red-green colour blindness**. Very rarely, blue cones are absent causing **blue weakness**. The exact mechanism of colour vision is not known. Many people challenge the trichromatic theory and several alternative theories have been proposed in recent years.

FIG. 16.12 (a) *Absorption spectra showing the wavelengths (colours) of light absorbed most by the iodopsin in the three main types of cones* (after Marks, Dobelle, MacNichol, Brown and Wald)

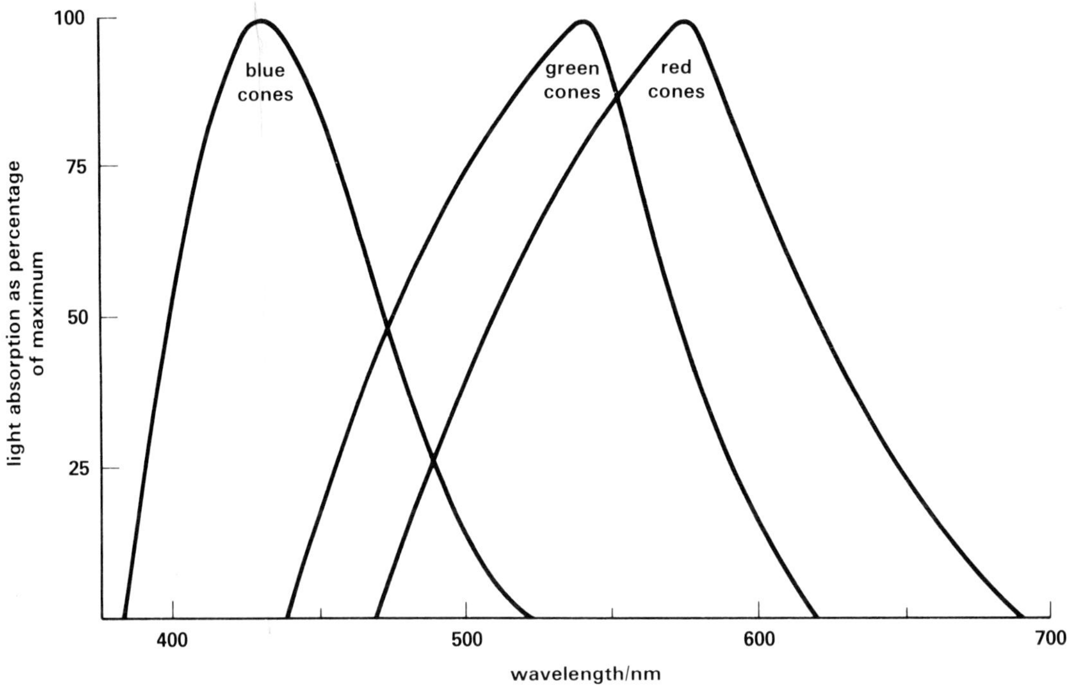

FIG. 16.12 (b) *Different colours are perceived in the brain from the sensory information received from the cones. Signals from combination of different cones produce the sensation of intermediate colours based on red, green and blue detected by the three primary cones*

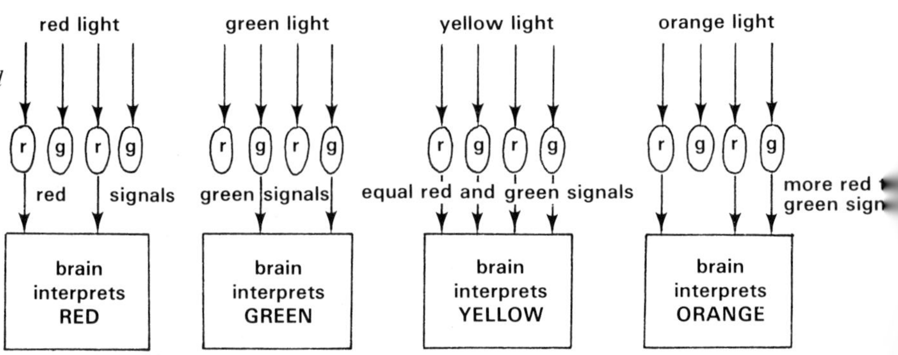

16.2 The mammalian ear

The ability to generate sounds, as well as receive and interpret them, is valuable as a means of communication between mammals. Such a form of communication is particularly well developed in human language. Sound waves trigger off the transmission of sensory nerve impulses from the ear to the cerebral cortex of the brain.

The mammalian ear also performs another, equally important function. It transmits to the brain information about the body's relative position in space.

16.2.1 Structure of the ear

The mammalian ear is divided into three main regions, the **outer ear**, **middle ear** and **inner ear** (Fig. 16.13). The outer ear channels sound waves from the surrounding air into the middle ear where the energy of sound waves is converted to mechanical vibrations. In the inner ear nerve impulses are generated in response to vibrations received from the middle ear and to changes in position of the head.

FIG. 16.13 *Structure of the human ear*

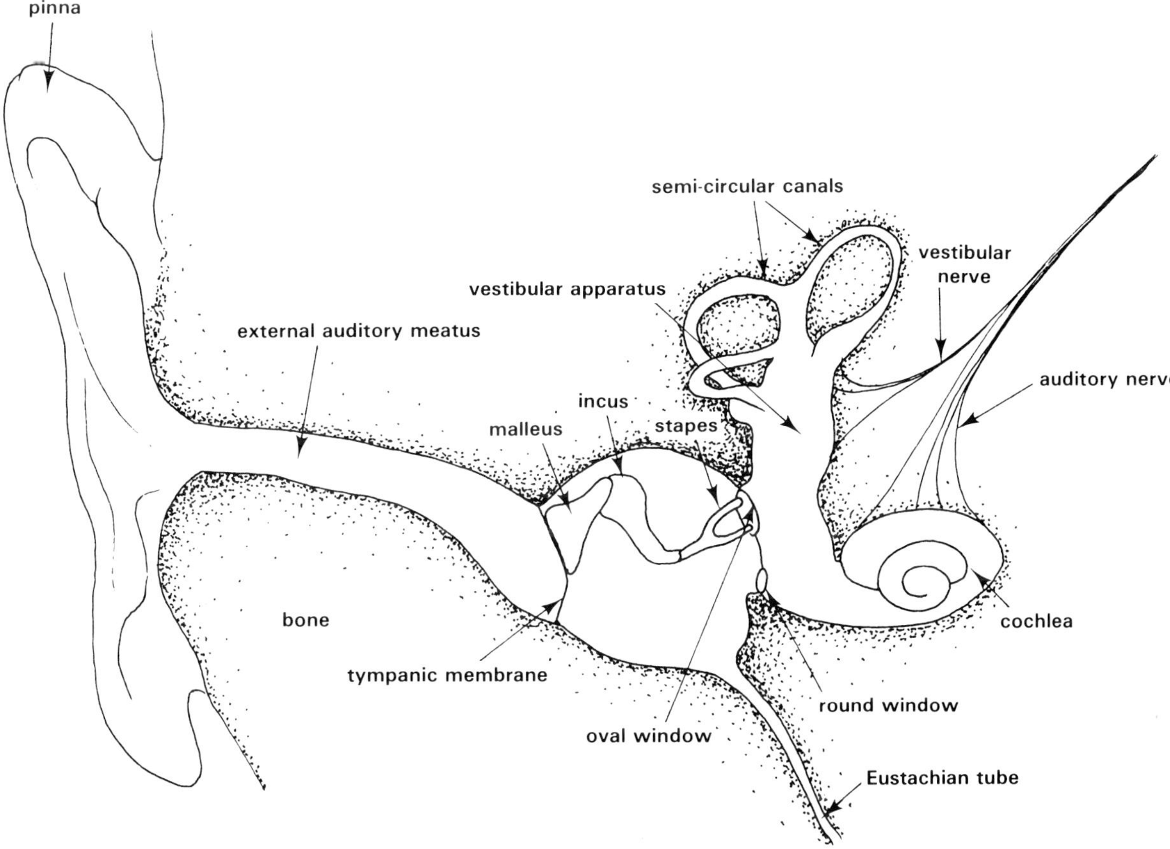

16.2.2 Hearing

Sound waves enter the ear along a short tube called the **external auditory meatus**. The external flap of skin, the **pinna**, helps in directing sound waves from the environment into the meatus. Some mammals have large and mobile pinnae which enable them to locate the source of sound without moving the head. At the inner end of the external auditory meatus is an elastic membrane called the **tympanic membrane** or eardrum.

Bridging the middle ear are three small bones called **ossicles** held in place by muscles and tendons. The ossicles are the **malleus**, **incus** and **stapes**. Sound waves entering the ear vibrate the tympanic membrane which in turn vibrates the ossicles. The innermost ossicle, the stapes, is connected to another membrane called the **oval window** which is part of the inner ear. The membrane of the oval window is less than five per cent of the area of the tympanic membrane. Consequently vibrations of the tympanic membrane are amplified about 20 times in the oval window. Amplification makes it easier for vibrations to pass through the dense liquid in the inner ear.

An air-filled canal, called the **Eustachian tube**, connects the middle ear with the pharynx. The air pressure in the external air and in the middle ear is normally the same. Should there be a sudden large increase in external air pressure there is a possibility that the eardrum will burst. However, this danger is usually prevented when air taken in from outside enters the Eustachian tube during swallowing. In this way the air pressure on either side of the eardrum is equalised.

The oval window transmits the vibration of the ossicles into a coiled, fluid-filled tube called the **cochlea** (Fig. 16.14). The cochlea contains three canals separated from each other by two flexible longitudinal membranes. The upper **vestibular canal** is connected to the oval window. Between the vestibular canal and the **median canal** is **Reissner's membrane**. The **basilar membrane** separates the median canal from the lower **tympanic canal**.

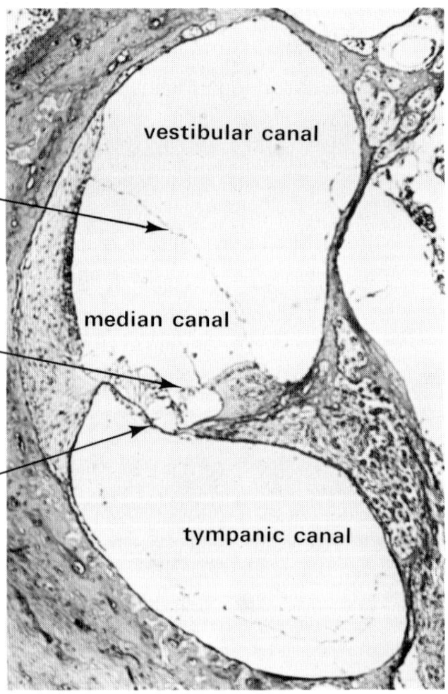

FIG. 16.14 (a) *Photomicrograph of a transverse section of cochlea from a guinea-pig, ×70*

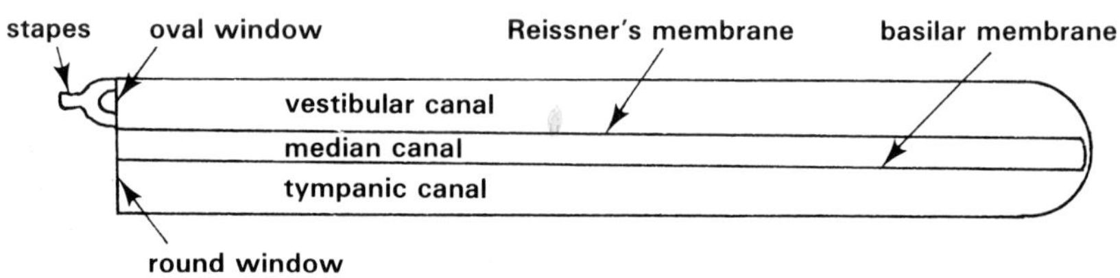

FIG. 16.14 (b) *Diagram of the cochlea 'straightened out' to show the three canals and their separating membranes*

FIG. 16.14 (c) *Diagram of the cochlea in transverse section.* Compare with Fig. 16.14 (a)

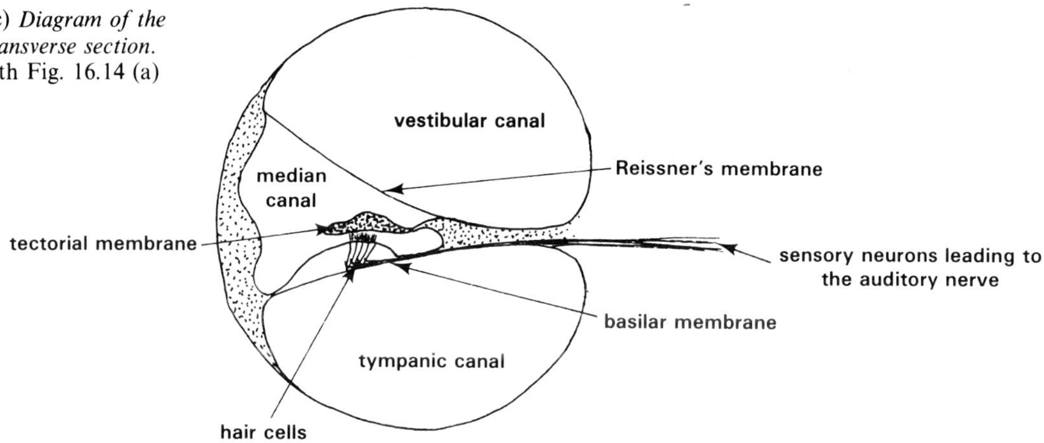

Vibrations of the oval window generate pressure waves in the fluid filling the vestibular canal. The waves cause Reissner's membrane to vibrate which in turn causes pressure waves to pass through the fluid in the median canal. The pressure waves in the median canal eventually bring about vibration of the basilar membrane. The tympanic canal is connected to a circular membrane called the **round window** just beneath the oval window. Pressure waves in the fluid inside the tympanic canal cause vibration of the round window. This arrangement causes the basilar membrane to vibrate in response to vibrations transmitted to the cochlea by the ossicles of the middle ear (Fig. 16.15).

The sensory region of the cochlea is the **organ of Corti** in the median canal (Fig. 16.14(c)). The organ contains many hair cells which are rooted in the basilar membrane. Short sensory hairs project from the free ends of these cells and touch the **tectorial membrane**. Vibrations of the basilar membrane cause the hair cells to move towards the tectorial membrane, deflecting the sensory hairs. Consequently nerve impulses are generated in sensory neurons which synapse with the hair cells. The impulses are transmitted to the brain along the auditory nerve.

FIG. 16.15 *Vibrations of the stapes move the oval window back and forth. The oscillations of the oval window generate pressure waves in the cochlear fluids and vibrations in the cochlear membranes. Note the effects of the vibrations on the round window,* (a) *when the oval window is 'pushed' and* (b) *when the oval window is 'pulled'*

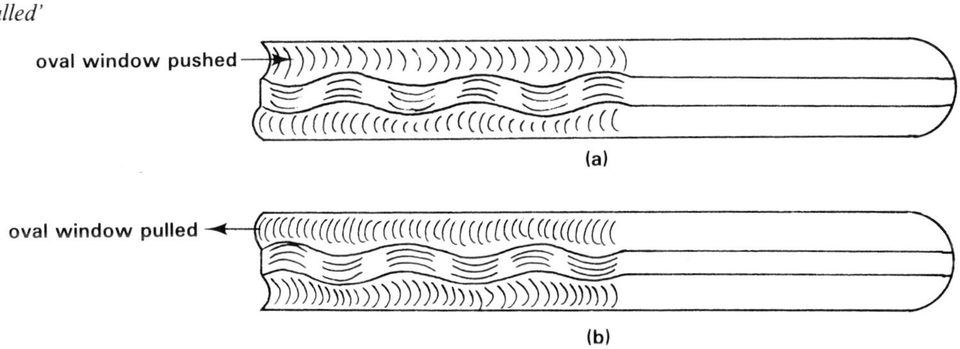

Vibrations of the basilar membrane are crucial to the conversion of sound into sensory nerve impulses. The basilar membrane is about 2·5 times wider at the apex of the cochlea than it is at its base, between the oval and round windows. Sound waves of short wavelength which have a relatively high frequency vibrate just a short portion of the basilar membrane. Only the hair cells near the oval window are thus stimulated. The

FIG. 16.16 *Different sound frequencies resonate the basilar membrane at different points along the cochlea. The resonance characteristics of the basilar membrane set the limit on the range of audible frequencies* (after Guyton)

impulses arriving at the brain are interpreted as sounds of a high pitch. A greater length of the basilar membrane is vibrated by sound waves of long wavelength. Hair cells further along the membrane now generate impulses in the auditory nerve. The brain interprets these impulses as sounds of a low pitch. Sounds of intermediate wavelength stimulate the middle part of the basilar membrane (Fig. 16.16).

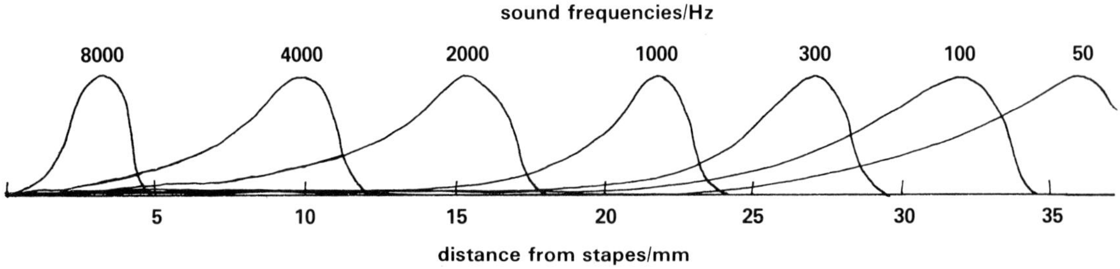

The intensity of sound is discerned according to the intensity with which appropriate sections of the basilar membrane are vibrated. Weak sounds generate fewer nerve impulses than loud sounds. The interpretation of sounds takes place in the cerebral cortex of the brain (Chapter 15).

16.2.3 Balance

Just above the cochlea and connected to it by a short tube is the **vestibular apparatus** (Fig. 16.17). The vestibular apparatus consists of two lymph-filled sacs called the **saccule** and the **utricle**. Projecting from the top of the utricle are three **semicircular canals**, also containing lymph.

FIG. 16.17 *The vestibular apparatus of the human ear*

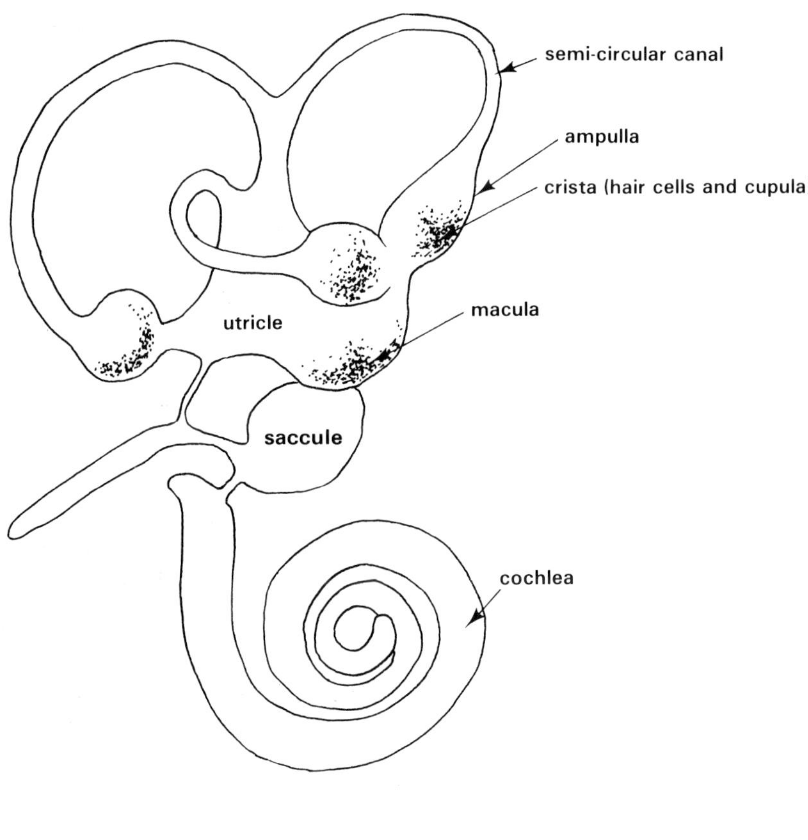

The saccule and utricle contain receptors called **maculae** which are sensitive to gravity. Small hairs project from the receptor cells into the lymph. The hairs are attached to calcium carbonate granules called **otoliths** (Fig. 16.18). Gravity causes the otoliths to distort the sensory hairs in a direction dictated by the position of the head. In response to the distortion, nerve impulses pass along the vestibular nerve to the brain. If the head is moved to a different position the otoliths distort the sensory hairs in a different direction. Information about the head's new position is interpreted in the brain.

FIG. 16.18 (a) *Structure of the macula from the utricle*

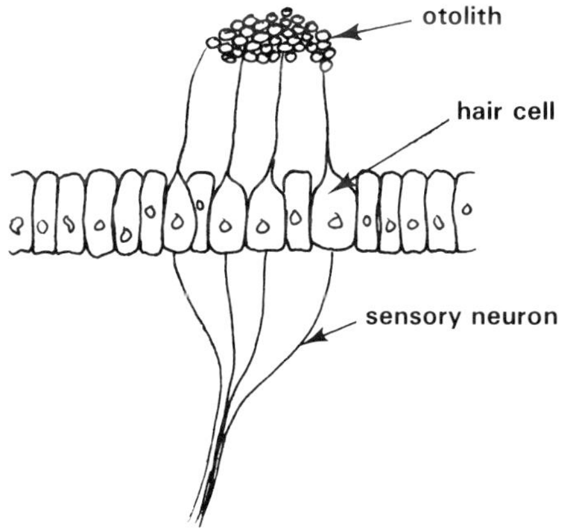

FIG. 16.18 (b) *The otolith deflects the sensory 'hairs' in a direction dictated by gravity and the position of the head in relation to the earth*

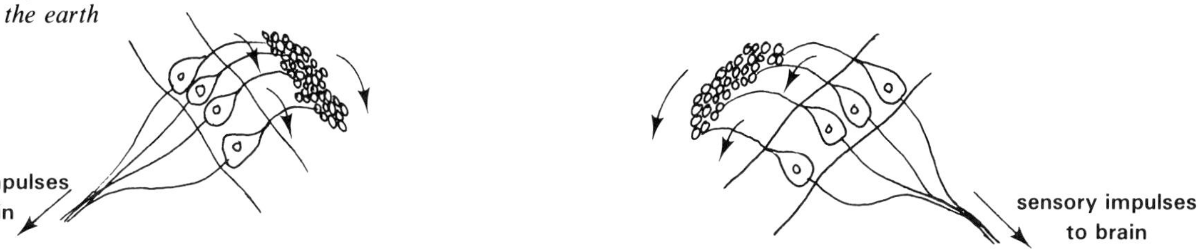

The semicircular canals provide information about head movements rather than the position of the head when it is stationary. The ends of the canals are enlarged to form an **ampulla**. Each ampulla contains a receptor, consisting of hair cells similar to those of the maculae. The ampullary hairs, however, project into a gelatinous mass called a **cupula** which is suspended in the lymph inside the ampulla (Fig. 16.19(a)).

Any movement of the head of course moves the semicircular canals in the same direction. The lymph inside the canals, however, lags behind and pushes the cupulae in the opposite direction (Fig. 16.19(b)). As a result, the hairs projecting into the cupulae are bent and nerve impulses are sent to the brain along the vestibular nerve. There are three semicircular canals and each is arranged at a right angle to the others. Consequently, at least one cupula is stimulated by lymph movements whatever direction the head is moved.

Information about the orientation and movement of the head is vital, especially when the whole body is moved. Visual information from the eyes also contributes to the body's awareness of spatial position. The information is used by the brain to co-ordinate movement and posture of the body.

16.2.4 Defects of the ear

The most common defects of the ear lead to hearing loss or **deafness**. Deafness can be caused by inability of the outer and middle ear to conduct vibrations to the cochlea. **Conductive deafness** is of this sort. One of the commonest causes of conductive deafness in man is blockage of the external auditory meatus with wax. Little is known of the function of wax which is secreted from the **ceruminous glands** in the skin inside the meatus. In some people the wax accumulates in the meatus and hardens, sometimes pressing against the eardrum. Normal hearing is usually restored after the hardened wax is removed with a special syringe.

FIG. 16.19 (a) *Structure of the receptors in the ampullae of the semi-circular canal*

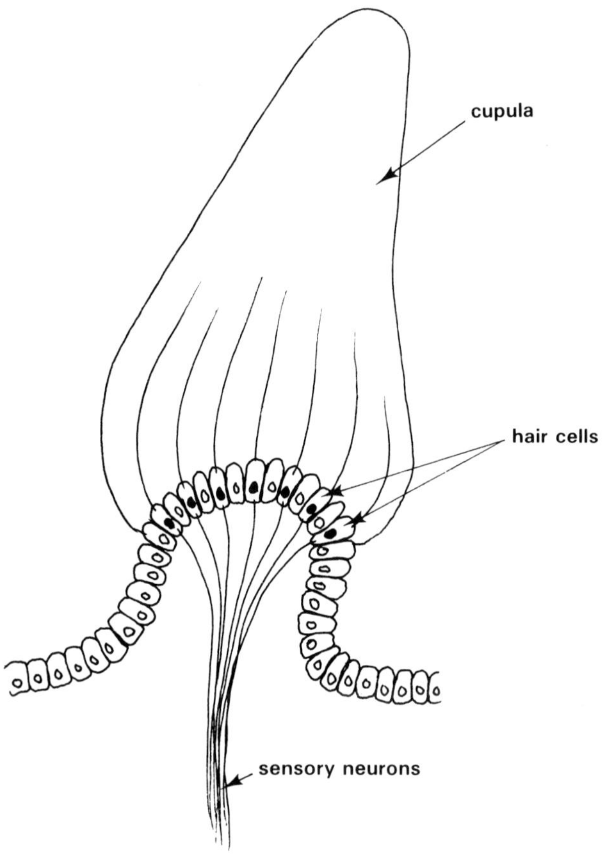

FIG. 16.19 (b) *Movements of the fluid inside the semi-circular canals, caused by movements of the head, displace the gelatinous cupula and sensory 'hairs'*

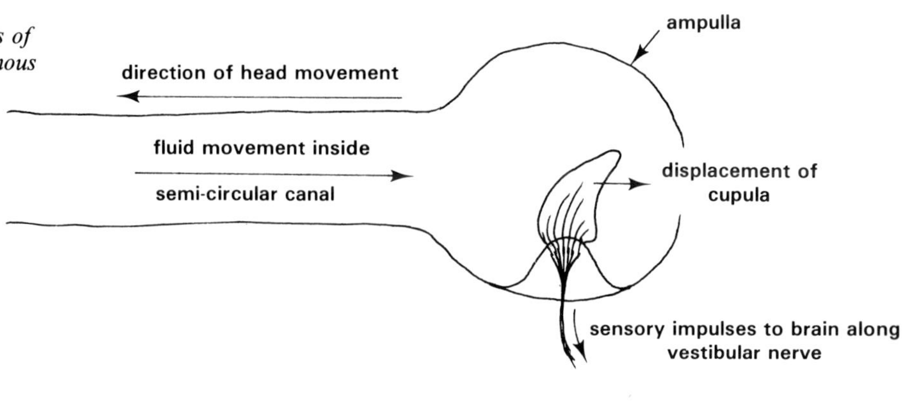

FIG. 16.20 *A 'behind-the-ear' hearing aid* (from DHSS booklet *General Guidance for Hearing Aid Users*)

Another cause of conductive deafness is a perforated eardrum. Perforation can be caused by infection in the middle ear or by mechanical injury resulting from a nearby explosion or a sudden blow to the head. Injury to the head can also cause the ossicles of the middle ear to become disconnected from one another thus breaking the conductive path to the cochlea. Patients with a conductive defect which does not respond fully to treatment can be helped with a hearing aid. This is a device which amplifies sound waves before they enter the inner ear (Fig. 16.20).

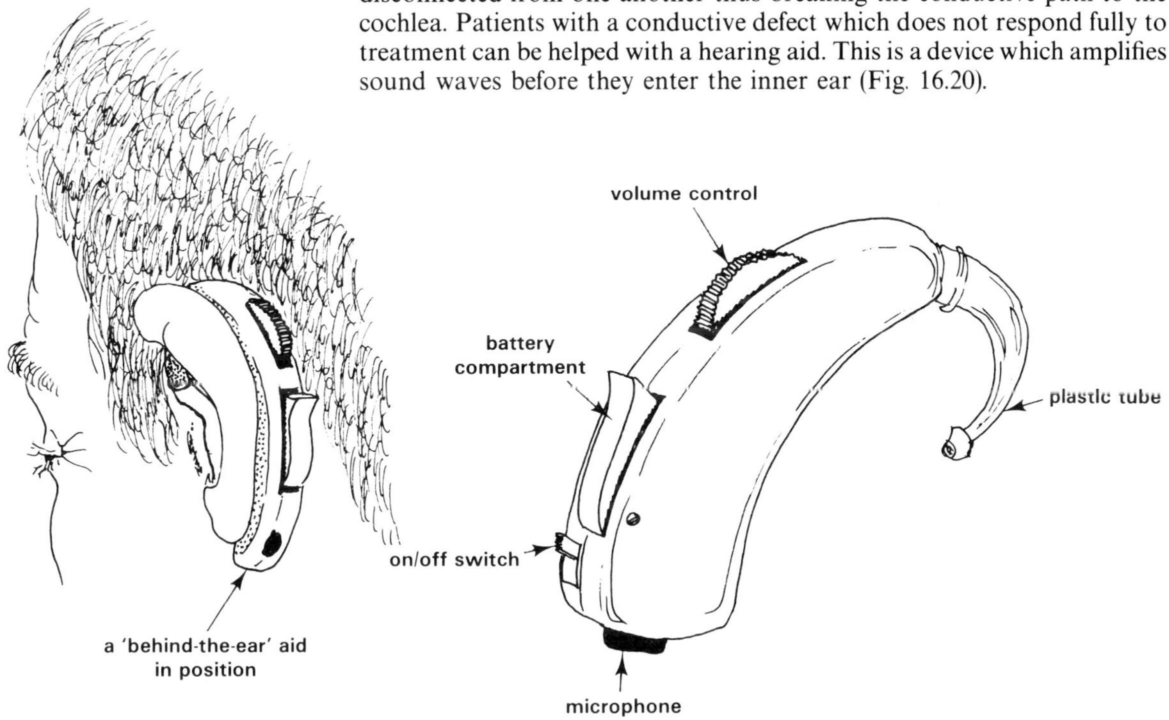

Malfunction of the cochlea and auditory nerve can be the cause of deafness even though vibrations are conducted perfectly into the inner ear. Such deafness is called **sensorineural (perceptive) deafness**. Sensorineural deafness can be inherited though it is often acquired. Acquired forms of the condition can result from infection, head injury, blast from explosions or exposure to excessive noise. Much concern has been expressed in recent years about the possible harmful effects on hearing of the very high noise levels in discotheques, at airports and where noisy machinery is used. So serious is the problem that people employed in extremely noisy places are encouraged to wear ear muffs to protect their hearing from permanent damage.

Complex though sense organs such as the eye and ear are, it is the interpretation of sensory information which ultimately limits their use. Information processing occurs in the brain by mechanisms which are, as yet, poorly understood.

Chapter 17

Thermoregulation in mammals

One of the many aspects of homeostasis is the regulation of body temperature. It is a characteristic feature of birds and mammals. These animals are called **endotherms**. They maintain a relatively high and constant body temperature which enables them to lead active lives even when the temperature of their surroundings is low. All other animals are called **ectotherms**. Their body temperature varies with temperature fluctuation of the environment (Fig. 17.1). Because the metabolic rate slows down when the body temperature is low, ectotherms are sluggish in cold weather. In these conditions they are less likely to succeed in obtaining food and avoiding predators (Fig. 17.2). Endothermy is thus of obvious survival value.

The regulation of body temperature is called **thermoregulation** and is brought about by balancing heat production in the body with heat loss to the environment.

17.1 Heat production

The main source of heat in a mammal is tissue respiration. Over 50 per cent of the energy released in respiration is heat energy (Chapter 5). The rate at which heat is produced is proportional to the metabolic rate which varies with the intensity of exercise. Humans produce about 250 kJ h^{-1} of heat energy when resting. Heat production increases to 1000 kJ h^{-1} during moderate exercise while the rate may be the equivalent of 8000 kJ h^{-1} in a few minutes of intense exercise.

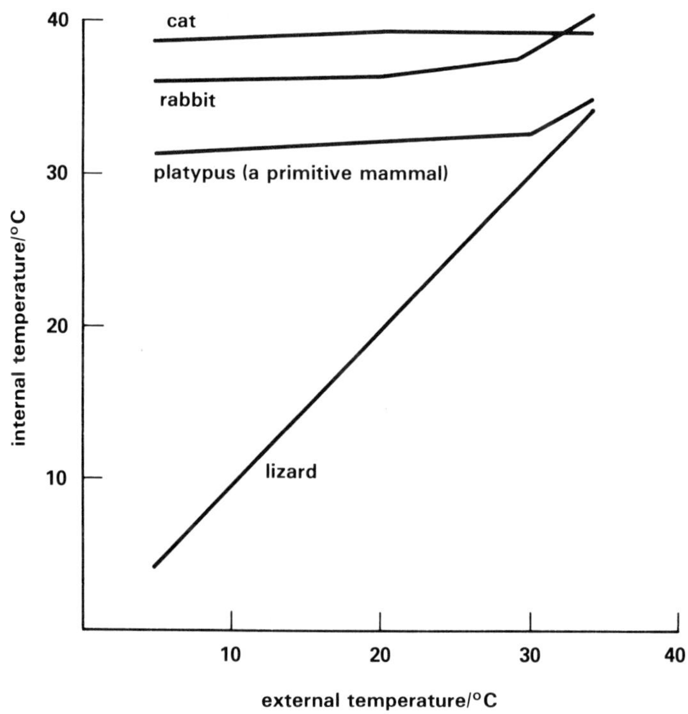

FIG. 17.1 *Effects of environmental temperature on the body temperatures of three mammals (endotherms) and the lizard (an ectotherm)*

FIG. 17.2 *Effects of temperature on metabolic rate.* Compare with Fig. 4.7

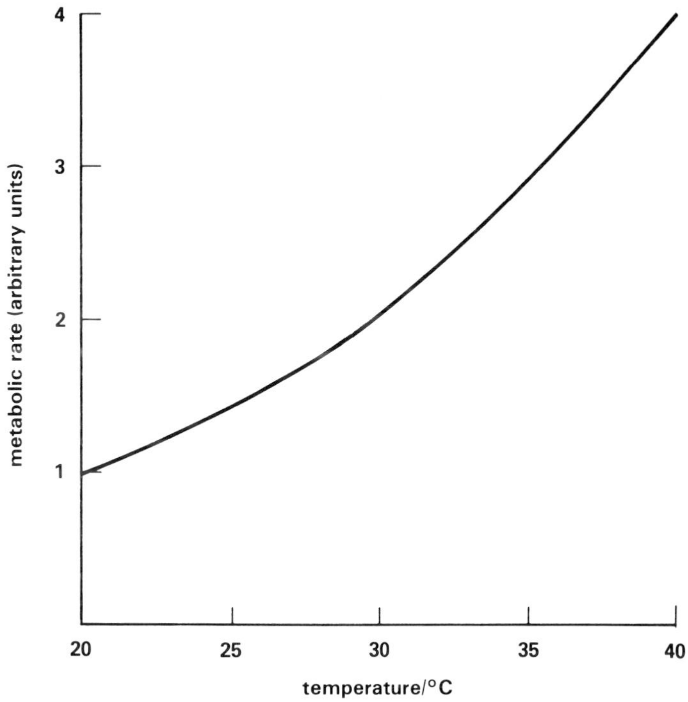

17.1.1 Measuring metabolic rate

When an animal is fasting energy is released in respiration of food reserves such as fat and glycogen in the body. When at rest nearly all the energy released in respiration is eventually given off as heat.

Measurement of the heat given off by a resting, fasting individual gives an indication of the energy required to maintain the body's vital functions.

FIG. 17.3 *A respirometer. The subject breathes through the mouthpiece. The oxygen consumed is recorded on a revolving kymograph drum as the level of the chamber falls. Exhaled carbon dioxide is removed by the soda lime*

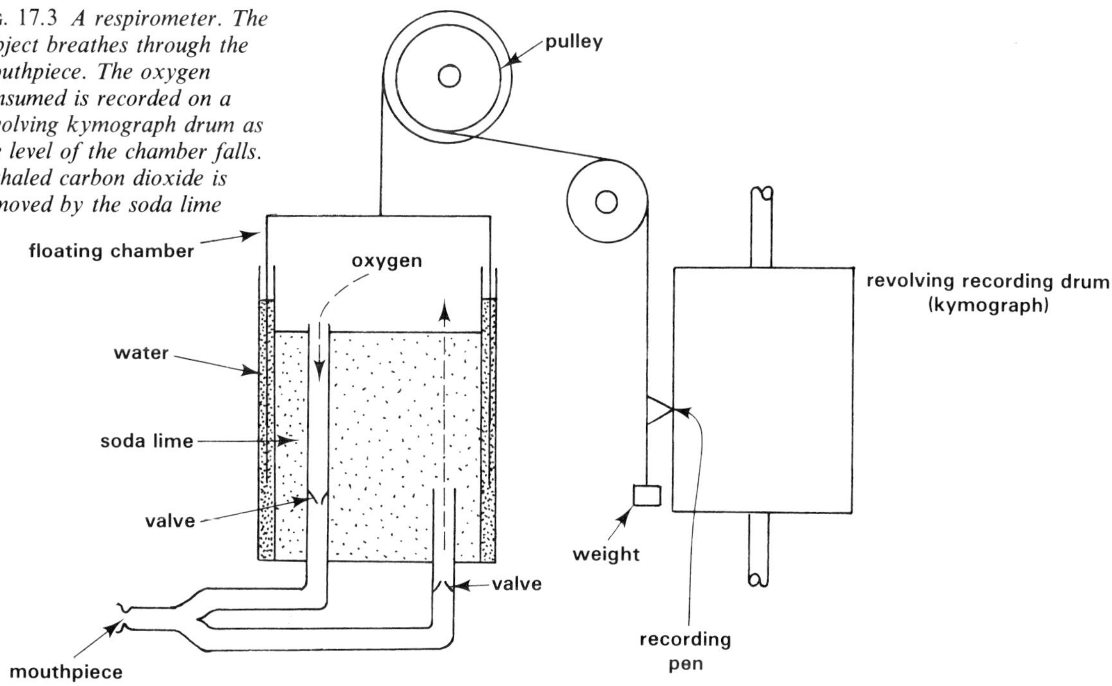

The rate at which the body respires to provide this amount of energy is called the **basal metabolic rate** (**BMR**). The BMR of a man can be measured using a **human calorimeter** which is an insulated room containing water-filled pipes. The temperature of the water entering and leaving the room through the pipes is recorded. So is the temperature of the air in the room. Heat lost from the body over a period of time causes a rise in temperature of the water and air. From the data the BMR can be calculated.

A much quicker way of calculating the BMR involves using a **respirometer** (Fig. 17.3). A respirometer allows the volume of oxygen taken in by the subject in a given period of time to be measured. For every 1 dm^3 oxygen used in respiration, approximately 20·17 kJ of heat energy are released. This is the average of the amount of heat energy released from the oxidation of carbohydrates, lipids and proteins. If a subject takes in 1·5 dm^3 oxygen in 5 minutes, which is equivalent to 18 $dm^3\ h^{-1}$, the rate at which heat energy is released is:

$$18 \times 20{\cdot}17 = 363{\cdot}06\ \text{kJ h}^{-1}$$
$$\text{Thus the BMR} = 363{\cdot}06\ \text{kJ h}^{-1}$$

The figure is generally adjusted to take into account differences in surface area of the body (section 17.2.4).

17.1.2 Distribution of body heat

Heat is produced unevenly in the body. Skeletal muscle releases a lot of heat during exercise. Another important source of heat is the liver (Chapter 14). Blood moving through the circulatory system has kinetic energy which is converted to heat energy when the blood meets resistance mainly in the arterioles. As blood flows through the skeletal muscles and liver it absorbs heat and distributes it to parts of the body where little heat is produced (Figs. 17.4 and 17.5). When blood flows near the body surface heat is lost through the skin.

FIG. 17.4 *Distribution of heat on the surface of the human body in a cold environment*

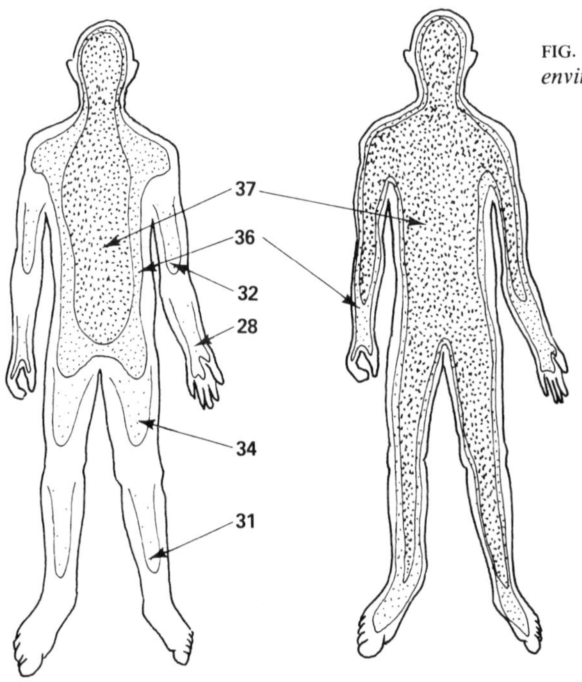

FIG. 17.5 *As 17.4 but in a hot environment. Figures are in °C*

17.2 Heat loss

Mammals lose body heat in three main ways, **radiation**, **evaporation** and **conduction**.

17.2.1 Radiation

Radiation is the emission of heat from a body to its surroundings, mostly the air. Except in tropical regions, the body temperature of mammals is generally higher than the surroundings. Mammals therefore radiate heat to their surroundings more rapidly than they gain heat back by the same means. It has been estimated that 60 per cent of the total heat loss from a naked man sitting in a room kept at 33°C is by radiation (Fig. 17.6).

Measurements of heat coming from the body as infra-red radiation are useful in the detection of certain types of tumour. The patient is kept in a room of constant temperature, generally between 18° and 20°C, to minimise fluctuations in skin temperature. Photographs are taken with a special camera which is sensitive to infra-red radiation coming from the body. Hot areas of the skin show up as light patches on the picture. Cool areas show up as dark patches. Hot spots occur in areas where blood flow and metabolism are increased, which may be diseased areas of the body. The technique is called **thermography** and is often used in the detection of breast cancer.

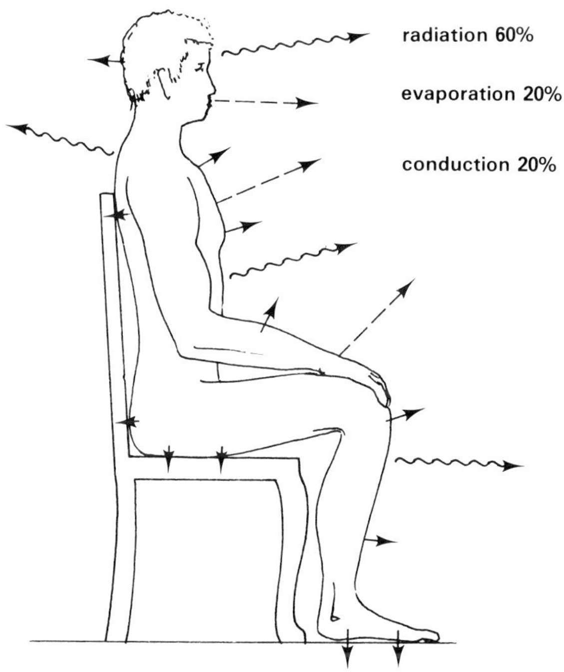

FIG. 17.6 *Approximate relative heat loss in man by radiation (wavy line) evaporation (broken line) and conduction (straight line)*

17.2.2 Evaporation

As water evaporates from a moist surface, energy is taken from the surface which consequently cools. The energy used is the **latent heat of vaporisation** (Chapter 2). The mammalian skin contains **sudorific glands** which secrete **sweat** on to the body surface when the body is overheated. Sweat is mainly water and when it evaporates the skin is cooled. Evaporation of body water also occurs from the moist linings of the nasal cavities, mouth, trachea and the extensive internal surface of the lungs. In very hot climates the surroundings often have a temperature higher than body temperature. In such conditions the body gains heat from the environment by radiation and conduction (section 17.2.3). Profuse sweating and subsequent evaporation of water from the skin's surface prevents overheating. A man can secrete up to 4 dm^3 of sweat per hour in very hot dry conditions. Dehydration of the body can then become a critical problem (Chapter 8).

Even in a moderately warm room when sweating is virtually nil, about 20 per cent of a man's total heat loss is due to evaporation. This is because even without sweating, small quantities of water vapour escape through the skin. Some of the heat loss is also due to evaporation from the mouth, nose, trachea and lungs (Fig. 17.6).

Many environmental factors affect the rate of evaporation and hence heat loss from the skin. Most notable are the water potential of the air in contact with the skin, the air temperature and air movement. They control the rate of evaporation from the mammalian body in much the same way that they influence transpiration from terrestrial plants (Chapter 11).

17.2.3 Conduction

Heat passes from a warm object to a cooler one in direct contact with it by **conduction**. The ground, if cooler than any part of the body in contact with it removes heat from the body by conduction. The greater the temperature difference between the body and other objects touching it, the greater is the rate of conductive heat loss. A cool breeze passing over the skin removes heat by conduction to the air. About 20 per cent of the total heat lost by the man illustrated in Figure 17.6 can be due to conduction.

17.2.4 Surface area and body volume

Heat is released in the body mainly in respiration. The amount of heat released depends on the **volume** of the body. Because most of the heat is lost through the skin, the amount of heat lost depends on the **surface area** of the skin.

As an animal grows, its volume increases in three dimensions whereas its surface area increases only in two dimensions. Consequently, relative to its volume its surface area increases at a slower rate. In terms of heat exchange, a bulky animal has a larger volume of tissues in which heat is released, but relative to this, a smaller surface through which heat is lost to the environment. The **surface area to volume (SA/V) ratio** is the area of skin per unit of body volume. A deer of volume 150 000 cm^3 and 19 000 cm^2 surface area has a SA/V ratio of:

$$\frac{19\,000}{150\,000} = 0{\cdot}127\ \text{cm}^2\ \text{cm}^{-3}$$

In comparison, a squirrel of 625 cm^3 volume and 550 cm^2 surface area has a SA/V ratio of:

$$\frac{550}{625} = 0{\cdot}88\ \text{cm}^2\ \text{cm}^{-3}$$

In other words, each cm^3 volume of the squirrel has about seven times the skin area available for heat loss compared with the bulkier deer (Fig. 17.7).

Such considerations highlight one of the factors which limits the extremes of size in terrestrial mammals. Bulky animals face overheating while small ones lose heat rapidly. Experimenting with small mammals, Pearson in 1957 obtained data for the metabolic rate of a variety of shrews. He related the metabolic rate to body mass (Fig. 17.8). The rate of metabolism controls the rate of heat production. It is, therefore, not surprising that the smaller shrews which have a greater relative surface area through which heat is lost show the highest metabolic rate. However, there is a limit to which increased metabolism can compensate for heat loss. It is estimated that a mammal smaller in size than the smallest species of shrew would be unable to make energy quickly enough from its food to make good the rate at which heat is lost through its body surface.

FIG. 17.7 *A fallow deer and a squirrel, two mammals with different rates of heat loss resulting from different body sizes*

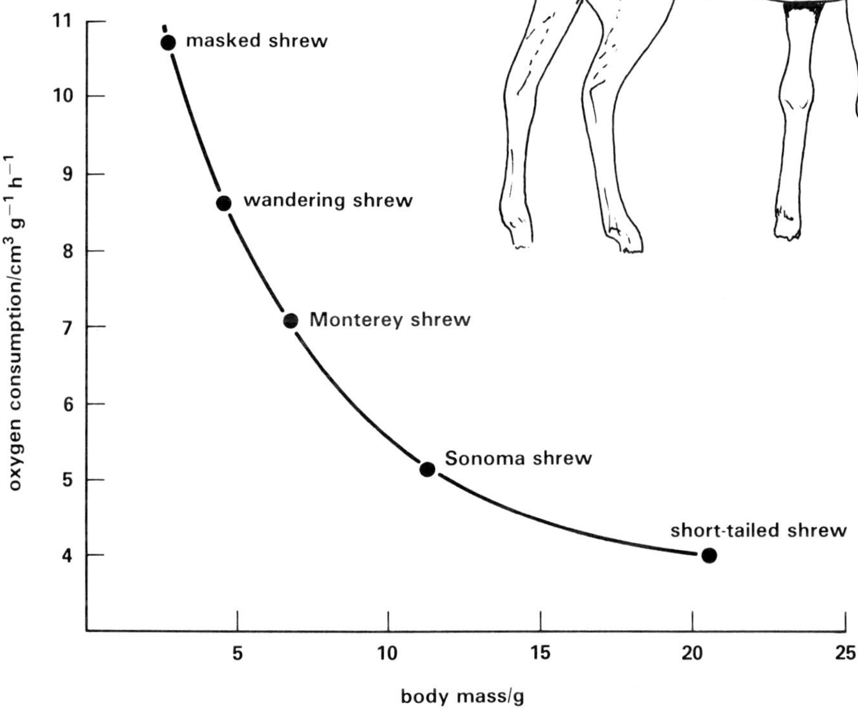

FIG. 17.8 *Relationship of metabolic rate (oxygen consumption) and body size in a variety of shrews* (after Pearson)

Since metabolic rate and surface area can be related in this way, measurements of BMR are usually expressed in units which take account of surface area. Expressing BMR in this way allows comparison to be made between animals of different sizes. In man, for example, the BMR is expressed in kJ $m^{-2}h^{-1}$. The surface area of a human is difficult to measure directly but it can be calculated from measurements of height and mass (Fig. 17.9).

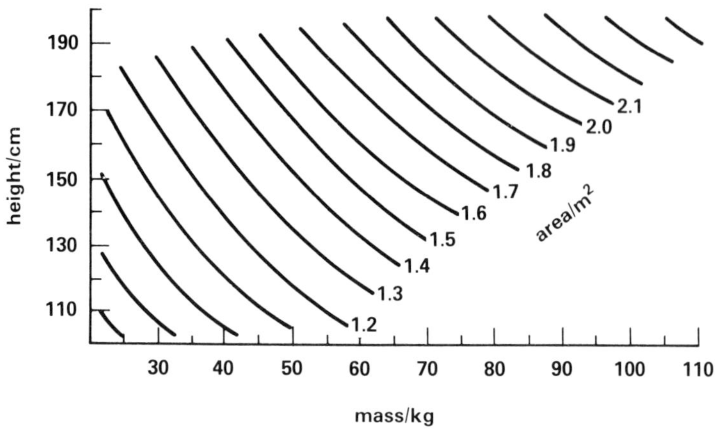

FIG. 17.9 *Relationship between height, mass and surface area in man*

17.3 Thermo-regulation

The regulation of body temperature in mammals is brought about by balancing heat production and heat loss.

17.3.1 The thermo-regulation centres

Thermoregulation takes place in response to changes in body temperature, but the changes must first be detected. This function is performed by specific parts of the hypothalamus in the forebrain (Chapter 15). In the hypothalamus are two **thermoregulation centres**. The **cold centre** responds to blood which has a temperature less than normal by triggering off responses which increase heat production and decrease heat loss. The **heat centre** responds to blood which has a temperature higher than normal by triggering off responses which reduce heat production and increase heat loss (Fig. 17.10).

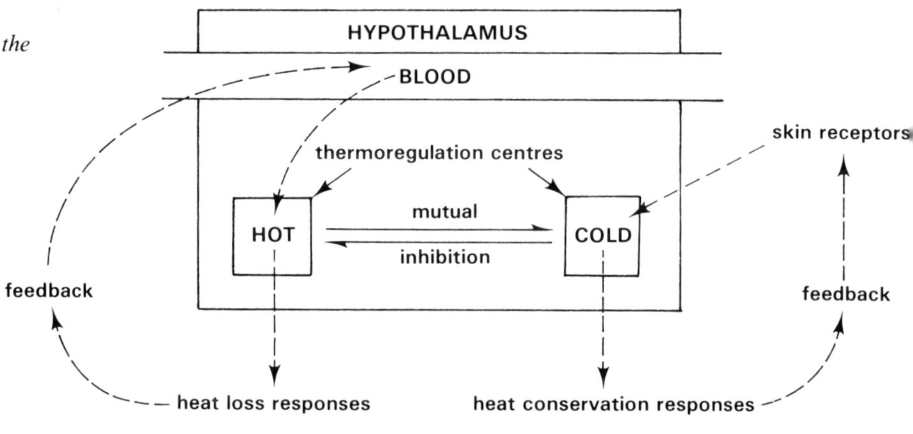

FIG. 17.10 *Action of thermoregulation centres in the hypothalamus*

The heat centre acts like a **thermostat**. It switches on heat loss mechanisms when the temperature of the blood is higher than normal. Conversely it switches on heat conservation mechanisms when the temperature of the blood is lower than normal. The cold centre is inhibited by the heat centre, but becomes active when receptors in the skin signal that the environment is getting cooler. Heat production mechanisms are then switched on and heat conservation mechanisms are switched on too.

In this way the body temperature is kept constant even though the environmental temperature varies. The cold centre also receives information about potential body temperature changes. The information travels along sensory neurons from the receptors in the skin which are sensitive to temperature changes outside the body. It is an early warning system which enables the thermoregulation centres to trigger off appropriate responses before external changes alter the internal body temperature too much.

17.3.2 Regulating heat production

Heat release in the body is ultimately limited by the availability of food. Assuming food to be adequate, other factors become important. Among these is production of the hormone **thyroxin** which controls the BMR (Chapter 18). Increased thyroxin output can double the BMR in man, but the response takes several days to come into effect. A similar but more immediate response is brought about by **adrenalin** made in the adrenal glands and **noradrenalin** secreted by sympathetic nerve endings (Chapters 15 and 18).

When the environmental temperature is very low considerable heat can be generated by **shivering**. Shivering is very rapid alternate contraction and relaxation of the skeletal muscles.

17.3.3 Regulating heat loss

There are several means by which mammals can alter the rate at which heat is lost from the body. Nearly all involve the **skin**. The mammalian skin acts as a physical barrier which prevents excessive loss of heat and water from the body and stops foreign matter and pathogenic microbes gaining access to the underlying tissues and organs. The skin has a thin outer layer called the **epidermis**, one of the main functions of which is to replace cells which are constantly lost from the surface. Below the epidermis is a much thicker layer, the **dermis**. The dermis contains blood vessels and a variety of receptors sensitive to heat, cold, pressure, touch and pain. Also in the dermis of many mammals are the **sudorific glands** which produce sweat.

FIG. 17.11 (a) *Photomicrograph of a vertical section through the skin from the human scalp,* ×20

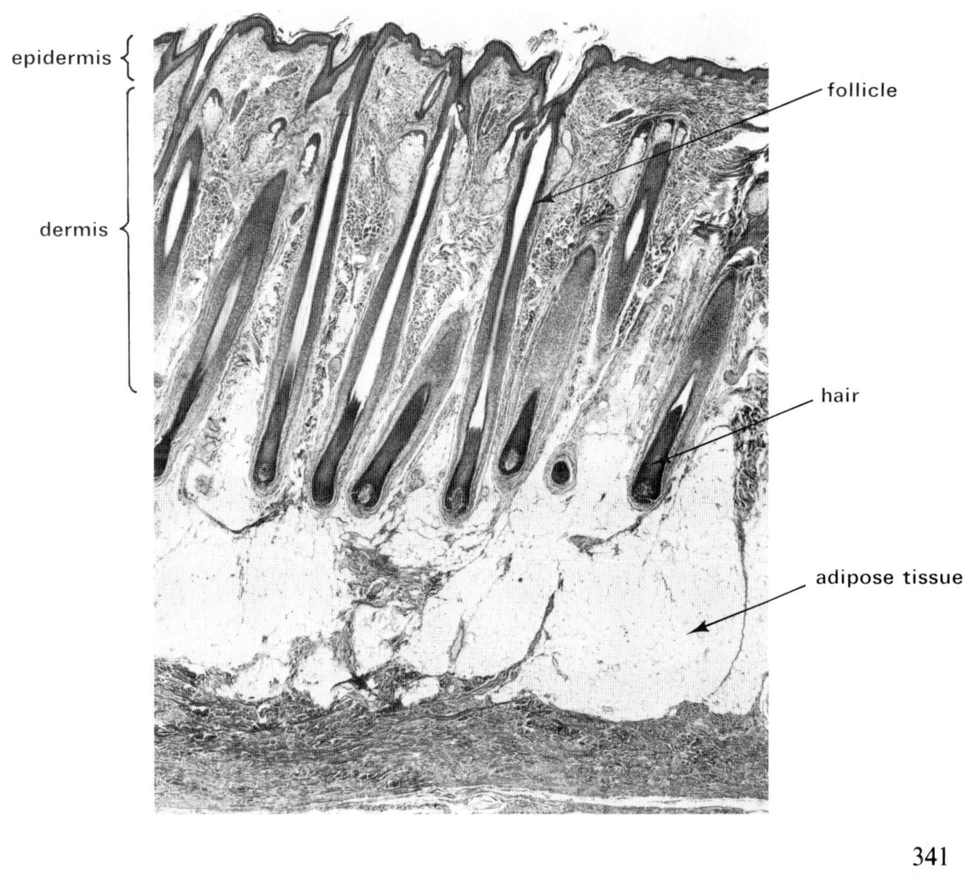

FIG. 17.11 (b) *Diagram showing some of the components of mammalian skin*

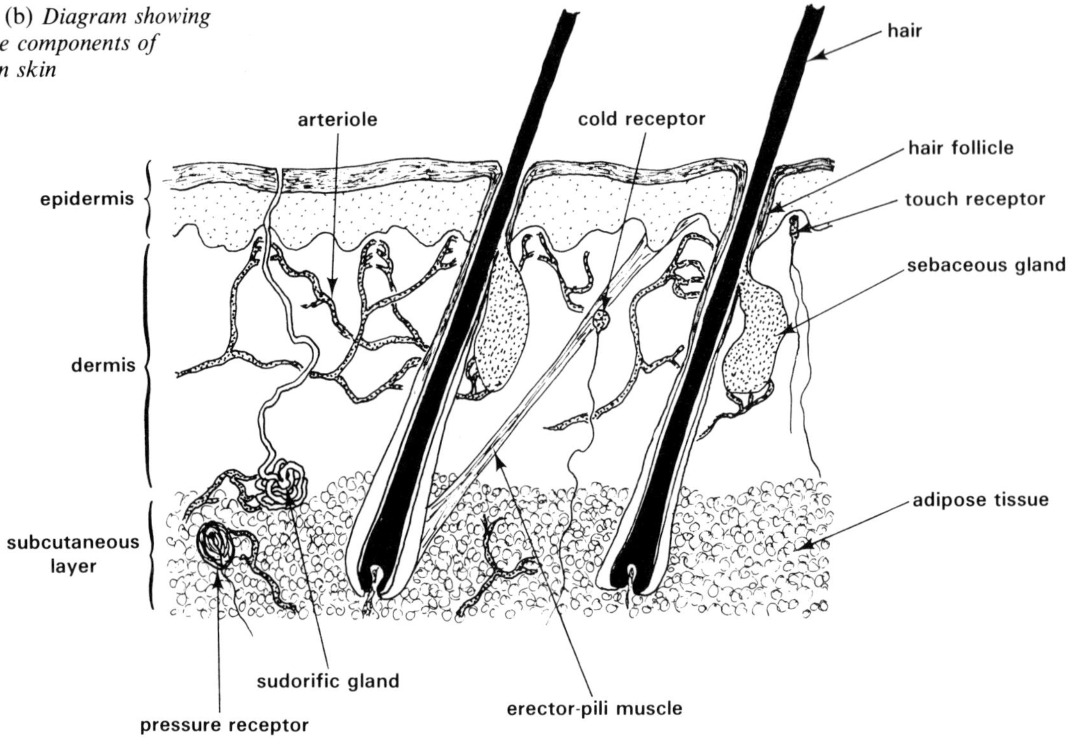

The sweat glands are coiled structures, each with a duct leading through the epidermis to the surface.

Hairs originate in the dermis and grow in pits called **follicles**. The bases of hairs are attached to small **erector-pili muscles**, the contraction of which can raise the hairs projecting from the surface. Beneath the dermis are fat deposits contained in **adipose tissue** (Fig. 17.11).

1. ADIPOSE TISSUE

Fat is a poor conductor of heat and **adipose tissue** is an effective thermal insulator. Heat is taken into the dermis by blood in numerous arterioles and capillaries. When the flow of blood is rapid, heat is lost quickly through the epidermis. Parasympathetic stimulation of the arterioles leading to the capillaries causes **vasodilation**, increasing blood flow in the skin and promoting heat loss (Fig. 17.12(a)). The nerve impulses which bring about vasodilation originate in the heat centre of the brain. Alternatively, **vasoconstriction** of the arterioles directs blood away from the skin, thereby reducing heat loss. The blood flow in human skin can be reduced by vasoconstriction to about one hundredth of the volume which flows when the arterioles are dilated (Fig. 17.12(b)). Sympathetic stimulation of the arterioles by nerve impulses from the cold centre of the brain causes vasoconstriction. Prolonged constriction of the arterioles resulting from long exposure to intense cold, deprives the dermis of the oxygen and nutrients it requires to maintain its metabolic functions. The tissues in the skin may then die or degenerate. This is the cause of frost bite.

2. HAIR

Most mammals are covered with **hair** which helps thermoregulation by keeping a layer of air next to the skin. Since it is kept in contact with the

FIG. 17.12 (a) *Vasodilation in the skin leading to heat loss through the epidermis;* (b) *vasoconstriction in the skin reducing epidermal heat to a minimum*

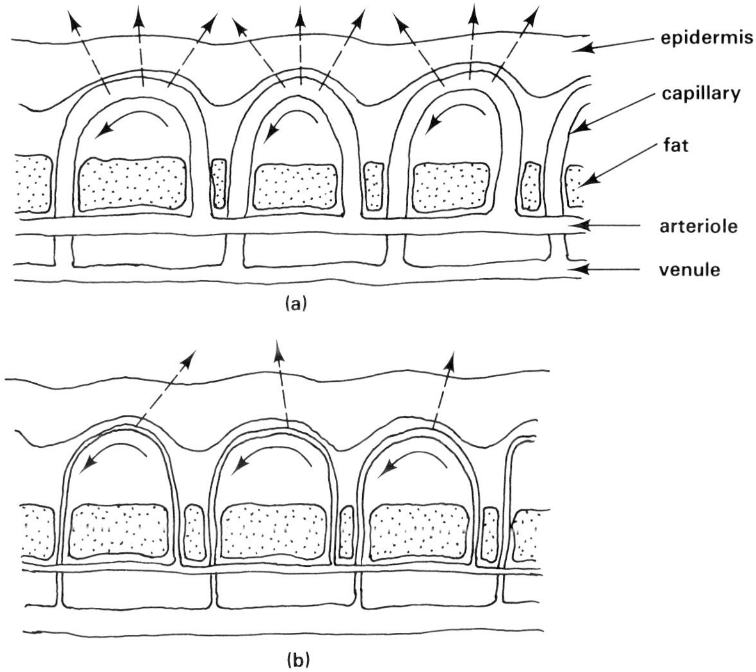

FIG. 17.13 *Variation in heat exchange with the atmosphere caused by elevation and depression of the hair on the skin in* (a) *a relatively cold environment,* (b) *a relatively warm environment and* (c) *a relatively hot environment*

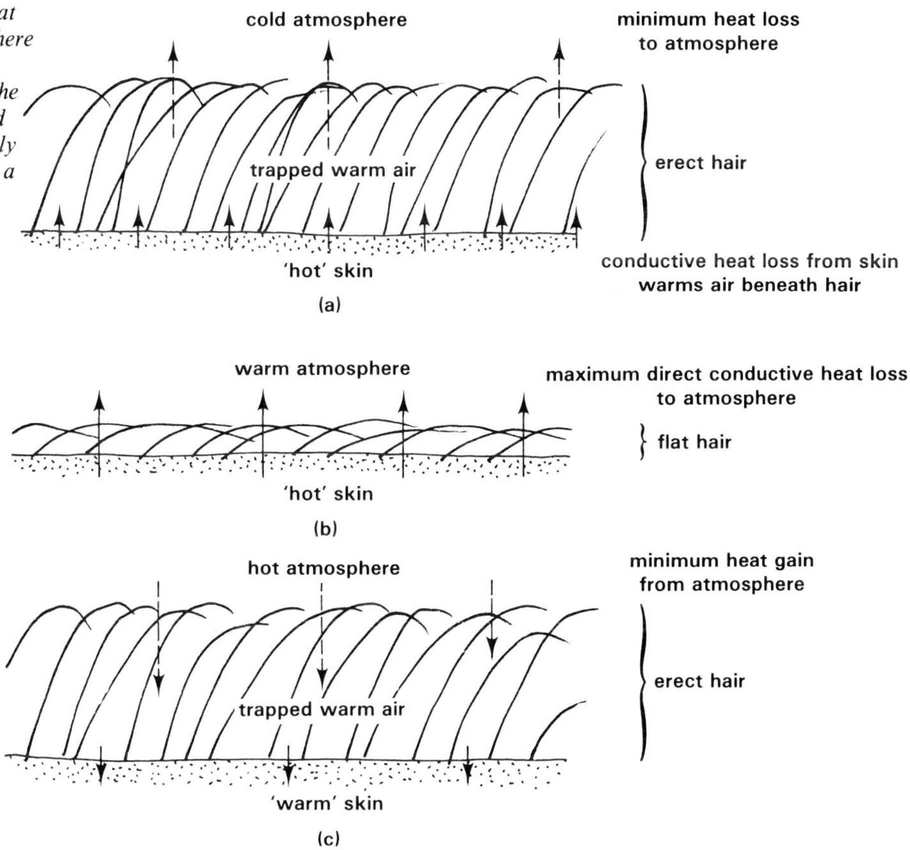

temperature. The maximum upper limit which the human body can survive is about 45°C and the lower limit is about 24°C. Nevertheless, permanent damage can be done to the tissues near to the upper and lower critical temperatures.

Figure 17.16 summarises the mechanisms of thermoregulation. Reference is made in Chapter 15 to the reflexes involved.

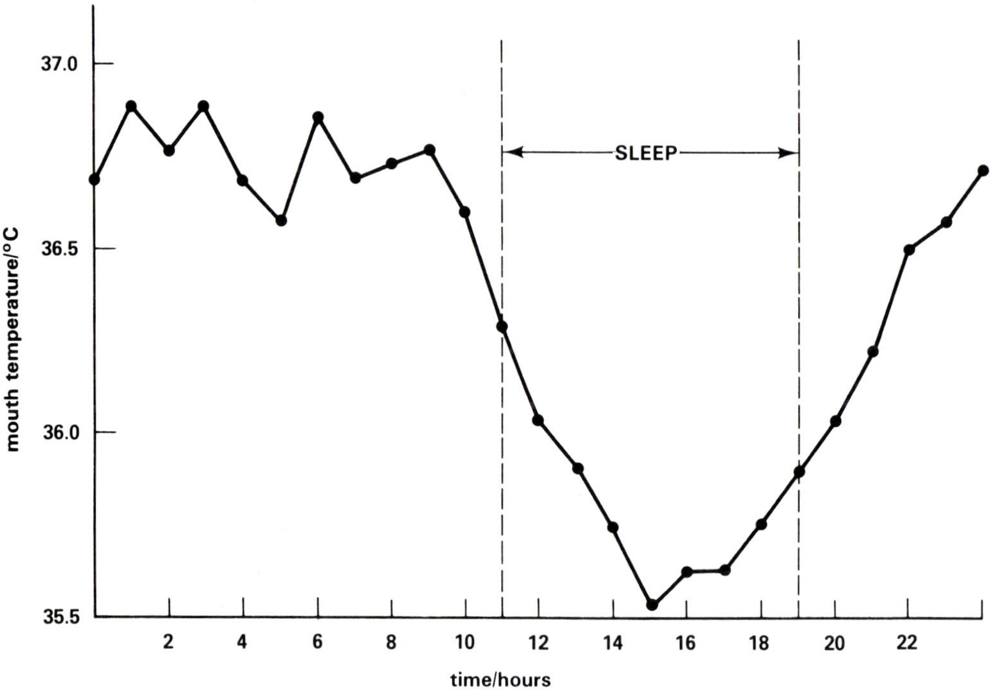

FIG. 17.15 *Average daily fluctuations in human body temperature*

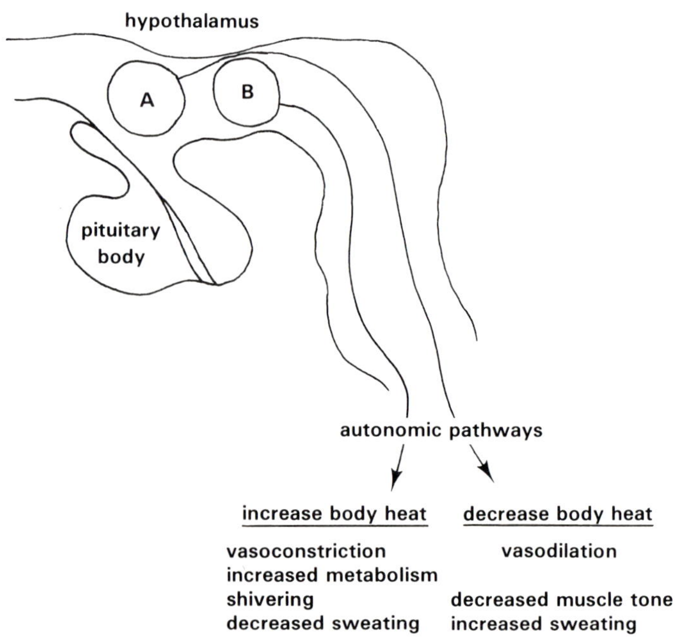

FIG. 17.16 *Summary of the main thermoregulatory mechanisms in mammals (A = hot centre; B = cold centre)*

17.3.4 Hibernation

Many endothermic animals become inactive in cold weather and enter a prolonged sleep. In this condition, called **hibernation**, the metabolic rate, oxygen consumption, heart and breathing rates are very low. The body temperature falls to only a few degrees above that of the surroundings, yet it is still kept fairly constant (Table 17.1). Hibernation is a means of surviving long periods of cold weather when food is scarce. Reserves of food in the body provide the energy needed to maintain the slow rate of metabolism during hibernation. When the climate becomes warmer, hibernating animals become aroused very rapidly. In some species, the oxygen consumption necessary to increase their metabolic rate can increase several thousand times in a few hours. Some large mammals, including grizzly bears, have a period of hibernation sometimes called **winter sleep**. The body temperature remains high, even when the surroundings are intensely cold. It is thought that hibernation of some mammals is brought on by a peptide hormone secreted by the hypothalamus. During hibernation, urination and defaecation stop, so helping to conserve body heat.

Several desert-living mammals have a form of hibernation which is of value in surviving long periods of drought rather than cold. Hibernation of this kind is called **aestivation**. During severe drought food is not likely to be plentiful. The reduced rate of breathing during aestivation is of survival value, since even a moderate rate of breathing results in considerable water loss which could lead to desiccation (Chapter 8).

Table 17.1 Comparison of some body functions in active and hibernating marmots (from Hughes 1965)

FUNCTIONS	ACTIVE	HIBERNATING
body temperature/°C	34–39	3–8
basal metabolism/kJ $m^{-2}day^{-1}$	1714	113
heart rate/beats min^{-1}	80	4–5
breathing rate/ventilations min^{-1}	25–30	0·2

Chapter 18 Endocrine control in mammals

Many functions of the mammalian body are co-ordinated and controlled by **hormones** which are produced by **endocrine glands**. Endocrine glands are **ductless** and secrete hormones directly into the body fluids, mainly the blood. The endocrine glands are distributed throughout the mammalian body (Fig. 18.1). Because they are transported in the blood, hormones can control body functions taking place some distance from the endocrine glands. This distinguishes endocrine glands from exocrine glands which have ducts to channel their products into nearby regions without using blood for transport (Fig. 18.2).

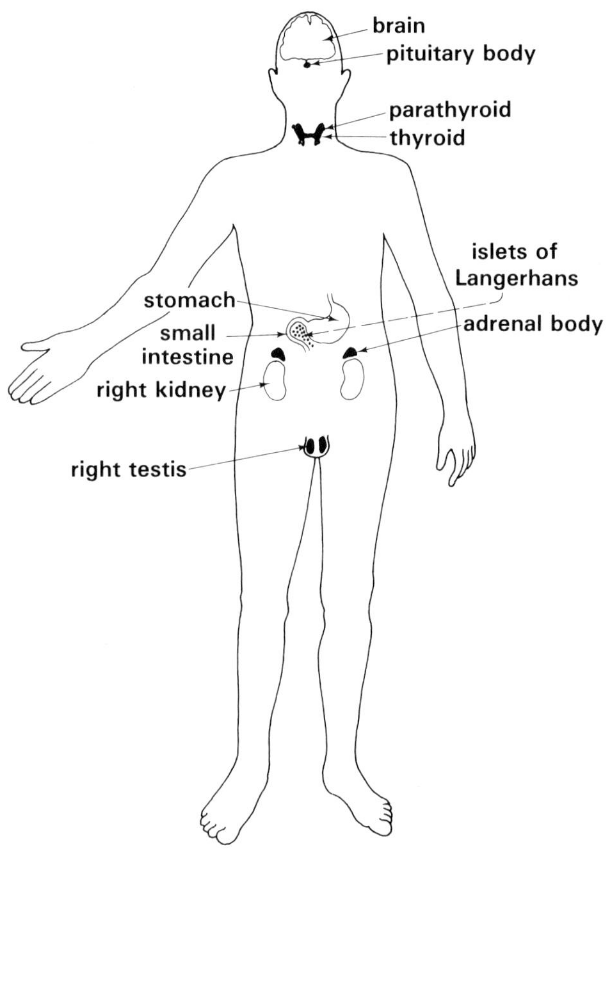

FIG. 18.1 *The main endocrine glands in man*

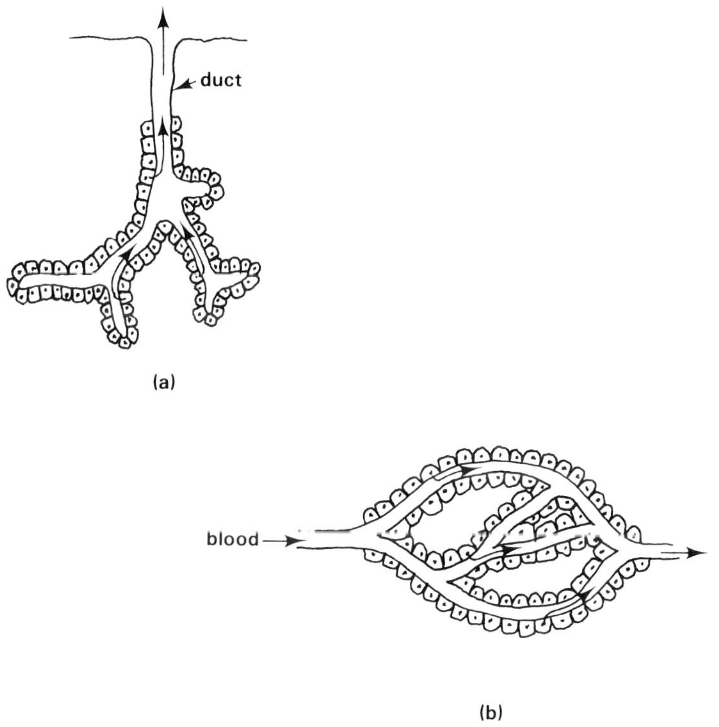

FIG. 18.2 *Basic construction of* (a) *an exocrine gland such as a digestive gland in the gut and* (b) *an endocrine gland*

Although only small amounts of hormones are found in blood their effects on the body tissues are very great. Once in the blood, hormones are bound to plasma proteins which carry them to their sites of activity called **target organs**. Activity of most endocrine glands is controlled by the nervous system (Chapter 15).

18.1 The thyroid and parathyroid glands

18.1.1 The thyroid gland

The mammalian **thyroid gland** is found in the neck close to the larynx (Fig. 18.1). Under the microscope the thyroid gland is seen to be composed of cells arranged in globular groups called **follicles** (Fig. 18.3). The closely packed follicles are made of cubical epithelium and are held together by connective tissue supplied with blood vessels. The epithelial cells secrete thyroid hormones into the cavities of the follicles where they are temporarily stored before they are taken into the blood.

The thyroid gland continuously removes relatively large quantities of iodine from the blood. The iodine ultimately comes from the diet. In the thyroid gland iodine is combined with the amino acid tyrosine, to produce mono-and diiodotyrosine then tetra- and finally triiodothyronine (Fig. 18.4). **Triiodothyronine (T_3)** and **tetraiodothyronine (T_4)** in a ratio of about 1:9 in man are the **thyroid hormones**. T_4 is usually called **thyroxin**.

The thyroid hormones affect all tissues of the body and have two main functions. First, they regulate growth and development by controlling the growth and differentiation of cells. It is thought that the hormones modify the activity of appropriate genes. The second main function of thyroid hormones is to control the basal metabolic rate (Chapter 17). When the body is at rest thyroid hormones adjust the basal metabolic rate to a level suitable for survival.

FIG. 18.3 *Photomicrograph of a thin section of cat thyroid, ×400*

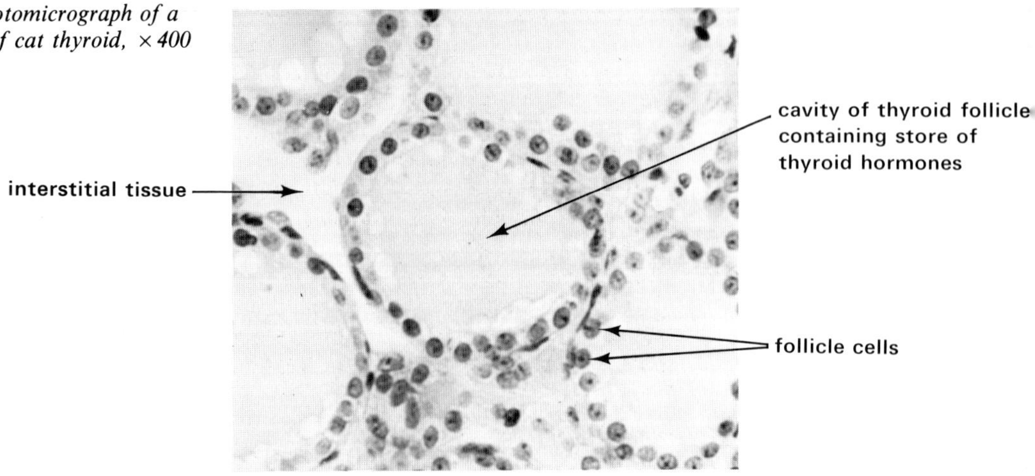

FIG. 18.4 *Pathway of thyroxin production*

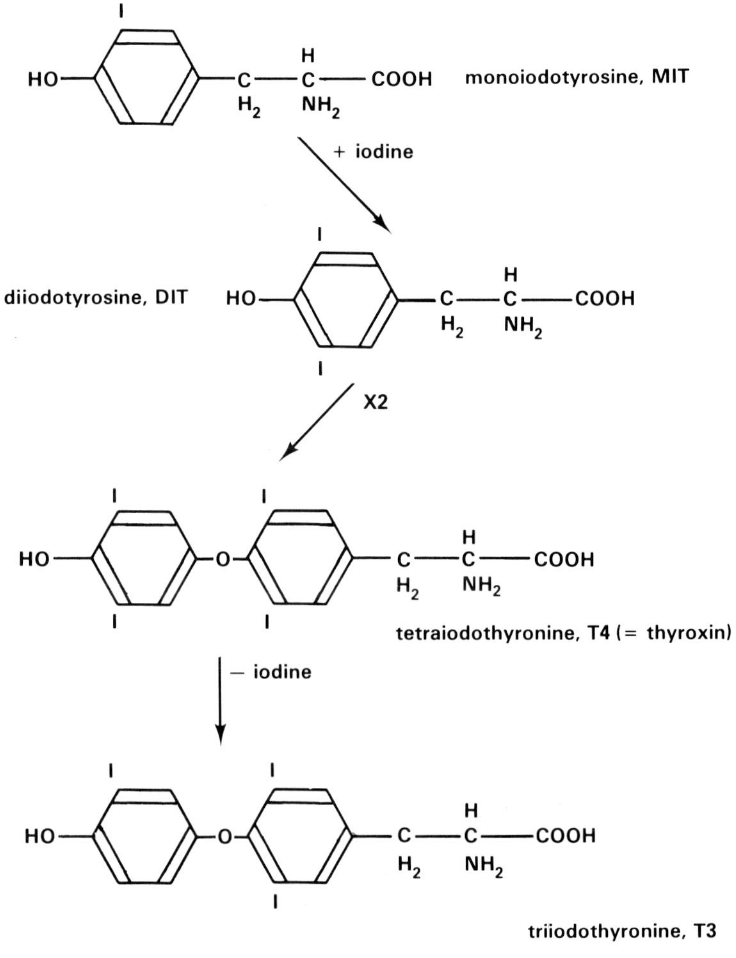

18.1.2 Control of thyroid activity

As with several other endocrine glands, growth and secretion of the thyroid gland are controlled by the **pituitary body** (Fig. 18.1). The pituitary body secretes a number of **tropins** which affect other endocrine glands (section 18.5.1). The trophic hormones include **thyrotropin (TSH)**. Growth of the thyroid gland and its output of hormones is stimulated by TSH. Secretion of TSH is in turn depressed by the thyroid hormones. The interaction is a **negative feedback control** mechanism. Another hormone controls the release of TSH. This hormone is called **thyroliberin**. It is made in the **hypothalamus**, the part of the brain immediately above the pituitary body (Fig. 18.5). Such control ensures that growth and activity of the thyroid gland meets the body's needs at any time. It is a homeostatic device which helps maintain the stability of the body's internal environment. Other comparable examples are described in the remainder of the chapter.

FIG. 18.5 *Mechanism controlling thyroid activity*

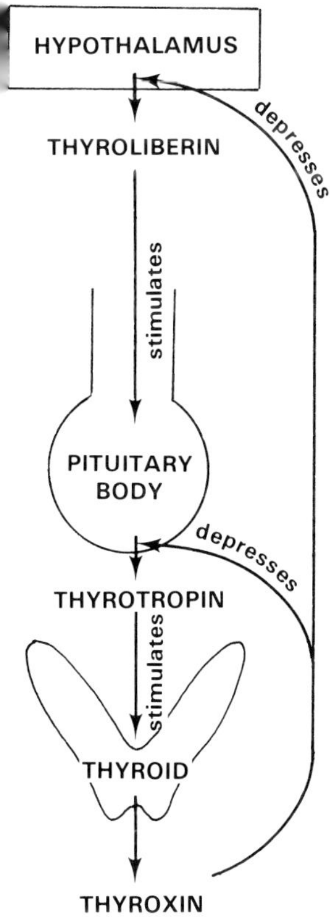

FIG. 18.6 *The fate of ingested iodine*

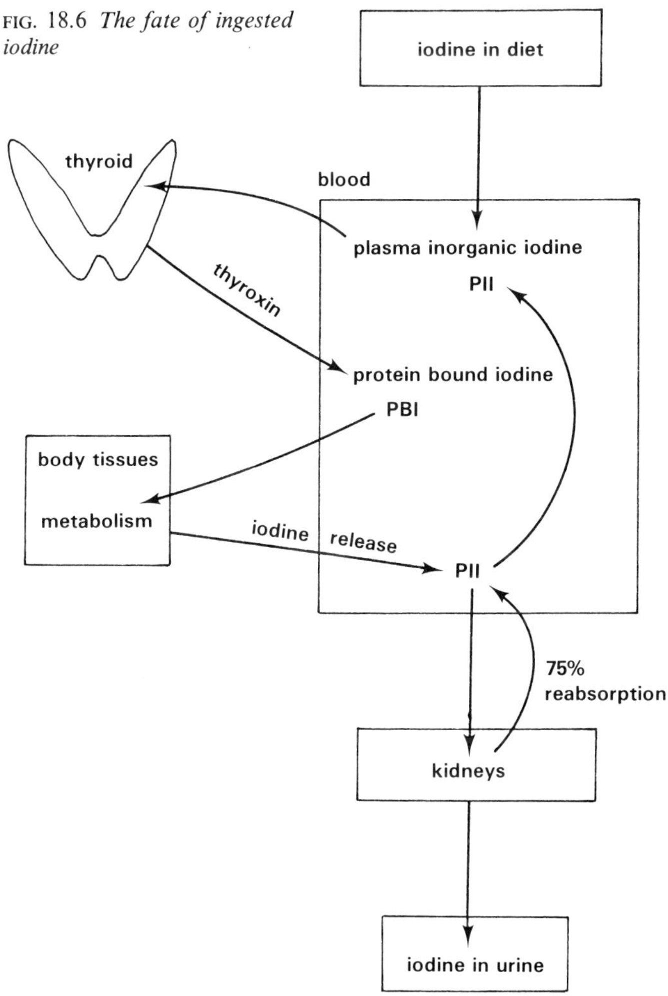

18.1.3 Measurement of thyroid activity

Human thyroid activity can be measured with the use of **radioactive isotopes** of iodine. Sodium iodide containing ^{125}I, ^{131}I or ^{132}I is given orally in doses which produce harmless levels of radiation to the patient. The radio-iodine circulates in the plasma as **plasma inorganic iodine (PII)**. Much of the iodine in PII is normally absorbed by the thyroid gland and used to make thyroid hormones. The hormones are secreted into the blood where the radio-iodine is carried as **protein bound iodine (PBI)**. When the hormones have performed their functions in the tissues iodine is released back into the blood to be absorbed once more by the thyroid gland. Some of the body's total **iodine pool** including the radioisotopes is excreted in the urine (Fig 18.6). There is a well-defined relationship between the amounts of radio-iodine in the plasma, thyroid gland and urine following a dose of the isotope (Fig. 18.7(a)). Consequently, measurements of the radiation in the thyroid gland, samples of blood and urine are useful in detecting abnormal activity of the thyroid gland (Fig. 18.7(b)).

FIG. 18.7 *Relationship between the levels of iodine in the thyroid gland, blood and urine after oral administration of radioactive iodine in man* (after Greig, Boyle and Boyle)*:* (a) *normal and* (b) *thyrotoxic*

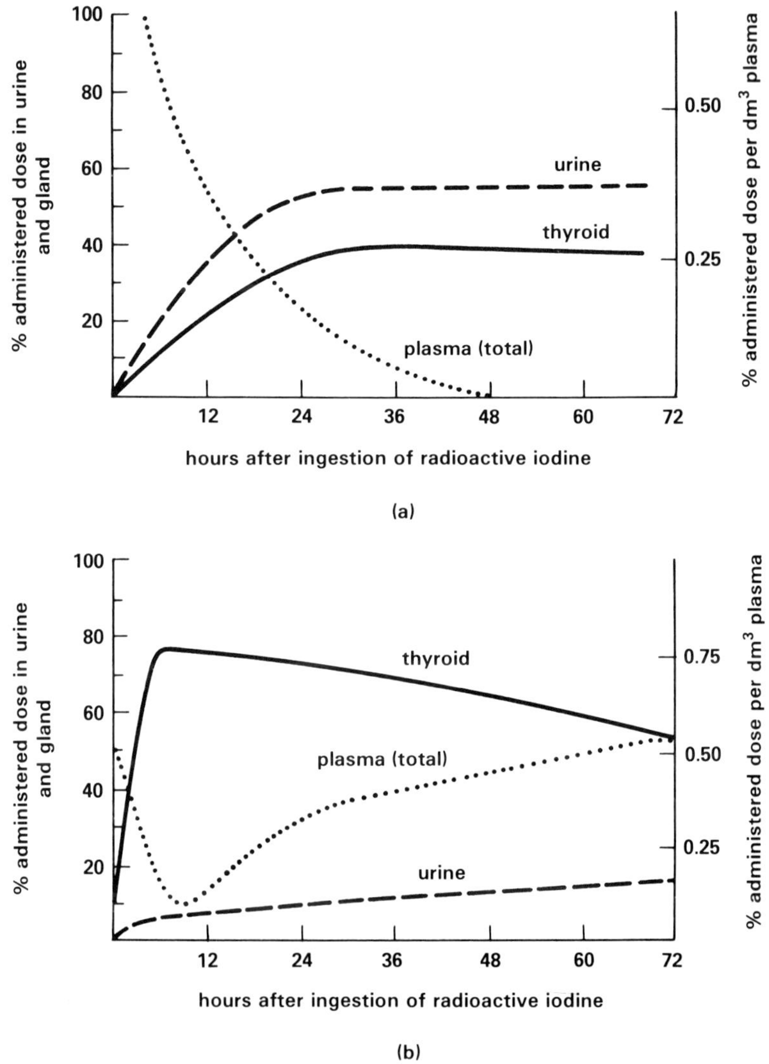

18.1.4 Malfunction of the thyroid gland

Overactivity of the thyroid gland is called **hyperthyroidism**. The condition can result from a failure of the TSH—thyroid control mechanism resulting in increased thyroxin output. Another cause of hyperthyroidism is secretion of thyroid hormones by a thyroid tumour. Either way an increase in basal metabolism occurs with increased heart rate, extreme irritability and loss of body mass. Removal of part of the thyroid gland may be necessary to check the condition. A common side-effect of an overactive thyroid gland is the secretion of exophthalmos-producing substance by the pituitary body. This substance causes excessive growth of the tissues immediately behind the eyes. Consequently protrusion of the eyes called **exophthalmos** often accompanies hyperthyroidism (Fig. 18.8).

Underactivity of the thyroid gland is called **hypothyroidism**. In adult humans hypothyroidism is the cause of a condition called **myxoedema**. The effects on basal metabolism are the opposite to those of hyperthyroidism. The BMR slows down, a smaller proportion of the energy-rich ingredients in the diet are respired, hence body mass increases. Mental activity also slows down so the patient is less alert than normal. At one time hypothyroidism was common in parts of Derbyshire and the Swiss Alps. Here the local soil and water supply are deficient in iodine and the population was thus deprived of an essential requirement for the synthesis of thyroid hormones. Addition of traces of iodine to commercial table salt has largely overcome the problem.

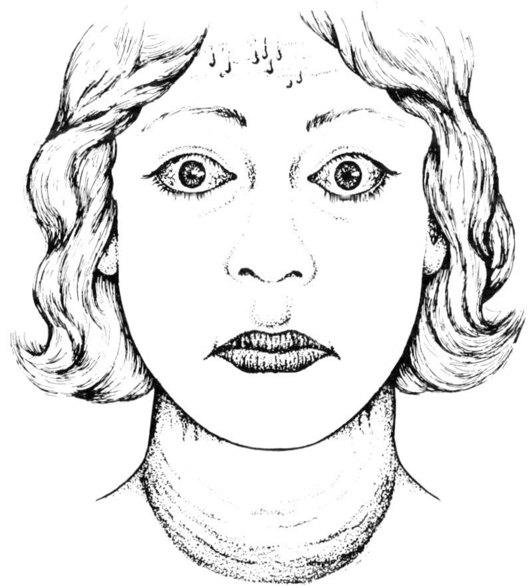

FIG. 18.8 *Facial characteristics of a person with thyrotoxicosis. Note the goitre and protruding eyes*

The abnormal growth and development which accompanies an underactive thyroid gland is particularly distressing in infants. **Cretinism** is the name given to the effects of thyroid deficiency in children. The main symptoms are retardation in mental, physical and sexual development.

Both hyper- and hypothyroidism usually result in excessive growth of the thyroid gland. The enlarged thyroid gland is called a **goitre** which causes swelling of the neck.

18.1.5 The parathyroid glands

In man the **parathyroid glands** are four small oval bodies embedded in the thyroid gland (Fig. 18.9). The parathyroid glands make a polypeptide hormone called **parathyrin** (**PTH**) which has a profound effect on the calcium ion content of the blood and other body fluids. PTH elevates the amount of calcium in the blood which, by negative feedback control, regulates PTH output (Fig. 18.10).

FIG. 18.9 *Position of the parathyroid glands in man*

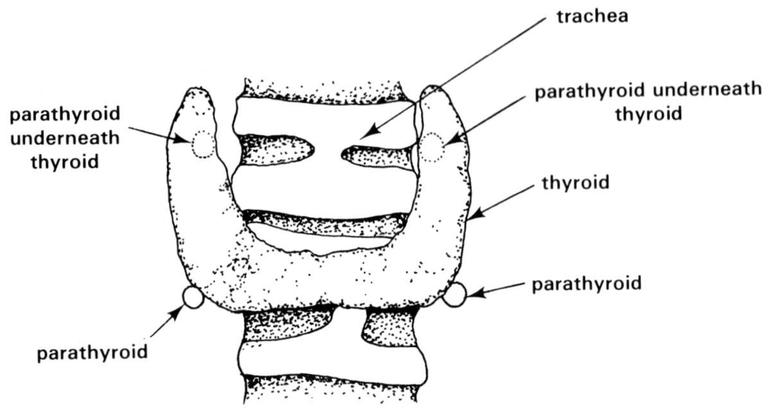

FIG. 18.10 *Mechanism regulating the output of parathyrin, PTH*

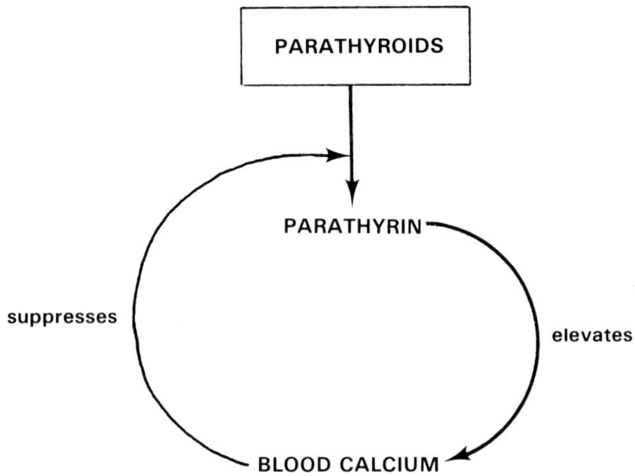

Calcium is an important constituent of body fluids. It participates in many body functions including coagulation of the blood (Chapter 9), nerve and muscle activity (Chapter 15) and teeth and bone formation. These functions depend not just on the presence of calcium ions but on a precise concentration of calcium ions. It is therefore important that the amount of calcium is regulated within narrow limits. Calcium is one of the most precisely regulated constituents of the mammalian body. The concentration of calcium ions in normal human blood serum ranges between only 9 and 11 mg per 100 cm^3.

PTH affects blood calcium in several ways:

1. RELEASE OF CALCIUM FROM BONE

Bone contains calcium salts, especially calcium phosphate. Calcium and phosphate(V) ions are continuously released from bones into the tissue fluids and redeposited in bones. Clearly the composition and structure of bone depends on regulating this reversible process (Fig. 18.11). By stimulating the **release of calcium** and phosphate ions from bone, PTH helps maintain normal concentrations of calcium and phosphate ions in blood.

FIG. 18.11 *Dynamic equilibrium between the calcium and phosphate in bone and that in the tissue fluid and blood*

2. REABSORPTION OF CALCIUM FROM THE URINE
Calcium and phosphate ions are filtered from the blood in the kidney nephrons. PTH promotes **reabsorption of calcium** ions from the filtrate in the proximal convolutions at the expense of phosphate ions which are excreted (Chapter 10). PTH thus elevates the concentration of calcium ions in the blood while lowering the concentration of blood phosphate ions (Fig. 18.12). The inverse relationship between calcium and phosphate ions in blood

$$[Ca^{2+}] \propto \frac{1}{[PO_4{}^{3-}]}$$

prevents the accumulation of unwanted calcium phosphate in the blood and tissues.

FIG. 18.12 *Effect of parathyrin on calcium and phosphate in the kidney nephrons*

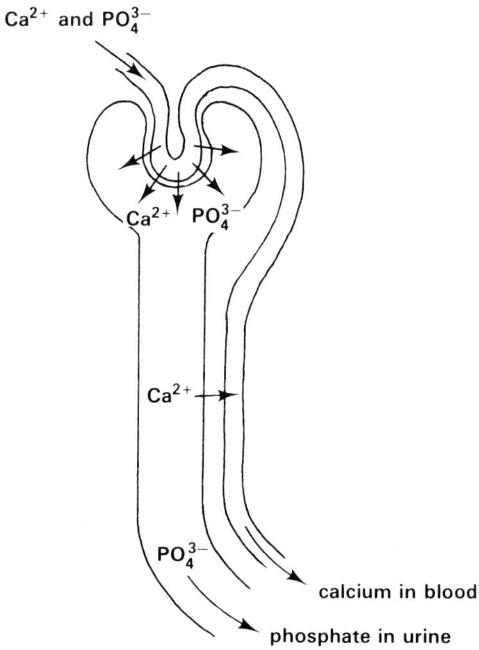

3. ABSORPTION OF CALCIUM FROM THE GUT
PTH is also thought to promote **absorption of calcium** ions from the gut, thus helping to maintain the normal concentration of calcium ions in the blood.

18.1.6 Role of the thyroid gland in calcium control

As well as PTH from the parathyroid glands, another hormone called **calcitonin** affects the calcium ion concentration of blood. Calcitonin is secreted from **C cells** in the thyroid gland. Its effect is to lower the concentration of calcium ions in blood by causing the deposition of calcium phosphate in bone. Calcitonin has been found in mammals and fish.

Salmon calcitonin is one of the most potent of biological compounds with a strength over 40 times that of human calcitonin. In experiments on rats, a dose of salmon calcitonin of 0·000000002 g kg^{-1} of rat lowered the concentration of calcium ions in blood by 10 per cent.

Thus it is the combined effects of PTH and calcitonin which regulate calcium and phosphate ions to the concentrations necessary for many physiological functions to take place normally (Fig. 18.13).

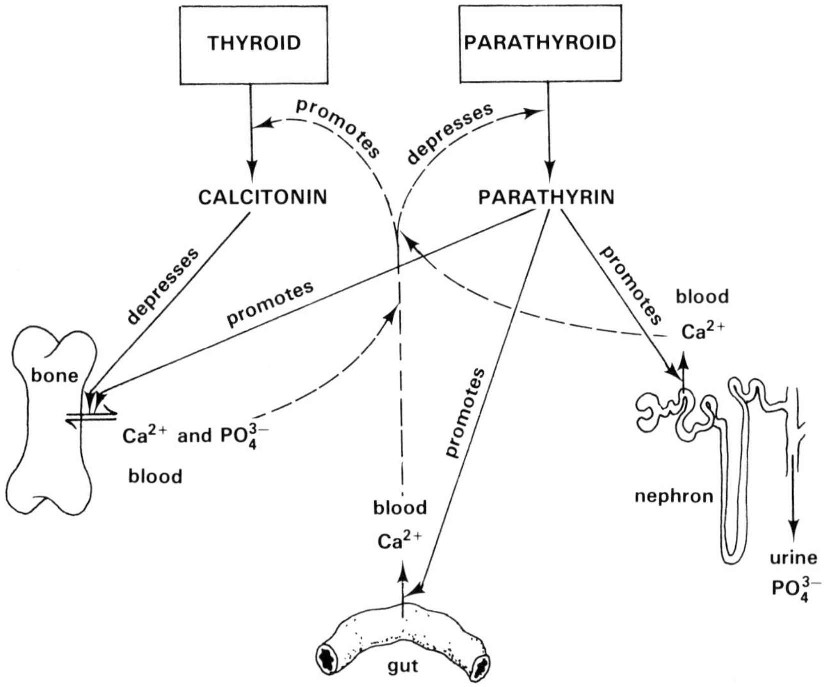

FIG. 18.13 *Summary of the effects of PTH and calcitonin on blood calcium and phosphate*

18.1.7 Malfunction of the parathyroid glands

Underactivity of the parathyroid glands, **hypoparathyroidism**, results in a lowering of the concentration of calcium ions and an elevation of the concentration of phosphate ions in blood. The condition is called **hypocalcaemia**. If the concentration of calcium ions in human blood serum drops below 7 mg per 100 cm^3 a condition called **tetany** results. Tetany is characterised by increased excitability of the nervous system. Muscular activity becomes spasmodic and uncontrolled.

Surgical removal of the parathyroid glands from dogs results in tetany within three days. Subsequent injection of parathyroid extract quickly corrects the condition but the effect is short-lived. Maintenance of normal concentrations of calcium ions in the blood of experimental dogs requires continued treatment with PTH (Fig. 18.14).

Overactivity of the parathyroid glands, **hyperparathyroidism**, can result in breakdown of bone structure and consequent elevation of the concentration of calcium ions in blood. The condition is called **hypercalcaemia**. Recent work indicates that the decalcifying activity of PTH increases in post-menopausal women. Before the menopause PTH is inhibited by oestrogen hormones secreted by the ovaries (Chapter 22). After the menopause oestrogen production stops. This explains why the bones of older women are often fragile.

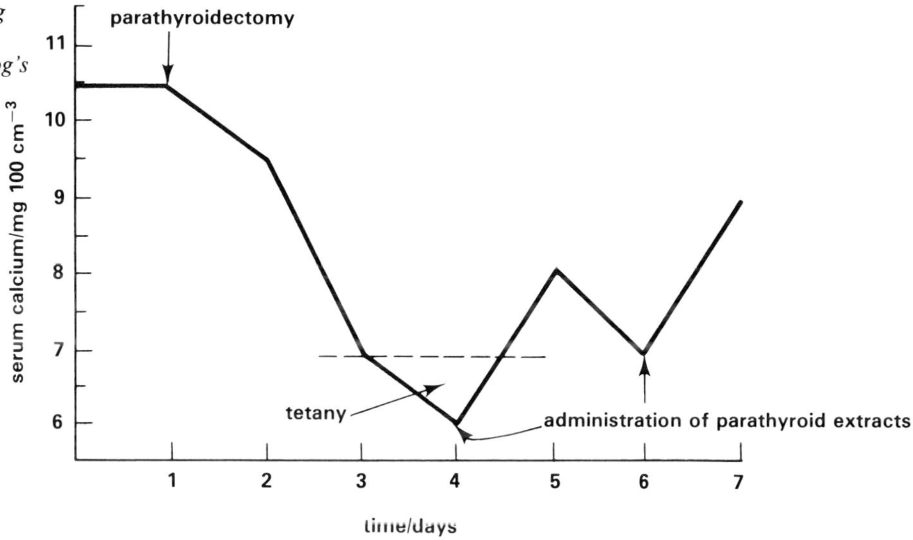

FIG. 18.14 *Effects of removing the parathyroids on the concentration of calcium in dog's blood*

18.2 Control of blood glucose

Carbohydrate is the main source of free energy released in respiration (Chapter 5). Nearly all the carbohydrate absorbed from the gut circulates in the blood as **glucose** and it is this sugar which is the main respiratory substrate. It is therefore vital that the blood maintains a constant and adequate supply of glucose to all the tissues. It is equally important, however, that the concentration of glucose in blood and tissue fluids is not excessive. Abnormally high concentrations of glucose in the tissue fluid would draw water from cells by osmosis (Chapter 2). Furthermore the water content of the body as a whole can be affected by the concentration of glucose in the blood. Normally the concentration of glucose in blood is sufficiently low for all the glucose in the renal filtrate to be reabsorbed into the blood in the kidneys (Chapter 10). Thus glucose is not usually excreted in urine. Since the reabsorption of water from the nephrons depends on the water potential gradient between the renal filtrate and the blood, any glucose remaining in the filtrate would minimise the gradient and reduce water reabsorption. Thus as well as tissue dehydration, a high concentration of glucose in blood could cause total body dehydration.

In the mammalian body mechanisms exist which regulate the concentration of glucose in the blood so that the tissues' metabolic needs are met without adversely affecting the body's water content. A number of hormones help to control the concentration of glucose in blood.

18.2.1 Insulin and glucagon

The mammalian pancreas is an exocrine gland which secretes pancreatic juice into the gut (Chapter 14). It is situated in a loop of the small intestine just below the stomach (Fig. 18.1). Embedded in the pancreas and sometimes also in the wall of the small intestine is a large number of microscopic patches of endocrine tissue called the **islets of Langerhans** (Fig. 18.15). Histochemical studies show that the islets consist of two types of cells called α- and β-cells. They are responsible for the production and secretion of two hormones called **glucagon** and **insulin** respectively. The hormones are discharged directly into the islets' blood capillaries. The rest of the pancreas and its exocrine ducts are not involved in hormone production or secretion. Experimentally tying off the pancreatic ducts prevents secretion of pancreatic digestive enzymes but has no effect on hormone secretion.

Insulin lowers the concentration of blood glucose while glucagon raises it. Output of the pancreatic hormones is regulated by the concentration of glucose in blood (Fig. 18.16).

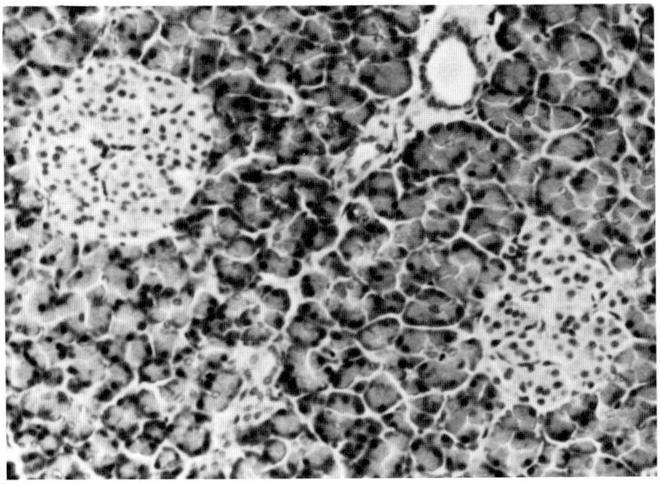

FIG. 18.15 *Photomicrograph of two islets of Langerhans seen in a thin section of monkey pancreas, × 100*

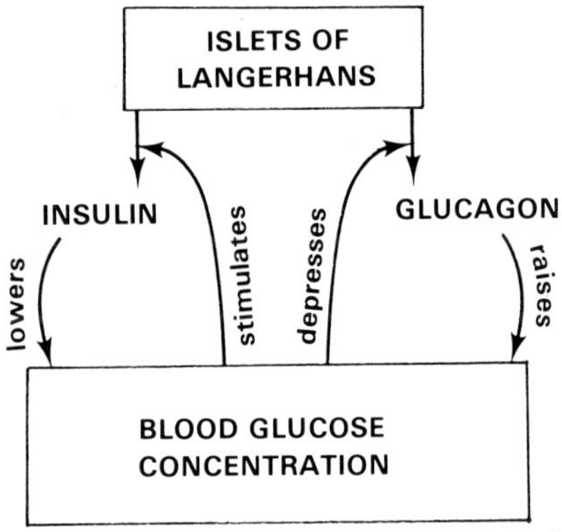

FIG. 18.16 *Effects of insulin and glucagon on the level of blood glucose*

1. THE FUNCTIONS OF INSULIN

Insulin performs two main functions in mammals. The first is to regulate the concentration of glucose in the blood. On the one hand glucose is used by the tissues at varying rates dependent on the rate of metabolic activity. More glucose is used during exercise than when the body is at rest. On the other hand the body's input of glucose varies depending on what has been eaten. The concentration of glucose in the blood draining the gut can double after a meal. The problem then is to reconcile the variable input and respiration of glucose with a relatively constant concentration of glucose in the blood. In dealing with this problem the liver, insulin and glucagon play vital roles.

Blood leaving the gut contains the absorbed products of digestion and passes through the hepatic portal system into the liver (Chapter 14). The liver cells contain enzymes which under the control of insulin promote the synthesis of **glycogen**, a polymer of glucose. It is as glycogen that much of the glucose absorbed from the gut is stored in the liver. Some glycogen is also stored in the skeletal muscles. Insulin therefore prevents any undue rise in the concentration of glucose in the blood. Glucose removed from the blood for respiration is replaced from the glycogen stores. Glucagon has the opposite effect to insulin. It stimulates the conversion of glycogen to

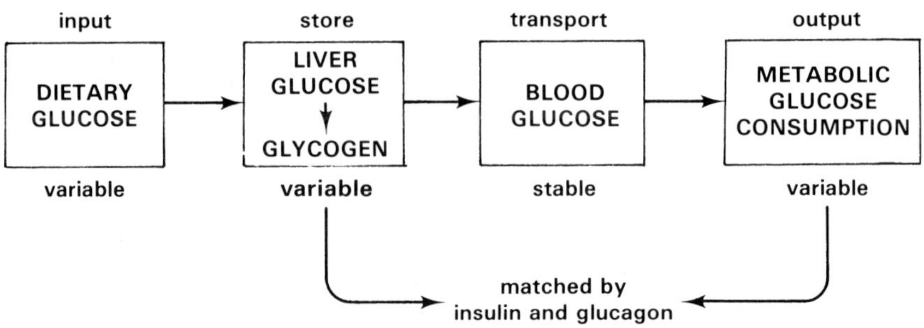

FIG. 18.17 *Summary of the fate of glucose in the mammalian body*

glucose. The balance between the effects of the two hormones results in regulation of the concentration of glucose in blood (Fig. 18.17). The **negative feedback relationship** between the hormones and glucose in blood ensures that glucose is released from the glycogen stores at a rate sufficient to match its uptake from the blood by respiring tissues.

The second main function of insulin is to affect the **rate of entry** of glucose into respiring cells. Glucose is taken into living cells by **active absorption**. Insulin greatly increases the rate of glucose absorption, possibly by triggering off a membrane carrier mechanism or by acting as a carrier itself. In a normal healthy man a concentration of about 50 to 80 mg glucose per 100 cm^3 blood is sufficient to meet the requirements of respiring cells. In the absence of insulin, this concentration would have to increase by between ten and twenty times for glucose to enter the cells at the same rate by diffusion (Fig. 18.18).

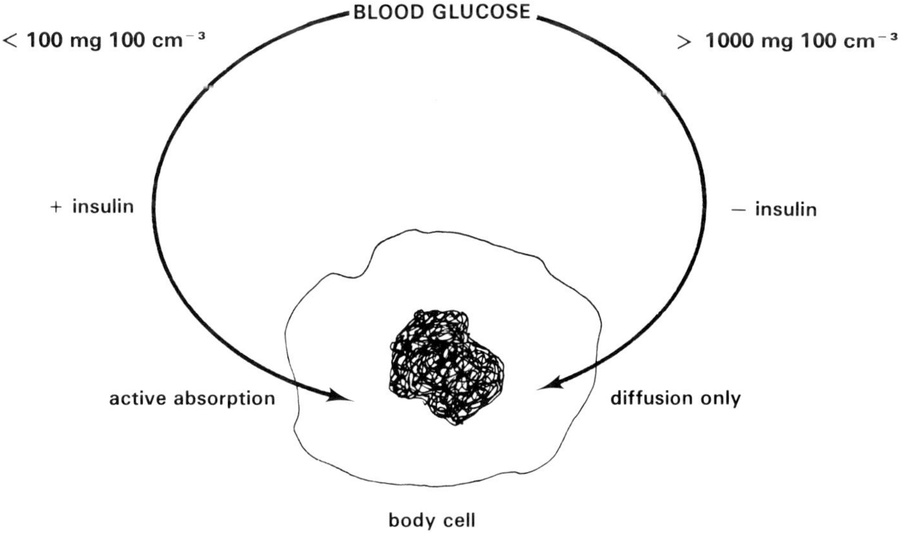

FIG. 18.18 *Insulin promotes the entry of glucose into body cells. In the absence of insulin the amount of intercellular glucose must rise to about 10 times its normal concentration for glucose to enter the cells at the same rate*

2. MALFUNCTION OF THE ISLETS OF LANGERHANS

Underactivity of the islets of Langerhans results in reduced secretion of insulin and is the cause of **diabetes mellitus**. This should not be confused with diabetes insipidus (Chapter 10). In diabetes mellitus the glucose concentration in blood rises. The condition is called **hyperglycaemia**, and glucose exceeds the maximum concentration which can be totally reabsorbed from the renal filtrate in the kidneys. Consequently glucose is excreted in the urine, a condition called **glycosuria**. The presence of glucose in the urine disturbs the water potential gradient which normally results in water reabsorption from the nephrons. Large volumes of dilute urine are thus produced, a condition called **diuresis**. Diuresis is dangerous because it brings about dehydration of the body. Since the breakdown of glycogen is uninhibited in diabetes mellitus the stores of glycogen in the liver and muscles are quickly used up. Body fats and proteins are then used as respiratory substrates causing a rapid loss of body mass.

The condition can be rectified by regular doses of insulin and by eating a carefully controlled diet. A clinical test often used in hospitals to assess whether insulin production is normal involves measurement of **glucose tolerance**. Patients are made to fast for several hours before ingesting 50 g of glucose in 150 cm^3 water. The concentration of glucose in the patient's blood is then measured immediately and at 30-minute intervals over a period of two to three hours. If necessary the urine is also analysed for glucose at hourly intervals. The concentration of glucose in the blood is plotted against time and a glucose tolerance curve is obtained (Fig. 18.19). In a healthy individual there is a slight rise in blood glucose concentration after the glucose drink. Insulin then brings the concentration of glucose in the blood down to its original value within about two hours and no glucose is excreted in the urine.

FIG. 18.19 *Glucose tolerance curves*

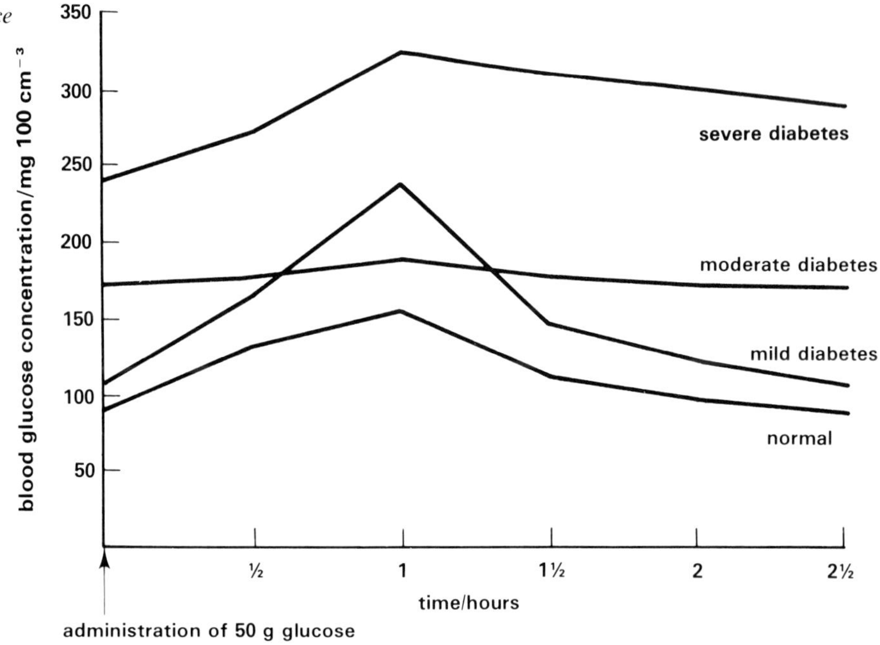

During late pregnancy the renal threshold for glucose may be lower than normal. Thus even though the concentration of glucose in the blood is normal and only slightly rises after a meal, the rise may be sufficient for some glucose to be excreted in the urine. Glycosuria during pregnancy therefore does not necessarily mean that the mother is suffering from diabetes mellitus.

18.2.2 Cortisol

The reserves of glycogen in the mammalian body are limited and in certain conditions fats and proteins can be converted to glucose to supply metabolic demands. The conversion is influenced by a number of steroid hormones called **glucocorticoids** secreted by the **adrenal bodies**, a pair of glands lying close to the kidneys (Fig. 18.1). Each adrenal body is divided into an inner **medulla** and an outer **cortex** (Fig. 18.20(a)). It is in the cortex that glucocorticoids are made. The most abundant of these hormones is **cortisol** (Fig. 18.20(b)).

Cortisol stimulates the conversion of fats and proteins to glucose and is thus involved in regulating the glucose concentration in blood. Output of cortisol is controlled by a trophic hormone from the pituitary body. The hormone is called **corticotropin** (**ACTH**). Secretion of ACTH is affected by the concentration of cortisol in the blood, another example of a negative feedback control mechanism (Fig. 18.21). The combined effects of insulin, glucagon and cortisol in regulating the glucose concentration in blood are summarised in Figure 18.22.

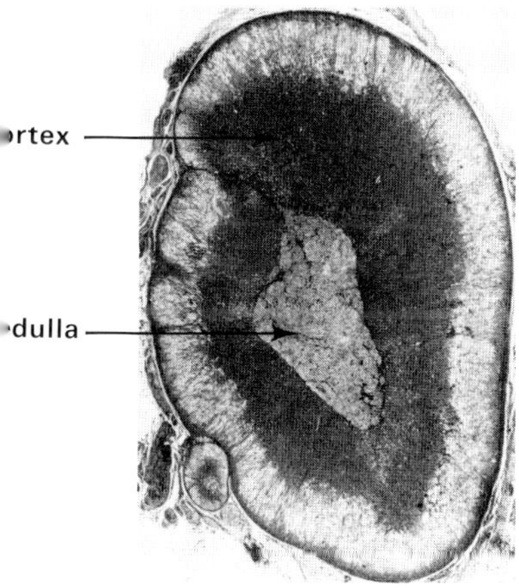

FIG. 18.20 (a) *Photomicrograph of a transverse section of an adrenal body from a cat, ×11*

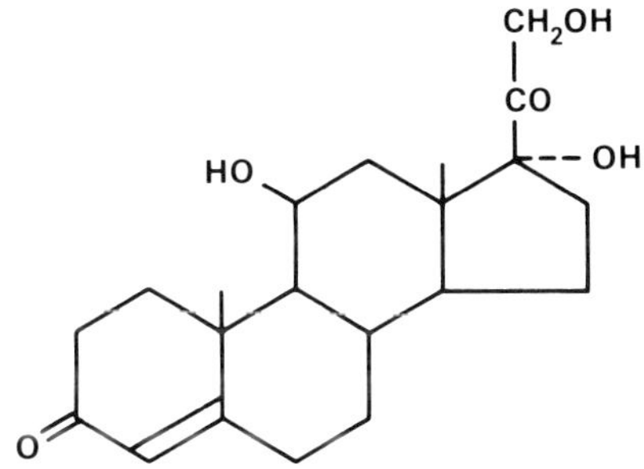

FIG. 18.20 (b) *Molecular structure of cortisol*

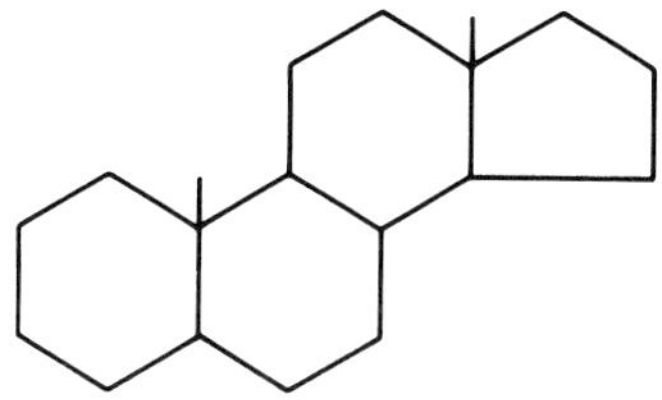
FIG. 18.20 (c) *The basic structure of a steroid*

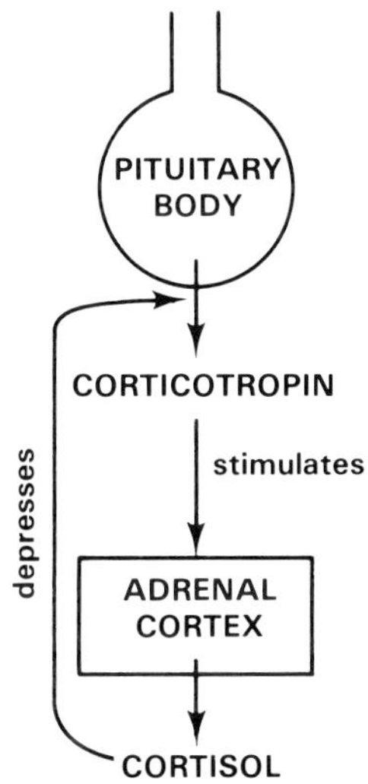

FIG. 18.21 *Mechanism regulating cortisol production*

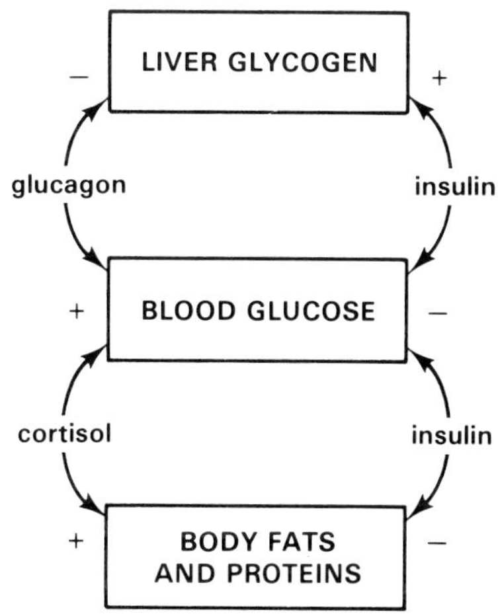

FIG. 18.22 *Combined effects of insulin, glycogen and cortisol on blood glucose*

Another important function of cortisol is its ability to depress autolysis of damaged body cells by lysosomes (Chapter 1). Cortisol-like drugs are valuable in promoting the repair of body organs damaged in degenerative diseases such as arthritis. One of the effects of adrenalin, secreted by the medulla of the adrenal glands, is to increase ACTH output (section 18.5.1). This partly explains the increased secretion of cortisol which normally accompanies mental and physical stress.

18.3 Control of blood sodium and potassium

Sodium and potassium salts, especially chlorides, participate in a variety of body functions, particularly nerve and muscle activity. Consequently the maintenance of stable concentrations of sodium and potassium ions in the blood is vital for normal physiological activity (Chapter 15). Furthermore, because sodium and potassium salts are soluble in water they affect the osmotic potential of the body fluids. The concentrations of sodium and potassium ions in the body are regulated by **mineralocorticoid hormones** made in the adrenal cortex.

18.3.1 Aldosterone

The most important mineralocortoid hormone is **aldosterone** (Fig. 18.23). This steroid is strikingly similar in molecular structure to cortisol (Fig. 18.20(b)). Nevertheless their functions are very different. Aldosterone promotes reabsorption of sodium ions (Na^+) into the blood from the filtrate in the renal nephrons (Chapter 10). Chloride ions (Cl^-) usually accompany the sodium ions, probably because of electrostatic attraction. Uptake of sodium ions depresses reabsorption of potassium ions (K^+). This is why potassium ions are found in urine. Output of aldosterone is inhibited by a high concentration of sodium ions in the blood, yet another example of a feedback mechanism which assists homeostasis (Fig. 18.24).

FIG. 18.23 *Molecular structure of aldosterone*

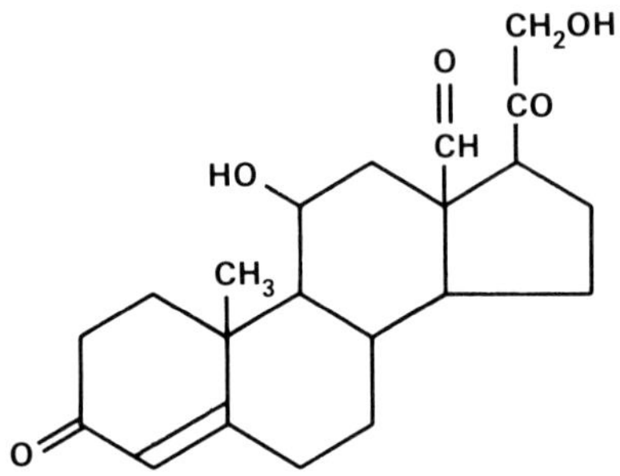

FIG. 18.24 *Aldosterone stimulates the reabsorption of sodium chloride by the nephrons*

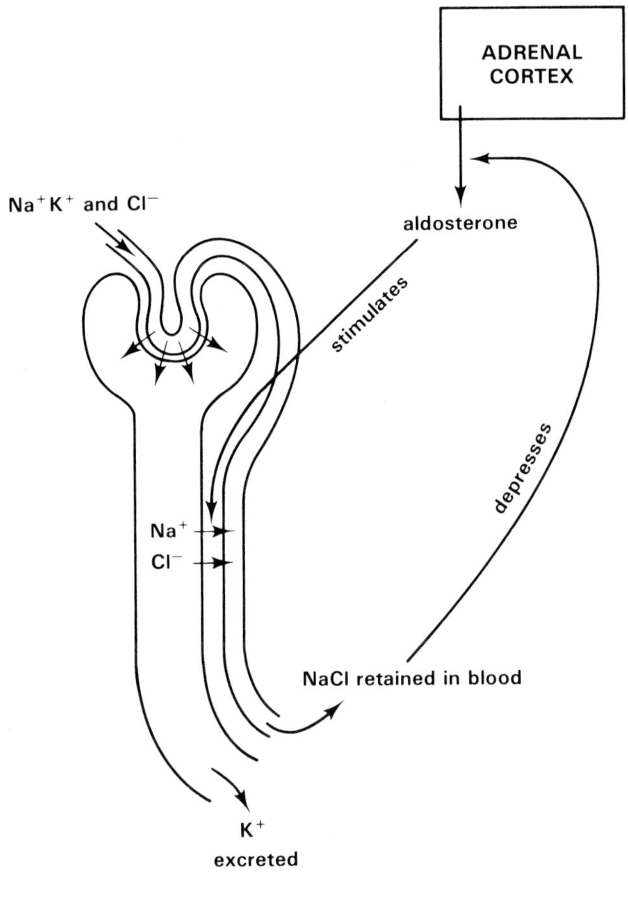

Depressed output of aldosterone can cause excessive excretion of water by the kidneys resulting in a fall in the blood volume. One effect of the fall is the secretion into the blood of the enzyme **renin** from special kidney cells. Renin activates the conversion of a plasma protein called **proangiotensin** into an active derivative **angiotensin**. Angiotensin stimulates secretion of aldosterone thereby aiding water reabsorption by the kidneys. Angiotensin also stimulates the brain to trigger off impulses which create the sensation of **thirst** (Fig. 18.25). These are appropriate responses to too little water in the body fluids, and providing water is consumed the body's state of hydration is rectified.

FIG. 18.25 *Effect of aldosterone on water reabsorption by the nephrons. Angiotensin stimulates the thirst centre in the brain as well as aldosterone secretion*

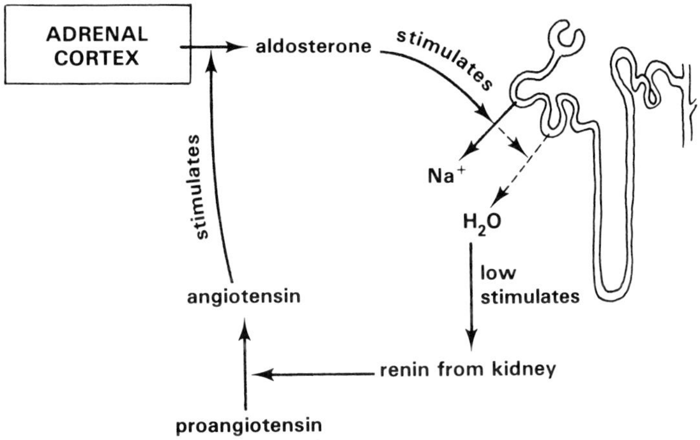

18.4 The adrenal medulla

The centre of each adrenal gland, the **medulla**, is derived from the same embryonic tissue which gives rise to sympathetic nerve ganglia. For this reason the medulla of the adrenal glands can be regarded as a modified part of the sympathetic nervous system. Sympathetic nerves, as part of the autonomic system play an important role in regulating many body functions (Chapter 15). Hormones secreted into the blood by the adrenal medulla have similar effects to stimulation of sympathetic nerves.

18.4.1 The medullary hormones

FIG. 18.26 *Structure of* (a) *noradrenalin and* (b) *adrenalin. These hormones belong to a group of chemicals called catecholamines*

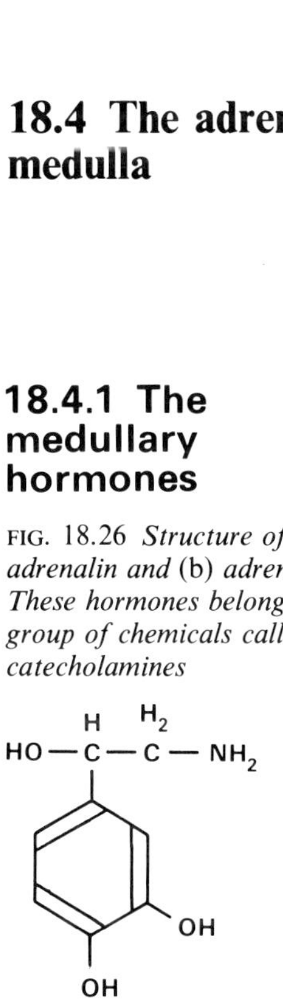

(a)

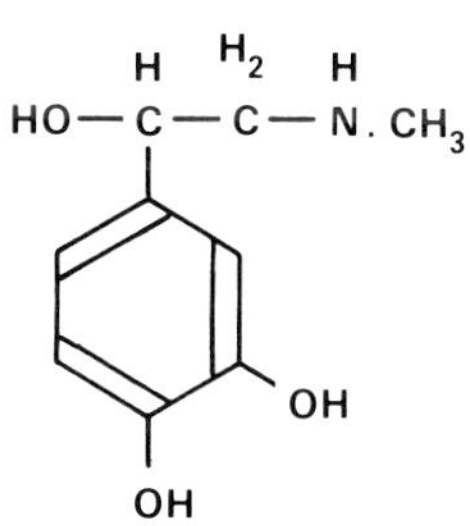

(b)

Two hormones are made in the adrenal medulla of mammals, **adrenalin** and **noradrenalin** (Fig. 18.26). Noradrenalin is the neuroeffector transmitter secreted by sympathetic nerve endings. However, adrenalin is the main secretion of the medulla. The effects of both hormones are similar and like sympathetic activity generally, they prepare the body to expend a lot of energy quickly. In fact, stimulation of the sympathetic nerves activates the medulla and promotes secretion of adrenalin.

Normally the adrenal medulla secretes small amounts of adrenalin and noradrenalin into the blood. However, following increased activity of the sympathetic nerves which usually accompanies physical and mental stress, larger quantities are released. Because the medullary hormones prepare mammals to run away from or to face an enemy, they are sometimes called the **flight or fight hormones**. In many respects this is an appropriate description. The effects of adrenalin and noradrenalin can be summarised as follows:

1. EFFECTS ON THE GUT AND RESPIRATORY SYSTEM

The smooth muscle of the gastro-intestinal tract relaxes and the bronchi become dilated. The thorax is enlarged because the diaphragm can now be pushed down further into the abdomen. The net result is that volumes of air larger than normal can be drawn in and out of the lungs, thereby increasing the rate of oxygen uptake by the blood.

2. EFFECTS ON THE CARDIOVASCULAR SYSTEM

The heart rate and the power of cardiac contractions increase with consequent rise of blood pressure. Arterioles in the skin and gut become constricted while the vessels supplying the skeletal muscles dilate. These effects, together with increased ventilation of the lungs, ensure an adequate supply of oxygenated blood to organs such as muscles which produce energy for movement.

3. EFFECTS ON BLOOD GLUCOSE

Glycogen stored in liver and skeletal muscles is converted to glucose, thus providing the source of energy required for increased muscular activity. Adrenalin stimulates secretion of ACTH and hence cortisol. Some of the extra glucose may therefore come from fats and proteins (section 18.2.2).

4. EFFECTS ON THE NERVOUS SYSTEM

Adrenalin increases sensitivity of the nervous system thereby increasing the speed with which the body reacts to environmental stimuli. This is of obvious advantage to a mammal in flight or fight. The various effects of the medullary hormones are illustrated in Figure 18.27.

FIG. 18.27 *Summary of the effects of adrenalin*

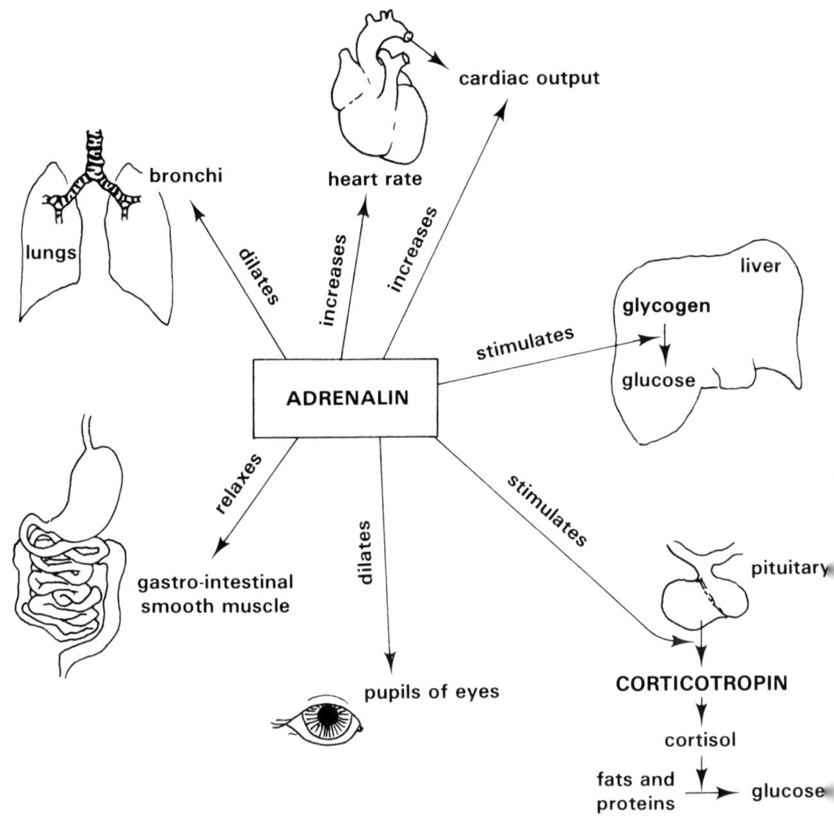

18.5 The pituitary body

Projecting downward from the base of the forebrain and almost totally enclosed by bone is the **pituitary body**, also called the **hypophysis**. It consists of two functional glands called the **anterior pituitary**, derived from the embryonic pharynx and the **posterior pituitary**, derived from the hypothalamus in the forebrain (Fig. 18.28).

18.5.1 The anterior pituitary

The anterior pituitary secretes several hormones including the various **tropins** referred to earlier in the chapter. **TSH** controls the secretion of thyroid hormones while **ACTH** controls the output of cortisol from the adrenal cortex. Other tropins affecting mainly the testes and ovaries are called **gonadotropins**. They are also produced by the anterior pituitary. The activities of **follitropin** (**FSH**) and **lutropin** (**LH**) are described in Chapter 22.

IG. 18.28 (a) *Position of the ituitary body beneath the ypothalamus*

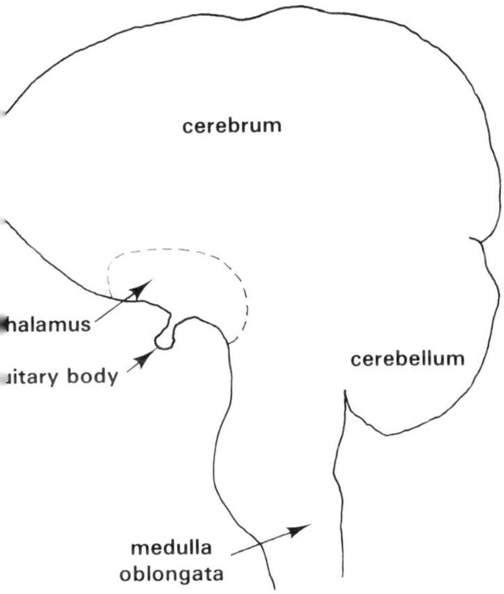

FIG. 18.28 (b) *Anterior and posterior components of the pituitary body*

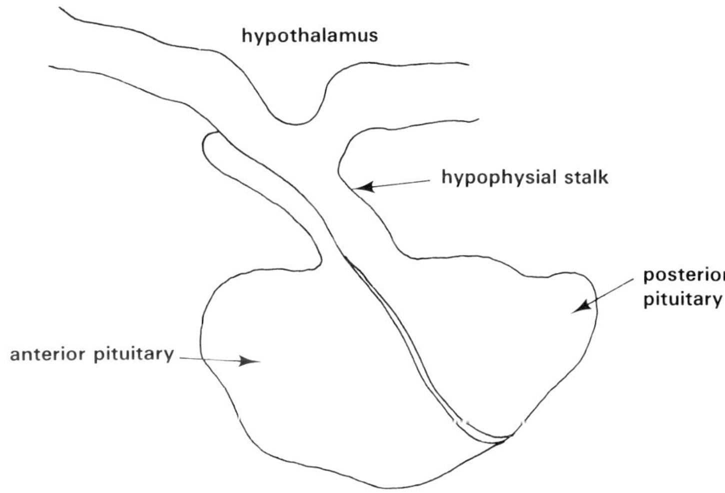

IG. 18.28 (c) *Photomicrograph of vertical section through the uman pituitary body* (× *10*)

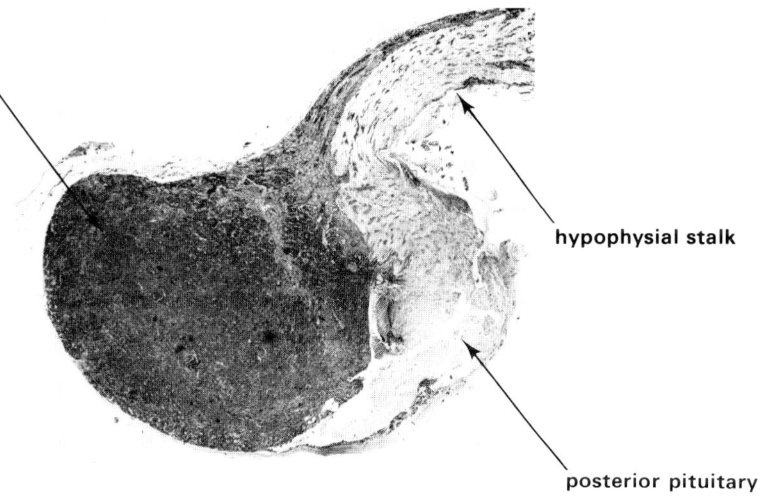

Another hormone made in the anterior pituitary is called the growth hormone or **somatotropin (STH)**. Growth is also controlled by thyroxin (section 18.1.1). STH is not strictly a tropin since it affects the tissues directly rather than through secretions of other endocrine glands. However, STH enhances the activities of the other hormones from the anterior pituitary. The main function of STH is to promote the growth of the body's tissues and organs by stimulating the synthesis of macromolecules, especially proteins. The precise mechanism of the stimulation is unknown but it may involve promoting the absorption of vital nutrients, especially amino acids by body cells from tissue fluid, and activation of the genes which control growth.

Secretion of STH occurs throughout life but diminishes after the growing period. The way in which its secretion is controlled is unknown.

Oversecretion of STH leads to **gigantism**, while undersecretion causes **dwarfism** (Fig. 18.29). In man, oversecretion of STH during adulthood when normal growth is complete leads to **acromegaly**. Many of the internal organs become enlarged as do the hands and feet. The most striking characteristic is the lower jaw which often grows to protrude forward rather noticeably (Fig. 18.30). The overall body height does not usually increase since after adolescence the limb bones are normally incapable of further growth in length.

FIG. 18.29 *Diagram showing gigantism* (left) *and dwarfism* (right) *contrasted with normal growth* (centre)

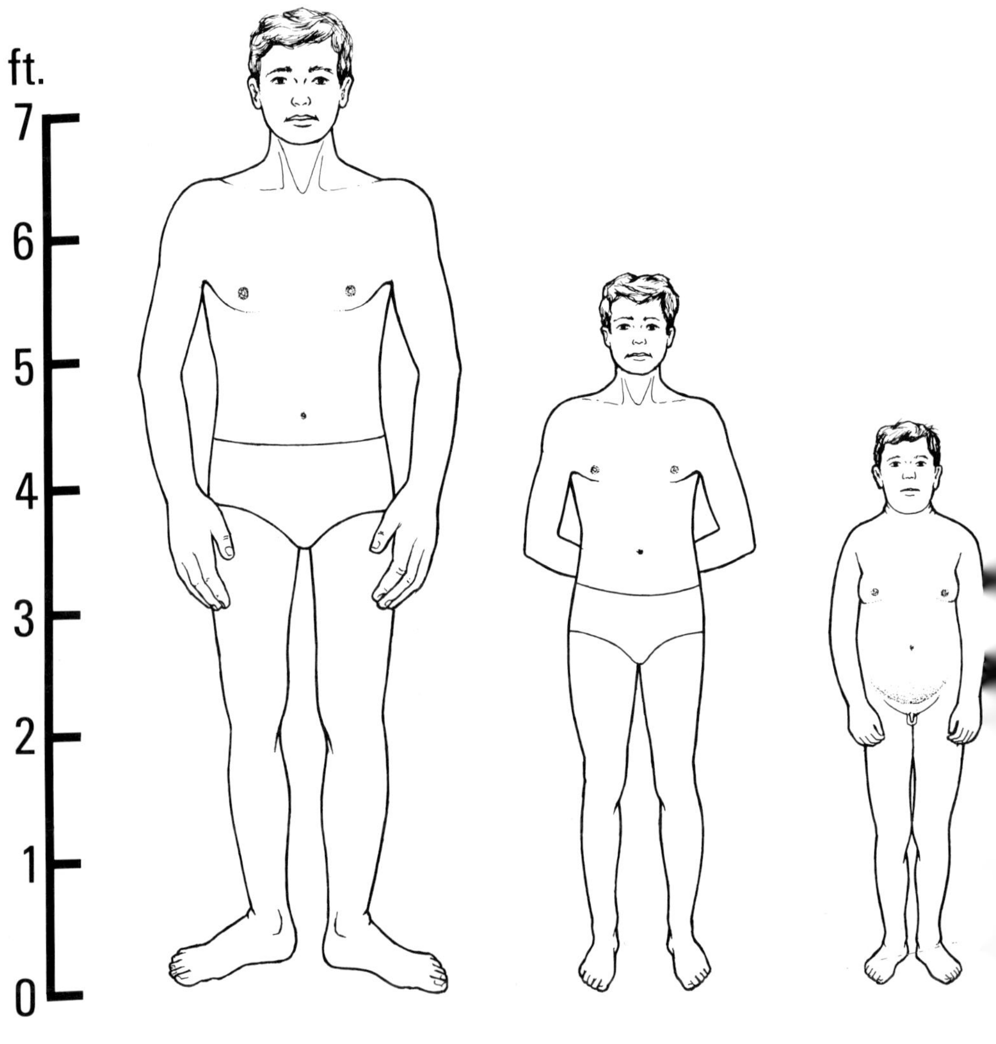

FIG. 18.30 *Facial characteristics of acromegaly. Note the protruding jaw and forehead*

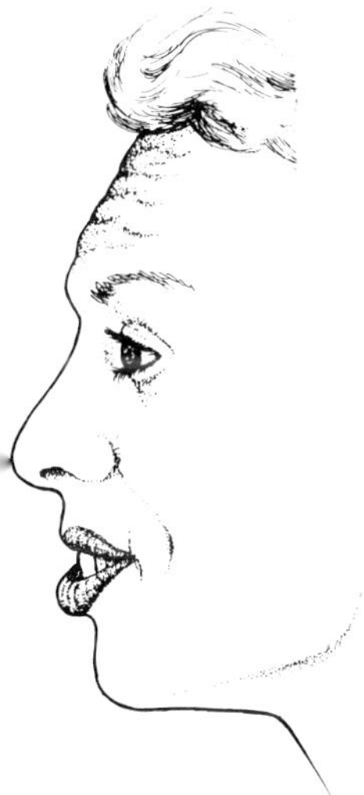

Secretion by the anterior pituitary is partly controlled by a variety of substances from the hypothalamus. The secretions are carried from the hypothalamus into the anterior pituitary in blood vessels (Fig. 18.31). One secretion is **thyroliberin**. Thyroliberin stimulates the release of TSH which in turn stimulates secretion of the thyroid hormones (Fig. 18.5). Other hormones made in the hypothalamus control the release of the rest of the hormones made in the anterior pituitary.

FIG. 18.31 *The hypothalamic–hypophysial portal system responsible for transporting tropin hormones made in the hypothalamus down into the anterior pituitary*

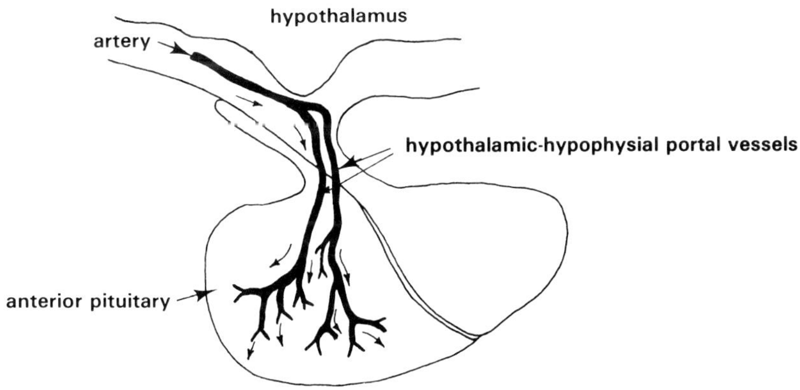

18.5.2 The posterior pituitary

The **posterior pituitary** produces two hormones. These are **vasopressin** and **ocytocin**. Both are polypeptides consisting of nine amino acids. Vasopressin (VP) and ocytocin are made by neurons in the hypothalamus and migrate in the axons of nerve fibres to the posterior pituitary where they are stored. When the neurons connecting the hypothalamus and posterior pituitary are stimulated, VP and ocytocin are released into the blood (Fig. 18.32).

Ocytocin affects smooth muscle and is particularly important in female mammals at the end of pregnancy when it brings about rhythmical contraction of the uterine wall during birth. This function and its role in controlling the ejection of milk from the mammary glands are described in Chapter 22. Vasopressin plays an important role in the regulation of water reabsorption by the renal nephrons (Chapter 10).

FIG. 18.32 *Hypothalamic–hypophysial neurons responsible for transporting vasopressin and ocytocin from the hypothalamus down into the posterior pituitary*

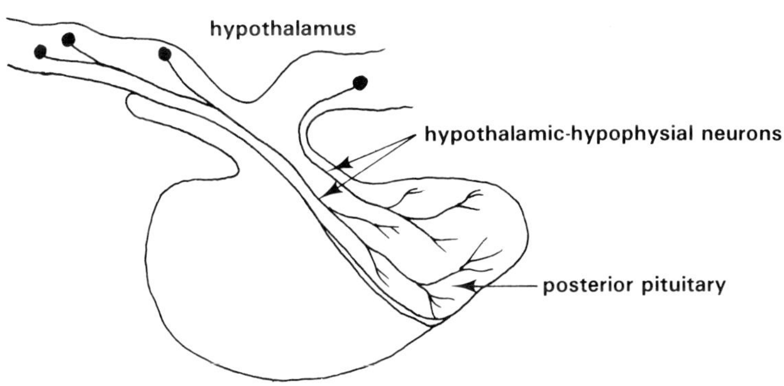

Chapter 19

Reproduction in flowering plants

Reproduction is the formation of new individuals. It is the means whereby successive generations are produced resembling their parents to a greate or lesser extent. The transmission of hereditary material from parent to offspring is an essential feature of reproduction. In flowering plants the transmission can occur in one of two main ways. In **sexual reproductio** male and female sex cells called **gametes** are produced. The gametes come together and nuclear fusion takes place. The genome of a sexually produced organism is a mixture of genes from two sources. In **asexual reproduction** offspring are formed in a number of ways but fusion of nuclea material does not take place. Offspring produced asexually nearly alway have an exact replica of the genome of their parent. Many species o flowering plants reproduce both sexually and asexually. Most flowering plants are **hermaphrodite** yet most species cross-breed.

Man is highly dependent on the end products of flowering plant reproduction. Seeds and fruits, tubers and bulbs figure prominently in our die and in the diets of our domesticated stock.

19.1 Sexual reproduction

In flowering plants male gametes develop in **pollen grains**, female gamete in **ovules**. Pollen grains and ovules are produced in **flowers**.

19.1.1 Flower structure

Following a period of vegetative growth, most flowering plants produc flowers. Annual plants flower in their first season of growth, biennials in their second season. After flowering both types die leaving seeds to germinate the following year. Perennial species generally flower every yea when established. Some angiosperms, for example the tulip, produce larg **solitary flowers** but others such as the dandelion have small flowers masse together in an **inflorescence**.

Flowers develop from apical meristems which previously gave rise t leafy shoots. Some of the factors which regulate the switch from a vegetative to a reproductive function are described in section 19.5. As a flowe bud opens it is possible to see four kinds of floral organs in most flower On the outside are the **sepals**, usually green in colour. Collectively th sepals of a flower are called the **calyx**. Immediately inside the calyx ar the **petals**, collectively called the **corolla**. The petals of many species c flowering plants are coloured. Yellow, blue and red are the most commo colours in wild flowers. Next inwards are the **stamens**, each consisting of **filament** and an **anther** in which pollen is produced. The term **androecium** i used to describe the collection of stamens in a flower. At the centre of th flower are found one or more **carpels**, collectively known as the **gynoeciur** or **ovary**. Each carpel or group of carpels contains one or more ovules an has a **stigma** and a **style**.

The apex of the flower stalk from which the floral organs arise is calle the **receptacle**. The numbers, size, colour and arrangement of the variou organs vary from one species to another, although the flowers of close related species are very similar in appearance. Figure 19.1 shows a range c flower structures of a few common British species.

FIG. 19.1 (a) *Half-flower of strawberry (a radially symmetrical flower)*

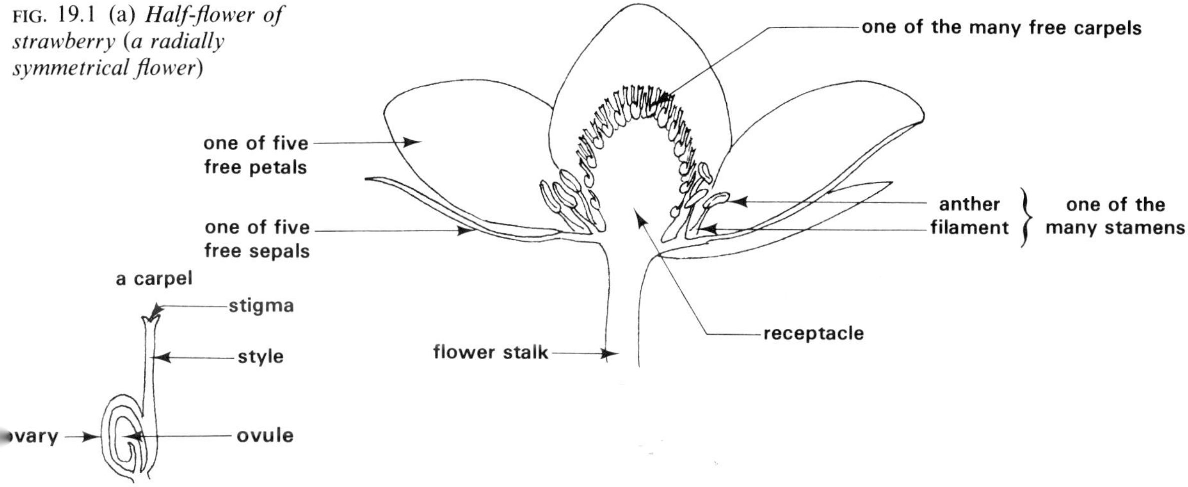

FIG. 19.1 (b) *Half-flower of broom (a bilaterally symmetrical flower)*

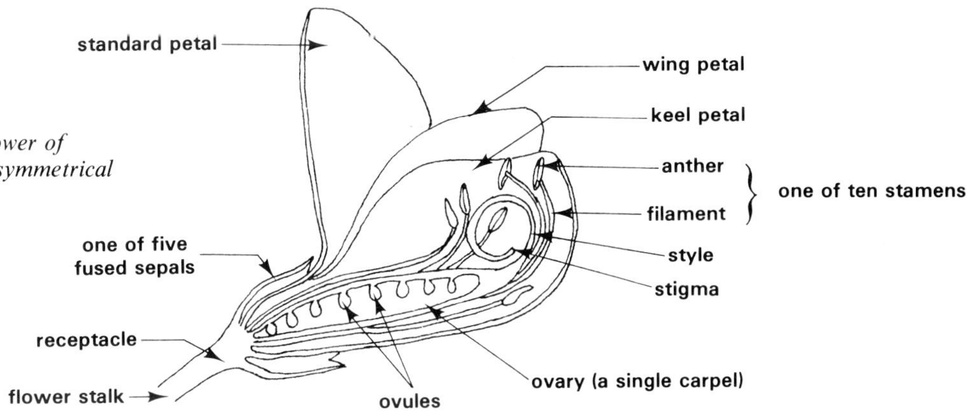

FIG. 19.1 (c) *Flowers of dandelion*

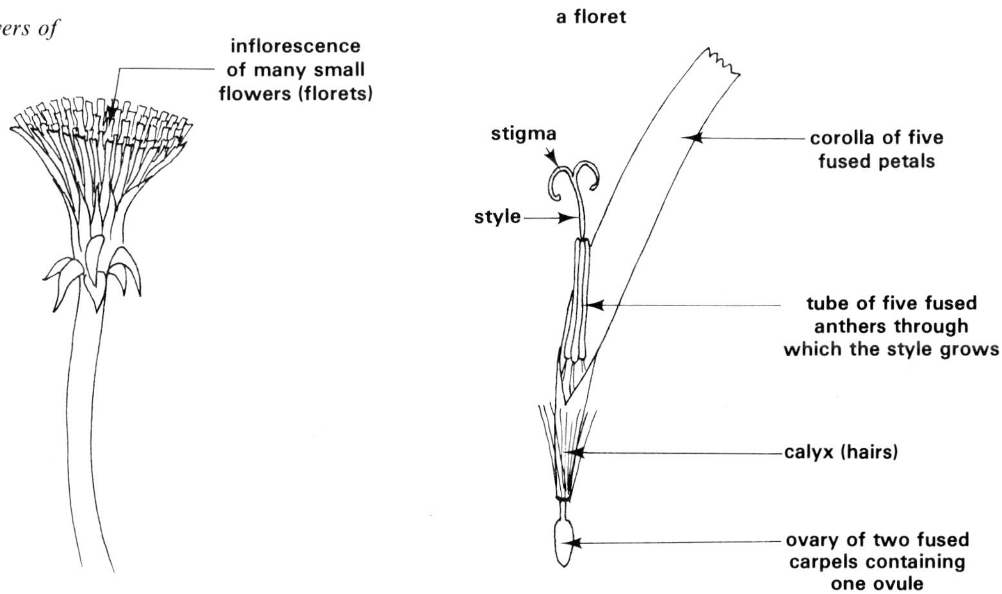

19.1.2 Development of pollen and ovules

Sexual reproduction cannot occur without the formation of sexual cells called **gametes**. In flowering plants male gametes are formed in the **pollen grains**. Female gametes are formed in the **ovules**.

1. POLLEN FORMATION

Pollen production takes place in the anthers (Fig. 19.2). Early in their development anthers are elongate masses of parenchyma tissue enclosed in an epidermis. In transverse section a young anther is seen to have two or four lobes according to the species. A row of cells extending the whole length of each lobe becomes organised into a central mass of **pollen mother cells** surrounded by several layers of flattened cells. The layer immediately surrounding the pollen mother cells is called the **tapetum**. Soon the mother cells undergo meiosis to produce tetrads of haploid **pollen grains**, also called **microspores**. Each pollen grain secretes a thick wall and its haploid nucleus divides by mitosis to form a **generative cell** and a **tube nucleus**.

FIG. 19.2 *Development of anther and pollen*
(a) *T.s. young anther*

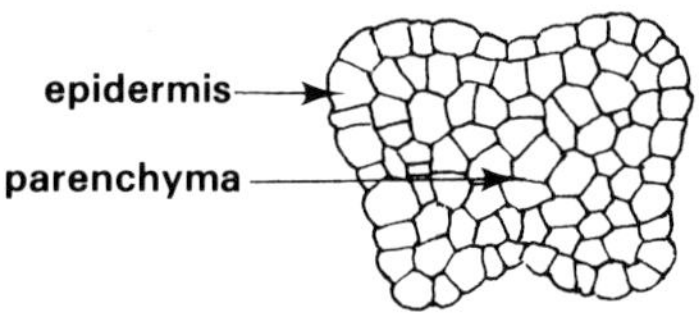

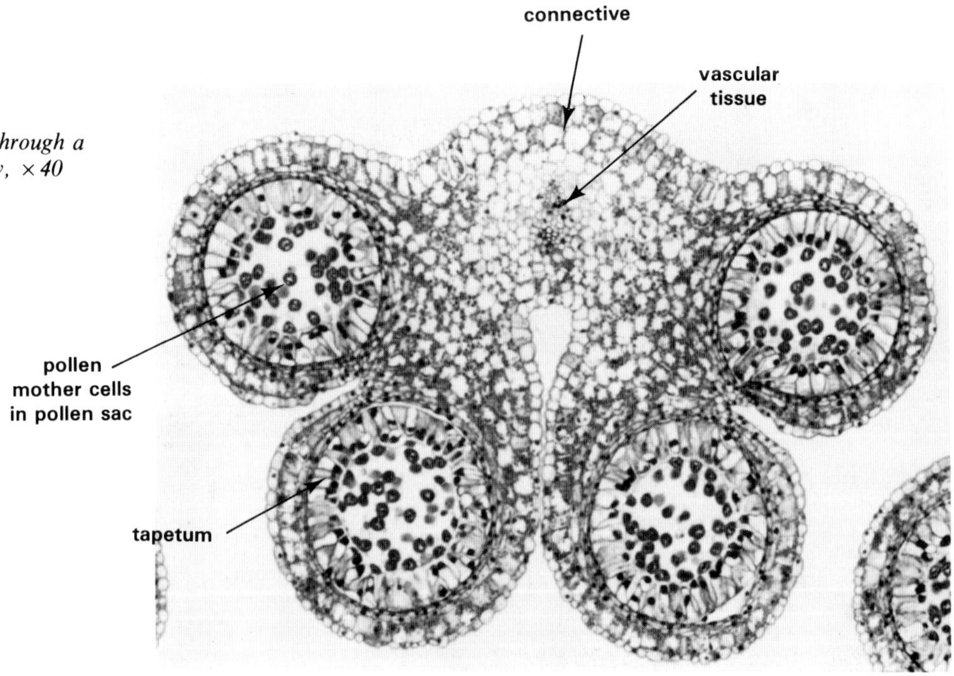

FIG. 19.2 (b)

(i) *transverse section through a young anther of lily, ×40*

While these changes are going on the anther grows considerably in size and depending on the species, two or four pollen sacs become prominent The cells around each sac become thickened with bands of lignin forming a **fibrous layer**. On drying out the fibrous layer shrinks causing the pollen sacs to rupture. Usually they open by splitting lengthwise down each side of the anther, though in some species pores or valves are formed instead

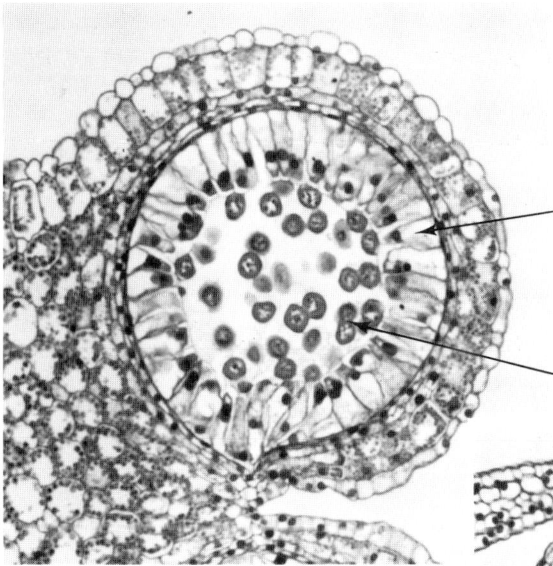

(ii) *pollen mother cell stage, × 70*

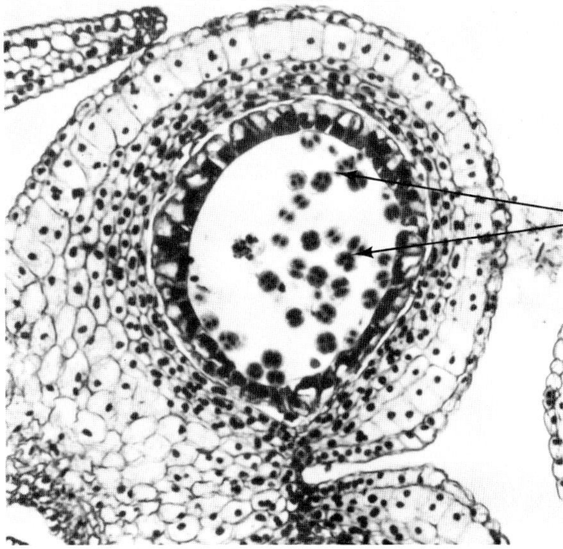

(iii) *tetrad stage, × 70*

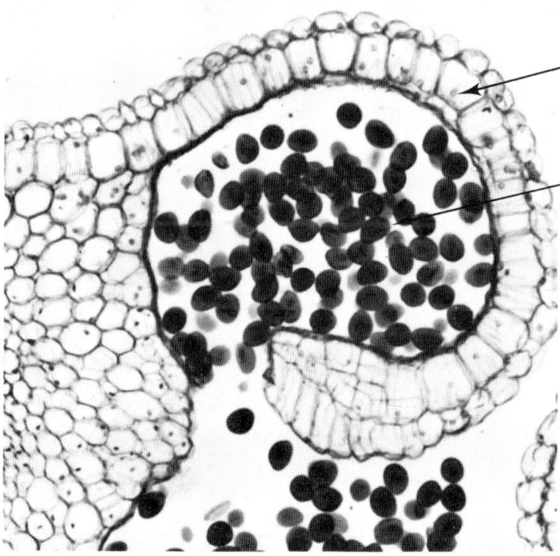

(iv) *dehiscent anther stage, × 70*

FIG. 19.2 (c) *Development of pollen grains*

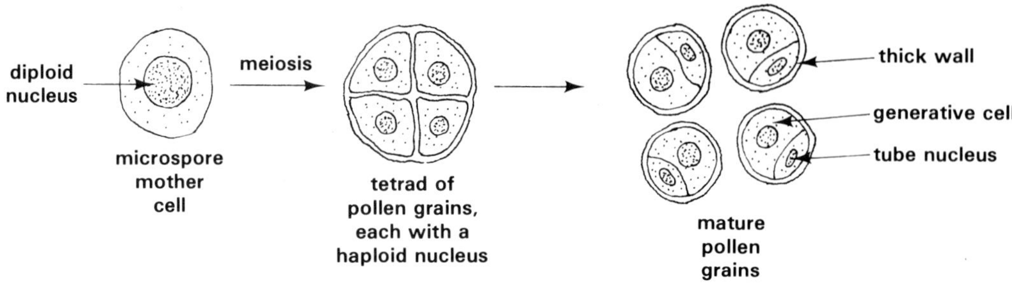

(vi) *section through mature pollen grains, × 400*

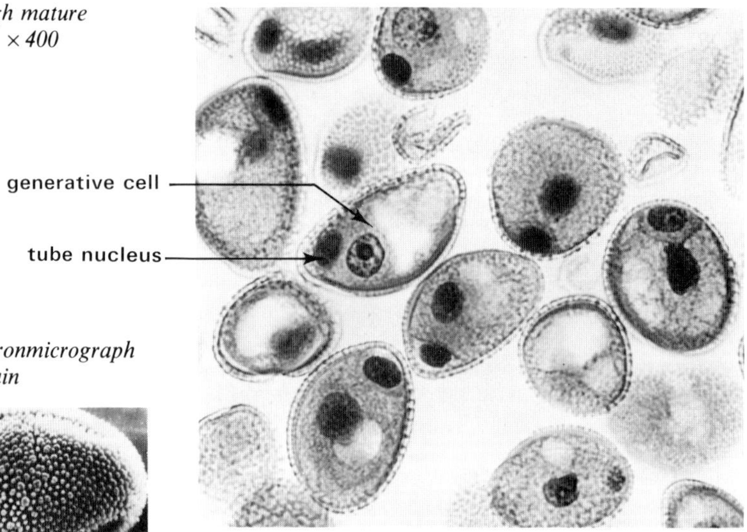

(v) *scanning electronmicrograph of a pollen grain*

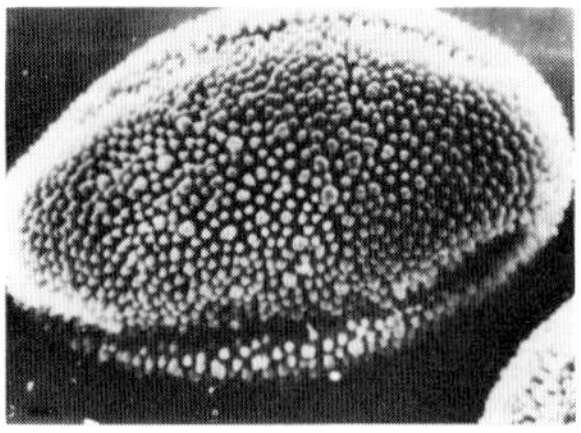

FIG. 19.2 (d) *T.s. dehisced anther*

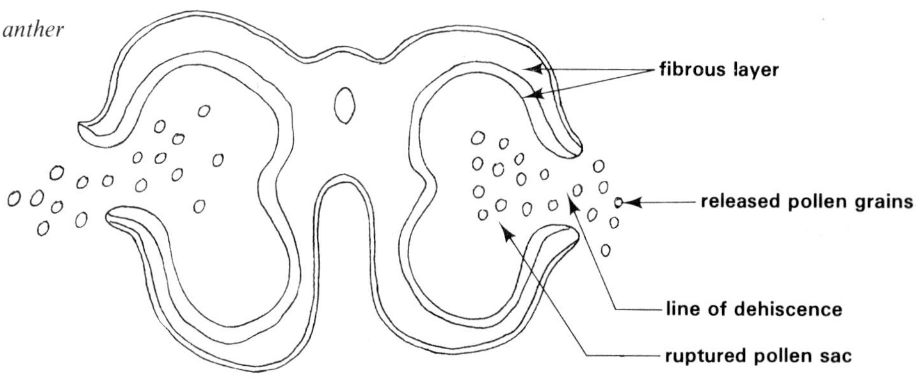

2. OVULE FORMATION

Ovules are formed inside the carpels. Depending on the species, one or more ovules develop in each carpel. In all species, however, an ovule grows from a pad of carpellary tissue called the **placenta** to which it is attached by a short stalk called a **funicle**. At first the young ovule is just a bulge of parenchyma tissue called the **nucellus**. As it enlarges the nucellus is enclosed by two layers called **integuments** which grow up from the funicle. When fully developed the integuments completely surround the nucellus except for a tiny pore called the **micropyle**. Meanwhile, near the tip of the nucellus a cell divides by mitosis to form an outer **parietal cell** and an inner **megaspore mother cell**. The latter divides by meiosis to form a row of four haploid **megaspores**. Only the innermost megaspore usually develops further. It grows considerably in size and its nucleus undergoes three mitotic divisions. The eight haploid nuclei which are formed become arranged in a characteristic fashion (Fig. 19.3). The resulting structure is called an **embryo sac**.

FIG. 19.3 (a) *Development of an ovule*

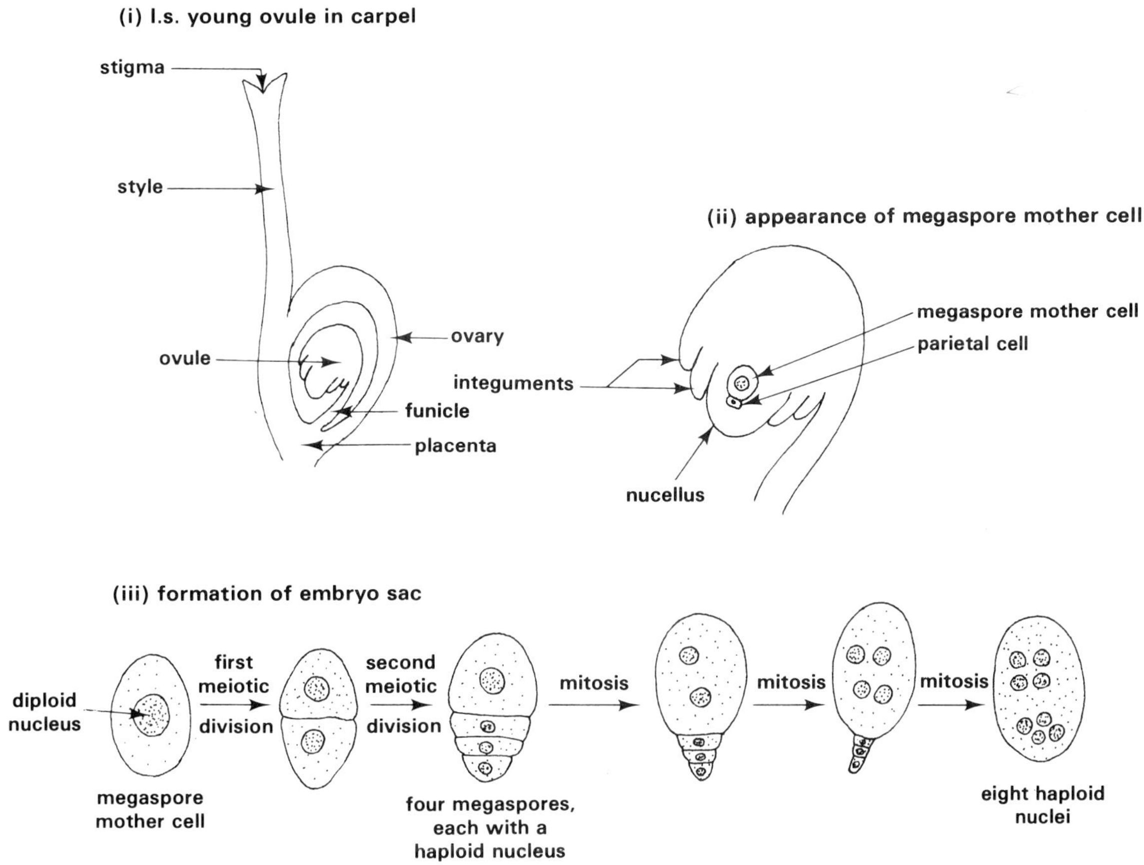

(iv) l.s. mature ovule

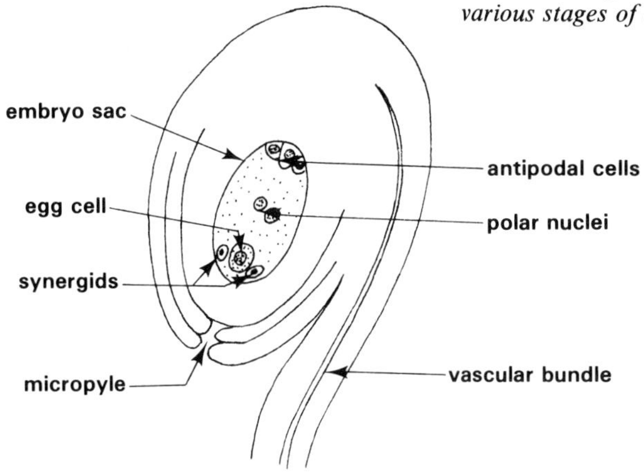

FIG. 19.3 (b) *Longitudinal sections through ovules at various stages of development*

(i) *megaspore mother cell stage, × 250*

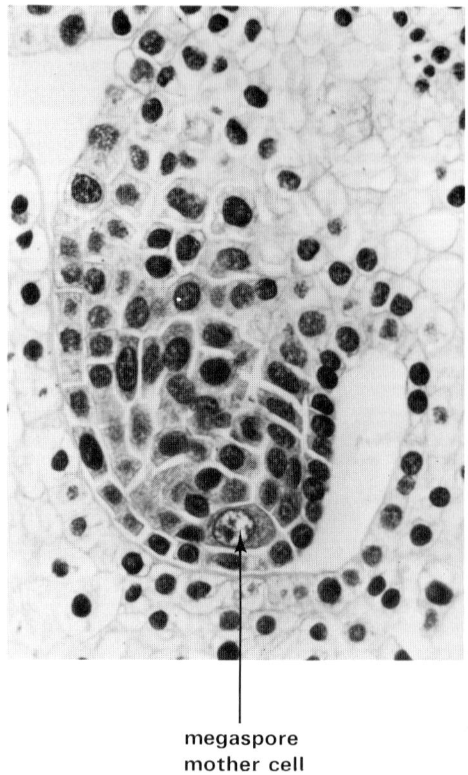

(ii) *embryo sac stage, × 125*

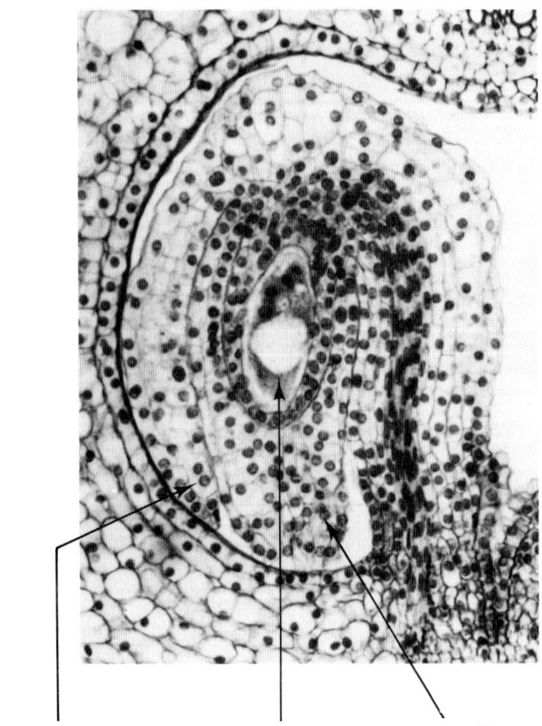

(iii) *young embryo sac, × 400, four nuclei stage*

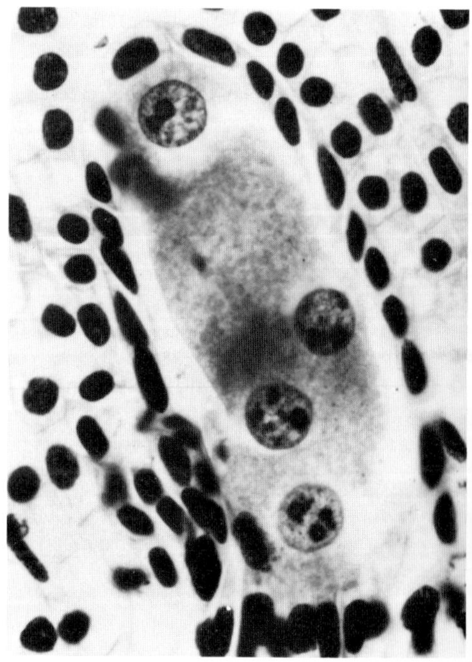

(iv) *mature embryo sac, ×300, eight nuclei stage*

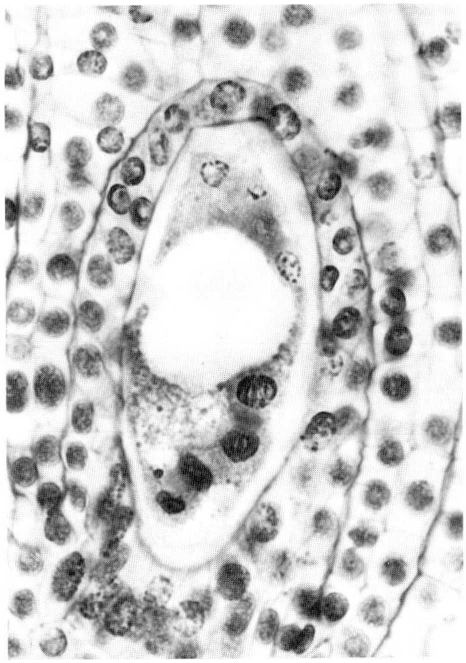

19.1.3 Fertilisation and its consequences

If fertilisation is to occur the male and female sexual cells must be brought together. The first step in bringing the gametes near to each other is **pollination** (section 19.3). Wind and insects are the main pollinating agents. They carry pollen from the anthers to the stigmas.

FIG. 19.4 (a) *Germinating pollen grains*

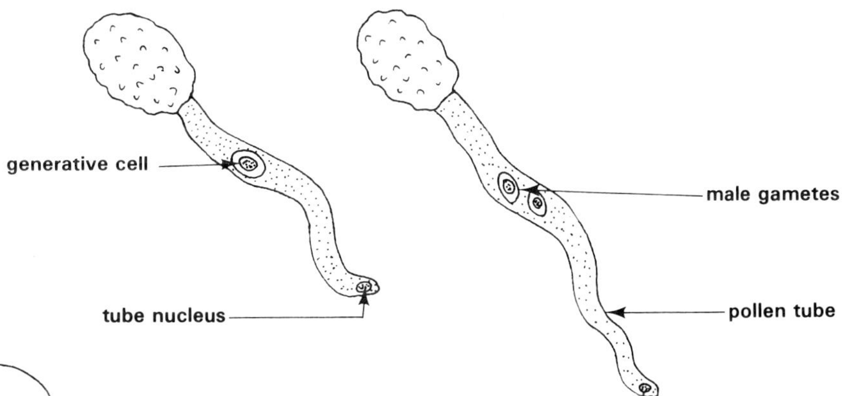

FIG. 19.4 (b) *Fertilisation*

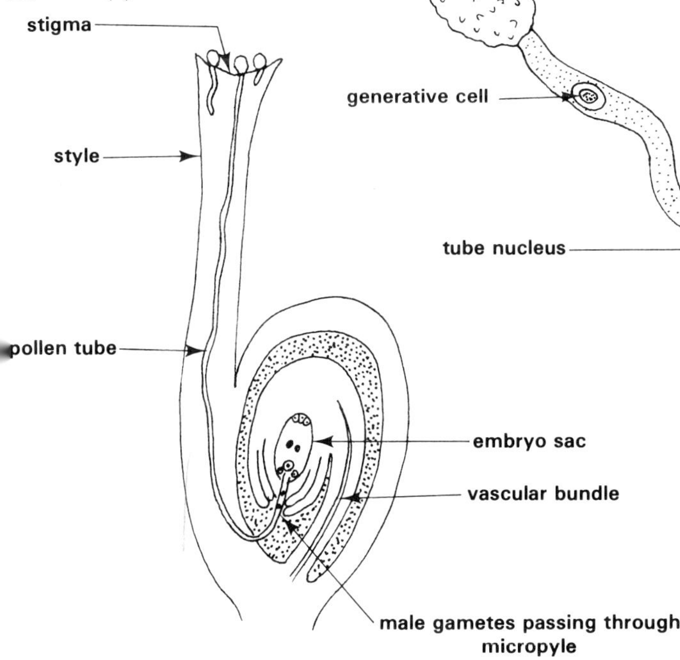

FIG. 19.4 (c) *Pollen grains germinating on the stigma of evening primrose, ×400*

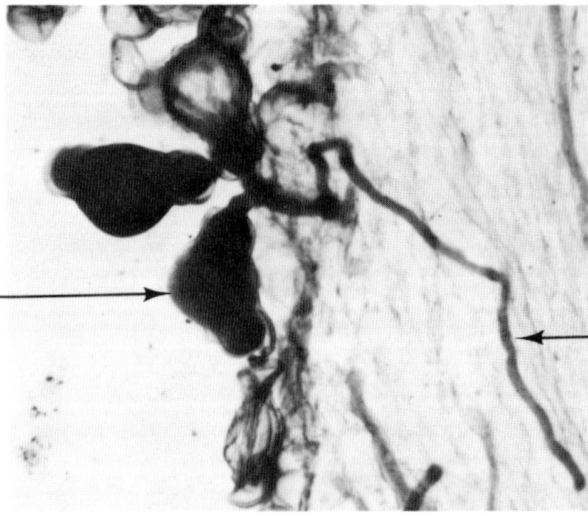

The **egg cell** of each embryo sac is a **female gamete**. Following the transfer of pollen to the stigma a **pollen tube** is formed from each pollen grain. As the tube grows down into the style the tube nucleus is situated at its tip. The generative cell then enters the tube and divides by mitosis to form two cells which are **male gametes** (Fig. 19.4). In some species the male gametes are formed before the generative cell enters the pollen tube. On reaching the ovule the pollen tube grows through the micropyle and nucellus to the embryo sac where its tip opens out. The tube nucleus disintegrates and the two male gametes enter the embryo sac. One of the gametes fuses with the nucleus of the egg cell to form a **diploid zygote**. The other fuses with the diploid nucleus formed by the fusion of the two polar nuclei. The result is a **triploid fusion nucleus**. This **double fertilisation** is unique to flowering plants. Following fertilisation the ovules develop into **seeds** and the ovary of the flower into a **fruit**.

1. SEED FORMATION

The subsequent events leading to seed production vary from one species to another. Essentially what happens is that the zygote develops into an **embryo plant** which is nourished as it grows by **endosperm** formed from the triploid fusion nucleus.

In shepherd's purse, mitosis of the zygote produces a short chain of cells. The first division is at right angles to the long axis of the ovule. The cell furthest away from the micropyle eventually becomes the embryo. The rest of the chain called the **suspensor** elongates, pushing the **embryonic cell** deeper into the embryo sac. Successive divisions of the triploid fusion nucleus produce a large number of triploid nuclei lying in the embryo sac. The nuclei may or may not become separated by cell walls forming a tissue called **endosperm** which surrounds the developing embryo. The embryonic cell divides to form a multicellular embryo with its **radicle**, the embryonic root, pointing towards the micropyle. In shepherd's purse the long axis of the mature embryo is bent. The two cotyledons with the **plumule**, the embryonic shoot, tucked between them point in the same direction as the radicle. During its development the embryo goes through globular, heart-shaped and torpedo stages. As the embryo grows the endosperm gradually disappears. Ultimately no endosperm remains so the seeds of shepherd's purse are **non-endospermic** (Fig. 19.5). However, in some flowering plants such as grasses, some of the endosperm is still present when the embryo is fully developed. These seeds are described as **endospermic** (Chapter 20).

During the final stage in the formation of a seed some of the integument cells usually become lignified, forming a tough protective seed coat called the **testa** perforated only by the micropyle. Gradual dehydration of the entire seed takes place so that eventually as little as 5–10 per cent of its mass is water. The embryo is now in a state of **dormancy** (Chapter 20).

FIG. 19.5 (a) *Stages in the development of an embryo of shepherd's purse*

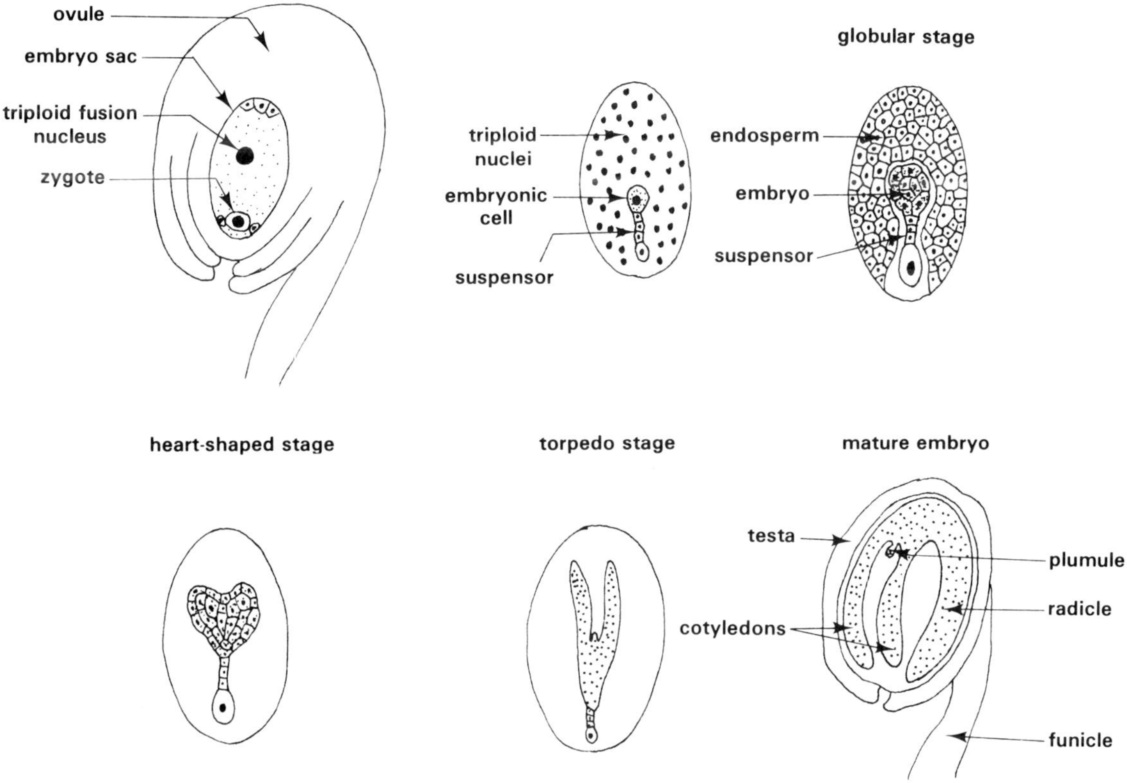

FIG. 19.5 (b) *Stages in the development of an embryo of shepherd's purse*

(i) *globular stage,* × *150*

(ii) *torpedo stage,* × *100*

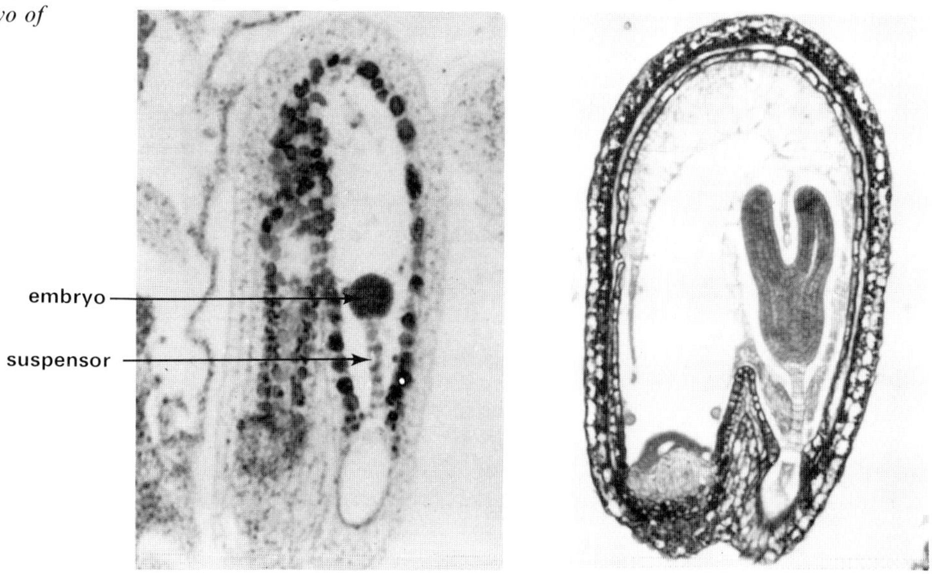

(iii) *mature embryo, × 100*

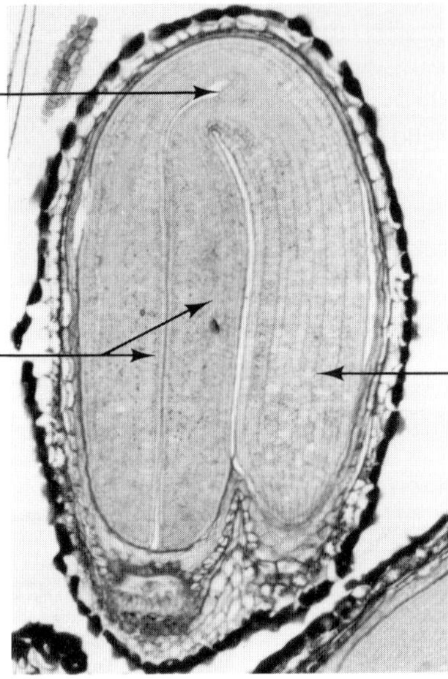

2. FRUIT FORMATION AND SEED DISPERSAL

While the seeds are developing, changes take place in the surrounding carpels. Growth of the carpels keeps pace with enlargement of the developing seeds. At maturity the seeds are completely enclosed and protected by carpellary tissue called the **pericarp**. The gynoecium has now developed into a **fruit**, the structure of which depends on the number and arrangement of carpels in the flower and on the changes taking place after fertilisation.

In many species the pericarp dries out at the same time as the seeds. The **dry fruits** which result often open by valves or pores through which the seeds are released when the fruit is shaken by wind. The pods of leguminous plants such as gorse and broom open by splitting along the dorsal and ventral edges and the seeds are shot out (Fig. 19.6(a)). In small-seeded dry fruits the pericarp often has an extension enabling the fruit to remain airborne for some time after its release from the parent. Dandelion fruits, for example, have a parachute-like pappus (Fig. 19.6(b)). In the dandelion and in many other flowering plants the seeds are not released. The pericarp splits open when the seeds germinate in the soil.

Some flowering plant species produce fleshy, **succulent fruits**. The fleshiness is sometimes due to growth of the pericarp as in plums and cherries. In other species another part of the flower enlarges instead. In the strawberry for example the receptacle swells considerably after fertilisation, pushing the tiny one-seeded carpels apart so that they are eventually scattered over the surface of the fruit (Fig. 19.6(c)). Fleshy fruits are often part of the diets of many animals. Although the seeds may be eaten they come to no harm unless crushed by the animals' teeth. This is because they are protected by the tough pericarp which is undigested in its passage through the animal's gut. By the time the animal has egested the seeds in its faeces they have probably been carried some distance from the parent plant.

There are many other patterns of fruit development but the end-product is generally structured so that the seeds are self-dispersed or are dispersed by wind, animals, or, occasionally, water. Dispersal helps to avoid overcrowding and competition which occurs if a large number of seeds germinate in a confined area. It also provides opportunities for species to colonise territories where previously they have not grown and where they may thrive.

FIG. 19.6 *Fruits*

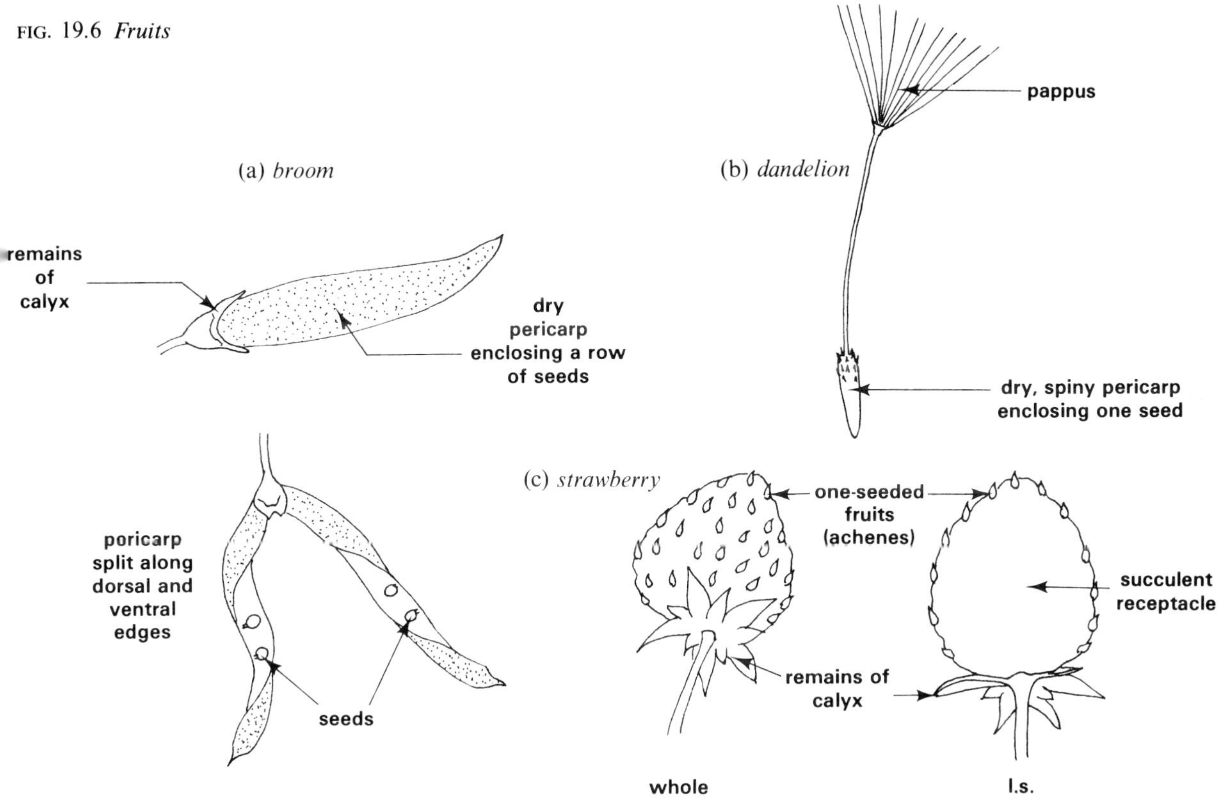

19.2 The life cycle of a flowering plant

The reproductive function of flowers involves the formation of two kinds of spores. Pollen grains are sometimes called **microspores** and the anthers in which they are produced can be called **microsporangia**. The larger **megaspores** are formed in the ovules or **megasporangia**. Thus a diploid spore-forming flowering plant is a **sporophyte** and produces two types of haploid spores. On developing further the spores give rise to gamete-bearing structures called **gametophytes**. The germinated pollen grain is a **male gametophyte** from which two male gametes arise whilst an embryo-sac is a **female gametophyte** in which a female gamete is formed. The life cycle is completed when an embryo sporophyte plant is produced in the seed following fertilisation (Fig. 19.7).

In the life cycle of a flowering plant there is thus an **alternation of generations.** Such an alternation of sporophyte and gametophyte is also found in other groups of terrestrial plants. In flowering plants, however, the gametophytes are vestigial and rely entirely on the sporophyte for their development. The situation is rather different in ferns where the sporophyte and gametophyte are independent plants and where the gametophyte has distinctive sexual organs. It is also different from the life cycle of a moss where the gametophyte is the free-living plant on which the sporophyte develops.

A feature of flowering plant reproduction is the development of the young sporophyte inside the carpel of the parent sporophyte. The young sporophyte thus has ideal conditions in which to develop. Because of this the chances that the next generation will be produced are very good. The development of seeds may be one of the reasons for the success of flowering plants compared with other groups of land plants.

FIG. 19.7 *Life-cycle of a flowering plant*

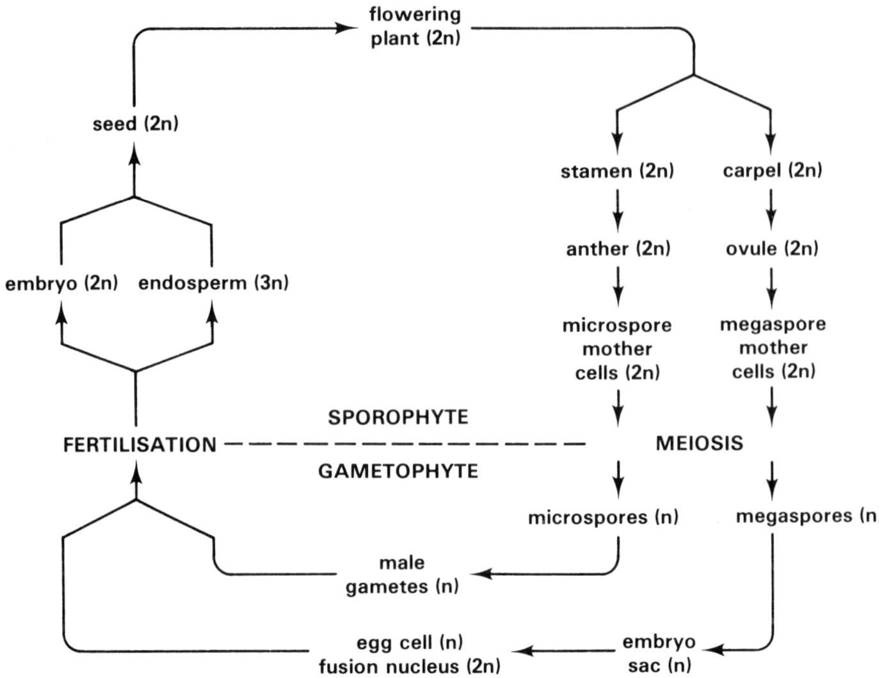

19.3 Pollination

The transfer of ripe pollen from an anther to the stigma of a flower of the same species is called **pollination**. **Self-pollination** occurs when pollen is carried from an anther to the stigma of the same flower or to the stigma of another flower on the same plant. When pollen is transferred from one plant to another of the same species, **cross-pollination** has taken place.

The two forms of pollination have very different genetic consequences. Self-pollination leads to **self-fertilisation**, cross-pollination to **cross-fertilisation**. Self-fertilised species depend on random assortment and crossing over (in meiosis leading to pollen grain and embryo sac production) and on mutation to bring about variation in the genomes of male and female gametes. Self-fertilised species therefore display less **genetic variation** than cross-fertilised species which are produced from gametes from two different individuals. Plants which are self-pollinated are called **inbreeders** while cross-pollinated plants are called **outbreeders**.

Inbreeding has its virtues because it can preserve particularly good genomes which may be suited to a relatively stable environment. Outbreeding is of greater evolutionary significance because it continually produces a variety of genomes. In the struggle for survival some genomes are more successful than others. Although a few species never outbreed it is interesting, in view of its potential evolutionary advantage, to find that most flowering plants do. In fact many flowering plant species have evolved a variety of mechanisms to ensure that cross-fertilisation usually takes place.

19.3.1 Mechanisms for ensuring outbreeding

When the stamens and ovules of flowers do not ripen at the same time pollen has to come from another plant of the same species if fertilisation is to occur. In the wood-sage the anthers discharge their pollen before the style has completed its growth and the stigma is receptive. The condition is called **protandry** (Fig. 19.8(a)). It contrasts with the behaviour of the rib-wort plantain in which the styles protrude from the flowers and the stigmas are ready to be pollinated before the stamens have grown. The latter condition is called **protogyny** (Fig. 19.8(b)). Some angiosperms such as willows and poplars have separate plants for the production of pollen and ovules. They have no option but to cross-fertilise. The primrose has two types of flower, pin-eyed and thrum-eyed (Fig. 19.8(c)). As you can see the structure of the pin-eyed flowers prevents them being self-pollinated. If pollen from thrum-eyed flowers falls on to their own stigmas the pollen will not germinate.

FIG. 19.8 (a) *Protandrous flowers of wood-sage*

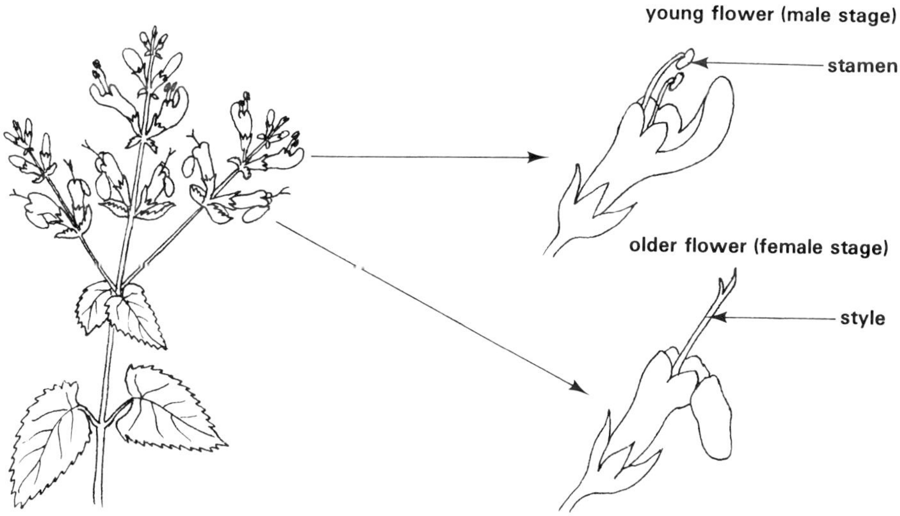

FIG. 19.8 (b) *Protogynous flowers of ribwort plantain*

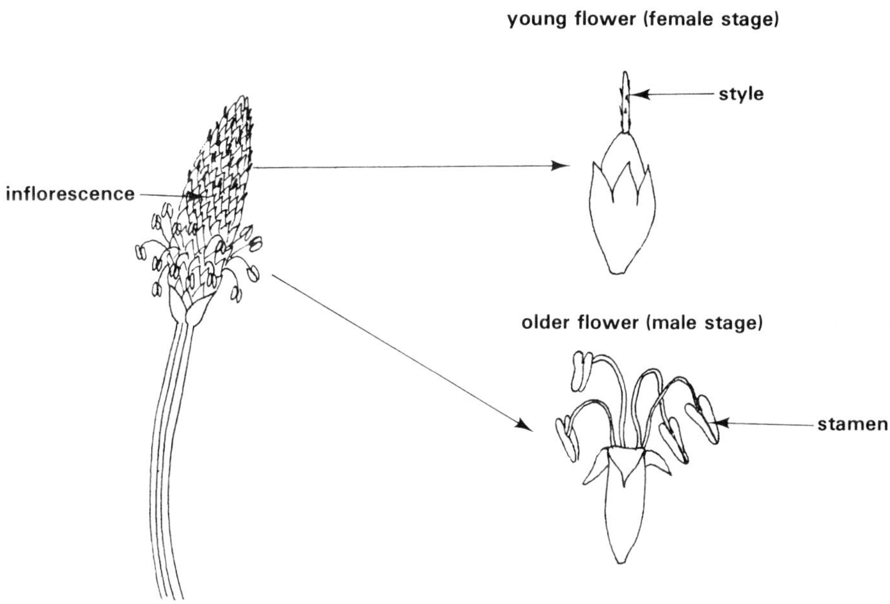

Other flowers, although producing both pollen and ovules, are **self-sterile**. When transferred to the stigma pollen will not germinate unless it comes from another plant of the same species. Self-sterility is a genetic trait. It is the reason why many varieties of apple, pear and cherry will not set fruit unless another variety is growing nearby to act as a **pollinator**.

FIG. 19.8 (c) *Flowers of primrose*

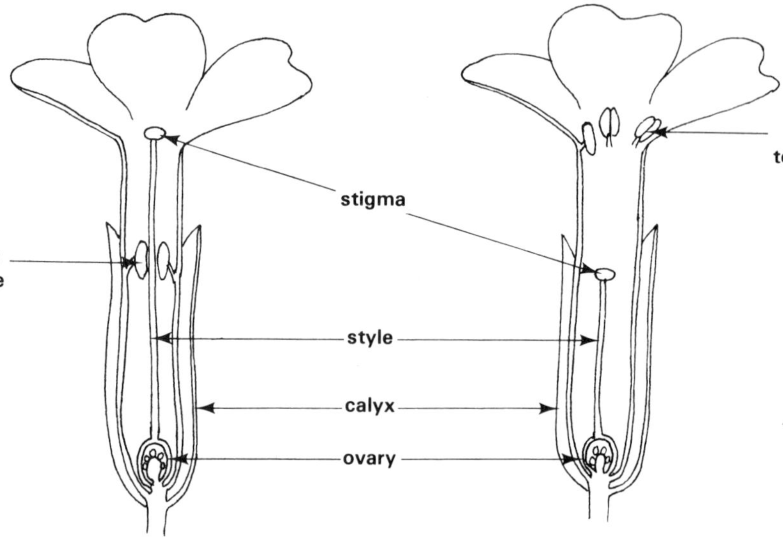

19.3.2 Pollination mechanisms

A number of agencies bring about pollination, the two most common being **wind** and **insects**.

1. WIND-POLLINATED FLOWERS

The flowers of **wind-pollinated** species often show a complete lack of petals and sepals. They have no means of attracting insects (Fig. 19.9). The flowers are often borne in inflorescences which either appear before the leaves as in trees such as ash, and shrubs such as hazel, or well above the leaves as in grasses and some plantains. In this way the leaves do not interfere with air movements around the flowers.

FIG. 19.9 (a) *Wind-pollinated flowers of rye-grass*

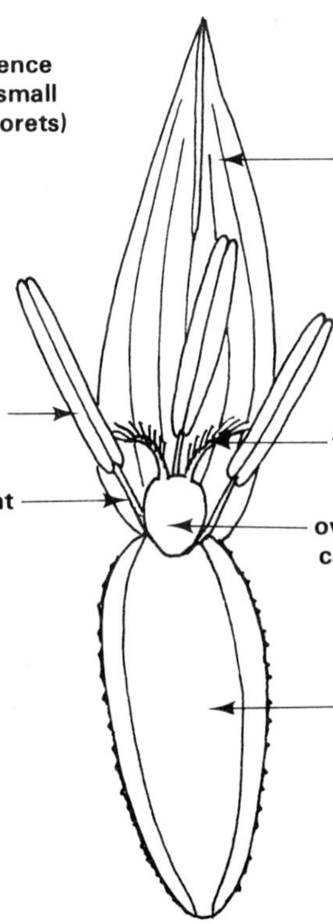

FIG. 19.9 (b) *Grass flowers. Notice the pendulous stamens*

The long, feathery and often sticky stigmas which protrude into the air improve the chances of pollination. The anthers are often hinged on to the filaments and hang out of the flower where the slightest air movement shakes out the pollen. The pollen grains are extremely light, often with air bladders, so that they remain suspended for long periods in the atmosphere. Many people suffer from hay-fever and similar allergies during the summer when the density of airborne pollen is high (Chapter 9). Grass pollen makes a large contribution to the pollen count.

FIG. 19.10 *Head and legs of worker bee*

front view of head

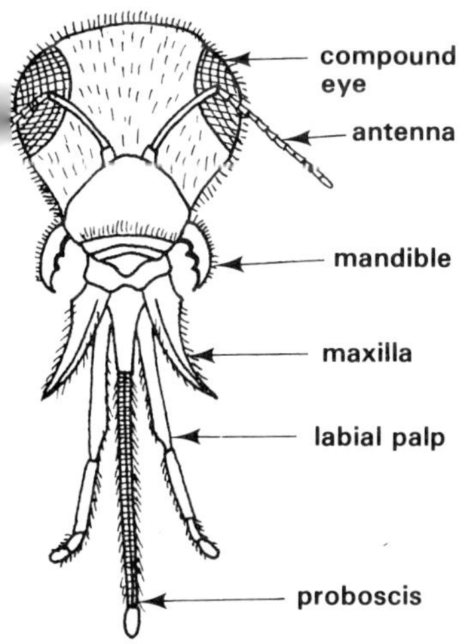

The proboscis is used as a suction tube to draw nectar into the mouth.

legs

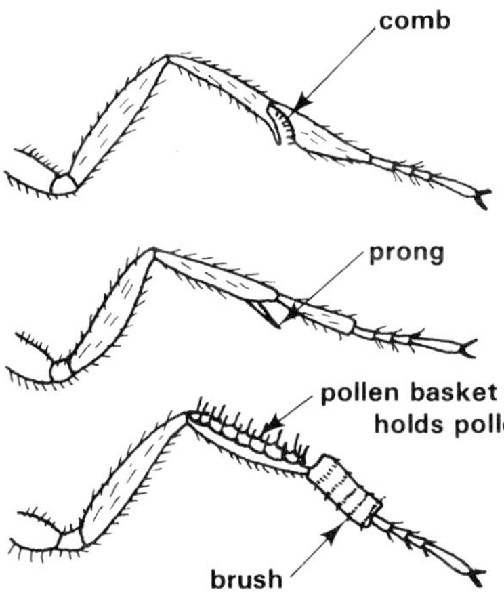

The comb removes pollen from the hairs on the front end of the body to the pollen basket. The brush transfers pollen from hairs on the rest of the body to the basket. The prong is used to dig out pollen from the basket when the bee returns to the hive.

2. INSECT-POLLINATED FLOWERS

One of the most remarkable facets of plant biology is the way in which certain insects and flowers of many species have evolved to their mutual advantage. **Insect-pollinated** flowers offer food. While taking it insects transfer pollen. Insects, like all animals, must have a balanced diet and many flowers provide carbohydrate, protein and lipids. The carbohydrate is found in **nectar**, a sugary solution secreted by special glands called nectaries which are often situated at the base of the petals. Pollen contains the other main dietary ingredients. Some insect-pollinated flowers such as poppies offer pollen only. Nectar and pollen have very little smell so are unlikely to be found by insects, except by chance. Flowers pollinated by insects have powerful insect attractants. Two senses which are highly developed in insects are smell and sight. It is not surprising therefore that insect-pollinated flowers are often highly scented. They are often relatively large and so easily seen. If small, they are grouped into conspicuous inflorescences. They are also brightly coloured. Significantly, the most common flower colours, yellow, blue and red, are those to which insects respond most readily.

The mouth-parts of the insects involved, such as bees and wasps, are adapted for sucking up nectar. Their legs are often modified to collect pollen (Fig. 19.10). Often the insects are social creatures and in co-operating in their search for food they increase the chances of pollination. Although pollen is collected as food by insects, insect-pollinated flowers are generally so structured that some pollen is transferred to the stigma by a foraging bee or wasp. This condition is seen at its extreme in zygomorphic flowers. The structure of zygomorphic flowers ensures that insects stand only in one position while feeding. Consequently pollen is dusted on to a specific site on the insect's body. In the white dead nettle it is the insect's back which receives the pollen. In gorse and broom it is its belly. Often the heavier bees operate a lever mechanism which brings the anthers down on to the body (Fig. 19.11). When visiting another flower of the same species the pollen is then at just the right position to make contact with the stigma.

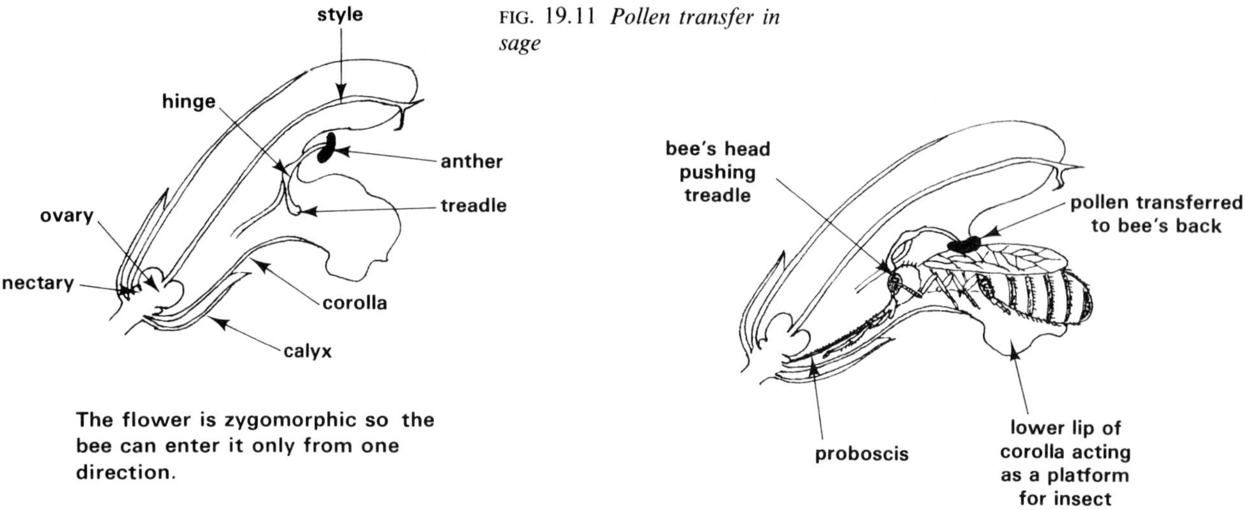

FIG. 19.11 *Pollen transfer in sage*

The flower is zygomorphic so the bee can enter it only from one direction.

19.4 Asexual reproduction

Some plants which produce flowers can produce seeds without sexual fusion taking place as previously described. The production of seeds without fertilisation is called **parthenogenesis**. It occurs in a number of ways.

19.4.1 Diploid parthenogenesis

Diploid parthenogenesis gives rise to seeds with normal diploid embryos. In the dandelion the megaspore mother cell invariably does not undergo meiosis and develops into an embryo without fertilisation. In the blackberry, embryos develop from a diploid cell in the nucellus.

19.4.2 Haploid parthenogenesis

Haploid parthenogenesis results in the formation of seeds with haploid embryos. This occurs when an unfertilised egg cell grows into an embryo, or more rarely when a male gamete on reaching the embryo sac does so. Examples of this form of reproduction have been reported in the thorn apple and the evening primrose. However, because a complete set of chromosomes is lost the plants which grow from the seeds are sterile.

19.4.3 Vegetative propagation

Many angiosperms can produce offspring by means other than seed formation. In these plants progeny are formed by proliferation of part of the vegetative body of the parent. Species which have **vegetative propagation** usually flower too. The garden strawberry, for example, flowers in early summer and produces fruit. Later, axillary buds on the parent plant grow over the soil surface. At the tip of each **runner** is a terminal bud. Along the length of the runner are scale leaves in the axils of which are axillary buds. One or more of the axillary buds produces roots which grow into the soil, and leaves grow up into the air. When the internodes of the runner decay several new plants are independent of the parent (Fig. 19.12).

FIG. 19.12 *Vegetative propagation in strawberry*

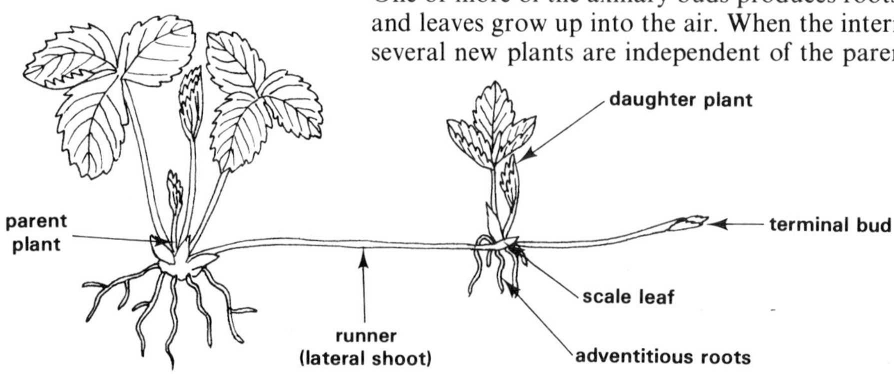

FIG. 19.13 *Organs of perennation and vegetative propagation*

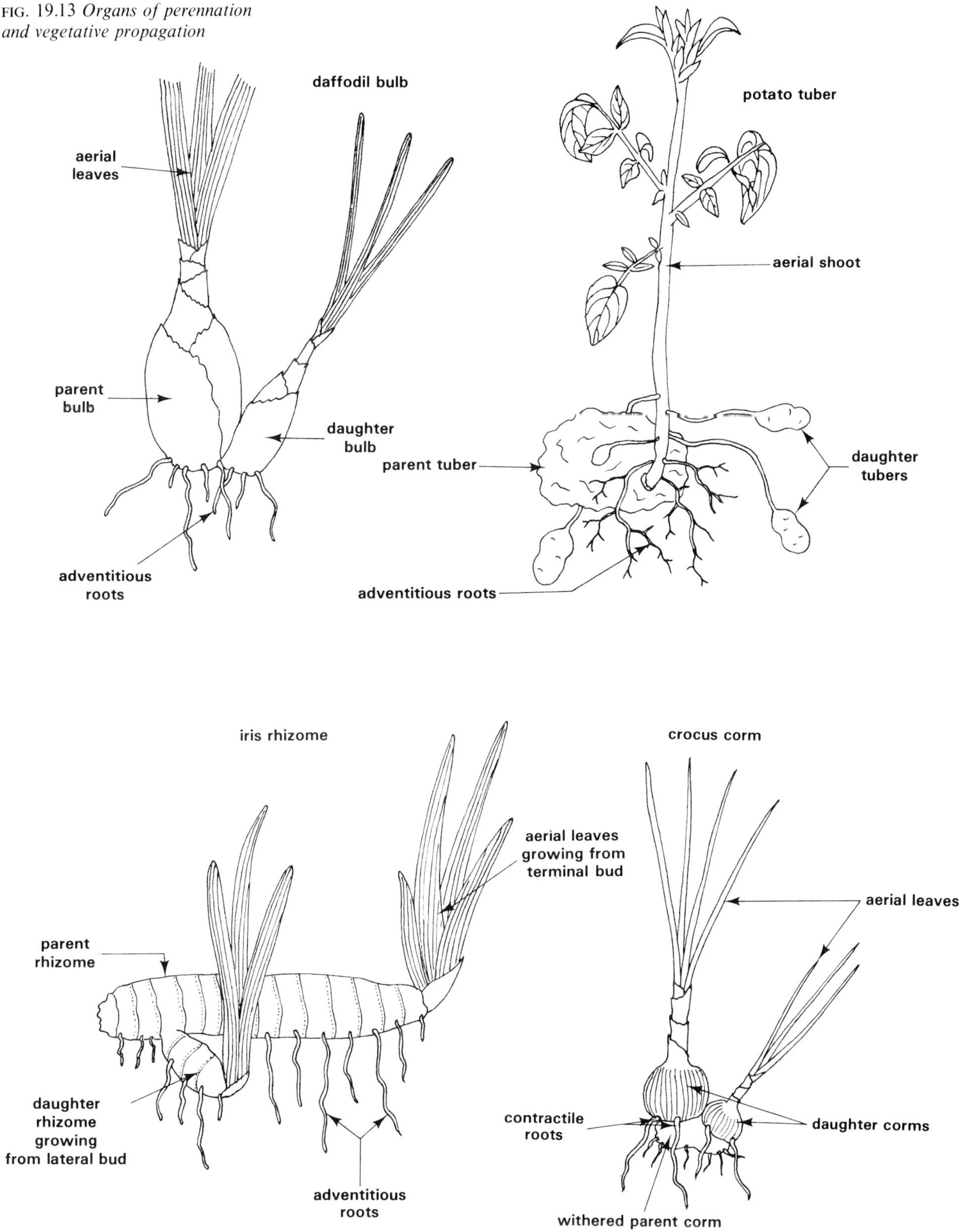

Many other methods of vegetative propagation are seen in wild and cultivated plants. Often propagation is coupled with a means of survival in adverse seasons. **Rhizomes**, **corms**, **bulbs** and **tubers**, for example, are frequently swollen with reserves of food which are used to establish new growth when the weather is suitable. As growth proceeds, lateral buds develop into daughter organs which later give rise to new plants (Fig. 19.13).

The various forms of asexual reproduction observed in flowering plants are often collectively called **apomixis**.

19.4.4 The consequences of asexual reproduction

In section 19.3 the differences between inbreeding and outbreeding were described and the genetic consequences were explained. All forms of asexual reproduction are examples of **inbreeding**. They are a means whereby genomes are passed with little or no change from parent to progeny. In fact asexual reproduction gives less scope for genetic variation than self-fertilisation where some change in the genomes of gametes will result from random assortment and crossing-over in meiosis. There is a tendency therefore for asexual reproduction to give rise to progeny of **genetic uniformity**. Such a group of plants is called a **clone**. Even so, the ability of many cultivated plants to reproduce by vegetative propagation is of great advantage to humans. It ensures that the genomes of useful varieties of plants are kept unchanged. Nevertheless occasional mutants, called **sports** by gardeners, appear among plants which propagate vegetatively.

Very few species of wild plants reproduce by asexual methods only. However, plants which can produce asexually are more versatile than those which rely entirely on sexual reproduction. It means that progeny can be produced even when seed production fails.

19.5 The physiology of angiosperm reproduction

Earlier in the chapter an orderly sequence of events beginning with the development of flowers and ending with the formation of seed-containing fruits is described. We will now examine some of the reasons for the changes. What causes a vegetative shoot to produce flowers and what controls the development of fruits and seeds? Why does a pollen tube grow towards an embryo sac when a pollen grain germinates on the stigma?

19.5.1 The physiology of flowering

The flowers of wild and cultivated plants grown outdoors appear at a particular time of the year. Daffodils, snowdrops, crocuses and hyacinths produce flowering shoots in early spring. Grasses and roses flower in summer, chrysanthemums and Michaelmas daisies flower in the autumn. This suggests that climate controls the times of flowering in different species. Among the more obvious seasonal changes of climate in temperate zones are **day-length** and **temperature**.

1. EFFECT OF DAY-LENGTH

The number of hours of light each day varies from one time of the year to another. In mid-winter the sun rises at about 8 am in southern England and dusk occurs at about 4.30 pm. This contrasts with mid-summer when dawn is at 5 am and sunset at 10 pm. British vegetation is thus exposed to little more than 8 hours of sunlight each day in winter and as much as 17 hours in summer. From December to June the number of daylight hours gradually increases while from June to December they gradually decrease.

The effect of day-length in controlling the time of flowering was discovered in America in the 1920s. It was found that a variety of tobacco flowered much more readily if the plants were given as little as five hours light a day compared with longer periods of light. The light had to be above a certain intensity for it to be effective. Since then it has been shown that many other species behave in the same way. They flower after exposure to several days when the number of light hours or **photoperiod** is small. Other species flower only after exposure to a number of days with long photoperiods. A third group are unaffected by daylength. Thus we have three categories of **photoperiodic response**:

(i) SHORT-DAY PLANTS which flower after a number of photoperiods of less than twelve hours, as occurs in Britain during autumn and winter. This group of plants includes chrysanthemums, rice and cotton.

(ii) LONG-DAY PLANTS which flower only after a succession of long photoperiods of more than twelve hours. In this group are many important crop plants such as wheat, clover and lettuce.

(iii) DAY-NEUTRAL PLANTS which produce flowers regardless of the length of photoperiod to which they are exposed. They include tomato, cucumber and dandelion.

The number of photoperiods required to induce the conversion of vegetative apices to floral apices varies from one species to another. The cocklebur requires only one **inductive photoperiod**. Most plants need about ten consecutive photoperiods of suitable length. It may then take several days or even weeks for vegetative apices to change into floral apices. A plant must be at a certain stage in its development when it receives the photoperiod treatment if eventually it is to flower. In some species the plant can be at the seedling stage. In others several mature leaves must be present.

It is now known that the length of the photoperiod is less critical than the length of the **dark period** in a daily cycle. If the photoperiods are interrupted with short periods of darkness, flowering still follows. However, if the dark period is interrupted by as little as one minute's exposure to light, flowering is prevented. Red-light is most effective in this respect. Yet the effect of red-light treatment can be overcome if the plant is immediately exposed to infra-red light. This suggests that a flower-inducing substance is made in darkness and is broken down by red light. Flowering plants produce a pigment, **phytochrome**, which is affected in this way (Chapter 20). Phytochrome may therefore play a part in regulating flowering. In what way is still unknown, but phytochrome may stimulate production of gibberellic acid (GA). GA has been shown to enhance flowering when applied to long-day plants grown in short-days. Grafting experiments strongly indicate that hormones are involved in regulating flowering and that the leaves perceive the stimulus of day length (Fig. 19.14).

2. EFFECT OF TEMPERATURE

As well as a suitable photoperiod treatment some plants require an appropriate temperature treatment if they are to flower. Winter varieties of wheat and barley sown in autumn in Britain will flower the following year, but if sown in spring they do not flower unless the seedlings are exposed to a temperature of between 1 and 5°C for several days. This shows that cold weather has an effect in regulating flowering of some species. Low temperature treatment induces flowering in many biennial species. In the first year of growth biennial plants such as the carrot and parsnip grow vegetatively and build up a reserve of food which is stored in their swollen taproots.

FIG. 19.14 *Some aspects of photoperiodism in a flowering plant*

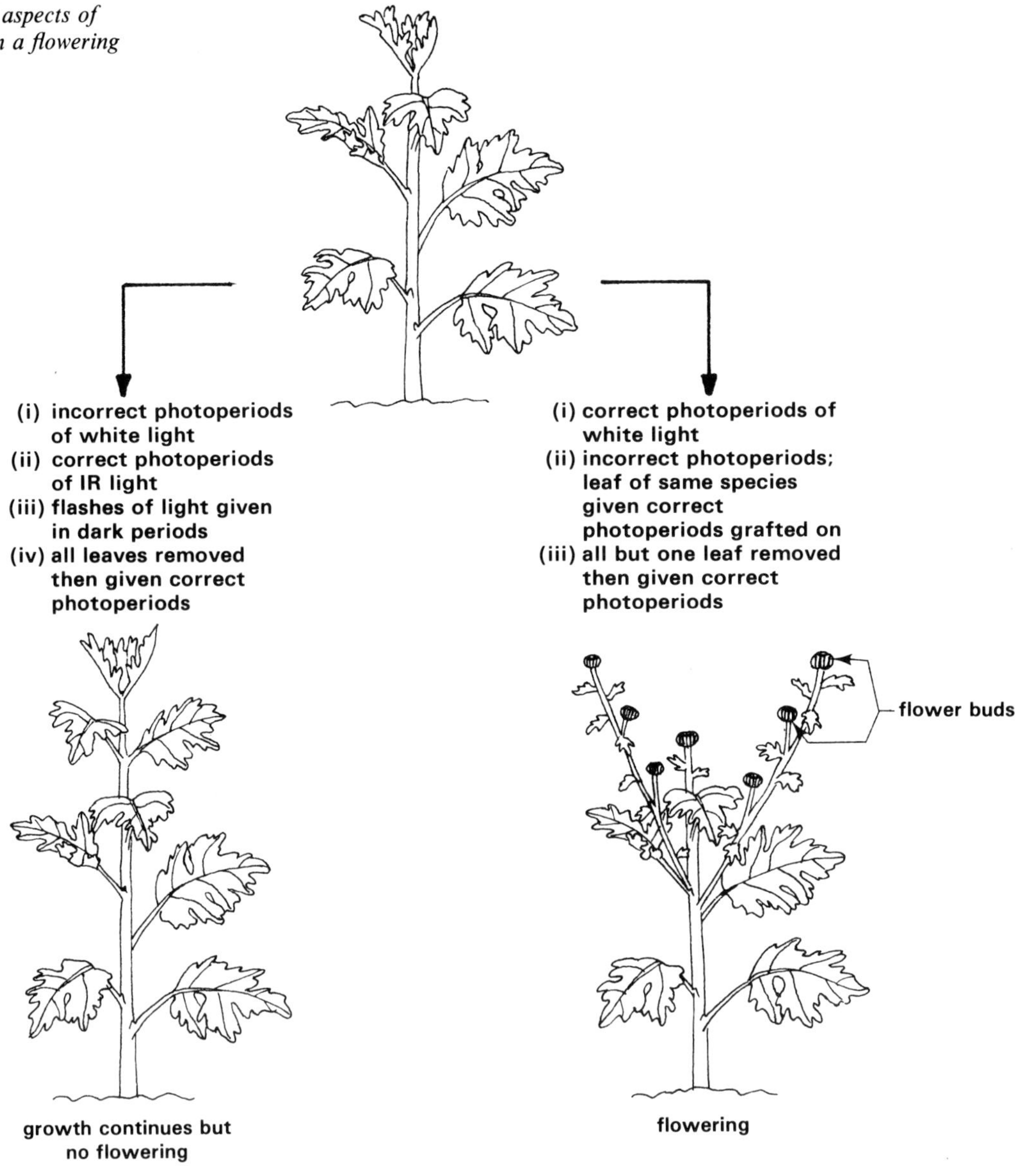

Next year, if the plants are left out of doors, a flowering shoot is produced using the stored food (Fig. 19.15). However, if they are kept over winter in a warm greenhouse they continue to grow vegetatively.

The cold-requirement for initiation of flowers is called **vernalisation**. How exposure to low temperatures promotes flowering is still poorly understood. It is likely, however, that it changes the hormone balance in the plant, possibly by promoting gibberellic acid production. Biennial plants treated with gibberellic acid will flower without vernalisation.

It is possible to investigate the involvement of hormones in flowering using tissue culture techniques. When floral apices are grown in a culture medium, floral organs differentiate if auxin, gibberellic acid and cytokinin are added (Chapter 21). The cucumber has been much studied in this respect. Application of auxin to male flower buds causes them to produce female flowers. Gibberellic acid has the opposite effect. Studies of this kind suggest that protandry, protogyny and the existence of separate male and female flowers on the same plant may be due to changes in hormone balance at different stages of growth.

FIG. 19.15 *A beetroot plant in the first and second year of its growth*

19.5.2 Physiology of pollen growth

A lot has yet to be learned about the reason why pollen tubes transfer male gametes with such accuracy into embryo sacs. The very fact that the tips of pollen tubes so frequently find the micropyle suggests that the nucellus or embryo sac secretes substances to which the pollen tube is sensitive. Growth of the tube is probably an example of **positive chemotropism**. However, there has been little success in identifying the substance or substances involved. More is known of the conditions which encourage germination of pollen grains. Whereas the pollen of some species will germinate in pure water, others need the presence of sugars, amino acids and other ingredients all of which are present in stigmatic and stylar tissues. The required concentrations of these substances is often quite high. Up to 15 per cent sucrose is needed in some cases. The trace element boron also stimulates pollen tube growth (Chapter 13).

Early growth of the pollen tube uses materials stored in the pollen grain. There is evidence that digestion of stylar and carpellary tissues by pectinase and cellulase enzymes takes place when the pollen tube grows further. Even so, pollen may fail to germinate despite successful pollination. Incorrect amounts of stimulants in the stigma and style, secretion of inhibitory materials by the stigma, style and ovules and inability of the pollen tube to produce enzymes which help the pollen tube penetrate the stigmatic surface are among the reasons for this.

A better understanding of the physiology of pollen tube growth could enable plant breeders to break down sterility barriers between varieties of flowering plant species. By bringing together genetic material from two different sources some of the hybrid progeny could be superior to existing varieties. This could mean higher yields of crop and go some way to alleviate the existing world food shortage.

19.5.3 Physiology of seed and fruit formation

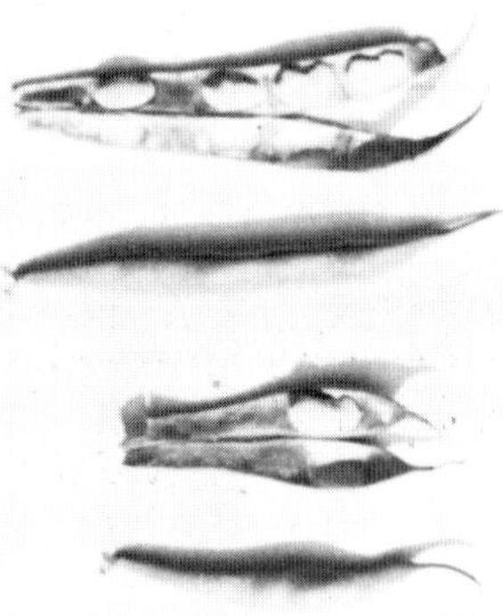

FIG. 19.16 *Effect of seed growth on growth of pericarp. In the small pod only one ovule was fertilised. Several ovules were fertilised in the larger pod.*

Some information of the conditions required for embryo growth has been obtained by analysing the endosperm which surrounds the embryo during its natural development. The coconut produces a large volume of liquid endosperm, commonly called coconut 'milk'. The milk is rich in sugars, minerals and plant hormones such as cytokinins and auxin. Recently young embryos of shepherd's purse have been grown successfully in a synthetic mixture of sucrose, various minerals, indole-3-acetic acid, kinetin and adenine. As the embryos develop they become less reliant on organic substances in their surroundings. Older embryos continue to develop if supplied with carbon dioxide, water, minerals and light. Other than this and the fact that embryos respire actively as they grow, little is known about the physiology of embryo development.

Simultaneous rapid growth of ovules and pericarp occur immediately after fertilisation. This indicates that growth of the various parts of the fruit are synchronised. Expansion of the fruit is stimulated by pollination in some species (Fig. 19.16). If auxin or gibberellic acid is sprayed on to unpollinated flowers, fruit will form. Yet the pollen of most species contains only a little auxin. It appears that pollination triggers off hormone synthesis in the ovules and carpels so that growth of seed and pericarp go 'hand in hand' (Fig. 19.17). Production of hormones in the growing fruit also inhibits the development of an abscission layer in the fruit stalk. The ovaries of unpollinated flowers usually fall away like the leaves of deciduous trees in autumn.

FIG. 19.17 *Growth of a plum*

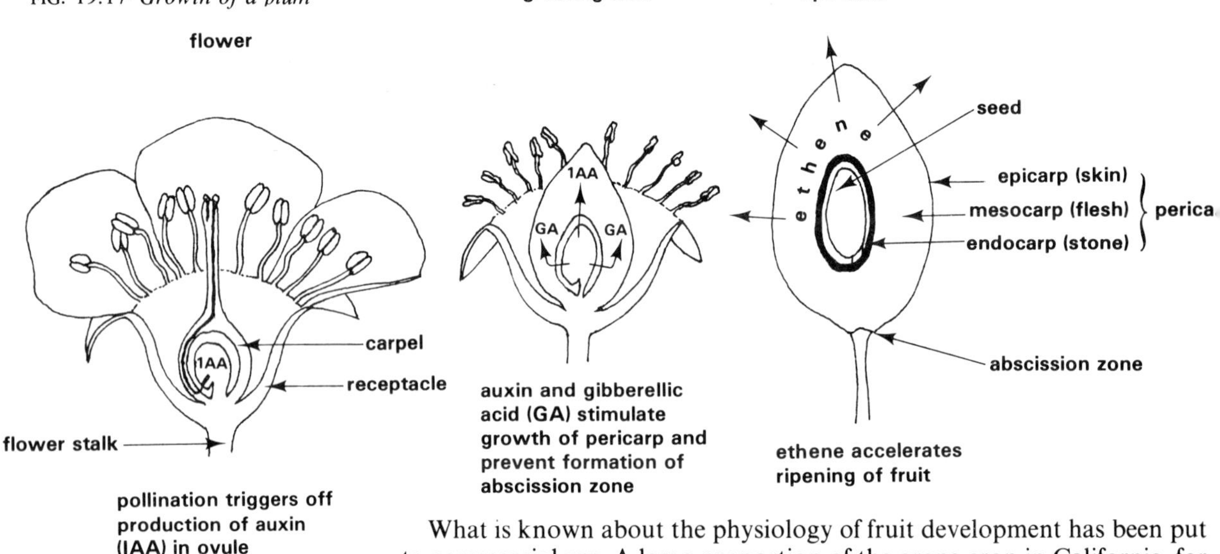

What is known about the physiology of fruit development has been put to commercial use. A large proportion of the grape crop in California, for example, is sprayed with gibberellic acid. Spraying does away with dependence on insects for pollination and ensures that more fruit develop. Seedless fruit develop because fertilisation does not occur. The development of seedless fruit is called **parthenocarpy**. Parthenocarpic fruits are produced naturally by some cultivated plants such as the banana and pineapple. Here fertilisation generally does occur but soon after their formation the embryos abort. Not, however, before they have supplied the necessary stimulus to the pericarp for its expansion.

19.5.4 Physiology of fruit ripening

The pericarps of dry fruits quickly lose water when their growth is finished. Drying is usually accompanied by lignification of the pericarp, forming a structure which helps disperse the seeds and protects them until they germinate. The ripening of fleshy fruits is accompanied by many chemical changes in the swollen pericarps or receptacles, making them attractive and palatable to animals. Unripe fruits are generally sour because they contain high concentrations of carboxylic acids. On ripening, the acids together with starch are converted to sweet-tasting sugars. Simultaneously the fruit becomes softer as pectinase and cellulase enzymes digest cell wall materials such as pectin and cellulose. The extent to which this occurs varies between species. In ripe plums for instance there is a lot of unchanged pectin while in cherries there is little. For this reason jam made from plums usually sets readily, the pectin acting as a gelatinising agent, but cherry jam does not set unless extra pectin is added.

Pigment changes are also common. Green unripe fleshy fruit become red, yellow and orange as chlorophyll is broken down and xanthophylls and carotenes predominate. Volatile aromatic oils may be synthesised giving the fruit a pleasant odour. The changes make the fruit attractive to some animals which help in dispersal of the seeds inside the fruit.

The many chemical conversions use energy from ATP made during respiration. Ripening fruit thus show a marked increase in respiratory rate. They also exhibit an increased output of ethene gas which accelerates ripening.

Knowledge of some aspects of fruit ripening is put to practical use. The ability to delay ripening has obvious advantages because it enables us to store fruit for long periods of time after it has been picked, thus avoiding wastage. Ripening can be delayed in a number of ways, all of which are aimed at minimising the respiration rate of the fruit. Storage at low temperatures or in an atmosphere containing a low concentration of oxygen and a high concentration of carbon dioxide is usually effective. It may be necessary to ripen fruit when it is taken out of storage. Ripening can be stimulated by placing the fruit in an atmosphere containing ethene.

Chapter 20

Seed structure and germination

Few species of flowering plants fail to produce seeds. Indeed, the evolutionary success of flowering plants can to some extent be attributed to seed production. New genomes arise when seeds are produced. Seeds also provide a resting stage which can be maintained for long periods. It is not uncommon for seeds to germinate after being stored for up to fifty years. The longest life span for seeds recorded to date is that of the Arctic lupin, *Lupinus arcticus*. Seeds of this species, discovered in frozen silt at Miller Creek, Yukon, Canada, in 1954, were later successfully germinated. Radiocarbon dating methods showed the seeds to be 10 000 to 15 000 years old. The longevity of seeds is due mainly to their extremely low metabolic rate and to the presence of a reservoir of energy in the form of stored food. Humans have long known of the food reserves in seeds and a great deal of time and effort has been spent in improving and cultivating crops such as cereals and legumes which produce edible seeds.

Although biologists are a long way from a complete understanding of many aspects of seed germination we shall see that the physiology of seeds is largely controlled by their environment.

20.1 Seed structure

A **seed** is an **embryo plant** together with its **store of food**. The whole structure is encased in a seed coat called the **testa**. The embryo consists of an immature shoot, the **plumule**, and an undeveloped root, the **radicle**. In the seeds of monocotyledonous plants such as grasses and maize the embryo is attached to a single seed leaf called the **cotyledon**. There are two seed leaves in dicotyledonous plants. The food reserve is stored in swollen cotyledons in sunflower and bean seeds. In maize, food is stored in a separate tissue called **endosperm** (Figs. 20.1, 20.2 and 20.3).

20.2 Morphological aspects of seed germination

Germination is the first step in the development of a mature plant from the embryo of the seed. The appearance of a seedling plant marks the end of germination. However, the way in which this happens differs from one species to another. The various patterns of germination can best be appreciated by studying the germination of seeds of several species.

20.2.1 Germination of broad bean

The seeds of the broad bean develop as a single row inside an elongated pod-shaped **pericarp**. Each seed is attached to the pod by a stalk, called the **funicle**, at the base of which is a tiny hole, the **micropyle**. When a seed is detached from its funicle a scar called the **hilum** is seen at one end of the testa. Each seed has two very large cotyledons packed with starch and protein. The embryo is tucked between the cotyledons to which it is attached by two short stalks (Fig. 20.1(a)).

If placed in moist soil at a suitable temperature the seed quickly swells as it absorbs water. Shortly afterwards the radicle elongates and pushes its way through the micropyle, bursting open the testa as it does so. As the

FIG. 20.1(a) *Seed of broad bean*

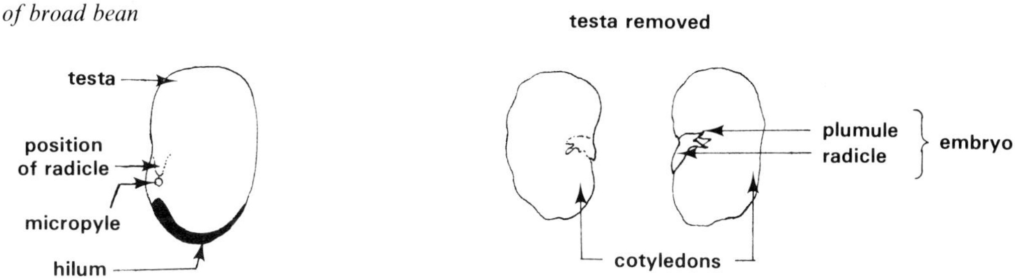

FIG. 20.1(b) *Germination of broad bean*

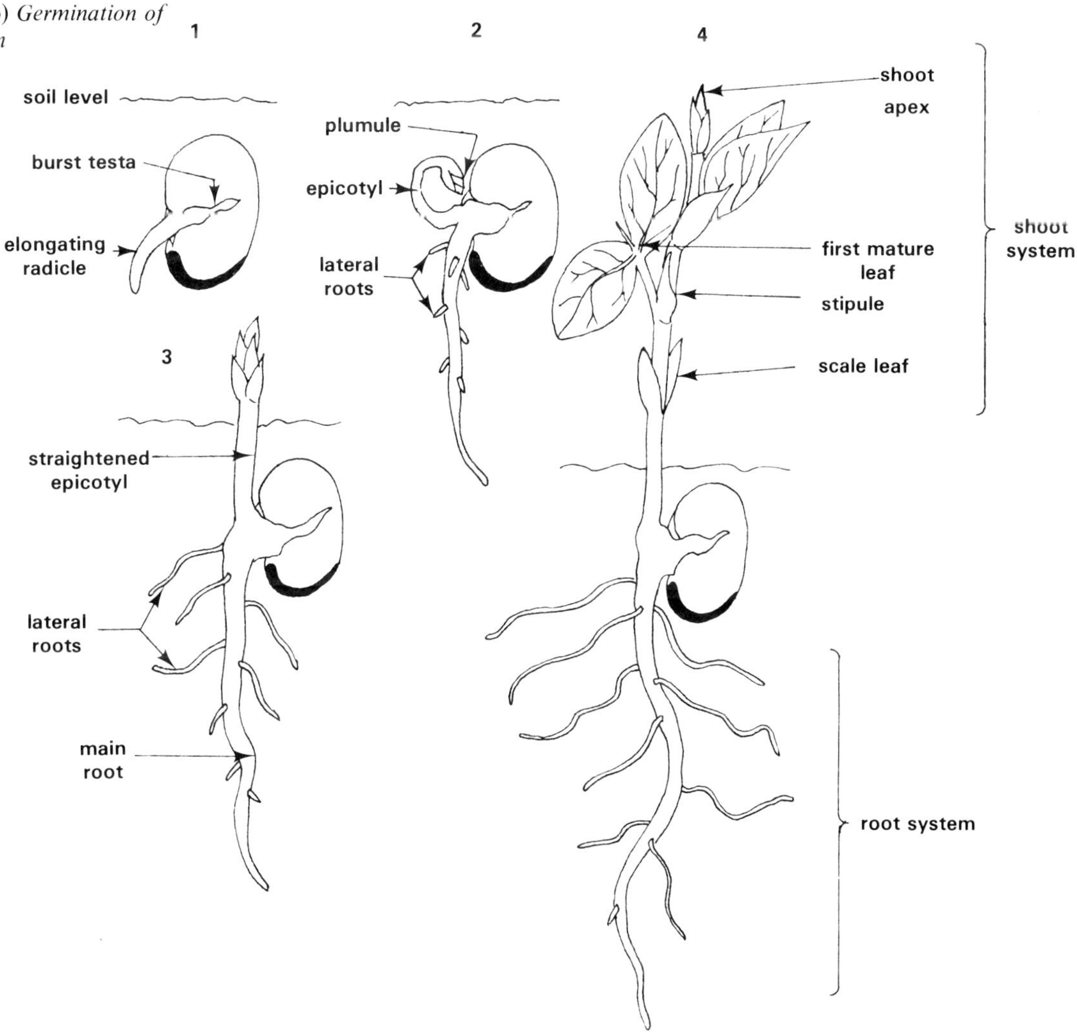

radicle extends down into the soil a number of lateral roots appear, forming a branched root system. While the radicle emerges the base of the plumule called the **epicotyl** also elongates and becomes hook-shaped as it grows between the cotyledons into the surrounding soil. Eventually the plumule reaches the soil surface where the epicotyl straightens and grows vertically. The embryonic leaves expand and develop into the large green compound leaves typical of the broad bean.

The cotyledons gradually shrink as the food reserves are used up. Such a pattern of germination where the cotyledons remain below the surface of the soil is called **hypogeal** (hypo = below; ge = earth) (Fig. 20.1(b)).

20.2.2 Germination of sunflower

Each sunflower seed is surrounded by a testa and a leathery pericarp and is therefore a one-seeded fruit called an **achene**. At the tapering end of the achene there is a small scar showing where it was attached to the flower stalk during its development. As in the broad bean there is no endosperm. The food reserve mainly of starch and oil is stored in the swollen cotyledons (Fig. 20.2(a)).

FIG. 20.2 (a) *Seed of sunflower*

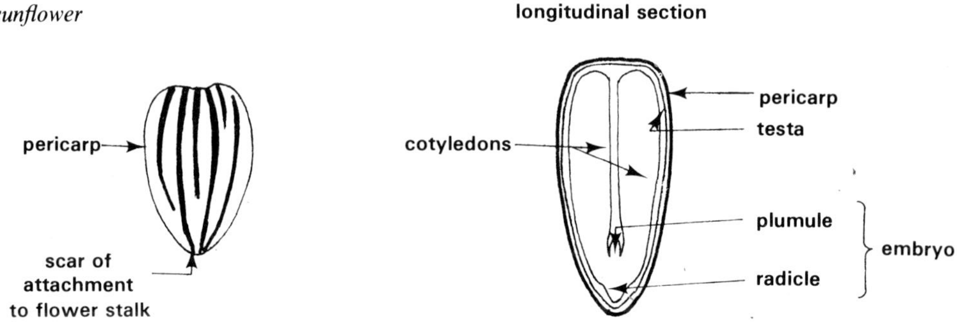

FIG. 20.2 (b) *Germination of sunflower seed*

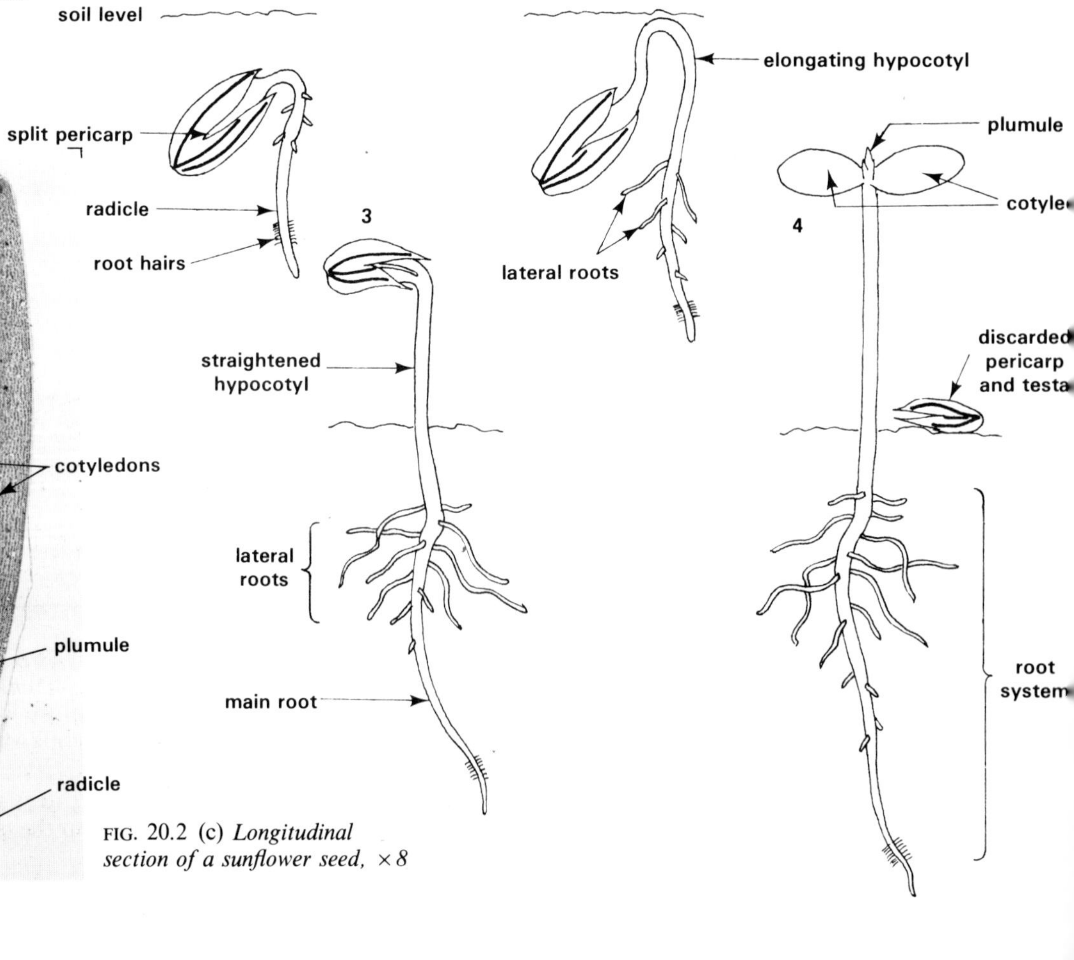

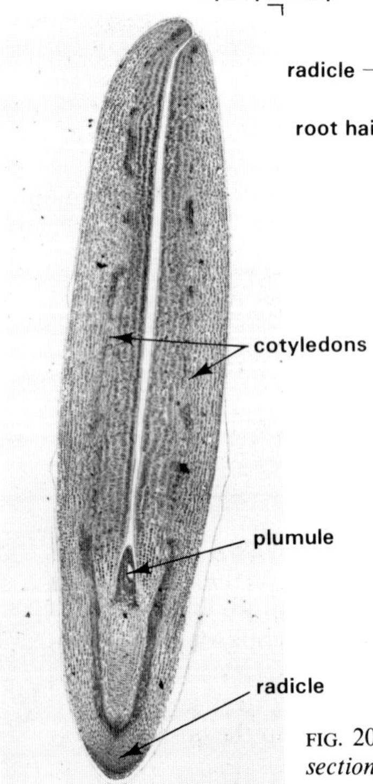

FIG. 20.2 (c) *Longitudinal section of a sunflower seed,* ×8

Despite the basic similarity in structure between the sunflower and broad bean seeds there are differences in the patterns of germination. After the absorption of water and subsequent emergence of the radicle, the **hypocotyl**, the part of the embryo between the cotyledon stalks and the radicle, begins to elongate. As it grows it becomes hook-shaped and the cotyledons with the tiny plumule tucked between them are dragged above soil level where the hypocotyl straightens. The cotyledons, by now shrunken because their food reserves have been used up, become green and start to photosynthesise. At this stage the plumule elongates and the first simple mature leaves appear. This type of germination where the cotyledons appear above soil level is called **epigeal** germination (epi = above) (Fig. 20.2(b)).

20.2.3 Germination of maize

A maize seed is enclosed in a tough pericarp which is fused with the testa. This type of one-seeded fruit is called a **caryopsis** and develops with several hundred others on a cob. At the tapered base of the fruit is a scar showing its point of attachment to the cob. On one of the broader sides of the fruit a lighter oval area can be seen under which the embryo is found. The radicle is enclosed in a hollow tube called the **coleorhiza**. The plumule is surrounded by a similar structure called the **coleoptile**. There is a small triangular cotyledon, the **scutellum**, to one side of which the embryo is attached. At its other side the scutellum is fused to the endosperm which stores starch, protein and oil (Fig. 20.3(a)).

FIG. 20.3(a) *Seed of maize*

FIG. 20.3 (c) *Longitudinal section of a maize seed, × 12*

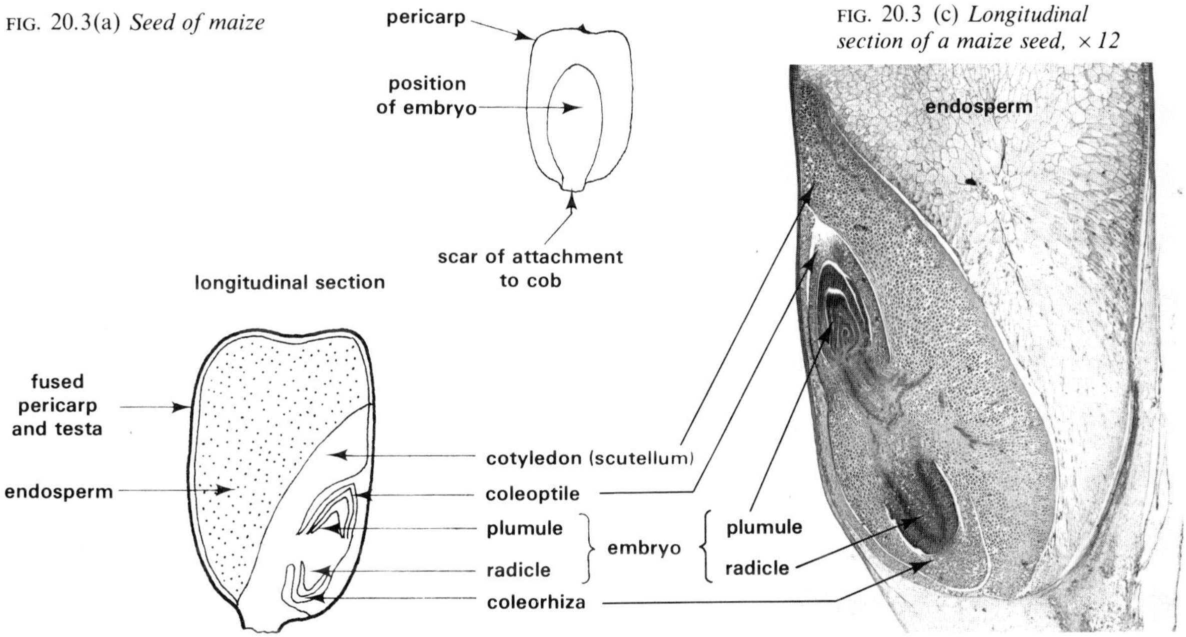

Soon after water uptake the radicle emerges, piercing the coleorhiza as it grows. Shortly afterwards the coleoptile appears, enclosing the plumule as it grows upwards through the soil. Growth of the coleoptile is mainly from its base which is called the **mesocotyl**. Once through the soil surface the coleoptile soon stops growing and the first long, strap-shaped leaf bursts through its tip. Adventitious roots grow from the mesocotyl and form a fibrous root system. Because the cotyledon remains below the soil level the germination of maize is **hypogeal** (Fig. 20.3(b)).

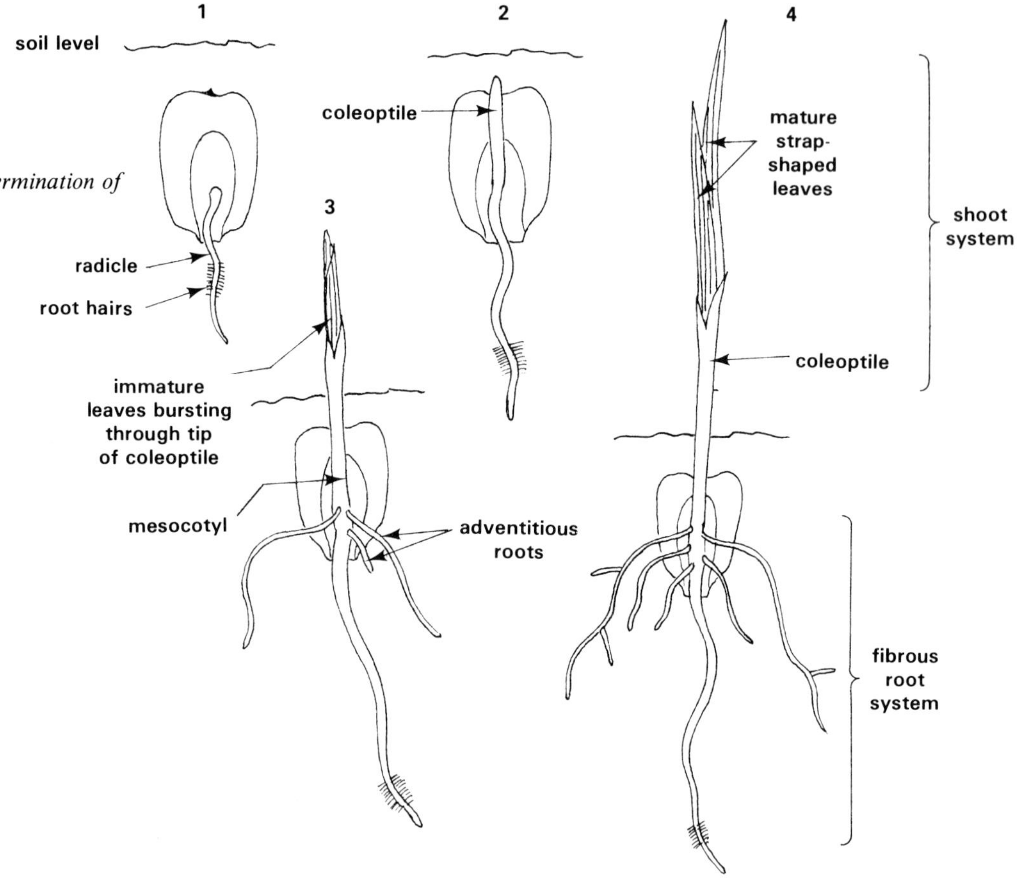

FIG. 20.3 (b) *Germination of maize seed*

20.3 Physiology of germination

The structural changes described so far are the consequences of physiological changes occurring inside the cells and tissues of the germinating seed. The first changes are mainly the result of **cell expansion** following the uptake of water (Section 20.3.2). Later changes involve the **growth** of new cells and tissues at the apices of the radicle and plumule. Growth requires raw materials and energy and initially it occurs at the expense of energy-rich molecules such as starch and lipids stored in the seed. Once the leaves of the young plant have expanded the seedling photosynthesises.

20.3.1 Mobilization of stored food

Table 20.1 gives an indication of the main materials stored in a variety of seeds. Because of their richness in **carbohydrates**, **lipids** and **proteins**, seeds feature prominently in the diets of many animals including man. Food reserves in seeds are insoluble in water and cannot be transported in the seedling. They must be broken down into relatively simple, soluble substances which dissolve in water to be moved to the growing apices of the plumule and radicle. As in the mammalian gut (Chapter 14), hydrolytic enzymes catalyse the breakdown of proteins, lipids and polysaccharides such as starch.

Table 20.1 Chemical composition of seeds

	PERCENTAGE DRY MASS		
SPECIES	CARBOHYDRATES	LIPIDS	PROTEINS
maize	50–75	5	10
wheat	60–75	2	13
rice	65–70	2	10
broad bean	57	2	36
sunflower	2	45–50	25
peanut	12–33	40–50	20–30
pea	34–46	2	20

1. CARBOHYDRATES

The hydrolysis of **starch** into the soluble disaccharide sugar **maltose** is catalysed by a complex of enzymes called **amylase**. The conversion of starch to maltose is used to produce malt for the brewing industry. Barley seeds are germinated for a few days and the sprouted grain then dried and ground into powder. When later steeped in water the maltose dissolves and provides the source of energy for yeast cells in the fermentation stage of brewing. In seeds germinating under natural conditions maltose is further hydrolysed by the enzyme **maltase** to **glucose** which is converted to **sucrose** for transport to the growing apices of the embryo. At the apices sucrose is used for the synthesis of cellulose, hemicelluloses and pectic compounds, the main components of plant **cell walls**. Some sucrose is **respired** to provide free energy for growth.

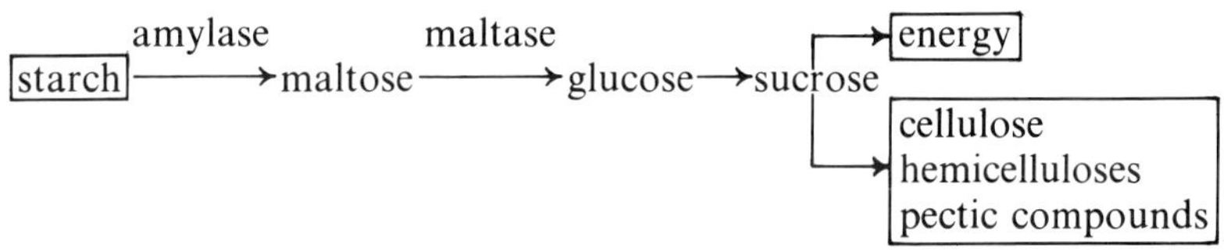

2. PROTEINS

Proteins are hydrolysed to polypeptides and **amino acids** by **peptidase enzymes**. Some amino acids are moved in solution to the embryo. Most are transported as **amides**. At the growing points of the plumule and radicle the amides are de-aminated and the amino acids are used to synthesise structural and enzymic **proteins**.

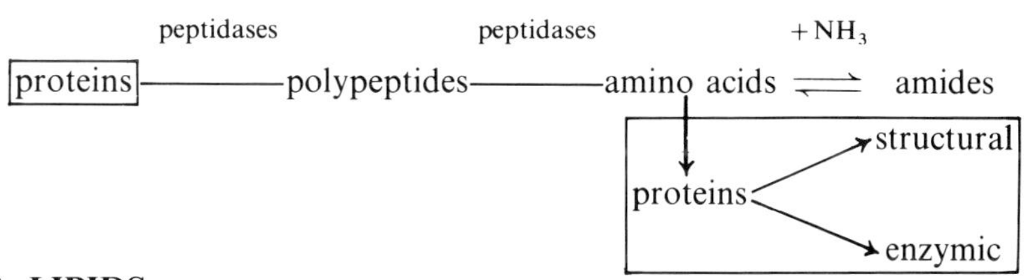

3. LIPIDS

Fats and oils are first hydrolysed to **glycerol** and **fatty acids** by **lipase** enzymes. The fatty acids may be oxidised to release energy or converted to sucrose ready for transport. Glycerol, which is only a small part of a lipid molecule, is also converted to transportable sugars.

Some of the changes described above are shown for wheat seeds in Table 20.2. The general picture is a gradual depletion of reserves in the food storage areas and an increase in dry mass of the embryo (Fig. 20.4).

Table 20.2 Changes in dry mass of maize seedlings during germination

	DRY MASS/mg g^{-1}		
TIME/DAYS	WHOLE SEEDLING	ENDOSPERM	EMBRYO
0	225	200	2
1	210	189	3
2	208	188	5
3	206	155	5
4	175	115	15
5	155	84	23

FIG. 20.4 *Changes in dry mass of embryo and endosperm during germination*

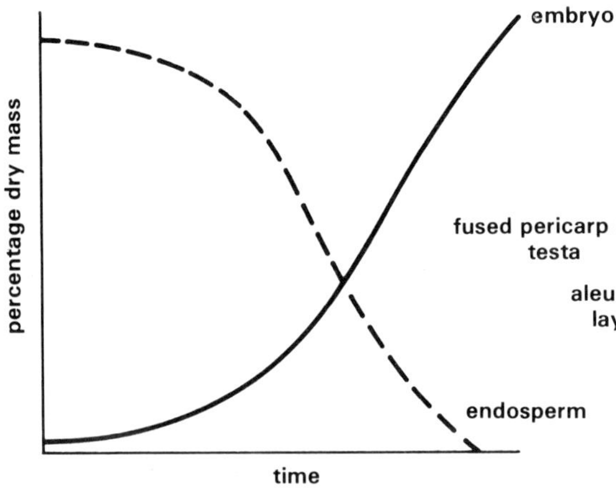

FIG. 20.5 (b) *Summary of the physiology of food mobilization in a barley seed*

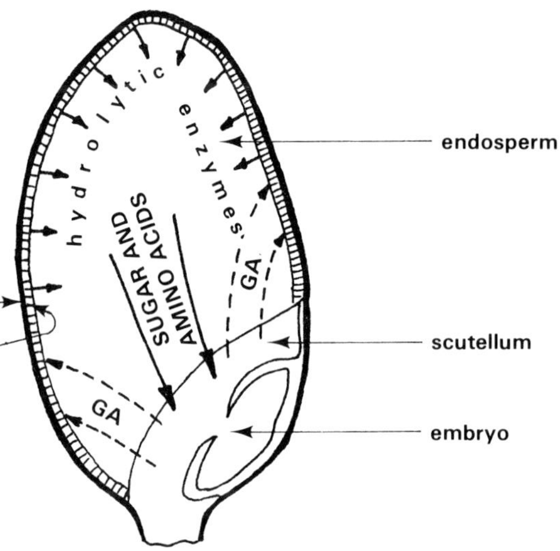

FIG. 20.5 (a) *An experiment to investigate the effect of the embryo on the release of the starch-hydrolysing enzyme amylase by the aleurone layer of barley seeds*

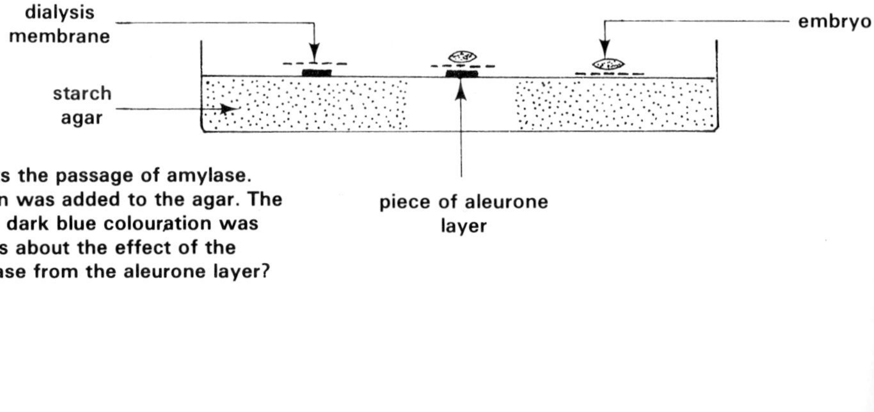

The dialysis membrane prevents the passage of amylase. After a few days iodine solution was added to the agar. The stippled area indicates where a dark blue colouration was observed. What does this tell us about the effect of the embryo on the release of amylase from the aleurone layer?

What causes such changes to occur? Studies with cereal grains show that the secretion of hydrolytic enzymes is triggered off by the hormone **gibberellic acid (GA)** made by the embryo (Fig. 20.5(a)). In cereals the release of enzymes takes place from the **aleurone layer** surrounding the endosperm. After absorption of water by the grain there is a marked rise in embryonic production of GA which diffuses into the endosperm where food reserves are hydrolysed (Fig. 20.5(b)). In some seeds the hydrolytic enzymes are found in lysosomes in the food-storing cells. Other hormones, notably **cytokinin** and **indole-3-acetic acid (IAA)** promote cell division and enlargement at the growing apices of the embryo. IAA also controls differentiation of vascular tissue in the developing shoot and root of the seedling (Chapter 21).

20.3.2 Factors affecting seed germination

If a gardener or farmer sows seeds at the wrong time of the year, few if any will germinate. **Environmental factors** can thus influence seed germination. Instructions concerning the best time of year to plant seeds are usually given on seed packets. For many outdoor crops of vegetables the most suitable time for sowing seeds in Britain is spring and early summer when the temperature is higher than in winter. In preparing a seed bed an experienced gardener ensures that the soil has a good crumb structure and is moist but not waterlogged. Too much water fills pore spaces in soil which are normally filled with air which contains oxygen. Thus a suitable **temperature**, **water** and **oxygen** have to be available for successful seed germination. Some seeds also require **light** before they germinate.

1. TEMPERATURE

Many of the physiological changes which take place in germination are catalysed by **enzymes**. The effect of temperature on enzyme activity is described in Chapter 4. For the seeds of each species of flowering plant there is an **optimum temperature** at which the germination rate is at its highest, providing no other factor is limiting germination (Fig. 20.6). The fact that seeds of most plants germinate early in the year if sown in a warm greenhouse is used by nurserymen in preparing trays of bedding plants for sale in early summer.

The seeds of many species such as red fescue grass, peach and apple germinate only if they have been subjected to a period of low temperature after they have absorbed water. A temperature between 0–5°C is normally

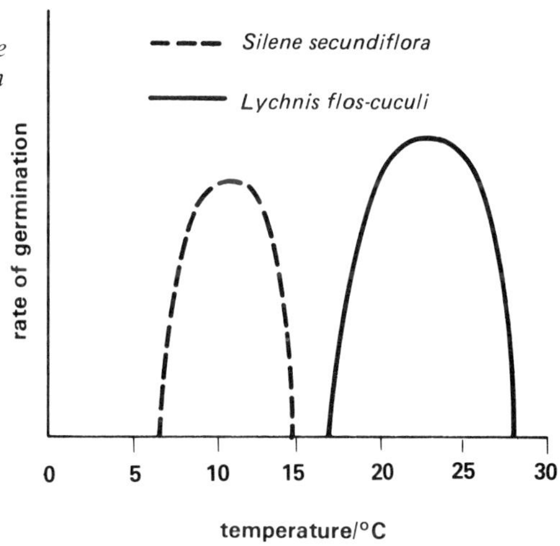

FIG. 20.6 *Effect of temperature on the rate of seed germination*

S. secundiflora **inhabits the Mediterranean coastal area. The seedlings of this species avoid the hot, dry summer weather because the seeds germinate in the cooler, moister winter months. This is reflected in its relatively low optimum germination temperature.**
L. flos-cuculi **is widespread in temperate deciduous forest areas including Britain. How does the higher optimum germination temperature for this species reflect the climate of its habitat?**

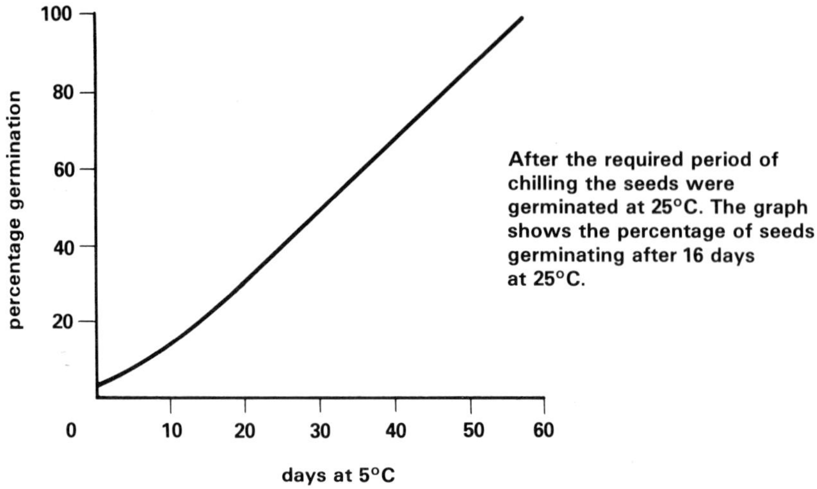

FIG. 20.7 *Effect of chilling on the rate of germination of apple seeds*

sufficient, the period of time varying from a few days to several weeks (Fig. 20.7). **Chilling** reduces the abscissic acid content of the seed coat and enables the embryo to make gibberellic acid (Fig. 20.8). In Britain the cold weather of winter provides the chilling requirement of seeds in the wild.

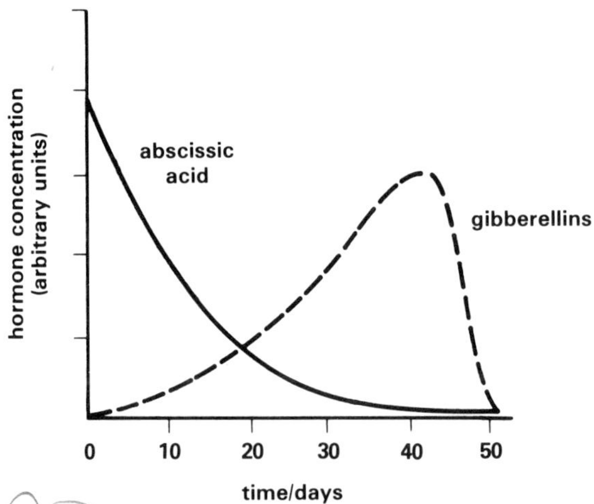

FIG. 20.8 *Effect of chilling on hormone concentrations in the seeds of sugar maple*

2. WATER

The water content of many types of seeds is as little as 5–10 per cent of their dry mass, far too low for rapid **metabolic activity**. Water is also needed for **vacuolation** of cells and for **transport** during germination.

It is normal practice to store seeds in an atmosphere which keeps them dry and prevents germination. When placed in water, seeds quickly swell enormously, often doubling their mass in a few hours. The initial absorption of water is largely by **imbibition**, the attraction between hydrophilic colloids such as membrane-bound proteins in the seed and water molecules (Chapter 2). Later the roots absorb water by **osmosis**.

In natural circumstances the water content of many seeds does not remain low for long. Most seeds are dispersed as soon as they are formed and on reaching the soil they absorb water. Even so, few seeds germinate at this stage. It is therefore evident that factors other than water content normally control germination.

3. OXYGEN

The synthesis of new cellular components at the apices of plumule and radicle requires free energy. Energy is supplied by ATP produced in **respiration** from stored energy-rich compounds such as carbohydrates and lipids. The manufacture of ATP occurs most efficiently when oxygen is available and aerobic respiration can occur (Chapter 5). As germination proceeds there is rapid intake of oxygen through the seed coat (Fig. 20.9).

Some of the energy in the reserves of food is liberated as heat, so it is possible to detect a rise in temperature of germinating seeds, particularly if kept in bulk. This is a problem farmers frequently encounter when grain with too high a water content has been stored. In these conditions the seeds begin to germinate, and **self-heating** occurs as heat energy is released. The temperature reached is so high that enzyme denaturation occurs and the

FIG. 20.9 *Intake of oxygen by dormant and non-dormant seeds*

Both sets of seeds were first soaked in water. An initial increase in oxygen intake is observed even in dormant seeds. However the rate of oxygen intake continues to increase only in the non-dormant seeds.

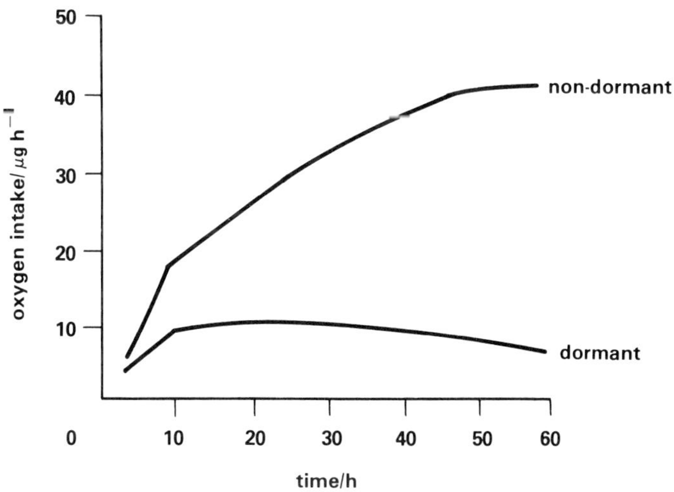

FIG. 20.10 *Respiratory quotients of seeds of pea and castor oil*

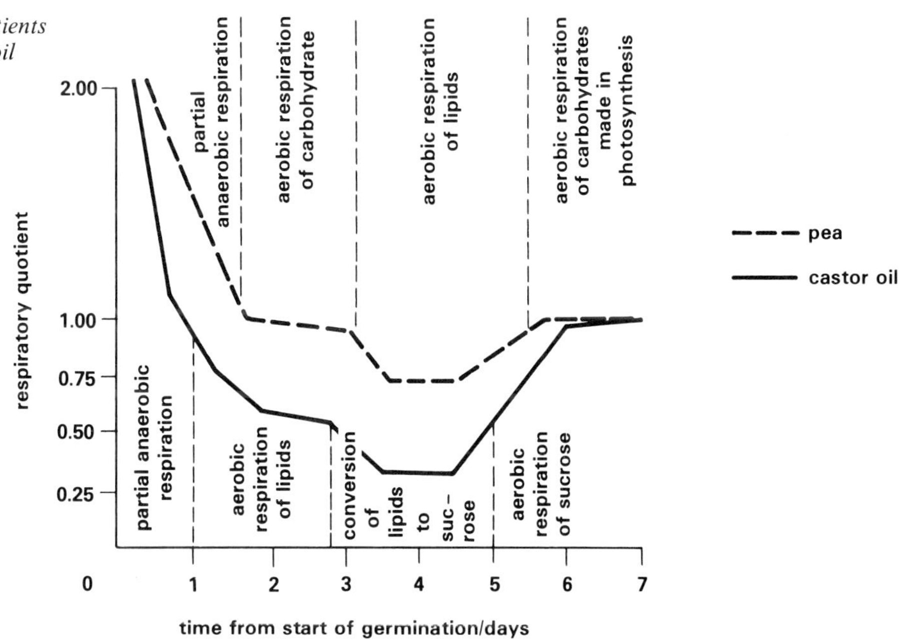

embryos die. Self-heated grain is useless as seed for a potential crop and its value as fodder is considerably reduced because much of the food reserve has been spent.

Carbon dioxide is a product of respiration. The ratio of carbon dioxide given off to oxygen used in a given period of time is called the **respiratory quotient** (Chapter 5). Figure 20.10 shows the respiratory quotients of two types of seeds at various stages in germination. The quotients give an indication of the type of substrate oxidised and whether aerobic respiration, anaerobic respiration, or both is taking place.

The testa of some seeds is relatively impermeable to oxygen so they may respire anaerobically at the start of germination. Large, bulky seeds such as broad beans have a small surface area to volume ratio which may result in an inadequate supply of oxygen to respiring cells and consequently some anaerobic respiration. For these reasons the RQ can be greater than 1·0 during the first 24–48 hours of germination. The RQ of most seeds then falls to 0·7. This is because lipids are now respired aerobically. If large quantities of lipids are stored, as in castor-oil seeds, the RQ at this stage may drop to as little as 0·35 owing to the conversion of lipids to sucrose.

$$\underset{\text{lipid}}{C_{16}H_{40}O_6} + 11O_2 \longrightarrow \underset{\text{sucrose}}{C_{12}H_{22}O_{11}} + 4CO_2 + 9H_2O$$

$$RQ = \frac{4}{11} = 0{\cdot}35$$

In carbohydrate-rich seeds the RQ soon climbs to 1·0 as aerobic respiration of sugar gets under way. When the seedling eventually photosynthesises the RQ is 1·0 as in the mature plant. Aerobic respiration of carbohydrates made in photosynthesis now takes place. At this stage RQ measurements have to be made in darkness. In the presence of light, carbon dioxide released in respiration is used for photosynthesis, while some of the oxygen made in photosynthesis is used for respiration.

4. LIGHT

Although the seeds of many plants can germinate in total darkness, others such as tobacco and some varieties of lettuce germinate only after exposure to **light**. The time of exposure varies from several seconds to a few days. Light-treatment is effective only if the seeds have absorbed water. The light need only be of low intensity and it is the red part of the spectrum which is required. Infra-red light inhibits germination, even though the seeds have previously been subjected to red light. The cause of this behaviour is the effect of light on the pigment **phytochrome**. Phytochrome exists in two forms, P_r which absorbs mainly red light and P_{ir} which absorbs mainly infra-red light (Fig. 20.11). Both P_r and P_{ir} are present in seeds. On absorbing red light, P_r is converted to P_{ir} while P_{ir} is reconverted to P_r when it absorbs infra-red light.

$$P_r \underset{\text{infra-red}}{\overset{\text{red}}{\rightleftharpoons}} P_{ir}$$

When a seed contains more than a certain amount of P_{ir} germination can proceed.

Sunlight, to which seeds are naturally exposed, contains both red and infra-red light. The proportion varies from time to time and place to place. Generally there is sufficient red light for the formation of enough P_{ir} to trigger off germination. The effect of P_{ir} accumulation is not certain but it

FIG. 20.11 *Absorption spectra of phytochromes*

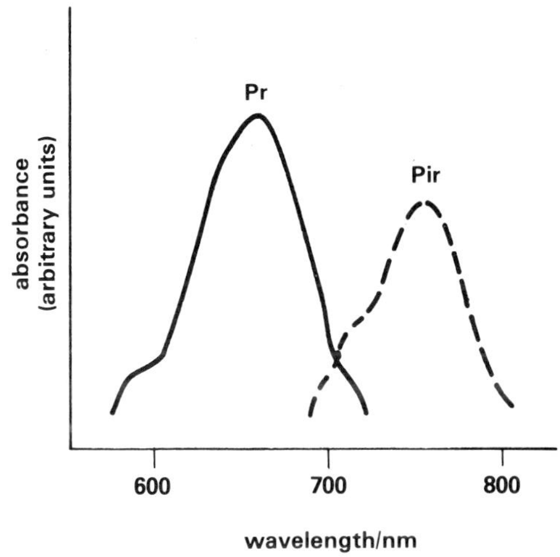

may stimulate the production of gibberellic acid. Seeds which can germinate in darkness seem to have sufficient P_{ir} and thus do not require light.

Many light-dependent seeds are small. If they germinated too deeply in soil the embryonic shoot system would not reach the soil surface. Their dependence on light ensures that they germinate only when at or near the soil surface where there is a reasonable chance of the seedlings' aerial system becoming established. Ploughing and digging bring the light-dependent seeds of weeds to the soil surface where their dormancy is broken. Another ecological aspect of light-dependence is seen in deciduous forests and woodlands where in summer the canopy of leaves on the trees absorbs much red light. The light reaching the ground is then proportionally richer than normal daylight in infra-red light. In these conditions seeds accumulate P_r which inhibits germination. Germination of the seeds of woodland herbs therefore normally takes place in spring before the leaf canopy appears. The intensity of light in the wood is then also favourable for seedling growth.

20.3.3 Seed dormancy

Even when provided with water, a suitable temperature, oxygen and light, the seeds of many species fail to germinate and remain dormant. There are a number of reasons for **seed dormancy**.

1. IMMATURITY OF THE EMBRYO

The embryo may be **structurally immature** when the seeds are dispersed from the parent plant. This has been shown to be so in the ash and the wood anemone. In some species such as hazel the embryo is unable to synthesise gibberellic acid. This means that the hydrolytic enzymes needed for mobilising food reserves are not produced. This is an example of **physiological immaturity**. Figure 20.12 shows the effect of gibberellic acid in stimulating germination of dormant hazel seeds.

2. IMPERMEABILITY OF THE SEED COAT

The seed coat may be impermeable to oxygen and water or is too hard for the swelling embryo to burst through. This is so in many leguminous species such as lupin, clover and sweet pea. If the testa is chipped or removed, dormancy is broken if the seeds are given conditions suitable for germination. In bulky fruits such as apples the thick wall of the fruit restricts the diffusion of oxygen to the seeds. In natural conditions the seed coat and fruit wall are gradually broken down by microbial activity in the soil.

FIG. 20.12 *Effect of gibberellic acid on germination of hazel seeds*

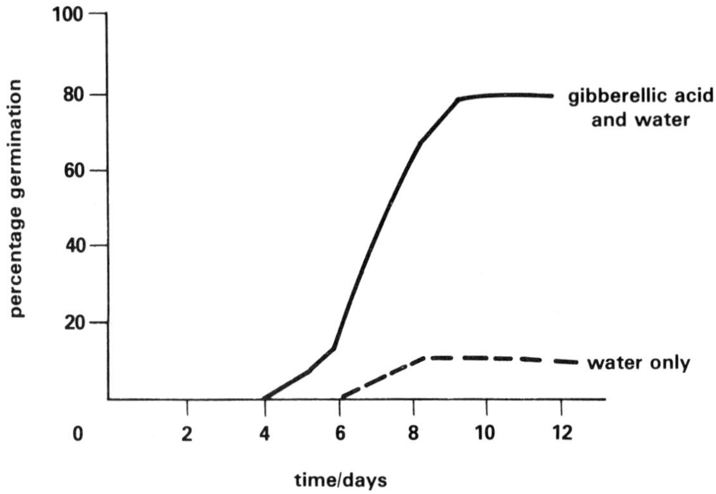

3. GERMINATION INHIBITORS

Seeds of plants with succulent fruits such as tomatoes develop in an environment which seems ideal for germination. They fail to germinate because of **inhibitor** chemicals in the sap of the fruit. In other species such as birch and rose the inhibitor is in the testa and can be removed by immersing the seeds in several changes of water. In natural conditions rainfall probably slowly leaches out the inhibitor. The most important natural inhibitor so far discovered is **abscissic acid** (Fig. 20.13).

FIG. 20.13 *Effect of abscissic acid on germination of rye grass seeds*

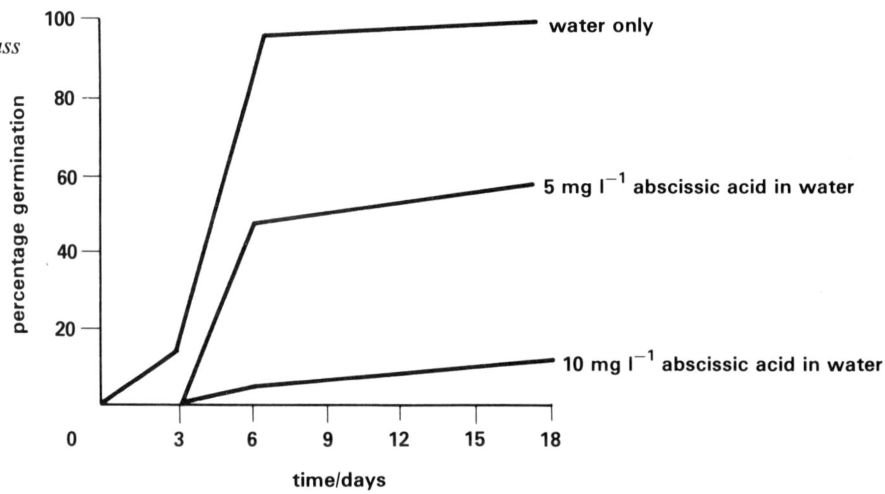

Although the various factors responsible for seed dormancy have been considered separately it is often a combination of factors which generally keeps the seeds of most species dormant. Figure 20.14 shows the combination of dormancy-imposing mechanisms which operate in the European ash.

The few aspects of dormancy considered here demonstrate the subtle interactions between seed and environment and show how germination is controlled so that it usually takes place when there is a reasonable chance that successful growth will follow. In Britain most flowering plants produce their seeds in summer. If germination took place immediately the seeds are

FIG. 20.14 *Combination of dormancy-imposing mechanisms in the European ash*

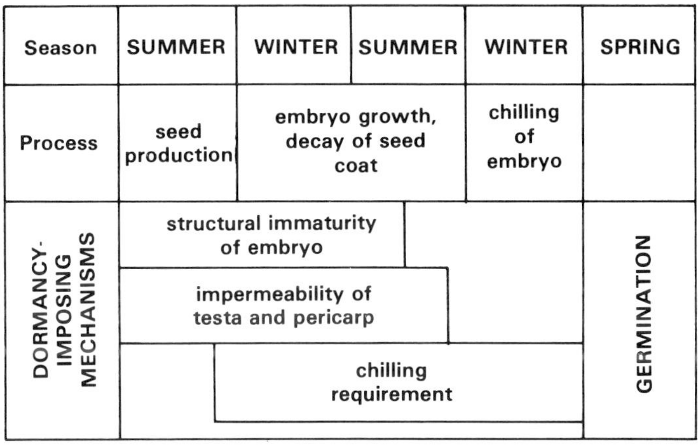

dispersed, large numbers of seedlings would compete for the available space and light during autumn. Few would become established properly before the cold weather of winter. Because germination is delayed until the following spring or summer, subsequent growth is much more likely to be successful with a long spell of favourable weather about to begin. The reasons for dormancy vary between species and the time required for inhibitory factors to disappear also varies. Thus germination is usually spread out over a long period of time whereby the effects of competition between seedlings is diminished and adverse climatic conditions are avoided.

Chapter 21

Growth and development of flowering plants

Growth, which can be thought of as an increase in mass, and **development**, an increase in complexity, go hand in hand in all living organisms. In flowering plants growth and development begin when a seed germinates and ends when a mature plant has grown. Trees can take many years to reach maturity yet a few weeks is sufficient for some annual plants. It is well known that plants kept in greenhouses grow more quickly than similar plants growing outdoors. It is also known that oak trees and not dandelions appear if we sow acorns. This is because **environment** and **heredity** control the pattern and the rate of growth and development.

Over the past twenty years especially, a good deal of effort has been made in an attempt to unravel the physiological basis of plant growth. It is now apparent that growth and development of plants are the consequences of subtle interactions between many **external** and **internal factors**. With this knowledge it may soon be possible for humans to control plant growth more effectively than at present. As a result there could be significant improvements in the production of food, timber and other essential plant products.

21.1 Morphological and anatomical aspects of growth and development

In the previous chapter, seed germination and the subsequent establishment of a small immature plant called a seedling is described. How does a seedling grow and develop into a much larger and more complex mature plant? Mature plants have many more cells than seedlings. It is therefore evident that somatic cell division, mitosis (Chapter 7), is an integral part of growth. But the adult plant is more than a large number of identical cells. It has a variety of cell types, each type adapted to perform specific physiological and mechanical roles. The changes which take place to produce several types of cells is called **differentiation**.

21.1.1 Primary growth and development

In seedling plants mitosis is mainly confined to groups of cells at the tips of radicles and plumules. These areas of somatic cell division are called **apical meristems**. They produce the cells which differentiate into the tissues of the **primary plant body**.

1. THE PRIMARY SHOOT SYSTEM

A thin longitudinal section cut through the middle of a shoot tip reveals, at the apex, a mass of closely packed cells with conspicuous nuclei. The thin cell walls consist largely of pectic substances and the cytoplasm lacks any large vacuoles. Some of the cells are undergoing mitosis (Fig. 21.1). This is the apical meristem of the shoot.

(i) THE APICAL MERISTEM OF THE SHOOT. It is usually possible to distinguish an outer zone of cells called the **tunica** and an inner mass of cells called the **corpus** in the apical meristem of a shoot. The tunica, which can be one to several cells thick, is characterised by the fact that during mitosis cross walls are laid down at right angles to the surface of the shoot apex. Its main task is to enlarge the surface area of the shoot. The outermost layer of cells derived from the tunica later differentiates into the **epidermis** of the primary shoot system. Division of the corpus cells occurs

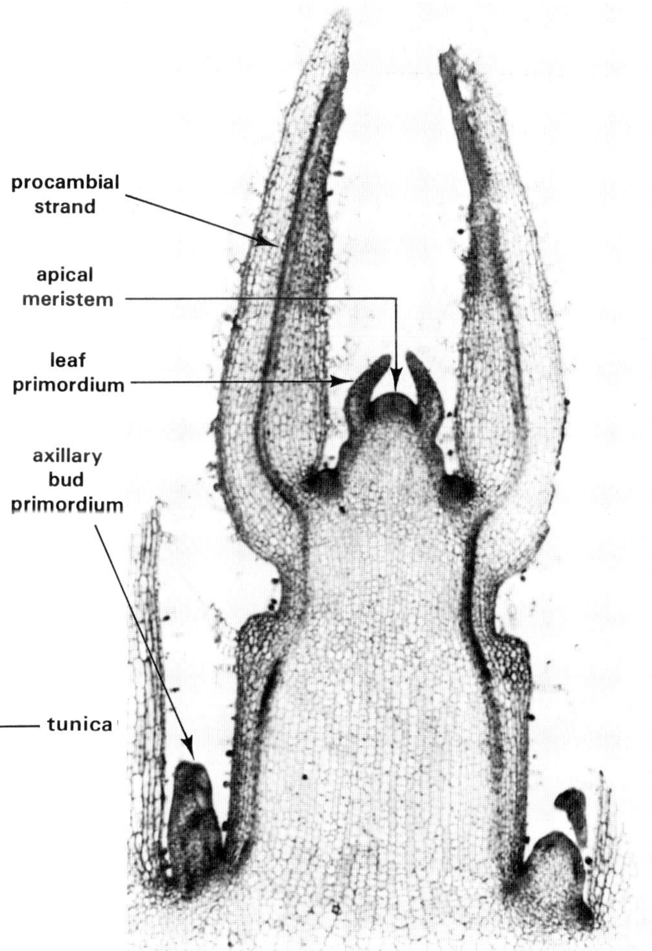

FIG. 21.1 (a) *Longitudinal section through the shoot apex of a dicotyledonous plant, × 30*

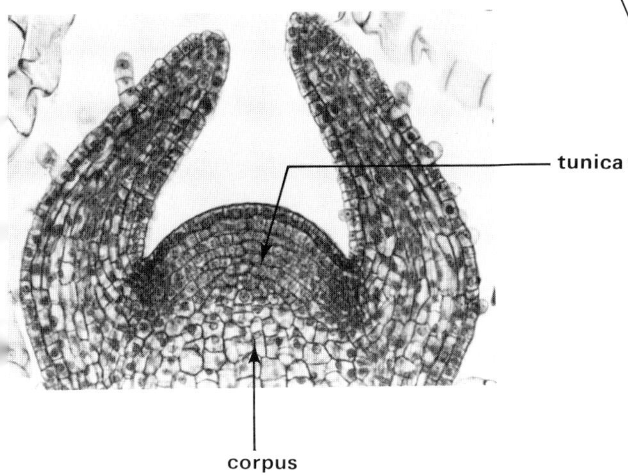

FIG. 21.1 (b) *Close-up view of apex, × 160*

in several planes. An internal mass of cells is thus produced, the size of which keeps pace with the ever-increasing surface layer formed by the tunica. Cells derived from the corpus differentiate into the tissues of the **cortex**, **vascular bundles** and **pith** of the primary stem.

Both tunica and corpus take part in the formation of swellings which arise at regular intervals on the surface of the shoot apex. The swellings are called **leaf primordia**. Their growth is so rapid that the earlier formed primordia soon enclose the apical meristem at the tip of the shoot. Mature leaves gradually differentiate from the older primordia, new primordia constantly being formed at the tip of the shoot as apical growth continues. The spatial arrangement of the leaf primordia determines the positions of mature leaves on the shoot. Paired primordia for example give rise to pairs of leaves on the mature stem. **Axillary bud primordia** which have the potential to grow into lateral shoots are generally seen in the axils of developing leaves near the shoot apex (Fig. 21.2). The tunica and corpus again produce the axillary bud primordia. The superficial origin of lateral shoots contrasts with the deep-seated origin of lateral roots Fig. 21.9).

FIG. 21.2 *The shoot apex of a dicotyledonous plant*

(a) *Longitudinal section* (b) *Transverse sections*

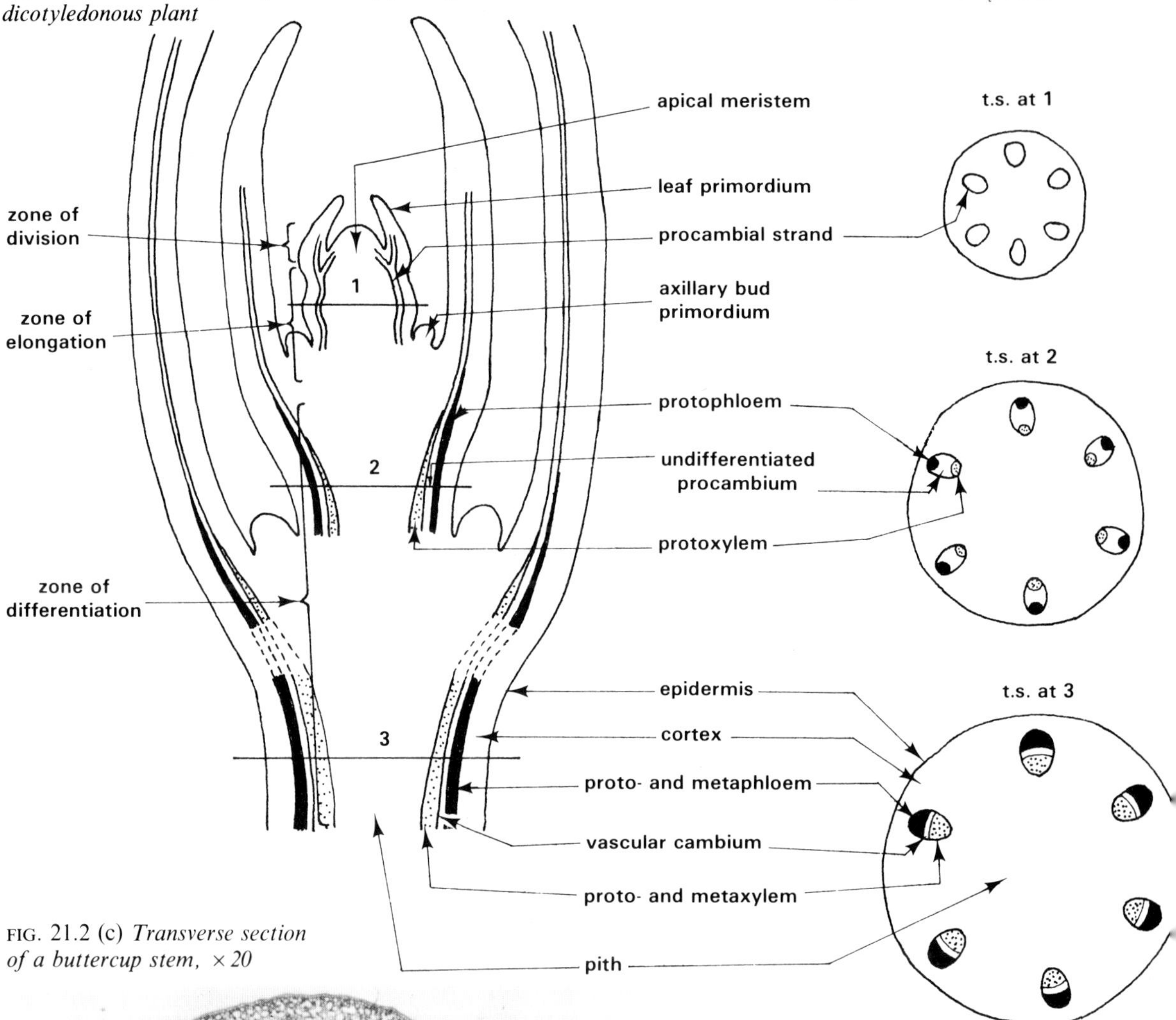

FIG. 21.2 (c) *Transverse section of a buttercup stem, ×20*

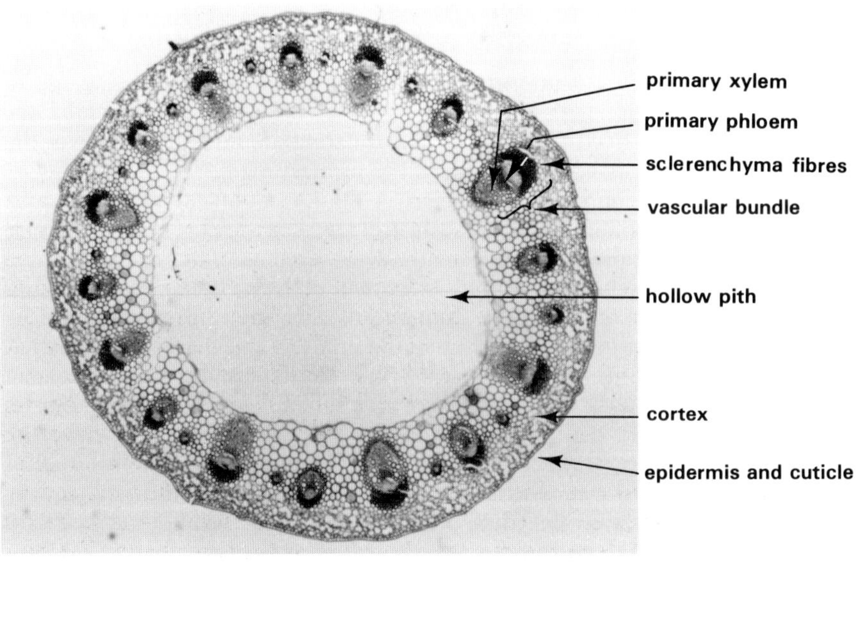

FIG. 21.2 (d) *Enlarged view of one of the vascular bundles, × 120*

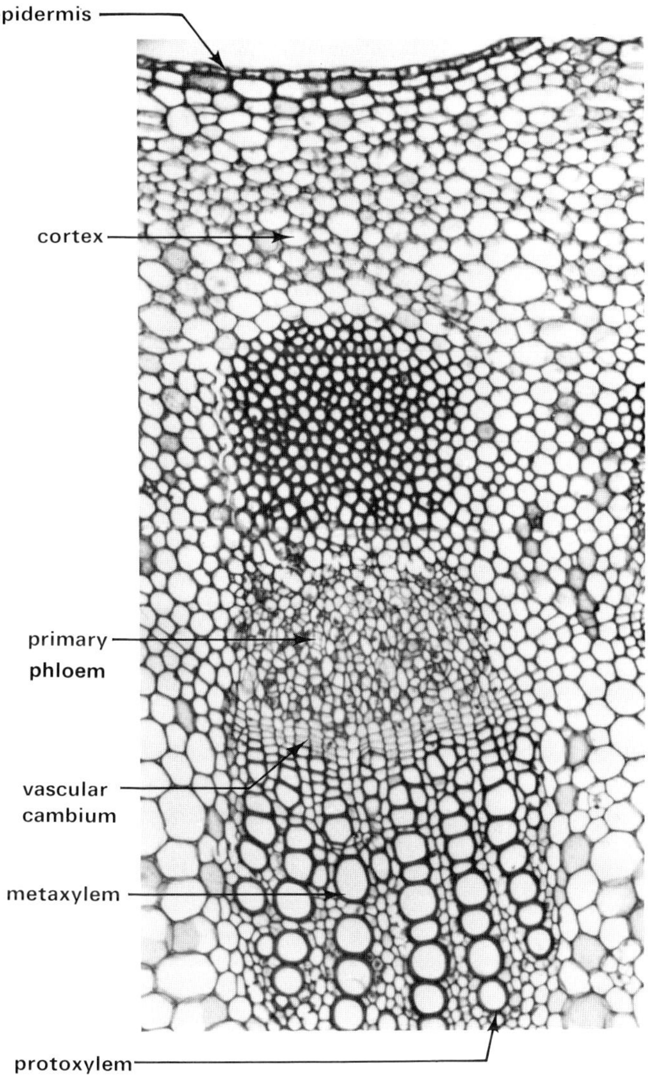

(ii) TISSUE DIFFERENTIATION IN THE STEM. Just behind the apical meristem the first signs of **tissue differentiation** are seen. Conspicuous vacuoles appear in the cytoplasm of cells cut off from the tunica and corpus. The effect is to cause considerable increase in length and girth of the cells. **Vacuolation** accounts mainly for elongation of the shoot at this stage. However, there is an increase in the protein and nucleic acid content of the cells. Cellulose is also laid down in the expanding cell walls.

Not all of the apically-derived cells undergo the changes outlined above. Several strands of cells extending backwards from the apex remain narrow with pointed ends. Although they elongate they do not develop large vacuoles. They also retain the power to divide even when the surrounding cells can no longer do so. Thus a number of discrete bundles of tissue called **procambial strands** appear among the vacuolate ground tissue. The positions of the strands are determined by the leaf primordia, one strand developing below each primordium.

The outermost cells of the procambial strands differentiate into the first formed cells of primary phloem called **protophloem**. First there is an unequal longitudinal division of each procambial cell. The smaller of the derivatives differentiates into a companion cell. At the same time the larger cell differentiates into a sieve-tube element. Sieve tubes transport organic substances in solution to all parts of the plant including the growing shoot apex (Chapter 12). Shortly afterwards the first formed water-carrying tissue called **protoxylem** differentiates from the innermost cells of each procambial strand. The main changes in protoxylem differentiation are loss of the protoplast, breakdown of the end walls of adjacent cells and secretion of a lignified secondary wall as annular or spiral bands inside the primary cell wall (Fig. 21.3(a)). The primary walls of protoxylem cells can continue growing for some time keeping pace with elongation of surrounding tissues. The secondary wall gives the necessary support to keep the lumen of each xylem element open for water transport.

While the changes outlined above are taking place the shoot apex continues to grow upwards. The part of the shoot where protophloem and protoxylem have formed now stops elongating and further differentiation occurs in the procambial strands. The procambial cells immediately inside the protophloem differentiate into **metaphloem** sieve-tubes and companion cells. The procambial cells immediately inside the protoxylem differentiate into **metaxylem** cells. The main changes in the formation of metaxylem cells are loss of end walls. The primary walls of metaxylem cells become covered internally by scalariform, reticulate or pitted, lignified secondary walls (Fig. 21.3(b)). The lack of plasticity compared with protoxylem cells reflects the cessation of elongation in this part of the shoot.

FIG. 21.3 (a) *Differentiation of protoxylem*

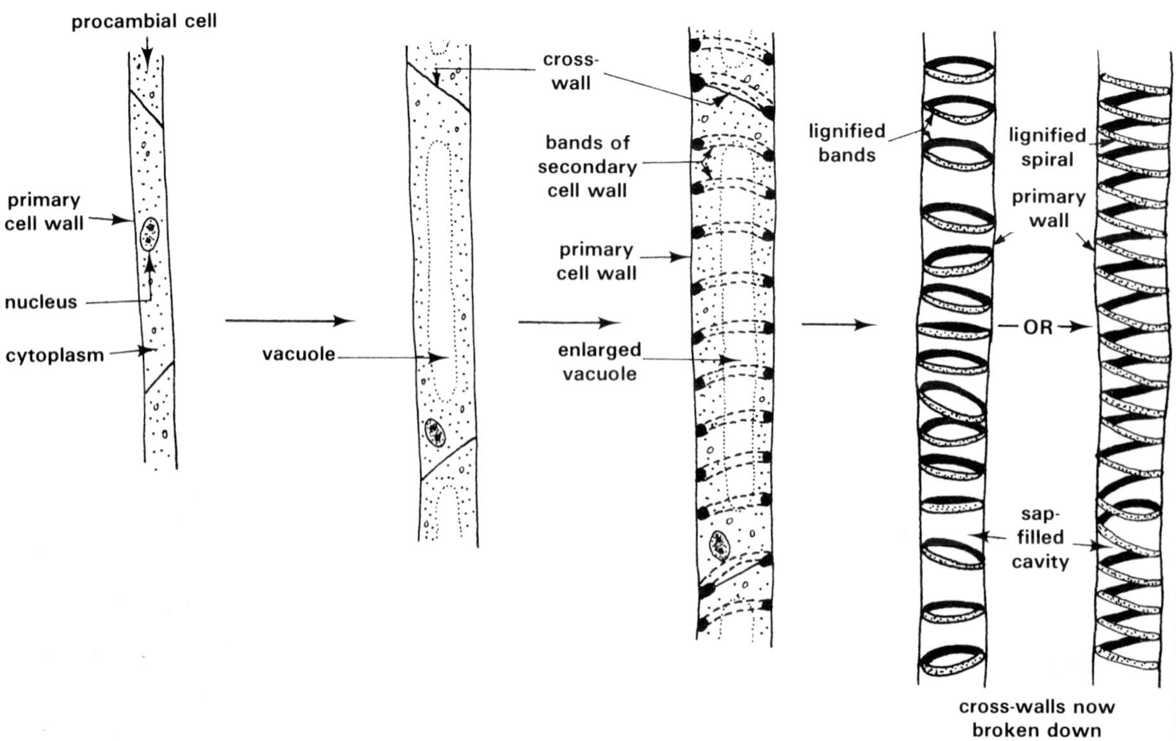

FIG. 21.3 (b) *Metaxylem cells*

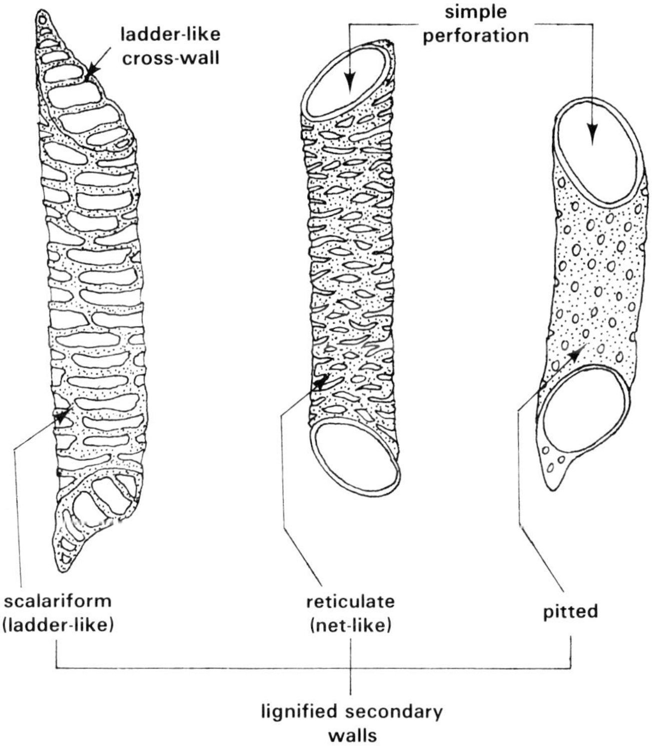

FIG. 21.3 (c) *Longitudinal section of protoxylem, × 120*

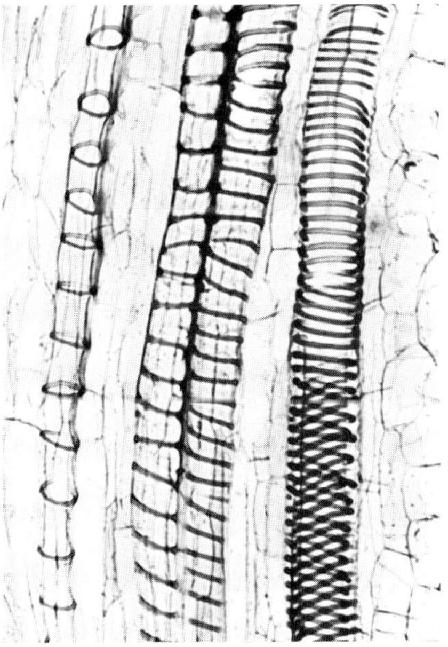

The cells of much of the ground tissue of the stem, (the cortex and pith) show less obvious changes as they differentiate into a tissue called **parenchyma**. The main changes are enlargement in girth and length, the development of thin cellulose walls and extensive vacuolation of the cytoplasm. The changes prepare the parenchyma cells for the storage of large quantities of sap which helps maintain turgidity of the young shoot. Starch grains too are frequently stored in parenchyma. In the outer cortex the cell walls often become thickened with stiff, yet plastic, deposits of cellulose

FIG. 21.4 (a) *Parenchyma*

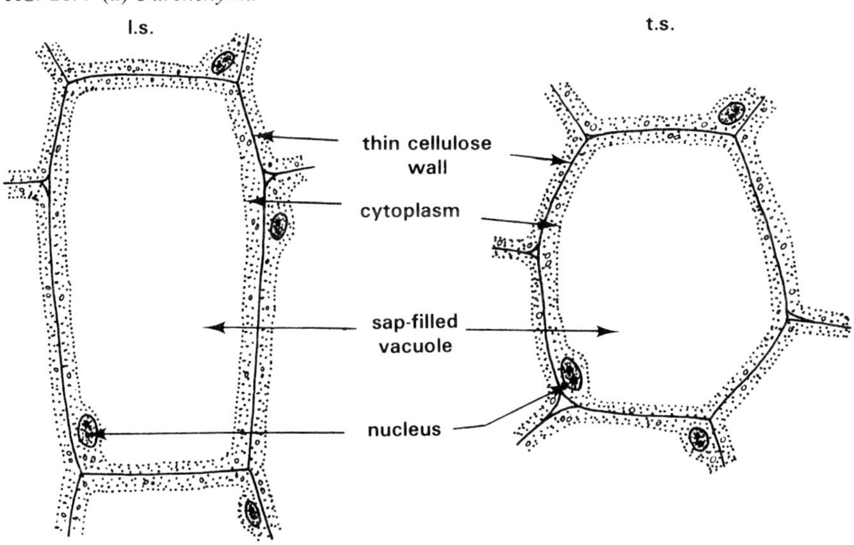

Parenchyma cells near the surface of the stem usually contain chloroplasts

(i) *transverse section of parenchyma, × 300*

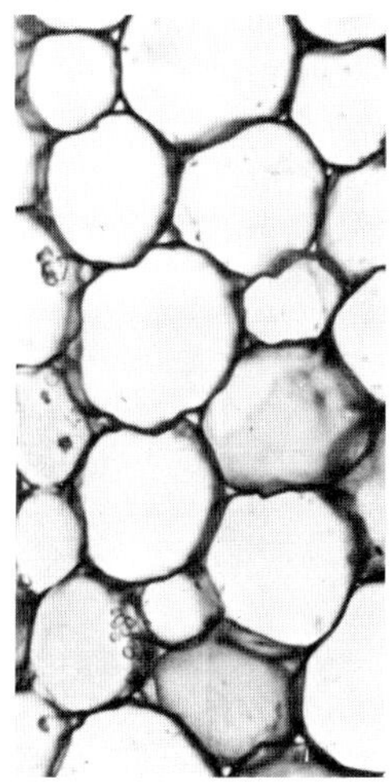

FIG. 21.4 (b)

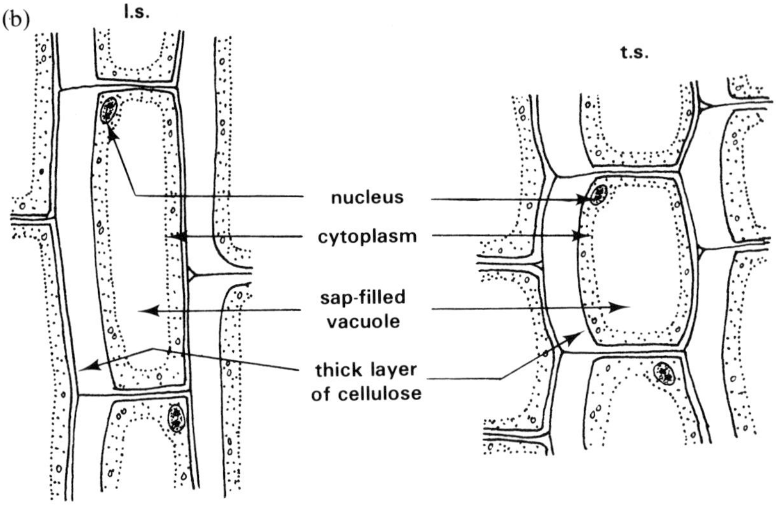

(ii) *transverse section of collenchyma,* × *300*

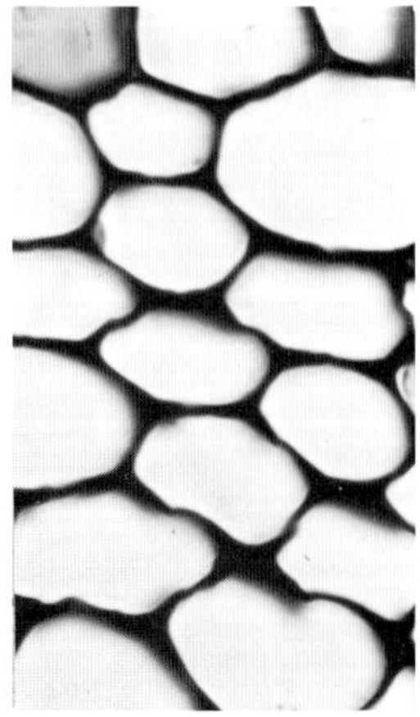

The position of the thick deposit of cellulose varies from one type of collenchyma to another

FIG. 21.4 (c) *sclerenchyma fibres*

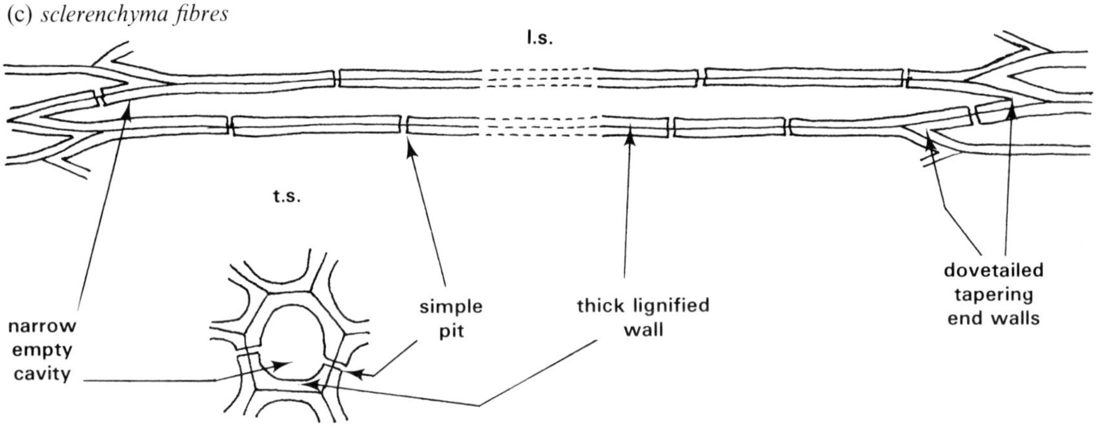

(iii) *sclerenchyma: transverse and longitudinal sections, both* × *300*

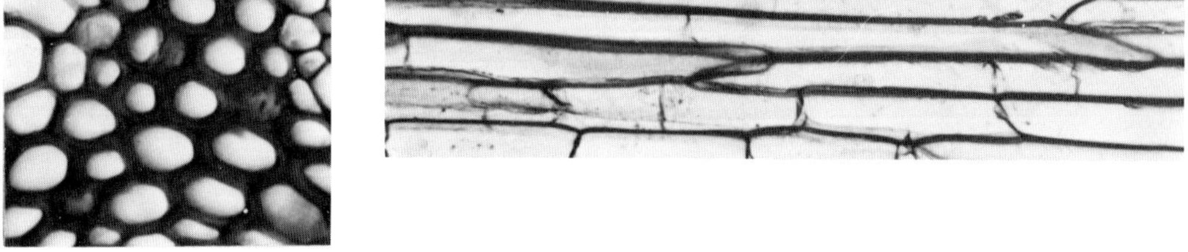

forming a supporting tissue called **collenchyma**. Parenchyma and collenchyma cells retain the ability to divide and often contain chloroplasts. Some cortical cells, particularly those immediately around each vascular bundle, become extremely elongated and have tapering end walls. They develop extremely thick, lignified secondary walls. These are **sclerenchyma fibres**, the ends of which dovetail together and form a very efficient supporting tissue (Fig. 21.4). The epidermal cells derived from the tunica secrete a waxy material called **cutin** over their outer surface making the **epidermis** waterproof. Some epidermal cells become modified into **guard cells** of **stomata** which are used for gas exchange (Chapters 11 and 12).

(iii) DEVELOPMENT OF LEAVES AND LATERAL SHOOTS. A leaf primordium grows initially into a peg-like outgrowth with an **adaxial meristem** on its lower surface. Division of the cells of the adaxial meristem produces a thicker peg containing procambial strands continuous with those in the stem. The peg later differentiates into the tissues of the leaf midrib. **Marginal meristems** appear on either side of the peg and divide to produce cells which differentiate into the epidermis, mesophyll and vascular tissue of the leaf blade (Fig. 21.5). The spatial arrangement or **phyllotaxis** of leaves on the mature stem is therefore determined by the positions of the leaf primordia at the stem apex. In Figure 21.5 it can be seen that the developing leaves are so close to each other at the shoot apex that they overlap and form a terminal **bud**. Growth and differentiation of the primary stem separates the older leaves as elongation of the **internodes**, the length of stem between successive leaves, occurs. Separation of the mature leaves allows efficient gas exchange and light absorption, important for photosynthesis, the main physiological function of leaves (Chapter 12).

FIG. 21.5 (a) and (b) *Stages in the early development of a leaf*

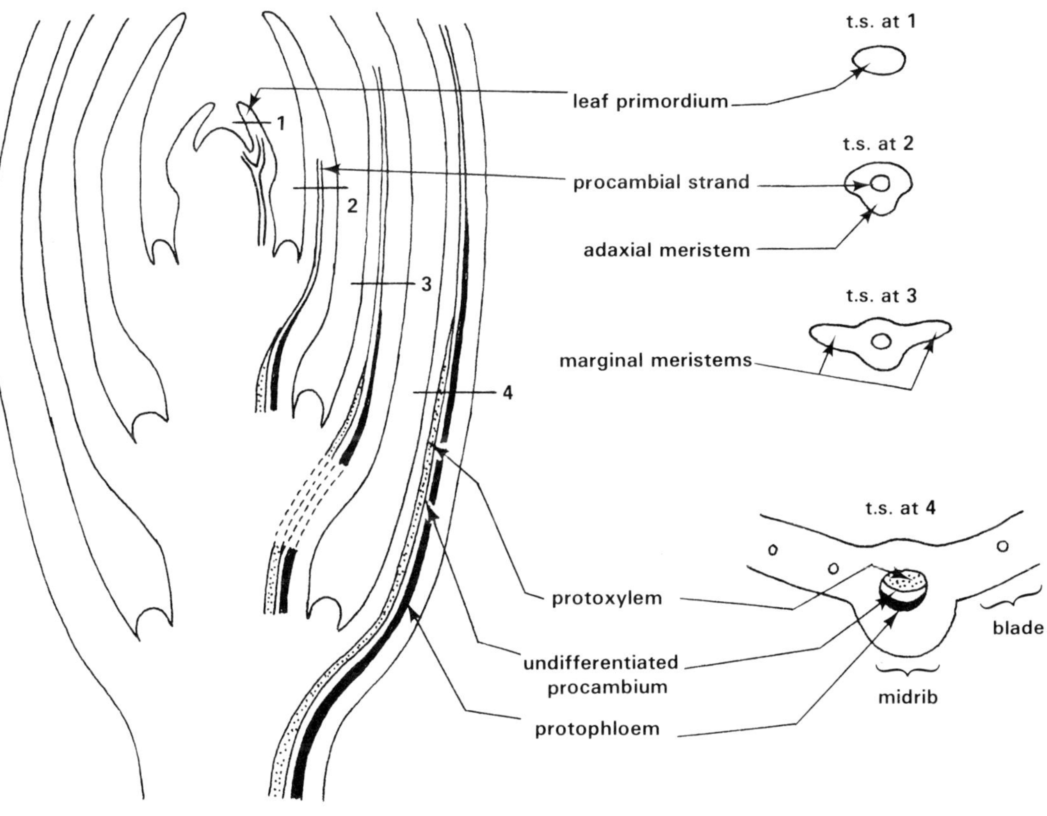

FIG. 21.5 (c) *Transverse section of a mature leaf, × 30*

Lateral buds in the axils of leaves may grow into side shoots. Development of side shoots is the same as described earlier for the main shoot.

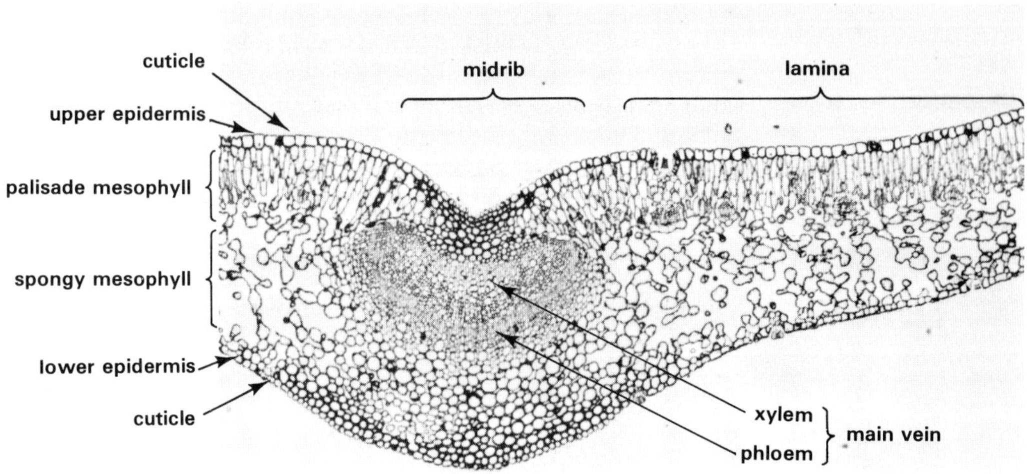

FIG. 21.6 *Longitudinal section through the apex of an onion root × 100*

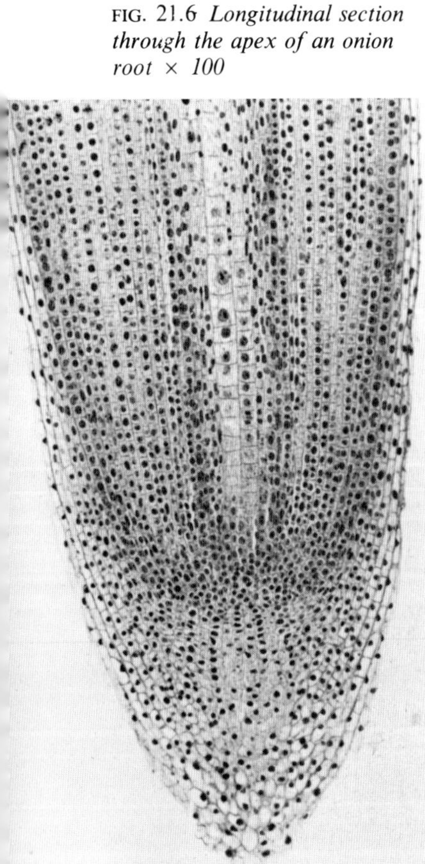

2. THE PRIMARY ROOT SYSTEM

(i) THE APICAL MERISTEM OF THE ROOT. The most obvious difference in appearance between longitudinal sections of stem and root apices is the absence of bulges comparable to leaf and bud primordia on the root apex. The root apex is also covered by a **root cap** (Fig. 21.6). There is, however, a marked similarity in appearance and behaviour of the apical cells which constantly divide by mitosis. In most roots it is possible to distinguish a number of zones of cells at the apex. The outermost zone is called the **protoderm**. It produces cells which differentiate into the root epidermis and root cap. Inside the protoderm is the **ground meristem** which produces cells which differentiate into the root cortex. Just behind the root apex a single **procambial strand** can be seen at the centre of the root. Some roots have an additional meristematic layer, the **calyptrogen**, which gives rise to the cells of the root cap. The meristematic zones radiate from a clump of cells called the **quiescent centre** situated immediately behind the root cap. The significance of the quiescent centre is not as yet fully understood. Its cells divide slowly and it is probably the site from which the meristematic layers arise (Fig. 21.7).

(ii) TISSUE DIFFERENTIATION IN THE ROOT. Differentiation of vascular tissue begins near the root apex. Several strands of sieve-tube elements and companion cells appear near the outside of the procambial strand. Shortly afterwards a similar number of strands of protoxylem cells alternating with the primary phloem strands differentiate. Metaxylem cells differentiate last of all at the centre of the procambial strand. The outermost procambial cells undergo little change and retain their ability to divide. They become the **pericycle** which may later produce lateral roots.

The derivatives of the ground meristem differentiate into parenchyma cells of the **root cortex** which are used mainly for the storage of starch and the transport of water and dissolved minerals from the soil solution to the root vascular tissue. The cortical cells of the root do not usually develop chloroplasts as do the outer cortical cells of the stem. The innermost layer of the root cortex differentiates into a special band of cells called the **endodermis**. Early in development the endodermal cells secrete a suberised

FIG. 21.7 *The root apex of a dicotyledonous plant*

(a) *longitudinal section*

(b) *transverse sections*

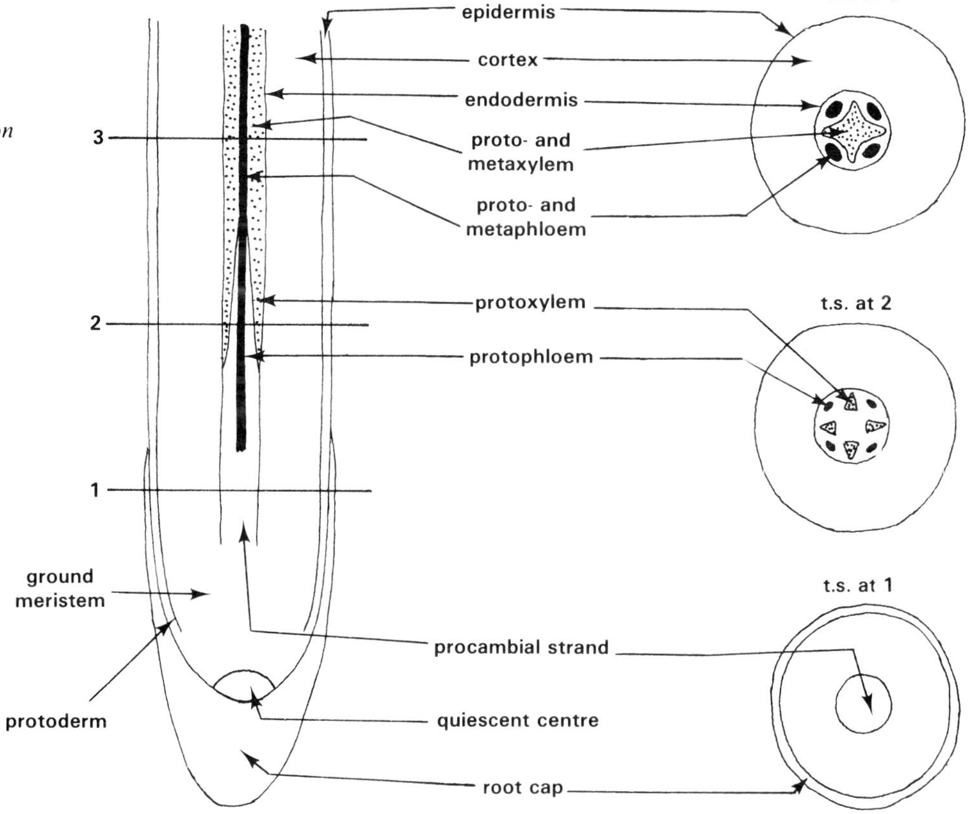

FIG. 21.7 (c) *Transverse section of a mature primary root of a dicotyledonous plant,* $\times 70$

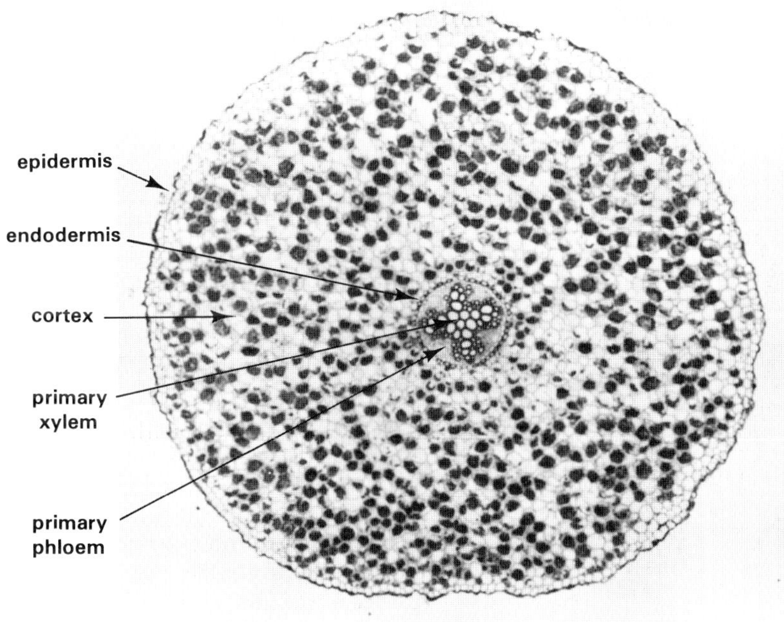

21.1.2 Secondary growth and development

Whereas some plants do not develop further than the primary stage, others can add secondary tissues to the primary body. The **secondary plant body** is derived from **lateral meristems**, the most important of which are the **vascular cambium** and **cork cambium**.

1. THE VASCULAR CAMBIUM

In plants which undergo secondary growth not all the procambial cells in the primary body differentiate into vascular tissue. What remains is called **vascular cambium** and is situated between the primary xylem and phloem of stems and roots. The vascular cambium consists of two types of cells, **ray and fusiform initials** (Fig. 21.10), and usually begins its activity during the first year of the plant's life.

FIG. 21.10 *The vascular cambium*

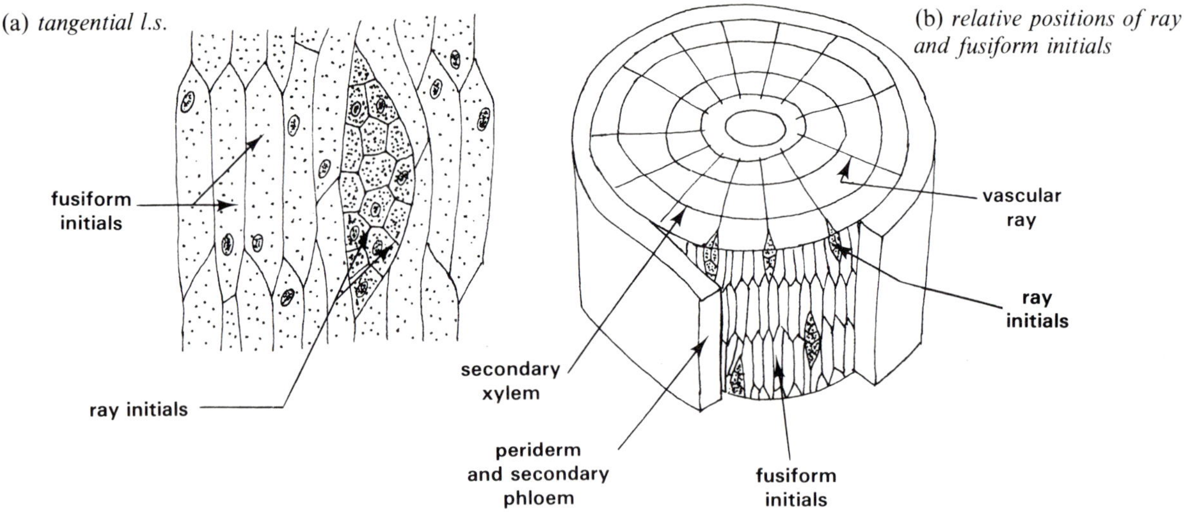

FIG. 21.11 *Stages in the differentiation of secondary xylem and phloem* (modified from Ray, 1963)

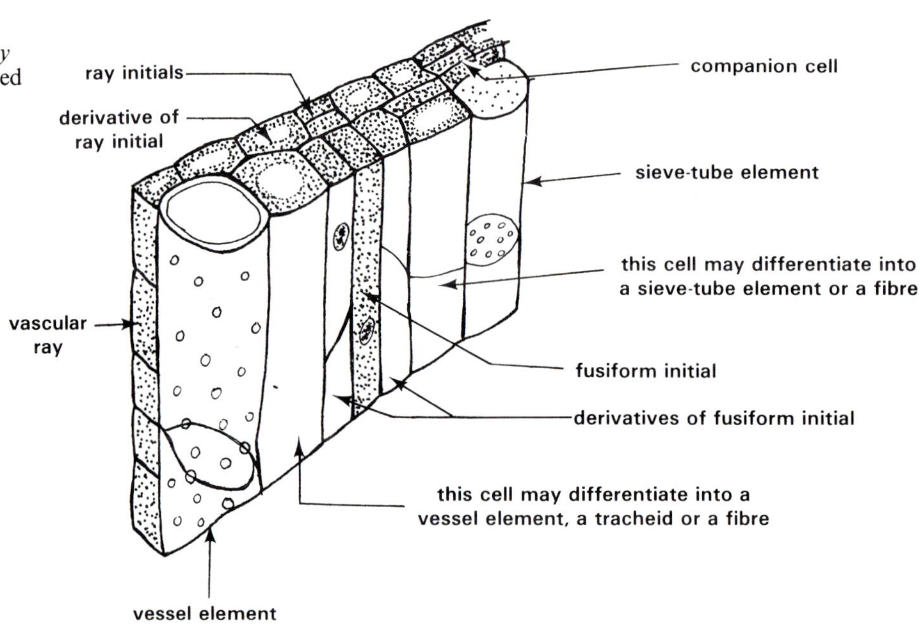

In the stem of a dicotyledonous plant the vascular cambium is at first confined to the vascular bundles. However, a complete cylinder of vascular cambium is formed as parenchyma cells between the bundles become meristematic. The main plane of division of the ray and fusiform initials is tangential. Derivatives cut off from the fusiform initials to the inside of the cylinder of vascular cambium **differentiate** into xylem vessel elements, tracheids and fibres. Those cut off to the outside become sieve-tube elements, companion cells and phloem fibres. Derivatives of the ray initials differentiate into parenchyma cells which cross the secondary xylem and phloem as radial **vascular rays** (Fig. 21.11). Occasionally the ray and fusiform initials divide by radial walls so that the circumference of the cylinder of vascular cambium increases, accommodating the growing amount of secondary xylem it encloses.

FIG. 21.12 *Stages in the secondary growth of a dicotyledonous stem as seen in transverse section*

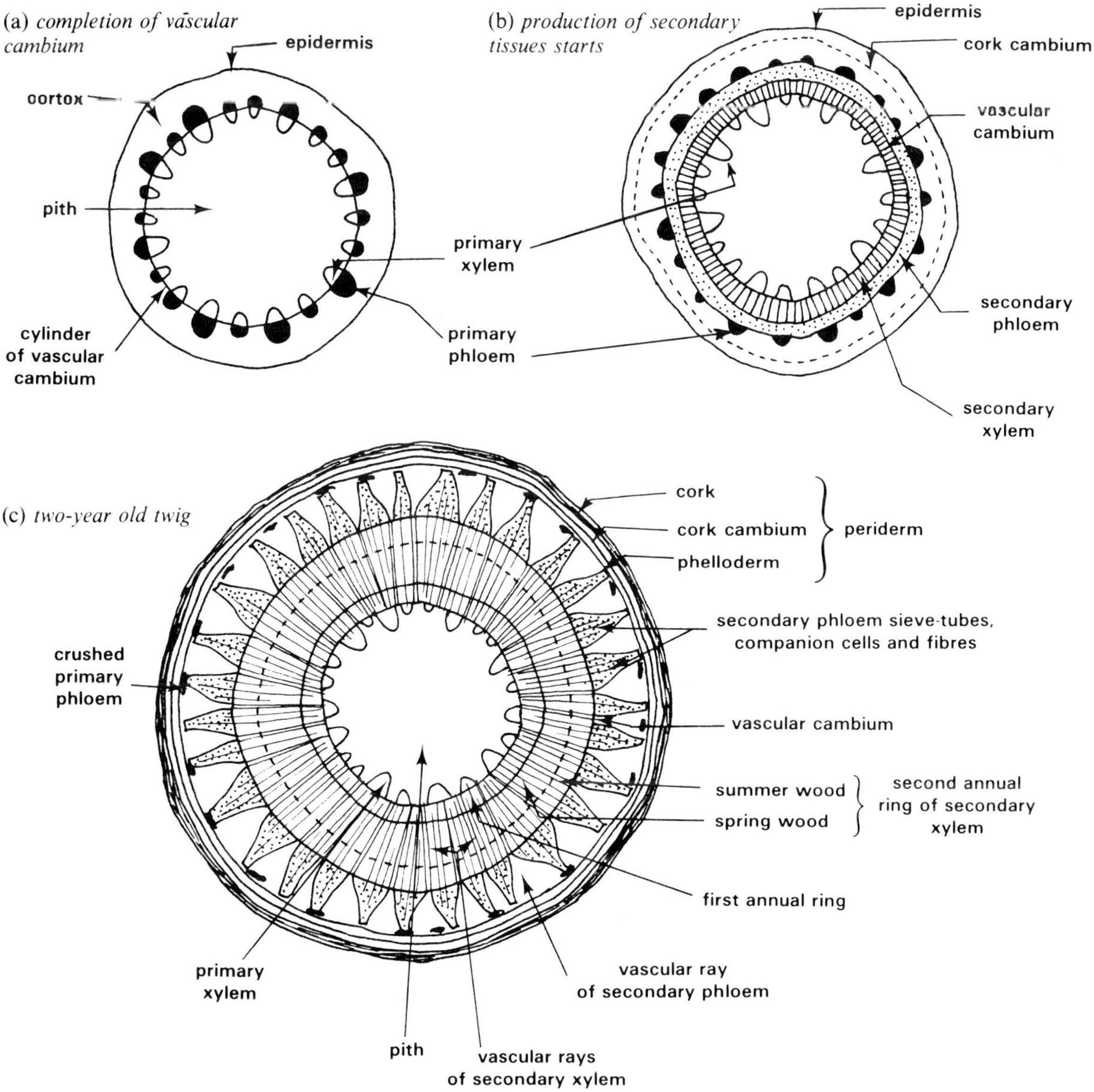

FIG. 21.12 (d) *Transverse section through a 5-year-old twig of lime, × 15*

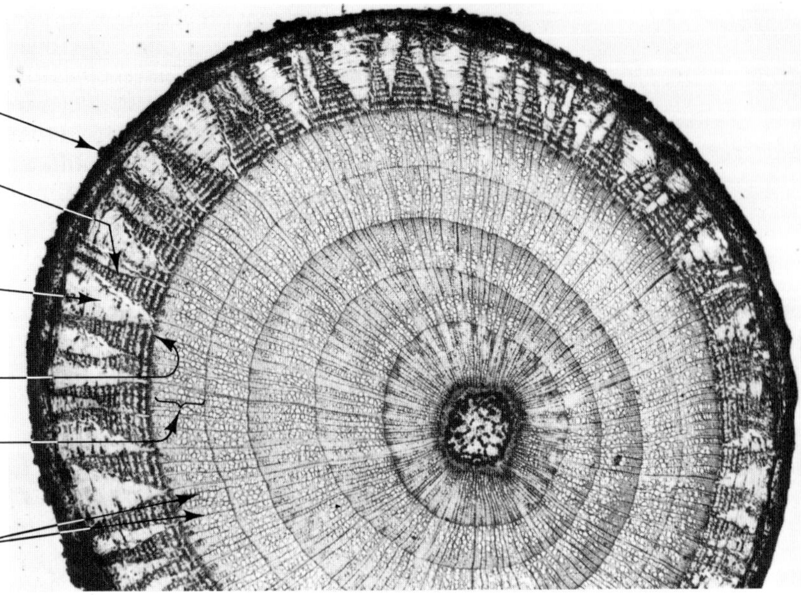

The vascular cambium is seasonal in its activity. It is dormant in winter and active in spring and summer. A cylinder of secondary xylem called an **annual ring** is added each year to the existing plant body. Vessels produced early in the growing season are generally larger in diameter than those arising later. Each annual ring thus consists of two distinct regions, **spring wood** on the inside and **summer wood** on the outside. The age of a shrub or tree can be found by counting the number of annual rings of secondary xylem in a cross-section of the main stem or trunk. There is no obvious layering in the secondary phloem. Here the vascular ray cells often undergo further division by radial walls so that wide, wedge-shaped phloem rays separate groups of sieve-tubes, companion cells and fibres (Fig. 21.12).

2. THE CORK CAMBIUM

The increase in girth resulting from the addition of secondary vascular tissue imposes a strain on the outer tissues of the stem. If the primary cortex and epidermis remained, the stem would split open with the risk of desiccation. This is prevented by the development of tissues called the **periderm** which replace the outer tissues of the primary stem.

A cylinder of **cork cambium** arises, usually from parenchyma cells in the outer cortex. In transverse section the cells of the cork cambium are uniformly rectangular in shape. As in the vascular cambium, mitotic division in a tangential plane cuts off derivatives to the outside and to the inside. The outer derivatives secrete a layer of waxy material called suberin in their secondary walls after which their protoplasts disappear. They are now **cork cells** and form an effective waterproof barrier which prevents dehydration of internal tissues. Here and there the cork cells are loosely arranged, forming **lenticels** which allow gas exchange between the outer tissues and the atmosphere. The small number of derivatives cut off internally undergo little change and remain as a narrow band of uniform cells called **phelloderm** (Fig. 21.13). The cells of the cork cambium now and again divide by radial walls to enlarge the circumference of the meristem, thereby keeping pace with the increase in girth caused by the activity of the vascular cambium.

A comparable pattern of secondary growth also happens in the roots of many dicotyledonous plants. The vascular cambium originates from strands of undifferentiated procambium lying between the primary xylem and phloem. It then develops into a cylinder from which annual rings of secondary vascular tissue are produced as in the stem. The cork cambium often originates from the pericycle so that early in its secondary growth the root becomes temporarily much thinner when the endodermis, cortex and epidermis are lost.

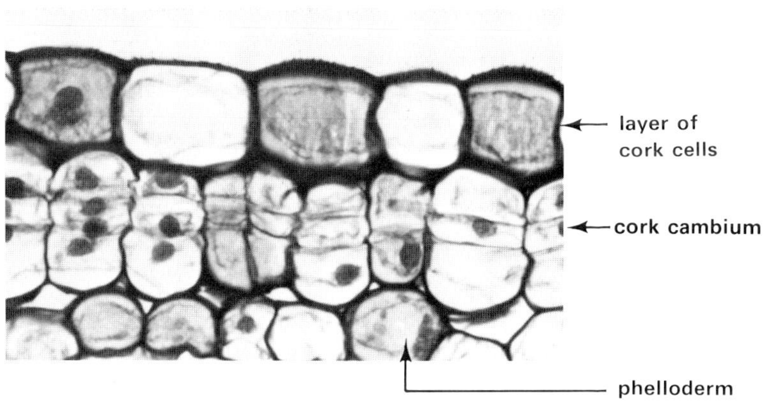

FIG. 21.13 (a) *Transverse section through the periderm of elder, ×360*

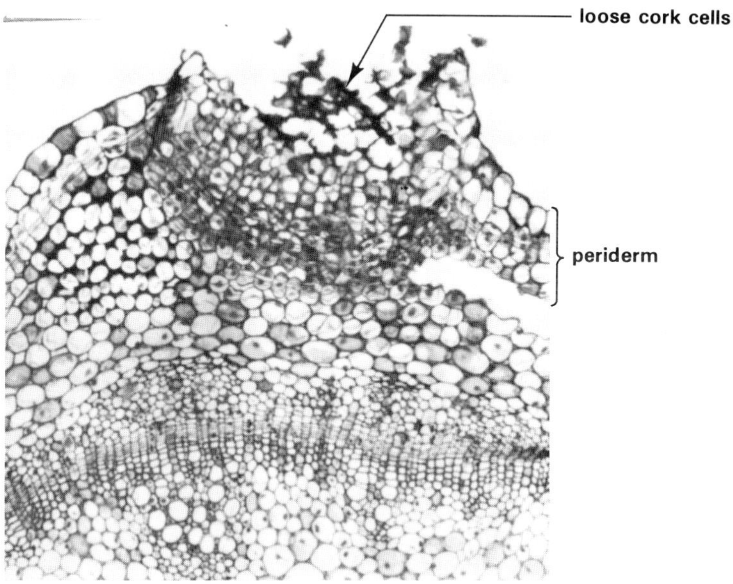

FIG. 21.13 (b) *Transverse section through a lenticel of elder, ×80*

Few monocotyledonous species undergo secondary growth. However, in plants of the grass family shoot growth is not entirely dependent on the apical meristem. In grasses, tissues at the bases of the internodes remain meristematic even though the rest of the internode is fully differentiated. Each internode thus has its own growth zone called an **intercalary meristem** (Fig. 21.14). The activity of the intercalary meristem is one of the reasons why grass shoots regenerate rapidly after being severely damaged in haymaking, lawnmowing and animal grazing.

FIG. 21.14 *Intercalary meristems in a grass shoot*

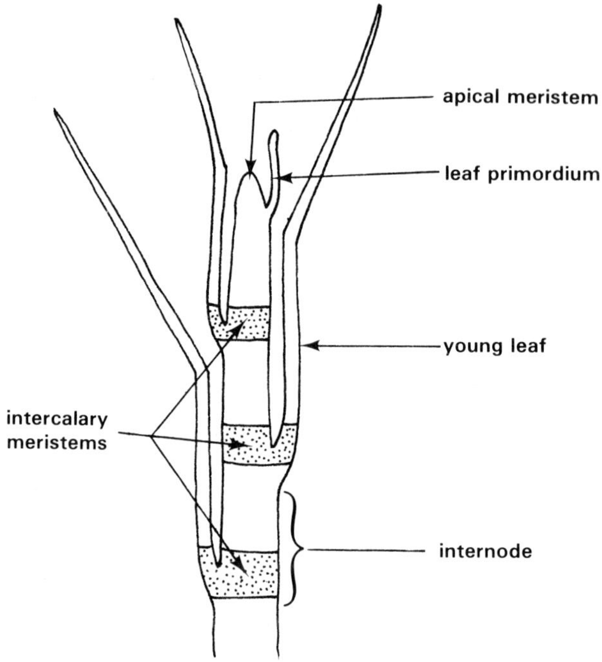

21.2 Physiological aspects of growth and development

A seedling becomes established using the reserve of food stored in the seed (Chapter 20). When the food reserve has been used up continued growth and development depend on the young plant obtaining alternative sources of energy and raw materials. The capture of energy in sunlight and its conversion to chemical bond energy is described in Chapters 5 and 12, while the roles of minerals in plant metabolism are dealt with in Chapter 13. There are, however, many other physiological aspects of plant growth. What for example causes roots to grow down into the soil and shoots to grow up into the air? What controls the orderly sequence of cell division and differentiation at the apices of roots and shoots? Why do deciduous trees shed their leaves in autumn, why do buds spurt into growth in spring and summer and why is the vascular cambium seasonal in its activity?

Climate plays some part in controlling plant growth. The metabolism of green plants occurs efficiently only if such factors as temperature, light intensity and water availability are at an optimum. Nevertheless many species of flowering plants stop growing even when environmental factors are ideal. This suggests that there is an inbuilt growth control mechanism which causes plants to enter a period of dormancy at certain times of the year. Thus **external** and **internal factors** must be examined if we are to find a physiological explanation for the morphological and anatomical changes described earlier.

21.2.1 External factors

1. LIGHT

When the **compensation point** (Chapter 12) has been passed a green plant begins to increase in dry mass as it stores the synthesised energy-rich substances, mainly carbohydrates like starch. Some of the energy released from the food reserves as high energy phosphate bonds of ATP is used in growth for building up the many complex constituents of the protoplasm and walls of new cells. The **intensity of light** largely determines the time required to reach the compensation point each day. If a plant cannot build up sufficient food reserves in a day to provide for energy-requiring processes such as growth, it cannot remain active for long and must either die or undergo a period of dormancy.

In a temperate climate the length of time a plant is subjected to light each day varies from season to season. Flowering plants respond to changes in **daylength**. Growth takes place in seasons of favourable climate and stops when winter approaches. This response is called **vegetative photoperiodism**. It accounts for leaf fall and bud dormancy in deciduous trees and the production of storage organs, such as bulbs, tubers, corms and taproots by herbaceous perennials.

The pattern of growth is affected by the **wavelength of light** to which green plants are exposed. Kept in total darkness shoot systems soon begin to show signs of **etiolation**. The internodes become abnormally long and the leaves remain embryonic and do not develop chlorophyll (Fig. 21.15). Red light alone can prevent etiolation. Red light converts the inactive form of phytochrome P_r to the active form P_{ir} (Chapter 20). P_{ir} promotes leaf expansion and inhibits internode elongation and the normal growth pattern of the shoot is established.

Both vegetative photoperiodism and prevention of etiolation are good examples of the ways in which light controls the balance of growth promotors and inhibitors in plants. The **direction** from which light is received by shoots and roots also affects their direction of growth by altering the distribution of growth promotors (section 21.2.2).

FIG. 21.15 *Etiolation in pea seedlings*

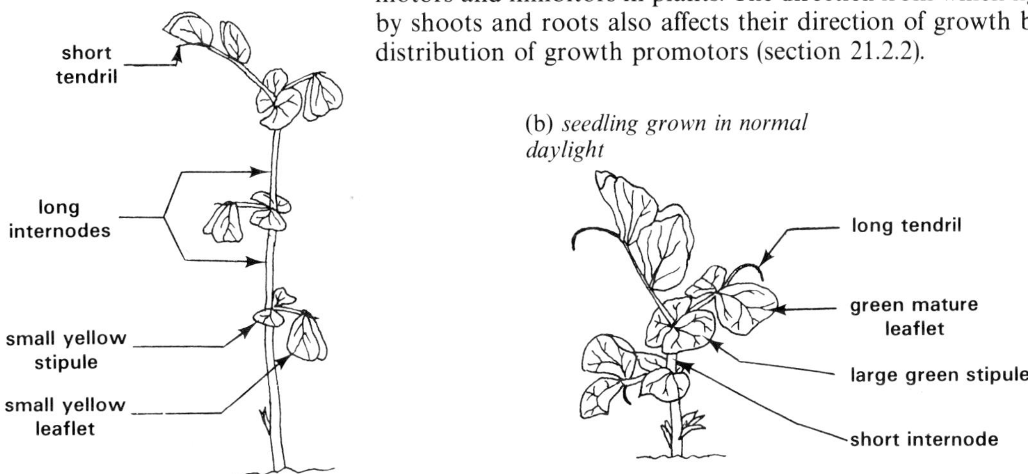

(a) *etiolated seedling grown without light*

(b) *seedling grown in normal daylight*

Both seedlings are of the same variety and of the same age

2. TEMPERATURE

Because growth depends on biochemical reactions catalysed by enzymes, it is affected by **temperature**. In the tropics the average yearly temperature is high enough to allow plants to grow for most of the time. In temperate zones growth is seasonal and often stops altogether in the winter because of low temperatures. In winter annual plants survive as **seeds**, herbaceous perennials as **bulbs**, **corms**, **tubers** and **rhizomes** or by the production of some other kind of fleshy storage organ. Deciduous shrubs and trees develop **dormant winter buds**.

Exposure to a period of **low temperature** is essential to break the dormancy of perennating organs and winter buds (Fig. 21.16). As with seeds, the effect of chilling is thought to reduce the amount of growth inhibitors. This ensures that growth normally occurs when the more suitable weather conditions of spring and summer are about to follow.

FIG. 21.16 *Effect of chilling in breaking the dormancy of* Gladiolus *corms* (after Ginzburg, 1973)

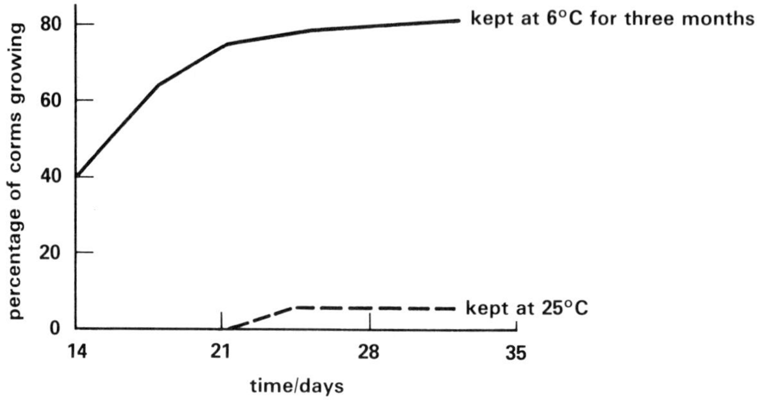

3. GRAVITY

Gravity affects the distribution of growth promotors at root and shoot apices thus influencing the direction in which they grow (section 21.2.2).

4. OXYGEN

Higher plants are aerobic organisms and can produce sufficient free energy for growth only if **oxygen** is available (Chapter 5). Root growth of most plants is inhibited in waterlogged soils where oxygen is scarce. Flowering plants which live totally or partly immersed in water are called hydrophytes. They often have special **aerating tissue** which stores oxygen made in photosynthesis. The storage of oxygen helps hydrophytes to overcome the relative scarcity of dissolved oxygen in water.

5. WATER AVAILABILITY

Elongation of cells during the primary growth of roots and shoots is mainly due to vacuolation. **Water** is essential for **vacuolation** and the subsequent maintenance of **turgidity** of young growing organs. The direction of root growth too is affected by water availability (section 21.2.2).

The synthesis of new cellular components, an essential feature of growth, takes place in water like all enzyme-catalysed reactions (Chapter 4). It is in water that the raw materials for growth are **absorbed** and **circulated** inside plants.

6. CARBON DIOXIDE

Carbon dioxide is essential for photosynthesis (Chapters 5 and 12). If growth is to occur beyond the seedling stage carbon dioxide must be available in sufficient quantities.

7. MINERAL ELEMENTS

Minerals are required for many facets of plant metabolism on which growth depends (Chapter 13). When higher plants are exposed to mineral-rich effluents, growth is not always stimulated even though the minerals are essential for plant growth. Growth is promoted when air containing moderate concentrations of sulphur dioxide comes into contact with flowering plants. However, a high concentration of sulphur dioxide is toxic to higher plants. Copper acts as a trace element in plant metabolism yet land plants do not readily colonise spoil tips rich in copper (Chapter 13).

8. BIOTIC FACTORS

In natural conditions a state of equilibrium exists between the trophic levels of every ecosystem. The balance is necessary for self-perpetuation of ecosystems. There are many well-known examples of the consequences of imbalance in ecosystems. Overgrazing in East Africa has converted productive natural grassland into desert. Removal of forest trees has led to serious soil erosion in China. Significantly, humans have usually been at the heart of these problems. People are the most potent **biotic factor** affecting the growth of plants. Enormous tracts of natural vegetation have been destroyed by man and replaced by farmland and forestry. The growth of plants on a substantial area of the earth's surface is therefore controlled by man.

21.2.2 Internal factors

Plants contain **growth promotors** and **inhibitors**. Because an understanding of the ways in which they work could enable man to control plant growth more efficiently, much effort has been put into investigations concerning these substances which are generally called **plant hormones**. The more important plant hormones so far identified are **auxins**, **gibberellins**, **cytokinins** and **abscissic acid**.

1. AUXINS

Indole-3-acetic acid (IAA) is the main **auxin** made in plants (Fig. 21.17). Produced at the apices of shoots from the amino acid tryptophan, IAA is transported backwards to the zones of elongation in roots and shoots, where it regulates **cell extension** and the **differentiation** of vascular tissues. Auxin transport is uni-directional or **polar** (Fig. 21.18). In coleoptiles IAA is carried in parenchyma tissue but in mature roots and shoots the main transporting tissue is probably the phloem.

FIG. 21.17 *Indole-3-acetic acid*

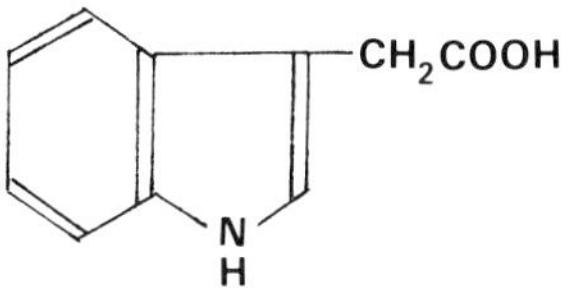

FIG. 21.18 *Polar transport of IAA*

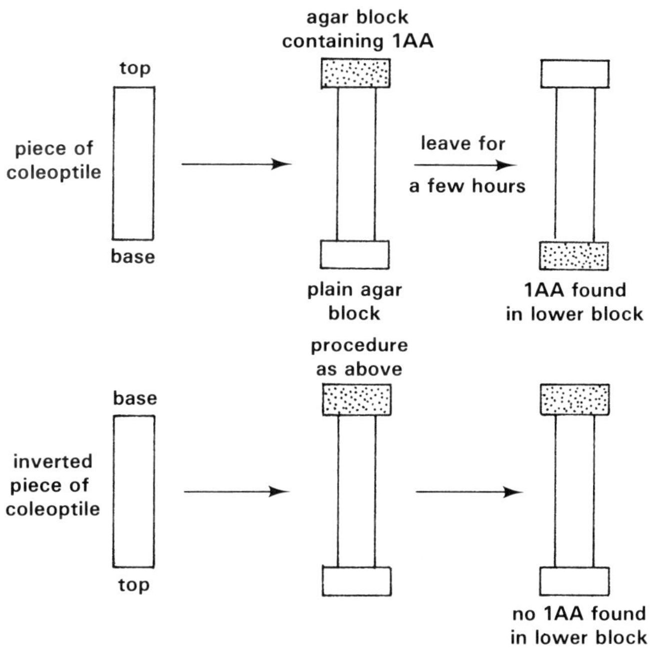

The IAA made by apical buds usually inhibits lateral buds from growing into side shoots, a phenomenon called **apical dominance** (Fig. 21.19). **Leaf expansion** is IAA-controlled (Fig. 21.20) as is the **growth of fruits and seeds** (Chapter 19). The **positions of procambial strands** at shoot apices too are determined by IAA made in leaf primordia (section 21.1.1). IAA released from the expanding buds of woody plants during spring **triggers the vascular cambium** into activity. IAA also **stimulates translocation** of organic substances in the phloem (Chapter 12). It is therefore apparent that the general shape of a plant, its orderly internal growth and development and its rate of growth are very much affected by auxins.

FIG. 21.19 *Demonstration of the role of IAA in apical dominance*

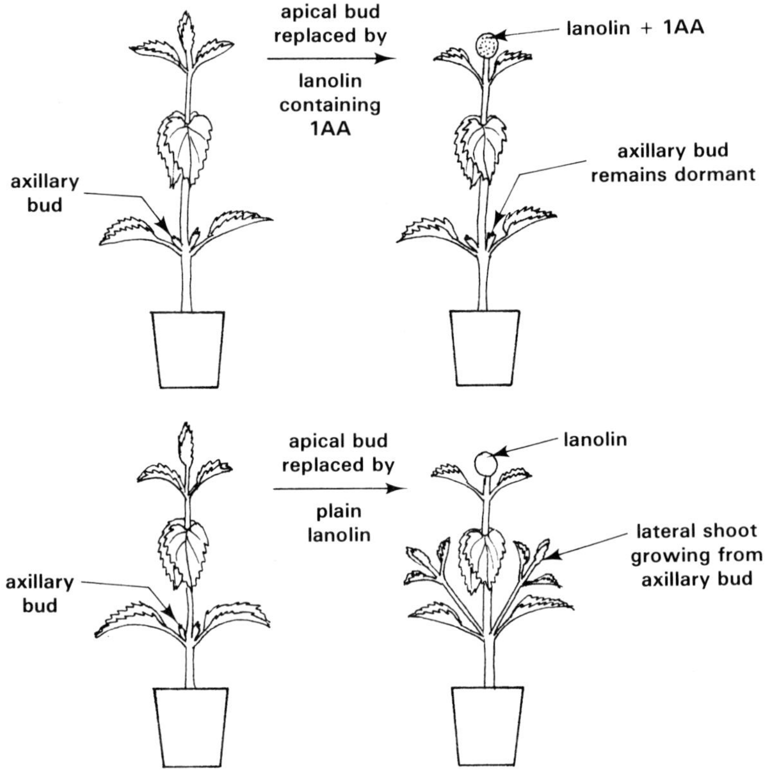

FIG. 21.20 *Correlation between auxin concentration and the growth of* Osmunda *fronds* (after Steeves and Briggs, 1960)

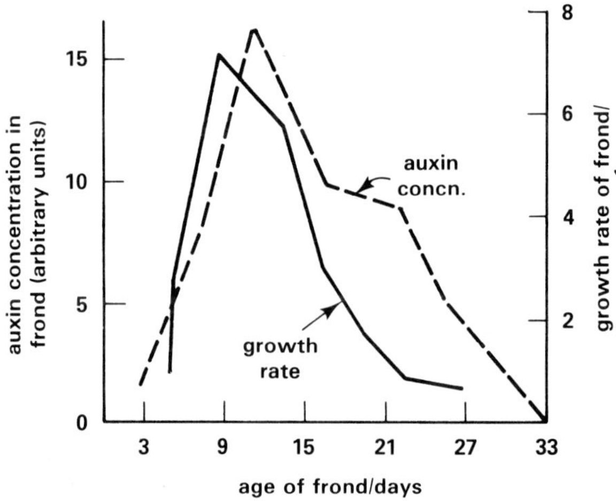

FIG. 21.21 *Some important landmarks in the discovery of auxins* (after Wareing and Philips, 1970)

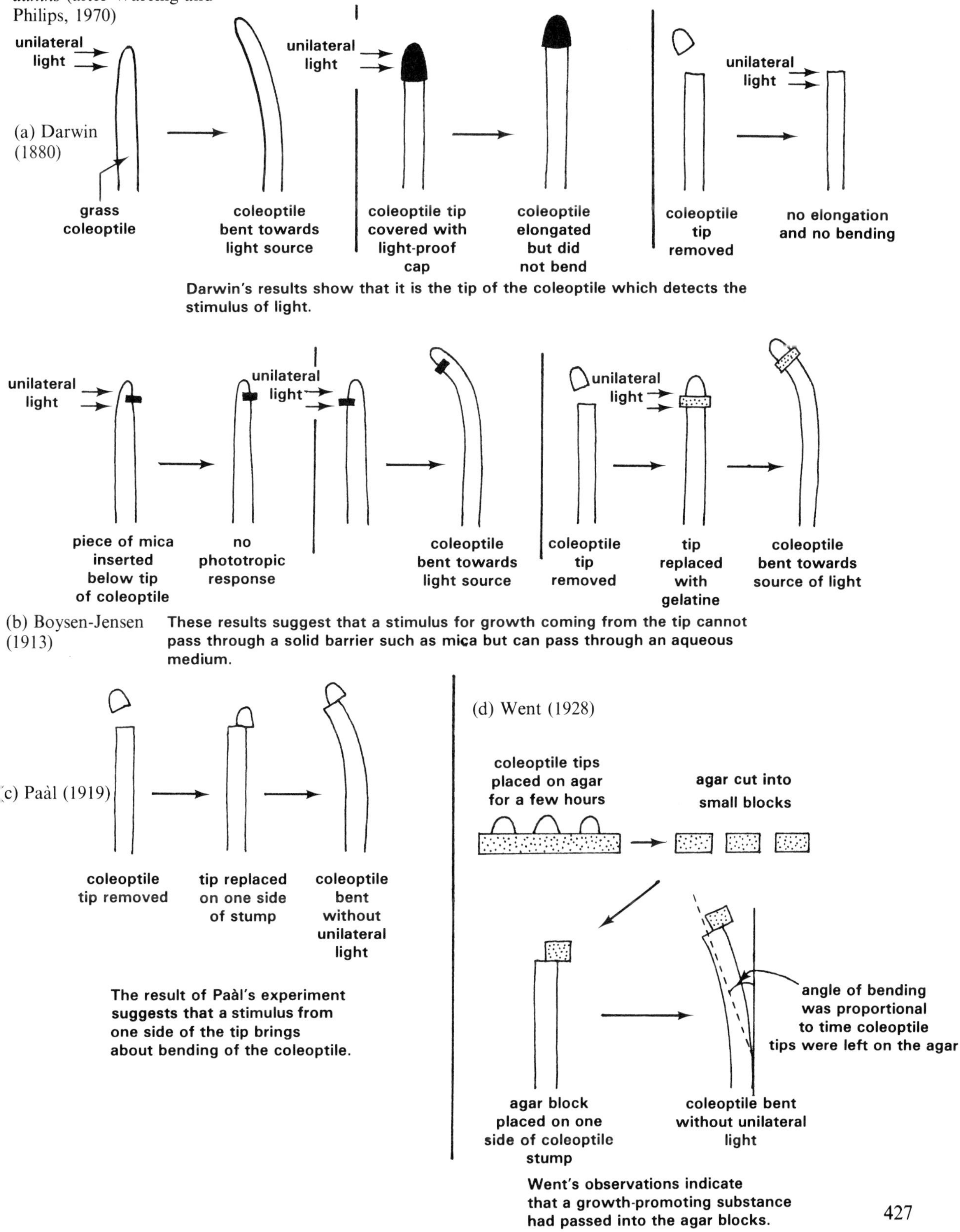

The discovery of auxins resulted from investigations into the tendency of shoot systems to grow towards a source of light (Fig. 21.21). The behaviour is called **positive phototropism**. Although there is still much to be understood of the underlying mechanism, auxins almost certainly play a key role. The effect of unilateral light on a shoot apex is to cause more auxin to be present on the shaded side. Thus more IAA is transported to the elongating zone on the shaded side of the shoot. The result is that the shaded side grows more rapidly and the shoot bends towards the source of light (Fig. 21.22).

FIG. 21.22 (a) *Effect of light on distribution of IAA at the apex of an oat coleoptile*

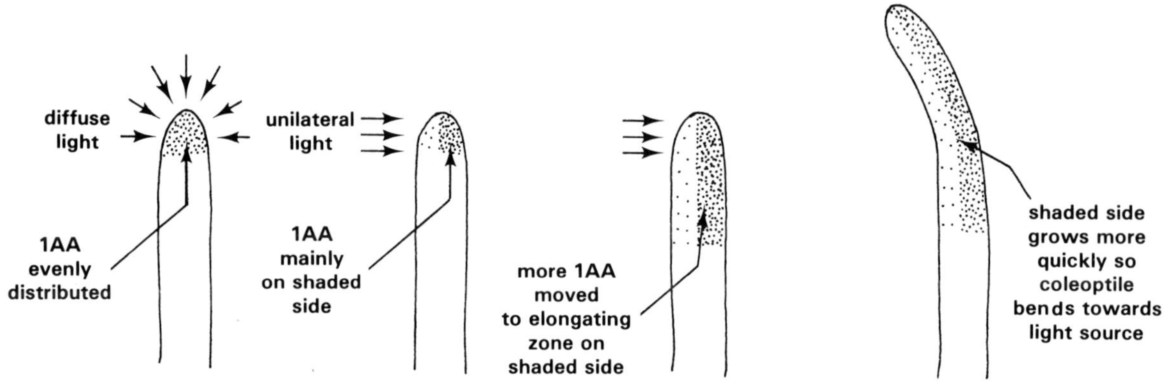

FIG. 21.22 (b) *Phototropic response of the shoots of pea seedlings*

Roots are usually **negatively phototropic** and grow away from a light source. The effect of unilateral light on auxin distribution at the root apex is similar to that at a shoot apex. What then causes the shaded side of a root treated in this way to grow less quickly than the side exposed to light? Experiments have shown that whereas relatively high concentrations of auxin stimulate shoot growth, roots grow quickest when given relatively low concentrations of IAA (Fig. 21.23). Thus the small amount of IAA transported to the elongating zone on the illuminated side of a root causes more rapid growth than on the shaded side so the root gradually bends away from the source of light.

FIG. 21.23 *Effect of IAA on root and shoot growth* (after Audus, 1959)

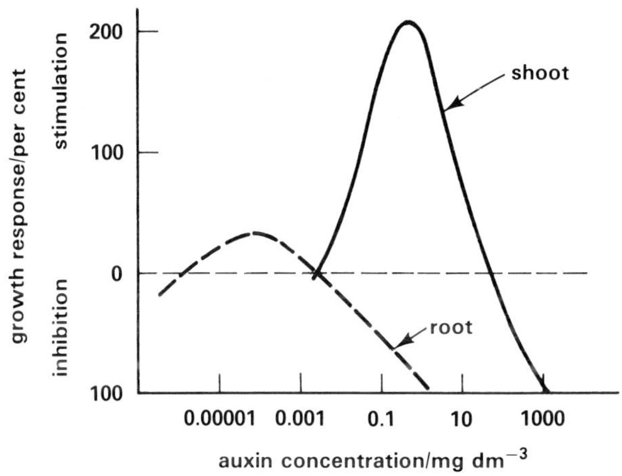

Having explained the phototropic response in terms of changes in auxin distribution it is much more difficult to determine why uni-directional light has such an effect. Blue light of wavelength 440–460 nm is more effective than any other in stimulating a phototropic response (Fig. 21.24). The **action spectrum** for phototropism also has a minor peak at 360 nm and resembles combined absorption spectra for carotene and riboflavin. If, or how, these substances could affect auxin distribution is not yet known. Little is known too of the way in which IAA affects cell growth. Some workers think that auxins soften the cell wall substances causing rapid cell enlargement by vacuolation as water is absorbed. Auxins may also stimulate cell growth by helping the unloading of metabolites from phloem sieve-tubes.

FIG. 21.24 *Action spectrum for phototropism in oat coleoptiles*

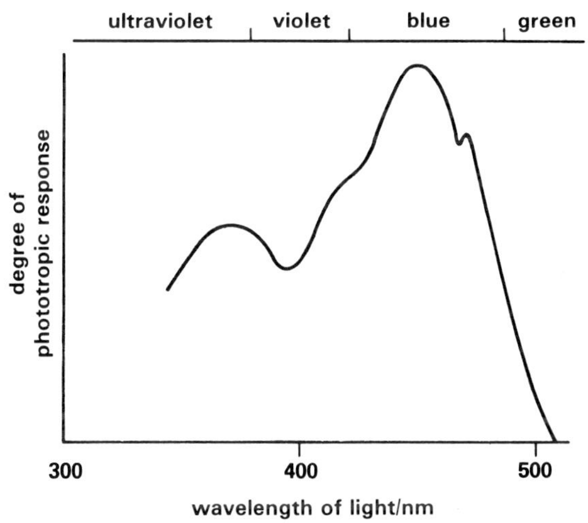

Roots and shoots also react to a unilateral stimulus of gravity. Shoots are usually **negatively geotropic**, growing away from a gravitational pull, while roots show **positive geotropism**. Changes in the normal pattern of auxin distribution are again thought to account for the responses (Fig. 21.25). Why gravity should bring about such changes is still not at all clear. Roots are also **positively hydrotropic**, growing towards a source of water, but again the reasons for this are still something of a mystery.

FIG. 21.25 *Geotropism in pea seedling*

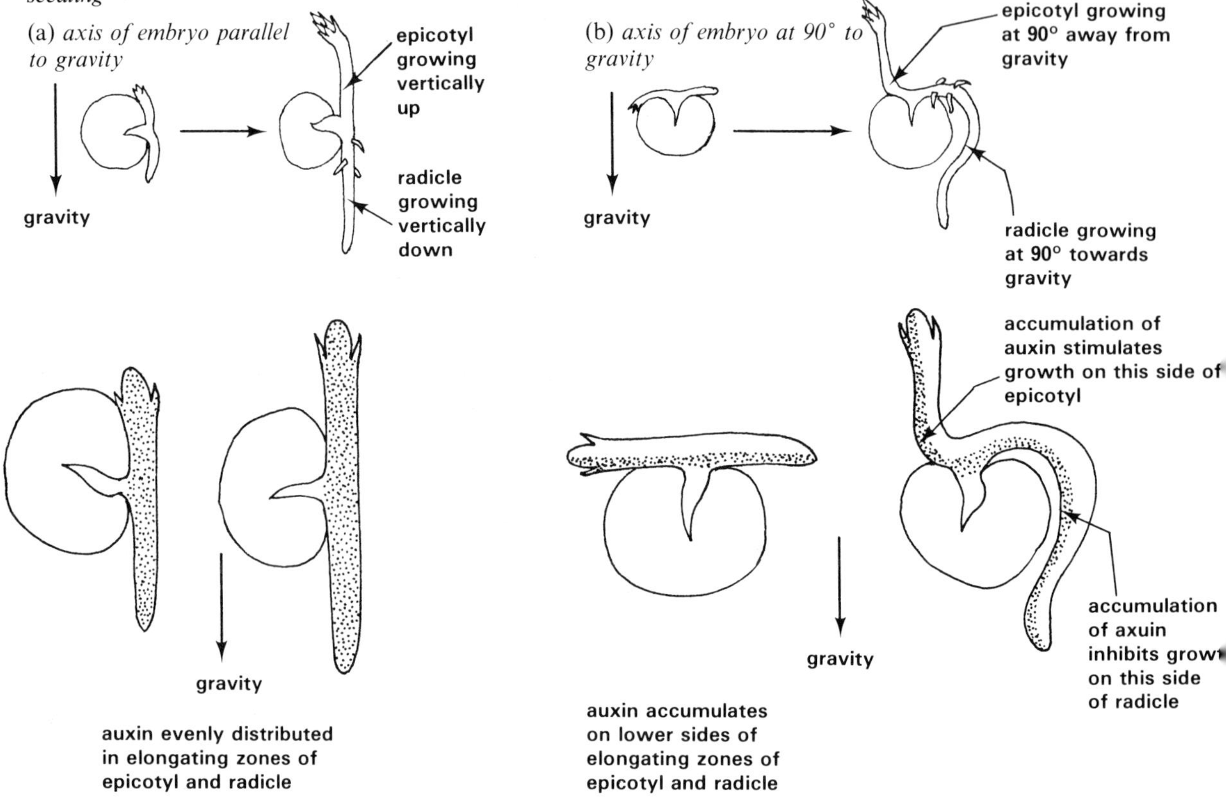

FIG. 21.26 *Gibberellic acid*

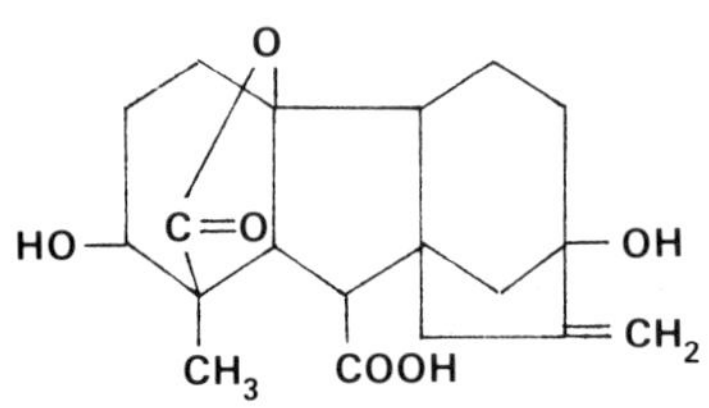

2. GIBBERELLINS

Gibberellins take their name from the fungal parasite *Gibberella fujikuroi* which causes a disease of rice plants known as 'foolish seedling'. Seedlings which are attacked by the fungus develop very long internodes so that the shoot systems are much taller than those of healthy plants. By the late 1920s Japanese workers showed that a growth-promoting substance called gibberellin was present in a liquid medium in which the fungus had been grown in pure culture. However, the chemical nature of gibberellin was unknown until the 1950s when British and American biochemists showed it to be **gibberellic acid** (Fig. 21.26).

Since then a number of closely related substances having similar effects have been isolated from higher plants. They are synthesised at the apices of roots and shoots but little is known of the way in which they are transported. The best known effect of gibberellic acid (GA) is to bring about **internode elongation**. GA also stimulates **enzyme production** during seed germination (Chapter 20) and plays a role in **cell division** and **tissue differentiation**. When applied to woody stems GA promotes division of the vascular cambium, but the derivatives fail to differentiate into mature xylem elements unless IAA is added. However GA on its own brings about differentiation of mature phloem elements. This suggests that the order in which primary xylem and phloem appear in root and shoot may be governed by the ratio of IAA : GA passing back from the apical meristems.

FIG. 21.27 *Zeatin*

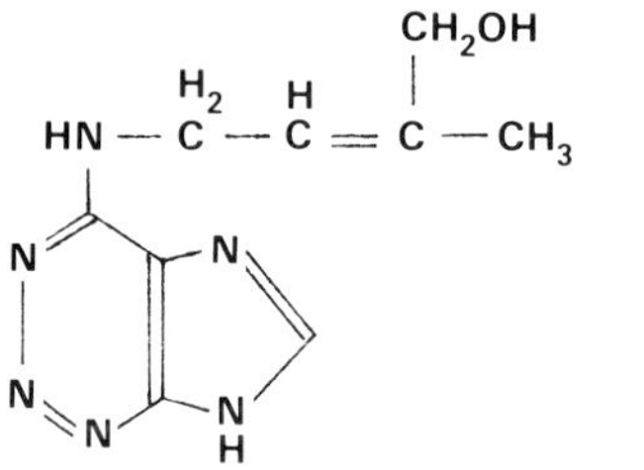

3. CYTOKININS

Interest in the **cytokinins** began in the 1950s when **kinetin** was found to affect the growth of plant tissue in sterile culture media. Kinetin is DNA which has been autoclaved in an acid solution. Kinetin closely resembles adenine, one of the nitrogenous bases of DNA and RNA, but it has not yet been isolated from higher plants. **Zeatin** is one of several similar compounds having comparable effects which has been extracted from a number of plants in recent years (Fig. 21.27).

Cytokinins are frequently found in xylem sap and are thought to be synthesised in the roots from where they are carried to other parts of the plant in the transpiration stream. Production of cytokinins is at its highest when a plant is growing rapidly and falls off as ageing begins.

Much of what is known about cytokinins comes from tissue culture experiments. Small samples of living cells called **explants** are taken from plant organs and aseptically transferred to sterile growth media containing sugar, minerals, vitamins and hormones. Growth of the transplanted tissue follows, but the pattern of growth depends on the composition of the medium, in particular the plant hormones present. With no cytokinin but IAA present the tissue grows into a mass of similar large multinucleate cells. When a small amount of cytokinin is added, a **callus** of uninucleate cells appears indicating that cytokinins have an effect on cell division. By changing the ratio of IAA to cytokinin the first signs of **organ differentiation** are seen. Roots appear on the explant if the ratio of auxin to cytokinin is high while shoots develop if the ratio is low. With no hormones, growth of the explant does not take place (Fig. 21.28).

FIG. 21.28 (a) *Root formation from callus tissue of cowpea,* $\times 4$

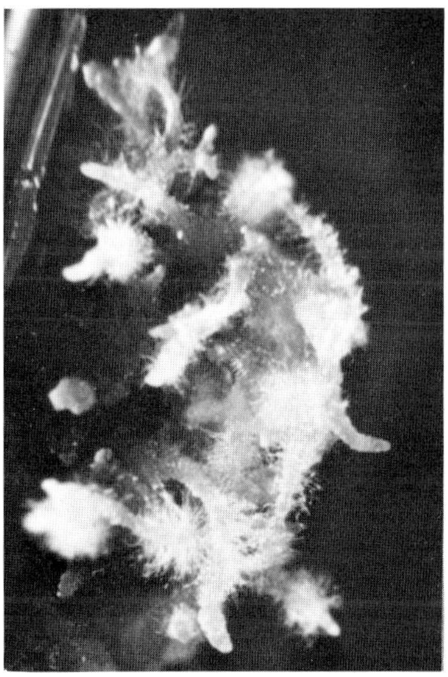

FIG. 21.28 (b) *Shoot formation from callus tissue of tobacco,* $\times 2{\cdot}5$

If these findings reflect what happens in intact plants then cytokinins evidently play a significant role in various aspects of plant growth. Particularly important are the ways in which cytokinins and other plant hormones interact in controlling plant growth.

4. ABSCISSIC ACID

Plant cells contain many substances which inhibit some process or another. One of the best known compounds which inhibits growth is **abscissic acid** (Fig. 21.29). Abscissic acid (ABA) was discovered in 1964 and has also

FIG. 21.29 *Abscissic acid*

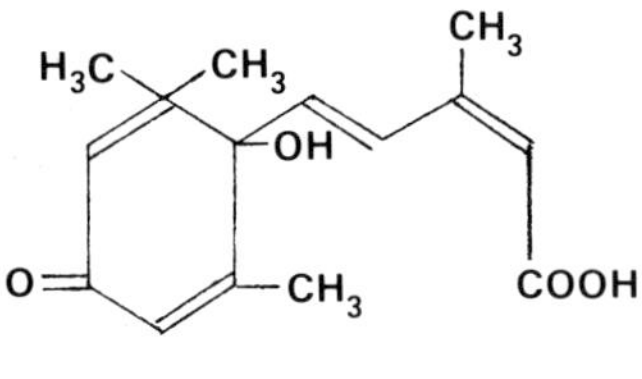

been called abscissin and dormin. The quantity of ABA in the leaves of deciduous trees increases in the shorter days of autumn. The accumulation of ABA slows down the growth rate of shoots and stimulates the **formation of dormant winter buds**. Soon leaf fall, **abscission**, occurs (Fig. 21.30). In this way the plant is prepared for winter conditions. The quantity of ABA in the shoot system falls after a period of cold weather. Dormancy of winter buds is then broken and growth follows in spring and summer. Once again it can be seen that hormone balance is controlled by climate and growth generally occurs only when a spell of good weather is about to follow.

FIG. 21.30 (a) *Longitudinal section through an abscission zone of sycamore, × 10*

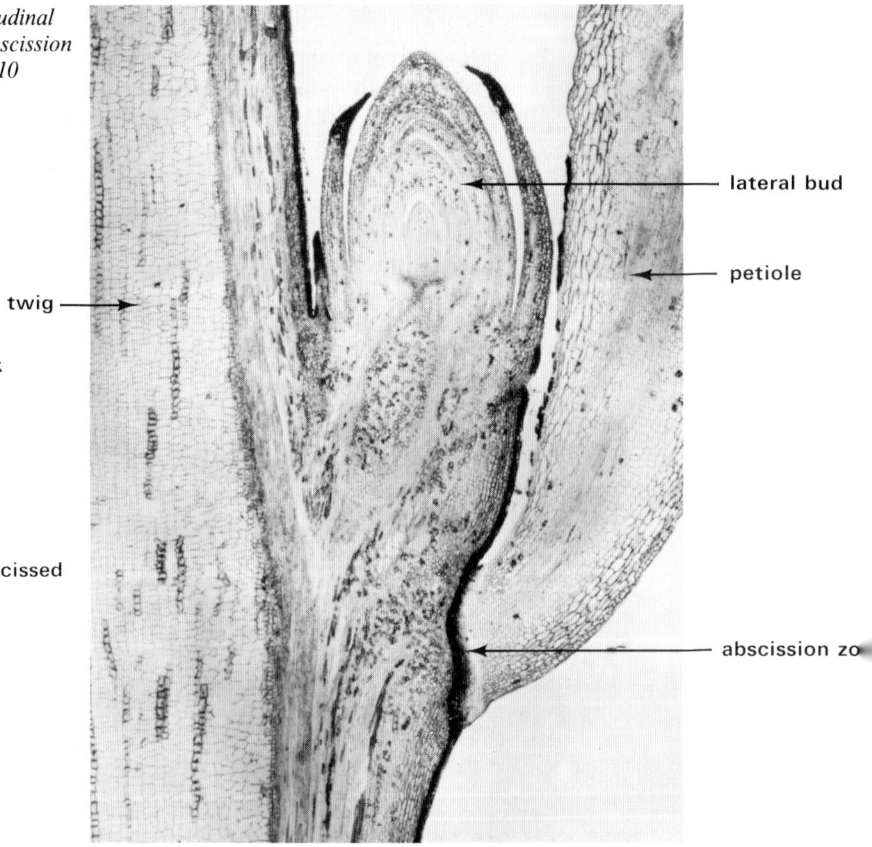

FIG. 21.30 (b) *Winter twig of sycamore. All the buds are dormant*

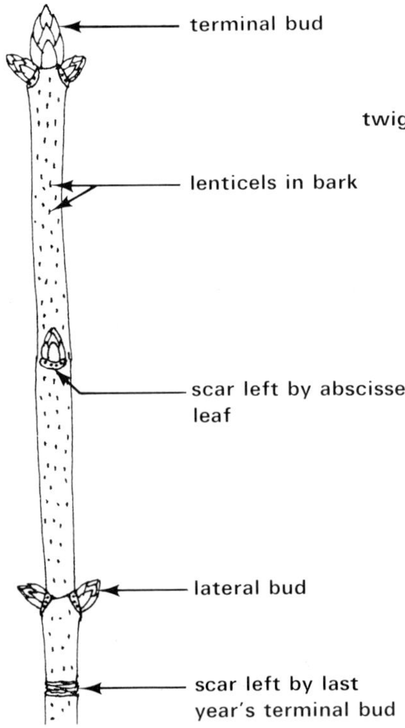

21.2.3 Practical uses of plant hormones

With the explosion of information obtained about growth-regulating substances over the past twenty years or so it is not surprising that some of the knowledge has been put to practical use. There are many synthetic compounds with auxin-like effects now in common use in agriculture and horticulture. They include various **phenoxyacetic acids** such as 2:4D (Fig. 21.31). 2:4D stimulates the formation of adventitious roots at the bases of cut shoots (Fig. 21.32) and is an invaluable aid to horticulturalists in accelerating the **striking of cuttings**. Many species of ornamental plants such as carnations and chrysanthemums are propagated by means of cuttings. Synthetic auxins also encourage the formation of wound tissue which knits together parts of plants after **grafting**.

FIG. 21.31 *2,4-dichlorophenoxy-acetic acid*

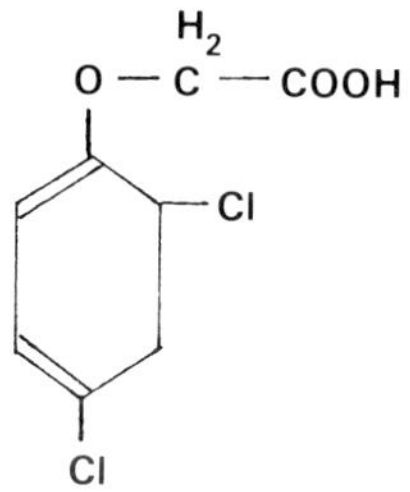

When sprayed on to fruit trees after flowering the phenoxyacetic acids prevent young fruit from dropping off. Large increases of apple and pear crops have been achieved in this way (Chapter 19).

Perhaps the most widespread use of synthetic auxins has been as **weed killers** applied to fields of cereal crops, pasture and lawns. The roots and shoots of the same plant respond differently to a particular concentration of auxins (section 21.2.2). It has also been found that different groups of plants vary in their reaction to applications of similar concentrations of synthetic auxin. Dicotyledonous plants such as dandelions and thistles are more sensitive to 2:4D than are monocotyledons such as grasses, wheat and maize. When sprayed on to an area of mixed species, for example a weedy lawn or a field of wheat infested with thistles, the dicotyledons are stimulated into abnormal growth. The internodes become grossly elongated, sieve-tubes become blocked and cells with unbalanced chromosome numbers arise. Distortion of the root system also occurs with the net result that the growth pattern is thrown completely out of control and death quickly follows. Meanwhile the monocotyledons are unaffected and are thus freed from unwanted competitors.

FIG. 21.32 *Effect of synthetic auxin on the striking of chrysanthemum cuttings*

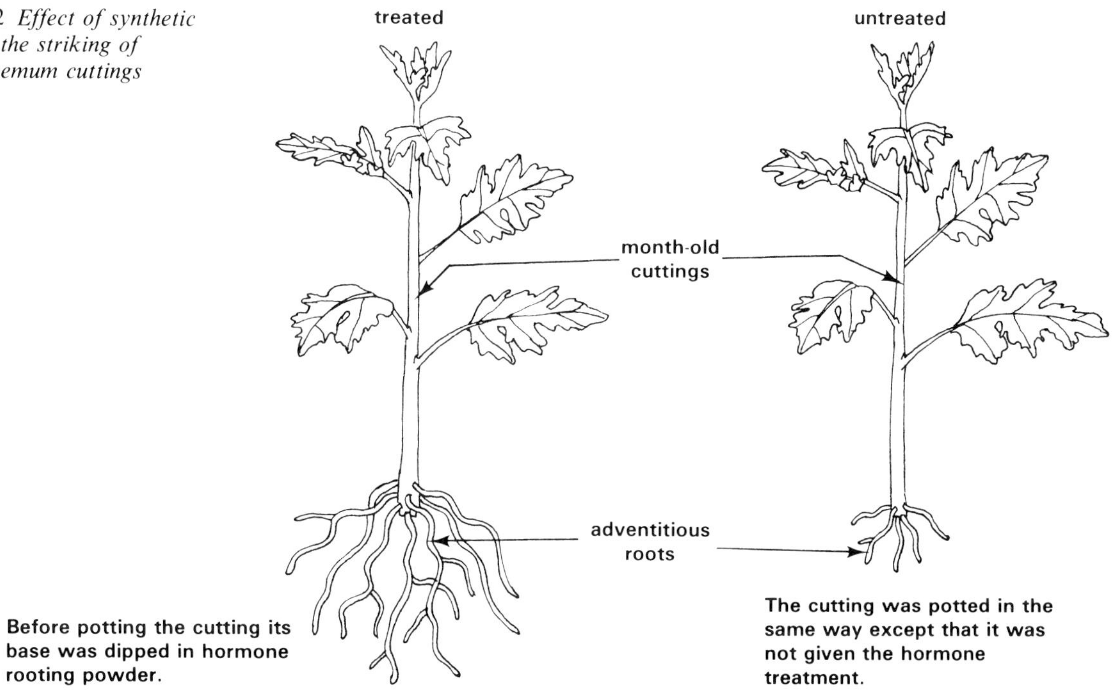

Despite the many practical benefits which result from their uses, synthetic auxins can cause serious ecological problems if used indiscriminately. Some are toxic to insects and have been known to kill large numbers of useful insects such as bees with considerable economic loss. Many weeds are the food plants of pollinating insects which starve when weeds are destroyed. Finally some weeds have evolved auxin-resistant varieties which are virtually impossible to eradicate by treatment with synthetic auxins.

Chapter 22

Mammalian reproduction

Whereas most flowering plants are hermaphrodite (Chapter 19) all mammals are **unisexual**. This means that mammalian gametes are produced in separate male and female animals and **cross-fertilisation** is inevitable. Consequently genetic variation among the offspring of mammals is ensured.

For sexual reproduction to occur successfully gametes have to be mature at the right time. Males and females have to be in the same locality and attracted to each other. Fertilisation must occur and the resulting embryo must be protected and provided with food for it to survive and develop properly.

Reproduction in mammals is a carefully regulated process although the controlling mechanisms vary in different species. An important feature of mammalian reproduction is that it occurs in such a way that the effects of chance and adverse environmental conditions are minimised. A successful outcome to sexual reproduction is therefore more likely in mammals than it is in many other groups of animals. Mammalian gametes are made in sex organs called **gonads**. The **testes** are the male gonads, the **ovaries** the female gonads. **Gametogenesis** is the process which gives rise to male and female **gametes**.

22.1 Testes

The production and maturation of **spermatozoa** (sperm) which are the male gametes, takes place in a pair of compact **testes**. The testes originate in the abdomen from the embryonic tissue which also gives rise to the urinary system. Indeed the urethra through which urine passes to the outside also provides the route for sperm to leave the male reproductive system (Fig. 22.1). As well as making sperm the testes produce male sex hormones.

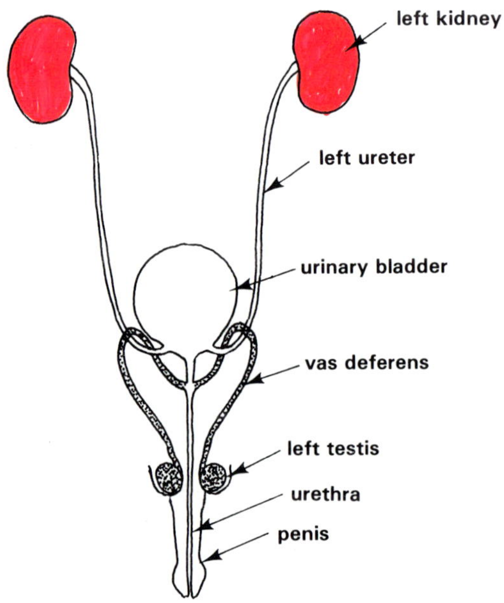

FIG. 22.1 *Diagram of the male uro-genital system in man*

22.1.1 Structure of the testes

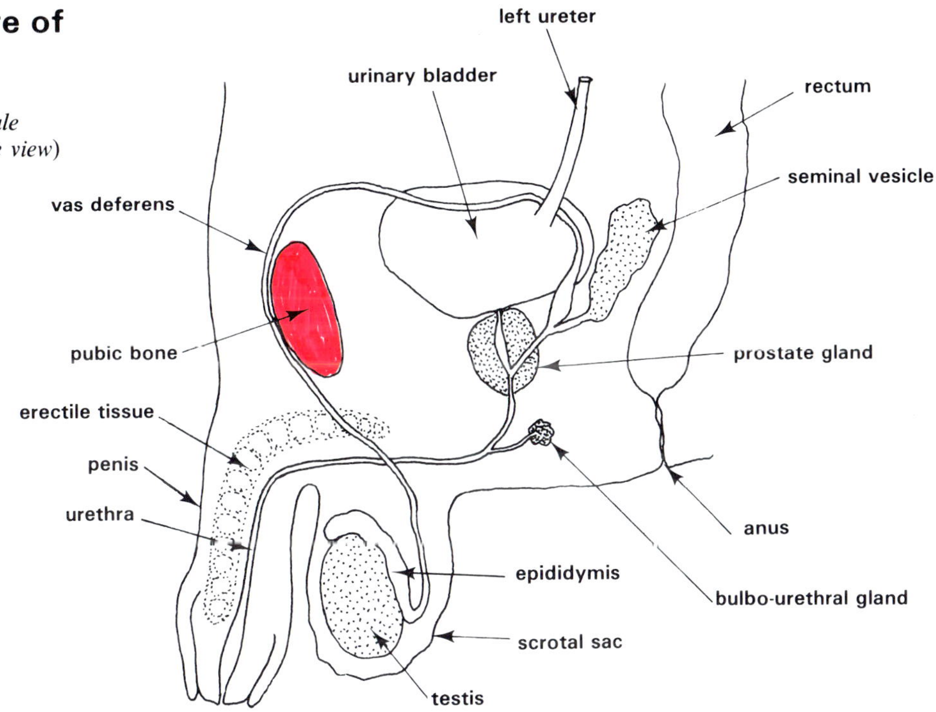

FIG. 22.2 *The human male reproductive organs (side view)*

The testes of most mammals descend from the abdomen into two sacs of skin called **scrotal sacs**. Under the microscope a thin section of a testis is seen as thousands of very fine, highly coiled **seminiferous tubules**. It is in the tubules that sperm are produced. The seminiferous tubules are continuous with other tubules called the **vasa efferentia**, **epididymes** and **vasa deferentia**. The sperm travel through the system of tubules on their way to the **seminal vesicles** where they are stored before passing out of the body through the **urethra** (Fig. 22.2). Cutting the vasa deferentia prevents the passage of sperm to the outside The operation which is called **vasectomy** is now commonly used to sterilise men.

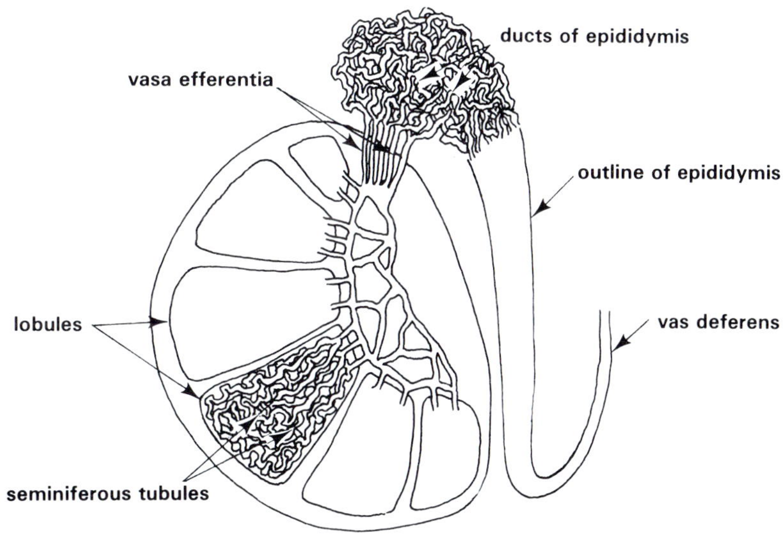

FIG. 22.3 (a) *Vertical section through testis. The seminiferous tubules have only been shown in one lobule*

FIG. 22.3 (b) *Photomicrograph of a seminiferous tubule seen in transverse section, from a rat, ×400*

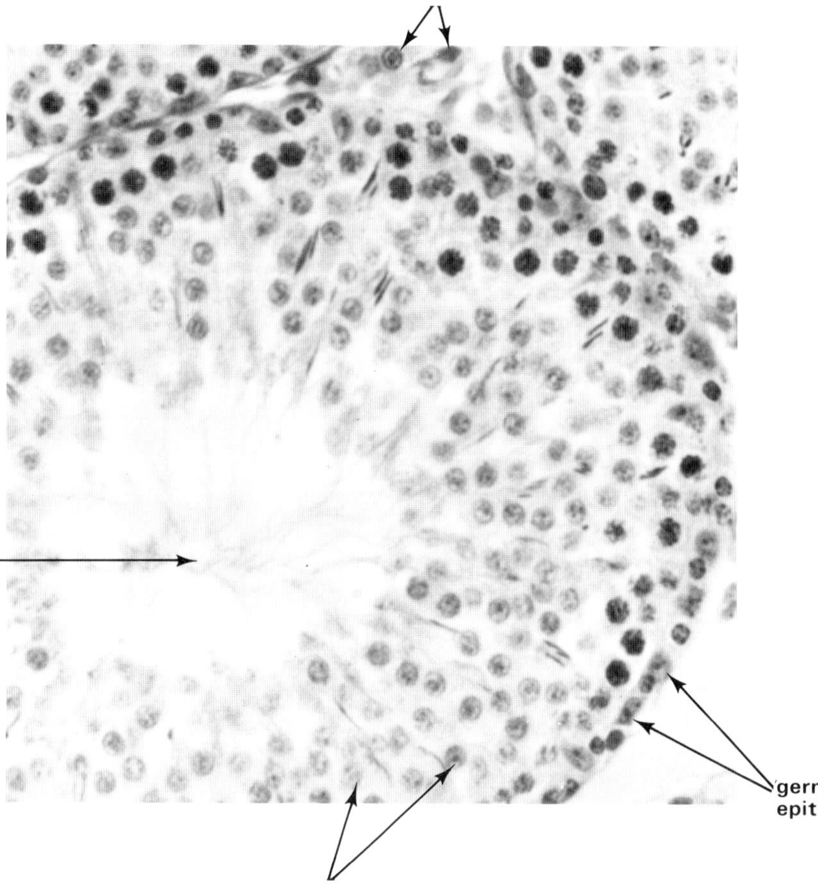

The walls of the seminiferous tubules consist of a layer of cells called the **germinal epithelium** from which sperm originate (Fig. 22.3). Sperm at different stages of development are found inside the seminiferous tubules. As they mature the sperm become attached to the relatively large **Sertoli cells**. The tubules are held together by connective tissue which contains **interstitial (Leydig) cells**, nerve fibres, blood and lymphatic capillaries.

22.1.2 Spermatogenesis

Spermatogenesis is the process whereby sperm are made. The production of sperm begins with divisions of the **primordial germ cells** which make up the germinal epithelium. The first divisions are mitotic (Chapter 7) and produce many genetically identical cells called **spermatogonia**. Next the spermatogonia increase in size and mass without dividing to become **primary spermatocytes**. The primary spermatocytes then divide by meiosis (Chapter 7). The first meiotic division produces **secondary spermatocytes**, two from each primary spermatocyte. The second meiotic division gives rise to **spermatids**, two from each secondary spermatocyte (Fig. 22.4). The final stage of spermatogenesis is differentiation of **spermatozoa** from the spermatids.

A mature spermatozoon has a **head** which contains a nucleus. Attached to the head is a long **tail** (flagellum) which the sperm uses to swim. Human sperm can swim at a rate of 1–4 mm per minute. At the base of the tail

FIG. 22.5 (a) *Diagram of a human sperm*

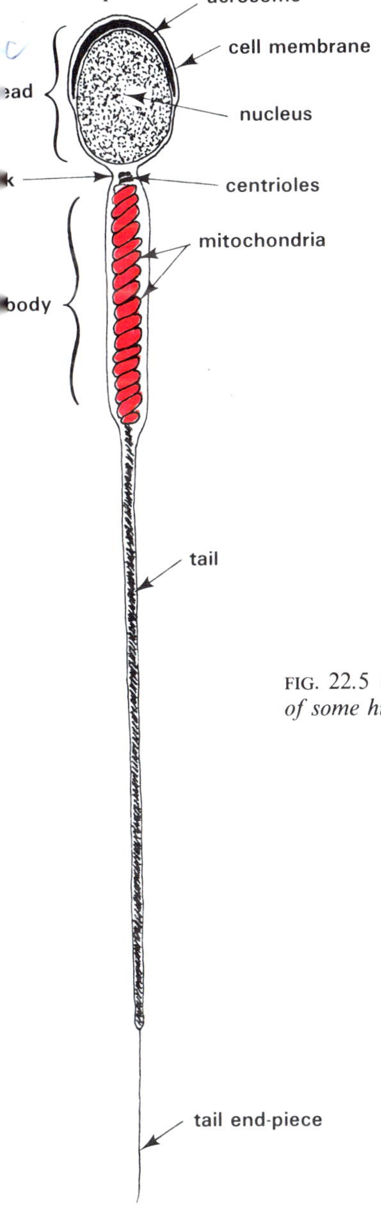

where it joins the sperm head, there are many mitochondria (Fig. 22.5). Maturing sperm cluster around the Sertoli cells from which they obtain materials essential for differentiation.

FIG. 22.4 *Spermatogenesis*

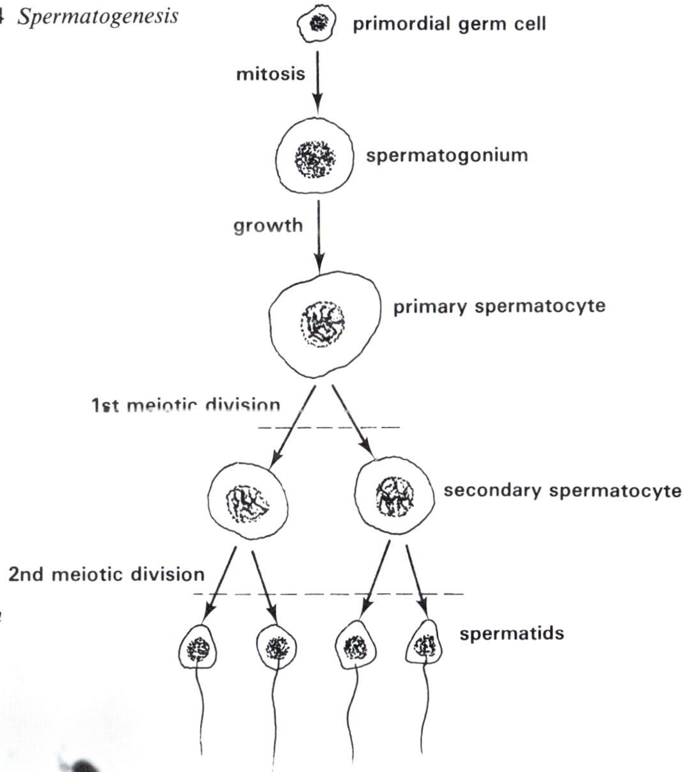

FIG. 22.5 (b) *Photomicrograph of some human sperm,* $\times$ *1000*

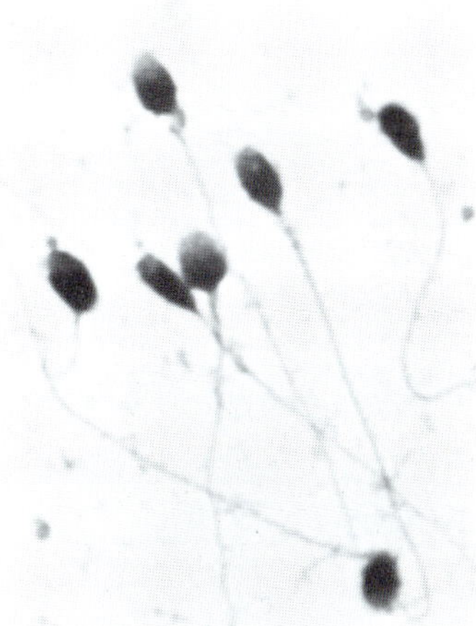

Spermatogenesis is inhibited by heat. Because the testes are located in the scrotal sacs where the temperature is lower than in the abdomen, production of sperm is normally encouraged. Before the development of efficient methods of contraception, it used to be common for men to take a very hot bath before sexual intercourse. However, it is questionable whether this practice had the desired contraceptive effect.

22.1.3 Male hormones

Spermatogenesis is stimulated by a hormone called **follitropin** (**FSH**) produced by the anterior pituitary (Chapter 18). FSH gains its name from the action it has in the female (section 22.2.3). In both male and female, FSH stimulates gametogenesis.

FIG. 22.6 *Mechanism controlling testosterone secretion*

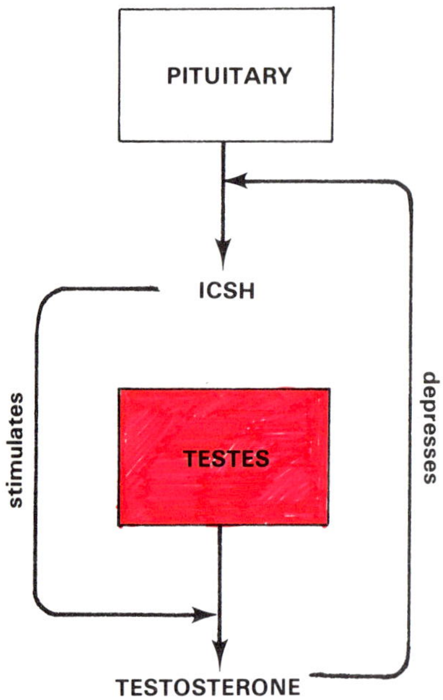

Another gonadotropin hormone made in the anterior pituitary is **lutropin (LH)**. LH is also named because of the effect it has in the female (section 22.2.3). In the male, LH is alternatively called **interstitial cell stimulating hormone (ICSH)**. As the name suggests ICSH stimulates the interstitial cells which respond by secreting a male sex hormone called **testosterone**. ICSH and testosterone interact in a negative feedback control mechanism so that the output of testosterone is kept relatively constant (Fig. 22.6).

Male sex hormones are collectively called **androgens**. The functions of androgens are twofold. First, they regulate the development of the male **accessory sex organs**. They include the vasa efferentia, epididymes, vasa deferentia, penis and scrotal sacs. The second main function of androgens is to control the development and maintenance of the **secondary sexual characteristics** which in man include growth of facial and pubic hair, breaking of the voice and general muscular development. Androgens are also partly responsible for a number of behavioural characteristics such as aggressiveness.

Castration, removal of the testes, does not necessarily lead to loss of secondary sexual characteristics in males. How can this be so when maintenance of the secondary sexual characteristics is an important function of androgens made in the testes? Androgens are steroids (Figs. 22.7 and 18.20(b)). Following castration there is increased output of steroids similar to androgens from the adrenal cortex (Chapter 18). This explains why eunuchs outwardly appear as normal males.

The development of male secondary sexual characteristics and the production of sperm begin in man at a period of life called **adolescence**. The point at which sexual maturity is reached is called **puberty**. The testes also produce female sex hormones, but their function in males is not clear.

22.2 Ovaries

Female gametes are called **ova**. Their production and maturation take place in the **ovaries**. The ovaries also produce **female sex hormones**. In female mammals a pair of ovaries lie in the abdominal cavity (Fig. 22.8).

22.2.1 Structure of the ovaries and oogenesis

Spermatogenesis in the testes (section 22.1.2) is paralleled in the ovaries by **oogenesis**, the production of ova. Unlike the testes, ovaries do not contain tubules but consist mainly of connective tissue. Like the testes, however, ovaries have a **germinal epithelium**. The ovarian germinal epithelium is on the outside of the ovaries. **Primordial germ cells** in the germinal epithelium divide by mitosis to form many **oogonia**. The oogonia become surrounded by **follicle cells**, also derived by mitosis from the germinal epithelium. The follicle cells and enclosed oogonia are called **primary follicles**. They migrate to the centre of the ovary.

At birth there are up to 400 000 primary follicles in a human ovary where they remain dormant until **puberty**. Hormones from the pituitary gland then start the process of oogenesis. In women only about 400 primary follicles normally mature over a reproductive lifetime of about 30–40 years. The end of this period, when follicle development stops, is called the **menopause**. The remaining primary follicles degenerate into cyst-like **atretic follicles** and remain in the ovaries.

In women, ova usually develop one at a time. Each oogonium grows into a **primary oocyte** which by now is surrounded by several layers of follicle cells. Between the dividing follicle cells cavities appear, filled with **follicular liquid**. The follicle becomes surrounded by two layers derived from the

FIG. 22.7 *Structure of testosterone*

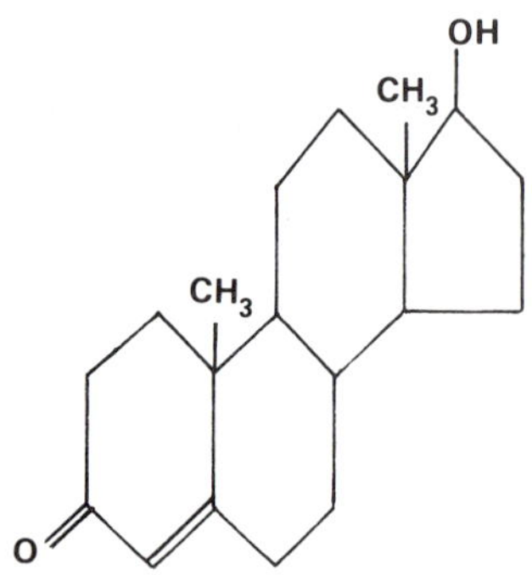

ovarian connective tissue. An outer fibrous **theca externa** encloses an inner vascular **theca interna** (Fig. 22.9). The mature follicle is called a **Graafian follicle** and can usually be seen bulging at the surface of the ovary (Fig. 22.10). During development the follicles of women grow from about 0·05 mm to about 12 mm in diameter.

FIG. 22.8 *The human female reproductive organs (ventral view)*

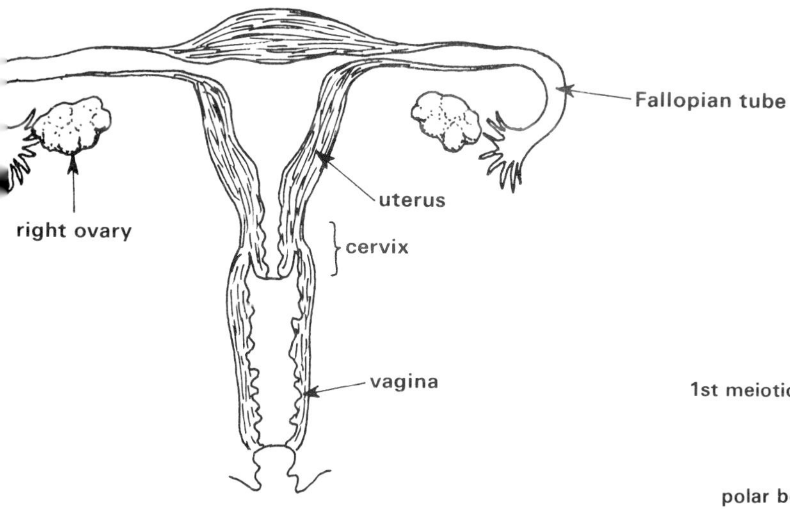

FIG. 22.9 *Oogenesis*

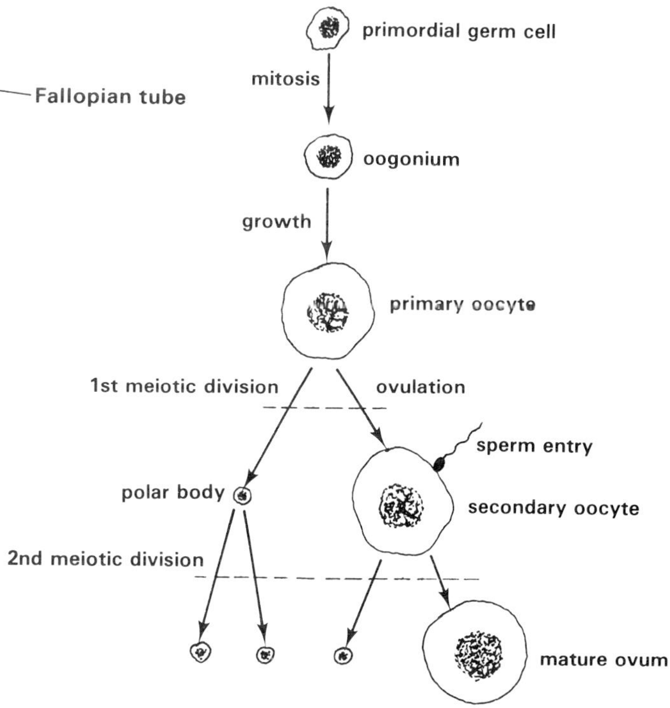

FIG. 22.10 *Photomicrograph of a thin section of ovary, from a rat, ×50*

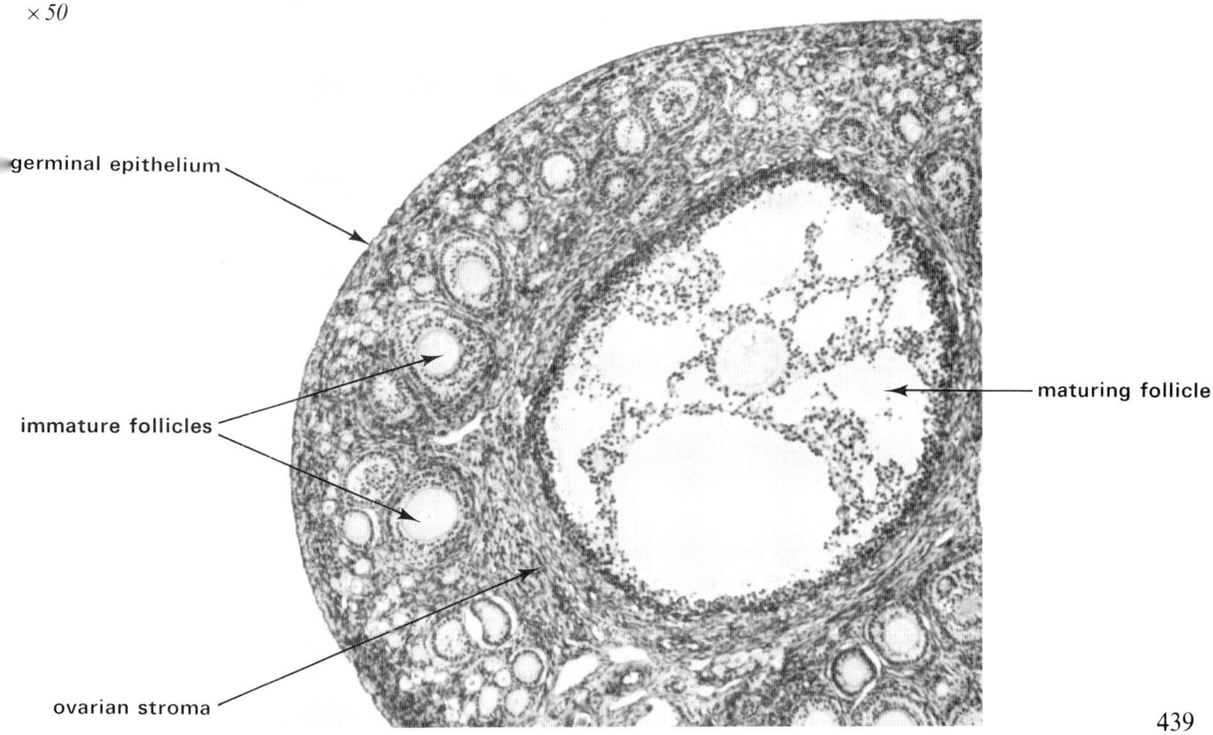

The primary oocyte inside the follicle now divides by meiosis. The first meiotic division which occurs just before ovulation produces a **secondary oocyte** and attached to it, a small cell called a **polar body**. **Ovulation** is the release of the secondary oocyte from the ovary into the abdominal cavity (sections 22.2.2 and 22.3.2). The second meiotic division usually occurs following fertilisation, just after a sperm nucleus enters the secondary oocyte. The secondary oocyte then produces the **ovum** and another small polar body. The second meiotic division also gives rise to two more polar bodies from the polar body produced in the first meiotic division. The polar bodies have no known function.

During oogenesis only one functional ovum arises from each primary oocyte, whereas spermatogenesis produces four functional sperm from each primary spermatocyte (section 22.1.2).

22.2.2 Hormonal control of ovulation

As in the male, gametogenesis in the female mammal is influenced by hormones from the anterior pituitary, particularly **follitropin (FSH)**. Unlike spermatogenesis, however, oogenesis is not a continuous process. It is a characteristic of mammals that the embryos develop inside the mother's reproductive tract for a period prior to birth. This period is called the **gestation period**. Since there is limited space in the mother for embryo development, there is a limit to the number of embryos which can develop at a time. The number of embryos carried by a mother during the gestation period is usually determined by the number of ova released at a time from the ovaries. In women only one ovum normally leaves the ovaries at each ovulation.

For many mammals living in the wild, it is advantageous to mother and offspring if birth occurs when food is plentiful and the weather is mild. In many species this is ensured by the seasonal secretion of FSH. Secretion of FSH in **seasonal reproducers** is influenced by day-length. In some species such as ferrets, FSH output is stepped up in spring when the number of hours of light in a day increases. In sheep, production of FSH increases in autumn when the day-length shortens. Other mechanisms such as **delayed implantation** (section 22.3.2) can also determine the time of year when birth takes place.

Secretion of FSH in some species is triggered off by the nervous stimulation of copulation. The mechanism is called **induced ovulation** and occurs, for example, in rabbits. Induced ovulation ensures that ripe ova are provided immediately after sperm have been introduced into the female tract (section 22.3.1). Since fertilisation is then likely to occur it is not surprising that rabbits have gained a reputation as prolific breeders.

Many mammals produce ova at regular intervals by a mechanism in which FSH interacts with ovarian hormones to produce a rhythm of activity. The rhythm is called the **oestrus** or **menstrual cycle**. This internal method of controlling ovulation is largely independent of external influences.

22.2.3 The oestrus cycle

Since the oestrus cycle is a sequence of events which repeats itself regularly in a cyclical fashion, there is no fixed beginning or ending. For convenience of description we shall begin with the onset of follicle development. Follicle development is stimulated by FSH from the anterior pituitary. FSH also causes the ovary to secrete a female sex hormone, an **oestrogen**. The most prominent oestrogen is called **estradiol**. Estradiol has several effects in the female body, some of which are described later (section 22.2.4). Among these is a negative feedback effect on FSH (Fig. 22.11).

FIG. 22.11 *Mechanism controlling estradiol secretion*

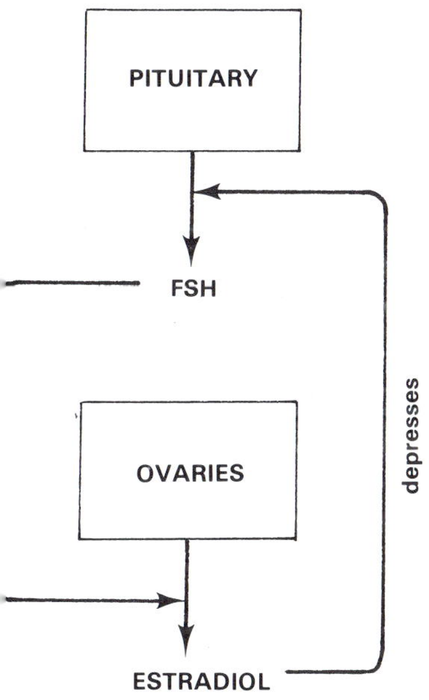

FIG. 22.13 *Mechanism controlling progesterone secretion*

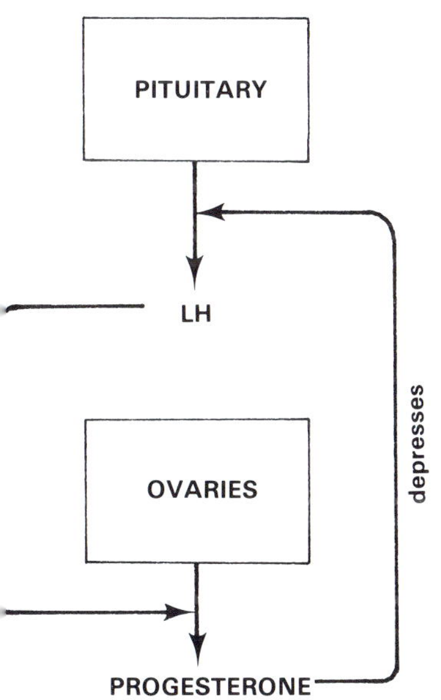

Another effect of estradiol is to cause the anterior pituitary to secrete **lutropin (LH)** which brings about ovulation. In women, ovulation usually occurs 14 days after a follicle starts to form. LH has a second function which is to stimulate the development of the **corpus luteum** from the remains of the ovarian follicle. As it grows the corpus luteum secretes a hormone called **progesterone** which is similar in structure to estradiol and testosterone (Figs. 22.12 and 22.7). Progesterone stimulates growth of the **endometrium**, the lining of the uterus, and its blood supply. Progesterone also inhibits the release of FSH and LH from the anterior pituitary (Fig. 22.13). What happens next depends on whether or not the ovum has been fertilised and implanted in the uterine wall.

FIG. 22.12 *Structure of* (a) *estradiol and* (b) *progesterone*

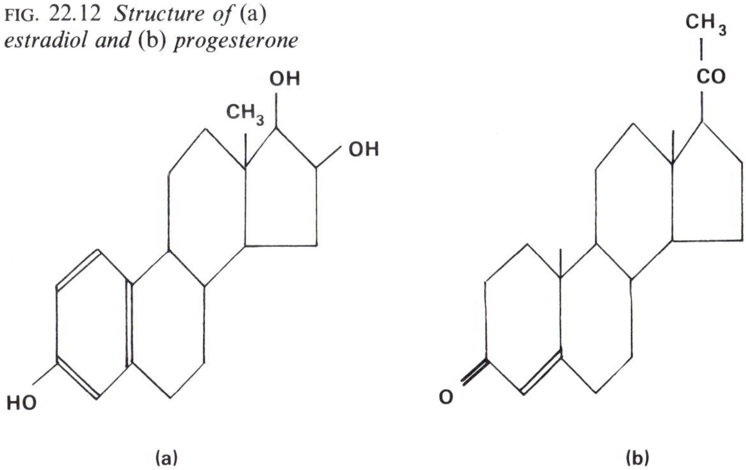

If fertilisation occurs, then a new source of progesterone develops, the **placenta** (section 22.3.3). Continued production of progesterone inhibits FSH secretion, so the development of new follicles during gestation is prevented. This is an important aspect of pregnancy. The well-being of an embryo or several embryos conceived at the same time, depends partly on their simultaneous development and birth. If follicles continue to appear and ovulation occurs after the first conception it may happen that other embryos would be conceived later on. A number of embryos at different stages of development would then be present in the uterus and a severe physiological burden would be placed on the mother. In addition, relatively violent muscular contractions of the uterine wall occur at birth. Embryos which are not ready to be born are unlikely to survive the contractions. Maintaining progesterone secretion during pregnancy is important for another reason. Progesterone stimulates growth and improves the blood supply of the endometrium. Maintenance of the endometrium is necessary for successful implantation of a fertilised ovum and subsequent attachment of the placenta.

If fertilisation does not occur the lack of LH from the anterior pituitary causes the corpus luteum to degenerate and progesterone production by the ovary then stops. Growth of the endometrium which is promoted by progesterone cannot now be maintained. Consequently the endometrium breaks down and passes through the vagina to the outside as the **menstrual flow**. Menstruation normally lasts for about 4 or 5 days in women. It is not a feature of the oestrus cycle of all mammals.

Lack of progesterone in the blood also means that FSH secretion from the anterior pituitary can begin once more. The cycle restarts with the development of a new follicle. In women, about 14 days elapse between ovulation and the start of a new cycle. With ovulation marking the mid-point, the oestrus cycle takes about 28 days to complete. The length of the cycle varies from woman to woman, and may be different for the same person at different times.

The prevention of unwanted pregnancies in women has been achieved for many years with the **contraceptive pill**. The pill contains chemicals which have effects similar to estradiol and progesterone. In particular, they prevent FSH secretion from the anterior pituitary. Consequently no follicles develop in the ovaries and fertilisation is impossible.

Figure 22.14 summarises the hormonal interactions which regulate the oestrus cycle and their effects on the ovary and uterus.

FIG. 22.14 *Summary of the main factors involved in the oestrus cycle*

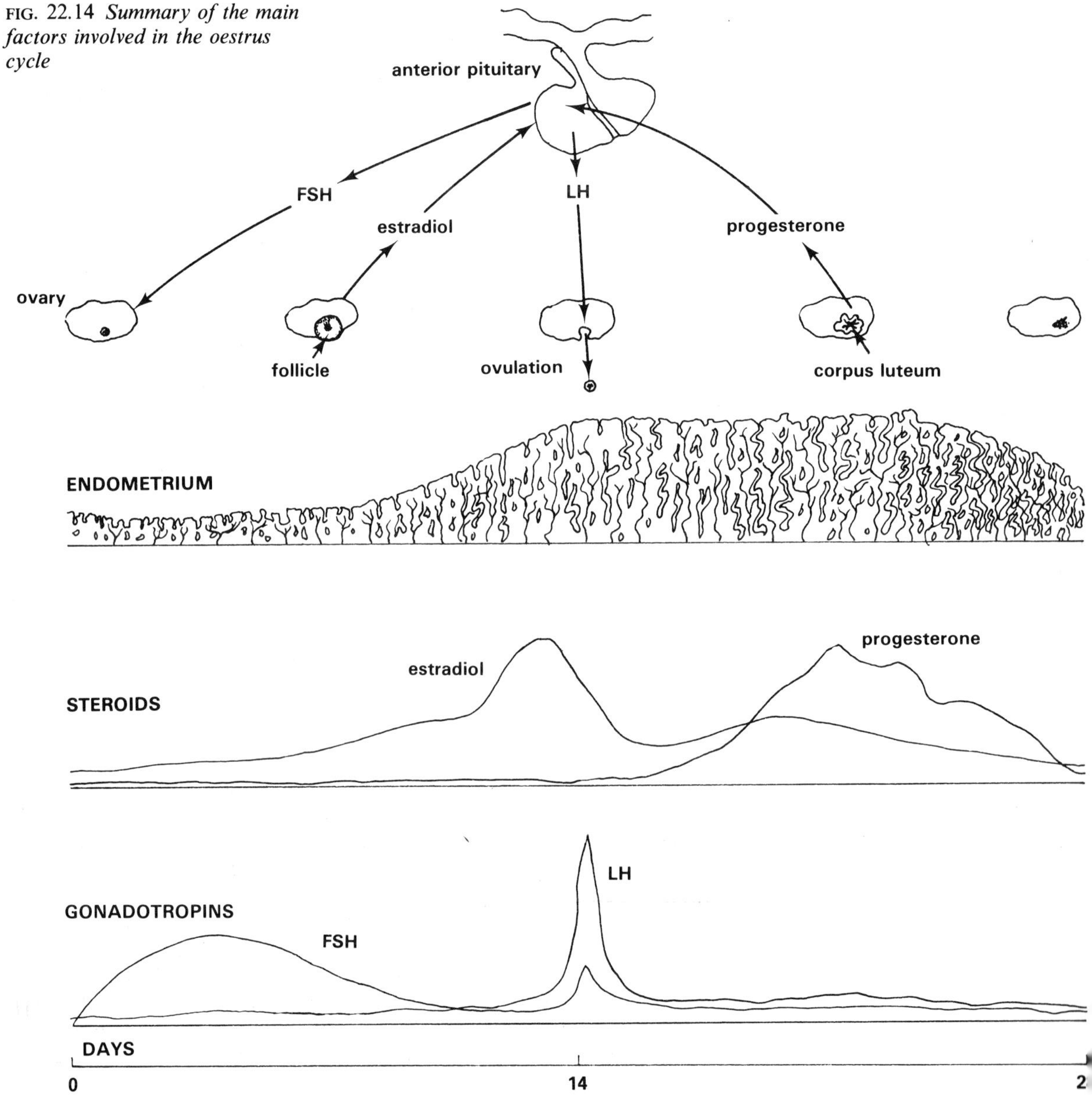

22.2.4 Other effects of female hormones

Like androgens in males, oestrogens in females regulate the development of the **accessory sex organs**. These organs include the **Fallopian tubes**, **uterus**, **vagina** and **clitoris**. Oestrogens also control the development and maintenance of the **secondary sexual characteristics** which in women include growth of pubic hair, development of the mammary glands and a relatively broad pelvic girdle.

It has been known for many years that the ovaries secrete androgens as well as oestrogens and that testes secrete oestrogens as well as androgens. The roles of androgens in females and oestrogens in males remain a mystery. However, an important effect of oestrogens in both sexes has been recently discovered. In the United States of America a number of doctors developed a method aimed at revitalising the sexual appetite of older women. The women had reached the menopause yet it was observed that their youthful sexual vitality could be restored if they were treated with oestrogens. Their ovaries of course had stopped secreting oestrogens at the menopause. Many women subscribed to the oestrogen treatment and a curious fact came to light. The treated women had significantly fewer bone fractures following accidental falls than other women of similar age who had not received oestrogen. In some way oestrogen strengthens the bones, or rather prevents them from deteriorating. After the menopause, the skeleton of women can diminish in mass by as much as two per cent each year. Oestrogens inhibit the action of **parathyrin (PTH)** which stimulates the absorption of calcium phosphate from bone into blood and tissue fluid (Chapter 18). After the menopause when oestrogen secretion stops, output of PTH is uninhibited and bone deterioration sets in. Men have no such problems because their testes secrete oestrogens as well as androgens throughout life.

22.3 Reproduction

In many animals fertilisation takes place outside the bodies of the parents and the embryos develop externally. This reproductive behaviour is called ovipary and such animals are **oviparous**. Reptiles, birds and a few primitive mammals such as the duck-billed platypus are **ovoviviparous**. In these animals fertilisation occurs inside the mother's body. However, the embryo, which is usually inside a shelled egg, develops externally after the egg is laid. Most mammals are **viviparous**, that is fertilisation and subsequent development of the embryo occur inside the mother's body. Internal fertilisation requires the introduction of sperm from the male into the female's reproductive tract where the ova are found after ovulation. The transfer of sperm from male to female takes place in an elaborate pattern of behaviour called **copulation**.

22.3.1 Copulation

Before copulation the male and female usually interact so that each partner becomes sexually aroused. Sexual excitation of the male results in erection of the penis. The penis is made mainly of spongy **erectile tissue**. Entry of blood into the cavities of the tissue causes **erection**. Activation of appropriate parts of the male's parasympathetic nervous system in response to stimuli from the female triggers off the sequence of events leading to erection. When erect the penis can be pushed into the vagina, the wall of which also contains erectile tissue. Appropriate excitation of the female causes this tissue to become gorged with blood enabling the penis to be gripped as it is pushed back and forth during copulation. The to and fro motion of the penis in the vagina is helped by mucus secretions. In the male the secretions come from the **bulbo-urethral glands** at the upper end of the urethra and from mucus glands along the length of the urethra (Fig. 22.2).

In the female mucus comes from glands inside the vagina.

When sexual excitation reaches a peak in the male, sympathetic nervous stimulation of the genitalia brings about **ejaculation**. Ejaculation is caused by rhythmic constriction of the genital ducts beginning in the testes and progressing to the penis. The peristaltic wave pushes sperm from the testes to the urethra of the penis and into the vagina. The ejaculated fluid is called **semen**. Semen consists of sperm suspended in mucus and a milky fluid from the **prostate gland**. The prostate fluid stimulates sperm to swim. Most of the ejaculated fluid comes from the seminal vesicles. In man approximately 350 000 000 sperm are normally present in each ejaculation.

During copulation the female is also excited. The to and fro motion of the penis rubs against the clitoris, a piece of erectile tissue at the top of the vulva. When sexual excitement reaches a peak in the female, peristalsis occurs in her reproductive tract. The direction of peristalsis is opposite to that in the male and it may help to carry sperm into the Fallopian tubes. In this way sperm are propelled efficiently to the regions where the ova are found.

The likelihood of successful fertilisation is increased in many wild animals because they normally copulate when ovulation has just occurred or is about to occur (section 22.2.2). In mammals whose ovulation is controlled by an oestrus cycle, the female usually copulates with the male only at this time. She is then said to be **in oestrus** or **on heat**. The frequency of oestrus depends on the length of the oestrus cycle. The cycle takes only four to five days in mice. In women the cycle lasts for about 28 days.

22.3.2 Fertilisation and implantation of the embryo

Following ovulation, secondary oocytes are sucked from the abdominal cavity into the **Fallopian tubes** by the action of cilia lining the tubes. In women oocytes die if they are not fertilised between 8–24 hours after ovulation. By this time they have been wafted only a short distance down the Fallopian tubes. Consequently fertilisation normally takes place in the upper regions of the Fallopian tubes. In some women the tubes are blocked. Until recently such women had no hope of having their own children. However, much research has recently developed a technique whereby an ovum is removed from the woman, fertilised externally and the resulting embryo placed in its mother's uterus. The technique which was first performed successfully with humans in 1978 in Britain produces what are popularly called **test tube babies**.

1. FERTILISATION

Fertilisation involves entry of the sperm nucleus into the secondary oocyte. The oocyte is usually surrounded by many small cells called the **corona radiata**. The corona is dispersed by the enzyme **hyaluronidase** secreted by the sperm when they arrive near an oocyte. Although an oocyte is approached by many thousands of sperm, only one usually enters it. The head of the successful sperm penetrates the oocyte's outer membrane, the sperm tail being left outside. The oocyte's membrane now becomes impermeable to the entry of other sperm. Entry of additional sperm is undesirable as it could produce a zygote with more chromosomes than normal. This could have adverse consequences for the embryo (Chapter 7).

When the sperm head enters, the secondary oocyte undergoes the second meiotic division to become the ovum proper. Only at this point are both gametes haploid (Chapter 7). Fusion of the sperm and ovum nuclei produces a **diploid zygote**. It is from the zygote that the embryo develops.

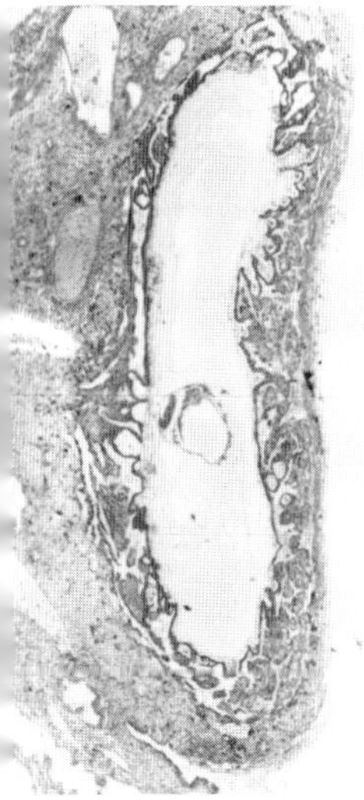

FIG. 22.15 *Photomicrograph of a 15-day human embryo embedded in the uterine wall, × 30*

Sometimes the zygote divides into two separate cells from which two individuals develop. These individuals are called **monozygotic twins**. Monozygotic twins, coming from the same sperm and ovum, are almost identical. Small differences appear as the twins develop. **Dizygotic twins** result from two different zygotes produced from two ova fertilised at the same time. Consequently dizygotic twins are usually quite different from one another.

2. IMPLANTATION

The zygote undergoes several divisions, producing a ball of 16 or 32 cells by the time it reaches the uterus. It is in this form that the embryo is **implanted** in the endometrium (Fig. 22.15). Peptidase enzymes from **trophoblast cells** on the outside of the embryo digest part of the endometrium, making space for the embryo. The products of digestion are absorbed by the trophoblasts and are used as nutrients by the embryo. Meanwhile the trophoblasts along with surrounding endometrial cells divide to form the placenta and foetal membranes.

Implantation of the embryo is delayed after fertilisation in some mammals. In deer for example, ova fertilised in the autumn rut are implanted in late December. The delay ensures that the fawns are born in midsummer when the weather favours survival.

22.3.3 The placenta

Considerable growth and development of the embryo, now called the **foetus**, takes place inside the uterus. Growth and development require the provision of oxygen and nutrients and the removal of waste materials. Oxygen and nutrients are supplied to the foetus by the mother's blood which also serves to remove foetal wastes. However, the foetal blood and the mother's blood do not mix. The two circulations come near to each other in the **placenta** (Fig. 22.16). Materials are exchanged between the blood of the mother and foetus across the placenta almost entirely by diffusion. The arrangement of the blood vascular systems of the mother and foetus is described in Chapter 9.

The placenta is formed by growth of some of the **foetal membranes** and part of the uterine wall in which the foetus is implanted. At an early stage several foetal membranes develop. They are the **yolk sac**, **allantois**, **amnion** and **chorion** (Fig. 22.17). The yolk sac is an extension of the embryo's hind

FIG. 22.16 *Ultrasonic B-scan showing a foetus inside the uterus of a pregnant woman*

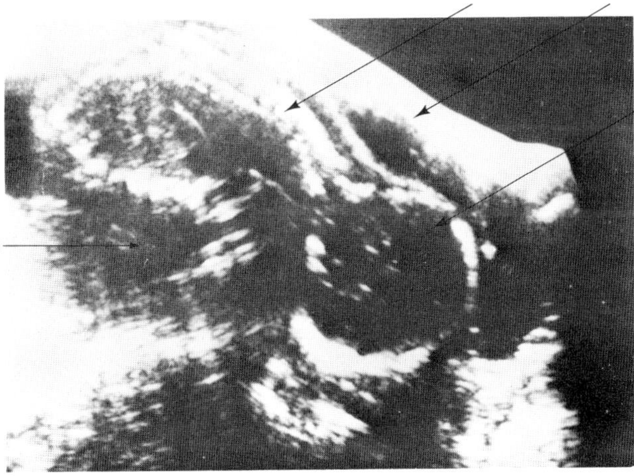

gut. In birds and reptiles yolk is the source of nutrients for the embryo. This is also the case in primitive mammals such as the duck-billed platypus which lay reptile-like eggs. In marsupial mammals also, the yolk sac provides nutrients for the embryo. In placental mammals, however, the yolk sac is relatively small. Nevertheless it is important in some mammals because antibodies pass through it into the embryo from the uterus. The antibodies provide the developing foetus with passive immunity (Chapter 9). Like the yolk sac, the allantois projects from the embryonic gut.

FIG. 22.17 *Development of the embryonic membranes in the mammal*

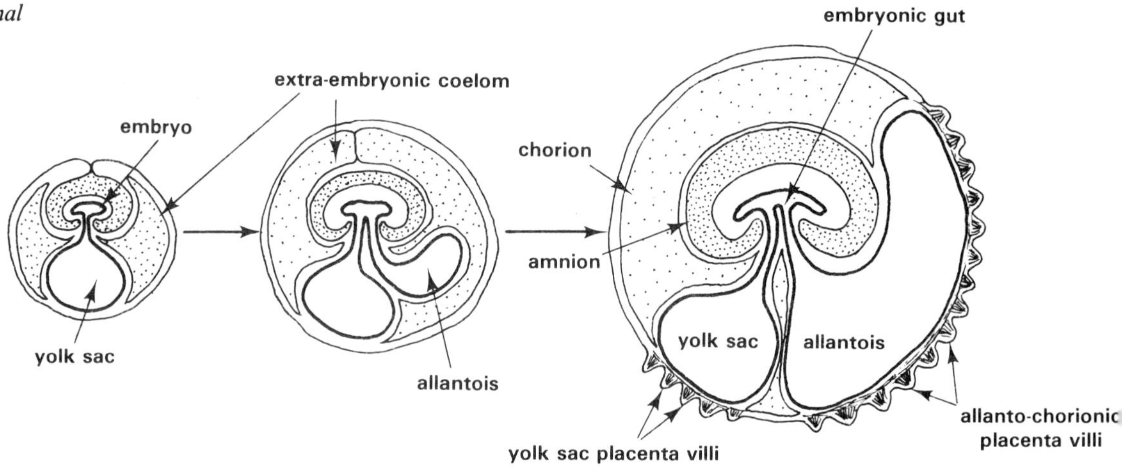

In reptiles, birds and egg-laying mammals, the allantois acts as a bladder, collecting wastes. The allantois is important in these animals, since the embryo, encased in its shell, has no means of disposing of solid wastes. In these animals too the allantois acts like a lung. Respiratory gases are exchanged across the allantoic membrane between the allantoic fluid and the atmosphere (Fig. 22.18). The amnion and chorion are membranes which grow to enclose the whole embryo. They are derived from the outermost layers of the embryo which by now lies in a fluid-filled cavity called the amniotic cavity. The chorion has a great number of **villi** which are attached to the uterine wall. The blood vessels of the allantois project into the chorionic villi and it is this vascular structure which becomes the **placenta** (Fig. 22.19).

FIG. 22.18 *Embryonic membranes of a reptilian egg*

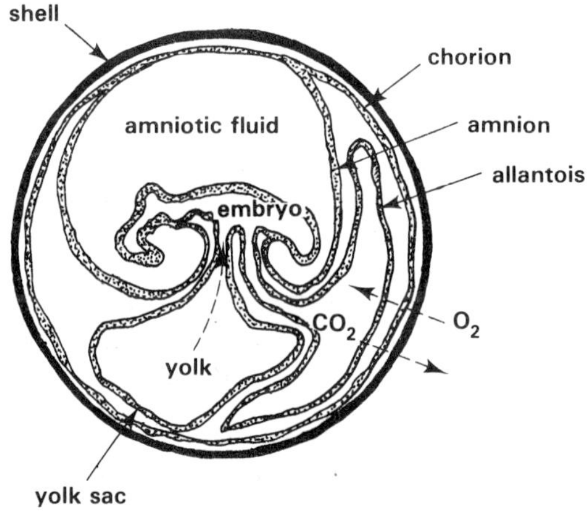

FIG. 22.19 *Blood vessels in the placenta*

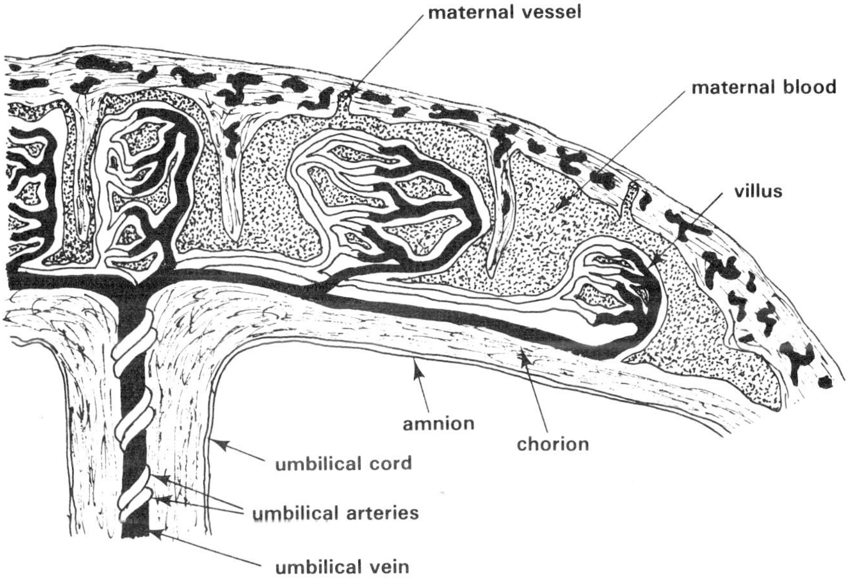

The chorionic villi provide a large surface area across which materials can be exchanged between maternal and foetal blood. Exchange of materials is further aided by the pattern of blood flow in the placental vessels. The maternal and foetal vessels are arranged in the placenta in such a way that maternal blood is close to the blood of the foetus (Fig. 22.20). Only substances of low relative molar mass can cross the placental barrier. Essential metabolites such as oxygen, sugars, amino acids, minerals, water and vitamins are transported from the mother's blood into that of the foetus. Antibodies which provide passive immunity in the foetus also pass from the mother across the placenta. Carbon dioxide, urea and other waste products made by the foetus move in the opposite direction. Most substances pass through the placenta by diffusion, though there is evidence that some sugars are moved by active transport.

FIG. 22.20 *Opposite blood flow in maternal and foetal vessels in the placenta*

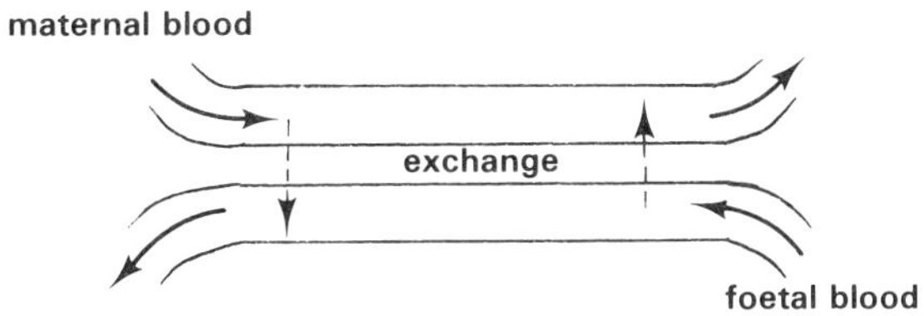

As well as acting as a route by which materials are exchanged between maternal and foetal blood, the placenta performs other vital functions. Among its other functions is the secretion of hormones. By about the second month of pregnancy in women the chorion secretes **choriogonadotropin**. This hormone is present in the urine of pregnant women and its detection is the basis of modern pregnancy tests. Small latex beads which are coated with an antibody specific to **human choriogonadotropin (HCG)** are added to a sample of urine. If the urine contains HCG the beads clump together due to the binding of HCG with the antibody. Some tests are more complicated and work by preventing the clumping of latex beads (Fig. 22.21).

FIG. 22.21 *Principle of the HCG agglutination inhibition test*

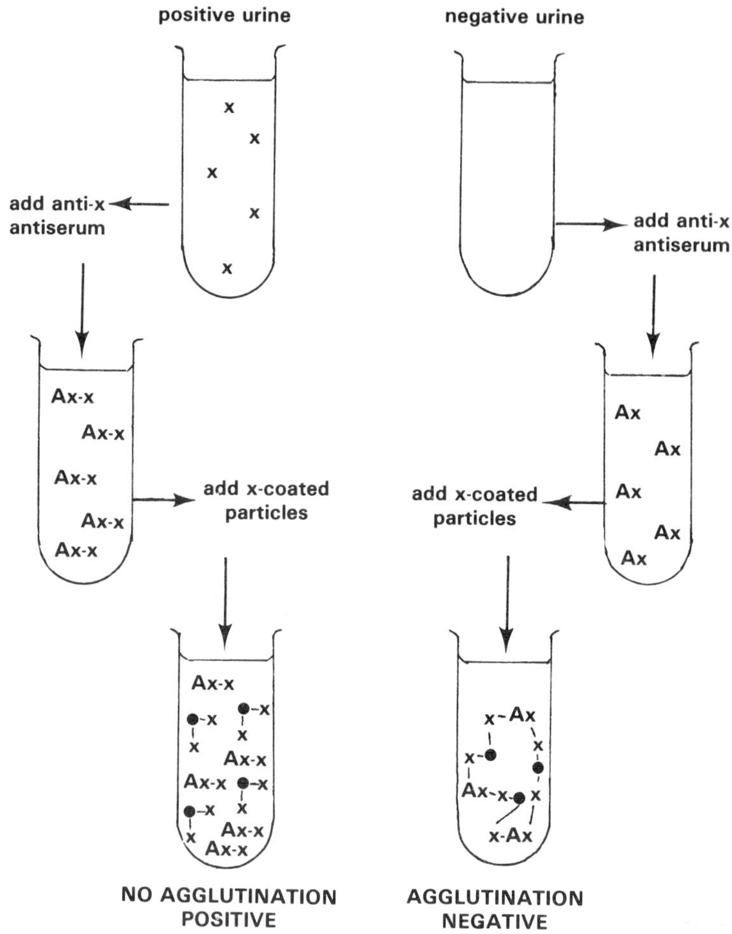

Estradiol and progesterone are also secreted from the placenta (section 22.2.3). These hormones prevent output of FSH from the anterior pituitary, thus stopping the development of new follicles in the ovaries. They also maintain the endometrium during pregnancy. Relatively high concentrations of progesterone in the uterus also keep the smooth muscle of the uterus relaxed, so protecting the developing embryos from premature birth.

22.3.4 Birth and lactation

Birth or **parturition** normally occurs when the foetus is fully developed at the end of the gestation period. Sudden and powerful intermittent contractions of the uterine wall mark the start of parturition. The smooth muscle of the uterus responds to at least two hormonal signals. One is the sudden drop in progesterone output from the placenta. Progesterone inhibits smooth muscle contraction. The other signal is a sudden increase in output of **ocytocin** from the posterior pituitary (Chapter 18). Ocytocin causes contraction of smooth muscle. Birth can be induced artificially by injecting the mother with ocytocin.

Ocytocin also brings about expulsion of milk from the mammary glands. The release of milk is an active muscular process and is a reflex response. Tactile stimulation of the nipples by a suckling infant generates nerve impulses which are transmitted in sensory neurons from the mammary glands to the hypothalamus in the brain. Ocytocin is released into the blood from the posterior pituitary. The hormone causes contraction of the smooth muscle lining the milk ducts in the mammary glands. Constriction of the ducts causes the milk to be ejected actively from the nipples into the infant's mouth.

FIG. 22.22 *The milk-expulsion reflex*

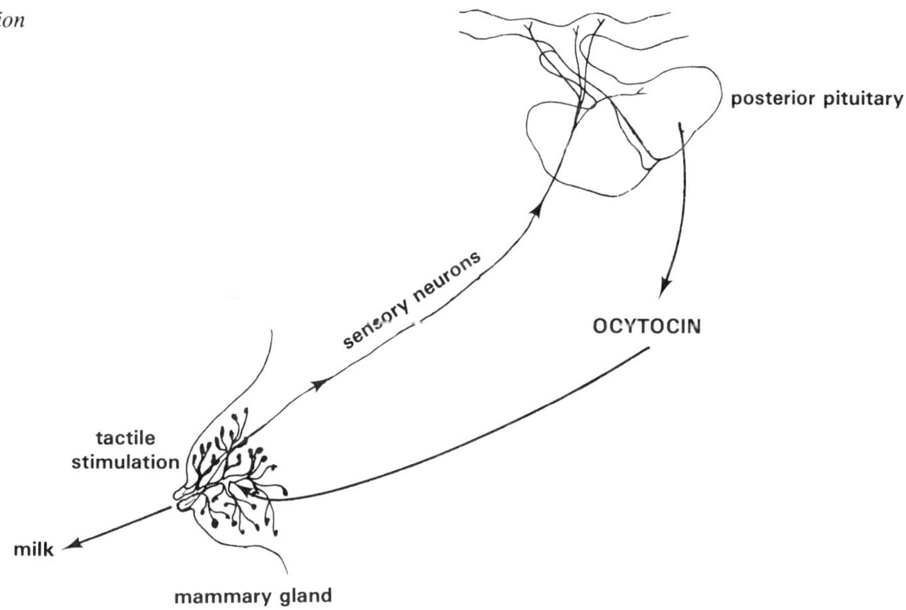

Milk production called **lactation**, is caused by the action of other hormones. During pregnancy, estradiol and progesterone from the placenta bring about growth of the milk ducts and secretory tissue in the mammary glands. At birth the placenta is released from the uterus as the **afterbirth**. The amounts of estradiol and progesterone in the mother's blood then quickly fall, causing the anterior pituitary to secrete the hormone **prolactin**. Prolactin stimulates the secretory tissue to produce milk. Milk is the normal source of nutrients for newly-born mammals. It also contains antibodies which give passive immunity in the digestive system of newly-born mammals. When sufficiently mature young mammals are weaned on to solid food.

Chapter 23 Genetics

Genetics is the science of **inheritance**, the way in which characteristics are passed from parent to offspring. All organisms closely resemble their parents. Progeny created asexually are likely to resemble their parents more closely than those arrived at by sexual reproduction. This happens because mitotic nuclear division, which gives rise to progeny asexually, reproduces the genetic material with little or no variation. Meiotic nuclear division is an integral part of the life cycle of every creature which reproduces sexually and allows scope for genetic variation (Chapter 7).

Before studying the ways in which characteristics are inherited, it would be useful to acquaint yourself with some commonly used genetical terms:

Gene: part of a DNA molecule which codes the synthesis of a protein (Chapter 6). The characteristics of organisms are largely determined by the types of enzymic and structural proteins they are able to synthesise.

Genotype (genome): the combination of genes an organism possesses.

Phenotype: the characteristics shown by an organism.

Alleles: each of the characteristics of an organism is usually determined by a pair of genes called alleles. The genotype thus consists of a number of alleles.

Homozygote (pure-breeding): an individual in which both of the alleles of a gene pair are similar.

Heterozygote (hybrid): an individual in which the alleles of a gene pair are dissimilar.

An organism may be heterozygous for some characteristics and homozygous for others.

Dominant and **recessive**: an individual which is heterozygous for a gene normally displays the characteristic determined by one of the allelic pair. This is called the dominant allele; its allelic partner is called the recessive allele. When an individual is homozygous for the recessive allele the characteristic determined by the recessive gene is displayed. The terms should be more meaningful when you have studied examples of various patterns of inheritance.

FIG. 23.1 (a) *Gregor Johann Mendel* (B&B photos)

23.1 Autosomal inheritance

The chromosomes in diploid cells exist in **homologous pairs** (Chapter 7). In many organisms one pair are the sex chromosomes (section 23.2), the rest are called **autosomes**. Gregor Johann Mendel, an Austrian monk, was the first to discover how genes carried by autosomes are inherited. He collected the seeds of a number of varieties of the garden pea and devised a procedure for following the passage of characteristics from parents to progeny. Between 1857 and 1864, he experimented in the monastery garden. In 1865, Mendel presented the results of his studies to the local Natural History Society. A year later, his findings were also published in the Annual Proceedings of the Society. They lay neglected until the beginning of this century, when several geneticists confirmed his conclusions and extended his methods to other species.

23.1.1 Monohybrid inheritance

Mendel's first experiments were designed to follow the inheritance of one well-defined characteristic. His procedure was to cross-pollinate pure-breeding varieties of the garden pea, collect the seeds and sow them the following year. The plants which grew were then allowed to self-pollinate and the seeds were again collected. The characteristics of the plants which grew from these seeds a year later were carefully noted.

One of the characteristics Mendel experimented with in this way was flower colour. In one investigation, he crossed a pure-breeding variety having red flowers with a pure-breeding white-flowered variety. All the progeny (F_1) had red flowers, but when selfed they gave rise to 705 red-flowered plants and 224 white-flowered F_2 plants, a ratio of approximately 3 red: 1 white (Fig. 23.1). This is known as a **monohybrid ratio**. About one-third of the red-flowered F_2 plants were found to be pure-breeding. The remainder on selfing gave rise to red-flowered and white-flowered progeny.

FIG. 23.1 (b) *Inheritance of flower colour in the garden pea*

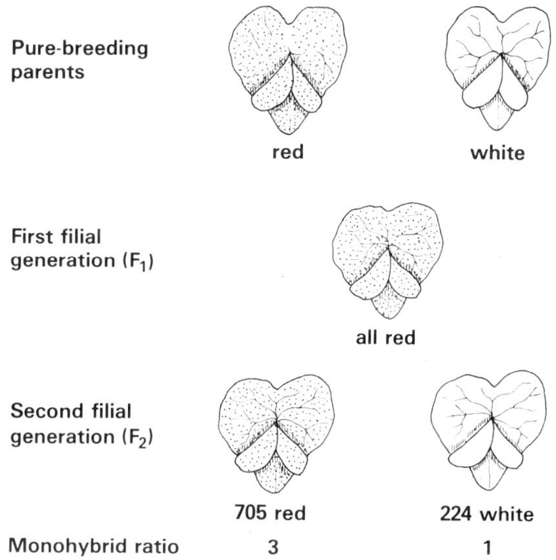

PURE-BREEDING PARENTS

RR homozygous red — *rr* homozygous white

GAMETES: *R* and *r*

F_1 HYBRIDS *Rr* heterozygous red

F_1 GAMETES: *R* or *r*

♀ \ ♂	*R*	*r*
R	*RR*	*Rr*
r	*rR*	*rr*

F_2

RR — homozygous red; *Rr*, *rR* heterozygous red — 3 red

rr — homozygous white — 1 white

PARENTS

Rr hybrid red — *rr* pure-breeding white

GAMETES: *R* or *r* — *r*

♀ \ ♂	*R*	*r*
r	*rR*	*rr*

rR : *rr*

1 red : 1 white

These observations led Mendel to formulate his **First Law of Inheritance**, which stated:

Of a pair of contrasting characters only one can be represented in the gametes.

The law can be more easily understood if symbols are used to represent the genes which determine the characteristics in question. Because all the F_1 plants had red flowers, it may be assumed that the allele for red colour (*R*) is dominant to the allele (*r*) for whiteness. The experiment may then be depicted as shown on the left.

The fact that plants of the genotype *Rr* are hybrids can be detected by crossing them with pure-breeding recessive parent plants. This is called a **back-cross** or **test-cross**.

The 1:1 ratio obtained is called a **back-cross ratio**.

Mendel observed that seven other characteristics of the garden pea were inherited in a comparable way.

An example of a human characteristic which follows the same pattern of inheritance is the Rhesus blood group (Chapter 9). The allele for Rhesus positive (*R*) is dominant to the allele for Rhesus negative (*r*). The genotype of a Rhesus positive person may thus be *RR* or *Rr*, whilst that of a Rhesus negative individual is *rr*. If both parents are heterozygous for the Rhesus group, what probability is there that a child they produce would be Rhesus negative?

CHROMOSOME BEHAVIOUR AND MONOHYBRID INHERITANCE

Organisms which reproduce sexually form gametes. In flowering plants the female gamete is the egg cell in the embryo sac, while the male gametes arise from the generative cell in germinated pollen grains (Chapter 19). The gametes of mammals are sperm and ova (Chapter 22). Gametes of flowering plants, mammals and many other groups of organisms are produced by meiotic nuclear divisions which cause them to have a haploid chromosome number (Chapter 7). In other sexually produced organisms, meiosis may take place at another stage in the life cycle (Chapters 25–27).

Mendel's First Law of Inheritance is also called the **Law of Segregation**, because alleles separate or segregate when gametes are formed. A study of the behaviour of chromosomes in meiosis shows how segregation of alleles occurs (Fig. 23.2). See also Figure 7.9.

FIG. 23.2 *Segregation of alleles in meiosis* (for clarity only one pair of autosomes is shown)

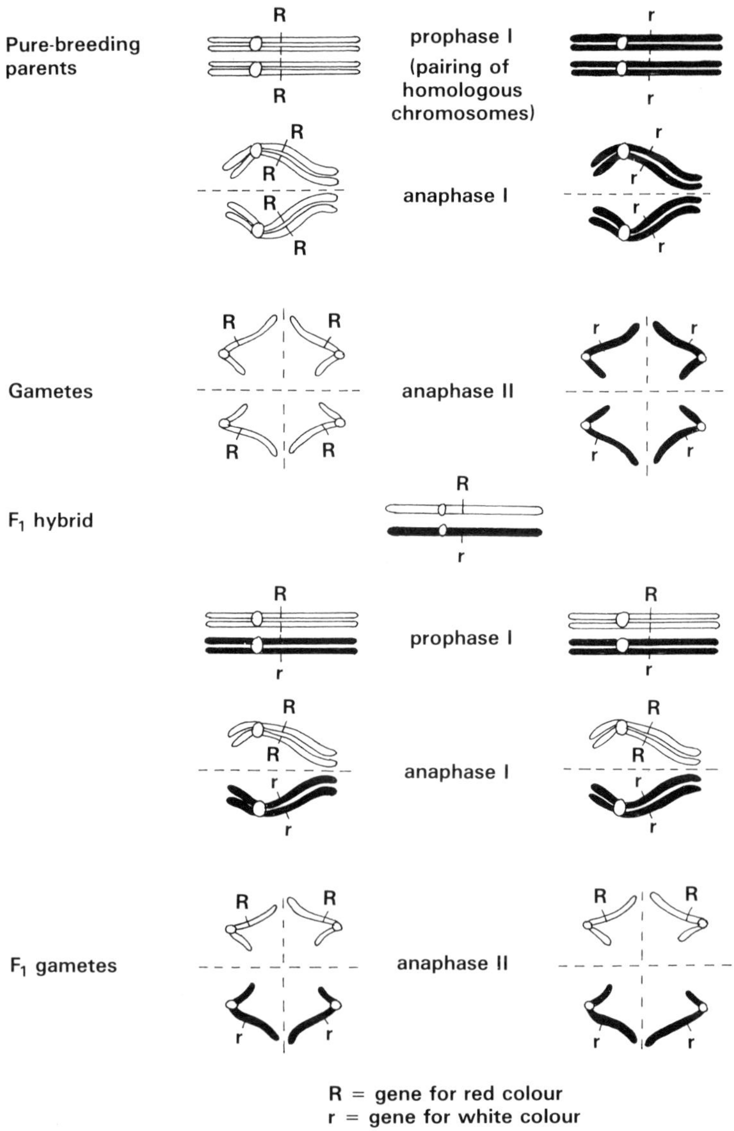

23.1.2 Dihybrid inheritance

Mendel also studied the simultaneous inheritance of two characteristics in the garden pea. In one of his experiments, he followed the inheritance of seed colour and texture. He first crossed a pure-breeding variety having round and yellow seeds with another pure-breeding variety having wrinkled and green seeds. All the F_1 plants had round yellow seeds. The F_1 plants were then allowed to self-pollinate and the colour and texture of the seeds of the F_2 plants were noted. Mendel's results are illustrated in Figure 23.3.

FIG. 23.3 *Simultaneous inheritance of two characteristics in the garden pea*

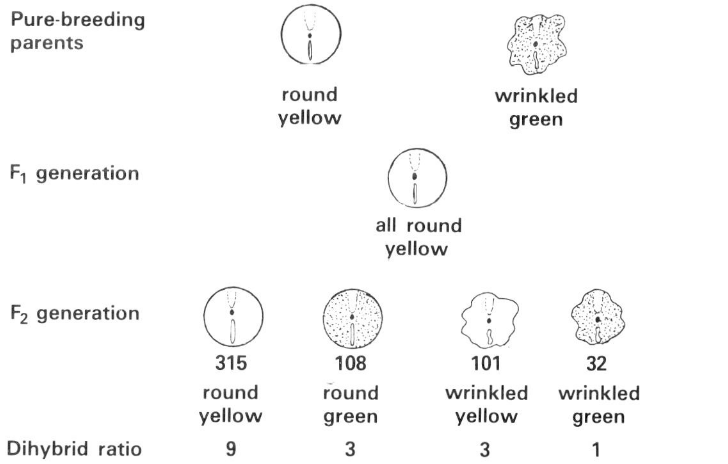

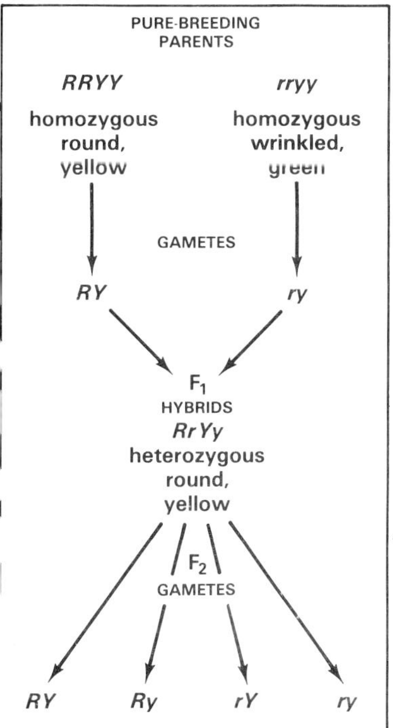

♀\♂	*RY*	*Ry*	*rY*	*ry*
RY	*RRYY*•	*RRYy*•	*RrYY*•	*RrYy*•
Ry	*RRyY*•	*RRyy**	*RryY*•	*Rryy**
rY	*rRYY*•	*rRYy*•	*rrYY*†	*rrYy*†
ry	*rRyY*•	*rRyy**	*rryY*†	*rryy*■

F_2

9 • round, yellow
3 * round, green
3 † wrinkled, yellow
1 ■ wrinkled, green

The results led Mendel to formulate a **Second Law of Inheritance**, which stated:

Each of a pair of contrasting characteristics segregates independently of those of any other pair.

Once more it is easier to understand the law using symbols to represent the genes which determine the characteristics under consideration. Because the F_1 plants had round and yellow seeds, it may be assumed that the allele for round (R) is dominant to the allele for wrinkled (r), and the allele for yellow (Y) dominant to the allele for green (y). The experiment may then be depicted as shown on the left.

Mendel observed that several other pairs of characteristics of the garden pea were inherited in a comparable way. Many other species show a similar pattern of dihybrid inheritance.

CHROMOSOME BEHAVIOUR AND DIHYBRID INHERITANCE

Once again a study of the behaviour of chromosomes in meiosis reveals how non-allelic genes segregate independently. The genes which determine the two contrasting features are located on different homologous autosomes (Fig. 23.4). Because the chromosomes of a homologous pair separate independently of those of another pair, the genes carried on the chromosomes segregate independently of each other.

23.1.3 Polyhybrid inheritance

Tracing the simultaneous inheritance of more than two contrasting characteristics is more complex. Nevertheless, Mendel's principle of independent segregation still applies. Thus the number of combinations of genes in the gametes of hybrid F_1 individuals increases, producing an even greater variety of genotypes in the F_2 generation (Table 23.1).

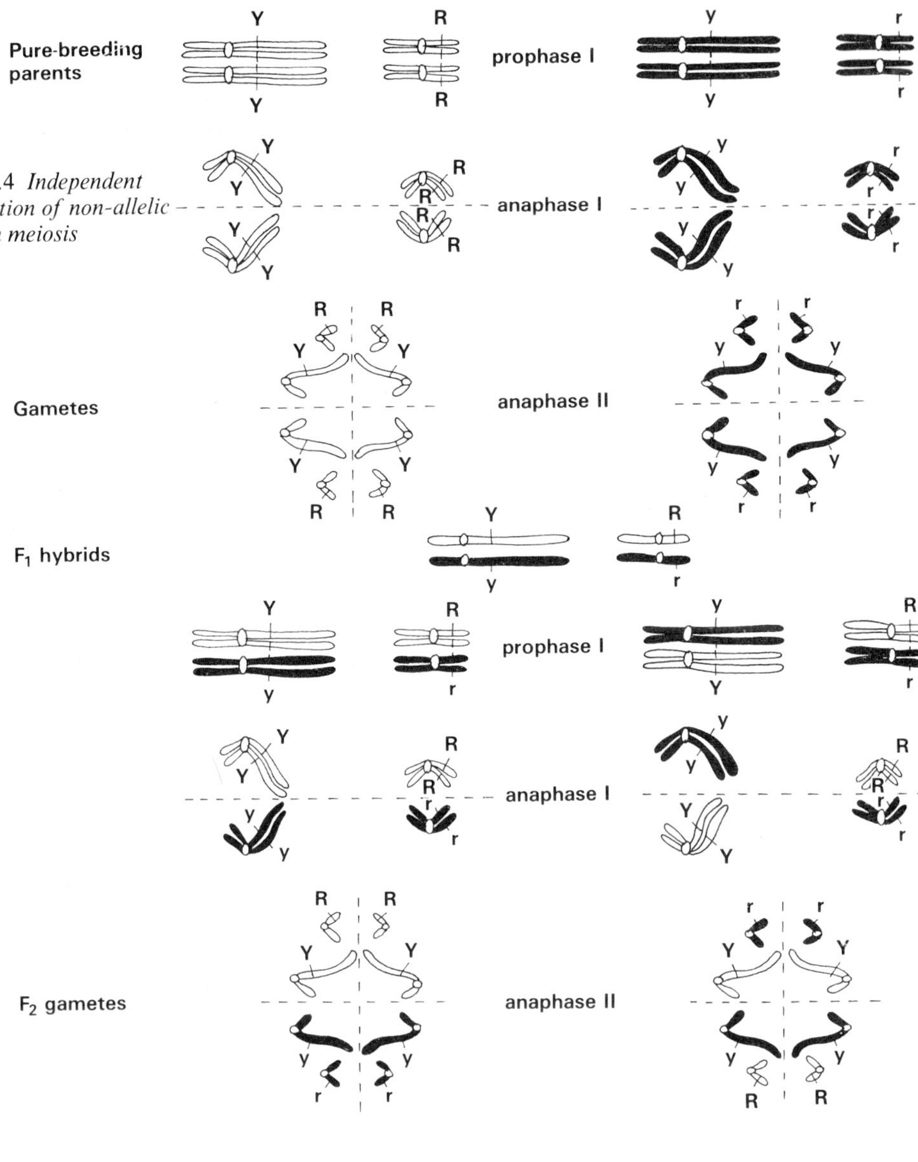

FIG. 23.4 *Independent segregation of non-allelic genes in meiosis*

Table 23.1 Relationship between number of alleles and F_2 genotypes

NO. OF ALLELES	NO. OF GENE COMBINATIONS IN F_1 GAMETES	NO. OF GENOTYPES IN F_2 GENERATION
1	$2^1 = 2$	$3^1 = 3$
2	$2^2 = 4$	$3^2 = 9$
3	$2^3 = 8$	$3^3 = 27$
n	2^n	3^n

23.1.4 Co-dominance and incomplete dominance

Complete dominance is not always observed in contrasting genes of an allelic pair. In people who belong to blood group **AB**, both allelic genes express themselves equally (section 23.1.5) and are said to be **co-dominant**. In other instances, one of the allelic genes may show **incomplete dominance** over its partner. A typical example is seen in people who suffer from thalassaemia (Mediterranean anaemia). The condition is caused by an allele (t) which is only partially dominated by the allele (T) which controls the production of normal haemoglobin. It means that people who are heterozygous for the condition (Tt) have a mild form of anaemia (thalassaemia minor). Individuals who are homozygous for thalassaemia (tt) suffer from very severe anaemia and usually die in childhood.

23.1.5 Multiple alleles

The examples of inheritance described so far all involve the segregation and expression of two alternative forms of a gene. Many characteristics of most organisms are determined by such alleles. There are, however, some characteristics which are determined by several forms of an allele known as **multiple alleles**. A good example is seen in the genotypes of people belonging to one of the four blood groups of the **ABO** system. As described in Chapter 9, the grouping is based on the presence or absence of **A** and **B** antigens on the red blood cells and **anti- A** and **anti- B** isoantibodies in the plasma. The alleles (I^A and I^B) which code the production of **A** and **B** antigens are co-dominant (section 23.1.4). Both are dominant to the allele (i) which does not code for antigen production (Table 23.2).

Table 23.2 Genotypes of A, B, AB and O blood groups

GROUP	ANTIGENS	GENOTYPES
A	**AA** or **AO**	I^AI^A or I^Ai
B	**BB** or **BO**	I^BI^B or I^Bi
AB	**AB**	I^AI^B
O	none	ii

It is evident that if a mother and her baby belong to group **O**, the father could belong to groups **O**, **A** or **B** but not to **AB**. Evidence of this kind is sometimes used in legal cases where the paternity of a child is in question. If a mother's blood group was **B** and her child of group **AB**, which group(s) could the father belong to?

23.1.6 Gene interaction

Alleles from different genes sometimes **interact** to give rise to unusual phenotypic ratios. Each of the common breeds of fowl has one of four comb shapes—rose, pea, walnut or single. Fowls with rose and pea combs are true-breeding, but when crossed give rise to F_1 fowls with walnut combs. If the F_1 birds are selfed, the phenotypic ratio among the F_2 fowls is 9 walnut: 3 rose: 3 pea: 1 single (Fig. 23.5). The 9:3:3:1 ratio indicates that this a case of dihybrid inheritance. However, it is an unusual case of dihybrid inheritance, because:

(i) the F_1 fowls have a comb form which neither of the parents had, and
(ii) a fourth comb form, single, appears in the F_2 generation.

The genes are inherited in typical Mendelian fashion. A walnut comb is produced when the alleles for pea (P) and rose (R) interact. A pea comb arises when the P allele is present without the R allele. When the R allele is present without the P allele, a rose comb appears. In the absence of both R and P alleles, a single comb develops:

FIG. 23.5 *Inheritance of comb form in fowls*

PURE-BREEDING PARENTS

RRpp homozygous rose — *rrPP* homozygous pea

GAMETES

Rp — *rP*

F_1 HYBRIDS

RrPp heterozygous walnut

F_2 GAMETES

RP *Rp* *rP* *rp*

♀ \ ♂	*RP*	*Rp*	*rP*	*rp*
RP	*RRPP* •	*RRPp* •	*RrPP* •	*RrPp* •
Rp	*RRpP* •	*RRpp* *	*RrpP* •	*Rrpp* *
rP	*rRPP* •	*rRPp* •	*rrPP* †	*rrPp* †
rp	*rRpP* •	*rRpp* *	*rrpP* †	*rrpp* ▪

F_2

9 • walnut
3 * rose
3 † pea
1 ▪ single

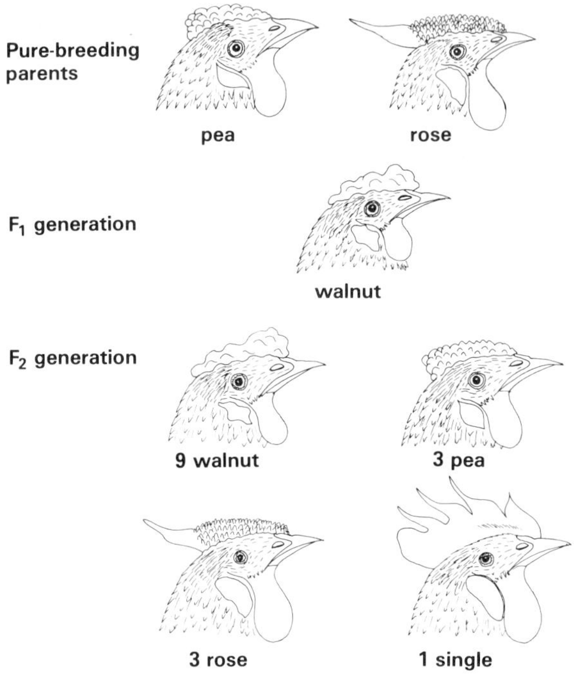

How would you detect whether or not:
(i) the fowls with walnut combs are heterozygous for both alleles, and
(ii) the fowls with single combs are homozygous for both alleles?

Gene interaction is known to occur in humans. Two alleles determine the type of haptoglobin, a plasma protein, in human blood. People who are homozygous for the two alleles have genotypes Hp^1Hp^1 or Hp^2Hp^2 and have different varieties of haptoglobin. In heterozygotes, the alleles Hp^1 and Hp^2 interact to form a third variety of haptoglobin.

23.1.7 Linkage

Up to now we have considered cases where the genes are located on separate autosomes and segregate independently. At the beginning of this century, geneticists came across examples of inheritance which clearly did not follow the typical Mendelian pattern.

In 1922, C. B. Hutchinson published the findings of some breeding experiments with maize. One of his crosses was between a variety homozygous for dominant genes which caused the seeds to be coloured and smooth, and a variety homozygous for recessive genes which gave colourless, shrunken seeds. As anticipated, the F_1 plants all had coloured, smooth seeds. The F_2 plants did not, however, show the expected 9:3:3:1 dihybrid ratio. Instead, Hutchinson noted that most of the F_2 plants had seeds similar to those of the pure-breeding parents. See diagram on left.

PURE-BREEDING PARENTS → F_1 → F_2

Coloured, smooth seeds × Colourless shrunken seeds → Coloured smooth seeds → 4032 coloured, smooth; 149 coloured shrunken; 152 colourless, smooth; 4038 colourless, shrunken

In 1925, T. H. Morgan wrote about crosses carried out on the fruit fly, *Drosophila* (Fig. 23.6(a)), in which comparable results were obtained. One of Morgan's experiments involved mating pure-breeding fruit flies having grey bodies and vestigial wings with another pure-breeding variety having black bodies and normal-sized (long) wings. All the F_1 flies had grey bodies and long wings showing that the alleles *G* and *L* for these characteristics were dominant. When F_1 females were crossed with pure-breeding males having black bodies and vestigial wings, the expected phenotypic ratio was equal numbers of grey and vestigial, grey and long, black and vestigial, black and long. Instead he got:

41·5% grey, vestigial	8·5% grey, long	8·5% black, vestigial	41·5% black, long

Morgan suggested that the results could be caused by the genes in question being on the same autosome: This was a perfectly reasonable assumption, because every organism has many more characteristics than it has chromosomes. It is therefore reasonable to deduce that each chromosome carries a number of genes. Such genes are said to be **linked**. The number of groups of linked genes in an organism is obviously the same as its haploid number of chromosomes.

FIG. 23.6 (a) Drosophila *with* (i) *long and* (ii) *vestigeal wings* (B&B)

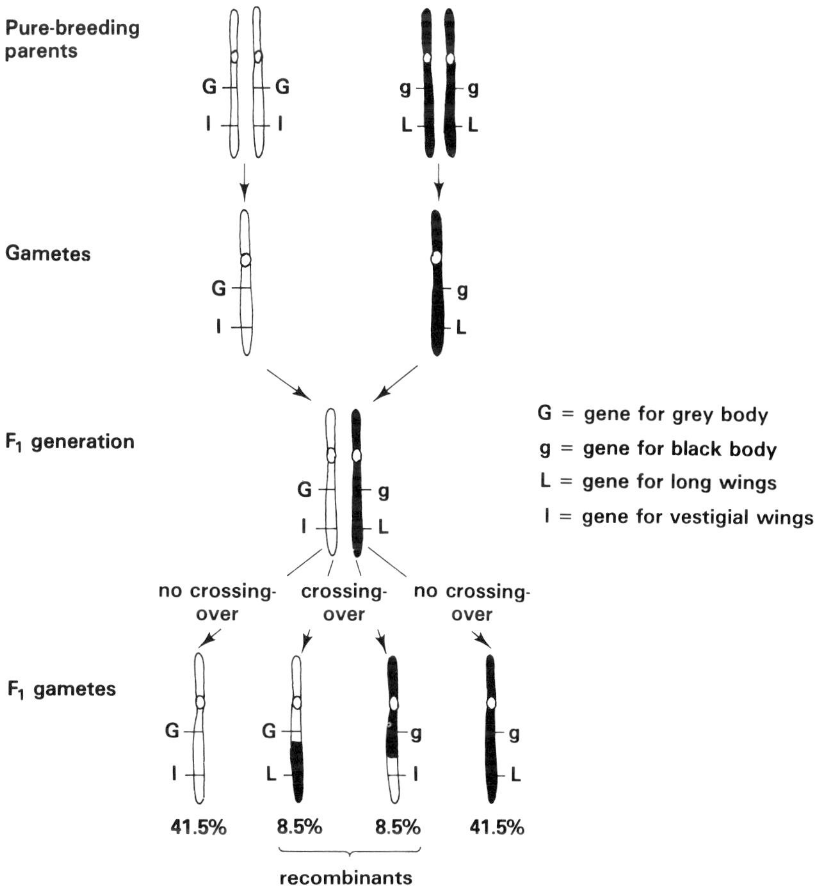

FIG. 23.6 (b) *Linkage in* Drosophila

In meiotic nuclear division, linked genes are passed *en bloc* to the gametes, so that most of the F_2 progeny inherit the characteristics determined by the linked genes. When crossing-over occurs in metaphase I of meiosis, an opportunity is provided for linked genes to be separated and give rise to **recombinants** (Fig. 7.13(a)). However, crossing-over may take place in only a small proportion of the cells undergoing meiosis. Hence few of the gametes will contain recombinant genes (Fig. 23.6(b)). Thus most of the progeny will exhibit the parental characteristics:

♀ \ ♂	gametes			
	41·5% *Gl*	8·5% *GL*	8·5% *gl*	41·5% *gL*
All *gl*	*Ggll* 41·5%	*GgLl* 8·5%	*ggll* 8·5%	*ggLl* 41·5%
F_2	grey, vestigial	grey, long	black, vestigial	black; long

Use the above example to work out how the linked genes for seed colour and texture in maize referred to earlier are inherited.

Several human characteristics are known to be determined by linked genes. They include the genes for **ABO** blood grouping and the **nail–patella syndrome**. People with the nail–patella (N–P) syndrome have small, discoloured nails, especially on the thumb, index fingers and the first and second toes. The patella (knee-cap) is missing or small and pushed to one side of the knee-joint. The life span and fertility of such individuals is quite normal. The abnormalities are caused by a dominant allele. The *N–P* gene is on the same autosome which carries the genes for ABO blood grouping.

Table 23.3 Relationship between ABO blood groups and N–P syndrome

BLOOD GROUP	A	O	B	AB
% normal	49·4	38·4	8·5	3·7
% with N–P	38·1	44·6	14·4	2·9

Most people with the N–P syndrome belong to the two most common blood groups, A and O (Table 23.3). Examination of the pedigrees of families in which the N–P syndrome has occurred clearly reveals that the ABO and *N–P* genes are linked (Fig. 23.7).

FIG. 23.7 (a) *Pedigree of a family showing linkage between genes for blood group and nail-patella syndrome* (after Fraser Roberts 1973)

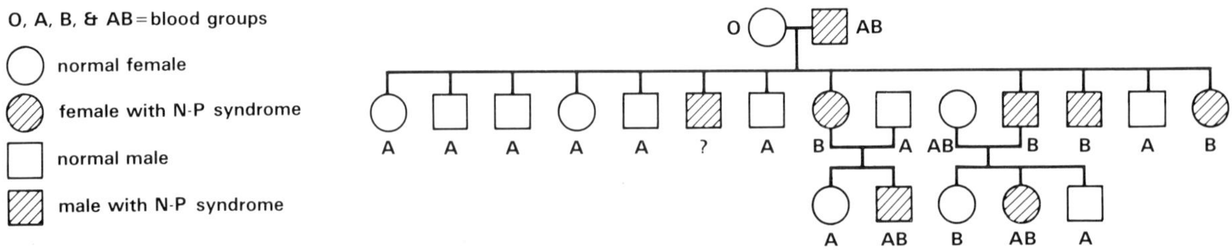

Linkage is normally tested for by back-crossing individuals which are heterozygous for both characteristics with the double recessive parent. What ratio of phenotypes would be expected in such a cross?

23.1.8 Chromosome maps

In the previous section we saw that the gametes produced by an individual who is heterozygous for linked genes are less likely to contain recombinant than parental genes. The frequency of recombination is constant and specific for any pair of linked genes. T. H. Morgan was the first to suggest that the frequency is proportional to the distance along the chromosome between the linked genes in question. Thus the further apart they are, the greater is the chance that a chiasma will form between them when homologous chromosomes associate in metaphase I of meiosis and the greater is the probability that they will be separated.

FIG. 23.7 (b) *Inheritance of linked genes for blood group and nail-patella syndrome*

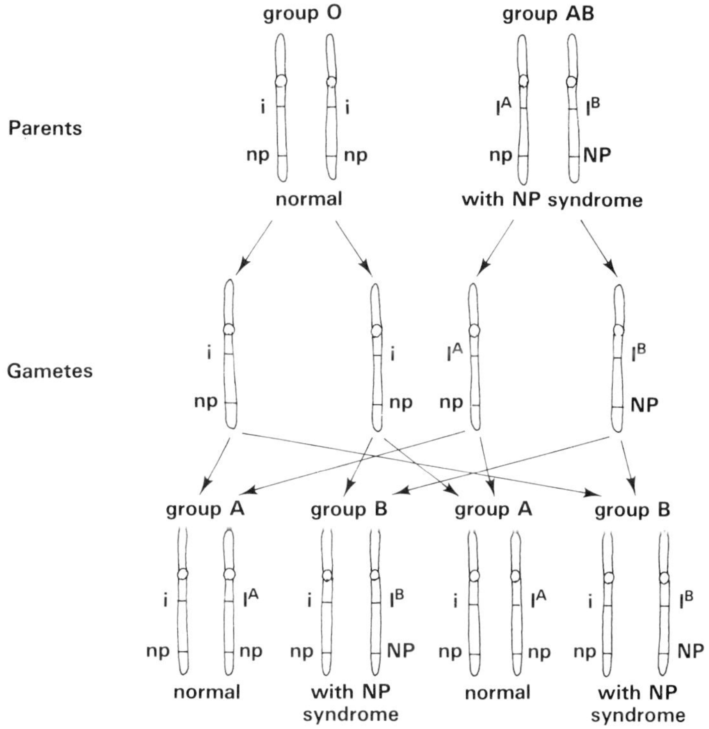

To test this assumption, Morgan and his colleagues carried out a number of breeding programmes involving linked genes in *Drosophila*. One of the investigations first involved crossing pure-breeding grey-bodied flies having normal eye colour with pure-breeding black-bodied flies having purple eyes. All the F_1 flies had grey bodies and normal eye colour. The F_1 females were then back-crossed with males having black bodies and purple eyes. The researchers obtained the following results:

grey, normal	250
black, purple	234
black, normal	15
grey, purple	16
	515

The proportion of recombinants was

$$\frac{15 + 16}{515} \times 100 = 6{\cdot}02\%.$$

Such a **cross-over value** indicated that the genes for black body and purple eye-colour were about 6 map units apart on one of the autosomes.

Next, pure-breeding flies having grey bodies and long wings were crossed with pure-breeding flies having black bodies and vestigial wings. The F_1 female flies were again back-crossed as described in the previous experiments. The progeny showed the following characteristics:

grey, long	192
black, vestigial	170
black, long	43
grey, vestigial	39
	444

The cross-over value was $\frac{43 + 39}{444} \times 100 = 18{\cdot}5\%$.

It indicated that the genes for black body and vestigial wings were 18·5 map units apart on the same autosome. The linear order of the genes could thus be:

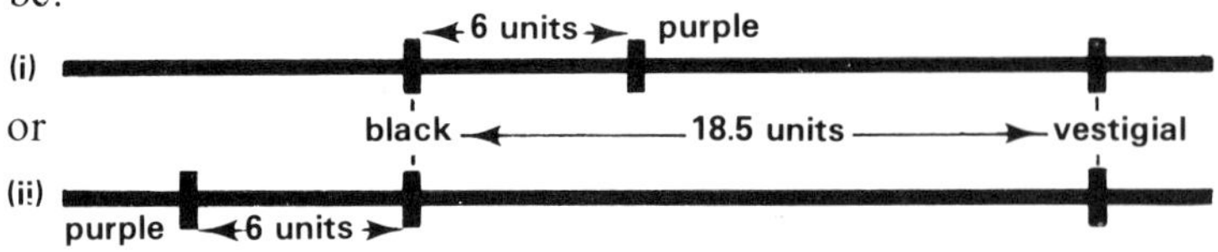

If it is the former, then the cross-over value for purple and vestigial should be about 18·5 − 6·0 = 12·5%; if the latter, the cross-over value should be 18·5 + 6·0 = 24·5%.

To find out which of the two orders is correct, Morgan and his colleagues carried out a further experiment in which they crossed pure-breeding normal-eyed, long-winged flies with pure-breeding flies having purple eyes and vestigial wings. Once more the F_1 flies were back-crossed as in the two previous investigations. The results were:

normal, long	230
purple, vestigial	200
purple, long	32
normal, vestigial	28
	490

The cross-over value was $\frac{32 + 28}{490} = 12{\cdot}2\%$.

It was therefore evident that the linear order of the genes on the homologous autosomes was:

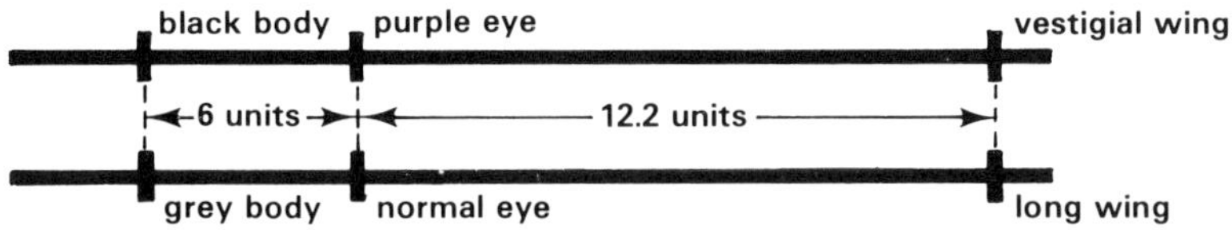

In more recent times, similar procedures have been used to map the chromosomes of a wide variety of living organisms.

23.2 Non-autosomal inheritance

The homologous pairs of chromosomes of a human are shown in Figure 7.1(b). Pairs 1–22 are the autosomes. The twenty-third pair are the **sex chromosomes**. They carry the genes which control the sexual development of an individual.

23.2.1 Inheritance of sex

In a male mammal, the sex chromosomes are different in size and shape and are called *X* and *Y* chromosomes. Female mammals have two *X* chromosomes (Fig. 23.8). Note that much of the longer arms of the *X* chromosomes has no counterpart in the *Y* chromosome.

FIG. 23.8 *The sex chromosomes of humans*

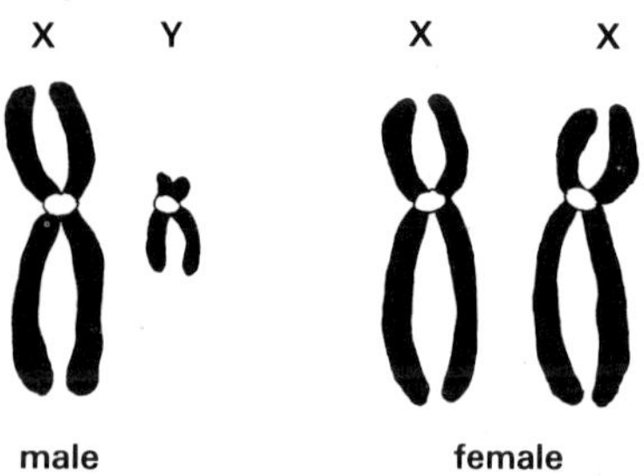

In the first nuclear division of meiosis, the sex chromosomes pair and then segregate just as the homologous pairs of autosomes do (Chapter 7). As a result, half of the gametes of a male mammal have 22 autosomes and an *X* sex chromosome; the other half have 22 autosomes and a *Y* sex chromosome. For this reason, the male is known as the **heterogametic sex**. All the gametes produced by females will normally have 22 autosomes and one *X* sex chromosome. This is why the female is called the **homogametic sex**.

When an ovum is fertilised, there is a 50 per cent chance that the sperm carries an *X* chromosome, in which case the zygote will be *XX* and develop into a female; there is also a 50 per cent chance that the sperm carries a *Y* chromosome and the *XY* zygote will develop into a male (Fig. 23.9). It is therefore the sperm which determines the sex of the progeny.

Many plants have a similar mechanism of sex inheritance. However, in birds, butterflies, most reptiles, some fish and amphibians, the female is heterogametic (*XY*) and the male homogametic (*XX*).

FIG. 23.9 *Inheritance of sex in a mammal*

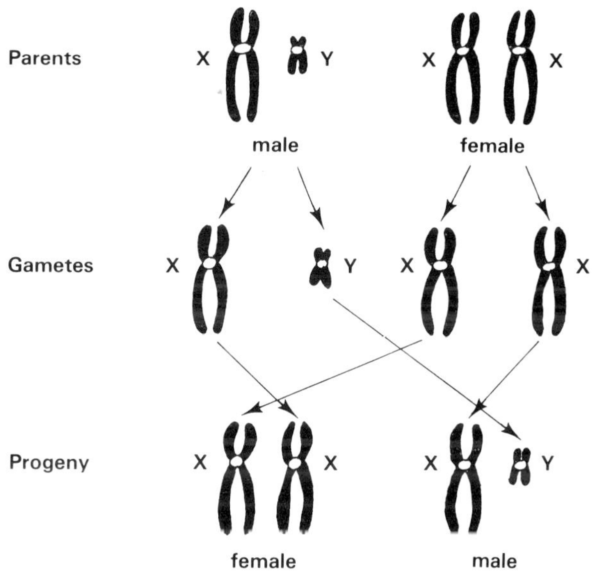

23.2.2 Sex linkage

As well as carrying genes which control sexual development, the sex chromosomes, especially the *X* chromosome, carry genes which determine other characteristics. Such genes are said to be **sex-linked**. When they occur on the longer arms of the *X* chromosome, their presence is bound to be apparent in males even when the alleles are recessive. This is because there are no corresponding alleles on the *Y* chromosome. In female mammals, the other *X* chromosome may carry dominant alleles which would mask any recessive alleles on this part of the sex chromosome (Fig. 23.10).

FIG. 23.10 *Sex linked genes*

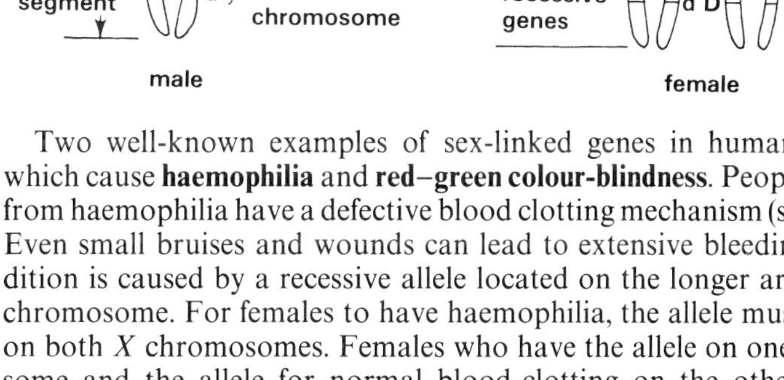

Two well-known examples of sex-linked genes in humans are those which cause **haemophilia** and **red–green colour-blindness**. People who suffer from haemophilia have a defective blood clotting mechanism (section 9.2.3). Even small bruises and wounds can lead to extensive bleeding. The condition is caused by a recessive allele located on the longer arms of the *X* chromosome. For females to have haemophilia, the allele must be present on both *X* chromosomes. Females who have the allele on one *X* chromosome and the allele for normal blood-clotting on the other are called **carriers**. They do not have the disease, but can transmit the recessive allele to their children (Fig. 23.11).

Perhaps the most publicised pedigree showing the inheritance of the gene for haemophilia is that of the descendants of Queen Victoria (Fig. 23.12).

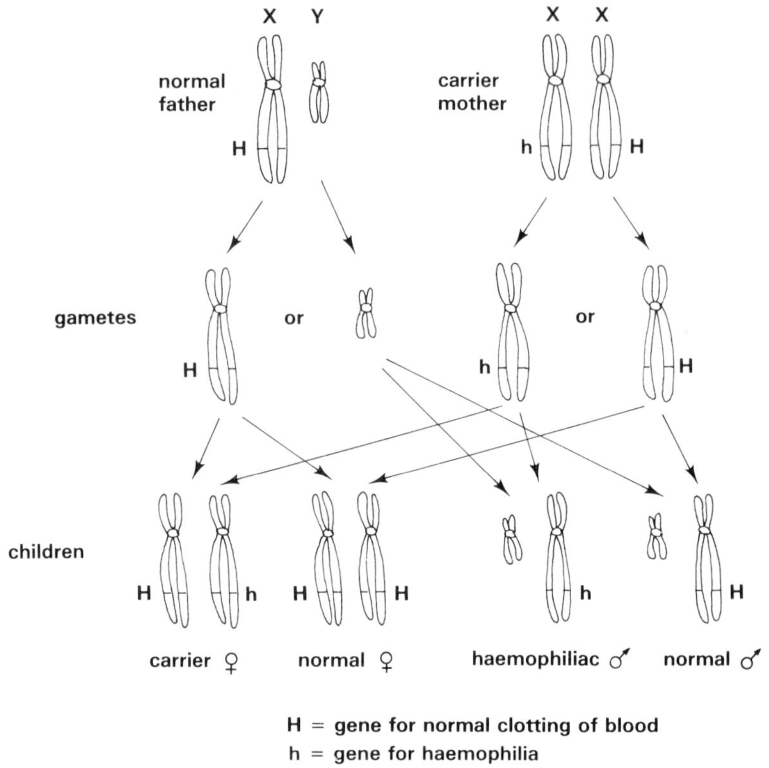

FIG. 23.11 *Inheritance of the gene for haemophilia*

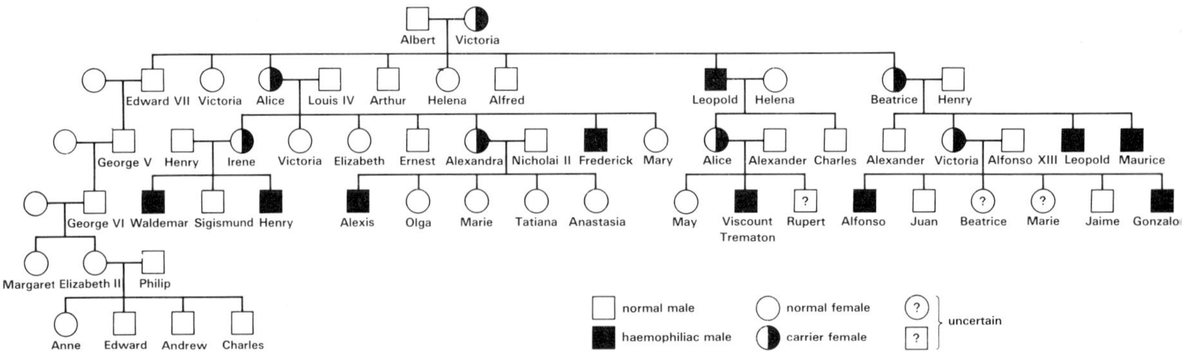

FIG. 23.12 *Pedigree of descendents of Queen Victoria* (after Pedder and Wynne 1972)

23.3 Inheritance of quantitative characteristics

Quantitative characteristics are usually determined by several genes. If the height of a large number of humans of the same age and sex is measured and the data plotted graphically, a curve similar to that in Figure 23.13 is obtained. It is called a **normal distribution curve**. Most of the individuals are of medium height. There are many fewer who are very short or very tall. This **continuous variation** is quite typical of quantitative characteristics.

The observations can be explained by assuming that characteristics such as height are determined by several genes. Let us suppose that three genes, *Aa*, *Bb* and *Cc*, control the height of a human and let us also assume that each of the dominant alleles is responsible for the addition of two units of height, while each recessive allele allows for 1 unit. The tallest individual will have the genotype *AABBCC* (12 units) and the shortest *aabbcc* (6 units).

FIG. 23.13 *Frequency distribution curve for height of men in South East England* (from Carter 1962)

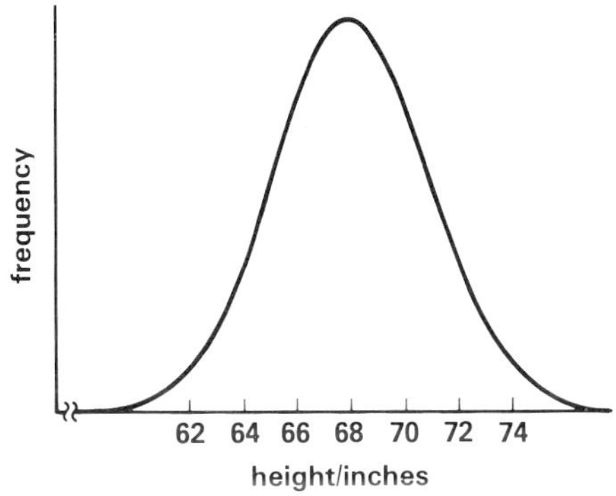

Individuals heterozygous for all three genes (*AaBbCc*) will have a height exactly halfway between the extremes (9 units). The distribution of height among the progeny of such heterozygotes can be worked out as follows:

gametes	*ABC*	*ABc*	*AbC*	*aBC*	*Abc*	*aBc*	*abC*	*abc*
ABC	12	11	11	11	10	10	10	9
ABc	11	10	10	10	9	9	9	8
AbC	11	10	10	10	9	9	9	8
aBC	11	10	10	10	9	9	9	8
Abc	10	9	9	9	8	8	8	7
aBc	10	9	9	9	8	8	8	7
abC	10	9	9	9	8	8	8	7
abc	9	8	8	8	7	7	7	6

FIG. 23.14 *Distribution curve for stature, assuming that the alleles with the properties stated in the text determine this characteristic*

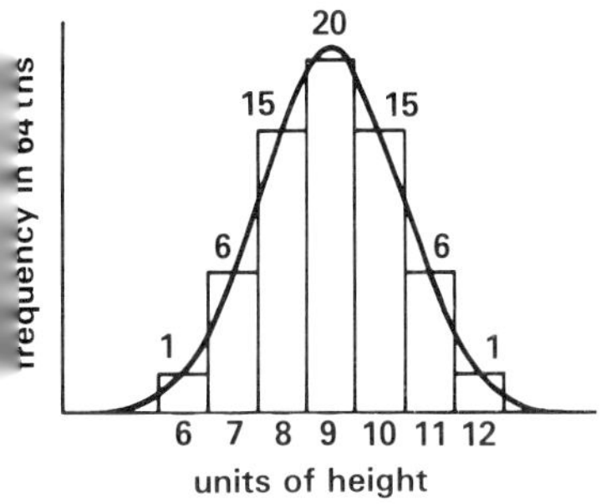

When displayed as a graph, the data appear as in Figure 23.14. Note the similarity between this curve and the normal distribution curve. The resemblance supports the idea that continuously variable characteristics are mainly determined by the additive effects of several genes.

23.4 Population genetics

A **population** is a group of individuals of the same species living in the same locality. No two individuals of the same species are alike. Identical twins (Chapter 22) are not the same even at birth, despite the fact that they are derived from the same zygote and thus have the same genotype. This is because they did not develop in identical environments. One of the twins may have been in a better position in the uterus to obtain nourishment from the placenta. Consequently it could grow more rapidly during gestation and would be larger at birth. Equally well, if you planted a batch of seeds in a fertile soil and another batch of the same variety in barren soil, the plants grown in the fertile soil should bear a much better crop. Thus the full genetic potential of any organism is realised only in an ideal environment. **Environmental differences** are the cause of some of the variations observed among individuals of the same species. However, much of the variation we see is due to **genetic differences**.

23.4.1 Inbreeding and outbreeding

The genes of organisms which reproduce sexually are passed in the gametes to the next generation. Gametes are usually formed by meiotic nuclear division which brings about recombination of parental genes (Chapter 7 and sections 23.1.2 and 23.1.7). Mating is normally at random, so the genes of the progeny come from a common **pool of parental genes**. All of the individuals in a population have many alleles in common, but they have some alleles which are different from other individuals. The process is repeated generation after generation and genetic variation constantly occurs among the progeny. This is what is known as **outbreeding**. It is the main reason for the variation of characteristics seen in populations which reproduce sexually.

Inbreeding limits the amount of genetic variation, because fertilisation is not at random (section 19.3). It also increases the number of homozygous alleles in a population (Fig. 23.15). In most organisms, an increase in homozygosity causes a reduction in vigour of the population. Such a loss of vigour is unlikely to occur among human populations, because religious and cultural barriers prevent marriage between close relatives. Another effect of inbreeding is to create genetically distinct lines of pure-breeding individuals. Some are homozygous dominant, others homozygous recessive for a given gene (Fig. 23.15). The two lines can be distinguished phenotypically and maintained separately. Inbreeding is practised when it is desirable to have a large number of genetically uniform organisms for a specific purpose. For example, if a newly produced drug is to be tested on experimental animals to find out whether or not it is suitable for use on humans, it is important that the test animals should be as identical as possible to one another. The variation in reaction to the drug is much less than occurs in a batch of random-bred animals and the results are much more reliable.

FIG. 23.15 *Effect of successive inbreeding on the proportion of homozygous alleles in a population*

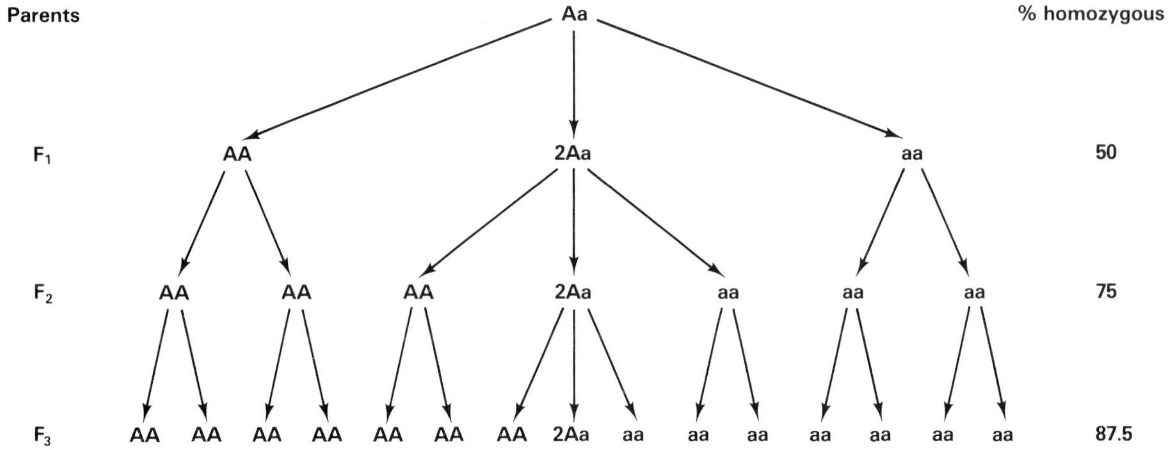

In the wild, occasional inbreeding among organisms which normally outbreed, perhaps as a consequence of physical isolation, may result in a new line which is unable to breed with the parent stock. This could be a way in which new species arise.

23.4.2 Clones

Organisms which reproduce asexually give rise to progeny by mitotic nuclear division which normally produces exact copies of the parental genotype (Chapter 7). Bacteria and protozoa which reproduce by fission (Chapter 25) and flowering plants which multiply by parthenogenesis or by vegetative propagation usually have identical genotypes too. Populations of individuals having the same genotypes are called **clones**. Cloning is useful because it preserves genotypes which may be very well suited to a particular environment. Gardeners frequently maintain clones of desirable varieties of plants by vegetative propagation (section 19.4).

23.4.3 The Hardy–Weinberg law

Each characteristic of an individual is usually determined by a gene pair, the alleles of which often occur in dominant and recessive forms. When a population breeds at random, the progeny consist of homozygous dominant, homozygous recessive and heterozygous individuals.

The proportions of individuals of each kind in the population will depend mainly on the frequency of the allelic genes in question. Consider an allele *A* and its recessive form *a*. Individuals of genotypes *AA*, *Aa* and *aa* are present in the population and contribute their genes to a large pool of gametes. If the frequency of gametes with gene *A* is **p** and the frequency of gametes with gene *a* is **q**, the proportions of genotypes among the progeny can be worked out as follows:

♂ / ♀	gametes	
	A(**p**)	*a*(**q**)
A(**p**)	*AA*($\mathbf{p}^2$)	*Aa*(**pq**)
a(**q**)	*Aa*(**pq**)	*aa*($\mathbf{q}^2$)

Now $AA + 2Aa + aa = 100\%$ or $1{\cdot}0$
Thus $\mathbf{p}^2 + 2\mathbf{pq} + \mathbf{q}^2 = 1{\cdot}0$
[therefore $(\mathbf{p} + \mathbf{q})^2 = 1{\cdot}0$ and $\mathbf{p} + \mathbf{q} = 1{\cdot}0$]

This is known as the **Hardy–Weinberg equation**. The relative proportion of the three genotypes in successive generations remains constant, provided:
(i) there is no migration into or out of the population,
(ii) mating is at random,
(iii) there is no natural selection, so that all three genotypes are equally capable of producing progeny, and
(iv) there is no mutation of the alleles.

The equation has been verified in populations of many species, including humans. People vary in their ability to taste phenylthiocarbamate (PTC). Some are unable to taste PTC, others experience a bitter taste when a small amount of it is placed on the tip of the tongue. The allele for tasting (*T*) is dominant to that for non-tasting (*t*). Non-tasters must therefore have the genotype *tt*, whereas tasters could be *TT* or *Tt*.

Table 23.4 Frequencies of tasters and non-tasters of PTC among American parents in Ohio (after Snyder 1932)

PHENOTYPE	NUMBER	PERCENTAGE	FREQUENCY
taster	1139	71·2	0·712
non-taster	469	28·8	0·288
total	1608	100	1·000

In the early 1930s, Snyder tested a large number of North American parents for their ability to taste PTC. His results are summarised in Table 23.4. Applying the Hardy Weinberg equation:

$$\mathbf{p}^2 + 2\mathbf{pq} = 0{\cdot}712$$
$$\text{and}\quad \mathbf{q}^2 = 0{\cdot}288$$
$$\mathbf{q} = \sqrt{0{\cdot}288}$$
$$= 0{\cdot}537$$

$$\begin{aligned} \text{Now} \quad \mathbf{p} + \mathbf{q} &= 1{\cdot}000 \\ \mathbf{p} + 0{\cdot}537 &= 1{\cdot}000 \\ \text{and} \quad \mathbf{p} &= 1{\cdot}000 - 0{\cdot}537 \\ &= 0{\cdot}463 \end{aligned}$$

The proportion of genotype $TT(\mathbf{p}^2)$ is therefore:

$$(0{\cdot}463)^2 = 0{\cdot}214 \text{ or } 21{\cdot}4\%$$

and the proportion of $Tt(2\mathbf{pq})$ is:

$$2(0{\cdot}463 \times 0{\cdot}537) = 0{\cdot}497 \text{ or } 49{\cdot}7\%$$

In this way the proportions of the genotypes of the parents were determined. Snyder also detected the same ratio of tasters and non-tasters among their children. It was therefore apparent that there had been no change in the proportions of individuals of the three genotypes in successive generations. This is known as the **Hardy–Weinberg equilibrium**. Disturbance of the equilibrium occurs when
(i) mating is non-random,
(ii) there is natural selection against one of the genotypes,
(iii) the alleles in question mutate, and
(iv) when migration occurs between populations.

23.4.4 Genetic polymorphism

In natural populations, the four provisions listed above rarely prevail. Instances occur when a particular genotype prevents its possessor from reproducing, thus bringing about a change in the frequency of the allelic genes concerned. For example, the genotypes for haemoglobin production among people of African origin are *SS* (homozygous normal), *Ss* (heterozygous) and *ss* (homozygous recessive for sickle-cell haemoglobin). Those who are homozygous recessive suffer from **sickle-cell anaemia** (section 8.3.4) and do not normally survive to reproductive age. Their genes are thus not passed on to the next generation. On the other hand, people who are homozygous dominant are more susceptible to malaria than heterozygous individuals. The loss of *s* genes to the next generation is therefore counterbalanced by the loss of *S* genes in people dying from malaria before they reach reproductive age. For these reasons the heterozygotes are more likely to survive and breed and the gene frequency remains stable. It explains why a harmful gene may be retained at a relatively high frequency in some populations.

New genes constantly arise by mutation (Chapter 6). However, the mutated gene is only retained in the population and their progeny if it is advantageous or neutral in terms of survival value. The increase in frequency of disadvantageous genes is usually checked at an early stage, perhaps by preventing the individual with the gene from reproducing. Thus, although a gene may mutate, it is not necessarily passed on to succeeding generations.

Preserving two or more forms of a gene in a population by means other than mutation is known as **genetic polymorphism**. Sickle-cell anaemia and the **ABO** blood groups are typical examples of how alternative forms of a gene may be preserved at higher frequencies than would occur by mutation alone. The gene for sickle-cell anaemia is advantageous in helping heterozygous individuals to resist malaria. The multiple alleles for **ABO** blood grouping appear to be neutral so far as survival is concerned.

Chapter 24 The origin and evolution of life

The earth is populated by an enormous variety of plant and animal life (Chapters 25–27). Some organisms clearly resemble others and there is little difficulty in accepting the fact that they are closely related. Others are so different in appearance that it would seem that they are unrelated. Evolution implies that all living organisms, however unalike, arose from common ancestors. They are the descendents of previous forms of life and in this sense they are related to each other.

For centuries people have wondered how life originated and how the diversity of living organisms evolved. Scientists can still only speculate about the origin of life. Much more is known about how life evolved, mainly due to the work of Charles Darwin and Alfred Russel Wallace in the nineteenth century and to the findings of twentieth-century geneticists and biochemists.

24.1 The origin of life

Radioisotope methods of dating (section 24.2.1) indicate that the earth was formed about $4{\cdot}6 \times 10^9$ years ago, whereas the oldest fossils are only $3{\cdot}2 \times 10^9$ years old. The first $1{\cdot}4 \times 10^9$ years of the earth's history are thus something of a mystery. Assuming that the ancestors of today's living organisms originated on earth, the way in which it happened has to be the subject of informed guesswork.

The British biochemist J. B. S. Haldane appears to have been the first to propose that life originated when the earth's atmosphere was devoid of oxygen gas. In 1929 he suggested that an atmosphere lacking oxygen would have no ozone layer which today stops the penetration of most of the ultraviolet radiation from the sun. Ultraviolet light is assumed to have provided energy for organic molecules to be made from atmospheric gases such as carbon dioxide, ammonia and water vapour. The organic molecules gradually accumulated in the oceans, in Haldane's words, as a *dilute soup*.

A few years later, the Russian biochemist A. I. Oparin came up with similar ideas as to how life began. There was little interest at the time in Haldane's and Oparin's suggestions. However, with present-day knowledge, it is reasonable to assume that the main steps in the evolution of life were probably:

1. **Synthesis of organic monomer molecules** such as amino acids, nitrogenous bases and sugars.
2. **Formation of organic polymers** such as proteins and nucleic acids.
3. **Isolation of the polymers** from the non-living environment.
4. **Replication of polymers**.

24.1.1 Monomer synthesis

An indication of the kinds of organic **monomers** that can be synthesised from simple gases came in the early 1950s. Harold Urey and Stanley Miller in the USA carried out a series of laboratory experiments in which they subjected a variety of gas mixtures to ultraviolet light and an electric spark (Fig. 24.1). The electric spark simulated lightning flashes. These may have been an additional or alternative source of energy for the synthesis of organic molecules in the earth's early atmosphere. Urey and Miller observed that gas mixtures such as hydrogen, methane, ammonia and water

FIG. 24.1 *Apparatus used by Miller and Urey to simulate monomer synthesis*

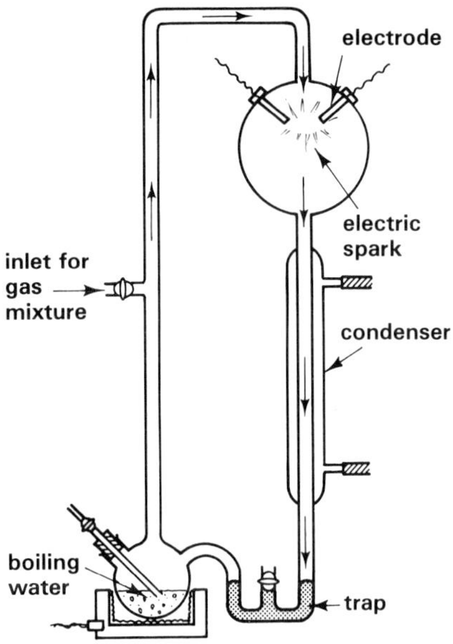

vapour gave rise to aldehydes, amino acids and carboxylic acids. Other mixtures—for example, carbon dioxide, carbon monoxide, nitrogen and water vapour—gave similar results.

Amino acids were possibly formed in the following way, known as the **Strecker synthesis**:

In the atmosphere:

$$\underset{\text{aldehyde}}{R.CHO} + \underset{\text{ammonia}}{NH_3} \xrightarrow{-H_2O} \underset{\text{imine}}{R.CH.NH} \xrightarrow{+HCN} \underset{\text{aminonitrile}}{R.CH.NH_2CN}$$

In the ocean:

$$\underset{\text{aminonitrile}}{R.CH.NH_2CN} + \underset{\text{water}}{2H_2O} \xrightarrow{-NH_3} \underset{\text{amino acid}}{R.CH.NH_2COOH}$$

Several of the amino acids formed in the experiments performed by Urey and Miller are found in the proteins of living organisms. To make nucleic acids, purine and pyrimidine bases are required, as well as the pentose sugars ribose and deoxyribose (Chapter 6). The purine base adenine can be readily synthesised from hydrogen cyanide. It is not so easy to predict how the other bases may have been formed. The pentose sugars can be made from methanal (formaldehyde) in the **formose reaction**:

$$\underset{\text{methanal}}{5H.CHO} \longrightarrow \underset{\text{ribose}}{C_5H_{10}O_5} \xrightarrow{-O} \underset{\text{deoxyribose}}{C_5H_{10}O_4}$$

24.1.2 Polymer synthesis

When amino acids join by peptide linkages to form proteins, water is one of the products of the reaction (Chapter 3). The same happens when nitrogenous bases and pentose sugars join to make nucleic acids. They are both examples of **polymerisation** by condensation reactions. It is difficult to see how condensation reactions could readily occur in the earth's primaeval oceans. Here water was abundant and would have kept the monomers apart. Bernal has suggested that the amount of water in the vicinity of the monomers may have been reduced by their adsorption on to clay or mica particles. Katchalsky has shown experimentally that polypeptides will form on clay minerals from esters of amino acids and AMP. Freezing and drying are alternative methods which may have concentrated the monomers prior to polymerisation.

24.1.3 Polymer isolation and replication

In living cells, the energy required to build polymers from monomers comes from ATP (Chapter 5). In prebiological systems, it may have come from ultraviolet light.

Oparin in the Soviet Union and Fox in the USA have closely studied some of the ways in which natural polymers may have become separated from their surroundings. The tendency of biological polymers to form polymer-rich droplets called **coacervates** has been examined by Oparin. He reports that coacervates are readily formed from aqueous suspensions of proteins and polysaccharides, and proteins and nucleic acids. Some coacervates are unstable and quickly sediment from suspension. Oparin has shown that such coacervates can be made stable by adding enzymes to the suspensions. The enzyme molecules concentrate in the coacervates, where they are able to catalyse biochemical reactions. One such enzyme is phosphorylase which catalyses the polymerization of glucose phosphate to form starch (Fig. 24.2). As starch accumulates, the coacervates grow and eventually break up into smaller coacervates which continue to grow in the

FIG. 24.2 *Polymerisation of starch in a coacervate*

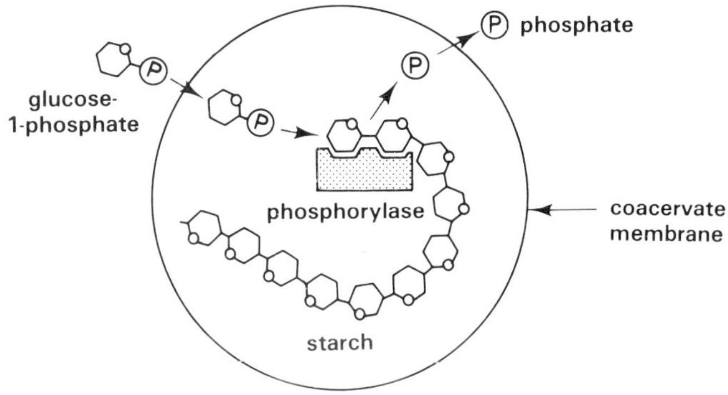

same way. Could this be the way in which biological polymers were first replicated?

In addition to condensation reactions, Oparin has shown that coacervates can also bring about electron transport. For example, coacervates containing dehydrogenase enzymes will reduce redox dyes such as methyl red when an electron carrier such as NADH is added to the suspension. Furthermore, he has succeeded in getting coacervates containing chlorophyll to develop a reducing power when exposed to visible light. This is comparable to the way in which chloroplasts reduce NADP in photosynthesis (Chapter 5).

Fox has worked mainly with protein coacervates. When heated in water at 130–180°C, they aggregate spontaneously into spheres 1–2μm in diameter. The spheres have a boundary which resembles the structure of a unit membrane, though it lacks the double phospholipid layer (Chapter 1). They grow by absorbing protein dissolved in the surrounding water and split in the same way as bacteria multiply by fission (Chapter 25). In addition, they are able to catalyse a variety of biochemical reactions, for example esterification, glucose oxidation and peroxidase activity. The experiments of Oparin and Fox show that biological polymers may form stable systems capable of catalysing biochemical reactions. Such systems may well have been the forerunners of living cells.

24.1.4 The first cells

The first cells to evolve were possibly unicellular organisms. Because oxygen gas was absent in the earth's oceans at the time, they probably acquired energy by fermenting some of the organic monomers synthesised from atmospheric gases. In many ways they were probably similar to anaerobic bacteria living today. The capacity of the earth to support **consumer organisms** of this kind was limited by the rate at which monomers were formed. When photosynthetic organisms evolved, the earth's capacity to support life became greatly enhanced. Such **primary producers** probably used hydrogen sulphide as a source of hydrogen for reducing carbon dioxide. This form of photosynthesis is used by some bacteria today. At a later stage, organisms able to use water instead of hydrogen sulphide in photosynthesis appeared. They were probably similar to blue-green algae (Chapter 25). It is these organisms which are found as microfossils in rocks at least $3{\cdot}2 \times 10^9$ years old.

The release of oxygen as a photosynthetic product resulted in a gradual but dramatic change in the composition of the earth's atmosphere. An important consequence of the change was the formation of the ozone layer in the upper atmosphere which reduced the penetration of ultraviolet light from the sun. It ended the non-biological production of organic matter. From this time on, synthesis of organic molecules was brought about mainly by photosynthesis.

24.2 Evidence of evolution

The reason why biologists believe that the enormous variety of life has evolved from simple ancestors is based on three main sources of evidence. They are the evidence from **fossils**, from **affinities** between organisms and from the **geographical distribution** of organisms.

24.2.1 Fossils

A **fossil** is any buried object which points to the existence of prehistoric life. Fossils are formed in various ways. One of the commonest is where a hard part of an animal, such as the shell or skeleton, immersed in water, has become infiltrated or replaced by minerals causing it to become **petrified** (changed to stone). In other instances, the body of an organism has become embedded in mud which hardened to form a **mould** when the body subsequently decayed. When the mould later filled with minerals brought in by water, a stoney **cast** was formed, similar in shape to the organism. Casts of the burrows of mud-dwelling invertebrates have been formed in this way. Alternatively, an **impression** of the shape of the body or its surface structure may be left in material which later changed into rock (Fig. 24.3).

FIG. 24.3 *Various types of fossils*

FIG. 24.4 *Rock strata at Aberystwyth, Wales*

Most fossils are found in **sedimentary rocks** formed from mud and silt deposited in lakes and on the sea bed millions of years ago. Earth movement later raised many sedimentary rocks above sea level. Often the rocks are in **strata**, the oldest at the bottom and the most recently formed at the top (Fig. 24.4). Some indication of the course of evolution can be obtained by comparing the sorts of fossils in the strata.

It is also possible to age the rocks by **radioisotope dating**. Nearly all elements exist as several **isotopes**, that is as atoms having slightly different atomic masses e.g. C^{12} and C^{14}. Some isotopes are unstable and decay by releasing sub-atomic α- and β-particles until they become more stable. Some examples are as follows:

$$\text{uranium}^{238} \longrightarrow \text{lead}^{206}$$
$$\text{potassium}^{40} \longrightarrow \text{calcium}^{40} + \text{argon}^{39}$$
$$\text{carbon}^{14} \longrightarrow \text{carbon}^{12}$$

The time required for half a given quantity of an unstable isotope to break down into a stable form is its *half-life*. Physicists have determined the half-lives of many unstable isotopes. It is thus possible to estimate accurately the age of a fossil by measuring the ratio of unstable:stable isotopes, for example U^{238}:Pb^{206} in the rock in which the fossil was found. If the ratios of several isotopes are measured at the same time, the dating is cross-checked and thus reliable. The order in which living organisms were evolved can thus be determined. It usually coincides with the order suggested from rock strata studies.

Other information of the kinds of living organisms which existed in past times comes from **amber**, the hardened resin of primitive seed-bearing trees, in which whole insects have been trapped. The **frozen bodies** of mammoths and woolly rhinoceroses found in Siberia, and the **pollen-grains** trapped in peat bogs, have also provided valuable information.

It is important to realise that fossils provide only a sketchy history of previous life. Many fossils have been found purely by chance when rocks have been disturbed in mining, quarrying and in the construction of roads, bridges and buildings. Many more lie as yet undiscovered. Fossils of soft-bodied organisms are not particularly plentiful. This is presumably because the organisms quickly decayed after death. For some forms of life such as fungi there is hardly any fossil evidence.

1. THE FIRST FOSSILS

Rocks over 6×10^2 million years old belong to the **Precambrian** geological period. Until quite recently there was no fossil evidence of life as far back as this. In the 1950s, two American geologists, Barghoorn and Tyler, reported the presence of fossil micro-organisms called **stromatolites** in Precambrian rocks near Lake Superior, Ontario. The fossils which are 3×10^3 million years old resemble bacteria and blue-green algae. Living stromatolites have since been found in the coastal waters of Western Australia. They are layered communities of bacteria and blue-green algae (Fig. 24.5).

FIG. 24.5 (a) *General view of stromatolites* (B&B)

FIG. 24.5 (b) *Section of fossil stromatolites* (B&B)

Living blue-green algae are able to photosynthesise and some can fix atmospheric nitrogen. If the stromatolite microbes were also able to do this, they may have had a profound influence on the course of evolution. By releasing oxygen gas, a product of photosynthesis, they may have created the conditions in which aerobic organisms first evolved. Before this time the earth's atmosphere contained very little oxygen gas (section 24.1).

2. ANIMAL AND PLANT FOSSILS

The oldest animal and plant fossils suggest that the earliest forms of life were simple and probably aquatic. Fossil burrows have been found in rocks of the late Precambrian period, less than 7×10^2 million years old.

FIG. 24.6 (a) Rhynia, *a psilophyte*

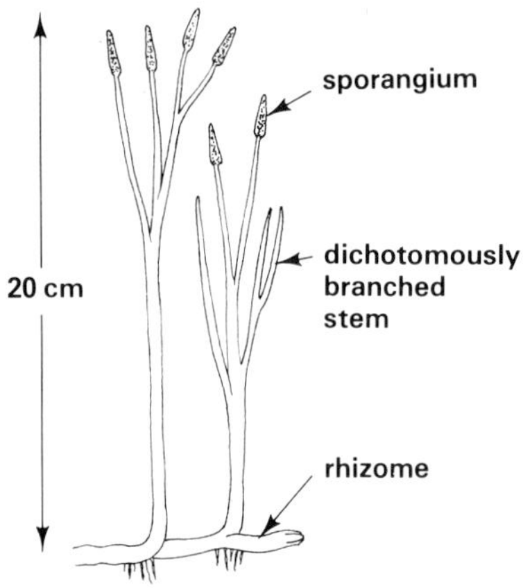

Psilophytes were the earliest vascular terrestrial plants. None survive today

Living invertebrate animals which form similar burrows are worm-like creatures. They use their hydrostatic skeleton to bore through mud and soil (Chapter 26). It is likely that the fossil burrows were formed by animals of this kind. Precambrian rocks dated as 6·8–5·8 × 10^2 million years old contain fossils which resemble **jellyfish** and **annelids**. Fragments of fossil invertebrate skeletons have also been found in rocks of the late Precambrian period. However, it is impossible to say to which group of invertebrates they belong. These earliest animals probably lived near the bottom of the oceans where they fed on particles of organic debris suspended in the water or deposited on the mud.

By the end of the **Cambrian** period, a wide variety of invertebrate groups had evolved. Some later became extinct, others have living descendants. One of the groups resembled **sponges**, another looked like **molluscs**. Another of the groups were **agnathans** (jawless fishes) which fed by ingesting particles filtered from the water through their gills. The plant life which existed at the time resembled **algae**. Some are single cells, others multicellular. They enriched the oceans with oxygen and detritus which may have stimulated evolution of the range of consumer organisms. During the **Ordovician** period, the first **bryophytes** appeared.

FIG. 24.6 (b) *T S stem of* Rhynia major (B&B)

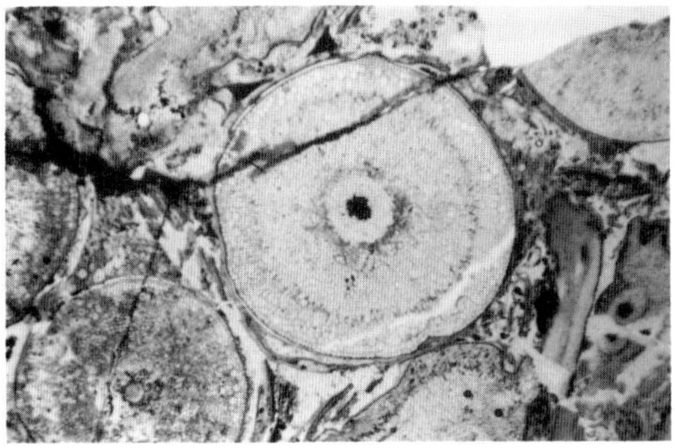

FIG. 24.7 *Tree-sized pteridophytes, now extinct*

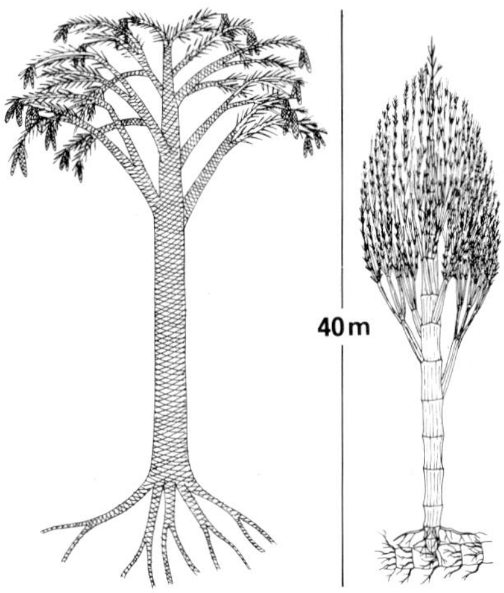

In the **Silurian** period, the first **jawed fishes** evolved, giving these animals a wide choice of food. It may have been the reason for the greater variety of fish which lived in the succeeding **Devonian** period. At this time the first vascular land plants had appeared. They were **psilophytes**, a group of extinct pteridophytes (Fig. 24.6) which most likely grew in soil covered with a shallow layer of water. As plants began to make their way on to land, invertebrates such as **annelid worms** and **arthropods** probably followed.

Amphibians were well-established by the **Carboniferous** period. Many were fairly large, omnivorous animals which fed on the evolving terrestrial plant and animal life. They used water for fertilisation and embryo development as do living members of this group (Chapter 27). Later amphibians were smaller and consequently less noticeable to predatory vertebrates which were beginning to emerge. It was from the smaller amphibians that present-day amphibians probably descended. At this time, vascular land plants were abundant. They included many of the larger extinct **pteridophytes** such as the giant horsetails and tree ferns (Fig. 24.7). Primitive **spermatophytes** called the pteridosperms had also evolved by this time. Some of them secreted resin which attracted terrestrial insects. Some of the insects have become fossilised in amber formed from the resin.

The earliest known **reptiles** appeared in the **Permian** period. Like living reptiles, they probably did not depend on water for reproduction and were able to colonise the land quickly. Here they preyed on and competed with the larger amphibians. Most were lizard-like and some had extremely large dorsal fins (Fig. 24.8). In the **Triassic** period, they were replaced by the **dinosaurs** which survived well into the **Cretaceous** period, over $1{\cdot}5 \times 10^2$ million years later. They were the most successful of terrestrial vertebrates to evolve up to this time and they exploited every ecological niche. Some, such as the **pterodactyls** were the first known vertebrates to fly (Fig. 24.9). Other dinosaurs were awesome predators, while some were herbivores of enormous size (Fig. 24.10). Some people believe that one of the reasons for the success of the dinosaurs was because they were warm-blooded. Rocks of the Triassic period also contain fossils of small animals which clearly had mammalian features. During the **Jurassic** period, the terrestrial vegetation included a wide range of **gymnosperms**. It was at this time that the first known **angiosperms** appeared. Although the dinosaurs still remained dominant among the terrestrial vertebrates, **birds** and **egg-laying mammals** began to emerge.

FIG. 24.8 *A pelycosaur* Dimetrodon *one of the earliest known reptiles*

FIG. 24.10 (a) Tyrannosaurus, *a predatory dinosaur, and* (b) Brontosaurus, *a herbivore*

FIG. 24.9 *A pterodactyl*

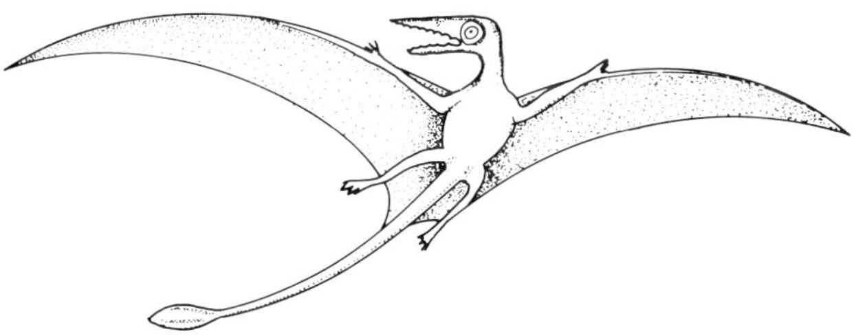

The dinosaurs became extinct in the **Cretaceous** period. There has been much speculation as to the cause of their demise. One suggestion is that their numbers probably outgrew the carrying capacity of their environment. By then a variety of **placental mammals** had evolved, including what is thought to be man's ancestors. The diversity of angiosperms also increased at this time.

The variety of **pollinating insects** which evolved in the subsequent **Tertiary** period reflects the fact that **spermatophytes** became the dominant vegetation on land at the time. Simultaneously there was an increase in the variety of birds and terrestrial mammals.

The major phases of evolution described to date are summarised in Table 24.1.

Table 24.1 Summary of the main phases of evolution from the fossil record.

Millions of years	Era	Period	Fossils
	CENOZOIC	Quaternary	Human
	CENOZOIC	Tertiary	Diverse mammals, birds and insects. Angiosperms dominant on land.
1×10^2	MESOZOIC	Cretaceous	First placental mammals; extinction of dinosaurs. Gymnosperms decreasing; diverse angiosperms.
	MESOZOIC	Jurassic	Dinosaurs abundant; first birds and egg-laying mammals. Diverse gymnosperms; first angiosperms.
2×10^2	MESOZOIC	Triassic	First dinosaurs; reptiles dominant; early mammals. First gymnosperms.
	PALAEOZOIC	Permian	Early reptiles. Pteridosperms extinct.
3×10^2	PALAEOZOIC	Carboniferous	Diverse amphibians; first reptiles and insects. Pteridosperms, giant horsetails and tree ferns.
	PALAEOZOIC	Devonian	Diverse jawed fish; first amphibians. First pteridophytes (psilophytes).
4×10^2	PALAEOZOIC	Silurian	Jawed fish. Bryophytes established.
	PALAEOZOIC	Ordovician	Jawless fish. First bryophytes.
5×10^2	PALAEOZOIC	Cambrian	Diverse invertebrates including sponges and molluscs. Diverse algae.
6×10^2 7×10^2 3×10^3	ARCHAEOZOIC	Precambrian	Jellyfish and annelids; fragments of invertebrate skeletons. Bacteria and blue-green algae. Worm burrows and tracks. Stromatolites.

3. EVOLUTION OF MAN

Primates of the early **Cenozoic** era were small, squirrel-like, tree-dwelling creatures. They had binocular vision and used their forelimbs for grasping. Their descendants, from which man evolved, moved from the trees to the forest floor to forage. These creatures had relatively small brains and walked with their knuckles touching the ground. Knuckle-walking enabled them to move while grasping sticks and stones in their hands. The sticks may have been used for threat or self protection and the stones for cracking nuts. Later they began to live at the edges of forests adjacent to open country.

Fossils from East Africa show that a man-like primate called *Australopithecus* lived 4×10^6 years ago. The shape of his pelvic girdle indicates that he had a stooping posture and walked on his hind legs. His brain was probably bigger than that of his predecessors, because his cranium was larger. The presence of small heaps of smooth pebbles with the fossils suggest that *Australopithecus* used them, possibly for hunting.

The first human, *Homo erectus*, appeared about $1{\cdot}5 \times 10^6$ years ago. Fossils of this primate suggest that he had an upright posture and he used more sophisticated hunting tools, such as spears made from pointed sticks. Fossils of *Homo sapiens* in the form of **Neanderthal man** are $1{\cdot}0 \times 10^5$ years old. He had a large projecting lower jaw and a recessed forehead. However, his cranium was slightly bigger than that of modern man. He used flint flakes, probably for opening carcasses and cutting up flesh.

Modern man, *Homo sapiens sapiens*, arrived on the scene about 40 000 years ago. Needles, awls and spearheads have been found with human

FIG. 24.11 *Main phases in man's evolution* (after Washburn 1978)

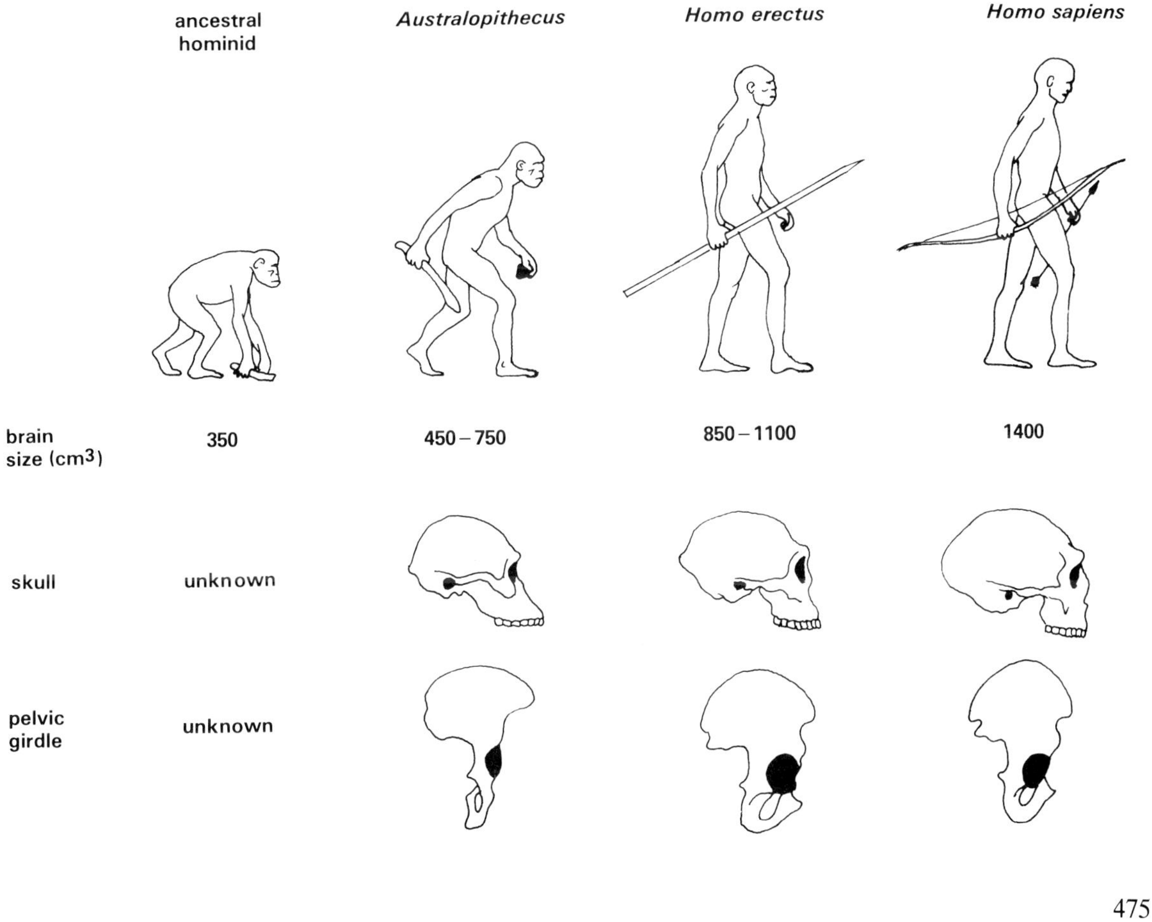

fossils of this age. It would therefore appear that hunting was an important part of his life, an activity requiring socialisation. Even greater social development was required when the transition from hunting to farming began some 10 000 years ago. The ability to construct boats and shelters enabled the growing human population to spread. Such activities require the ability to communicate. The development of language played a vital role in this respect. Man's capacity to adapt to and manipulate the environment have been potent forces in his evolution. The main phases of human evolution are shown in Figure 24.11.

24.2.2 Affinities

All living organisms have common features. Some have features which are virtually identical to those of another organism. In other words, they have a close **affinity** to each other and for this reason they are classified in the same group (Chapters 25–27). Among the features which indicate that all living organisms are related by descent are **anatomical**, **physiological**, **embryological**, **immunological**, **biochemical** and **behavioural** affinities. The relationship is more reliably established when a number of the features are common.

1. ANATOMICAL AFFINITIES

When the anatomy of various animals, which superficially appear to be unrelated, is compared, similarities may be evident which suggest a common ancestry. During the course of evolution, vertebrate limbs have become adapted to serve a variety of purposes. For example, the forelimbs of a whale are used as paddles, the forelimbs of birds for flight and the hands of humans for grasping and manipulating objects. Even so, the limbs of all vertebrates develop from the same embryonic tissues and fit a common plan known as the **pentadactyl limb** (Fig. 24.12). For this reason they are called **homologous structures**.

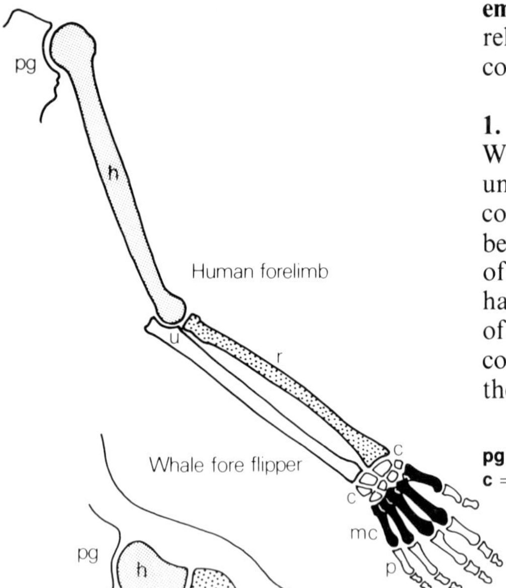

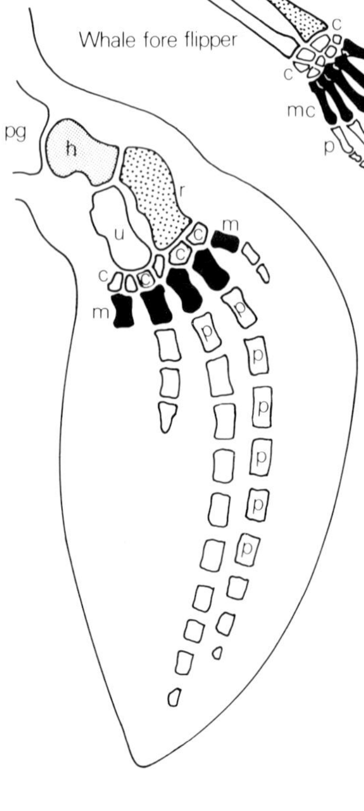

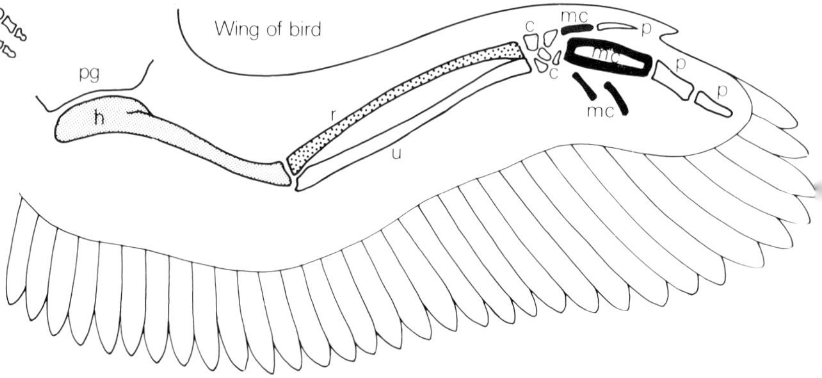

FIG. 24.12 *Forelimbs of* (a) *man,* (b) *whale and* (c) *bird*

pg = **pectoral girdle** **h** = **humerus** **r** = **radius** **u** = **ulna**
c = **carpals** **mc** = **metacarpals** **p** = **phalanges**

Insect mouthparts vary in function and appear to be quite different in structure. The mouthparts of locusts are used for biting vegetation, those of butterflies and bees for sucking nectar, whilst those of fleas are used for piercing skin and siphoning blood. Yet they all have a common structural plan (section 26.7.4).

Some animals have **vestigial structures** which in other related creatures are fully developed. For instance, whales have pelvic girdles but lack hind limbs. This suggests that whales in common with other vertebrates have evolved from the same ancestors.

The examples given above show how structures of similar origin have become adapted for different roles in various creatures. They illustrate **adaptive radiation** and are examples of **divergent evolution**. There are instances where structures of quite different origin have evolved to carry out similar functions. The wings of insects and birds are both organs used for flight yet they do not have the same origin. They are **analogous structures** which illustrate that **convergent evolution** can also occur.

2. PHYSIOLOGICAL AFFINITIES

The composition of the **body fluids** of animals, both aquatic and terrestrial, is fundamentally similar. Furthermore, the composition of body fluids resembles that of sea water in which life is thought to have originated (Table 24.2). Transport of oxygen to respiring tissues is often enhanced by the presence of oxygen-binding pigments in the blood (Chapter 9). **Haemoglobin** is found in all vertebrates and in many invertebrates.

Table 24.2 Concentrations of ions in seawater and in the body fluids of a variety of aquatic and terrestrial organisms (from Hollingsworth and Bowler 1972)

	Concentration (m mol l^{-1})				
	Na^+	K^+	Ca^{2+}	Mg^{2+}	Cl^-
seawater	460	10	10	52	540
squid blood	460	24	11	57	590
sea-urchin blood	444	10	10	50	522
crab blood	468	12	18	24	524
crayfish blood	142	4	8	4	140
mammalian serum	145	6	3	2	116

3. IMMUNOLOGICAL AFFINITIES

In 1904, George Nuttall devised a procedure based on immunological methods for determining the relationship between animals. When, for example, the serum of a human is injected into an experimental animal, the latter forms **antibodies** against the proteins in human serum (Chapter 9). If the serum from the experimental animal is then mixed with human serum, the antibodies combine with **serum proteins** which caused their production to form a precipitate. Should the serum from the experimental animal be mixed instead with serum from another animal, the amount of precipitate formed is a measure of the affinity between the human and the other animal. Such methods suggest that humans are more closely related to the chimpanzee than to other primates (Table 24.3).

Table 24.3 Precipitin reactions with human serum (from Marshall 1978)

SERUM	PERCENTAGE PRECIPITATION
human	100
gorilla	64
baboon	29
deer	7
kangaroo	0

FIG. 24.13 *Computer predicted relationship between a variety of organisms based on differences in the amino acid sequence of their cytochrome* C (after Ayala 1978)

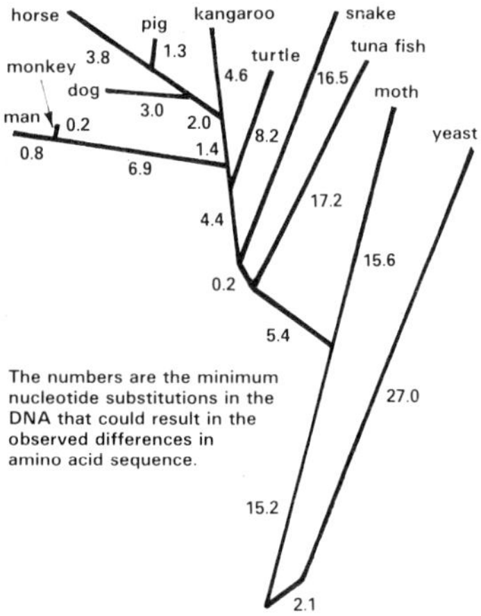

FIG. 24.14 *Chimpanzee suckling its young* (London Zoological Society)

4. BIOCHEMICAL AFFINITIES

When the sequence of amino acids in **haemoglobin** from different animals is determined, there is less difference between man and chimpanzees than that of man and other primates. This again points to man and chimpanzees having a common ancestor more recently than man and other primates.

Another protein which has been studied in this respect is **cytochrome C**, a respiratory co-enzyme (Chapter 5). The amino acid sequence of cytochrome C has been determined for organisms as diverse as bacteria, yeasts, invertebrates and vertebrates. The variations are caused by slight differences in the nucleotide sequence of DNA which codes the production of the co-enzyme (Chapter 6). In this way it is possible to compute the minimum number of nucleotide differences between the genes which code the synthesis of cytochrome C in various organisms. A comparison of the differences shows how closely the organisms are related (Fig. 24.13). The results agree well with the fossil record.

5. EMBRYOLOGICAL AFFINITIES

Examination of the embryos of vertebrates, which as adults are very different, reveals similarities in development. The shapes and positions of the brain, eyes, nostrils, limbs and tail are comparable in animals as remotely related as fish, amphibians, reptiles, birds and mammals. At some stage in development each of the embryos has gill slits or pouches to which deoxygenated blood is pumped from the heart. With the exception of fish, the gill slits later degenerate. Annelids and molluscs also have a common embryonic form called the **trochophore larva** (Chapter 26).

6. BEHAVIOURAL AFFINITIES

Organisms whose patterns of behaviour are similar are more likely to be closely related than those whose behaviour is very different.

Jane Goodall in Tanzania has observed many aspects of chimpanzee behaviour. Apart from man, chimpanzees are the most habitual users of simple tools. They use sticks for attacking, exploring, poking and teasing. They collect ants and termites using small twigs and blades of grass. They clean themselves with leaves and use stones to crack nuts. The play behaviour of adult and juvenile chimpanzees resembles that of humans. Before it is weaned, a young chimpanzee is also held by its parents in a way comparable to the way in which human babies are nursed (Fig. 24.14). The observations further substantiate the claim that chimpanzees and humans have common ancestors.

24.2.3 Geographical distribution

Each of the main land masses of the world has its characteristic plant and animal life. Marsupials are confined to Australia and South America, elephants to Africa and India.

FIG. 24.15 *World-wide distribution of species of mammals and birds* (from Marshall 1978)

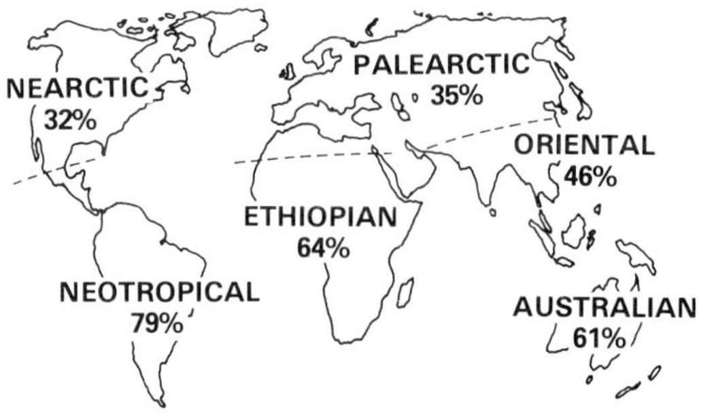

The figures show the percentage of the world's total number of species endemic to each area

Wallace was one of the first naturalists to survey the world-wide distribution of birds and mammals. He noted that there are six major land masses separated from each other by natural barriers such as mountain ranges and oceans. The number of species native to Africa, Australia and South America is about twice as great as in Asia, Europe and North America (Fig. 24.15). It is thought that the first mammals evolved in Asia and migrated into Africa and Europe. From here they spread into Australia and the Americas using bridges of land which at that time connected the continents. **Continental drift** (movement of the land masses) caused Australia and South America to become cut off in the Cretaceous period (Fig. 24.16). It is assumed that placental mammals were just beginning to evolve at this time and explains why many of the mammals in these areas are marsupials. Africa and North America became separated from Europe later on, by which time a large range of placental mammals had evolved. They are more successful than marsupials and therefore they are more prevalent in Asia, Africa, the Americas and Europe. Because Asia did not drift apart from Africa, migration is still possible between these land masses. It is the reason why elephants are found in both Africa and Asia.

FIG. 24.16 *Continental drift*

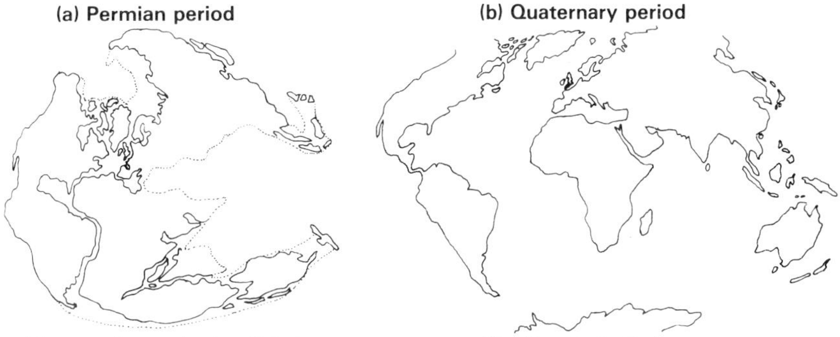

24.3 How evolution came about

There have been many attempts to explain how life evolved into the enormous variety of living organisms which now inhabit the earth. The theories of **Lamarck**, **Darwin** and **Wallace** are particularly important.

24.3.1 Lamarckism

Jean-Baptiste Lamarck (1774–1829), a French naturalist, was the first modern biologist to propose how the variety of living organisms has evolved. His theory was based on two main premises:

(i) That organisms **acquired new features** because of an *inner need*.

(ii) That the **acquired features are inherited** by future generations.

Lamarck's ideas are often illustrated with reference to the evolution of the giraffe's long neck. According to Lamarck, the ancestor of the giraffe was a short-necked creature whose *inner need* to eat the leaves of trees caused it to stretch higher and higher so that its neck became progressively longer. The offspring of these animals inherited the longer neck so they could feed in the same way.

Living organisms may acquire new characteristics during their life time. For example, a blacksmith acquires large biceps because of the nature of his work. However, the children of a blacksmith have biceps which are normal in size. It is therefore evident that acquired characteristics are not inherited.

24.3.2 Darwinism

FIG. 24.17 (a) *Charles Darwin*

Charles Darwin (1809–1882) was well acquainted with the variety of life. Between 1831 and 1836 he worked as a naturalist on HMS *Beagle* on its voyage around the world (Fig. 24.17). He made careful records of the diversity and distribution of living organisms, particularly in South America, the Pacific Islands and Australia. Darwin was also a keen geologist. He made an extensive collection of fossils from various parts of the world.

After many years of observation and experiment, Darwin's theory of evolution was presented in a paper to the Linnaean Society of London in 1858. At the same meeting, a paper written by **Alfred Russel Wallace**, an English naturalist who had recently explored the East Indies and Australia, was also read. Darwin and Wallace had arrived independently at the same conclusions. Darwin's theory of evolution, illustrated by numerous examples, was published in 1859 in *The Origin of Species by Means of Natural Selection.* It was based on the following observations and deductions:

(i) Most organisms have the potential to produce very large numbers of progeny. For example, a female cod lays about 85×10^6 eggs in a season, a frog $1–2 \times 10^3$ eggs, an orchid produces $1{\cdot}7 \times 10^6$ seeds. There must be intense **competition**, because the numbers of organisms remain fairly stable.

FIG. 24.17 (b) *Darwin's voyage in HMS Beagle*

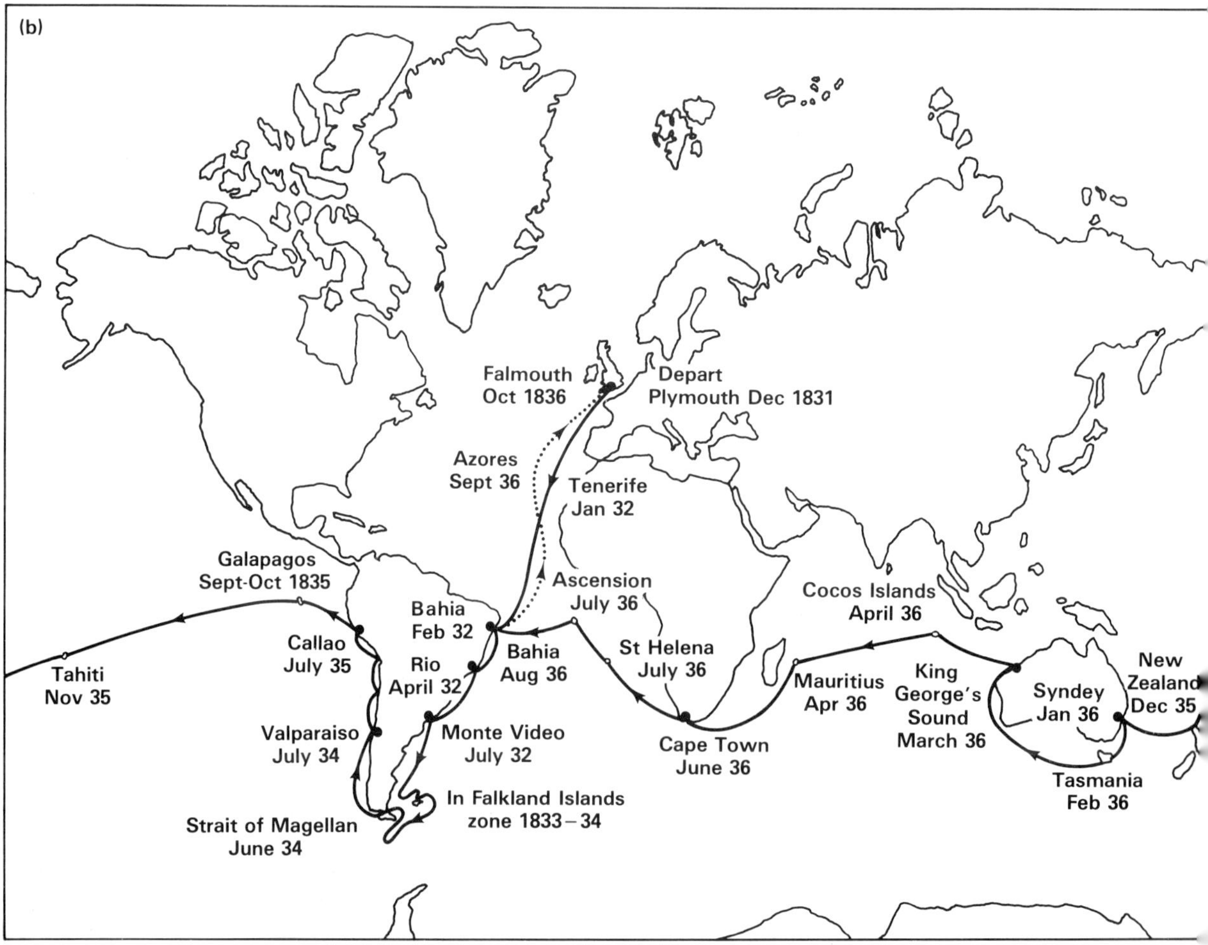

(ii) All organisms, even members of the same species, **vary**. You have only to look at your classmates to notice that this is so!
(iii) The progeny which are most likely to survive competition are those which have the combination of features which enable them to cope best with their environment. This is called **survival of the fittest by natural selection**.
(iv) The features favoured by natural selection are **inherited**. Darwin's interpretation as to how the long neck of the giraffe was evolved would go something like this:

Among the ancestors of the giraffe were animals with a range of neck lengths. Those with long necks could browse on the leaves of trees. In this way they could also avoid the competition with other herbivores which ate vegetation growing nearer the ground. The short-necked ancestors succumbed to the competition and became extinct. The long-necked variety survived and gave rise to long-necked progeny which are the ancestors of the modern giraffe.

24.3.3 Variation

Darwin had no idea of the origin and causes of variation (Chapters 6 and 7). Nor did he know how characteristics were inherited. Mendel's work (Chapter 23), though published in Darwin's life-time, was neglected until 1900, well after Darwin's death.

Inheritable variation is of two kinds, **continuous** and **discontinuous**. Continuous variation is caused by the random assortment of many genes which affect some characteristics such as height. Discontinuous variation occurs where two alternative forms of a gene exist (Chapter 23). The discovery of the nucleic acids and their functions have made it possible to explain the causes of discontinuous variation (Chapter 6). Changes in the genetic code are known as **gene mutations**. All genes mutate, but some do so more frequently than others. **Chromosome mutations** are caused by an alteration in the number of chromosomes or by fragmentation of chromosomes. Because they are inherited, mutations which occur in sex cells are more important than somatic mutations.

1. GENE MUTATIONS

Proteins perform numerous functions in living organisms (Chapter 3), so they determine many of an organism's characteristics. The role played by a protein is determined largely by its **primary structure**, the sequence of amino acids in its molecule. The primary structure affects the three-dimensional structure, the **conformation** of the protein molecule. It is the conformation which determines the protein's function. For example, the type of substrate which binds to the active centre of an enzyme depends on the conformation of the enzyme molecule. If the primary structure of the enzyme is abnormal, its conformation may be so altered that substrate molecules cannot bind to the active centre.

The sequence of amino acids in proteins is precisely regulated by the **genetic code** (Chapter 6). Any change in the code, a **gene mutation**, will cause abnormal proteins to be made. Sometimes the change is harmless. It may even be beneficial. If this is so, the new gene may confer an advantage on its possessor. As a consequence, it may increase in frequency in a population, especially if it is a dominant gene. Usually gene mutations are harmful, because the abnormal proteins which are synthesised are unable to perform their normal functions. Such individuals may not survive to reproductive age, so the mutation is not passed to the next generation.

Gene mutations are the cause of **haemophilia** and **sickle-cell anaemia** in humans (Chapter 9). Oddly enough, people who are heterozygous for sickle-cell anaemia are resistant to malaria, so it is more likely that they will survive to childbearing age than normal individuals. It is for this reason that the gene for sickle-cell anaemia is frequent among people who live in countries where malaria is endemic.

2. CHROMOSOME MUTATIONS

During meiosis, one or more chromosomes may break. The fragments of broken chromosomes can behave in a variety of ways:
(i) they may become lost (**deletion**),
(ii) they may become attached to the end of another chromosome (**translocation**),
(iii) they may become turned round and rejoin the chromosome from which they broke off (**inversion**),
(iv) they may become inserted into another chromosome (**duplication**).
Clearly, these changes may alter the complement of genetic material in the gametes.

Exposure to ultraviolet light is one of the causes of chromosome fragmentation. Nucleic acids strongly absorb UV light. New varieties of moulds such as *Penicillium* are produced by irradiation with UV light. Many new strains of crop plants have been developed by exposing their seeds to γ radiation.

Sometimes a pair of homologous chromosomes fails to separate in meiosis, giving rise to gametes with one chromosome less and one chromosome more than normal. The progeny formed from such gametes are called **polysomics**, having fewer or more chromosomes than normal. **Down's syndrome** in humans is caused by an extra chromosome (Chapter 7).

In other instances, whole sets of homologous chromosomes do not separate in meiosis, so that diploid gametes are produced. Fusion with a normal haploid gamete gives rise to progeny with a triploid chromosome number. This condition is called polyploidy and is more often observed in plants than in animals. **Polyploids** are usually more vigorous than their diploid counterparts.

An example of how polyploidy can give rise to new species of plants is seen in the cord grass, *Spartina*. In 1870, a new variety of cord grass was observed growing in Southampton Water. It was named *Spartina townsendii*. Before this time two species of cord grass, *S. maritima* and *S. alterniflora*, were known in the locality. It is thought that *S. townsendii* is a polyploid hybrid of the other two species (Fig. 24.18). In the past hundred

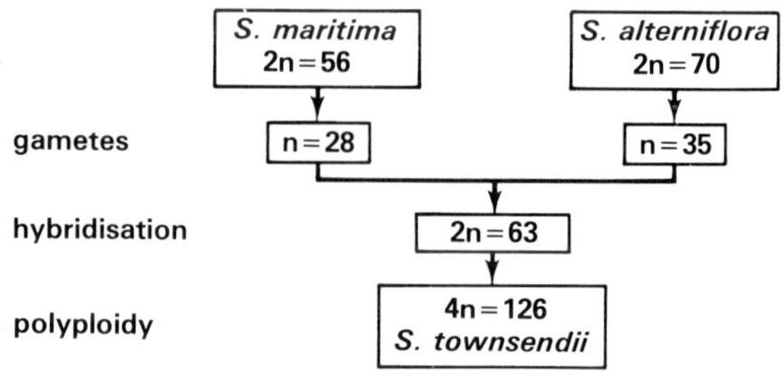

FIG. 24.18 *Evolution of a new species of cord grass* Spartina townsendii

years it has spread to many other parts of the coast of England. Its vigorous growth is of great help in building up mud flats which can be reclaimed from the sea to provide useful farmland (section 29.2.1).

24.3.4 Selection

Darwin saw the important role of **selection** as an evolutionary force. In *The Origin of Species by Natural Selection* he described many examples of both natural and artificial selection.

1. NATURAL SELECTION

A number of experimental and field studies carried out this century have provided an insight into how selection works in natural conditions. One of the first studies was of the peppered moth, *Biston betularia*. Collections of preserved peppered moths show that up to the middle of the nineteenth century the only variety known had the speckled, light colour of pepper dust. In 1845, a black moth of the same species was caught in Manchester. By the end of the eighteen-hundreds, the black variety made up 98 per cent of the population of the moth in the Manchester area.

The change in frequency of the gene for black colour coincides with the spread of heavy industry in the locality. Before the Industrial Revolution, the air in and around Manchester was clean. The bark of trees growing in the area was covered with lichens. Against such a background the speckled variety of the moth is camouflaged (Fig. 24.19). Insectivorous birds

FIG. 24.19 *Non-melanic and melanic varieties of the peppered moth* (Biophotos)

presumably had difficulty in seeing it, so the moth had a good chance of surviving and reproducing. The soot and smoke generated by heavy industry polluted the air and was deposited on the bark of trees. Many of the lichens were killed by the high concentrations of sulphur dioxide in the atmosphere. Against a dark background the speckled moth would be seen easily and taken by insect-eating birds. In contrast, the black form would be less conspicuous. It would be less likely to be taken as part of the diet of insectivorous birds. Consequently its survival was favoured. It was for this reason that the gene for black colour gradually became more frequent in subsequent generations.

To prove that natural selection was the cause of the changed gene frequency, Dr H. B. D. Kettlewell bred large stocks of the two varieties of the peppered moth, which were marked and then released in two areas:
(i) in polluted Birmingham where over 90 per cent of the peppered moth population was the black variety, and
(ii) in an unpolluted rural area of Dorset where none of the peppered moths was black.
He observed and filmed insectivorous birds such as robins, redstarts and hedge sparrows feeding in the two localities. The birds were particularly

severe on the variety of moth which was not camouflaged by its background. Kettlewell also recaptured the surviving marked moths (Table 24.4). The experimental fieldwork confirmed that natural selection was the cause of the increase in frequency of the gene for blackness among peppered moths in industrialised areas. This is an example of **industrial melanism**. It has since been observed among many other types of moth in Britain, Europe and the USA.

Table 24.4 Natural selection of the peppered moth in two localities (from Marshall 1978)

	NON-MELANIC	MELANIC
Dorset, 1955 (unpolluted)		
released	496	473
recaptured	62	30
% recaptured	12·5	6·3
Birmingham, 1953 (polluted)		
released	137	447
recaptured	18	123
% recaptured	13·1	27·5

Another example of natural selection which has come to light even more recently is seen in the flora of disused mine tips. Professor A. D. Bradshaw and his colleagues have studied the vegetation of such tips in North Wales, where the spoil contains high concentrations of heavy metals such as copper, tin and zinc. Even though the tips are over fifty years old, little vegetation grows on them (Fig. 24.20). However, a few species of plants have slowly colonised the tips. They are often called **metallophytes** (Chapter 13) because of their ability to grow in soil containing high concentrations of metal ions. Grasses such as *Agrostis tenuis* and *Festuca ovina* are exceptionally tolerant of heavy metals. It has been proved by experiment that their tolerance is genetically controlled. The frequency of the gene for tolerance to heavy metals is much higher among metallophytes than in

FIG. 24.20 (a) *Spoil heaps of an abandoned lead mine at Cwmystwyth, Wales* (b) *A metallophyte* Festuca ovina *growing on the spoil*

(a) (b)

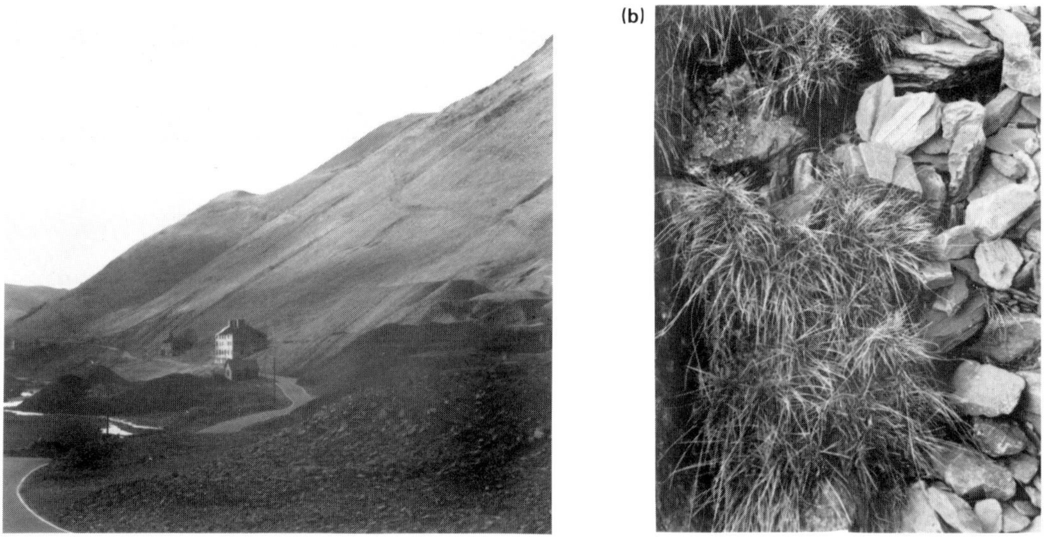

populations of the same species growing in normal soils. The vegetation of spoil heaps has therefore been naturally selected from non-tolerant populations of plants growing nearby.

2. ARTIFICIAL SELECTION

For centuries man has selected livestock and crop plants because they have desirable features such as resistance to disease and increased yield. Where this happens it is called artificial selection. In *The Origin of Species*, Charles Darwin quoted many examples of how livestock had been improved by artificial selection.

A well-documented example of the influence of man in selection is seen in the evolution of wheat. In wild wheats, the ripe ear is brittle and breaks up to release each seed-containing spikelet separately. It brings about efficient dispersal of the seeds. This type of wheat is of little use for cultivation, because the ear breaks off when the grain is harvested. Over the past 10 000 years or so man has selected non-brittle varieties of wheat for agriculture. One of the first was Einkorn wheat, *Triticum monococcum*, from Iran with a diploid number (2n) of 14 (genome *AA*). It was widely cultivated in Neolithic times. Einkorn wheat is, however, a low-yielding variety, so it was later replaced by Emmer wheat, *Triticum dicoccum*, a tetraploid with a chromosome number of 28 (genome *AABB*). Half of its chromosomes (*AA*) are thought to have come from Einkorn wheat. The other half (*BB*) probably came from a grass *Agropyron*. Emmer wheat was grown for thousands of years by the Ancient Egyptians. It is still cultivated on a small scale in a few parts of India and Russia. One of its disadvantages is that it is difficult to remove its seeds from the chaff in threshing. For this reason 'naked' wheats have been selected in more recent times. Bread wheat, *Triticum aestivum* (2n = 42, genome *AABBDD*) is the most widely grown naked wheat today. It is a hexaploid, probably a hybrid of Emmer wheat and the grass *Aegilops* (Fig. 24.21).

FIG. 24.21 *Evolution of bread wheat* Triticum aestivum

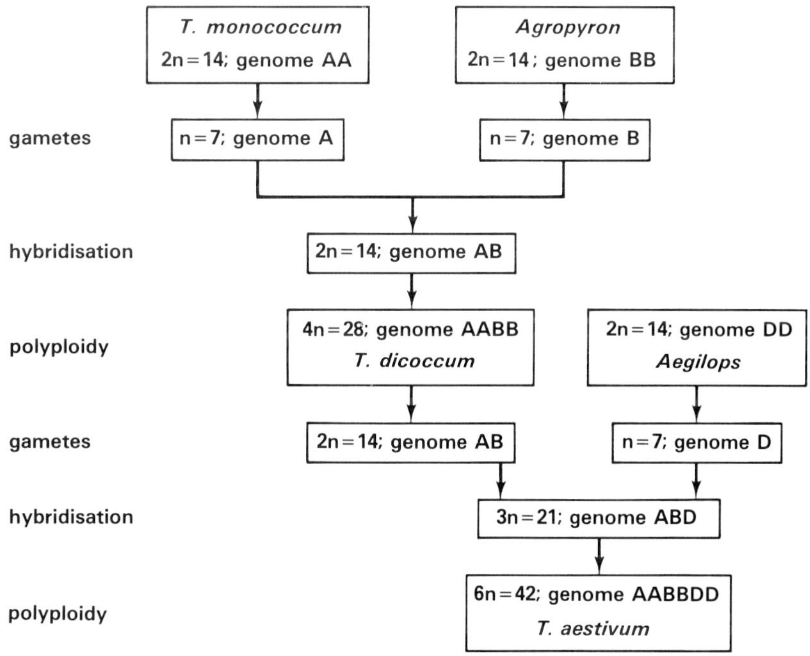

24.3.5 Isolating mechanisms

A **species** can be defined as *a natural population, the individuals of which are actually or potentially capable of breeding with each other to produce fertile progeny, and which do not interbreed with members of other species*. Not all individuals in a natural population have the same chance of breeding with one another. Every species is thus made up of a number of breeding sub-units called **demes**. When demes become isolated, they may in time lose their ability to breed with other demes of the same species. They may then be thought of as new species. There are several ways in which isolation can occur.

1. GEOGRAPHICAL ISOLATION

One of the most striking examples of how new species can arise when demes become spatially separated was observed by Darwin. On his journey in HMS *Beagle*, Darwin visited the volcanic islands of the Galapagos archipelago, west of Ecuador. He noticed that there were just twenty-four species of birds on the islands, most of which he had not seen on the South American mainland. Fourteen of the species were finches belonging to four genera. In his account of the journey in *Voyage of the Beagle*, Darwin referred to the finches as follows:

> 'One might really fancy that from the original paucity of birds on this archipelago, one species had been taken and modified to different ends.'

The species of Darwin's finches can be distinguished by their feeding habits and the shapes of their beaks. Finches are usually ground-dwelling, seed-eating birds. However, on the Galapagos Islands the finches eat a variety of foods (Fig. 24.22). Some are seed-eaters, others feed on cacti. Of

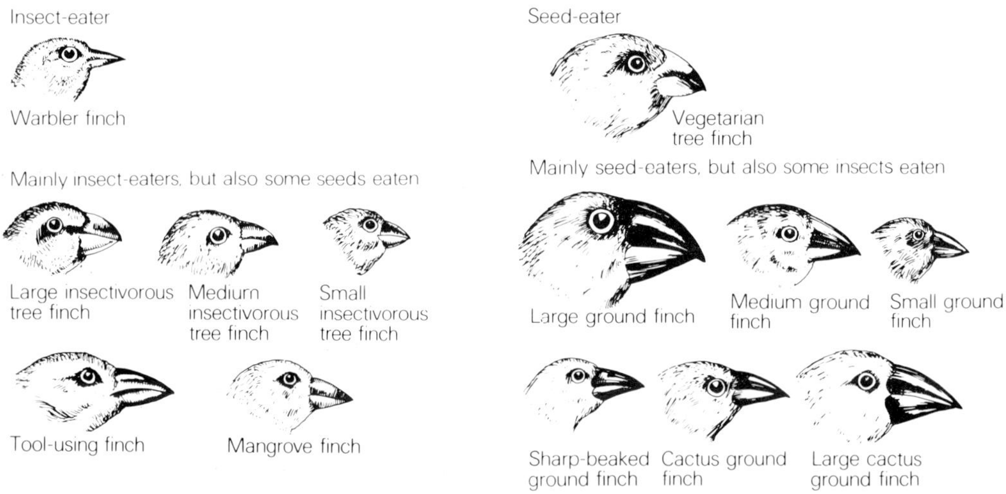

FIG. 24.22 *Galapagos finches*

the insectivorous finches, one feeds like a woodpecker. Subsequent studies of the anatomy and reproductive behaviour of the finches have revealed the supposed evolutionary relationship between the species (Fig. 24.23).

It is assumed that sometime after the Galapagos Islands were formed by volcanic eruption, seed-eating finches flew across from the mainland of nearby South America. The vegetation on the newly formed islands was sparse, so seeds were scarce and the finches were forced to adopt new eating

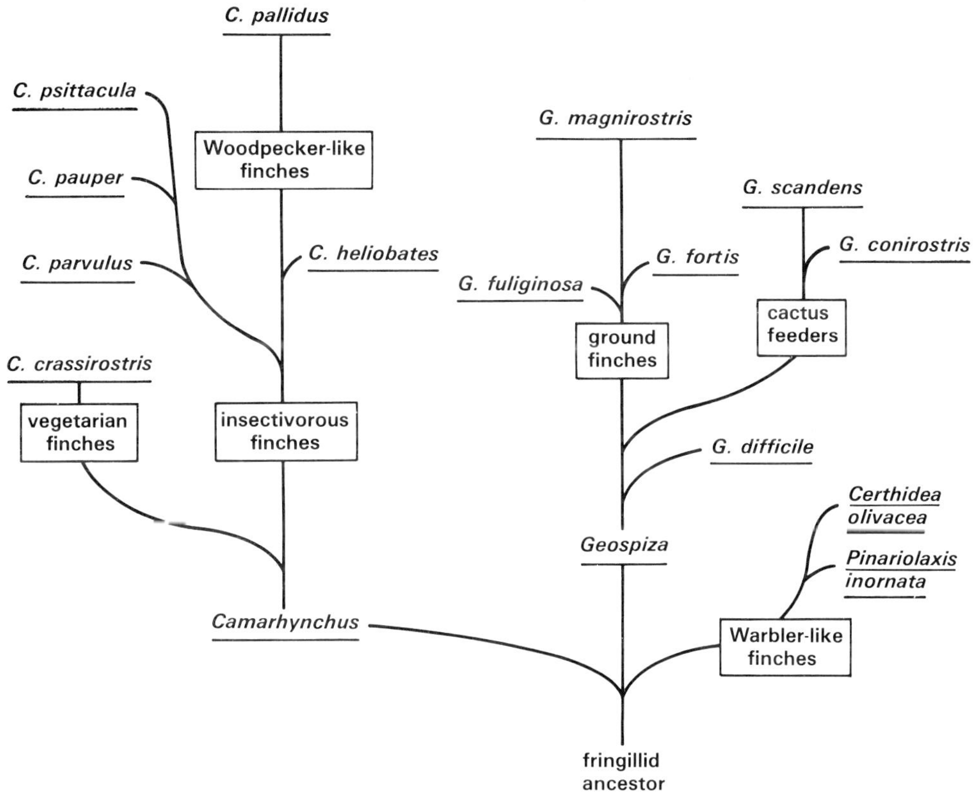

FIG. 24.23 *Probable evolutionary relationships of Galapagos finches* (after Lack, 1947)

habits. This is another example of **adaptive radiation**. In time the demes of finches became sufficiently different in their general habits that they no longer interbred. As a result, fourteen new species gradually evolved from the single species which first colonised the islands.

Comparable patterns of evolution have been observed in island populations in Britain. The mainland, Hebridean and Shetland forms of the British wren are slightly different in colour and wing length and do not interbreed. At the moment they are considered to be varieties of the same species. The Orkney vole exists as five sub-species on different islands off the coast of Scotland.

2. REPRODUCTIVE ISOLATION

Even when related demes live in the same locality, they do not always breed with each other. The causes of this are twofold:

(i) PRE-FERTILISATION

(a) **Seasonal barriers**. Many flowering plants and mammals reproduce seasonally because of different responses to daylength (Chapters 19 and 23). It is probable that some species have evolved from demes which reproduce at a different time of the year from other demes in a population. For example, viable hybrids can be obtained by crossing *Pinus radiata* and *Pinus attenuata*. However, they do not normally occur naturally because they produce pollen at slightly different times of the year.

(b) **Behavioural barriers**. The plumage of male finches living on the Galapagos Islands is so similar that it is difficult to identify the species to which they belong. However, female finches have no problems in identifying a male of the same species. During courtship the male passes food to the female in his beak. It is the shape of the male's beak which enables the female to recognise her mate. In this way interbreeding between demes is avoided.

(c) **Mechanical barriers**. The genitalia of male and female animals in related demes may be different in size. It is often assumed that this may prevent copulation. However, this has not been confirmed by observation.

An example of how a mechanical barrier can prevent interbreeding between related demes is seen in the orchid *Ophrys*. Its flowers are pollinated by male bees of the genus *Andrena*. The male bees are attracted to the flowers because they resemble female bees of the same genus. In attempting to copulate with the flowers, male bees become dusted with pollen. When the bees subsequently attempt mating with another flower of the same species, cross-pollination takes place. Transfer of pollen to other closely related species of orchid is avoided because their flowers do not resemble female bees of the genus *Andrena*.

(d) **Physiological barriers**. Many related demes of flowering plants are reproductively mature at the same time and there are no spatial, behavioural or mechanical barriers. Pollination may occur, yet they do not interbreed. The reason is that the stigma and style of the recipient flower does not provide suitable physiological conditions for germination of pollen grains from a related deme.

(ii) POST-FERTILISATION. Some demes intermate, but do not produce viable progeny. Among the reasons for this are:

(a) **Hybrid inviability**. Fertilisation and embryo development occur when cross-mating takes place between many species. However the progeny are not viable. The reasons for this are not fully known.

(b) **Hybrid sterility**. Mules are produced by crossing a horse with a donkey. Because the chromosomes from the parents do not pair at meiosis, the gametes of mules are non-viable. It is for this reason that mules are sterile. In this way the genes of horses and donkeys remain isolated.

24.3.6 The formation of species

Once a deme has been **isolated** from the rest of its species, **natural selection** acts on variants within the deme, changing the frequency of genes. The genomes of isolated demes may as a result become so different from the genomes of other demes that some degree of **sterility** exists. After prolonged isolation total sterility may develop, so that the isolated deme becomes a new species.

The stages in the formation of a new species are as follows:

(i) **variety**—a recognisable type within a deme,
(ii) **race**—members of partially isolated demes,
(iii) **sub-species**—partially fertile with original species,
(iv) **species**—infertile with original species.

The process is not irreverisble. Where it has not gone to stage (iv), interbreeding may take place if the barriers preventing it are removed.

Evolution is a controversial subject of which much is still to be learned. Darwin compared it with trying to unravel the story of a novel of which only one page was available with half the lines missing and in each line half the words missing. Shortly after the publication of *The Origin of Species*, Darwin was severely criticised by members of the Church who favoured the idea of Special Creation. However, in the hundred years since Darwin's death many new and important biological and geological discoveries have served to confirm his ideas of how the variety of life we see today has come into being.

Chapter 25

Variety of life: Micro-organisms and plants

Biological classification tries to make order and sense out of the great variety of living things. Biologists are constantly revising classifications and there is much argument and controversy on the subject of taxonomy. The following outline of micro-organisms and the plant kingdom and that of the animals in chapters 26 and 27 is a widely used system of classification with which most biologists are familiar.

25.1 Nomenclature and classification

Naming things is one of the fundamental functions of language. It enables us to identify objects in our surroundings and to tell other people about the objects we see. Stone-Age man identified animals that were important to him. He made elaborate cave paintings of the animals he hunted and the predators he avoided. The Ancient Greeks went a stage further. They divided things into large groups which had common features. Animals were distinguished from plants.

A problem with naming things, however, is the language used. An organism may have several different names, even in the same language, let alone the names given it by people who speak another language. For example, *man* in English may also be called *people* or *humans* or even *folk*. To overcome this problem in biology, Latin has been used to name living things.

The system of naming organisms used by biologists today was devised in the eighteenth century by Carolus Linnaeus, Professor of Medicine at the university of Uppsala in Sweden from 1741 to 1778. Linnaeus published several editions of *Systema naturae*. In his writings he used a **binomial system** which gives animals and plants two names. The first is the **generic name**, that is, the **genus** to which the organism belongs. A genus is a small group of closely related organisms. The second name is the **specific name**. A **species** may be defined as a group of very closely related organisms which interbreed and produce fertile offspring. *Homo sapiens* (*L*) is the binomial name for man. Including (*L*) after the specific name means that Linnaeus first described the organism by that name.

As well as naming organisms, biologists classify them. The branch of biology concerned with classifying organisms is **taxonomy**. Organisms can be classified merely for reference and filing. For example, all flowers with yellow petals can be grouped together. This is **artificial** classification. Alternatively, the system most useful to biologists is a **natural** classification in which closely related organisms are collected into groups. The largest of the groups are kingdoms. The simplest classification contains two kingdoms, **Animalia** and **Plantae**. The animal kingdom is subdivided into **phyla**, the plant kingdom into **divisions**. Phyla and divisions are sub-divided into **classes**, **orders** and **families**. Generally the smaller the group, the more closely related are the organisms in it. By closely related we mean organisms which have many fundamental features in common.

When choosing **diagnostic features** for classification, biologists look for features that are characteristic of the whole group. Superficial features such as colour are of little use in natural classifications. Crocuses, for example exist in white, yellow and blue-flowered forms yet they all belong to the same species. We must also beware of **analogous** structures that adapt basically different organisms to a similar habit. Bats, birds and

can increase the nitrogen content of soils, thereby promoting soil fertility (Chapter 29).

4. INDUSTRIAL USES OF BACTERIA

(a) MANUFACTURE OF DAIRY PRODUCTS

(i) **Butter** is prepared by churning cream, which causes fat globules in the cream to coalesce into granules. The liquid part of the cream, called buttermilk, is then drained off and the granules are compressed to make butter. In Britain nearly all butter is made from pasteurised milk in which the natural microflora is killed. However, the cream is sometimes soured by inoculating it with starter cultures of *Streptococcus lactis* and *Leuconostoc citrovorum*. The streptococci ferment milk sugar, lactose to lactic acid, while the leuconostocs produce volatile substances which give the butter flavour and aroma.

(ii) **Cheese**. Pasteurised milk is generally used in the commercial production of cheese. Starter cultures of *Streptococcus lactis* or *S. cremoris* are added to the milk, and changes in pH and texture are monitored as the milk is curdled by the bacteria. The enzyme rennin, in rennet prepared from calves' stomachs, is usually added. This speeds up curdling by coagulating the milk protein casein. Soft cheeses are made by allowing the liquid called whey to drain from the curd. In making hard cheeses, the curd is compressed. Common salt is mixed with the curd or applied to its surface to prevent the growth of undesirable micro-organisms and to add flavour.

(iii) **Yoghurt** was originally prepared from buttermilk produced in butter-making. In Britain it is now manufactured from pasteurised milk. In Eastern Europe and Asia, it is frequently made from the milk of goats, sheep and mares. The milk is inoculated with a mixed starter culture containing *Streptococcus thermophilus* and *Lactobacillus bulgaricus* and kept at 42–45°C. The bacteria ferment lactose to lactic acid, so curdling the milk and giving it a sour taste. The flavour of natural yoghurt made in this way can be altered by adding fruit pulp and fruit juices.

(b) PRODUCTION OF ANTIBIOTICS. **Antibiotics** are chemicals produced by micro-organisms which, at very low concentrations, have the capacity to inhibit or destroy other micro-organisms. They are of medical and veterinary importance, because they can be used to kill pathogenic micro-organisms in humans and livestock without adversely affecting the patient. Antibiotics are made by moulds and by bacteria. Some are effective against several pathogens (broad-spectrum), others act on only one or two (narrow-spectrum). **Streptomycin** is a broad-spectrum antibiotic made by the actinomycete bacterium *Streptomyces griseus*. It is used extensively to treat humans and livestock suffering from tuberculosis and bacterial pneumonia. **Chloramphenicol** (chloromycetin) is another broad-spectrum antibiotic made by *S. venezulae*. This antibiotic is used in the treatment of venereal diseases, typhoid fever and skin infections. Apart from their use in treating diseases, antibiotics are widely used to stimulate the growth of livestock. When added to animal feedstuffs, antibiotics kill micro-organisms including pathogens in the gut and promote protein synthesis in the body.

(c) PRODUCTION OF VINEGAR. **Ethanoic acid** is formed when ethanol is partially oxidised:

$$CH_3CH_2OH + O_2 \longrightarrow CH_3COOH + H_2O$$

A number of species of bacteria can bring about the conversion. Some are responsible for the natural souring of wine, giving it a flavour like vinegar. The manufacture of vinegar makes use of two genera of bacteria, *Acetomonas* and *Acetobacter*. In Britain, most vinegar is made from fermented malt wort or from cider which is allowed slowly to trickle down tall towers called acetaters packed with woodshavings. A starter culture of *Acetobacter* is added. It soon forms a film of large surface area on the shavings. Within four or five days, partial oxidation of the ethanol is complete and vinegar is tapped off from the base of the acetater.

(d) MANUFACTURE OF AMINO ACIDS AND PROTEINS

(i) **Amino acids**. In recent years, amino acids have increasingly been produced commercially with the aid of bacteria. It is possible to make amino acids by hydrolysing proteins or by chemical synthesis. However, microbial production is more economical and the product is of better quality. When *Micrococcus glutamicus* is grown in a liquid medium containing glucose, minerals, vitamins and peptone, about 15g dm^{-3} of the amino acid lysine appear in the medium within 3–4 days. Substantial amounts of other amino acids such as glutamic acid, valine, tryptophan and alanine appear when other species of bacteria are used. Some of the acids are 'essential' amino acids and are used to supplement animal feedstuffs containing protein of low biological value.

(ii) **Enzymes**. **Amylase** enzymes from *Bacillus polymyxa* are used to convert starch into malt for use in the brewing industry. **Peptidases** from *B. subtilis* are used in the leather industry to remove blood and hair from hides and to soften skins. Peptidase enzymes produced by *B. subtilis* have also been used on a large scale in recent years in the manufacture of **biological detergents**. The enzymes destroy the proteins of such things as egg yolk and blood which are difficult to remove from fabrics washed with conventional detergents or with soap. However, people involved in the production of biological detergents as well as people using them sometimes develop skin allergies and dermatitis. For this reason commercial production of bacterial peptidases has now slackened.

(iii) **Single Cell Protein (SCP)**. A good deal of work is being carried out in the production of protein from a variety of micro-organisms including fungi, bacteria and algae. So far, SCP makes only a small contribution to the world's protein supply. In the near future, as the human population grows and the shortage of protein becomes more acute, SCP is likely to become increasingly important. Compared with meat production, the manufacture of SCP is much more rapid and efficient. A bullock weighing 500 kg produces 0·45 kg of protein per day, while the same amount of yeast, for example, yields 50 tonnes of protein per day. Comparable results are obtained with bacteria. What is even more advantageous is that by-products of the petroleum and natural gas industries are among the raw materials required to grow SCP on a large scale.

(e) RETTING OF FIBRES. Linen and hemp are manufactured from the fibres in the stems of flax and hemp plants. The stems are immersed in water at 30°C and bacteria such as *Bacillus subtilis* and *Clostridium butyricum* in the water secrete pectinase enzymes which hydrolyse the middle lamella holding the fibres together. Consequently the fibres are separated and can then be freed from the rest of the tissues. The separation of the fibres by microbial activity is called **retting**.

(f) MAKING OF SILAGE. **Silage**-making is important to British agriculture, because it enables farmers to store grass over winter without having to dry it. In many summers it is virtually impossible to make hay, and drying grass indoors is expensive. In making silage, fresh-cut grass is compressed in a large silo or a pit. Bacteria such as *Lactobacillus* and *Streptococcus* on the grass ferment sugars in the plant juices and release fatty acids such as butyric, propionic and ethanoic acid. These give the silage its characteristic flavour and smell.

(g) TREATMENT OF SEWAGE. The decomposition of organic matter in **sewage** and the conversion of the breakdown products into harmless ions such as nitrate and sulphate are brought about by saprophytic and chemo-autotrophic bacteria. Their activities are similar to soil bacteria. The treatment of sewage in this way prevents gross pollution of inland watercourses and helps to minimise the spread of enteric diseases.

5. FOOD SPOILAGE

Foods with high protein content are often decomposed by bacteria. The smell of rotten eggs is caused by the release of hydrogen sulphide by protein-digesting species of *Pseudomonas*. Fresh and cooked meat and fish can be putrefied by a number of different species of proteolytic bacteria, including *Achromobacter*. Untreated milk is soon soured by lactic acid-producing bacteria. Canned foods may be spoiled by bacteria such as *Clostridium* and *Bacillus* which survive as spores during the process of canning.

Vast sums of money are invested in preserving food from spoilage by micro-organisms. The methods used are numerous and range from traditional processes such as boiling, salting, smoking, drying and pickling to relatively recent developments such as freezing, refrigeration, freeze-drying, canning and pasteurisation. All are aimed at preventing the growth of bacteria and other microbes in food.

FIG. 25.9 (a) *The death cap,* Amanita phalloides, × $\frac{2}{3}$ (b) *a puff-ball,* Lycoperdon caelatum, × $\frac{2}{3}$ (c) *a bracket fungus,* Trametes versicolor, × *1*

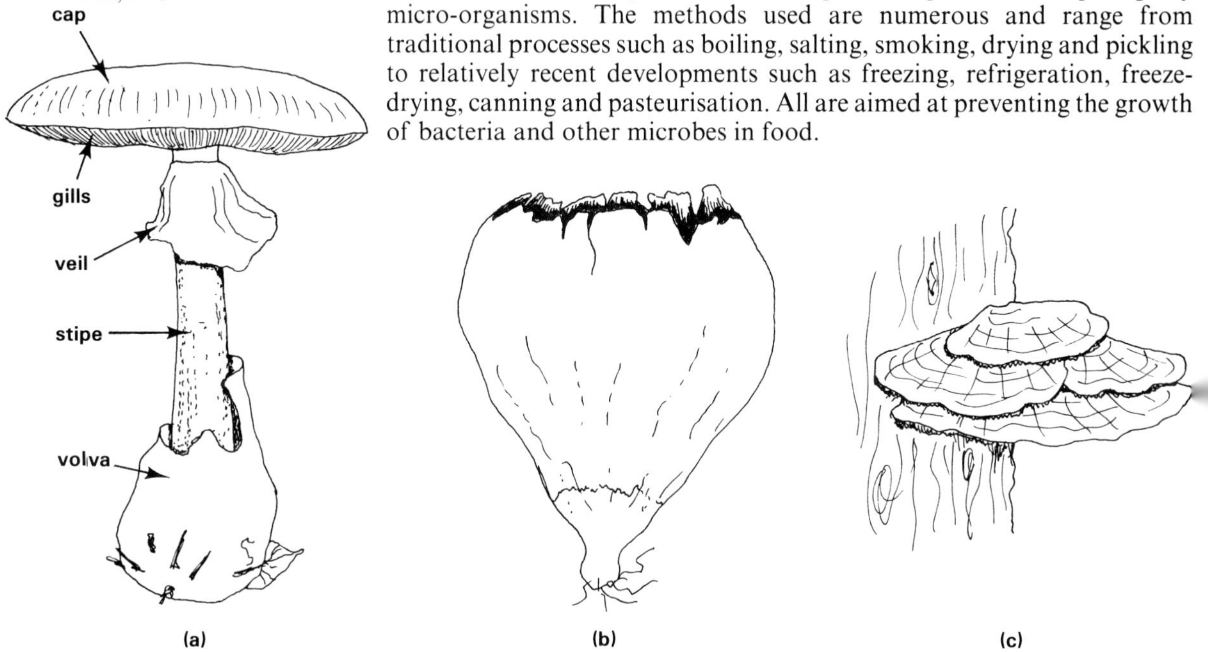

25.4 Fungi (*Eumycophyta*)

Fungi range in size from microscopic forms to the bracket fungi, toadstools and puffballs which are easily seen with the unaided eye (Fig. 25.9).

25.4.1 Structure

Some fungi are **unicellular**, such as the yeast *Saccharomyces*. More often they exist as a **mycelium** made of a network of branching multicellular threads called **hyphae** (Fig. 25.10). Fungal hyphae are bounded by a fibrous **cell wall** made largely of glucans, mannans and chitin. The protoplasm inside contains a **nucleus**, or more often many nuclei, each bounded by a nuclear membrane. Chromosomes appear when the nucleus divides

FIG. 25.10 (a) *Yeast,* Saccharomyces *sp. budding,* × *1000* (b) *aseptate hyphae* (c) *septate hyphae*

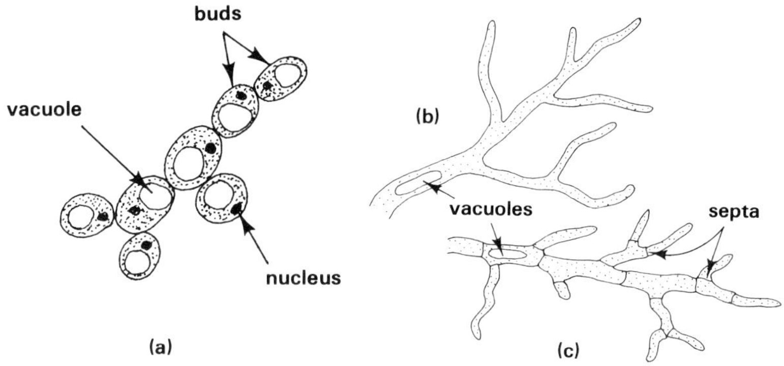

Also present are **mitochondria** and **endoplasmic reticulum**. All these structures distinguish fungi from bacteria.

Fungi are divided into four classes on the basis of hyphal structure and mode of reproduction (Table 25.3). Hyphae may be either septate or aseptate. **Septate** hyphae have cross-walls called **septa** which divide the protoplast into cells containing one or more nuclei. Septa are absent from **aseptate** hyphae, where a single **coenocytic** protoplast containing very many nuclei is present in the mycelium. A mycelium grows by apical elongation and branching of the hyphae.

Table 25.3 Classification of fungi (from Williams and Shaw 1982)

FUNGI (*MYCOPHYTA*)

- Mycelium unicellular or of aseptate hyphae
  - Class *Phycomycetes**
    Includes
    water moulds: *Saprolegnia*
    pin moulds: *Mucor*
    late blight fungus: *Phytophthora*
    downy mildews: *Peronospora*
- Mycelium unicellular or of septate hyphae
  - Reproduce by sexual and asexual methods
    - Sexual spores produced inside an ascus
      - Class *Ascomycetes* (*Ascomycotina*)
        Includes
        yeasts: *Saccharomyces*
        powdery mildews: *Erysiphe*
        blue-moulds: *Penicillium, Aspergillus*
        flask fungi: *Sordaria*
        cup fungi: *Aleuria*
    - Sexual spores produced on a basidium
      - Class *Basidiomycetes* (*Basidiomycotina*)
        Includes
        mushrooms: *Agaricus*
        toadstools: *Coprinus*
        puffballs: *Lycoperdon*
        stinkhorns: *Phallus*
        bracket fungi: *Polyporus*
        rust fungi: *Puccinia*
  - Sterile fungi or reproduce only by asexual methods
    - Class *Deuteromycetes* (*Deuteromycotina*)
      Includes
      grey mould: *Botrytis*
      green mould: *Cladosporium*
      brown rot fungi: *Monilia*

* Recent classifications divide the *Phycomycetes* into the *Mastigomycotina* (zoosporic fungi) and the *Zygomycotina* (zygosporic fungi) which are equal in rank to the *Ascomycotina*, *Basidiomycotina* and *Deuteromycotina*.

25.4.2 Nutrition

A major difference between fungi and higher plants is the absence of chlorophyll in fungi. All fungi are **heterotrophic**, depending on organic matter as a source of energy and nutrients. **Saprophytic** fungi such as *Mucor* use dead organic matter. Digestive enzymes are secreted by the growing tips of hyphae. The extra-cellular enzymes convert the organic substrate on which the fungus is growing into soluble products which are absorbed by the hyphae.

Parasitic fungi such as *Phytophthora* absorb soluble organic matter from the cells of their host using haustoria (Chapter 28). The fungi of lichens and mycorrhizae are **symbionts** obtaining organic matter from their partners.

25.4.3 Reproduction

Fungi produce **spores** when they reproduce. The method of spore production may be asexual or sexual and varies from class to class. In favourable conditions, spores germinate to form a new mycelium.

FIG. 25.11 *Asexual reproduction in fungi* (a) Saprolegnia × *200* (b) Mucor, × *200* (c) Erysiphe, × *400* (d) Aspergillus, × *400* (e) Penicillium, × *400*

1. ASEXUAL SPORES

These are formed after mitotic nuclear division. They normally give rise to progeny which are similar to the parent.

(a) *PHYCOMYCETES* produce asexual spores in **sporangia**. Some species, such as *Saprolegnia*, are aquatic and produce flagellate **zoospores** (Fig. 25.11(a)). The flagella allow dispersal by swimming through water. In the appropriate conditions, the zoospores germinate and new hyphae emerge. Non-aquatic species such as the pin-mould *Mucor* produce aerial sporangia. They are borne on vertical branches of the mycelium called **sporangiophores** (Fig. 25.11(b)). The spores are unicellular but without flagella and are called **aplanospores**. Aplanospores are released from the sporangia into the air and are dispersed by air currents.

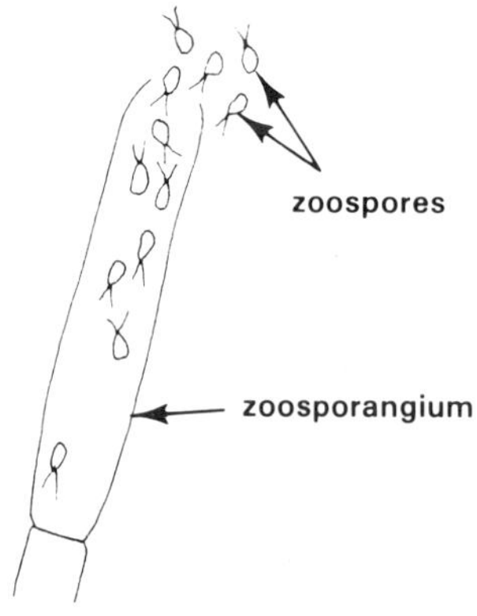

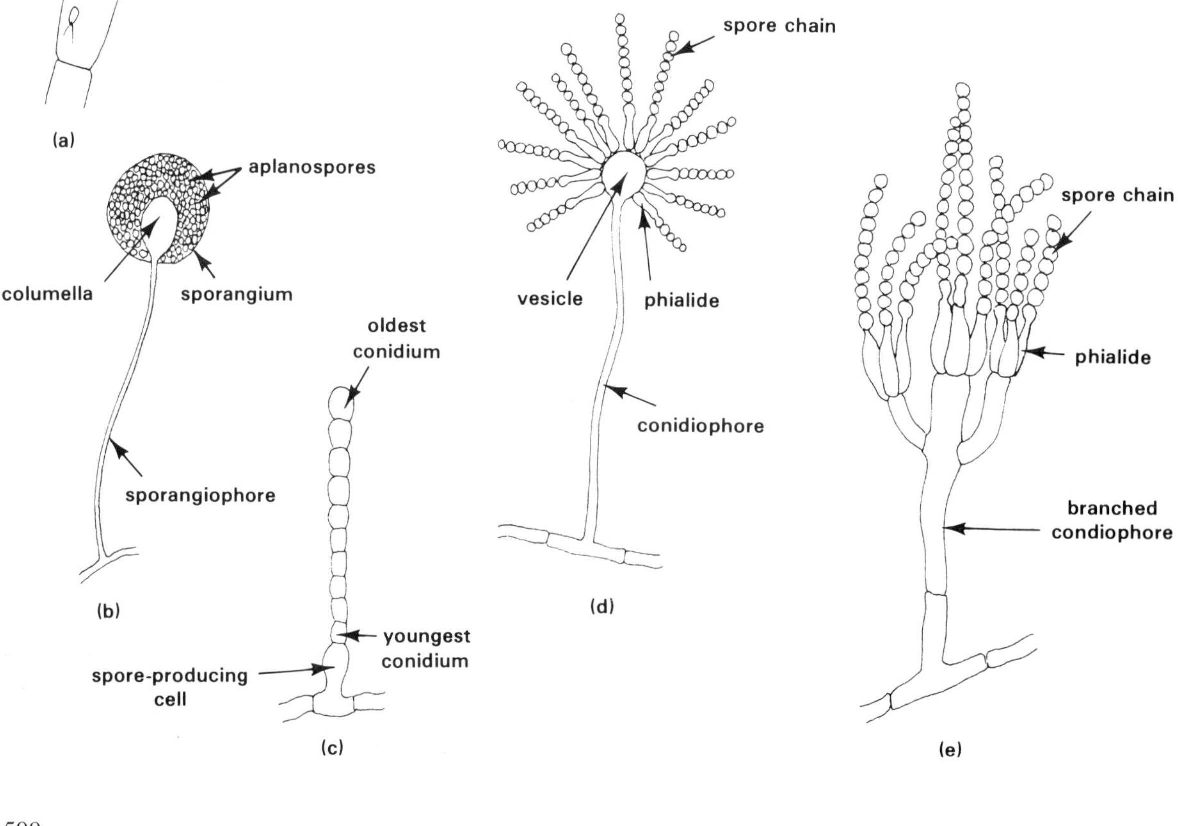

(b) *ASCOMYCETES* produce asexual spores called **conidia**. Conidia are often formed in chains from special hyphae called **conidiophores** (Fig. 25.11(c)–(e)). Yeasts such as *Saccharomyces* reproduce asexually by **budding**.
(c) *BASIDIOMYCETES*. Asexual spore production is not often seen in this class. When formed, the asexual spores are similar to conidia.
(d) *DEUTEROMYCETES*. Most members of this class produce **conidia**.

2. SEXUAL REPRODUCTION

This is common in fungi and involves the fusion of nuclei followed by meiosis. It results in genetic variation among the offspring.
(a) *PHYCOMYCETES* produce gametes in unicellular sexual organs known as **gametangia**. The male gametangium is called an **antheridium**, the female an **oogonium**. Most aquatic phycomycete fungi are **homothallic**, male and female gametangia arising on the same mycelium. The self-fertilised eggs develop into thick-walled **oospores** (Fig. 25.12(a)). *Mucor* is

FIG. 25.12 *Sexual reproduction in* (a) Saprolegnia (b) Mucor (c) Mucor *zygospores*, × *80*

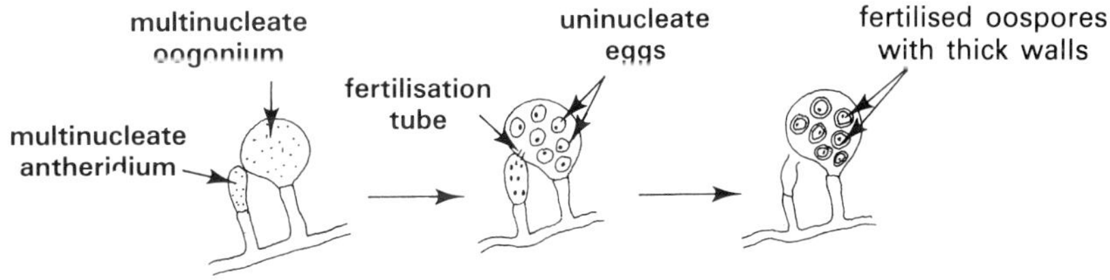

(a)

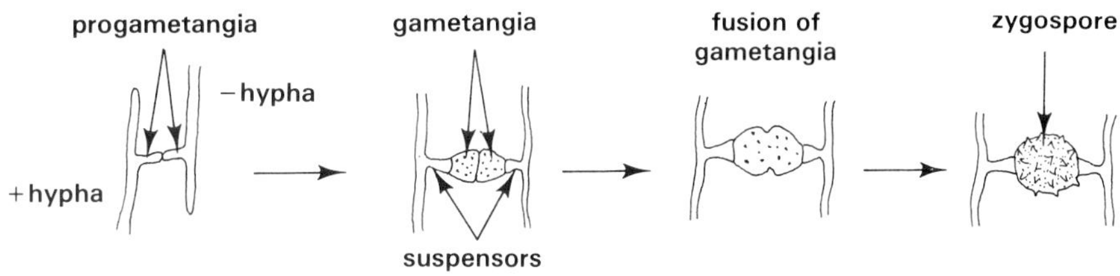

(b)

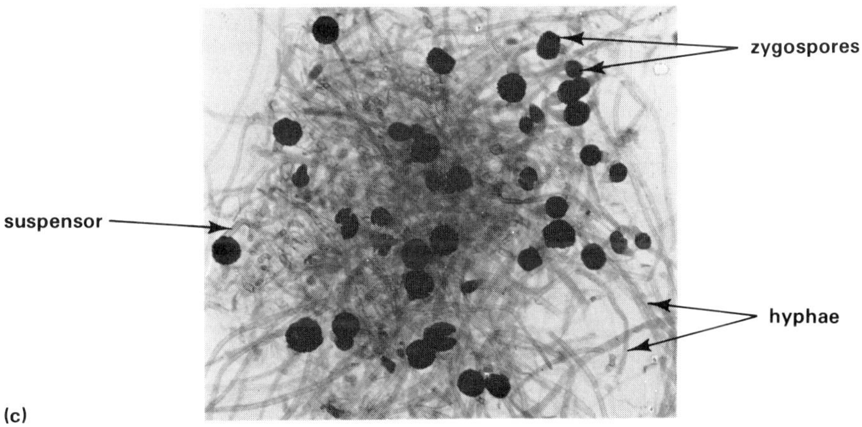

(c)

heterothallic, and cross-fertilisation occurs between two genetically different mycelia. Gametangia arise from adjacent mycelia on hyphal branches called suspensors. The mycelia and gametangia are identical to look at and are usually described as + and − rather than male and female.

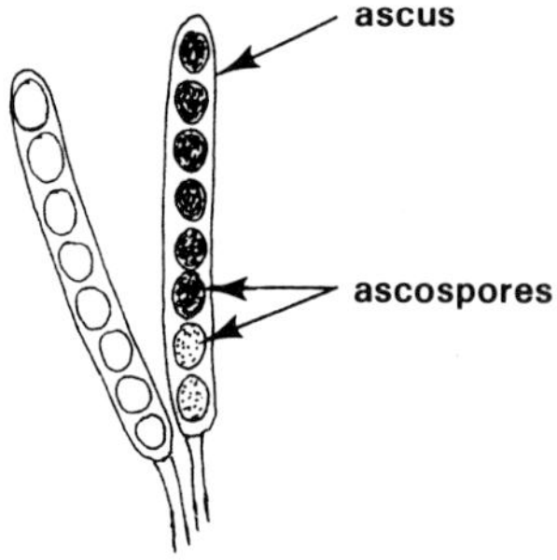

FIG. 25.13 *Ascospores of* Sordaria fimicola, × *150*

Gametangia join to form a **zygospore** in which fusion takes place between + and − nuclei (Fig. 25.12(b) & (c)). Meiosis follows, restoring the normal haploid chromosome number in each nucleus. After a period of rest, the zygospore germinates. A **promycelium** grows from the zygospore and supports a sporangium. The sporangium contains either + or − asexual spores.

(b) *ASCOMYCETES* are heterothallic. The sexual organs are unicellular, a male **antheridium** and a female **ascogonium**. The male nuclei pass into the ascogonium through a fertilisation tube. Nuclear fusion takes place and **ascospores** develop inside **asci** (Fig. 25.13). They may be surrounded by a protective **ascocarp** made of sterile hyphae from the surrounding mycelium. The ascospores are shot out of the ascocarp or released when the ascocarp decays.

(c) *BASIDIOMYCETES* are heterothallic, but there are no sexual organs. **Conjugation** occurs between adjacent hyphae from different mycelia. A new **secondary mycelium** develops containing nuclei from each of the parent mycelia. The secondary mycelium gives rise to a **basidiocarp** (Fig. 25.14)

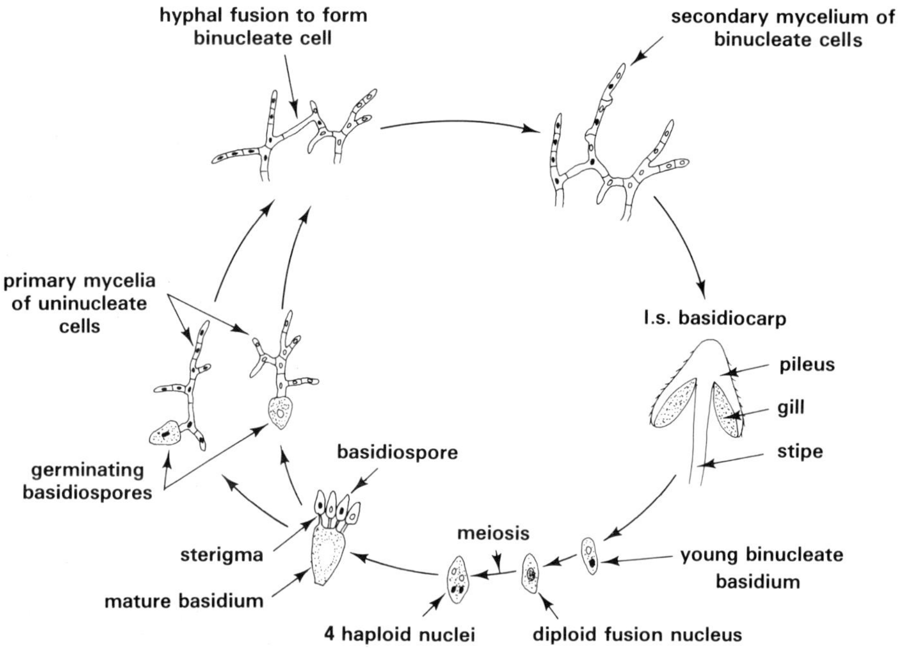

FIG. 25.14 *Life cycle of* Coprinus lagopus (after Williams and Shaw 1982)

consisting of a vertical **stipe** supporting a cap-shaped **pileus**. Beneath the pileus is a number of radiating gills called **lamellae** which bear spore-producing **basidia**. Nuclear fusion followed by meiosis occurs in the basidia. The resulting **basidiospores** are released and may be dispersed by air currents, water, insects or other animals.

(d) *DEUTEROMYCETES* do not reproduce sexually.

25.4.4 Importance of fungi to man

1. PARASITIC FUNGI

Some fungi are plant and animal **pathogens**. Ringworm, thrush and athlete's foot are examples of human diseases caused by fungi. A much larger number of fungi are plant pathogens. One of the most notorious of the parasitic fungi is *Phytophthora infestans*, the cause of late blight of potatoes. In the 1840s this fungus ravaged the European potato crop, leaving millions of starving peasants in its wake. Between 1841 and 1851, the population of Ireland alone was thus reduced, by starvation and emigration, by one and a half million people.

2. SAPROPHYTIC FUNGI

Many **saprophytic** fungi, together with bacteria, decompose plant and animal remains to form **humus** in the soil. Humus is rich in minerals and is able to hold moisture. It is therefore a valuable component of all fertile soils. Plant remains contribute most of the material from which humus is formed (Chapter 29).

Not all saprophytic fungi benefit mankind. Prepared food readily becomes mouldy, making it unpalatable. Mouldy food may be lethal if eaten, because some saprophytic fungi release poisons called **mycotoxins** on to the substrate on which they are growing. Saprophytic fungi attack the buildings in which we live. Dry rot of timber, for example, is caused by the basidiomycete fungus *Merulius lachrymans*. Other saprophytic fungi destroy wallpaper and fabrics in damp houses.

3. FUNGI AS FOOD

In most countries, some of the larger fungi are collected for human consumption. A few species such as the edible mushroom *Agaricus bisporus* are cultivated on a large scale. The protein content of mushrooms is insufficient to consider growing them as a basic foodstuff. However, yeasts such as *Torulopsis* and *Candida* produce substantial amounts of protein. They can be grown on factory waste such as molasses, woodpulp and whey, or on by-products of the petroleum and natural gas industries. The term **single cell protein (SCP)** is used to describe protein made in this way. The efficiency with which yeasts synthesise protein is remarkable compared with traditional methods of protein-production using livestock. For example, one hectare of maize yields 4000 kg of grain. When fed to cattle, this produces 85 kg of lean meat. If used to make SCP, the yield is 360 kg of protein.

4. FOOD MODIFIED BY FUNGI

A great variety of cheeses is ripened by moulds and sometimes yeasts. Such cheeses differ from non-ripened cheeses in digestibility, vitamin content, appearance and palatability.

5. PRODUCTION OF ETHANOL AND ORGANIC ACIDS

The production of alcoholic beverages is a huge industry. Brewing, winemaking and distilling have gone on for centuries. At one time, most of the industrially-used ethanol was also prepared by fermentation, but it is now made mainly by chemical synthesis.

In the manufacture of **alcoholic beverages**, a carbohydrate-rich substrate is fermented by the brewer's yeast *Saccharomyces cerevisiae*. Malt is the substrate used in brewing and in the production of some distilled beverages such as whisky. The malt comes from barley grains which are germinated so that the starch they contain is converted to the disaccharide sugar maltose. The grain is then dried, ground up, steeped in warm water and brewer's yeast is added. The mixture is kept short of oxygen so that the yeast respires anaerobically, fermenting the sugar into ethanol and carbon dioxide. Fruits, especially grapes, leaves, seeds and vegetables provide the sugar for wine production. Fermentation is also employed in the manufacture of various organic acids, mainly citric acid.

6. PRODUCTION OF ANTIBIOTICS

Many **antibiotics** made by fungi have been isolated and tested, but medical and veterinary use is confined so far to **penicillin**, **cephalosporin** and **griseofulvin**.

Penicillin was discovered almost accidently by Alexander Fleming in 1928 when he was working at St Mary's Hospital, Paddington. A plate culture of staphylococci, the bacteria which infect wounds, had become contaminated in his laboratory with a mould. He noticed that there were areas where the bacteria had apparently been destroyed by some unknown substance produced by the mould. Later the mould was identified as *Penicillium notatum*. Fleming published his observations, but nobody took much notice until the Second World War. The large number of injuries gave impetus to a search for drugs which would help heal infected wounds. Howard Florey and Ernst Chain succeeded in isolating the anti-bacterial substance, now called penicillin. It was found to be effective against many different species of bacteria.

Some of the earliest-produced penicillin eventually proved to be less effective, mainly because resistant strains of bacteria evolved. However, modern production methods have made it possible to make modifications to the original penicillin molecule. The newer penicillins are more effective. Today the main producer mould is *P. chrysogenum* which is grown aerobically in a liquid medium in huge tanks of several hundred thousand litres' capacity. By altering the composition of the medium, the mould can be made to release different kinds of penicillin, which can be extracted from the medium and prepared for medicinal use.

7. GIBBERELLIN PRODUCTION

Gibberellin is made by the fungus *Gibberella fujikuroi*. The main use of gibberellin is in the production of malt from germinated barley grain for the brewing industry. Barley grains make their own gibberellin (Chapter 20) but if extra gibberellin is given, the production of maltose is considerably speeded up.

8. VITAMIN PRODUCTION

Brewer's yeast, *Saccharomyces cerevisiae*, synthesises a range of **vitamins** of the B-group. For this reason yeast products such as brewer's yeast tablets are taken by humans to supplement diets deficient in these vitamins. Animal feedstuffs are supplemented by riboflavin (vitamin B_2) which is made by the yeast *Ashbya gossypii*.

9. STEROID TRANSFORMATIONS

Pharmaceutical interest in **steroids** has increased enormously in recent years. This results from the discovery of the value of **cortisone** and its derivatives in the treatment of arthritis. Other steroids are used as **oral contraceptives**. When plant steroids are added to a culture medium in which fungi can grow, high yields of the finished steroid drugs are achieved. Among the fungi which are used for this purpose are *Rhizopus nigricans*, *Fusarium culmorum* and *Trichoderma viride*.

10. ENZYME PRODUCTION

Recently, enzymes produced by fungi have become widely used.

(a) **Amylase**. Large-scale production of amylase from *Asperillus niger* now takes place. The fungus is grown in a medium containing starch and minerals. A major use of fungal amylase is in brewing. In all brewing processes, the first step is to hydrolyse cereal starch. The traditional way is to convert starch to maltose by germinating barley grain. Now, many maltsters are using ground grain to which fungal amylase is added. The main advantage of the new procedure is that it is much more efficient and therefore more economical.

(b) **Peptidases**. In cheese production, milk is first clotted using rennin from calves' stomachs. Recently, peptidase enzymes from *Mucor pusillus* and *M. miehei* have been used in the commercial production of some cheeses to coagulate the milk.

(c) **Pectinases**. Pectinase enzymes, mostly from species of *Penicillium* and *Aspergillus*, are now prepared commercially. Their main use is in clearing fruit juices by hydrolysing pectin which causes cloudiness.

11. BIOLOGICAL CONTROL

One successful use of fungi in biological control is the control of *Heterobasidion annosum* by *Peniophora gigantea* (section 29.1.3)

25.5 Algae

Algae are primitive plants which contain chlorophyll and can photosynthesise. Algae were once considered as a single group within the plant kingdom. Today, however, most biologists recognise several **divisions** of algae including the *Cyanophyta*, *Chlorophyta*, *Phaeophyta*, *Rhodophyta*, *Bacillariophyta* and *Euglenophyta*.

25.5.1 *Cyanophyta (Myxophyta)*

FIG. 25.15 *Two cyanophytes*
(a) Gloeothece, × *750 a unicell*
(b) Nostoc, × *850 a simple filament*

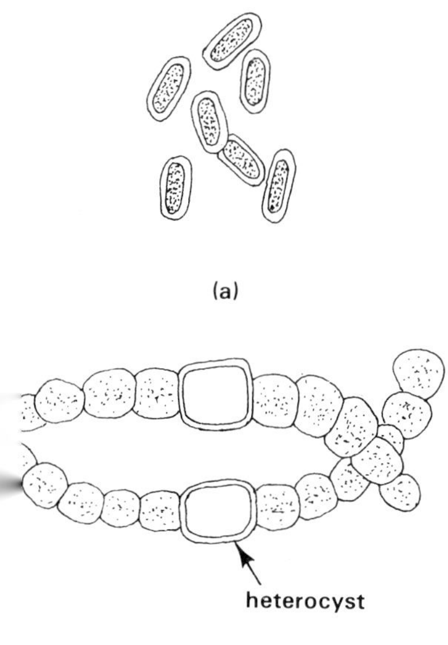

The cyanophytes are the **blue-green algae**. Fossil evidence suggests that the first living organisms on earth were very like the blue-green algae (Chapter 24). Many features of the group are similar to bacteria, and for this reason they are often classified together. One of the characteristics of blue-green algae is that they are pigmented. The pigments include **chlorophyll**, **carotene**, **xanthophyll**, **phycocyanin** (blue) and **phycoerythrin** (red). Various combinations of pigments result in the wide range of colours seen among the cyanophytes. Most, however, are blue-green.

Blue-green algae have a relatively simple structure, being either **unicellular** or simple **filaments** (Fig. 25.15). The cells or filaments are usually surrounded by a sticky film of mucilage. The cell wall is made of mucopeptide similar to that of bacteria. Also like bacteria, blue-green algae are **prokaryotic**. Nuclear material is not enclosed in a nuclear membrane. The photosynthetic pigments are located in cytoplasmic lamellae. Food reserves such as cyanophycin granules, oil and glycogen are stored in the cytoplasm. There are no mitochondria. Gas vacuoles in the cytoplasm of some aquatic species enable the cells to float, placing the algae in the best position for light absorption. Some filamentous species form **heterocysts**, thick-walled cells with a clear protoplast.

Blue-green algae do not reproduce sexually. Asexual reproduction is by **fission** similar to that seen in bacteria or by fragmentation of filaments. Some species form thick-walled resistant spores called **akinetes**.

Many cyanophytes are found in **symbiotic** relationship with higher plants. Others are the algal component of lichens (Chapter 28). As well as producing carbohydrate by photosynthesis, many cyanophytes can also use atmospheric nitrogen to make amino acids and proteins. Nitrogen fixation takes place in heterocysts. These properties enable blue-green algae to colonise regions hostile to other organisms. Cyanophytes are often the first to appear on bare ground.

25.5.2 *Chlorophyta*

FIG. 25.16 *Three chlorophytes* (a) Chlamydomonas, × *1000 unicell* (b) Spirogyra, × *150 filament* (c) Ulva, × $\frac{1}{2}$ *thallus*

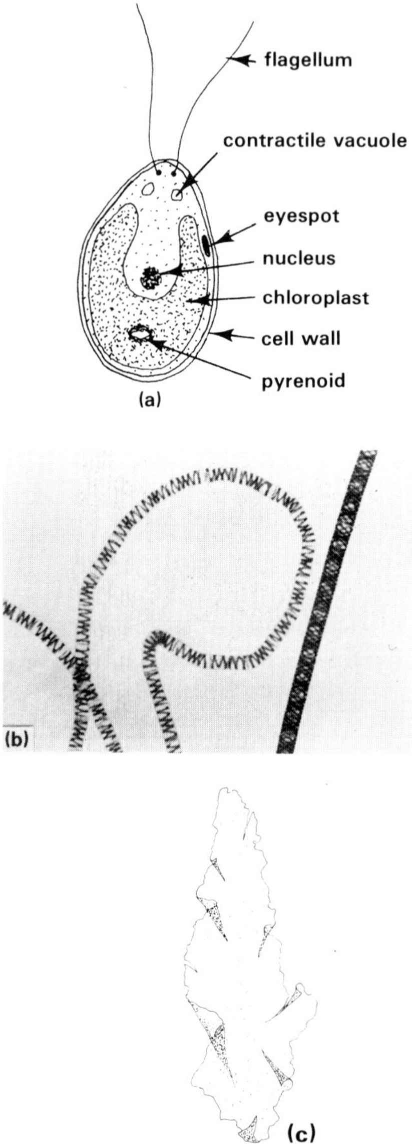

The chlorophytes are the **green algae**. They are nearly all aquatic plants, a few are terrestrial. Green algae include **unicells**, **colonies**, **filaments** and **thalloid** forms (Fig. 25.16). A thallus is a multicellular plant body not differentiated into roots, stems and leaves. The cells are **eukaryotic**, having extensive internal membranes, including a nuclear membrane. **Chlorophylls a** and **b**, **carotene** and **xanthophyll** are found in chloroplasts. **Starch** and **oil** are the main food reserves and **cellulose** is the main component of the cell wall. **Zoospore** formation is the usual method of asexual reproduction. The **sex organs are unicellular** and the male gametes are motile. In many green algae the female gametes are motile too.

The *Chlorophyceae* is the main class of green algae. It contains many orders, including the *Volvocales* and *Zygnematales*.

1. *VOLVOCALES*

Nearly all the members of this order live in fresh water as unicells or as colonies. A typical example is *Chlamydomonas*. It is a flagellated unicellular green alga, each cell having two or four flagella according to the species. The oval protoplast is enclosed in a thin cellulose wall and contains a large cup-shaped chloroplast. A haploid nucleus is suspended in the cytoplasm (Fig. 25.17). Asexual reproduction is by mitotic division of the nucleus followed by cleavage of the protoplast. Two, four or eight haploid **zoospores** are formed and released when the wall of the parent cell ruptures.

Chlamydomonas produces gametes prior to sexual reproduction. In some species, any haploid cell can act as a gamete. Because their gametes are similar in size and appearance, these species are **isogamous**. The gametes join in pairs at their flagellated ends. Nuclear fusion soon follows to produce a diploid zygote which secretes a thick protective wall. Before germination, the nucleus of the zygote divides by meiosis. Four, eight or sixteen haploid nuclei are formed. The protoplast cleaves into a similar number of pieces, each with a nucleus. The new cells are released when the zygote wall splits open. They quickly develop flagella and start swimming about. Some species are **anisogamous**, producing motile male and female gametes of unequal size. Others are **oogamous**, forming motile male gametes and larger female gametes which have no flagella.

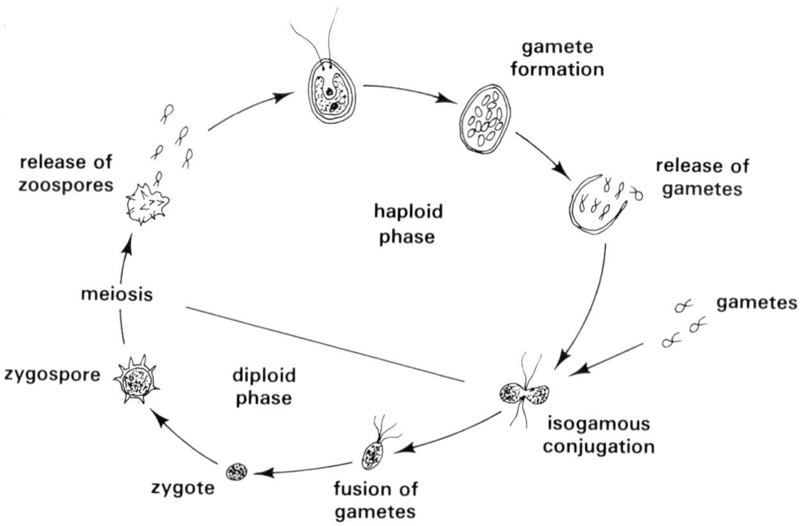

FIG. 25.17 *Sexual cycle in* Chlamydomonas. *In some species, male and female gametes are different sizes and gamete conjugation is anisogamous*

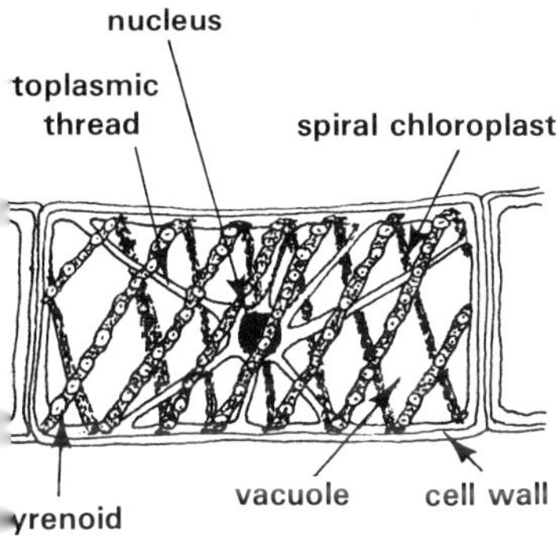

FIG. 25.18 Spirogyra, × *500*

2. *ZYGNEMATALES (CONJUGALES)*

Members of this order live in fresh water as single cells or unbranched filaments. An example is *Spirogyra*, which grows as unbranched filaments made of cylindrical cells. The cellulose cell wall is enclosed in a layer of mucilage. Large fluid-filled vacuoles occupy much of the intracellular space. One or more spiral chloroplasts lie in the cytoplasm (Fig. 25.18). The haploid nucleus is suspended at the centre of the cell by cytoplasmic threads.

Cell division causes the filaments to grow in length, after which they fragment into short chains of cells. **Fragmentation** is a form of asexual reproduction.

Sexual reproduction is by **conjugation**. Two or more filaments come to lie next to each other with their cells aligned. Short bulges grow from adjacent cells and elongate, gradually pushing the filaments apart. The cross walls between the bulges break down and the filaments are now joined by **conjugation tubes** (Fig. 25.19(a)). The filaments are therefore **gametophytes**.

FIG. 25.19 Spirogyra
(a) *conjugation,* × *300*
(b) *zygospore formation,* × *300*

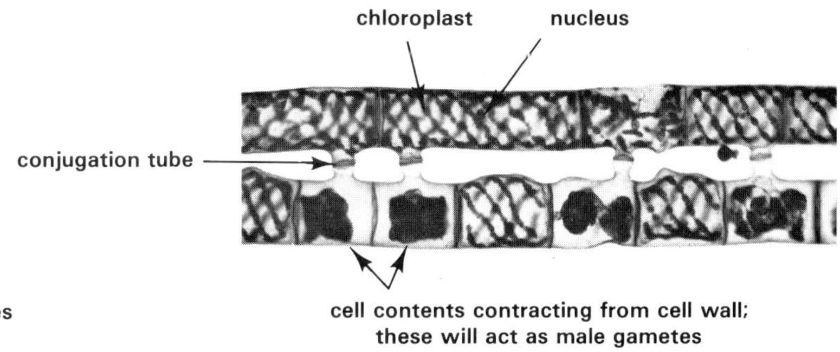

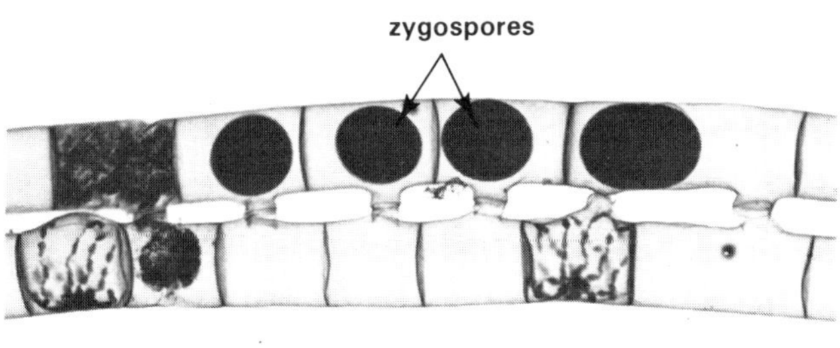

Because the gametes are similar in size, *Spirogyra* is **isogamous**. The protoplasts of one filament become amoeboid and pass through the conjugation tubes into the adjacent filament. The nuclei of the gametes fuse to form diploid zygotes which develop a resistant wall to become **zygospores** (Fig. 25.19(b)). Zygospores are released when the parent filaments decay. The zygospore nucleus divides by meiosis. Three of the resulting four nuclei degenerate. In favourable conditions when the zygospore germinates, a haploid cell emerges. It divides by mitosis to form a new filament (Fig. 25.20).

FIG. 25.20 *Haplontic life-cycle of* Spirogyra

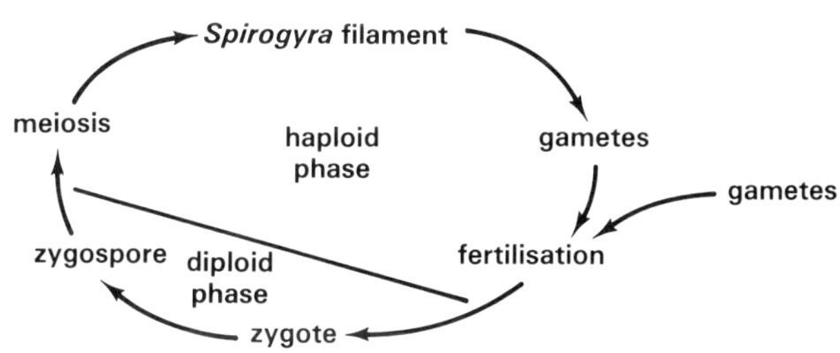

25.5.3 *Phaeophyta*

The phaeophytes are the **brown algae**. They include **filamentous** forms and the **thalloid** macroscopic marine seaweeds. Their yellow or brown colour is caused by **xanthophyll** and **fucoxanthin** although **chlorophylls a** and **c** are present too. The pigments are located in chloroplasts. **Laminarin**, a soluble polymer of glucose, is the main food reserve. Cell walls have an inner layer of cellulose and an outer gelatinous layer made of **algin**. The cells are **eukaryotic**. Most brown algae produce **unicellular sex organs**. Many also reproduce asexually by forming **zoospores**.

FIG. 25.21 *The bladder wrack,* Fucus vesiculosus
(a) *vegetative thallus,* $\times \frac{1}{3}$
(b) *female conceptacle* $\times$ *75*
(c) *male conceptacle,* $\times$ *75*

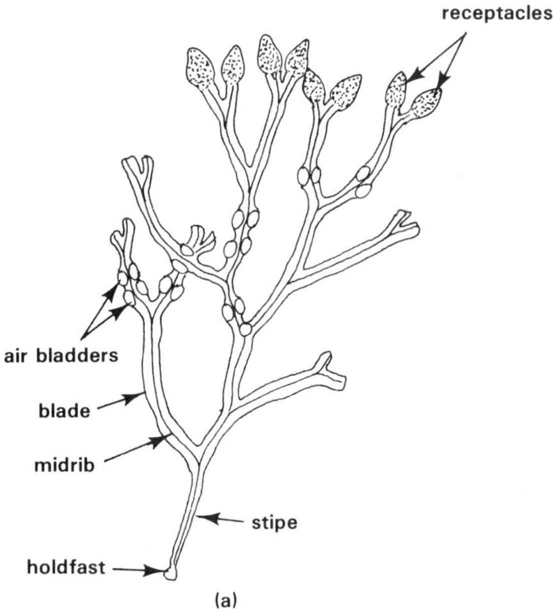

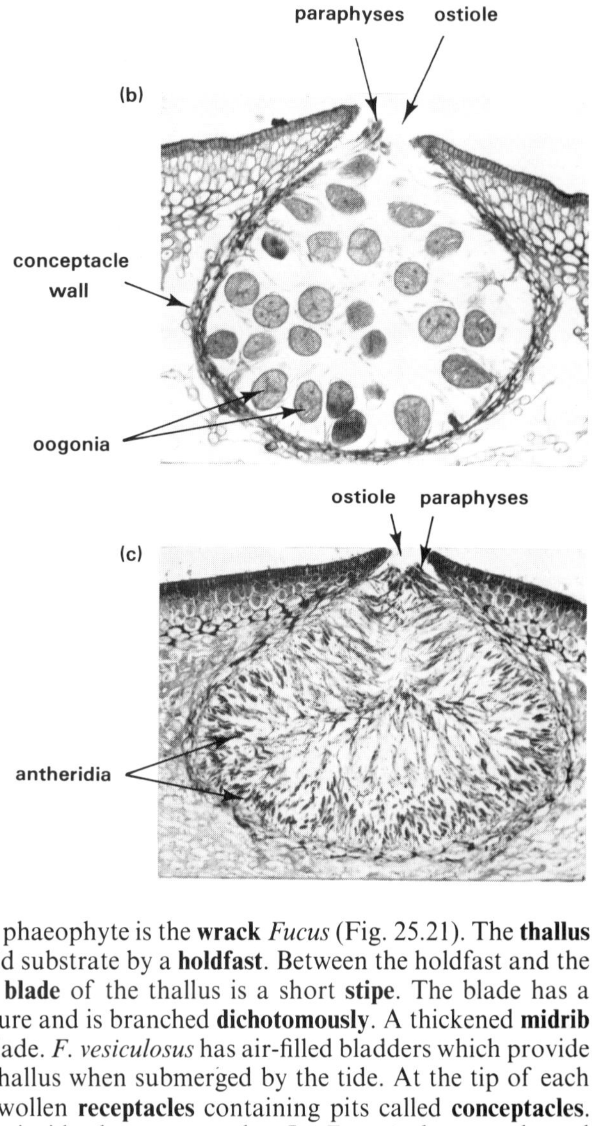

An example of a phaeophyte is the **wrack** *Fucus* (Fig. 25.21). The **thallus** is attached to a solid substrate by a **holdfast**. Between the holdfast and the extensive flattened **blade** of the thallus is a short **stipe**. The blade has a tough leathery texture and is branched **dichotomously**. A thickened **midrib** is present in each blade. *F. vesiculosus* has air-filled bladders which provide buoyancy for the thallus when submerged by the tide. At the tip of each branch there are swollen **receptacles** containing pits called **conceptacles**. The sex organs are inside the conceptacles. In *F. vesiculosus*, male and female conceptacles are in separate plants. Conceptacles open to the outside by pores called **ostioles**. The male organs are **antheridia**, which produce the flagellate male gametes called **antherozoids**. The female organs are **oogonia**. They produce the non-motile female gametes called **oospheres**. *Fucus* is therefore **oogamous**. The thallus is the gametophyte stage of the life cycle. Unlike the chlorophytes, the gametophyte of *Fucus* is diploid.

FIG. 25.22 *Life cycle of* Fucus vesiculosus

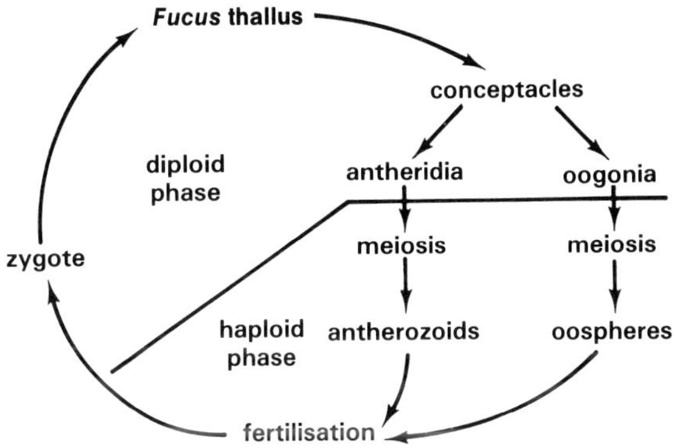

FIG. 25.23 Laminaria digitata, × $\frac{1}{10}$

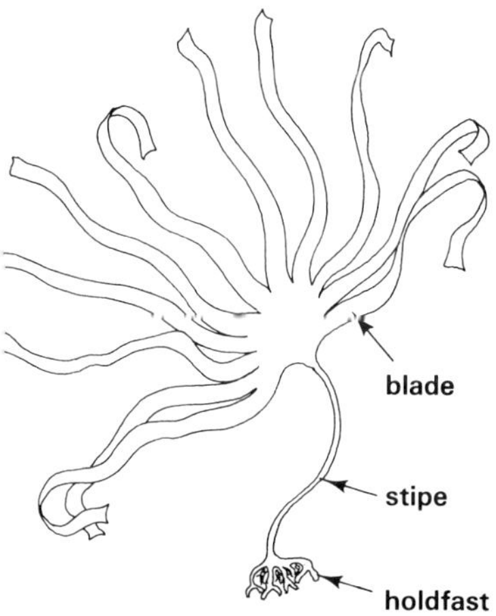

Gametes are produced by meiosis, so the antherozoids and oospheres are haploid. Fertilisation occurs in the surrounding water. The diploid zygote develops into a new diploid thallus and the cycle is completed (Fig. 25.22). *Fucus* does not reproduce asexually.

Another phaeophyte is the **kelp** *Laminaria* (Fig. 25.23). The diploid plant is differentiated into a holdfast, stipe and one or more strap-like blades. It reproduces asexually, forming flagellate haploid zoospores. For this reason, the diploid plant is the **sporophyte** part of the life cycle. Zoospores germinate into microscopic **gametophyte** filaments which have unicellular sex organs. Because the sporophyte and gametophyte are different in appearance, the life cycle of *Laminaria* has a **heteromorphic alternation of generations**.

25.5.4 *Rhodophyta, Bacillariophyta and Euglenophyta*

The rhodophytes are the **red algae**, nearly all of which are marine and **thalloid**. Their colour is caused by the presence of relatively large amounts of **phycoerythrin**. An example is *Chondrus* (Fig. 25.24).

The bacillariophytes include the **diatoms**. They are found in almost all aquatic habitats and constitute much of the **phytoplankton** in the world's oceans. Diatoms are important producers in marine ecosystems (Chapter 29). They live as single cells or as small colonies (Fig. 25.25). The cell wall is **silicified** and often highly sculptured. It is divided into two tightly-fitting parts, one slightly larger than the other. Asexual reproduction is by mitotic division. Since the cell wall is composed of two unequally-sized parts, the products of asexual reproduction are of slightly different sizes.

The euglenophytes include many unicellular flagellated algae which are often also classified as *Protozoa*. An example is *Euglena* (section 26.1.2).

FIG. 25.24 Chondrus crispus × *1*

FIG. 25.25 *A variety of diatoms,* × *100*

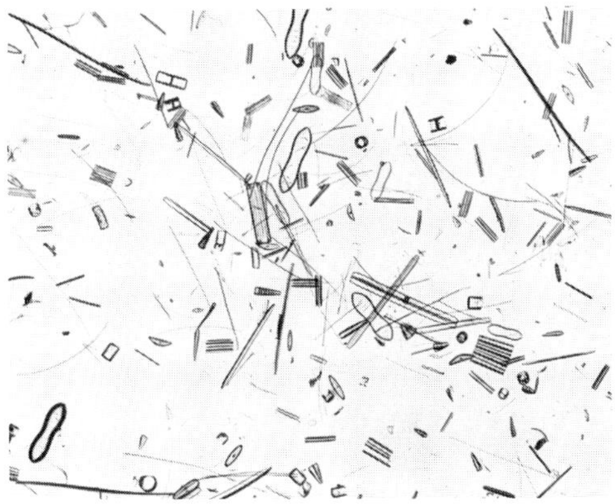

25.6 *Bryophyta*

The bryophytes are **liverworts** and **mosses**. They are green plants, nearly all terrestrial. Most are restricted to damp regions because they need water for fertilisation and they lack a waterproof cuticle. Bryophytes have a **heteromorphic alternation of generations** in which the dominant generation of the life cycle is the haploid **gametophyte**. The gametophyte of many liverworts is thalloid. In mosses and many liverworts, the gametophyte is differentiated into stem and leaves. Fine threads called **rhizoids** hold the gametophyte to the substrate. There is no vascular tissue.

FIG. 25.26 Marchantia polymorpha (a) *whole plant showing gemma cups, × 2* (b) *vertical section through gemma cup, × 35*

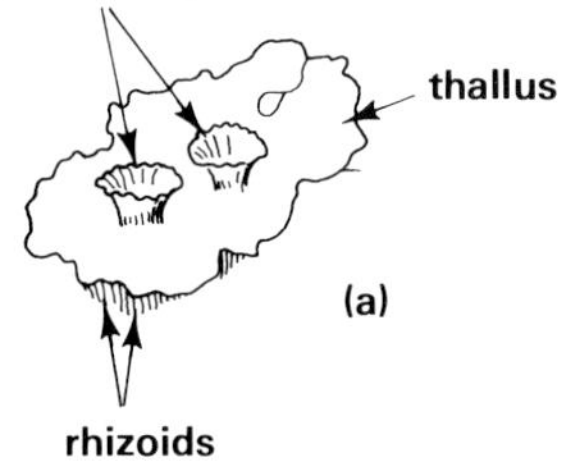

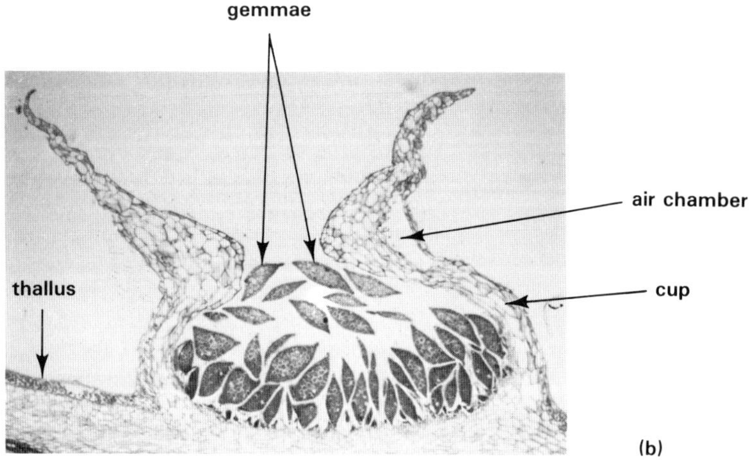

Many liverworts and some mosses reproduce asexually by means of **gemmae**. Gemmae are multicellular, microscopic structures, often produced in **gemma cups** (Fig. 25.26). Raindrops falling into the cups scatter the gemmae, which may germinate to produce new gametophyte plants. Bryophytes are **oogamous**, because they produce small flagellated male gametes and large non-motile female gametes. The **sex organs are multicellular**. The diploid **sporophyte** never exists as an independent plant and remains attached to the gametophyte.

The bryophytes are divided into two classes, *Hepaticae* and *Musci*.

25.6.1 *Hepaticae*

The *Hepaticae* are the **liverworts**. They are usually found in moist environments such as rocks moist with freshwater and on wet soil.

Pellia is a **thalloid** liverwort (Fig. 25.27). The thallus is flattened and dichotomously branched. It is attached to the substrate by numerous **unicellular rhizoids** on the underside of the thallus. The thallus is the

FIG. 25.27 *A thalloid liverwort,* Pellia epiphylla, *× 3*

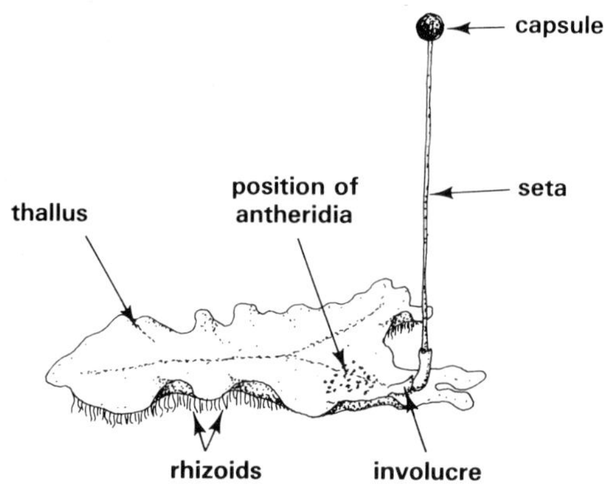

FIG. 25.28 Pellia, *sporogonium*, × 50

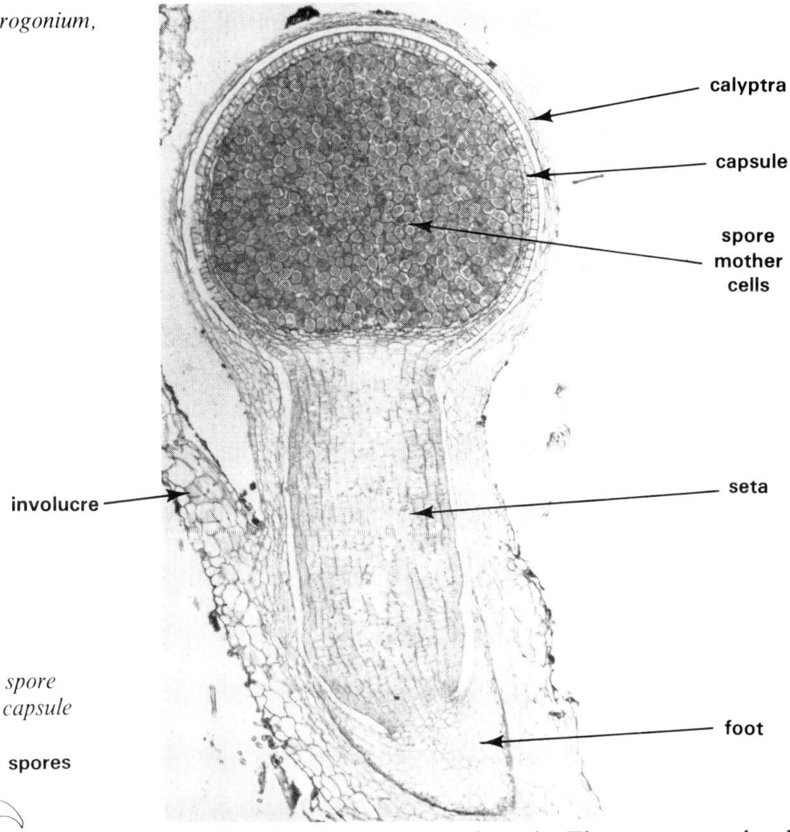

FIG. 25.29 Pellia (a) *spore release from bursting capsule* (b) *elater*

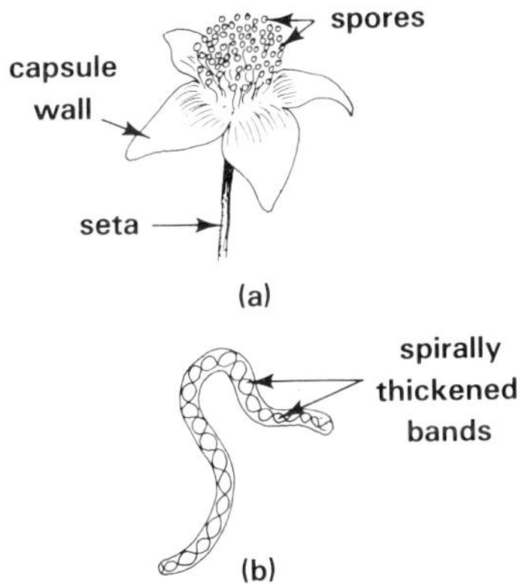

FIG. 25.30 *A leafy liverwort,* Marsupella emarginata × *3,* (after Watson 1959)

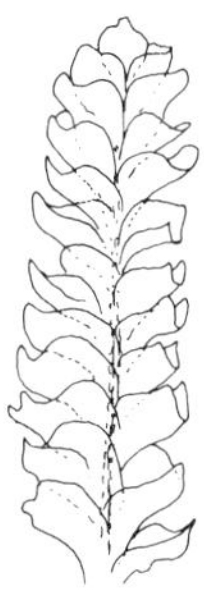

gametophyte phase of the life cycle. The sex organs develop on the upper surface of the thallus near the tip of the branches. The female organs, called **archegonia**, are in small pockets covered by a flap of tissue called an involucre. Mature archegonia each contain a haploid female gamete called an egg cell or oosphere. A little behind the archegonia are pits in which the male organs, **antheridia**, develop. The antheridia produce unicellular haploid male gametes called antherozoids. The antherozoids are flagellated and, in wet conditions, swim and seek out an oosphere. They are attracted to the female gametes by sucrose secreted from the necks of the archegonia. The movement of unicells towards a chemical stimulus is called **chemotaxis**. A diploid zygote produced by fertilisation divides and forms a multicellular embryo which becomes the sporophyte. As it develops, the **sporogonium** stays inside the remains of the archegonium, the wall of which grows to form a **calyptra**. The mature sporogonium consists of a **foot**, **seta** and a large **capsule** in which diploid spore mother cells undergo meiosis to produce haploid spores. The sporophyte rests in this form over winter. During the following spring, the spore capsule is pushed upwards by elongation of the seta (Fig. 25.28). Growth of the sporophyte is entirely dependent on nutrients absorbed from the gametophyte by the foot of the sporogonium. The capsule wall splits into four parts as it dries out (Fig. 25.29). Within the spore mass lie many **elaters**, long cells with spirally-thickened walls. The elaters twist as they dry out, helping to dislodge the spores which are dispersed by air currents. New haploid thalli arise from germinated spores.

An example of a **leafy** liverwort is *Marsupella* (Fig. 25.30). It has an erect stem bearing two rows of trough-shaped leaves.

25.6.2 *Musci*

The *Musci* are the **mosses**. Like liverworts, most mosses inhabit damp places. However, mosses are more tolerant of desiccation and can survive in fairly dry places such as sand dunes and on dry stone walls. Each plant has a simple **stem** attached to the substrate by **multicellular rhizoids**. Simple **leaves** are usually arranged spirally along the stem. Antheridia and archegonia, usually on separate plants, arise from the growing tips of the stems. As in liverworts, the sporophyte is attached to the parent gametophyte plant.

FIG. 25.31 (a) Funaria hygrometrica, × *2*
(b) Polytrichum *sp.* × $\frac{1}{2}$

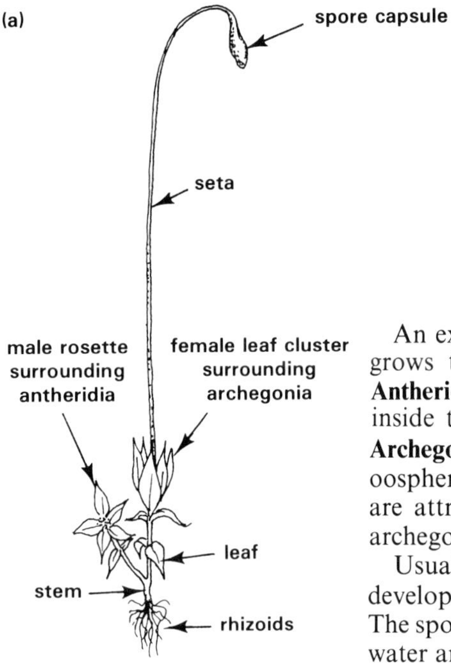

An example of a moss is *Funaria* (Fig. 25.31). Each plant is erect and grows to a few centimetres in height, often with a branching stem. **Antheridia** arise at the tip of the main stem. Repeated mitotic divisions inside the antheridia produce many haploid biflagellated antherozoids. **Archegonia** develop at the tip of a side-branch. There is a single haploid oosphere inside each archegonium. The antherozoids are chemotactic and are attracted to the oospheres by proteins secreted from the necks of archegonia. On fertilisation, a diploid zygote is formed.

Usually only one zygote develops further at each stem apex. The development results in a **sporogonium** with a long seta bearing a capsule. The sporogonium is attached to the gametophyte by a **foot**, through which water and nutrients are absorbed. However, the sporophyte is not totally dependent on the gametophyte. The **seta** and **capsule** become green and make organic materials by photosynthesis. The developing sporogonium is enclosed at first by the remains of the archegonium. As the seta elongates, the capsule is carried upwards. A cap called the **calyptra**, the remnant of the archegonium, covers the capsule (Fig. 25.32). The capsule contains a

FIG. 25.32 Funaria,
(a) *archegonia, × 20*
(b) *developing sporophyte*
(c) *antherozoids*

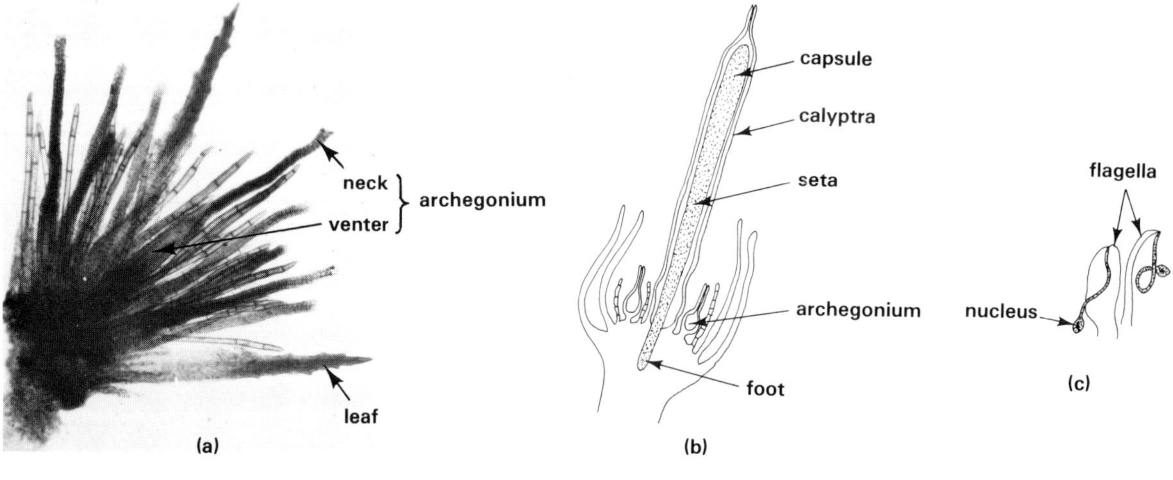

central tissue mass called the **columella**, surrounded by sporogenous tissue which produces the spores. Spore formation involves meiosis, and the haploid spores eventually occupy most of the space inside the capsule. The capsule is topped by the **peristome** covered by an outer domed cap, the

FIG. 25.33 Funaria, *capsule* (a) *V S, × 15* (b) *peristome teeth, × 30*

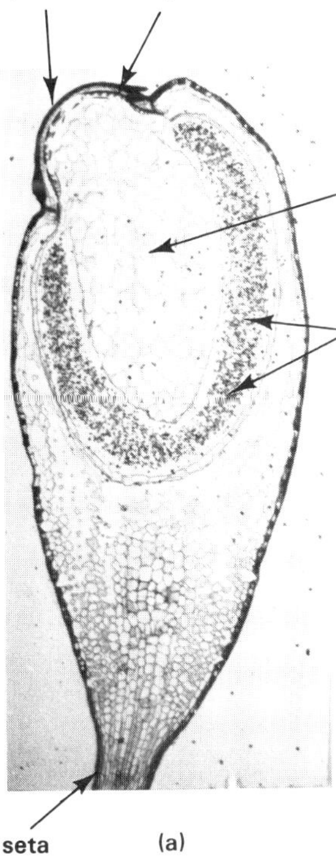

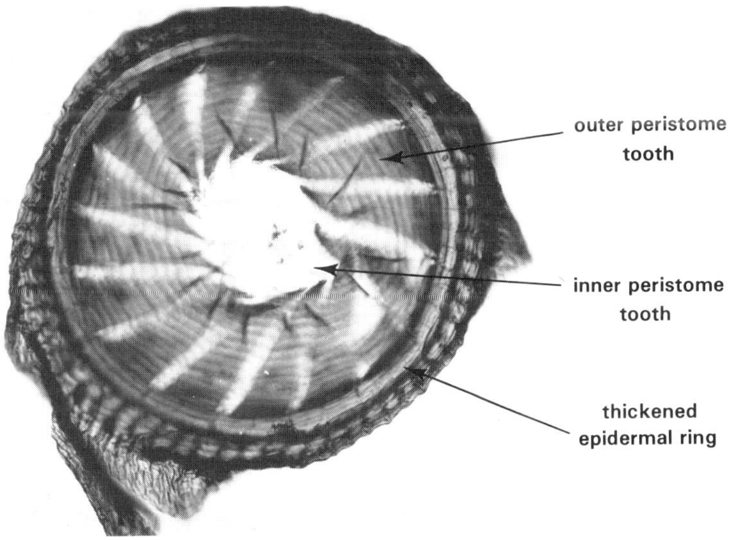

operculum (Fig. 25.33). As the spores mature, the columella disappears and the capsule dries out. The calyptra and operculum fall away, exposing the teeth of the peristome to the air. The peristome teeth are hygroscopic, bending open when dry and closing back when wet. When open, the ripe spores fall out, because the spore capsule is usually held upside down. Spores are dispersed by air currents. In suitable conditions, the spores germinate to produce a branching filament called the **protonema**. Haploid moss plants develop from 'buds' on the protonema and the life cycle is completed.

25.7 *Pteridophyta*

The pteridophytes include **clubmosses**, **horsetails** and **ferns**. Pteridophytes have a **heteromorphic alternation of generations**. The diploid sporophyte is the dominant phase and is independent of the haploid gametophyte. Unlike the algae and bryophytes, pteridophytes have **vascular tissue** containing **tracheids** or **xylem vessels** and **sieve cells**. The sporophyte plant is differentiated into **roots**, **stems** and **leaves**; the shoot system is covered by a **waterproof cuticle**. These features represent a greater adaptation to terrestrial life than is seen in the bryophytes. In the Carboniferous period, about three hundred million years ago, pteridophytes were the dominant plants on land. Their fossilised remains are useful to us as coal. The pteridophytes include the orders *Selaginellales*, *Equisetales* and *Filicales*.

25.7.1 *Selaginellales*

The *Selaginellales* include the **clubmoss** *Selaginella* (Fig. 25.34). *S. selaginoides* grows in upland pastures in the north and west of Britain. Most other species are tropical. In *S. kraussiana*, the sporophyte plant has a prostrate branching stem. Four rows of leaves, two small and two large,

FIG. 25.34 *Clubmoss,* Selaginella kraussiana (a) *whole plant,* × *1* (b) *strobilus* × *70* (c) *antherozoid*

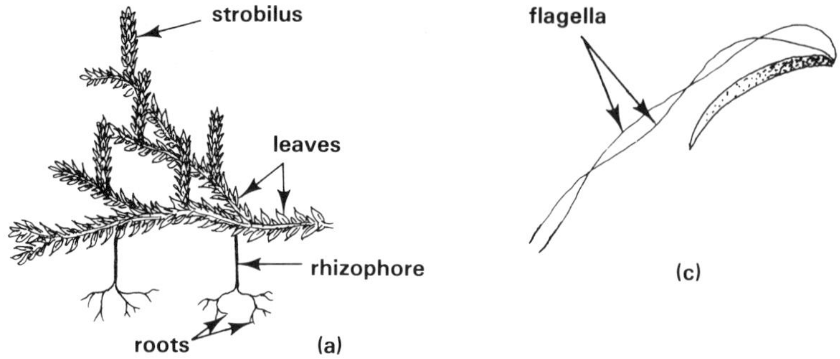

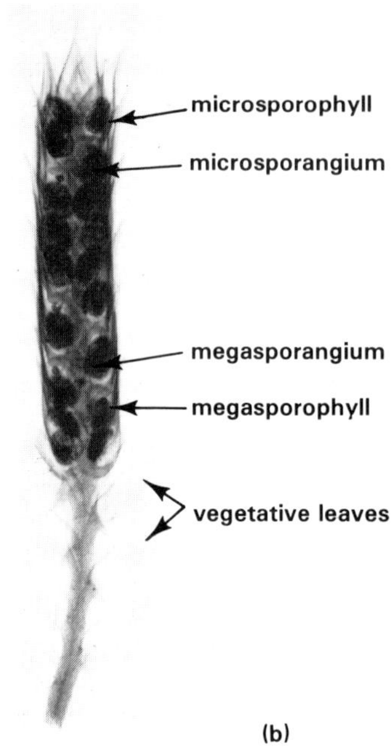

project laterally and the stem is anchored to the soil by roots. The roots develop from rhizophores which grow down from the stem.

In a mature **sporophyte**, cones called **strobili** develop at the ends of the shoots. Each strobilus carries modified leaves called **sporophylls**, in the axils of which develop the sporangia. Two kinds of sporangia are formed in the same strobilus. Each **microsporangium** produces many small **microspores**. Four large **megaspores** usually develop inside each **megasporangium**. For this reason *Selaginella* is **heterosporous**. Meiosis occurs in the production of spores and each spore is haploid. When ripe, the sporangia split open and the spores are released into the air. A **male gametophyte** which produces many biflagellated antherozoids develops inside each microspore. The antherozoids are released by rupture of the microspore wall. A **female gametophyte** develops inside each megaspore. This is made up of a cellular prothallus, on which archegonia develop at one end. An oosphere appears in each archegonium. As the archegonia develop, the megaspore wall splits, exposing the apex of the gametophyte. Fertilisation of the oosphere by an antherozoid produces a diploid zygote which develops into a new sporophyte plant to complete the life cycle.

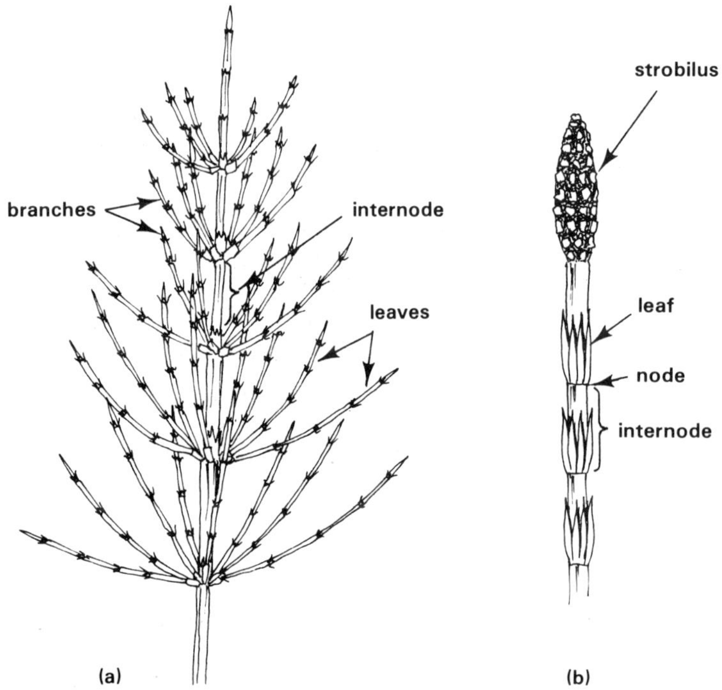

FIG. 25.35 *Common horsetail,* Equisetum arvense (a) *sterile aerial branch,* × $\frac{1}{2}$ (b) *fertile aerial branch,* × *1* (c) *spores with coiled and uncoiled elaters*

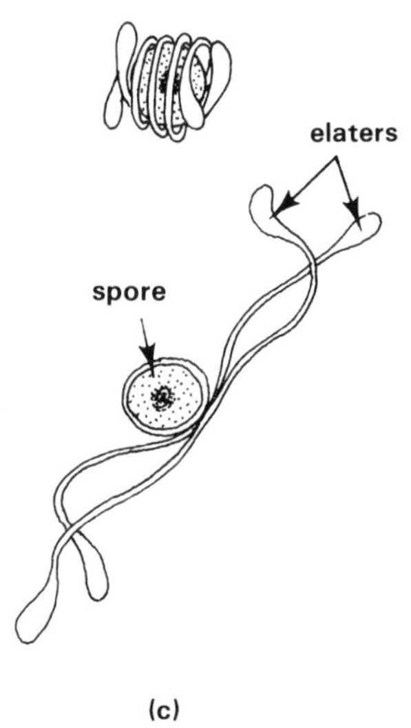

25.7.2 *Equisetales*

The *Equisetales* are represented by a single living genus, *Equisetum*, the **horsetail** (Fig. 25.35). The stem of the **sporophyte** is a root-like rhizome which grows horizontally in the soil. Whorls of small scale-like leaves arise at nodes on the rhizome. Adventitious roots also arise at the nodes where the rhizome may be branched. In *E. arvense*, two kinds of aerial shoots grow from the rhizome. Sterile shoots are green and much-branched at the nodes. Photosynthesis occurs in the stem, the whorls of leaves at each node being scale-like and colourless. Fertile shoots are colourless, unbranched and have a single **strobilus** at the apex. The strobilus is made up of several whorls of sporangiophores. Each consists of a stalk with a disc on the outside which supports the **sporangia**. Meiosis occurs in the production of spores. Each haploid spore secretes a wall containing four coiled strips. The strips are hygroscopic and spring open when dry, thus helping to free the spores.

Spores are short-lived and germinate in suitable conditions to produce the **gametophyte** generation. Each gametophyte is a small green lobed thallus less than a centimetre across, attached to the soil by rhizoids. Antheridia and archegonia develop on the thallus, and zygotes are formed when oospheres are fertilised by motile antherozoids. The zygotes develop into new sporophyte plants.

25.7.3 *Filicales*

The *Filicales* are the **ferns** such as *Dryopteris* (Fig. 25.36). The **sporophyte** plant has an underground rhizome. A tangled mass of adventitious roots grows from the rhizome, which is usually covered by the bases of old leaves from previous years' growth. The apex of the rhizome projects above the surface of the soil. From it arise compound leaves called **fronds**. Each frond has a main axis called the **rachis**, from which arise numerous lateral **pinnae**. Each pinna is divided into many green **pinnules**. Fronds develop over two years. They begin as coiled structures and gradually unroll as growth proceeds.

FIG. 25.36 *The male fern,* Dryopteris filix-mas (a) *whole plant* (b) *two fronds*

(a) (b)

The pinnules of mature fronds have **sporangia** on their lower surface. Sporangia are in clusters called **sori** and are covered by a protective flap of tissue called the **indusium** (Fig. 25.37). The indusium degenerates as the sori

FIG. 25.37 Dryopteris,
longitudinal section sorus, × 150

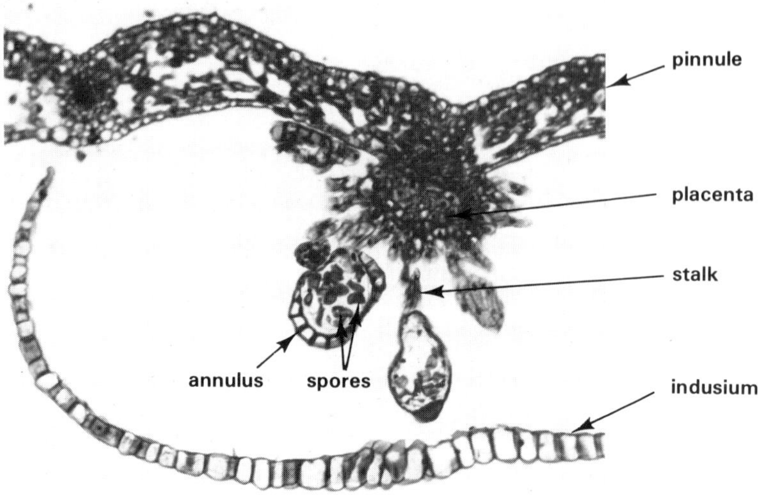

FIG. 25.38 Dryopteris
sporangium (a) *mature*
(b) *dehisced with annulus bent back* (c) *annulus recoil propelling spores into the air*

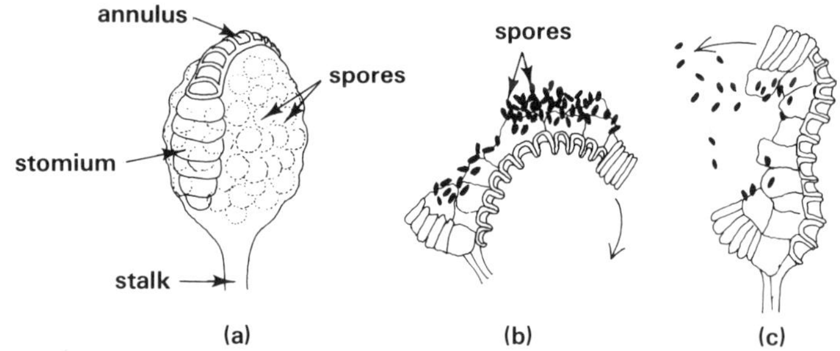

FIG. 25.39 Dryopteris
(a) *photomicrograph of prothallus, × 20* (b) *antheridium, × 600* (c) *antherozoid, × 1000*
(d) *archegonium, × 650*

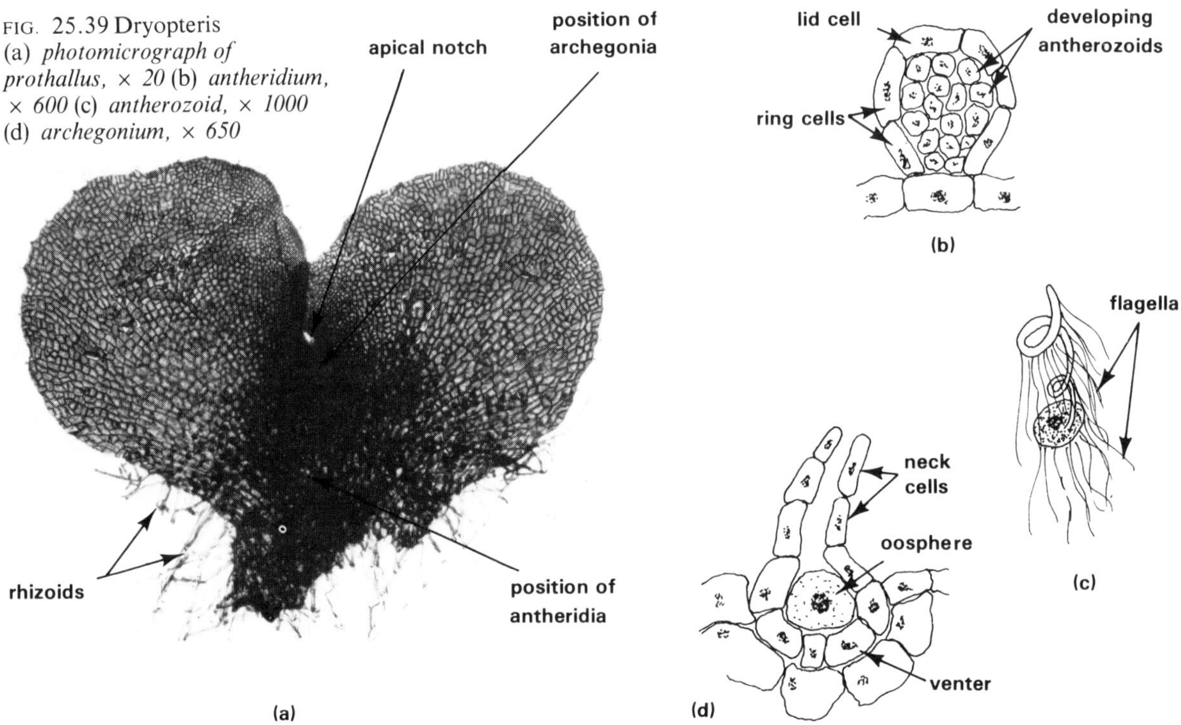

FIG. 25.40 Dryopteris, *developing sporophyte,* × *15*

develop, exposing the ripe sporangia to the air. Each mature sporangium consists of a flat spore-containing capsule attached by a stalk to the **placenta**. A row of cells with partially thickened walls extends three-quarters of the way around the capsule. These cells make up the **annulus** (Fig. 25.38(a)). Next to the annulus is a row of large thin-walled cells which make up the **stomium**. Dehiscence of a sporangium occurs when the annulus cells dry out and shrink. The thinner-walled stomium ruptures and the annulus springs back to reveal the haploid spores. As the annulus cells dry out more, their ability to hold the annulus in its sprung position fails. The annulus suddenly recoils and many of the spores are catapulted away to be dispersed by air currents (Fig. 25.38(b) and (c)).

After a short dormant period, the haploid spores germinate to produce the **gametophyte** generation. The gametophyte is a flat heart-shaped **prothallus** about a centimetre long. It is green and attached to the soil by **rhizoids** (Fig. 25.39). Sex organs develop on the underside of the prothallus. Spherical antheridia are found among the rhizoids. Antherozoids are coiled and flagellated. Archegonia develop some distance away from the antheridia on the central cushion near the apical notch of the prothallus. Each archegonium has a cup-shaped **venter** from which projects a short **neck**. The venter encloses a single oosphere. Chemotaxis by the antherozoids brings them towards the archegonia; the attractant is malic acid, secreted by the necks of the archegonia. Antherozoids swim down the archegonial necks and fuse with the oospheres to form diploid zygotes. Usually only one zygote develops further on each prothallus to give rise to a new sporophyte generation (Fig. 25.40).

25.8 *Spermatophyta*

The **spermatophytes** are the **gymnosperms** and **angiosperms**. They dominate the earth's terrestrial vegetation. Except in a few genera, there are no motile antherozoids such as are found in the bryophytes and pteridophytes. Consequently, spermatophytes do not require water for fertilisation. The male gametes are haploid nuclei inside resistant **pollen**. **Seeds** contain and protect the embryo (Chapter 19). The main phase of the life cycle is the diploid **sporophyte** (Fig. 25.41), usually with well-developed roots, stem

FIG. 25.41 *Life cycles of* (a) *a bryophyte* (b) *a pteridophyte and* (c) *an angiosperm*

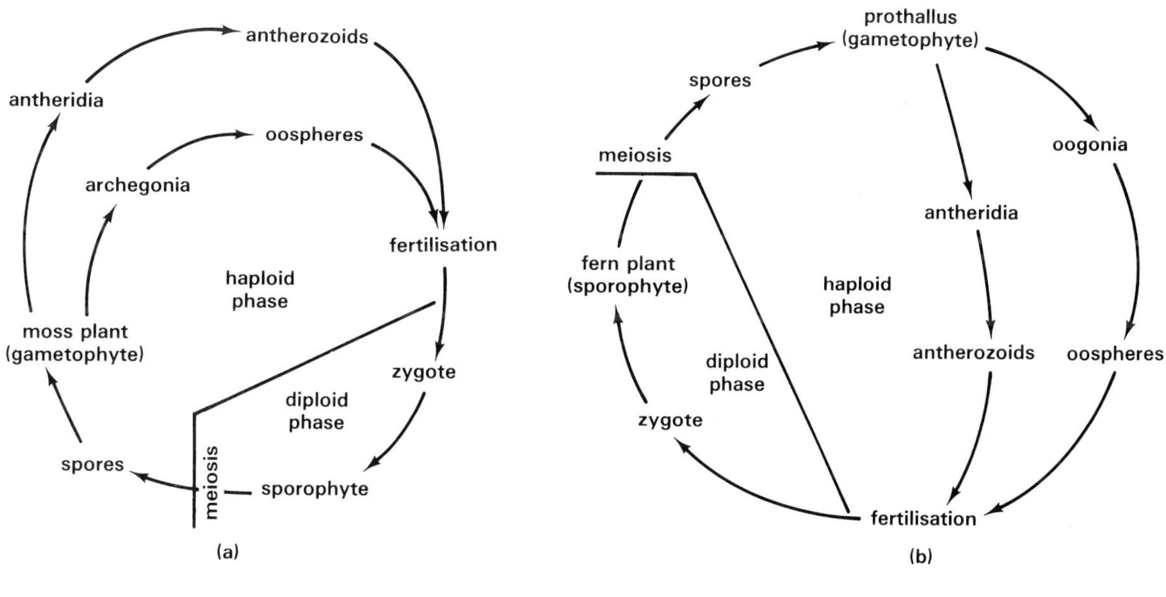

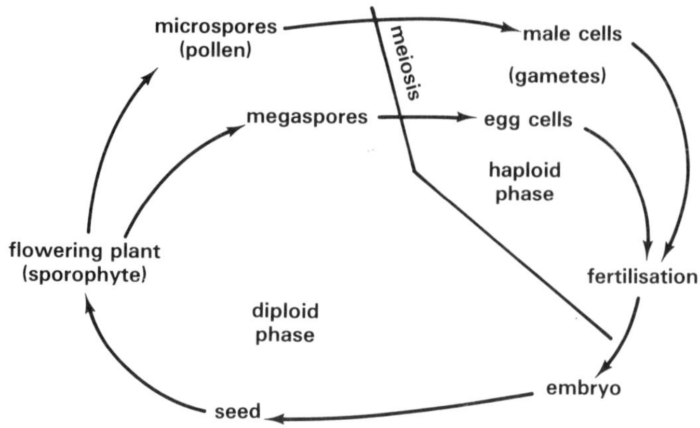

(c)

and leaves. Efficient **vascular tissue** is present (Chapter 11) and the aerial parts of the sporophyte are protected from desiccation by a **waterproof cuticle**. The development of **woody tissue** in many spermatophytes enables them to grow to considerable size (Fig. 11.12). These features are largely responsible for the relative success of spermatophytes as terrestrial plants.

The spermatophytes contain two main classes, *Gymnospermae* and *Angiospermae*.

25.8.1 *Gymnospermae*

The gymnosperms contain **cycads** and **conifers**. The seeds of gymnosperms are naked and not enclosed in a pericarp as in angiosperms. **Tracheids** (Chapter 11) are the water-transporting cells, and **sieve cells** carry organic materials. Secondary vascular tissue is always present. The gymnosperms contain several orders, including the *Coniferales*.

FIG. 25.42 *The Scots pine,* Pinus sylvestris, $\times \frac{1}{120}$

1. *CONIFERALES*

The Scots pine, *Pinus sylvestris* (Fig. 25.42) is a conifer. It is a tall tree, growing to a height of 30 m or more. Underground it has a branched system of roots which arise from a vertical tap root. Old roots are woody and give sturdy anchorage. As a pine tree grows, it loses its lower branches, leaving the bottom of the shoot as a straight trunk. A pyramidal mass of branches grows from the upper part of the trunk. Photosynthetic leaves are restricted to lateral dwarf or spur shoots which are eventually shed from the tree. The dwarf shoots develop from buds in the axils of brown scale-like leaves on the main shoot. Each spur shoot consists of a short stem, a series of overlapping deciduous bud scales and two needle-like leaves (Fig. 25.43). The thick cuticle of the leaves helps prevent drying out in windy and in arid conditions. The leaves also tolerate frost.

Pinus is **monoecious** and **heterosporous**, bearing male and female cones on the same tree. **Male cones** take the place of dwarf shoots and arise in clusters on young long shoots, just behind the terminal buds. A male cone has many **microsporophylls**, each bearing two **microsporangia** on the underside. Haploid **microspores (pollen grains)** are formed by meiosis. When mature, they each contain an incomplete male gametophyte and have two air-filled sacs. When they have shed their pollen, male cones wither and drop off the tree (Fig. 25.44).

Female cones take the place of long shoots. On the axis of the cone are small spirally-arranged **ovuliferous scales**, under each of which is a **bract scale** (Fig. 25.45). Each ovuliferous scale bears two **ovules** on its upper

FIG. 25.43 Pinus *twig, growing tip*

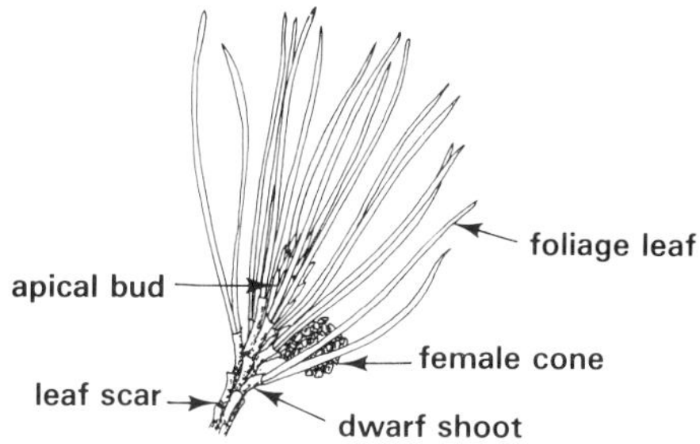

FIG. 25.44 Pinus (a) *cluster of male cones* (b) *longitudinal section of male cone, × 5* (c) *pollen grains, × 80*

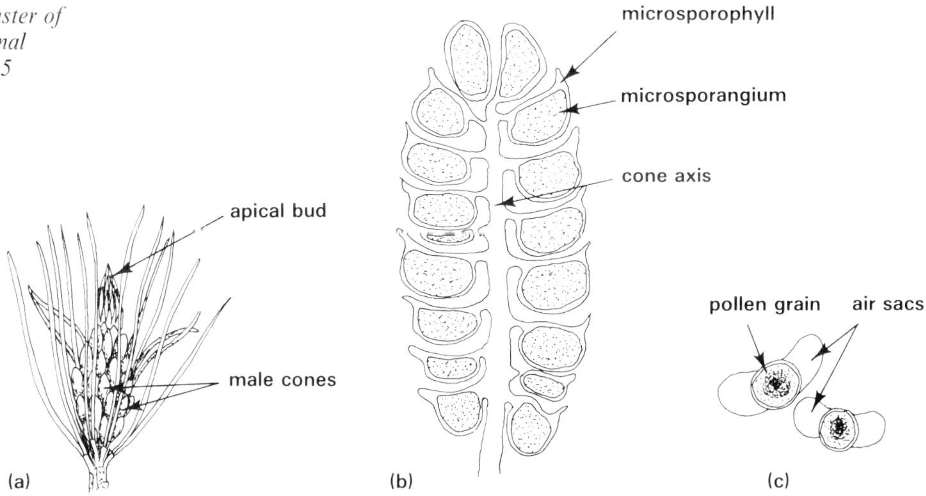

FIG. 25.45 Pinus *female cone* (a) *beginning of second year* (b) *two ovules, × 10*

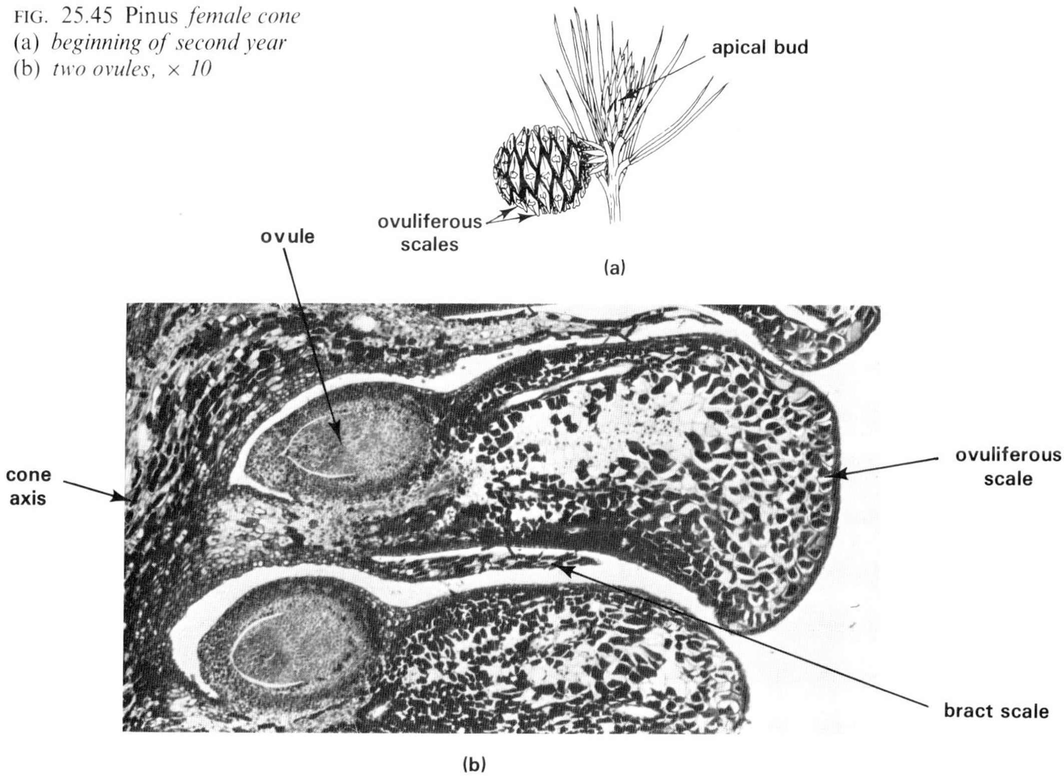

FIG. 25.46 Pinus, *longitudinal section of ovule at fertilisation stage* (from photomicrographs, × 5)

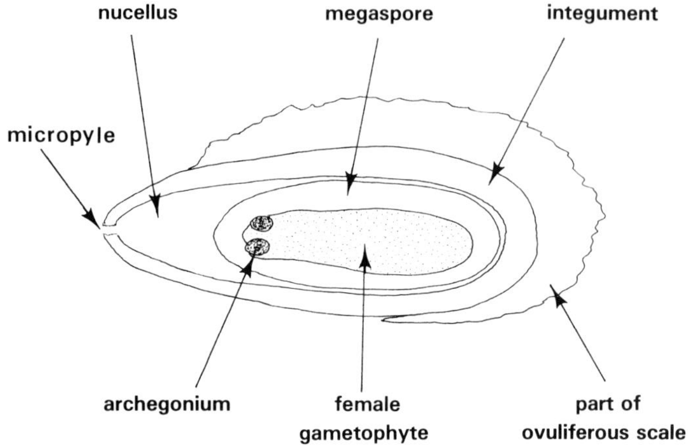

FIG. 25.47 Pinus *development of pollen grain* (a) *just before shedding* (b) *at the time of shedding* (c) *the following spring* (d) *just before fertilisation*

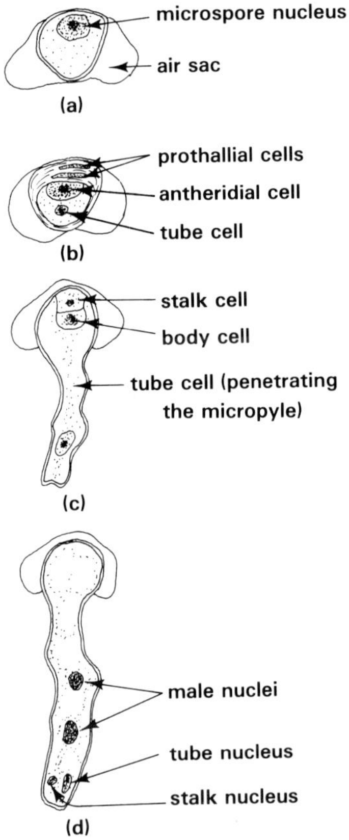

surface. Ovules contain a mass of tissue, called the **nucellus**, which is equivalent to a **megasporangium**. It is covered by an **integument**. At one end is a small pore, the **micropyle**. A single haploid **megaspore** develops inside each ovule.

Pollination, the transfer of pollen grains from male cones to female cones, is by wind. The air sacs keep the pollen grains suspended for long periods in the air. Pollen is drawn into the ovule through the micropyle. After pollination, the development of the male and female gametophytes proceeds slowly and is interrupted by winter. In the following spring, the **female gametophyte** (prothallus) becomes cellular, and three or four **archegonia** are formed (Fig. 25.46). The **male gametophyte** completes its development, and the male gametes are carried through the nucellus to the archegonia by growth of the **pollen tube** (Fig. 25.47).

Fertilisation occurs when the male nucleus from the pollen fuses with the female nucleus in the oosphere. A diploid zygote is formed. Usually only one zygote develops in each ovule to produce an **embryo**. The integument becomes a hard testa and protects the embryo inside the **seed**. Each seed has a thin papery wing, part of the ovuliferous scale (Fig. 25.48). Maturing of the seeds ready for release from the female cones takes a further year. Female cones therefore require three years to complete their seed-producing function. Ripe seeds are dispersed by the wind and germination is epigeal (section 20.2).

FIG. 25.48 Pinus (a) *female cone, third year* (b) *seed* (c) *longitudinal section of embryo,* × 7

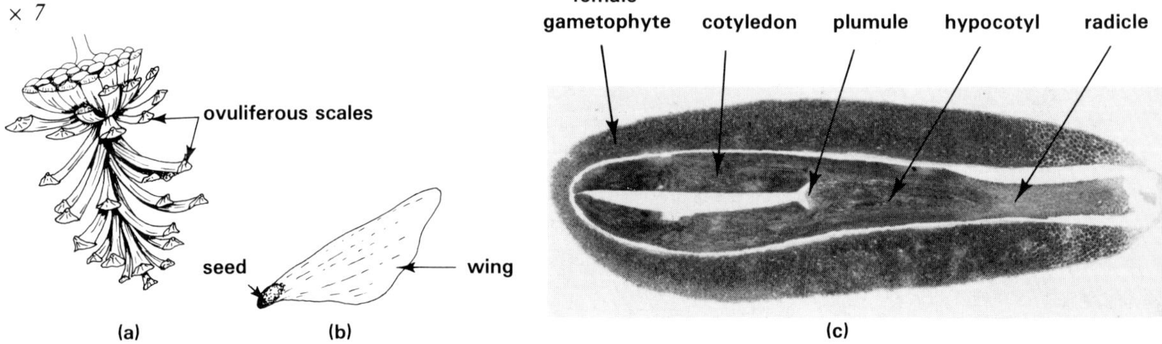

25.8.2 *Angiospermae*

The angiosperms are the **flowering plants**. The sexual reproductive organs are found in **flowers** and the seeds are enclosed in a **pericarp**. The ovules with two integuments are borne within a structure called the **carpel**. The female gametophyte is an **embryo sac** lacking archegonia. It develops from a megaspore produced by the nucellus of the ovule. The microspores (pollen) which are produced in anthers germinate on a special region of the carpel called the **stigma**. Pollination is by wind, water, insects and sometimes birds. **Double fertilisation** occurs, producing a zygote and usually a triploid endosperm nucleus. The vascular system consists of **vessels** and **tracheids** and **sieve tubes** with **companion cells** (Chapters 11 and 12). These elements are more effective at transportation than the tracheids and sieve cells of gymnosperms. Secondary vascular tissue is often present.

For details of angiosperm anatomy and reproduction refer to Chapters 19, 20 and 21. There are two subclasses, *Monocotyledones* and *Dicotyledones*.

1. *MONOCOTYLEDONES*

These produce seeds with a **single cotyledon**. The vascular tissue in the leaves is arranged in **parallel veins** (Fig. 25.49). In the stem, the vascular

FIG. 25.49 *Some monocotyledons* (a) *wild oat* Avena fatua (b) *common sedge,* Carex nigra (c) *maize, Zea* mays

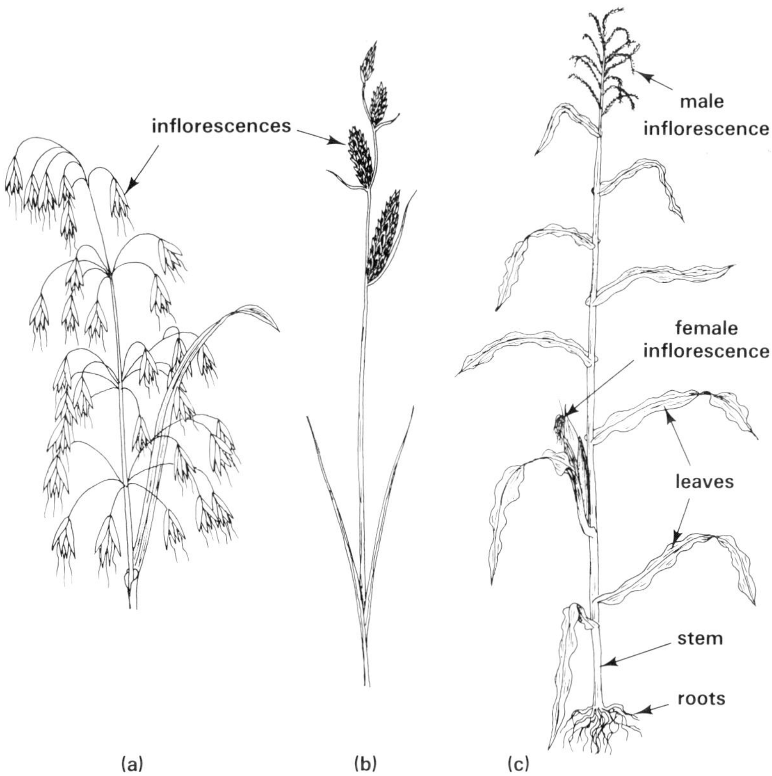

bundles are scattered (Fig. 25.50). The floral parts are usually arranged in **threes** or multiples of three (Fig. 25.51). Secondary growth (Chapter 21) occurs in only a few species. For this reason, monocotyledonous plants are mainly **herbaceous**. Some perennate by forming bulbs, corms and rhizomes, which are also a means of propagation (Chapter 19).

FIG. 25.50 *Transverse section of monocotyledonous stem,* Zea mays, × *5*

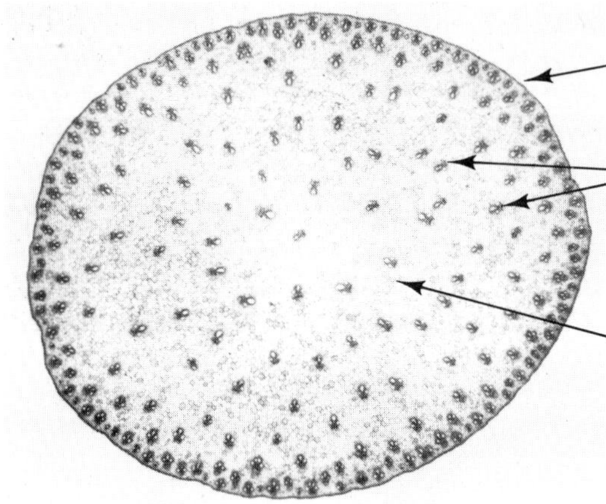

FIG. 25.51 *Grass floret* (after Gill and Vear)

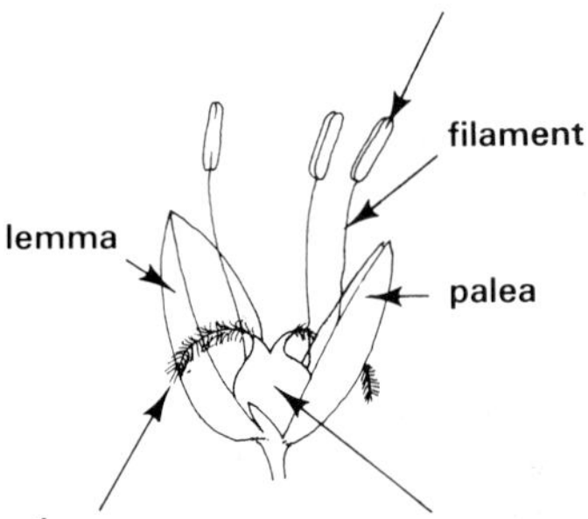

Among the monocotyledonous plants most important to man are the cereals, such as barley, oats, maize, rice and wheat, and the grasses. Grasses make up most of the vegetation in pastureland.

2. *DICOTYLEDONES*

These produce seeds with **two cotyledons** (Fig. 25.52). The vascular tissue in the leaves is net-like (Fig. 11.1). In the stem, the vascular bundles are arranged in a circle between the cortex and pith (Fig. 21.2). The floral parts are generally in **fours** or **fives** or in multiples of these numbers (Fig. 19.1).

FIG. 25.52 *Some dicotyledons* (a) *common buttercup,* Ranunculus acris (b) *dandelion,* Taraxacum officinale (c) *oak* Quercus robur, × $\frac{1}{100}$

Secondary growth occurs in many dicotyledons, which grow as **shrubs** and **trees**. The climax vegetation in most parts of Britain comprises dicotyledonous deciduous trees, such as elm and oak, and shrubs such as the hawthorn. In autumn they lose their leaves, and their woody twigs survive the winter (Fig. 21.30). There are many herbaceous dicotyledonous species including **annuals** which overwinter as seeds, and **perennials** which survive unfavourable conditions as tubers and swollen tap roots (Figs. 19.13 and 19.15). Biennial and perennial dicotyledons such as beetroot, carrots, parsnips and potatoes are an important part of the diet of humans, as are the seeds of some annuals such as peas and beans.

Spermatophytes make up the bulk of the earth's terrestrial vegetation. Among the reasons for their success is their enormous variety of habit, independence of water for fertilisation and the ability of many species to tolerate and survive desiccation. For these reasons there are few terrestrial habitats where flowering plants are not found.

Chapter 26

Variety of life: Non-chordate animals

Non-chordate animals include the single-celled *Protozoa* and a wide variety of multicellular groups. None of them has a dorsal notochord, which is characteristic of the chordate animals. Non-chordate animals are often called **invertebrates**, as they do not have vertebrae either. However, some chordate animals are also invertebrate (Chapter 27).

26.1 *Protozoa*

Protozoans are micro-organisms whose bodies consist of a single cell and are thus **unicellular**. Some biologists see the protozoan body as not being divided into cells. From this point of view, protozoans are sometimes described as **acellular**. The phylum *Protozoa* is divided into four classes: *Sarcodina*, *Mastigophora*, *Ciliata* and *Sporozoa*.

26.1.1 *Sarcodina (Rhizopoda)*

The sarcodines are protozoans which have cytoplasmic extensions called **pseudopodia** (Fig. 26.1). *Amoeba's* body changes shape constantly because pseudopodia are formed. When the body touches a solid surface, the cytoplasm changes viscosity, becoming a liquid **sol** at the rear of the body. The **plasmasol** flows forward into the leading edge of the animal as it advances. When the plasmasol enters the pseudopodia, it becomes a more viscous **plasmagel**. Each pseudopodium extends further as more plasmasol

FIG. 26.1 *Some sarcodines*
(a) *Amoeba,* × *100*
(b) *Actinophrys,* × *900*
(c) *Difflugia,* × *175*
(d) *Entamoeba,* × *1000*

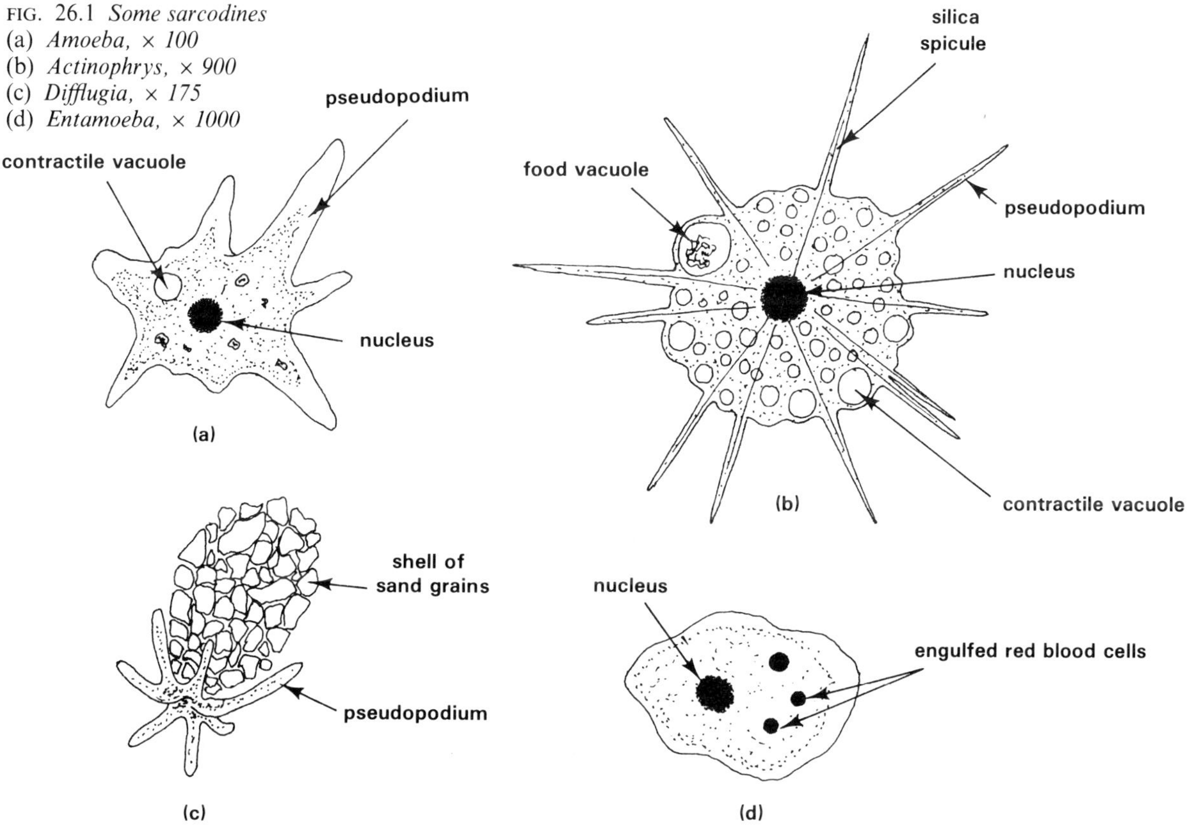

FIG. 26.2 *Changes occuring in the cytoplasm during amoeboid movement*

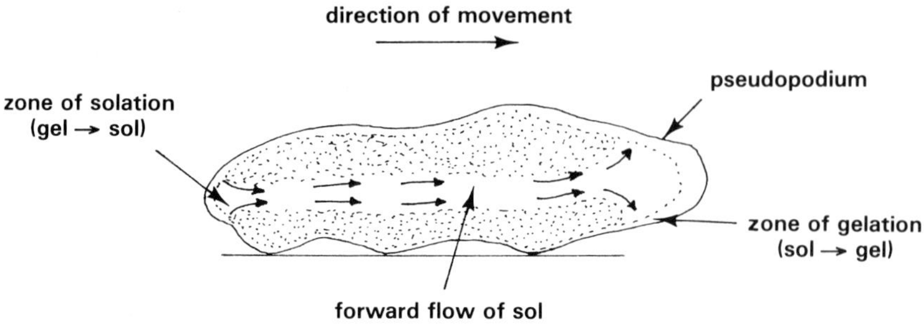

flows in from behind (Fig. 26.2). There is no permanent front or rear. *Amoeba* can stop suddenly and reverse its direction of movement. This often happens if the animal meets an obstruction. The use of pseudopodia for locomotion is called **amoeboid movement**. Amoeboid movement is also seen in some of the white blood cells of multicellular animals (Fig. 9.22). Pseudopodia are also used for capturing prey. The pseudopodia are extended over the prey, which are engulfed into food vacuoles in the cytoplasm. The process is called **phagocytosis** (section 9.2.2). The pseudopodia of some sarcodines are supported by thin rods such as the silica spicules of *Actinophrys*. In others the entire body is surrounded and supported by a shell through which the pseudopodia project. An example of a shelled sarcodine is *Difflugia*. Two groups of shelled sarcodines, the *Foraminifera* and the *Radiolaria*, are abundant in the sea. When they die, their shells sink to the sea bed, forming thick **oozes** which have given rise to limestone and siliceous rocks.

Reproduction in the sarcodines is mainly by **binary fission** in which mitosis occurs. The parasitic *Entamoeba histolytica* produces resistant cysts which are egested in the faeces of an infected host and bring about the spread of amoebic dysentery. Sexual reproduction occurs in many sarcodines, but not *Amoeba*. Most sarcodines are free-living in the sea, freshwater ponds and lakes or in thin films of water in soil and on vegetation. In freshwater species, water is constantly taken in by osmosis. It accumulates in one or more vacuoles which increase in size as the water enters. At intervals they expel the water to the outside through the body surface. Because they pulsate doing this, they are called **contractile vacuoles**.

26.1.2 *Mastigophora (Flagellata)*

Protozoans which have one or several **flagella** belong to the *Mastigophora*. Flagella are whip-like organelles, relatively long compared with cilia, but with the same ultrastructure (Fig. 26.3). They are used in locomotion.

FIG. 26.3 *Electronmicrograph, transverse section of cilia × 50 000. Cilia contain longitudinal fibrils, two in the centre surrounded by nine outer pairs. Contraction of the fibrils causes bending of the cilia*

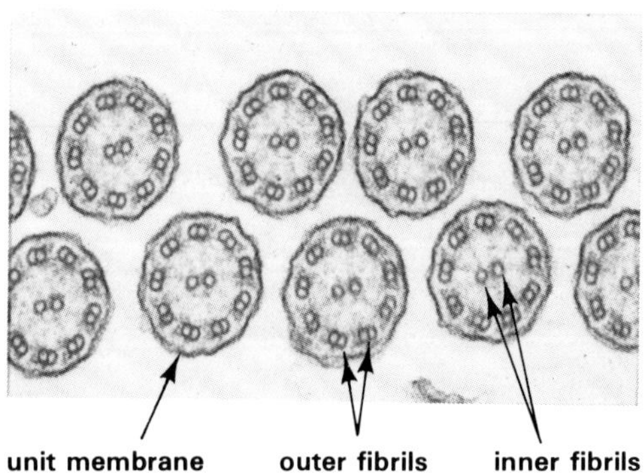

Euglena, for example, has a single locomotory flagellum (Fig. 26.6). A second very short flagellum is found at the base of the main flagellum inside a cup-shaped reservoir at the anterior end of the body. Waves of contraction spread along the locomotory flagellum from the base to the tip. Spiral movements of the flagellum pull the animal through the water in a helical path (Fig. 26.4(a)). Locomotion may also be brought about more slowly by pulsation of the whole body, called **euglenoid movement**, in which contractile plates in the flexible pellicle are used (Fig. 26.4(b)).

FIG. 26.4 (a) *Flagellate swimming in* Euglena
(b) *Euglenoid movement*

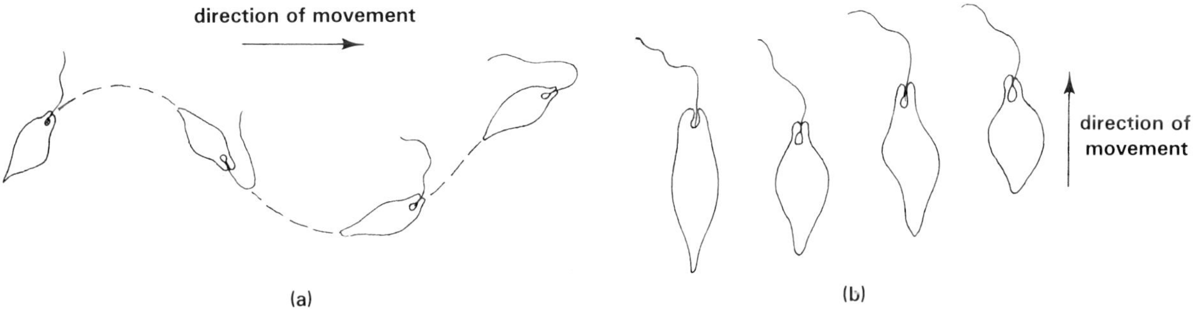

FIG. 26.5 *Binary fission in* Euglena

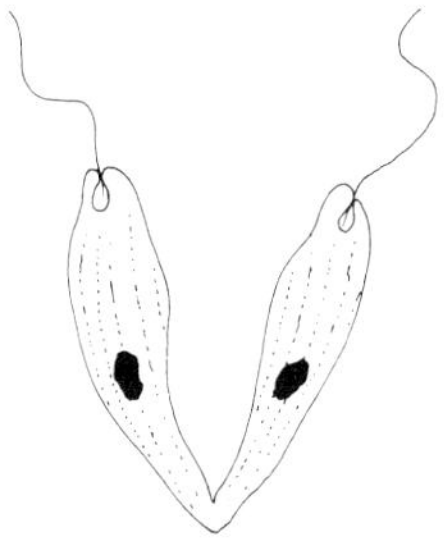

Euglena is **phototactic**, moving towards light to photosynthesise. A **photoreceptor** near the base of the long flagellum and a **stigma** in the adjacent cytoplasm are involved in the phototactic response. Contractile vacuoles regulate the water potential of freshwater flagellates.

Reproduction is by **binary fission**. Mitosis occurs and the protoplast divides longitudinally (Fig. 26.5). In adverse conditions the flagellum may withdraw and a resistant **cyst** is secreted around the protoplast. Fission may occur inside cysts. Several new individuals then emerge when the cysts burst in favourable conditions.

The *Mastigophora* is divided into two sub-classes, *Phytomastigina* and *Zoomastigina*.

1. *PHYTOMASTIGINA*

These include *Euglena* and *Ceratium* (Fig. 26.6). Their main feature is the presence of **chlorophyll**, contained in **chloroplasts**. It enables them to

FIG. 26.6 *Two green flagellates*
(a) Euglena, × *400*
(b) Ceratium × *300*

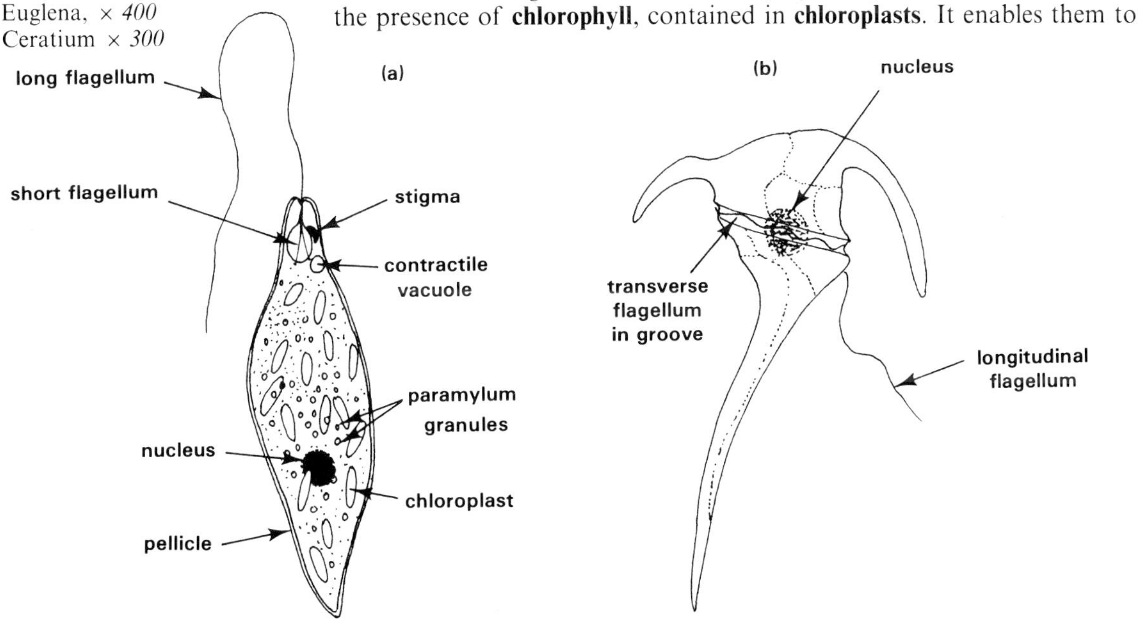

photosynthesise (**autotrophic** nutrition), although many are capable of **heterotrophic** nutrition in the dark. The presence of chlorophyll is a distinctly plant-like feature, and for this reason members of the *Phytomastigina* may also be classified among the **algae** (Chapter 25). The chloroplasts contain **pyrenoids** which store the product of photosynthesis, a starch-like carbohydrate called **paramylum**. Granules of paramylum may also be found free in the cytoplasm (Fig. 26.6(a)).

2. *ZOOMASTIGINA*

These are flagellates which do not have chlorophyll, so their nutrition is **heterotrophic**. They include *Trypanosoma*, a parasite which is the cause of sleeping sickness in mammals, and *Trichonympha*, a cellulose-digesting symbiont which lives in the gut of termites (Fig. 26.7).

FIG. 26.7 *Two non-green flagellates* (a) Trypanosoma, × *2000* (b) Trichonympha, × *2500*

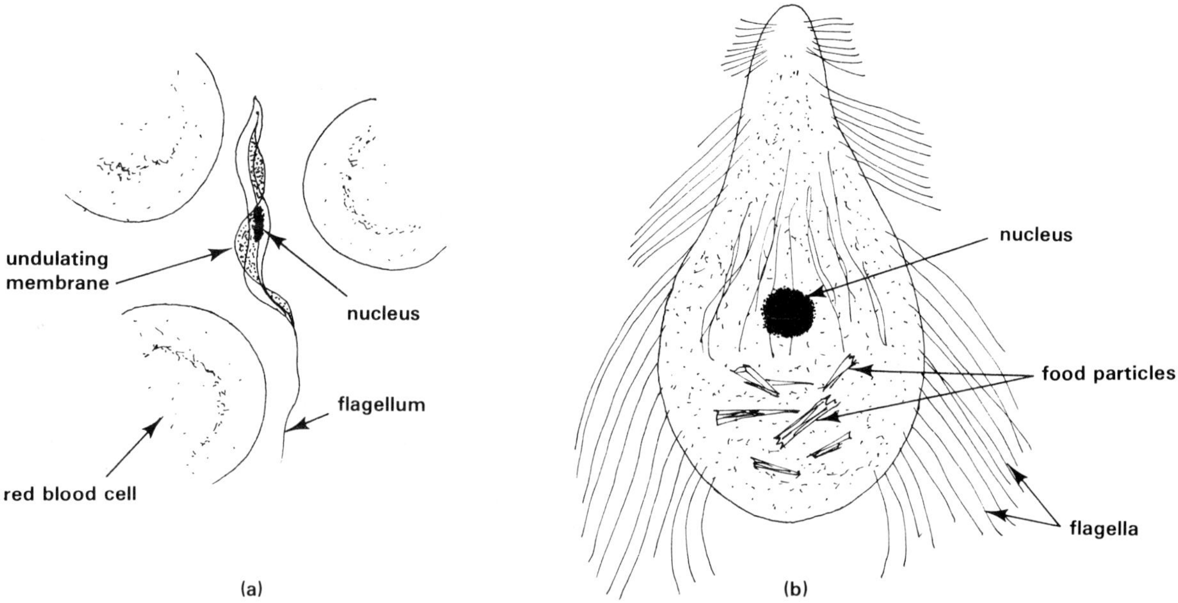

26.1.3 *Ciliata Ciliophora*

Paramecium and a variety of stalked protozoa such as *Vorticella* are **ciliates** (Fig. 26.8). Their main characteristics are the presence of numerous **cilia** and two nuclei, a small **micronucleus** and a large **meganucleus**.

FIG. 26.8 *Two ciliates*
(a) Paramecium × *200*
(b) Vorticella × *150*

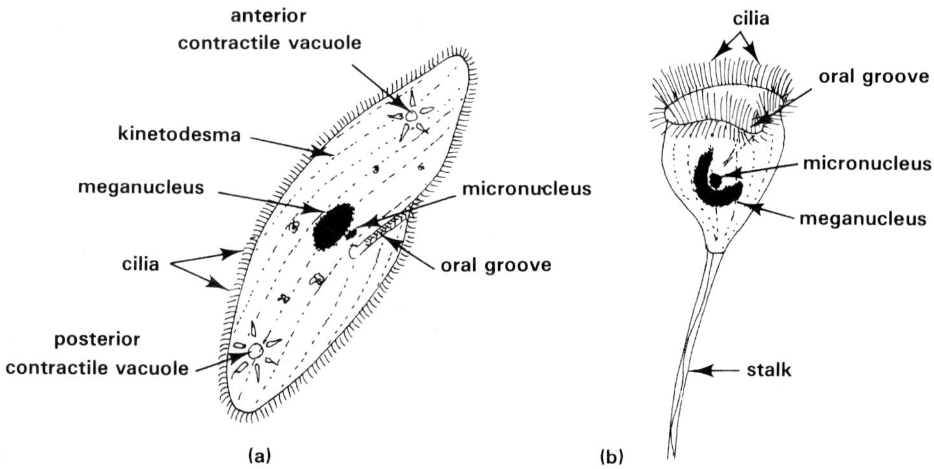

FIG. 26.9 (a) *part of the pellicle of* Paramecium (after Vickerman and Cox)
(b) *metachronal rhythm*

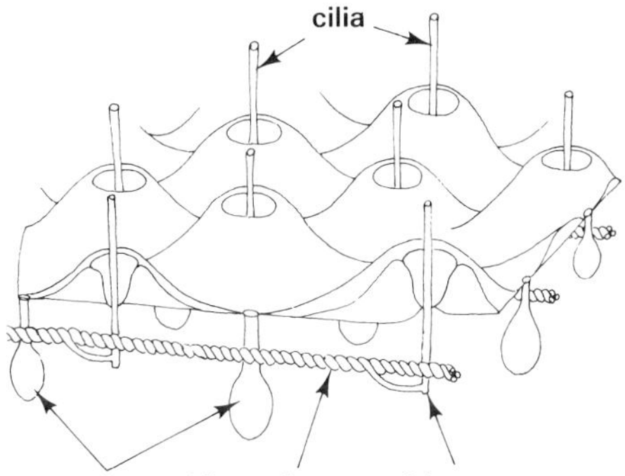

FIG. 26.10 *Path of food vacuoles in* Paramecium

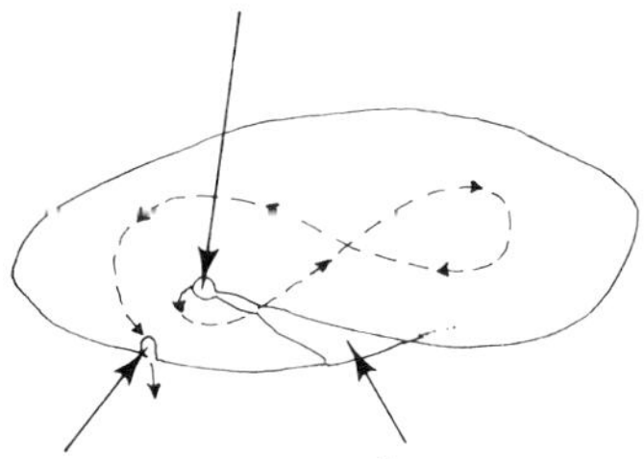

FIG. 26.11 *Binary fission in* Paramecium (compare with *Fig. 26.5*)

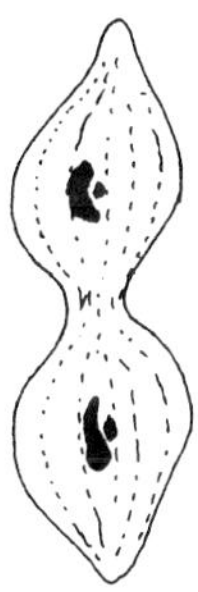

FIG. 26.12 *Conjugation in* Paramecium, × *160*

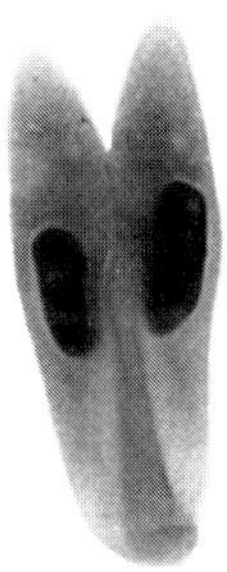

The cilia may be all over the body as in *Paramecium* or in patches as in *Vorticella*. Each cilium is attached to a **kinetosome** or **basal body** in the pellicle (Fig. 26.9). The kinetosomes are linked in rows by fine threads called **kinetodesmata** arranged longitudinally under the pellicle. Just beneath the pellicle in many ciliates are numerous sacs called **trichocysts**. They contain threads which may be discharged outwardly and used to capture prey, for defence against predators or the attachment of the body to a solid surface.

Cilia are often used for locomotion. In *Paramecium*, the cilia are arranged in tracts across the pellicle. Each cilium beats rhythmically and slightly out of phase with the adjacent cilia. This is called **metachronal rhythm** and creates a thrust against the surrounding water. *Paramecium* usually moves in a straight path, the body rotating about the longitudinal axis. If an individual meets an obstruction, reversal of the metachronal rhythm brings about a change of direction.

Cilia may also help in the capture of food. *Paramecium* has an **oral groove** on one side of its body. Small food particles such as bacteria are sucked down the oral groove by the beating of cilia. The food is engulfed into the cytoplasm by phagocytosis at the **cytostome** at the end of the oral groove. Food vacuoles produced in this way circulate in definite paths in the cytoplasm. Digestion occurs within the vacuoles from which the products are absorbed into the cytoplasm. Eventually, the unused contents of the vacuoles are discharged to the outside through the pellicle at the **cytoproct** (Fig. 26.10). The stalked ciliates such as *Vorticella* live attached by contractile stalks to solid surfaces such as larger animals, rocks or aquatic weeds. The cell is capped by rings of cilia. Rhythmic beating of the cilia helps to direct food into the oral groove. **Contractile vacuoles** regulate the water potential of freshwater ciliates (Fig. 2.12).

Ciliates reproduce both asexually and sexually. The asexual process of **binary fission** involves mitosis of the micronucleus, fission of other organelles and transverse division of the body (Fig. 26.11). Sexual reproduction occurs by **conjugation**, a complex process resulting in genetic variation among the offspring because of nuclear transfer and meiosis (Fig. 26.12). Self-fertilisation, called **autogamy**, occurs in some ciliates. This is a process in which conjugation occurs in a single individual.

26.1.4 *Sporozoa*

All the members of this class are parasitic. An example is *Plasmodium*, several species of which cause malaria in man. The main characteristics of the *Sporozoa* result from their parasitic way of life. They include a complex life cycle, a relatively simple body form and an absence of locomotory organelles. The name *Sporozoa* refers to the production of **spores** which often occurs in sporozoan life cycles.

Plasmodium will be described as an important example of the group. Three species of *Plasmodium* infect humans. *P. vivax* (Fig. 26.13) causes benign tertian malaria, *P. falciparum* malignant tertian malaria and *P. malariae* quartan malaria. All species are dispersed by the mosquito *Anopheles* which acts as a **vector** and **secondary host**.

FIG. 26.13 *Life cycle of* Plasmodium vivax

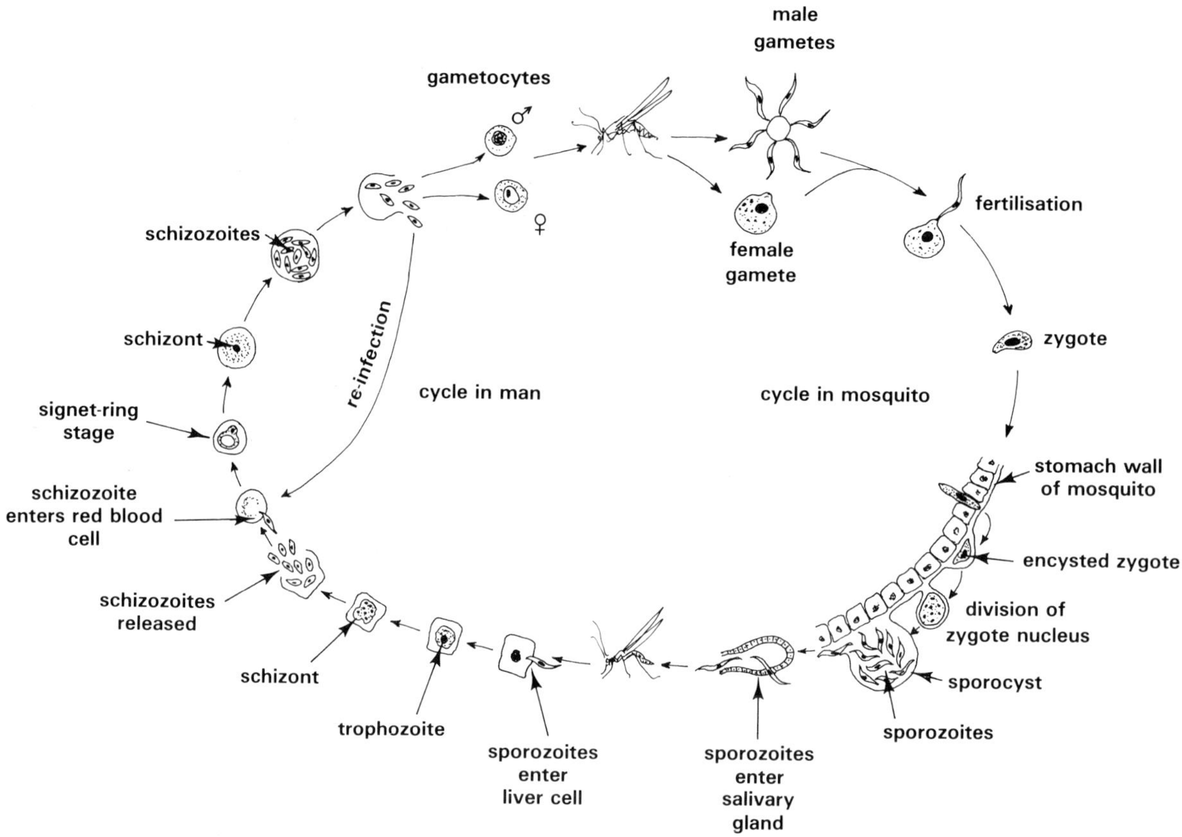

Malaria is the most common cause of death among humans. In the 1940s over three million people, mainly Asians and Africans, died of malaria annually. Today the figure has fallen to about two million. The reduction has come about by a combination of measures which are based on a knowledge of the life cycle of *Plasmodium* and its vector. Denying the anopheline mosquito access to humans prevents transmission of the disease. Spraying of human dwellings with insecticides such as DDT has proved effective in this respect. However, there is evidence that strains of *Anopheles* resistant to DDT have evolved in some countries where malaria is on the increase. The vector has an aquatic larval and pupal stage. Draining off, oiling or poisoning swamps and marshes reduces the mosquito's breeding territory. This approach has been very effective in recent years in China.

26.2 *Porifera*

Poriferans are commonly known as **sponges**. All sponges are sessile and aquatic, mostly marine. The body wall encloses a cavity into which water is drawn through numerous pores. The water is returned to the surroundings through larger pores called **oscula** (Fig. 26.14). The body wall consists of two parts, an outer **dermal layer** and an inner **gastral layer** (Fig. 26.15). On the inside, lining the body cavity are many **choanocytes**. These are cells, each with a collar and flagellum projecting into the body cavity. The beating action of the flagella creates the water current that provides the organism with oxygen and food, and eliminates its wastes. Particles of food such as plankton are engulfed and digested by the choanocytes. On the outside, the dermal layer consists largely of flat cells called **pinacocytes**.

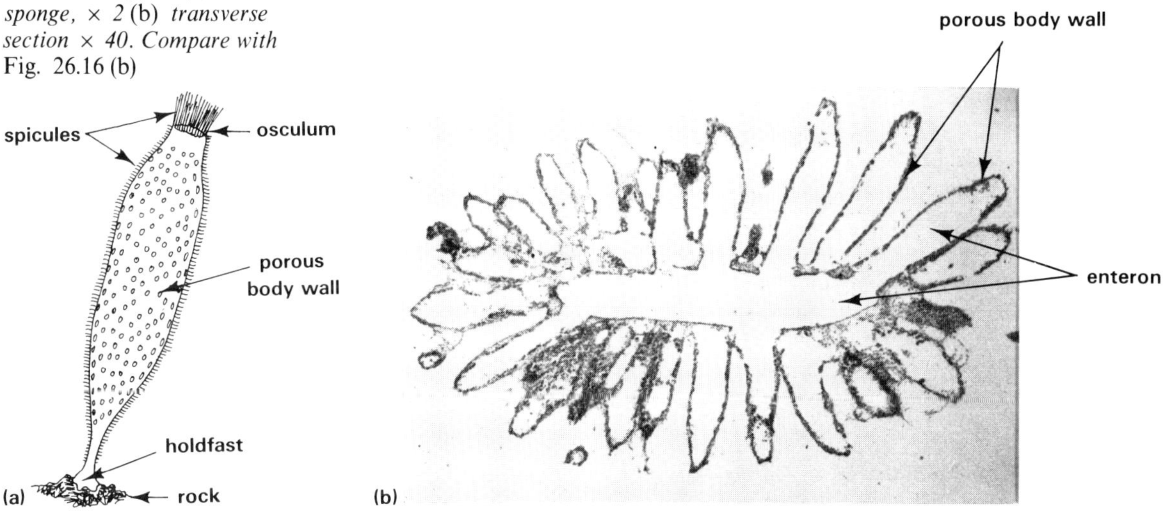

FIG. 26.14 Sycon (a) *whole sponge,* × *2* (b) *transverse section* × *40. Compare with* Fig. 26.16 (b)

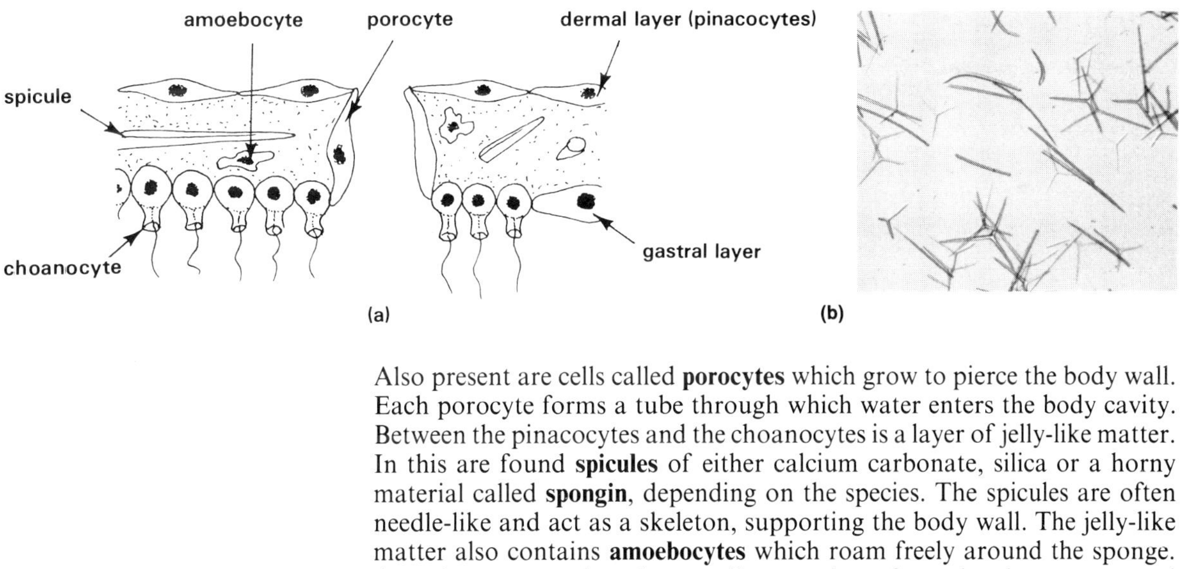

FIG. 26.15 *Sponge wall structure* (a) *diagram of a section showing cell types* (b) *spicules,* × *150*

Also present are cells called **porocytes** which grow to pierce the body wall. Each porocyte forms a tube through which water enters the body cavity. Between the pinacocytes and the choanocytes is a layer of jelly-like matter. In this are found **spicules** of either calcium carbonate, silica or a horny material called **spongin**, depending on the species. The spicules are often needle-like and act as a skeleton, supporting the body wall. The jelly-like matter also contains **amoebocytes** which roam freely around the sponge. Amoebocytes are thought to collect nutrients from the choanocytes and transport them to other parts of the sponge. Amoebocytes also produce the gametes for reproduction. Sponges contain no nervous system or sense organs.

The sponge shown in Figure 26.14 has a simple structure. In more complex sponges the body wall is folded into canals lined with chambers of choanocytes (Fig. 26.16).

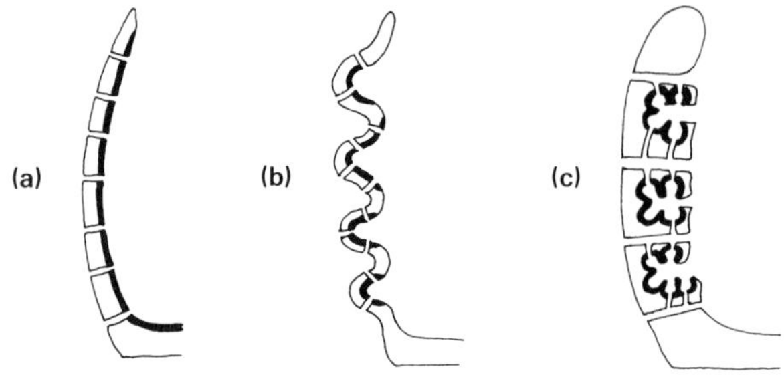

FIG. 26.16 *Grades of sponge wall* (a) *asconoid* (b) *syconoid* (c) *leuconoid*

26.3 *Cnidaria*

The *Cnidaria*, along with another phylum *Ctenophora*, are commonly called **coelenterates**. *Hydra*, *Obelia*, sea anemones, corals and jellyfish are cnidarians. Like sponges, they are aquatic. The body wall is of two layers of cells enclosing a central water-filled cavity called the **enteron**. Cnidarians exist in two basic forms, the **hydroid** and the **medusa** (Fig. 26.17). Each form has a single opening to the outside surrounded by **tentacles**. Through the opening food is brought into the enteron. Wastes are discharged from the enteron through the same opening. Coelenterates are said to be **diploblastic**, because the body is derived from two tissue layers. The outer layer is called the **ectoderm** and is separated from the **endoderm** by a jelly-like **mesogloea**. The diploblastic state is sometimes called the **tissue level of development** (Fig. 26.38). The ectoderm and endoderm consist of a variety of cells which perform specific functions. However, the tissues are not aggregated into organs. All coelenterates are **radially symmetric** (Fig. 26.29).

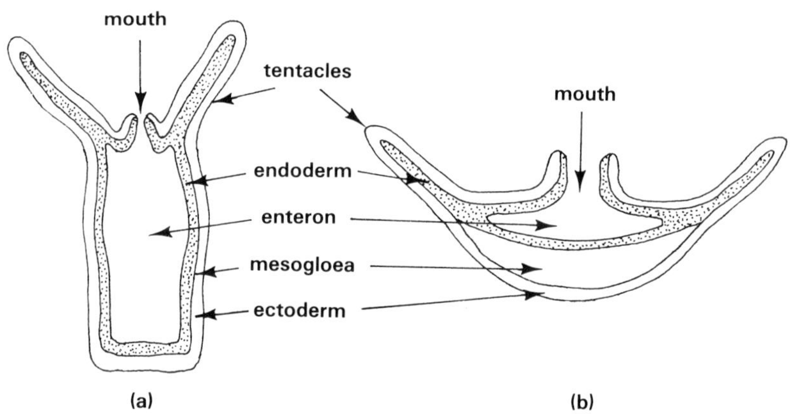

FIG. 26.17 *Cnidarian body forms* (a) *hydroid* (b) *medusoid*

26.3.1 Cell differentiation in cnidarians

1. MUSCLE CELLS

These cells are not like those of mammals (Chapter 15). However, they do contain contractile fibres. In the ectoderm, the fibres are arranged along the axis of the body. In endodermal muscle cells, they are arranged in a circle around the body (Fig. 26.18). The longitudinal and circular fibres act **antagonistically**. Contraction of one set is accompanied by relaxation of the other set and vice versa. The effect is to elongate or shorten the body. Many cnidarians are sessile and are supported by a hard skeleton, so body

FIG. 26.18 *The main cell types in the cnidarian body wall*

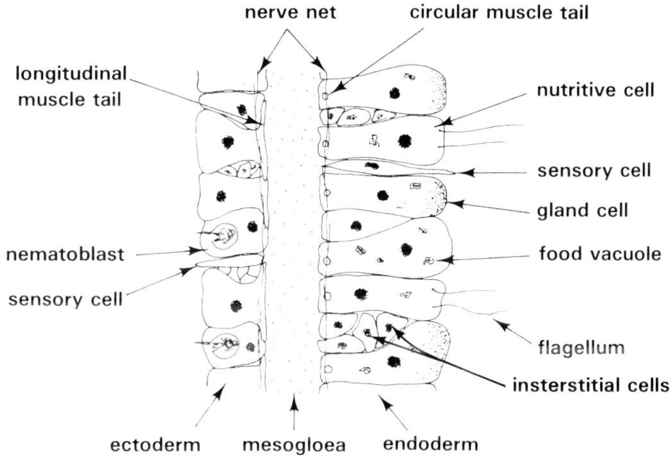

movement is restricted to retraction or extension of feeding tentacles. In others, such as jellyfish, rhythmic activity of the contractile fibres causes a pulsating movement of the whole body. *Hydra* moves by looping and somersaulting (Fig. 26.19).

FIG. 26.19 *Cnidarian movement*
(a) *pulsation in a jellyfish*
(b) *somersaulting in* Hydra

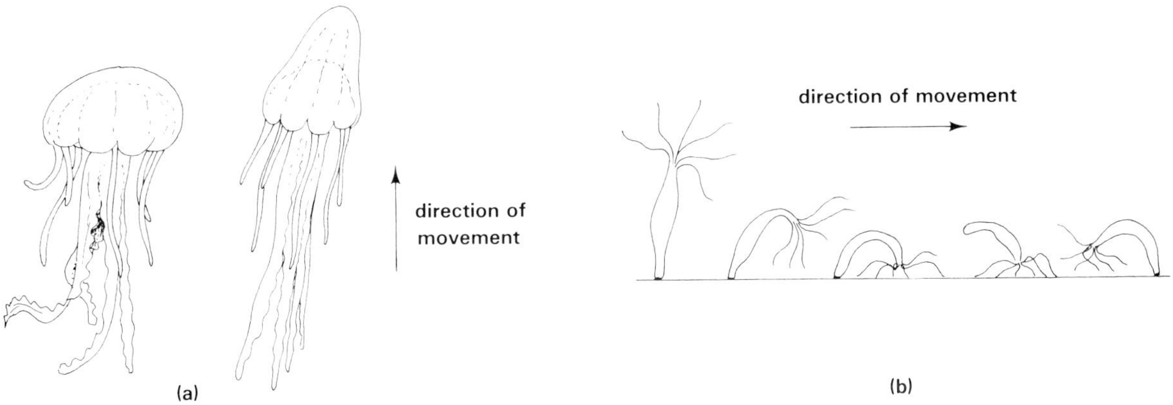

FIG. 26.20 *Nematocyst*
(a) *coiled* (b) *discharged (note the thread turns inside out)*

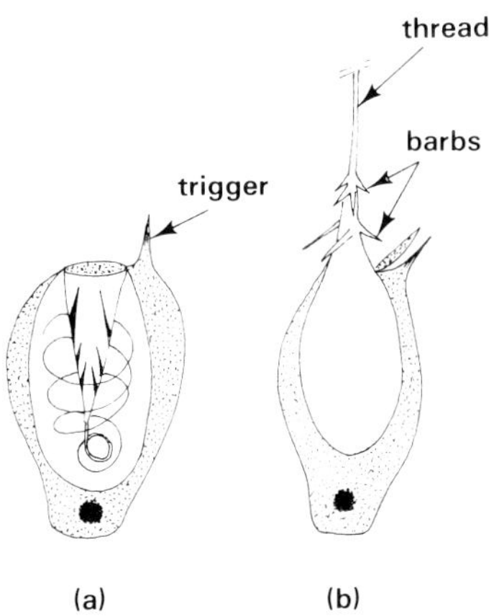

2. NEMATOBLASTS

These are also called **cnidoblasts** and are found in groups in the ectoderm, especially in the tentacles. Nematoblasts are used to capture prey. They contain a coiled and often barbed thread inside a structure called a **nematocyst**. The thread uncoils and quickly projects from the cell when it is triggered. The triggering device is on the outer surface of the nematoblast and may be activated by touch and chemical stimulation (Fig. 26.20).

3. INTERSTITIAL CELLS

These are small undifferentiated cells which may develop into any of the other kinds of cells in the cnidarian body wall.

4. GLAND CELLS

These are found in the ectoderm at the base of cnidarians such as *Hydra* and sea anemones. They secrete a sticky substance by which the animal adheres to the substrate. Gland cells in the endoderm secrete a juice of hydrolytic enzymes into the enteron. Some digestion of food occurs in the enteron which for this reason is often called the **gastrovascular cavity**.

FIG. 26.21 *Nerve net in* Hydra

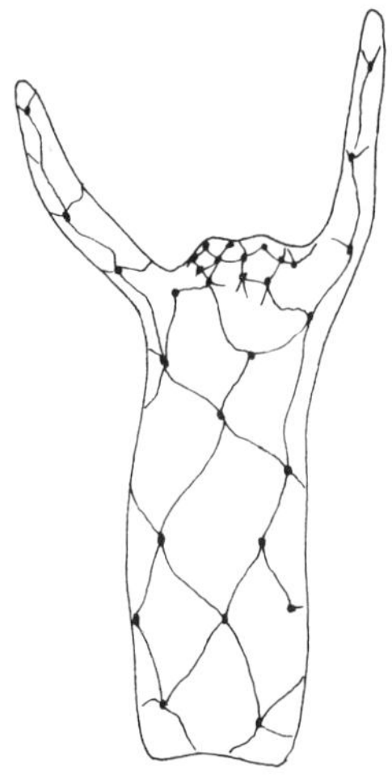

5. NUTRITIVE CELLS

These are muscle cells in the endoderm. They form pseudopodia which engulf food particles from the enteron. Digestion is intracellular. Nutritive cells may also have flagella, the beating of which causes water to enter and leave the enteron through the mouth.

Some cnidarians, especially reef-building corals, have **symbiotic** unicellular green or brown **algae** in the endoderm layer. Sugars made photosynthetically by the algae are used by its partner as an energy source. When food is scarce, up to 50 per cent of the cnidarian's energy comes from the algae. Amino acids made by the algae are also used by the cnidarians for protein synthesis. The benefit derived by the algae from the association is obscure.

6. SENSORY CELLS

These connect to a **nerve net** which extends through the ectoderm and endoderm (Fig. 26.21). It enables the cnidarian to sense its surroundings and respond to stimuli in an appropriate way. Responses may be to attack prey or avoid danger by retracting the body from a predator.

26.3.2 *Variety of cnidarians*

The *Cnidaria* are divided into three classes: *Hydrozoa*, *Anthozoa* and *Scyphozoa*.

1. *HYDROZOA*

These are single, free-moving organisms such as *Hydra*, or more usually colonial, sessile organisms such as *Obelia*. The main body form is the **hydroid**.

Hydra reproduces sexually and asexually. In sexual reproduction, sperms are made in **testes** and ova in **ovaries**. The sexual organs are ectodermal in origin and often arise on the same individual. *Hydra* is thus

FIG. 26.22 Hydra (a) *showing testes, × 80* (b) *budding, × 120*

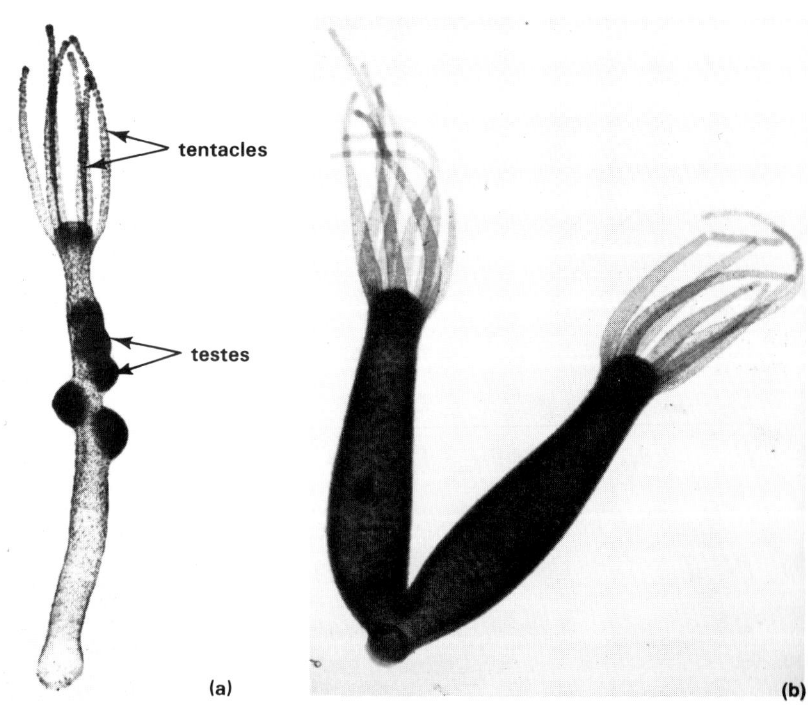

hermaphrodite. However, the gonads mature at different times and cross-fertilisation is usual between different individuals. In asexual reproduction, a new *Hydra* is formed by **budding** on an established hydroid. When full-grown, the junction between the bud and parent is constricted and the new *Hydra* is released (Fig. 26.22). Budding involves mitosis of interstitial cells followed by cell differentiation. While it is developing, the enteron of the bud and parent are joined.

Obelia is a colonial organism made of very many hydroids joined together by a system of branching tubes called the **coenosarc**. The colony is surrounded by a chitinous exoskeleton called the **perisarc**. At the ends of the colony's branches, hydroids, called **hydranths** or **polyps**, project into the surrounding water. Their main function is food capture (Fig. 26.23).

FIG. 26.23 Obelia (a) *colony, × 25* (b) *medusa, × 15*

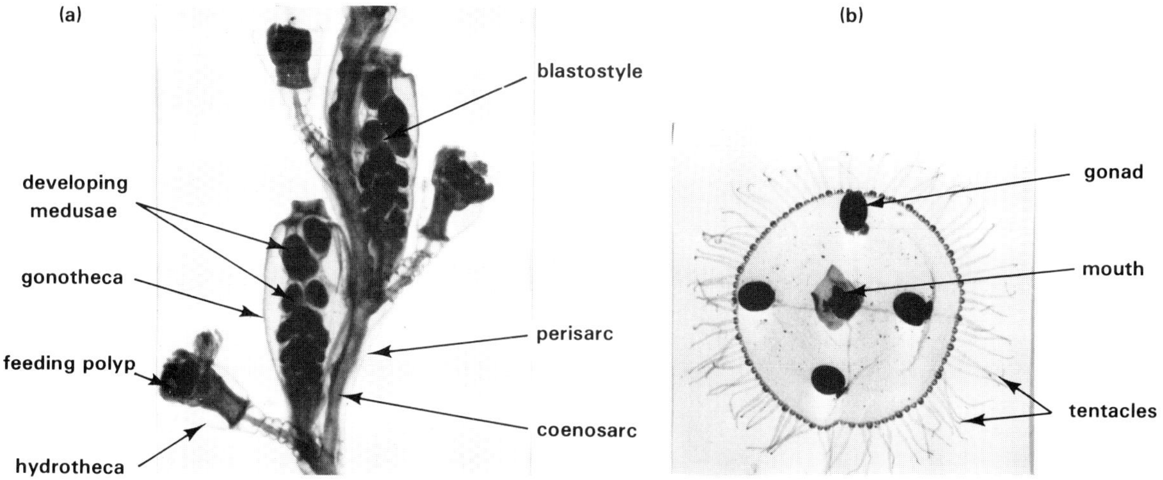

Asexual reproduction in *Obelia* involves the budding of medusae from reproductive polyps called **blastostyles**. Medusae are small jellyfish-like structures which break free from the parent colony. Each has gonads, from which arise the gametes used in sexual reproduction. The product of fertilisation is a **planula larva** which settles and grows into a new colony.

2. *ANTHOZOA (ACTINOZOA)*

These are **hydroids** which do not have a medusoid stage in the life cycle (Fig. 26.24). **Sea anemones** and **corals** are anthozoans. The sea anemone

FIG. 26.24 *Sea anemone* (a) *longitudinal section; body plan* (b) *life cycle*

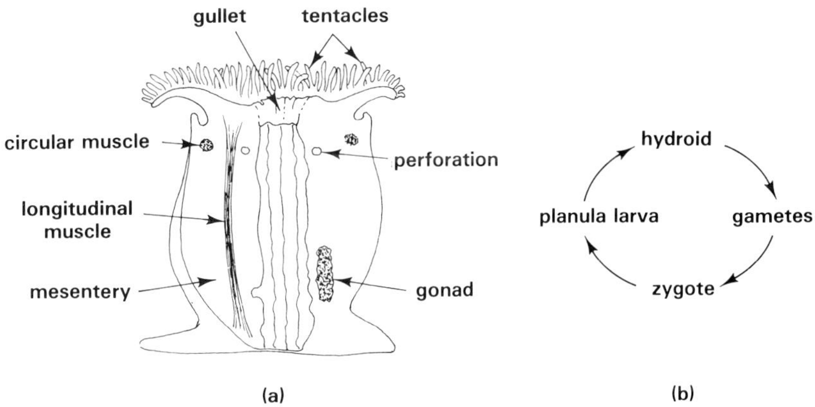

Actinia lives on the British shoreline between high and low tide marks. Its mouth is ringed by numerous tentacles covered in nematocysts which are used for food capture. In the rim of the mouth are ciliated grooves. Rhythmic beating of the cilia creates movement of water which enters and leaves the enteron through the mouth. The endoderm grows into the enteron to form folds called **mesenteries** (Fig. 26.25). They provide a large internal surface area for the absorption of food from the enteron. *Actinia* retracts its whole body when longitudinal muscle fibres in the mesenteries contract. When this happens, only the ectoderm is exposed to the drying air between tides.

FIG. 26.25 Actinia *T. S. through gullet* × 6

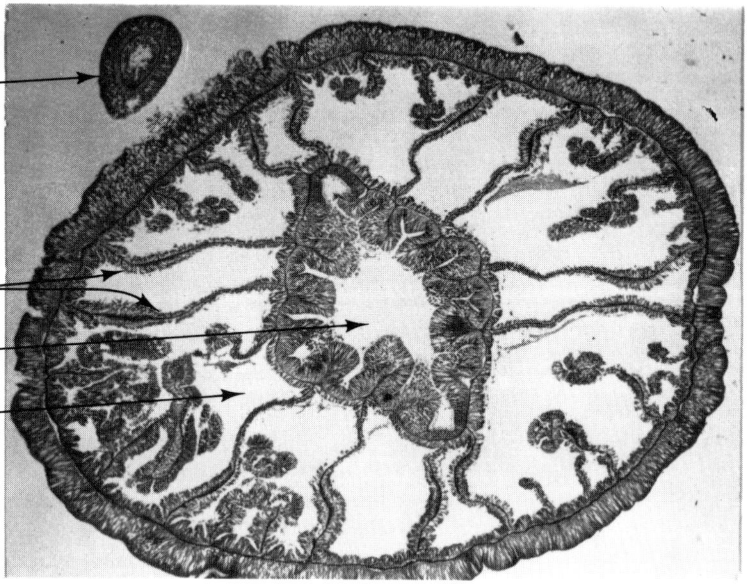

The gonads are found on the mesenteries of separate male and female animals. Gametes are released to the outside and fertilisation occurs in the sea, or occasionally in the enteron of females. A planula larva arises from the zygote and is the **dispersal phase** of the life cycle. When the larva settles, perhaps miles away from its parents, a new hydroid develops, providing the surroundings are suitable.

Corals are colonial organisms which secrete a hard supportive and protective skeleton of limestone (Fig. 26.26). Corals living in the same area often form a **reef**. A reef is built up by new corals growing on layers of old skeletons left by past colonies. The Great Barrier Reef of Australia stretches for more than 2000 kilometres (Fig. 26.27). An **atoll** is a circular coral reef which developed around the coast of an island that has since sunk beneath the surface of the sea.

FIG. 26.26 *Underwater view of corals* (James Davies photographs)

3. *SCYPHOZOA*

These are **medusoid** cnidarians, the hydroid stage being absent from the life cycle. They include **jellyfish** such as *Aurelia* which swims in the surface waters of the sea around Britain (Fig. 26.28). The bell-shaped medusa has a ring of small tentacles around the rim. The mouth is at the centre on the underside. Projecting from the mouth are four frills of tissue called **oral arms**, which are used in the capture and ingestion of prey. The mouth leads

FIG. 26.27 *Great Barrier Reef, Australia* (James Davies photographs)

FIG. 26.28 (a) *Life cycle of the common jellyfish,* Aurelia (b) *ephyra larva,* × *10*

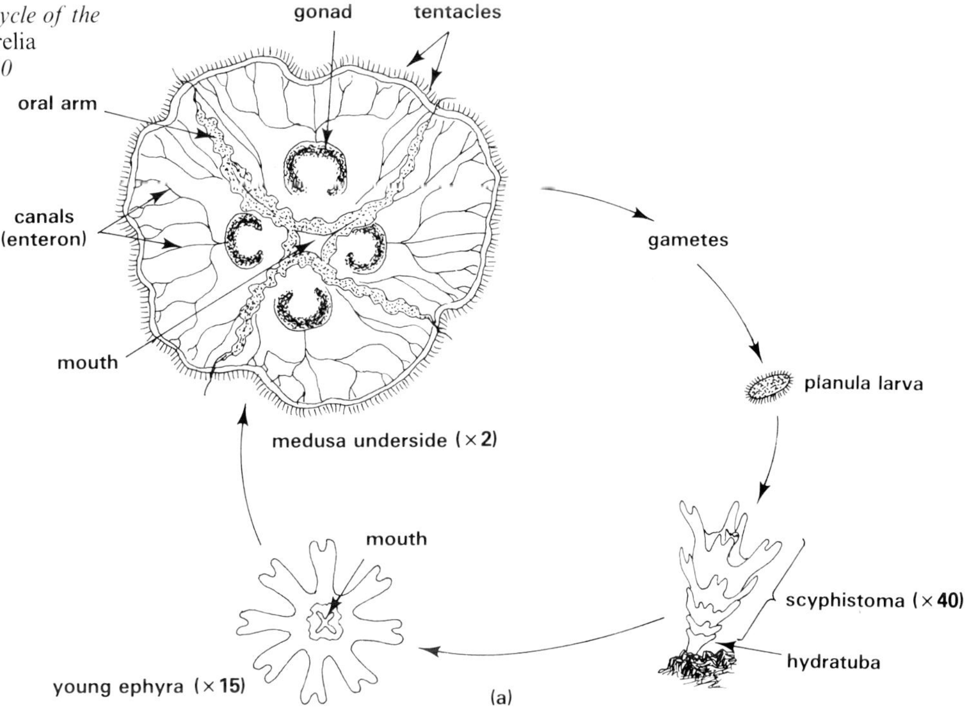

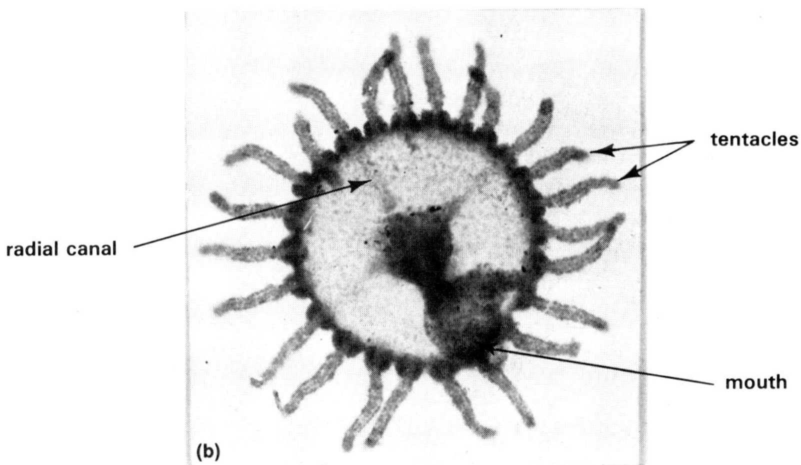

into a lobed enteron called the **gastric cavity**, which radiates as a system of narrow branched **canals** to the edge of the medusa. In the canals, food and oxygen are brought to all parts of the body. Much of the upper part of the medusa is mesogloea, hence the jelly-like consistency of jellyfish. The sexes are separate and the gonads develop in the gastric cavity. Ova are fertilised in the frills of the oral arms and planula larvae are formed. When the larvae settle, they develop into a small hydroid-like polyp from which small **ephyra larvae** are released by budding into the sea. Each ephyra is a small medusa and develops into an adult jellyfish.

26.4 *Platyhelminthes*

Flukes, tapeworms and turbellarians are **flatworms** belonging to the phylum *Platyhelminthes*. The flatworm body is **triploblastic**, originating from three tissue layers; an inner endoderm, separated from an outer ectoderm by a solid middle layer called the **mesoderm**. Flatworms are **acoelomate**, because there is no body cavity or coelom in the mesoderm. Reproductive, nervous and excretory organs develop in the mesoderm, so the triploblastic condition is sometimes called the **organ level of development**. This is a distinct advance on the body form of poriferans and coelenterates. Flatworms are **bilaterally symmetric**, whereas poriferans and coelenterates are radially symmetric (Fig. 26.29). There is a distinct head,

FIG. 26.29 *Planes of symmetry* (a) *radial* (b) *bilateral*

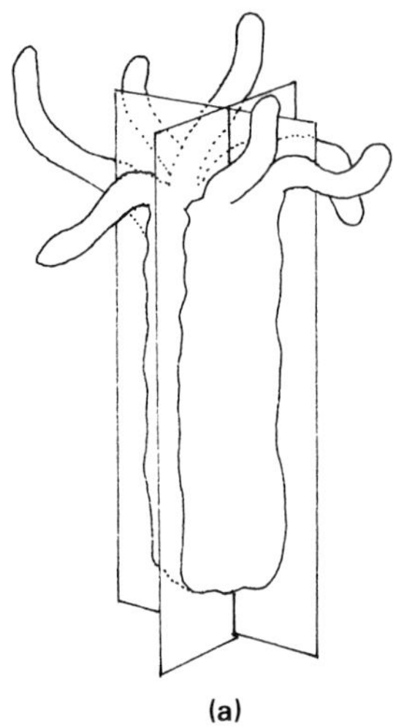

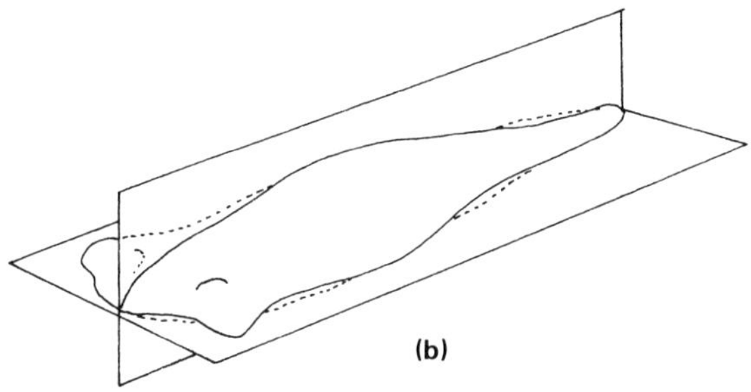

often with sense organs and a primitive internal brain. The development of complex structures in the head is called **cephalisation**. Flatworms have no blood system. An extensively branched gut is usually present and delivers food to all parts of the body. As in coelenterates, there is a single gut opening through which food enters and wastes leave the body.

The *Platyhelminthes* is divided into three classes; *Turbellaria*, *Trematoda* and *Cestoda*.

26.4.1 *Turbellaria*

Turbellarians are mainly free-living, aquatic flatworms such as *Dendrocoelum* and *Planaria* (Fig. 26.30). They move by an undulating action brought about by antagonistic longitudinal and circular muscles beneath the ectoderm. The ectoderm cells on the underside of the body are ciliated.

FIG. 26.30 Dendrocoelum, × 7

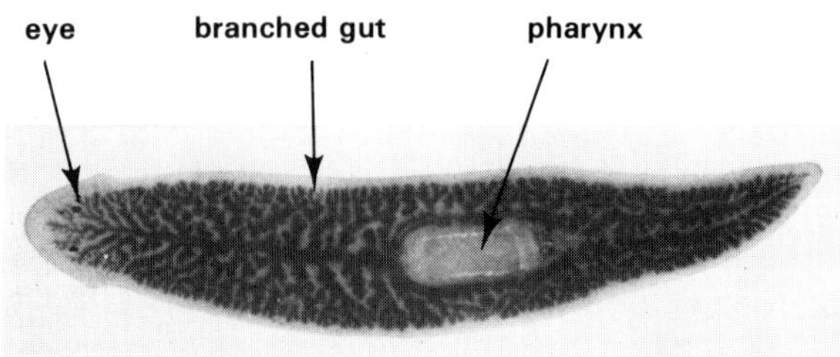

Turbellarians glide over solid surfaces when the cilia beat. The mouth is at the end of a muscular, tubular **pharynx**, which is extended from the ventral surface when feeding (Fig. 26.31(a)). *Planaria* feeds on small animals and secretes a digestive juice on to the prey through the extended mouth. A pumping action of the pharynx then sucks small pieces of partly digested food into the gut. Secretory cells lining the gut produce enzymes which complete the digestion of the food. Metabolic wastes are removed by a system of **excretory canals** fed by **flame cells**. The cells have flagella which create a current in the excretory system. The excretory canals open on to the body surface by several pores, through which the wastes are discharged to the outside (Fig. 26.31(b) and (c)).

FIG. 26.31 *Body systems in* Planaria (a) *digestive* (b) *excretory* (c) *flame cell* (d) *nervous* (e) *reproductive*

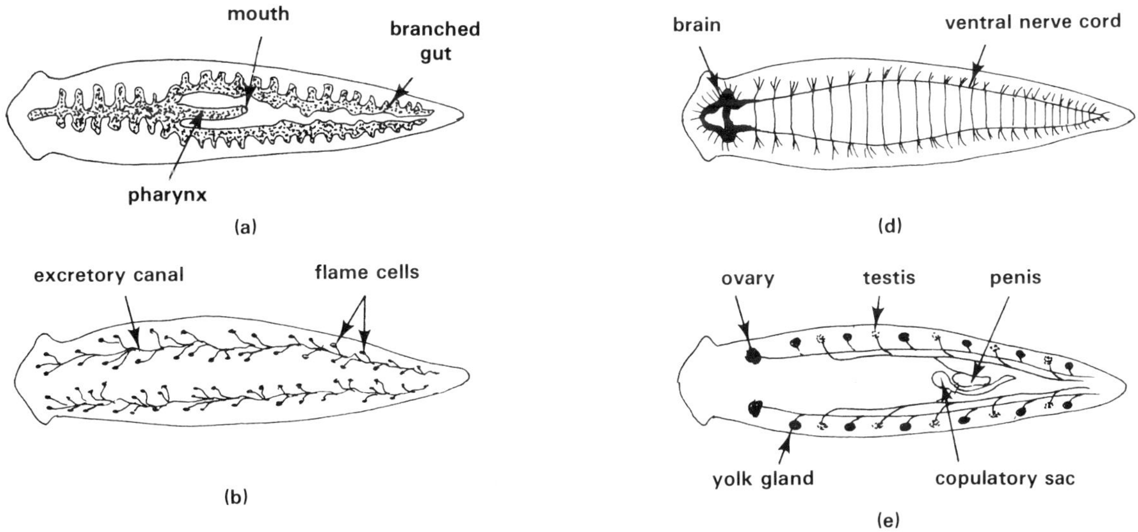

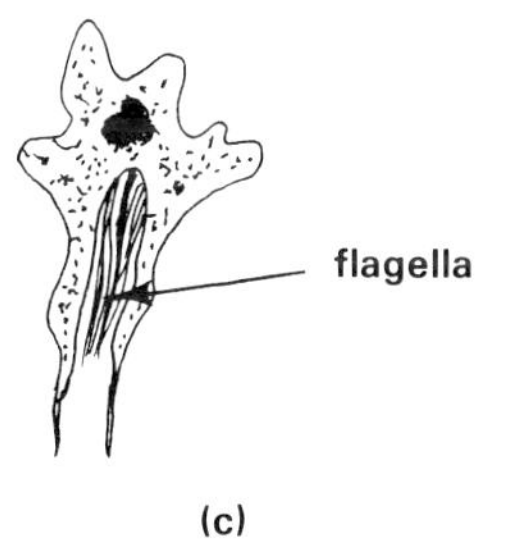

Turbellarians have **eyespots**, usually on the dorsal surface of the head. As far as can be judged, turbellarians cannot perceive clear images. However, the eyespots can distinguish between light and dark and may be able to detect movement. On the leading edge of the head there are groups of **chemoreceptors**. Turbellarians use them to detect the presence and location of food.

The nervous system is more organised than the simple nerve net of coelenterates. There are two longitudinal bundles of nerve fibres making a primitive **nerve cord**, which is positioned ventrally in the mesoderm. In the head, the double nerve cord joins to form a concentration of nervous tissue which acts as a simple **brain** (Fig. 26.31(d)).

Although turbellarians are **hermaphrodite**, they engage in copulation which ensures **cross-fertilisation**. Two animals come to lie with their ventral surfaces facing each other. The penis of each animal is inserted into the genital pore of the other (Fig. 26.31(e)). Sperms are exchanged and fertilisation is internal. The fertilised eggs, together with yolk cells, are enclosed in a shell as an egg capsule. The capsules are shed to the outside to hatch after some weeks, releasing small flatworms. There is no larval stage in the life cycle. Some turbellarians reproduce asexually by splitting into two halves, anterior and posterior. Each half then grows into a new adult. Many also show remarkable powers of **regeneration**. If a turbellarian is cut into many pieces, a new individual may grow from each of the severed parts.

26.4.2 *Trematoda*

The trematodes are the **flukes** such as *Echinostoma*, *Fasciola* and *Schistosoma* (Fig. 26.32). Many of the body features of flukes result from their parasitic way of life. Most are **endoparasites** living inside their hosts. There are no external cilia in the adult. A protective **cuticle** covers the outer surface of the body. There are usually one or more **suckers** by which the fluke clings to its host. The mouth leads into a branched gut. Flame cells linked to a system of excretory tubes remove metabolic wastes. There is a well developed nervous system, but no sense organs.

FIG. 26.32 Echinostoma revolutum, × 10

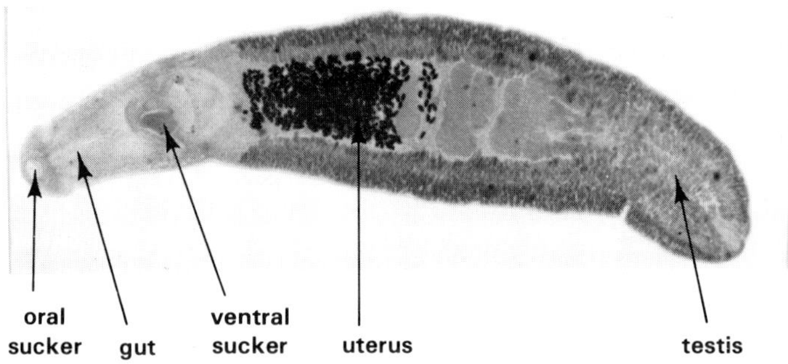

A significant feature of flukes is the well developed reproductive system. Individuals are usually **hermaphrodite**. The life cycle is often complex and may involve more than one host.

Fasciola hepatica is the **liver fluke** which lives in the bile ducts of its primary hosts, sheep and cattle. It has a pair of testes and a single ovary (Fig. 26.33). Although the fluke is hermaphrodite, **cross-fertilisation** takes place. The yolky fertilised eggs have a protective shell and are egested in the faeces of the primary host. In water, each egg develops into a ciliated **miracidium larva**. Miracidia swim by ciliary action and enter the secondary host, usually the freshwater snail *Limnaea truncatula*. The miracidia change into **sporocysts**, from which arise another larval form called **rediae**. Each redia changes into yet another larval form called a **cercaria**, which passes into the pulmonary cavity of the snail and from there to the outside. The cercariae wriggle on to vegetation and become encased in a cyst. Here they may lie dormant for many months before being eaten by the primary host. In the host's gut the cysts hatch into small flukes which migrate into the body cavity. They find their way to the liver, where they cause considerable damage. The flukes eventually come to lie in the bile ducts, grow to maturity and the life cycle is completed (Fig. 26.34).

FIG. 26.33 Fasciola, *reproductive system*

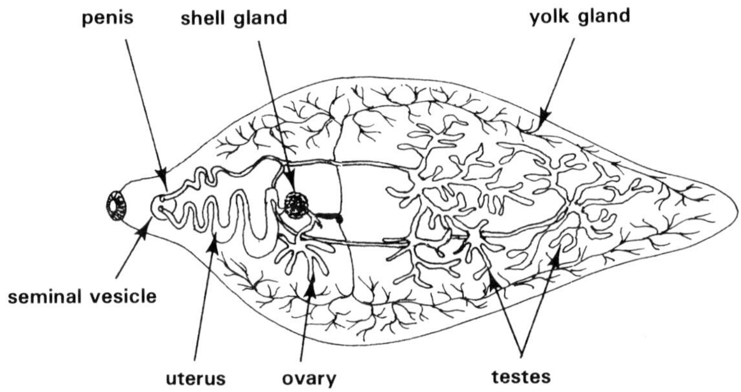

FIG. 26.34 *Life cycle of* Fasciola hepatica

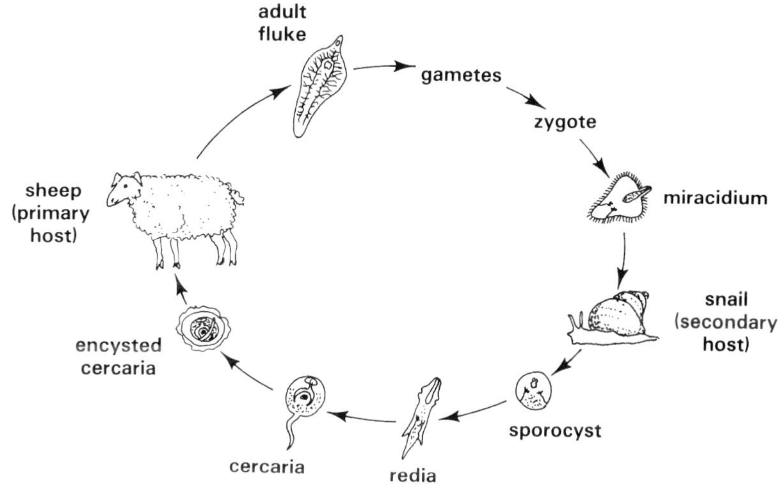

Schistosoma lives in the abdominal veins of humans. It is called the **blood fluke**. The sexes are separate, the female lying permanently in a groove along the surface of the male's body (Fig. 26.35). The life cycle involves several larval stages as in *Fasciola* and the secondary host is also a water snail. The disease caused by *Schistosoma* is called **bilharzia** and is very common in some parts of the world, such as China and the Middle East. Bilharzia is not usually a fatal disease, but it causes people to become extremely lethargic and unable to work.

FIG. 26.35 *The blood fluke,* Schistosoma, × *20*

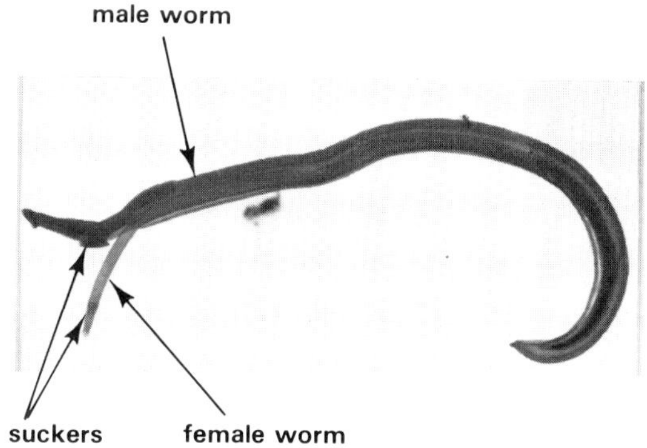

26.4.3 *Cestoda*

The cestodes are **tapeworms** such as *Taenia*. All tapeworms are **endoparasites**. Many of their body features reflect the parasitic way of life. There are no sense organs or gut, and the excretory and nervous systems are degenerate. The body is covered by a tough cuticle which protects it from the host's digestive juices. Nearly all the space inside tapeworms is occupied by reproductive organs.

Tapeworms live in the gut of their host, often growing to great lengths. *Taenia solium*, the pork tapeworm of man, for example, may become over 4 metres long. The head is called the **scolex** and has a ring of **hooks** and **suckers** by which it clings to the inside of the host's intestine (Fig. 26.36). Behind the head the tapeworm produces a great number of **proglottides**. As the proglottides mature, they move further away from the scolex and develop reproductive organs. Eggs are fertilised by sperms from the same proglottis. The fertilised eggs are then provided with yolk and a thin shell. Each egg develops into a small six-hooked embryo encased in a resistant **onchosphere**. Ripe proglottides containing onchospheres become detached from the tapeworm and pass to the outside in the host's faeces. If the onchospheres are eaten by a suitable secondary host, in this case a pig, further development takes place. The embryo is released from its case in

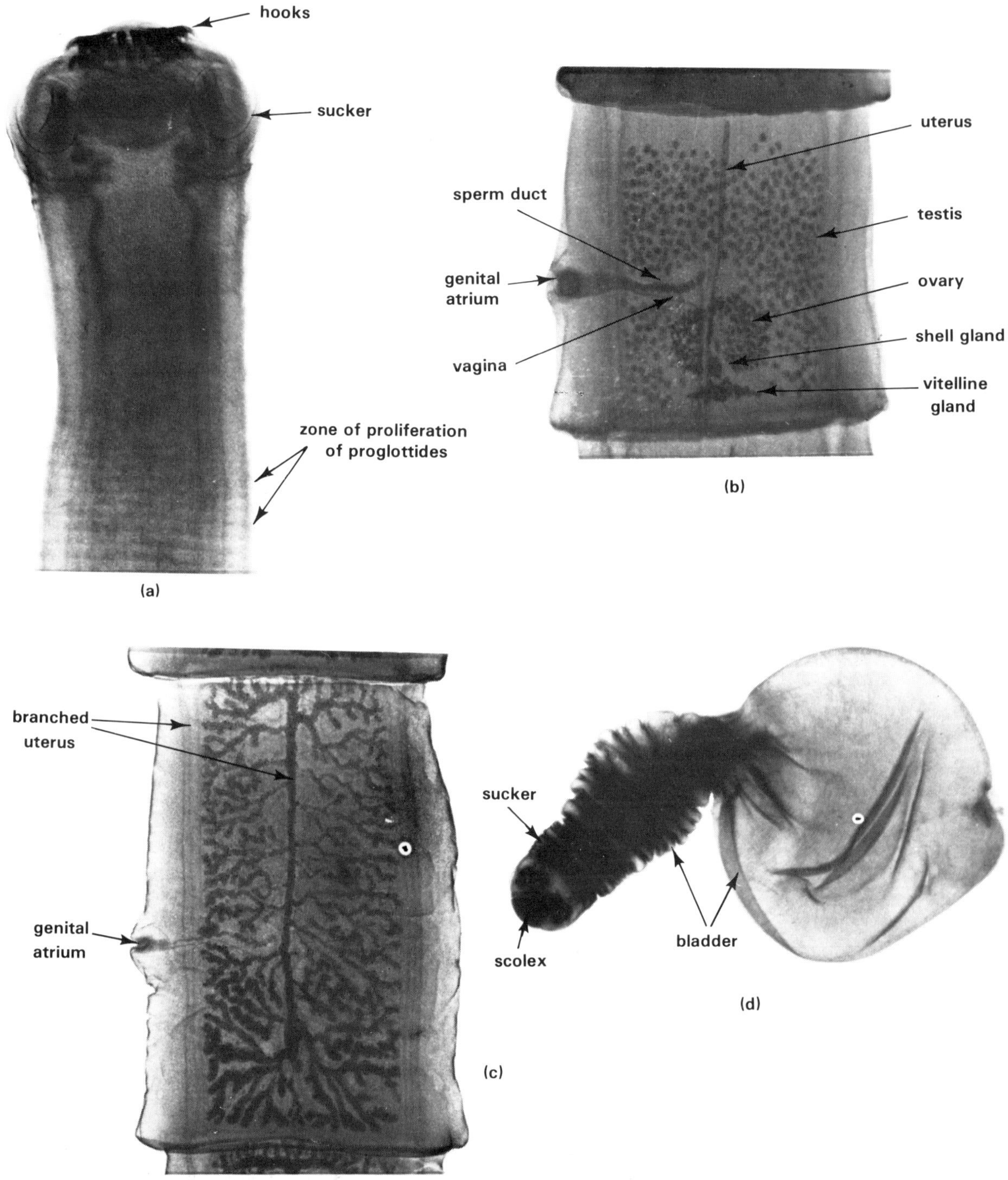

FIG. 26.36 Taenia (a) *scolex, × 15* (b) *proglottis showing reproductive organs, × 25* (c) *gravid proglottis just before shedding, × 20* (d) *bladderworm, × 10*

the host's stomach and bores its way into a blood vessel. Eventually the embryo becomes encysted, usually in the host's muscles, where it develops into a fluid-filled **cysticercus** or **bladderworm**. Should pork infected with bladderworms be eaten without sufficient cooking to kill them, the worm attaches itself to the gut wall and develops into a new adult tapeworm. Pork tapeworms are rare in developed countries where meat is inspected for parasites before it can be sold for human consumption.

Taenia saginata, the beef tapeworm, is another cestode that lives in man. Over half the adult population of many North African and Middle Eastern countries are parasitised by it.

26.5 *Nematoda*

The nematodes are **roundworms** such as *Ascaris lumbricoides* which lives in the small intestine of man (Fig. 26.37). Many nematodes are parasites. Most kinds of multicellular plants and animals act as hosts.

Nematodes are all thread-like animals almost devoid of external features. The body is covered by a cuticle and there are no cilia. The **gut** has two openings, the **mouth** and **anus**. This is an advance on the single opening to the enteron seen in coelenterates and flatworms, because food moves through the gut in one direction, making feeding, digestion and absorption more efficient. Longitudinal muscles beneath the ectoderm enable movement of the body. The absence of circular muscles, however, permits only a

FIG. 26.37 (a) Ascaris *sp.* × *1*
(b) *transverse section* × *30*

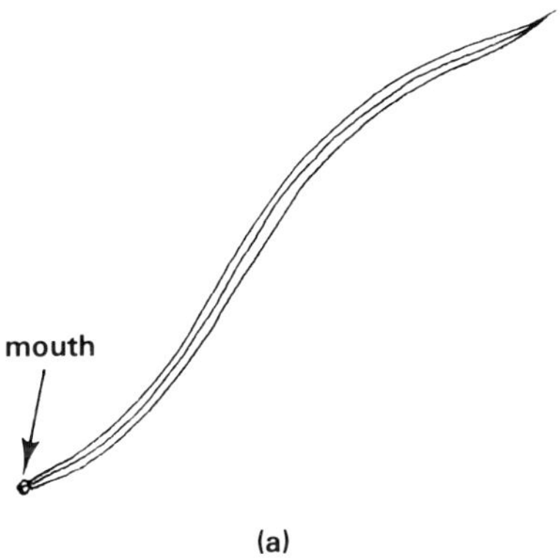

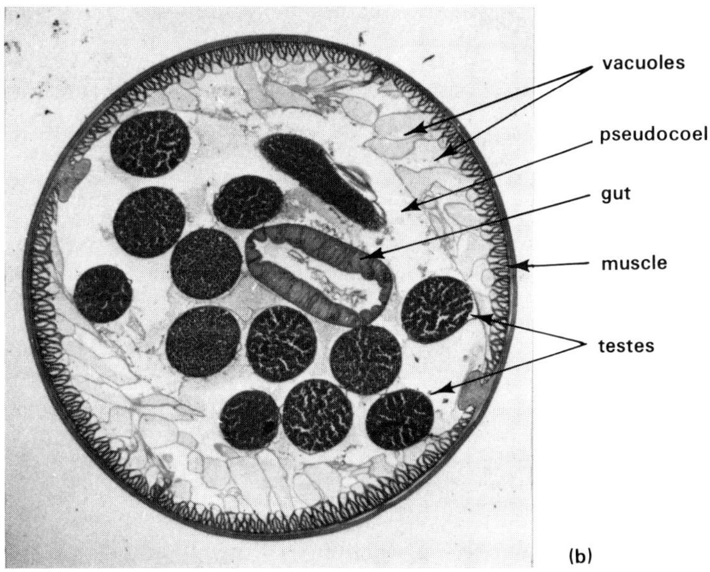

back-and-forth thrashing motion, so movement from place to place is relatively inefficient.

The many cells making up the ectoderm have no plasma membranes. For this reason it is a **syncitium**. When viewed microscopically, the ectoderm appears as a mass of separate nuclei. Between the muscles and gut there is a fluid-filled cavity formed from the vacuoles of giant cells in the mesoderm. Consequently, the cavity is not a coelom but is a **pseudocoel**. The excretory system consists of canals which open to the outside by an excretory pore. There are no flame cells. Sensory cells, probably chemoreceptors, are found around the mouth. They may be used to locate food. Nearly all nematodes are **dioecious**. The reproductive organs are found in the pseudocoel.

26.6 *Annelida*

The phylum *Annelida* includes the bristleworms, fanworms, earthworms and leeches. Annelids are **triploblastic**. However, unlike the flatworms and nematodes, the mesoderm is split into two parts by a fluid-filled cavity called the **coelom** (Fig. 26.38). It is thought that the coelom may have evolved primarily as a space for storing gametes. Another suggestion is that it evolved to store excretory products prior to their elimination from the body. In living annelids, the coelom performs both these functions and is an advance on the acoelomate condition. The body of annelids is divided internally by partitions called **septa** into many co-ordinated compartments.

FIG. 26.38 *Three grades of organisation* (a) *diploblastic* (b) *triploblastic acoelomate* (c) *triploblastic coelomate*

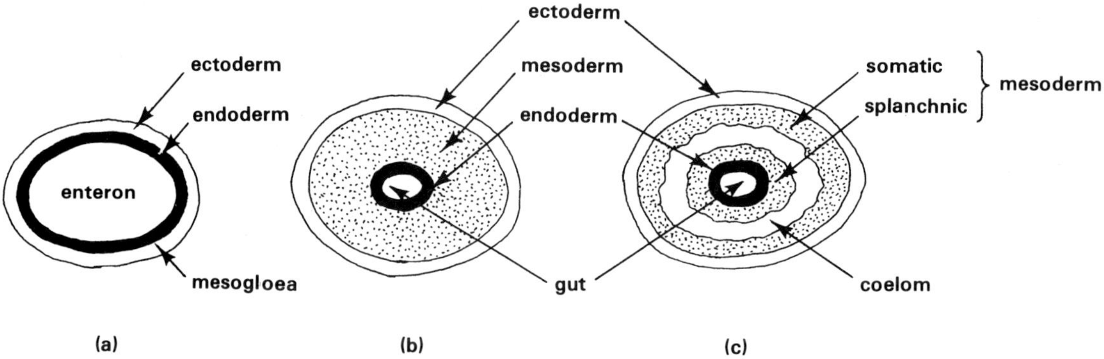

This kind of structural organisation is known as **metameric segmentation**. Annelids have a tubular gut with a mouth and anus at opposite ends of the body. The excretory organs are coiled tubes called **nephridia** arranged one pair per segment. They remove wastes from the coelomic fluid through a ciliated funnel called the nephrostome. The wastes are discharged to the outside through small openings called nephridiopores.

Annelids show advanced cephalisation. There is a primitive brain which consists of a pair of **dorsal nerve ganglia** at the anterior end. They are connected by a ring of nerves around the pharynx to a pair of nerve fibres, making the **ventral nerve cord** which runs the length of the body. Paired nerves arising from the cord supply the organs of each segment. The nerve cord of many annelids contains **giant nerve cells** which conduct impulses very rapidly (section 15.1.5). Annelids also have a variety of simple sense organs which detect changes in light intensity and temperature. They are located in the epidermis mainly at the head end of the body.

The circulatory system consists of closed vessels containing blood. Blood moves through the vessels by the pumping action of some of the vessels. Annelid blood often contains respiratory pigments such as **haemoglobin** and **chlorocruorin** which enable the transport of relatively large volumes of oxygen (Fig. 28.12). Gills are found in some annelids.

Another annelid feature is the presence of **chaetae**, bristle-like structures composed of **chitin**, which project from the body surface. Chaetae are often used in locomotion, which is achieved by the antagonistic action of circular and longitudinal muscles.

The annelids are divided into several classes, including the *Polychaeta*, *Oligochaeta* and *Hirudinea*.

26.6.1 *Polychaeta*

The polychaetes are so called because they have many chaetae. They include the **bristleworms** and **fanworms**. All are aquatic, mostly marine.

The **ragworm**, *Nereis diversicolor* (Fig. 26.39) lives in U-shaped burrows in the mud along the coast of Britain, often in estuaries. The chaetae project from flaps called **parapodia** on the sides of the body (Fig. 26.39(b) and (f)).

FIG. 26.39 Nereis (a) *whole animal,* × ½ (b) *transverse section* × *20*
(c) *head, mouth extended*
(d) *V. S. eye* (e) *trochophore larva*
(f) *parapodium* × *45*

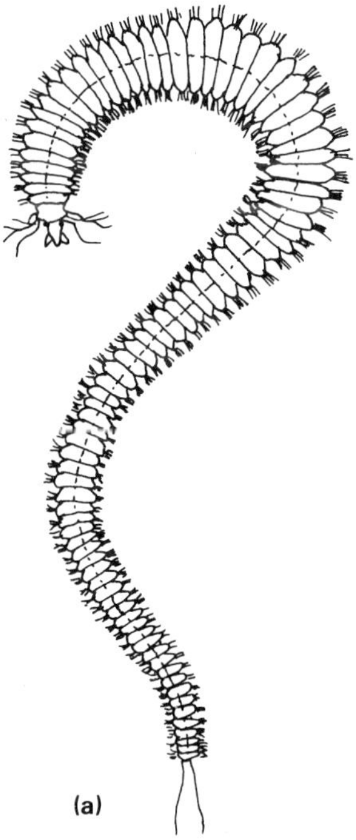

(a)

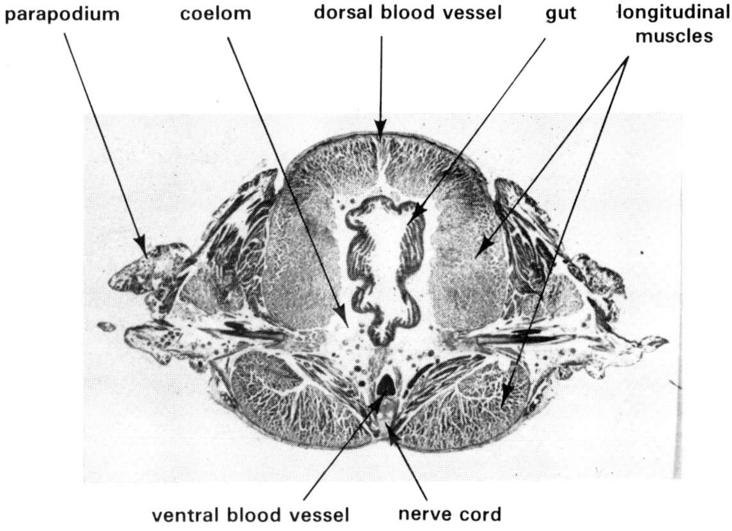

(b)

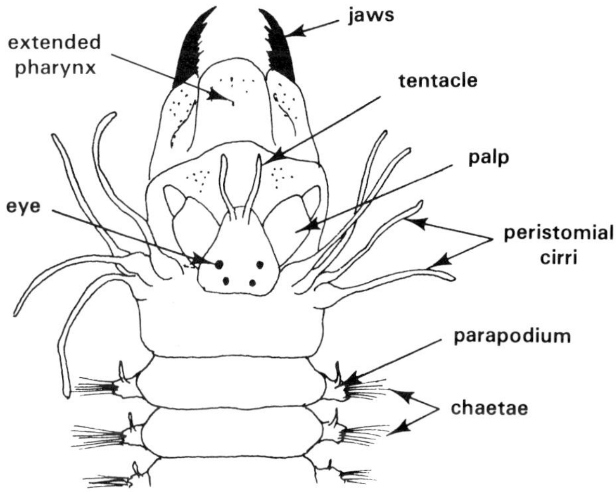

(c)

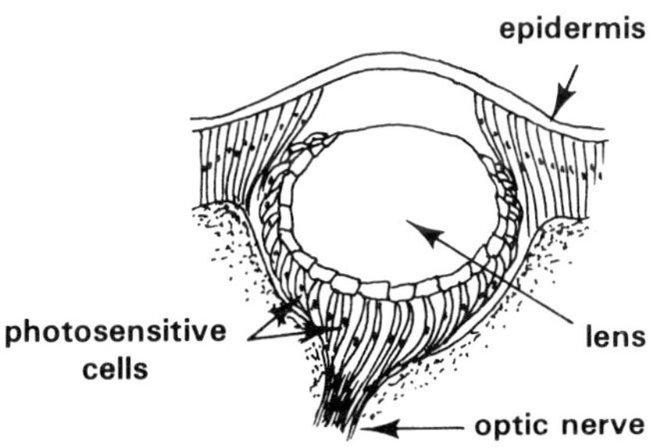

(d)

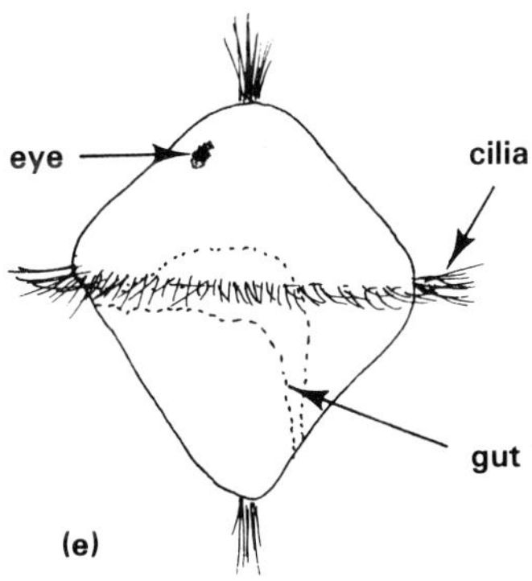

(e)

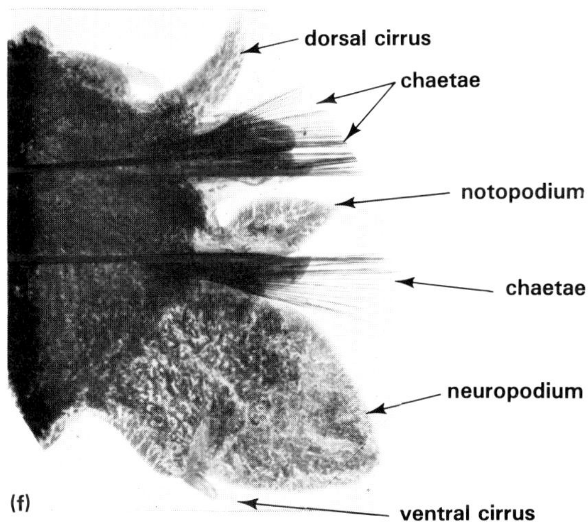

(f)

Ragworms use the parapodia to set up water currents in their burrows. The currents bring in food and oxygen and eliminate wastes from the burrow. Projecting from the head are sensory **tentacles** and **palps**. They are thought to detect food, which is grabbed by the jagged jaws on the protrusible pharynx (Fig. 26.39(c)).

Nereis has well-developed **eyes**. These consist of a cup of photosensitive cells beneath a gelatinous lens. It is doubtful that they can perceive images, but *Nereis* certainly detects movements in its surroundings. Respiratory gas exchange occurs through the body surface. In some polychaetes such as the **lugworm** *Arenicola*, gills are present (Fig. 26.40(a)).

FIG. 26.40 *Two polychaetes*
(a) *the lugworm,* Arenicola, × ½
(b) *a fanworm,* Sabella, × ¼

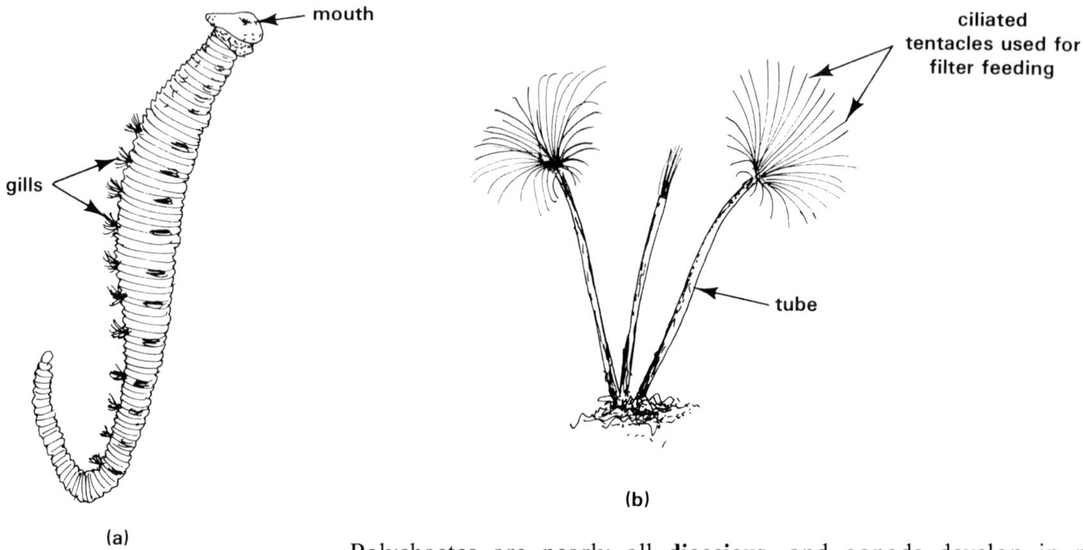

Polychaetes are nearly all **dioecious**, and gonads develop in most segments. Very often segments containing ripe gametes break away from the parent worm and fertilisation is external. Ripening and release of gametes from males and females are co-ordinated so that sperms and eggs mix together in the sea. Swarming is seen in some polychaete worms prior to fertilisation. A famous example of swarming is shown by *Leodice viridis*, the Pacific palolo worm. It takes place exactly at dawn on the day of the last quarter of the October–November moon. The rear halves of the worms project from their burrows and break away. They rise to the surface and writhe in large numbers, eventually releasing their gametes for fertilisation to occur. A **trochophore** larva is typical of polychaetes (Fig. 26.39(e)).

Fanworms, such as *Sabella*, live in tubes which the worms secrete. Extensive tentacles on the head project into the sea from the mouth of the tube. The action of cilia on the tentacles creates water currents which bring small food particles into the fanworm's mouth (Fig. 26.40(b)).

26.6.2 *Oligochaeta*

The best known of the oligochaetes are the **earthworms** (Fig. 26.41(a)). Oligochaetes have few chaetae. In *Lumbricus terrestris*, four pairs of chaetae project from each segment. There are no parapodia. Earthworms are terrestrial, commonly found burrowing in soil. The chaetae are used to grip the sides of the burrow while the action of longitudinal and circular muscles pushes the worm through the soil. During movement, the coelomic fluid acts as a **hydroskeleton**. It is squeezed by the muscles, causing the body to become shortened or lengthened (Fig. 26.41(b)).

Excretion is by means of paired **nephridia** (Fig. 26.41(c)). There is

FIG. 26.41 *Earthworm* (a) *whole animal,* × $\frac{2}{3}$ (b) *movement involving elongation of anterior segments, anchorage by chaetae to walls of soil burrow and finally drawing posterior part of body up to the front* (c) *nephridium* (d) *transverse section intestinal region,* × *10* (e) *dissected anterior segments displaying reproductive organs; dorsal view with seminal vesicles on the right removed* (f) *mating and sperm transfer*

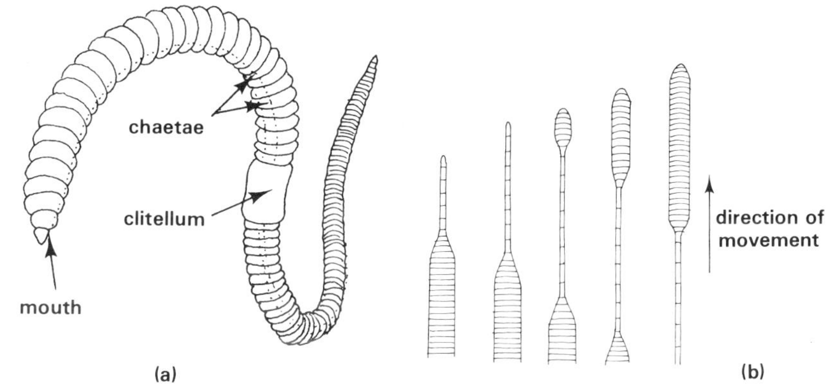

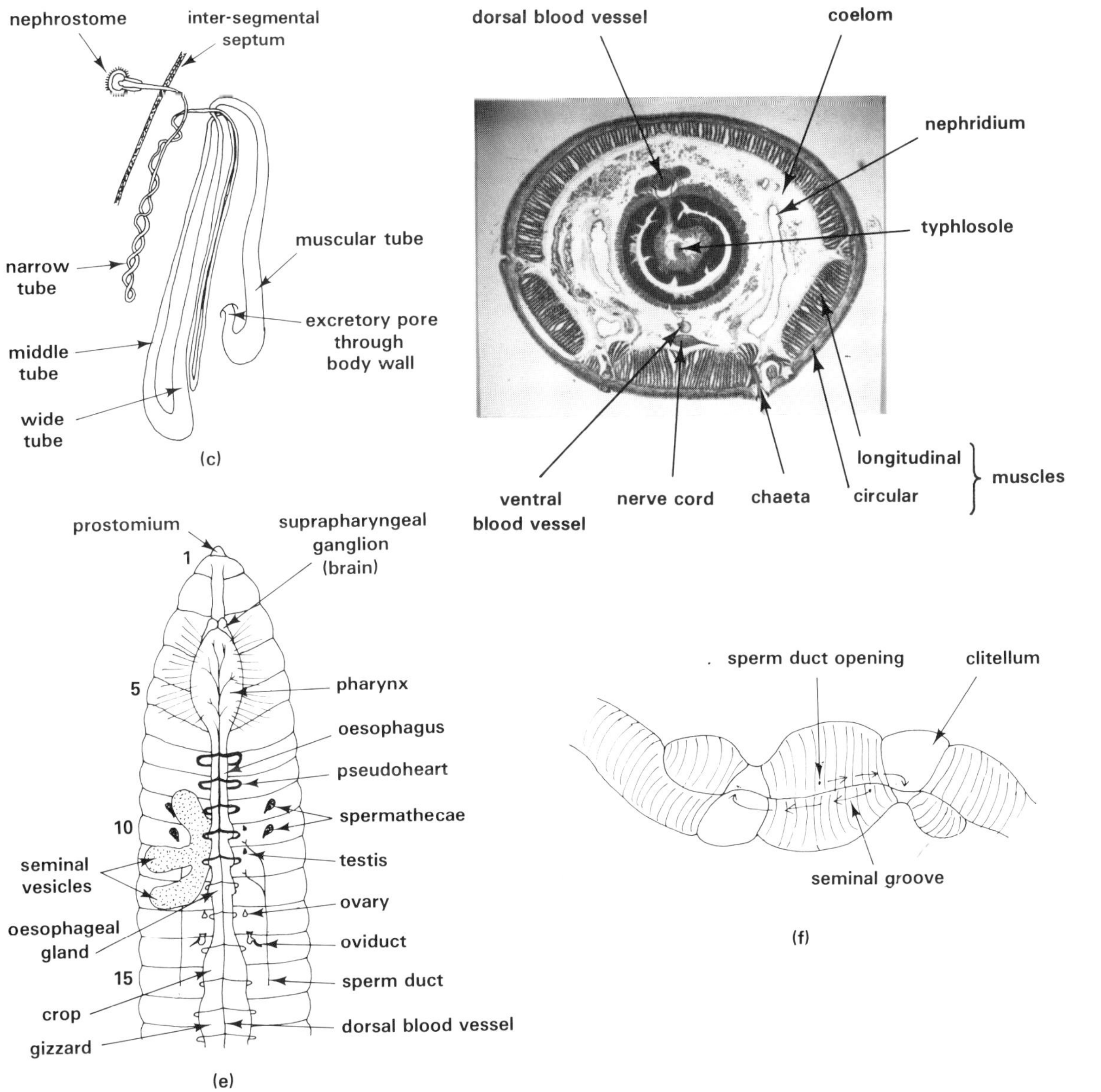

evidence that substances are selectively reabsorbed into the coelom from the nephridia in much the same way that reabsorption occurs in the nephrons of vertebrate kidneys (Chapter 10). In this way, nephridia help to regulate the chemical composition of the coelomic fluid.

Earthworms ingest soil and detritus which they take into their burrows. Food enters the mouth by the sucking of the muscular pharynx. The food then passes into the oesophagus, where **oesophageal glands** secrete calcium carbonate. In this way the food is made alkaline. The oesophagus leads into a thin-walled sac called the **crop** and then into a muscular, toothed **gizzard** which breaks the food into small fragments. Secretory cells in the intestine produce a digestive juice containing enzymes. The dorsal part of the intestine extends into the intestinal cavity as a longitudinal ridge called the **typhlosole**, which increases the area for absorption of digested food (Fig. 26.41(d)).

Blood flows the length of the body towards the head in a contractile dorsal vessel and towards the rear in a ventral vessel. Circular vessels connect the dorsal and ventral vessels in each segment. In some of the anterior segments, thicker-walled, contractile circular vessels are found. They are called **pseudohearts** and help keep the blood circulating.

The reproductive organs are restricted to a few segments in the anterior part of the body (Fig. 26.41(e)). Although hermaphrodite, earthworms copulate in pairs so cross-fertilisation takes place. When mating, two individuals come together with their ventral surfaces touching, their bodies pointing in opposite directions. Segments 9 to 11 of one worm lie opposite the **clitellum** of the other (Fig. 26.41(f)). The clitellum of each worm secretes **mucus** which ensheaths the two worms in the region of the sex organs. Sperms are ejected from the **sperm ducts** which open on to the surface of segment 15. The sperms are then transported forwards in **seminal grooves** on the ventral surface and enter the **spermathecae** on segments 9 and 10 of the mating partner. After sperms have been exchanged, the worms separate. Later, the clitellum secretes a band of mucus which glides forward over the worm. As it passes segment 14, the **oviducts** deposit several ripe eggs into the mucus. Sperms stored from a previous mating are then added to the eggs as the mucus passes the spermathecae. Fertilisation takes place and the band of mucus slips off the worm's head to form a protective **cocoon**. After a period of development, young worms escape from the cocoon. There is no larval stage in the life cycle of oligochaetes.

26.6.3 *Hirudinea*

Leeches are the best known hirudineans (Fig. 26.42). Many leeches are ectoparasites, sucking blood from their hosts. Others are free-living carnivores, preying on small animals. Leeches are dorso-ventrally flattened and the coelom is filled with connective tissue. There are usually two **suckers**, one at each end of the body. They are used to cling to the host, to stones and other solid structures. Leeches have no chaetae. The numerous annulations on the outer surface do not correspond to the 33 internal segments.

FIG. 26.42 *A leech,* Hirudo, $\times 1\frac{1}{2}$

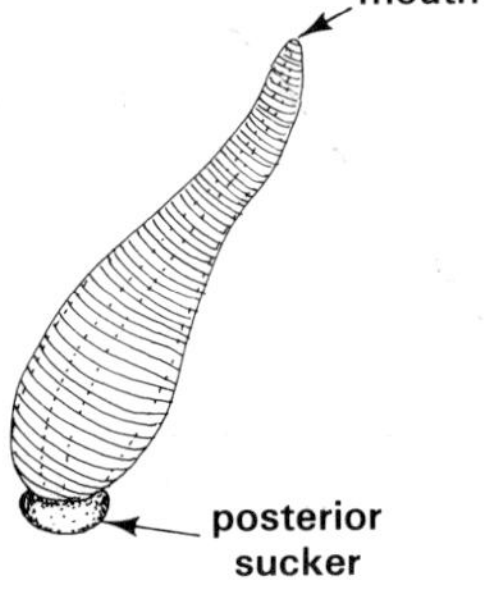

Inside the mouth is a group of tooth-like jaws. Parasitic leeches use them to puncture the host's skin before sucking blood. Blood-sucking leeches secrete in their saliva an anticoagulant called **hirudin** which prevents the blood from clotting as they feed.

Although many leeches are parasitic, they have simple sense organs and a well-developed nervous system. Leeches are hermaphrodite, but reproduction involves cross-fertilisation and a cocoon is formed. As in the oligochaetes, there is no larval stage in the life cycle.

26.7 *Arthropoda*

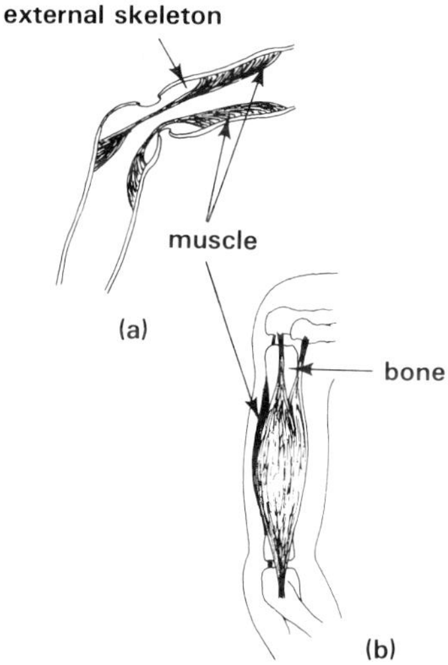

FIG. 26.43 *Comparison of limb joints* (a) *arthropod* (b) *vertebrate* (section 15.1.9)

The *Arthropoda* includes **crustaceans**, **spiders**, **centipedes**, **millipedes** and the most numerous of all animal groups, the **insects**. Arthropods are bilaterally symmetrical, metamerically segmented, triploblastic, coelomate animals. The body is divided basically into a **head**, **thorax** and **abdomen**. Projecting from some of the body segments are pairs of **jointed limbs** (arthron = joint: podos = foot).

The outermost layer of cells secretes a thick **cuticle**, which consists largely of chitin and makes up an **exoskeleton**. The cuticle of most terrestrial arthropods is often covered with a waterproof layer of **wax** which prevents excessive water loss. To allow a degree of movement in the body and limbs, the exoskeleton is jointed. Joints are regions where the cuticle is flexible. Internal muscles operate at a joint to cause movement of the limb or body segments (Fig. 26.43). The limbs of arthropods are modified to perform a variety of functions including walking, swimming, jumping, feeding, reproduction and, where present, ventilation of the gills.

The exoskeleton is fixed in size and does not grow with the animal. This contrasts with our endoskeleton which increases in size as our bodies grow. When an arthropod grows to the limit imposed by its exoskeleton, the cuticle is moulted, a process called **ecydsis**. A new flexible cuticle is secreted which inflates and hardens to a larger size than the old one. The animal's soft tissues grow until the new cuticle needs replacing. In insects a hormone called **ecdysone** (section 26.7.4) regulates ecdysis, which may occur many times in the life cycle (Fig. 26.44).

FIG. 26.44 *Growth curves of* (a) *locust, an arthropod* (b) *a vertebrate*

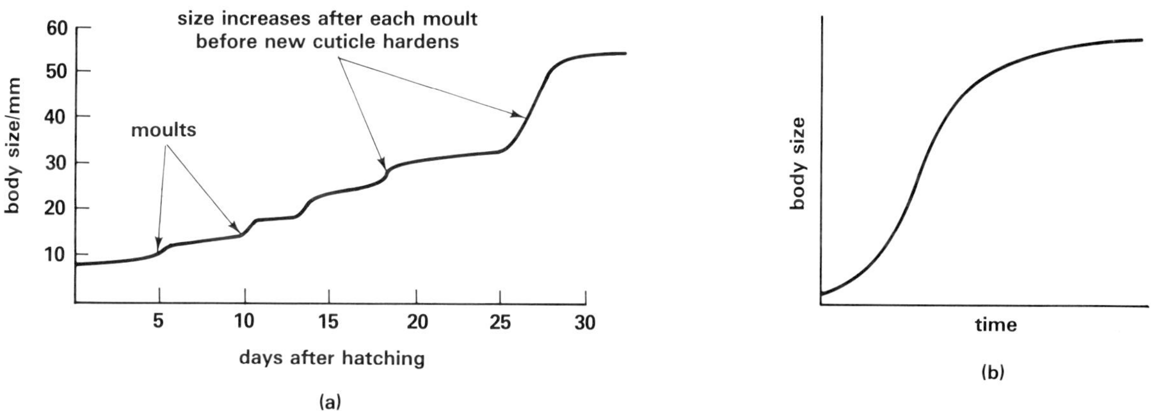

Arthropods are more cephalised than annelids. The head often bears complex mouthparts and sense organs. Internally, the brain is relatively well developed. Many arthropods have **compound eyes** consisting of very many photoreceptors called **ommatidia** (Fig. 26.45). Since the ommatidia all point in a slightly different direction, each looks at a slightly different part of the environment. It is assumed that the animal perceives a mosaic image of its surroundings.

Arthropods have an open blood vascular system. Blood circulates in vessels which open into a large mesodermal cavity called the **haemocoel**. The coelom is reduced in size compared with annelids. There is usually a **dorsal tubular heart** which pumps blood forwards towards the head. Blood is collected from the haemocoel through pairs of holes called **ostia** in the sides of the **heart** (Fig. 26.46).

FIG. 26.45 (a) *Photomicrograph V. S. compound eye of a locust,* × *15* (b) *diagram of an ommatidium* (c) *in dimly lit conditions the pigment in the pigment cells may recede enabling more light to reach the photosensitive rhabdome*

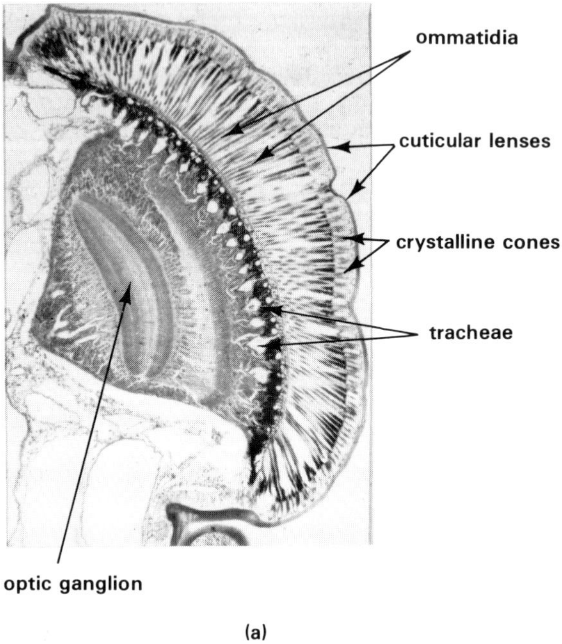

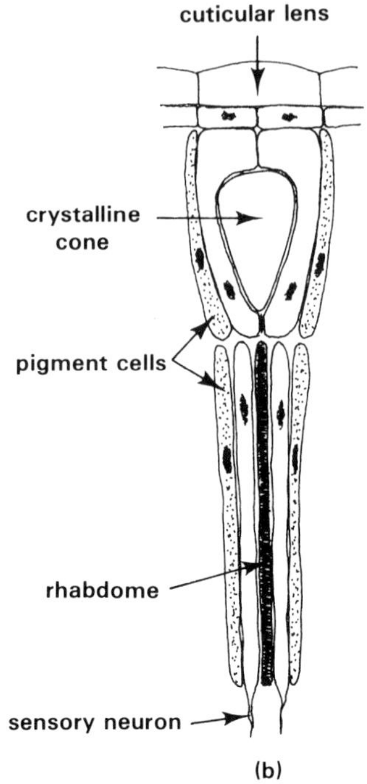

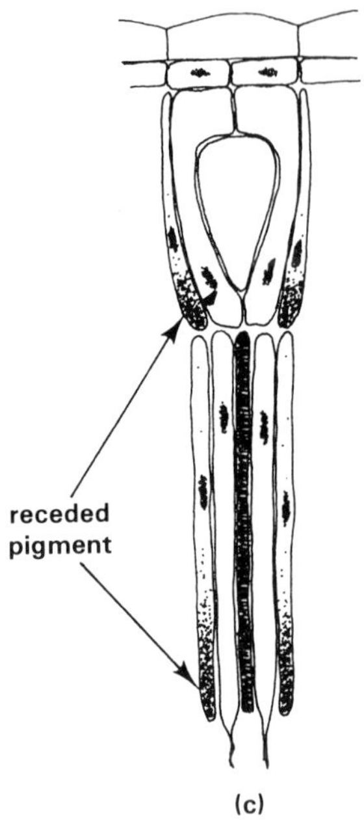

FIG. 26.46 *Arthropod heart. The arrows indicate the direction of blood flow*

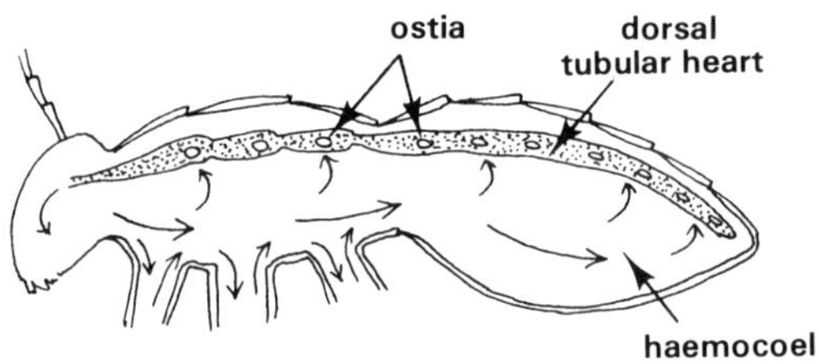

The arthropods are traditionally divided into several classes including the *Onychophora*, *Crustacea*, *Myriapoda*, *Insecta* and *Arachnida*. Some authorities consider the arthropods to have had several different origins. They place the *Crustacea* in one phylum, the *Arachnida* in another and the rest in a phylum called *Uniramia*.

26.7.1 *Onychophora*

The best known onychophoran is *Peripatus* (Fig. 26.47). *Peripatus* is a worm-like animal which has annelid as well as arthropod features. The *Onychophora* may represent an evolutionary link between the annelids and the arthropods.

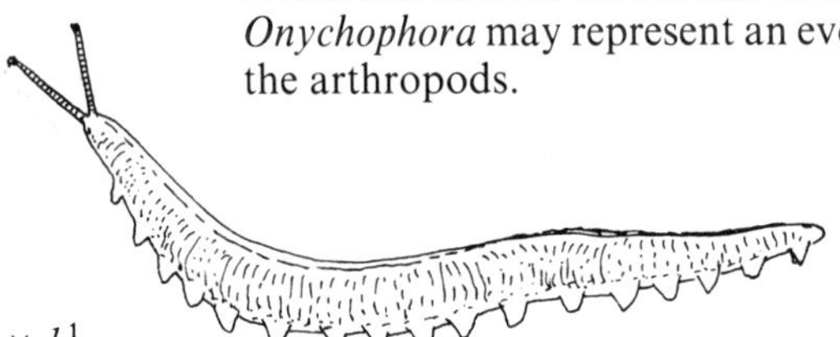

FIG. 26.47 Peripatus, × $1\frac{1}{2}$

26.7.2 *Crustacea*

Crustaceans include **waterfleas**, **barnacles**, **woodlice**, **crabs**, **shrimps**, **prawns**, **crayfish** and **lobsters**. **Woodlice** are the only truly terrestrial crustaceans (Fig. 26.48), the rest being aquatic, mostly marine.

Crustaceans have a thick, often calcareous exoskeleton. The head is often fused with a number of thoracic segments to form a **cephalothorax**. Sometimes a large fold called the **carapace** develops from the posterior edge of the head and grows to cover much of the anterior part of the body (Fig. 26.49). The carapace protects the anterior region of the body and often encloses gills (Fig. 26.49(b)). In lobsters, crayfish and crabs (Fig. 26.50) a current of oxygen-laden water is made to flow over the gills by the wafting action of modified mouthparts. In small forms such as waterfleas (Fig. 26.51), respiratory gas exchange may occur through the body surface. The blood of some crustaceans contains a respiratory pigment called **haemocyanin**.

FIG. 26.48 *Woodlouse* Oniscus, $\times 1\frac{1}{2}$

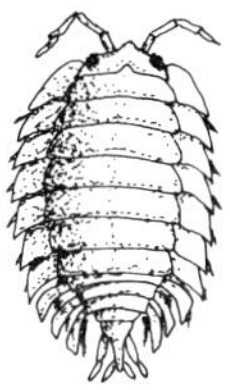

FIG. 26.49 *Crayfish,* Astacus (a) *whole animal,* $\times \frac{3}{4}$ (b) *T. S. thorax*

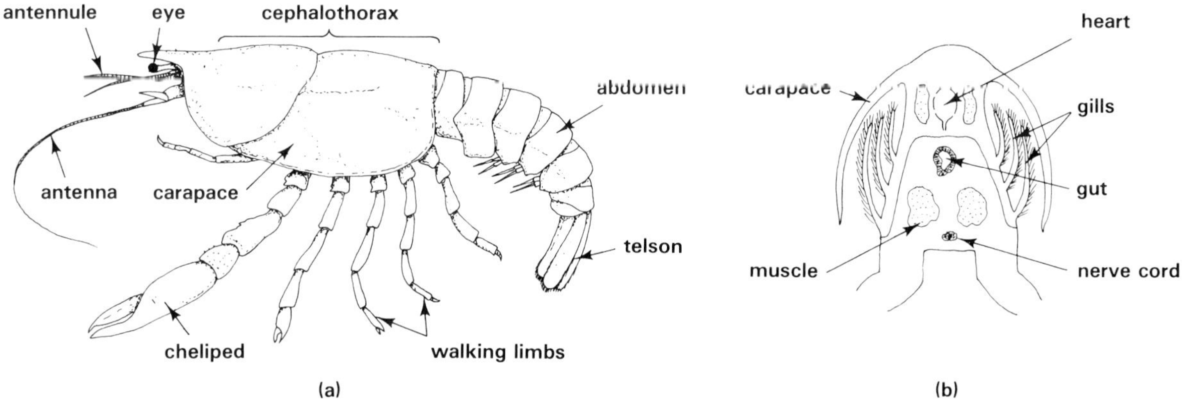

FIG. 26.50 *Edible crab,* Cancer pagurus, $\times \frac{1}{4}$ (a) *adult* (b) *zooea larva,* $\times$ *50*

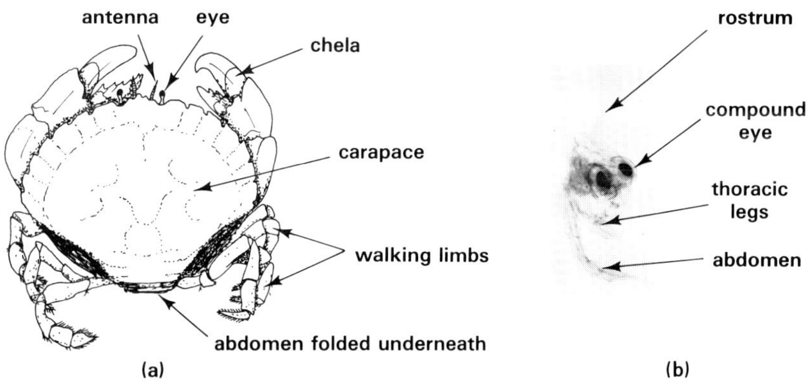

FIG. 26.51 Daphnia, $\times$ *25*

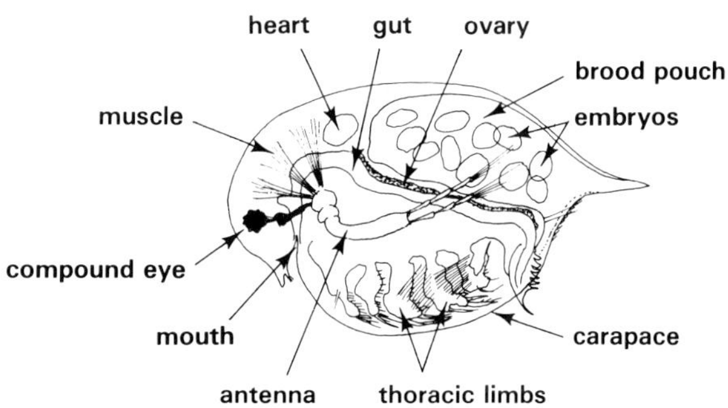

FIG. 26.52 *Crustacean mouthparts, basic plan*

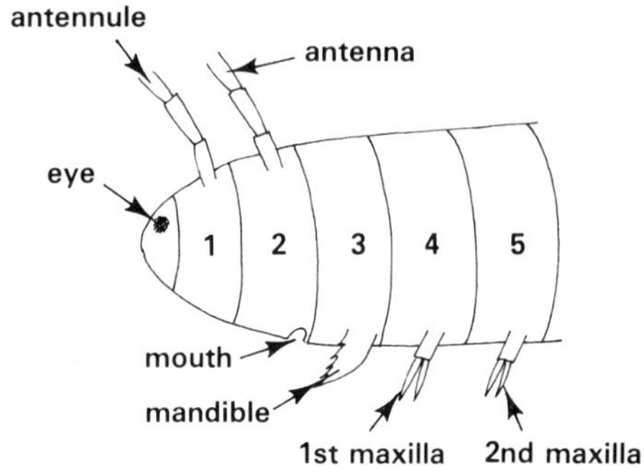

Crustaceans have five pairs of appendages on the head (Fig. 26.52). There are two pairs of **antennae**. The first pair are often small and are called **antennules**. The antennae are tactile sense organs, used to feel the surroundings or food before ingestion. A pair of **mandibles** is used to bite or chew food. Finally there are two pairs of maxillae sometimes called **maxillules** and **maxillae**, which may be used to manipulate food during feeding. In the shore crab *Carcinus*, as many as three pairs of legs are modified to form **maxillipeds** which help in feeding. Many crustaceans have compound eyes.

FIG. 26.53 *Barnacle,* Balanus, × *2*

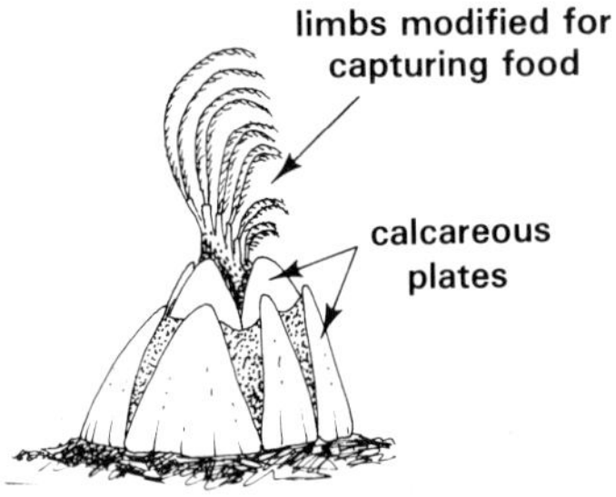

The basic body plan of some crustaceans is highly modified to suit the requirements of a specialised way of life. An example is the barnacle, *Balanus*, which lives stuck to rocks in the intertidal zone. The body is encased in calcareous plates which open on the top of the body. Food is captured by modified thoracic limbs covered in cirri, which project from the opening and filter small organisms from the sea and transfer them to the mouth (Fig. 26.53).

Crustaceans are usually dioecious and the life cycle often includes a larval stage called a **nauplius** (Fig. 26.54).

FIG. 26.54 *Nauplius larvae*

26.7.3 *Myriapoda*

FIG. 26.55 *Centipede,* Lithobius, × $1\frac{1}{2}$

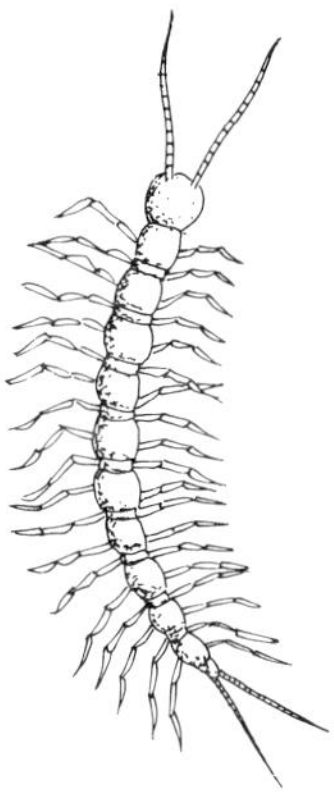

The myriapods include **centipedes** and **millipedes** (Fig. 26.55). They have elongated, narrow bodies in which the thorax and abdomen are difficult to distinguish externally. The head bears antennae, mandibles and maxillae. There are many pairs of walking legs, one or two pairs per segment (centi = hundred; milli = thousand; podos = foot). Gas exchange occurs through holes called **spiracles** on the side of the body. As in insects the spiracles lead into a system of branched air-tubes called **tracheae** (section 26.6.4). Another insect-like feature of the myriapods is the presence of **Malpighian tubules** which are used for excretion.

Myriapods are terrestrial animals. The sexes are usually separate and there is no larval stage in the life cycle.

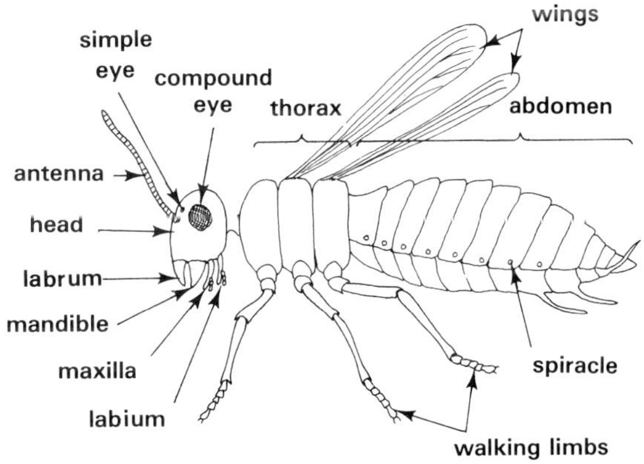

FIG. 26.56 *Insect body, basic plan* (from Buchsbaum, after Snodgrass)

26.7.4 *Insecta*

The class *Insecta* includes **ants**, **aphids**, **bees**, **beetles**, **butterflies**, **house flies**, **locusts**, **mosquitoes** and **moths**. Insects occupy most habitats, however, there are no truly marine insects. There are at least twice as many different kinds of insects as all the other animals put together.

The body of an adult insect is clearly divisible into a **head**, **thorax** and **abdomen**. A pair of antennae and compound eyes are usually present on the head. The thorax bears three pairs of jointed limbs (Fig. 26.56).

Many insects have **wings** and are good fliers. The wings are flat, dorsal extensions of the second and third thoracic segments. They contain air-filled tubes (tracheae) which give strength and rigidity. Gas exchange is by **gills** in aquatic insects and **tracheae** in terrestrial forms. Tracheae are air-filled tubes that open to the air by paired **spiracles** on the sides of each segment. Resting insects rely on diffusion to take in oxygen and to get rid of carbon dioxide. Abdominal movements ventilate the tracheae during activity. The tracheae branch to supply all the major internal organs of the body (Fig. 26.57). Gas exchange occurs in the terminal tracheal branches called **tracheoles**. The role of the blood as an oxygen carrier is less important than in non-tracheate arthropods.

The gut of insects is divisible into three main parts: fore-, mid- and hindgut (Fig. 26.58). At the junction of the foregut and midgut is a ring of finger-like projections called **caeca** which secrete digestive juices. Digestion and absorption take place in the midgut. At the junction of the midgut and hindgut is a mass of narrow excretory tubes called **Malpighian tubules**. They collect metabolic wastes from the haemocoel and discharge them into the gut. Nitrogenous waste in the form of potassium urate is absorbed from the blood by the tubule cells. In the tubules, potassium urate, water and carbon dioxide react to form potassium hydrogen carbonate and **uric acid**. The potassium hydrogencarbonate is reabsorbed

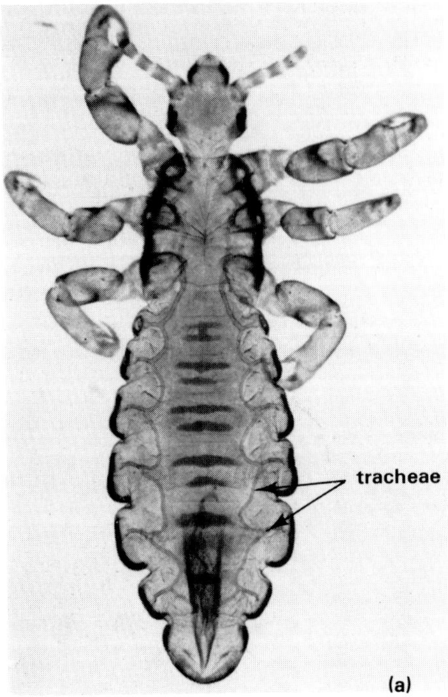

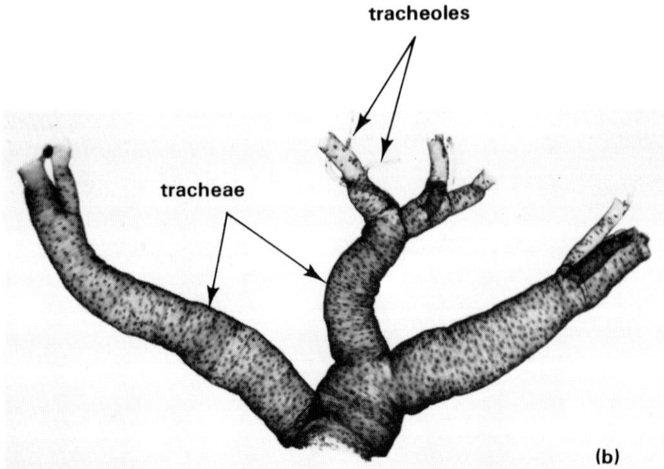

FIG. 26.57 (a) *Human body louse,* Pediculus humanus corporis *showing tracheal system,* × *12* (b) *branched tracheae dissected from an insect,* × *40*

FIG. 26.58 *Insect gut*

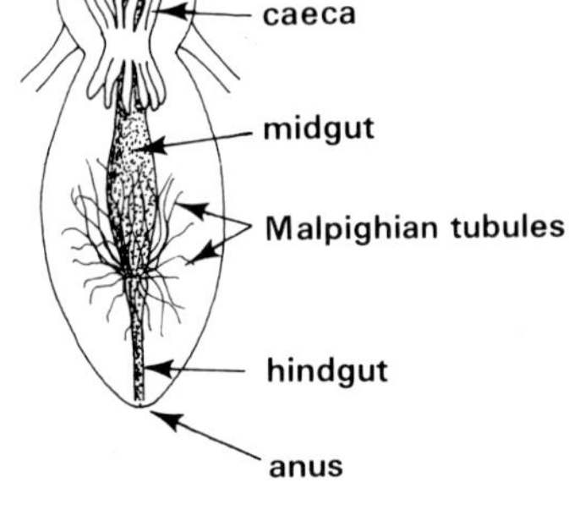

into the blood and the uric acid is discharged into the gut. Uric acid is almost insoluble in water which is absorbed into the blood from the Malpighian tubules and the hindgut. The faeces and nitrogenous excretory products are relatively dry. Conservation of water in this way helps insects resist desiccation and is one reason why they are able to live in very dry habitats.

Insects undergo metamorphosis in their life cycles. **Complete metamorphosis** is shown by some species such as the housefly, bee and butterfly (Fig. 26.62). Fertilised eggs hatch into **larvae**, which give rise to **pupae**. In a pupa, the larval tissues are metamorphosed into an **imago**, the adult insect. Larval and pupal stages are missing in the life cycles of insects such as cockroaches and locusts, which display **incomplete metamorphosis**. Their fertilised eggs hatch into **nymphs**, which are like the adult insect but smaller and sexually immature. After several moults, the nymphs grow into imagos.

Moulting and metamorphosis are regulated by hormones. The **moulting hormone**, **ecdysone**, is secreted by the **ventral gland** in the head of some insects and by the **prothoracic gland** in others. The gland is stimulated to do so by neurosecretions from the **cerebral ganglion**. Release of the neurosecretions occurs in some species when the abdomen is stretched after feeding. In others it is the act of swallowing. When the imago stage is reached the ecdysone-producing gland degenerates and moulting stops. The role of hormones in incomplete metamorphosis has been carefully worked out in the blood-sucking bug *Rhodnius*. In the first four larval stages **juvenile hormone**, **neotenin**, is secreted by the **corpus allatum** just behind the cerebral ganglion. Neotenin interacts with ecdysone keeping the soft, juvenile cuticle between moults. When the fifth larval stage is reached secretion of neotenin ceases and the hard, adult cuticle develops. In species which have complete metamorphosis the pupal stage develops when the

FIG. 26.59 *Beetle,* Geotrupes, × *2*

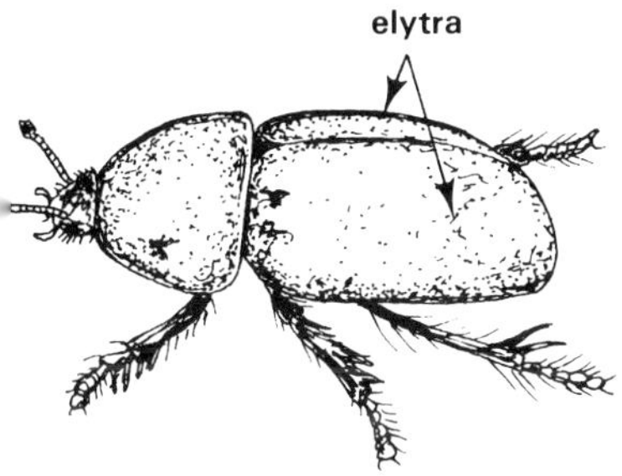

output of neotenin begins to fall. When it stops completely the imago stage develops.

The class *Insecta* is divided into many orders, including:

1. *COLEOPTERA*

Beetles are in this order (Fig. 26.59). The forewings are two horny shields called **elytra** which cover the hindwings. In flight, the elytra project sideways. The mouthparts are modified for chewing solid food.

2. *DIPTERA*

Flies and mosquitos are dipterans. The hindwings are a pair of **halteres** which act as stabilisers during flight. The mouthparts are modified for sucking and sometimes for piercing and biting (Fig. 26.60).

FIG. 26.60 *Heads and mouthparts* (a) *house fly,* Musca, × *9* (b) *mosquito,* Anopheles, × *14*

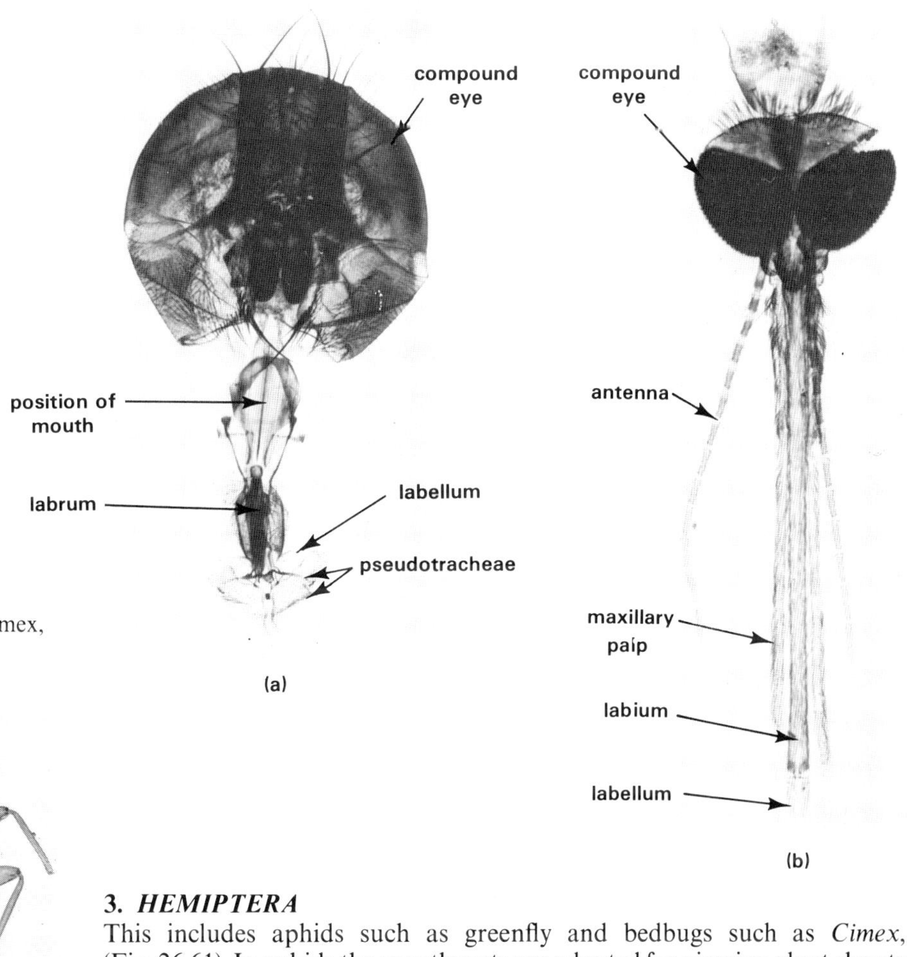

FIG. 26.61 *The bed bug,* Cimex, × *10*

3. *HEMIPTERA*

This includes aphids such as greenfly and bedbugs such as *Cimex*, (Fig. 26.61). In aphids the mouthparts are adapted for piercing plant shoots and sucking sap from the phloem (Figs. 12.12 and 12.17). Bedbugs suck the blood of mammals.

4. *LEPIDOPTERA*

Butterflies and moths are lepidopterans. The maxillae form a long protrusible **proboscis** which is used for sucking liquid food such as nectar. Both pairs of wings are large and covered with flat scales (Fig. 26.62).

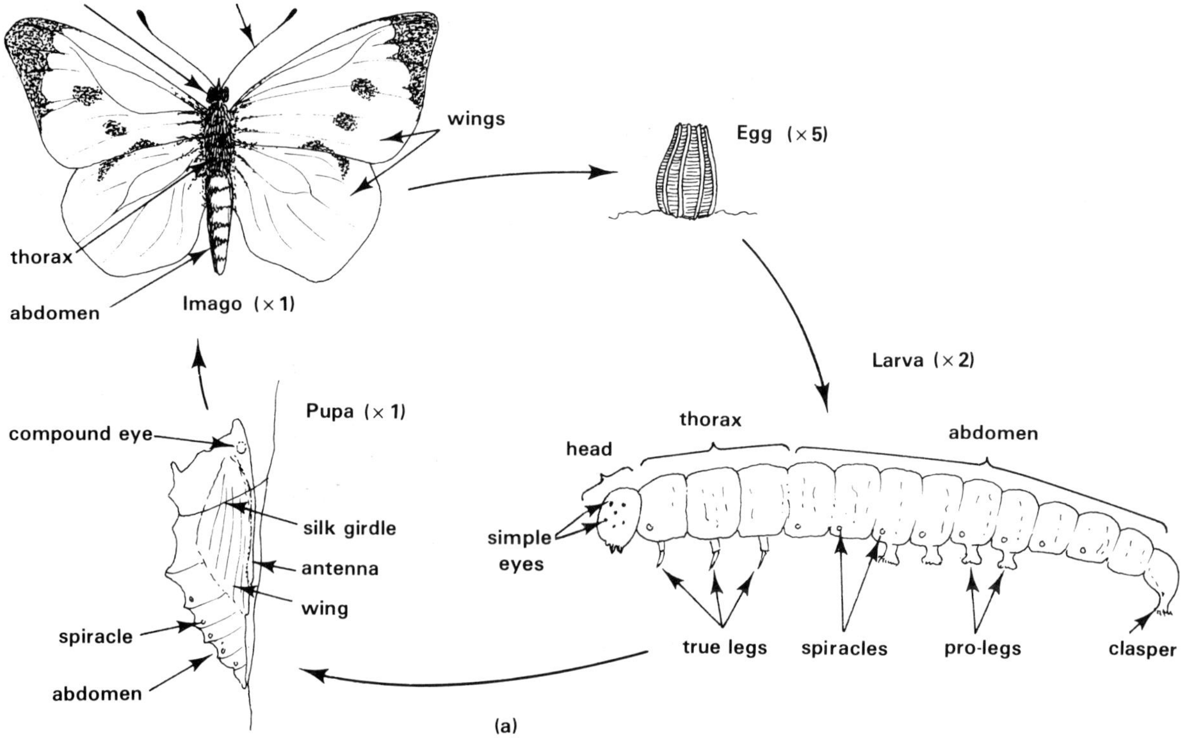

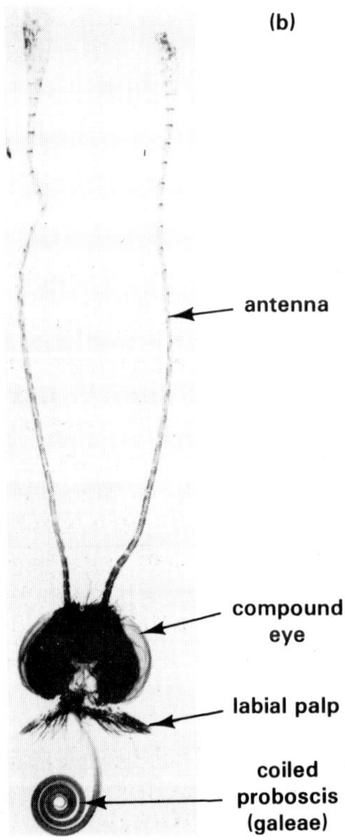

FIG. 26.62 (a) *Life cycle of the large white butterfly,* Pieris brassicae (b) *photomicrograph of butterfly mouthparts, × 7*

5. *ORTHOPTERA*

This includes locusts, grasshoppers and crickets. The mouthparts are modified for biting. The third pair of legs are elongated for jumping. On them are ridged **stridulation organs** which are rubbed to produce a chirping sound. It attracts the opposite sex prior to mating (Fig. 26.63).

FIG. 26.63 *Locust, × 1*

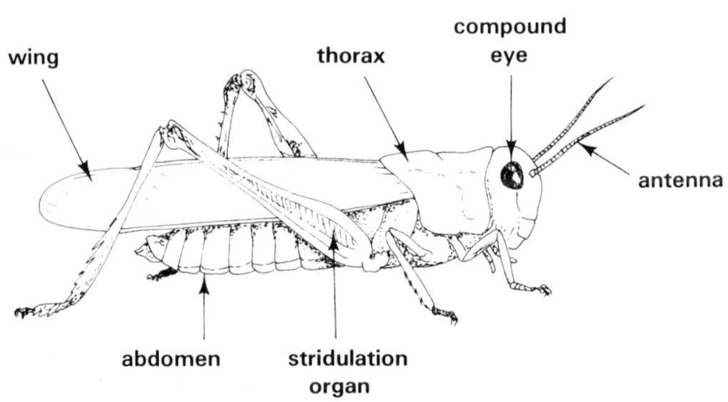

6. *HYMENOPTERA*

Ants, bees and wasps are in this order. They have biting or sucking mouthparts. The two pairs of wings are linked by a row of hooks on the leading edge of the hindwings which engage a groove on the trailing edge of the forewings. The first abdominal segment is fused with the thorax.

Many hymenopterans live in **social colonies** sometimes containing many thousands of individuals. The colony contains several forms or **castes**. In the honey bee, for example, the colony is centred on a single large female called the **queen** (Fig. 26.64). Her eggs are fertilised by males called **drones**.

FIG. 26.64 *Honey bees* (a) *queen* (b) *drone* (c) *worker* (d) *hive cells* (e) *worker mouthparts,* × 9

(a)

(b)

(c)

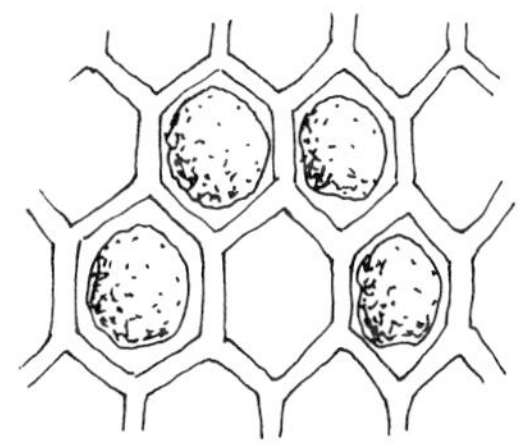

(d)

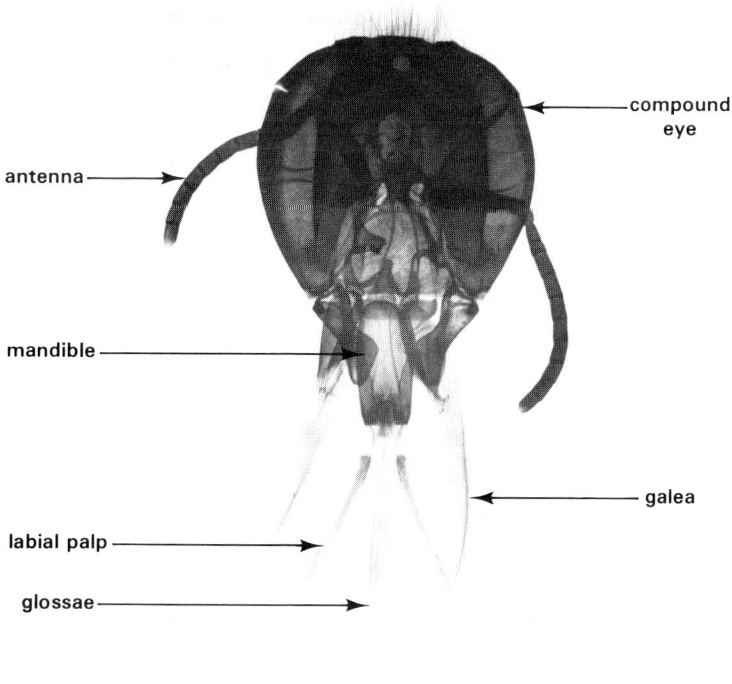

(e)

Fertilising the queen's eggs is their only function. The queen lays eggs one at a time in hexagonal wax cells in the **hive**. Any unfertilised eggs give rise to drones. Fertilised eggs produce either new queens or sterile females called **workers**. The workers feed the queen and build the wax cells which house the colony's larvae and pupae. Queen larvae are fed a special material called **royal jelly**. Other larvae are fed a mixture of pollen and honey. After moulting, the pupae develop inside a silk **cocoon** from which the adult emerges after a few days. The queen kills new queen larvae with her sting. Sometimes the workers prevent her doing this and a new queen grows to maturity. The old queen may leave the hive with a swarm of workers and establish a new colony elsewhere.

While collecting food for the colony, worker bees are important to flowering plants in distributing their pollen. The workers' legs are modified for the carriage of pollen (Fig. 19.10).

26.7.5 *Arachnida*

The arachnids include **spiders**, **scorpions**, **mites** and **ticks**. Most are terrestrial. The body is divided into two parts. The first six segments make up the **prosoma** which bears the head and four pairs of walking legs. The

FIG. 26.65 *Spider,* Epeira, × *4*

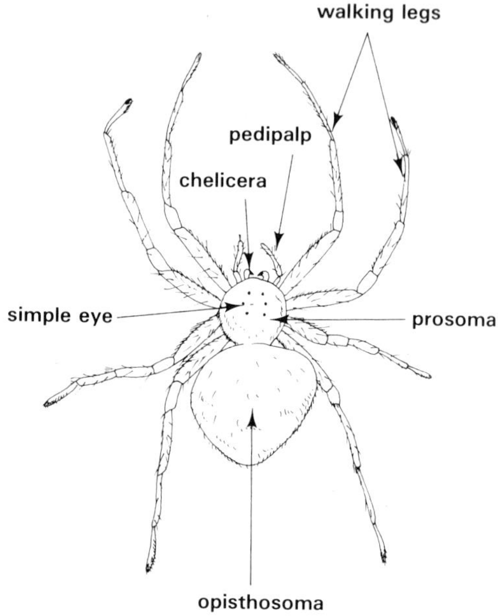

posterior part of the body is called the **opisthosoma** and usually has no appendages (Fig. 26.65).

Gas exchange in many arachnids involves the use of **lung books**. These are air-filled chambers containing many flaps of blood-filled tissue called lamellae. The lung books are rather like enclosed gills. In spiders there is also a tracheal system, but it is not as extensive as in insects. Consequently the blood of arachnids is important in the transport of oxygen in the body.

There are no antennae nor mandibles in arachnids. Instead, the mouthparts include paired **chelicerae** and **pedipalps**. The chelicerae each have a sharp claw which may be used to pierce prey. A paralysing poison flows through tubes inside the chelicerae and into the wound. The pedipalps are sensory appendages which may also be used by males to transfer sperms to the female during mating. **Malpighian tubules** are used to excrete nitrogenous wastes (section 26.7.4). There are no compound eyes, but simple eyes are often present. In spiders, a **web** is produced by three pairs of **spinnerets**, found on the posterior tip of the opisthosoma. Using a web to catch prey is unique to spiders. The sexes are usually separate and the life cycle has no larval stage.

Ticks and mites are ectoparasites found on the skin, usually feeding on the blood of their host. Their bodies are rounded, and the division between prosoma and opisthosoma is lost. They have no spinnerets (Fig. 26.66). Scorpions are ferocious predators which attack their prey using the sting at the tip of their arched tails.

26.8 *Mollusca*

The phylum *Mollusca* includes **snails**, **slugs**, **whelks**, **winkles**, **limpets**, **mussels**, **octopuses**, **cuttlefish** and **squids**. Molluscs are coelomate, but the coelom is much reduced. The heart consists of a single ventricle and two lateral atria. Like arthropods, the blood flows in a **haemocoel**.

Molluscs are not segmented. The body is divided into three parts, the **head**, **foot** and **visceral hump**. The visceral hump is covered by a soft skin called the **mantle** which usually secretes a hard **calcareous shell**.

FIG. 26.66 *A tick,* Dermacentor, × *7*

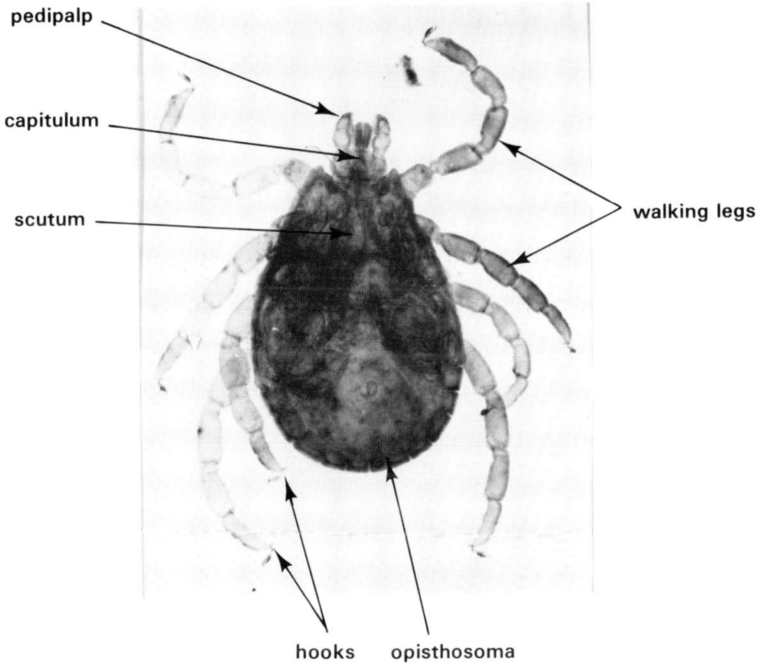

FIG. 26.67 *Radula of* Helix, × *50*

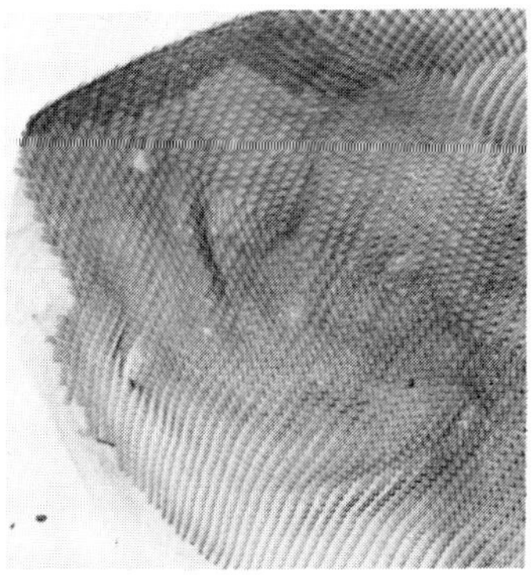

FIG. 26.68 *Veliger larva of a gastropod mollusc*

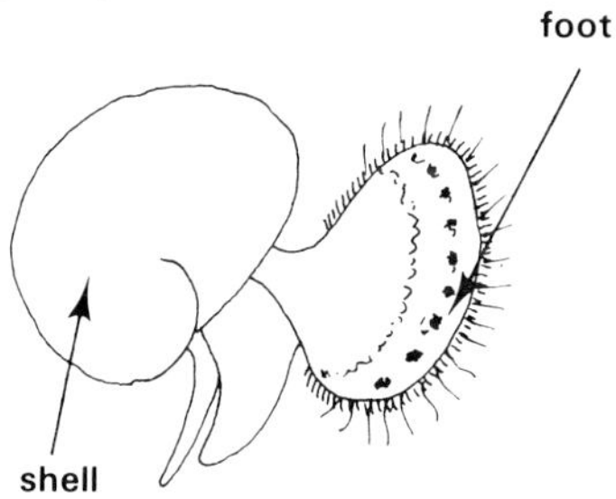

Most molluscs are aquatic and exchange respiratory gases by means of gills called **ctenidia** which are found in the **mantle cavity** beneath the shell. In terrestrial forms such as snails, the mantle cavity is air-filled and acts as a simple lung. It has a vascular roof and opens to the air by a small pore called the pneumostome. The blood of molluscs contains the oxygen-carrying pigment **haemocyanin**.

In the mouth of many molluscs is a structure called the **radula** which has many rows of small teeth. The radula is used for scraping food off solid surfaces, such as algae from rocks, and for rasping vegetation (Fig. 26.67).

The central nervous system consists of cerebral ganglia and a circum-oesophageal ring. Nerve fibres called pedal cords supply the foot; visceral loops pass to the visceral hump.

Molluscs are hermaphrodite, and in marine forms the life cycle includes a **trochophore** larva similar to that seen in polychaetes (section 26.6.1). It changes into a **veliger larva** from which the adult develops (Fig. 26.68).

Molluscs are divided into several classes including the *Gastropoda*, *Lamellibranchia* and *Cephalopoda*.

26.8.1 *Gastropoda*

Snails, slugs, limpets, whelks and winkles are gastropods. They have a distinct head, usually with eyes and prominent **tentacles**. The muscular foot is flattened and brings about a sliding form of movement. In most gastropods the visceral hump is twisted and the shell is coiled to accommodate the twisted body. The visceral hump also displays **torsion**; in addition to being twisted it is turned 180° on the foot (Fig. 26.69).

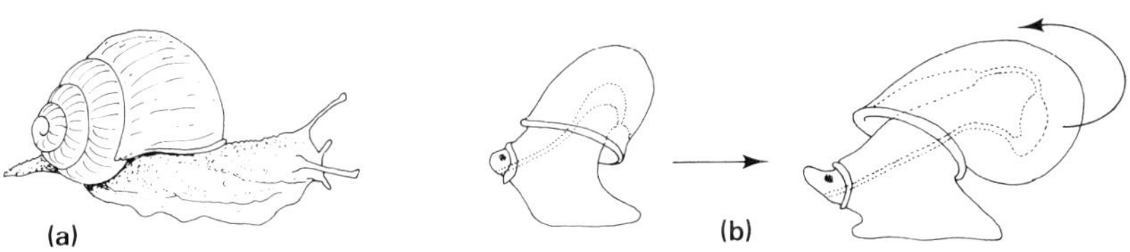

FIG. 26.69 (a) *Common garden snail,* Helix aspersa, × $\frac{2}{3}$
(b) *torsion*

26.8.2 *Lamellibranchia (Bivalvia)*

This includes mussels, razorshells, clams and scallops. The body is laterally flattened and **bilaterally symmetrical**. The shell develops as two **valves** which are hinged along one edge. The head is much reduced. Eyes, tentacles and radula are absent. The foot may be extended and used for burrowing in sand or mud (Fig. 26.70). Other bivalves such as the edible mussel, *Mytilus edulis*, live attached to rock surfaces by **byssus threads** (Fig. 26.71). The mantle cavity contains large gills which have many cilia arranged in tracts on their surfaces. The beating of the cilia causes oxygen and food-carrying water to flow over the gills. **Palps** near the mouth filter food particles out of the current of water.

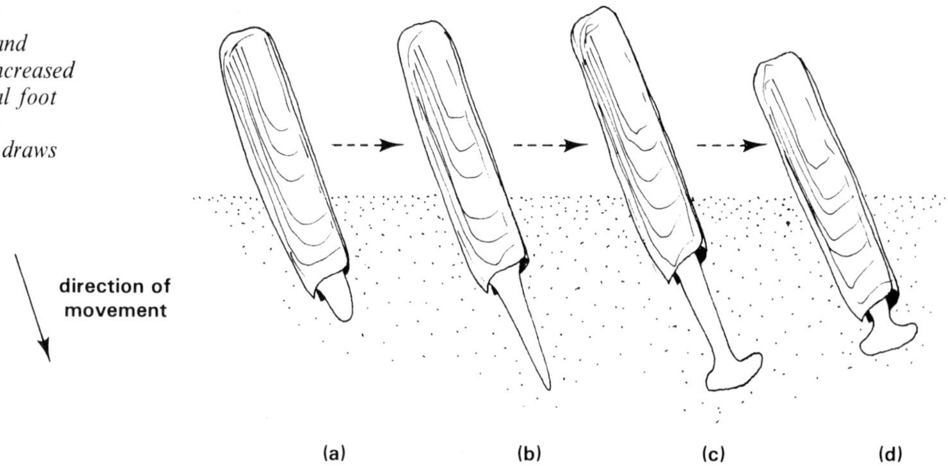

FIG. 26.70 *Razor shell burrowing in sand* (a) *and* (b) *foot extended by increased blood pressure* (c) *distal foot expands like an anchor* (d) *muscle contraction draws shell down*

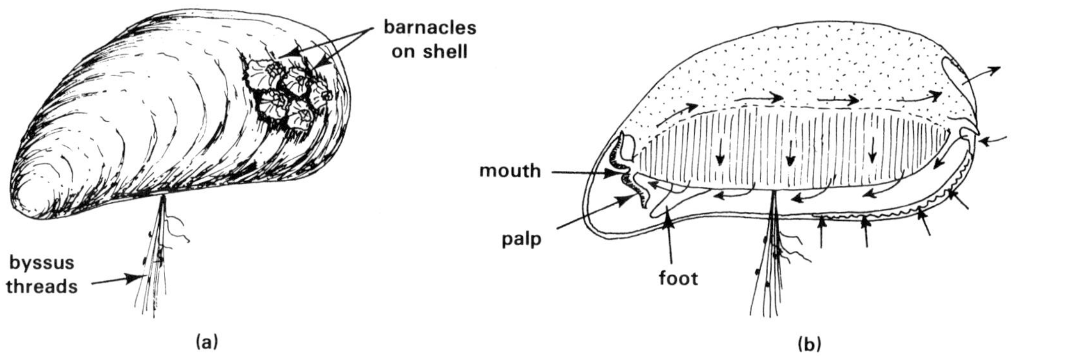

FIG. 26.71 (a) *The common mussel,* Mytilus edulis, × *1* (b) *feeding currents in* Mytilus, *shell removed*

26.8.3 *Cephalopoda*

Octopuses, **squids** and **cuttlefish** are cephalopods. The head is well developed and surrounded by a ring of **tentacles**. The nervous system is well developed, and the eyes of cephalopods are remarkably similar to those of vertebrates (Fig. 26.72). A **siphon** connects the mantle cavity with the sea water outside. When muscle action applies pressure to the water inside the mantle cavity, the water is squirted out through the siphon and the animal is propelled rapidly in the opposite direction. This action is often used as an escape mechanism when danger threatens. As another defence mechanism, some cephalopods secrete a dark fluid called **sepia** from an **ink sac**. Some cephalopods, such as *Nautilus*, have a coiled external shell containing chambers. In the squid and cuttlefish, the shell is internal and greatly reduced, while the shell is absent altogether in the octopus (Fig. 26.73).

FIG. 26.72 *Vertical section eye of cuttlefish, × 10*. Compare with Fig. 16.1

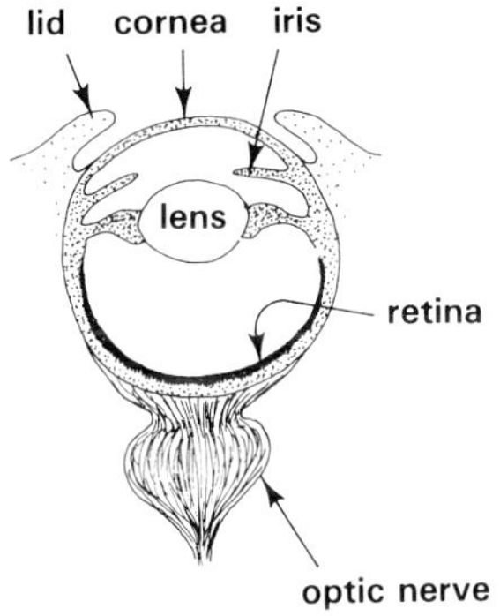

FIG. 26.73 *Octopus swimming, × $\frac{1}{8}$*

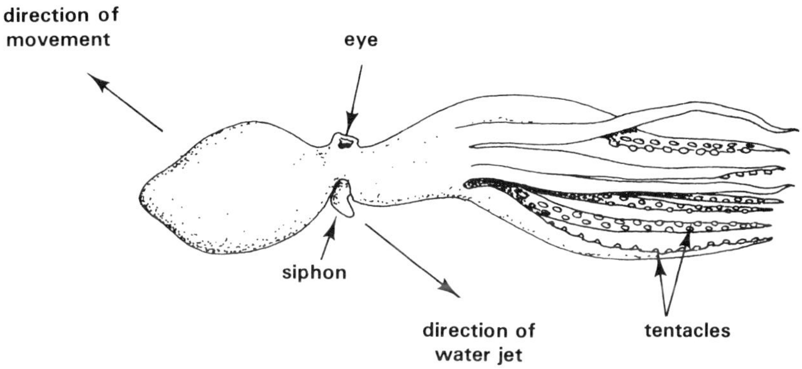

26.9 *Echinodermata*

The phylum *Echinodermata* includes **starfish** and **sea urchins**. One of the most striking features of echinoderms is their **radial symmetry**. This is often **pentamerous**, that is radiating in five directions from the centre. Adult echinoderms are coelomate. They are not segmented and there is no head. The mouth is on the **oral surface** underneath the animal, the anus is on the upper, **aboral surface**. Numerous **spines** usually project from the skin, which contains calcareous plates. Some spines are arranged in groups and may act as pincers. They are called **pedicellariae** and may be used for defence or for gripping and cutting prey. Some have poison glands attached to them.

Another feature peculiar to echinoderms is the **water vascular system**, a complex system of water-filled coelomic tubes which radiate throughout the body. Sea water enters the system through a perforated calcareous plate called the **madreporite** on the aboral surface near to the anus. The action of cilia maintains a current of water in the tubes. From the system, rows of many **tube feet** perforate the skin and project to the outside. The tube feet are kept inflated by the pressure of water in the water vascular system. Muscles in the tube feet enable them to be used to move the whole animal (Fig. 26.74). The area covered by the tube feet is called the **ambulacrum** and is on the oral surface.

FIG. 26.74 *Starfish* (a) *water vascular system* (b) *transverse section arm. Tube feet are moved by the action of internal muscles*

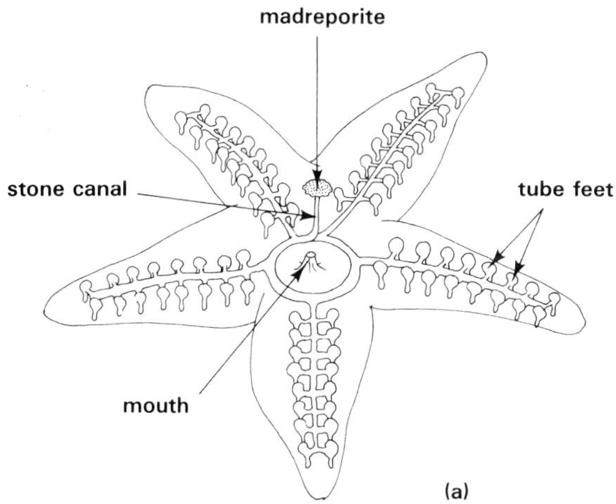

(a)

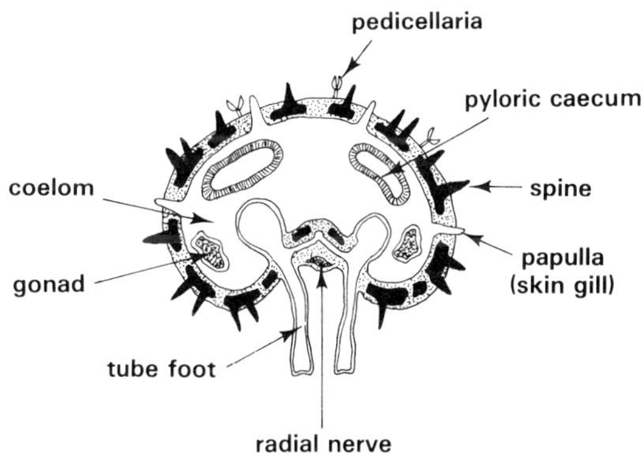

(b)

FIG. 26.75 *Pluteus larva,* × *70*

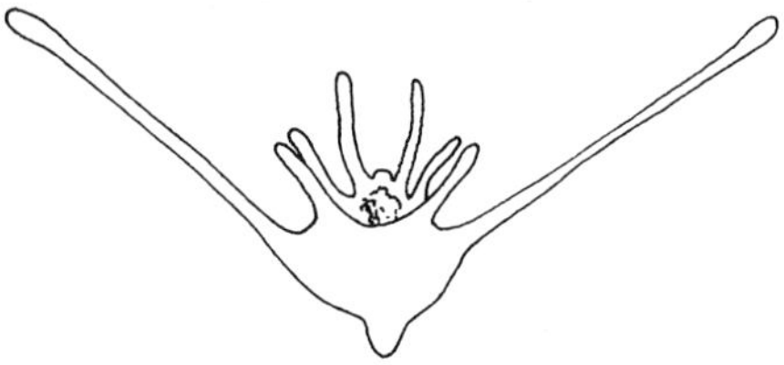

The simple nervous system consists of a ring of fibres around the mouth and a series of radiating branches. There is no brain. The blood vascular system is much reduced and probably plays little part in the circulation of materials in the body.

The sexes are separate and fertilisation is external. The life cycle involves a free-swimming, bilaterally symmetrical **pluteus larval** stage (Fig. 26.75). The structure and development of echinoderm larvae is similar to that seen in primitive chordates (section 27.1). For this reason it is thought that echinoderms and chordates evolved from a common stock.

The echinoderms are divided into four classes, including the *Asteroidea* and *Echinoidea*.

26.9.1 *Asteroidea*

Starfish such as *Asterias* belong to this class (Fig. 26.76). The body is star-shaped with a photosensitive eyespot at the tip of the ambulacral groove on each arm. It is usually raised on the leading arm when the starfish is moving. The calcareous plates are spaced out in the skin, so the arms are flexible. On the oral surface, small thin-walled outgrowths called **papullae** project from the skin. They act as gills and may also be the sites of nitrogenous excretion.

Starfish use their tube feet as suction pads to pull open the shells of bivalve molluscs. The stomach can be everted through the mouth to take in the soft bodies of their prey. Extensions of the gut called **pyloric caeca** project into the arms (Fig. 26.74(b)).

FIG. 26.76 *Common starfish,* Asterias rubens, × *1*

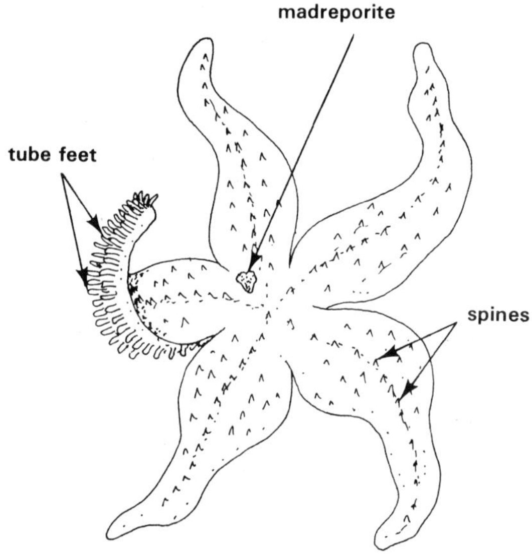

FIG. 26.77 *Common sea urchin,* Echinus esculentus, × $\frac{1}{2}$

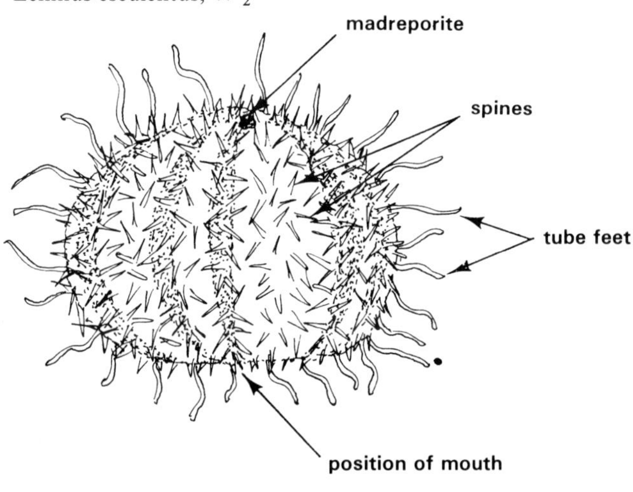

26.9.2 *Echinoidea*

This includes the sea urchins such as *Echinus* (Fig. 26.77). It has no arms. The calcareous plates in the skin are fused to form a spherical shell. Long, movable spines and pedicellariae project from most of the body surface. While feeding, urchins use a complex apparatus called **Aristotle's lantern**. It consists of five calcareous plates called pyramids from which teeth project. Muscle action causes a chewing movement of the pyramids and teeth.

Chapter 27 Variety of life: Chordate animals

Chordates are **bilaterally symmetrical, coelomate** animals. Their name is derived from the dorsal rod of cells called the **notochord** which extends the length of the body. The notochord is relatively rigid and provides support. Dorsal to the notochord is a **hollow nerve cord**, usually with a well-developed brain in the head. The heart is placed ventrally and pumps blood forwards. At some stage in the life cycle, chordates have pairs of **gill clefts** in the sides of the pharynx and a solid **post-anal tail** (Fig. 27.1).

FIG. 27.1 *Chordate body plan*

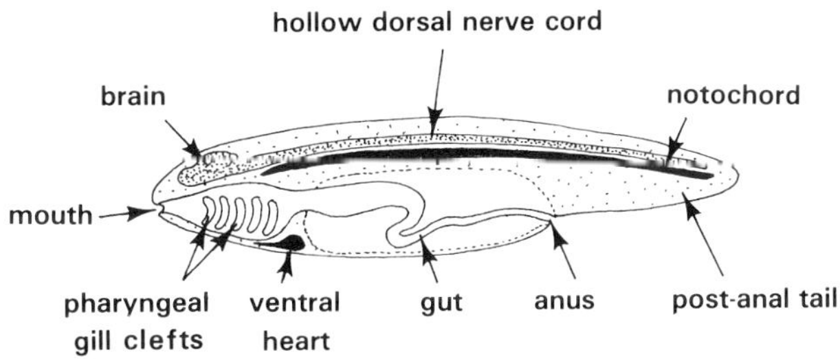

The phylum *Chordata* has three sub-phyla, the *Urochordata*, *Cephalochordata* and the *Vertebrata*. The urochordates and cephalochordates are sometimes called protochordates.

27.1 Protochordates

Protochordates are **invertebrate chordates**. They are primitive animals and are thought to be the modern remnants of stock from which all chordates evolved. The *Urochordata* is divided into several classes, including the *Ascidiacea*. The *Cephalochordata* has a single class called the *Cephalochorda*.

27.1.1 *Ascidiacea*

FIG. 27.2 Ciona (a) *internal structure*, × *1* (b) *larva* (compare with Fig. 27.1)

The ascidians include the **sea squirts** such as *Ciona* ((Fig. 27.2(a)). Sea squirts are sessile, **non-segmented** and without a coelom. In the adult, the notochord is lost and the nerve cord is degenerate. A large proportion of the body is occupied by the pharynx. Ciliary action on the **gill bars** between the gill clefts sets up currents of food-carrying water. Food particles are directed towards the mouth. Water passes through the gill clefts and out via a cavity called the **atrium**. The gill bars act as a food filter. A ciliated groove called the **endostyle** is present along one wall of the pharynx. It secretes a thyroxin-like compound containing iodine. The endostyle is thought to have given rise to the thyroid gland seen in other chordates (Chapter 18).

The entire body is surrounded by a **tunic** composed of **tunicin**, a substance similar to cellulose. Ascidian larvae have typical chordate characteristics (Fig. 27.2(b)).

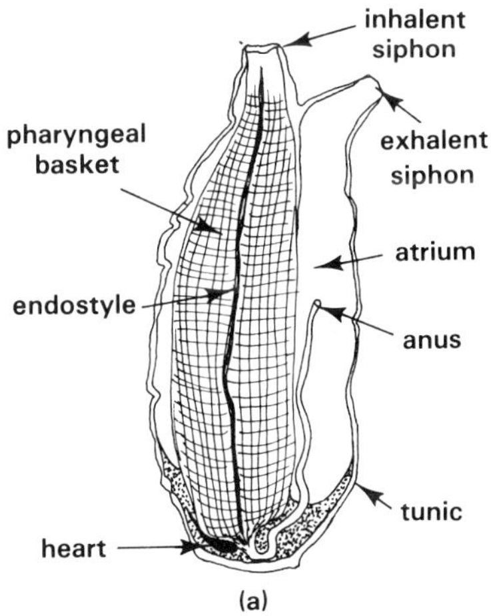

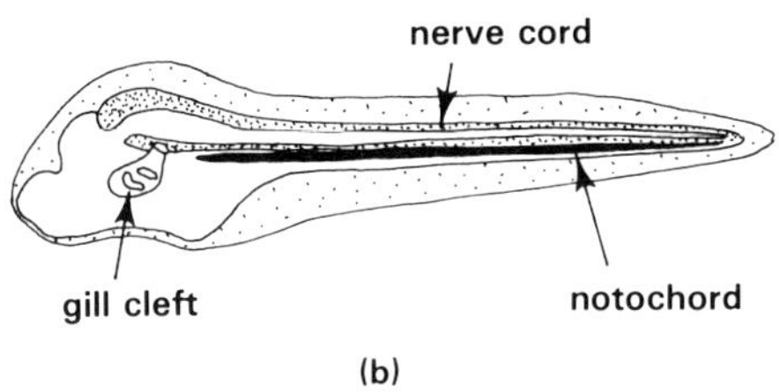

27.1.2 *Cephalochorda*

The cephalochordates include the **lancelets** such as *Branchiostoma* (*Amphioxus*) (Fig. 27.3). Lancelets are small fish-like animals, living in the sea. Their name is derived from the notochord, which runs the length of the body and into the head. Lancelets are **metamerically segmented**. They are capable of swimming by alternate contraction and relaxation of muscles on each side of the body. The muscles are arranged in V-shaped segmented blocks called *myotomes*. The notochord allows bending of the body. Swimming is not efficient, however, since there are no well-developed fins. Lancelets spend most of their time partially buried in sand with the head protruding from the burrow.

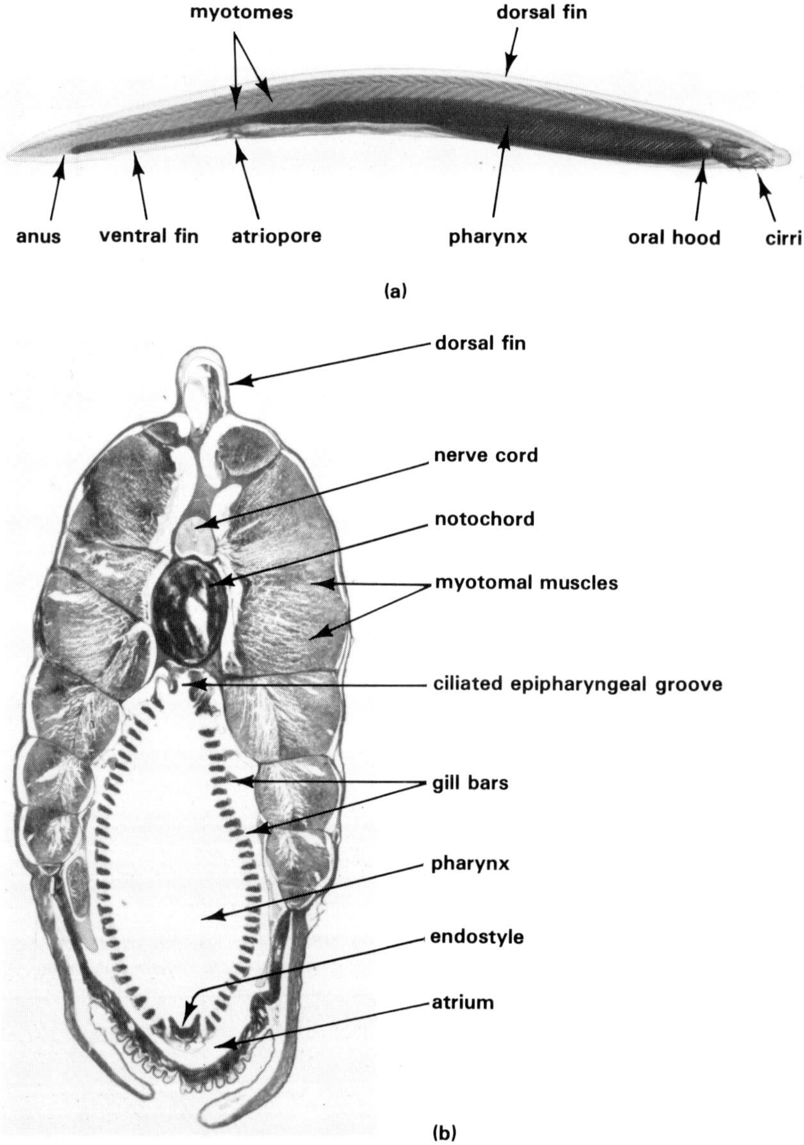

FIG. 27.3 Branchiostoma (a) *whole animal,* × *4* (b) *transverse section through pharynx,* × *25*

Like sea squirts, lancelets are **filter feeders**. The pharyngeal gill bars are lined with cilia and there is a well-developed endostyle. At the entry to the mouth is a ring of **tentacles** which acts as a strainer. Only food particles of

FIG. 27.4 Branchiostoma; *flow of mucus and oxygen-bearing water through the pharynx*

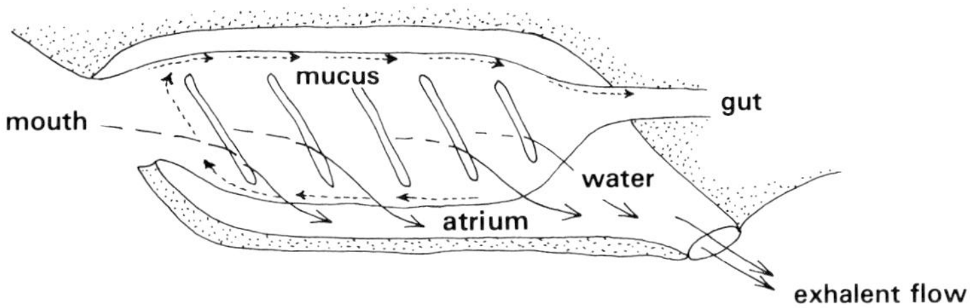

manageable size enter the pharynx and are trapped on the gill bars before being directed to the gut. The roof of the mouth and the endostyle secrete mucus which helps movement of food along the ciliary tract of the pharynx. Oxygen-carrying water flows through the gill clefts into a cavity called the **atrium**. From here the water is expelled through a ventral opening (Fig. 27.4). Oxygen is absorbed into the blood in the gill bars. The blood contains no respiratory pigments and there is no heart. The ventral blood vessel is contractile and pumps blood forwards and up into the gill bars.

Pairs of **nephridia** in the pharyngeal segments are used for excretion. The nephridia are similar to those in annelids, except that they contain **solenocytes** (Fig. 27.5) which are very like the flame cells of flatworms. The lancelet's nephridia empty into the atrium.

FIG. 27.5 Branchiostoma (a) *nephridium* (b) *solenocyte* (compare with Fig. 26.31 (c))

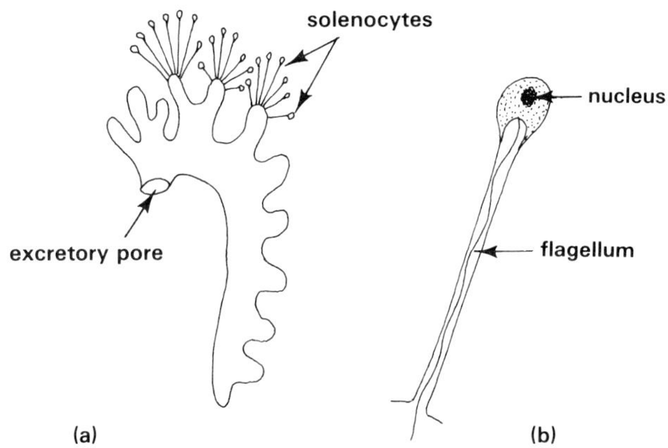

Cephalochordates have no brain. This feature and the lack of sense organs is thought to be a degenerate condition resulting from the animals' way of life. There are separate sexes. The gonads are arranged segmentally and grow into the atrium.

27.2 Vertebrata (Craniata)

The vertebrates are chordates in which the notochord is strengthened by cartilage, or more usually bone, forming a **vertebral column** divided into vertebrae. In the head the brain is surrounded by a skeletal case called the **cranium**.

Vertebrates are divided into several classes—*Agnatha, Chondrichthyes, Osteichthyes, Amphibia, Reptilia, Aves* and *Mammalia.*

27.2.1 *Agnatha*

The agnathans are **jawless fish** such as lampreys (Fig. 27.6). They are the few living representatives of the class from which all other vertebrates are thought to have evolved. Lampreys are ectoparasites. They use suckers

FIG. 27.6 *Lamprey*, × $\frac{1}{3}$

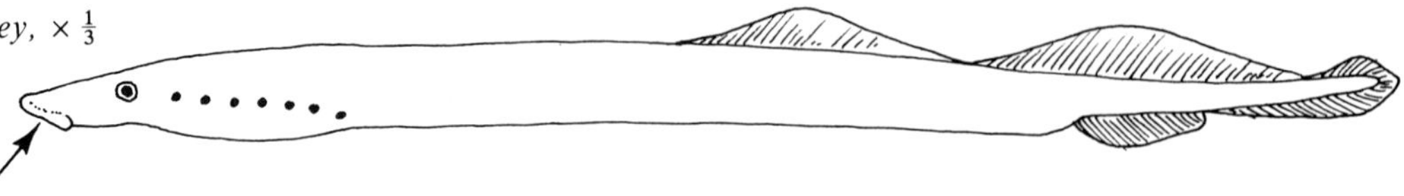

around their mouths to attach themselves to other fish. They perforate the skin of the host from which they suck blood. The skeleton is cartilaginous and the skin has no scales.

27.2.2 *Chondrichthyes (Elasmobranchii)*

The chondrichthyans are **cartilaginous fish** such as dogfish, sharks, rays and skates (Fig. 27.7). Nearly all live in the sea. They have strong jaws lined with teeth and the skeleton is made of cartilage. The skin is thick and

FIG. 27.7 (a) *blue shark*, Carcharius, × $\frac{1}{40}$ (b) *skate*, Raja, × $\frac{1}{8}$, (c) *mermaid's purse, egg case of the lesser spotted dogfish*, × $\frac{1}{2}$

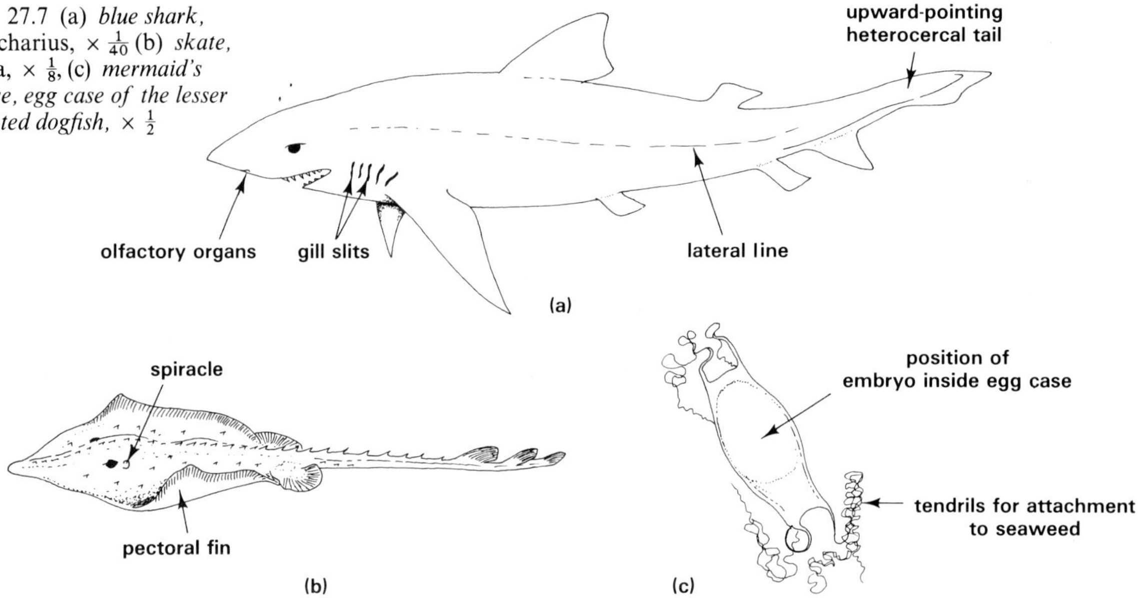

covered by many tooth-like **placoid scales** (Fig. 27.8). These are thought to be the evolutionary remains of the external armour that once covered their ancestors. The body is **dorso-ventrally flattened**. Beneath the tip of the head is a pair of well-developed olfactory organs. Sharks are well known for their keen sense of smell. The highly developed eyes are similar to those of mammals (Chapter 16). Running the length of the body on each side is a **lateral line system**. It consists of a long canal just beneath the skin connected with the sea through numerous perforations in the skin. In the canal are many small hair cells which are sensitive to vibrations in the surrounding water. The lateral line enables cartilaginous fish to detect movements in their surroundings.

FIG. 27.8 *Placoid scales of dogfish*, × *10*

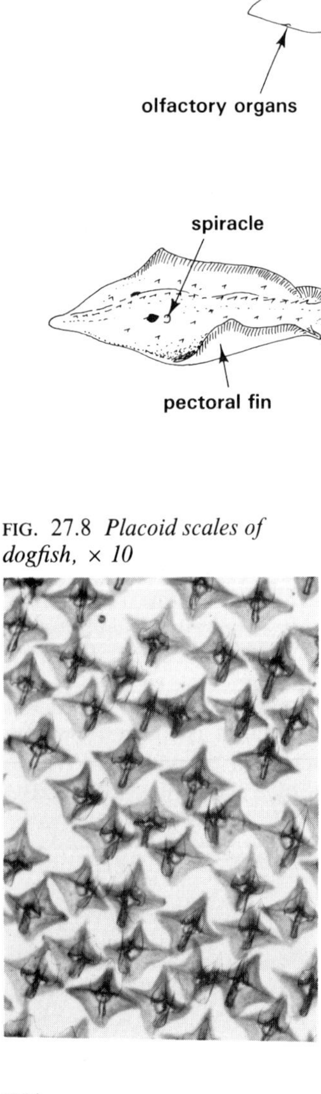

Gill clefts, usually five pairs, open at **gill slits** just behind the head. Water taken into the mouth is forced through the gill slits when the floor of the mouth is raised. Blood passing through the gills travels in much the same direction as the sea water. Gas exchange in such a **parallel-flow** arrangement is relatively inefficient (Fig. 27.16(b)). A pair of small openings called **spiracles** is found just behind the eyes. In rays and skates, the spiracle allows oxygen-carrying water into the pharynx while the animal is partially buried in sand when water cannot enter the mouth (Fig. 27.7(b)).

Cartilaginous fish are powerful swimmers. Alternate contraction and relaxation of **myotomal muscles** flex the body sideways, first one way then the other. The sides of the body and the fin of the **heterocercal tail** push against the water, giving forward thrust. The body is stabilised by the **rigid fins.** They help prevent rolling, pitching and yawing (Fig. 27.9). There is no swim bladder. Rays and skates are greatly flattened and mostly live on the sea bottom. Their pectoral fins are very extensive, allowing them to glide over the sea bed in an undulating fashion.

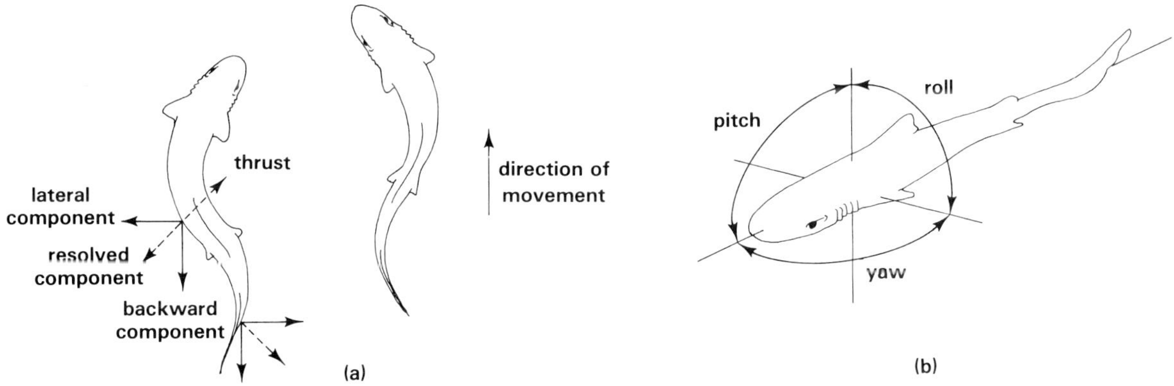

FIG. 27.9 *Mechanics of swimming in dogfish* (a) *lateral flexing* (b) *deviations of motion*

Just behind the olfactory organs on the ventral surface is the mouth, which leads into a large bilobed stomach. The intestine is relatively short. The distance food travels through it, however, is greatly increased by a **spiral valve** which also increases the absorptive surface area of the intestine (Fig. 27.10).

Blood containing haemoglobin circulates in a system of closed vessels. The ventral vessel leads to an S-shaped heart between the pectoral fins. The heart has four chambers. A single ventricle pumps deoxygenated blood

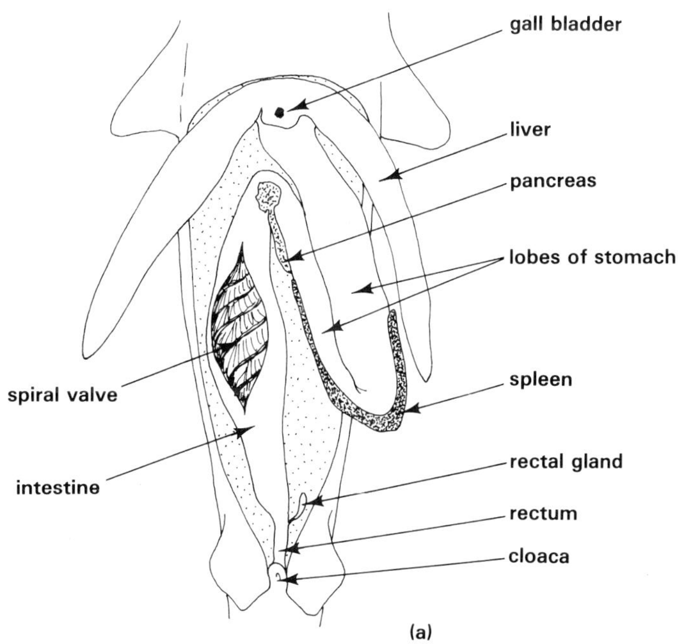

FIG. 27.10 *Dogfish* (a) *gut dissected to reveal the spiral valve* (b) *transverse section* × *10*

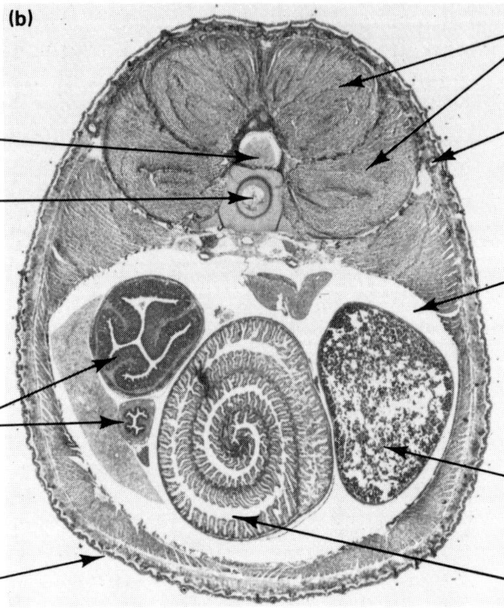

FIG. 27.11 *Dogfish heart and branchial blood supply. The direction of blood flow is indicated by arrows*

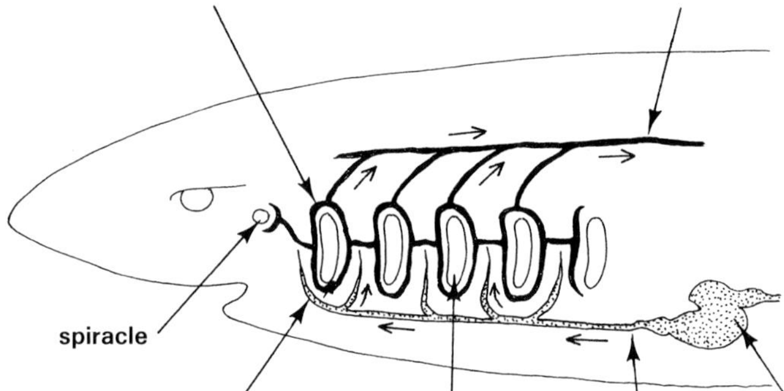

forward towards the gills (Fig. 27.11). Fish have a **single circulation**, blood flowing once through the heart on each complete circuit of the body (Fig. 27.21(a)). A peculiar feature of cartilaginous fish is the presence in their blood of urea in concentrations which would be toxic to other vertebrates. The large amount of urea makes the water potential of their blood similar to that of sea water. Paired **kidneys** are used to eliminate nitrogenous and ionic wastes. Urine is produced by many microscopic tubules called nephrons.

The sexes are separate and reproduction involves copulation. The male has a pair of **claspers** between the pelvic fins. Claspers are used to introduce sperms into the oviducts of the female. After fertilisation, the eggs are enclosed in a tough case and released into the sea (Fig. 27.7(c)). Coiled threads trailing from the egg cases become entangled in seaweeds. When sufficiently developed, the young fish break free from the **egg case** and swim away. In some sharks and rays, development of the young takes place in the mother's body.

27.2.3 *Osteichthyes*

The osteichthyeans are **bony fish** (Fig. 27.12). They inhabit fresh and brackish water as well as the sea and are by far the most numerous of aquatic vertebrates. There are about seven times more species of bony fish than cartilaginous species.

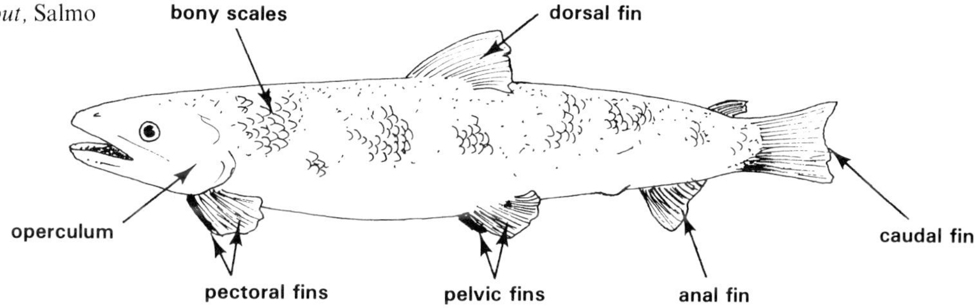

FIG. 27.12 *Brown trout,* Salmo trutta, $\times \frac{1}{5}$

The internal skeleton consists of bone and the skin is covered by many thin **bony scales**. Along each side of the body is a **lateral line canal**. There is no spiracle and the gills are covered by a bony flap called the **operculum**. The body is usually **laterally flattened**, the fins are flexible and the tail fin is **homocercal**.

One of the unusual features of most bony fish is the **swim bladder**, an air-filled sac close to the pharynx. It is thought that the lungs of air-breathing vertebrates may have evolved from swim bladders. In **lung fish**, the swim bladder is a paired structure connected to the pharynx and used for gas exchange (Fig. 27.13). In most bony fish, the swim bladder is used in maintaining buoyancy. The gas, mainly oxygen, inside the bladder forces the fish upwards towards the surface of the water. The body mass drags the

FIG. 27.13 *Australian lungfish,* Neoceratodus (a) *whole animal,* $\times \frac{1}{6}$ (b) *position of lungs*

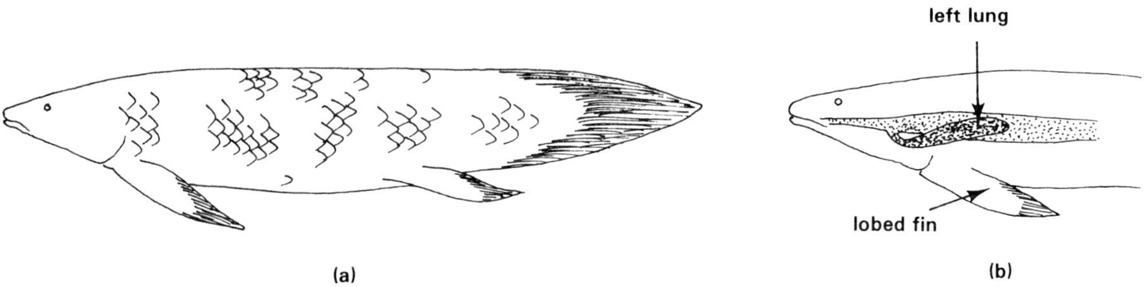

fish downwards under the influence of gravity. The wall of the bladder is highly vascular. Gas may be absorbed from the bladder by the blood or discharged into the bladder from the blood. In this way, bony fish can alter their density, enabling them to swim at an appropriate depth with the minimum of muscular effort (Fig. 27.14). Mackerel do not have a swim bladder. They swim continuously to maintain their preferred level in the water.

The **fins** in bony fish are thin sheets of skin supported by rays of bone. The pelvic fins are usually well forward and used with the pectoral fins in diving, rising, turning and braking (Fig. 27.15). The rigid fins of cartilaginous fish do not allow the range of movements seen in bony fish. In some bony fish, forward thrust is provided solely by flapping movements of the fins. During fast swimming, myotomal muscles flex the body providing extra thrust. The streamlined shape of many bony fish also aids swimming by reducing friction and drag.

FIG. 27.14 *Swim* (air) *bladders in bony fish* (a) *position in the herring,* (b) *maintenance of buoyancy at different depths by inflation or deflation of the swim bladder. Neutral buoyancy is achieved when the fish neither rises nor sinks*

FIG. 27.15 *Use of the pectoral fins in bony fish* (a) *cornering* (b) *braking* (c) *skeleton*

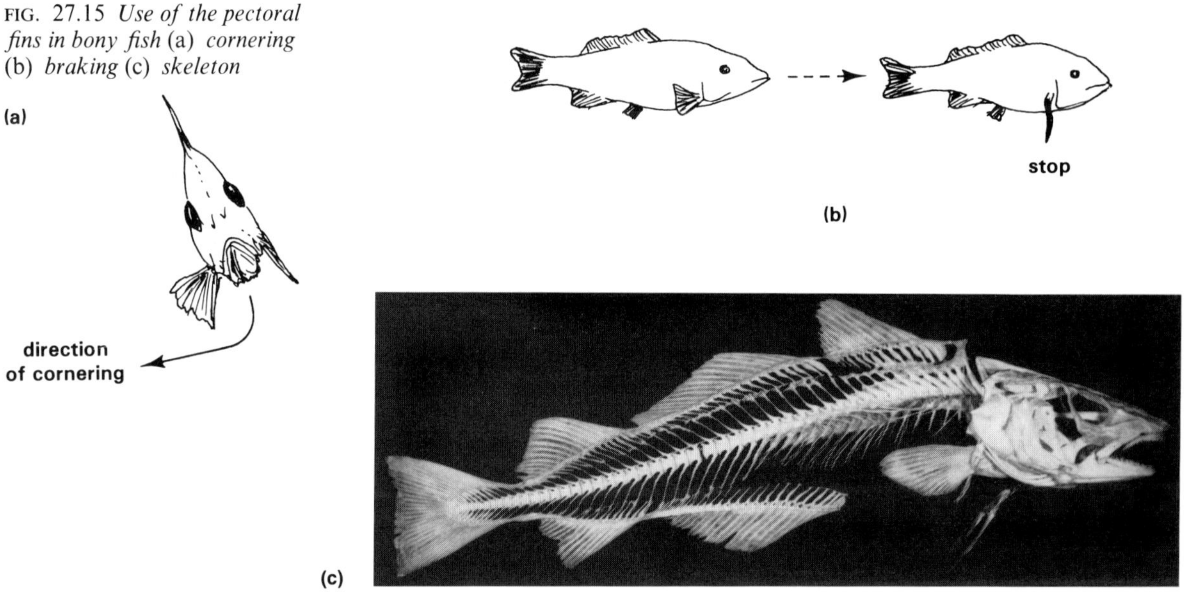

Respiratory gas exchange occurs at the **gills**, which are well supplied with blood and supported by bony gill bars. As in cartilaginous fish, there are usually five pairs of gill clefts. Each gill is composed of very many thin plates called **lamellae**. There is thus a considerable surface area for gas exchange, which helps offset the relatively low oxygen content of water, less than 1 per cent by volume. Water is forced over the gills when the floor of the mouth is raised. The gill lamellae are arranged so that blood and water flow in opposite directions. Gas exchange in such a **counterflow** arrangement is much more efficient than in the parallel flow mechanism seen in cartilaginous fish (Fig. 27.16). Osmoregulation in bony fish is described in Chapter 28.

Reproduction in bony fish usually involves external fertilisation. The large numbers of eggs laid by females helps compensate for the losses caused by predators and other hazards. In one season, for example, a female cod may produce as many as ninety million eggs. Reproduction may also involve complex behaviour of mating pairs, nest-building, care of the

FIG. 27.16 (a) *Gill structure in bony fish.* See Fig. 8.9 *The lamellae are arranged so that the water flows over them in the opposite direction to that of the blood within them. This counter flow enables maximum gas exchange.* (b) *Section through a gill of dogfish. The blood-water counter flow is less efficient than in bony fish because the water flows mostly along the lamellae rather than between them.*

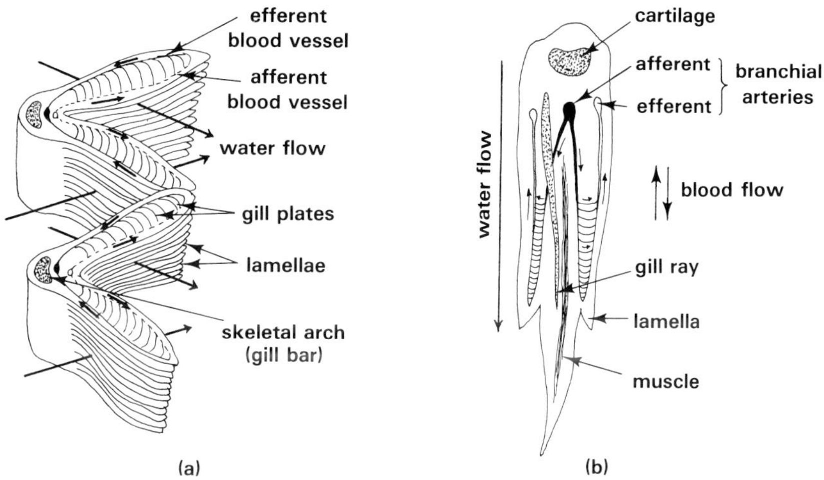

young, shoaling and long migrations. The salmon, for example, normally returns to the river where it was hatched, after swimming several thousands of miles across the oceans.

The class *Osteichthyes* is divided into two main sub-classes, *Sarcopterygii* and *Actinopterygii*. The sarcopterygians are the lobe-finned fish. There are only a few living representatives, including lungfish and the **coelacanth**, *Latimeria* (Fig. 27.17). The first land vertebrates may have evolved from coelacanth-like ancestors. The lobed fins are thought to have given rise to legs. The actinopterygians include the infra-class *Teleostei*, to which most of the bony fish living today belong.

FIG. 27.17 *Coelacanth,* Latimeria $\times \frac{1}{10}$

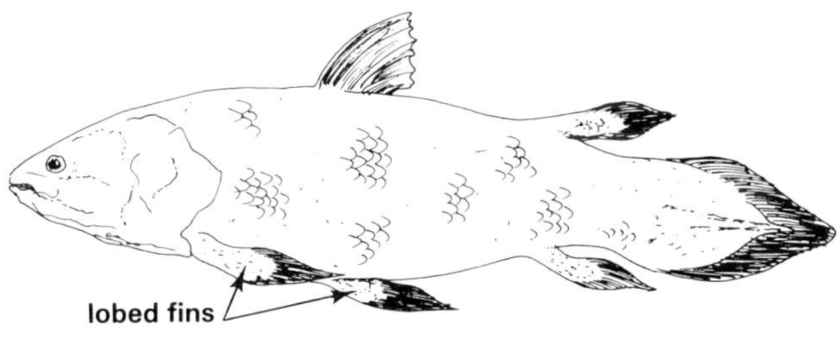

27.2.4 *Amphibia*

The **amphibians** include **frogs, toads, newts** and **salamanders** (Fig. 27.18). Amphibians were probably the first vertebrates to colonise land. They are thought to have evolved at a time when widespread seasonal droughts were common. The theory is that some lobe-finned fish used their fins as primitive legs and crawled to neighbouring ponds when their own pond dried out. The skeleton of amphibians has evolved to support the body on land. The vertebral column acts as a suspension girder from which the thoracic and abdominal organs hang. The force of gravity acting on the body mass is transmitted to the ground through strong **pectoral** and **pelvic girdles** and the limbs. Swimming in amphibians is a fish-like side to side flexing of the body (Fig. 27.19). Amphibian skeletons contain bone and

FIG. 27.18 (a) *Common newt,* Triturus vulgaris, × *1* (b) *common frog,* Rana temporaria, × *1*

FIG. 27.19 (a) *The main components of the amphibian skeleton* (b) *fish-like locomotion in an amphibian* (compare with Fig. 27.9 (a))

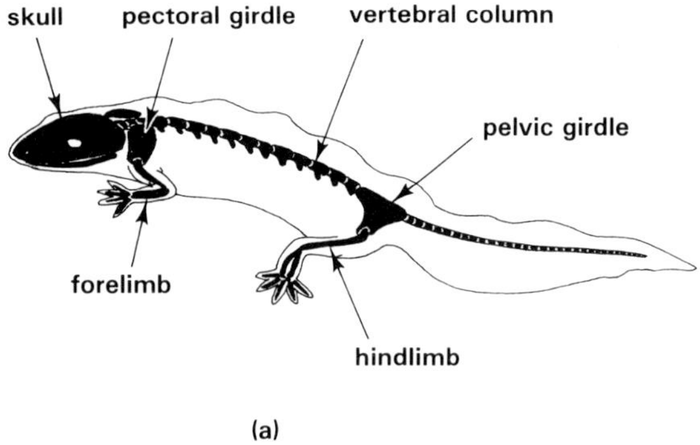

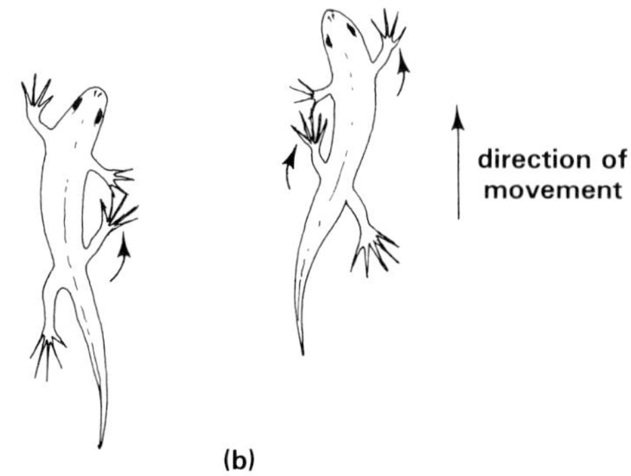

often a lot of cartilage. The bones of the limbs are arranged in a characteristic fashion. The limbs are **pentadactyl**, usually terminating in five digits (Fig. 27.20). In the forelimbs of amphibians, the number of digits is usually reduced. The presence of pentadactyl limbs in amphibians, reptiles, birds and mammals points to a common ancestry (Fig. 24.12).

FIG. 27.20 *Pentadactyl limb, general plan.* See Fig. 24.12

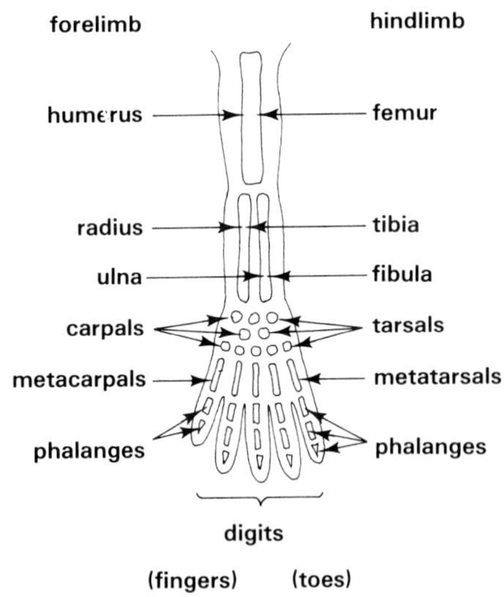

FIG. 27.21 *Blood circulation in the vertebrates* (a) *single type in fish* (b) *double type in other vertebrates in which the blood flows twice through the heart during each complete circuit*

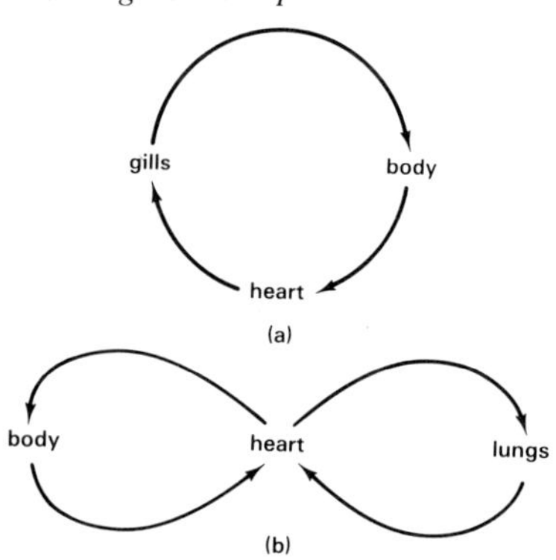

About 21 per cent of the volume of the earth's atmosphere is oxygen. The problem faced by air-breathers is to extract the oxygen from the atmosphere without losing too much water. Respiratory surfaces must be moist to allow oxygen gas to dissolve before the oxygen can diffuse into the blood. As the respiratory surface must also be exposed to the atmosphere, inevitably it loses moisture by evaporation (section 8.1). The lungs of

FIG. 27.22 *Amphibian heart. The spiral valve may help to separate oxygenated* (continuous arrows) *from deoxygenated* (dotted arrows) *blood*

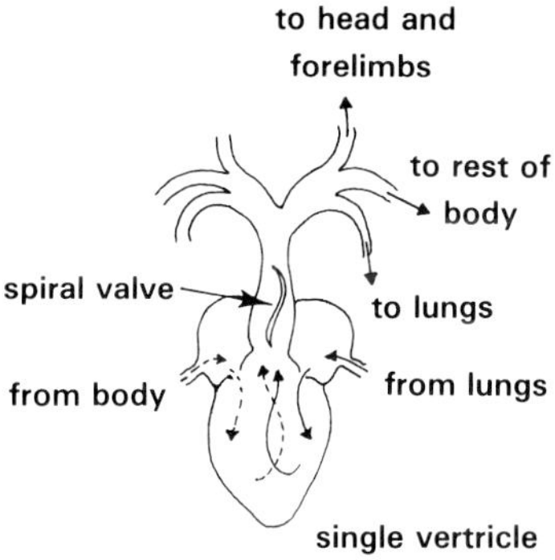

amphibians are relatively simple air-filled sacs (Fig. 8.5). Most amphibians use their **smooth moist skin** as an accessory respiratory surface. Larval amphibians use **gills**.

Amphibians have a **double circulation**, blood travelling through the heart twice on each circuit of the body (Fig. 27.21). The amphibian heart has a **single ventricle** in which oxygen-carrying blood mixes with deoxygenated blood (Fig. 27.22). Delivery of oxygen to the tissues is thus somewhat inefficient. It is offset to some extent by absorbing oxygen through the skin. Most amphibians are restricted to damp habitats, because water constantly evaporates from the moist skin.

Another important reason why most amphibians live in moist habitats is that they require water for fertilisation and larval development. Amphibian **larvae** are fish-like and usually have gills. The transition from larva to adult involves great changes in body form, known as **metamorphosis** (Fig. 27.23).

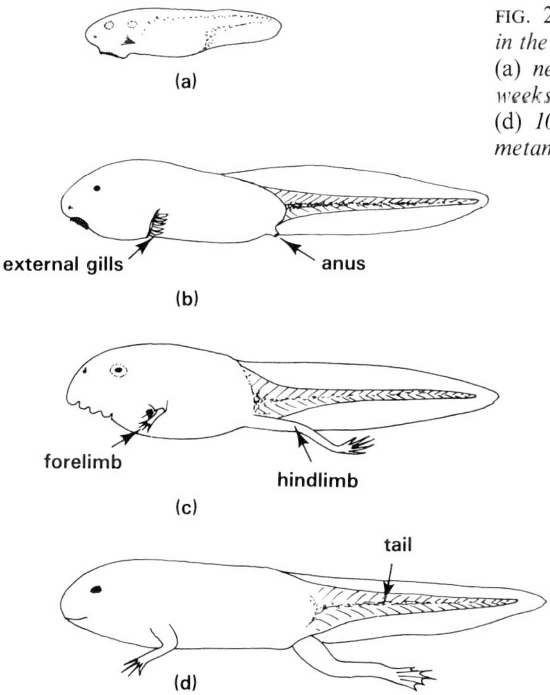

FIG. 27.23 *Some tadpole stages in the development of the frog* (a) *newly-hatched,* × *5* (b) *2 weeks,* × *8* (c) *7 weeks,* × *2* (d) *10 weeks, just before final metamorphosis,* × *3*

In some amphibians the adult remains aquatic. Others are **neotenous**, the larval body form persisting throughout life (Fig. 27.24). A lateral line system is present in aquatic amphibians.

FIG 27.24 *The axolotl,* Sirenodon mexicanum, × $\frac{2}{3}$

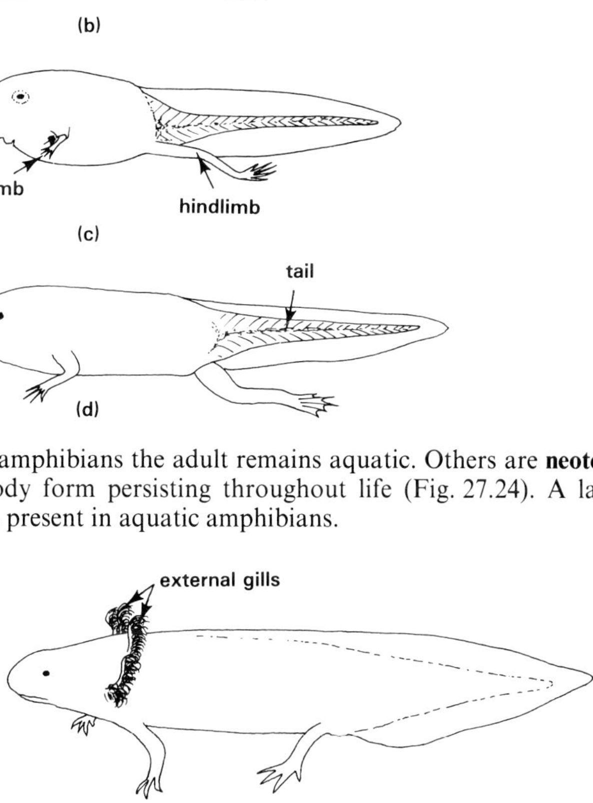

The *Amphibia* is divided into several orders including *Apoda, Urodela* and *Anura*. The apodans are legless burrowing amphibians which live in the tropics. The urodeles include newts and salamanders. They have a fish-like body with a long tail. Urodeles are thought to resemble the earliest amphibians. Some urodeles such as the axolotl are neotenous. The anurans include frogs and toads. On land, the highly developed back legs of anurans are used for jumping. In water, they are used for swimming. The much-shortened vertebral column, fused bones and lack of a tail are all part of a body design which allows anurans to leap.

27.2.5 *Reptilia*

Crocodiles, **lizards**, **snakes** and **turtles** are **reptiles** (Fig. 27.25). The few present-day reptiles are descendents of a once very successful group of animals, including the **dinosaurs**, which dominated the land about 200 million years ago. Many extinct reptiles were **bipedal**, walking upright on the hind limbs. A few **pterosaurs** even took to the air. Their forelimbs supported flaps of skin rather like the wings of bats (Fig. 24.9).

FIG. 27.25 *Green lizard,* Lacerta viridis, × $\frac{2}{3}$

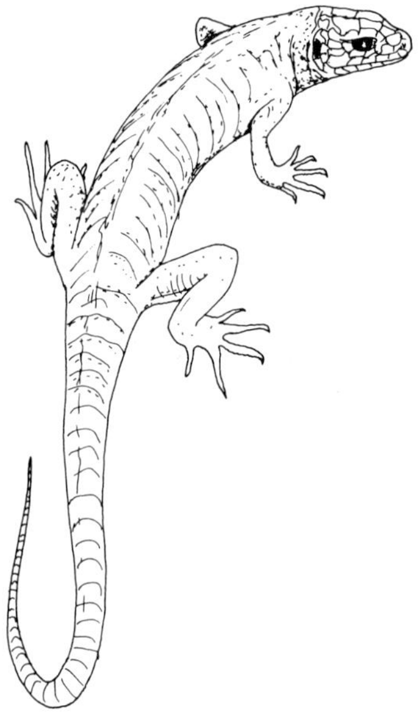

FIG. 27.26 *The gait of* (a) *amphibians* (b) *reptiles*

Most of the features of reptiles make them better suited to life on land than amphibians. The distal parts of the limbs are bent downwards, raising the body clear of the ground (Fig. 27.26). Reptiles can thus move on all four limbs without the trunk of the body touching the ground. Pairs of **ribs** project from the vertebrae. They give support to and protect the soft organs in the body cavity. Movements of the ribs, brought about by contractions of **intercostal muscles**, are used to ventilate the **lungs**. The lungs of reptiles have a more complex internal structure than those of amphibians (Fig. 8.5). Ingrowths of tissues increase the inner surface area for gas exchange.

The **skin is dry** and covered by **horny scales**. Beneath these in the skin there may be **bony plates**. They provide a tough armour in some reptiles. Little evaporation takes place through the skin. Transport of oxygen in the blood is aided by the partial division of the heart's ventricle into two chambers. In the crocodile, the division is complete and there are two ventricles (Fig. 27.27).

FIG. 27.27 *Reptile heart*

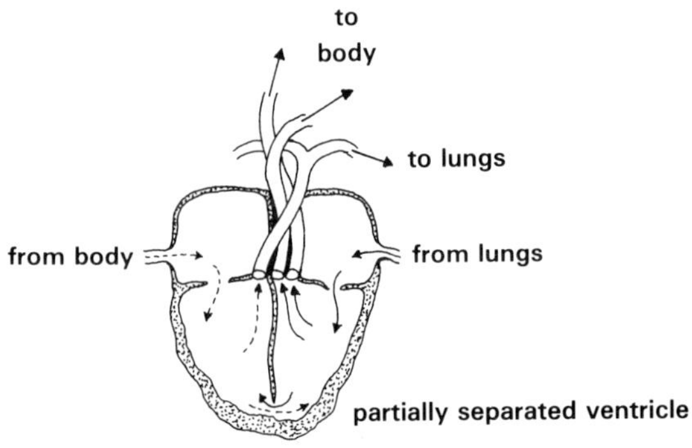

The kidneys of reptiles are capable of producing a concentrated urine and thus help to retain body water. **Uric acid** is the main nitrogenous waste. It requires the minimum of water for its elimination. Marine reptiles have **salt excretion glands** in the orbits of the skull. They discharge tears rich in salts which the reptiles have absorbed from seafood.

Reptiles usually have rows of identical teeth. This **type** of dentition is called **homodont** (homos = same; dens = tooth). **Salivary glands** are also present. They represent an adaptation to the terrestrial way of life and are absent from fish and amphibians. The main function of saliva is to lubricate food when it is taken into the gut. Water performs this function in most aquatic vertebrates.

The nervous system and sensory organs of reptiles display several advances over those of amphibians. The forebrain is more developed, especially the cerebral hemispheres (Fig. 15.40). The eyes are focused by changing the shape of the lens as in mammals (section 16.1.2). In fish and amphibians, the lens is moved towards or away from the retina. The reptilian eye is strengthened by a ring of bones called **ossicles** surrounding the iris (Fig. 27.28). Eyelids are present, including a third eyelid called the nictitating membrane. In amphibians the lower eyelid is the **nictitating membrane**, the upper lid is fixed. Movements of the eyelids remove abrasive particles from the front of the eye.

FIG. 27.28 *Vertical section lizard's eye*. Compare with Figs 16.1 and 27.38

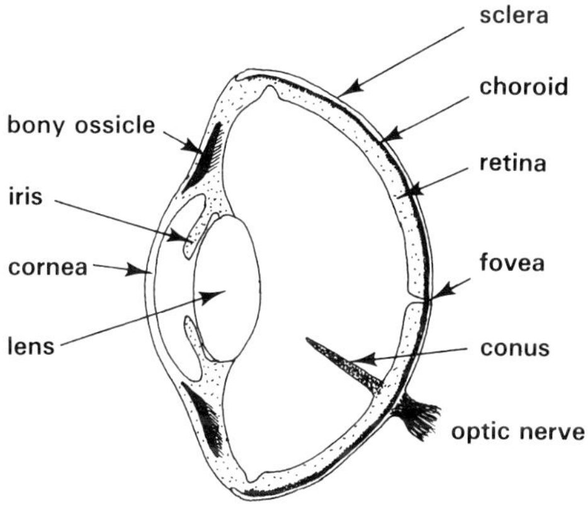

Copulation and **internal fertilisation** are features of reptilian reproduction. The embryo develops inside a membraneous fluid-filled compartment called the **amnion** where it is protected from desiccation. Eggs are often laid in nests or buried in sand or soil, where they are hidden from predators. A few reptiles retain the eggs inside the female's body. The **amniote egg** is a feature of reptiles, birds and mammals (Fig. 22.18). The embryo obtains food from a **yolk sac** attached to its gut. Wastes are discharged into another sac called the **allantois** which enlarges during development and eventually comes close to the shell.

The shell of most reptilian eggs is leathery in texture and respiratory gases pass through it. The allantois aids in gas exchange between the atmosphere and the embryo. Because the embryos of reptiles are protected from predation the chances of survival are greater than in fish and amphibians which leave the eggs to fend for themselves. The enormous losses of fish and emphibian embryos are offset by the large numbers of eggs produced.

Reptiles are divided into several orders including the *Chelonia*, *Squamata* and *Crocodilia*. Chelonians include terrapins, tortoises and

FIG. 27.34 *Wings of vulture* (a) *soaring upwind, gaining height* (b) *upwind on level* (c) *downwind, losing height* (d) *gliding flight* (From J. Z. Young, after Ahlborn)

sufficient to keep the bird aloft. Birds may use moving air to **glide** or **soar** simply by holding their wings still and extended at the appropriate angle. Birds of prey often soar in circles at great height while looking out for prey. They use warm upcurrents of air called **thermals** to provide lift. The shape and proportions of the wing are also important in soaring, which requires little energy (Fig. 27.34). In **flapping flight**, the wings are forcibly moved up

FIG. 27.35 *Wing flapping in the pigeon showing the* (a) *downstroke* (b) *upstroke* (from photographs after Brown)

FIG. 27.36 *Skeleton of a pigeon*

and down. Lift is generated as the wings push down on the air. The angle of the wing is changed to minimise drag as the wing is raised (Fig. 27.35). Flapping requires a great deal of energy. The relatively large flight muscles are attached to a flat sternal plate called the **keel** (Fig. 27.36).

The tail is much reduced in birds, although the tail feathers may be long. Lowering and fanning out the tail feathers increases lift when the bird is flying slowly while landing.

Birds, like mammals, are **endothermic** (Chapter 17). They regulate their body temperature by physiological means. A relatively high and constant body temperature enables respiration to occur at a rate rapid enough to provide energy for flight. Maintaining a relatively high body temperature also enables birds and mammals to be active even in very cold environments. Animals, other than birds and mammals, are ectothermic. Their body temperature changes with that of their environment (Fig. 17.1). Ectotherms may regulate their body temperature to a certain degree by behavioural means such as basking in the sun, seeking shade or burrowing.

Large volumes of oxygen are needed to provide the energy for flight. Ventilation of the lungs in birds is far more efficient than in other vertebrates. It is assisted by a system of **air sacs** connected to the lungs (Fig. 27.37). Some of them connect with the air spaces in the pneumatic bones. When a bird breathes in, any air which remains in the lungs from previous ventilations is sucked into the sacs. The lungs are filled with fresh air, avoiding the dead space that occurs in the lungs of other vertebrates (section 8.2.1). Ventilation of the lungs and air sacs is brought about by movements of the ribs and sternum. There is no diaphragm. During flight, the action of the flight muscles ventilates the lungs at the same rate as movements of the wings. In some diving aquatic birds such as penguins, the

FIG. 27.37 *Air sacs in a bird from the side* (after Goodrich)

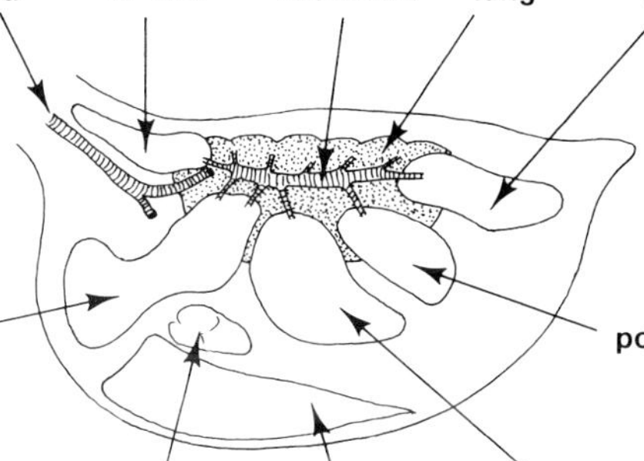

air sacs may provide buoyancy, acting like the swim bladder of bony fish (section 27.2.3). The lungs of birds are spongy organs with an internal structure similar to that of mammals (Chapter 8).

As in all other vertebrates, the carriage of oxygen in the blood is aided by haemoglobin. The heart has four chambers and oxygenated blood is completely separated from deoxygenated blood.

The nervous system is well developed, especially the brain. Birds display more complex behaviour than reptiles. Bird behaviour usually includes the formation of flocks, pairing and mating, seasonal migration, communication between individuals and the rearing of young. Birds are especially vocal and songs are generated by a structure called the **syrinx** in the trachea. The inner ear is comparable to that of mammals. Its sensitivity to sound enables birds to communicate vocally.

The eyes of birds are comparable to those of other vertebrates. A feature of birds' eyes, however, is the **pecten**, a vascular rod, often branched, which projects from the retina into the vitreous humour (Fig. 27.38). The

FIG. 27.38 *Vertical section; bird's eye.* Compare with Figs 16.1 and 27.28

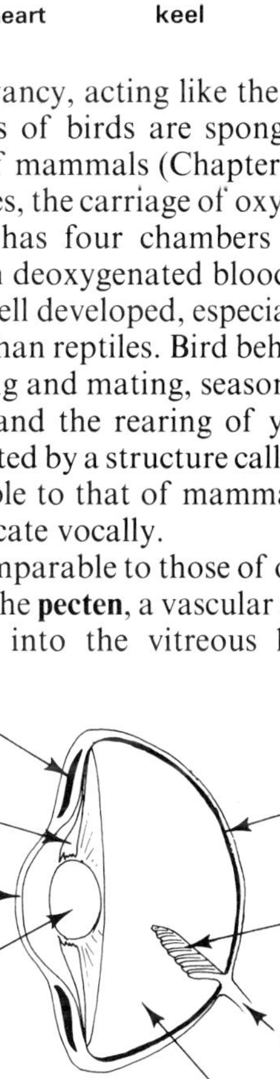

function of the pecten is not clear. One theory is that it throws a shadow on to the retina and interrupts the image seen by the eye. Slight movement in the field of view may thus be exaggerated by the on–off effect as an object moves into or out of the pecten's shadow. Certainly, vision is a dominant sense in birds. As in reptiles, there is a ring of **optic ossicles** at the front of the eye. They may help protect the eye against rapid air movement during flight. Also as in reptiles there is a **nictitating membrane**. Focusing is achieved by altering the curvature of the lens, as in mammals (section 16.1.2).

Birds have no teeth. The jaws are drawn out into a horny **beak**. In many birds the beak has evolved to make use of a particular type of food (Fig. 27.39).

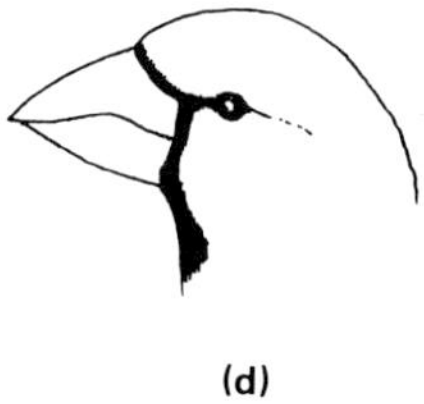

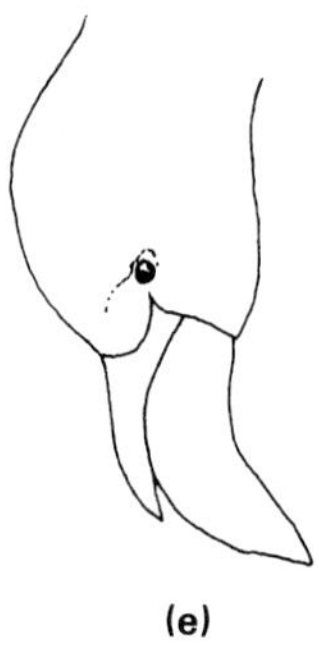

FIG. 27.39 *Variety of birds' beaks* (a) *cormorant, catching fish* (b) *harrier, gripping and ripping flesh* (c) *oyster catcher, picking food from mud* (d) *hawfinch, crushing seeds* (e) *flamingo, filtering water*

The kidneys of birds are very similar to those of mammals and excrete hypertonic urine (Chapter 10). **Uric acid** is the main nitrogenous excretory material. In marine birds, excess salts are excreted through the nose from **salt glands** behind the eyes.

Birds reproduce in much the same way as reptiles. Copulation followed by internal fertilisation leads to the development of **amniote eggs** (Fig. 22.18). Birds' eggs, like those of reptiles, are **cleidoic**. They are protected from desiccation and predators by a tough **calcareous shell**. The eggs are usually laid in a nest, where they are incubated by one or both parents. The young are cared for after hatching.

There are very many orders of birds. *Falconiformes* are birds of prey such as buzzards, eagles, hawks, kestrels and vultures. Unlike owls, they hunt by day. They have hooked beaks for tearing flesh and strong claws with which to capture prey. Their keen sense of vision enables them to spot prey while soaring high above the ground. *Passeriformes* are perching birds such as finches, rooks, sparrows, starlings, swallows, thrushes, tits and wrens. It is by far the largest order, containing about half the total number of known bird species. They have adapted to a wide variety of habitats. The feet of perching birds are adapted for gripping branches. Their behaviour is often complex and great use is made of vocal communication.

27.2.7 Mammalia

Mammals include the platypus, kangaroo, antelopes, bats, cattle, cats, dogs, elephants, horses, sheep, shrews, rodents, whales and man. Features typical of mammals include:
(i) **hair** and **sweat glands** in the skin which assist **endothermy** (Chapter 17),
(ii) a muscular **diaphragm** separating the thorax from the abdomen (Chapter 8),
(iii) a highly **developed brain** and **intelligent** behaviour involving **learning** and **memory** (Chapter 15),
(iv) **well-developed sense organs** (Chapter 16),
(v) **heterodont dentition** and a bony roof to the mouth called the **palate** (Chapter 14),
(vi) development of the embryo inside the mother's body, the offspring being provided with **milk** from well-developed **mammary glands** (Chapter 22).

The limbs of terrestrial mammals are positioned beneath the body, enabling them to travel very rapidly over land. Greyhounds can run at speeds of about 59 km h^{-1}, while cheetahs have been reported to reach 112 km h^{-1} for short periods (Fig. 27.40). Some mammals, such as whales and dolphins, are efficient swimmers (section 8.4); others, such as bats, are capable of flight.

FIG. 27.40 (a) *Skeleton of a cat* (b) *cheetah running at high speed*

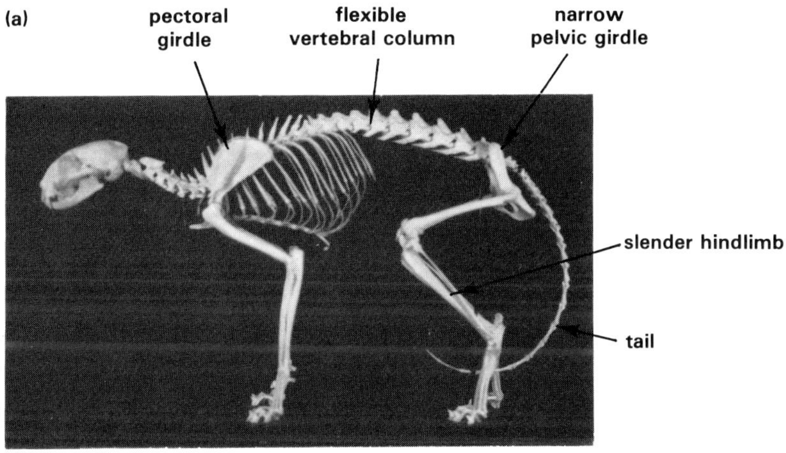

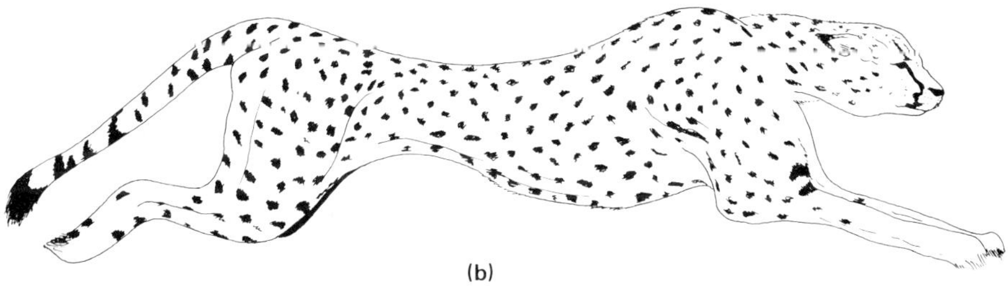

Mammals are divided into several sub-classes:

1. *PROTOTHERIA*

This has a single order, the *Monotremata*. There are two **monotremes**, the spiny anteater and the platypus (Fig. 27.41). They are primitive mammals and are thought to be the remains of an early mammalian stock. Monotremes have hair and sweat glands, although their body temperature fluctuates more so than in other mammals (Fig. 17.1). They care for their young and have simple mammary glands. Among their reptilian features is the laying of **amniote eggs**. They are deposited in a nest by the platypus and carried in a skin pouch by the spiny anteater. The urine ducts and anus have a common opening called the **cloaca**.

FIG. 27.41 (a) *Platypus*, Ornithorhyncus, × $\frac{1}{3}$ (b) *spiny ant-eater*, Tachyglossus, × $\frac{1}{8}$

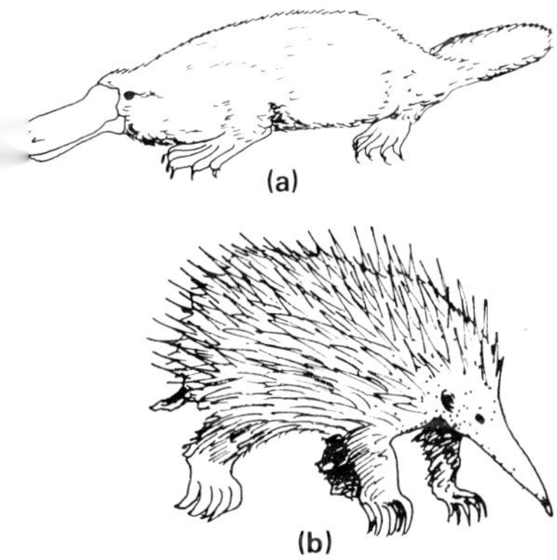

2. *THERIA*

Therians are divided into two infra-classes:

(i) *METATHERIA* includes the order *Marsupiala*. **Marsupials** are found mainly in Australia. Their evolution there has been due to Australia's geographic isolation from other land masses (Chapter 24). Adaptive radiation of marsupials in Australia is comparable with that of other mammals elsewhere (Fig. 27.42). In marsupials, the embryos emerge from their mother's reproductive tract very early and enter a **pouch** on the mother's abdomen. Further development of the offspring takes place in the pouch, where they suck milk from mammary glands. There is no placenta. As in monotremes and reptiles, the urinogenital tract opens into a **cloaca**.

(ii) *EUTHERIA* are the **placental mammals**. The embryos of eutherians develop within the mother's uterus, where nutrients are supplied and wastes removed by a **placenta** (section 22.3.3). After birth, the young are nourished by milk from **mammary glands**.

FIG. 27.42 *Three marsupials*
(a) *opossum*, Marmosa, $\times \frac{1}{5}$
(b) *kangaroo*, Macropus, $\times \frac{1}{25}$
(c) *wombat*, Phascolomis, $\times \frac{1}{15}$

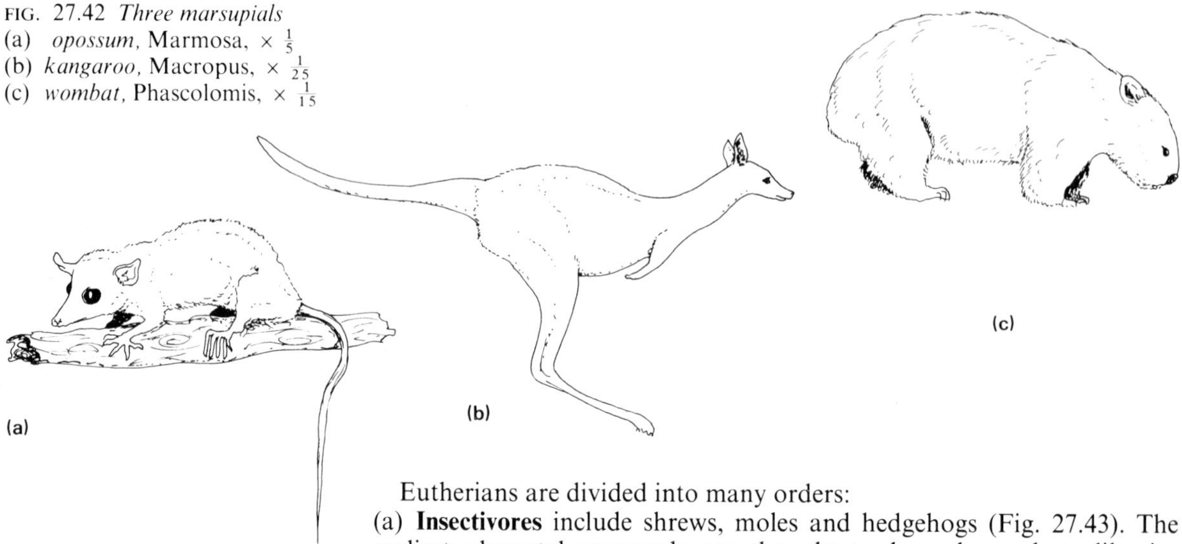

FIG. 27.43 *Common shrew*, Sorex araneus, $\times \frac{2}{3}$

FIG. 27.44 *Black rat*, Rattus rattus, $\times \frac{1}{4}$. *See Fig. 14.11* (a)

FIG. 27.45 *Common wolf*, Canis lupus, $\times \frac{1}{14}$

Eutherians are divided into many orders:

(a) **Insectivores** include shrews, moles and hedgehogs (Fig. 27.43). The earliest placental mammals are thought to have been shrew-like insectivores. Most modern insectivores are small and nocturnal. Insects form a large part of their diet, hence the name given to the order. The sense of smell is relatively well developed and the long snout may be pushed into holes or crevices in search of insects. Insectivores have a full mammalian dentition (Fig. 14.10). Shrews are among the smallest of all mammals. Small size leads to excessive heat loss (Fig. 17.8). Many insectivores overcome this problem by hibernating in winter (section 17.3.4).

(b) **Rodents** are the most numerous of all mammals and include beavers, mice, rats, squirrels and voles (Fig. 27.44). They are nearly all herbivorous, having a single pair of incisors on each jaw. Open roots allow continuous growth of the incisors, which are used to gnaw food (Fig. 14.11(a)). The large caecum contains cellulolytic bacteria which aid the digestion of vegetation (section 14.3.5).

(c) **Carnivores** include bears, dogs, seals, walruses, wolves and cats such as cheetahs, lions and tigers (Figs. 27.40 and 27.45). They are flesh-eaters whose dentition is specialised for gripping, piercing, ripping and tearing flesh (Fig. 14.4). The digits have strong claws which are often retractable. Carnivores often form complex social groups, usually hunting in packs. Secretions from well-developed anal glands are used frequently for recognition and to mark territory. Some carnivores, such as seals, have become successful swimmers. They are capable of diving to great depths and for long periods in search of food (section 8.4).

(d) Mammals with hoofs are called **ungulates** (ungula = hoof). They are relatively large herbivores, often able to run at great speeds to escape predators. They are often grazing animals and collect into large herds. In many species the pupil of the eye is horizontal, giving a wide angle of vision. The pinnae are often long and mobile. The neck is usually long, so that individuals can keep watch for predators while chewing food. The young are relatively well developed at birth. Their survival often depends on being able to run with the herd within a few minutes of being born.

(i) **Artiodactyls** are the **even-toed ungulates** such as antelopes, camels, cattle, deer, hippopotamuses, pigs and sheep (Fig. 27.46). They have feet with two toes forming a **cloven hoof**. The dentition is modified for grazing, grinding vegetation and cud-chewing (Fig. 14.6–8). Cellulolytic bacteria are found in a large multichambered stomach (section 14.3.3).

FIG. 27.46 *Impala*, Aepyceros, $\times \frac{1}{10}$

(ii) **Perrisodactyls** are the **odd-toed ungulates** such as horses, zebras and rhinoceroses (Fig. 27.47). The digits are reduced to a single long toe. As in artiodactyls, the teeth are modified for grinding food. However, the bacteria necessary for digesting vegetation are found not in the stomach but in the caecum (section 14.3.5).

FIG. 27.47 *Grant's zebra,* Equus burchelli boehmi, $\times \frac{1}{15}$

(e) **Chiropterans** are bats (Fig. 27.48). In many respects bats are similar to insectivores. Many bats eat insects, but some are fruit-eaters, while vampire bats drink the blood of other vertebrates. Bats are the only mammals capable of true flight. Their wings consist of flaps of skin supported by four long fingers, the legs and even the tail. There is a **keel** on the sternum for the attachment of flight muscles. When resting, bats often hang upside down, clinging to something solid with their clawed toes. Bats cool down when not flying and many species hibernate in winter. They have an elaborate **echolocation** system which is used to avoid obstacles during flight and to locate insects.

FIG. 27.48 *Greater horseshoe bat,* Rhinolophus ferrumequinum, $\times \frac{1}{3}$ (a) *in flight* (b) *roosting*

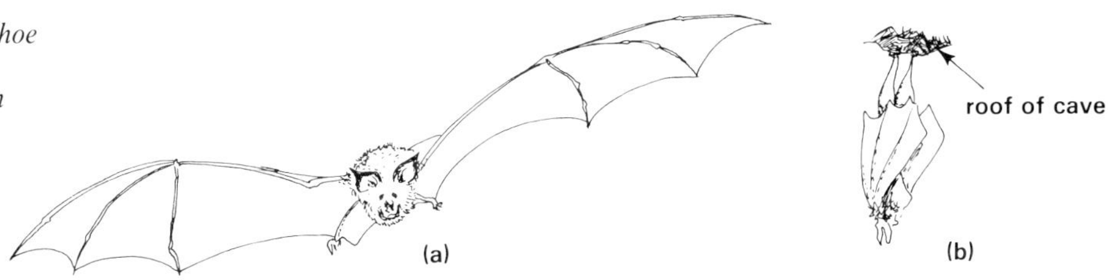

(f) **Cetaceans** include dolphins and whales (Fig. 27.49). They are marine mammals capable of diving to great depths for long periods (section 8.4).

FIG. 27.49 *Blue whale,* Balaenoptera musculus, $\times \frac{1}{145}$ *See Fig. 14.12*

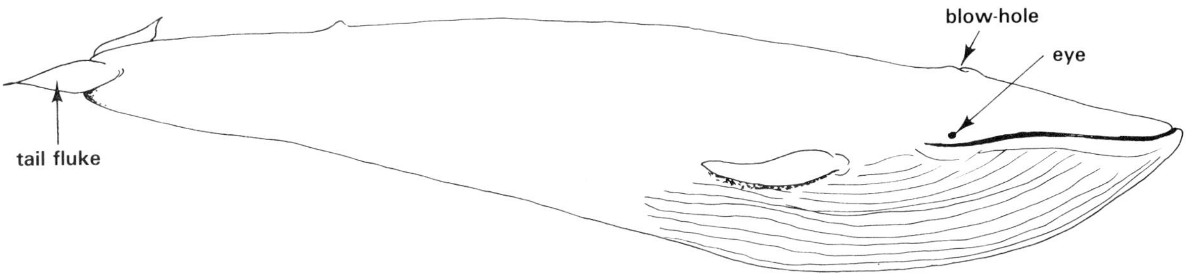

FIG. 27.50 *Slender loris*, Loris tardigradus, × $\frac{1}{3}$

FIG. 27.51 *Gibbon*, Hylobates, × $\frac{1}{8}$

The short neck and a tapered outline enable these creatures to slip easily through water. The forelimbs are modified to form **flippers** which, together with a well-developed dorsal fin, are used as stabilisers while swimming. The hind limbs are absent altogether. The tail is also modified as a fin with horizontal **flukes**. The main thrust in swimming is provided by an up-and-down movement of the body and the tail flukes. It contrasts with the lateral movement of the body and tail in fish. The skin of cetaceans is smooth and there is generally no hair. Heat loss is minimised by a thick layer of fat called **blubber**. The large body mass of whales relative to surface area also helps to reduce heat loss (section 17.2.4).

The blue whale is the largest animal ever seen on earth. Specimens have been known to measure 32 metres long and weigh about 150 tonnes. The nostrils of cetaceans are on the dorsal surface of the head and are used as a **blow-hole** in breathing. Dolphins and **toothed whales** eat fish and other marine animals (Fig. 14.12(a)). **Whalebone whales** feed on small organisms such as the shrimp-like krill which form part of the plankton of the sea. Whalebone whales filter the plankton from the sea using a complex system of **baleen plates** as a sieve (Fig. 14.12(b)). Dolphins have a well developed **echolocation** system similar to that of bats. Dolphins and whales are also known to communicate with members of their own species by a complex system of sounds. The cetaceans have large brains and are among the most intelligent of mammals.

(g) **Primates** are divisible into two sub-orders. The *Prosimii* includes the aye-aye, bush babies, lemurs, lorises and tarsiers (Fig. 27.50). The *Anthropoidea* includes apes, marmosets, tamarins, a variety of monkeys and, in the family *Hominidae*, man (Fig. 27.51).

Most primates live in trees. They have hands and feet, and sometimes a **prehensile tail** capable of grasping branches. The digits have **nails** instead of claws. The eyes are usually at the front of the head, each eye seeing the same field of view but from a slightly different angle. This is **stereoscopic vision** and makes it possible for the distance of objects to be judged.

Primates often form complex social groups in which communication between individuals may be very detailed. There is considerable care of the young. Egg production by the ovaries is cyclical and involves a complex hormone control (section 22.2) There are usually few offspring. The period of development and growth is very long in primates compared with other mammals, up to 20 years in man. The brain is relatively large, especially the cerebral hemispheres (section 15.2.3). Intelligent behaviour involving teaching, learning, memory, abstraction and prediction occurs in primates to a far greater degree than in other animals. Primates are nearly all **omnivorous**, with an **unspecialised dentition** (Fig. 14.9).

Two main features of the human body have enabled man to evolve as the dominant mammal on earth. Man's inquisitive nature and an ingenuity in solving problems is probably attributable to the **large cerebral hemispheres** of the brain. The other feature is the **manipulative ability of the hands**. The adduction of the thumb and index finger enables man to handle and shape things with great skill. Manufacture of tools and comfortable houses, the development of agriculture and the domestication of other animals have contributed greatly to man's evolution. The organisation of social groups into states, the making of laws and the development of art have all contributed to man's **civilisation**. Unfortunately, man has also developed the capacity to destroy the world as well as improve it for himself.

Chapter 28

Ecology 1: Distribution of organisms; associations

Ecology is the study of the interaction of living organisms with each other and with their surroundings. Plants and animals inhabit land up to a height of about 6 km above sea level. In water they live as far down as 11 km below the surface. The total volume of the earth in which life permanently exists is called the **biosphere**, in which there are four major **habitats**—marine, estuarine, freshwater and terrestrial. On land there are several **biogeographical zones**, in each of which there is characteristic plant and animal life. They are called **biomes** and include temperate deciduous forest, tropical rain forest and grasslands such as steppe and savanna (Fig. 28.1).

28.1 Factors affecting the distribution of organisms

One of the questions constantly asked by ecologists is, 'Why is this organism found in this habitat and not elsewhere?' The factors which determine where an organism can live are either **biotic** (living) or **abiotic** (chemical and physical) and are often seasonal.

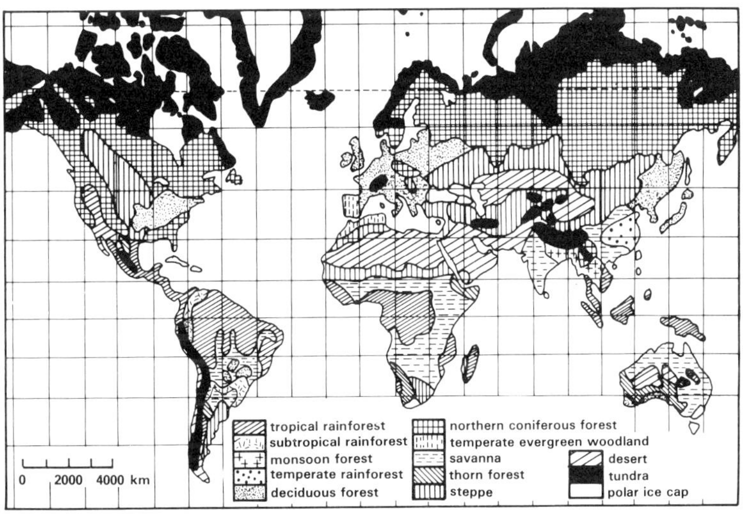

FIG. 28.1 (a) *Distribution of the earth's biomes* (from Sands 1978)

FIG. 28.1 (b) *Tropical rain forest* (Biophotos)

FIG. 28.1 (c) *Tundra* (Biophotos)

(b)

(c)

28.1.1 Biotic factors

The creatures which co-exist in a habitat determine to a large extent each other's success in the community. Living organisms affect each other in a variety of ways. They may **compete** for the same resources. **Grazing** animals may eradicate certain species of plants and encourage the growth of others. Many organisms are very particular what they eat and will live only where their **food source** is available.

1. COMPETITION

Plants compete for light, carbon dioxide, water, minerals, pollinators and sites for spores and seeds to germinate. Animals compete for food, mates, breeding sites and shelter from predators. Intraspecific **competition** is the name given to competition between individuals of the same species. Competition between individuals of different species is known as interspecific competition.

(i) **Intraspecific competition** among flowering plants has been studied by sowing seeds at known densities and later measuring the yield of the plants. The total dry mass produced per unit area of soil is the same over a wide range of sowing density. This may come about because many seedlings die when seeds germinate close to each other. The few plants that survive then have an adequate share of resources, so they grow quite well. Alternatively, most of the seedlings may survive and grow into mature plants, but each plant has a lesser share of resources so is smaller than normal. In contrast, seed production is reduced when plants are overcrowded, because many fail to flower and set seed (Fig. 28.2).

FIG. 28.2 *Effect of sowing density on* (a) *yield* (dry crop) *of clover and* (b) *seed production by shepherd's purse* (from *Solomon*, "Population Dynamics", Inst. Biol. "Studies in Biology" published by Edward Arnold)

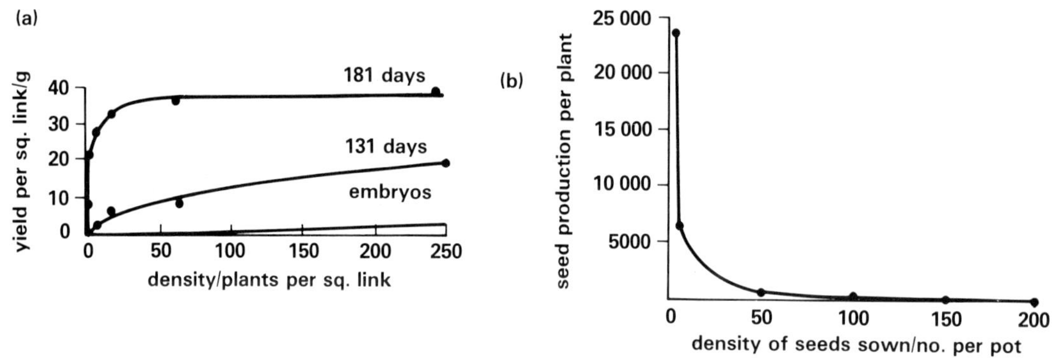

FIG. 28.3 *Effect of population density on* (a) *egg production by* Drosophila (from Solomon as above) *and* (b) *mortality rate of brown trout* (from Open University 1974)

A reduction in the reproductive rate is also frequently noted in dense colonies of animals. The fruit fly *Drosophila* lays fewer eggs when surrounded by too many of its own kind. The mortality rate of young fish increases at high densities (Fig. 28.3). In bird colonies, higher numbers of

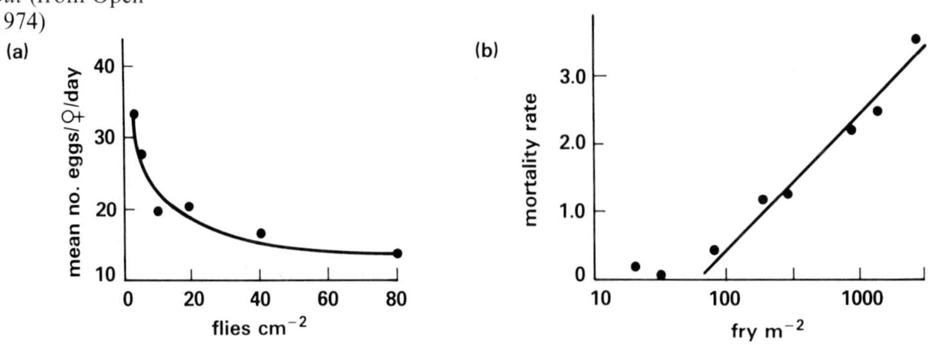

fledglings are reared when the adult population density is low. Mammals have fewer live births in crowded conditions. Competition for food is likely to be the main cause of these effects. However, experiments with mammals show that fewer young are reared at high densities even when food is unlimited. It is thought that an increase in aggression may in part be the cause of the fall in the rate of reproduction. Rats and hamsters have been seen to cannibalise their young when living in overcrowded conditions.
(ii) **Interspecific competition** among plants is seen wherever crops are grown. Weeds grow in the crop and compete for space, light, water and nutrients. It is often in the early growth of the crop that weeds are very effective competitors. Unless kept in check, they can seriously reduce the yield of the crop (Fig. 28.4). Many kinds of weeds germinate rapidly and

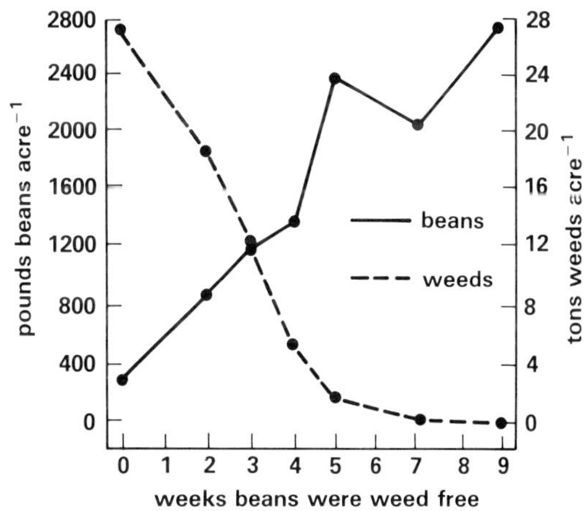

FIG. 28.4 *Effect of weed density on the yield of field beans* (from Hill, "The Biology of Weeds", Inst. Biol. "Studies in Biology" published by Edward Arnold)

grow quickly at the beginning of the crop's growth. By establishing themselves at this stage, they use up space in which a crop plant might have grown. Their shoot systems often intercept light which the crop would otherwise use. When the crop plants reach maturity, they may be taller than the weeds. By this time, however, the weed plants will have flowered and set seed (Fig. 28.5).

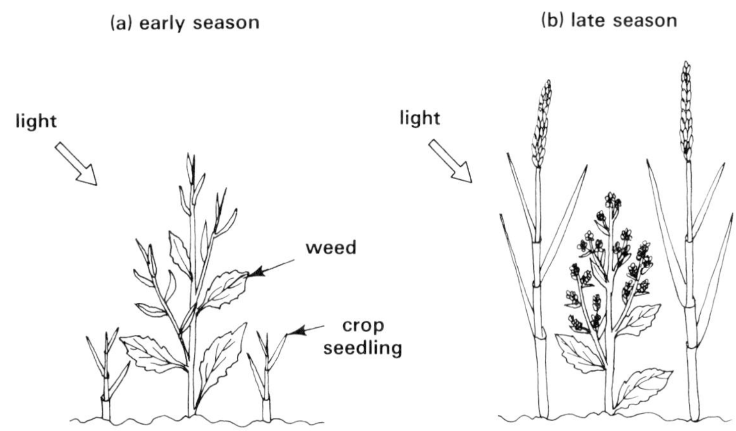

FIG. 28.5 *Competition between weed and crop plants*

The blackbird and song thrush inhabit parkland and gardens in Britain. Both compete for the same type of food, which includes slugs, earthworms, insects and fruit. They are able to co-exist partly because the thrush eats

FIG. 28.6 *Flour beetles* (a) T. confusum (B&B photos) (b) T. castaneum (B&B photos)

(a)

(b)

about five times more animal food than the blackbird. Most of it comes from snails, the shells of which thrushes crack open on large stones called thrushes' anvils. Blackbirds do not have the ability to do this.

The examples described above show that interspecific competition allows communities of different species to exist in a particular habitat. This is possible because different species make use of different resources of the habitat or use the resources at different times. On the other hand, intraspecific competition is more likely to affect the distribution of species, because organisms of the same species have similar niches and thus compete for the same resources at the same time.

(iii) **Competitive exclusion**. No two species can co-exist in a community if they have the same demands on the resources of the habitat. This is known as the **competitive exclusion principle**. Competitive exclusion has been studied using two species of flour beetle, *Tribolium castaneum* and *T. confusum* (Fig. 28.6). They can be kept in the laboratory in bottles of flour which is food and habitat for them. The outcome of competition between the two species is governed by temperature and humidity (Table 28.1). At high temperatures (34°C) and in very humid conditions (70% RH) *T. castaneum* succeeded better, while at low temperatures (24°C) and in dry conditions (30% RH) *T. confusum* did better. Whatever the conditions, only one of the species survived in the end.

Table 28.1 Interspecific competition between flour bettles (after Park 1954)

TEMP. °C	% RH	PERCENTAGE REMAINING	
		T. castaneum	*T. confusum*
34	70	100	0
34	30	10	90
29	70	86	14
29	30	13	87
24	70	29	71
24	30	0	100

2. GRAZING

Cattle, sheep, horses and rabbits are examples of grazers. Their natural habitat is pastureland, where they feed on growing grass and herbs. **Grazing** affects some plant species more than others. Grasses are tolerant of grazing, because their intercalary meristems (section 21.1.2) enable their shoots to regrow quickly after being nibbled. Some grassland herbs grow so close to the ground that they avoid being grazed to any large extent. Others are unpalatable to livestock, so they are left uneaten.

The effects of grazing by rabbits on grassland vegetation have been closely studied. Rabbits were brought into Britain about 850 years ago to be bred for their meat and fur. The number of wild rabbits was fairly small until the middle of the last century. By the 1950s, they were a serious pest to farmers. At this time a lethal viral disease of rabbits, myxomatosis, was introduced in an attempt to reduce the number of wild rabbits. The campaign was very effective and by 1960 the wild rabbit population had severely declined. Observations of the vegetation in grassland areas before and after the outbreak of myxomatosis showed that the absence or reduction in grazing by rabbits had three general effects:

(i) the overall height of the vegetation increased,

FIG. 28.7 *The ragwort* Senecio jacobaea

(ii) there was a greater variety of dicotyledonous herbs, and
(iii) woody species such as bramble, heather and tree saplings started to grow in the pasture.

However, there were some notable exceptions to these trends. Two dicotyledonous herbs, wild thyme and ragwort (Fig. 28.7) virtually disappeared. Wild thyme is a low-growing plant which is not intensively grazed by rabbits. In tall vegetation, however, it is a poor competitor, and gradually died out. Ragwort is a much taller plant, but again is not an effective competitor among tall herbs. The reason why it was abundant before the outbreak of myxomatosis is because rabbits dislike its taste. Where the vegetation is kept short by grazing, the ragwort is able to compete reasonably well.

3. FOOD SOURCE

The distribution of many plant-eating animals is confined to places where their food plants grow. Some animals have specialist methods of feeding off plants. The crossbill, for example, has a beak which can prise open pine and spruce cones (Fig. 28.8). Not surprisingly, it lives mainly in mature plantations of conifers. Animals able to eat a variety of plant food are more widely distributed.

FIG. 28.8 *Crossbill* (R.S.P.B.)

We saw in the previous section that grazing determines which plants grow in grassland communities. Animals also help in the dispersal of some species of plants. The fruits of some flowering plants are hooked and catch in the fur of mammals as they move through vegetation. Succulent fruits are often taken as food by animals. The seeds are later egested unharmed (Fig. 28.9). Migratory birds can disperse seeds over great distances in this way.

Predatory animals (section 29.1) are found where their prey is abundant. Parasites, commensals and symbionts (section 28.2) normally live only where their hosts or partners are located.

FIG. 28.9 *Fruits dispersed by animals*

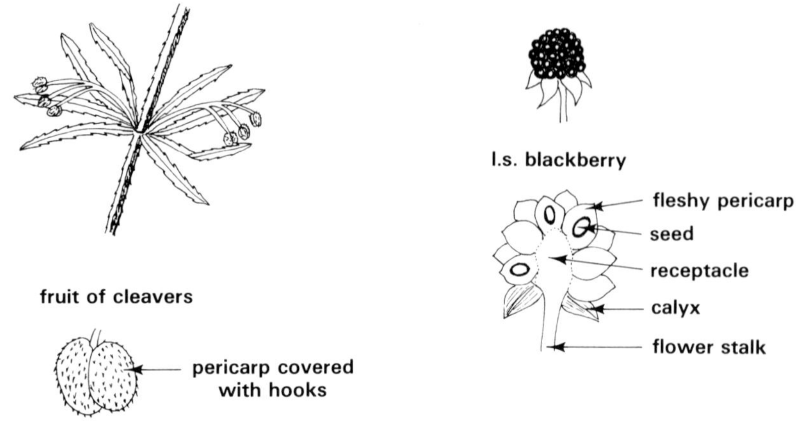

4. ANTIBIOSIS

Plants and animals often deter other creatures by releasing toxic substances into their surroundings. The substances may affect other organisms of the same species or those of other species.

(i) INTRASPECIFIC ANTIBIOSIS. **Pheromones** produced by many vertebrates which live on land are used to mark out their territory. Male rabbits are often seen rubbing their chins on the ground. This activity brings about the release of a pheromone from the submandibular salivary glands. The pheromone warns other bucks that the territory is occupied.

Older tadpoles of the frog *Rana pipiens* release a substance into water which inhibits the development of younger tadpoles. It avoids overcrowding of the habitat.

(ii) INTERSPECIFIC ANTIBIOSIS. Saprophytic soil fungi such as *Penicillium* are well known as producers of **antibiotics** in the laboratory (section 25.4.4). Antibiotics kill or prevent the growth of many kinds of bacteria. Soil has been shown to contain antibiotics, so it is reasonable to assume that fungi which make antibiotics release them into their natural environment. Here they enable them to compete effectively with saprophytic bacteria.

Washings from heather roots have been shown to inhibit the growth of fungi which form mycorrhizae with spruce and birch trees (section 28.2.2). It may be that heather prevents mycorrhizal formation and explains the inability of such trees to thrive in heathland areas.

5. MAN

Homo sapiens is undoubtedly the most potent biotic force in the world today. Much of the vegetation on land is not natural. It has been grown there by man in his capacity as a farmer, forester, landscaper and gardener. Man is also a predator and has hunted many animals to the point of extinction (section 29.1.3). Pollution of the environment is largely due to the industrial and domestic waste created by man (Chapter 30).

28.1.2 Abiotic factors

Climate determines the biogeographical regions of the world. Temperature, solar radiation, rainfall and air movement are the main factors which influence climate. The availability of gases for respiration and photosynthesis, and mineral nutrients, are other important abiotic factors which affect the distribution of organisms.

1. TEMPERATURE

Ectotherms are inactive in cold habitats (Fig. 28.10). Birds and mammals are endothermic and can thus be active even in very cold parts of the earth.

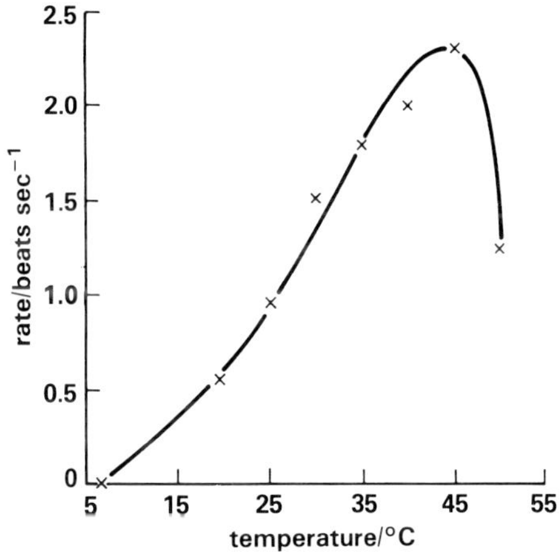

FIG. 28.10 *Effect of temperature on locusts' heart rate* (from Simpkins 1973)

There is little fluctuation in temperature in lakes, seas and oceans because water has a high specific heat capacity. This is partly why aquatic habitats are suitable for many kinds of ectothermic creatures. Radiant heat from the sun does not penetrate water very far, so the temperature of deep waters is fairly low (2–3°C) but constant.

Extremes of temperature occur on land. On the fringes of polar areas, the air temperature for much of the year is nearly always below freezing point. Only lichens, mosses, a few flowering plants and one or two endothermic animals such as penguins and polar bears can tolerate such conditions. For the same reason, high mountains have a typical alpine flora and fauna.

In desert areas the daytime temperature is very high and causes water to evaporate very quickly. Here a major problem faced by living organisms is how to resist or tolerate desiccation. Xerophytic plants such as cacti, insects and a few mammals, notably camels, are able to do this.

Even in temperate regions of the world the mean summer and winter temperatures may differ by as much as 20°C. It is this difference which is partly the cause of the seasonal activity of plants and animals in such areas.

2. SOLAR RADIATION

Any self-sustaining community must have access to sunlight, because light is essential for photosynthesis (Chapter 5). Although many heterotrophic organisms can and do live in total darkness, they rely on organic molecules made by photo-autotrophs as an energy source.

In the ozone layer of the earth's atmosphere, much of the ultraviolet light from the sun is absorbed. Solar radiation passing through this layer is about 10 per cent ultraviolet, 45 per cent visible light and 45 per cent infra-red. Infra-red radiation is the earth's external source of heat. Clouds of water vapour and dust reduce the amount of radiation arriving at the earth's surface. The intensity of solar radiation is highest near the equator, which is closer to the sun than any other part of the earth. This explains why tropical areas have higher mean annual temperatures than elsewhere on earth. The combination of intense light, high temperature and abundant rainfall is why vegetation grows so vigorously in the tropics.

FIG. 28.1.1 *Penetration of water by visible light* (after Lucas and Critch 1974)

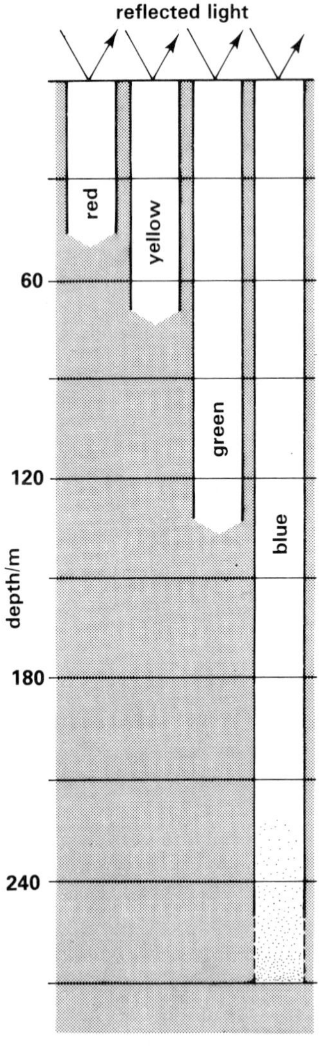

The time of year when certain terrestrial mammals breed and when flowering plants reproduce is to some extent governed by the number of hours of light each day (Chapters 22 and 19).

The shorter wavelengths of light penetrate water deepest. Most of the red light is absorbed in the first 50 m. Only blue light reaches a depth of 250 m. Blue light reflected from the sea bed gives the sea its blue colour when the sun shines. Beyond 200 m, there is total darkness (Fig. 28.11). It is for this reason that green algae which require a high intensity of red and blue light for photosynthesis live mainly near the sea surface. Brown algae which can survive at lower intensities of red light live between 10 and 25 m, while red algae which use mainly blue light can grow deeper down. As with the atmosphere, the amount of light which penetrates water can be seriously reduced by the presence of suspended particles.

3. AVAILABILITY OF OXYGEN

Most living organisms are **aerobes** and require oxygen gas for the release of energy in respiration (Chapter 5). At sea level, the atmosphere contains about 20·9 per cent oxygen gas by volume. At high altitudes there is the same proportion of oxygen present, but its partial pressure is less (Table 8.4). This means that oxygen is less readily absorbed by living organisms. Given time, mammals produce extra erythrocytes which enable them to carry enough oxygen to their tissues when at high altitudes (Table 8.5). Others such as the llama, which normally live at such heights, have a variant of haemoglobin with an exceptional affinity for oxygen. Even so, there is a limit to the ability of any terrestrial animal to compensate for the lack of oxygen gas in habitats of this kind. Together with low temperature, it explains why there is very little mountain fauna above a height of about 4·5 km, where the partial pressure of oxygen is roughly half that at sea level.

Oxygen gas is relatively scarce in water. The amount present depends on its solubility, the temperature (Table 28.2), the partial pressure of oxygen in the air, the amount of solutes dissolved in the water and on the rate at which it is consumed by aquatic organisms. Even when fully saturated with oxygen, water contains less than 1 per cent by volume of the gas. Oxygen is thus much less accessible to aquatic organisms. Some aquatic animals require relatively high concentrations of dissolved oxygen to survive. Others can manage where there is much less (Table 28.3).

Near the surface of a lake or sea where the water is in contact with air, the water may be saturated with oxygen. Photosynthetic plants help to maintain high concentrations of dissolved oxygen. Deeper down, where there are no photo-autotrophs and because oxygen diffuses very slowly through water, much less dissolved oxygen is present. Thermal convection currents help to carry some oxygen downwards from the upper layers.

Table 28.2 Effect of temperature on concentration of dissolved oxygen in water

TEMP. °C	PERCENTAGE OXYGEN BY VOLUME
10	0·796
15	0·723
20	0·649
25	0·593
30	0·548

Table 28.3 Effect of dissolved oxygen concentration on survival of freshwater fish (after Open University 1972)

SPECIES	DISSOLVED OXYGEN ($mg\ dm^{-3}$)*
rainbow trout	3·7
perch	1·2
roach	0·8
tench	0·7

* The concentrations are the minimum required for 7 days' survival at 16°C.

However, in the deepest waters there may be little or no oxygen gas available. Here only invertebrates whose oxygen-carrying pigments become saturated at very low oxygen tensions (Fig. 28.12) and anaerobic bacteria can survive.

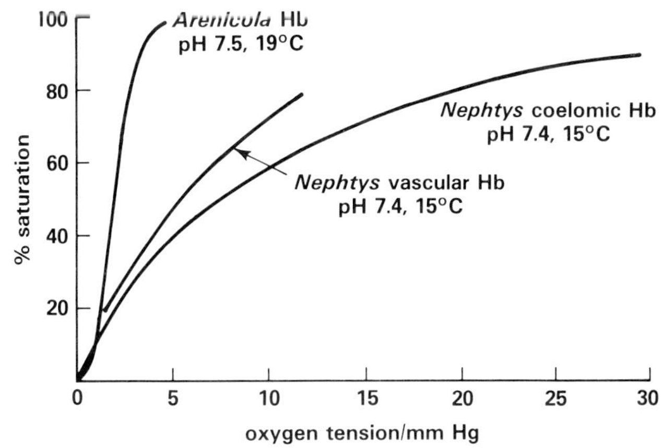

FIG. 28.12 *Oxygen dissociation curves for haemoglobin of* Arenicola *and* Nephtys (from Jones 1955)

Aquatic habitats may become seriously depleted of dissolved oxygen when polluted by organic matter. The organic matter encourages the growth of decomposer micro-organisms which use up the oxygen at a rate quicker than it can be replaced. The reduction in dissolved oxygen may render the water unfit for cleanwater fish such as salmon and trout (Chapter 30).

4. AVAILABILITY OF CARBON DIOXIDE

Carbon dioxide is one of the raw materials essential for **photosynthesis** (Chapter 5). At sea-level, the earth's atmosphere contains about 0·03 per cent by volume of carbon dioxide. When light intensity is high, it is this small amount of carbon dioxide which limits the rate of photosynthesis. As with oxygen, the partial pressure of carbon dioxide gas at high altitudes is less. It is mainly this, and the lower temperatures, which prevents, plants growing at a height of more than 6 km in mountainous areas.

Carbon dioxide is nearly forty times more soluble in water than oxygen. However, because the partial pressure of carbon dioxide in the air is 700 times less, the volume of carbon dioxide dissolved in water is generally small compared with oxygen. Even so, aquatic plants are never short of carbon dioxide for photosynthesis. This is because water contains vast quantities of carbonate and hydrogen carbonate ions which are formed when carbon dioxide reacts with water:

$$CO_2 + H_2O \rightleftharpoons \underset{\text{carbonic acid}}{H_2CO_3} \rightleftharpoons H^+ + \underset{\text{hydrogen carbonate}}{HCO_3^-} \rightleftharpoons 2H^+ + \underset{\text{carbonate}}{CO_3^{2-}}$$

The ions can be used as a source of carbon dioxide. As dissolved carbon dioxide, HCO_3^- and CO_3^{2-}, sea water contains the equivalent of 4·7% carbon dioxide. This is 150 times more than in the earth's atmosphere.

FIG. 28.13 *Effect of altitude on atmospheric pressure* (from Hollingsworth and Bowler, "Principles and Processes of Biology" published by Chapman & Hall)

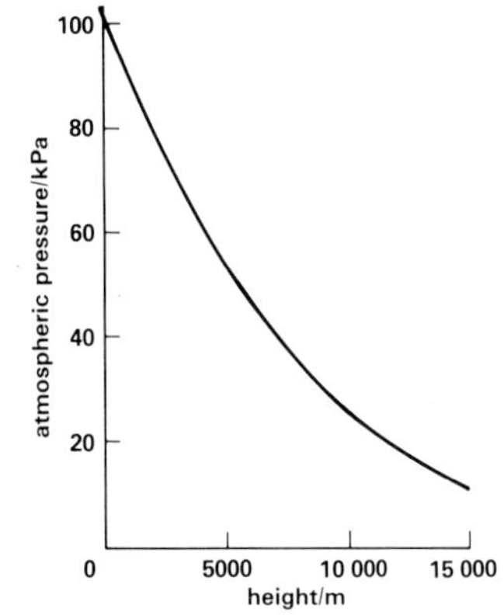

5. PRESSURE

At sea-level, the pressure of the air is 101·4 kPa (1 atm), but it reduces with altitude (Fig. 28.13). Cold and the low partial pressures of oxygen and carbon dioxide prevent organisms living permanently above a height of about 6 km.

In water, the pressure increases by about 100 kPa for each 10 m in depth (Fig. 8.23). At 11 km below the oceans' surface, the greatest depth at which aquatic organisms live permanetly, the pressure is over 1000 times that at sea level. Simple forms of life such as bacteria appear to be unaffected by aquatic organisms live permanently, the pressure is over 1000 times that at magnitude by floating at an appropriate depth. Bony fishes have **swim bladders** which enable them to adjust the depth and hence the pressure at which they swim (section 27.2.3). Whales and seals store large amounts of **blubber** which gives them buoyancy. Freshwater plants have **aerating tissue** which retains oxygen and carbon dioxide (Fig. 28.14). Seaweeds often have buoyant **air-bladders**. The oils stored in diatoms help to keep them afloat. The lift provided by such adaptations ensures that many aquatic plants float near the surface where light, oxygen and carbon dioxide are more plentiful.

FIG. 28.14 *Transverse section stem of pondweed* Potomageton (B&B photos)

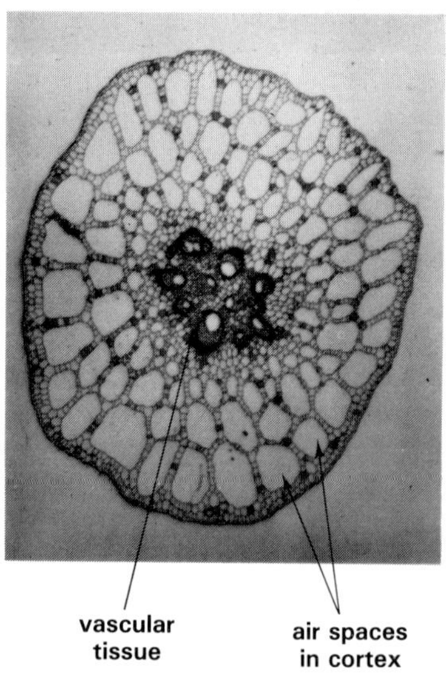

6. WATER POTENTIAL

Water is vital for many of the activities of living organisms (Chapter 2). In most terrestrial habitats, the water potential of the air is much less than that of living organisms. Consequently, organisms which live on land constantly lose water by **evaporation**. The external surfaces of most land-dwelling organisms are waterproofed and evaporation of water into the air is minimised. Animals which live on land conserve water by reabsorption in the renal system and hind gut. Insects, birds and mammals minimise water loss by producing solid or semi-solid faeces. Even so, they continually lose water vapour through their respiratory surfaces. When the stomata of terrestrial plants are opened to take in carbon dioxide for photosynthesis, water vapour is lost by **transpiration**.

In aquatic habitats there are three possibilities:

(i) the water potential of an organism is less than (hyperosmotic/hypertonic to) the surroundings,

(ii) the water potential is greater than (hyposmotic/hypotonic to) the surroundings,

(iii) the water potential is the same as (isosmotic/isotonic with) the surroundings.

Table 28.4 Comparison of ionic composition of fresh water and freshwater organisms (after Hollingsworth and Bowler 1972)

	CONCENTRATION (m mol dm^{-3})				
	Na^+	K^+	Ca^{2+}	Mg^{2+}	Cl^-
fresh water	0·5	0·06	2·7	0·4	0·9
crayfish blood	142	4	8	4	140
Nitella sap	86	59	19	22	107

Fresh water contains only small amounts of dissolved solutes (Table 28.4) so usually has a higher water potential than the organisms which live in it. It means that freshwater plants and animals constantly absorb water by **osmosis**. The wall pressure of plant cells limits the intake of water Freshwater animals have to eliminate the excess water. In simple animals such as protozoans, **contractile vacuoles** serve this purpose (section 2.4). More complex animals such as fish have elaborate osmoregulatory devices. Bony fish which inhabit ponds, streams, rivers and freshwater lakes absorb water by osmosis through their gills. They regulate their water potential by producing large volumes of dilute urine. Their renal tubules are very efficient in reabsorbing mineral ions from the renal filtrate. Any loss of minerals in the urine is made good partly by the fishes' diet and also by the active absorption of salts by the **chloride cells** of the gills.

Sea water is relatively rich in dissolved solutes and has a lower water potential than the body fluids of marine bony fish. As a consequence they constantly lose water by osmosis through their gills. They drink sea water to make good the loss of water. Excess sodium, potassium and chloride ions are excreted through the chloride cells of the gills (Fig. 28.15). The low glomerular filtration rate of the kidneys ensures little water is passed in their urine.

FIG. 28.15 *Osmoregulation in fish* (a) *freshwater bony fish* (trout) (b) *a marine bony fish* (cod)

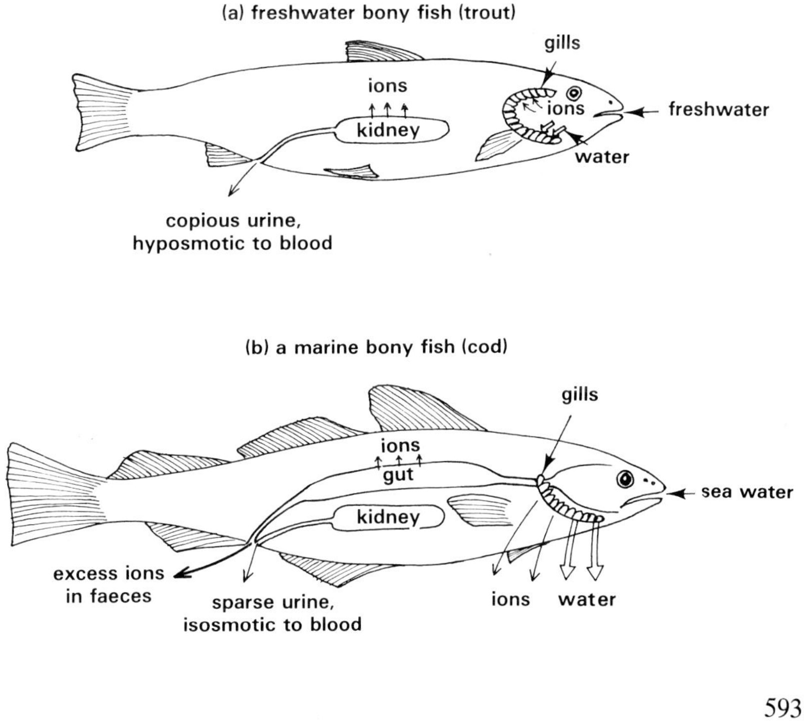

Most marine animals maintain their body fluids isosmotic with sea water by regulating their intake of solutes (Table 24.2). Aquatic animals which live in estuaries where the sea and river waters mix are often able to do this over a wide range of water potential (Fig. 28.16). They are said to be

FIG. 28.16 *Effect of water potential of the external medium on the water potential of the body fluid of three aquatic animals* (after Ramsay 1968)

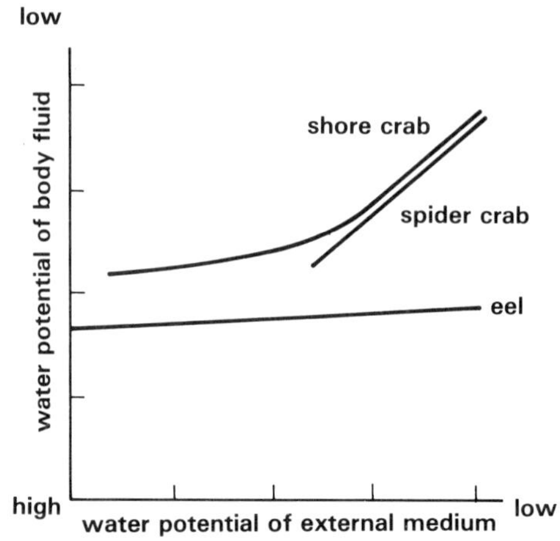

How do the differences reflect the habitats of the animals?

euryhaline. The majority of marine animals have limited powers at doing this and are said to be **stenohaline**. Migratory fish such as the salmon and eel change their method of osmoregulation when they move from the sea to rivers, and vice versa. The ability to adapt to changes of water potential enables such creatures to exploit a wider range of habitat than those which cannot do so.

7. MINERAL AVAILABILITY

A variety of minerals is required for the healthy growth of plants and animals (Chapters 13 and 14). In upland rivers, lakes and reservoirs the water contains such sparse amounts of minerals that there is hardly any plant growth. Aquatic plants are more likely to be found in lowland lakes and rivers which are often enriched with minerals reaching them in drainage water from farmland. The sea contains an ample supply of minerals which encourage the growth of marine algae.

FIG. 28.17 *The stinging nettle* Urtica dioica *growing in a farmyard*

Fertilisers and manures are applied regularly to cultivated soils to produce healthy crops. In contrast, many natural soils are deficient in minerals, phosphate in particular. The stinging nettle can be used to assess the relative amount of phosphate in soil, because its growth rate is proportional to phosphate concentration. It probably explains why this species grows well in abandoned farmyards where there are high concentrations of phosphate left by animal droppings (Fig. 28.17).

The availability of minerals in soil is affected by many factors. One of the most important of these is pH. In fairly acid soils (pH less than 6·5), deficiencies of Ca, Mg, K and P are often observed, whereas Mn, Al and Fe are frequently present in such high concentrations that they are toxic to plant growth. Chlorosis caused by iron deficiency may occur in alkaline soils. The spoil heaps of derelict mines often contain concentrations of Pb, Cu, Ni, and Zn which are toxic to most plants. There are however certain species, grasses especially, which can grow successfully in such habitats. They are sometimes called **metallophytes** (Chapter 13 and Fig. 24.20).

8. WATER MOVEMENT

It is in fast-flowing streams and rivers, in wave action at the surface of lakes and seas, on sea shores and in estuaries that **water movement** is most apparent. Turbulent water is likely to be well **oxygenated**, as it is constantly brought into contact with air. Still, deep water is often deficient in oxygen.

Living organisms cope with the mechanical effect of moving water in a variety of ways. Submerged aquatic plants have tough but flexible bodies. This enables them to bend with the current without being damaged (Fig. 28.18). Attachment organs such as the **holdfast** of seaweeds prevent such plants from being washed away.

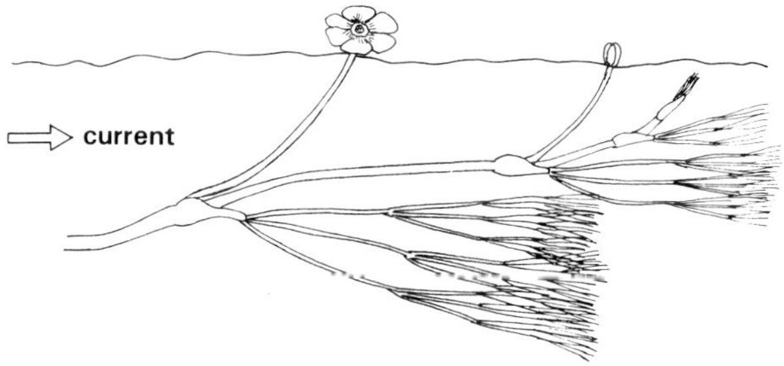

FIG. 28.18 *River crowfoot* Ranunculus fluitans

The ways in which aquatic animals withstand or avoid moving water are just as varied. Shore crabs hide under seaweeds and in rock crevices. Sea anemones, limpets and barnacles are firmly fixed to rock surfaces. In streams and rivers, caddis fly larvae are weighed down by their stony cases, snails by their shells (Fig. 28.19). Many estuarine animals such as lugworms and cockles burrow into mud and thus avoid being moved by tidal currents.

The larvae of fixed aquatic animals, the spores of non-flowering aquatic plants and the seeds of a few species of flowering plants are **dispersed** by moving water. Many of the larger fish and aquatic mammals are strong swimmers and often migrate long distances against tides and river currents.

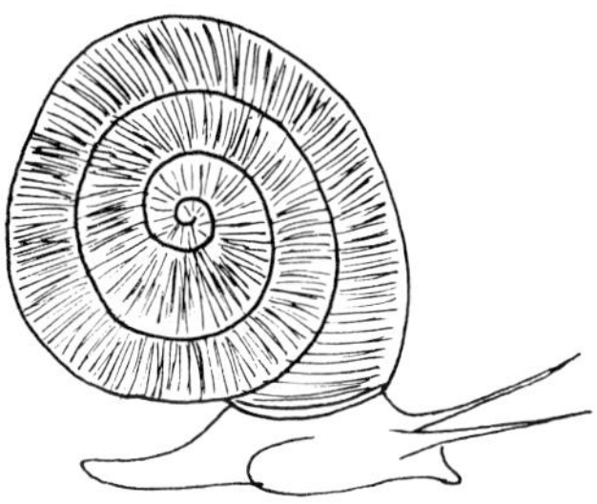

(a) Ramshorn snail

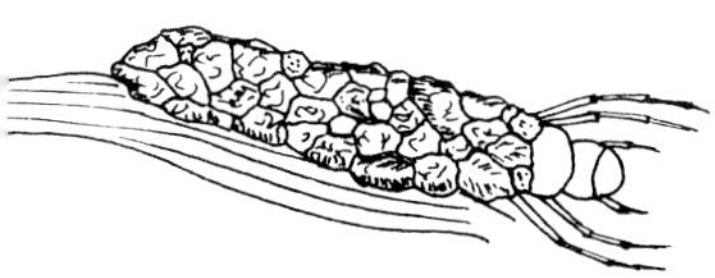

(b) larva of caddis fly

FIG. 28.19 (a) *Ramshorn snail* (b) *larva of caddis fly*

9. AIR MOVEMENT

Moving air encourages **evaporation** of water. It is a factor in determining the distribution of terrestrial plants. Windy habitats are often colonised by plants which can minimise transpiration (Chapter 11).

Wind also aids in the **dispersal** of plants and animals. Birds are the masters of the air. They can fly long distances against strong winds. Insects are not usually very strong fliers. They are often blown from place to place. The same applies to plant spores and seeds. Spores are very light and remain suspended in the air for long periods. Seeds sometimes have wing-like extensions, which help their dispersal by moving air (Fig. 28.20).

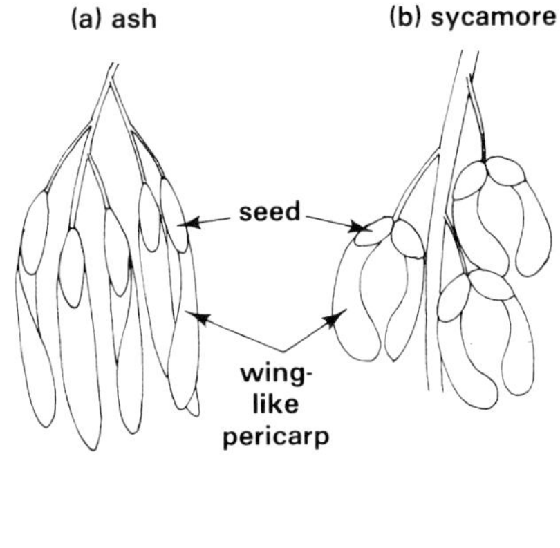

FIG. 28.20 *Winged fruits*

10. EDAPHIC FACTORS

The distribution of many terrestrial organisms is affected by soil conditions. Factors which affect soil conditions are known as **edaphic factors**. They are discussed in section 29.3.5.

28.1.3. The factor complex

FIG. 28.21 *Zonation on a rocky shore* (a) *chanelled wrack and* (b) *spiral wrack in upper zone* (c) *barnacles and limpets and* (d) *knotted wrack in middle zone*

It is unusual for a single factor to determine the distribution of a species. More often it is a complex of interacting factors. A study of the distribution of the inhabitants of rocky seashores around Britain helps to illustrate the **factor complex**. Between high and low water marks is the littoral belt, in which brown algae and invertebrates are clearly zoned (Fig. 28.21). Tufts of channelled wrack, *Pelvetia canaliculata*, cling to the rocks near the high-water mark on sheltered shores. A little further down the shore are clumps of spiral wrack *Fucus spiralis*. Among the algae and in

rock crevices in this **upper zone** is a gastropod mollusc, the winkle, *Littorina saxatilis*. Patches of rock are occupied by the barnacle *Chthamalus stellatus*. Next is a **middle zone** of heavy masses of knotted wrack, *Ascophyllum nodosum*, in which the predatory dog whelk *Nucellus lapillus* lurks. Another barnacle, *Balanus balanoides*, and the limpet, *Patella vulgata*, adhere to the rocks in this zone. At the bottom of the shore is a **lower zone** of serrated wrack, *Fucus serratus*, and bladderwrack, *Fucus vesiculosus*.

The upper limit of each species on the shore is possibly a measure of its ability to resist desiccation when exposed to air at low tide. Species in the lower zone are exposed for a shorter time than those living higher up the shore. It may be that the species of the upper zone can retain moisture better and are thus able to tolerate longer exposures to drying air.

A more difficult question to answer is what determines the lower limit of each species. Is it a measure of the ability to survive immersion in sea water and buffeting by the waves? Do competition, grazing and predation have a bearing on the zonation?

An insight into the complex of factors which affect the distribution of the two species of barnacles has been obtained by moving rocks on which they live to other zones. In one investigation, rocks covered with *Chthamalus* were moved downshore to the middle zone occupied by *Balanus*. The moved barnacles survived for a long time, showing that they could tolerate the conditions lower down the shore. Eventually, larvae of *Balanus* settled on the stones and, as they grew, *Chthamalus* gradually disappeared. One of the reasons why *Chthamalus* does not do well in the middle zone may therefore be that it does not compete well with *Balanus* for space on the rocks. Predation by the dog whelk and smothering of the rocks by knotted wrack may be contributory factors.

28.2 Associations between organisms

Plants and animals often associate temporarily or permanently with organisms belonging to a different species. The **associations** are often a means of providing food for one or both of the partnerships.

28.2.1 Parasitism

A **parasite** is an organism which gets part or all of its food from another species called the **host**. The activities of parasites are usually harmful and they are often the cause of their hosts' death. However, hosts are sometimes carriers of parasites without coming to any harm. A good many parasites live permanently on or in their host. Others visit their hosts only to feed. Whereas the majority are **obligate parasites**, a few such as *Pythium*, a fungus which causes *damping off* of seedlings, are **facultative parasites**. After killing seedlings, the fungus lives as a saprophyte on their dead remains.

Parasites belong to a wide range of living organisms. Those which are most successful are protozoans, platyhelminths, nematodes, arthropods, fungi, viruses and bacteria. The general characteristics of these groups of plants and animals are described in Chapters 25–27. Parasitic micro-organisms are often called **pathogens**.

Parasites are sometimes thought of as **degenerate organisms**. This is because they often lack some of the features of their free-living relatives. Flatworm parasites, for example, often have no digestive system or sensory organs. They also have limited powers of movement and co-ordination. Parasitic flowering plants have no roots and may lack chloroplasts. However, it is probably better to think of parasites as **specialists**. Their morphology, biochemistry, physiology, methods of reproduction and dispersal are specially adapted for a parasitic existence.

1. HABITAT

Ectoparasites live on the surface of the host's body. The skin, mouth, nostrils and gills of animal hosts and the epidermis of plant hosts are the usual places where they are to be found. Ectoparasites of animals often cling to their hosts using claws, suckers or hooks (Fig. 26.57(a)). Ectoparasites of plants have attachment organs called **haustoria** (Fig. 28.22).

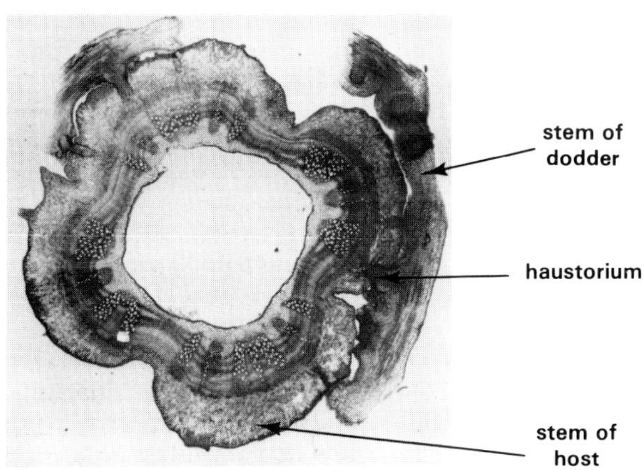

FIG. 28.22 *Haustoria of the dodder* Cuscuta

Endoparasites live inside their hosts' bodies. Many endoparasites of plants have a preference for young, active tissues such as the mesophyll of leaves. Endoparasites of animals frequently inhabit the digestive tract or body fluids of their hosts. Gut parasites often have hooks and suckers which attach them to the gut wall (Fig. 26.36). In this way their movement along the digestive tract by peristalsis is prevented.

2. ACCESS TO HOST TISSUES

A **vector** is an animal which carries parasites from one host to another. **Blood-sucking insects** are the most notorious vectors of a range of human parasites. Millions of people are infected annually with yellow fever and malaria, which are transmitted by mosquitoes (section 26.1.4). The tsetse fly is the vector of sleeping sickness, black flies carry river blindness, while typhus is transmitted by the body louse. **Sap-sucking insects** such as aphids are the vectors of many viral diseases of crops. Enormous sums of money are spent each year on insecticides in an attempt to prevent insect vectors coming into contact with humans and crops. Stopping the vector from breeding is often an effective alternative strategy.

Other parasites enter their hosts through damaged outer tissues or through natural openings such as stomata, the nasal openings and the mouth. Some can even penetrate unbroken skin. An example is the fluke *Schistosoma* which is passed in a larval form to man from water snails. The disease caused by the fluke is bilharzia (section 26.4.2). It is prevalent in countries where crops are irrigated, as in rice-growing. Molluscicides can be used to kill the snails, thus denying the fluke access to human tissues.

Parasites are often very **invasive** when they enter a host. They may secrete **enzymes** enabling them to penetrate healthy tissues. Fungal parasites invade plant tissues by secreting pectinase and cellulase enzymes. Some pathogenic bacteria attack hyaluronic acid, the material which cements animal cells to each other, by secreting the enzyme hyaluronidase. *Schistosoma* secretes the same enzyme to penetrate human skin. Once in the body, it invades body organs, especially the liver, through blood and lymph capillaries.

3. HOST REACTION

Microbial parasites of animals trigger the host's **immune system** into action (Chapter 9). However, the parasite often has time to become established before the system comes into action. Phagocytosis also helps to ward off infections caused by microbes. Defence mechanisms of these kinds are ineffective against larger parasites such as helminths and nematodes. It may be expected that the host's digestive enzymes would attack gut parasites. However, these parasites have very tough outer coverings which resist damage by gut enzymes.

Plants do not have an immune system. Nevertheless, they can resist infection in a variety of ways. When infected, many species of plants produce chemicals called **phytoalexins** which protect healthy tissues from attack by the parasite. Others have high concentrations of toxic substances, notably phenols, in their external tissues.

4. FEEDING

Many parasites have very exacting nutritional requirements. This partly explains why a parasite often has a specific host or can live in only a limited range of hosts.

Insect and nematode parasites frequently have mouthparts adapted

FIG. 28.23 *Spread of* Peronospora tabacina *through European tobacco crops* (from Deverall, "Fungal Parasitism", Inst. Biol. "Studies in Biology" published by Edward Arnold)

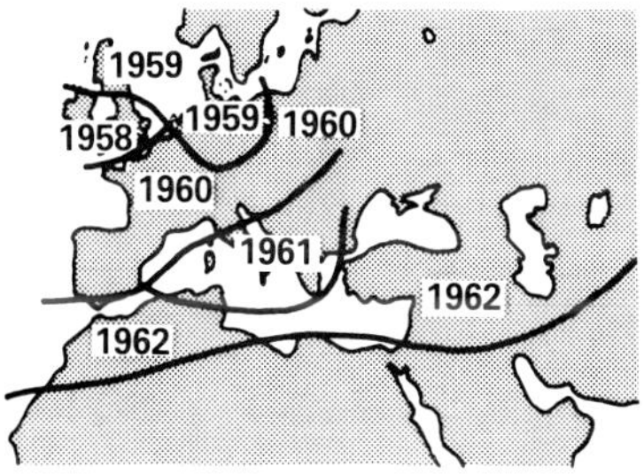

FIG. 28.24 *Anopheline mosquito, the vector of malaria*

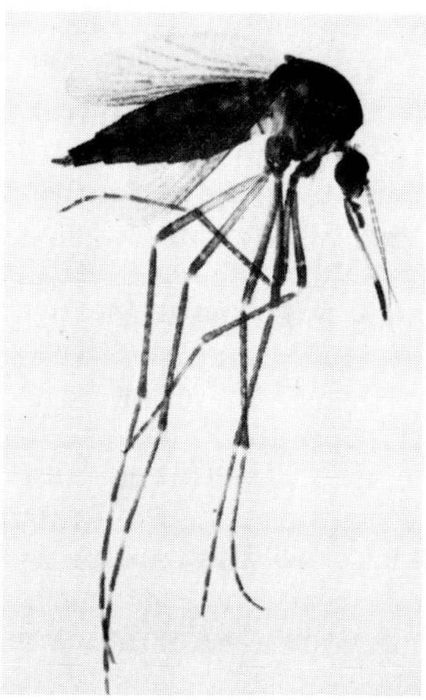

for piercing the host's outer tissues and sucking blood or phloem sap (Figs. 26.60 and 12.12). Microbial parasites such as viruses, bacteria and protozoa absorb soluble materials through their body surfaces by active transport and diffusion from the body fluids and cells of the host. Gut parasites take in food which has been made soluble by the digestive enzymes of the hosts. Many endoparasites have a relatively large surface area through which nutrients are absorbed.

The haustoria of parasitic plants also provide a large area of contact with the host. In addition, they make the membranes of the host cells permeable to nutrients, allowing food to pass into the parasite. Some parasitic flowering plants, such as mistletoe, have green leaves and can thus photosynthesise. Others, such as the dodder, have scale leaves which lack chloroplasts. They rely entirely on the host for organic nutrients.

5. RESPIRATION

Parasites which live where there is a high oxygen tension release energy by **aerobic respiration**. They include ectoparasites and endoparasites which inhabit well-oxygenated tissues such as the mesophyll of leaves and the blood of vertebrates. The intestines of animals have a low oxygen tension, so gut parasites respire anaerobically. The relative inefficiency of **anaerobic respiration** in releasing energy (Chapter 5) is compensated for by the abundant supply of respiratory substrates in the host's food.

6. REPRODUCTION AND TRANSMISSION

The chance of most parasites finding a new host is maximised because they have a prolific rate of reproduction. Both asexual and sexual reproductive methods are used.

Endoparasitic fungi release huge numbers of asexual spores from hyphae on the outside of the host. They are carried by air currents over vast areas (Fig. 28.23). This is why many diseases of crop plants spread so rapidly. Asexual spores produced by protozoan parasites which inhabit blood are carried to new hosts by blood-sucking insect vectors. This is how the malarial parasite is transmitted by the mosquito, *Anopheles* (Fig. 28.24). Extremely large numbers of sexually-produced cysts and eggs of gut parasites pass to the outside world in the faeces of their host (Table 28.5). They are able to resist desiccation and can survive for years. A fresh host usually becomes parasitised when consuming infected food or water. Cysts and eggs of gut parasites are often stimulated to hatch by intestinal enzymes (Fig. 28.25). In this way they remain dormant until they reach an appropriate host.

Table 28.5 Number of eggs produced by selected parasites (after Marshall 1978)

SPECIES	No. PRODUCED
Taenia solium (pork tapeworm)	800×10^6 (total production)
Ascaris (roundworm)	200×10^3 per day
Ankylostoma (hookworm)	35×10^3 per day
Diphyllobothrium (fish tapeworm)	1×10^6 per day

FIG. 28.25 *Effect of intestinal enzymes on the hatching of cysts of the dog tapeworm* (after Smyth 1967) *Hanks is a physiological solution with a composition similar to intestinal fluid but it contains no enzymes*

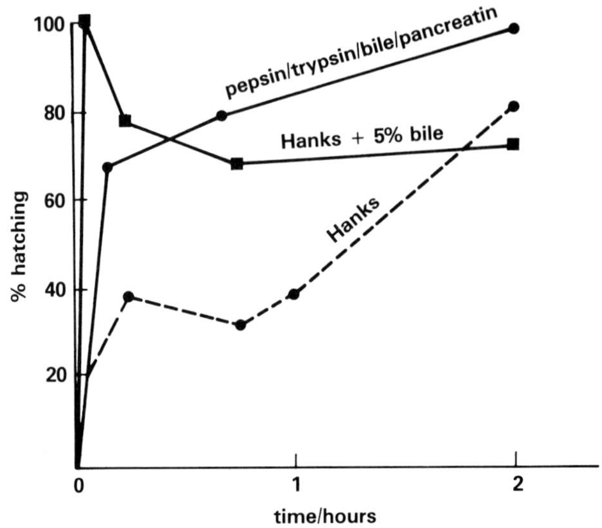

Some parasites have **secondary hosts** in which they spend part of their life cycle. The rabbit is the secondary host of the dog tapeworm. Others have **alternative hosts**. Many game animals in Africa are alternative hosts to humans for the malarial parasite. Additional hosts of these kinds improve the survival chances of such parasites.

7. EFFECT ON HOST

Parasites sometimes have no detectable effect on their hosts. Humans can be **carriers** of parasites, such as the bacterium which causes typhoid fever, without any ill-effects. However, there are many instances when the harmful effects of parasites are all too apparent.

Physical damage to important organs such as the brain and liver is caused by the hydatid cysts of flatworm parasites. Gut parasites sometimes damage the intestinal mucosa, causing haemorrhage. **Enzymic damage** of host tissues by invasive bacteria and fungi is quite common. Bacterial and protozoan parasites of the bloodstream frequently bring about haemolysis of the host's red blood cells. Substances which are toxic to the host are secreted by many parasites. Probably the best-known of these are bacterial **toxins**. Tumorous growth of the host is a feature of some parasitic diseases. Fungal parasites of plants are known to produce plant hormones, which are thought to be the cause of swollen organs in diseases such as club-root of brassicas (Fig. 28.26). Gut parasites often absorb sufficient food for the host to be undernourished. Blood-suckers may take enough blood for the host to become anaemic.

The general effect of parasites is to bring about a loss in fitness of the host. Even though the host may survive, its inability to thrive when parasitised may mean that it competes less favourably or that it is more easily taken by predators.

FIG. 28.26 *Cabbage with club root* (Biophotos)

28.2.2 Symbiosis

Symbiosis is an association between organisms of different species in which each partner benefits. There is thus a mutual advantage for the partners, which are called **symbionts**. For this reason, symbiosis is alternatively known as **mutualism**. Symbionts are often so dependent on each other that they are unable to live independently. One or both symbionts of other partnerships are sometimes found as free-living organisms.

1. MYCORRHIZAE

A **mycorrhiza** consists of a fungus and the root of a higher plant. In **ectotrophic** mycorrhizae, the fungus forms a sheath which covers the lateral roots of forest trees such as oak, beech and conifers. The fungus is often a basidiomycete unable to hydrolyse lignin and cellulose, the most abundant energy-rich substrates in soil. It depends on photosynthesis by the tree to provide organic materials. Experiments in which $^{14}CO_2$ was fed to mycorrhizal pine seedlings have shown that up to 10 per cent of the products of photosynthesis pass into the fungus. Even so, mycorrhizal plants grow more rapidly than those without the fungal partner (Table 28.6).

Table 28.6 Comparison of growth of mycorrhizal and non-mycorrhizal plants (after Harley 1971)

	MEAN DRY MASS (g) OF SEEDLINGS OR CUTTINGS	
	non-mycorrhizal	mycorrhizal
Pinus strobus	0·303	0·405
Quercus robur	1·14	1·69
Eucalyptus macrorhiza	7·8	11·3

Endotrophic mycorrhizae have most of the fungus inside the root (Fig. 28.27). Phycomycete, basidiomycete and imperfect fungi have been found in this type of mycorrhiza. The partner includes trees and orchids, as well as a wide range of important crop plants. Some of the fungi rely on photosynthesis by the partner to provide organic materials. Others can digest lignin and cellulose in the soil and pass the end-products into the roots of the plant. In this way growth of the plant is stimulated. Some orchids are unable to photosynthesise and rely entirely on the fungus for organic materials.

FIG. 28.27 *Transverse section of an endotrophic mycorrhiza*

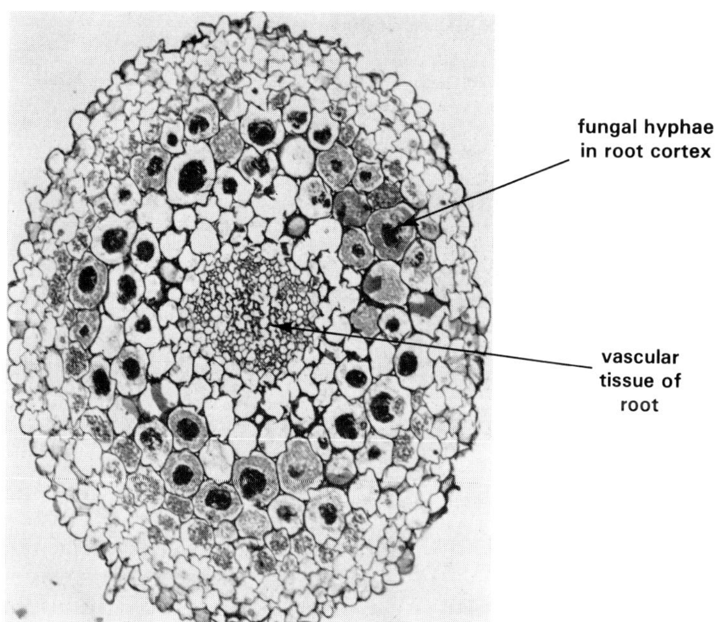

Table 28.7 Growth of mycorrhizal and non-mycorrhizal plants in soil with high (H) and low (L) phosphate content (after Harley 1971)			
		MEAN DRY MASS (g)	
		non-mycorrhizal	mycorrhizal
strawberry	L	6·69	16·04
	H	18·83	17·04
tomato	L	0·09	0·39
	H	0·70	0·74

The more vigorous growth of most mycorrhizal plants is thought to be due to their efficiency at absorbing minerals even from mineral-deficient soils (Tables 13.7 and 28.7). It enables them to compete more effectively with other plants in places where soils are infertile and allows them to become established in poor soils. The benefit to the fungus is apparent where it uses the plant's photosynthetic products. The advantage is less obvious where the fungus is not reliant on its partner for such materials.

2. LICHENS

A **lichen** is an association between an **alga** (phycobiont) and a **fungus** (mycobiont). Lichens are often found as crust-like, leaf-like or shrub-like growths on stones, roof tiles and tree bark (Fig. 28.28). More than 90 per cent of the dry mass of most lichens is made up of the fungus. The algal cells are scattered near the surface of the lichen, where light can penetrate.

FIG. 28.28 (a) *Crustose lichens growing on bare rock*
(b) *transverse section of a lichen* Xanthoria

(a)

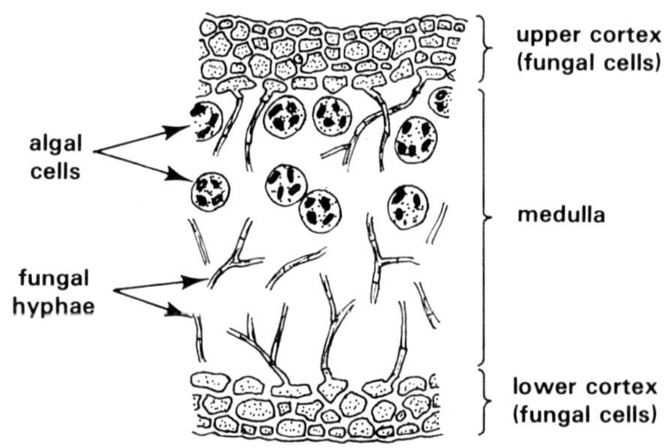

(b)

The unicellular green alga *Trebouxia* is most commonly the phycobiont. An ascomycete fungus is nearly always the mycobiont. Neither have been known to live independently. Some phycobionts such as *Nostoc* are, however, free-living. It is able to use nitrogen gas in the same way as nitrogen-fixing bacteria.

Experiments with $^{14}CO_2$ show that between 40 and 70 per cent of the photosynthetic products of the algal partner pass into the fungus. Where the alga is a nitrogen-fixer, most of the nitrogenous compounds it makes are also taken up by its partner. It is therefore quite obvious how the fungus gains from the association. The advantages to the alga are less apparent. It may be protected by the fungus from intense sunlight and from desiccation. It has also been suggested that minerals absorbed by the fungus are transferred to the alga, but there is no experimental proof that this occurs.

3. ROOT NODULES AND NITROGEN-FIXING BACTERIA

Probably the best-known of this type of association is between nitrogen-fixing bacteria of the genus *Rhizobium* and the roots of leguminous plants such as clover. The bacteria get into the roots through root hairs. They then cause the cortex cells to divide, forming **nodules** in which the bacteria multiply (Fig. 28.29). *Rhizobium* reduces nitrogen gas to form ammonia:

$$N_2 + 3H_2 \longrightarrow 2NH_3$$

A substantial amount of the ammonia is used by the legume to make amino acids, proteins and nucleic acids. In return, the bacteria are supplied with sugars and vitamins and have a sheltered habitat.

FIG. 28.29 (a) *Root system of broad bean plant,* × $\frac{3}{4}$
(b) *Section through a root nodule,* × *30*

(a)

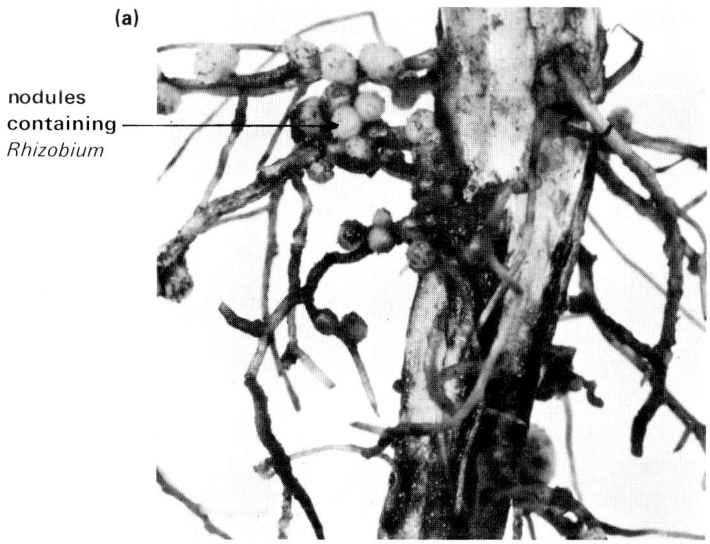

(b)

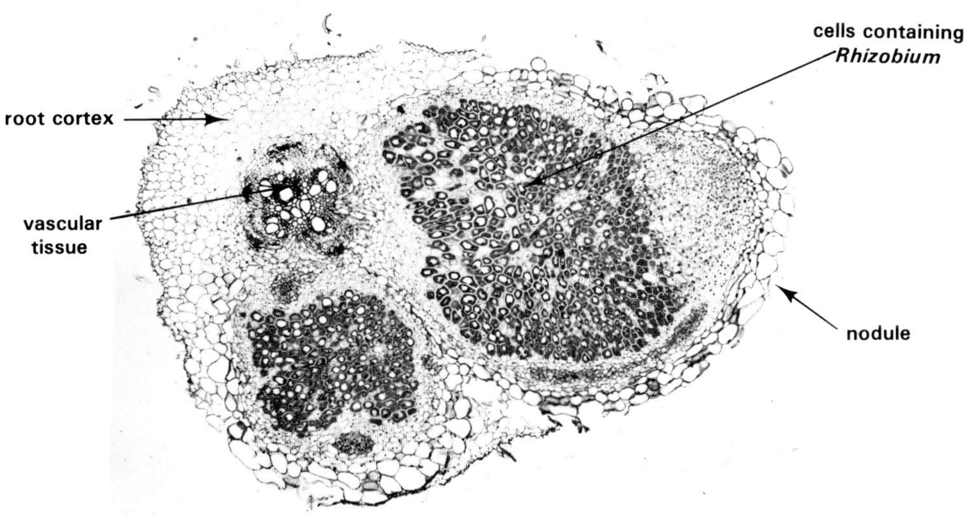

Apart from growing more vigorously in partnership with nitrogen-fixing bacteria, plants with root nodules are able to grow in soils deficient in ammonia and nitrates. This makes them very competitive in poor soils.

4. HERBIVOROUS ANIMALS AND GUT MICROBES

Ruminant mammals such as cattle, goats and sheep have a complex stomach (Chapter 14). One of the chambers is the **rumen**. It is here that a variety of bacteria and protozoa live in millions. They are anaerobic and obtain energy by fermenting carbohydrates and proteins in herbage. About 60–90 per cent of the carbohydrates in herbage are fermented in the rumen. The main products are volatile fatty acids such as ethanoic, lactic, butyric and propionic acids, as well as carbon dioxide and methane gas. The gases are belched out, but the acids are absorbed into the ruminant's bloodstream. Up to 70 per cent of the animal's energy requirements come from the absorbed acids. What is even more significant is that without the rumen bacteria very little of the carbohydrate in herbage could be used by the ruminant. This is because no mammal produces an enzyme capable of breaking down cellulose, the main ingredient of plant cell walls. Unless the cell wall is destroyed, starch grains, sugars and proteins inside the cells are inaccessible to enzyme attack. Rumen protozoa are mainly ciliates and a few flagellates. They ferment starch, forming the same end-products as the bacteria.

Between 40 and 50 per cent of the proteins in herbage are hydrolysed by rumen bacteria into amino acids. A small proportion is used by the bacteria and protozoa for protein synthesis. The remainder is fermented to form fatty acids and ammonia. Most of the ammonia is taken into the bloodstream and used for making ruminant proteins.

The environment in the rumen is ideal for microbial growth. It is warm and moist, and there is an abundance of food. As a consequence, the microbes multiply quickly. Their numbers are kept in check, because every time food passes from the rumen into the other chambers of the stomach some of the microbes are taken along too. In the abomasum they are digested and are a significant part of the ruminant's source of protein, B-vitamins and vitamin K. Similar activities take place in the caecum and colon of ruminants and also in non-ruminants.

5. CLEANER ANIMALS

Many species of African game, such as antelopes and zebras, are groomed by **oxpecker birds** which remove ticks and blood-sucking flies from their hides (Fig. 28.30). When predators come near the birds alert the game by calling and flying off.

FIG. 28.30 *Oxpeckers on African buffalos* (Eric and David Hoskins)

Egyptian plovers and sandpipers have been observed taking leeches from inside the open mouths of basking crocodiles on the River Nile. The birds are safe because crocodiles do not feed while they are lying out in the sun.

Barber fish or **cleaner fish**, as they are alternatively called, play an important role in keeping many species of larger fish in good health. They do this by picking off lice, parasitic fungi and bits of dead skin. The fish which is being cleaned allows the barber fish to go into its mouth and even into its gill chamber to do its job.

In all the cleaning associations described above the groomer obtains a supply of food. The groomed animal is relieved of harmful parasites and is thus more likely to thrive.

28.2.3 Commensalism

Commensalism is the association between organisms of different species in which one species benefits but does no apparent harm to its partner.

Living on the skin, in the mouth and respiratory passages of mammals are millions of coccoid bacteria. The large intestine teams with bacilli such as *Escherichia coli*. The bacteria have a permanent source of food and are sheltered from the outside world. Laboratory investigations have shown that some species of commensal skin bacteria can produce antibiotics which are effective against pathogenic bacteria. Whether they do this while living on the skin is yet to be determined. A common feature of all commensal bacteria is that they take up sites in the mammalian body which disease-causing microbes might otherwise occupy. In this way they may help to reduce the incidence of microbial diseases among mammals.

Another commensal partnership is seen between the hermit crab *Eupagurus bernhardus* and the sea anemone *Adamsia* (Fig. 28.31). The crab is a scavenger and lives in the abandoned shells of gastropod molluscs such as whelks. As it tears up its food, small pieces float away and are picked up by the anemone. The tentacles of the anemone have a sharp sting and protect the crab from would-be predators.

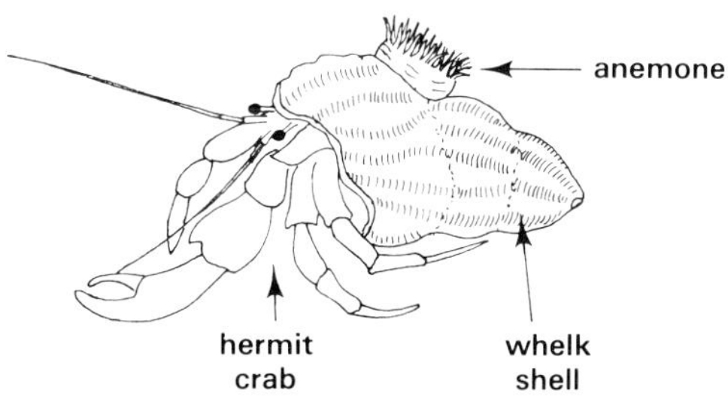

FIG. 28.31 *Commensal partnership between hermit crab and the anemone* Adamsia

Attempts to define associations sometimes fall down. This is because there is a very delicate balance in many partnerships. Given appropriate circumstances, an association can change from one kind to another. Hospital staff frequently carry pathogenic staphylococci in their nasal passages without coming to any harm. Does it mean that in these people the bacteria are commensal? Conversely, commensal bacteria can become pathogenic if given the opportunity. *E. coli* is quite safe in our bowel, but if it gets into our urinary tract it causes a severe infection.

The nitrogen-fixing bacterium *Rhizobium* is a symbiont so long as its host plant thrives. However, when its supply of carbohydrate slows down, it starts attacking the root cells of the legume. In contrast, root cells in mycorrhizal associations sometimes appear to digest some of the hyphae of the fungal partner. This has led some biologists to believe that such relationships may in fact be examples of *controlled parasitism*.

Chapter 29

Ecology 2: Populations, communities and ecosystems

An **ecosystem** is part of a biome such as a pond, stream, woodland or seashore, each inhabited by a typical **community** of living organisms. A **population** is a group of individuals of the same species living in the same place at the same time. The place in which they live is called a habitat. An organism's **niche** is the role it plays in a community.

29.1 Populations

The number of organisms of the same species in a habitat at any time is determined by innumerable factors. Many are those which affect the distribution of the species (section 28.1). One of the factors, called the **key factor**, is more important than any other. **Density-independent factors** affect a population, whether it is dense or sparse. Those which have a greater effect on a dense population are known as **density-dependent factors**. To find out how such factors regulate the size of a population, it is useful to look at a model of population growth.

29.1.1 Population growth

Growth of a population can be studied by inoculating a fixed volume of nutrient broth with bacteria, incubating the culture at the optimum temperature and counting the number of bacteria at known time-intervals. Four phases of population growth are seen (Fig. 29.1).

FIG. 29.1 *Growth of a population of bacteria*

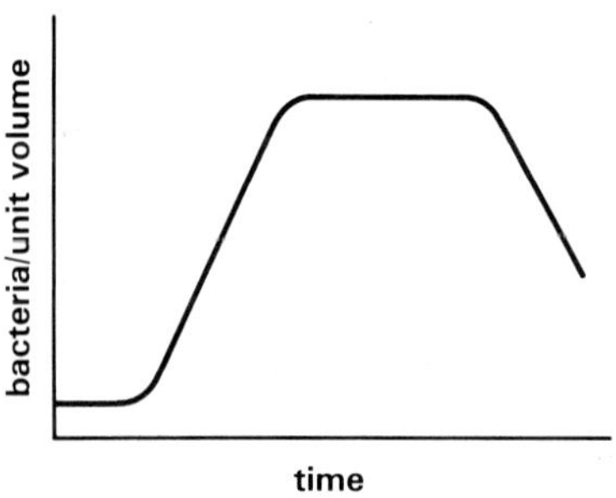

FIG. 29.2 *Effect of temperature on the growth of a population of bacteria*

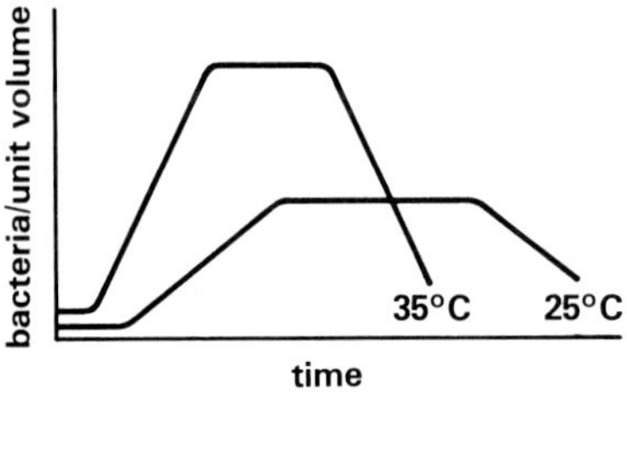

1. LAG PHASE
In this phase the population grows rather slowly. There are several reasons for the slow growth. The bacteria may have been in a dormant state, and time is required before their metabolism begins to work efficiently. They may have been growing previously in a different medium and have to adjust to their new diet.

2. LOG (EXPONENTIAL) PHASE
Here the population increases at its most rapid rate. There are no factors limiting growth. Nutrients and oxygen are in plentiful supply and there is ample space. It is called the log phase because a straight line is obtained if the logarithm of the number of bacteria is plotted against time.

3. STATIONARY PHASE
By this time the population size is stable and does not increase further. There is a limit to which any habitat can support a population. It is called the habitat's **carrying capacity**. The key factors here are density-dependent factors such as the amount of nutrients and supply of oxygen. The shortage of nutrients and oxygen prevents any further increase in the density of the population. This is what is known as **environmental resistance**.

4. DEATH PHASE
At this stage the carrying capacity of the environment has declined. It is unable to support such a high density of bacteria and they begin to die. They may die of starvation, a shortage of oxygen, or waste products may be present in toxic amounts.

If the investigation was repeated at 10°C lower, the growth rate would be about half of what was seen at the optimum temperature. The change in temperature has this effect whatever the density of the population (Fig. 29.2). It is a density-independent factor. Remember that the laboratory model does not necessarily indicate what happens in populations outdoors. It has not allowed for the possibility of resource renewal, competition with other species, disease, predation and climatic changes. Nevertheless, there are two very important conclusions to be drawn from such studies. The first is that the density of a population will increase up to the carrying capacity of its environment. Secondly, as the carrying capacity alters, so does the population density (Fig. 29.3).

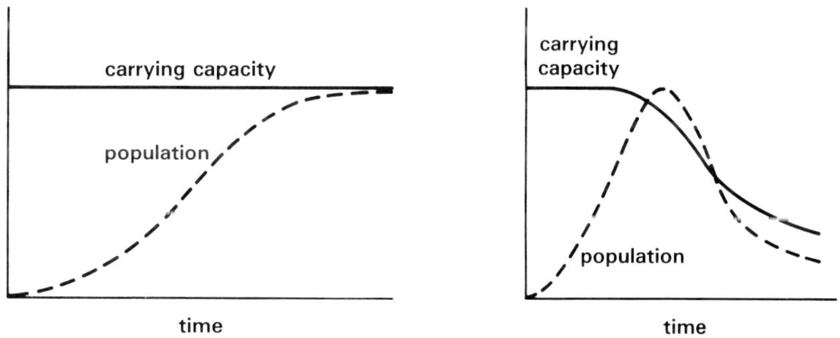

FIG. 29.3 *Effect of population on the carrying capacity of the environment* (from Owen, "What is Ecology?" published by OUP) (a) *stability resulting from pressures exerted by carrying capacity* (b) *decrease in population caused by reduction of carrying capacity*

29.1.2 Growth of human populations

FIG. 29.4 *Cabbage seed weevil* (B&B photos)

Over the years there have been fluctuations in the density of the human population in many localities. Between 1845 and 1847, the population of Ireland fell by over 1·5 million people, due to starvation and emigration. It was caused by a fungal disease known as late blight of potatoes. Bad weather has often been the cause of crop failures and subsequent human **starvation**. Competition occurs between humans and animal pests for the crops we grow. Locusts are notorious pests of crops in tropical countries. They swarm in millions over vast areas, devouring everything green within sight. Plagues of locusts often last for years. Even when crops are safely harvested they may be consumed by **pests** such as the seed weevil (Fig. 29.4). **Disease** is the most frequent cause of human deaths. Today over 2 million people die annually of malaria. **Wars** have accounted for intermittent but drastic reductions in the number of humans. There were about 22 million deaths in the Second World War between 1939 and 1945.

Table 29.1 shows the probable number of humans on earth over many centuries. The figures before 1800 are estimates based mainly on archeological and historical evidence. Censuses provide the more reliable figures for the more recent times. Use the data to plot a graph with time as the horizontal axis and the logarithm of the number of people as the vertical axis. Your graph should show that humans appear to be in the **log phase** of population growth. Between 70 and 80 million humans are added each year to the existing population. It means that the birth rate is greater than the death rate. But how has this come about?

1. BIRTH RATE

Each British mother gave birth on average to 7·6 children in 1890. In 1975, it was down to 2·3. The downward trend is seen in many countries. Better education and more reliable methods of **contraception** have been mainly responsible for the declining birth rate. Even so, until only recently the birth rate in Britain was higher than the death rate. In many countries more children are born each year than people dying (Table 29.2).

Table 29.1 Estimated number of people on earth (after Sands 1978)

YEAR	NUMBER
1 000 000 BC	125 000
300 000	1 000 000
25 000	3 340 000
8 000	5 320 000
4 000	86 500 000
3 000	150 000 000
0	250 000 000
AD 1 000	350 000 000
1 650	500 000 000
1 750	730 000 000
1 800	800 000 000
1 850	1 100 000 000
1 900	1 600 000 000
1 950	2 500 000 000
1 970	3 600 000 000

Table 29.2 Birth and death rates per 1000 population in various countries (mainly after Solomon 1976)

	1932	1959	1960	1970	1971	1972	1978
Britain							
birth rate	15·8	16·9	–	–	–	14·9	12·0
death rate	12·3	11·7	–	–	–	11·9	12·0
USA							
birth rate	17·4	–	23·6	21·0	–	15·6	15·0
death rate	10·9	–	9·5	10·9	–	9·4	9·0
Chile							
birth rate	34·0	35·4	–	29·6	–	–	–
death rate	22·7	12·5	–	9·4	–	–	–
Japan							
birth rate	32·9	17·5	–	–	19·2	–	–
death rate	17·7	7·4	–	–	6·6	–	–

2. DEATH RATE

Improved **hygiene**, **sanitation**, **diet**, **disease control** and **medical care** are some of the more important reasons why the human death rate has declined. In the 1940s, about 3 million people died of malaria each year. Now it is about 2 million. There were 162 infants among every 1000 deaths in Britain in 1900. Today it is 29 per thousand. Modern medical practice has greatly increased the chance of diagnosing and curing many human diseases. Disease prevention by vaccination and immunisation is now widely practised. Such measures have been so successful that killer diseases, for example smallpox, have been virtually eradicated.

3. LIFE EXPECTANCY

Females born in Britain in 1870 could expect to live for about 45 years on average. A hundred years later, their life expectancy was 75 years. The trend is the same worldwide. It means that now more women survive their full reproductive span. This is one reason why the birth rate is higher.

4. THE OUTLOOK

The earth has finite resources and there is a limited amount of space. If it continues to grow at its present rate, the human population could soon outgrow the earth's carrying capacity. Humans are adaptable and intelligent creatures. They have the ability to avert the dire consequences of unlimited population growth. However, there is a limited number of options. The most obvious of these is to reduce the birth rate. Increased food production is another possibility, but it will only delay the inevitable if growth of the human population is not kept in check.

29.1.3 Population dynamics

Long-term studies of wild populations show successive growth curves of the kind we have just studied (Fig. 29.5). There are many possible causes of such fluctuations. Spells of very cold weather kill many individuals (Fig. 29.6). Epidemics of disease and fluctuations in food supply have comparable effects. Predation is a key factor in the ups and downs observed in some animal populations.

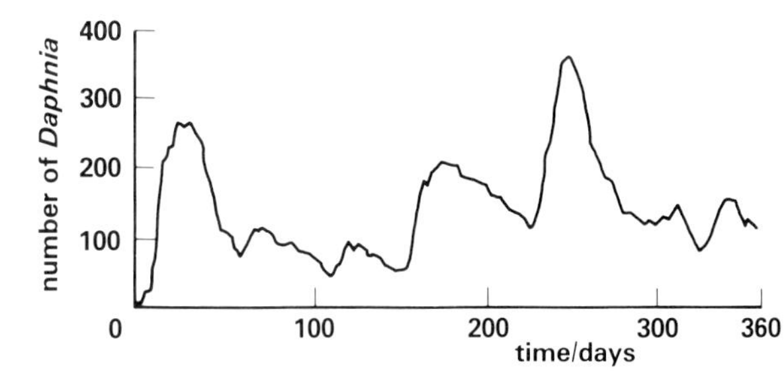

FIG. 29.5 *Fluctuations in numbers of the water flea* Daphnia *with time* (from Sands 1978).

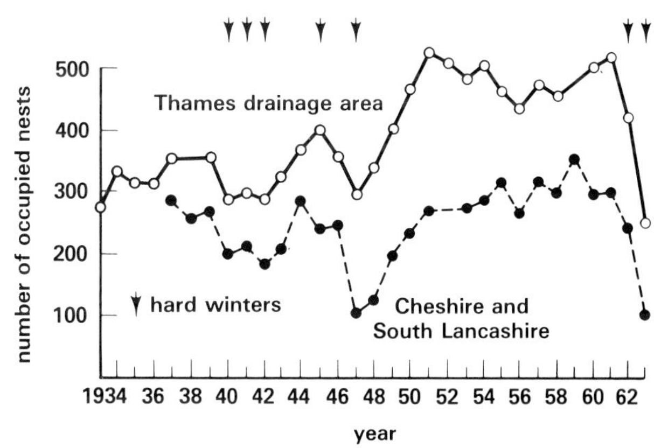

FIG. 29.6 *Numbers of breeding pairs of grey heron in two areas of England* (from Owen, "What is Ecology?" published by OUP)

1. PREDATION

A **predator** is an animal which captures and rapidly kills live animals, called **prey**, for its food. Repeated fluctuations in numbers of predators and their prey have been seen over a fairly short time in laboratory studies. The density of predators is slightly out of phase with the number of prey. A peak in the number of prey is followed by an increased density of predators. When the numbers of predators increase, there is a fall in the density of the prey (Fig. 29.7).

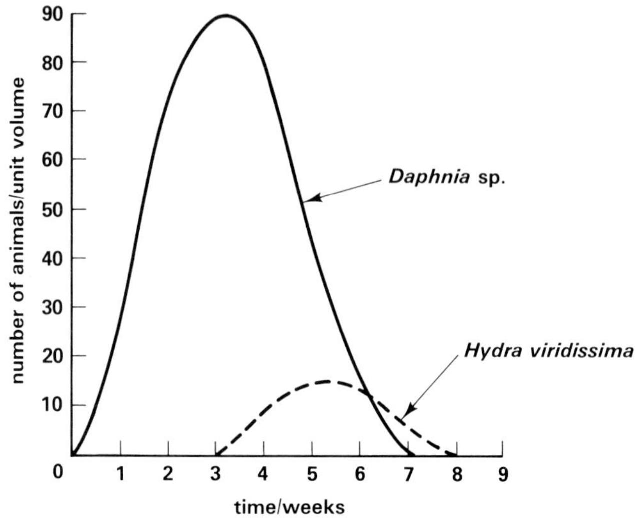

FIG. 29.7 *Relationship between the density of a predator* Hydra *and its prey* Daphnia (from Brown, "Ecology of Fresh Water" published by Heinemann)

Similar fluctuations are thought to occur in wild populations. Perhaps the best-documented outdoor study is of the snowshoe hare and its predator the lynx in Canada between 1845 and 1935 (Fig. 29.8). The

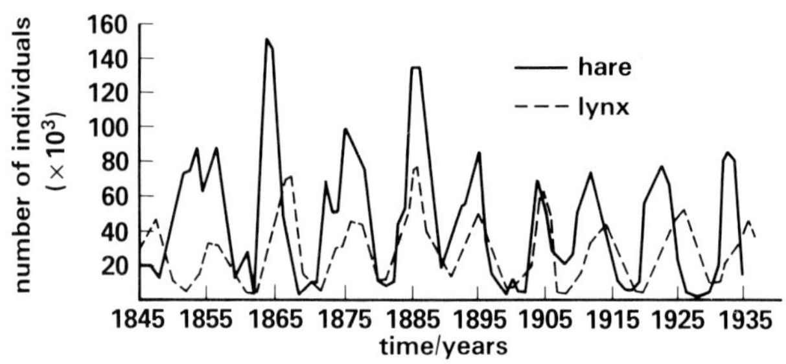

FIG. 29.8 *Fluctuation in abundance of the lynx and snowshoe hare in Canada* (from Odum, "Fundamentals of Ecology" published by Saunders)

density of the hare and lynx populations was estimated from the numbers of their pelts received by the Hudson Bay Company, from information provided by trappers and from field observations. Fluctuations in each of the populations occurred every 9–10 years. In other predator-prey relationships, the interval may be larger or smaller.

Predation is a **density-dependent factor**. Changes in prey density usually have a delayed effect on the density of predators. Food supply, weather, the incidence of disease and the predation rate are among the factors which determine the numbers of prey. Specialist predators which eat a limited variety of prey either starve or are forced to migrate when prey is scarce. General predators can turn to other kinds of prey.

The relationship between predators and prey helps to maintain the biological fitness of animal populations. Young, old or infirm prey are more easily captured by predators. When prey is in short supply, predators which are low in the pecking-order are likely to go without food. In these ways the fittest of the prey and predators survive.

2. HUMANS AS PREDATORS

Humans kill many species of animals as part of their omnivorous diet. Domesticated stock such as pigs, sheep, cattle and fowl are farmed to maintain a stable supply for market. Wild prey also make up part of our food supply. Marine animals, notably fish and whales, figure prominently in the diets of many humans.

The seas are generally thought of as a common resource which anyone may fish. Improved fishing methods have meant that more and more fish have been taken in recent years from the world's seas and oceans (Table 29.3). Fishing vessels now travel over a thousand miles from their home ports. Echo-sounders, sonar equipment and helicopters are used to spot shoals of fish. Factory ships stay at sea for months, processing the catch from fishing fleets. Intensive fishing sooner or later results in a fall in the catch. The fleet then moves to other fishing grounds. It often takes many years for **overfished** areas to recover. There is the fear that, in the not-too-distant future, fish stocks generally will become so depleted that the oceans will soon be unable to meet the demand placed on them.

Table 29.3 Amounts of fish taken from the world's oceans in recent years (after Lucas and Critch 1974)

YEAR	GLOBAL CATCH (TONNES)
1940	20×10^6
1963	46×10^6
1970	70×10^6

Fluctuations in fish numbers are sometimes due to natural causes. Many food fish eat plankton. Their numbers depend to some extent on the amount of plankton available to them. It has been suggested that the decline of the herring shoals in the North Sea during the 1930s may have been caused partly by overfishing and partly by a fall in phosphate concentration. Phosphate stimulates growth of plankton. Recovery of the herring population in the 1960s was probably because the fish had overcome the intensive fishing of earlier days and also because of increased phosphate concentration. The phosphate came from domestic detergents which became popular at that time.

There is no doubt that predation by humans has been the main cause of the dramatic fall in numbers of many species of whale this century. Following the severe decline in the numbers of blue whales in the 1940s, by which time they had been hunted almost to the point of extinction, whaling fleets switched to catching fin whales. When the fin whale population slumped in the 1950s from overhunting, whalers took to capturing sei whales. In a little more than a decade the sei whale population fell drastically (Fig. 29.9).

FIG. 29.9 (a) *Numbers of five species of whale caught over a 25 year period* (from Lucas and Critch 1974) (b) *Fin whales* (Eric and David Hoskins)

(a)

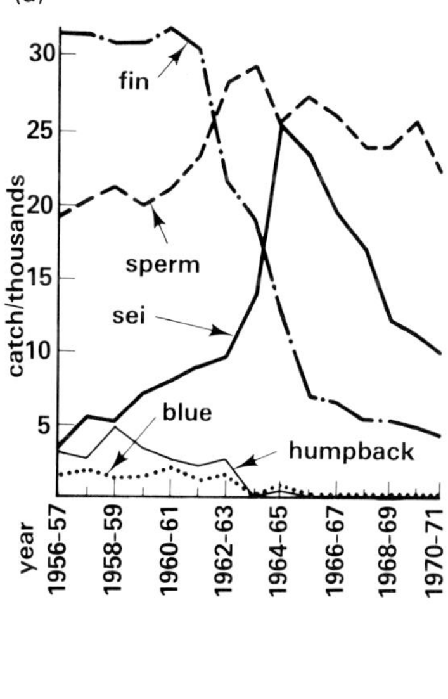

(b)

3. REGULATION OF POPULATION SIZE

Studies on wild populations have made it possible to find out how the sizes of natural populations are regulated. The findings should enable us to control the size of wild populations to our advantage. To keep the population size stable, the rate at which mature stock is harvested must be equalled by replacement from immature stock (Fig. 29.10). In this way the

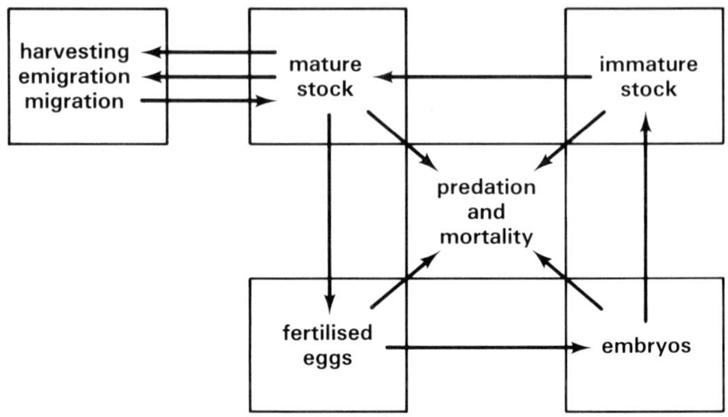

FIG. 29.10 *Model of population regulation*

population is kept in the log phase of growth and the carrying capacity of the environment is not overstretched. If the population reaches the stationary phase before it is harvested, it may take a long time for the population to recover its optimum number.

Managing this in a massive habitat such as the sea is easier said than done. Up to now there has been little serious attempt to regulate populations of marine fish. Shoals are usually a mixture of mature and young stock. If a net with a small mesh is used, many young fish are caught, leaving too few to allow populations to recover rapidly.

Various measures have been taken to try to conserve whale and fish stocks. Worldwide bans on the hunting of humpback whales came into being in 1966. A similar measure was taken to protect the blue whale in 1967. A ten-year ban on the capture of any whales was proposed at the International Whaling Commission in 1972 but was turned down. Catch quotas of overexploited species of fish have been set by international agreement. Much still needs to be done to rectify the mistakes of the past. Had the blue whale been maintained at its optimum population density, a sustained catch of 6000 individuals a year could have been achieved. The amount of meat alone would have provided three million people with a 200 g steak every day!

4. BIOLOGICAL CONTROL

The dispersal of plants and animals to new habitats often upsets the equilibrium of the community to which they have moved. Introduced species often increase in numbers very quickly. It happens because the factors which checked their numbers in their previous habitat are absent or less strong in their new environment. In other words, there is less **environmental resistance**. The key factor is often the absence of any natural enemies.

When the prickly-pear cactus, *Opuntia stricta*, was taken to Australia from North America in 1900, it soon spread to grassland. Within 25 years it covered millions of acres and was a serious nuisance to farmers. In its natural habitat the cactus population was kept down by the browsing larvae of a moth, *Cactoblastis*. When the moth was introduced into Australia from Argentina, its caterpillars soon stopped the spread of the cactus. Within a few years most of the lost farmland was reclaimed.

Heterobasidion annosum a basidiomycete fungus, is a killer of pines and other conifers in many countries. The main source of the infection is from tree stumps left after felling, on which the fungus grows and sporulates. Growth of *H. annosum* is prevented if the stumps are inoculated with the spores of another basidiomycete fungus, *Peniophora gigantea*. The inoculum is prepared commercially and is used on a large scale in Britain by the Forestry Commission.

There are many other instances of the successful **biological control** of pests. The advantage of regulating populations of pests in this way is that the control is very specific, so that useful organisms are unaffected. In contrast, pesticides are often unable to distinguish between the target organism and other closely related but desirable species (Chapter 30).

29.2 Communities

Only a few hundred years ago, much of the British countryside was covered with deciduous forest inhabited by wild boar, fallow deer and woodland birds. Deciduous forest is the **climax community** for most low-lying areas of Britain (Fig. 29.11). Today vast tracts of land are intensively cultivated and trees are confined to hedgerows and copses. However, if arable land is neglected, it eventually reverts to forest. The sequence of changes which occur in arriving at a climax community is called **succession**. It occurs wherever plants have an opportunity to colonise bare ground.

29.2.1 Succession

Primary successions begin where vegetation has never grown previously. Bare rock, sand and mud are examples. **Secondary successions** occur where vegetation has grown but has since been destroyed by fire, farming or by flood.

FIG. 29.11 *Oak forest, the climax vegetation of much of Britain*

1. PRIMARY SUCCESSIONS

The three successions described here are seen on bare rock, sandy beaches and in the mud of river estuaries around Britain. Such habitats are fairly accessible to most students of Biology.

(i) BARE ROCK. Crustose **lichens** such as *Xanthoria parietina* cling by their rhizoids to the surface of bare rock. Though they grow rather slowly, lichens are very hardy organisms. They endure the wide fluctuations of temperature and dryness of bare rock. Lichens overcome the lack of available nutrients on the rock face by absorbing minerals dissolved in moisture from the air. When lichens die, they add organic matter to the particles of rock eroded by weathering. Tufts of small **mosses** such as *Tortula muralis* are now able to grow on the rock. They can tolerate long spells of drought and retain moisture like a sponge when rain falls. The organic matter they add to the weathered rock attracts saprophytic microbes and detritivores such as nematodes, molluscs and arthropods.

At this stage the rock is covered with a thin layer of soil in which seedlings of **herbaceous flowering plants** become established. Their roots penetrate fissures in the rock and prise it apart into pieces. As the developing soil deepens, large-rooted **shrubs** and eventually **trees** are able to colonise the area (Fig. 29.12). This is the primary succession which occurs in the development and colonisation of sedentary soils. The process may take thousands of years. Climate mainly determines the climax community which eventually appears.

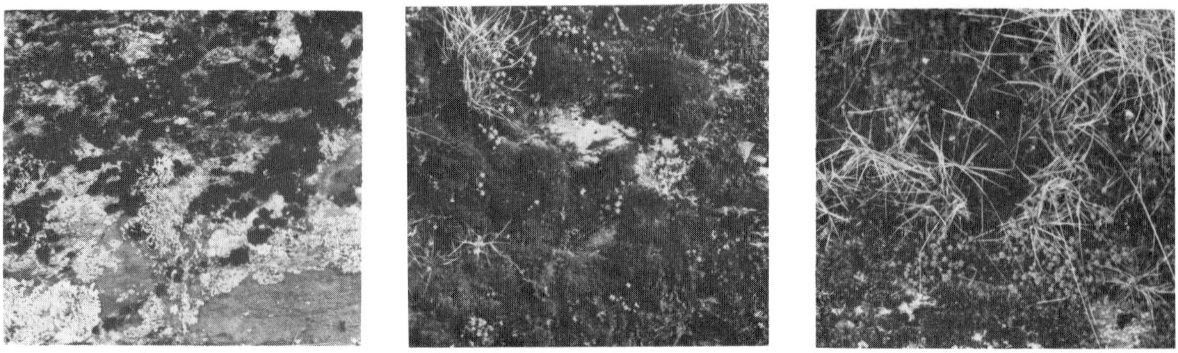

FIG. 29.12 *Succession on bare rock* (a) *mainly lichens and mosses* (b) *mainly mosses and seedlings of herbaceous angiosperms* (c) *mainly herbaceous angiosperms.*

FIG. 29.13 *Succession on a sandy shore at Ynyslas, Wales* (a) *embryo dune colonised by prickly saltwort* (left) *and sea rocket* (b) *yellow dune colonised by marram grass*

(a)

(b)

(ii) SAND. Sandy beaches are found in many places around the coast of Britain. When exposed to the sun and wind, the sand dries and is blown onshore. On the upper part of the beach, just beyond the reach of the highest tides, annual flowering plants, notably the prickly saltwort *Salsola kali* and the sea rocket *Cakile maritima*, grow. They can withstand abrasion by blown sand, the salinity and dryness of the beach and wide fluctuations in temperature. Around them, blown sand forms small hummocks which become colonised by sand couch grass, *Agropyron junceiforme*. The spear-like leaves of the couch grass gather more sand, which is consolidated by the plant's fibrous roots. It prepares the way for the xerophyte marram grass, *Ammophila arenaria*, whose spiky shoots trap large amounts of blown sand. The sand builds up quickly to form **yellow dunes** which are stabilised by the long rhizomes of the marram grass. They are called yellow dunes because fresh sand is continually deposited between the tufts of marram grass. As the marram grass spreads, the spaces between the tufts become smaller and more stable. They become colonised by ground-hugging angiosperms such as sea holly *Eryngium maritimum* and sea bindweed *Calystegia soldanella*. The organic matter in the top few centimetres of sand increases as the dunes become clad in vegetation. It encourages the growth of lichens such as *Cladonia*, mosses such as *Tortula ruraliformis* and flowering plants, the sand sedge *Carex arenaria* and red fescue grass *Festuca rubra*.

In winter, the maturing dunes look grey when the shoots of the vegetation die back. For this reason they are now called **grey dunes**. By now a crust of peat-like organic matter lies on the surface of the sand. Rain leaches the organic crust of lime, and acid-loving plants such as heathers are able to compete successfully with the dune plants. The **heathland** so formed eventually gives way to scrub vegetation and finally to **forest** (Fig. 29.13).

(iii) MUD. Clay and silt carried down by rivers often settle as mud in estuaries. When the mud is sufficiently thick, it is exposed to the air at low tide and colonisation by plants begins. In Britain, the first plants to grow in the saline mud are halophytes such as the glasswort *Salicornia europaea* and cord grass *Spartina townsendii*. When the tide comes in, their shoots are immersed in brackish water and speed up the sedimentation of mud. Sea aster *Aster tripolium* and sea poa grass *Puccinellia maritima* now begin to colonise the mud. The fibrous roots of the grass help to stabilise the mud. As the mud thickens, it is covered less frequently by tides and begins to dry out.

The drier conditions enable red fescue, *Festuca rubra*, to compete with *Puccinellia*. In many parts of Britain the vegetation is grazed by sheep and cattle, causing the succession to stop at this stage. Where the natural sequence is allowed to go on, the mud continues to thicken and the salt marsh vegetation is now covered only by high spring tides. Organic matter accumulates and sea pink *Armeria maritima*, sea lavender *Limonium vulgare*, and sea plantain *Plantago maritima* thrive. They are finally supplanted by the sea rush, *Juncus maritimus*, which in turn may give way to **heathland** and **forest** (Fig. 29.14).

FIG. 29.14 *Succession on saline mud at Gibraltar point, Lincs.* (a) *glasswork* (b) *sea lavender* (c) *cord grass*

(a) (b) (c)

An interesting feature of primary successions is that at each stage the inhabitants change the habitat, making it amenable to more competitive organisms which eventually oust the previous community. The process is repeated over and over until the climax community develops.

2. SECONDARY SUCCESSIONS

Burning of heather, *Calluna vulgaris*, is part of the management of grouse moors. It causes the heather to produce young, tender shoots which make up the bulk of the diet of grouse. Burning also prevents trees from growing among the heather. Strip-burning is the normal practice, leaving stands of old, tall heather for the birds to nest in and take cover from predators.

FIG. 29.15 *Heather moor* (a) *before burning and* (b) *after burning* (B&B)

(a) (b)

After a strip of heather has been burned, charred heather stems stick out of the bare peat. The heather roots are unaffected, and buried in the peat at the bases of the charred stems are reserve buds which soon spurt into growth. Gelatinous **green algae** such as *Zygogonium* and **lichens** such as *Lecidia uliginosa* colonise patches of bare peat. They are followed by other lichens, especially *Cladonia*, **mosses**, notably *Polytrichum*, and **heather seedlings**. Wavy hair grass, *Deschampsia caespitosa*, and crowberry, *Empetrum nigrum*, may later dominate the vegetation, but the heather plants soon outgrow the other species and within a year or two the community is back to normal (Fig. 29.15).

Secondary successions are much more rapid than primary successions. This is because the soil is already developed and contains the spores, seeds and vegetative organs of propagation of the colonising plants.

29.3 Ecosystems

An **ecosystem** is a more or less self-sufficient community of organisms in equilibrium with each other and with their environment. Energy and matter are exchanged between ecosystems and their surroundings. The activities of the community cause **energy to flow** through the ecosystem. The community consists essentially of producers and consumers, which remove matter from the environment, and decomposers, which return it. The way in which producers, consumers and decomposers interact ensures that **matter is cycled** in ecosystems.

29.3.1 Trophic relationships

Green plants are the lifeblood of every ecosystem. They make organic molecules by photosynthesis from simple inorganic molecules. For this reason they are called **producers**. Organic substances are eaten mainly by animals which are the **consumers** in ecosystems. **Primary consumers** are mainly herbivorous animals which feed on green plants. Predators, scavengers and many parasites are **secondary consumers**. They feed on primary consumers. **Tertiary consumers** feed on secondary consumers, and so on. When producers and consumers die, their bodies are broken down by **decomposers** such as bacteria and fungi, which also dispose of animal faeces. Dead organic matter is also consumed by animals called **detritivores**. Millipedes, woodlice and earthworms feed mainly on dead vegetation in soil ecosystems. In aquatic ecosystems, particles of dead organic matter suspended in the water are eaten by detritivores such as bivalve molluscs and lugworms.

FIG. 29.16 *Trophic levels in a food chain*

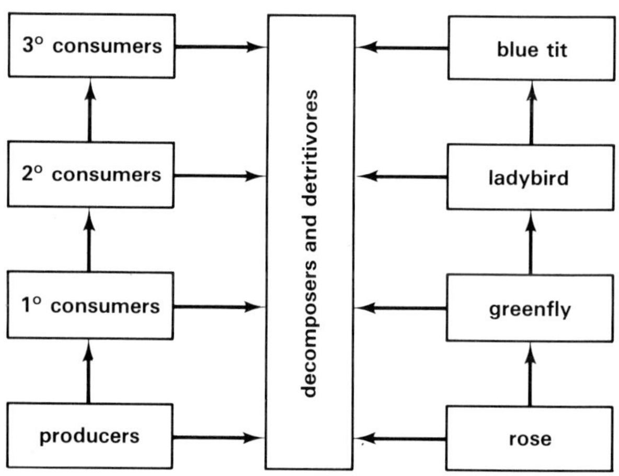

It is convenient to think of the feeding relationships in ecosystems as a **food chain** with several **trophic levels** (Fig. 29.16). In reality, feeding relationships are rarely as simple as this. Insectivorous plants, for example, are producers and also consumers. Omnivores can be primary, secondary and tertiary consumers, so too can decomposers and detritivores. It is therefore more informative to show feeding relationships as **food webs** (Fig. 29.17). This gives a much clearer picture of what happens to food in a community.

FIG. 29.17 *Food web in a freshwater ecosystem* (after Owen 1974)

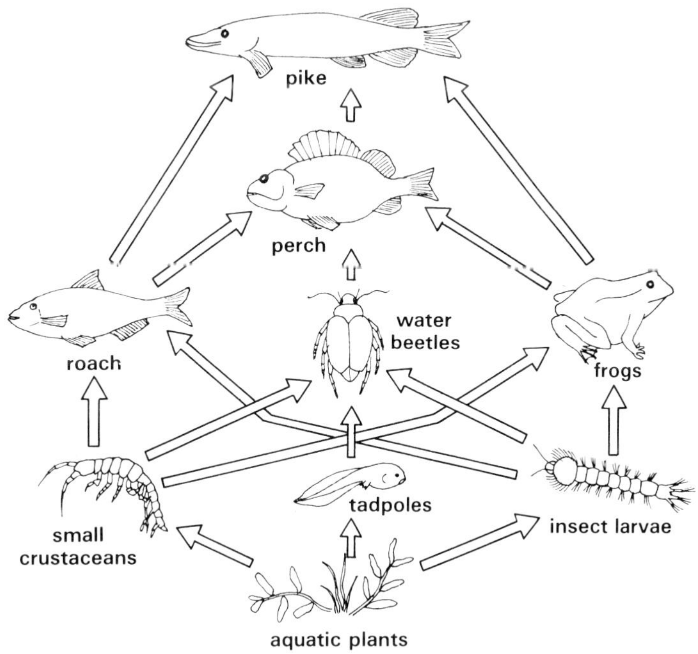

29.3.2 Energy flow

Energy can be transformed from one form to another. Green plants, for example, convert the energy in sunlight into the chemical bond energy of photosynthetic products. When energy is converted from one form to another, some energy always appears as heat. A proportion of the energy in respiratory substrates is released as heat energy.

The energy source for all ecosystems is the sun. About 641×10^4 kJ m^{-2} y^{-1} of solar energy reaches the earth's atmosphere. A good deal of solar energy does not, however, penetrate the atmosphere. It is reflected or absorbed and radiated back into space by the ozone layer, dust particles and clouds. The precise amount reaching the earth's surface depends on geographical location. Britian gets about 105×10^4 kJ m^{-2} y^{-1}, which is roughly a third of the energy received in tropical countries. Between 90 and 95 per cent of the energy getting to the surface of the earth is reflected by vegetation, soil and water or absorbed and radiated to the earth's atmosphere as heat. It means that only between 10 per cent and 5 per cent is left for producers to make use of.

1. PRODUCERS

Let us assume that 100 units of energy per unit time reach the leaves of a crop plant. What exactly happens to the energy? About half is not of an appropriate wavelength to be absorbed by chloroplast pigments. Roughly a quarter of what is absorbed ends up as chemical bond energy in photosynthetic products such as starch. The rate at which the products are formed is called **gross primary productivity** (GPP). A substantial amount of the **gross production** is respired by the plant. What is left, in this example just 5·5 per cent of the energy reaching the leaf, is **net production** (Fig. 29.18). The rate at which the products of photosynthesis accumulate is known as **net primary productivity** (NPP). The factors which affect NPP in crop plants are discussed in Chapter 12.

FIG. 29.18 *Fate of solar energy reaching the leaf of a crop plant* (data from Hall 1979)

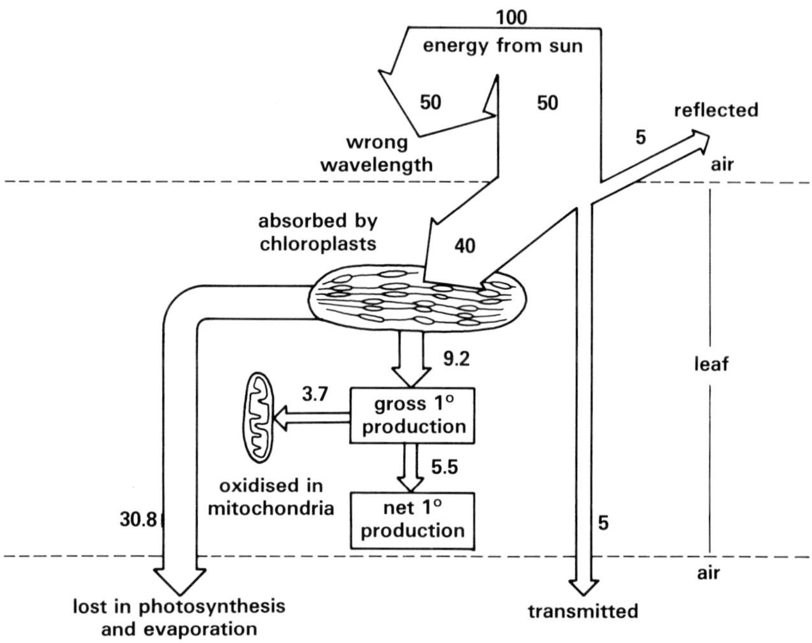

In winter, fields often have no crops growing in them. During the early growth of a crop, a good deal of sunlight is absorbed or reflected by the soil. It is only when plants are fully grown that their leaves absorb the maximum amount of sunlight. When the NPP is averaged for the whole year, it is therefore much less than in the growing season. In natural ecosystems where the climate allows plants to grow all year, the NPP is higher. In others, climatic factors limit the rate of photosynthesis, so the NPP is lower (Table 29.4).

Table 29.4 Net primary productivity of some of the world's ecosystems (after Whittaker 1975)

	NPP ($g\,m^{-2}\,y^{-1}$)	
ECOSYSTEM	RANGE	MEAN
open ocean	2–400	125
lakes and streams	100–1500	250
continental shelf	200–1000	360
temperate grassland	200–1500	600
temperate forest	600–2500	1250
tropical forest	1000–3500	2000

The NPP determines the amount of energy available to the consumers in the community. Thus the ability of any ecosystem to support consumers is determined by the NPP of its plants.

2. CONSUMERS

Let us consider the transfer of energy from producers to primary consumers. **Secondary productivity** is the rate at which consumers accumulate energy in the form of cells and tissues. The first point to bear in mind is that **herbivores** do not eat all the vegetation in an ecosystem. Cattle grazing a meadow will eat the grasses and palatable weeds such as buttercups. They leave inedible weeds such as nettles and thistles. Even the plants that are grazed are not eaten entirely. The roots are inaccessible and part of the shoot system is also left uneaten. It means that only part of the NPP of the ecosystem is transferred to the primary consumers. The amount depends to some extent on the variety and density of primary consumers. In pasture grazed by cattle it is about 30–45 per cent.

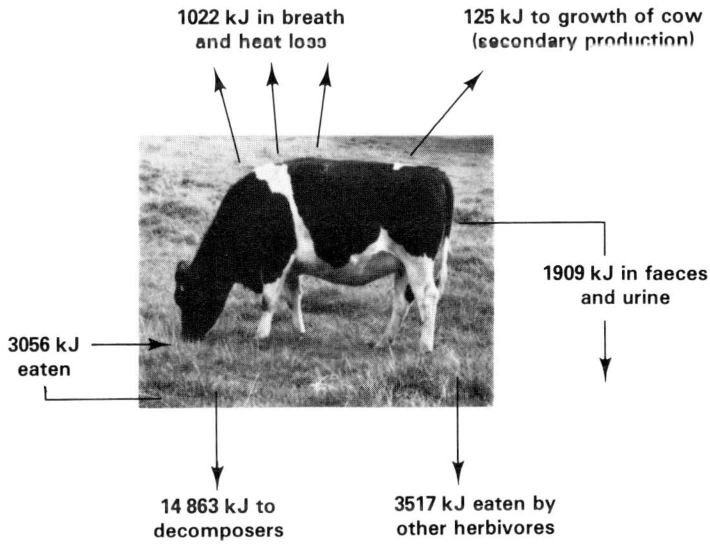

FIG. 29.19 *Fate of energy in a year's growth of grass from 1 m² of pasture* (data from Nuffield Study Guide in Advanced Biology 1974)

Figure 29.19 shows the fate of energy consumed by a bullock grazing on pasture. Nearly two thirds of the energy $\left(\frac{1909}{3056}\text{ kJ}\right)$ is excreted in urine and egested in the faeces. The remaining third $\left(\frac{1147}{3056}\text{ kJ}\right)$ is absorbed into the circulatory system. Roughly 90 per cent of the absorbed energy $\left(\frac{1022}{1147} \times 100\right)$ is lost as heat or is belched out as methane gas. Only about 10 per cent of the absorbed energy $\left(\frac{125}{1147} \times 100\right)$ is used to synthesise new cells and tissues. The secondary production of the bullock is thus only 0·6 per cent $\left(\frac{125}{21\,436} \times 100\right)$ of the NPP of the pasture. Keeping cattle in warm buildings reduces the amount of heat lost through the skin. It also limits the amount of energy used in movement. Such methods are used to improve the productivity of livestock for human consumption.

Carnivores have a much higher secondary productivity. This is because their protein-rich diet is more readily and efficiently digested. Flesh-eating animals do not have energy-consuming symbiotic microbes in their digestive tracts and their faeces contain much less undigested matter. Only about 20 per cent of the energy intake is lost in the faeces and urine of carnivores. They absorb almost twice as much energy per unit mass of food compared with herbivores.

The proportion of absorbed energy released in respiration is determined by the activity of the consumer and whether or not it maintains a constant body temperature. **Endotherms** have a stable temperature because the energy in absorbed food makes good the energy lost as heat to their surroundings. In cold weather, more absorbed energy is used for this purpose. **Ectotherms** do not use energy in this way and are thus able to direct a higher proportion of absorbed energy into secondary production. The most productive consumers are thus likely to be inactive, carnivorous and ectothermic (Table 29.5).

Table 29.5 Production of a range of animals (mainly after Open University 1974)

			% ABSORBED	% RESPIRED	% PRODUCED
endotherms	herbivores	rabbit	50·0	47·4	2·6
		cow	37·5	33·4	4·1
ectotherms	carnivores	trout	86·0	55·9	30·1
		spider	91·0	62·0	29·0
	herbivores	grasshopper	37·0	24·0	13·0
		caterpillar	41·0	17·6	23·4

3. DECOMPOSERS AND DETRITIVORES

The proportion of the primary production used by herbivores varies from one ecosystem to another. Up to 90 per cent of the phytoplankton in the oceans is eaten by microphagous animals. About 50 per cent of the primary production of pastureland is grazed, whereas as little as 10 per cent is consumed by herbivores in forests. The faeces of herbivores and most of what is left of the primary production are used as an energy source by **decomposers** and **detritivores**.

Some idea of the roles of decomposers and detritivores in energy flow in terrestrial ecosystems has been obtained by burying leaf discs contained in nylon bags of various mesh sizes in soil. The mesh size determined which decomposers and detritivores had access to the leaf discs (Table 29.6). The

Table 29.6 Effect of mesh size of nylon bags on access to leaf discs by soil organisms (after Phillipson 1966)

MESH SIZE (mm)	ORGANISMS WITH FREE ACCESS
7·000	Decomposers, detritivores
1·000	Decomposers and detritivores except earthworms
0·500	Decomposers and small detritivores such as mites, springtails and enchytraeids
0·003	Decomposers only

FIG. 29.20 *Effect of detritivores on the disappearance of buried oak leaf discs* (from Phillipson, "Ecological Energetics", Inst. Biol. "Studies in Biology" published by Edward Arnold)

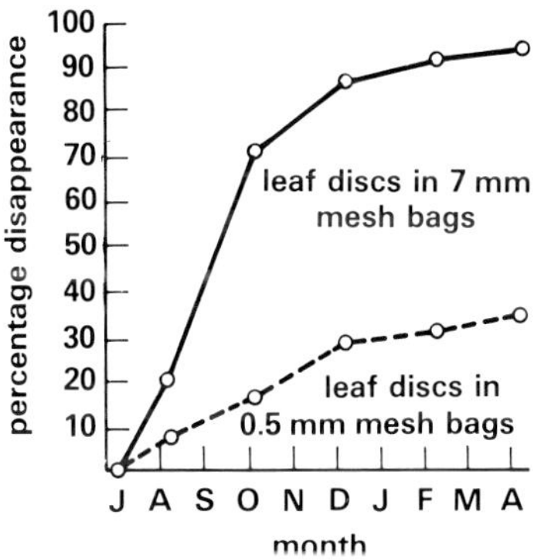

bags were dug up at regular intervals to measure the rate at which the discs were broken down. In the large mesh bags, which earthworms could get into, the discs were broken down three times faster than in any of the others. Where only microbes could enter, the discs showed little signs of deterioration over the nine months the investigation lasted (Fig. 29.20). The investigation fails to show what proportion of the energy in the leaf discs is used by the detritivores and how much is used by the decomposers. Detritivores are herbivorous animals which, as we saw earlier, egest much of the energy they consume in their faeces. A millipede feeding on dead hazel leaves, for example, absorbs only 10 per cent of the energy in the leaf material. Evidence of this kind points to the decomposers as the main users of energy in dead organic matter. So why are the detritivores apparently so important? Dead plant material is often deficient in nitrogen which limits microbial activity. The faeces of detritivores contain more nitrogen and moisture than the dead vegetation they eat. When altered in these ways, the plant material is used much more readily by decomposer bacteria and fungi.

One ecosystem in which the energy flow through decomposers has been determined is a salt marsh in Georgia, USA (Table 29.7). The primary production available to the animals and decomposers living in the marsh is $34\,354 - 15\,370 = 18\,984$ kJ $m^{-2}y^{-1}$. The proportion used by the decomposers is $\frac{16\,287}{18\,984} \times 100 = 85{\cdot}8\%$. It is thought that this is a reflection of the energy flow through the decomposers in most ecosystems.

Table 29.7 Energy flow in a Georgia salt-marsh (after Teal 1962)

PROCESS	ENERGY (kJ $m^{-2}y^{-1}$)
gross production	152 323
producer respiration	117 969
net production	34 354
decomposer respiration	16 287
export from marsh	15 370
primary consumer respiration	2 495
secondary consumer respiration	201

4. WHOLE ECOSYSTEMS

In most ecosystems there are many species, and feeding relationships are often poorly known. The few ecosystems where the flow of energy is known in detail are fairly simple. A freshwater spring is a simple ecosystem. The producers are diatoms, green filamentous algae and small flowering plants such as duckweed. When they die, the producers become detritus and sink to the water bed. Some of the detritus is carried away by the current. Detritus also enters the spring with the incoming water. The detritivores include freshwater lice, bivalve and gastropod molluscs and small crustaceans. Larvae of the caddis fly feed on larger pieces of dead vegetation. Predatory turbellarians and midge larvae are the consumers.

The flow of energy between the various groups of organisms is shown in Figure 29.21. The first important thing to notice is that the energy leaving the system mainly as heat is the same as the amount of solar energy coming in. The second is that the rate at which energy passes into the animals at each trophic level is about 10 per cent of that entering the previous level. For example, the secondary consumers in the spring receive

FIG. 29.21 *Flow of energy in Silver Springs, Florida* (after Odum 1957)

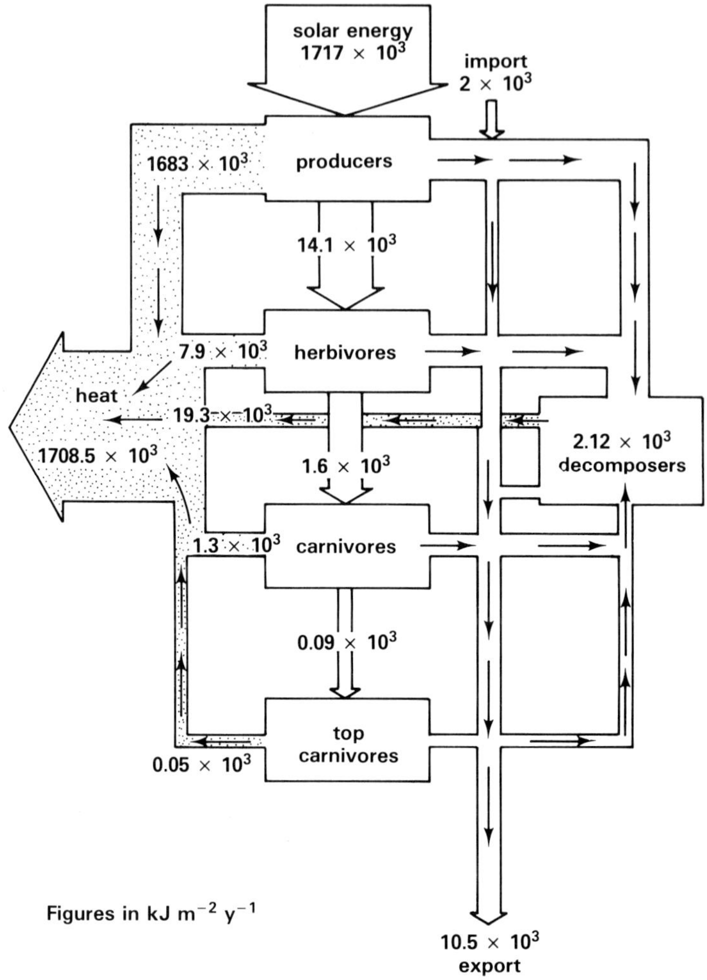

1605 kJ m^{-2} y^{-1} from the primary consumers which get 14 120 kJ m^{-2} y^{-1} from the producers. The rate at which energy passes to the secondary consumers compared with the rate it enters the primary consumers is thus $\frac{1605}{14\,120} \times 100 = 11{\cdot}4\%$. This is called the **gross ecological efficiency**. Because only about 10 per cent of the energy passes from one level of consumers to the next, the number of levels is limited to two or three in most ecosystems.

29.3.3 Ecological pyramids

The food and energy relationships in ecosystems can be displayed as bar diagrams. The producers are placed at the bottom, the primary and secondary consumers in the middle and tertiary consumers at the top. Diagrams of this kind often have the shape of a pyramid. Decomposers and detritivores are not often shown on **ecological pyramids**, which are of three types:

1. PYRAMIDS OF NUMBERS

These show the numbers of organisms at each trophic level. The length of each bar is proportional to the number of organisms. A major drawback of number pyramids is that they fail to distinguish between the sizes of organisms. A mature tree in a forest ecosystem is counted the same as a diatom in a lake. A cow in a meadow is equated with a leaf-eating caterpillar in a woodland. For this reason, number pyramids are bulged at the middle when the producers are large and few in number as in forest ecosystems. They are inverted when the consumers carry parasites. For example, a single rose bush may support thousands of aphids, which in turn may be the hosts for millions of parasites (Fig. 29.22).

FIG. 29.22 *Pyramids of numbers*

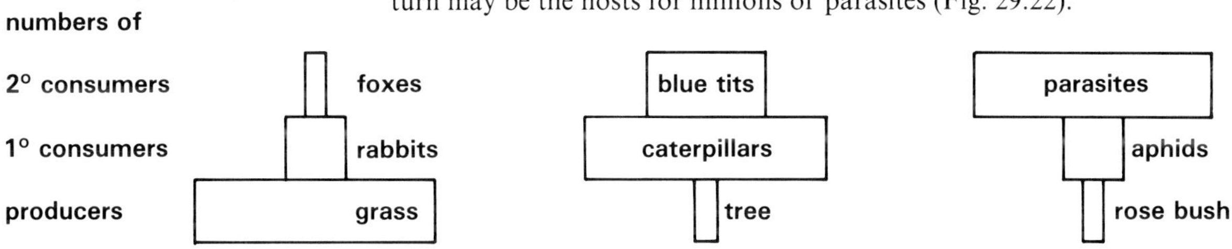

2. PYRAMIDS OF BIOMASS

These show the dry mass of the organisms in the trophic levels at a particular point in time. The length of the bars is proportional to the biomass in each level. They tell us what is called the **standing crop**. One of the problems with this approach is that it does not allow for changes in biomass at different times of the year. Deciduous trees, for example, have a larger biomass in summer than in winter when they have shed their leaves. Another difficulty is that the rate at which the biomass accumulates is not taken into account. A mature tree has a large biomass which increases slowly over many years. In comparison, the standing crop of diatoms in a lake is very small, yet production is high because their turnover rate is so rapid. This is why inverted pyramids of biomass are obtained for aquatic ecosystems (Fig. 29.23).

FIG. 29.23 *Pyramids of biomass* (a) *a field in Georgia, U.S.A.* *and* (b) *the English Channel*

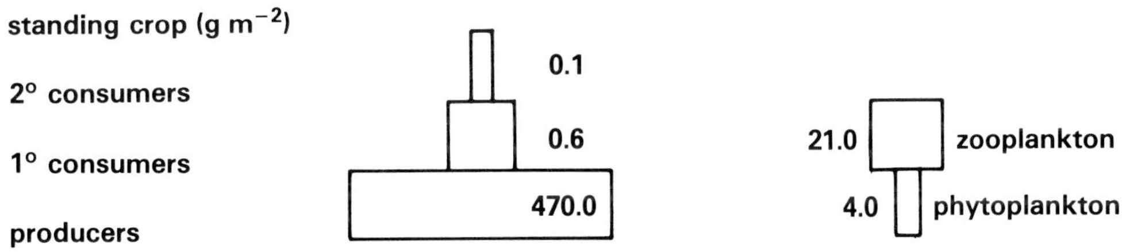

3. PYRAMIDS OF ENERGY

These show how much energy passes from one trophic level to the next. The length of the producer bar is proportional to the amount of solar energy used annually in photosynthesis. The other bars show the rate at which energy passes along the food chain (Fig. 29.24). Note that the transfer of energy from producers to primary consumers is less efficient than between the other trophic levels. Energy pyramids are more informative than pyramids of numbers and biomass. They tell us how much energy is required to support each trophic level. Because only a proportion of energy in a level is transferred to the next, energy pyramids are never inverted nor do they have a central bulge.

FIG. 29.24 *Pyramid of energy in Silver Springs, Florida*

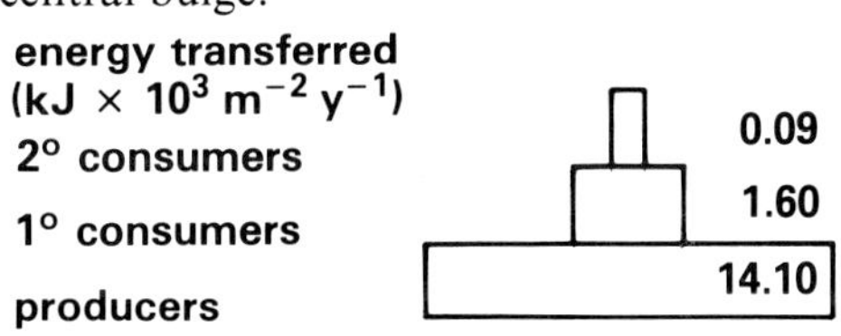

29.3.4 Cycling of matter

Energy comes into ecosystems from the sun and is lost as heat to the surroundings. In contrast, matter is cycled between organisms and their environment. The availability of minerals, especially nitrogen, carbon dioxide and water affects the distribution and abundance of plants and hence animals. For this reason a study of the cycling of nitrogen, carbon and water is important.

1. THE NITROGEN CYCLE

Nitrogen is vital to plants and animals for the synthesis of amino acids, proteins and nucleic acids. The earth's atmosphere contains over 78 per cent by volume of nitrogen gas, yet in this form it is useless to most living organisms. Plants take in nitrogen as ammonium and nitrate(V) ions. On a global scale, farmers add about 75×10^{12} g of ammonium and nitrate fertilisers to cultivated soils each year. Treating fields with nitrogen fertilisers is essential, because most of the nitrogen previously in the soil is removed in the crop at harvesting. In uncultivated soils, the crop is returned each year as dead leaves, roots, animal carcasses and faeces. Nitrogen in the detritus is converted to ammonium and nitrate(V) ions and is absorbed once more by the vegetation. The cycling of nitrogen takes place in several steps (Fig. 29.25).

FIG. 29.25 *The nitrogen cycle*

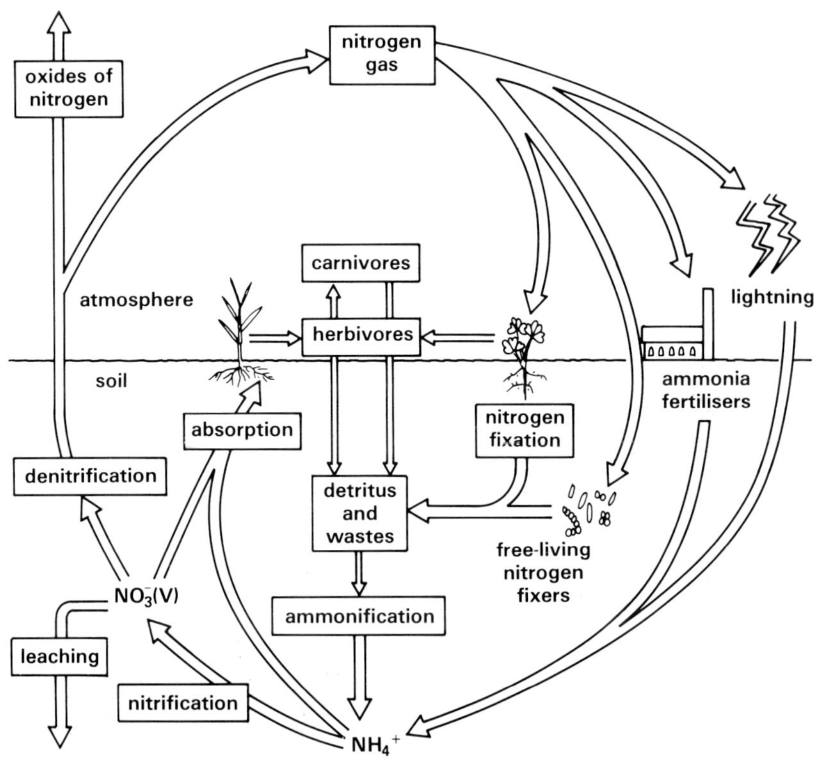

(i) AMMONIFICATION. A wide range of **saprophytic soil bacteria** and **fungi** decompose detritus. Peptidase enzymes released by the decomposers hydrolyse proteins to amino acids, some of which are absorbed and used to synthesise microbial protein. Unwanted amino acids are deaminated in a way comparable to that which occurs in the mammalian liver and ammonia is released. As much as $7000–10\,000 \times 10^{12}$ g of nitrogen enter soil annually in this way. Some ammonia escapes into the atmosphere, but much of it is converted to nitrate(V) ions by nitrifying bacteria.

(ii) NITRIFICATION. Well-aerated soil contains chemo-autotrophic **nitrifying bacteria**. They oxidise ammonia to nitrate(V) ions in two stages. The first stage is the conversion of ammonia to nitrate(III) ions, mainly by bacteria of the genus *Nitrosomonas*. Nitrate(III) ions are toxic to plants, but they are oxidised as quickly as they are formed into nitrate(V) ions by bacteria of the genus *Nitrobacter*.

Plants absorb nitrate(V) ions, but these are also rapidly leached from soil by rain water. In anaerobic conditions as in waterlogged soils nitrate(V) ions are reduced to nitrate(III), ammonia, nitrogen and oxides of nitrogen by **denitrifying bacteria** such as *Pseudomonas denitrificans*.

(iii) NITROGEN FIXATION. Something like 200–300 × 10^{12} g of soil nitrogen are lost each year by leaching, denitrification and ammonification. The loss is made good by **nitrogen-fixing bacteria** and **blue-green algae**. They are able to reduce nitrogen gas to ammonia which they use to form amino acids. Free-living bacteria such as *Azotobacter* and *Clostridium* and blue-green algae such as *Nostoc* account for 170–270 × 10^{12} g of nitrogen fixed annually. The rest is fixed by symbiotic bacteria, notably *Rhizobium* which lives in the nodules of legume roots (section 28.2.2). Before artificial fertilisers were generally available, farmers and gardeners boosted soil fertility by growing legumes in rotation with other crops.

2. THE CARBON CYCLE

The earth's atmosphere contains 2·5 × 10^{18} g of carbon dioxide. The oceans contain 150 times more. Terrestrial and aquatic organisms exchange about 100–200 × 10^{12} g of carbon dioxide annually with their surroundings. The exchange is mainly brought about by three activities (Fig. 29.26).

FIG. 29.26 *The carbon cycle*

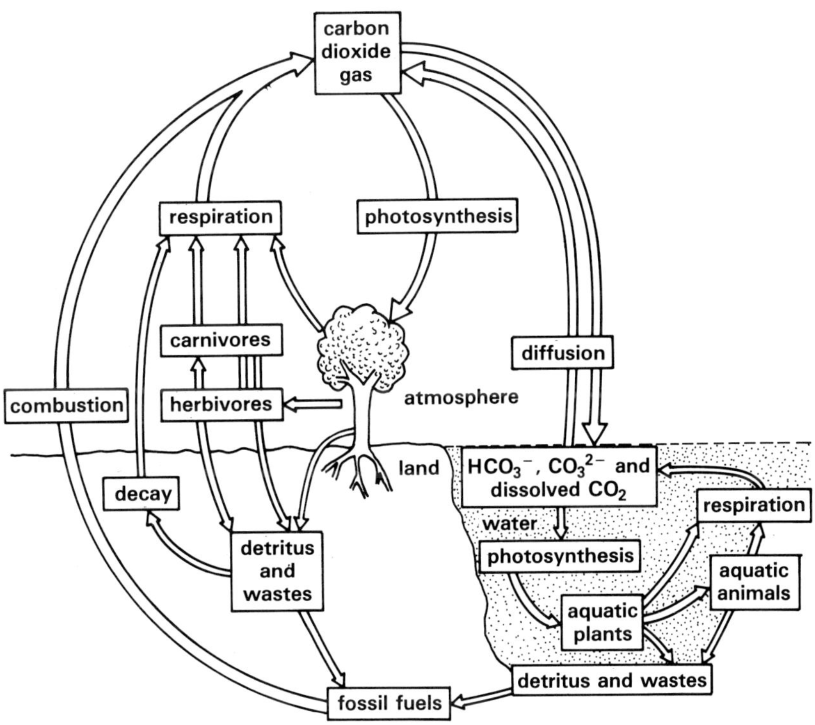

(i) PHOTOSYNTHESIS. Producers use carbon dioxide in photosynthesis. Each year, terrestrial plants remove between 50 and 100 $\times$ 10^{12} g of carbon dioxide from the atmosphere. Marine algae use about the same amount from the oceans. The standing crop of plants is an enormous reservoir of carbon. They hold about twice as much carbon as is contained in the atmosphere. Carbon fixed in photosynthesis millions of years ago, especially during the Carboniferous period, is preserved in vast reserves of fossil fuels such as coal, oil and natural gas. Peat is a recently-formed fossil fuel.

(ii) RESPIRATION. Living organs make carbon dioxide as a respiratory product. The amount of respiratory carbon dioxide released by producers is over half the amount they fix in photosynthesis. Consumers contribute about 10 per cent and decomposers and detritivores roughly 40 per cent of the carbon dioxide returned to the environment as a product of respiration.

(iii) COMBUSTION. Carbon dioxide is released when fossil fuels are burned. It is estimated that about 1–10 $\times$ 10^{12} g of carbon dioxide enter the atmosphere annually in this way. The amount of fossil fuels burned each year has increased over the past century. It is thought to be one of the reasons why the mean concentration of carbon dioxide in the earth's atmosphere is slowly rising (Fig. 30.1). The cutting-down of vast tracts of tropical forest may be another cause, because there is now less vegetation to remove atmospheric carbon dioxide in photosynthesis.

Ecologists have speculated on the possible effects of the increased carbon dioxide in the air. One possible consequence is what is called the **greenhouse effect**. The surface of the earth reflects some of the heat from the sun, thus warming the earth's atmosphere. When the atmosphere is enriched with carbon dioxide, it reduces the amount of heat escaping into space just as the glass in a greenhouse does. The consequence would be a rise in air temperature world-wide and much of the ice at the poles would melt. The resulting rise in sea levels would flood huge areas of farmland and most of the world's capital cities. An alternative possibility is that a rise in temperature would cause increased evaporation, making the earth's atmosphere more cloudy. Less heat from the sun could then reach the earth's surface, so compensating for the greenhouse effect. The fact that the outcome is the subject of great controversy tells us how little is known of the rates of the processes which bring about the cycling of carbon.

3. THE WATER CYCLE

Water has many roles in living organisms and life is impossible without it (Chapter 2). The total mass of water vapour in the atmosphere is equivalent to a mean rainfall of 2·5 cm a year over the earth's surface. The average rainfall is 90 cm a year, so water in the atmosphere is cycled

$$\frac{90}{2{\cdot}5} = 36 \text{ times a year.}$$

Rain does not fall evenly throughout the world. The amount falling on land determines to a large extent the abundance and distribution of terrestrial plants. Two processes are the cause of the cycling of water (Fig. 29.27).

(i) EVAPORATION. The earth's atmosphere has a lower water potential than living organisms, aquatic habitats and all but the driest of environments. Consequently, water constantly evaporates into the air. Most **evaporation** occurs over the oceans, from which about 1500 $\times$ 10^6 m^3 of water vapour pass into the atmosphere each day. This compares with approximately 200 $\times$ 10^6 m^3 each day from the land, roughly half from

FIG. 29.27 *The water cycle*

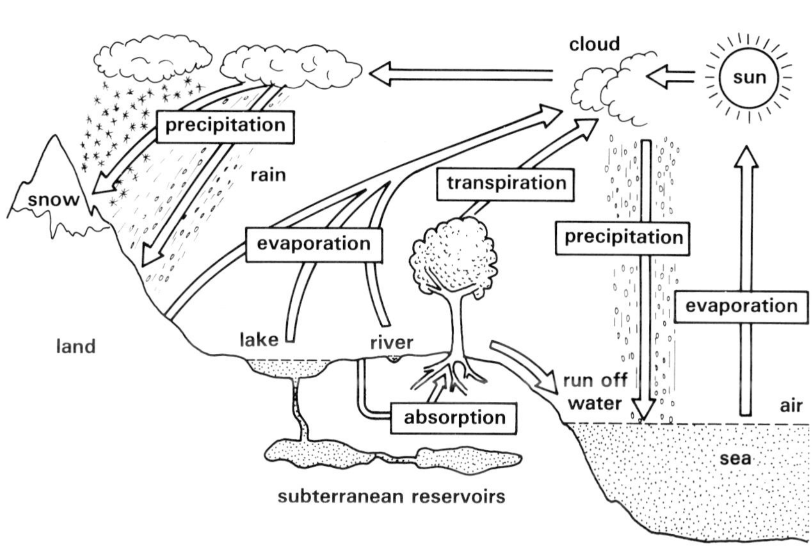

the soil and half from vegetation. Water vapour is less dense than air, so it rises to the upper atmosphere where the temperature is lower. Here it condenses, forming clouds of water droplets. Most clouds form over the oceans, where evaporation is greatest. Clouds sometimes evaporate when they absorb heat from the sun. Alternatively they are blown elsewhere, often over land where water precipitates from them.

(ii) PRECIPITATION. Water precipitates from clouds as rain, hail or snow. The mean daily **precipitation** over land is about 100×10^6 m^3 more than that lost by evaporation. The difference is because this amount of water runs off the land into the oceans in streams and rivers every day. The total precipitation of water over the earth is, however, the same as the amount evaporated, so the mean water vapour content of the atmosphere remains constant.

It is important to realise that evaporation and precipitation are uneven in different parts of the world. It explains why some terrestrial habitats are constantly wet, whereas others are arid. In many areas, precipitation is also seasonal and wet spells alternate with dry ones.

The rate at which water is cycled causes the rapid removal of a variety of atmospheric pollutants. The clearing of a haze after a shower is because dust, soot, smoke and other particles suspended in the air have been washed out. Rain also dissolves other atmospheric pollutants, such as sulphur dioxide.

The cloud cover in the atmosphere affects the earth's **heat balance**. Rain clouds reflect or absorb about 20 per cent of the radiation from the sun, mainly infra-red rays. Clouds also reflect heat radiating from the earth back to the earth's surface. The greenhouse effect is comparable to what we saw earlier with atmospheric carbon dioxide. It helps to prevent the loss of too much heat to outer space.

29.3.5 Soil as an ecosystem

Soil is a mixture of mineral particles and organic matter. It is the habitat for hordes of decomposers, detritivores and carnivores, as well as the roots of green plants which are the producers in the soil ecosystem. In addition to providing nutrients for its inhabitants, soil is their source of air, heat and water. Many of the stages in the cycling of matter also take place in soil.

FIG. 29.28 (a) *Soil profile under heather moorland*
FIG. 29.28 (b) *Profiles of* (i) *podsol, and* (ii) *brown earth*

(a)

1. SOIL PROFILES

When a deep trench is dug in soil, it is usual to see the soil in horizontal layers called **horizons**. The layering, which varies from one type of soil to another, is known as a **soil profile** (Fig. 29.28). Freshly deposited **detritus**, mainly leaves, twigs and fruits, make up the topmost horizon. Beneath it is a layer of partly decomposed detritus, then a well-rotted horizon of **humus**. In soils where earthworms are plentiful, humus is thoroughly mixed with the underlying horizon of mineral particles. Horizons L–A are the **topsoil**. It lies on the lighter-coloured B horizons which make up the **subsoil**. The roots of plants grow mainly in the topsoil.

(b)

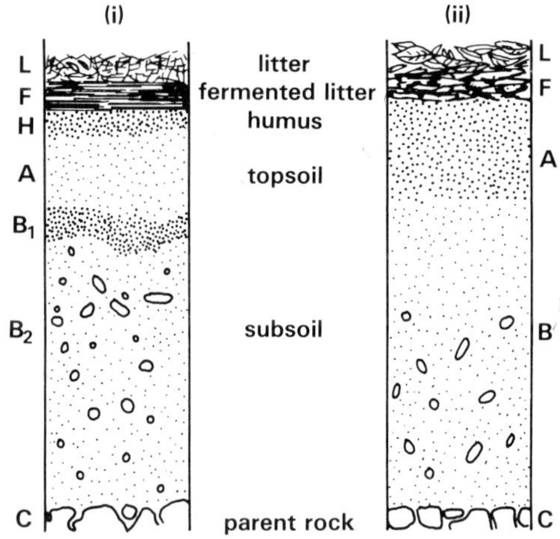

2. MINERAL PARTICLES

Sand, **silt** and **clay** are the mineral particles in soil. They are derived from rock by weathering and are of different sizes (Table 29.8). The mineral particles of **sedentary soils** come from the underlying rock. The parent rock of **sedimentary soils** may be a long way off, the particles having been carried by water before settling as a sediment. Sand and silt are made of silica, a material which is physically and chemically inert. Clay is composed of layers of aluminosilicates which can attract and hold mineral ions and water. The ions can be displaced by others in a process called **ion exchange**. They are then available for absorption by soil inhabitants and plant roots.

Table 29.8 Sizes of soil particles (International Society of Soil Science scale)

PARTICLE	DIAMETER (mm)
coarse sand	2·00–0·200
fine sand	0·20–0·020
silt	0·02–0·002
clay	< 0·002

The proportion of sand, silt and clay determines the feel or **texture** of a soil and also its **structure**. The mineral fraction of sandy soils contains more than 80 per cent sand particles by weight. When rubbed between the fingers, sandy soils have a friable gritty texture. Clay soils contain more than 40 per cent clay particles and have a clinging soapy texture. The structure of a soil is the way in which the particles bind into larger units called **aggregates**. A high proportion of clay usually causes the mineral particles to stick together in large **clods**. They make it difficult to obtain a fine tilth which is desirable for seedling growth. Loam soils contain small aggregates called **crumbs** in which clay, silt and sand are bound by humus and fungal hyphae. Adding lime to soils encourages crumbs to form by causing the **flocculation** of clay particles. Good crumb structure improves drainage and aeration of soil.

3. PORE SPACE AND AIR CAPACITY

Between the mineral particles are pores filled with air or water. The pores are the spaces in which the soil inhabitants live and plant roots grow. Clay soils have a large **pore space** but a low capacity for retaining air, because many of the pores are extremely fine and hold water even when drainage has occurred. In contrast, the **air capacity** of sandy soils is higher, despite the fact that the pore space is smaller than in clay soils. This is because water drains more easily through the coarser pores, which then become filled with air.

4. SOIL AIR

The air in the pore space is continuous with the earth's atmosphere, and gas exchange occurs between the two. **Soil air** in the uppermost horizons is little different in composition from the atmosphere. Deeper down, soil air generally contains more carbon dioxide and less oxygen (Table 29.9). The differences come about because of respiration by plant roots and the soil inhabitants. The extra carbon dioxide encourages autotrophic micro-organisms such as nitrifying bacteria. Aerobic micro-organisms use oxygen gas at such a rate that air-filled pores may become anaerobic. This explains why anaerobic nitrogen-fixing bacteria such as *Clostridium* thrive even in well-aerated soils.

Table 29.9 Comparison of composition of the atmosphere and soil air (after Russell 1961)

	% OXYGEN	% CARBON DIOXIDE
arable land (fallow)	20·4–21·1	0·02–0·38
grassland	16·7–20·5	0·30–3·30
atmosphere	20·97	0·03

Soil air is usually saturated with water vapour which helps to prevent desiccation of soil inhabitants.

FIG. 29.29 *Common rush* Juncus communis *growing in poorly-drained pasture*

5. SOIL MOISTURE

The moisture content of well-drained soils fluctuates mainly according to rainfall. After prolonged heavy rain, the pore space is filled with water and the soil is waterlogged. If a soil is **waterlogged** for a long time, anaerobic bacteria flourish. They include denitrifying and sulphate-reducing bacteria. Sulphate-reducers produce hydrogen sulphide which is toxic to roots. Root growth and mineral absorption are also inhibited in waterlogged soils. A few species of plants, such as the common rush, *Juncus communis*, can tolerate such conditions (Fig. 29.29). Waterlogging also slows down the rate at which organic matter is decomposed. This is why thick layers of partly decayed detritus accumulate in bogs and marshes as peat.

In places which are well-drained, gravity causes water to percolate through soil. The amount of water retained when **gravitational water** has drained away is the **field capacity** of the soil. A soil's ability to retain water draining through it depends on its structure and organic content. The smaller pores in clay soils hold moisture better than the coarser pores of sandy soils. Organic matter holds moisture like a sponge. The water-holding capacity of sandy soils can be improved by digging in organic matter in the form of peat or compost.

Water is held in the soil pores by capillarity. It is **capillary water** that is mainly accessible to plant roots and the inhabitants of soil. Capillary water is lost by evaporation and root absorption. If it is not replaced by rainfall or irrigation, a point is reached when the water potential of the soil is so low that roots are unable to absorb water. At this point plants begin to wilt. There is still **hygroscopic water** in the soil, but it is strongly held by clay particles and organic matter.

Soil water contains dissolved mineral ions and gases which soil organisms and plant roots may absorb.

6. ORGANIC MATTER

Small amounts of organic matter are made in soils by autotrophic micro-organisms. However, the quantities are insignificant compared with **detritus** in the form of dead leaves, twigs, fruits and roots from vegetation. In well-aerated soils, detritus is acted on by decomposers and detritivores and converted to black, amorphous **humus**. The type of humus which forms depends on the nature of the detritus and the soil inhabitants which break it down. **Mull humus** develops where deciduous trees grow in soils with a high calcium content. Earthworms, which abound in calcium-rich soils, pull enormous numbers of dead leaves into the soil. The humus which forms is thus thoroughly mixed with mineral particles in the topsoil, where a good crumb structure develops. **Mor humus** is acidic and is formed where coniferous trees or heathers grow in sandy soils with a low calcium content. Earthworms are scarce in such soils, so little detritus is mixed with the mineral particles. Most of the detritus stays on the surface of the soil, where it is humified.

Very thick deposits of **peat** accumulate in places where water stands permanently, such as bogs and fens. Peat is partly decayed detritus. Bog peat is very acidic, fen peat less so.

7. SOIL pH

The pH of a soil is governed primarily by the amount of calcium it contains. Calcium-rich mineral particles are formed when calcareous rocks such as limestone are weathered. Siliceous rocks such as sandstone and granite are weathered to form particles lacking calcium.

Some plant species, for example beech, *Fagus sylvaticus*, are tolerant of a wide range of soil pH. It grows in British soils with a pH ranging from 3·8 to 8·8. However, soil pH is an important factor governing the distribution of many species of plants. **Calcifuge** species such as heather, *Calluna vulgaris*, thrive in acid, calcium-deficient soils. Calcifuges can be grown in calcareous soils, provided plenty of acid peat is dug in first. **Calcicole** species such as dog's mercury, *Mercurialis perennis*, do best in alkaline soils where calcium is plentiful. Some calcicoles fail to thrive in acid soils because there is not enough calcium present. Others do not do well because they are poisoned by the high concentrations of aluminium and manganese in acid soils. Dressing acid soils with lime enables calcicoles to be grown.

The pH of soil also affects the distribution of soil organisms. Fungi are more tolerant of acid conditions than bacteria. A few species of earthworm are acid-tolerant but most prefer neutral or alkaline soils (Fig. 29.30).

FIG. 29.30 *Effect of soil pH on earthworm distribution* (after Satchell 1955)

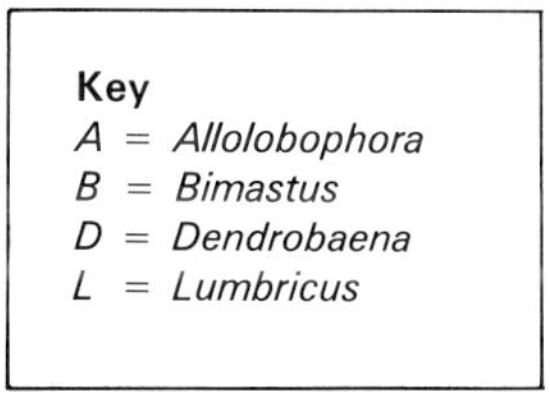

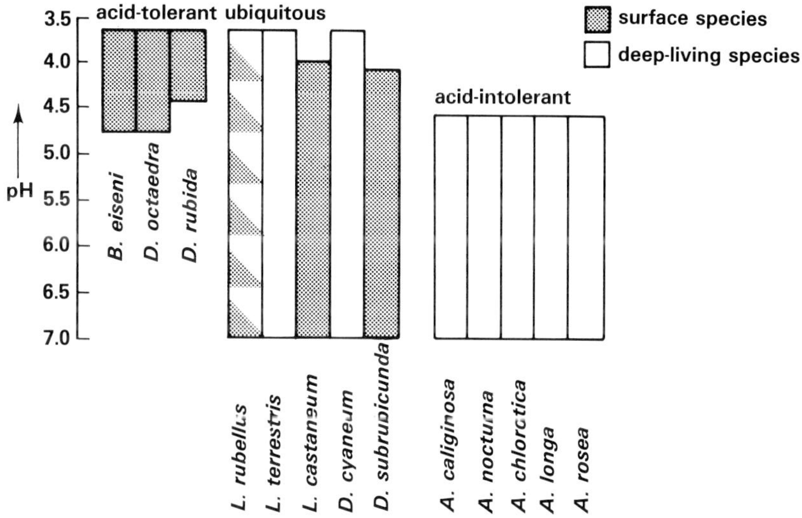

FIG. 29.31 *Temperature fluctuations in air and soil* (from Brown, "Ecology of Soil Organisms" published by Heinemann Educational Books)

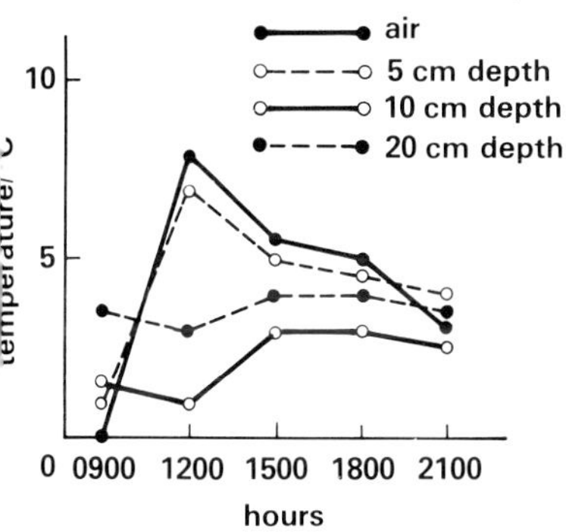

FIG. 29.32 *Effect of temperature on leaf burial by* Lumbricus terrestris (data from Edwards and Lofty 1972)

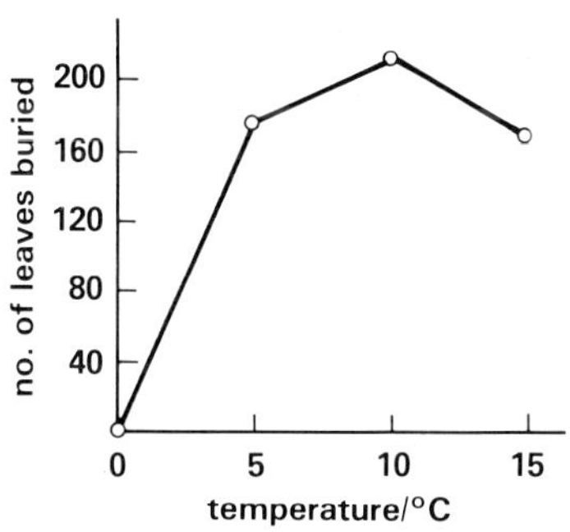

8. SOIL TEMPERATURE

The **temperature** of soil depends mainly on how much solar radiation reaches the soil's surface and how well the radiation is absorbed and conducted. Where vegetation forms a dense canopy, little radiation reaches the soil. Dark soils absorb heat better than light-coloured soils. However, a thick layer of dark detritus on the surface may absorb heat so well that little is transferred to the underlying horizons. Soils with a high moisture content absorb heat well, but do not warm up a great deal because water has a high specific heat capacity (Chapter 2). Nevertheless, water conducts heat better than air. Soils which are dry at the surface may therefore be cold deeper down.

Soil temperatures vary from season to season. In the upper horizons there are daily fluctuations in temperature too, whereas the temperature of the lower horizons is fairly stable (Fig. 29.31). Seeds fail to germinate and roots stop absorbing water and minerals if the temperature falls below 5°C. The activity of earthworms is also affected by temperature (Fig. 29.32). Much is still to be learned about the effect of temperature on many of the soil's inhabitants. Most are thought to be dormant at low temperatures.

9. SOIL MICROFLORA

Soil is the natural habitat for representatives of all the main groups of **micro-organisms**. Their activities are vital to the cycling of matter (section 29.3.4).

(i) BACTERIA are the most numerous of soil microbes. A gram of soil may contain as many as 1×10^9 bacteria. They have a live mass of up to 90 g in a square metre. Soil bacteria feed in two main ways:

(a) **Autotrophs. Photo-autotrophic bacteria** which use carbon dioxide as a source of carbon and solar radiation as an energy source live near the soil surface where sunlight is available. They photosynthesise in a way comparable to green plants. **Chemo-autotrophs** include nitrifying, denitrifying and sulphate-reducing bacteria. The quantity of organic material made by autotrophic bacteria is very small in comparison with the amount of detritus entering the soil. Their activities in the cycling of matter are much more important.

(b) **Heterotrophs**. The most abundant of heterotrophic bacteria in soil are the **decomposers**. They feed saprophytically, using a wide range of organic substances in detritus as a source of energy and nutrients. Some are able to decompose organic pesticides. Other heterotrophic soil bacteria are primary consumers. They feed as **parasites** on plant roots or as **symbionts**. The best-known of the symbionts are the nitrogen-fixing bacteria.

(ii) FUNGI are just as abundant as bacteria in neutral and alkaline soils. In acid soils, fungi are more plentiful. All soil fungi are heterotrophs. The majority are **decomposers** feeding saprophytically on detritus. As a source of energy they use a wide variety of organic compounds including lignin and cellulose which few bacteria can break down. Saprophytic soil fungi are therefore effective in decomposing woody detritus. Others are primary consumers living **symbiotically** as mycorrhizae or as root **parasites**. A few soil fungi are **predators** catching protozoans with sticky discs on their hyphae or lassooing nematodes in hyphal nooses.

(iii) ALGAE are found in all soils, but they are not very abundant. They are most plentiful near the surface of moist, undisturbed soils. In acid soils, unicellular and filamentous **green algae** are most plentiful. Neutral and alkaline soils are preferred by **diatoms**. **Blue-green algae** are often found in large numbers in soils which are waterlogged for lengthy periods of time. Their nitrogen-fixing ability is important in maintaining the fertility of paddy fields. Algae are producers, but they add little to the organic matter in soil.

(iv) VIRUSES are parasites. Those found in soil are mainly the cause of plant diseases and the bacteriophages which lyse bacteria.

FIG. 29.33 *Head ends of various nematodes* (a) *plant parasite,* (b) *detrivore,* (c) *predator*

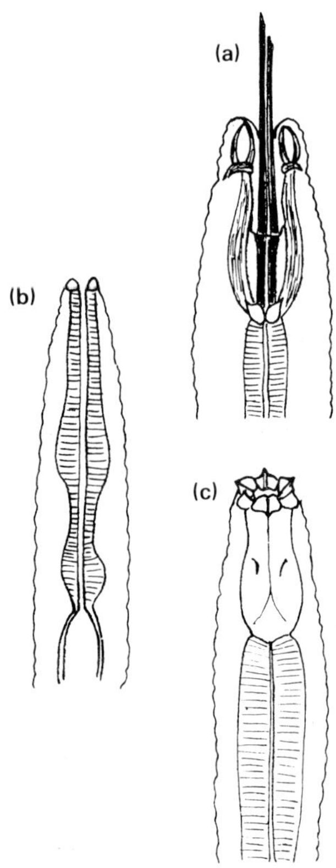

10. SOIL FAUNA

There are many animals which are found nowhere else but in soil. It is convenient to group them according to size.

(i) MICROFAUNA are only visible with a microscope. Flagellate, ciliate and rhizopod **protozoans** are common in most soils (Figs. 26.1–26.12). A few, such as *Euglena*, can photosynthesise and are producers. Some are detritivores consuming small fragments of detritus. The majority are primary consumers feeding on the plentiful supply of soil bacteria.

(ii) MESOFAUNA are soil animals between 0·2 and 10 mm long. A hand lens is required for the smallest of them to be seen clearly. The most abundant of the mesofauna are **nematodes**. Some are detritivores using their muscular pharynx to suck in small particles of detritus suspended in water. Many are primary consumers feeding as parasites on the juices of plant roots, which they pierce using sharp stylets. They often live permanently in roots and frequently are the vectors of viral diseases of plants. A few soil nematodes are predators on small soil animals, which they grasp using the tooth-like structures around their mouths (Fig. 29.33).

Arthropods are well-represented in soil (Fig. 29.34). Collembolans, commonly called **springtails**, are small wingless insects. They are called springtails because of the springing organ which is folded under the abdomen while the animal is at rest. When extended, it acts as a lever causing the insect to spring into the air. Many species of springtails are detritivores. Predatory **spiders** live near the surface of soil where they catch insect larvae, small centipedes and millipedes. The most ferocious of soil arthropods are the **false scorpions**, which are found mainly in detritus where they prey on spiders and springtails. **Mites** are the most abundant of

FIG. 29.34 *Soil mesofauna*

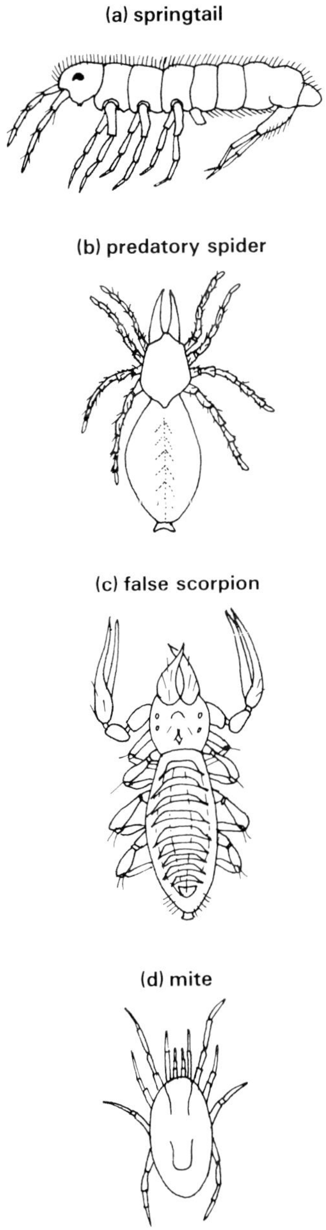

soil arthropods. They have a range of feeding habits. Some are detritivores using their blunt mandibles to chew dung and detritus. Others have a preference for fungal mycelia. Predatory mites capture nematodes and springtails, while spiders are the hosts for parasitic species.

(iii) MACROFAUNA are soil animals bigger than 10 mm in length. The arthropods are again well represented (Fig. 29.35). Many are **insects** or

FIG. 29.35 *Soil macrofauna*

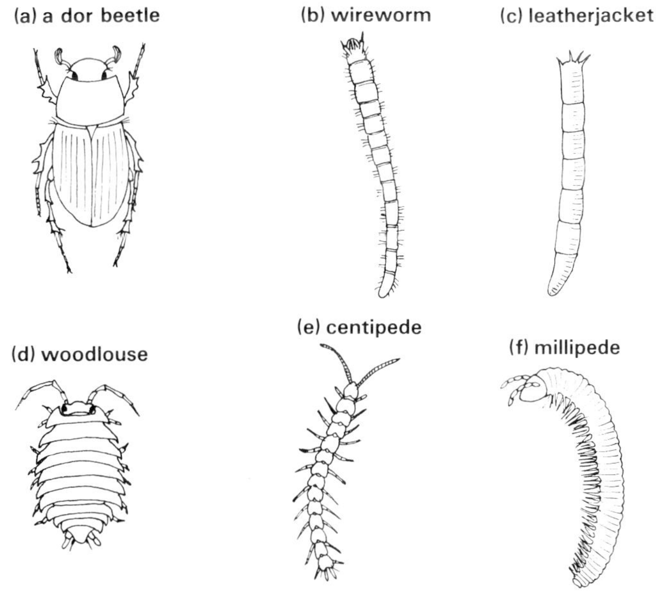

insect larvae. They include predators such as **ground beetles** which prey on mites, detritivores such as **rove beetles** which feed on carrion and **dorbeëtles** which eat cowpats. Primary consumers such as **wireworms** (larvae of the click beetle) and **leatherjackets** (crane fly larvae) which browse on plant roots are also present. **Crustaceans** are relatively few in soil; the most frequent are **woodlice** which are detritivores. **Chilopods** are represented by carnivorous **centipedes** which prey on mites and springtails. **Millipedes** are burrowing diplopods which are detritivores feeding mainly on leaf-litter.

Molluscs of the macrofauna are slugs and snails. They are best known as consumers of living plant material which they rasp away using their file-like radula (Fig. 26.67). However, many are omnivorous, eating detritus and carrion, while a few species of slugs are carnivorous, preying on annelids.

The best-known of soil **annelids** are the **earthworms**. There are twenty five species of earthworm in Britain. Ten are common in farmland and in gardens. Earthworms are detritivores feeding mainly on partly decayed leaves which they drag into their burrows. In this way they help to mix the mineral particles of soil with organic matter. Their burrows also help to aerate and drain the soil. Earthworms eat their way through soil as they burrow. The soil they egest is deposited underground or as casts on the soil surface. Casts are small piles of very fine soil rich in ammonia which improve the tilth and fertility of soil. Charles Darwin estimated that casting produced a top layer of soil 5 mm thick each year in his garden. In cultivated soils earthworms are fewer because many are killed by ploughing and are eaten by birds which follow the plough. Smaller than earthworms are the **enchytraeids**, commonly known as **potworms**. These annelids are detritivores feeding mainly on partly decayed detritus. They are present in larger numbers than earthworms in acid soils. Unfortunately, they are much less beneficial because they do not burrow.

11. DISTRIBUTION OF SOIL ORGANISMS

The types and numbers of soil inhabitants vary from one soil type to another (Table 29.10). As we have seen, soil moisture content, aeration and pH have an important bearing on the organisms present. Within the same soil, however, there is usually a **vertical distribution** of soil organisms. More of the inhabitants are found in the upper layers than in the deeper horizons (Fig. 29.36). Little has been done to find out the reasons for vertical distribution. However, it is possible to speculate on what the causes may be.

Table 29.10 Effect of soil type on earthworm populations (after Guild 1951)

SOIL TYPE	WORMS m^{-2}	NO. OF SPECIES
light sandy	57	10
medium loam	56	9
clay	40	9
peaty soil	14	6

FIG. 29.36 *Vertical distribution of some soil arthropods* (data from Jackson and Raw 1966)

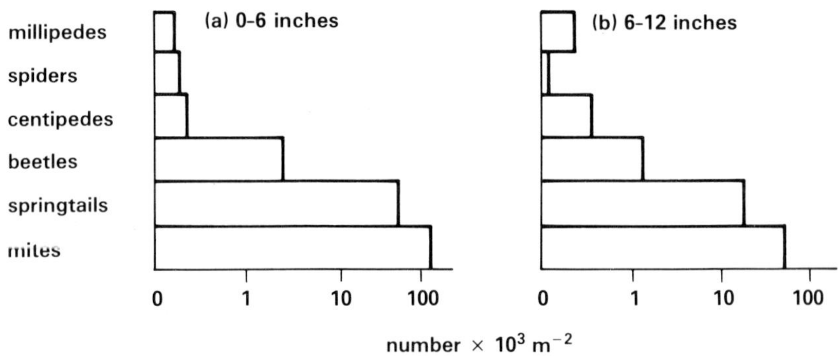

Algae and photo-autotrophic bacteria can only flourish where **light** is available. This is probably why they are active only at the surface of soil. The majority of soil organisms respire aerobically. It is possibly for this reason that many of them inhabit the upper horizons where **oxygen** is more abundant.

Many of the larger soil animals are unable to burrow, so are confined to the upper horizons. Smaller species may use the **burrows** of earthworms to get to the deeper layers, or they may be washed downwards by water percolating through the soil. Burrowing enables earthworms to inhabit the moister lower horizons where desiccation is less likely.

There is some evidence that availability of suitable **food** may account for the vertical distribution of different species of springtails. **Temperature** preference may be another factor influencing vertical distribution. Some species of mite move up and down in the soil in order, it is thought, to keep near to their optimum temperature. **Predation** and **competition** must also have a bearing on the vertical distribution of all soil organisms, but so far these factors have been little investigated.

One aspect about which rather more is known is the **rhizosphere** effect. As roots grow, surface cells are rubbed off by rough mineral particles. Young roots exude sugars and amino acids into the soil The effect is to encourage the activity of soil micro-organisms in the immediate vicinity of growing roots. The rhizosphere is a zone extending several millimetres from the root surface. In it soil microbes are many times more numerous than elsewhere. They compete with plant roots for nutrients, but are generally beneficial to plants. Some of them produce auxins which stimulate root growth, others are symbionts which may form an association with the roots. It is also possible that they keep parasites at bay.

12. DECOMPOSITION

Precisely what happens when detritus is broken down varies from one type of soil to another. It depends mainly on the nature of the detritus, decomposers and detritivores. The detritus in a meadow is mainly the soft leaves, stems and roots of grasses. Earthworms are usually abundant. In a coniferous forest, woody twigs and cones make up part of the detritus which consists mainly of tough, spiky leaves. Earthworms are scarce.

Very few comprehensive studies have been made of the decomposition process. Detritus usually contains a large proportion of cellulose and hemicelluloses. In woody detritus the cellulose is lignified. The amounts of starch, sugars and protein are usually small, because these materials are withdrawn from leaves before they fall and are stored elsewhere in plants. However, minerals are usually present, often in substantial amounts.

The decomposition of pine needles occurs in a number of stages:

Stage 1 Colonisation by fungi; needles dark brown but still intact.

Stage 2 Mesophyll collapsed, containing fungal hyphae and faeces of detritivores; needles greyish but still intact.

Stage 3 Needles fragmented and mixed with hyphal fragments and faeces of detritivores.

Stage 4 Needles humified and mixed with mineral particles.

Detritus usually has a high carbon: nitrogen ratio. As it is consumed by soil organisms the ratio falls. This is because the decomposers and detritivores use some of the carbon compounds for respiration, and carbon dioxide is released to the air. While the detritus is attacked by soil organisms it is leached of minerals by falling rain. The minerals are then available for absorption by plant roots. Eventually the only materials left are those resistant to decomposition or which cannot be digested by detritivores. Humus is an amorphous mixture of such compounds. Clearly the composition of humus varies according to the type of detritus and the way in which it has been decomposed.

13. FOOD WEBS IN SOIL

The **producers** of soil ecosystems are the vegetation, micro-organisms are the **decomposers**, and the soil fauna are the **consumers** (Fig. 29.37). As in most ecosystems, the **food web** is imperfectly known, mainly because much has still to be learned about the food preferences of the soil fauna.

14. NUTRIENT CYCLING AND ENERGY FLOW

Many of the stages in the cycling of **carbon** and **nitrogen** take place in soil

FIG. 29.37 *Food web in soil* (simplified)

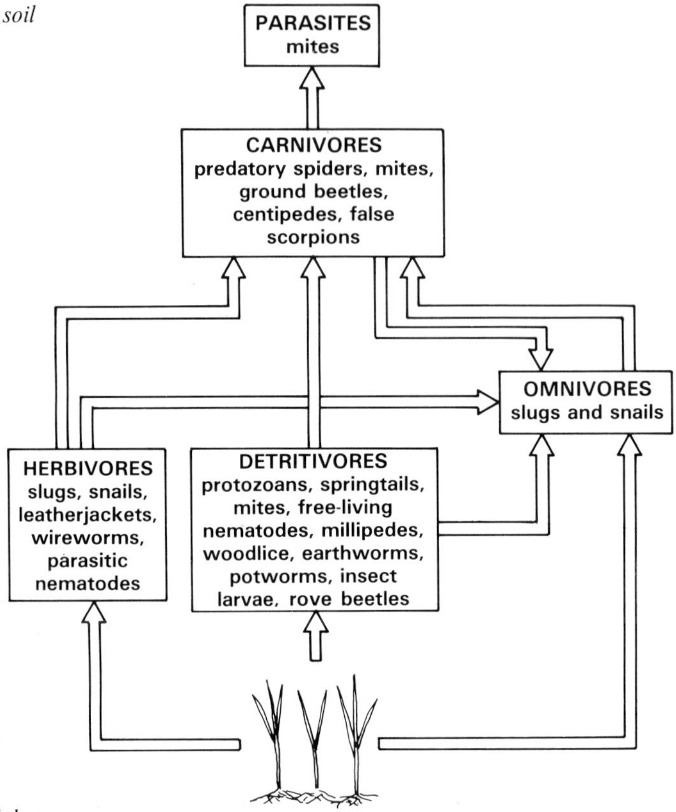

FIG. 29.38 (a) *The sulphur cycle* (b) *The phosphorus cycle*

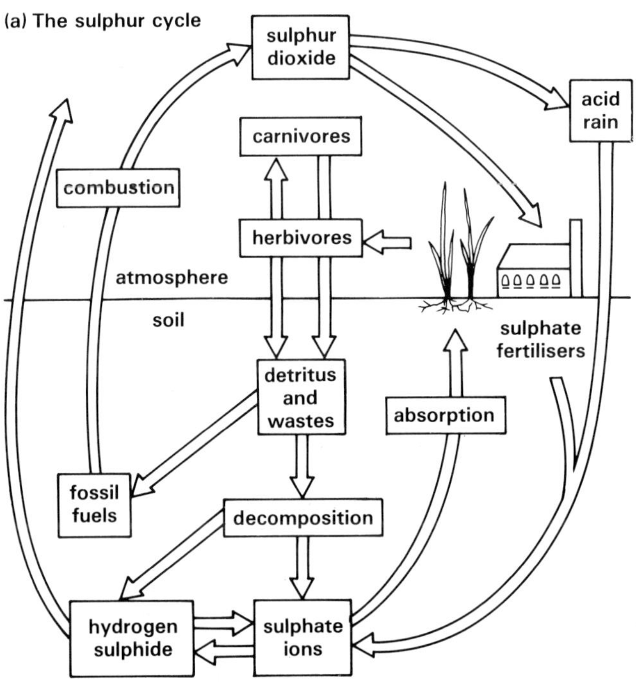

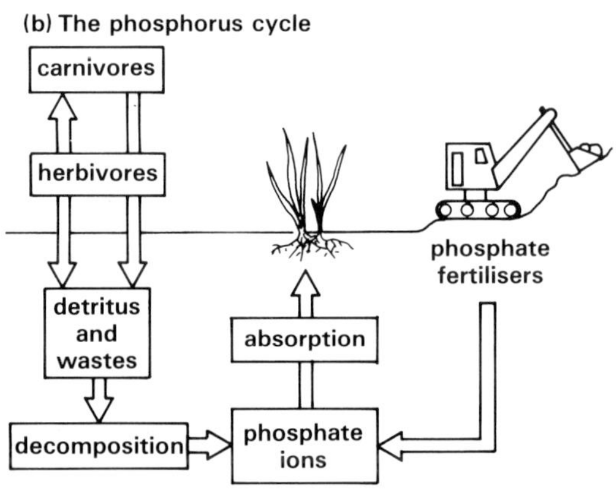

FIG. 29.39 *Annual cycling of five nutrients in a Belgian forest* (after Mason 1976)

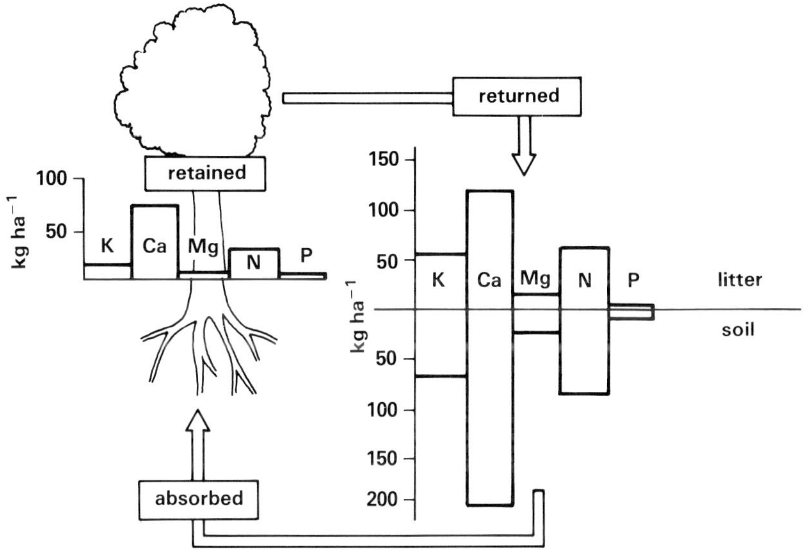

(section 29.3.4). Soil micro-organisms also play vital roles in the cycling of **phosphorus** and **sulphur** (Fig. 29.38). The repeating cycles of growth, death and decay ensure that minerals are constantly circulated among the soil community. Soil usually contains a much larger reservoir of minerals than the vegetation growing in it (Fig. 29.39).

In the past, ecologists concentrated mainly on counting the numbers of various kinds of organisms in soil samples. Today, interest is centred around their activities and in particular the **flow of energy** through the soil community. The few investigations which have been completed show that many of the detritivores are inefficient converters of energy (Table 29.11).

Table 29.11 Assimilation efficiencies of some detritivores (after Mason 1976)

DETRITIVORE	EFFICIENCY (%)
earthworms	1·00
millipedes	6–15
woodlice	15–30
mites	10–65
molluscs	50–75

The assimilation efficiency is $\frac{C - F}{C} \times 100$ where C = mass of food consumed and F = mass of faeces produced

This is because they are unable to digest much of the plant material they consume. Symbiotic microbes in the intestines of some detritivores may assist digestion in much the same way as in herbivorous mammals. A few detritivores, notably molluscs, produce cellulase enzymes in their digestive juices which considerably boost their efficiency of energy conversion. Nevertheless, the faeces of most detritivores contain much undigested plant material which decomposers can break down. Decomposers are also usually active in detritus before it is eaten by detritivores. It is for these reasons that it is presently thought that decomposers account for over 80 per cent of the energy entering the soil ecosystem.

Chapter 30

Pollution and conservation

There are many toxic substances in the biosphere. They are part of the natural cycling of matter (Chapter 29). For example, when volcanoes erupt they discharge poisonous gases and ash is scattered for miles around. However, the amounts of toxic materials arising from natural events are often small in comparison with those released into the environment by man. A good many toxic substances are man-made and are of recent origin. Some are the products of industry and man's attempt to eradicate or control pests on a large scale. Others are the results of people living close to each other in towns and cities. In such places, the sheer mass of domestic waste poses disposal problems.

Substances introduced into the environment by man which adversely affect living organisms, man included, are called **pollutants**. Growth of the human population, industry and agriculture are at the heart of many aspects of pollution.

30.1 Pollution of the atmosphere

The earth's atmosphere is a mixture of gases which is about 2000 km thick. The lowermost layer, about 10 km thick, is called the **troposphere**. It is with this layer that gas exchange occurs between the atmosphere and living organisms. Above it is the **stratosphere**, which contains ozone, a gas which absorbs ultraviolet and infra-red radiation from the sun. In this way terrestrial organisms are protected from excessive exposure to such forms of radiation. Ultraviolet radiation is one of the causes of mutations, while infra-red radiation raises the temperature of living organisms and can be the cause of sunstroke and sunburn.

Table 30.1 shows the composition of the troposphere at sea level in a clean-air area. Variable amounts of other gases such as neon, helium, krypton, xenon, methane, carbon monoxide, hydrogen, ammonia, sulphur dioxide, hydrogen sulphide, nitric and nitrous oxides are also present. They are there as part of the natural cycling of matter. Man's industrial activities have altered the amounts of the atmosphere's natural constituents. In recent times, man's technology has also caused new ingredients to enter the atmosphere. There is growing evidence that such changes are harmful to life.

Table 30.1 Composition of the troposphere at sea level

GAS	VOLUME (%)
nitrogen	78·08
oxygen	20·96
argon	0·93
carbon dioxide	0·03

The amount of water vapour varies from 0 to 4 per cent

30.1.1 Carbon dioxide

The burning of fossil fuels such as coal, oil and natural gas provides people with most of the energy they require for domestic, industrial and agricultural purposes. When such fuels are burned, **carbon dioxide** is released into the air. Data obtained from widely-spaced sampling points

FIG. 30.1 *Annual mean concentration of CO_2 in the air at three widely spaced sites* (from Spedding, "Air Pollution" published by OUP)

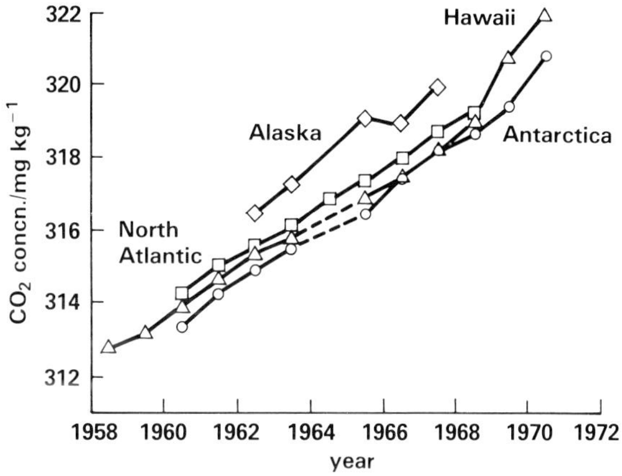

indicate that the amount of carbon dioxide in the air is increasing (Fig. 30.1). Two major effects of increasing atmospheric carbon dioxide are possible:

(i) It may stimulate photosynthesis by plants. However, this is unlikely, as other factors such as scarcity of minerals and light limit photosynthesis.

FIG. 30.2 *Temperature changes, measured and estimated in the northern hemisphere* (from Spedding as above)

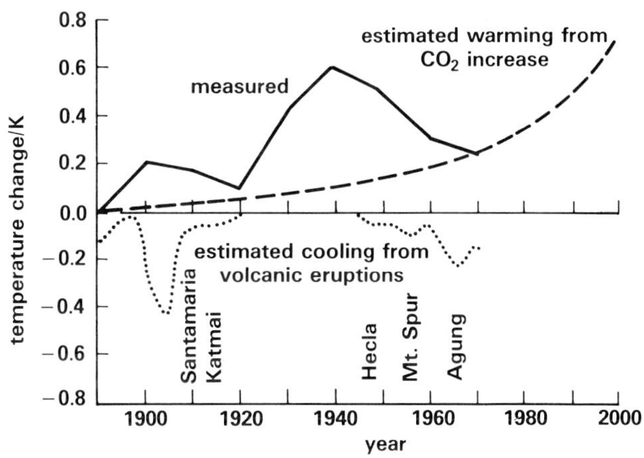

(ii) The greenhouse effect (section 29.3.4). Figure 30.2 shows the predicted change in world temperature up to the year A.D. 2000, based on present emissions of carbon dioxide. Of course, the use of alternative sources of energy such as nuclear fuels may in the near future bring about a reduction in the emission rate. The falls in measured temperature are thought to be due to increases in particulate matter in the atmosphere from industry and volcanic eruptions. Modern industries release less dust, soot and smoke, so any future falls in the measured temperature are more likely to be caused by natural events. If, however, the overall result is a gradual increase in temperature, it will bring about melting of the polar ice-caps, thus raising the level of the oceans. One of the consequences of this would be a flooding of large areas of low land on which many modern cities have been built.

30.1.2 Sulphur dioxide

Sulphur dioxide is released into the air when fossil fuels are burned and in the smelting of ores (Table 30.2). The *background* concentration is between 0·3 and 1·0 $\mu g\ m^{-3}$, but in areas near heavy industry the concentration is as high as 3000 $\mu g\ m^{-3}$. The effects can be beneficial or harmful.

Table 30.2 Annual sulphur dioxide emissions for Britain in 1965 (after Robinson and Robbins 1970)

SOURCE	EMISSION × 10^6 (TONNES)
coal	102·0
petroleum	28·5
copper smelting	12·9
lead smelting	1·5
zinc smelting	1·3

1. BENEFICIAL EFFECTS

Sulphur dioxide is oxidised to sulphate ions in the air. When precipitated in rainfall, sulphate can be absorbed from the soil by plant roots. Sulphur is an essential nutrient for plant growth, so its absorption as sulphate stimulates the growth of crops. The effect could be important in poor countries where chemical fertilizers are not used for economic reasons.

2. HARMFUL EFFECTS

(i) HUMAN HEALTH. The main danger occurs when humans are exposed to high concentrations of sulphur dioxide in combination with smoke arising from the combustion of fossil fuels (Fig. 30.3). The increased

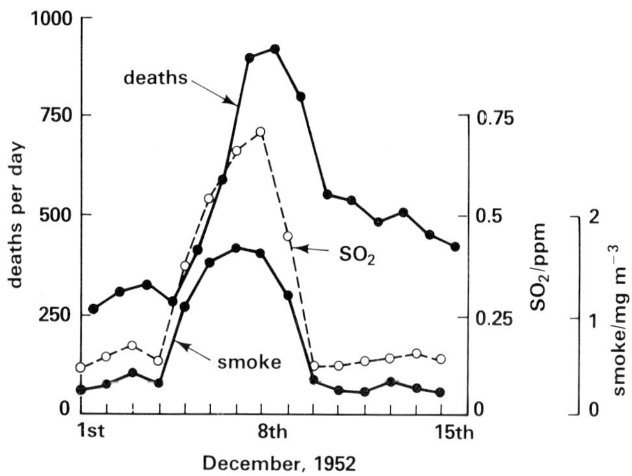

FIG. 30.3 *Human death rates and pollution of the air with soot and SO_2 in London* (from Mellanby, "The Biology of Pollution", Inst. Biol. "Studies in Biology" published by Edward Arnold)

number of deaths when these factors were present was mainly due to bronchitis, pneumonia and heart failure. Laboratory experiments indicate that sulphur dioxide slows down ciliary activity in the respiratory tract. Particulate matter is then not cleared in the usual way and reaches the alveoli, where it causes irritation and interferes with gas exchange. Bronchitis is the main cause of death in men over 45 years of age in Britain. About 30 million working days a year are lost by people who suffer from the condition.

(ii) EFFECTS ON PLANTS. Plants absorb sulphur dioxide through their stomata. The leaves of some important crop plants such as barley, wheat and cotton are damaged by high concentrations of sulphur dioxide in the air. Others such as potatoes, maize and onions are resistant. Lichens are especially sensitive and have been used as indicators of aerial pollution (Fig. 30.4).

FIG. 30.4 *Distribution of lichens in the Newcastle-on-Tyne area* (after Gilbert 1970)

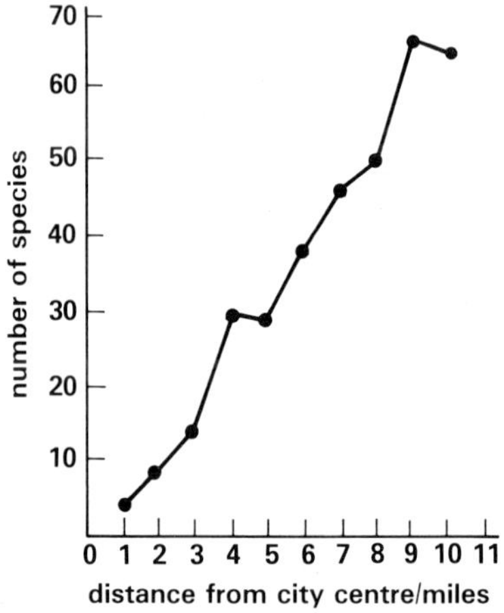

FIG. 30.5 *Soot and SO_2 emissions in London air after the passing of the Clean Air Act* (from Mellanby, "The Biology of Pollution" Inst. Biol. "Studies in Biology" published by Edward Arnold)

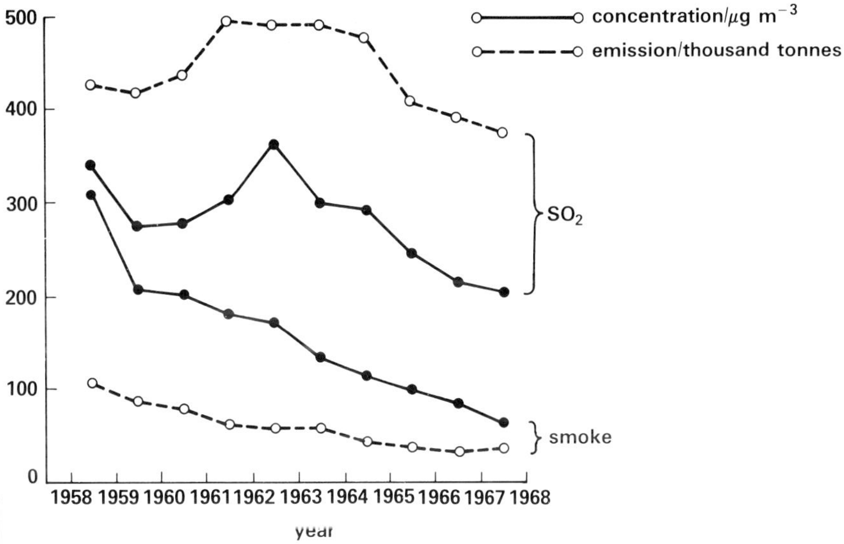

FIG. 30.6 *Accumulation of acid rain over Southern Norway* (from Ottaway, "The Biochemistry of Pollution" Inst. Biol. "Studies in Biology" published by Edward Arnold)

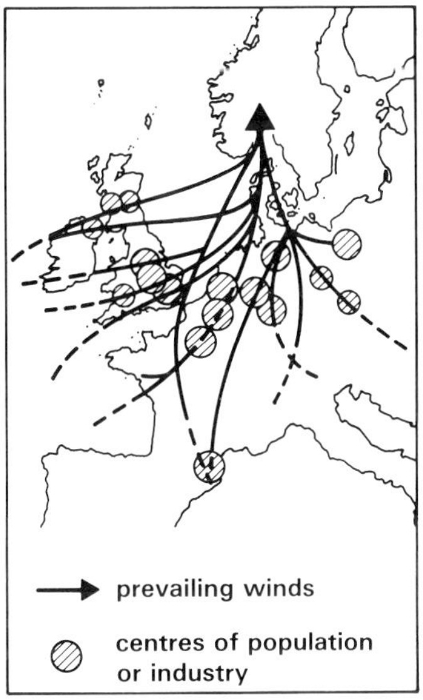

The implementation of the Clean Air Act 1956 has done much to reduce the amounts of sulphur dioxide and smoke in the air around and in British towns and cities in recent years (Fig. 30.5). Such improvements can only contribute to a reduction of some of the harmful effects mentioned. Even so, something like 30 million tonnes of sulphur dioxide are still released into the air in western Europe each year. It is blown by the prevailing winds to Scandinavia, where it falls as sulphuric acid in **acid rain** (Fig. 30.6). A high concentration of sulphur dioxide in the air is toxic to plants. Acid rain also lowers the pH of soil, bringing toxic elements such as aluminium into solution. The extensive damage to plantations of conifers in Sweden and Germany in recent years is probably due to a combination of such factors. The high concentration of aluminium leached from soils receiving acid rain is thought to be the reason for the massive decline in fish populations in Norwegian lakes in the past decade. So serious is the threat from acid rain that it was the sole topic at the 1982 Conference on the Environment held in Stockholm.

30.1.3 Particulate matter

The most obvious effect of the presence of particles in the air is a reduction in visibility. The smogs of the 1950s contained large amounts of smoke particles. **Smoke**, **soot** and **ash** particles are released into the air when fossil fuels are burned and ores refined. Ash and soot particles are heavy and are deposited near to their source of release. The smaller smoke particles remain suspended in the air for much longer. They are breathed in and may permanently blacken the alveoli, where they cause irritation and interfere with gas exchange. It was this which contributed to the increase in human deaths in the London smogs of the 1950s. Smoke particles may also contribute to the various forms of pulmonary ailments which are common among smokers.

30.1.4 Carbon monoxide

Haemoglobin has a much higher affinity for **carbon monoxide** than oxygen. Breathing in high concentrations of carbon monoxide reduces the blood's ability to carry oxygen to respiring tissues. Many people suffer from oxygen deficiency in their tissues when the carbon monoxide haemoglobin content in their blood reaches 5 per cent. Cigarette smokers often have up to 10 per cent carbon monoxide haemoglobin in their blood. It is this which is thought to be the cause of babies born to mothers who smoke heavily being smaller than those of non-smokers.

30.1.5 Oxides of nitrogen

Nitrogen oxides play an important role in the formation of **photochemical smog** which was first recognised in Los Angeles, USA. Both nitric oxide and nitrogen dioxide, as well as hydrocarbons, are present in the exhaust gases of motor vehicles. In sunny weather they become trapped near the ground by thermal inversion, causing a severe reduction in visibility. Ozone and **peroxyacyl nitrates** (PANs) are formed in the smog and cause eye and lung irritation, in addition to damage to vegetation and motor-vehicle tyres.

30.1.6 Metals

At the present time lead is considered to be the most serious metal pollutant in the atmosphere (section 30.2).

30.2 Pollution by heavy metals

Heavy metals are those with relative atomic masses above 100. **Lead**, **mercury** and **cadmium** are in this category. They accumulate in living organisms, reaching concentrations which inhibit enzyme activity.

30.2.1 Lead

Not all environmentalists agree that the present concentration of lead in our surroundings is harmful to life in general. However, there are many pieces of evidence which show that the amount of lead in the environment is increasing. There is lead in the air we breathe, in the water we drink and in the food we eat.

1. LEAD IN THE AIR

Combustion of petrol in motor vehicles accounts for over 80 per cent of the lead in air. Lead is added to petrol as **tetraethyl lead** (TEL) which serves as an **anti-knock compound**. It improves the efficiency with which petrol is burned in internal combustion engines. Most of the lead comes out in the exhaust gases as lead chloro-bromide (PbClBr). In rural areas, about 20 per cent of the lead taken in by humans comes from the air. It is over 50 per cent in towns and cities. People who work close to motor vehicles have higher concentrations of lead in their blood than those who do not (Table 30.3).

Table 30.3 Concentrations of lead in the blood of people in Cincinnati, USA (after Lagerwerff 1972)

OCCUPATION	LEAD CONCENTRATION (μg per 100 ml blood)
office worker	19
policeman	21
postman	23
parking attendant	34
garage mechanic	38

2. LEAD IN WATER

Tributaries of some Welsh rivers such as the Rheidol and Ystwyth are devoid of fish life. They receive water from disused **lead mines**. In places, the concentration of lead is more than 0·5 ppm, which is toxic to freshwater fish. Only a few species of algae and insects survive.

Lead poisoning was common among Ancient Romans. It happened because **lead tanks and pipes** were used to supply drinking water. The water pipes in many older houses today are made of lead. They contribute substantially to the intake of lead by some people.

3. LEAD IN FOOD

Lead in the air is washed out by falling rain. Soil near to busy roads is more likely to be polluted in this way than elsewhere (Fig. 30.7). **Composts** made

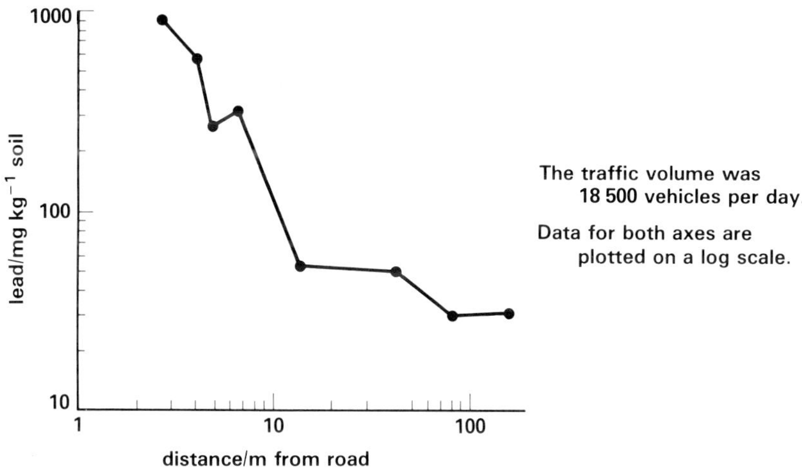

FIG. 30.7 *Lead in surface soil as a function of distance from a highway* (after Harrison and Laxen 1981)

from sewage sludge may also contain relatively high concentrations of lead. Plant roots absorb lead from polluted soil. Foliage may also take in lead from the air. Either way, the amount of lead in plants may impair human health if the contaminated plants are eaten. The amount of lead in **canned foods** is higher than in fresh foods. This is because lead solders are used to seal cans.

4. LEAD IN MAN

Whether inhaled or ingested, lead is absorbed into the blood and **accumulates** in the liver, kidneys and bones. About 90 per cent of lead in the body is in the bones and teeth. The amounts of lead absorbed from air, food and water have been measured in the USA (Table 30.4). Food is the main source, wherever people live. In urban areas, lead from air makes up a large proportion of absorbed lead. Most of it is thought to have come from car exhausts. There is evidence that the **mental development** of children in urban areas may be affected by the lead they breathe in. For this reason, it is policy in Britain to reduce lead in petrol by two-thirds in 1985.

Tobacco smokers take in more lead than non-smokers, because nicotine is thought to stimulate the absorption of lead by the lungs.

Table 30.4 Average daily intake of lead by people in USA (after Walker 1975)

SOURCE	LEAD ABSORBED PER DAY (μg)
food	17·0
water	1·0
urban air	10·4
rural air	0·4
tobacco smoke	9·6

30.2.2 Mercury

Mercury is as hazardous to living organisms as lead. An estimated 230 tonnes of mercury reach the oceans from natural sources, mainly the weathering of rocks. Worldwide production of mercury for industrial and agricultural uses amounts to more than 7000 tonnes annually, of which 25 to 50 per cent is believed to be discharged into the environment. Mercury is used extensively as a floating electrode in the production of chlorine and caustic soda from brine. It is also used as a catalyst in the manufacture of vinyl plastics. Organic mercury fungicides are used to preserve wood pulp and as seed dressings to ensure good germination.

1. MERCURY IN THE AIR

When coal and oil are burned, mercury is released into the air. Ore-refining is another source of aerial mercury. Mercury also evaporates from the earth's crust. High concentrations of atmospheric mercury detected by *sniffer* aircraft are valuable indicators of where ores of mercury can be found.

2. MERCURY IN WATER

Rain picks up mercury as it falls through the air. Waste water from paper mills and factories making vinyl plastics also contains mercury. Most of the mercury accumulates in mud at the bottom of rivers, lakes and seas. There it is converted to **methyl mercury** by methane-producing bacteria. Methyl mercury is volatile and very toxic. It is absorbed by aquatic organisms which may be part of a food web involving man.

3. MERCURY IN FOOD

In the recent past, **sprays** and **seed dressings** containing mercury were used a great deal to prevent and to control many plant diseases caused by pathogenic fungi. The annual usage of mercury worldwide for this purpose was 140 tonnes in 1967. It fell to about half this amount by 1970 and the trend is still downward.

Mercury is retained in the upper layers of well-drained soils. From here it is absorbed by the roots of plants. Mercury in sprays is taken in through the leaves. Translocation to the fruit and other edible parts of plants ensues. Mercury poisoning has occurred in wood pigeons consuming dressed seed. In Sweden, Canada and the USA freshwater fish have been shown to contain much higher concentrations of mercury than marine fish (Table 30.5). It is thought to have entered lakes in the waste water from **wood pulp mills**. The pollution is so bad in parts of North America that commercial fishing in some lakes has been banned in the past few years.

Table 30.5 Concentrations of mercury in Swedish freshwater and marine fish (after Walker 1975)

SPECIES	HABITAT	MERCURY CONCENTRATION (ppm)
mackerel	marine	0·06–0·08
herring		0·03–0·11
cod		0·15–0·19
pike	freshwater	5·00

4. MERCURY IN MAN

The appalling events at Minamata and Niigata, Japan, in the 1950s underlined the danger to man of pollution by mercury. At Minamata 111 people were seriously affected by mercury poisoning and 46 of them died. Shellfish caught in Minamata Bay made up a large proportion of their diet. It was later discovered that a vinyl plastics factory had for some time discharged waste water into the bay. Table 30.6 shows the concentrations of mercury in the seawater and in marine organisms from Minamata Bay in 1960. Note how the mercury had **accumulated** higher up the food chain.

Table 30.6 Concentrations of mercury in seawater and marine organisms from Minamata Bay in 1960

SOURCE	MERCURY CONCENTRATION
seawater	1·6– 3·6 ppb
plankton	3·5–19·0 ppm
shellfish	30–102 ppm

Post-mortem examinations revealed high concentrations of mercury in the kidneys, liver and brain of those poisoned (Table 30.7). At Niigata, 120 people were poisoned by mercury in similar circumstances. The victims had eaten up to three fish meals a day. At both places the survivors were partially or totally paralysed and had lost most forms of sensation. Many were blinded. Mothers who three years earlier had shown no signs of mercury poisoning bore infants who suffered from mental retardation and cerebral palsy. The developing foetuses had evidently accumulated mercury from their mothers' blood.

Table 30.7 Concentrations of mercury in body organs of Minamata victims[1] and a control group[2] of humans

ORGANS	MERCURY CONCENTRATION	
	1	2
kidneys	106 ppm	1·0 ppb
liver	42 ppm	3·0 ppb
brain	21 ppm	0·1 ppb

30.2.3 Other heavy metals

Copper enters streams and rivers in drainage water from copper mines and in the liquid effluent from copper-plating works. It is a very toxic metal. Freshwater plants and fish are killed by less than 1 ppm of copper. Fish absorb it through their gills. The rate at which water passes over the gills therefore determines how much copper is absorbed in a given time. In water containing a low concentration of dissolved oxygen, gill ventilation is rapid. In such conditions fish are more quickly killed by copper polluting the water.

Copper also pollutes the spoil heaps of copper mines. Its presence limits the vegetation to copper-tolerant metallophytes (Chapter 13). Pollution of soil by copper has occurred in some English orchards. It gets there from copper-containing fungicides, such as Bordeaux mixture, which have been sprayed on the trees for over a hundred years. The polluted soil is devoid of most kinds of animal life. The absence of earthworms is thought to be the reason why a thick layer of poorly decayed detritus has accumulated on the soil surface.

Zinc appears in streams and rivers in the effluent from zinc mines. Water boatmen and the larvae of caddis and stone flies tolerate up to 500 ppm.

Freshwater fish are killed by less than 1 ppm. As with copper, fish are more quickly killed in poorly aerated water. Most terrestrial plants can tolerate up to 7 ppm of zinc in soil. The spoil heaps near zinc mines contain much more than this and are inhabited by zinc-tolerant metallophytes.

The air in the vicinity of zinc smelters is polluted with oxides of zinc and cadmium. Humans absorb **cadmium** from the air through their lungs and there is some evidence that people working and living near smelters suffer from acute cadmium poisoning. Cadmium concentrates in the kidneys, causing renal damage and high blood pressure. The drainage water from zinc mines also contains cadmium. In the Jintsu Basin of Japan, where riverwater containing such effluent is used to irrigate paddy fields, people suffer from a chronic form of cadmium poisoning called *itai-itai*. Minerals are withdrawn from the bones and there is severe pain. Cadmium is taken up by the rice crop, which is a staple part of the diet of the Japanese. They therefore ingest much more cadium then people living in unpolluted areas.

30.3 Pesticides

A wide range of toxic chemicals called **pesticides** is used by man to control or eradicate pests.

30.3.1 Herbicides

Herbicides make up about 40 per cent of the world's production of pesticides. They are used to control or eliminate weeds. Gardeners use herbicides to get rid of daisies, dandelions, plantains and other weeds growing in lawns. Farmers use them to eliminate weeds such as thistles, docks and poppies, which grow among cereal crops and in pastures. Herbicides are also used in forestry to kill forest weeds such as rhododendrons and gorse. Railways are kept free of weeds by spraying herbicides on the track.

Many herbicides are similar to auxins (Chapter 21). Auxin-like herbicides are biodegradable and are soon broken down to harmless products by soil bacteria. For this reason they seldom cause environmental problems. However, an impurity which is present in one group of herbicides has recently given cause for concern. Several widely-used herbicides are derivatives of trinitrophenol, for example 2:4:5 trichlorophenoxyacetic acid (2:4:5T). In manufacturing trinitrophenol, an impurity called **dioxin** is formed and this is usually present in 2:4:5T. Dioxin has been shown to be harmful to humans. It is so potent that half a gram of it can kill 3000 people. Although it is normally present in only small amounts in 2:4:5T, dioxin is a potential threat because a good deal of the herbicide is released into the environment. In the USA, over 3000 tonnes of 2:4:5T are used annually, mainly in forestry. In the UK, about 3 tonnes are used each year, chiefly by British Rail and the Forestry Commission.

The effects of dioxin on humans and its potential effects have been studied in three main ways:

1. LABORATORY STUDIES

When small amounts of dioxin are painted on to the ears of rabbits, the treated area develops a very severe form of acne known as **chloracne**. When given to animals in their food and water, dioxin has been shown to be one of the most potent of poisons (Table 30.8). The animals which died in these experiments showed general wastage of body tissues and organs. **Tumours** and **cancer** were frequent. A number of serious **teratological defects** (defects of the foetuses) were observed when dioxin was given to pregnant animals. They included cleft palate, kidney malfunction, enlarged livers

Table 30.8 Minimum dose of dioxin required to kill 50% of a batch of animals (LD 50 values)

SPECIES	LD 50 (ppm)
rat	0·0005
mouse	0·1000
guinea pig	0·0006

and internal haemorrhage. In monkeys, whose anatomy and physiology are very similar to those of humans, spontaneous abortion, haemorrhage, difficulty in conception, gangrene of the fingers and toes and loss of hair occurred even at the lowest dosage tested.

2. VIETNAMESE AND AMERICAN FORESTS

Eleven million gallons of 'Agent Orange' (50 per cent 2:4:5T) were sprayed by the Americans onto the forests of Vietnam in the 1970s. The herbicide defoliated the trees, making it easier to observe enemy movements. It has since been shown that defects among children born in the contaminated areas are much higher than normal. USA servicemen working in the area later fathered children with **physical and mental handicaps**. Dioxin was found in the bodies of the fathers. More recently, **miscarriages** in women living in the forests of Oregon, USA, where 2:4:5T has been used for several years, have been greater than expected. It has led to a temporary ban on the use of the herbicide in this part of the USA. For these reasons there has also been a campaign to stop the use of 2:4:5T in Britain.

3. FACTORY ACCIDENTS

There have been several major explosions at factories where trinitrophenol is produced. One of the most recent was at Seveso, Italy, in 1976. Cats and dogs died in large numbers. There were 400 cases of **chloracne** in children alone. **Miscarriages** and **cancer** rates were higher than normal. Chloracne among workers and their families, abnormal liver function and higher incidences of skin and heart disease followed an explosion at Bolsover, England in 1968. The effects of an accident at Nitro, West Virginia, USA in 1949 are still unknown. Recently, a comprehensive survey of the health of the affected people has been carried out. The results are awaited and could be vitally important because some conditions such as cancer often have a long latent period. There is little doubt that some dioxin was released in the explosions and was taken into the bodies of workers and people living nearby by absorption through the skin and lungs and by swallowing.

30.3.2 Fungicides

Compounds containing mercury and copper are the most serious pollutants of the **fungicides**. Their environmental effects are discussed in section 30.2.

30.3.3 Insecticides

Chemicals which kill insects have been known for a long time. Before 1940, the **insecticides** most widely used were natural products such as pyrethrum and nicotine. Since then, two groups of synthetic insecticides, organochlorine and organophosphorus compounds, have replaced the older insecticides. Like pyrethrum and nicotine, organophosphorus insecticides are biodegradable and are quickly broken down into harmless products in the environment. Although very toxic, they are not pollutants if used in a responsible way. In contrast, **organochlorine insecticides** persist for many years in the environment. Their persistence has been the cause of pollution.

The best-known of the organochlorine insecticides is **DDT** (dichloro-diphenyl trichloroethane). It was first made nearly a century ago, but its insecticidal powers were not realised until the Second World War. Its non-toxicity to man and its effectiveness in killing insects led people to believe that DDT would soon eradicate insect pests. Malaria, yellow fever and other insect-borne diseases would become a thing of the past. Organo-chlorine insecticides such as **aldrin**, **dieldrin**, **heptachlor** and **lindane** were just as effective in eradicating insect pests of crops. Hopes were high that the agricultural use of such compounds would eliminate starvation in developing countries. Today the widespread use of DDT and some of the other organochlorine insecticides has been banned in many developed countries. People die in their millions each year of insect-borne diseases and crops are still ravaged by insect pests. What has gone wrong?

1. OVERUSE

Rachel Carson's aptly titled book, *Silent Spring* (1963) publicised the ecological effects of the **overuse** of organochlorine insecticides in the USA. In places where farmers were grossly exceeding the recommended dose rate, there were hardly any songbirds. Some had been killed by breathing in air containing large amounts of organochlorine insecticides or by eating contaminated food. The massive reduction of the songbird population was, however, mainly caused by the insecticides reducing their fertility. Many of the eggs which were laid failed to hatch. Enough of the insecticides had also been leached from the land to kill fish in nearby rivers and lakes.

Table 30.9 Persistence of some organochlorine insecticides (after Walker 1975)

COMPOUND	TIME FOR 95% LOSS (YEARS)
Dieldrin	4–30
DDT	5–25
Lindane	3–10

2. PERSISTENCE

Organochlorine insecticides are very stable substances. They persist unchanged for a long time in the environment (Table 30.9). **Persistence** increases the chances of poisoning non-target organisms. In the 1950s, thousands of seed-eating birds were poisoned after eating cereal grain dressed with aldrin and dieldrin. Endotherms convert DDT to less toxic DDE; aldrin to dieldrin. The amounts of DDE and dieldrin in the flesh and eggs of birds provide an estimate of the extent of pollution of the environment by organochlorine insecticides. Such a survey was carried out between 1960 and 1965 in Britain after reports of a severe decline in the numbers of predatory birds such as the peregrine falcon and golden eagle (Fig. 30.8). The survey showed that predatory birds had higher concentrations of DDE and dieldrin in their bodies than other species (Fig. 30.9). The insecticides had probably entered the flesh-eating species along a food chain.

Because they are insoluble in water, the organochlorine compounds are stored in fatty tissues instead of being excreted. In this way they **accumulate**

FIG. 30.8 (a) *Distribution of peregrine falcons in Britain in 1961* (from Mellanby, "The Biology of Pollution" Inst. Biol. "Studies in Biology" published by Edward Arnold)
(b) *Peregrine falcon* (B&B photos)

The first number shows the percentage of territories occupied, the second (in box) the percentage in which young were reared (from Mellanby 1967 after Ratcliffe)

(a)

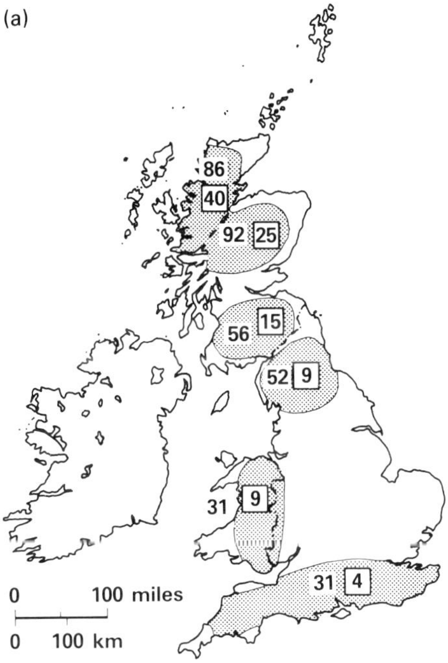

(b)

FIG. 30.9 *Residues of organochlorine insecticides in British birds* (from Walker 1975)

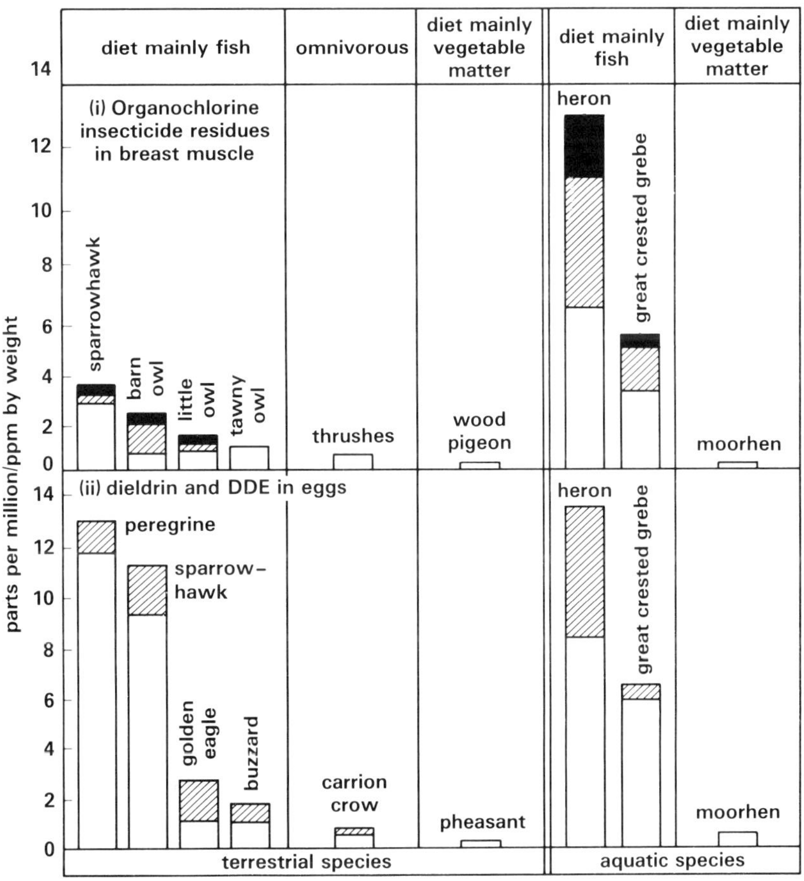

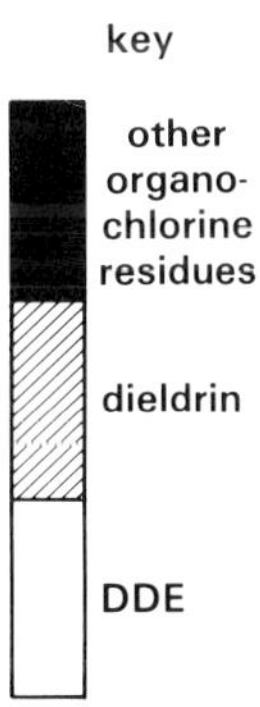

at each trophic level. Toxic amounts of DDE and dieldrin are probably released into the bloodstream when fat reserves are used at times of food shortage and at egg-laying. Laboratory experiments show that sublethal amounts of organochlorine insecticides cause birds to lay eggs with thin, fragile shells. When incubated by the parents, they are likely to be broken. A study of the eggshells of peregrine falcons showed that they had become significantly thinner after organochlorine insecticides came into general use in Britain in the 1940s (Fig. 30.10). Circumstantial evidence of this kind led

FIG. 30.10 *Change in time of the eggshell index of the peregrine falcon in Britain* (from Ratcliffe Journal of Applied Ecology, Vol. 7, published by Blackwell Scientific Publications Ltd)

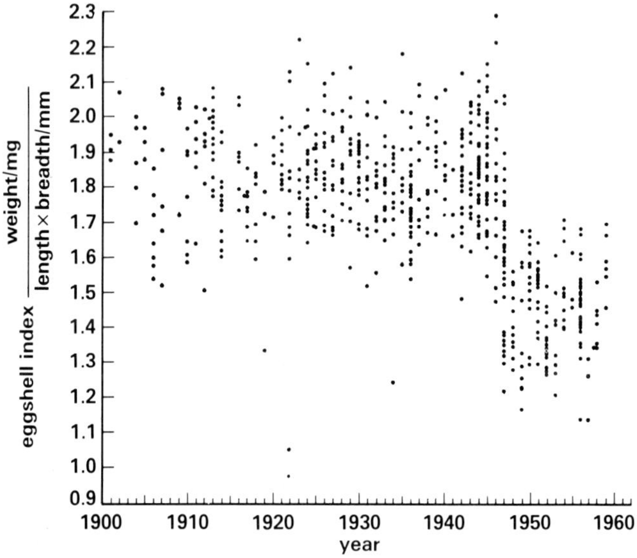

to a restriction of the use of organochlorine insecticides for agricultural purposes in the USA. Britain and other western countries adopted similar measures in the late 1960s. Subsequently there has been a marked improvement in the breeding success of predatory birds.

3. RESISTANCE

Soon after DDT was introduced, houseflies in Italy were found to be unaffected by it. They had acquired a means of converting DDT to less toxic DDE. It is now known that over 100 species of insect vectors have developed a **resistance** to organochlorine insecticides (Fig. 30.11). It is for this reason that any hope of eradicating malaria in the near future has

FIG. 30.11 *The number of insects of public health importance which have developed resistance to insecticides* (from Ottaway, "The Biochemistry of Pollution" Inst. Biol. "Studies in Biology" published by Edward Arnold)

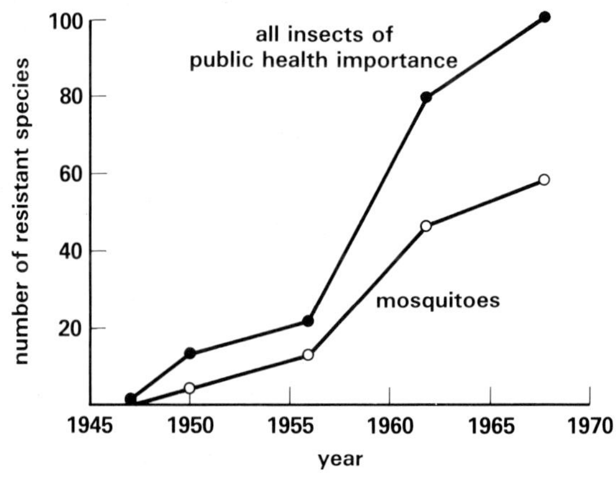

subsided. More than 200 species of insects which are pests of crops are also resistant. Whilst this is not a pollution problem, it does give cause for concern to those who have to control insect pests and insect-borne diseases.

The adverse environmental effects of pesticides have often presented the latter in a rather bad light. However, it is important to take an objective view. There is little doubt that they have saved millions of people from disease and starvation. Much of the publicity centred around them has stimulated research into producing safer pesticides and alternative ways of pest control. There is now a move towards **integrated control** of pests. It involves using natural methods of control where possible and resorting to the use of pesticides only when necessary. A typical example is the control of the red spider mite, a pest of greenhouse plants such as tomatoes and cucumbers. Its numbers can be kept in check by introducing another species of mite which preys on red spider mites. Unfortunately, the predator does not do well near the roof where the temperature is high. Any red mites here can be killed with a pesticide spray. The amount of pesticide used is much less than required if it was the only control available.

30.4 Radiation

Ever since life evolved, living organisms have been subjected to various forms of **radiation**. The most obvious is visible light. The sun radiates ultraviolet and infra-red waves. Radiation also comes from outer space as cosmic rays, and from radioactive minerals in rocks. Natural forms of radiation are not thought of as pollutants. Radiation introduced into the environment by man is a form of pollution.

30.4.1 Forms of radiation

The forms of radiation which pose a threat to the well-being of living organisms fall into two categories:

1. ELECTROMAGNETIC WAVES

Gamma-rays are **electromagnetic waves** with a wavelength of about 10^{-12} m. Their very short wavelength gives them considerably more energy than visible light and consequently much better powers of penetration. Gamma-rays are emitted when radioactive atoms (**radionuclides**) distintegrate or when atomic nuclei are bombarded with sub-atomic particles.

2. SUB-ATOMIC PARTICLES

Alpha-particles are given off when radionuclides break down. They are positively charged, consisting of two protons and two neutrons. When they collide with anything solid, α-particles lose a good deal of energy. **Beta-particles** are electrons and have a negative charge. They are not very penetrating. Like α-particles, they soon lose energy when they hit something solid. It is for this reason that α- and β-particles are biologically among the most damaging forms of radiation. However, they are unlikely to do very much damage unless inside a living organism. **Neutrons** have no net charge. Each neutron consists of one proton and one electron. They are emitted when certain elements are bombarded with α-particles or with γ-rays. Neutrons are more penetrating than α- and β-particles. Like γ-rays, they can do a great deal of harm even when outside living organisms.

Some radionuclides give off radiation for only a short time. Others do so for many years. The time required for a radionuclide to emit half its radiation is called its **half-life** (Table 30.10). The half-life and type of radiation emitted determine the degree of danger.

Table 30.10 Half lives of some radionuclides (after Ottaway 1980)

NUCLIDE	RADIATION	HALF-LIFE
^{90}Sr	β-particles	28y
^{129}I	β-particles γ-rays	16×10^6y
^{131}I	β-particles γ-rays	8 days
^{137}Cs	β-particles γ-rays	30y
^{237}Np	α-particles	$2{\cdot}2 \times 10^6$y
^{239}Pu	α-particles γ-rays	$2{\cdot}4 \times 10^4$y

The unit of radiation most meaningful to biologists is the gray (Gy). 1 Gy is equal to 1 J of radiation energy absorbed by 1 kg of body mass.

30.4.2 Sources of radiation

Natural sources account for more than 80 per cent of the radiation absorbed by humans (Table 30.11). There is little that can be done about **natural radiation**. Living organisms have had to cope with it since life began. What is of concern is the radiation released by man's activities.

Table 30.11 Radiation absorbed by people in Britain (after Mellanby 1980)

SOURCE	ANNUAL DOSE (μGy)	PERCENTAGE
natural background	870	83·8
medical	140	13·5
nuclear fallout	21	2·02
miscellaneous	7	0·67
radioactive waste	0·1	0·01

Though **man-made radiation** presently accounts for a relatively small amount of the total, it is on the increase and adds to the risks created by natural sources. Two of man's activities which release radiation into the environment are the use and testing of **nuclear bombs** and the use of **nuclear fuels**. Both are emotive subjects to people the world over.

In the early 1960s there was a dramatic increase in the amount of ^{90}Sr in the milk consumed in Britain. It followed the testing of nuclear weapons by the USA and USSR. Soon after the Nuclear Test Ban Treaty, contamination by ^{90}Sr reverted to normal and has stayed there since (Fig. 30.12).

Thermal nuclear reactors use natural uranium, a mixture of ^{235}U and ^{238}U. When bombarded with neutrons, uranium decays into a variety of **fission products**, including ^{90}Sr, ^{129}I, ^{131}I, ^{137}Cs and ^{239}Pu. **Fast reactors** use ^{239}Pu from thermal reactors mixed with ^{238}U. When bombarded with electrons, the ^{238}U is converted to ^{239}Pu. The conversion produces more ^{239}Pu than was present at the start. For this reason, fast reactors are sometimes called **breeders**. Like ^{235}U, the ^{239}Pu disintegrates into lead, but

FIG. 30.12 *Average ratio of* ^{90}Sr *to Ca in milk in Britain* (from Mellanby, "The Biology of Pollution" Inst. Biol. "Studies in Biology" published by Edward Arnold)

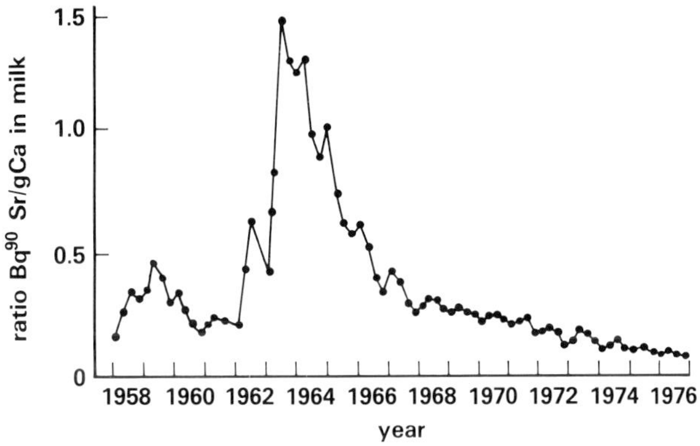

more quickly. There is more danger of environmental pollution from fast reactors, because the ^{239}Pu is processed twice.

The fission products which are potentially most dangerous to living organisms are ^{90}Sr, ^{129}I, ^{131}I and ^{137}Cs. Radioactive iodine absorbed by grasses and eaten by cows appears in their milk. Humans drinking contaminated milk concentrate radio-iodine in the thyroid gland. In this way the thyroid can be exposed to high doses of radiation. ^{90}Sr accumulates in bone adjacent to the marrow. Its long half-life means that it irradiates dividing bone marrow cells for years. Caesium is taken up by soft tissues, especially muscle.

Accidents have happened at nuclear power plants, spilling fission products into the surrounding countryside. The chief risk is failure of the cooling system in a reactor. The build-up of heat could be enough to melt a reactor. Partial failure of the cooling system in a fast reactor caused an explosion at Three Mile Island near Pittsburg, USA, in 1979. The effects are still being assessed. The worst nuclear accident in Britain happened at Windscale, Cumbria, in 1957 when ^{131}I and ^{137}Cs were released. As a precautionary measure, milk produced for several weeks within 5 km^2 of the nuclear station was declared unfit for consumption.

Another problem faced by the nuclear fuel industry is what to do with spent reactor cores which are still radioactive. If stored indefinitely, the fission products decay and become harmless. The difficulty is in deciding where they should be kept. Dumping at sea and storage in underground caverns are the disposal methods used at present.

30.4.3 Biological effects of radiation

The effects of radiation on living organisms are two-fold.

1. GENETIC EFFECTS

Living cells are very sensitive to radiation at interphase. It is at this stage in the cell cycle that replication of DNA occurs. Radiation alters the genetic code by breaking hydrogen bonds between the pairs of nitrogenous bases in the DNA molecule. Bases may be lost or reassembled in a way different from that in the original DNA. Such changes are called **gene mutations** (section 6.1.4). The faulty DNA then codes the synthesis of abnormal proteins which may be defective in function. Gene mutations may be passed to future generations in gametes.

Intense doses of radiation cause chromosomes to fragment (section 7.3). Chromosome fragments do not behave as normal chromosomes in nuclear division. They often fail to become attached to the spindle and are lost when the cytoplasm cleaves. The ends of large chromosome fragments may

FIG. 30.13 *Possible behaviour of fragmented chromosomes*

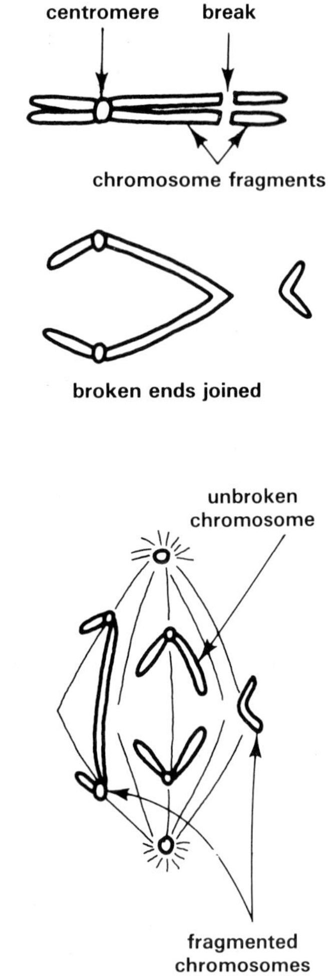

join up. It is then impossible for the chromatids to separate at anaphase (Fig. 30.13). Such changes are **chromosome mutations**.

Muller in 1927, using the fruit-fly *Drosophila*, was the first to demonstrate that radiation was a cause of gene mutations. He also showed that the mutation rate was proportional to the dosage of radiation (Fig. 30.14).

FIG. 30.14 *Effect of X-rays on the mutation rate of* Drosophila

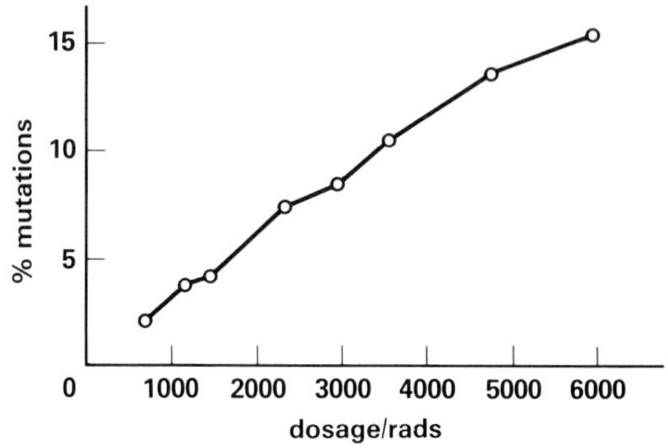

The probability of a mutation occurring increased with each exposure. The critical exposure period for any organism is when it is producing offspring. It is then that mutations may occur in cells which give rise to progeny formed asexually or in gamete-forming cells. For women the critical period extends over thirty child-bearing years. It has been estimated that the rate of mutation among humans would double if women absorbed an additional 0·5 Gy over their reproductive life span. If the increase was only 0·01 Gy each generation the mutation rate would increase by 1·5 per cent.

2. SOMATIC EFFECTS

Table 30.12 summarises the observations made on Japanese people exposed to very high doses of whole-body radiation following the nuclear bomb explosions at Hiroshima and Nagasaki in 1945, and on fishermen from the Marshall Islands exposed to radioactive fall-out near a nuclear-weapon testing station in the Pacific Ocean in 1954. The children of pregnant women exposed to radiation at Hiroshima and Nagasaki weighed much less than normal, had smaller brains and many suffered from severe mental and physical handicaps. Survivors at Hiroshima were more likely to have leukaemia if they were near the centre of the explosion (Fig. 30.15).

Table 30.12 Somatic effects of radiation

DOSAGE (Gy)	DEATH WITHIN	GENERAL EFFECT	SPECIFIC EFFECTS
> 100	1 day	CNS syndrome	Vomiting, diarrhoea, convulsions, brain damage, coma
10 – 100	2 weeks	GI syndrome	Gut lining not replaced, inability to digest food, vomiting, diarrhoea, emaciation
2 – 10	3–4 weeks	BM syndrome	Blood cells not replaced, anaemia, fever, vomiting, haemorrhages, loss of hair
< 2	unknown	life-shortening	Inability to make antibodies, small wounds remain septic for long periods.

CNS = central nervous system GI = gastro-intestinal BM = bone marrow

FIG. 30.15 *Relationship between the incidence of leukaemia and distance from centre of the atomic explosion at Hiroshima, Japan*

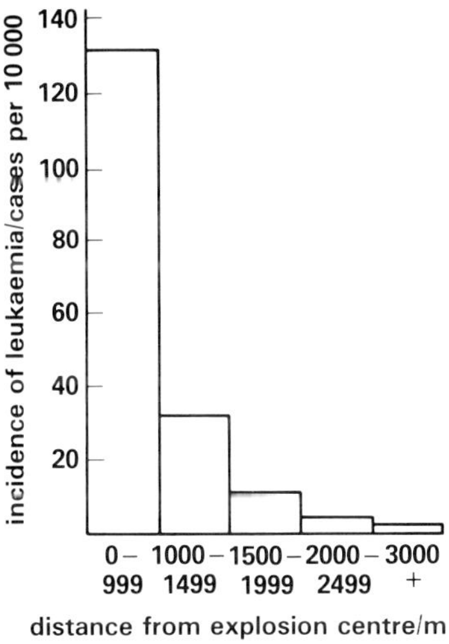

Fall-out of ^{90}Sr from the testing of nuclear weapons may well have been the cause of the increased number of cases of leukaemia in Britain in the 1960s.

As with pollution by pesticides, it is important to try to see the threat from radiation in perspective. Reserves of fossil fuels are being used at such a rate that it is predicted they will be exhausted in the foreseeable future. At present, nuclear fuel offers the main alternative source of energy for industrial and domestic use. As more nuclear power plants are built, the risk of radiation pollution is likely to increase. So far, rigorous safeguards have been taken. Although accidents have happened and some radiation has escaped from nuclear power stations, there has been little immediate danger to human life. However, the amount of radioactive waste to be disposed of is growing rapidly. There is concern about the safety of dumping at sea where the containers may eventually corrode. Nuclear waste buried underground may escape if earth tremors occur. The very long half-lives of some fission products increase the possibility of contamination. Future generations could then inherit the hazard of pollution by the radioactive wastes of today's nuclear fuel industry.

A worse hazard would come from the wide-scale use of nuclear weapons. The radiation released by explosions of nuclear bombs worldwide would kill most of us immediately and many parts of the earth could be uninhabitable for a very long time.

30.5 Pollution of aquatic habitats

The more obvious of society's waste products, such as plastic containers, glass bottles and tin cans which are often dumped in streams, rivers, lakes and the oceans, are eyesores. There is little evidence that they harm organisms. Agricultural, domestic and industrial wastes are the main pollutants of aquatic habitats.

30.5.1 Freshwater pollution

1. RIVERS

The pollution of rivers in Britain by **heavy metals** is described in section 30.2. Other industrial wastes such as **ammonia** and **cyanide** are also toxic to aquatic life. **Particulate matter** released by industry can pollute rivers too. Coal washings and china clay settle on the beds of rivers, fouling the spawning places of salmon and trout. When suspended in water, the particles reduce penetration of light for aquatic plants and asphyxiate fish by blocking their gills.

Sewage is the biggest polluter of fresh water. It is the waterborne waste of society. Sewage is over 99 per cent water. The remainder is a mixture of organic and inorganic substances which varies in composition from place to place, depending mainly on the industries in a locality. Sewage also contains bacteria, some of which are pathogenic. The pathogens come from the faeces of people with intestinal diseases such as cholera, dysentery and typhoid fever.

The effects of discharging untreated sewage into a river have been studied by Hynes (Fig. 30.16). One of the most striking features is a substantial and immediate drop in the amount of oxygen dissolved in the water. It happens because organic matter stimulates decomposer organisms, especially bacteria, which break down suspended solids in the sewage. As they respire, the decomposers use up dissolved oxygen. The amount of oxygen used in breaking down the organic matter into simple soluble products, such as ammonia, sulphate and phosphate, is the **biochemical**

FIG. 30.16 *Effects of organic effluent on* (a) *physical changes* (b) *chemical changes* (c) *flora* (d) *fauna of a river* (from Hynes, "The Biology of Polluted Waters" published by Liverpool University Press, 6th imp. 1978)

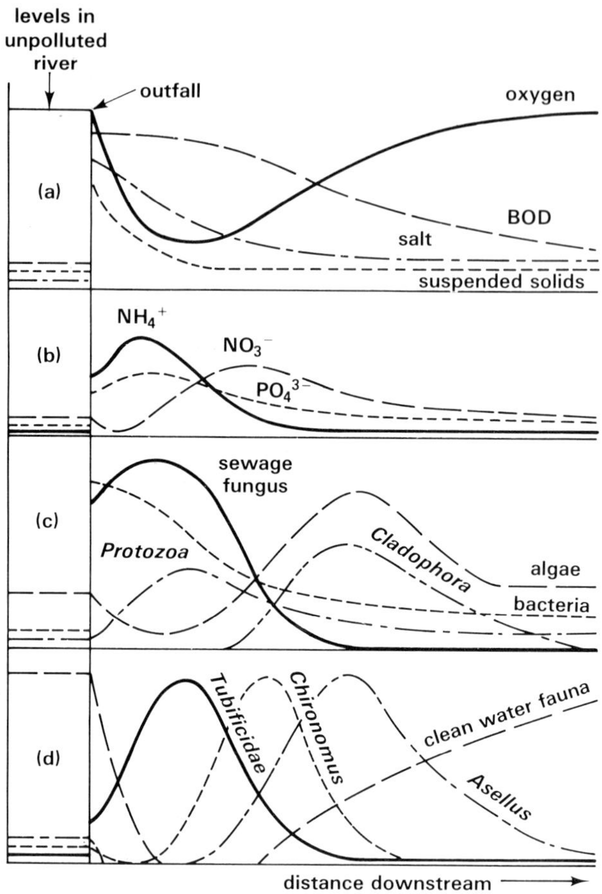

oxygen demand (BOD) of the sewage. The ammonia is quickly oxidised to nitrate(V) by nitrifying bacteria. Some of the phosphate may have come from detergents in the sewage. Downstream from the sewage outfall, the dissolved oxygen concentration returns to normal as oxygen is absorbed by the river from the air. A gradual fall in BOD occurs simultaneously as the decomposers are dispersed by the flowing water.

Changes in the flora and fauna of the river accompany the chemical changes. Filamentous bacteria called **sewage fungus** thrive near the outfall. They are anaerobic and tolerate the high concentration of ammonia which makes the water alkaline. Algae, *Cladophora* in particular, are sensitive to pollution by sewage. Downstream they flourish, stimulated by the minerals released from the decomposed organic matter. Their numbers then return to normal as the minerals are used up or diluted by water from tributaries. The fauna most tolerant of sewage are annelids of the family *Tubificidae* (tubifex worms). Their blood contains a form of haemoglobin with an exceptional affinity for oxygen. It enables them to extract oxygen even when the concentration of dissolved oxygen in water is very low. Larvae of the midge *Chironomus* are the next most tolerant. They too have a type of haemoglobin which binds very efficiently with dissolved oxygen. The water louse *Asellus* begins to appear when the dissolved oxygen begins to recover. **Clean-water fauna** such as the freshwater shrimp *Gammarus* and larvae of the caddis fly, stonefly and mayfly are wiped out by sewage. They reappear when the amount of dissolved oxygen is back to normal (Fig. 30.17).

FIG. 30.17 *Changes in the fauna of a polluted river* (from Sands 1978)

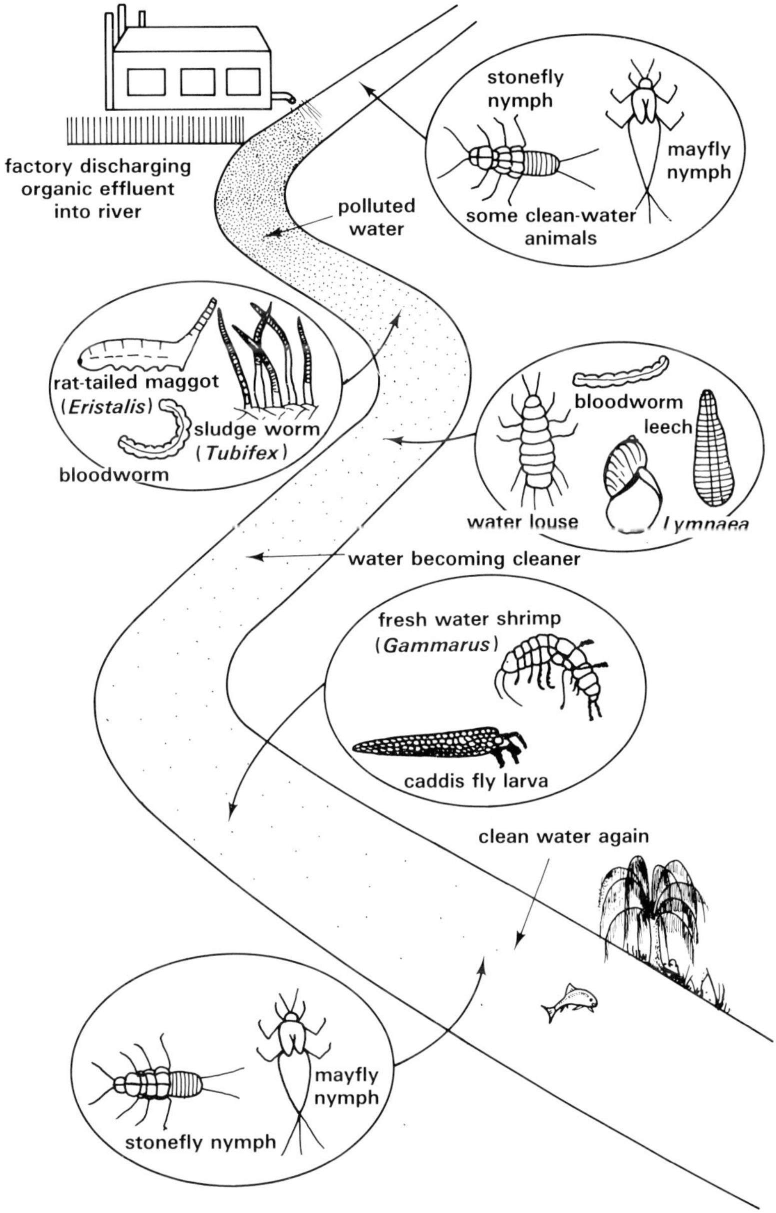

The numbers and types of animals at different sampling points in a river provide a useful guide to the extent and type of pollution. Given time, a river cleans itself in the way described. However, if it receives successive outfalls of sewage close to each other, the stretches of water between the outfalls do not have time to recover. In these circumstances the water becomes deoxygenated. Anaerobic bacteria partly decompose the sewage, releasing toxic ammonia and hydrogen sulphide. Rivers as badly polluted as this have an obnoxious smell and contain little flora and fauna.

A hundred years ago, many rivers flowing through British towns and cities were like this because they were used as open sewers. The discovery that they were the cause of the spread of cholera and typhoid fever led to the construction of **sewage-treatment plants**. The aim of sewage treatment is to lower the BOD of sewage such that an effluent can be discharged into the rivers without grossly upsetting the ecological balance. At the same time, the number of intestinal bacteria is reduced so that the river is not a hazard to bathers and may even be used as a source of water for human consumption. As the human population has grown, many older treatment plants are now unable to cope with the amount of sewage they receive. Some raw and partly treated sewage is discharged into many of our rivers. A few years ago, stretches of the River Thames flowing through London were so badly polluted with sewage that the water was devoid of dissolved oxygen. Today the water is clean enough for salmon to survive. Cleaning the river was achieved mainly by properly treating London's sewage in newly-constructed sewage-treatment plants.

A good deal of water is taken from rivers to cool industrial machinery. The biggest user of water for cooling purposes in Britain is the Central Electricity Generating Board. When returned, the water is hotter than when it was removed. In an unpolluted river, the increase in temperature lowers the amount of dissolved oxygen (Table 28.2). At the same time, it increases the metabolic rate of aquatic organisms and therefore raises their oxygen demand. Up to now no gross changes in the flora and fauna have been observed in Britain, because the increase in temperature is modest. In other parts of the world, salmon and trout have disappeared from stretches of clean rivers which have been warmed to a greater extent. Ironically, cooling water returned to polluted rivers accelerates their return to normal. While cascading down cooling towers (Fig. 30.18), water takes up a good

FIG. 30.18 *Cooling towers of the electricity generating station at Farndon, Notts. with River Trent in foreground*

deal of oxygen from the air, so the water returned to polluted rivers contains more oxygen than the water extracted. The increase in temperature and oxygen also encourages decomposers to break down organic matter more quickly. In this way the BOD returns to normal sooner.

2. LAKES

Lakes are fairly still bodies of water. For much of the year there is a boundary called the **thermocline** about 16 m below the surface of deep lakes. It separates the warmer upper layer, the **epilimnion**, from the colder **hypolimnion** beneath. The temperature of the epilimnion fluctuates according to air temperature. When it cools to 4°C, water becomes more dense and sinks from the epilimnion into the hypolimnion. In this way the hypolimnion is kept permanently at about 4°C and mixing between the two layers is confined to cold seasons. At other times of the year the epilimnion floats on the denser hypolimnion and there is no mixing (Fig. 30.19). Phytoplankton as it photosynthesises oxygenates the epilimnion. Photosynthesis is inhibited in the hypolimnion, because less light penetrates

FIG. 30.19 *Temperature zones in a lake*

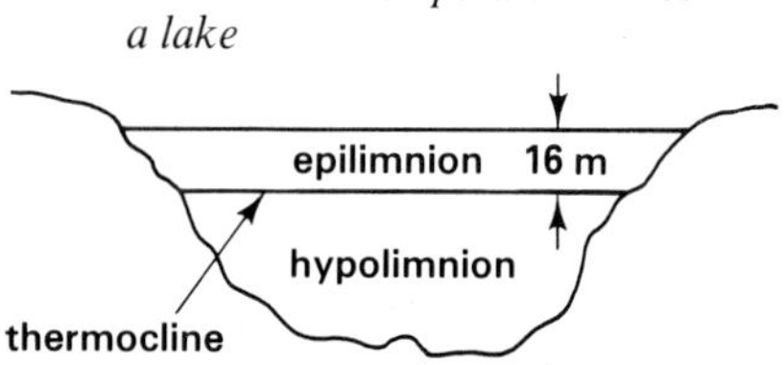

below 16 m. It means that the hypolimnion relies on the epilimnion for oxygen. Recharging the hypolimnion with oxygen, however, can only occur when the two layers mix in cold weather.

Reference has already been made to pollution of lakes by **acid water** draining from land polluted with sulphur dioxide and by **mercury** in industrial effluent (sections 30.1.2 and 30.2.2). In unpolluted lakes, the water contains only small amounts of dissolved minerals. The low mineral content limits the growth of aquatic plants. In such **oligotrophic** lakes there is consequently little organic matter to be decayed. For this reason the water has a low BOD and remains well oxygenated. When polluted with sewage or with drainage water from nearby arable land, the water is enriched with minerals. The water is now **eutrophic** and growth of phytoplankton is stimulated. Blooms of algae, blue-greens especially, quickly appear. Some of them release toxins which kill fish. When the algae die, they contribute substantially to the dead organic matter which sinks to the bed of the lake. Here it creates a high BOD, and what oxygen there is in the hypolimnion is soon used by decomposers. When this point is reached, anaerobic bacteria release ammonia, methane and hydrogen sulphide, making the water unfit for most forms of aquatic life. If there is a large amount of organic matter to be decayed, anaerobism may extend to the epilimnion.

There are two ways in which the effects of such pollution can be reversed. One is to dredge the lake bed. Clearly this is too large a task for all but the smallest lakes. The other is to oxygenate the hypolimnion so that decomposers break down the organic matter. This expensive approach is presently being tried in an attempt to clean up Lake Geneva in Switzerland. For some of the world's largest lakes it seems that the effects of eutrophication are irreversible. The flora and fauna of large parts of Lake Erie in Canada are pollution-tolerant species. Masses of decaying algae and dead fish are regularly washed up on the lake's shore. The water is unfit for bathing and the local fishing industry has virtually collapsed.

30.5.2 Marine pollution

Unlike the water in a lake, sea water moves continuously. In some seas the movement brings about a rapid turnover of water. The turnover is two years in the North Sea. For this reason pollutants are soon carried away and dispersed. The effects of pollution are more likely to be serious in shallow, enclosed seas. Here the turnover may take hundreds of years and marine organisms soon concentrate toxic pollutants. This was a major contributory factor in the poisoning of people with **mercury** at Minamata, Japan (section 30.2.2).

Eutrophication has been another cause of pollution in enclosed seas. Within the past 30 years, parts of the southern Baltic Sea have been made anaerobic in the same way as an enriched lake (section 30.5.1). Enrichment with phosphate fertiliser coming from surrounding agricultural land is mainly to blame. Eutrophication also occurs when raw or partly-treated **sewage** is discharged at sea, a common feature of many coastal towns on the Mediterranean Sea. Though rather unpleasant, sewage-tainted seawater is unlikely to be a health risk to bathers. However, humans have contracted typhoid fever after eating shellfish from sewage-contaminated water.

Shellfish also concentrate **organochlorine insecticides** in their tissues. Oysters, for example, accumulate DDT by a factor of 70 000 times more than in seawater. As little as 0·001 ppm of DDT in seawater reduces the growth of oysters. Organochlorine insecticides pass from one trophic level to another in the sea as in other ecosystems and with comparable effects. The decline of predatory marine birds such as the herring gull, the osprey and brown pelican in various parts of North America in the 1960s is thought to have occurred because they accumulated high concentrations of DDT residues in their bodies.

Marine organisms concentrate **radionuclides** in their tissues too. They are often used as a measure of the amounts of radionuclides in the environment near coastal nuclear power plants. So far the evidence indicates little danger to marine life or to humans eating seafood.

Oil has captured the headlines as one of the most serious forms of marine pollution. When the *Torrey Canyon* went aground off Land's End in 1967, about 60 000 tonnes of crude oil were spilled. Much of it was washed up on Cornish beaches. The rest was blown across the English Channel and ended up on the French coast. The foundering of the *Amoco Cadiz* off the coast of France in 1978 caused 200 000 tonnes of crude oil to be released. Much of the oil came up on the beaches of Brittany. There have been many other similar incidences elsewhere. Large spillages have also occurred more recently from oil rigs in the North Sea and at oil terminals in the Shetland Islands. It has been estimated that up to 10 million tonnes of crude oil are released annually into the world's seas and oceans.

FIG. 30.20 *Guillemot polluted with oil* (RSPB)

The worst casualties of oil pollution are fish-eating birds. From the air, oil slicks resemble patches of plankton where fish are likely to be feeding. Attracted by what looks like a good source of food, the birds settle on the slick or dive through it. Their feathers become clogged with oil, stopping the birds from flying (Fig. 30.20). Oil-soaked feathers are poor insulators of body heat, so many of the birds die of hypothermia. The birds attempt to rid themselves of the oil by preening, but in doing so they swallow crude oil and are poisoned. Something like 100 000 sea birds, especially guillemots, were killed by the oil spillage from the *Torrey Canyon* alone.

Crude oil also kills seaweeds, molluscs and crustaceans when it is washed up on rocky shores. The seaweeds grow again quite quickly, often better than before. Browsing molluscs which keep them in check are slower to return, but within two years the shore is more or less back to normal. The oil disappears, because it is broken down by aerobic bacteria. Concerned by the possible harm to their tourist industries, British and French authorities tried various measures to deal with the oil from the sunken tankers. In Britain the polluted shoreline was sprayed with detergents to disperse the oil. Recovery of littoral organisms was slower when this was done, because detergents are toxic to marine life. The French sprinkled chalk and sawdust on the slicks to sink the oil before it could be washed up on the shore. Molluscs on the seabed were poisoned by the oil and their numbers have still not returned to normal.

The world's oceans contain over 14×10^{18} m^3 of water. The earth's atmosphere extends up to 2000 km. It is tempting to believe that such huge volumes can absorb all the wastes of human activities without any ill-effects. Indeed, there is a catchphrase which says, 'dilution is the solution to pollution'. Unfortunately, aerial pollutants are concentrated by natural forces such as precipitation. Marine pollutants do not become evenly dispersed. Some of the world's largest freshwater lakes have been unable to take man's wastes without irreversible and undesirable effects. Living organisms have the knack of accumulating toxic materials and passing them on to others. The unwanted products of some of man's activities are the problems of others.

30.6 Conservation

Early man lived by hunting, fishing and gathering food. His numbers were few and he led a nomadic existence. The resources he took from his surroundings had time to recover as he moved from place to place. It was when he settled as a farmer in Neolithic times that man's impact on the environment was first felt. He cut down forest to provide land on which to grow crops. As the human population grew, more forest was cleared and marshland was drained to be used for growing crops and rearing livestock. Habitat destruction has gone on to such an extent that the wildlife in many areas is now impoverished and some species of plants and animals are near to extinction. It has led to the **conservation** of habitats in which living organisms are managed and protected from man's excesses.

30.6.1 The case for conservation

FIG. 30.21 *The number of exterminated mammal and bird forms over the past 300 years* (from Spellerberg, "Ecological Evaluation for Conservation" Inst. Biol. "Studies in Biology" published by Edward Arnold)

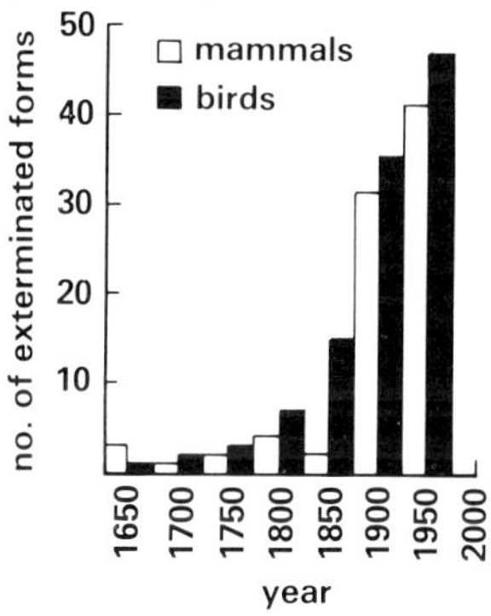

During the past 300 years, animal species have disappeared at an alarming rate (Fig. 30.21). It has been estimated that about 25 000 species of plants are now near to extinction. **Destruction** of natural habitats and **over-exploitation** by man are the main causes of extermination. Natural forest and woodland have been chopped down, wetlands have been drained and heathland burned to provide more land for growing crops. Large areas have been flooded to provide water for industrial and domestic use. Birds and mammals have been mercilessly hunted. Wild grasslands have been overgrazed and turned into desert.

Environmentalists argue that it is **morally wrong** for humans to condemn other species to extinction. Many people derive **pleasure** from observing wildlife. There are also good practical reasons for conserving all existing forms of life. Many species of wild plants are the sources of **medicinal drugs**, but so far only 2 per cent have been screened for the useful products they may yield. Many wild species may be **hardier** and more resistant to disease than their domesticated relatives. It may be desirable in future to transfer the genes for these characteristics to domesticated stock. Many pests are kept in check by wild animals which are their **natural enemies**. If they are eradicated, we could be overrun by pests. Other species are useful as **monitors of pollution** and alert us to potential hazards to man's health. Many species of wild animals are more **productive** than domesticated livestock in natural ecosystems. They could be managed to provide a valuable supply of meat for human consumption.

Conserving wildlife is also important for present-day economic reasons. The big game reserves of African countries attract many **tourists**. Fishing and shooting are important sources of income locally in many developed countries.

The aim of conservation is to **manage** wildlife so that it benefits mankind. It means that viable populations of all existing species should be maintained.

30.6.2 Conservation in action

The need for conservation of wildlife was realised nearly a century ago in a number of countries. **National Parks** were established in various parts of the world where wild species could exist without man's interference. The first to be created was the Yellowstone National Park, USA, in 1876. Protection societies were founded and legislation was passed to help preserve wildlife. In Britain, the **Royal Society for the Protection of Birds** was founded in 1889, the National Trust in 1895. After the passing of the National Parks and Countryside Act 1949, the **Nature Conservancy** was set up to establish and manage British nature reserves. National Parks were designated and Sites of Scientific Interest identified. In 1973, the Nature Conservancy became the **Nature Conservancy Council** (NCC).

International bodies have also helped to promote and co-ordinate conservation projects. The **International Union for Conservation of Nature** (IUCN) was founded by UNESCO in 1956. More recently, the **World Wildlife Fund** has done much to conserve endangered species in developing countries. In 1980, the **World Conservation Strategy** was launched to set out the aims of conservation and to identify the obstacles which might prevent it happening.

Perhaps the biggest problem confronting conservationists is in identifying which species need protection. One way of doing so is to determine the population sizes of threatened species. Measures which can be taken to sustain viable populations in their natural environments can then be suggested. This approach was initiated by Sir Peter Scott in the mid-1960s. The information is collected from many parts of the world and documented in **Red Data Books** kept at the IUCN headquarters at Morges, Switzerland. Protective legislation aimed at conserving endangered species in Britain includes the Protection of Birds Acts 1954 and 1967, Badgers Act 1973, Conservation of Wild Creatures and Plants Act 1975 and Wildlife and Countryside Act 1981. Every five years the NCC is required to review lists of species under threat.

1. TERRESTRIAL SITES

Evaluating the worth of an ecosystem for conservation purposes is an elaborate exercise. The NCC has taken particular interest in the conservation of old woodlands in Britain. Deciduous woodland is the natural climax vegetation for much of this country and contains a wide variety of native flora and fauna. Today, deciduous woodland covers about 10 per cent of the land area of Britain, mainly in fairly small patches surrounded by farmland (Fig. 30.22). Small woods are constantly being chopped down

FIG. 30.22 *English landscape showing pockets of woodland* (B&B photos)

and the land used for other purposes. The NCC often has to decide which woods are worth conserving, so that measures can be taken to protect them. The first thing to be done is to make a list of all the species. The next is to identify **indicator species**. According to Peterken (1977), a typical indicator species of old woodland helps create the canopy of the wood, can tolerate the shade of a closed woodland canopy or requires woodland conditions to survive. On this basis the species indicative of old British woodland include wood sorrel, wood millet, sedges and columbine. If they are present, the flora of the wood and probably the fauna too is likely to be diverse. Conserving such a wood maintains viable populations of a wide range of plant and animal species. Other criteria of importance in evaluating a site are:

(i) AREA. Every species requires a minimum area for its survival. If the aim is to conserve a population of large herbivores, a very large area of habitat is required. In general, the larger the area the more diverse is the flora and fauna. Nevertheless, small areas may be worth maintaining if the aims of conservation are more modest.
(ii) STRUCTURAL DIVERSITY. An area with a diversity of habitats is more valuable for conservation purposes than a homogeneous area. Banks, paths, rides and streams in a wood provide places where a wide range of species can survive.
(iii) RARITY. Some sites are the last refuges of rare species. Although the site may lack other desirable features, it is worth conserving. Otherwise the species could be lost for ever.
(iv) VULNERABILITY. Some sites may be near to urban areas and are likely to be interfered with by trespassers. Others may be close to industry and there is a risk of pollution.
(v) COST. Money has to be found to purchase sites. Some are more expensive than others. Conserving a site also means that it has to be **managed**. Access to visitors may have to be controlled. If the vegetation is not the natural climax, succession will occur if the site is left to its own devices and the flora and fauna will change. At many sites it may be desirable to prevent succession. In this way diverse sites can be maintained supporting viable populations of a large range of species. This is a key distinction between preservation and conservation. However, it does mean that some sites are more costly than others to conserve.

2. MARINE CONSERVATION

The territorial waters of most countries extend 5 km from the coast. In 1961, the government of Iceland enlarged its territorial waters to a distance of 20 km and in 1972 they were extended to 75 km. The Icelandic government's reason for doing so was to conserve fishing grounds. Catches of fish in Icelandic waters have fallen in recent years, probably through overfishing. Because Iceland's main export is fish, it is vital to her economy to have a guaranteed supply of fish in nearby waters. The protective action gave rise to friction between Iceland and countries whose fishing fleets had used the area for many years. The British were particularly hard-hit, as about 25 per cent of Britain's fish catches had been caught in the seas around Iceland.

Stocks of fish in many fishing grounds have become seriously depleted by overfishing. When this happens, fishing fleets usually move elsewhere. Over-exploited fishing grounds eventually recover, although it may take years. There is no evidence that overfishing has caused the extinction of any marine organisms, although several species of whale have come near to it. Conservation is clearly required if the living resources of seas and oceans are to provide us with a sustained supply of food. Some of the measures which have been taken to protect whales from over-exploitation are described in section 29.1.3. International agreements limit the catches of fish which can be taken from territorial waters. However, the open seas belong to nobody. Their stock is fished with scant regard for the future. It would be a great catastrophe if nothing could be done to conserve marine wildlife. The oceans are potentially the richest source of protein in the world.

Questions

The questions have been arranged so that they can often be answered after the appropriate chapter has been studied. In some instances it may be necessary to use information from more than one chapter.

JMB = Joint Matriculation Board Examinations Council
London = University of London Examinations Council
ONC and OND = Joint Committee for Ordinary National Diplomas and Certificates
B = Biology Bot = Botany Z = Zoology

Chapter 1

1 Write concise notes on each of the following:
(a) mitochondria, (b) nucleoli,
(c) endoplasmic reticulum.
How has electron microscopy changed our views on the structure of cells? (London: June 1975) B

2 Describe how tissues are prepared for observation under either (a) the light microscope or (b) the electron microscope. Include each step of the procedure, and explain why it is necessary. (London: January 1974) Z

3 (a) Make a labelled diagram to illustrate chloroplast structure as revealed by the electron microscope.
(b) Describe, with the aid of diagrams, the structural and functional characteristics of
(i) the endoplasmic reticulum, and
(ii) the Golgi apparatus.
(c) (i) What are lysosomes, where are they formed, why are they sometimes referred to as 'suicide bags'?
(ii) Suggest a possible reason for the occurrence of large numbers of lysosomes in phagocytic cells.
(JMB: June 1976) B

4 (a) (i) Give three differences, in working, between the light microscope and the electron microscope.
(ii) What are the relative ranges of magnification and resolving power of a light microscope and an electron microscope?
(iii) Give two disadvantages in the use of an electron microscope as compared with that of a light microscope.
(b) Using diagrams, compare what is revealed of the structure of any three components of the cytoplasm of a given cell seen under the light microscope with that seen under the electron microscope. (JMB: June 1974) B

5 Give a brief account of the distribution of membranes within a generalised cell. Describe the structure and functions of the surface membrane (the plasmalemma) of cells.
(JMB: June 1973) B

Chapter 2

1 Consider this statement: 'When a plant cell is placed in a sugar solution which is stronger than the cell sap, plasmolysis occurs.'
(a) What does the word 'stronger' mean in this context?
(b) Draw a fully labelled diagram of a plant cell which has undergone plasmolysis.
(c) Describe a method involving plasmolysis and using sucrose solution by which you could determine the osmotic potential (or osmotic pressure) of the cell sap of the cells of a plant. Use the outline below for your answer.
(i) The preparation of suitable tissue of a named plant for investigation.
(ii) The procedure to be followed.
(iii) The results you would expect. State how these may be used to determine the osmotic potential (or osmotic pressure) of the cell sap.
(JMB: June 1978) B

2 (a) What is meant by
(i) osmotic pressure, (ii) turgor pressure,
(iii) suction pressure or diffusion pressure deficit or water potential, (iv) plasmolysis.
(b) Discuss whether a plant membrane should be considered to be semi-permeable or differentially permeable.
(c) Explain what you would expect to happen when a plant cell having an osmotic potential equivalent to 5 atmospheres and a suction pressure of 2 atmospheres is
(i) immersed in pure water,
(ii) immersed in a hypertonic sucrose solution,
(iii) immersed in strong acid.
(London: January 1977) B

3 Discuss the importance of water to living organisms.
(London: June 1974) B

4 Mammalian red blood cells are sensitive to a change in salt concentration of the external solution. If they are transferred from plasma to a less concentrated solution they swell and, if they swell sufficiently, may burst, in which case they are said to be haemolysed. In an experiment to find the percentage of human red cells haemolysed at different concentrations of salt solution, the following results were obtained:

percentage salt concentration g 100 cm^{-3}	0.33	0.36	0.38	0.39	0.42	0.44	0.48
percentage red cells haemolysed	100	90	80	68	30	16	0

(a) Plot the results on graph paper, using the horizontal axis for the percentages of salt concentration.
(b) Explain why red cells swell and burst when placed in a dilute salt solution.
(c) At what percentage salt solution is the proportion of haemolysed to nonhaemolysed cells equal?
(d) Suggest a hypothesis to account for the red cells haemolysing over a range of salt concentrations rather than at one particular salt concentration.
(e) What is the significance of these observations in relation to the functioning of the human body? (ONC: 1978)

Chapter 3

1 Discuss the importance of proteins within cells.
(London: January 1977) B

2 Give an account of the ways in which reserve food materials are stored and utilised in plants and animals.
(London: January 1973) B

3 Discuss the ways in which the use of each of the following has contributed to advances in biological knowledge and understanding.
(a) the electron microscope. (b) chromatography.
(c) radioactive isotopes. (London: June 1978) B

4 What is the chemical nature of fats and oils that occur in plant tissues? How do (a) protein and (b) starch differ from fats and oils? Describe precisely how you would investigate whether sucrose and protein are present in carrot root tissue.

(London: June 1975) Bot.

5 (a) Distinguish
   (i) between sucrose and maltose, and
   (ii) between starch and glycogen.
(b) How could you obtain from a powder containing sucrose, starch and cellulose, cellulose with minimum amounts of the others as contaminants?
(c) (i) What are the two main products formed by the hydrolysis of fats?
   (ii) What general term is given to the reaction leading to the formation of fats?
   (iii) Give two reasons why fats (oils) are important as storage compounds.
   (iv) How would you demonstrate that a castor-oil seed contains an appreciable amount of fat?
(d) (i) Proteins have been called 'biological polymers'. Explain what this means.
   (ii) Name two elements likely to be found in proteins but not in carbohydrates or fats.
   (iii) Give one simple physical or chemical test which would suggest that an unknown substance was a protein.
   (iv) Proteins form what are termed 'hydrophilic colloids'. Explain what this means.
   (v) What is imbibition? Give one biological process in which imbibition occurs.
(e) Name the two main chemical constituents of the plasmalemma and show by means of a diagram, how they are thought to be arranged. (JMB: June 1975) B

Chapter 4

1 Discuss the role of enzymes in the regulation of cellular activities. (JMB: Special Paper June 1978) B

2 (a) What is an enzyme?
(b) List the factors which affect the rate of an enzyme-controlled reaction.
(c) Describe an experiment to investigate the effect of one factor on the rate of an enzyme-controlled reaction.
(d) What is meant by a co-enzyme? Discuss briefly the role of co-enzymes in metabolism.

(London: January 1977) B

3 (a) What is meant by (i) specificity and (ii) denaturation of an enzyme?
(b) Discuss the ways in which (i) temperature and (ii) pH may affect the activity of an enzyme.
(c) How may starch be converted to glucose? Would you expect the same enzymes to be involved in the synthesis of starch? Give reasons for your answer.

(London: June 1976) B

4 Enzymes may be described as biological catalysts. Give an account of (a) their catalytic and (b) their other properties. Explain briefly why enzymes are essential to living organisms.

(London: January 1974) B

5 (a) Give an account of the factors affecting the rate of enzyme reactions, relating the action of these factors to the nature and properties of enzymes.
(b) Outline a method you might use to determine the effect of one of these factors on the rate of a named reaction.

(JMB: June 1975) B

6 (a) State four properties you would expect an enzyme to possess.
(b) What is meant by:
   (i) an enzyme activator?
   (ii) an enzyme inhibitor?
Give a named example of each.
(c) (i) For each numbered enzyme 1–6 below write down the letter of the reaction A–F which it catalyses:
   1. diastase (α-amylase) 2. cytochrome oxidase
   3. a dehydrogenase 4. phosphorylase
   5. invertase 6. phosphatase.

Reactions:
   A. glucose-phosphate + water $\rightleftharpoons$ starch + inorganic phosphate.
   B. starch $\rightleftharpoons$ dextrins.
   C. sucrose $\rightleftharpoons$ glucose + fructose.
   D. glucose-1-phosphate $\rightleftharpoons$ glucose + inorganic phosphate.
   E. acid I ($C_4H_6O_3$) $\rightleftharpoons$ acid II ($C_4H_4O_4$).
   F. transfer of electrons to molecular oxygen during aerobic respiration.
   (ii) Briefly indicate the physiological significance of any four of these reactions. (JMB: June 1973) B

Chapter 5

1 In aerobic respiration the energy contained in a molecule of glucose is made available to the cells by three main processes: glycolysis, tricarboxylic acid cycle, electron-transfer system.
(a) Explain concisely the essential features of each of these processes.
(b) In what ways does the anaerobic respiration of glucose differ from aerobic respiration of the same substrate?

(JMB: June 1977) B

2 Give an account of the fixation and utilisation of carbon in plants which is sufficiently detailed to explain the following statements.
(a) (i) The first product of carbon dioxide fixation is 3-phosphoglyceric acid (PGA).
   (ii) Light energy is required only to provide the ATP and electron donors (reduced coenzymes) needed to reduce PGA and maintain a supply of ribulose diphosphate.
   (iii) There are alternative uses for ATP and the electron donors in addition to those of carbon dioxide fixation.
(b) (i) Starch grains begin to grow close to grana.
   (ii) The formation of cellulose and pectins occurs near to the plasmalemma. (JMB: June 1978) B

3 (a) Give an outline of the biochemical processes which occur doing aerobic respiration in a cell.
(b) Briefly differentiate between aerobic and anaerobic respiration.
(c) Explain why (i) a yeast cell and (ii) a muscle fibre need not take up oxygen during respiration.

(London: January 1978) B

4 (a) What is the main function of ATP in cell metabolism? State briefly how it fulfils this function.
(b) Explain, in outline only, how ATP is generated by the cells of a green plant in the light and in darkness.

(JMB: June 1976) B

5 In an experiment with mitochondria a medium which contained inorganic phosphate and oxidisable substrates was used. The medium was saturated with air at the start. The

experiment determined the fall in oxygen concentration in the medium when firstly mitochondria, and then ADP, were added.

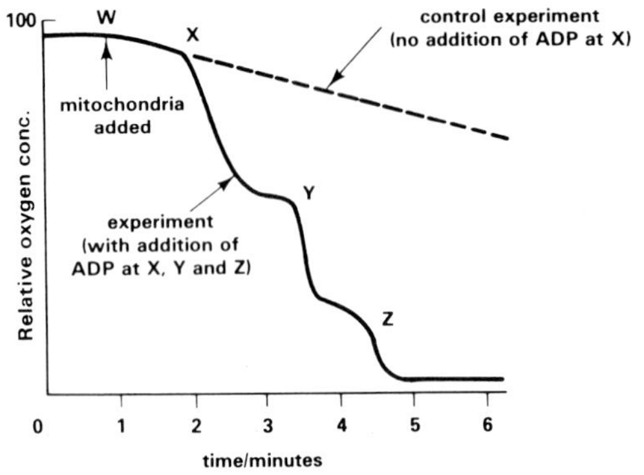

The letters used below refer to those on the graph. In the experiment, mitochondria were added at W. A standard amount of ADP was added at X, a similar amount at Y, and at Z.

In a control experiment, mitochondria were added at W. No ADP was added.

The results are shown in the graph.

(a) State one function of the phosphate in the medium.

(b) Account for
  (i) the slight drop in oxygen concentration when the mitochondria were added at W.
  (ii) the shape of the graph when the ADP was added at X and Y.

(c) Why does the graph become horizontal shortly after the addition of ADP at Z?

(d) Briefly explain what effect the following additions might have.
  (i) The addition of excess ADP at X.
  (ii) The addition of cyanide at X as well as the excess ADP. (JMB: June 1977) B

6 The apparatus drawn below can be used to measure the rate of respiration of small organisms.

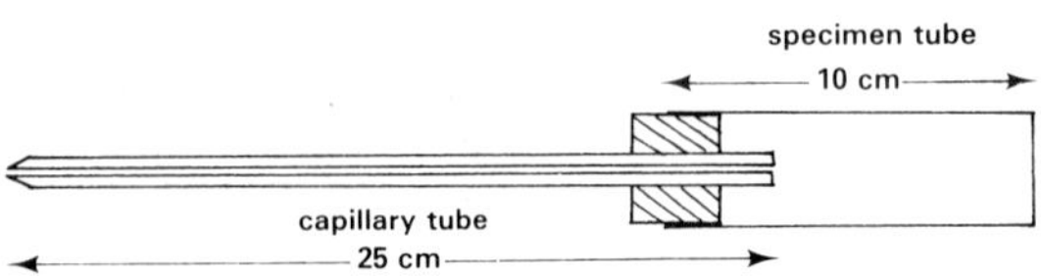

(a) Name any two organisms which could be used in this apparatus.

(b) To measure oxygen consumption, you would need to put a chemical into the specimen tube. Write down.
  (i) which chemical you would use.
  (ii) the function it performs in the investigation.
  (iii) how you would place it in the tube, keep it in position, and isolate it from the organisms.

(c) Explain how you would proceed to use the apparatus to measure the uptake of oxygen by an organism.

(d) Could this apparatus be used to measure the rate of anaerobic respiration? Explain your answer.

(e) The apparatus provides a very simple device to measure the rate of respiration. Give any two sources of error which might arise when using it. (JMB: June 1977) B

Chapter 6

1 (a) Explain concisely, those features of the structure of DNA which enable it to
  (i) serve as a store of genetic information, and
  (ii) transmit identical information to the cells produced as a result of mitosis.

(b) (i) What is a gene and what is a gene mutation?
  (ii) Explain why mutations may appear
    (A) immediately (somatic),
    (B) in the first generation.
    (C) not until several generations of offspring have appeared. (JMB: June 1978) B

2 Give an illustrated account of the structure of DNA. How is DNA involved in the synthesis of proteins.? Indicate the genetic significance of changes that may occur in the structure of a DNA molecule. (London: January 1976) B

3 (a) Describe the structure of DNA.

(b) Bacterial cells were grown in a medium containing radioactive nitrogen. On division the DNA strands of the daughter cells were radioactive. The daughter cells were placed in a normal medium and when division occurred half of the DNA contained labelled nitrogen. How can this be explained? (OND: 1974)

4 (a) Mouse cells grown in culture were exposed for 30 minutes to radioactive uracil, then either (A) fixed or (B) grown on for an additional 4 hours in a medium containing non-radioactive uracil and then fixed. The distribution of the radioactivity was determined by autoradiography and the results of such an experiment are given below.

	PERCENTAGE OF RADIOACTIVITY OVER		
	NUCLEOLUS	REST OF NUCLEUS	CYTOPLASM
(A) 30 minutes	54	41	5
(B) 30 minutes + 4 hours	14	19	67

  (i) Give a brief outline of the principles of the technique of autoradiography.
  (ii) From these data and your knowledge of the functioning of the nucleus, account for the distribution of radioactivity after 30 minutes and after 30 minutes plus 4 hours.
  (iii) Supposing the cells had been growing continuously for $4\frac{1}{2}$ hours in radioactive medium, what then would have been the likely distribution of radioactivity within the cell?

(b) The following experiment was devised to see whether newly-synthesised protein molecules go directly from the endoplasmic reticulum-bound ribosomes into the cavity of the endoplasmic reticulum or whether they are first freed into the cytoplasm and later picked up by the endoplasmic reticulum.

A microsome fraction was prepared by differential centrifugation of homogenised tissue and was suspended in a medium which can be regarded as being equivalent to the cytoplasm of the cell. The microsome fraction consists chiefly of fragments of the rough endoplasmic reticulum. A radioactive amino acid was added to the medium containing the microsomes. At successive intervals samples were taken and treated with a detergent which frees the ribosomes and disperses the membranes. Radioactivity protein was determined separately for the ribosomes, the detergent-dispersed fractions, and the medium. The results were as follows.

TIME IN MINUTES	RADIOACTIVITY IN C.P.M.		
	DETERGENT-DISPERSED FRACTION	RIBOSOMES	MEDIUM
1	10	65	30
2	40	100	50
3	80	116	60
5	150	115	70
10	200	115	70

(i) Plot a graph of these data.
(ii) Interpret these results as fully as you can, indicating whether they show that newly-synthesised protein follows one or other of the routes described in the aims of the experiment.
(JMB: Special Paper June 1977) B

5 (a) Briefly describe one piece of experimental evidence which directly supports the view that DNA is the molecule of heredity.
(b) Give three chemical features of DNA which render this molecule particularly suitable to be the vehicle of heredity.
(c) By using the following keywords in an appropriate context construct a simple account of protein synthesis in living cells. The account need be no longer than is necessary to include all of the keywords which may be used in any order. Keywords: codon (triplet), messenger RNA, transcription, enzyme, polypeptide, ribosomes, nuclear membrane, amino acids, proteins. (JMB: June 1974) B

Chapter 7

1 (a) Give an illustrated account of mitosis.
(b) Where does meiosis occur in a mammal and in a flowering plant? What is its significance?
(c) List four differences between mitosis and meiosis.
(London: January 1978) B

2 'It is sometimes said that meiosis consists of two mitotic divisions.' Discuss the validity of this statement.
(London: January 1974) Z

3 What are the functions of a nucleus in a non-dividing cell? Make fully labelled diagrams showing the stages of mitosis in a plant cell, the nucleus of which contains four chromosomes.
(London: January 1975) Bot.

4 In vegetative cells the cycle of the main stages of cell division can be represented by the following scheme:

⟶ interphase ⟶ mitosis ⟶ interphase
↑ cytoplasmic division

(a) (i) At what stage does DNA synthesis occur?
(ii) Give an example of nuclear division proceeding in the absence of cell division.
(b) Give an account of the structural changes which take place as a cell passes through this cycle and note any difference between plant and animal cells.
(JMB: June 1974) B

5 (a) Suppose you are given an onion bulb. Outline the procedure you would follow in order to be able to see its chromosomes.
(b) The relative amounts of DNA were measured in the cells of the plant *Tradescantia* during meiosis and mitosis. The results are given below:

PHASE OF NUCLEAR CYCLE	DNA CONTENT PER CELL
Mitosis: Early interphase	2·0
Prophase	4·0
Late telophase	2·0
Meiosis 1: Leptotene	4·0
Diplotene	4·0
Meiosis 2: Telophase	1·0

(i) Account for the differences in DNA content between
(A) mitosis early interphase and mitosis prophase.
(B) mitosis prophase and mitosis late telophase.
(C) meiosis 1 diplotene and meiosis 2 telophase.
(D) meiosis 2 telophase and mitosis early interphase.
(ii) What would you estimate the DNA content of cells at meiosis 1 telophase to be?
(c) A diploid cell contains three pairs of chromosomes in the nucleus. Draw a labelled diagram to show the appearance of the cell at anaphase of a mitotic division.
(JMB: June 1977) B

Chapter 8

1 Describe the mechanism of (a) ventilation and (b) gaseous exchange in a mammalian lung. Explain how the oxygen concentration of the blood is maintained under varying degrees of physical activity. (London: June 1976) B

2 The table below gives the percentage saturation with oxygen of the blood of three animals at different pressures of oxygen:

OXYGEN PRESSURE (mm OF MERCURY)	SATURATION OF BLOOD WITH OXYGEN		
	HORSE	FOETAL HORSE	LLAMA
10	20	10	20
20	40	50	60
30	50	70	80
40	70	80	90
50	80	90	90
60	80	90	—

Plot these data in such a way that the graphs (oxygen dissociation curves) can be compared. Given that the llama lives at a high altitude, in the Andes, explain the differences between these graphs. What do you think the oxygen dissociation curves might be like for (a) horses normally kept at sea level but used to take travellers across high mountains, and (b) horses used for ploughing, and (c) race horses, and (d) llamas in zoos, and (e) foetal llamas?
(London: June 1971) Z

3 (a) Describe the mechanism involved in the ventilation of the lungs in a mammal.
(b) Explain how these breathing movements are controlled.
(JMB: June 1974) B

4 Write a detailed account of the carriage of the blood gases in mammals, including reference to environmental effects.
(JMB: Special Paper June 1978) B

5 (a) State briefly what you consider to be the main properties and requirements of surfaces used for gaseous exchange.
(b) How are these requirements achieved in
(i) a terrestrial flowering plant, and
(ii) a terrestrial mammal? (JMB: June 1976) B

Chapter 9

1 Describe the structure, mode of action and function of the heart in a mammal. (London: June 1977) B

2 Explain how the structure and operation of the mammalian heart enable it to function as a pump in the circulatory system. What effects do the aorta, other arteries, capillaries and veins have on the flow of blood? (London: June 1968) Z

3 (a) Describe the mode of action of a mammalian heart.
(b) Explain how the heart beat is regulated according to the demands of the body. (JMB: June 1978) B

4 (a) What do you understand by the terms antigen and antibody? State their general importance in mammals.
(b) Explain, with *one* example, how antigen/antibody responses in man have been used in the fight against infectious disease.
(c) Explain how antigen/antibody responses in man (other than that given in answer to (b)) have led to medical problems. Describe how these problems have been or are being overcome. (JMB: June 1978) B

5 The table below gives some of the characteristics of various types of blood vessels in man.

	DIAMETER OF LUMEN	THICKNESS OF WALL	APPROX. TOTAL CROSS-SECTIONAL AREA FOR ALL VESSELS OF EACH TYPE (cm^2)	PERCENTAGE OF TOTAL BLOOD CONTAINED IN ALL VESSELS OF EACH TYPE
Aorta	25 mm	2 mm	4·5	2
Artery	4 mm	1 mm	20	8
Arteriole	30 μm	20μm	400	1
Capillary	6 μm	1μm	4500	5
Venule	20 μm	2μm	4000	
Vein	5 mm	500μm	40	50
Vena cava	30 mm	1·5 mm	18	

(a) (i) Comment on any relationships you observe in this table, and explain them as far as you can.
(ii) Discuss the distribution of the total blood volume in the light of the figures given in the right-hand column above.
(b) The figure below gives diagrammatic curves, drawn to different scales, for total cross-sectional area, mean velocity of blood flow, and mean pressure in each type of blood vessel. Deduce which curve is which.

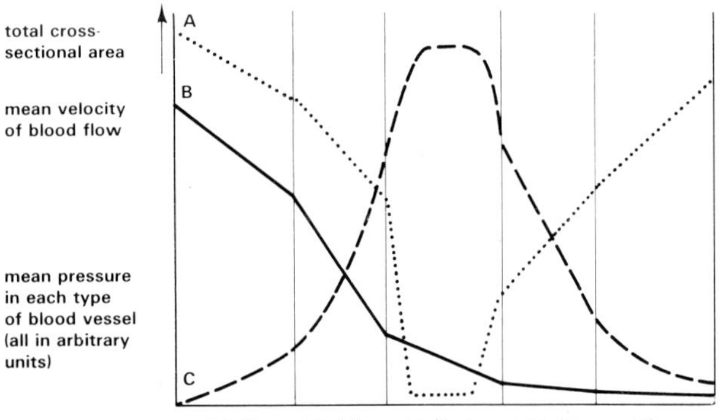

(c) (i) Make a diagram of the heart labelled to show the route of the excitation wave which accompanies the heart beat.
(ii) Give two pieces of evidence which show that the sino-atrial node is the pacemaker of the heart.
(iii) Give two pieces of evidence which show that the origin of the heart beat is myogenic. (JMB: Special Paper June 1975) B

Chapter 10

1 Make large, fully labelled diagrams to show
(a) the general internal structure of a mammalian kidney, and
(b) the detailed structure of a nephron.
Explain how the kidney controls the water content and the urea content of the body. (London: June 1975) B

2 What are the functions of the mammalian kidney? Explain how the structure of the kidney is specialised for the performance of the functions you have described. (London: June 1967) Z

3 Give an account of the histology of the mammalian kidney, with special reference to high-power detail, to show how structure is related to function. (London: June 1975) Z

4 The graph shows the effects of a temporary constriction of the renal artery in a mammal.
(a) (i) On which side of the constriction would these effects be shown?
(ii) What corresponding changes would you expect to find in the blood pressure on the opposite side of the constriction?
(iii) What immediate effect would this constriction have on the rate of glomerular filtration?
(iv) Predict, giving your reasons, the effect on the composition of the urine of lowering the temperature of the kidney from 37°C to 25°C.

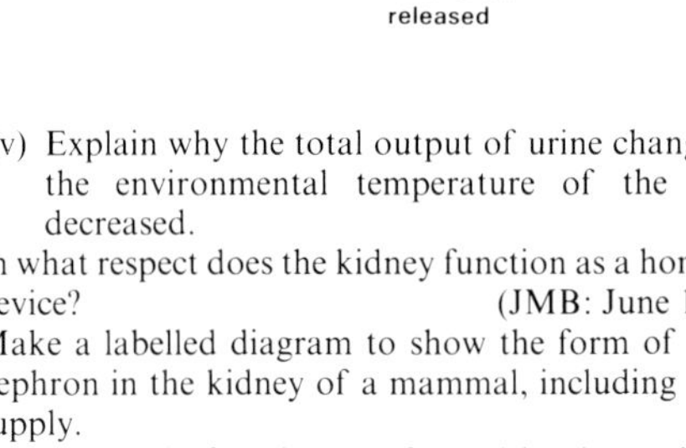

(v) Explain why the total output of urine changes when the environmental temperature of the body is decreased.
(b) In what respect does the kidney function as a homeostatic device? (JMB: June 1974) B

5 (a) Make a labelled diagram to show the form of a typical nephron in the kidney of a mammal, including its blood supply.
(b) State the main functions performed by the nephron and relate these, as far as possible, to specific regions. (N.B. Physical and chemical details of how these functions are carried out are not needed.)
(c) The figure below indicates the osmotic pressures of dissolved mineral salts and of urea in the blood of three

different fishes, compared with the osmotic pressures of fresh water and of sea water. Assuming that the structure of the fish kidney is essentially the same as that of the mammalian kidney, what differences, if any, would you expect to find between:

(i) the amount of urine produced,
(ii) the concentration of urine produced, and
(iii) the form of the nephrons in these three fishes?

Explain your answer. (JMB: June 1975) B

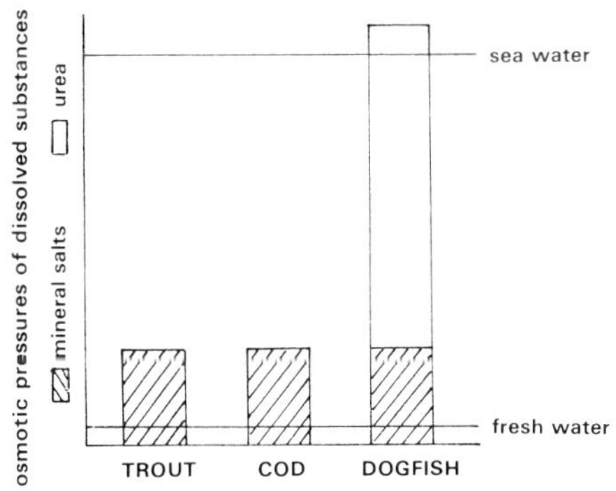

Chapter 11

1 (a) Explain, concisely, the basis of the 'root pressure' and 'cohesion-tension' hypotheses which have been proposed to explain the transport of water from roots to leaves. For each hypothesis, outline the supporting experimental evidence.
(b) (i) Give an illustrated account of the structure of the tissue in which the upward movement of water occurs in the stem.
(ii) Describe one experiment which would show that the upward movement of water does occur in this tissue. (JMB: June 1978) B

2 The graph below shows the relationship between stomatal aperture and water loss from a leaf, for a plant in still air.

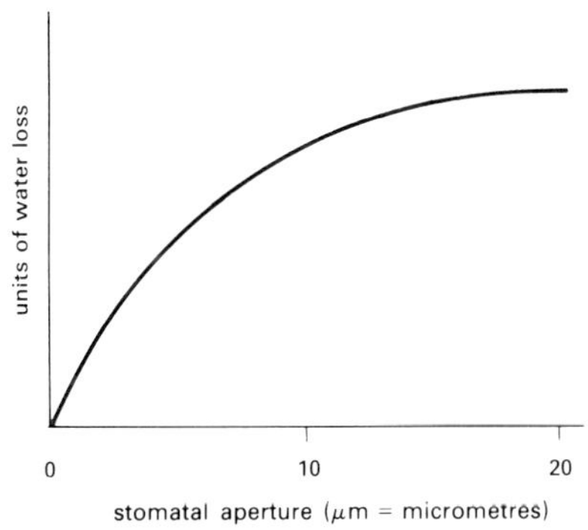

(a) Describe the relationship shown by the graph.
(b) What is the effect on the rate of water loss when the stomatal aperture reduces from 20 to 10 μm?
(c) How do other factors influence the loss of water vapour from a leaf?
(d) Discuss which of these factors you would expect to have the greatest influence over a 24-hour period in hot summer weather.
(e) Draw a curve to show how the shape of the graph would change if the plant was transferred to and left in moving air. (London: June 1976) B

3 By means of a fully labelled diagram describe the movement of water from the soil solution into the vacuole of a parenchyma cell of the root cortex. What effect does the endodermis of the root have on water movement into the stele?

Explain, as fully as you are able, how water enters xylem vessels in the root. (London: June 1975) Bot.

4 Briefly compare the functions of phloem and xylem in a flowering plant. What kinds of cells are found in the xylem and how is their structure related to the functions of the tissue? (London: June 1975) B

5 (a) Describe one method of measuring the velocity of flow of sap in the xylem tissue of either an intact plant or a cut shoot.
(b) The efficiency of the wood of different species in water conduction can be compared by measuring their specific conductance. This is done by measuring the quantity of water which passes through a standard length (15 cm) of stem under a pressure of 30 cm of mercury in 15 minutes. This quantity divided by the area of cross-section of the conducting tract gives a value which is called the specific conductance.

For a stem of a larch tree, in which the xylem is largely composed of tracheids, the specific conductance was 14.5 and for a beech tree it was 65.

Comment upon this difference as fully as you can.
(c) The graph below records the variation in the velocity of flow of sap during the course of a single day in the xylem of intact trees of the same two species.
(i) What is the force which moves the sap through the plant?
(ii) Why does the rate of flow rise to a peak at noon and then decline?
(iii) How do you explain the continued flow of sap in late evening?

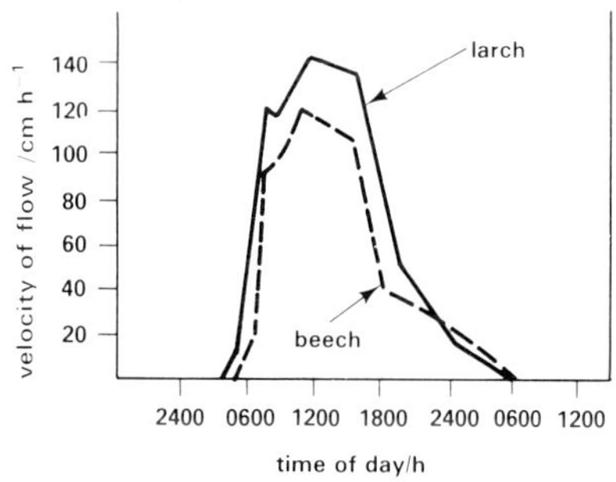

(d) The values recorded in the graph appear not to agree with the values for specific conductance given in (b). Explain why both sets of values can be correct and compatible with each other. (JMB: Special Paper June 1977) B

Chapter 12

1 A shoot of pond weed was submerged in pond water at 15°C and placed on a bench in daylight. The bubbles of gas which escaped from the cut end of the shoot were collected and their

volume was measured at intervals of time. The experiment was repeated with the shoot submerged in pond water held at temperatures of 25°C, 35°C and 45°C. The results are given below.

(a) Express these results graphically in what you consider to be the most satisfactory way.

(b) (i) Calculate a typical Q_{10} for photosynthesis as shown in this experiment.

TEMPERATURE °C	TOTAL VOLUME OF GAS IN mm³ COLLECTED AFTER			
	15 MINUTES	30 MINUTES	45 MINUTES	60 MINUTES
15	0·7	1·5	2·2	3·0
25	1·4	3·0	4·3	5·7
35	2·5	4·8	6·7	8·3
45	4·0	6·3	7·1	7·3

(ii) Explain your choice of data for the calculation.

(c) (i) Give one possible reason for the levelling-off of gas production with time at 45°C.

(ii) Suggest one experiment, or modification of the experiment described here, to test if this reason is valid.

(JMB: June 1978) B

2 (a) The following table shows the rates of carbon dioxide diffusion through membranes perforated with holes of different diameters. In each case the area of membrane perforated by the holes was the same and the number of perforations per unit area of membrane was also similar.

Diameter of holes (mm)	22·7	12·06	6·03	3·23	2·00
cm³ CO_2 diffusing h^{-1}	0·24	0·10	0·06	0·04	0·02

Use the data to construct a graph showing the rate of diffusion of the gas per unit area of hole.

(b) Relate your findings to the exchange of gases between the leaves of a terrestrial plant and its surrounding atmosphere.

(c) Write a brief account of the mechanism of stomatal movement. (OND: 1977)

3 Explain the idea that stomatal movement is a turgor phenomenon and describe how this can be tested by experiment. Describe and explain the effect on stomatal aperture of changes in the rate of photosynthesis in (a) the leaf mesophyll and (b) the guard cells.

(JMB: Special Paper June 1978) B

4 Write an account of the ways in which external factors may influence the rate of photosynthesis in a green plant. Describe carefully how you would measure

(a) the rate of photosynthesis, and

(b) the effect of one external factor on this rate.

(London: January 1976) B

5 Compare the structure of a xylem vessel with that of a sieve-tube. Show how differences between them may be related to their different functions in the plant.

(London: January 1977) B

6 Leaf discs (1 cm diameter) were punched from the mature leaves of a shrub at two-hour intervals during a warm, sunny day. The dry mass of each sample was determined. The results are given below. From the measurements, the changes in dry mass per two hours were calculated.

1	2	3
TIME OF DAY	DRY MASS OF LEAF DISCS (g)	CHANGE IN DRY MASS SINCE PREVIOUS SAMPLE (g)
5·00	3·006	—
7·00	3·028	0·022
9·00	3·148	0·120
11·00	3·390	0·242
13·00	3·650	0·260
15·00	3·782	0·132
17·00	3·936	0·154
19·00	4·008	0·072
21·00	3·992	−0·016

(a) Make a graph of the changes in dry mass (column 3) during the course of the investigation.

(b) Briefly account for the changes in dry mass recorded in each of the periods below.

(i) From 07·00 hours to 13·00 hours.

(ii) From 13·00 hours to 15·00 hours.

(iii) From 15·00 hours to 17·00 hours.

(iv) From 17·00 hours to 21·00 hours.

(JMB: June 1976) B

Chapter 13

1 A green plant synthesises hexose sugar in its leaves and absorbs ammonium ions by its roots. What further processes of transport and synthesis must occur, and in what tissues, before some of the organic nitrogen compounds synthesised from these raw materials will be exported from the roots?

(JMB: June 1977) B

2 Radioactive ^{32}P was simultaneously supplied to the roots of two similar plants, one of which had a ring of phloem removed as shown on the diagram. At the same time the leaves of both plants were in an atmosphere containing $^{13}CO_2$.

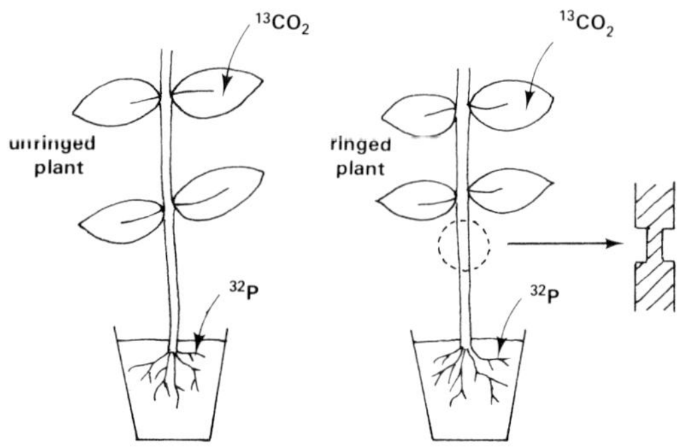

The concentrations of ^{32}P and ^{13}C after 24 hours are given in the table.

	UNRINGED PLANT	RINGED PLANT
^{32}P in roots	100·0	100·0
^{32}P in leaves	2·2	1·7
^{13}C in roots	0·09	0·00
^{13}C in leaves	0·10	0·99

What do these results show? Comment on the physiological processes involved. (London: January 1976) Bot.

3 Give an account of the mechanism of mineral ion absorption by the roots of higher plants. For three different mineral ions, discuss their importance in nutrition and indicate the deficiency symptoms which develop in their absence.
(London: June 1978) Bot.

4 An experiment was carried out to measure the uptake of water, potassium and oxygen by different zones of the root in a barley plant. The root of an intact plant was immersed in dilute potassium nitrate solution and measurements were made when the plant was transpiring at a high rate. The results (in arbitrary units) are shown below.:

DISTANCE FROM ROOT TIP (mm)	UPTAKE OF		
	WATER	POTASSIUM	OXYGEN
0–25	16	5	7
25–50	29	13	3
50–75	24	10	2

(a) Plot, by drawing three lines on one graph, the uptake of (i) water (ii) potassium (iii) oxygen.
(b) Suggest explanations to account for the differences in uptake of
  (i) water in the different zones of the root.
  (ii) oxygen in the different zones of the root.
(c) What is meant when an uptake process is said to be
  (i) active, (ii) passive?
(d) (i) Do the data suggest that the uptake of potassium is
    (A) mainly active (B) mainly passive
    (C) neither A nor B?
  (ii) Give two reasons for your answer to (i).
(JMB: June 1977) B

5 The diagrams (Figs. A and B) are of the aerial parts of kidney bean plants grown in culture solution. Ten days after germination a radioactive isotope, either ^{45}Ca or ^{32}P, was placed in the culture solution. After one hour the plants were removed and the roots washed. They were then returned to a normal culture solution and allowed to grow for a number of hours; this is shown on each diagram. After this time they were taken from the culture solution, dried quickly and autoradiographed. In the diagrams the intensity of shading is proportional to the concentrations of radioactivity found in each leaf of the plant. Note that in this plant the first leaves are a pair of heart-shaped primary leaves, the trifoliate (3-leaflets) leaves subsequently formed being borne singly. Losses by radioactive decay in the course of the experiment can be ignored.
(a) Give two assumptions which must be made concerning the absorption and distribution of radioactive isotopes in plants when interpreting data such as these.
(b) Which leaves of the plant show the greatest concentration of
  (i) calcium after 6 hours, and after 96 hours?
  (ii) phosphorus after 6 hours, and after 96 hours?
(c) (i) It was suggested that when calcium had been translocated into a given leaf it remained there. Does Fig. A support this hypothesis? Give your reasons.
  (ii) How do you account for the apparent decrease in radioactivity in leaf X (Fig. A) during the time of the experiment?
(d) Give an explanation for the changes in the distribution of radioactive phosphorus in the plant in Fig. B.
(e) (i) Using these experimental results, explain where you would expect deficiency symptoms to show when (A) calcium and (B) phosphorus is lacking in the culture medium.
  (ii) Give (A) one role of calcium and (B) one role of phosphorus in the plant. (JMB: June 1974) B

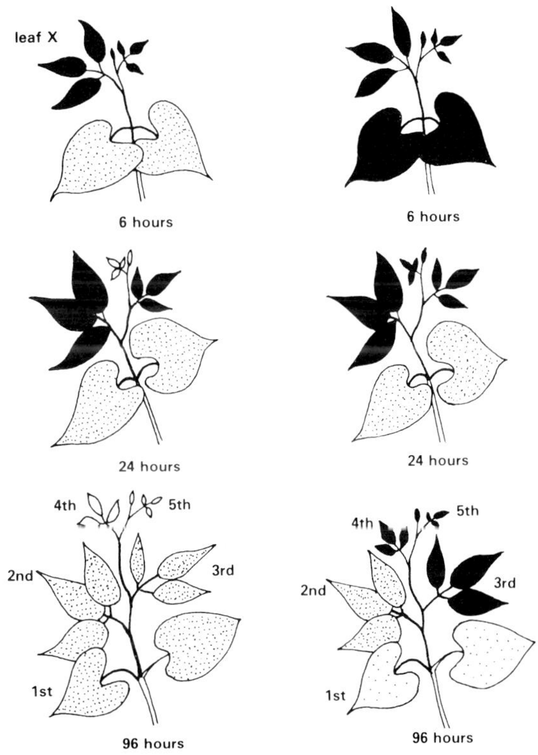

Fig. A. Distribution of ^{45}Ca.
Fig. B. Distribution of ^{32}P.

Chapter 14

1 Describe the following processes in a mammal:
(a) food ingestion and mastication,
(b) digestion in the duodenum,
(c) absorption in the ileum,
(d) production of the faeces. (London: January 1976) B

2 Why do animals require a source of nitrogen in their diet? In what forms do animals obtain nitrogen? Describe how animals process nitrogen-containing compounds and make the products available to the cells of the body.
(London: June 1978) Z

3 What is an enzyme? Describe the roles of enzymes in the digestion of proteins in a mammal making reference to those factors which are likely to influence enzyme activities.
(London: January 1978) Z

4 'The liver has a strategic role in the metabolism of carbohydrates, fats and proteins and, in addition, performs several other key functions.' Discuss this statement.
(JMB: Special Paper June 1977) B

5 Give a full account of any four proteolytic enzymes of the human digestive system. For each state:
  (i) its site of production (be as precise as you can in locating this),
  (ii) the form in which it is secreted (actual chemical formulae are not required),

(iii) its effect on the substrate molecule on which it acts,
(iv) the particular event or condition which stimulates its production and release. (JMB: June 1977) B

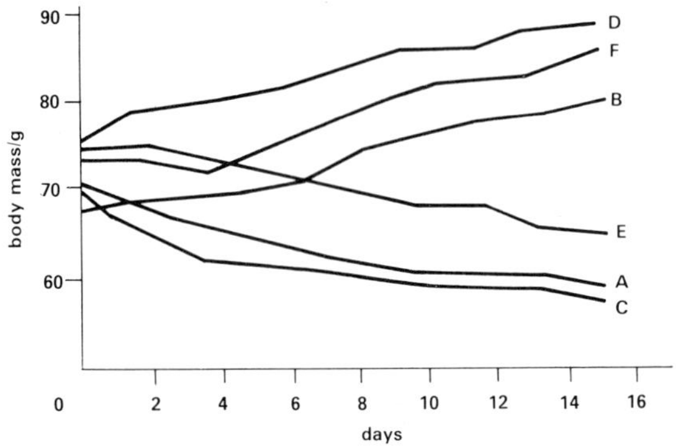

6 (a) The graph above shows the results of six experiments on the nutritional requirements of young rats in which the following modifications of a complete diet were used:

Curve A. The only protein given was zein, a protein found in maize.
Curve B. The only protein given was zein and the amino acids lysine and tryptophane were added.
Curve C. The only protein given was zein and the amino acid lysine was added.
Curve D. The amino acid cystine was omitted.
Curve E. The amino acid methionine was omitted.
Curve F. The level of methionine was reduced and cystine was omitted. At day 4 cystine was added.

(i) What conclusions can you make regarding
(A) zein as a source of amino acids for rats?
(B) the nutritional importance to rats of the amino acids lysine, tryptophane, cystine and methionine?
(C) the ability of rats to synthesise these amino acids?
(ii) Name and describe the process by which mammals can synthesise amino acids.

(b) Measurements were taken of (A) rate of production of urine, (B) concentration of urine, of a dog which had drunk its fill of water. Ten minutes after these observations had commenced a saline solution, hypertonic to the blood plasma, was injected into the carotid artery of the dog. The results of the investigations are shown in the graphs below.

A. Rate of urine production

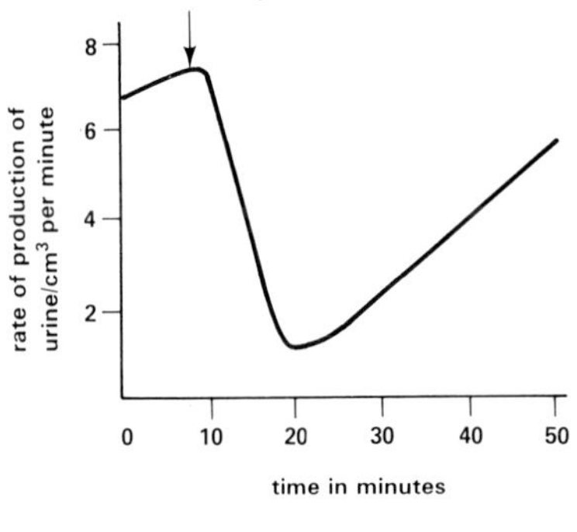

B. Concentration of urine

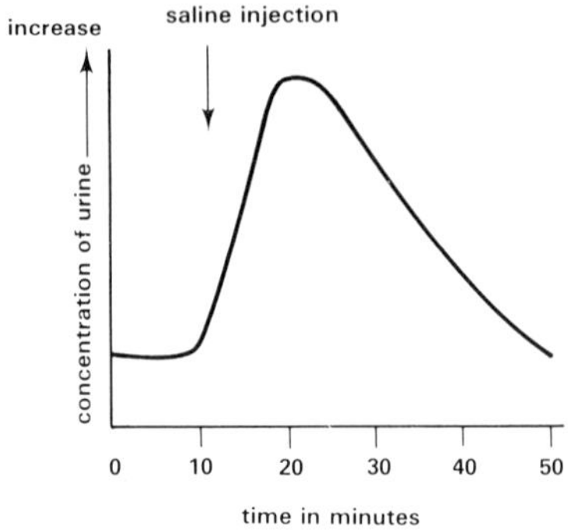

(i) Explain (A) the change in rate of production of urine,
(B) the change in concentration of the urine,
(ii) When the experiment was repeated but with the saline solution injected into a vein in the neck of the dog, it had no effect on the amount of urine produced. Explain this observation.
(JMB: Special Paper June 1975) B

Chapter 15

1 (a) Make a fully labelled diagram to show the main parts of a mammalian brain.
(b) Briefly explain the functions of the main parts of the brain in a mammal.
(c) Give an illustrated account of the way in which nerve impluses are conducted in a mammalian nerve fibre.
(London: June 1977) B

2 Outline the major pathways of the reflex arc. Describe the way in which a nerve impulse is transmitted along a fibre and across a synapse. (London: June 1975) Z

3 What is the nature of the nerve impulse? Describe
(a) how an impulse is transmitted between neurons, and
(b) what happens when an impulse reaches a striated muscle.
(London: June 1973) Z

4 Give a comparative account of the histology of striated (skeletal) and smooth muscle.

By reference to named organs explain how each type of muscle is related to the particular function of the organ concerned. (London: June 1978) Z

5 (a) Write an account of the nature, initiation and transmission of the nerve impulse.
(b) What are the main points of difference in function between the parasympathetic and sympathetic parts of the autonomic nervous system? (JMB: June 1975) B

6 The processing of information in the mammalian brain is assisted by special types of neuronal circuitry. Read the following information carefully, then answer the questions relating to the two diagrams. You should assume that a single impulse arriving at a synapse is sufficient to generate an impulse in the neuron or neurons on the other side of the synapse. If futher inputs maintain excitation above threshold, repetitive discharges will occur until excitation falls. Remember that transmission across a synapse involves a short delay.
(a) (i) If the input to Circuit A were to be a single impulse, what would be the output?
(ii) Explain how this effect is achieved.

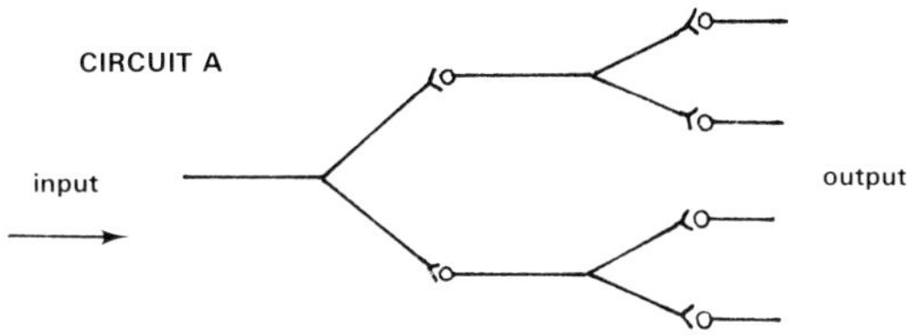

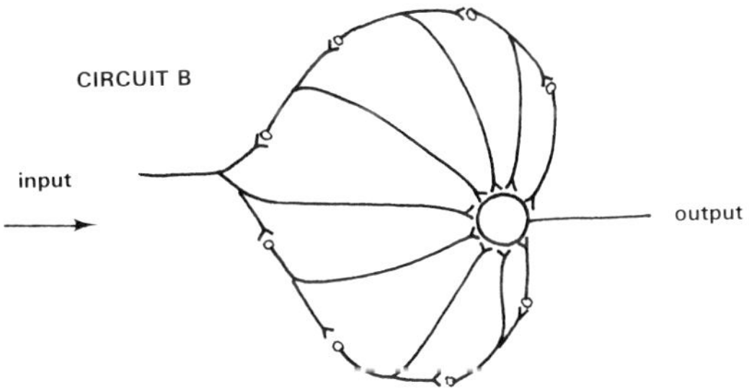

(b) (i) If the input to Circuit B were to be a single impulse, what would be the output?
(ii) Explain how this effect is achieved.
(JMB: June 1976) B

Chapter 16

1 Make a large, fully labelled diagram of the eye of a mammal in section. Write explanatory notes on each of the following.
(a) retina (b) accommodation.
(London: January 1974) B

2 Make a large, clearly labelled diagram of the ear of a mammal. Describe how those parts of the ear concerned with (a) balance and (b) hearing carry out their functions.
(London: June 1974) B

3 (a) What are the biological advantages of (i) sight, and (ii) colour vision, to animals?
(b) Make a large, clearly labelled diagram of the mammalian eye as seen in section.
(c) Briefly describe how accommodation for distance and light intensity is brought about.
(London: January 1977) B

4 (a) Make a labelled drawing of a representative portion of the cochlea of a mammal to show the internal structure of the channels in cross section.
(b) Give a brief account of how
(i) the vibrations on the oval window of the inner ear are transmitted to the sensory cells of the cochlea.
(ii) pitch discrimination may be achieved.
(c) Explain briefly why
(i) in nocturnal mammals the eyes often have
(A) a wide pupil
(B) a tapetum (a reflecting structure situated behind the visual cells)
(C) a retina containing numerous rod cells which function in groups,
(ii) in tree-dwelling mammals the eyes are usually located at the front of the head. (JMB: June 1974) B

5 This question refers to the mammal.
(a) Make a labelled diagram of a section through the cochlea to show the arrangement of the sensory cells and their surrounding structures and canals.
(b) Explain how mechanical vibrations at the tympanic membrane are transmitted to the sensory cells in the cochlea.
(c) Briefly describe how the direction of the source of a sound of short duration may be located.
(JMB: June 1976) B

6 (a) Describe the structure and functions of the human retina.
(b) What is colour blindness and why does it occur?
(ONC: 1978) B

Chapter 17

1 What is meant by the statement that mammals are warm-blooded while all invertebrates are cold-blooded? How is warm-bloodedness maintained, and what advantages does it confer on a mammal? (London: January 1969) Z

2 The following results were obtained when a group of students measured their mouth temperatures.

TEMPERATURE IN °C	NUMBER OF STUDENTS	TEMPERATURE IN °C	NUMBER OF STUDENTS
35·0	1	36·5	7
35·5	4	37·0	3
36·0	4	37·5	1

(a) (i) Calculate the average temperature of this group.
(ii) Give two possible reasons why the average differs from the quoted national average of 36·9°C.
(iii) Give two possible reasons why the mouth temperatures of the individuals differ.
(b) Describe briefly how the body detects and reacts to an increase in the external temperature.
(c) What are the advantages of having a constant body temperature?
(d) Explain the causes of the following observations:
(i) The application of heat to a man's unclothed arm may cause a rise in the temperature of the skin of the feet.
(ii) There can be a skin temperature gradient from 35°C to 15°C from the unclothed shoulder to the finger tip when the environmental temperature is 15°C.
(JMB: June 1973) B

3 (a) The graphs below show how the human body responds to an increase in the air temperature. The measurements were made on unclothed, resting male subjects in still air. The relative humidity of the air was low.

GRAPH I

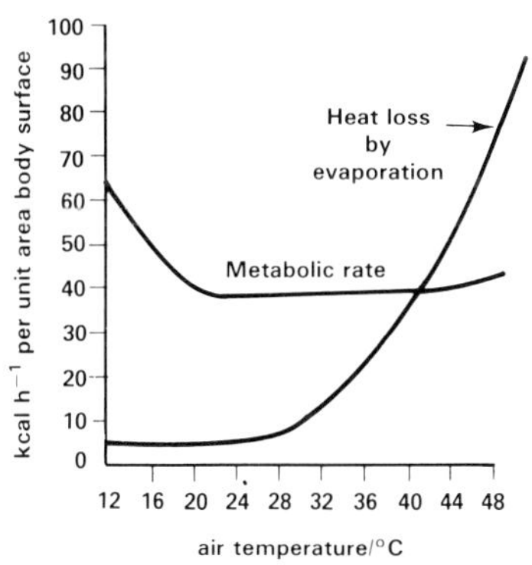

GRAPH II

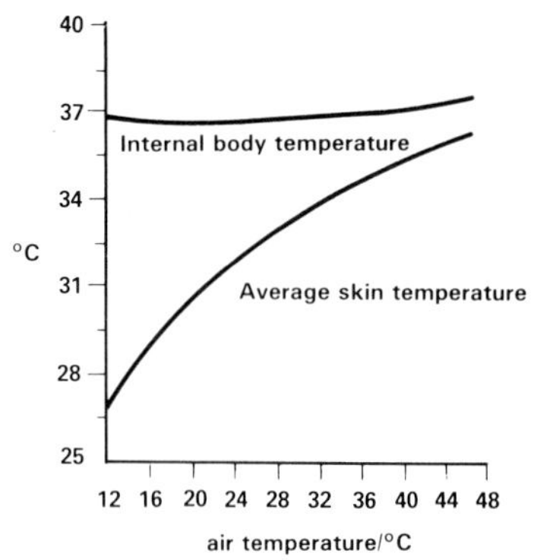

(i) Account for the changes in slope in the curves in Graph 1 which occur:
(A) at about 22°C for Metabolic rate and
(B) at about 28°C for Heat loss by evaporation.
(ii) Account for the differences, in Graph II, between the curves for Internal body temperature and Average skin temperature.
(iii) State two ways, other than by evaporation of sweat, by which heat is lost via the skin.
(iv) Name two DIFFERENT external factors: one of which (A) could decrease loss of heat by evaporation of sweat and the other (B) which could increase loss of heat by evaporation of sweat.

(b) (i) One arm of a human subject was immersed in hot water while the other arm was left exposed to the air. The exposed arm soon began to sweat and to turn pink.
State two ways in which the responses of the exposed arm could have been brought about.
(ii) When the blood flow from the heated arm was stopped, the exposed arm ceased sweating and lost its pink colour. What does this allow you to deduce about the method of thermo-regulation of the exposed arm? (JMB: June 1975) B

4 (a) (i) Give a fully-labelled diagram of a generalised vertical section of the skin of a mammal to show the structures visible under a light microscope.
(ii) The skin is not a uniform structure. Describe three different ways in which the skin is specialised at named locations in the human body.
(b) (i) Name the physical processes by which heat can be lost from exposed skin and comment briefly on their relative importance.
(ii) Discuss the role of the skin in the regulation of overall body temperature in mammals.
(JMB: June 1978) B

Chapter 18

1 What is homeostasis? Indicate the part played by each of the following in the homeostatic mechanisms of a mammal:
(a) skin, (b) pancreas and
(c) heart and blood vessels. (London: June 1974) B

2 (a) Show the position of, and label, eight different endocrine glands on a large outline drawing of a human male.
(b) Give an account of the role of two hormones which play a part in carbohydrate metabolism in the mammal.
(JMB: June 1974) B

3 The pituitary is said to be a 'master gland' within the endocrine system of a vertebrate. Using specific examples of the hormones which it produces, describe instances of its activities which you feel reflect this description of the gland.
To what extent do you consider that the statement might misrepresent the pituitary gland in relation to other endocrine organs? (London: June 1978) Z

4 This question refers to the mammal.
(a) What are the sources of the glucose found in the blood? How and where does glucose enter the blood? What processes lead to a loss of glucose from the blood?
(b) Describe how a constant level of blood glucose is maintained. (JMB: June 1977) B

5 A person suspected of having diabetes mellitus may take a glucose tolerance test as follows. After several hours of fasting he or she ingests 50 g glucose dissolved in 150 cm^3 water. The blood glucose is estimated at the same time, and subsequently every half hour for two and a half hours.
The graph gives glucose tolerance data for three people who had undergone the test.
(a) Using the graph suggest
(i) why the blood glucose is estimated as frequently as every half hour.
(ii) why the testing was continued for only two and a half hours.

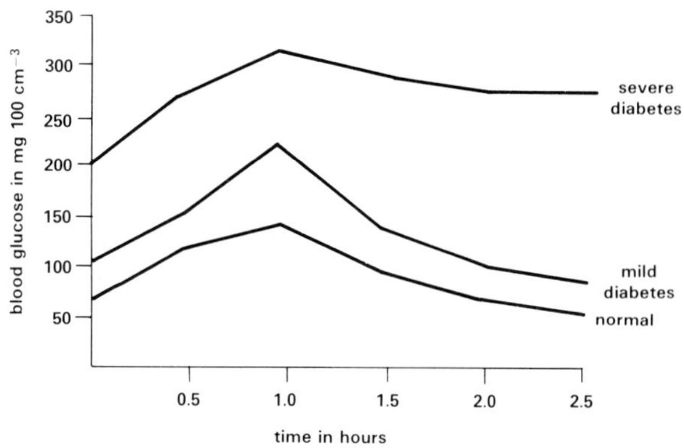

(b) The kidney starts to excrete glucose when the blood glucose level exceeds about 180 mg per 100 cm^3. Glucose in the urine (glycosuria) is therefore a common symptom of diabetes mellitus.
Using the graph, explain whether a test would or would not reveal glucose in the urine of a mild diabetic.
(i) at half an hour after the start of the test.
(ii) at two hours after the start of the test.
(c) Treatment of experimental animals with the drug alloxan produces similar symptoms to those of diabetes mellitus. Alloxan selectively destroys particular secretory cells of the body. Give the location and function of the cells which it destroys. (JMB: June 1978) B

Chapter 19

1 (a) Make a large labelled drawing of a longitudinal section of the mature ovule of a flowering plant.
(b) Describe the structural and physiological events which occur after pollination up to and including the formation of the fruit in a flowering plant. (JMB: June 1977) B

2 Distinguish between pollination and fertilisation in a flowering plant. Describe the pollination mechanism of a named insect-pollinated flower. To what extent do insects and flowering plants depend on each other? (London: January 1977) B

3 It is increasingly the practice to grow genetically-uniform plants; breeds of farm animals are also tending to become more uniform genetically.
(a) Explain, with examples, the various means by which such genetic uniformity is obtained.
(b) Discuss, with examples, the advantages and disadvantages of this uniformity. (JMB: Special Paper June 1977) B

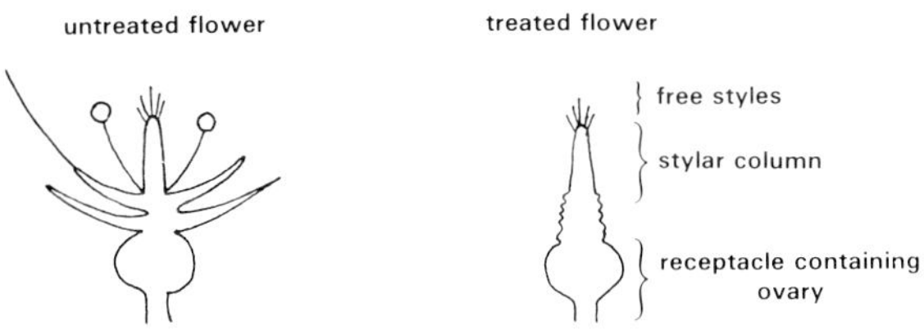

4 The diagram above shows the design of an experiment to assess the relative effectiveness of insect and wind pollination in apple trees. The weather during the experiment was suitable for both wind and insect pollination. The variety of apple tree used was self-incompatible (when self-pollinated the pollen tubes made little growth in the stigma and style). A large number of untreated and treated flowers were exposed for two days for pollination to occur. The flowers were then protected from further pollination. The extent of pollination was evaluated seven days later by considering the number and penetration of pollen tubes. These data are shown in Table. 1

TABLE I

REGION	AVERAGE NUMBER OF POLLEN TUBES		FLOWERS (AS % OF TOTAL INVESTIGATED) IN WHICH REGION LISTED CONTAINED THE POLLEN TUBES	
	UNTREATED	TREATED	UNTREATED	TREATED
Free styles	158	25	40	21
Stylar column	86	8	15	4
Ovary	38	4	12	3

(a) (i) Give two reasons which could explain why there are so many more pollen tubes in the free styles than in the ovary.
(ii) What is the significance of the presence of pollen tubes in the ovary?
(iii) Give two ways in which treatment (shown in the diagram) may affect the pollination of the flower.
(iv) From the data, state, giving two reasons for your answer, whether wind or insect pollination is more effective.
(b) The data in Table II refer to two varieties of apple.

Table II

	Variety A	Variety B
Longevity of unfertilised ovule measured from the time of flower opening	8 days	12 days
Time required for the growing pollen tube to reach the ovule	5 days	5 days

(i) Calculate the number of days from flower opening during which pollination can be effective for each of the two varieties.
(ii) Which variety is likely to be the most fruitful (taking no account of other factors)? (JMB: June 1978) B

5 (a) What structure gives rise to the flower in higher plants?
(b) A short-day plant, species P, and a long-day plant, species Q, both flower when grown in cycles of 13 hours light/11 hours dark. Copy the table below (the three columns shown in bold type on the right only) and indicate the likely flowering responses of these plants in the daylengths shown. Use a tick for flowering and a cross for non-flowering.

Daylength (hr) Light	Dark		**Flowering response Species P**	**Species Q**
9	15	**A**		
11	13	**B**		
13	11	**C**	√	√
15	9	**D**		
17	7	**E**		

(c) The critical daylength is that daylength which lies at the boundary between inductive and non-inductive daylengths. The critical daylength for flowering in species X is 14 hours light/10 hours dark and in species Y is 13 hours light/11 hours dark. Do these critical daylengths show that
A species X is a long-day plant and species Y a short-day plant?
B species X is a short-day plant and species Y is a long-day plant?
C both species are long-day plants?
D both species are short-day plants?
E each species could be either a long-day plant or a short-day plant?
(Give one letter only).
(d) Cocklebur is a short-day plant which requires only one inductive cycle for flower formation. A plant grown under long days (18 hours light, 6 hours dark) does not flower. When subjected to a single inductive short day (10 hours light, 14 hours dark) it subsequently flowers.
(i) When an additional 0·5 hours exposure to white light is given in the middle of the dark period to a plant grown under 9·5 hours light, 14 hours dark, the plant does not flower. What does this suggest about the relative importance of the light and dark periods?
(ii) Wavelengths of light in the red region of the spectrum are more effective in inhibiting flowering when given as a light treatment in the middle of the dark period. What pigment is likely to be the receptor for this response?
(iii) Plants maintained under long daylengths flower when the lamina of a single leaf attached to the plant is enclosed and given short-day conditions. How does this observation support the concept of a flowering hormone? (JMB: June 1974) B

Chapter 20

1 (a) Describe the chemical interactions which exist
(i) between the seed coat and the embryo, and
(ii) between the endosperm and the embryo.
For each case, describe one such chemical interaction and show how the interaction could be demonstrated practically.
(b) (i) How, in nature, are the barriers to germination removed?
(ii) How does the possession of mechanisms of seed dormancy benefit plant species?
(JMB: June 1978) B

2 Write a concise account of the following aspects of the seeds of flowering plants:
(a) the significance of seed size,
(b) mechanisms and significance of dormancy,
(c) mobilisation of storage materials at germination.
(JMB: June 1976) B

3 (a) (i) Give one external factor which affects the rate of respiration of a plant and say how it affects the rate.
(ii) Give two places in, or parts of, a higher plant where you would expect the rate of respiration to be high, and two where you would expect it to be low.
(iii) Suggest one method, giving reasons, by which ripe apples could be stored for as long as possible.
(b) (i) Give a labelled diagram to show the apparatus you would use to measure the respiratory quotient (RQ) of germinating seeds.
(ii) Describe how you would use this apparatus to measure the oxygen intake and carbon dioxide production of the seeds. State what control you would use.
(iii) The following results were given by germinating seeds under standard time and conditions in such an experiment.
Volume of O_2 used = 1·60 cm^3
Volume of CO_2 given out = 1·15 cm^3.
Calculate the RQ. What type of substrate was being respired?
(iv) What other measurements would you need in order to calculate (A) the respiratory rate and (B) the Q_{10} for respiration of germinating seeds?
(JMB: June 1974) B

4 Examine the graph of amylase activity in germinating barley grains and answer the questions that follow:

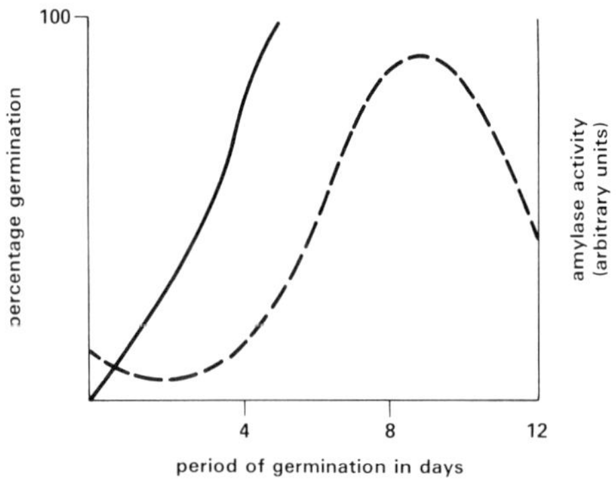

(a) What is the time interval in days between all the barley grains having commenced germination and the peak in amylase activity?
(b) What reaction does amylase catalyse and what is the product of the reaction?
(c) Suggest reasons for the change in amylase activity after the eighth day of germination.
(d) Make a large, labelled drawing of a longitudinal section of a cereal grain.
Mark on your drawing one site of amylase activity, and one destination for the product of the reaction.
(e) Explain the effect of an increase in temperature from 15° to 45°C on amylase activity.
(London: January 1976) Bot.

5 The graphs below show changes which occur in (I) dry matter, (II) area and (III) photosynthetic activity, with time from the

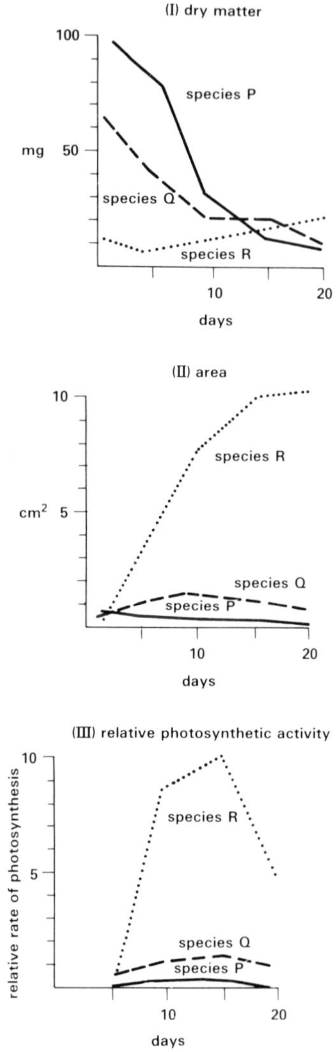

start of germination, in the cotyledons of the seeds of three species of plant, Species P, Species Q and Species R.
(a) Distinguish briefly between the meanings of the terms hypogeal and epigeal, as used to describe germination. Give one named example of each.
(b) Of the three species, P, Q and R, which one shows hypogeal germination? Give two reasons for your choice.
(c) Using the information in the graphs, together with your knowledge of germination, explain what processes may account for the following:
(i) the fall in cotyledon weight with time in Species P,
(ii) the fact that the fall in cotyledon weight with time in Species Q is proportionately less than that in Species P,
(iii) the fact that cotyledon weight in Species R
(A) increases
(B) that the increase is very small.
(iv) the fact that the photosynthetic activity of the cotyledons of Species R
(A) rises sharply between day 5 and day 10 and
(B) falls after day 15.

(d) Is it reasonable to suggest that, of the two species which have epigeal germination, one is better adapted to this condition than the other? Briefly explain your answer. (JMB: June 1975) B

Chapter 21

1 Give an account of shoot elongation in flowering plants, showing how it is regulated by external and internal factors. (JMB: Special Paper June 1977) B

2 (a) (i) What is bioassay?
(ii) Outline a technique which can be used to bioassay auxin.
(iii) State four effects which auxins may produce in living cells, tissues or organs.
(b) (i) Describe how you would attempt to propagate a plant from a stem cutting, outlining the optimum conditions and the ideal procedure for success.
(ii) What anatomical changes occur in the vicinity of the wounded surface of a stem cutting during successful propagation?
(iii) What is meant by polar transport of auxin?
(iv) What, for stem cuttings, are the consequences of the polar transport of auxin?
(v) With what other category of plant hormones do the auxins which are important for the establishment of the cutting interact and what is the outcome of such interaction? (JMB: June 1976) B

3 Describe the various ways in which light affects the growth and development of plants (omitting photosynthesis). (London: June 1974) B

4 Give an explanation of each of the following:
(a) Trees near a street lamp sometimes flower earlier than similar trees elsewhere.
(b) The shoots of plants placed on a window sill grow towards the light.
(c) The removal of the terminal bud of a plant may lead to the development of the lateral buds. (London: January 1976) B

5 Write about the root and shoot system of flowering plants under the following headings:
(a) A comparison of the structure of the root and shoot apical regions.
(b) The sites of initiation and early development of lateral roots and lateral buds.
(c) The factors which affect the direction of growth of roots and shoots. (JMB: June 1973) B

Chapter 22

1 Describe how the following intermittent actions are initiated and controlled in a mammal:
(a) secretion of gastric juice, (b) ovulation.
Discuss the main control principle shown by both of these examples. (JMB: June 1973) B

2 (a) For mammals:
(i) state three features of the placenta which facilitate the exchange of materials,
(ii) give a brief account of the endocrine functions of the placenta.
(b) In the foetus, oxygenated blood from the placenta passes via the umbilical vein and posterior vena cava to the right atrium (auricle). There is an opening in the septum between the left and right atria, the foramen ovale. This usually closes over at birth.
(i) What function may be served in the foetus by the foramen ovale?
(ii) What malfunction might be expected in the circulatory system of the infant if this opening did not seal?
(iii) Mammalian foetal haemoglobin usually takes up oxygen at partial pressures at which the maternal haemoglobin gives up oxygen. What is the advantage of this?
(c) (i) The table below shows the calcium (Ca) requirements of three women:

	Ca requirements (mg day $^{-1}$)
Adult female	680
Pregnant female	1600
Nursing mother	2000

Explain these differences in the daily requirement of calcium.
(ii) Briefly explain why the enzyme rennin is found predominantly in young mammals.
(iii) The young of grazing mammals open their eyes shortly after birth and can soon move around independently. In many carnivorous mammals the young do not open their eyes for some time after birth, they are often quite helpless and have a much longer period of dependence and association with their parents. What relationship does there appear to be between the situation given above and the ways of life of the animals? (JMB: June 1975) B

3 (a) Give an account (using graphs and or diagrams if you wish) of the events which occur in
(i) the ovary, and (ii) the uterus
of a non-pregnant human female during the monthly reproductive cycle.
(b) Describe how these events are controlled by hormones, stating, for each hormone, its precise effect and its site of production. (JMB: June 1976) B

4 (a) Make a fully-labelled plan diagram of a transverse section of a mammalian testis and indicate where and how spermatogenesis occurs.
(b) Explain the importance of mitosis and meiosis in spermatogenesis. (ONC: 1978)

5 What are the essential features of the process of fertilisation in plants and animals? Consider the variety of means by which fertilisation is accomplished. (JMB: Special Paper June 1977) B

6 Compare and contrast the processes of gametogenesis in a male and female vertebrate. Show how the differences described are related to the nature of the gametes produced. (London: June 1976) Z

Chapter 23

1 In tomatoes, tall plants are produced by the dominant gene *D*, and its recessive allele *d* produces short plants. Hairy stems are produced by the dominant gene *H*, and hairless (smooth) stems by its recessive allele *h*. Red stems are produced by the dominant gene *A*, and non-red (green) stems by its recessive allele *a*.
(a) What are the possible genotypes of plants which are:
(i) tall, hairy and green-stemmed,
(ii) short, smooth and red-stemmed?
(b) On crossing a plant which was short, hairy and green-stemmed, with one that was short, smooth and red-stemmed, the following progeny were obtained:
29 short, hairy, red;
25 short, hairy, green;
28 short, smooth, red;
30 short, smooth, green.

What were the genotypes of the parents? Give a reasoned explanation of your answer.

(c) What is meant by a back-cross (test-cross)? Explain how such a back-cross could be used to show whether a tall, smooth, green-stemmed plant was heterozygous or homozygous for the 'tall' gene. (London: June 1976) B

2 (a) Briefly describe, with the aid of one example in each case, what you understand by the following:
(i) chromosome mutation,
(ii) incomplete dominance,
(iii) sex linkage.

(b) Blood groups **ABO** in humans are under the control of genes (I), which occur in three forms, I^A, I^B, I^O; any two of these can occur together:

BLOOD TYPE	GENOTYPE
O	I^OI^O
A	I^AI^A or I^AI^O
B	I^BI^B or I^BI^O
AB	I^AI^B

A baby has blood type **B**, his mother has blood type **A**, his paternal grandfather has blood type **A**, and his paternal grandmother has blood type **B**. Determine (i) the genotype of the baby and (ii) the possible genotype of the baby's father. Use symbols as above to show how you reach your conclusions (London: June 1977) B

3 'Black-and-tan' is a characteristic in mice in which the development of black fur is restricted to the top side of the body.

A pure-breeding black-and-tan female mouse with long ears was crossed with a pure-breeding black, short-eared male. The offspring had black-and-tan fur and long ears. These F_1 mice were interbred and the following progeny obtained.

	BLACK-AND-TAN, LONG EARS	BLACK, LONG EARS	BLACK-AND-TAN, SHORT EARS	BLACK, SHORT EARS
females	16	7	6	2
males	20	5	4	2
total	36	12	10	4

(a) Is there any evidence from the data to suggest that the characters of fur colour and ear length in mice are sex-linked?

(b) Explain your answer given in part(a) above.

(c) What else can be deduced from the data about the nature and location of the genes which control fur colour and ear length?

(d) Construct a diagram to explain the probable result of a cross between an F_1 individual and its short-eared parent. (London: June 1980) B

4 (a) A number of rats with longer tails than normal are discovered in a wild population. Describe clearly how you would determine experimentally whether or not tail length is:
(i) a discontinuously variable character,
(ii) an heritable character.

(b) Assuming that tail length is a discontinuous character controlled by a single gene with two alleles, describe clearly how you would determine whether or not
(i) the allele determining long tail is dominant,
(ii) the gene is located on the X chromosome.

(c) (i) What is a gene pool?
(ii) Suppose the previous experiment had shown tail length to be a character with two alternative forms (short and long) controlled by a single autosomal gene with two alleles, the allele for long tail being dominant. A sample of 100 rats is taken from the wild population of which 36 are long-tailed. Use the Hardy–Weinberg equation to calculate the frequency of the tail-length alleles. Explain your deductions clearly.
(iii) The Hardy–Weinberg equation assumes genetic equilibrium in a population. Describe three factors which can disturb this equilibrium.
(JMB: June 1982) B

5 (a) Make large, labelled drawings to show one pair of chromosomes in a cell at
(i) metaphase of mitosis,
(ii) metaphase I of meiosis,
(iii) metaphase II of meiosis.

(b) How is sex genetically determined in man?

(c) In humans, a gene responsible for clotting blood is carried on the X chromosome. People who carry only the recessive gene bleed easily and are called haemophiliacs. The diagram below shows the occurrence of haemophiliacs in a certain family. Indicate the genotype for each individual numbered in the diagram below.
(London: June 1981) B

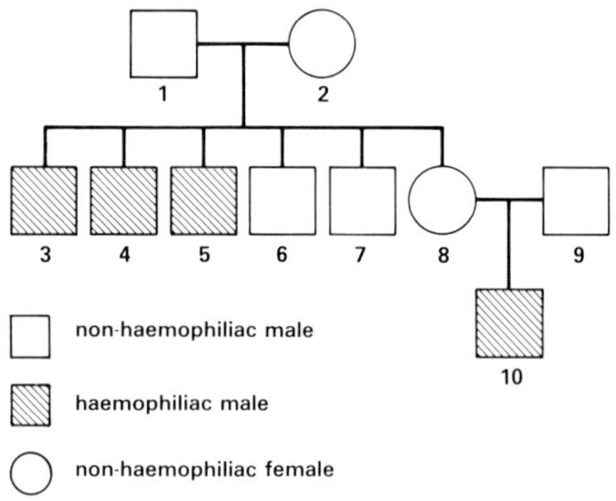

6 Two genes in the mouse interact to control three possible coat colours: grey, black and chocolate. The two genes are located on different chromosomes (autosomes), each gene having two alleles. A is dominant to a, B is dominant to b.

Examples of four genotypes and their phenotypes are given in the table below.

GENOTYPE	PHENOTYPE
AABb	grey
Aabb	grey
aaBb	black
aabb	chocolate

(a) What colour coat would you expect each of these genotypes to give?

AABB *AaBb*
AAbb *aaBB*

(b) An *AABB* female was crossed with an *aabb* male.
(i) Give the genotype of the F_1.
(ii) Give the phenotypes of the F_2 and the ratio in which they are produced.

(c) A female from the F_1 in b(i) above was crossed with a chocolate male. For this cross, give the phenotypes and the ratio in which they are produced. (JMB: June 1981) B

Chapter 24

1 Write an account of either the theories of the origin of life or the evidence for evolution in the plant and animal kingdoms. (London: January 1977) B

2 Discuss the ways in which genetic variation, natural selection and isolation mechanisms may produce evolutionary change and speciation. (London: June 1977) B

3 Discuss critically the importance of the following to the theory of evolution:
(a) geographical distribution of organisms,
(b) fossils,
(c) a knowledge of chromosomes. (London: June 1978) B

4 State the theory of evolution put forward by Darwin and cite the evidence he used in formulating this theory. In what ways has this theory been modified by more recent evidence? (London: January 1980) B

5 (a) Why is it difficult to arrive at a satisfactory definition of the term 'species'?
(b) How does genetic variation arise and how is it maintained in a population?
(c) Discuss the roles of natural selection and isolation in the evolution of species. Illustrate your answer by reference to named examples. (JMB: June 1981) B

6 Melanism in a species of moth is controlled by a gene with two alleles, one coding for melanic form (*M*, dominant), the other for the non-melanic form (*m*, recessive). In areas of atmospheric pollution a change in the frequency of non-melanic forms relative to melanics may occur. The graph shows the percentage frequency of melanic types in two populations over twenty generations. At the end of this time, population A lives in a heavily polluted environment, population B in a much less polluted environment.

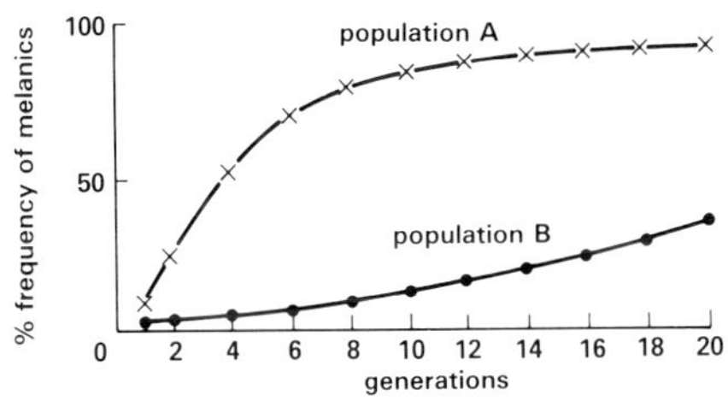

(a) (i) Explain how natural selection may be operating on population A.
(ii) Why are the results shown in the graph for population B different from those for population A?
(b) If the pollution affecting population A was entirely stopped during generation 21, what would be the effect on the relative frequency of melanic individuals in this population in subsequent generations? Explain your answer.
(c) Generation 14 of population B has a 19 per cent frequency of melanic phenotypes. Using the Hardy–Weinberg formula, calculate the frequency of the three genotypes in this generation. (JMB: June 1980) B

Chapter 25

1 (a) What is alternation of generations?
(b) Write an illustrated account of alternation of generations in the life cycle of a moss.
(c) How does alternation of generations in a fern and a flowering plant differ from that in a moss? (London: January 1979) B

2 Give an account of the economic importance of viruses and bacteria. (London: June 1977) B

3 Discuss the value of external features in the construction of a natural classification of plants and animals. (London: June 1977) B

4 Gymnosperms and angiosperms are classified as subdivisions of the same major group of plants. What are the features which allow these two groups to be classified.
(a) in the same major group
(b) as separate sub-groups? (London: June 1978) B

5 Write an essay on viruses. (JMB: June 1980) B

6 Compare the gametophyte generation of *Selaginella* with that of a named moss. (JMB: June 1980) B

7 (a) Describe the gametophyte generation of a fern under the following headings.
(i) habitat
(ii) growth and structure
(iii) nutrition
(iv) reproduction.
(b) Briefly compare the fern gametophyte with the female gametophyte of a conifer. (JMB: June 1982) B

Chapter 26

1 Discuss the range of feeding methods in animals. (London: January 1980) B

2 (a) State briefly the difference between sexual and non-sexual reproduction.
(b) How are large increases in numbers brought about in
(i) a named protozoan,
(ii) a named coelenterate,
(iii) a mammal, other than man,
(iv) a fern?
(c) Suggest why populations of most plants and animals remain fairly constant despite the production of large numbers of offspring. (London: June 1982) B

3 (a) Name the phylum to which each of the following belongs:
(i) a ciliate, (iii) a starfish,
(ii) a polychaete, (iv) an anuran.
(b) Give three reasons why a hydroid and a jellyfish are classified in the same phylum.
(c) Give three ways in which a hydroid differs from a planarian. (London: Specimen paper 1978) B

4 (a) What type of life cycle is shown by the organism illustrated below?
(b) Name the stages A, B, C and D.

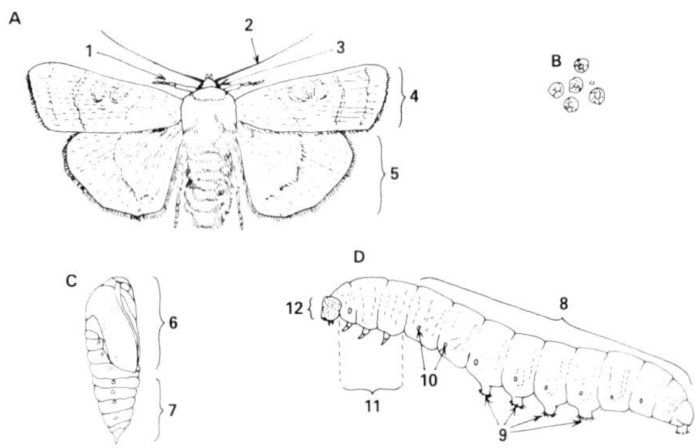

(c) Name the parts numbered 1 to 12.
(d) Describe the functions of the parts indicated by 10.
(e) What part do hormones play in the life cycle of this organism? (London: June 1980) B

5 Name four freshwater invertebrates which employ different methods of locomotion. Give a detailed and illustrated account of the mechanism of locomotion in each of the species. (JMB: June 1980) B

Chapter 27

1 (a) What are the distinguishing features of chordate animals?
(b) Using a named example of (i) a fish, (ii) an amphibian and (iii) a bird, describe the ways in which their external features show adaptation to their environments. (London: June 1979) B

2 (a) Give three reasons why a frog and a mammal are classified in the same phylum.
(b) Give three ways in which a frog and a lizard differ structurally from each other.
(c) State three features of birds that have contributed to the success of this group. (London: June 1982) B

3 The following diagram shows:
A a dogfish in side view (X indicates the centre of gravity)
B a dorsal view of a dogfish tail during a phase of locomotory activity
C a posterior view of the tail in a comparable phase of activity.

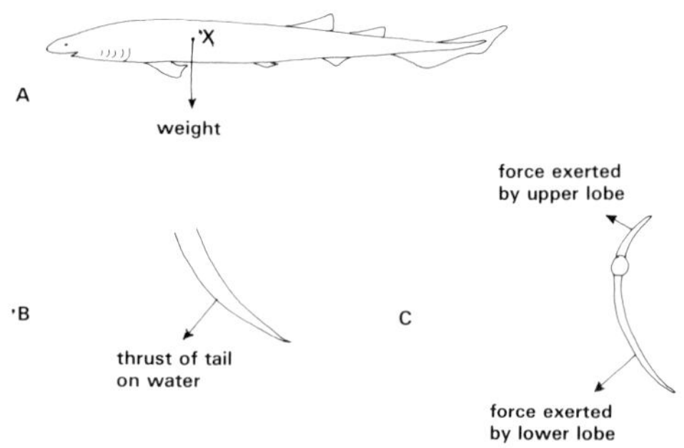

(a) What form of tail does the dogfish possess?
(b) By adding arrows to diagrams B and C, resolve the reactions to the forces indicated.
(c) On the basis of these analyses show by the addition of arrows to diagram A:
(i) the result of the reaction to the force exerted in B; indicate by an arrow numbered 1.
(ii) the resultant effect of the reactions to the sets of forces exerted in C; indicate by an arrow numbered 2.
(iii) the overall resultant effect of both sets of forces in B and C; indicate by an arrow numbered 3.
(d) How may the net effects of the forces represented by your arrows 2 and 3 be countered?
(e) Briefly describe how the results of the various forces described and illustrated contribute to the mode of life of the dogfish. (London: June 1982) Z

4 (i) Select from the following jumbled list of diagnostic characters six features which you regard as appropriate to the identification of an arthropod and six features which you regard as appropriate to the identification of a bony fish:
(a) paired fins
(b) lacks cilia
(c) exoskeleton with bony scales
(d) brain derived from hollow dorsal nervous system
(e) skin moist, glandular and ciliated
(f) respiratory surface a tracheole
(g) branched enteron with single aperture
(h) jointed appendages
(i) acoelomate
(j) normally winged
(k) flame cells
(l) cuticular exoskeleton
(m) body cavity coelomic
(n) hermaphrodite
(o) respiratory surface a gill
(p) nervous system comprising nerve ring and lateral nerve cords
(q) body cavity haemocoelic
(r) notochord present at some stage.
Arrange these features in two logical sequences, six characters for each particular animal.
(ii) Classify these two animals as far as you are able.
(iii) Give your reasons for selecting and arranging the data and for classifying these two animals in this way.
(iv) Abstract the remaining six features from the above list, arrange them in a logical sequence, and, giving your reasons, classify the animal as far as you are able. (London: June 1981) Z

5 (a) State three ways in which the ability to fly has contributed to the success of birds.
(b) Explain the principles of flight and show how the structure of birds' wings permits both gliding and powered flight. (JMB: June 1982) B

Chapter 28

1 Discuss the ways in which the distribution of organisms is affected by climate, edaphic (soil) and biotic factors. (London: June 1981) B

2 Write an essay on close associations between individual organisms of different species. (JMB: Special Paper June 1982) B

3 (a) What are the similarities and differences between parasitic and symbiotic modes of life?
(b) Give an account of the relationships between two members of (i) a named symbiotic association, and (ii) a named parasite-host association. (JMB: June 1978) B

4 Discuss, with examples, the reasons why plants and animals are not uniformly distributed through a named habitat you have studied. (London: January 1977) B

5 Explain why osmotic control is important to animals. Describe the ways in which fish and mammals regulate the water and salt content of their bodies. (London: June 1977) B

Chapter 29

1 (a) Explain what is meant by an ecosystem.
(b) Explain the meaning of the following, giving examples all chosen from *one named* ecosystem.
(i) pyramid of biomass
(ii) ecological niche
(iii) energy flow through an ecosystem
(iv) trophic levels
(v) food web. (London: January 1982) B

2 Many fresh leaves were picked from oak trees and cut up into squares of area 4 cm^2. Fifty such squares were placed in each

of three muslin bags having a fine mesh (0·5 mm) and another three sets of fifty squares were placed in bags of coarse muslin (5 mm mesh). The bags were half-buried in the leaf litter of an oak wood near to one another. Each month the percentage leaf area remaining was measured for each bag and the bags were put back into position in the ground. The experiment was conducted for 10 months and the results obtained are tabulated below.

	MEAN PERCENTAGE LEAF AREA REMAINING	
MONTH	0·5 mm MESH BAGS	5 mm MESH BAGS
July	97	96
Aug.	93	80
Sept.	90	60
Oct.	84	30
Nov.	80	20
Dec.	76	16
Jan.	74	14
Feb.	73	11
Mar.	71	8
Apr.	67	4

(a) Present these results in graphical form
(b) Attempt to explain the results as fully as possible.
(c) Suggest a further investigation that could test the validity of the explanations you have given.
(London: June 1977) B

3 Give an account of the factors which control the size of populations, commenting on these factors in relation to the human population. (JMB: Special Paper June 1982) B

4 By referring to particular ecosystems, distinguish between the following pairs of ecological terms:
(i) zonation and succession,
(ii) producer and consumer,
(iii) grazing food web and detritus (decomposer) food web,
(iv) biotic and abiotic factors. (JMB: June 1982) B

5 The energy content of a grassland has been estimated for each trophic level as follows:

	KILO-JOULES* PER SQUARE METRE
primary producers	5033
herbivores	122
omnivores	12
carnivores	10

*1 kilo-calorie is equivalent to 4·2 kilo-joules.

(a) Comment on the biological significance of these data.
(b) What is meant by 'primary producer' in this habitat?
(c) Discuss the factors that would affect the net production of the grassland's primary producers.
(d) The table below gives figures for two species of arthropod that live in the same grassland habitat. Plot graphs to show the numbers of each species against time.

TIME (WEEKS)	NUMBERS OF INDIVIDUALS species A	species B
1	0	50
2	5	100
3	50	500
4	100	1000
5	500	2000
6	2100	1000
7	800	400
8	400	80
9	10	50
10	50	500
11	150	1000
12	500	2000

(e) What deductions can be made from the graphs concerning the biological interrelationships of the two species? Outline an experiment which might be carried out to provide further information in support of your deductions. (London: January 1977) B

6 (a) What is meant by a soil?
(b) Explain why a loam soil is a fertile soil.
(c) What are the effects of adding to a soil
(i) animal manure, (ii) lime?
(London: June 1980) B

Chapter 30

1 What principles would you apply to the observation of a woodland or a freshwater habitat? Why is conservation of natural habitats of importance to man?
(London: June 1976) B

2 Discuss the uses and abuses of pesticides and herbicides.
(London: January 1977) B

3 Discuss the effects the following might have if they entered a slow flowing river (a) untreated sewage, (b) excessive run-off from agricultural land, (c) hot water from the cooling towers of a power station.
(London: January 1977) B

4 The graphs below show the effect on a stream of untreated sewage.
(a) Graph A shows physico-chemical effects (ammonia, nitrate, dissolved oxygen, suspended solids). Identify each of the lines 1–4 and give your reasoning.

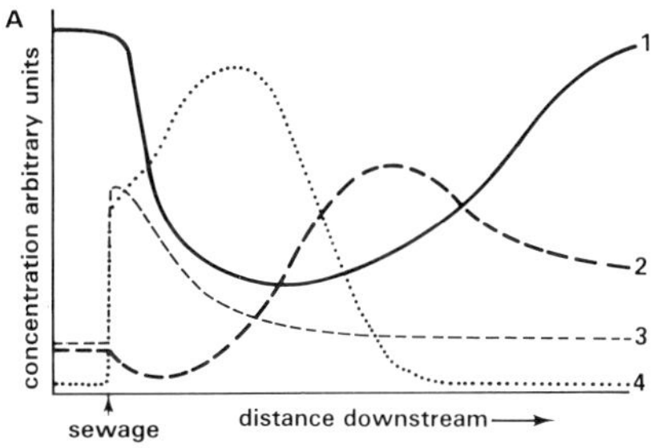

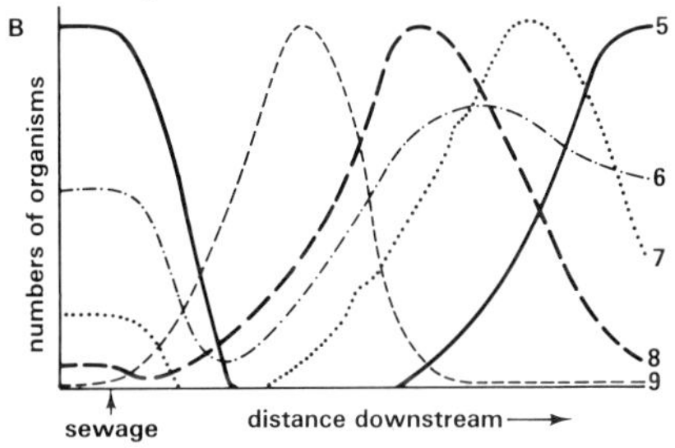

(b) Graph B shows changes in flora and fauna (algae, *Chironomus*, clean-water invertebrates, *Tubifex*, *Asellus*). Identify each of the lines 5–9 and give your reasoning.
(c) Draw a sketch graph to indicate the effect of sewage on the number of bacteria in the stream. Explain the shape of your curve. (JMB: June 1980) B

5 Discuss the impact of man's agricultural activity on the biosphere. (London: January 1981) B

6 Discuss the biological hazards of physical and chemical pollutants in the environment.
(JMB: Special Paper June 1982) B

Index

Note: The bold numbers denote figure references.

abdomen 547, **26.49, 26.56,** 551, **26.62, 26.63**
Abiotic factors 28.1.2, 588–96
ABO blood groups, inheritance 455, 458, 466
abomasum 270, **14.22,** 495
ABO system 179–80, **Tables 9.3–4**
abscissic acid, effect on seed germination 404, **20.13**
in leaf abscission, 431–2
structure 432, **21.29**
abscission 432
absorption and action spectra, photosynthesis 88
absorption, gut 275–6, **Table 14.2**
absorption of minerals, flowering plants 246–9
absorption of water, flowering plants 208–9, **11.11, 11.14, 11.21**
measuring rate of 206, **11.10(a)**
absorption spectra, chloroplast pigments 90–1, **5.15**
phytochromes 403, **20.11**
acetylcholine 160, **9.9(b),** 295, **15.18,** 300, **15.23(b),** 307–8, **15.34**
acetyl co-enzyme A 83
achene 394
acid-base balance 193
pair 33
acid rain 641
Acids, Bases and Buffers 2.3.1, 33–4
acoelomate 536, **26.38**
acromegaly 366–7, **18.30**
acrosome 437, **22.5(a)**
Actinozoa 533
action potential 286–7, **15.7,** 289, **15.9**
action spectrum, photosynthesis 89, **5.13**
phototropism 429, **21.24**
actin 297–8, **15.20(c)–21**
activation energy 68–9, **4.2**
activation, nucleic acids 108
activator, of enzymes 71
active absorption, gut 276, **Table 14.2**
active centres, enzymes 69
active immunisation 178
active transport, minerals in plants, 250–1, **13.14**
active uptake, minerals by plants 248–9, **13.10–11, 13.14**
Adaptations to High Altitude 8.33, 144–6
adaptive immunity 173
adaptive radiation 477
adaxial meristem 413, **21.5**
adenine 79, 98–9, **6.2**
adenosine-5′-diphosphate (see ADP)
adenosine-5′-monophosphate (see AMP)
Adenosine-5′-triphosphate 5.1.1, 78–9
adipose tissue 51, **3.17,** 342, **17.11(b)**
ADP 79
adrenal bodies 349, **18.1,** 360–1, **18.20(a)**
adrenal cortex 360–3, **18.20(a), 18.24–5**
adrenalin 160, **9.9(b),** 300, **15.23(b),** 363–4, **18.26(b), 18.27**
adrenal medulla 361–3, **18.20(a), 18.21**
adrenergic 307–8, **15.34**
adsorption chromatography 60
adventitious roots 385, **19.13,** 395, **20.3**
aerating tissue 424, 592, **28.14**
aerobes 78, 590
aerobic respiration 88
aerofoil 575, **27.33**
aestivation 347
afferent arterioles, kidney 185–6, **10.4**
afferent nerves 302
Affinities 24.2.2, 476–8
afterbirth 449
agglutination 177, 448, **22.21**
***Agnatha* 27.2.1, 563**
air capacity, soil 629
air sac 576, **27.37**
air movement, effect on transpiration, 201, **11.4**
air spaces, leaves 188–9, **11.2,** 221
air vapour pressure 202, **Table 11.2**
alanine 53–4, **3.21–2, Table 3.3**
alcoholic fermentation 80–1, **5.2(b)**
aldose sugars 41
aldosterone 362–3, **18.23–5**
aleurone layer 398–9, **20.5(b)**
***Algae* 25.5, 505–9**
alkaline solution 20
allanto-chorionic placenta villi 446, **22.17**
allantois 445–6, **22.17–18,** 573
alleles 450
allergen 178
Allergy 9.4, 178
all-or-none effect 286–7, **15.7**
alternation of generations 379, **25.41**
alveoli 133–4, **8.4**
ameloblast cells 256–7, **14.1**
amino acid pool 280
Amino Acids 3.3.1, 53–5
amino acids, biochemical tests 59–60
classification 54, **Table 3.3**
essential 254
in proteins 53, **Table 3.2**
non-essential 254
separation 61, **3.29**
structure 53, **3.20, 3.21,** 55, **3.24**
ammonia 195, **10.16,** 280, **14.32**
amnion 445–7, **22.17–19,** 573
amniote egg **22.18,** 573, 578, 579
amniotic fluid 445, **22.18**
Amoeba 523, **26.1**
amoebocyte 529, **26.15**
amoeboid movement 170, 524, **26.2**
AMP 79
***Amphibia* 27.2.4, 569**
amphions 54, 59
Amphioxus 562
amphoteric 54
ampulla 330–2, **16.17, 16.19(b)**
amylase, in germinating seeds 397–8, **20.5(a)**
in mammal 266, 272
amylopectin 46, **3.10**
amylose 46, **3.9**
anaemia 147, 169
anaerobes 78
anaerobic respiration 88
analogous structures 477
anaphase, meiosis 124–6, **7.9–10**
mitosis 118–19, **7.3**
androecium 368
androgens 438
angiosperm life cycle 380, **19.7**
***Angiospermae* 25.8.2, 521–2**
Angiosperm Reproduction, Physiology 19.5, 386–9
angiotensin 362–3, **18.25**
angle of aperture 23, **1.23**
***Annelida* 26.6, 542–6**
annual rings 419–20, **21.12(c), (d)**
annulus **25.37–38,** 517
Anopheles 528, **26.60**
antagonistic activity 306, **15.32,** 530
antenna **26.49–52,** 550, **26.56, 26.60, 26.62–4**
antennule **26.49, 26.52,** 550
anterior pituitary 365, **18.28(b), (c),** 367, **18.31,** 442, **22.14**
anther, dehiscence 372, **19.2(b) (iv)**
development 370, **19.2, 25.51**
antheridium 501, **25.12,** 502, 508, **25.21, 25.27,** 511, **25.39,** 517
antherozoid 508, **25.32, 25.34, 25.38–39,** 517
Anthozoa 533
anti-A 179–80, **Table 9.4, 9.32**
anti-B 179–80, **Table 9.4, 9.32**
antibiosis 588
antibiotics 496, 504
antibodies 166, 173–4, 176–8, 181, **9.17,** 447, 477
antibody reactions 176–7
anticoagulants 173
anticodon 101, **6.7,** 108–9, **6.18,** 111, **6.21**
anti-D 179–81, **9.32**
antidiuresis 189, **10.9,** 192
antidiuretic hormone, ADH 192
antigens 174–81, **9.28–9**
antiserum 178
Anura 571
anus 265, **14.14,** 277
aorta 152–3, **9.2, 9.3(a), (b),** 156, **9.6**
aortic valve 153, **9.3(b),** 156, **9.6**
apex, root 414, **21.6**
shoot 407, **21.1**
aphids 230–1, **12.12,** 236, **12.17,** 551, 553
apical dominance 425–6, **21.19**
apical meristem, root 414–15, **21.6, 21.7(a)**
shoot 406–7, **21.1(b), 21.2**
apical meristems 406
aplanospore 500, **25.11**
Apoda 571
apomixis 386
aqueous humour 318–19, **16.1(b)**
Aqueous Solutions Chapter 2, 26–40
aqueous solution 31
Arachnida 555
archegonium 511, **25.32, 25.39,** 517, 520, **25.46**
Arenicola 544, **26.40**
arteries 152–3, **9.2,** 163–4, **9.14(a), (b)**
arterioles 153, 162–3, **9.11, 9.12, 9.14(a)**
artefacts 3, 23
***Arthropoda* 26.7, 547–56**
Artiodactyls 580
Ascaris 541, **26.37**
ascending chromatography 61, **3.29**
ascending limb, loop of Henle 189–90, **10.11**
***Ascidiacea* 27.1.1, 561**
Ascomycetes 501–2
asconoid **26.16**
ascorbic acid 255
ascospores **25.13,** 502
ascus **25.13,** 502
Asexual Reproduction, Flowering Plants 19.4, 384–6
Aspergillus **25.11,** 504–5
Associations 28.2, 597–605
aster 118–19, **7.3(b)**
***Asteroidea* 26.9.1, 560**
asthma 178
astigmatism 322
atmometer 207, **11.10(b)**
atmospheric humidity, effect on transpiration 201–2, **11.5**
Atmospheric pollution 30.1, 638–42
atomic model, DNA 100, **6.5(a)**
ATP 15, 78–9
ATP, in chloroplasts 92, **5.16,** 95, **5.20**
in guard cells 223
in muscle 298–9
in protein synthesis 108
production 83–4, **Table 5.1**
structure 79
atmospheric pressure 144, **Table 8.4,** 592, **28.13**
atretic follicles 438
atria 151–3, **9.1–3(a), (b)**
atrial systole 155, **9.5(a),** 158
atrio-ventricular node 155, **9.5(b)**
atrio-ventricular valves 153–4, **9.3(b)**
atrium 561, **27.2–4,** 563
auditory nerve 327, **16.13,** 329, **16.14(c),** 333
autoimmune diseases 174
autolysis 13
autonomic nervous system 307–8, **15.33, Table 15.3**
autophagosomes 12–13, **112(b)**
autoradiographs, photosynthetic products 94, **5.18**
autoradiography 93
Autosomal inheritance 23.1, 450–60
autosomes 450
autotrophs 526, 631
auxins 425–30
***Aves* 27.2.6, 574**
axillary bud primordia 407–8, **21.2(a)**
axolotl **27.24**
axon 284–91, **15.3–9, 15.12,** 293, **15.14**

***Bacillariophyta* 25.5.4, 509**
back-cross 451
***Bacteria* 25.3, 492–8**
bacteria, cellulolytic 275
nitrogen-fixing 114–15, **6.24,** 495
phagocytosis of 170, **9.22**
bacteriophage 490, **25.1**
Balance 16.2.3, 330–1
baleen 264, **14.12(b),** 582
B-antigen 179–80, **Tables 9.3–4**
barleyseed, food mobilisation 398, **20.5(b)**
barnacle 549, **26.53**
baroreceptors 138–9, **8.10–11,** 161–2, **9.10, 9.12**
basal metabolic rate, BMR 336, 339, 350, 353
basement membrane 186–7, **10.6**
bases 33
nitrogenous 98–9, **6.2, 6.4**
Basidiomycetes 501–2
basidiospore 502, **25.14**
basilar membrane 328–30, **16.14, 16.16**
basophils 170
bat 133, **27.48**
β-cells 357
β-carotene 89–90, **Table 5.2, 5.14(b), 5.15,** 255
beak **27.29,** 578, **27.36, 27.39**
bed bug **26.61**
bee, 383, **19.10,** 551, 555, **26.64**
beetle 551, 553, **26.59**
beetroot 389, **19.15**
bends 150
beri-beri 255
bilateral symmetry 536, **26.29,** 558, 561
bile 271, 274, **14.27**
bile duct 271, **14.23,** 278–9, **14.31,** 281–2
bilharzia 539
bilirubin 281, **14.33**
bimolecular leaflet 52, **3.19**
binary fission 494, **25.7,** 525, **26.5,** 527, **26.11**
binomial system 489
biochemical oxygen demand 656
Biochemical Techniques 3.4, 60–65
biochemical tests, amino acids 59–60
cellulose 49
fats and oils 51
glycogen 47
phospholipids 52
proteins 59–60
starch 46
sugars 46
biogeographical zones 483
biological control 612–13
biomes 583, **28.1**
biosphere 483
Biotic factors 28.1.1, 584–8
biotic factors effects on plant growth 425
birth 367, 448
Birth and Lactation 22.3.4, 448–9
biuret test 60
***Bivalvia* 26.8.2, 558**
bladder sphincter 182–3, **10.2**
bladderworm 541, **26.36**
bladder wrack 508, **25.21**
blastostyle 533, **26.23**
blind spot 318, **16.1(b),** 323
blood cells 168–71, **Table 9.2, 9.20–3,** 173, **9.25,** 177, **9.31**
blood fluke 539, **26.35**
blood groups 179–81, **Table 9.3, 9.32**
Blood Lymph and Circulation Chapter 9, 151–81
blood pH 193, 195
blood pressure, 158–9, **9.8,** 161–3, **9.12–14(a)**
blood vessels 152, **9.2,** 154, **9.3(c),** 163, **9.14(a)**
blood volume 153–4, **Table 9.1,** 160
blubber 344, 582
blue cones 326, **16.12**
blue-green algae 505
B-lymphocytes 174–6, **9.28**
body temperature 334–5, **17.1,** 337, 340, 345–7, **17.14, 17.15, Table 17.1**
Bohr effect 143
bolus 266, **14.16**
bone 299, **15.26–9,** 300, 354–6, **18.11, 18.13,** 443
bone marrow 169–71, **9.23(a),** 175–6, **9.28,** 281–2, **14.33,** 300, **15.26, 15.28–9**
bony fish 567
bordered pit, electronmicrograph 21, **121(b)**
Bowman's capsule 182, 185–7, **10.3(c), 10.4, 10.6**
bract scale 518, **25.45**
brain 301, **15.2,** 307–14, **15.33, 15.35–15.41, 15.43,** 537, **26.31, 26.41,** 578
Branchiostoma 562, **27.3–5**
Breathing 8.2, 133–9
breathing control 137–8, **8.10**
brewing 503–4
Broad Bean, Germination 20.2.1, 392–4
bronchi 134–5, **8.3, 27.37**
bronchioles, 134–5, **8.3**
broom, flower 369, **19.1**
fruit 379, **19.6**

brown algae 508
Brunner's glands 273, 276–7, **14.29(b), 14.30**
***Bryophyta* 25.6, 510–13**
bud 413
  winter 432, **21.30**
budding 501, 533, **26.22**
buffer, isotonic 24
  thermal 29
buffering capacity, acid-base pair 33
  amino acids 55
  proteins 59
bulb 385, **19.13**, 521
bulbo-urethral gland 435, **22.2**, 443
bundle of His 155, **9.5(b)**
buttercup 408, **21.1(c), 25.52**
butterfly 551, 553, **26.62**
byssus threads 558, **26.71**

caecum 265, **14.14**, 274–5, **14.28**, 495, **26.58**
calcicole 630
calcifuge 630
calcitonin 355–6, **18.13**
calcium, in plant growth 244
  in mammals 353–7, **18.13, 18.14**
callose 233–4, **12.15**
callus 431
calorimeter 84–5, **5.6**, 336
Calvin cycle 95, **5.19**
calyptra 511, **25.28, 25.32**
calyptrogen 414
calyx 368
cambium, cork 420–1, **21.13**
  vascular 418–20, **21.10**
Cambrian period 472
camel 132, **Table 8.1**, 192, 344
canaliculus 278–9, **14.31**, 301, **15.27**
canines 258–63, **14.4, 14.6, 14.9–11(a), (b)**
capillaries, blood 153, 163–4, **9.14(a), (c)**
  lymphatic 166, **9.17**
capillarity, water 29, 206–7, 210, 215
capsid 490
capsule 492, **25.27–28**, 511, 512, **25.32–33**
capsule, Bowman's 182, 185–7, **10.3(c), 10.4, 10.6**
carapace 549, **26.49–51**
carbohydrate metabolism 280
Carbohydrates 3.1, 41–8
carbohydrates 254, 397
carbon atom, asymmetric 42
carbon cycle 625–6, **29.26**
carbon dioxide availability 591
carbon dioxide, diffusion 220–1, **Tables 12.1–2**
  effect on photosynthesis 225, **12.6**
  effect on plant growth 424
  evolution, measuring rate of 87, **5.10**
  exchange, by leaves 227, **12.10**
  fixation 93–5
  in mammals 142, **Table 8.3, 8.16**, 144
  inside leaves 222
  tension 143, **817**
Carbon dioxide, pollution 30.1.1, 638–9
Carbon Dioxide Uptake by Leaves 12.1.3, 219–21
carbonic acid 142, **8.16**, 193, **10.14**
carbonic acid-hydrogencarbonate 142, **8.16**, 193, **10.14**
carbonic anhydrase, in leaves 221
  in mammals 142, **8.16**
Carboniferous period 472
carbon monoxide haemoglobin 141
Carbon monoxide, pollution 30.1.4, 641–2
carboxylases 77
carboxyl group 49–50, **3.15(b)**, 53, **3.20**, 55, **3.23**
cardiac centre 160–2, **9.9(a), 9.10, 9.13**, 311
cardiac cycle 154–5, **9.5**
cardiac muscle 299–300, **15.24**
cardiac output 146, 159–60, 364, **18.27**
cardiovascular system 363
carnassial teeth 258–9, **14.4**
carnivores 258–9, **14.5**, 580, 620
carpels 368, 521
carrier molecules 249, 284, 359
carrier proteins, in cell membrane 9
carrot, tap root 230, **12.11**
carrying capacity 606–7, **29.3**
cartilage 299, **15.25**
Cartilage, bone and joints 15.1.9, 299–302
cartilaginous fish 564
caryopsis 396
casein 267–8, **14.19**
Casparian band, strip 210–11, **11.15**, 250, 416, **21.8**
catecholamines 363, **18.26**
cathode ray oscilloscope, CRO 286–7, **15.5, 15.7**, 289, **15.9–10**
C-cells 355
cell cycle 120–2, **7.6**
Cell Division Chapter 7, 116–31
cell division, meiosis 123–9
  mitosis 117–23
Cell Fractionation 1.4, 24–5
Cell Membranes 1.2.1, 8–9
cell plate 120–1, **7.5(a)**
Cell Structure Chapter 1, 1–25
Cell Ultrastructure 1.2, 5–21, 1.5
Cell Wall 1.2.11, 20–1
cellular immunity 174, 176, **9.28**
cellulolytic bacteria 270, 275
cellulose 48–9, **3.13–14**
Cenozoic era 475
centipede 551, **26.55**
central canal 303, **15.27**, 309
central nervous system, CNS 283, **15.2**, 301–2, **15.25**, 304, **15.29**, 309
central sulcus 314, **15.43**
central vein 278–9, **14.31**
centrifugation, differential 25, **125**
centrioles 13–14, **1.13**
centromere 119
Centrosomes 1.2.7, 13–14
cephalisation 536
***Cephalochorda* 27.1.2, 562**
***Cephalopoda* 26.8.3, 558**
cephalothorax 549, **26.49**
cercaria 538, **26.34**
cerebellum 308–12, **15.35, 15.37, 15.39–40**, 314, **15.43(a)**
cerebral cortex 314, **15.42, 15.43(a)**
cerebral hemispheres 309, 582
cerebro-spinal fluid, CSF 303, **15.27**, 309
cerebrum 308–10, **15.35, 15.37**, 312–13, **15.40–1**
ceruminous glands 332
cervix 439, **22.8**
***Cestoda* 26.4.3, 539**
cetaceans 344, 581
C_4 pathway 96, **5.21**
C_4 plants 96–7, 205
chaetae 542, **26.39, 26.41**
chela **26.50**
chelicera 556, **26.65**
cheliped **26.49**
Chelonia 573
chemical transmitters 293–6, **15.16–17**
chemoreceptors 138, **8.10**, 161, **9.10**, 537
chemotaxis 170, 511
chemotropism, pollen grains 389
  roots 429
chiasmata, 125, 128, **7.13(a)**
chilling, breaking corm dormancy 423–4, **21.16**
  of seeds 400, **20.7–8**
chiropterans 581
chitin 542
Chlamydomonas 506, **25.16–17**
chloride shift 142–3, **8.16**
chlorocruorin 542
chlorophyll 89–90, **Table 5.2, 5.14(a)**, 505–6, 508, 525
chlorophylls, absorption spectra 90, **5.15**
***Chlorophyta* 25.5.2, 506**
chloroplast pigments 89, **Table 5.2**
Chloroplasts 1.2.9, 16–18
chloroplasts, functions 88–97
  location 217–18, **12.1(a)**, 525
  ultrastructure 16–18, **1.16–17**
chlorosis 243–4
choanocyte 529, **26.15**
cholesterol 172, 281
choline 51, **3.18**, 295, **15.18**
cholinergic 307–8, **15.34**
cholinesterase 295, **15.18**
***Chondrichthyes* 27.2.2, 564**
chondroblast 300, **15.25**
choriogonadotropin, HCG 447–8, **22.21**
chorion 445–7, **22.17–19**
chorionic villi 446
choroid 317–18, **16.1(b), 16.2, 27.28**
chromatids 119
chromatin 4, 19
chromatography, adsorption 60
  column 62–3, **3.30**
  gas-liquid 63–4, **3.31**
  ion-exchange 64–5, **3.32**
  paper 60–2, **3.29**
  partition 60
  thin-layer 63
chromatophore 492
Chromosome maps 23.1.8, 458–60
chromosome mutation 129–30, 481–2
chromosomes 4, 116–17, **71**
  homologous pairs 116–17, **7.1(b)**
  human 116–17, **7.1(a), (b)**
  mongol 131, **7.15(a)**
  random orientation 128–9, **7.13(b)**
  replication 122–3, **7.8**
chyle 275
chyme 270, 274, **14.27**
chymotrypsin 273, **14.26**
chymotrypsinogen 272–3, **14.26**
  structure 67, **41**
cilia 325, **16.11**, 444, **26.3**, 526, **26.8–9, 26.39**
ciliary body 317–19, **16.1(a), (b)**, 321
***Ciliata* 26.1.3, 526**
Ciliophora 526
Circulation of Blood and Lymph 9.1, 151–68
Circulation in the Mammalian Foetus 9.1.4, 167–8
circulation, minerals in plants 250–1, **13.14**
cirrus **26.39, 27.3**
cisternae 11, **1.11**
Cladophora 88–9, **5.12**
clasper **26.62**, 566
classification 489
cleaner animals 604, **28.30**
cleavage, cytoplasmic 120–1, **7.5**
Climate, Effect on Transpiration 11.2.1, 199–202
clitellum **26.41**, 546
clitoris 443
cloaca **27.10**, 579
clone 386
Clones 23.4.2, 464
clot 171–3, **9.25**
clubmoss 513, **25.34**
clubroot 600, **28.26**
***Cnidaria* 26.3, 530–6**
cnidoblast 531
coacervates 469
coagulation 171–3
cobalt 256
cochlea 327–30, **16.13–15, 16.17**, 333
cocoon 546, 555
Co-dominance 23.1.4, 455
coelenterates 530–6
coelocanth 569, **27.17**
coelom 542, **26.38–39, 26.41, 26.74, 27.10**
coelomate 542, **26.38**, 561
coenosarc 533, **26.23**
co-enzymes 71
codon 101, 111, **6.21**
codon-anticodon binding 109–11, **6.18, 6.21**
Co-factors, Enzyme 4.3.1, 71
cohesion, water 206
cold centre 340, **17.10**
cold receptors 302, 304, **15.29, 340, 17.10**
Coleoptera 553
coleoptile 395–6, **20.3**
coleorhiza 395–6, **20.3**
collagen, 58, **3.26**, 300
collecting duct 182, 184–5, **10.3(b), 10.4**, 189–90, **10.10**, 192
collenchyma 412–13, **21.4**
Colligative Properties, Aqueous Solutions 2.3.2, 34–5
colloidal state 32
  suspension 59
colloid osmotic potential 163
colon 265, **14.14**, 274, **14.28**, 277
colour blindness 326, 461
colour vision 325
columella **25.11**, 513, **25.33**
Commensalism 28.2.3, 605
Communities 29.2, 613–16
community 606, 613
companion cells 233–5, **12.15**, 521
compensation period 227
  point 227, 422
competition, interspecific 585, **28.4–5**
  intraspecific 584, **28.2–3**
competitive exclusion 586
competitive inhibitors 71
complement 177, **9.30**
compound eye 547, **26.45, 26.50–1, 26.56, 26.60, 26.62–3, 26.64**
compound microscope 1–2, **1.2(a)**
composts 246
concave lens 321, **16.6(b)**
concentration gradient 188–9, **10.7**
conceptacle 508, **25.21**
condensation 133, **8.2**
condenser 21
conditioned reflex 305, **15.31**
Conduction 17.2.3, 338
cone cells 322–6, **16.9–10, 16.12**
conidium **25.11**, 501
Coniferales 518
Conjugales 507
conjugation 502, **25.17**, 507, **25.19**, 527, **26.12**
Conservation 30.1, 661–3
consumers 78, 469, 616
continental drift 479
continuous flow ventilation 137, **8.9**
continuous variation 463
contour feathers **27.30**, 575
contraceptive pill 442
contractile vacuole 39–40, **2.12, 26.1**, 524, **26.6, 26.8**, 527
contraction, of muscle 297–9, **15.21**
convex lens 322, **16.7(b)**
co-ordination 283
Copulation 22.3.1, 443–4
copulatory sac **26.31**
corals 530, 534, **26.26**
cork cambium 420–1, **21.13(a)**
cork cells 420–1, **21.13(a)**
corm 385, **19.13**, 521
cornea 317–19, **16.1, 16.3, 27.28, 27.38**
corolla 368
corona radiata 444
coronary thrombosis 172
corpus 406–7, **21.1**
corpus luteum 441–2, **22.14**
cortex, adrenal 361–3, **18.20(a), 18.21, 18.24–25**
cortex, kidney 182–4, **10.3**, 190, **10.12**
cortex, root 209–10, **11.13(a)**
Corti, organ of 329
corticotropin, ACTH 361, **18.21**
Cortisol 18.2.2, 360–1
cotyledon 392, **25.48**, 521–2
counter-current multiplication system 190, **10.11**
counterflow 568, **27.16**
crab 549, **26.50**
cranial nerves 310–11, **15.39**
***Craniata* 27.2, 563–82**
crayfish 549, **26.49**
creatine 297
crenation 39, **2.11**
Cretaceous period 473
cretinism 353
cristae 14–15, **1.14**
Crocodilia 573
crocus, corm 385, **19.13**
crop **26.41**, 546, **26.58**
cross-fertilisation 380, 537–8
  pollination 380
crossing-over 127–8, **7.13(a)**
cross-over value 459
crown, of tooth 256, 258, **142**
***Crustacea* 26.7.2, 549**
crypt of Lieberkühn 273, 276–7, **14.29(b), 14.30**
C_3 plants 97
cud 270
cupula 331–2, **16.19**
current, electric 288, **15.8**, 292, **15.13**, 294, **15.16**
curvature, of lens 321
cuticle 52, 198, **11.2(b)**, 204–5, **11.9(a)**, 513, 518, 538, 547
cuticular transpiration 197
cutin 21
cuttings 432–3, **21.32**
cuttlefish 558, **26.72**
***Cyanophyta* 25.5.1, 505**
cyclic photophosphorylation 92–3, **5.16(b)**
Cycling of matter 29.3.4, 624–7
cysteine 53–4, **3.21**
cysticercus 541
cytochrome oxidase 83, **5.5**
cytochromes 83, **5.5**, 92, **5.16(a)**
cytokinins 399, 431
cytoplasm 5

Cytoplasmic Cleavage 7.1.2, 120–1, 7.5
cytoproct 527, **26.10**
cytosine 98-9, **6.2**
cytostome 527, **26.10**

daffodil, bulb 385, **19.13**
dandelion, flower 369, **19.1, 25.52**
fruit 379, **19.6**
Danielli-Davson membrane model 8. **1.6**
D-antigen 179–81. **Table 9.3**
Daphnia **26.51**
dark-adapted eye 325
dark period 387
Darwin 130, 427, **21.21,** 479
Darwinism 24.3.2, 480–1
Darwin's finches 486–7, **24.22, 24.23**
day-length, effect on flowering 386–8
mammals 440
plant growth 423
day-neutral plants 387
DDT 528, 648–9, 659
dead space 136
deafness 332–3
deamination 280–1, **14.33**
death phase 606
decomposer organisms 245, 495, 616, 620, 632
decompression sickness 149–50
Defects of the Ear 16.2.4, 332–3
Defects of the Eye 16.1.3, 321–2
defence against disease 170, 173, 178
deficiency of nutrients, mammals 255–6
symptoms, plants 243–5, **13.3–5, 13.7**
dehydration, cells 2, 6
in mammals 359
dehydrogenases 76, 82
delayed implantation 440
denaturation, enzymes 72
proteins 59
dendrites 284–5, **15.3,** 293–4, **15.14–15**
Density and Viscosity, Water 2.2.2, 29
density-dependent factor 606, 610
density-independent factor 606
dental formula (see dentition)
dentine 256–8, **14.1–2**
dentition, dog 259, **14.4**
elephant 264, **14.13**
hedgehod 262, **14.10**
man 261, **14.9**
rabbit 263, **14.11(b)**
rat 262, **14.11(a)**
sheep 260, **14.6**
toothed whale 263, **14.12(a)**
deoxyribonucleic acid (see DNA)
deoxyribose 99, **6.1, 6.3**
depolarisation 286–8, **15.6, 15.8,** 294, **15.16,** 298
depression of freezing point 34
dermal layer 529, **26.15**
dermis 341–2. **17.11**
descending limb, of loop of Henle 189–90, **10.11**
detection, of stimuli 283, 317
detoxification 282
detritivores 616, 620
detritus 628
Deuteromycetes 501, 502
Development of Flowering Plants Chapter 21, 406–33
development, anther 370–3, **19.2**
lateral roots 416–17, **21.9**
lateral shoots 413–14, **21.5**
leaves 413–14. **21.5**
mammals 348, 353, 445
ovule 371–5, **19.3**
plant embryo 376–8, **19.5**
pollen 370–2, **19.2**
diabetes insipidus 192
diabetes mellitus 359–60, **18.19**
dialysing fluid 195–6, **10.18**
diaphragm 133–5, **8.3, 8.6,** 578
diaphysis 300, **15.26**
diastema 258, 260, **14.6**
diastole 158
diatoms 509, **25.25**
***Dicotyledones* 522, 25.52**
diet 254
differential centrifugation 25, **1.25**
differentiation, plant tissues 406
in mammals 348
stem tissues 409–13, **21.2–4**
secondary xylem and phloem 418–19. **21.11**
root tissues 414–16
diffraction pattern 57
diffusion 9, 40
of carbon dioxide, plants 220–1. **Tables 12.1–2**
of minerals, plants 247–8, **13.9,** 251, **13.14**
of respiratory gases, mammals, 133
of sodium ions 284–6, **15.4,** 290, **15.11**
of water vapour, plants 198–9, **11.2(b),** 216, **11.21**
diffusion shells 203
Digestion 14.3, 264–75
digestive enzymes 264, 273, **Table 14.1**
digestive system 265, Fig 14.14
Dihybrid inheritance 23.1.2, 453
dinosaurs 473, **24.10,** 572
dioxin 646–7
diploblastic 530, **26.38**
diploid 127, 376
Diploid Parthenogenesis 19.4.1, 384
Dipodomys 133, **8.1–2**
Diptera 553
disaccharide sugars 44–5, **37–8,** 266
discrimination sensory 324, **16.10**
disperse phase 32
dispersion medium 32
dissociation curves, myoglobin 148, **8.22**
oxyhaemoglobin 141, **8.15,** 143, **8.17,** 145–6, **8.19(a), 8.20, 28.12**
Dissociation of Water 2.2.5, 30–1
distal convolution 182, 185, **10.4,** 189–92, **10.10, 10.13**
distribution curve, normal 463, **23.13, 23.14**
disulphide bridges, in proteins 55–6, **3.24,** 58, **3.28,** 67, **4.1,** 174, **9.26**
diuresis 189, **10.9,** 192
Diving and Man 8.4.2, 149–50
dizygotic twins 445
DNA 18, 98–100, 490, 492
DNA, as Hereditary Material 6.1.3, 102–4
changes in mitotic division 122, **7.7**
recombinant 114
replication 105–6, **6.12,** 122, **7.6–7**
role in protein synthesis 107–11
structure 99–100, **6.1–4**
synthetase 105
dogfish 564, **27.8–11**
Dormancy of Seeds 20.3.3, 403–5
dorsal root 302–3, **15.27**
double fertilisation 376
down feather 574, **27.30**
Down's syndrome 482
drone 555, **26.64**
Dryopteris 515, **25.36–40**
ductless glands 348
ductus arteriosus 167–8, **9.19**
ductus venosus 167–8, **9.19**
duodenum 265, **14.14,** 267, **14.17,** 270–6. **14.22–3, 14.29(b)**
dwarfism 366, **18.29**

ear 317, **16.13,** 327
eardrum 327
earthworm 544–6, **26.41**
ecdysone 547, 552
ecdysis 547
***Echinodermata* 26.9, 559–60**
***Echinoidea* 26.9.2, 560**
echolocation 581, 582
Ecological pyramids 29.3.3, 622–4
ecology 583, 606
Ecosystems 29.3, 616–37
ecosystem 606, 616
Ecosystem, Soil as 29.3.5, 627–37
ectoderm 530, **26.17, 26.18, 26.38**
ectoparasites 597
ectotherms 333–5, **17.1,** 620
edaphic factors 596
effectors 139, **8.12(a),** 283, **15.1–2,** 302, **15.26,** 304, **15.29**
efferent arterioles 185–6, **10.4**
efferent nerves 302
egg cell, flowering plant 374, **19.4(d),** 376
ejaculation 444
***Elasmobranchii* 27.2.2, 564**
elastic recoil, of arteries 159
elater 511, **25.29**
electrocardiogram, ECG 157–8, **9.7**
Electrochemical Basis of Nervous Activity 15.1, 283–300
electroencephalogram, EEG 315–16, **15.45(a), (b)**
electromagnetic waves 651
electron microscope 5, **1.4(a),** 21–3, **1.22**
electron transfer, in chloroplasts 91
electron transport chain 83, **5.5**
electronmicrographs 22
electro-osmosis 238–9, **12.20(a)**
Electrophoresis 3.4.2, 66
elevation of boiling point 34
Elodea 224, **12.4**
elution 62
elytra 553, **26.59**
embolism 173
embryo, flowering plant 376–8, **19.5**
mammal 444–6, **22.15, 22.17–18**
sac 373–4, **19.3(c),** 521
embryonic cells, flowering plant 376–8, **19.5(a)**
emulsification 271–2, **14.24**
enamel 256–60, **14.1–2, 14.7,** 263
enamel organ 257, **14.1**
Endocrine Control in Mammals Chapter 18, 348–67
endocrine glands 348–9, **18.1–2**
endoderm 530, **26.17, 26.18, 26.38**
endodermis 210–11, **11.15**
endometrium 441–2, **22.14,** 445, 448
endoparasites 538, 539, 598
endoplasmic reticulum, rough 9–10, **1.9**
smooth 9, 499
endosperm 376, 392, 395, **20.3,** 397–8, **Table 20.2, 20.4**
endospores 494, **25.8**
endostyle 561, **27.3**
endotherms 334–5. **17.1,** 576, 578, 620
Energy flow 29.3.2, 617–22
energy flow, in soil 637, **Table 29.11**
enterocrinin 274, **14.27**
enterokinase 272–3, **14.26**
enteron **26.14,** 530, **26.17, 26.25, 26.28**
environmental resistance 606, 612
Enzyme Action 4.2, 68
enzyme activators 71
active centre 69
Enzyme Catalysis 4.2.1, 69
Enzyme Classification 4.4, 75–7
enzyme, co-factors 71
Enzyme Concentration, 4.3.5, 74
Control 4.2.4, 70
Enzyme Inhibitors 4.3.2, 71–2
enzyme production, effect of gibberellic acid on 398–9, **20.5**
Enzyme Specificity 4.2.3, 70
Enzyme Structure 4.1, 67–8
Enzyme, Factors Affecting 4.3, 70–5
enzyme-substrate complex 69, **4.3**
eosinophils 169–70, **9.20(d),** 178
ephyra **26.28,** 536
epicotyl 393–4, **20.1**
epidermis, leaf 198, **11.2,** 204, **11.9(a),** 217–20, **12.1(a), 12.2**
root 209, **11.13,** 212, **11.16**
stem 409, **21.2(d),** 413
epididymis 435, **22.2–3(a)**
epiglottis 265–6, **14.14–15**
epilimnion 658
epiphysis 300, **15.26**
***Equisetales* 25.7.2, 515**
erectile tissue 435, **22.2,** 443–4
erector-pili muscles 303–4, **15.29,** 342, **17.11(b)**
Erythrocytes 9.2.1, 169–70
erythropoiesis 144, **8.18,** 169
Escherichia coli, DNA replication 106, **6.14**
genetic engineering 115
protein synthesis in 110–11
essential amino acids 254
esterification 50, **3.16**
estradiol 440–2, **22.11–12(a), 22.14,** 448–9
ethanoic acid 33
ethanol 79–81, **5.2(b)**
etiolation 423, **21.15**
Euglena 509, 525, **26.4–6**
euglenoid movement 525, **26.4**
***Euglenophyta* 25.5.4, 509**
***Eumycophyta* 25.4, 498**
euryhaline 594
Eustachian tube 327–8, **16.13**
Eutheria 579
evaporation 40, 132–3, **8.2,** 197, 200, 216, **11.21**
Evidence of evolution 24.2, 470–9
evolution, convergent 477
evolution, divergent 477
Evolution, Evidence of 24.2, 470–9
evolution of bread wheat 485, **24.21**
evolution of man 475, **24.11**
excretion 182, 282
excretory canal 537, **26.31**
exocrine glands 348, **18.2**
exodermis 209
exophthalmos 353
exoskeleton 547
expiratory reserve volume 136, **8.8**
exponential phase 606
extensor muscle 306
external auditory meatus 327–8, **16.13,** 332
eye 317–18, **16.1(a), (b), 16.2,** 320–2, **16.5–7, 26.72, 27.28, 27.38**
eyepiece lens 2, **1.2(a),** 22, **1.22**
eye spot 537, **26.30**

facilitated transport 249, **11.13(b)**
Factor complex 28.1.3, 596–7
facultative anaerobes 494
FAD 71, 83, **5.5**
FADH 83, **5.5**
faeces 277
Fallopian tubes 439, **22.8,** 443–4
fanworm 542, **26.40**
Fasciola 538, **26.33, 26.34**
fats 49, 255, 272–3, **14.24–5, Table 14.1**
Fats and Oils 3.2.1, 49–51
fat-soluble vitamins 255
fatty acids 49–51, **3.15(b),** 272–3, **14.25, Table 14.1,** 275
feather 574, **27.30**
feedback 70, 139, **8.12,** 172, 283–4, **15.1–2,** 340, **17.10,** 351, 353 359, 360, 440
Fehling's test 42
female cone 518, **25.43, 25.45, 25.48**
fermentation, alcoholic 80–1, **5.2(b),** 494
lactic 80–1, **5.2(b)**
fern 513, 515, **25.36–41**
ferritin 281–2, **14.33**
Fertilisation and Implantation of the Embryo 22.3.2, 444–5
Fertilisation, Flowering Plants 19.1.3, 375–6
fertilisers 240, **13.1,** 246
fibrin 171–3, **9.24–5**
fibrinogen 171–2, **9.24**
fibrinolysin 172
fibrous layer 371–2, **19.2(b)(iv)**
fibrous protein 57
***Filicales* 25.7.3, 515**
filtrate, glomerular 186–90, **10.6(b), 10.10, Table 10.1,** 194
filtration, pressure 163–4
fixation, cells 2, 6
carbon dioxide 93–5
flaccid 36
flagella 493, **25.5,** 524, **26.6, 26.8, 26.18**
***Flagellata* 26.1.2, 524, 26.4–7**
flame cell 537, **26.31**
flatworm 536
flavin-adenine dinucleotide (see FAD)
flexor muscle 306
flight 574, 576, 27.34–5
flight or fight hormones 363
flipper **27.49,** 582
flower structure 369, **19.1,** 521
flowering, effect of day-length 386–8
effect of temperature 388–9
Flowering, Physiology 19.5.1, 386–9
fluke **27.49,** 582
Focusing 16.1.2, 319–21
foetal circulation 167–8, **9.19**
haemoglobin 146–7, **8.20,** 167
liver 169
membranes 445
foetus 167, **9.18,** 445, **22.16,** 447–8
follicle cells 438
follicle, hair 341–2, **17.11(a), (b)**
ovarian 438–42, **22.10, 22.14**
thyroid 349, 350, **18.3**
follitropin, FSH 364, 437, 440–2, **22.11, 22.14**
food chain 617
food web 617, **29.17,** 635, **29.37**
foot 511, **25.28,** 512, **25.32**
Foraminifera 524
forebrain 309, 313, 364
Fossils 24.2.1, 470–5, 24.3,
fovea 318, **16.1(b),** 324, **27.28**
Fractionation of Cells 1.4, 24–5

fragmentation, chromosomes 1.30, **7.14(a)**
frequency, of impulses 295
  of sound 330, **16.16**
frog **27.18**
frond 515, **25.36**
frontal lobes, of brain 314
fructose 41–3, **Table 3.1, 3.2, 3.4** 45, **3.7**
fruit formation 378–9
Fruit Formation, Physiology 19.5.3, 390
fruit growth 390, **19.17**
Fruit Ripening, Physiology 19.5.4, 391
fruits 378–9, **19.6**
Fucus vesiculosus 508, **25.21, 25.22**
Funaria 512, **25.31–33**
functional residual capacity 136, **8.8**
***Fungi* 25.4, 498–505**
Fungicides 30.3.2, 647
funicle 372–3, **19.3(a)**
fur 344
fusiform initials 418, **21.10–11**

Galapagos finches 456–7, **24.22, 24.23**
gall bladder 265, **14.14,** 271, **14.23,** 274 **14.27,** 281
gall stones 281–2
gametangia 501, **25.12**
gametes, flowering plants 375–6, **19.4(a)**
  mammalian 434
gametogenesis 434
gametophyte 379–80, **19.7,** 507, 509, 510, 514, 520, **25.46, 25.48**
Gas Exchange and Evaporation 8.1, 132–3
  in Mammals Chapter 8, 132–50
  in the Tissues 8.3.2, 142–4
gastral layer 529, **26.15**
gastric juice 267, 274, **14.27**
  mucosa 267
  pits 267–8, **14.18(a), (b)**
  secretin 274, **14.27**
gastrin 269, 274, **14.27**
***Gastropoda* 26.8.1, 557**
gastrovascular cavity 531, 536
gemmae 510, **25.26**
Gene interaction 23.1.6, 455–6
gene mutations 106–7, **6.15,** 129, 481, 653
  structural 112–13, **6.23**
  regulator 112–13, **6.23**
generations, alternation of 379–80, **19.7**
generative cell 370, 372, **19.2(b) (vi),** 375, **19.4(a)**
generator potential 324
genes 111–13, 450
Genetic Code 6.2.2, 110–11
genetic effects of radiation 653–4
Genetic Engineering 6.3, 114–15
Genetic polymorphism 23.4.4, 466
Genetics 450–66
Genetic Variation 7.3, 130–31
genital atrium **26.36**
genome 127, 129–30, 450
genotype 450
Geographical distribution 24.2.3, 478–9
germinal epithelium 436, **22.3(b),** 438–9, **22.10**
gestation period 440
geotropism 429–30
germination, epigeal 395
Germination, Factors Affecting 20.3.2, 399–403
germination, hypogeal 394, 396
  inhibitors 404
Germination of Seeds Chapter 20, 392–405
Germination, Physiology 20.3, 396–403
giant nerve cell 542
gibberellic acid 430
  effect on flowering 388
  effect on seed germination 398–9, **20.5(b),** 403–4, **20.12**
  structure 430, **21.26**
gibberellins, 430, 504
gigantism 366, **18.29**
gill cleft 561, **27.1, 27.2, 27.11**
gills **26.40, 26.49,** 551, 568, **27.16,** 571, **27.23, 27.24**
gizzard **26.41,** 546, **26.58**
gliding 576, **27.34**
globin 140, **18.13,** 147
globular protein, structure 58, **3.27–8**
globulin 175, **9.27(b)**
glomerulus 182, 185–6, **10.3(c), 10.4**
glucagon 357–8, **18.16,** 361, **18.22**
glucocorticoid hormones 360
glucose 41–3, **Table 3.1, 3.2–3,** 45–6, **3.7–8,** 48, 357
glucose tolerance 359–60, **18.19**
glutamic-oxaloacetic transaminase, GOT 280–1
glyceraldehyde 41–2, **Table 3.1, 3.1**
glycerol 49–51, **3.15(a), 3.16, 3.18,** 272–3, **14.25, Table 14.1,** 275
glycine 53, **3.21**
glycogen 47–8, **3.12**
glycolysis 80, **5.2(a)**
glycoproteins 11, 269
glycosidic linkages 44–6, **3.7–8, 3.10,** 48, **3.13,** 266, 272
glycosuria 359
goblet cells 269
goitre 353, **18.8**
Golgi Body 1.2.3, 11
  body, functions 11
  ultrastructure 11, **1.10–11**
gonadotropins 364, 438
gonads 434
Graafian follicle 439
grafting 432
grana 16–17, **1.16**
grasses **25.51,** 522
gravity, effects on the ear 331, **16.18(b)**
gravity, effect on plant growth 424, 429–30, **21.25**
grazing 586
Great Barrier Reef **26.27**
green cone 326, **16.12**
greenhouse effect 626
grey matter 302–3, **15.27**
Griffith's experiment 102–3, **6.9**
grinding 259–61, 14.7–8
gross ecological efficiency 622
gross productivity 618
ground meristem 414–15, **21.7(a)**
Growth and Development of Plants
  Chapter 21, 496–33
  Physiology 21.2, 422–33
growth hormone 365
Growth, Primary 21.1.1, 406–17
  Secondary 21.1.2, 418–21
guanine 98–9, **6.2**
guard cells 219–23, **12.2(a), (b), 12.3**
  photosynthesis by 222
  mineral concentration in 223, **12.3**
gut 264
guttation 212
***Gymnospermae* 25.8.1, 518–20**
gynoecium 368

habitats 583
haem 140, **18.13**
haematinic principle 282
haemocoel 547, **26.46,** 556
haemocyanin 549, 557
haemoglobin 139–43, **8.13, 8.16,** 146–7, 169–70, 477–8, 542
  analysis 112, **6.22**
haemoglobinic acid 143
haemolysis 39, **2.11,** 177, **9.31,** 179–80
haemolytic disease of the newborn, HDNB 181
haemophilia, inheritance 461–2, 482
haemosiderin 281–2, **14.33**
hair 341–4, **17.11(a), (b), 17.13,** 578
hair cells 329–32, **16.14(c), 16.18, 16.19(a)**
halteres 553
haploid 379
Hardy-Weinberg Law 23.4.3, 465–6
Hatch-Slack pathway 96, **5.21**
haustoria 597, **28.22**
Haversian canal 300, **15.27**
hay fever 178
Hearing 16.2.2, 327–30
hearing aid 333, **16.20**
Heart 9.1.1, 153–63
heart 151–5, **9.1–3, 9.5,** 160, **9.9(a),** 166, **9.17,** 168, **9.19,** 547, **26.46, 26.51, 27.2, 27.11, 27.22, 27.27, 27.37**
heart rate 159–62, **9.9(b), 9.10, 9.13**
heart sounds 159
heart valves 153, **9.3(b),** 155–6, **9.5–6**
heart (oestrus) 444
heat centre 340
Heat Loss 17.2, 337–40
Heat Production 17.1, 334–6
heavy metal pollution 642–6
hedgehog 262, **14.10**
helium 149
α-helix 57, **3.25**
hemicelluloses 49
Hemiptera 553
***Hepaticae* 25.6.1, 510**
hepatic artery 152, **9.2,** 278, **14.31(a)**
hepatic portal vein 278, **14.31(a)**
hepatic vein 152, **9.2,** 278, **14.31(a)**
Herbicides 30.3.1, 646–7
herbivores 258, 261, **14.8,** 604, 619
hermaphrodite 368, 533, 537–8
herring **27.14**
Hershey–Chase experiment 103–4, **6.11**
heterocercal tail **27.7,** 565
heterocysts 505, **25.15**
heterodont 258, 578
heteromorphic alternation of generations 509, 510, 513
heterotrophs 632
heterozygote 450
Hibernation 17.3.4, 347
high energy bonds 79
Hill reaction 91
hilum 393
hindbrain 309, 311
***Hirudinea* 26.6.3, 546**
histamine 178
histocompatibility (HL-A) system 181
histone 100–1
holdfast 508, **25.21, 25.23, 25.24, 26.14**
homeostasis, cellular 112
  mammalian 182, 283, 335, 351, 362
homocercal tail 567
homodont 573
homogametic 460
homologous structures 476
homozygous 450
Hormonal Control of Ovulation 22.2.2, 440
hormones, flowering plant 388–90, 398–9, 425–33
  mammalian 348
Hormones, Plant, Practical Uses 21.2.3, 432–3
horsetail 513, **25.35,** 514
human calorimeter 336
human chorionogonadotropin, HCG 447–8, **22.21**
human chromosomes 116–17, **7.1,** 130–1, **7.15(a)**
human dentition 261, **14.9**
humoral immunity 174, 176, **9.28**
humus 503, 628, 630
hydathodes 212–13, **11.18**
Hydra 530, **26.19,** 532, **26.21, 26.22**
hydrochloric acid 267–9, **14.19**
hydrogen acceptors, photosynthesis 91–3
  respiration 71, 81, 83
hydrogen bonds, in water 27–8, **2.3**
hydrogencarbonate 142–3, **8.16, Table 8.3,** 193–4, **10.14–16,** 196, 271
  ion 30
hydroid 530, **26.17,** 532
Hydrolases 4.4.1, 75–6
hydrolysis 75–6, **4.12(a), (b), (c)**
hydrolytic enzymes 75, 264, 396–8
hydrophilic colloid 32
hydrophytes 204
hydroskeleton 544
hydrostatic pressure, of blood 163, 186
hydrotropism 429
hydroxyl ion 30
Hydrozoa 532
Hymenoptera 555
hyperglycaemia 359
hypermetropia 321–2, **16.7**
hyperthyroidism 352
hypertonic solution 37
hypha 498, **25.10**
hypocotyl 394–5, **20.2(b), 25.48**
hypolimnion 658
hypophysial stalk 365, 18.28
hypophysis 364
hypothalamic-hypophysial neurons 367, **18.32**
  portal veins 367, **18.31**
hypothalamus 192, 310, **15.37,** 315, 340, **17.10,** 346, **17.16,** 365, **18.28**
hypothyroidism 353
hypotonic solution 36

IAA, effect on root and shoot growth 425–30
IAA, role in apical dominance 425–6, **12.19**
  role in tropisms 427–30, **21.22, 21.25**
IAA, structure 425, **21.17**
  transport 425, **21.18**
ileum 265, **14.14,** 271, 275, **14.29(a)**
image, formation in the eye 319–22, **16.4**

imago 552, **26.62**
imbibition 40, 400
immune response 176, **9.28**
immunity 173–5, 178
immunisation 178
immunoglobulins 174–6, **9.26, 9.27(b), 9.28**
impala **27.46**
implantation 444–5
impulse 286–90, **15.7–10,** 292, **15.13, Table 15.2,** 294, **15.16,** 298
Inbreeding 23.4.1, 463–4
inbreeding 380
incipient plasmolysis 37, **2.9**
incisors 258–64, **14.4, 14.6, 14.9–10, 14.11(a), (b), 14.13**
incompatible blood 179
incomplete dominance 455
incus 327–8 **16.13**
indicator species 662
indole-3-acetic acid (see IAA)
indusium 515, **25.37**
inflammation 178
inflorescence **25.49**
inheritance 450–66
Inheritance of sex 23.2.1, 460–1
Inheritance quantitative 23.3, 462–3
inhibitors, competitive 71, **4.6**
  effect on enzymes 70–2
  effect on plant growth 431–2
  germination 404
  muscle 298
  non-competitive 72
  non-reversible 72
  reversible 71
inhibitory synapses 295, 306, **15.32**
initials, ray and fusiform 418, **21.10–11**

innate immunity 173
  reflexes 304
inner ear 327, 333
Inorganic Nutrients, Mammal 14.1.3, 256
***Insecta* 26.7.4, 551–5**
Insecticides 30.3.3, 647–50
Insectivores 261, 580
insect-pollinated flowers 383–4, **19.11**
insulin 357–9, **18.16, 18.18, 18.22,** 361
Insulin and Glucagon 18.2.1, 357–60
insulin, structure 56, **3.24**
integuments 372–4, **19.3(b), (c) (ii),** 520, **25.46**
intercalary meristems 421–2, **21.14**
intercostal muscles 134, 137, **8.3,** 572
interferon 173
intermediate neurons 302–3, **15.27**
internode elongation 413, 423, **21.15**
interphase 117, **7.2**
interstitial cells, of Leydig 436, **22.3(b),** 438
interstitial cell stimulating hormone, ICSH 438, **22.6**
interventricular septum 153, **9.3(b),** 155
intestinal juice 273
intrinsic factor, IF 169–70, 276–7, **Table 14.2**
invertebrates 523
inverted image 319–20, **16.4(b)**
inverted retina 323
involucre **25.27, 25.28**
iodine 256, 348, 350–1, **18.4, 18.6**
iodopsin 325
ion exchange 628
ion-exchange, in soil 245
ion uptake, plants 246–9
ionic product, water 30
iris, eye 317–19, **16.1(a), (b), 26.72, 27.28, 27.38**
iris rhizome 385–6, **19.13**
iron, in mammal 256, 281
iron, in plant growth 224
islets of Langerhans 349, **18.1,** 357–9, **18.15–16**
isoantibodies 179–80
iso-electric point, amino acids 55
  proteins 59
Isolating mechanisms 24.35, 486–8
Isomerases 4.4.4, 77
isotonic solution 38
isotopes 470

Jacob–Monod hypothesis 112–14, **623**
jaundice 282
jejunum 271
jellyfish 530, 534–6, **26.28**
Jenner 178
joint 302, **15.29**, 547, **26.43**
Jurassic period 473
juvenile hormone 552

kangaroo **27.42**
kangaroo rat 133, **8.1–2**, 192–3
keel 576, **27.36, 27.37**, 581
kelp 509
ketose sugars 42
kidney 182–96, **10.1, 10.3, 10.12**, 566
kidney failure 195
Kidney Machines 10.5, 195–6
kinases 76
kinetin 431
kinetodesma 527, **26.9**
Krebs' TCA cycle 82–3, **5.4**
Küpffer cells 281

labium **26.56, 26.60**
labrum **26.56, 26.60**
lachrymal glands 319
lactation 448–9
lacteals 275–7, **14.30**
lactic acid 81, 149
lactic fermentation 80–1, **5.2(b) (i)**
lacuna 300, **15.27**
Lagomorpha 262
lag phase 606
Lamarckism 24.3.1, 479
lamellae, in chloroplasts 16–18, **1.16–17**
in rods 325, **16.11**
***Lamellibranchia* 26.8.2, 558**
lamprey 563, **27.6**
large intestine 277
latent heat of melting 28
of vaporisation 28, 337
latent period 490
lateral line 564, **27.7**, 567
lateral root, development 416–7, **21.9**
shoot, development 413
Lead, Pollution by 30.2.1, 642–3
leaf 512, **25.31**, 513, **25.49**
Leaf Area Index 12.3.1, 288
Leaf as a Photosynthetic Organ 12.1, 217–22
development 413, **21.5**
expansion 425–6, **21.20**
mosaic 218, **12.1(b)**
Leaf, Penetration by Light 12.1.1, 217–18
primordia 407–8, **21.2**, 413, **21.5**
structure 198, **11.2**, 204–5, **11.9**, 218–20, **12.1–2**
leaf scar **25.43**
Leaf Structure, Effect on Transpiration 11.2.2, 202–5
leaf suction 207
unit rate 229
venation 197, **11.1**
Leaf, Water Supply 12.1.2, 219
leaves, shade 218
leaves, sun 218
leech 546, **26.42**
lens 317–22, **16.1, 16.3–8, 26.39, 26.45, 26.72, 27.28, 27.38**
lens, eyepiece 2, **1.2(a)**, 22, **1.22**
objective 2, **1.2(a)**, 22, **1.22**
lenticles 420–1, **21.13(b)**
lenticular transpiration 197
Lepidoptera 553
Leucocytes 9.2.2, 170
leuconoid **26.16**
Leydig cells 436, 438, **22.3(b)**
lichens 500, 505, 602, **28.28**
Life Cycle, Flowering Plant 19.2, 379–80
ligaments, suspensory 318–9, **16.1(b)**, 321
Ligases 4.4.5, 77
light-adapted eye 324
light, effect on plant growth 422–3
effect on seed germination 402–3
penetration through leaves 217–18
penetration through water 29–30
Light-Dependent Reactions 5.2.1, 88–93
Light-Independent Reactions 5.2.2, 93–5
Light-Intensity, Effect on Photosynthesis 12.2.2, 226–7
light intensity, effects on eye 325
light-intensity, effect on transpiration 199–200, **11.3**
light microscope 2, **1.2(a)**, 22, **1.22**
light, penetration of water 590, **28.11**
lignin 21
limiting factors, law of 225
Linkage 23.1.7, 456–8
Linnaeus 489
lipase enzymes, in germinating seeds 397
in mammal 272, **14.25**, 273, **Table 14.1**
Lipoids 3.2, 49
lipid bilayer 8, **1.6**
lipid globules 51, **3.17(b)**
lipid hydrolysis 76, **4.12(c)**
lipids, in seeds 397
in mammals 255, 271, 281
lipid metabolism 281
Liver 14.5, 278–82
liver 265, **14.14**, 271, **14.23**, 278–82, **14.31**, 14.33
liver fluke 538
liverwort 510
lizard **27.25**
lobules, of liver 278, **14.31**, 279
Lock and Key Mechanism 4.2.2, 69
locust 551, 554, **26.63**
log phase 606
long-day plants 387
long-sightedness 321
loop of Henle 182, 185, **10.4**, 189–91
louse **26.57**
lugworm 544, **26.40**
Lumbricus 544, **26.41**
lung books 556
lungfish 567, **27.13**
lungs 133, **8.3–8.6, 27.13**, 572, **27.37**
lutropin, LH 364, 438, 441, **22.13**, 442, **22.14**
Lyases 4.4.6, 77
lymph 166, **9.17**
lymphatic capillaries 166, **9.17**
nodes 165–6, **9.16, 9.17**
system 165–6, **9.16, 9.17**
vessels 165–6, **9.16, 9.17**
Lymph Formation and Circulation 9.1.3, 165–6
lymphocytes 166, **9.17**, 168, **Table 9.2**, 169, **9.20(b)**, 170–5, 176, **9.28**, 181
Lymphocytes and Antibodies 9.2.4, 173–7
lysis 103
lysosomes, functions 12–13, **1.12(b)**
structure 12, **1.12(a)**
lysozyme 173
lytic cycle 103, **25.3**, 491–2

macrofauna, soil 633–4
macronutrients, in mammals 256
Macronutrients, Plant 13.2.1, 242–4
macula 330–1, **16.17, 16.18**
madreporite 559, **26.74, 26.76–7**
magnesium, in plant growth 244
maize, germination of 395–6, **20.3**
seed structure 395, **20.3(a), (c)**
malaria 147, 528
male cone 518, **25.44**
Male Hormones 22.1.3, 437–8
malleus 327–8, **16.13**
Malpighian body 182
Malpighian tubule 551, **26.58**, 556
maltase, in germinating seeds 397
in mammals 273, **Table 14.1**
maltose 44–5, **3.8**, 272–3, **14.25**, **Table 14.1**
***Mammalia* 27.2.7, 578**
mammary glands 448–9, 578–9
mandible 550, **26.52, 26.56**
manganese deficiency, plants 245, **13.7**
manometer, Warburg 85, **5.7**
simple 85–6, **5.8**
manures 246
Marchantia **25.26**
marram grass 205, **19.9(c)**
marsupials 446, 579, **27.42**
mass-flow 236–8
***Mastigophora* 26.1.2, 524**
Matter, Cycling of 29.3.4, 624–7
maxilla 550, **26.52, 26.56**
maxilliped 550
maxillule 550
median canal 328–9, **16.14**
medulla, adrenal 360–1, **18.2(a)**, 363
kidney 182, 184–5, **10.3**
medulla oblongata 137, 161, 309–12, **15.37, 15.40**
Medullary Hormones 18.4.1, 363–4
medusoid 530, **26.17**, 534, **26.28**
megakaryocytes 171, **9.23(a)**
meganucleus 526, **26.8**
megasporangia 379, 514, **25.34**, 520
megaspore mother cell 373–4, **19.3(b), (c)**, 380, **19.7**
megaspores 373, **19.3(c)**, 379–80, **19.7**, 514, **25.46**, 520
megasporophyll 514, **25.34**
Meiosis 7.2, 123–7
Significance 7.2.3, 127–9
melanin 323, 16.9
melanism, industrial 484
membrane carrier 248–9, **13.11**, 284, 359
Membrane Recovery 15.1.4, 289
Membranes, Cell 1.2.1, 8–9
membranes, functions 9
ultra structure 8–9, **1.6–1.8**
unit 8, **1.7**
memory 314
Mendel **23.1**, 450
Mendel's first law 451
Mendel's second law 453
meninges 309–10, **15.37**
menopause 438
menstrual cycle 440
flow 441
meristems, adaxial 413, **21.5(a), (b)**
apical 406–8, **21.1, 21.2**, 414–15, **21.6, 21.7(a)**
ground 414–15, **21.7(a)**
intercalary 421–2, **21.14**
lateral 418
marginal 413, **21.5(a), (b)**
mermaid's purse **27.7**
mesentery 534, **26.24–5**
mesocotyl 395, **20.3(b)**, 396
mesoderm 536, **26.38**
mesoflora, soil 632–3, **29.33, 29.34**
mesogloea 530, **26.17–18**
mesophytes 204
mesosome 492, **25.4**
messenger RNA 101, 108–9, 111
metabolism of absorbed food 280
metachronal rhythm 527, **26.9**
metallophytes 245, 485, 594
metameric segmentation 542, 562
metamorphosis 552, 571
metaphase, meiosis 124–6, **7.9, 7.10**
mitosis 118–19, **9.3**
metaphloem 408, **21.2(a), (b)**, 410, 415, **21.7(a), (b)**
Metatheria 579
metaxylem 408, **21.2(a), (b)**, 410–11, **21.3(c)**, 415, **21.7(a), (b)**
Michaelis' constant 75, **4.11**
microfauna, soil 632
microflora, soil 631
micronucleus 526, **26.8**
Micronutrients, Plant 13.2.2, 244–5
micropyle 374, **19.3(d)**, 392, **20.1(a)**, 520
microscope, compound 1–2, **1.2(a)**
electron 5, **1.4(a)**
light 2 3, **1.1, 1.2(a)**
phase-constrast 2
simple 1, **1.1**
Van Leeuwenhoek's 1, **1.1**
microsomes 24
microsporangia 379, 514, **25.34**, 518, **25.44**
microspore mother cells, 370–1, **19.2(b)**, 380, **19.7**
microspores 370, 379–80, **19.7**, 514, 518, **25.47**
microsporophyll 514, **25.34**, 518, **25.44**
microvilli 188, **10.8**
micturition 182
midbrain 309, 313
middle ear 327, 332
middle lamella 3, 7, **1.5(a)**, 20
milk 267–8, **14.19**, 449, **22.22**, 578
milk expulsion reflex 449, **22.22**
milk teeth 256–7, **14.1**, 258, **14.3**
millipede 551
mineralocorticoid hormones 361
minerals, plant 240
Minerals Absorption, Mechanisms 13.5.2, 247–9
Plants 13.5, 246–9
Mineral Circulation, plants 13.6.3, 250–1
content, leaves 246, **Table 13.6**
deficiency, effect on plant growth 242, **Table 13.3**, 243, **13.3–13.5**, 245, **13.7**
elements, effect on plant growth 243, **Table 13.4**
fertilisers 246
ion concentration, guard cells 223, **12.3**
Mineral Movement, into Shoot System 13.6.2, 250–1, 13.14
Mineral Nutrition, Plants Chapter 13, 240–53
Mineral Requirements, Plants 13.1, 240–2
Mineral Transport, Plants 13.6, 249–51
mineral uptake, roots 246–7, **13.8, Table 13.7**
Minerals, Functions in Plants 13.2, 242–5
Toxic 13.3, 245
miracidium 538, **26.34**
Mitochondria 1.2.8, 14–16
mitochondria distribution 15–16, **1.15**, 499
functions 83
mitochondria, ultrastructure 14–15, **1.14**
Mitosis 7.1, 117–20
Mitosis, Significance 7.1.3, 122–3
mitral valve 153, **9.3(b)**, 156, **9.6**
molars 258–64, **14.2, 14.4–14.13**
***Mollusca* 26.8, 556–9**
mongol child 131, **7.15**
chromosomes 131, **7.15**
***Monocotyledones* 521, 25.49**
monocytes 168, **Table 9.2**, 169–70, **9.20**
Monohybrid inheritance 23.1.1, 450–2
Monosaccharides 3.1.1, 41–3
monotremes 579
monozygotic twins 445
mosquito 528, **26.13**, 551, **26.60**, 599, **28.24**
moss 510
moth 551, 553
motor neurons 302–3, **15.27**
motor region, of forebrain 312, **15.40**, 314, **15.43**
Mouth 14.3.1, 265–6
mucin 268–9. **14.18(b)**
Mucor 500, **25.11**, 501, **25.12**, 505
mucosa gastric, 267
mucus 11, 563, **27.4**
Multiple alleles 23.1.5, 455
murmurs 159
***Musci* 25.6.2, 512**
Muscle and Contraction 15.1.8, 296–299
muscle, cardiac 299–300, **15.24**
skeletal 296–8, **15.20, 15.21**
smooth 298, **15.22**
muscle cell 530, **26.18**
mutation, chromosome 129–31, **7.14, 7.15**, 481, 654
gene 106–7, **6.15**, 111–12, **6.22**, 129, 481, 653
mutualism 600
mycelium 498
mycorrhiza 247, 601–2, **28.27**, **Tables 28.6–7**
mycotoxins 503
myelin sheath 289–92, **15.12, 15.13**, 293, **15.15**, 296, **15.19(b)**
myofibrils 296–7, **15.20**
myogenic activity 159, 298
myoglobin 147–8, **8.22**
structure 58, **3.27**
myopia 321, **16.16**
myosin 297, **15.20(c)**, 298, **15.21**
myotome 562, **27.3**, 565
***Myriapoda* 26.7.3, 551**
Mytilus 558, **26.71**
myxoedema 353
***Myxophyta* 25.5.1, 505**

NAD 71, **5.2**, 80–1, 83, **5.5**
NADH 80–1, **5.2**, 83, **5.5**, 84, **Table 5.1**
NADH, absorption spectrum 69, **4.4**
NADP 71, 91, **5.16(a)**, 92–3, **5.21**, 96, **5.19**, 95
NADPH 91, **5.16(a)**, 92–3, **5.21**, 96, **5.19**, 95
nail-patella syndrome 458
natural selection 481
nauplius 550, **26.54**
Neanderthal man 475
nectar 383
negative feedback, enzymes 70
nematoblast 531, **26.18**
nematocyst 531, **26.20**
***Nematoda* 26.5, 541**
neotony 571
nephridium 542, **26.41**, 544, 563, **27.5**
nephrons 182, 184–5, **10.3–10.5**, 355–6, **18.12, 18.13**, 362–3, **18.24, 18.25**

Nereis 542–4, **26.39**
nerve cells, see neurons
nerve cord 537, **26.31**, 542, **26.39**
Nerve Impulse 15.1.3, 287–9
nerve net 531, **26.21**
Nervous Control and Coordination in Mammals Chapter 15, 283–316
nervous system 284, 302, **15.25**, 308, **15.38**
Net Primary Productivity 12.3.3, 229
net primary productivity 229, 618 **Table 29.4**
Neuro-Effector Junctions 15.1.7, 296–7
neuro-effector junctions 295–6, **15.19**
neurogenic activity 298
neurons 284–5, **15.3**
neutral solution 30
neutrophils 168, **Table 9.2**, 169, **9.20(a)**, 170, **9.22**
newt **27.18**
niche 606
nicotinamide 255
nicotinamide-adenine dinucleotide (see NAD)
  phosphate (see NADP)
nicotinic acid 255
nictitating membrane 573, 577
nitrification 625
nitrogen cycle 624–5, **29.25**
nitrogen deficiency in plants 243, **13.3**
nitrogen fixing bacteria 603–4, **28.29**, 624
nitrogen, in plant growth 242–3
nitrogen narcosis 149
nitrogenous bases, in nucleic acids 98–9, **6.2**, 101, **6.7(a)**
nocturnal mammals 323
node of Ranvier 289–91, **15.12(c)**, 292, **15.13**
Nomenclature and classification 25.1, 489–90
Non-autosomal inheritance 23.2, 460–2
non-essential amino acids 254
non-reducing sugars 44
noradrenalin 307, 308, **15.34**, 363, **18.26(b)**
normal distribution curve 463, **23.13–14**
notochord 561, **27.1–3**
nucellus 372–4, **19.3**, 520, **25.46**
nuclear division, meiosis 123–7
  mitosis 117–20
nuclear membrane 18–19, **1.18**, **1.19**
Nucleic Acids 6.1, 98–107
nucleoid 493, **25.4**
nucleolar organiser 19
nucleolus 19
nucleoside 99
nucleotide 98–9, **6.3**
Nucleus 1.2.10, 18–20
Nutrient-Film Technique 13.7, 252–3
nutritional requirements, mammal 254
nutritive cell 532, **26.18**

oak **25.52**
Obelia 530, 532–3, **26.23**
objective lens 2, **1.2(a)**, 22, **1.22**
octopus 558, **26.73**
ocytocin 367, 448–9
odontoblasts 256, 257, **14.1**
oedema 166
oesophagus 265–7, **14.14**, **14.15**, **14.17**, 270–1, **14.22**, **14.23**
oestrogen 440
Oestrus Cycle 22.2.3, 440–2
oil pollution 660, **30.20**
oils 49, 272, 281
oleic acid 50, **3.15(b)**
***Oligochaeta* 26.6.2, 544**
oligotrophic 659
omasum 270, **14.22**
ommatidia 547, **26.45**
omnivores 260
onchosphere 540
***Onychophora* 26.7.1, 548**
oocyte 438–9, **22.9**
oogamy 506, 510
oogenesis 438–9, **22.9**
oogonia 438–9, **22.9**, 501, **25.12**, 508, **25.21**
oosphere 508, **25.39**, 517
oospore 501
open root 262
operculum 513, **25.33**, 567, **27.12**
opisthosoma 556, **26.65**, **26.66**
opossum **27.42**
opsin 324
optic nerve 317–9, **16.1**, **26.39**, **26.72**, **27.28**, **27.38**
oral groove **26.8**, **26.10**, 527
Ordovician period 472
organelles 6
organic matter, soil 630
organ level of development 536
organochlorine insecticides 647, 659
organ of Corti 329
Organ Transplantation 9.6, 181
Origin of Life 24.1, 467–9
ornithine cycle 280, **14.32**
Orthoptera 554
osculum 529, **26.14**
osmometer 34–5
osmoregulation centre 315
osmoregulation, fish 593, **28.15**
osmosis 34–5
Osmotic Behaviour, Animal Cells 2.4.2, 38–9
  Plant Cells 2,4.1, 35–8
osmotic potential 34
osmotic properties 34–5
ossicles 327–8, **27.28**, 573, **27.36**, 577
ossification 301, **15.28**
***Osteichthyes* 27.2.3, 567**
osteoblast **15.26**, 301
ostia 547, **26.46**
ostiole 508, **25.21**
otoliths 331, **16.18**
Outbrooding 23.4.1, 463–4
Outbreeding Mechanisms 19.3.1, 380–4
outer ear 327
oval window 327–9, **16.13–16.15**
Ovaries 22.2, 438–43
ovary, flower 368–9, **19.1**
  mammalian 439–42, **22.8**, **22.10–22.14**
overfishing 611
overheating 338
ovipary 443
ovovivipary 443
ovulation 440, 442, **22.14**
Ovule Development 19.1.2, 370–5
ovule 518, **25.45–6**
ovuliferous scale 518, **25.45–6**, **25.48**
ovum 438, 440
oxidases 76
Oxidation of Respiratory Substrates 5.1.2, 79–83
oxidation water 193
oxidative phosphorylation 83
Oxido-Reductases 4.4.2, 76
Oxygenation of the Blood 8.3.1, 139–42
oxygen carrying capacity 140, **Table 8.2**
Oxygen Debt 8.2.3, 139
  dissociation curves, haemoglobin 141–6, **8.15**, **8.17**, **8.19(a)**, **8.20**, 591, **28.12**
  myoglobin 148, **8.22**
oxygen dissolved in water 590, **Tables 28.2–3**
oxygen, effect on plant growth 424
  effect on seed germination 401
Oxygen Uptake and Carriage 8.3, 139–48
oxygen uptake by plant tissues 237, **Table 12.6**
  by seeds 401, **20.9**
oxyhaemoglobin 141
oxymyoglobin 147
oxyntic cells 267, **14.18(a)**, 268, **14.18(b)**

pancreozymin 273–4, **14.27**
Paramecium 526, **26.8–12**
parapodium 542, **26.39**
Parasitism 28.2.1, 597–600
parasite 490, 494, 500
Parathyroid Glands 18.1.5, 353–5
parenchyma 411, **21.4**, **25.50**
partition coefficient 60
passive immunity 178, 447
pathogen 502
pecten 577, **27.38**
pectoral girdle 569, **27.19**, **27.40**
pedicellaria 559, **26.74**
pedipalp 556, **26.65–6**
Pellia 510, **25.27–9**
pellicle **26.6**, **26.9**
pelvic girdle 569, **27.19**, **27.40**
penicillin 504
Penicillium 504–5
pentadactyl limb 476, **24.12**, 570, **27.20**
peppered moth 483, **24.19**
pericarp 392–5, 521
perichondrium 300
periosteum 300, **15.26**
Peripatus 548, **26.47**
Peripheral Nervous System and Reflexes 15.2.1, 302–6
perisarc 533, **26.23**
peristome 513, **25.33**
Permian period 472
perrisodactyls 581
persistance, insecticides 648
Pesticides 30.3, 646–51
***Phaeophyta* 25.5.3, 508**
phagocytosis 9, 120, **9.22**, 490, 524
phalanges **27.20**, **32**
phenotype 450
pheromones 588
phloem, meta 408, **21.2**, 410, **21.7(a)**, **(b)**, 415
  proto 408, **21.2**, 410, **21.5(a)**, **(b)**, 413, **21.7(a)**, **(b)**, 415
  role in translocation 230–2
  structure 233–5, **12.15**
  ultrastructure 234–5, **12.15**
phosphocreatine 79, 298
3-phosphoglyceraldehyde (PGAL) 95, **5.19**, 80–1, **5.2(a)**
Phospholipids 3.2.2, 51–2
phosphorus cycle 636, **29.38(b)**
phosphorus deficiency in plants 243, **13.4**
phosphorylation, oxidative 83, **5.5**
  photo- 92–3, **5.16**
photolysis 91–2
photomicrographs 22
photoperiodic response 387–8, **19.14**
photoperiodism, vegetative 423
photophosphorylation 92, **5.16(b)**
Photoreception 16.1.4, 322–6
photoreceptors 322–3, 525, **26.39**, **26.45**
photorespiration 97
photosensitive pigments 89, **Table 5.13**, 324–6
Photosynthesis 5.2, 88–97
photosynthesis 78
  effect of carbon dioxide concentration 225, **12.6**, 227, **Table 12.3**
  effect of light intensity 226–7, **12.9**
  effect of temperature 226, **12.8**
  factors affecting 223–8
  in guard cells 222
  measuring rate of 223–4, **12.4**
phototaxis 525
phototropism 428, **21.22**
phototropism, action spectrum 429
phragmoplast 120–1, **7.5(a)**
Phycomycetes 500–1
phyllotaxis 413
phytochrome 387, 402
phytochromes, absorption spectra 403
Phytomastigina 525
phytoplankton 509
Phytophthora 500, 502
pileus 502, **25.14**
pinacocyte 529, **26.15**
pinna, ear 327, **16.13**
pinna, fern 515, **25.36–7**
pinocytosis 9, 13, 40, 490
  reverse 9
Pinus sylvestris 518, **25.42–8**
pitch, of sound 330
pit, bordered 21, **1.21(b)**
pith 408, **21.2(a)**, **(b)**, 411
pits 20
Pituitary Body 18.5, 364–67
pituitary body 191–2, **10.13**, 310, **15.37**, 315
placcoid scale 564, **27.8**
Placenta 22.3.3, 445–8
placenta, flowering plant 371
  mammalian 147, 445–6, **22.16**, 447, **22.19**
  membranes 446
Planaria 536–7, **26.31**
plankton 263
plant communities 228
plantain, protogyny 381, **19.8(b)**
planula 533, **26.24**, **8**
plasma
  cells 174, 176, **9.28**
  inorganic iodine, PII 351, **18.6**
  membrane 3, **1.3**, 7–8, **1.5(b)**, 492, **25.4**
  proteins 163, 174–5, **9.27**, 348
plasmagel 523, **26.2**
plasmasol 523, **26.2**
plasmodesma 20, **1.20(b)**
Plasmodium 527–8, **26.13**
plasmolysis 37, **2.9**
platelets 171, **9.23**
***Platyhelminthes* 26.4, 536–41**
platypus **17.1**, 579, **27.41**
plumule 392–3, **20.1**, 395, **20.3**, **25.48**
pluteus 560, **27.75**
pneumatic bone 300, 595, **27.31**
polar body 439–40, **22.9**
polarisation 286
polar molecules 27
polar transport, auxins 425, **21.18**
pollen, formation 370–2, **19.2(a)**, **(b)**
  grains 370–2, 517–8, **25.44**, **25.47**, 520
  germinating 375–6, **19.4(a)**, **(b)**, **(c)**
pollen mother cells 370–1, **19.4(a)**, **(b)**, **(c)**
pollen tube 375–6, 520, **25.47**
Pollen Growth, Physiology 19.5.2, 389
Pollination 19.3, 380–4
Pollination Mechanisms 19.3.2, 382–4
pollutants 638
Pollution, of atmosphere 30.1, 638–42
Pollution, by heavy metals 30.2, 642–6
Pollution, of aquatic habitats 30.5, 655–60

***Polychaeta* 26.6.1, 542**
Polyhybrid inheritance 23.1.3, 453–4
polymer 46, 52, 98
polymorphism, genetic 466
polynucleotide 98–100
polyp 533, **26.23**
Polypeptides and Proteins 3.3.2, 55–60
polypeptides 55, 267, 268, **14.19**, 273, **14.26**, **Table 14.1**
polyploidy 130, 482
Polysaccharides 3, 1.3, 46–9
polysomes 108, 110, **6.19(b)**
  in protein synthesis 108–10
polysomy 130, 482
polyploids 482
population 463, 606
Population dynamics 29.1.3, 609–13, 295–10
Population genetics 23.4, 463–6
Population growth 606–9, 29.1.3
Populations 24.1, 606–13
pore density, effect on transpiration 203–4, **11.8**
  size, effect on transpiration 203
***Porifera* 26.2, 529–30**
porocyte 529, **26.15**
posterior pituitary 365, **18.28**, 367, **18.32**
postsynaptic membrane 293–4, **15.15**, **15.16**
potassium deficiency in plants 243, **13.5**
potassium, in plant growth 243
potato blight 500, 502
potato, tuber 385, **19.13**
potential difference 286
potometer 206, **11.10(a)**
Precambrian period 471
predation 609
preen gland 575
prefrontal lobotomy 315
pregnancy 180, 442
Pregnancy and Foetal Haemoglobin 8.3.4, 146–7
pregnancy test 447–8, **22.21**
premolars 258–63, **14.4–14.11(b)**
pressure changes, in the heart 158
pressure potential 36
  receptor 341
  root 212
  turgor 36
  wall 36
  waves, in ear 329, **16.15**
presynaptic terminals 293, **15.15**
primary colours 325
primary consumers 616
Primary Growth and Development of Plants 21.1.1, 406–17
primary producers 469
primary productivity 229, 618
primary root system 414–17
  shoot system 406–14
  stimulus 305, **15.31**
primary structure, proteins 56
primary wall 20
primates 582
primordia, axillary bud 407–8, **21.2**
  leaf 407–8, **21.1**, **21.2**
primordial germ cells 436–9, **22.4**, **22.9**
primrose, flower structure 381–2, **19.8(c)**
proangiotensin 362–3, **18.25**
proboscis 553, **26.62**

procambial strands 408–9, **21.2(a), (b),** 413–15, **21.5(a), (b), 21.7(a), (b)**
producer organisms 217, 616–19
Productivity of Plants 12.3.3, 229
profibrinolysin 172
progesterone 441–2, **22.12–22.14**
proglottides 539, **26.36**
prolactin 449
promitochondria 16
propagation, of nerve impulse 287
prophase, meiosis 124–5, **7.9,** 125–6, **7.10**
mitosis 118–19, **7.1(b)**
proplastids 18
prosoma 555, **26.65**
prostacyclin 171
prostate gland 435, **22.2,** 444
prosthetic group 67
protandry 380–1, **19.8(a)**
protein bound iodine, PBI 351–2, **18.6**
protein metabolism 280
Protein Synthesis 6.2, 107–14
proteins, biochemical tests 59–60
cell membrane 8–9, **1.6–1.8**
denaturation 59, 72
functions 59
properties 59
repressor 113, **6.23**
solubility 59
structure 56–8, **3.24–3.28**
prothallus **25.39–40,** 517
prothrombin 171–2, **9.24**
Protochordates 27.1, 561–3
protoderm 414–15, **21.7(a)**
protogyny 381, **19.8(b)**
protonema 513
protophloem 408, **21.2,** 410, **21.5(a), (b),** 413, **21.7(a), (b),** 415
protoplasm 3
protoplasmic streaming 238–9, **12.20(b)**
Prototheria 579
protoxylem 408, **21.2(a), (b),** 411, **21.3(c),** 413, **21.5(a), (b),** 415, **21.7(a), (b)**
differentiation 410, **21.3(a)**
***Protozoa* 26.1, 523–8**
proximal convolutions 182, 185, **10.3(c), 10.4,** 187–8, **10.8,** 189, 355, 362
pseudocoel 541, **26.37**
pseudoheart **26.41,** 546
pseudopodia 170, 523, **26.1, 26.2**
***Pteridophyta* 25.7, 513–7**
pterodactyl 473, **24.9**
puberty 438
pubic bone 435, **22.2**
pulmonary artery 153, **9.3,** 158
capillaries 134, **8.4**
valve 153, **9.3(b),** 155, 159
pulse 158
pupa 552, **26.62**
pupil 318–19, **16.1(b)**
purines 98
Purkinje fibres 155, **9.5(b)**
pyloric sphincter 267, **14.17,** 271
Pyramids, ecological 29.3.3, 622–4
pyramids of biomass 623, **29.23**
pyramids of energy 623, **29.24**
pyramids of numbers 622–3, **29.22**
pyrenoid 507, **25.18,** 526
pyrimidines 98
P-wave, ECG 157–8, **9.7(b), (c)**

Q10 (temperature coefficient) 73
QRS-complex (ECG) 157–8, **9.7(b), (c)**
quantasomes 16
quaternary structure, proteins 58
queen bee 555, **26.64**
quiescent centre 414–15, **21.7(a)**

rachis, feather **27.30,** 575
rachis, fern 515, **25.36**
radial muscles, of iris 319
radial symmetry 530, **26.29,** 559
Radiation, forms of 30.4.1, 651–2
radiation, of heat 337
Radiation, sources of 30.4.2, 652–3
radiation, solar 199, 589
radicle 392–5, **20.1–20.3, 25.48**
radio-iodine 351–2, **18.7**
radioisotope dating 470
radioisotopes, in carbon dioxide fixation 93–5, **5.17, 5.18, Table 5.3**
in chromosome replication 122–3, **7.8**
in DNA replication 106, **6.14**
in oxygen evolution 91
in translocation 231–5, **21.13**
Radiolaria 524
radionuclides 651, 660
radius **27.20, 27.32**
radula 557, **26.67**
ragworm 542, 544
random orientation, chromosomes 129, **7.13, 23.4**
Ranvier, node of 289–92, **15.12(c), 15.13**
razor shell 558, **26.70**
reabsorption 187–9, **Table 10.1, 10.7,** 191
reagins 178
receptacle, flower 368–9, **19.1(a), (b)**
receptacles 508, **25.21**
receptive sites 294
receptors 302, **15.26,** 317
recombinant DNA 114, **6.24**
recombinants 457
recovery, of membrane 290, **15.11**
red algae 509
red blood cells 139, 142, **8.16,** 144–5, **8.18, Table 8.5,** 168–9, **Table 9.2, 9.20, 9.21,** 173, **9.25**
red bone marrow 144, **8.18,** 169–70, **9.23(a)**
red cone 326, **16.12**
red-green colour blindness 326
redia 538, **26.34**
reducing sugars 44
reflex action 302–6, **15.30**
refraction, of light 319, **16.3**
refractory period 289, **15.10**
Regulating Heat Loss 17.3.3, 341–6
Regulating Heat Production 17.3.2, 341
regulation of the heart 159–61
Regulation of Nephron Function 10.2.3, 191–2
Reissner's membrane 328–9, **16.14**
rejection, of transplant 181
relative density, water 29
relay 302
renal artery 152, **9.2,** 182–4, **10.1, 10.3**
dialysis 195–6, **10.18**
pelvis 182, 184, **10.3(b)**
threshold, for glucose 360
vein 152, **9.2,** 182–4, **10.1, 10.3**
renin 362–3, **18.25**
rennin 267–8, **14.19,** 496
repressor, protein 113, **6.23**
reproduction, asexual in flowering plants 384–6
mammalian 434–449
sexual in flowering plants 368–79
***Reptilia* 27.25, 572**
resistance, environmental 606, 612
resistance, to insecticides 650–1, **30.11**
resolution 22
resolving power 22
Respiration 5.1, 78–88
respiration, germinating seeds 401–2
Respiration, Measuring Rate 5.1.4, 85–7
respiration, metabolic pathways 79–83
site of 15, 83
respiratory centre 137–9, **8.10,** 162, **9.13,** 311
Respiratory Physiology of Diving Mammals 8.4, 148–50
repiratory pigment 139
respiratory quotient (see RQ)
quotients, seeds 401–2, **20.10**
substrates 78
respirometer 335–6, **17.3**
simple 86, **5.8**
Warburg 85, **5.7**
response to stimulus 283–4, **15.1**
Resting Potential 15.1.1, 284–6
resting potential 286–9, **15.7, 15.9**
retardation factor (see Rf value)
retention time 63
reticular formation 310, **15.37,** 312–13, **15.40, 15.41**
reticulo-endothelial system 170
reticulum 270, **14.22**
retina 317–25, **16.1, 16.3–16.7, 16.9, 16.11, 26.72, 27.28, 27.38**
Rf value 62
rhesus monkey 179
system 179–80, **Table 9.3**
rhizoid 510, **25.27, 25.31,** 512, **25.39,** 517
rhizome 386, **19.13,** 521
rhizosphere 247
***Rhizopoda* 26.1.1, 523**
***Rhodophyta* 25.5.4, 509**
rhodopsin 324–5
riboflavin 255
ribonucleic acid (see RNA)
ribose 41, **Table 3.1,** 101, **6.7(a)**
ribosomal RNA 102
ribosomes 13, 102, 108–9, 492, **25.4**
ribulose 41, **Table 3.1**
ribulose 1.5-bisphosphate 95
ribs 134–5, **8.3, 8.6**
rickets 255
ringing experiments 232, **12.14**
RNA, messenger 101
ribosomal 102
RNA, role in protein synthesis 107–9
structure 101–2, **6.7, 6.8**
synthetase 107
transfer 101
rod cells 322–6, **16.9–16.12**
rodents 262, 580
root apex 414–15, **21.6, 21.7(a), (b)**
cap 414
cortex 414
hairs 209–10, **11.13(a), (b)**
lateral 416–17, **21.9**
nodules 603, **28.29**
Root Pressure 11.4, 212–13
root pressure manometer 213, **11.17**
structure 414–16, **21.7, 21.8**
system, primary 414
Roots, Mineral Absorption 13.5, 246–9
roots, of teeth 258, **14.2,** 262
rough endoplasmic reticulum 9–10, **1.9**
round window 327–9, **16.13, 16.14(b)**
roundworm 541
RQ 87, 401–2
rumen 270, **14.22,** 495
rumen, microbes 604
ruminants 270
Rumination 14.3.3, 270
runner, strawberry 385, **19.12**

Saccharomyces 498, **25.10,** 501–4
saccule 330–1, **16.17**
saliva 265–6
salivary amylase 266
glands 266, **14.15, 26.13, 26.58,** 573
sap 35
sap, composition of 230, **Table 12.4**
***Sarcodina* 26.1.1, 523, 26.1**
sarcomere 296–8, **15.20, 15.21**
saturation, of haemoglobin 141, **8.15,** 143, **8.17,** 145–6, **8.19(a), 8.20**
***Schizomycophyta* 25.3, 492**
schizont **26.13**
schizozoite **26.13**
Schwann cell 289–91, **15.12**
sclera 317–18, **16.1(b), 27.28**
sclerenchyma fibres, differentiation 412–13, **21.4**
scolex 539, **26.36**
Scots pine 518, **25.42–8**
scrotal sac 435, **22.2**
scurvy 255–6
scutellum 395–6, **20.3(a)**
Scyphozoa 534
sea anemone 530, 533–4, **26.24–5**
sea squirt 501, **27.2**
sea urchin 559–60, **26.77**
seasonal reproducers 440
secondary consumers 616
secondary growth, stem 418–21, **21.12, 21.13**
secondary growth, host 528, 538, **26.34**
secondary plant body 418, 522
sexual characteristics 438, 443
stimulus 305, **15.31**
structure, proteins 57
wall 20
secretin 274, **14.27**
section cutting, ultramicrotome 6, **1.4**
sedge **25.49**
sedimentary rock 470
seed dispersal 378–9, **19.6,** 595, **28.20**
Seed Dormancy 20.3.3, 403–5
seed formation 376–8, **19.5**
Seed Formation, Physiology 19.5.3, 390
Seed Germination, Factors Affecting 20.3.2, 399–403
Morphology 20.2, 392–6
Physiology 20.3, 396–405
Seed Structure 20.1, 392–6
seedlings, changes in dry mass 397, **Table 20.2,** 398, **20.4**
seed 392, 517, 520, **25.48**
seeds, chemical composition 397, **Table 20.1**
food mobilisation 396–9
oxygen intake 401, **20.9**
respiratory quotients 401–2, **20.10**
segregation 452
Selaginella 513, **25.34**
***Selaginellales* 25.7.1, 513**
Selection 24.3.4, 483–5
self-sterility 381
semen 444
seminal groove **26.41,** 546
semicircular canals 327, **16.13,** 330–2, **16.17, 16.19(b)**
seminal vesicles 435, **22.2,** 444, **26.33, 26.41,** 546
seminiferous tubules 435–6, **22.3**
sense organs 283, **15.2,** 302, 317
sensitised lymphocytes 174, 176, **9.28**
sensorineural deafness 333
sensory hairs 329–31
sensory neurons 302–3, **15.27,** 329, **16.14(c),** 331, **16.18,** 332, **161.9**
sensory region, of brain 313–14, **15.43**
sepals 368–9, **19.1(a), (b)**
septum, cardiac 153, **9.3(b),** 155
serotonin 171
Sertoli cells 436–7
serum proteins 175, **9.27,** 477
seta **25.27,** 511, **25.31**
sewage 498
sewage pollution 655–9, **30.16–17**
sex chromosomes 460
sex hormones 438, 440
Sex linkage 23.2.2, 461–2
Sexual Reproduction, Flowering Plants 19.1, 368–79
sexual reproduction, mammalian 443–449
shade leaves 218
shark **27.7**
shelled egg 446
shoot apex 407–8, **21.1, 21.2(a), (b)**
shoot system, primary 406–14
short-day plants 387
shrew 261, 339, **17.8, 27.43**
shivering 303–4, **15.29,** 341
short-sightedness 321
sickle cell anaemia 147, 170, 466, 482
sickle cell trait 147
sickle cells 147, **8.21**
sieve plates 233–4, **12.15**
sieve-tubes 233–4, **12.15,** 513, 518, 521
Silurian period 472
single cell protein 497, 503
sinu-atrial node 154–5, **9.5**
sinusoids 278–9, **14.31**
skate **27.7**
skeletal muscle 296–8, **15.19–15.21**
skeleton 443
skin 337–45, **17.11, 17.14,** 495
sleep 313
deprivation 313
Small Intestine 14.3.4, 271–4
smallpox 178
smooth muscle 298, 299, **15.22, 15.23**
snail 538, **26.34,** 557, **26.67, 26.69**
sodium-potassium exchange pump 284–5, **15.4,** 289
Soil, as a Source of Minerals 13.4, 245–6
Soil, as an ecosystem 29.3.5, 627–37
soil, air 629, **Table 29.9**
air capacity 629
fauna 632–4, **29.33–4**
food web 635, **29.37**
microflora 631
moisture 629–30
organic matter 630
particles 628, **Table 29.8**
pH 630–1
pore space 629
profiles 628, **29.28**
structure 628
temperature 631, **29.31**
texture 628
solar radiation, effect on transpiration 199–200
solenocyte 563, **27.5**
solution, hypertonic 37, **2.9,** 39, **2.11**
hypotonic 36–7, **2.9,** 39, **2.11**
isotonic 37–9, **2.9, 2.11**
solutions, depression of freezing point 34
elevation of boiling point 34
osmotic properties 34–5, **2.7**
solutions, true 32
solvent front 61–2, **3.29**
somatotropin, STH 365–6

sorus 515, **25.37**
sound waves 327–8
Species, formation of 24.3.6, 486
specific heat capacity, water 29
specificity, enzymes 70
spectrum, visible 88, **5.11**
spermatheca **26.41**, 546
spermatocytes 436–7, **22.3(b), 22.4**
Spermatogenesis 22.1.2, 436–7
spermatogonia 436–7, **22.4**
***Spermatophyta* 25.8, 517–22**
spermatids 436–7, **22.4**
spermatozoa 434, **22.3–22.5**, 436–7, 444
sphincters 267, **14.17**, 269, **14.21**, 271
sphygmomanometer 159, **9.8**
spicule **26.1**, 524, 529, **26.14–15**
spider 555, **26.65**
spinal canal 303, **15.27**
  cord 301–3, **15.25, 15.27**
spindle 118–19, **7.3(b)**
spindle fibres 14
spinneret 556
spiny ant-eater 579, **27.41**
spiracle 551, **26.56, 26.62**, 564
spiral valve 565, **27.10, 27.22**
Spirogyra **25.16, 25.18–20**, 507
spirometer 136–7, **8.7**
  tracing 136, **8.8**
spleen 169
sponge 529, **26.14**
sporangia 500, **25.11**, 514
sporocyst **26.13**, 538, **26.34**
sporophyll 514
sporophyte 379–80, **19.7**, 509–10, 515, 517, **25.32**
***Sporozoa* 26.1.4, 527**
sporozoite **26.13**
spring wood 419–20, **21.12(c)**
Squamata 573
stamens 368–9, **19.1**
stapes 327–8, **16.13, 16.14(b)**
staining cells 2, 6
starch, in chloroplasts 47, **3.11(a)**
  in germinating seeds 397
  in mammals 266, 272–3, **14.25, Table 14.1**
  in potato tuber 47, **3.11(b)**
  structure and properties 46
  test for 46
starfish 559, 569, **26.74, 26.76**
starling **27.29**
stem cells 175–6, **9.28**
stenohaline 594
stereoscopic vision 582
stereoisomers, amino acids 54, **3.22**
  glyceraldehyde 42, **3.1**
  sugars 43, **3.3, 3.4**
steroid hormones 360–1, **18.20(c)**, 438
  -secreting cells 9
Steroids and Sterols 3.2.4, 52
sternum 134, **8.3**, 169
sterols 52
stethoscope 159
stigma 368–9, **19.1**, 521, **25.51**, 525, **26.6**
stomach 265, **14.14**, 267–271, **14.17–14.23**
Stomata, Opening and Closing 12.1.4, 221–3
stomata, stem 413
  structure 219–20, **12.2**
stomatal density, effect on transpiration 203–4, **11.8**
  size, effect on transpiration 203
  transpiration 197
stomium **25.38**, 517
stone canal **26.74**
storage materials, cells 5
storage materials, seeds 396, **Table 20.1**
  organs 229, **12.11**
stratosphere 638
stridulation organ 554, **26.63**
striking, cuttings 432–3, **21.32**
striped muscle 296–8, **15.20, 15.21**
strobilus 514, **25.34–5**
stroke volume 160
stroma 16
stromatolites 471
style 368–9, **19.1**
subclavian vein 152, **9.2**, 165–6, **9.16**
subcutaneous layer 342, **17.11(b)**
suberin 420
suberisation 209–10
subsoil 628
substrate 69
Substrate Concentration, effect on enzymes 4.3.6, 74–5
Succession 29.2.1, 613–16, 29.12–14
sucrose 44–5, **3.7**
sudorific glands 337, 342, **17.11(b)**
sugars, aldose 41
  ketose 42
  non-reducing 44
  properties 41–4
  reducing 42, 44
  structure 42, **3.2**, 43, **3.3, 3.4**, 45, **3.7, 3.8**
sulphur cycle 636, **29.38(a)**
Sulphur dioxide pollution 30.1.2, 639–41
sulphur, in plant growth 244
summer wood 419–20, **21.12(c)**
sunflower, germination 394–5, **20.2(b)**
sunflower seed, structure 393–4, **20.2(a), (c)**
sun leaves 218
Surface Area and Body Volume 17.2.4, 338–40
surface area of lungs 132
  for reabsorption 188
  of red blood cells 169
  of skin 340, **17.9**
  of small intestine 275
  to volume ratio 338
Surface Tension of Water 2.2.3, 29
suspensions 32
suspensor 376–7, **19.5(a), (b)**
suspensory ligaments 318–21, **16.1(b)**
swallowing 266
sweat gland 578
sweating 344
swim bladder 567, **27.14**
syconoid **26.16**
symbionts 500, 505, 600
Symbiosis 28.2.2, 600–5
sympathetic nerves 301, **15.25**, 306–8, **15.33, 15.34, Table 15.3**
synapses 293–5, **15.14–15.18**, 308, **15.34**
synaptic cleft 293–4, **15.15**
Synaptic Transmission 15.1.6, 293–5
syncitium 541
synovial capsule 302, **15.29**
systole 155, **9.5**, 158

tactile stimulation 448–9, **22.22**
tadpole **27.23**
Taenia 539–41, **26.36**
tapetum 370–1, **19.2(a), (b)**
  of eye 323
tapeworm **26.36**
target organs 348
taxonomy 489
tears 173, 319
tectorial membrane 328–9, **16.14**
teeth 256–64, **14.1–14.3**
Teleostei 589
telophase, meiosis 124–6, **7.9, 7.10**
  mitosis 118–20, **7.3(b)**
temperature coefficient (Q_{10}) 73
Temperature, Effect on Enzyme Action 4.3.3, 72–3
temperature, effect on flowering 388–9
temperature, effect on heart rate 589, **28.10**
temperature, effect on photosynthesis 226, **12.8**
  effect on plant growth 423–4, **21.16**
  effect on seed germination 399–400, **20.6, 20.7**
  effect on transpiration 200–201
temperature, mammalian body 334, **17.1**, 336, **17.4**, 345–6, **17.14, 17.15**
Tensile Strength of Water 2.2.3, 29
tertiary consumers 616
Tertiary period 474
tertiary structure, proteins 58, **3.26**
testa 377, 392–3, **20.1(a), 20.2(a)**, 395, **20.3(a)**
test-cross 451
Testes 22.1, 434–8, 532, **26.22, 26.31–3, 26.36–7, 26.41**
testosterone 438, **22.6, 22.7**
test tube baby 444
tetanus 178
tetany 356, **18.14**, 357
tetraiodothyronine, T_4 349, 350, **18.4**
thalamus 310, **15.37**, 312, **15.40**
thallus 508, **25.26**
theca externa 439
theca interna 439
Theria 579
Thermal Properties of Water 2.2.1, 27–9
thermocline 656
thermography 337
Thermoregulation 17.3, 340–7
thermoregulation centre 304, **15.29**, 315, 340, **17.10**
Thermoregulation in Mammals 17, 334–47
thermostat 340
thiamin 255
thin-layer chromatography 63
thoracic ducts 165, **9.16**
thorax 133–4, **8.3**, 547, 551, **26.56, 26.62–63**
thrombin 171–2, **9.24**
thrombocytes 168, **Table 9.2**, 171–2, **9.23(b), 9.24**
Thrombocytes and Coagulation 9.2.3, 171–3
thrombocyte factors 171–2, **9.24**
thromboplastin 171–2, **9.24**
thrombosis 172
thrombus 172
Thunberg tube 82, **5.3**
thymine 98
thymus 175–6, **9.28**
thyroid gland 349–56, **18.1, 18.3, 18.5, 18.6, 18.9, 18.13**
thyroliberin, TRH 351, **18.5**, 367
thyrotoxic state 352–3, **18.7(b), 18.8**
thyrotropin, TSH 351, **18.5**, 364
thyroxin 341, 349, 350–1, **18.4–18.6**
tick 555, **26.66**
tidal volume 136, **8.8**
tissue differentiation, root 414–15
  stem 408–13, **21.2, 21.3**
  factors 171–2, **9.24**
  fluid 164, **9.15**, 166
T-lymphocytes 174–6, **9.28**
tonoplast 4, **1.3(a)**, 12, 36, **2.8**
tooth bud 256–7, **14.1**
toothed whale 263, **14.12(a)**
topsoil 628
torsion 557, **26.69**
total plasmolysis 37, **2.9**
toxins 166, **9.17**
trace elements, mammals 256
trace elements, plants 241
trachea 134–5, **8.3**, 265–6, **14.14, 14.15, 27.37**
tracheae **26.45**, 551, **26.57**
tracheids 214–15, **11.19**, 513, 518, 521
tracheole 551, **26.57**
transaminases 76, 280
transamination 77, **4.13**, 280
transcription 107–8, **6.16**
Transferases 4.3, 76
transfer cells, in leaf 235, **12.16**
  in root 250, **13.13**
transferrin 281–2, **14.33**
transfer RNA 101, **6.7**
transformation 103
transfusion, of blood 179–81
translation, genetic code 108–9, **6.18**
Translocation of Photosynthetic Products 12.4, 229–39
translocation, effect of auxin on 426
  measuring rate of 235–6, **12.17, Table 12.5**
Translocation Mechanisms 12.4.2, 235–9
  Pathway 12.4.1, 230–5
transmembrane potential 286, **15.5**
transmitters, chemical 293–5
Transpiration 11.1, 197–9
transpiration and water absorption 206–8, **11.10(a), 11.11**
Transpiration, Effects 11.3, 206–12
Transpiration, Factors Affecting 11.2, 199–205
transpiration stream 208
transpiration-cohesion-tension theory 209
transplantation, of organs 181, 195
***Trematoda* 26.4.2, 538**
triacylglycerol 50, **3.16**
Triassic period 473
tricarboxylic acid cycle 82–3, **5.4**
triceps muscle 306, **15.32**
trichocyst 527, **26.9**
trichromatic theory of colour vision 325
tricuspid valve 153, **9.3(b)**
triiodothyronine, T_3 349, 350, **18.4**
triplet code 110
triploblastic 536, **26.38**
triploid fusion nucleus 376
trophoblasts 445
tropins 364
tropisms 427–9, **21.21, 21.22**
trochophore 478, **26.39**, 544, 557
trophic levels 616–17, **29.16**
Trophic relationships 29.3.1, 616–22
trophozoite **26.13**
troposphere 638
trout **27.12**
Trypanosoma 526, **26.7**
trypsin 272–3, **14.26**
trypsinogen 272–3, **14.26**
tube feet 559, **26.74, 26.76, 26.77**
tube nucleus 375, **19.4(a)**
tuber, potato 385, **19.13**
tubule cells 193–4, **10.15, 10.16**
tunica 406–7, **21.1(a), (b)**
***Turbellaria* 26.4.1, 536**
turgid 36
turgidity 221, 411, 424
turgor pressure 36
tusks 263–4, **14.13**
T-wave, ECG 157–8, **9.7**
tympanic canal 328–9, **16.14**
  membrane 327, **16.13**
typhlosole **26.41**, 546
tyrosine 348, 350, **18.4**

ultracentrifuge 24, **1.24**
ultrafiltration 186–7, **10.6(b)**
ultramicrotome 6, **1.4(b)**
ultraviolet radiation 255
Ulva **25.16**
umbilical blood vessels 167–8, **9.19**, 447, **22.19**
umbilical cord 167, **9.18**, 447, **22.19**
ungulates 580
Uniramia 548
Unit Leaf Rate 12.3.2, 229
unit membrane, hypothesis 8
unit membrane, structure 8, **1.7**
Uptake and Loss of Water 2.4, 35–9
urea 187, **Table 10.1**, 280–1, **14.32, 14.33**
ureter 182–4, **10.1–10.3**, 434–5, **22.1, 22.2**
urethra 182, **10.1, 10.2**, 434–5, **22.1, 22.2**
uric acid 551, 573, 578
urinary system 183, **10.1**
urinary bladder 182–3, **10.1, 10.2**, 434–5, **22.1, 22.2**
urine 182, 187, **Table 10.1**, 189–90, **10.9, 10.10**
Urodela 571
uterus 367, 439, **22.8**, 441, 445, 448, **26.32–3, 26.36**
utricle 330, **16.17**

Vaccines 9.3, 178
vacuolation 409, 424
vacuole, contractile 39, **2.12**
Vacuoles 1.2.4, 12
vagina 439, **22.8**, 443–4
vagus nerve 159–60, **9.9(a)**, 307, **15.33**
Van Leeuwenhoek's microscope 1, **1.1**
Variation 24.3.3, 481–2
vasa deferentia 434–5, **22.1–22.3**, 438
  efferentia 435, **22.3(a)**, 438
vascular bundles, stem 408–9, **21.2(c), (d), 25.50**
vascular cambium 409, **21.2**, 418–19, **21.10–21.12**
  effect of auxin on 426
vascular rays 418–19, **21.10–21.12**
vasectomy 435
vasoconstriction 161–2, **9.11, 9.12**, 342–3, **17.12**
vasodilation 161–2, **9.11, 9.12**, 342–3, **17.12**
vasomotor center 161–3, **9.12, 9.13**
vasomotor control 161
vasopressin 191–2, **10.13**, 367
vector 490, 495, 528, 598
vegetative photoperiodism 423
Vegetative Propagation 19.4.3, 384–6
veins 152–2, **9.2**, 163–4, **19.14**
veliger 557, **26.68**
vena cava 152, **9.2**, 153, **9.3**
venter **25.32, 25.39**, 517
ventilation 137, **8.9**
ventricles, of brain 309–10, **15.37**
  of heart 152–6, **9.2, 9.3, 9.5(b), 9.6**
ventricular diastole 158
  systole 158, **9.5(b)**
venation 197, **11.1**